Housing Allocation and Homelessness

Second Edition

Housing Allocation and Homelessness

Second Edition

Jan Luba QC
Barrister, Garden Court Chambers

Liz Davies
Barrister, Garden Court Chambers

JORDANS

MT

Published by
Jordan Publishing Limited
21 St Thomas Street
Bristol BS1 6JS

British Library Cataloguing-in-Publication Data

A catalogue record for this book is available from the British Library.

ISBN 978 184661 155 1

Typeset by Letterpart Ltd, Reigate, Surrey

Printed in Great Britain by CPI Antony Rowe, Chippenham, Wiltshire

5/19/11

STOP PRESS

1. On the eve of the printing of this book, on 18 March 2010, the Tenant Services Authority (TSA) published the new national standards for social housing in England which will come into force on 1 April 2010.

2. Their arrival, foreshadowed at many points in this book, heralds a new era for the regulation of providers of social housing – whether local housing authorities or housing associations.

3. The standards are set out in *The regulatory framework for social housing in England from April 2010.*[1]

4. Directly relevant to Part One of this book, the new National Tenancy Standard includes the following new standard for allocation of social housing by *all* registered providers of social housing:

Allocations

Registered providers shall let their homes in a fair, transparent and efficient way. They shall take into account the housing needs and aspirations of tenants and potential tenants. They shall demonstrate how they:

- make the best use of available housing

- are compatible with the purpose of the housing

- contribute to local authorities' strategic housing function and sustainable communities.

There should be clear application, decision-making and appeals processes.

5. The details include 'Specific expectations' which deal with social housing allocation (and homelessness) in terms which require that:

1.1 Registered providers shall co-operate with local authorities' strategic housing function, and their duties to meet identified local housing needs. This includes assistance with local authorities'

---

[1] Tenant Services Authority, March 2010, available at: http://www.tenantservicesauthority.org/server/show/ConWebDoc.20175/changeNav/14567.

homelessness duties, and through meeting obligations in nominations agreements. Where, in exceptional circumstances, registered providers choose not to participate in choice-based lettings schemes in areas where they own homes, they shall publish their reasons for doing so.

1.2 Registered providers shall develop and deliver services to address under occupation and overcrowding in their homes, within the resources available to them. These services should meet the needs of their tenants, and will offer choices to them.

1.3 Registered providers shall provide tenants wishing to move with access to clear and relevant advice about their housing options. They shall participate in mobility schemes and mutual exchange schemes where these are available.

1.4 Registered providers' published policies shall include how they have made use of common housing registers, common allocations policies and local letting policies. Registered providers shall clearly set out, and be able to give reasons for, the criteria they use for excluding actual and potential tenants from consideration for allocations, mobility or mutual exchange schemes.

1.5 Registered providers shall develop and deliver allocations processes in a way which supports their effective use by the full range of actual and potential tenants, including those with support needs, those who do not speak English as a first language and others who have difficulties with written English.

1.6 Registered providers shall minimise the time that properties are empty between each letting. When doing this, they shall take into account the circumstances of the tenants who have been offered the properties.

1.7 Registered providers shall record all lettings and sales in the Continuous Recording of Lettings system.

6. From 1 April 2010, the TSA will enforce these new standards either on their own initiative, or in response to complaints from tenants and applicants, pursuant to powers conferred by the Housing and Regeneration Act 2008.

Jan Luba QC
Liz Davies
19 March 2010

PREFACE TO THE SECOND EDITION

When the first edition of this book was published, we noted that the number of homeless households temporarily accommodated by English local housing authorities under their homelessness duties was at an all time high of over 100,000. The government took urgent measures to reduce those numbers, announcing an ambitious target to halve that figure by 2010.

As at the end of September 2009, just under 57,000 homeless households were in temporary accommodation in England. A further 2,567 households were in temporary accommodation in Wales. Of course, this figure does not show the real number of homeless people in England or Wales. Indeed, it might be said that those households in temporary homes are the lucky ones. Not everyone who makes an application for homelessness assistance is entitled to accommodation and so the figures exclude those people who are not eligible for assistance, do not have a priority need or became homeless intentionally. Those are the people who have to fend for themselves, usually in the private rented sector, and may end up sleeping rough.

One of the reasons for the reduction has been the increased co-operation between local housing authorities and registered social landlords (RSLs), or registered providers of social housing as they will soon be called. More lettings of social housing homes in England are now made by RSLs than by local housing authorities. For this reason, we have included a new chapter on 'lettings by registered social landlords' (Chapter 6). We have done so with some trepidation since the Tenant Services Authority (TSA) is due to announce new national statutory standards for England in April 2010, after the publication of this book.

The English and Welsh governments have also encouraged local housing authorities to engage actively in homelessness prevention. Prevention policies are now so widespread that we have devoted a second new chapter to the subject (Chapter 8 on 'homelessness prevention'). Good use of prevention options can assist a potentially homeless household to find new accommodation, or to remain in existing accommodation, before that household comes close to having to make an application for homelessness assistance. Prevention options, in the form of rent deposits, mediation, etc, might also be used to assist a local housing authority to discharge any accommodation duty it has towards an applicant for homelessness assistance. However, prevention of homelessness should not be the prevention of *applications* for homelessness assistance and some of the arrangements employed by local housing authorities, in the name of homelessness prevention, have been held to be unlawful, or to constitute maladministration, by the courts and the Ombudsmen in England and Wales.

As we began planning this new edition, the homelessness scene in the UK lost one of its most valued contributors with the untimely passing of the unique and colourful Bob Lawrence. Bob had dedicated much of his working life to the interests of those without shelter. He most recently worked as a Special Adviser with Communities and Local Government and was a regular volunteer with Crisis at Christmas. We were proud that he was so enthusiastic about this book. The housing world will miss him greatly.

As always, we have received extraordinary support from the Jordans' team. Our publisher Tony Hawitt is patient, surprisingly flexible about deadlines and a pleasure to work with. The whole of the production team were extremely efficient and insightful.

We have also had the great benefit of comments and feedback from readers of the first edition. We are most grateful for that and would welcome a similar response to this new edition.

Our thanks to work colleagues, friends and family remain as before. Any errors are, naturally, our responsibility. The law is – we hope – up to date at the end of February 2010.

Jan Luba QC
Liz Davies

February 2010

BIOGRAPHICAL NOTES

Jan Luba QC is a barrister practising from Garden Court Chambers in London and a Bencher of the Middle Temple. He was called to the Bar in 1980 and in 2000 was made a Queen's Counsel and Recorder (part-time judge). He specialises in housing law with particular emphasis on housing management law, homelessness, allocation of social housing and housing conditions.

He is the author of *Housing & The Human Rights Act: A Special Bulletin* published by Jordans in October 2000. He is co-author of *Homelessness Act 2002: A Special Bulletin* (Jordans, 2002). He is also the co-author of *Defending Possession Proceedings* (Legal Action Group, 7th edn, 2010), the co-author of *Repairs: Tenants Rights* (Legal Action Group, 4th edn, 2010), and is the co-contributor to the monthly column 'Recent Developments in Housing Law' published in the magazine *Legal Action*.

Jan has considerable experience as a housing law trainer and has written widely on housing allocation and homelessness issues in both the legal and housing press. He is a patron of Croydon Housing Aid Society.

Liz Davies is a barrister practising at Garden Court Chambers, London. She specialises in all types of legal work for tenants, other occupiers and homeless applicants. Before coming to the Bar, she was a solicitor specialising in housing law.

With Jan Luba QC, she is co-author of *Homelessness Act 2002: A Special Bulletin* (Jordans, 2002). She is a contributing author to the *Housing Law Handbook* (Law Society, 2009).

In 2001, she published *Through the Looking Glass* (Verso, 2001), an account of her two years' membership of the Labour Party's National Executive Committee. She is Chair of the Haldane Society of Socialist Lawyers.

CONTENTS

PART II
HOMELESSNESS

Chapter 7
Local Housing Authorities' Homelessness Reviews and Strategies

Chapter 11
Homeless or Threatened with Homelessness 343

Chapter 12
Eligibility for Assistance 377

Chapter 21
Contracting out of Homelessness and Allocation Functions

Appendix 1
England: Allocation

TABLE OF CASES

References are to paragraph numbers.

TABLE OF STATUTES

References are to paragraph numbers.

TABLE OF STATUTORY INSTRUMENTS

References are to paragraph numbers.

TABLE OF EC LEGISLATION

References are to paragraph numbers.

PART I
ALLOCATION

Chapter 1

ALLOCATION OF SOCIAL HOUSING: AN OVERVIEW

'The allocation of social housing is a difficult and potentially controversial matter, which gives rise to very hard choices, at all levels of decision making, whether strategic, policy or specific.'[1]

USING THIS PART OF THIS BOOK

1.1 This Part of this book deals with the process of distributing long-term tenancies of council and housing association homes – the allocation of social housing. For those coming new to this subject, the rest of this chapter introduces the topic and relates some of its history. The chapter contains an outline of the present legal framework for allocation of social housing and some comment about its recent and possible future development.

1.2 Readers already involved in the process of distributing social housing, or advising those who seek a new home in social housing, will probably want more detailed information on one or more of the essential stages of the allocation process.

1.3 The starting point, addressed in Chapter 2, is to assemble the necessary information about local arrangements for allocation of social housing and make an application for consideration under those arrangements. That chapter deals with how applications are made, processed and decided.

1.4 The first hurdle for an applicant is to be accepted as eligible to be considered for allocation of a tenancy of social housing. Eligibility, and thus access to the local scheme, is the subject of Chapter 3.

1.5 Among those applicants who are eligible, there needs to be a process of sifting or assessment to determine respective priorities between them. That may be as simple as a date-ordered queue or as complex as a sophisticated individual assessment of each applicant's housing need. Every local housing authority will need a scheme for assessment or prioritisation by which it can work out who gets what in respect of available homes. Chapter 4 describes how such schemes are drawn up and amended, and the parameters within which they must be operated.

1.6 Once an applicant's priority has been identified, the next stage will be to determine whether, and on what terms, to make them an offer of a new home in social housing. Local arrangements may enable applicants to try to select homes for themselves, by bidding in response to advertisements ('choice based letting' or 'CBL'), or provide for staff to choose applicants for available properties. These processes and arrangements are described in Chapter 5.

1.7 In this second edition of the book we have added to this Part a wholly new Chapter 6 dealing with the discrete question of allocation of social

---

[1]   Lord Neuberger in *R (Ahmad) v Newham London Borough Council* [2009] UKHL 14 at [25].

housing by housing associations. Most of their available homes are let as a result of nominations made by local housing authorities by operation of the mechanisms described in Chapters 2 to 5. But Chapter 6 now additionally deals with applications made directly to housing associations for the allocation of their homes.

1.8 Readers seeking the primary sources on social housing allocation, rather than descriptive text, will find that we have gathered in Appendix 1 the essential statutory materials, the statutory Codes of Guidance and other relevant documents.

1.9 The authors are ever anxious to improve and make more accessible the content of this Part (and all parts) of this book. Comments on the content or structure are warmly welcomed, either direct to the authors or through the publishers.

INTRODUCTION

1.10 For the purposes of this book, 'social housing'[2] is taken to embrace the portfolio of residential accommodation held by local housing authorities, by registered social landlords[3] (such as housing associations and housing co-operatives) and by organisations such as housing action trusts, for letting to individual tenants. This Part of this book primarily focuses on how landlords in the first category (local housing authorities) allocate the homes that they have available to rent. But it also considers the most numerically significant form of letting by the second category (registered social landlords) – those lettings arising from nominations made by local housing authorities. Direct allocation of the remaining vacancies in RSL stock and the letting of properties by other social housing organisations are addressed in Chapter 6 of this book.[4]

1.11 Local housing authorities in many (but not all) areas face a difficult task in the distribution of their available rented homes. Demand for such social housing often far exceeds supply, and the supply of affordable housing has been generally diminishing.[5] Pressure on what remains of the stock is increasing.

---

[2]   A term now technically defined, for other purposes, by Housing and Regeneration Act 2008, s 68(1).

[3]   Hereafter abbreviated to 'RSLs'. The term 'registered social landlord' will shortly pass into history. The Housing and Regeneration Act 2008 will, when fully introduced, bring in the new term 'registered provider of social housing'.

[4]   See Chapter 10 of Alder & Handy *Housing Association Law and Practice* (Sweet & Maxwell, 4th edn, 2003) and Robert Latham *Allocating social housing: the registered social landlord context* (2008) October *Legal Action*, p 42.

[5]   In the 2008/09 financial year in England, 25,500 new units of affordable housing were completed by RSLs and 550 by local authorities; but another 3,860 were lost under the right to buy: see *Housing and Planning Statistics 2009* (Communities & Local Government [CLG], December 2009, at http://www.communities.gov.uk/publications/corporate/statistics/housing planningstatistics2009). The Government set a target of producing 'at least 45,000 new social

1.12 In each local housing authority's area, those seeking the allocation of social housing in order to provide themselves with a long-term home will include, among many others:

(1)   applicants for Housing Act 1996 (HA 1996), Part 7 ('Homelessness') assistance who are in temporary accommodation provided by the local housing authority;[6]

(2)   people staying with family or friends but needing a home of their own;

(3)   tenants in the private sector who occupy unsuitable accommodation or who want the relative permanence of a secure or assured tenancy in social housing;

(4)   the local housing authority's own tenants who may occupy unsuitable or overcrowded accommodation, or who may need to move for work or family reasons;

(5)   people from outside a local housing authority's own area needing to move into it; and

(6)   rough sleepers.

All of those people may apply to the local housing authority and ask that they be allocated somewhere suitable and secure to live.

1.13 Local housing authorities can meet some of that demand by selecting applicants for secure or introductory tenancies of properties from their own stock, or by nominating applicants to other local housing authorities or to RSLs. Each time a local housing authority selects an applicant, or nominates in this way, it has, in legal terms, 'allocated' accommodation.[7]

1.14 How does the local housing authority decide which deserving case gets priority over other deserving cases and therefore who should get the next available property? The answer, in broad terms, is that each local housing authority is free to draw up its own policy on how it will prioritise its list of applicants, provided that the policy adopted complies with certain statutory requirements and with basic legal principles of fairness and rationality. Before looking in somewhat more detail[8] at the current legal framework (to be found

---

homes a year by 2010–11' for England in the 2007 Green Paper *Homes for the future: more affordable, more sustainable* (http://www.communities.gov.uk/documents/housing/doc/Homes forthefuture.doc). In the summer of 2009 the Government made a commitment to invest an extra £1.5 billion towards building a total of 110,000 new affordable homes over the next 2 years: *Building Britain's Future* (HM Government, June 2009, at http://www.hmg.gov.uk/ buildingbritainsfuture.aspx).

6   See Chapters 7 and 19.
7   Subject to exceptions set out at HA 1996, s 159(5), s 160(2) and (3) and regulations; see **1.24–1.26**.
8   In Chapters 2 to 5.

largely in HA 1996, Part 6), the rest of this initial chapter offers a brief résumé of the relevant recent history of legal regulation in the allocation of social housing and a thumbnail outline of the current law.

HISTORY

Allocation law: a shifting landscape

1.15 Before 1 April 1997,[9] local housing authorities could organise the allocation of social housing as they saw fit, subject only to legal principles of rationality and fairness, their statutory duties towards applicants for homelessness assistance under HA 1996, Part 7,[10] and a long-standing statutory obligation to give reasonable preference to certain groups.[11] Provided that they complied with those obligations, the priority accorded to different groups of applicants was left to the discretion of each local housing authority.[12] They also enjoyed a general discretion as to when, and in what circumstances, they would exclude certain applicants from consideration for the allocation of social housing.[13] Commonly, local housing authorities would use this discretion to exclude applicants who were in rent arrears, or who had a history of nuisance behaviour. Many also operated policies suspending applicants from consideration if they refused a certain number of offers of suitable accommodation or for other reasons.

1.16 From 1 April 1997, HA 1996, Part 6 ('Allocation of Housing Accommodation') provided a new statutory basis for the allocation of social housing by local housing authorities. Almost 6 years later, in January 2003, HA 1996, Part 6 was, in its turn, very substantially amended by the Homelessness Act 2002.[14] Although local housing authorities' schemes for allocating accommodation are still governed by HA 1996, Part 6, those amendments were so substantial that local housing authorities now operate under a virtually new statutory regime. But before we outline that new scheme, it is necessary to describe the arrangements in place between 1997 and 2003, not least because much of the case law on social housing allocation turns on the provisions then in force.

---

9   When HA 1996, Part 6 came into force.
10   And, previously, Housing Act 1985, Part III, s 65.
11   Re-enacted as Housing Act 1985, s 22, giving reasonable preference to those occupying insanitary or overcrowded houses; those with large families, those living in unsatisfactory housing conditions; and applicants for homelessness assistance to whom they owed duties.
12   Housing Act 1985, s 21 vests the general management of its houses in a local housing authority.
13   *R v Canterbury City Council ex p Gillespie* (1986) 19 HLR 7, QBD.
14   Those amendments came into force on 31 January 2003 in England and on 27 January 2003 in Wales: Homelessness Act 2002 (Commencement No 3) (England) Order 2002, SI 2002/3114, art 3, and Homelessness Act 2002 (Commencement) (Wales) 2002, SI 2002/1736 (W 166), art 2(2).

Allocation law between April 1997 and January 2003

1.17 The big change that had been introduced on 1 April 1997 was the requirement for local housing authorities to maintain a 'Housing Register', one list that would contain all the different applicants entitled to be considered for an allocation of social housing except internal applicants for transfer. Within the list of applicants held on that register, local housing authorities were required to give reasonable preference to particular groups. Importantly, no specific preference was required to be given to applicants entitled to assistance under HA 1996, Part 7 ('Homelessness'), thereby abandoning the explicit statutory duty to that effect which had been contained in the earlier Housing Act 1985.[15] At the same time, HA 1996, Part 7 had introduced the concept that local housing authorities' duties to applicants for assistance under that Part (who had a priority need and had not become homeless intentionally) were simply to provide accommodation for a period of 2 years.[16] The idea was that applicants for assistance under HA 1996, Part 7 would be provided with safety-net accommodation, and during those 2 years they would either rise to the top of the list of those on the local housing register and be allocated social housing accommodation or would find their own accommodation in the private sector. Homelessness was no longer to be an automatic passport into long-term social housing. Some of that changed with the election of a new government (in May 1997), and from 1 November 1997 the effect of a ministerial order was that homeless people, who were in priority need and had not become homeless intentionally, were included among the groups of people to whom 'reasonable preference' had to be given in the allocation of social housing.[17]

1.18 Subject to those 'reasonable preferences', however, a local housing authority could draw up its own policies as to how to recognise – usually by a points system – the different types of need for an allocation of accommodation among those on the register. Local housing authorities could also continue to operate policies excluding certain categories of applicants, provided that they scrutinised each applicant's case individually and fairly.[18] Many local housing authorities therefore continued to operate policies, adopted before 1997, of excluding people with rent arrears and those who had committed acts of nuisance, and of suspending applicants who had refused offers of

---

[15] In its original form HA 1996, s 167(2) had required local housing authorities to give reasonable preference only to those occupying insanitary or overcrowded housing or otherwise living in unsatisfactory housing conditions; those occupying housing accommodation which was temporary or occupied on insecure terms; families with dependent children; households consisting of or including someone who was expecting a child; households consisting of or including someone with a particular need for settled accommodation on medical or welfare grounds; and households whose social or economic circumstances were such that they had difficulty in securing settled accommodation.

[16] HA 1996, s 193(2) prior to amendments made by the Homelessness Act 2002.

[17] Allocation of Housing (Reasonable and Additional Preference) Regulations 1997, SI 1997/1902.

[18] *R v Wolverhampton Metropolitan Borough Council ex p Watters* (1997) 29 HLR 931, CA.

accommodation.[19] They were also entitled to operate policies excluding applicants from outside their own areas.[20] Local housing authorities were additionally required by statute to exclude asylum seekers and other persons subject to immigration control from their registers.[21]

1.19 The housing register scheme did not apply to existing tenants seeking transfers within the same landlord's stock. As far as those transfers were concerned, local housing authorities retained the broad general discretion to operate any policy they wished, subject to public law considerations of fairness and rationality, and limited statutory requirements to consider housing need.[22] Many local housing authorities operated policies excluding tenants who had a certain level of rent arrears or who were accused of nuisance behaviour from being eligible for a transfer,[23] and suspending from transfer schemes those tenants who had refused an offer of a transfer.[24]

The move to the current statutory scheme

1.20 In January 2003, HA 1996, Part 6 ('Allocation of Housing Accommodation') was substantially amended by Homelessness Act 2002, ss 13–16.[25] The concept of a compulsory housing register was abolished and replaced by a requirement to have a comprehensive local housing allocation scheme. The categories of reasonable preference were altered. New codes of statutory guidance were issued: the *Allocation of Accommodation Code of Guidance for local housing authorities* in England;[26] and the *Code of Guidance for local housing authorities on allocation of accommodation and homelessness* for Wales.[27] Local housing authorities are required to have regard to the guidance when making allocation schemes and decisions on allocations.[28] Although barely referred to in the statutory amendments, running through the

---

[19] See e g *R (Giles) v Fareham Borough Council* [2002] EWHC 2951 (Admin), (2003) 35 HLR 36, Admin Court (acquiescence in nuisance behaviour) and *R v Southwark London Borough Council ex p Mason* (1999) 32 HLR 88, QBD (refusal of offers). One survey of 74 housing organisations found that 47 had an exclusions policy in place, with a further eight operating a deferral/refusal policy: *Exclusions from the housing register* (Northern Housing Consortium, May 2000).

[20] *R (Conway) v Charnwood Borough Council* [2002] EWHC 43 Admin, (2002) March *Legal Action*, p 16, QBD.

[21] HA 1996, s 161(2).

[22] *R v Newham London Borough Council ex p Watkins* (1993) 26 HLR 434, QBD.

[23] *R v Lambeth London Borough Council ex p Njomo* (1996) 28 HLR 737, QBD (rent arrears); *R v Southwark London Borough Council ex p Melak* (1996) 29 HLR 223, QBD (rent arrears); and *R v York City Council ex p Wilson* (1997) June *Legal Action*, p 18, QBD (nuisance).

[24] *R v Wandsworth London Borough Council ex p Lawrie and Heshmati* (1997) 30 HLR 153, QBD.

[25] In force from 27 January 2003 (Wales) and 31 January 2003 (England) – see fn 14.

[26] *Allocation of Accommodation: Code of Guidance for local housing authorities* (Office of the Deputy Prime Minister, November 2002) [English Code]. Parts of that Code were subsequently replaced by the further statutory guidance given in *Fair and flexible: statutory guidance on social housing allocations for local authorities in England* (Department for Communities and Local Government [CLG], December 2009) [English 2009 Code].

[27] *Code of Guidance for local housing authorities on allocation of accommodation and homelessness* (National Assembly for Wales, April 2003) [Welsh Code].

[28] HA 1996, s 169(1).

new approach to allocation of social housing is the concept that applicants should have a choice of accommodation, rather than be the subject of a take-it-or-leave-it allocation.[29]

OVERVIEW OF THE CURRENT STATUTORY SCHEME

1.21 The text of this part of this chapter necessarily provides only an introductory overview of matters that, as the cross-referencing to other parts of the text indicates, are given fuller treatment later in this Part of this book. It aims to do no more than introduce the reader to some of the key features of current provisions for the allocation of social housing.

The present statutory scheme in outline

1.22 HA 1996, Part 6 now applies to new applicants for social housing allocation and to existing local housing authority tenants seeking transfers.[30] When making an 'allocation', local housing authorities must comply with both the provisions of HA 1996, Part 6 and with their own local allocation schemes.[31] An 'allocation' is defined as occurring when the local housing authority selects a person to be its own secure or introductory tenant, nominates a person to be a secure or introductory tenant elsewhere, or nominates a person to be an assured tenant of an RSL.[32] Provided that the local housing authority has complied with HA 1996, Part 6 in drawing up its allocation scheme, and has treated all its applicants in accordance with the provisions of HA 1996, Part 6, it 'may allocate housing accommodation in such manner as they consider appropriate'.[33] However, the key rule is that an allocation can only be made which is in compliance with the terms of the local housing authority's own adopted allocation scheme.[34]

1.23 Whilst the requirement to keep a housing register has been abolished,[35] in practice local housing authorities need to maintain a list of applicants whom they have accepted as eligible for their local allocation scheme, and to organise that list so as to reflect the different applicants' relative priorities under the scheme.[36] Local housing authorities may call that list a 'register', a 'waiting list' or anything else, as they wish.[37]

---

[29]   A summary of the amendments was given in Chapter 2 of the English Code. That Chapter was
       replaced by the provisions of the English 2009 Code.
[30]   HA 1996, s 159(5).
[31]   HA 1996, ss 159(1) and 167(8).
[32]   HA 1996, s 159(2).
[33]   HA 1996, s 159(7).
[34]   HA 1996, s 167(8).
[35]   Homelessness Act 2002, s 14(1).
[36]   English 2009 Code, para 63; Welsh Code, para 5.1.
[37]   The Welsh Assembly Government has said: 'The 1996 Act also, somewhat curiously, abolishes
       any requirement for a local authority to maintain a register of housing applicants. Since it is
       difficult to imagine any effective administrative procedure that could operate without such a
       register, this Report assumes that all social landlords will, in practice, continue to maintain a

Circumstances where the normal allocation arrangements do not apply

1.24 The allocation provisions set out in HA 1996, Part 6 do not apply to each and every situation in which a person comes to be a tenant of social housing. The Codes helpfully each contain a list of common situations in which social housing can come to be occupied by a new tenant without the statutory provisions engaging at all.[38] Some of these exceptions are the result of express provisions in the HA 1996, Part 6 (and regulations made under them) and others are the result of the term 'allocation' in HA 1996 being narrowly defined as occurring only when an authority nominates or selects a person for a tenancy.[39] For example, the provisions of HA 1996, Part 6 do not apply where someone obtains a tenancy of social housing as a result of:

(1) vesting by succession of a periodic secure or introductory tenancy on the death of the tenant;[40] or

(2) devolution of a fixed term secure tenancy on the death of the tenant;[41] or

(3) assignment of a secure tenancy as part of a mutual exchange;[42] or

(4) assignment of a secure or introductory tenancy to a person who would have been qualified to succeed to the tenancy on the tenant's death;[43] or

(5) the vesting or disposal of a secure or introductory tenancy pursuant to a court order made under the specified provisions of three family law statutes identified in the Act;[44] or

(6) an order made under specified provisions of the Civil Partnership Act 2004 in relation to a secure or introductory tenancy;[45] or

(7) a transfer initiated by the landlord of a secure or introductory tenant (ie not initiated by the tenant making an application for a transfer).[46]

In none of these cases will there have been an 'allocation' for HA 1996, Part 6 purposes.

---

register, or "waiting list", of applicants': *A Review of Welsh Social Landlords' Approaches to Increasing Choice in Letting Accommodation* (Welsh Assembly Government, 2008), http://cymru.gov.uk/dsjlg/research/reviewofsociallandlords/reviewofsociallandlordse.doc.

38 English Code, Annex 1; Welsh Code, Annex 1.
39 HA 1996, s 159(2).
40 HA 1996, s 160(2)(a) and (3)(b).
41 HA 1996, s 160(2)(b).
42 HA 1996, s 160(2)(c).
43 HA 1996, s 160(2)(d) and (3)(c).
44 HA 1996, s 160(2)(e)(i)–(iii) and (3)(d)(i)–(iii).
45 HA 1996, s 160(2)(e)(iv) and (3)(d)(iv), amended by Civil Partnership Act 2004, s 81 and Sch 8, in force from 5 December 2005 (Civil Partnership Act 2004 (Commencement No 2) Order 2005, SI 2005/3175).
46 HA 1996, s 159(5).

1.25 In fact, HA 1996, Part 6 need not have expressly excepted most of these situations at all. In each category but the last, an existing tenancy has been transferred – by court order, vesting or deed – from one tenant to another, rather than by the local housing authority selecting the tenant from its list of applicants, and in the last case it is the local housing authority which, for its own purposes, wants the occupier to move. Another situation in which a social housing tenancy may pass to a new tenant without an allocation is on the making of a court order under the Family Law Act 1996, Sch 7, Part II. An order under those provisions moves the tenancy from the existing tenant to a new tenant by 'virtue of the order and without further assurance'. By the order the tenancy is 'transferred to, and vested in' the new tenant without any intervention by the local housing authority. There is, accordingly, no allocation for HA 1996, Part 6 purposes in that case.

1.26 HA 1996, Part 6 is also not applicable:

(8) where a tenant or owner-occupier has been displaced from his or her previous accommodation by a local housing authority and a local housing authority provides suitable alternative accommodation under the Land Compensation Act 1973, s 39; or

(9) where the local housing authority grants a secure tenancy to a former owner-occupier or a statutory tenant of a defective dwelling-house acquired by the local housing authority (under Housing Act 1985, ss 554–555).[47]

Allocation to non-tenant occupiers

1.27 Local housing authorities receive many requests for tenancy allocation from non-tenants who are occupying existing local housing authority accommodation and are seeking the grant of a tenancy for that particular property. Such an occupier may have no statutory right to the tenancy, but may have been occupying that accommodation as his or her home for some time and wish to remain there. The Codes give as examples:

• where one joint tenant has terminated the tenancy, by serving a notice to quit on the landlord, and the other former joint tenant remains in the home;[48] or

---

[47] HA 1996, s 160(4); Allocation of Housing (England) Regulations 2002, SI 2002/3264, reg 3; and Allocation of Housing (Wales) Regulations 2003, SI 2003/239 (W 36), reg 3.

[48] The factual scenario of *R (Dixon) v Wandsworth London Borough Council* [2007] EWHC 3075 (Admin), (2008) February *Legal Action*, p 40, Admin Ct.

- where a tenant has died and the remaining household member has no statutory succession rights, but has lived with the tenant for the preceding year, or was the tenant's carer, or needs to live in the property to care for the tenant's dependants.[49]

Those situations will be subject to HA 1996, Part 6 and will ultimately be governed by the terms of the local housing authority's allocation scheme. The Codes recommend that local housing authorities set out in their allocation schemes whether they will grant tenancies in those circumstances and, if so, on what basis.[50]

The local allocation scheme

Drawing up and amending the local scheme

1.28 When drawing up its local allocation scheme, or making any significant changes to it, a local housing authority is required to consult the RSLs with whom it has nomination arrangements.[51] The Codes also recommend that social services departments, health authorities, Supporting People teams, Connexions Partnerships, relevant voluntary sector organisations and other recognised referral bodies should be consulted.[52] A minimum consultation period of 12 weeks is recommended.[53] A local housing authority should take into account the findings and conclusions of its own homelessness review and strategy when settling upon (or amending) an allocation scheme and, conversely, the homelessness strategy should take into account the local allocation scheme.[54]

1.29 Once the local allocation scheme has been adopted, if there is any subsequent alteration reflecting 'a major change of policy' (such as a move to choice based letting),[55] the local housing authority is required to take such steps as it considers reasonable, within a reasonable period of time, to bring that alteration to the attention of those likely to be affected by it.[56] A 'major change of policy' is said by the Codes to include any amendment that would affect the relative priority of a large number of people, or any significant alteration to procedures.[57] In *R (A) v Lambeth London Borough Council*,[58] the Court of Appeal was asked to consider whether a change in the proportions of

---

49   The factual scenario of *R (Neville) v Wandsworth London Borough Council* [2009] EWHC 2405 (Admin), QBD, (2009) December *Legal Action,* p 17.
50   English Code, paras 3.9–3.10 (dealing with both joint tenancy termination and succession); Welsh Code, para 4.7 (succession only); and see the further discussion at **4.124–4.128**.
51   HA 1996, s 167(7). For detailed consideration of these requirements, see Chapter 4.
52   English 2009 Code, paras 7 and 43–45; Welsh Code, para 5.13.
53   Welsh Code, para 5.14, English Code, para 6.6 expressly endorsed that period but has been replaced by more general guidance in English 2009 Code, para 40.
54   English Code, para 1.5. See also **7.73–7.74** and **7.174–7.176**.
55   See **1.43–1.54** and **5.7–5.61**.
56   HA 1996, s 168(3).
57   English Code, para 6.3; Welsh Code, para 5.12. See also **4.10–4.16**.
58   *R (A) v Lambeth London Borough Council* [2002] EWCA Civ 1084, (2002) 34 HLR 57, CA.

accommodation to be allocated between different groups within the allocation scheme constituted 'a major change of policy'. The court held that the targets governing the distribution of offers between the different groups were not a published part of the allocation scheme and that amending them would not be 'a major change of policy' requiring consultation.[59]

1.30 What exactly those 'reasonable steps' required by the statute should be is not addressed in the English Code, although the Welsh Code recommends that current applicants should normally be informed of major policy changes by personal letter.[60]

Avoiding discrimination

1.31 The allocation scheme must not discriminate, directly or indirectly, on grounds of race, ethnicity, sex or disability.[61] These requirements are explored in Chapter 4.[62]

1.32 Housing authorities should ensure, when consulting in relation to allocation schemes, that views of groups which are currently under-represented in social housing are taken into account. Local housing authorities are encouraged to monitor the operation of their allocation schemes in order to identify and prevent discrimination and to review their schemes if particular groups are shown to be disadvantaged.

1.33 For their part, RSLs are required to co-operate with any requests from a local housing authority to offer accommodation to rent, to such extent as is reasonable.[63] Local housing authorities should be working with RSLs, other housing providers and voluntary agencies in order to meet housing needs, and with support services (Supporting People teams, health authorities, social services departments, police and probation services) to ensure that housing, care and support needs of vulnerable people are met.

Other features of allocation schemes

1.34 Local housing authorities may not contract out of ultimate responsibility for the local housing allocation scheme. Responsibility for adopting or altering the scheme, the principles of the scheme, consulting RSLs and ensuring that the allocation scheme is available for inspection by the public cannot be contracted out.[64] Local housing authorities may contract out the functions of:

59　[2002] EWCA Civ 1084, (2002) 34 HLR 57, CA at [26]–[28] per Collins J.

60　Welsh Code, paras 5.11–5.13.

61　Under the Race Relations Act 1976, the Sex Discrimination Act 1975 and the Disability Discrimination Act 1995. See English Code, para 5.28; Welsh Code, para 4.60.

62　See **4.129–4.132**.

63　HA 1996, s 170. See also English 2009 Code, paras 93–100; Welsh Code, pp viii–ix.

64　Local Authorities (Contracting out of Allocation of Housing and Homelessness Functions) Order 1996, SI 1996/3205, applying to both England and Wales. See also English Code, paras 7.1–7.6 and **21.30–21.39**.

- making inquiries into an application;

- making decisions as to eligibility;

- carrying out reviews of decisions;

- making arrangements to secure that advice and information and necessary assistance is available; and

- making the actual allocation decision, arranging the tenancy sign-up etc.

The local housing authority remains legally responsible for any acts or omissions of the contractor and for decisions made in its name.[65]

1.35 Elected councillors are prohibited from taking part in any decisions on an individual allocation if the accommodation is in their electoral ward or if the person subject to the allocation decision has a sole or main residence in their electoral ward. Elected members can, of course, seek and obtain information on behalf of their constituents, and participate in more general policy decisions that affect their wards.[66]

1.36 Even those local housing authorities which have transferred the whole of their housing stock, and no longer have any properties to allocate, are required to operate an allocation scheme, because they retain nomination rights to RSLs or other local housing authorities, and the exercise of those nomination rights constitutes an 'allocation'.[67]

Rights to information, advice and assistance[68]

1.37 The local housing authority must publish a summary of its adopted allocation scheme and provide a free copy of that summary to any member of the public who asks for one.[69] The whole scheme must be kept available for inspection by members of the public and a copy must be provided upon payment of a reasonable fee to anyone who asks for one.[70] Many local housing

---

[65] See **21.4**.
[66] Allocation of Housing (Procedure) Regulations 1997, SI 1997/483, reg 3(2) (England) and Local Housing Authorities (Prescribed Principles for Allocation Schemes) (Wales) Regulations 1997, SI 1997/45, reg 3, Sch 1, para 1. See also English Code, paras 6.14–6.15; Welsh Code, paras 5.17–5.18. A local housing authority's practice of inviting elected councillors to comment at the point of a potential allocation was criticised by the Public Service Ombudsman for Wales as giving the impression that there might be undue influence: *Housing Allocation and Homelessness in Wales: A Special Report by the Local Ombudsman for Wales* (February 2006), http://www.ombudsman-wales.org.uk/en/publications/?pID=76.
[67] English Code, paras 7.7–7.11.
[68] See **2.7–2.29** and **2.41–2.44**.
[69] HA 1996, s 168(1).
[70] HA 1996, s 168(2).

authorities publish their scheme on their websites. Provision of information in different languages is recommended by the Codes.[71]

1.38 Applicants to the local housing authority are entitled to receive advice and information about their right to make an application for an allocation of social housing, and the local housing authority must provide assistance free of charge to any person who is likely to have difficulty in making an application.[72] An applicant for an allocation has the right to general information to enable him or her to assess how the application is likely to be treated, whether housing accommodation appropriate to his or her needs is likely to be made available and, if so, how long it is likely to take.[73] He or she also has the right to request information setting out any facts taken into account when making a decision as to his or her eligibility or relative priority and has the right to request a review of any decision that he or she is not eligible for an allocation.[74]

Eligibility for allocation[75]

1.39 The amended HA 1996, Part 6 circumscribes the power of local housing authorities to exclude individuals, or classes of people, from their allocation schemes. Indeed, it abolishes the power to exclude by prescribing particular classes of applicant (eg non-residents, applicants owing debts to the local housing authority, etc) altogether. But local housing authorities *must* exclude from their allocation schemes people who are subject to immigration control and people who are not habitually resident in the Common Travel Area (CTA), or who only have limited rights of residence in the CTA under European Union law, *unless* they have been prescribed as eligible by regulations, or *unless* they are already secure, introductory or (in certain cases) assured tenants.[76] Local housing authorities *may*, but are not required to, choose to exclude people whose behaviour, or that of a member of their household, makes them unsuitable to be tenants.[77] If an applicant is ineligible (whether by reason of immigration status or past misconduct), he or she cannot be granted a sole tenancy or participate in taking a joint tenancy.[78] Local housing authorities cannot exclude applicants from their allocation schemes except on these narrow grounds.

---

[71] Welsh Code, para 4.61; the specific reference to this effect in English Code, para 5.31 has been replaced by more generalised guidance in English 2009 Code, para 47. The reference is maintained at English CBL Code, para 5.6 in relation to choice based letting schemes.

[72] HA 1996, s 166(1).

[73] HA 1996, s 167(4A)(a).

[74] HA 1996, s 167(4A)(b), (c) and (d).

[75] See Chapter 3.

[76] HA 1996, s 160A(3) and (4)–(6); Allocation of Housing and Homelessness (Eligibility) (England) Regulations 2006, SI 2006/1294, reg 3 (England); Allocation of Housing (Wales) Regulations 2003, SI 2003/239, regs 4–5 (Wales).

[77] HA 1996, s 160A(7) and (8). For an example see *R (Dixon) v Wandsworth London Borough Council* [2008] EWCA Civ 595, (2008) July *Legal Action*, p 22, CA.

[78] HA 1996, s 160A(1).

Identifying and prioritising different needs[79]

1.40 The classes of people to whom the local housing authority must award 'reasonable preference' within its allocation scheme are now:

(1) people who are homeless within the meaning of HA 1996, Part 7 ('Homelessness');

(2) people who are owed a duty by any local housing authority under HA 1996, ss 190(2), 193(2) or 195(2) (or the equivalent duties under Housing Act 1985), or who are occupying accommodation provided to them by a local housing authority under HA 1996, s 192(3);

(3) people who are occupying insanitary or overcrowded housing, or otherwise living in unsatisfactory housing conditions;

(4) people who need to move on medical or welfare grounds, including grounds relating to a disability;[80] and

(5) people who need to move to a particular locality in the district of the local housing authority, where failure to meet that need would cause hardship to themselves or to others.[81]

1.41 An applicant's circumstances, or the circumstances of his or her household, may fulfil more than one of the categories of reasonable preference. Until 2009 the categories had been treated as additional to each other, so that if an applicant's needs meant that he or she fell into more than one category, the allocation scheme had to ensure that all of those needs were reflected in the applicant's relative priority on the list of those to be considered for allocation: this was known as 'cumulative' or 'composite' assessment.[82] But in 2009 the House of Lords decided that the re-casting of HA 1996, s 167(2) by the Homelessness Act 2002 had removed any requirement to take a cumulative or composite approach.[83]

1.42 Within the preference categories, the local housing authority may award 'additional preference' to particular individuals, if they have 'urgent housing needs'. In determining the relative degree of preference, it can take into account

---

[79] See Chapter 4.
[80] Housing Act 2004, s 223 inserted the words '(including grounds relating to a disability)' and was brought into force in England from 27 April 2005; Housing Act 2004 (Commencement No 2) (England) Order 2005, SI 2005/1120. Extraordinarily, the provision has yet to be brought into force in Wales.
[81] HA 1996, s 167(2).
[82] *R (A) v Lambeth London Borough Council, R (Lindsay) v Lambeth London Borough Council* [2002] EWCA Civ 1084, (2002) 34 HLR 51, CA; *R v Islington London Borough Council ex p Reilly and Mannix* (1998) 31 HLR 651, QBD; *R v Tower Hamlets London Borough Council ex p Uddin* (2000) 32 HLR 391, QBD; *R (Cali) v Waltham Forest London Borough Council* [2006] EWHC 302 (Admin), (2007) 39 HLR 1; and *R (Ahmad) v Newham London Borough Council* [2008] EWCA Civ 140, (2008) April *Legal Action*, p 40, CA.
[83] *R (Ahmad) v Newham London Borough Council* [2009] UKHL 14, HL.

the applicant's financial resources available to meet his or her housing costs, any behaviour of the applicant or a member of his or her household, and any local connection between the applicant and the local housing authority's district. It may therefore decide whether to give the applicant additional priority (so as to put him or her higher on the list) or whether to give a lesser priority (move him or her lower down the list).[84] The local housing authority is entitled to give an applicant no preference at all if it concludes that his or her behaviour, or that of a member of his or her household, has been the type of behaviour that would have entitled the local housing authority to a possession order had the applicant been a tenant when that behaviour was carried out.[85]

Choice[86]

1.43 When the 1997–2001 Labour government first consulted on amending HA 1996, Part 6, it emphasised that one of its priorities was to offer more choice to applicants for social housing.[87] The aims of allocation policies were expressed as:

> '... to empower people to make decisions over where they live and exercise choice; help create sustainable communities; and encourage the effective use of the nation's social housing stock.'[88]

And the intention was that applicants:

> '... should have as much opportunity as possible for their views to be taken into account when they are seeking a new home.'

The 'choice' envisaged was to be:

- a free one (in that applicants should not be penalised for refusing offers);

- as wide as possible, both in respect of the types of tenancy on offer from different landlords and geographically; and

- well-informed.[89]

1.44 The government received a mixed response to these proposals and respondents' views tended to be influenced by whether they were in areas of high or low demand for affordable housing. Obviously, it is easier to provide

---

84   HA 1996, s 167(2A). See **4.91–4.100**.
85   HA 1996, s 167(2B), (2C). See **4.101–4.110**.
86   For a full discussion of Choice in the modern context of housing allocation see **5.7–5.23**.
87   *Quality and Choice: A Decent Home for All* (Green Paper, DETR April 2000), which led to the Homelessness Act 2002. Available at http://www.communities.gov.uk/archived/publications/housing/qualitychoice2.
88   *Quality and Choice: A Decent Home for All*, para 9.1.
89   *Quality and Choice: A Decent Home for All*, para 9.17.

applicants with 'choice' in areas of low demand, and respondents from those areas were more enthusiastic than those in areas of high demand for, and a limited supply of, affordable housing.

1.45 In the event, and notwithstanding the expressed policy intentions behind the introduction of the amended HA 1996, Part 6, there is hardly any reference to 'choice' in the statutory provisions, save for a requirement that the local housing authority must include a statement as to its policy on 'choice' within its allocation scheme, and provide a copy of that statement to each applicant for assistance under HA 1996, Part 7 to whom it has accepted a duty under HA 1996, s 193 or s 195.[90] The amended HA 1996, Part 6 permits local housing authorities to reserve allocation of particular accommodation in their stock either to a person who makes a specific application for that accommodation or to persons of a particular description. These provisions are the limited statutory vehicles for the government's policy that local housing authorities should offer 'choice'.[91]

1.46 There are a number of rationales behind the concept of 'choice based lettings'. One is to relieve the pressure on local housing authorities in areas of high demand for, and limited supply of, social housing. The government encourages local housing authorities to form regional and sub-regional consortia for social housing allocation, so that, for example, applicants in particular parts of the country may apply for accommodation elsewhere in their regions. Another rationale is to reduce the number of offers of accommodation that are rejected by applicants. If applicants select their own property, rather than being offered a property selected by the local housing authority, there are likely to be far fewer refusals. A further, associated, rationale is to increase the numbers of offers accepted by applicants by encouraging applicants to provide as much information as possible on the type and location of accommodation that they would accept, in advance of being offered a property.[92]

1.47 Constructing an allocation scheme based on the assessment of applicants' needs, and – commonly – prioritisation of applicants according to greater or lesser need, while also offering customer 'choice', is a difficult exercise, both conceptually and practically. It is the subject of a discrete additional statutory Code of Guidance directed to English local housing authorities seeking to establish choice based letting schemes.[93]

1.48 The original English Code and the English CBL Code advise that the government believes that choice should be provided wherever possible. If, however, the local housing authority continues to operate a scheme based on

---

90 HA 1996, s 167(1A), s 193(3A) and s 195(3A).
91 HA 1996, s 167(2E).
92 See Chapter 5 of this book for a more detailed description of 'choice based lettings' schemes and, at **5.7–5.23**, analysis as to their effectiveness in practice.
93 *Allocation of Accommodation: Choice-based Lettings – Code of Guidance for Local Housing Authorities* (CLG, August 2008) [The English CBL Code]. See Appendix 1.

need, rather than choice, the applicant should be allowed an opportunity to express his or her 'preference' about the location and type of accommodation to be offered. In areas of high demand and restricted supply, applicants should be encouraged to widen their preferences as much as possible. The hope is that the more information that is obtained from the applicant, and the more flexible the applicant is prepared to be, the more likely the local housing authority is to be able to satisfy the applicant with one single offer of accommodation.[94]

1.49 The Welsh Code suggests a more flexible approach. Local housing authorities should determine their local housing need and consider how they can best comply with the statutory requirements as well as with the policy emphasis on 'choice' and 'preference'. The Code describes and compares a number of different models: choice based schemes, needs based schemes, and midway schemes. It describes practical methods of meeting housing need within choice based schemes, or, alternatively, maximising choice and preference under needs based approaches.[95]

1.50 An early attempt to implement choice based lettings in the London Borough of Lambeth was scrutinised by the Court of Appeal and found to be so deficient that it was struck down as unlawful. The scheme failed to give reasonable preference to those entitled to it by HA 1996, Part 6. Lambeth had asked applicants to assess their own needs and this, too, was held to be unlawful.[96]

1.51 From April 2001, 27 local housing authorities participated in a pilot scheme to implement choice based lettings. The Office of the Deputy Prime Minister (ODPM)[97] funded De Montfort University to run a website (www.choicemoves.org.uk) which provides some analysis of the pilot project and an account of the implementation of choice based letting schemes in England and Wales.[98]

1.52 In October 2006 the government published *Monitoring the Longer Term Impact of Choice-based Lettings*.[99] The report presented findings from two research studies commissioned by the ODPM in 2004 and focuses on the longer-term impact of choice based lettings. It found that:[100]

- typically, CBL generates improved tenancy sustainment and this is testament to the effectiveness of the system in better matching people to properties and improving service user satisfaction with letting outcomes;

---

[94] English CBL Code, passim and English 2009 Code, paras 24–25.
[95] Welsh Code, paras 4.24–4.44.
[96] *R (A) v Lambeth London Borough Council, R (Lindsay) v Lambeth London Borough Council* [2002] EWCA Civ 1084, (2002) 34 HLR 57, CA.
[97] The government department responsible for housing and homelessness in England at the time. The relevant department is now Communities and Local Government: see www.communities. gov.uk.
[98] See **5.8–5.13** for an analysis of the pilot scheme.
[99] Available at http://www.communities.gov.uk/publications/housing/monitoringlonger.
[100] At para 9.62.

- similarly, the evidence of consumer responsiveness to variations in demand illustrates comprehension of CBL mechanisms on the part of housing applicants; and

- whilst most CBL landlords see their systems as 'simplified and transparent' by comparison with previous approaches, many applicants reportedly remain baffled on how competing bidders are ranked by priority.

1.53 The government's policy is that all local housing authorities in England and Wales should be implementing choice based lettings by 2010.[101] The new English CBL Code published in the summer of 2008 was intended, at least in part, to drive forward that policy among local housing authorities in England. The government has commissioned research to evaluate the success of the further waves of CBL schemes established in England beyond those included in the initial pilots.

1.54 In Wales, the Assembly Government commissioned a project to provide a review of letting systems currently in use by social housing landlords in Wales, which were either choice based or in which choice was an important component part. Its report found that, by the end of 2006/07, choice based lettings had become an increasingly significant feature of the social housing sector in Wales. Eleven local housing authorities and housing associations were letting the whole of their stock through CBL schemes, and an increasing number of housing associations had become partners in local housing authority-led CBL schemes. The report concluded that much work needed to be done and that, in particular, the provision of feedback to applicants was 'the area which requires the greatest improvement in CBL schemes'.[102]

How are the modern allocation schemes operating?

1.55 There has been no recent major national research programme to investigate or monitor the lawfulness or effectiveness of the scores of housing allocation schemes adopted and operated by the hundreds of local housing authorities across England. In 2007/08 the central government department responsible for housing allocation policy, Communities and Local Government, commissioned a small scale review by independent researchers. Its findings presented only a snapshot of practice across a relatively modest selection of housing authorities.[103]

---

[101] *Sustainable Communities: Homes for All*, paras 5.18–5.21 (ODPM, January 2005): extracts reproduced at **5.22** and available at http://www.communities.gov.uk/archived/publications/corporate/homesforall.

[102] *A Review of Welsh Social Landlords' Approaches to Increasing Choice in Letting Accommodation* (Welsh Assembly Government), at http://cymru.gov.uk/dsjlg/research/review ofsociallandlords/reviewofsociallandlordse.doc.

[103] *Exploring local authority policy and practice on housing allocations* (CLG, July 2009).

1.56 By contrast, in Wales, the much smaller number of local housing authorities, operating under essentially the same legal framework as those in England, has been subject to significant scrutiny and that scrutiny has thrown up issues equally relevant to social housing allocation by local housing authorities in England. For example, in February 2006, the Public Services Ombudsman for Wales published *Housing Allocation and Homelessness: A Special Report by the Local Government Ombudsman for Wales* containing an examination of how the modern legal structure for social housing allocation was operating in Wales.[104] The report found:

- that a significant number of Welsh local housing authorities had yet to adopt allocation policies that fully complied with the law and took account of the statutory guidance;

- in particular, that the changes introduced by the Homelessness Act 2002 had still not been sufficiently introduced, some 3 years after those changes had come into force;

- that, as a result, the lawfulness of each allocation decision since January 2003 was potentially questionable;

- that some local housing authorities continued to operate unlawful policies of blanket exclusions;[105] and

- that some local housing authorities were failing to accord preference to the categories of applicants entitled to a reasonable preference.[106]

1.57 Local housing authorities in Wales were asked to take expert legal advice and to review their allocation schemes as a matter of urgency. Some Welsh local housing authorities had already started that process as a result of the Public Services Ombudsman's investigations of individual complaints.

1.58 In response to the Ombudsman's Special Report, and to further letters of complaint being received by the Assembly Government and by Shelter, officials of the Welsh Assembly Government carried out a joint review with Shelter Cymru of the 22 local housing authority allocation schemes in Wales. That review was published in March 2007.[107] It found that all the allocation schemes scrutinised required some level of further review. Issues identified ranged from failure to adopt schemes meeting statutory requirements to the need to clarify or elaborate those schemes which did satisfy the legal basics. The report contained a series of recommendations for both the Assembly Government and for local housing authorities. The latter included a recommendation that every

---

[104] http://www.ombudsman-wales.org.uk/en/publications/?pID=76.

[105] See **1.39** and Chapter 3 of this book.

[106] See **1.40–1.42** and **4.20–4.90**.

[107] *Review of Local Authority Allocation Schemes (2006): report by Welsh Assembly Government and Shelter Cymru* (March 2007), http://www.sheltercymru.org.uk/shelter/uploads/pdf/Review_of_LA_Allocation_Schemes.pdf.

Welsh local housing authority 'undertake a fundamental review of their allocation schemes to ensure they are compliant with the law, Code of Guidance and good practice and review them annually thereafter'.

1.59 The response of the Welsh Assembly Government was to commit itself to 'undertaking a full review of allocation schemes every three years and to issue strengthened guidance to local housing authorities and housing associations on allocations' and to ensuring that the 'revised guidance addresses the issues raised by the Ombudsman'.[108] Sadly, the revised guidance had not materialised by the end of 2009, even as a consultation draft. That may be explained in part by the fact that in Wales the Code of Guidance covers both allocation *and* homelessness, and the revision of the Code has accordingly had to await the adoption of the new Welsh *Ten Year Homelessness Plan* which was the subject of a consultation exercise late in 2008 and was only finally adopted in July 2009.[109] However, in the consultation draft of its new National Housing Strategy for Wales, the Welsh Assembly Government states that it 'will review the impact of allocation policies'.[110] While the delay may therefore have a ready explanation, the need to address problems with allocation schemes operated by Welsh local housing authorities remains acute. In May 2008 the Chartered Institute for Housing in Wales reported that, at least in respect of the operation of provisions excluding applicants from social housing, 'not all the exclusion policies and procedures examined during the project were legal'.[111]

1.60 In England, in contrast, the focus of government-commissioned research has been on the operation of choice based letting schemes, where those have been adopted by local housing authorities, rather than upon the general operation of allocation schemes nationally.[112] It has fallen to advice agencies and others to identify general trends in allocation schemes. For example, in April 2006 Shelter found widespread poor practice in relation to access to social housing – and the operation of unfair exclusions from allocation schemes – in the North-East of England. Its report *Exclusions in Tyne and Wear: an investigation by Shelter's NEHAC into why applicants are excluded from social rented housing*[113] researched decisions that an applicant was not eligible to join an allocation scheme on the grounds of his or her 'unacceptable behaviour'.[114] It found that:

---

108 Leighton Andrews AM (National Assembly for Wales, Deputy Minister for Housing) answering WAQ50133 on 4 July 2007 in the Welsh Assembly.

109 *Ten Year Homelessness Plan for Wales* (Welsh Assembly Government, July 2009), at http:// wales.gov.uk/topics/housingandcommunity/housing/publications/homelessnessplan/?lang=en.

110 *Sustainable Homes: A National Housing Strategy for Wales, Consultation Draft* (January 2009), http://wales.gov.uk/docs/desh/consultation/090128housingstrategyen.pdf.

111 *Am I on the list? Exclusion from and reinclusion on social housing waiting lists* (CIH Cymru, May 2008).

112 The most recently published research on allocation schemes in England is *Exploring local authority policy and practice on housing allocations* (CLG, July 2009). For other research specifically directed to choice based letting see **1.51–1.54**.

113 Shelter, April 2006, http://england.shelter.org.uk/professional_resources/policy_library/policy_library_folder/exclusions_in_tyne_and_wear.

114 See **3.143–3.189** for the statutory test.

- blanket exclusions were continuing;

- many people were being excluded for low levels of rent arrears (which would not have resulted in an outright possession order);

- homeless families who were unlawfully excluded could be trapped in temporary accommodation, with detrimental effects particularly for any children in the household;

- the exclusions go against the government's target of reducing the use of temporary accommodation for the homeless by one half by the year 2010;

- young people were particularly subject to unfair exclusions;

- people with criminal records were unfairly excluded;

- in the vast majority of cases, the behaviour for which applicants were excluded had occurred at least a year earlier and no attempt was being made to apply the second limb of the behaviour test for eligibility;

- not all applicants who were excluded were given written notification of that decision; and

- where applicants were assisted by independent advisers on appeals, their appeals were successful.

1.61 The report recommended that:

- allocation schemes should provide realistic routes back into social rented housing;

- where applicants are excluded, they should be informed of the reasons for the decision and also what action they are expected to take so as to lift the exclusion in the future;

- anyone who is positively engaging with a recognised agency that provides support (in order to address the reasons for the behaviour that might lead to an exclusion decision) and which will continue to provide support if the applicant is housed should be allowed onto an allocation scheme;

- all housing staff involved in allocation decisions should be fully trained in the behaviour test;

- local housing authorities and RSLs should adopt a code of good practice involving assistance in applying for an allocation, referrals to independent advice, clear information about the test, written decisions and information about appeals;

- there should be regular audits to ensure that blanket exclusions are not being applied in practice; and

- a decision to exclude an applicant should be made by more than one officer, on undisputed and not hearsay evidence, with the applicant being given an opportunity to explain or provide evidence, and applying good practice 'in the round'.

1.62 On a more limited scale, an independent survey was conducted in 2004/05 of the allocation schemes operated by 12 local housing authorities in the London area.[115] Its conclusions were that:

- local housing authorities were not disclosing all aspects of their allocation procedures in their published allocation schemes as required by HA 1996, Part 6;[116]

- requests for copies of allocation schemes were not being met promptly by many housing authorities and in some cases copies of allocation schemes were only available under threat of litigation;

- there was an urgent need for the CLG to provide further guidance to ensure that local housing authorities comply with their statutory duties; and

- to ensure that social housing is allocated in a fair and transparent manner, targets must be set and outcomes monitored and published.[117]

1.63 These various reports demonstrate that, despite the wholesale restructuring of housing allocation law by the Homelessness Act 2002, too many local housing authorities have taken too long to catch up with the modern law of housing allocation and to devise and implement wholly lawful housing allocation schemes. In England, in particular, it has been left to inspectors, the courts and the Ombudsmen to turn up instances of poor or unlawful practices which may, in fact, be widespread. For example, an Audit Commission inspection of a major English city council's allocation arrangements found:

> 'the allocation policy and practice … is poor and lacks clarity, clear policies and procedures and there is no effective mechanism of control or audit to ensure the allocation of homes is done fairly and transparently.'[118]

---

[115] Robert Latham 'Allocating accommodation: reconciling choice and need', published in two parts at (2005) March *Legal Action*, p 16 and (2005) May *Legal Action*, p 15.

[116] HA 1996, s 167(1).

[117] R Latham 'Allocating accommodation: reconciling choice and need', (2005) May *Legal Action*, pp 18–19.

[118] *Nottingham City Homes – Nottingham City Council* (Audit Commission, March 2006).

1.64 Indeed, as recently as March 2009 the Local Government Ombudsman in England identified one local housing authority as not having operated a lawful allocation scheme since September 2002.[119]

THE FUTURE FOR SOCIAL HOUSING ALLOCATION

1.65 In England, the expectation is that during 2010 every local housing authority will reconsider the terms of its housing allocation scheme. In the English 2009 Code the Secretary of State expressly encourages all housing authorities to 'review their existing policies as soon as possible and to revise them, where appropriate' in the light of the guidance given in that Code.[120] Although some previous Ministers of Housing had suggested that the present Government might use its regulation-making powers to add to the categories of those entitled to a reasonable preference in housing allocation (for example, to expressly mention those under-occupying social housing), the current Minister indicated as recently as July 2009 that no further change to the categories was proposed.[121] The need to review allocation schemes in 2010 is not simply driven by the English 2009 Code but also by imminent changes in social housing regulation in England.

1.66 In April 2010, the Tenant Services Authority ('TSA') will start to exercise its new statutory functions. Established by the Housing and Regeneration Act 2008 (in which it is officially described as 'the Office for Tenants and Social Landlords'),[122] the TSA has power to set standards to be followed by the providers of social housing.[123] Those standards will require registered providers of social housing to comply with specified rules about criteria for allocating housing accommodation.[124] The Housing and Regeneration Act 2008 gives the TSA considerable powers of inspection and enforcement to ensure that the standards are complied with.[125] These new arrangements will take effect for both registered social landlords and local housing authorities from 1 April 2010. Statutory consultation on the content of the new standards was conducted from November 2009 until February 2010. A flavour of the likely final content of the standard for housing allocation is given by the draft published for statutory consultation in November 2009.[126] The draft suggested that the final housing allocation standard (part of a broader Tenancy standard) might be framed along the following lines:

---

[119] *Complaint against Medway Council* (08/008/647, 23 March 2009), Local Government Ombudsman, (2009) May *Legal Action*, p 30.

[120] English 2009 Code, para 8.

[121] Rt Hon John Healey MP, Minister for Housing and Planning, letter to local housing authorities in England, 31 July 2009.

[122] Housing and Regeneration Act 2008, s 81(1).

[123] HRA 2008, s 193(1).

[124] HRA 2008, s 193(2)(a).

[125] HRA 2008, ss 192–269.

[126] *A new regulatory framework for social housing in England: A statutory consultation* (TSA, November 2009), chapter 8, available at http://www.tenantservicesauthority.org/server/show/ConWebDoc.19730.

'The Tenancy standard

The required outcomes

Allocations

Registered providers must let their homes in a fair, transparent and efficient way. They must take into account the housing needs and aspirations of tenants and potential tenants. They should demonstrate how their allocations processes:

- make the best use of available housing
- contribute to local authorities' strategic housing function and sustainable communities

There should be clear decision making and appeals processes.

Specific requirements

1. Allocations

1.1   Registered providers will co-operate with local authorities' strategic housing function, and their duties to meet identified local housing needs. This includes assistance with local authorities' homelessness duties, and through meeting obligations in nominations agreements. Where in exceptional circumstances registered providers choose not to participate in choice-based lettings schemes in areas where they own homes, they justify their reasons for doing so publicly.

1.2   Registered providers will develop and deliver services to address under occupation and overcrowding in their homes, within the resources available to them. These services will meet the needs of their tenants, and will offer choices to them.

1.3   Registered providers will provide tenants wishing to move with access to clear and relevant advice about their housing options. They will participate in mobility schemes and mutual exchange schemes where these are available.

1.4   Registered providers will publish their allocations policies and outcomes, how this has made best use of available housing and contributed to sustainable communities. The published policies should include (where it applies) their participation in:

- common housing registers
- common allocations policies
- local lettings policies

Registered providers will clearly set out, and be able to give reasons for, the criteria they use for excluding actual and potential tenants from consideration for allocations, mobility or mutual exchange schemes.

1.5   Registered providers will develop and deliver allocations processes in a way which supports their effective use by the full range of actual and potential tenants, including those with support needs, those who do not speak English as a first language and others who have difficulties with written English.

1.6   Registered providers will work to make sure that the specific needs and aspirations of tenants and potential tenants with diverse needs are reflected in the choices available to them. This applies particularly to the development of local lettings policies.

1.7   Registered providers must minimise the time that properties are empty between each letting. When doing this, they must take into account the circumstances of the tenants who have been offered the properties.

1.8   Registered providers must record all lettings and sales in the Continuous Recording of Lettings system.'

The final version of the standard will be distributed by the TSA in March 2010 and will come into statutory effect on 1 April 2010.

1.67   In Wales, the Assembly Government is likely to embark in 2010 on a consultation exercise concerning revision of the Welsh Code, following completion of its consultation on a new National Housing Strategy.[127] In January 2010, the National Assembly for Wales began deliberations upon a draft Legislative Competence Order that, if adopted, would not only enable establishment of a new social housing regulator for Wales along the lines of the TSA in England but would also empower the Government and the Assembly in Wales to make new law on social housing allocation.[128]

---

[127] See **1.59**.
[128] The National Assembly for Wales (Legislative Competence) (Housing and Local Government) Order 2010, available at: http://www.assemblywales.org/bus-home/bus-legislation/bus-leg-legislative-competence-orders/bus-legislation-lco-2009-hlg-2.htm.

Chapter 2

INFORMATION, APPLICATIONS AND DECISION-MAKING IN RESPECT OF SOCIAL HOUSING ALLOCATION

'If applicants are to view the system as fair, they need to know how their application will be treated under the allocation scheme, what their rights and expectations are under the scheme, and they need reassurance that the scheme is being complied with and applied consistently across all applicants.'[1]

INTRODUCTION

2.1 Anyone considering applying for an allocation of social housing will want to understand, before applying, how the local scheme works and how his or her application is likely to be treated. An individual who then submits an application will want to know what is happening to his or her application, and may need advice. He or she will want an early indication, and a realistic one, about the prospects of being allocated a suitable home. When decisions are made on applications, applicants will want to have prompt notification and an explanation for any adverse findings. In short, access to straightforward information is crucial to applicants having confidence in the local housing allocation process.

2.2 Consequently, in the Housing Act 1996 ('HA 1996'), Part 6 ('Allocation of Housing Accommodation') there are specific obligations on local housing authorities to inform members of the public about the content of their allocation schemes, and to provide applicants with advice and information about their individual applications. In addition, local housing authorities are subject to the provisions of the Data Protection Act 1998 and the Freedom of Information Act 2000, which may respectively enable applicants to access records relating to their own applications and information about specific aspects of housing allocation locally.

2.3 HA 1996, Part 6 also makes reasonably detailed provision about the receipt and processing of applications, and the notification of decisions. Some applicants will, inevitably, be dissatisfied with decisions affecting their applications. In some, but not all, of those cases, HA 1996, Part 6 gives applicants the right to request a review of the decision. Applicants dissatisfied with the result of that review could bring judicial review proceedings to challenge the decision or the process by which it was reached. There is no provision within HA 1996, Part 6 for an appeal to the county court.

2.4 For those cases when reviews are not specifically provided for in HA 1996, Part 6, the local housing authority may provide an extra-statutory review. In any event, legal challenge to an initial decision, a statutory review decision, or an extra-statutory review decision can only be by way of judicial review.

2.5 Additionally, any complaint about the handling of an individual application can be made via the local housing authority's internal complaints procedure, or be raised with its monitoring officer or, ultimately, pursued with

---

[1]   *Fair and flexible: statutory guidance on social housing allocations for local authorities in England* (December 2009) ['English 2009 Code'], para 49. Reproduced at Appendix 1.

the Local Government Ombudsman. An applicant who is or has become a tenant of social housing could also complain to the Tenant Services Authority ('TSA') and seek redress if it appears that the local housing authority or another registered provider of social housing has not complied with the TSA's published standard for allocation of accommodation.[2]

2.6 This chapter reviews, in sequence, the statutory duties upon local housing authorities to inform applicants, to receive and process applications, and to notify decisions on those applications.

INFORMATION
General information and advice about local social housing allocation

2.7 HA 1996, Part 6 requires local housing authorities to ensure that advice and information about the right to apply for accommodation is available free of charge to everyone in their districts.[3] Although HA 1996, Part 6 elsewhere specifically requires the publication of a free summary of the allocation scheme, this general duty to make information and advice available goes much wider than that.

2.8 The information provided by local housing authorities should include information as to procedures and also stock availability. The English CBL Code advises that applicants should be informed about:

- the procedures for applying to join the local allocation scheme;

- how applicants are prioritised under the scheme;

- how successful applicants are selected;

- the rationale for advertising criteria, in any choice based letting scheme;

- review procedures; and

- whether any registered social landlord ('RSL') to which the local housing authority can nominate operates specific exclusion policies and, if so, what these are.[4]

Local housing authorities are also advised to provide general information about the profile of their stock, including the type, size and location of the stock, whether it is accessible or could be adapted, whether there is access to a

---

2   Housing and Regeneration Act 2008, s 238(2)(a); and see **1.65–1.66**.
3   HA 1996, s 166(1)(a).
4   *Allocation of Accommodation: Choice-based Lettings Code of Guidance for Local Authorities* (August 2008) ['English CBL Code'], para 5.6. Reproduced in Appendix 1.

shared or private garden, and how old it is. Where stock is in short supply, an indication of how frequently it is likely to become available would also be helpful.[5]

2.9   Care must be taken to ensure that this advice and information is accessible to all. Information should be easy to understand and should be available in translation, where relevant, and in alternative formats (Braille, large print, and audiotapes, etc).[6] Arrangements for access to information and advice will need to take account of the special needs of specific groups of prospective applicants, e g prisoners or travellers.[7] Local housing authorities are encouraged to make information available using a variety of media, including printed hard copy form, on a website or via the telephone.[8] The CRE Code of Practice on Racial Equality in Housing[9] includes this pertinent example of the care that needs to be taken in preparing information:

> 'A local council (or housing association) fails to make sure that information about its lettings services reaches people from all racial groups; for example, by not advertising the service in outlets which it knows are preferred by ethnic minority residents. This could amount to indirect discrimination' (Example 35).

2.10   Where the local housing authority is operating a choice based letting scheme, it is strongly encouraged to make available information in the form of 'feedback' on how properties have actually been allocated.[10] Indeed, whatever type of allocation scheme is being operated, local housing authorities can help actual or prospective applicants by:

> 'making available general information about the profile of their stock (amount, type, size, location and accessibility); together with information about how often property of that type/size/location becomes available and estimated waiting times. Information should be kept up-to-date and published on a regular basis. It should be widely available as it may be of interest to people who may be considering applying for social housing as well as those who are already on the waiting list.'[11]

2.11   Although the statutory focus is on information about the right to apply for social housing allocation, statutory guidance suggests that local housing authorities should take the opportunity also to furnish applicants with a range of information about other housing options.[12] This should include advice and assistance about:

---

5   English CBL Code, para 5.11.
6   English CBL Code, para 5.6.
7   English CBL Code, para 5.7.
8   English CBL Code, para 5.8.
9   See **4.130**.
10   English CBL Code, paras 5.14–5.18.
11   English 2009 Code, para 50. This new guidance followed publication of *Exploring local authority policy and practice on housing allocations* (Communities & Local Government [CLG], July 2009) which found that few local housing authorities routinely offer all applicants for allocations the same sort of housing options interview convened for those who are homeless.
12   English CBL Code, para 5.12.

- renting in the private sector;

- low cost home ownership options;

- mobility schemes which enable applicants to move out of the district;

- mutual exchange options for existing social tenants;

- home improvement schemes or adaptations services which enable applicants to remain in their existing accommodation; and

- supported/sheltered housing for older and disabled people.[13]

Prospective applicants may also have the right to obtain a broader range of information about social housing allocation under the Data Protection Act 1998 and the Freedom of Information Act 2000.[14]

2.12 For some enquirers, the provision of information will suffice. But the statutory duty under HA 1996, s 166 also provides that *advice* must be available free of charge. This can be particularly important where the local housing authority has adopted a choice based letting scheme that requires applicants to be pro-active in securing an allocation. The guidance suggests that suitable advice could be provided by the local housing authority, another social landlord, or the voluntary sector, and that it is likely to be most effective if the adviser 'has appropriate housing related experience and is properly trained to sensitively meet the needs of a diverse client group.'[15]

Information about a particular local allocation scheme

2.13 Each local housing authority is required by HA 1996, Part 6 to publish a summary of its allocation scheme and to make a copy of that summary available free of charge to 'any member of the public who asks for one'.[16] The request for a copy can come from 'any member of the public'. There is no requirement that the person making the request should also be an applicant under the local housing authority's allocation scheme, or even a prospective applicant. Indeed, there is no requirement that the person should have any connection with that particular local housing authority's district. Any member of the public, anywhere in the country, is entitled to receive a free summary of any local housing authority's allocation scheme on request. Obviously, it is this provision that allows advisers to collect summaries of any allocation schemes that might be useful to them in advising members of the public.

2.14 There is no requirement to publish the whole of the allocation scheme, although many local housing authorities do put their full scheme on their

---

13 English 2009 Code, para 25.
14 See **2.27–2.28**.
15 English CBL Code, para 5.13.
16 HA 1996, s 168(1).

websites.[17] However, each local housing authority must 'make the scheme available for inspection at their principal office'.[18] The principal office is usually the town hall, or the central address for the housing department. Members of the public do not, however, need to attend the principal office in person in order to see the full scheme. If they ask for a copy (in person, by post, by phone, or by email) and pay any required fee (which can only be a reasonable amount), the local housing authority 'shall provide' a copy of the full scheme.[19] The statutory guidance encourages local housing authorities to go beyond the statutory minimum requirements by publishing their allocation schemes on websites and by printing a stock of hard copies.[20] Again, advisers may consider purchasing copies of the allocation schemes operated by several local housing authorities, or may simply download them from websites.

2.15 Sadly, not all local housing authorities have readily embraced the statutory requirement to make the full scheme available for purchase on demand. The full scheme, which must cover 'all aspects of the allocation process',[21] will often be a substantial document, and there is not infrequently a degree of reticence in supplying copies. One limited exercise in requesting copy schemes from 12 local housing authorities in London produced only four responses within 14 days, five further responses within 28 days, and the remaining three only after complaints to the monitoring officer for each local housing authority and service of a pre-action protocol letter threatening judicial review proceedings.[22] A good deal of time and legal expense can be wasted when a failure to respond promptly to a request for a copy of the scheme leads to a claim for a mandatory order in judicial review proceedings.[23] Such claims never come to trial, for obvious reasons, but leave local housing authorities with substantial legal costs easily exceeding the expense of supplying a copy of the scheme promptly in response to the initial request.

2.16 The scheme adopted by the local housing authority must not only set out how the authority will prioritise applicants but additionally the *procedure* that it follows in allocating housing.[24] Where the local housing authority has adopted a choice based letting arrangement, the formal allocation scheme will need to set out the procedures and priorities as they apply not only to the initial

---

17 Local housing authority web sites are usually at the government's domain name: thus, a typical address would be www.anytown.gov.uk. In preparing the report *Exploring local authority policy and practice on housing allocations* (CLG, July 2009) researchers found that only 71% of local housing authorities surveyed had published the full scheme on their websites. Even among those operating CBL schemes, 15% had not done so (at para 4.2).

18 HA 1996, s 168(2).

19 HA 1996, s 168(2).

20 English CBL Code, para 5.8.

21 HA 1996, s 167(1).

22 Robert Latham 'Allocating accommodation: reconciling choice and need' (2005) March *Legal Action*, p 16 and (2005) May *Legal Action*, p 15.

23 As in *R (Onuegbu) v Hackney London Borough Council* [2005] EWHC 1277 (Admin), (2005) August *Legal Action*, p 17, Admin Ct.

24 HA 1996 s 167(1).

consideration of an applicant's application but also to the treatment of any bid made by the applicant for specific accommodation.[25]

2.17 Experience would suggest that there has often been a failure to grasp the significance of the fact that for these purposes 'procedure' includes 'all aspects of the allocation process, including the persons or descriptions of persons by whom decisions are to be taken'.[26] Too many allocation schemes simply set out broad policy statements, unlawfully leaving the mechanics to be detailed in unpublished procedure manuals or staff training materials. In short, the statutory requirement is that the published scheme deals with both 'how' and 'why' allocations are made.

2.18 The courts have not taken an altogether consistent line as to how much detail, on the prioritisation of applications or the procedures to be followed in processing them, is required in a local allocation scheme. The range of approaches taken by the courts is illustrated by the following examples:

- A scheme which did 'not explain what criteria apply or indicate that they will be applied' was held to be unlawful in that respect.[27]

- An allocation scheme provided for nominations by social services but did not explain what sort of communication from what part of social services would qualify as such a nomination. That was insufficient.[28]

- A scheme enabled an applicant to obtain substantially increased points if he was imminently required to give up accommodation leased from the private sector. It wrongly failed to indicate precisely at what stage the extra points would accrue.[29]

- A local housing authority had adopted targets for achieving allocations to particular classes of applicant. The targets were not part of the procedure of the scheme, so the scheme did not need to be amended each time they were changed.[30]

- On a challenge to the sufficiency of detail in a local housing authority's scheme, in respect of allocation to particular priority groups, a judge said:

---

[25] English CBL Code, para 3.7.

[26] HA 1996 s 167(1).

[27] *R (Cali, Abdi and Hassan) v Waltham Forest London Borough Council* [2006] EWHC 302 Admin, [2007] HLR 1, Admin Ct.

[28] *R (Yazar) v Southwark London Borough Council* [2008] EWHC 515 (Admin), (2008) May *Legal Action*, p 46, Admin Ct.

[29] *R (Lin) v Barnet London Borough Council* [2007] EWCA Civ 132, [2007] HLR 30, CA.

[30] *R (A) v Lambeth London Borough Council* [2002] EWCA Civ 2084, [2002] HLR 57, CA

'The scheme must set out all aspects of the allocation process but it is not
necessary to do more than ... explain what criteria apply to each group and
to indicate that an officer will allocate in accordance with those criteria
which may be general.'[31]

- An allocation scheme which was already 'very long and detailed' did not
  set out the precise criteria under which applicants in medical need were to
  be admitted to a particular priority category. That level of detail did not
  need to be added to the scheme.[32]

- A local housing authority operated a policy that, at shortlisting stage,
  bidders from the same bands would have the presence (or otherwise) of a
  local connection taken into account. The policy was not initially
  mentioned in the published allocation scheme but was added on a later
  revision. The court held that the matter was one of minor detail the
  omission of which was not unlawful.[33]

Information about applications

2.19   When anyone applies for an allocation of social housing, he or she must
be informed by the local housing authority of his or her relevant statutory
rights.[34] Those rights are:

- the right to request such general information as will enable the applicant
  to assess how his or her application is likely to be treated under the
  scheme, including whether he or she is likely to fall within any of the
  groups entitled to a reasonable preference;[35]

- the right to request such general information as will enable him or her to
  assess whether accommodation appropriate to his or her needs is likely to
  be made available and, if so, how long it is likely to be before an offer is
  made;[36]

- the right to be notified in writing of any decision that he or she is *not* to be
  given any reasonable preference that he or she would ordinarily have been
  entitled to receive, and of the reasons for that decision;[37]

---

[31]   *R (Lynch) v Lambeth London Borough Council* [2006] EWHC 2737 (Admin), [2007] HLR 15
       at [51].
[32]   *R (Ahmad) v Newham London Borough Council* [2008] EWCA Civ 140, (2008) April *Legal
       Action*, p 34, CA.
[33]   *R(Van Boolen) v Barking & Dagenham London Borough Council* [2009] EWHC 2196 (Admin),
       (2009) September *Legal Action*, p 34, Admin Ct.
[34]   HA 1996, s 166(2).
[35]   HA 1996, s 167(4A)(a)(i).
[36]   HA 1996, s 167(4A)(a)(ii).
[37]   HA 1996, s 167(4A)(b).

- the right to ask the local housing authority to inform him or her of any decision about the facts of his or her case which has been, or is likely to be, taken into account when considering whether to allocate accommodation;[38]

- the right to request a review of any decision that he or she is *not* to be given reasonable preference, any decision as to the facts of his or her case, or any decision that he or she is *not* eligible for an allocation;[39] and

- the right to be informed of a review decision and the grounds for that review decision.[40]

2.20 Such information must be given to every applicant and, plainly, the terms of the statutory provision indicate a policy intention that the information is provided when the application is first received, in a written acknowledgement of, or response to, the application or as accompanying information to the acknowledgement or response.

2.21 As is clear from the first two items in the list above, the applicant may request 'general information' which will enable him or her to assess how the application is likely to be treated, whether he or she will be entitled to any preference, whether he or she is likely to receive accommodation and, if so, after what period. There is no time limit specified within which this information must be requested. It follows, therefore, that the applicant may request this information *at any time*, once he or she has made the application. Of all the available information, it is this – a realistic appraisal of the prospects of obtaining a suitable local allocation – that the applicant is most likely to want. Many advisers will have drawn up pro-forma requests for this information, to enclose when writing to the local housing authority about individual applications.

2.22 The main statutory Codes of Guidance on social housing allocation[41] do not contain much guidance on what information the applicant could expect to receive, having made the request. The English Code recommends that local housing authorities maintain lists of properties earmarked for special groups (eg properties adapted for disabled use, etc), and that those lists should be made available to relevant applicants.[42] However, only a small number of applicants will benefit from that sort of information.[43] In late 2009, in reaction to evidence that the operation of allocation schemes was not well understood,

---

38   HA 1996, s 167(4A)(c).
39   HA 1996, s 167(4A)(d).
40   HA 1996, s 167(4A)(d).
41   *Allocation of Accommodation: Code of Guidance for local housing authorities for England* (Office of the Deputy Prime Minister, November 2002) [English Code], reproduced in Appendix 1; *Code of Guidance for local housing authorities on allocation of accommodation and homelessness for Wales* (National Assembly for Wales, April 2003) [Welsh Code], reproduced in the attached CD-ROM.
42   English Code, para 6.11.
43   See **4.111–4.119**.

the Secretary of State took the opportunity to put much greater emphasis in the statutory guidance on the broader publication and dissemination of information about how local schemes work and which groups of applicants actually receive offers of accommodation. In particular, a more expansive view has been adopted of the information that should be made available to actual or prospective applicants.[44]

2.23 For most applicants the information that they receive should include:

- whether or not they have been accepted as eligible for an allocation;

- the type of property they are likely to be allocated;

- the method that will be used in assessing their needs, whether by awarding points or by inclusion in a specific group or band, or otherwise;

- the number of other applicants with equal or greater priority; and

- an assessment of the likely time that they will have to wait to receive an offer (or to make a successful bid in a choice based letting scheme), by reference to average waiting time or to the number of lettings of similar properties in the previous year or quarter.

2.24 This sort of information allows the applicant an opportunity to assess his or her realistic (if sometimes depressing) chances of receiving an offer. It may usefully be accompanied by a copy of the free published summary of the particular local housing authority's allocation scheme.

Information about specific facts

2.25 The applicant has the right to ask the local housing authority to inform him or her of any decision about the facts of his or her case which are likely to be, or have been, taken into account in considering whether to allocate housing accommodation to him or her.[45] This right is similar in terms to a right previously contained in the Housing Act 1985.[46] The present right is greater in scope, but it is only triggered if the applicant requests the information; there is no automatic requirement on the local housing authority to give this information to the applicant as a matter of course. The right is to receive information 'about the facts of his [or her] case'.[47] The 'facts' relied upon by the local housing authority may have come from various sources: from the applicant, but also from housing officers, doctors, schools, other professionals or agencies, or even neighbours.

---

44 English 2009 Code, paras 47–52.
45 HA 1996, s 167(4A)(c).
46 Housing Act 1985, s 106(5).
47 HA 1996, s 167(4A)(c).

2.26 The right to factual information is not limited to the facts which the local housing authority takes into account in determining general issues about whether to allocate accommodation to the applicant, for example, as to his or her eligibility or priority. The wording is sufficiently broad to enable an applicant to ask whether he or she will be considered for, or why he or she was not considered for, a particular property.

2.27 Local housing authorities are subject to the information disclosure requirements of the Data Protection Act 1998, giving any individual the right of access to 'personal data' held either on computer or in manual files contained in a 'relevant filing system'.[48] The right of access means that an individual is entitled to know whether the local housing authority is processing any of his or her personal data and, if so, to be told what that data is, the source of the data, why it is being processed and to whom the data is being, or may be, disclosed. To constitute 'personal data', the information must have as its focus the individual involved, rather than the individual simply being mentioned peripherally in relation to some other individual or issue.[49] The data can be withheld where it identifies another person who has not consented to its disclosure, or it is reasonable to withhold it.[50] Local housing authorities may also refuse to supply the data which is 'unstructured' and where the costs of supplying the data are disproportionate.[51] Any request for data made under the Data Protection Act 1998 must be in writing and accompanied by a fee. The English CBL Code suggests that, if local housing authorities remain unclear about their obligations and responsibilities under the Data Protection Act 1998 in the context of social housing allocation, they may wish to contact the office of the Information Commissioner.[52]

2.28 Local housing authorities are also subject to the information disclosure provisions of the Freedom of Information Act 2000. An individual is entitled to make a written request to a public authority, which includes a local housing authority, and to be informed by the public authority whether it holds information of the description specified in the request and, if so, to have that information communicated to the individual, unless the information is exempt.[53] 'Personal data' is exempt from disclosure, as it is provided to the public authority in confidence.[54] The Freedom of Information Act 2000 can therefore be used to obtain the local housing authority's policies, procedures and other general information about social housing allocation, but not confidential information about a particular application. As the statutory guidance indicates, the duties imposed by the Freedom of Information Act 2000 are *additional* to the information-provision duties imposed by HA

---

48 Data Protection Act 1998, s 7.
49 *Durant v Financial Services Authority* [2003] EWCA Civ 1746, (2004) The Times, January 2, CA.
50 Data Protection Act 1998, s 7(4).
51 Data Protection Act 1998, s 9A.
52 English CBL Code, para 5.36. The Information Commissioner is at www.ico.gov.uk.
53 Freedom of Information Act 2000, s 1; exemptions are at ss 21–44 inclusive.
54 Freedom of Information Act 2000, s 40.

1996.[55] For example, an applicant may use a request under the Freedom of Information Act 2000 to obtain a list of local housing authority properties in a particular area or throughout a local housing authority's district in order to know what properties *might* become available.[56] However, where a local housing authority was asked to give the addresses of properties owned by an RSL operating in its area it was entitled to provide that information in a way that did not allow individual occupiers to be identified.[57]

Confidentiality

2.29 The applicant has the personal right to confidentiality, in that the fact that an application has been made cannot be divulged to any other member of the public without the applicant's consent.[58] Routinely, of course, local housing authorities request consent from applicants so that they can seek information from others, such as doctors or social workers, to help them determine the application. This consent should not, however, be treated as a general consent permitting the local housing authority to inform others, who do not need to know, that an application has been made. In practice, a considerable issue has arisen about the sharing of information between local housing authorities and RSLs about applicants nominated to RSLs for housing allocation. Although local housing authorities are encouraged to draw up information sharing protocols to cover such situations,[59] any sharing of personal information about an applicant can only be achieved by consent[60] and only in compliance with the Data Protection Act 1998.[61] To facilitate the drawing up of information-sharing protocols, the Housing Corporation published a national standard protocol on sharing information about applicants for re-housing.[62] That protocol has now been endorsed by the statutory guidance on housing allocation issued to local housing authorities in England.[63]

APPLICATIONS

Making an application

2.30 Local housing authorities are under no duty to seek out those most in need of any available social housing. Their statutory responsibilities are

---

[55] English CBL Code, para 1.10.
[56] See *Decision Notice concerning Mid Devon DC* [2006] 4 May, Information Commissioner Ref FS50082890, (2006) July *Legal Action*, p 26 and *Decision Notice concerning Braintree DC* (2006) 4 May, Information Commissioner Ref FS50066606, (2007) March *Legal Action*, p 13.
[57] *Turcotte v Information Commissioner* [2008] 12 June, Information Tribunal Case no EA/2007/0129.
[58] HA 1996, s 166(4).
[59] English CBL Code, para 5.35.
[60] Because even the simple fact that an applicant has applied to the local housing authority cannot be revealed except by consent: HA 1996, s 166(4).
[61] English CBL Code, para 5.36.
[62] *Access to Housing: Information sharing protocol* (Housing Corporation, November 2007) at http://www.housingcorp.gov.uk/server/show/ConWebDoc.12842.
[63] English 2009 Code, para 98.

confined to responding to, and considering, applications made to them by those seeking allocation of any available stock. So, for all those seeking social housing, everything turns on successfully making an application and then pursuing its proper consideration under the terms of the allocation scheme adopted by the local housing authority to which the application is made.

2.31 However, to ensure that the most vulnerable are not disadvantaged in gaining access to what might be available, each local housing authority must ensure that free advice and information is available in its district about the right to make an application for social housing.[64] Each local housing authority must also ensure that free assistance is provided to anyone who is likely to have difficulty in making an application.[65]

2.32 Many of those most in need of social housing will have sought the help of the local housing authority because they were homeless or facing the prospect of homelessness. An application for homelessness assistance (made under HA 1996, Part 7 'Homelessness') does not automatically count as an application for an allocation of social housing (under HA 1996, Part 6), and therefore local housing authorities receiving homelessness applications should attempt to ensure that applicants also complete any separate application forms required for their allocation schemes.[66]

2.33 Any person can apply to *any* local housing authority or, indeed, to *every* local housing authority for an allocation of social housing. Obviously, an applicant is more likely to be allocated accommodation quickly in areas where supply exceeds demand. But applications cannot be restricted or rejected because the local housing authority to which application has been made has little or no vacant housing currently available. The chosen local housing authority may not even own any property to rent, perhaps having disposed of its housing stock, but it must still receive and process applications under its allocation scheme and then 'allocate' by making nominations to local RSLs, or to other local housing authorities, under that scheme.[67]

2.34 There is no minimum age restriction on applications and nothing in the statutory scheme suggests that a person who is 'dependent' on another cannot apply.[68]

2.35 There is no national prescribed form for applications. The only requirement is that the application must be made in accordance with the

---

[64] HA 1996, s 166(1)(a); see **2.7–2.12**.

[65] HA 1996, s 166(1)(b); see **2.41–2.44**.

[66] Paragraph 6.7 of the *Homelessness Code of Guidance for Local Authorities*, July 2006, Department for Communities and Local Government, Department for Education and Skills, and Department of Health [the English Homelessness Code] suggests that an applicant for homelessness assistance is advised of the 'various housing options that might be available', including an application for an allocation of long-term social housing.

[67] HA 1996, s 159(2)(c).

[68] In contrast to a 'homelessness' application: see **9.28–9.31**. See also *R v Oldham Metropolitan Borough Council ex p Garlick* [1993] AC 509, HL.

procedural requirements (if any) set out in the allocation scheme of the local housing authority to which the application is directed.[69] If the scheme requires that a particular application form should be completed, the form should not be complicated to complete but might well be sufficiently detailed to enable a wide range of information to be obtained from the applicant (eg as to age, religion, sexual orientation, ethnicity, disability, gender and any support needs).[70] It will need to elicit the information necessary to enable the local housing authority not only to decide whether the applicant is eligible for an allocation but also whether the household includes any 'restricted persons'.[71]

2.36   Separate applications must be made to each local housing authority from which the applicant seeks consideration for an allocation. To make the process easier for applicants, local housing authorities and RSLs who are collaborating in regional or sub-regional allocation arrangements are encouraged to have a single application form that can be treated as constituting an application to them all.[72]

2.37   There are no statutory pre-conditions to the making of an application. The local housing authority cannot impose a charge for receiving an application or its consideration. The applicant need not already have an address in the local housing authority's district, nor satisfy any particular period of residence in the district. Even if the local housing authority believes that the applicant is highly likely to be found to be ineligible for an allocation, or is likely to be given a very low priority under the local scheme, it must still accept an application from anyone, whether that person is physically in its district or elsewhere, if the application is made in accordance with the relevant procedural requirements (if any) of the local housing authority's scheme.[73]

2.38   Again, so as to ensure that the most vulnerable are not excluded, local housing authorities are advised to ensure that applicants who have no fixed address can make applications.[74]

2.39   It is a criminal offence, when making an application, or when giving the local housing authority any further information, knowingly or recklessly to make a statement which is false in a material particular or knowingly to withhold information which the local housing authority reasonably requires the applicant to give.[75] A suitable warning to this effect should be included with the information that the applicant receives on, or prior to, making an application.

---

69   HA 1996, s 166(3).
70   English CBL Code, paras 5.19–5.21.
71   See **4.109–4.110**.
72   English CBL Code, paras 7.13–7.14.
73   HA 1996, s 166(3). See also Welsh Code, paras 3.27–3.29.
74   English Code, para 5.51, Welsh Code, para 3.30.
75   HA 1996, s 171.

2.40 Once the application has been made in a form which meets the procedural requirements of the local allocation scheme, the local housing authority is required to consider it.[76]

Assistance in making an application

2.41 As already explained,[77] local housing authorities are required to ensure that free *advice* and *information* about the right to make an application for an allocation of social housing is available to people in their districts.[78] But they are also required to ensure that free *assistance* is provided to anyone in their districts who is likely to have difficulty in making an application.[79] Local housing authorities may provide this assistance directly through their own staff (eg in Housing Advice Centres), or may contract the services out to independent advice agencies or other providers.[80]

2.42 The Codes recommend that the written advice and information available to those needing assistance should be available in a range of formats and languages, as appropriate to the needs of the area.[81] Those formats should presumably include audio tapes, large print versions or Braille copies, as well as copies in the different languages commonly used in the district.[82] Those likely to need specialist information will obviously also be more likely to need specialist support in making their application for an allocation. The local housing authority will need to have addressed these issues in its equality impact assessments (under the race relations and disability discrimination legislation) made in relation to the adoption of (or changes to) the allocation scheme.[83]

2.43 Particular issues arise where a local housing authority operates a choice based letting scheme requiring applicants to bid for advertised properties. The English CBL Code treats each 'bid' made in such a scheme as an application and, accordingly, advises that assistance must be made available to those who may need help to bid regularly. It suggests that the housebound, prisoners, and gypsies (and other travellers) may need special help to make applications, as they will not necessarily have access to the internet or be able to attend at pick-up points to collect free sheets describing available properties.[84] Local housing authorities are also specifically invited to consider how to meet the needs of applicants who are deaf, blind or partially sighted, who have learning disabilities or who cannot read English.[85] Obviously, any reasonable adjustment sought by an applicant on account of his or her disability should be made. For example, an applicant who could not read printed material could

---

[76] HA 1996, s 166(3).
[77] See **2.7–2.12**.
[78] HA 1996, s 166(1)(a).
[79] HA 1996, s 166(1)(b).
[80] See Chapter 21.
[81] English 2009 Code, para 47; Welsh Code, para 4.98.
[82] English CBL Code, para 5.6; Welsh Code, para 4.98.
[83] English CBL Code, paras 1.6–1.13; English 2009 Code, para 21; and see **4.129–4.132**.
[84] English CBL Code, para 5.7.
[85] English CBL Code, para 5.9.

require that the local housing authority advise him or her by telephone of suitable properties available. In a case in which the re-housing of a housebound disabled tenant depended on her husband and full-time carer checking every week what properties had been advertised under a local housing authority's scheme, the Local Government Ombudsman said that 'it was insensitive to expect someone in [his] position to devote time and energy to bidding for properties'.[86]

2.44 In *Housing and the Disability Equality Duty: A guide to the Disability Equality Duty and Disability Discrimination Act 2005 for the social housing sector* the former Disability Rights Commission suggested that when local housing authorities make impact assessments of choice based lettings arrangements, they should consider:

- Is advertising accessible?

- Are a property's accessible features advertised?

- Does a mechanism exist to identify the requirements of disabled applicants?

- Is there a mechanism to allow extra time for disabled applicants if they need it?

- Is there a mechanism for providing support in making applications?[87]

Processing applications

2.45 When an application has been received, the local housing authority will normally consider, first, whether an applicant is 'eligible' for an allocation of social housing under the terms of the statute and its own allocation scheme.[88] It is important that the local housing authority decides eligibility at the initial application stage, because an applicant permitted to engage with the allocation scheme (eg by being allowed to bid for properties in a choice based letting scheme) will have a legitimate expectation of full consideration for an allocation.[89] The issue of eligibility may be revisited just prior to any prospective allocation to take account of any changed circumstances since the initial application.[90]

2.46 If the local housing authority decides that the applicant *is* eligible, it should then consider:

---

[86]   *Complaint against Leeds CC* (05/C/13157), (2008) January *Legal Action*, p 37.
[87]   *Housing and the Disability Equality Duty: A guide to the Disability Equality Duty and Disability Discrimination Act 2005 for the social housing sector* (DRC, 2006), p 56.
[88]   See Chapter 3.
[89]   English CBL Code, para 3.10.
[90]   English CBL Code, para 3.10.

- whether he or she falls into any of the categories to which it must give reasonable preference;[91]

- whether he or she is entitled to any additional preference;[92]

- whether the applicant's behaviour permits the local housing authority to give him or her no preference at all;[93] and

- what priority the applicant is entitled to under the scheme.[94]

2.47 There is no statutory deadline or time limit within which the local housing authority must decide these questions once it has received an application, although a commitment to process applications within a particular period might well be made by a local housing authority in its own allocation scheme. If it becomes plain that the application is not being considered at all, the applicant may need to seek a mandatory order in a claim for judicial review. If the application is being considered, but progress is unduly slow, the applicant may wish to make a complaint under the local housing authority's own complaints procedure[95] or, if that proves unsatisfactory, seek the help of the Local Government Ombudsman.[96]

2.48 Where a local housing authority is operating a choice based letting scheme it may wish to make only a preliminary assessment of an initial application (in order to avoid expending resources examining in detail applications from applicants who have no realistic prospect of successfully bidding), and to reserve detailed scrutiny to a later stage (eg when an applicant has bid for and appears to qualify for the allocation of a particular property). This practice may, however, cause difficulties in complying with the notification and review requirements in respect of an applicant before letting the particular property to a different applicant.

2.49 The English CBL Code advises those local housing authorities operating choice based letting schemes to review applications *twice*, ie at both the initial application stage and again at the bidding stage.[97] On that model, at the second stage, the application will again be assessed to determine whether the applicant:

- is still eligible; and

- meets any specific letting criteria for the particular property; and

---

[91]   HA 1996, s 167(2). See also **4.20–4.86**.
[92]   HA 1996, s 167(2). See also **4.87–4.90**.
[93]   HA 1996, s 167(2B) and (2C). See also **4.101–4.110**.
[94]   HA 1996, s 167(2A). See also **4.91–4.100**.
[95]   Information about the local housing authority's own complaints procedure should be supplied to applicants by the authority itself: English 2009 Code, para 49.
[96]   See **2.82** and more generally www.lgo.gov.uk.
[97]   English CBL Code, paras 3.7 and 4.5.

- still has the appropriate priority for an allocation to be made; and

- that the applicant's household matches any size criteria for the property.[98]

Local housing authorities adopting this approach may find that they are required to notify decisions[99] on more than one occasion for each applicant and will need to include the detail of the procedures that will be operated at each stage in their allocation schemes.

2.50 The advice in the English CBL Code relating to double-testing for eligibility (at the stage of determining the initial application and at the pre-offer stage) does not sit happily with the drafting of the eligibility regulations.[100] At least in terms of transitional provisions, those regulations focus on the position when an applicant's *application* was first made.[101]

Applications from current tenants of social housing

2.51 Secure, introductory, or other tenants of social housing applying for transfers to alternative social housing accommodation have the same rights:

- to make applications,

- to have their applications considered,

- to be notified as to their rights to information and review, and

- for the fact of their applications to remain confidential,

as applicants who are not existing social housing tenants.[102] Applications to a local housing authority by current tenants of social housing can be made not only by tenants of that local housing authority but also by tenants of any other social landlord (whether a different local housing authority or an RSL).[103]

2.52 Their applications will be treated in the same way as all other applications, *except* that the local housing authority should not make inquiries into their eligibility on immigration or habitual residence grounds. That is because secure or introductory tenants, or assured tenants who obtained their current accommodation as a result of an allocation by a local housing authority, are eligible for a further allocation regardless of their immigration or habitual residence status.[104]

---

[98] English CBL Code, para 4.17.
[99] See **2.62–2.64**.
[100] See Chapter 3.
[101] Allocation of Housing and Homelessness (Eligibility) (England) Regulations 2006, SI 2006/1294, reg 8, reproduced in Appendix 2.
[102] English Code, para 3.6; Welsh Code, para 4.4.
[103] English Code, para 3.5.
[104] HA 1996, s 160A(6).

Procedure for handling applications

2.53 There is no prescribed national code for the way in which applications must be processed. The Secretary of State has the reserve power to prescribe by regulations the 'principles' that should govern allocation procedures, but the power has not been used.[105] The procedure being followed will therefore be that set out in the particular local housing authority's own allocation scheme. This must cover all aspects of the allocation process, including the identity (or description) of the staff by whom decisions will be taken.[106] From 1 April 2010, the Tenant Services Authority will seek to enforce new national standards for housing allocation issued in exercise of its powers under the Housing and Regeneration Act 2008.[107]

2.54 In dealing with an application for allocation of social housing, there is no duty upon the local housing authority to 'make ... inquiries' into the application (in contrast to the position in relation to applications for homelessness assistance).[108] The extent of any investigation of an application will be outlined in the local allocation scheme. It would be perfectly lawful for a local housing authority to confine its consideration of an application to the content of the application form. It does not have to investigate for itself, for example, any further medical or welfare needs an applicant's household may have. This makes it all the more important that application forms are comprehensive (as well as easy to complete) and that any advice given to a prospective applicant underscores the need to put forward all relevant information at the time the application is made.

Applications which trigger other responsibilities

2.55 It may be plain, from the terms in which the applicant has completed the local housing authority's application form, that there is a need for other assistance, even before consideration of the application for social housing allocation is completed.

2.56 If the form provides material which gives the local housing authority reason to believe that the applicant may be homeless or threatened with homelessness, it *must* make the enquiries necessary to establish whether it owes the applicant a duty under the homelessness legislation.[109] This is because an application for social housing is an application 'for accommodation', which may trigger the threshold for enquiries into any potential homelessness.[110]

---

[105] HA 1996, s 167(5).
[106] HA 1996, s 167(1).
[107] See **1.66**.
[108] See Chapter 10.
[109] HA 1996, Part 7 ('Homelessness').
[110] HA 1996, ss 183–184. Discussed further in Chapter 10; and see *R (Bilverstone) v Oxford City Council* [2003] EWHC 2434 (Admin), [2003] All ER (D) 170 (Oct), Admin Ct.

2.57 Likewise, if the local housing authority is also a social services authority or a childrens' services authority, the application may trigger responsibilities under community care or child care legislation.[111] For example, if the application reveals that:

(1) the applicant is under the age of 18, and

(2) she or he is seeking accommodation because the person with parental responsibility is unable to accommodate any longer,

the childrens' services authority may itself owe a statutory duty to accommodate under the Children Act 1989.[112]

Repeat applications

2.58 In principle, there is nothing to stop an unsuccessful applicant from making a further application at any stage. However, in practice, unless the applicant's circumstances have changed, the decision will be likely to be the same. HA 1996, Part 6 specifically provides that an applicant who has been treated as ineligible can make a fresh application at any time, and the Codes suggest that, if ineligibility arose from past misconduct, it will be for the applicant to show that his or her behaviour or circumstances have changed.[113]

DECISION-MAKING

Decisions on applications

2.59 As already noted, there is no statutory time limit within which a decision must be reached or within which the applicant must be notified of the outcome of the application (although any local housing authority may include such a provision in its local scheme). Nor is there a general statutory requirement that all decisions on applications be notified in writing, in any particular form or style (although, as will be seen later, adverse decisions often carry notification requirements). Again, the local allocation scheme might be expected to address such matters.

2.60 For the vast majority of applicants, the outcome of the application will be some form of notification of success. This may be a simple letter indicating that the applicant will in future be considered for an allocation based on the material provided in the application form or, where there is a local choice based letting system, that the applicant is free to make bids for available properties. What the applicant most probably wants to know, and may not have been

---

111 *R v Tower Hamlets London Borough Council ex p Bradford* (1997) 29 HLR 756, QBD.
112 Children Act 1989, s 20. See also *R (M) v Hammersmith and Fulham London Borough Council* [2008] UKHL 14, [2008] 1 WLR 535, HL, and *R (G) v Southwark London Borough Council* [2009] UKHL 26, [2009] 1 WLR 1299, HL; and see **20.55–20.82**.
113 HA 1996, s 160A(11). See also English Code, para 4.24; Welsh Code, para 3.19.

automatically told, is when, realistically, the application will result in an allocation of social housing (ie selection for the offer of a tenancy of a house or flat). The applicant is entitled to ask for information, in writing, about precisely that: whether housing accommodation is likely to be made available and, if so, how long it is likely to be before it is made available.[114]

2.61 For the minority of applicants, the notification will be that their application has been wholly or partly unsuccessful. The most serious adverse decision that an applicant could receive is that he or she is 'ineligible for an allocation'.[115] The legal framework for decisions on eligibility and the obligations when notifying such decisions are discussed in the next chapter.[116] Other adverse decisions, and the notification obligations attaching to them, are dealt with in this and successive chapters.

Notifying decisions

2.62 Curiously, while every local housing authority must accept applications for social housing made in accordance with its allocation scheme and determine them, there is no express statutory obligation on local housing authorities to give written notification of all decisions and/or to give reasons for them. No doubt these matters were thought so central to good administrative practice as not to require explicit mention in HA 1996, Part 6 because they will be included in the allocation scheme adopted by any local housing authority.

2.63 However, if a local housing authority decides that an applicant is 'ineligible' for its allocation scheme,[117] or that he or she is not to be given any preference on the grounds of unacceptable behaviour,[118] those decisions must be notified to the applicant in writing.[119] The applicant is also entitled to be given reasons for those decisions.

2.64 In each of those two cases, the decision must be 'notified' to the applicant, meaning that it should actually be received by him or her.[120] However, in the case of a decision that the applicant is not eligible, the decision is additionally treated as having been given to the applicant:

> '… if it is made available at the authority's office for a reasonable period for collection by him [or her] or on his [or her] behalf.'[121]

---

[114] HA 1996, s 167(4A)(a)(ii); see **2.21–2.23**.
[115] HA 1996, s 160A(9).
[116] See Chapter 3.
[117] See Chapter 3.
[118] See **4.101–4.110**.
[119] HA 1996, s 160A(9), (10), and s 167(4A)(b).
[120] '"Notify" requires the giving of a notice which imports a degree of formality sufficient to constitute the document, as it will usually be, a notice', per LJ May in *Ali v Birmingham City Council* [2009] EWCA Civ 1279 at [39].
[121] HA 1996, s 160A(10).

This treating provision only applies if the applicant does not actually receive the decision. If the applicant does receive the decision, any time limits run from the date of receipt, not from a notional date when the applicant could have collected the decision.

REVIEWS

Right to a review

2.65 An applicant has a statutory right, under HA 1996, Part 6, to request a review of the following three categories of decisions made by a local housing authority:

(1) that he or she is not to be awarded any reasonable preference, to which she or he would otherwise be entitled, on the grounds of unacceptable behaviour;[122]

(2) concerning the facts of his or her case which are likely to be, or have been, taken into account in considering whether to allocate accommodation;[123] and

(3) that he or she is not eligible for an allocation.[124]

The first and third categories of decisions listed here refer to decisions taken under specific statutory provisions, and the applicant will have been notified in writing of those decisions with reasons.[125]

2.66 The second category of decision carrying a right to a review is much more wide-ranging. From the wording, it is reasonable to assume that it includes decisions about:

(1) the type of property for which an applicant will be considered;

(2) the extent of the applicant's household to be considered for housing with him or her;[126]

(3) the applicant's medical condition or other welfare needs;

(4) other facts used to determine whether the applicant is entitled to a reasonable preference;

---

[122] HA 1996, s 167(4A)(b) and (d).
[123] HA 1996, s 167(4A)(c) and (d).
[124] HA 1996, s 160A(9) and s 167(4A)(d).
[125] HA 1996, s 160A(9) and s 167(4A)(b).
[126] *R (Ariemuguvbe) v Islington London Borough Council* [2009] EWCA Civ 1218, CA.

(5) whether the applicant should receive additional preference on the grounds of urgent housing needs or otherwise; and

(6) determining the applicant's priority, including his or her financial resources, behaviour (or that of his or her family), and local connection where the scheme renders any of these relevant.

This second category carrying a right to request a review, therefore, opens the door for an applicant to request an internal review, and consequent reconsideration, of nearly all the adverse decisions (if any) that are made on his or her application.

2.67 Unlike the decisions on unacceptable behaviour and eligibility, however, there is no automatic *notification* of the initial decision to the applicant in this second category of decisions. For the applicant even to access his or her right to request a review, he or she must first request the local housing authority to inform him or her of its decision about a particular fact, or set of facts, about his or her case.[127] Only having made that request, and received the response, can the applicant then sensibly request a review.

2.68 It is also important to note that in this second category, the review will not be of the decision itself, but solely a review of the facts taken into account when making the decision. Thus, a local housing authority's decision that the applicant is not entitled to any medical priority cannot be subject to a statutory review. But the local housing authority's decision on the facts of the applicant's medical condition can be subject to a review. It is the correctness of the facts, not the conclusions arising from the facts, that can be challenged. This is, obviously, a poor substitute for a general statutory right to review any decision made on an application.

2.69 The statutory rights to obtain a review of a decision on an application for allocation represent the legal minimum. There is nothing to prevent a local housing authority from adopting in its allocation scheme an extra-statutory commitment to allow a review of additional categories of adverse decisions or of all adverse decisions.

Procedure on review

2.70 There are no statutory provisions governing these rights to a review. There are, for example, no statutorily specified time limits within which a review must be requested and no statutorily prescribed form or procedure for making the request for a review.

2.71 Before HA 1996, Part 6 was amended by the Homelessness Act 2002, the right to request a review of decisions under HA 1996, Part 6 was contained in HA 1996, s 164. Regulations made under HA 1996, s 165 required the local

---

[127] See **2.25–2.28**.

housing authority to notify the person concerned that he or she had a right to make written representations and of the procedure involved. The local housing authority was required to notify the applicant of its decision on review within 8 weeks from the request, or any longer period as agreed between the parties in writing.[128] The reviewing officer, if employed by the same local housing authority which had made the original decision, had to be an officer who had not been involved in that original decision and had to be senior to the original decision-maker.[129] However, HA 1996, ss 164 and 165 were both repealed in January 2003.[130] The Secretary of State is now empowered to make regulations governing 'the procedure to be followed' on housing allocation, which appears, from the wording, to encompass any procedural matters under the allocation scheme, including any procedure relating to requests for review.[131] However, no regulations have been made in exercise of that power.

2.72 In this procedural vacuum, there is scope for uncertainty on all sides. Local housing authorities cannot insist that applications for review are promptly made, are put in writing or are accompanied by grounds. Applicants cannot insist on a review being determined within a specific time period from a request being made, or that the review should be considered by officers of a particular seniority. However, it is reasonable to assume that Parliament intended reviews within HA 1996, Part 6 to have the same function as reviews within HA 1996, Part 5 ('Conduct of Tenants')[132] and Part 7 ('Homelessness'), ie a reconsideration of all the relevant facts and law at the time that the review is decided, not a narrow review confining itself to the legality or fairness of the original decision.[133]

2.73 Applicants are, of course, entitled to the benefit of the usual public and administrative law protections of natural justice, procedural fairness etc and to expect high standards of administration from a local housing authority.[134] But one would ordinarily expect more detailed guidance. None is given in the English Code and the more recent English CBL Code includes nothing relating to review procedure. The English 2009 Code simply states that it is important that applicants have clear information about review rights as well as 'the procedure on review'.[135] When the main English Code was issued on

---

[128] Allocation of Housing and Homelessness (Review Procedures) Regulations 1999, SI 1999/71, regs 3–5. Reproduced in Appendix 2.

[129] SI 1999/71, reg 2.

[130] HA 1996, s 165(1) repealed by Homelessness Act 2002, Sch 2.

[131] HA 1996, s 167(5).

[132] HA 1996, s 129 gives an introductory tenant the right to request a review of his or her landlord's decision to seek an order for possession and the Introductory Tenancy (Review Procedures) Regulations 1997, SI 1997/72 regulate the procedure on review.

[133] For a discussion of the scope of reviews in the homelessness context see **19.102–19.109**.

[134] For examples of challenges to internal review arrangements on allocations see: *R v Tower Hamlets London Borough Council ex p Spencer* (1995) 29 HLR 64, QBD (a challenge brought under Housing Act 1985) and *R v Southwark London Borough Council ex p Mason* (2000) 32 HLR 88, QBD (a challenge to a review panel's decision on the suitability of accommodation offered under the allocation scheme).

[135] English 2009 Code, para 49.

11 November 2002, it was accompanied by a letter from the Office of the Deputy Prime Minister[136] (ODPM) to Directors of Housing in the following terms:

'The Code does not contain detailed guidance on the procedures which housing authorities should adopt when carrying out reviews of decisions under Part 6 of the 1996 Act. The issue of local authorities' review procedures under Parts 5 and 7 of the 1996 Act has been considered on more than one occasion recently by the Court of Appeal. We understand that one of those cases may be the subject of an appeal to the House of Lords. We will consider whether it would be appropriate to bring out further guidance to cover review procedures under Part 6 of the 1996 Act as the law continues to develop. In the meantime, housing authorities should ensure that the procedure for any review carried out at the request of an applicant as mentioned in paragraphs 4.30, 5.58 and 6.13 of, and annex 13 to, this guidance is fair and compatible with the Convention for the Protection of Human Rights and Fundamental Freedoms (commonly known as the European Convention on Human Rights) (see sections 1 and 6(1) of, and Schedule 1 to, the Human Rights Act 1998). In doing so, they will wish to have regard to relevant judgments of the domestic courts and the European Court on Human Rights.'[137]

2.74 In relation to adverse decisions on 'eligibility', or 'no preference', the Welsh Code recommends that local housing authorities adopt the following as 'fair procedure' in relation to reviews:

- ensuring that notifications of decisions include advice on the right to request a review, the time within which the request must be made, and sources of advice and assistance;

- ensuring that applicants have an opportunity to request further information about any decision about the facts of their case;

- advising applicants that they may request a review by way of an oral hearing or a written submission;

- ensuring that the review is carried out by a person who was not involved in the original decision and, if the reviewer is to be another officer, one senior to the original decision-maker;

- ensuring that the circumstances of the applicant at the time of the review, not just at the time of the original decision, are taken into account;

- if there is not to be a hearing, allowing the applicant to make written representations, and informing the applicant of the date by which those representations must be received, giving the applicant at least 5 clear days' notice;

---

[136] The government department responsible for housing and homelessness in England at the time. The relevant department is now Communities and Local Government (CLG).

[137] The full letter is reproduced in Appendix 1 of this book.

- if there is to be a hearing, giving at least 5 days' notice to the applicant of the date, time and place (unless the applicant consents to lesser notice);

- ensuring that the reviewer determines the procedure to be adopted for hearings, and that the procedure gives the applicant the right to be heard, to be accompanied, to be represented by a lawyer or other person, to call witnesses to give evidence, to put questions to any witness and to make written representations;

- ensuring that, if a person having been given notice should fail to appear at the hearing, the reviewer has regard to all the circumstances, including any explanation offered for the absence and should be able to proceed with the hearing or give any directions he or she thinks proper for the conduct of a further review;

- ensuring that the reviewer will allow applicants to be able to request an adjournment of a hearing, and will grant or refuse the request as the reviewer sees fit;

- ensuring that the reviewer should be able to adjourn the hearing at any time during the hearing on the applicant's application, or if the reviewer otherwise sees fit. If, at a re-scheduled hearing, the identity of the reviewer has changed, the hearing should be a complete re-hearing of the case;

- ensuring that, where more than one person is conducting the review, the review should only proceed in the absence of one of the reviewers if the applicant consents; and

- ensuring that the applicant is notified of the decision on the review and, if the decision confirms the original decision, of the reasons for it.[138]

2.75 In the absence of either explicit statutory provisions or statutory guidance as to review procedures, it has been left to the courts to scrutinise individual review decisions and review procedures on a case-by-case basis applying traditional administrative law principles (outlined in Chapter 19). The courts have developed some expertise in scrutinising the role of reviewing officers in reviews conducted of decisions made within the introductory tenancy and homelessness regimes of HA 1996,[139] so that the move to judicial scrutiny of review procedures in the housing allocation field has been relatively straightforward.

Notifying review decisions

2.76 Each allocation scheme must be framed in terms that provide for an applicant who has sought a review to be notified of the decision on review and

---

[138] Welsh Code, para 3.26.
[139] HA 1996, Part 5 'Conduct of Tenants' and Part 7 'Homelessness' respectively.

the grounds for it.[140] This requirement is interpreted as meaning that there should usually be provision in the allocation scheme for delivery of a written statement of the review decision and of the reasons for it.

2.77 In one case, in which the adequacy of the reasons given in a review decision was challenged, despite the decision being set out in a lengthy letter to the applicant, a judge said:[141]

'In my view proper, adequate and intelligible reasons are set out in the decision letter. The reasons are stated "in sufficient detail" to enable [the Claimant] to know what conclusion [the decision maker] has reached on the "principal important controversial issues" (*Bolton Metropolitan Borough Council v Secretary of State for the Environment* [1995] 3 PLR 37, 43C, Lord Lloyd; and see *William v Wandsworth LBC* [2006] HLR 42 at para 18). Moreover [the reviewing officer] balanced competing factors and explained why he concluded that some outweighed others.'

Challenges to review decisions and non-reviewable decisions about particular applications

2.78 Any legal challenges to review decisions, or to any decisions about individual applications that do not carry the right to request a review, can only be brought by judicial review, on the grounds that the local housing authority has infringed some requirement of public or administrative law, or has failed to comply with the duty to supply the grounds for the decision.[142]

2.79 Judicial review challenges to allocation decisions tend to fall into two distinct categories:

(1)   challenges to the allocation scheme itself; and

(2)   challenges to particular decisions made relating to particular applicants.

This part of this chapter is concerned only with the latter. Challenges to the contents of allocation schemes are dealt with in Chapter 5.[143] Of course, occasionally, both forms of challenge may be available in a particular case. For an example of a judicial review which, at least initially, involved both forms of challenge see *R (Ahmad) v Newham London Borough Council*.[144]

2.80 As far as individual decisions are concerned, an applicant seeking to challenge such a decision would have to show that it was contrary to the

---

[140] HA 1996, s 167(4A)(d).

[141] *R (Dixon) v Wandsworth London Borough Council* [2007] EWHC (Admin) 3075 at [26], (2008) February *Legal Action*, p 40, Admin Ct.

[142] The duty to supply reasons in an allocation case is set out at **2.63** and **2.76**. The classic grounds upon which judicial review claims can be mounted are discussed at **19.211–19.237**.

[143] See **4.133–4.137**.

[144] [2008] EWCA Civ 140, (2008) April *Legal Action*, p 34, CA (later determined by the House of Lords solely as a challenge to the structure of the allocation scheme at [2009] UKHL 14, HL).

provisions of HA 1996, Part 6, or of the local housing authority's allocation scheme, or had been reached applying an unfair or unlawful procedure, or was based on some other mistake of law or, in some circumstances, a mistake of fact.[145] In one unsuccessful case, the challenge to the decision of a reviewing officer (on eligibility for housing allocation) was described as containing 'the familiar complaints that he had misdirected himself, failed to take into account relevant circumstances, and/or failed to give adequate reasons'.[146]

2.81 Claims for judicial review have been particularly successful in relation to decisions on medical needs assessment for the purposes of allocation schemes. In one case, a local housing authority's assessment failed to address issues raised by the applicant's medical advisers and gave insufficient reasons for the refusal to accord the highest medical priority in the local scheme.[147] In another, the medical assessment was based on medical advice commissioned by the local housing authority, but that advice had failed to address particular points and specific materials put forward by the applicant's advisers.[148] In a third case, a local housing authority's decisions were:

> 'insufficiently reasoned as to the criteria applied as to how medical need can or fails to come within the doctrine of reasonable preference and how the evidence has been related to the criteria that are applied.'[149]

In a fourth case, the medical advisers engaged by the local housing authority had gone beyond their remit and advised as to the relative priority of the applicant to others in housing need. The local housing authority had wrongly taken into account those non-medical opinions and relied upon them.[150]

2.82 Where an applicant is dissatisfied either with the decision (or review decision) on his or her application, or with the procedure followed, but there is no arguable error of law, the applicant should invoke the local housing authority's own internal complaints procedure and, if still dissatisfied, then complain of maladministration to the Local Government Ombudsman.[151] Those dissatisfied applicants who are or who have become tenants of social housing can also seek redress through the compensatory powers of the Tenant Services Authority which will be available from April 2010.[152]

---

145 *E v Secretary of State for the Home Department* [2004] EWCA Civ 49, [2004] QB 1044, CA.
146 *R (Dixon) v Wandsworth London Borough Council* [2008] EWCA Civ 595, (2008) July *Legal Action*, p 22, CA.
147 *R (Sawalha) v Westminster City Council* [2008] EWHC 1216 (Admin), (2008) July *Legal Action*, p 22, Admin Ct.
148 *R (Ghandali) v Ealing London Borough Council* [2006] EWHC 1859 (Admin).
149 *R (Ahmad) v Newham London Borough Council* [2007] EWHC 2332 (Admin) at [24], (2007) November *Legal Action*, p 34, Admin Ct – not appealed on this point
150 *R (Bauer-Czarnomski) v Ealing London Borough Council* [2010] EWHC 130 (Admin), Admin Ct.
151 For the Local Government Ombudsman's Fact Sheet *Complaints about your housing application* (April 2009) see http://www.lgo.org.uk/complaints-about-housing-application/.
152 Housing and Regeneration Act 2008, ss 236–245.

2.83 Sadly, the most common source of dissatisfaction concerns the length of time that applicants have to wait before being made an offer of accommodation or succeeding in a bidding process in a choice based letting scheme. Invoking legal remedies, or complaints procedures, rarely cures that grievance where the root cause of it is an excess of demand over supply.

Chapter 3

ELIGIBILITY FOR ALLOCATION

AN OVERVIEW

3.1   Only two categories of applicant may be found ineligible for allocation of accommodation by a local housing authority. The first is dictated by Housing Act 1996 ('HA 1996'), Part 6, itself, the second by the exercise of local case-by-case discretion. Eligibility will be determined in accordance with the procedures in the local allocation scheme, which will indicate how the tests for each category of eligibility will be applied locally. If an applicant is found to be within one of the two categories, the local housing authority is statutorily barred from allocating housing accommodation to him or her.[1]

3.2   In the first category, the local housing authority *must* decide that people who are subject to immigration control (with limited exceptions), and other people who are to be treated as persons from abroad, are ineligible *unless* either:

(1)   they are currently secure, introductory or, in certain cases, assured tenants of social housing; or

(2)   they fall within one of the exceptional classes prescribed by regulations as being eligible for allocation notwithstanding their immigration or residence status.[2]

3.3   In the second category, the local housing authority *may* choose to adopt and apply a rule that applicants who have been guilty of unacceptable behaviour, serious enough to make them unsuitable to be tenants of the local housing authority, are ineligible for an allocation.[3] This is a discretionary power available to the local housing authority; it is not obliged to use it. If it does choose to use it, considers an applicant's behaviour, and concludes that the behaviour is *not* so serious as to make the applicant unsuitable to be a tenant, but that he or she should be penalised in some way, it could decide that the applicant *is* eligible for an allocation, but that he or she should receive a lower priority than other applicants.[4]

3.4   Each of the two categories of ineligibility is examined in detail later in this chapter.

3.5   Beyond the two statutory categories, local housing authorities are *not* permitted to treat any applicant as ineligible for an allocation.[5] The previous

---

[1]   Housing Act 1996, s 160A(1).
[2]   HA 1996, s 160A(3), (4), (5) and (6); Allocation of Housing and Homelessness (Eligibility) (England) Regulations 2006, SI 2006/1294, regs 3–4; Allocation of Housing (Wales) Regulations 2003, SI 2003/239 (W 36), regs 4–5.
[3]   HA 1996, s 160A(7) and (8).
[4]   HA 1996, s 167(2A). See **4.93–4.94**.
[5]   HA 1996, s 160A(2).

practices of some local housing authorities, in prescribing whole groups or classes of applicants as ineligible, by reason of age, residence, rent arrears, or otherwise,[6] would now be unlawful.

3.6 If an applicant is found by the local housing authority to be ineligible, that decision and the reasons for it must be notified to him or her in writing.[7] The applicant is then entitled to request a review of the decision and to be notified of the review decision and the reasons for it.[8] There is no provision for any appeal against the review decision to the county court, and so any challenge by legal proceedings could only be by judicial review.[9]

3.7 If an applicant is ineligible for an allocation of accommodation, he or she must not be allocated a sole tenancy, nor granted a joint tenancy with others under the allocation scheme.[10] So, if a couple apply for an allocation of a property to be let on a joint tenancy and only one of them is eligible, a joint tenancy cannot be granted. The tenancy can only be granted to the eligible applicant in his or her sole name.

3.8 The eligibility restrictions apply to *applicants*, not to their dependents or others in the household with whom they seek to be accommodated. However, as indicated below, the previous unacceptable behaviour of a household member may allow a local housing authority to treat the applicant himself or herself as ineligible.[11] If an eligible applicant has ineligible dependents, their needs must still be taken into account when the local housing authority considers the type and size of accommodation to be allocated.[12] However, a local housing authority is free to take into account the immigration status of family members in deciding whether they form part of an applicant's 'household' at all.[13] If an ineligible household member is a 'restricted person',[14]

---

[6]   See **1.15** and **1.18**.

[7]   HA 1996, s 160A(9) and (10).

[8]   HA 1996, s 167(4A)(d).

[9]   For three examples of challenges to eligibility decisions by way of judicial review see *R (McQ) v Bolton Metropolitan Borough Council* [2005] EWHC 1285 (Admin), (2005) August *Legal Action*, p 17, Admin Ct; *R (Dixon) v Wandsworth London Borough Council* [2008] EWCA Civ 595, (2008) July *Legal Action*, p 22 and *R (M) v Hackney London Borough Council* [2009] EWHC 2255 (Admin), (2009) May *Legal Action*, p 26

[10] HA 1996, s 160A(1). However, once a person has been granted a secure or assured tenancy, that tenancy does not come to an end, nor is the landlord entitled to apply for possession, simply because he or she is ineligible for a grant of a secure or assured tenancy. The landlord can only obtain possession under the grounds for possession at Housing Act 1985, Sch 2 (secure tenants) or Housing Act 1988, Sch 2 (assured tenants), or if the tenant loses his or her security of tenure (*Akinbolu v Hackney London Borough Council* (1997) 29 HLR 259, CA).

[11] See **3.161–3.163**.

[12] *R (Kimvono) v Tower Hamlets London Borough Council* (2001) 33 HLR 78, Admin Ct.

[13] *R (Ariemuguvbe) v Islington London Borough Council* [2009] EWHC 470 (Admin), (2009) April *Legal Action*, p 21, Admin Ct, upheld on appeal in *R (Ariemuguvbe) v Islington London Borough Council* [2009] EWCA Civ 1308, (2010) January *Legal Action*, p 35, CA.

[14] HA 1996, s 184(7). See **4.109–4.110**.

that fact will not render the otherwise eligible applicant ineligible, but it may affect his or her entitlement to a reasonable preference.[15]

3.9 Ineligible applicants are not prevented from acquiring a tenancy in cases where the provisions of the HA 1996, Part 6 do not apply, ie where the grant of a tenancy to them does not count as an allocation at all.[16]

THE FIRST CATEGORY: INELIGIBILITY ON THE GROUNDS OF IMMIGRATION STATUS

A summary

3.10 The provisions governing ineligibility on the basis of immigration status are tortuous and complicated. The Codes of Guidance[17] each have several annexes to help with the assessment of eligibility.[18] However, the chapter on eligibility in the English Code does not cover amendments to the provisions for assessment of eligibility for an allocation made on or after 2002, and therefore some of its guidance is considerably out of date.[19] In those circumstances, reference may be usefully made to chapter 9 and Annexes 8–13 of the Homelessness Code of Guidance (England) for up-to-date guidance on those aspects of the modern scheme of eligibility for allocation, which are broadly similar to those of eligibility for homelessness assistance.[20]

3.11 The immigration status of an existing secure or introductory tenant, or an assured tenant who was nominated to his or her landlord by a local housing authority, who has applied for an allocation (eg by way of a transfer) is irrelevant.[21] Those applicants are eligible for an allocation irrespective of their immigration status.

3.12 The general rule at HA 1996, s 160A(3)–(5) is that applicants who are 'people from abroad' are not eligible.[22] They fall into two distinct categories.

- those subject to immigration control—
  - they are *not eligible* for assistance

---

15   HA 1996, s 167(2ZA) and **4.109–4.110**.
16   HA 1996, s 160(2), (3) and (4). See also **1.24–1.26**.
17   *Allocation of Accommodation: Code of Guidance for local housing authorities for England* (Office of the Deputy Prime Minister, November 2002) [English Code] (see Appendix 1). *Code of Guidance for local housing authorities on allocation of accommodation and homelessness for Wales* (National Assembly for Wales, April 2003) [Welsh Code] (see CD-ROM).
18   English Code, Annexes 4–12 inclusive; Welsh Code, Annexes 4–15 inclusive.
19   Allocation of Housing and Homelessness (Eligibility) (England) Regulations 2006, SI 2006/1294, regs 3 and 4 apply to applications for an allocation made on or after 1 June 2006 (reg 8).
20   *Code of Guidance for Local Authorities* (Department for Communities and Local Government, Department for Education and Skills, Department of Health, July 2006) (the English Homelessness Code) (see Appendix 2).
21   HA 1996, s 160A(6).
22   HA 1996, s 160A(1)(a).

> – *unless* they fall within a class prescribed as 'eligible' in regulations made by the Secretary of State or the Welsh Assembly Government;[23]

- those not subject to immigration control but who are nevertheless prescribed by regulations as being 'persons from abroad'—
  - they are *not eligible* if they are not habitually resident in the Common Travel Area *unless* they are prescribed as exempt from the habitual residence test; or
  - they are *not eligible* if they are prescribed as ineligible because of their particular rights of residence under European Union law.[24]

3.13   The first sub-category, and the details of it, differ according to whether the application for an allocation is made to an English or a Welsh local housing authority. For applications made to English local housing authorities, the details differ according to whether the application was made before 1 June 2006, or on or after that date.[25] The details of the second sub-category also differ according to whether application is made to an English or a Welsh local housing authority and, for applications made to English local housing authorities, the details are different depending on whether application was made before 1 June 2006, or on or after that date.[26]

3.14   The Secretary of State and the Welsh Assembly Government[27] each have the power to make regulations exempting some people from abroad from the exclusory rule.[28] They each also have the power to make regulations excluding people who would otherwise be eligible. Each of these powers has been exercised several times, in both England and Wales.

3.15   For England, the Secretary of State has made the Allocation of Housing and Homelessness (Eligibility) (England) Regulations 2006,[29] which apply to all

---

23   HA 1996, s 160A(3).

24   HA 1996, s 160A(5).

25   And whether the application was made between 20 April 2006 and 31 May 2006, or on or before 19 April 2006.

26   And whether the application was made between 1 May 2004 and 31 May 2006, or on or before 30 April 2004.

27   This power was exercisable by the National Assembly for Wales until 25 May 2007. On that day (which was the day of the appointment of the First Minister after the May 2007 elections to the National Assembly for Wales), functions previously exercised by the National Assembly for Wales were transferred to the Welsh Assembly Government (Government of Wales Act 2006, s 161 and Sch 11, para 30).

28   They cannot designate as eligible any person who is excluded from entitlement to housing benefit by the Immigration and Asylum Act 1999, s 115 (HA 1996, s 160A(4)). Immigration and Asylum Act 1999, s 115 prescribes that 'a person subject to immigration control' is not eligible for housing benefit unless he or she falls within one of the classes of people prescribed by the Secretary of State. Classes of persons subject to immigration control who are entitled to housing benefit are prescribed in the Social Security (Immigration and Asylum) Consequential Amendment Regulations 2000, SI 2000/636, reg 2 and Sch 1, Part 1 and the Housing Benefit Regulations 2006, SI 2006/213, reg 10(3B).

29   SI 2006/1294. See Appendix 2 of this book.

applications for an allocation of social housing to local housing authorities in England made on or after 1 June 2006.[30] Those Regulations have since been amended by:

- the Allocation of Housing and Homelessness (Eligibility) (England) (Amendment) Regulations 2006;[31]

- the Allocation of Housing and Homelessness (Eligibility) (England) (Miscellaneous Provisions) Regulations 2006;[32]

- the Allocation of Housing and Homelessness (Eligibility) (England) (Amendment No 2) Regulations 2006;[33] and

- the Allocation of Housing and Homelessness (Eligibility) (England) (Amendment) Regulations 2009.[34]

Appendix 2 of this book contains the text of the Allocation of Housing and Homelessness (Eligibility) (England) Regulations 2006[35] as amended by all of the above Regulations.

3.16 In Wales, the National Assembly for Wales[36] made the Allocation of Housing (Wales) Regulations 2003,[37] which apply to all applications for homelessness assistance to Welsh local housing authorities made on or after 29 January 2003.

3.17 The Welsh Regulations have been amended by:

- the Allocation of Housing (Wales) (Amendment) Regulations 2006, reg 2;[38] and

---

[30] Any applications for an allocation of social housing made before 1 June 2006 to English local housing authorities are determined according to the Homelessness (England) Regulations 2000, SI 2000/701, amended by Allocation of Housing and Homelessness (Amendment) (England) Regulations 2004, SI 2004/1235 and further amended by the Allocation of Housing and Homelessness (Amendment) (England) Regulations 2006, SI 2006/1093. See **3.49–3.58** and **3.123–3.136**.

[31] SI 2006/2007, in force for applications to English local housing authorities made on or after 25 July 2006.

[32] SI 2006/2527, in force for applications to English local housing authorities made on or after 9 October 2006.

[33] SI 2006/3340, in force for applications to English local housing authorities made on or after 1 January 2007.

[34] SI 2009/358, in force for applications to English local housing authorities made on or after 18 March 2009.

[35] SI 2006/1294.

[36] Its functions were acquired by the Welsh Assembly Government on 25 May 2007. See fn 27.

[37] SI 2003/239 (W 36).

[38] SI 2006/2645 (W 226).

- the Allocation of Housing and Homelessness (Eligibility) (Wales) Regulations 2009.[39]

Appendix 3 of this book contains the text of the Allocation of Housing (Wales) Regulations 2003 as amended by both these Regulations.

3.18 The Regulations in both England and Wales set out classes of persons who are subject to immigration control, but are prescribed as nevertheless eligible. They also set out classes of persons who are not subject to immigration control, but are nevertheless ineligible.

3.19 Each of the two categories of persons from abroad (those subject to immigration control and those not subject to such control) needs careful examination. But first it is necessary to work out which sub-category an applicant is within. That depends on whether or not the applicant is 'subject to immigration control'.

3.20 This part of this chapter deals with:

- the first sub-category (persons subject to immigration control) as it applies to:
  - English local housing authorities for applications made on or after 1 June 2006, discussed at **3.35–3.48**; then
  - English local housing authorities for applications made before 1 June 2006, discussed at **3.49–3.58**; then
  - Welsh local housing authorities, discussed at **3.59–3.60**; and

- the second sub-category (other persons from abroad) as it applies to:
  - English local housing authorities for applications made on or after 1 June 2006, discussed at **3.65–3.122**; then
  - English local housing authorities for applications made before 1 June 2006, discussed at **3.123–3.136**; and then
  - Welsh local housing authorities, discussed at **3.137–3.139**.

It concludes with a review of the circumstances of those who would be eligible in only one of either England or Wales, at **3.140–3.142**.

3.21 Applications for an allocation made before 31 January 2003 (England) or 29 January 2003 (Wales) fall to be determined under HA 1996 and the Regulations in force at the time, ie before the amendments inserted by the Homelessness Act 2002.[40]

---

[39] SI 2009/393 (W 42).

[40] HA 1996, s 161(2) (now repealed) prohibited allocation to persons subject to immigration control except those prescribed as qualifying persons. For England, Allocation of Housing (England) Regulations 2000, SI 2000/702, reg 4 prescribed six Classes of persons (A–E(ii)) as eligible. The first four of these Classes were equivalent to the current Classes A–D (see **3.39–3.48**). The last two Classes, E(i) and E(ii), were equivalent to Classes D(i) and D(ii) in the Housing (England) Regulations 2002, SI 2002/3264 (see **3.50–3.58**). HA 1996, s 161(3) (now

3.22 The starting point, however, for either sub-category is consideration of who is and who is not, in the ordinary course of events, 'a person subject to immigration control'.

The meaning of 'subject to immigration control'

3.23 The starting point is with the special meaning of 'subject to immigration control'. The Housing Act 1996, s 160A(3) refers to:

'... a person subject to immigration control within the meaning of the Asylum and Immigration Act 1996.'

3.24 The Asylum and Immigration Act 1996 defines 'a person who is subject to immigration control' as being a person:

'... who under the 1971 Act requires leave to enter or remain in the United Kingdom (whether or not such leave has been given).'[41]

3.25 Tracing that route back to the Immigration Act 1971[42] reveals that:

- British citizens;

- Commonwealth citizens with the right of abode;

- European Economic Area (EEA) and Swiss nationals exercising certain Treaty rights;[43]

- family members and some extended family members of those EEA or Swiss nationals exercising certain Treaty rights; and

- certain people who are exempt from immigration control under the Immigration Acts (diplomats and their family members based in the UK, and some military personnel)

---

repealed) restricted allocation only to qualifying persons. Allocation of Housing (England) Regulations 2000, SI 2000/702, reg 5 prescribed three additional classes of persons (F–H) as qualifying. Allocation of Housing (England) Regulations 2000, SI 2000/702, reg 6 prescribed people who were not habitually resident in the Common Travel Area as not eligible for an allocation, with certain exceptions. These provisions were all applied to applications for an allocation to Welsh local housing authorities by the Allocation of Housing (Wales) Regulations 2000, SI 2000/1080 (W 73).

[41] Asylum and Immigration Act 1996, s 13(2).
[42] Immigration Act, ss 1–3.
[43] Immigration Act 1988, s 7; Immigration (European Economic Area) Regulations 2006, SI 2006/1003, regs 13–15. From 1 June 2002, Swiss nationals have had the same rights to freedom of movement and social security within the EEA as EEA nationals: Immigration (Swiss Free Movement of Persons) (No 3) Regulations 2002, SI 2002/1241. Swiss nationals fall within the definition of 'EEA nationals' at Immigration (European Economic Area) Regulations 2006, SI 2006/1003, reg 2. All references to EEA nationals therefore include Swiss nationals.

do *not* require leave to enter or remain in the UK and therefore cannot be persons 'subject to immigration control'.[44] Those applicants will be eligible *unless* they fall within the second sub-category of persons prescribed as being 'persons from abroad' and not eligible.[45]

3.26 The legal definition of 'The United Kingdom' and its related parts is given in Box 1.

Box 1

Key Geographic Terms:

England: counties established by Local Government Act 1972, s 1, Greater London area and the Isles of Scilly.[46]

Great Britain: England, Wales, and Scotland.[47]

United Kingdom: England, Wales, Scotland and Northern Ireland.[48]

Common Travel Area (CTA): England, Wales, Scotland, Northern Ireland, Republic of Ireland, Isle of Man, and the Channel Islands.[49]

3.27 Box 2 shows which countries are members of the European Union (EU) and/or members of the wider European Economic Area (EEA).[50] For these purposes, nationals of Iceland, Liechtenstein, Norway and Switzerland have the same rights to enter or reside as nationals of most of the EU member states.[51] Rights for nationals of the eight 2004 Accession States ('A8 states')[52] and for nationals of Bulgaria and Romania ('A2 states')[53] are slightly different from those enjoyed by nationals of other EEA states. We refer throughout this chapter to nationals of EEA member states, by which we mean all the EU member states, including the A8 and A2 states, plus the three additional EEA member states and Switzerland.

---

[44] Immigration Act 1971, ss 1–3; Immigration Act 1988, s 7; Immigration (European Economic Area) Regulations 2006, SI 2006/1003.

[45] HA 1996, s 160A(5); Allocation of Housing and Homelessness (Eligibility) (England) Regulations 2006, SI 2006/1294, reg 4 (as amended) and Allocation of Housing (Wales) Regulations 2003, SI 2003/239 (W 36), reg 5 (as amended).

[46] Interpretation Act 1978, s 5 and Sch 1.

[47] Union of Scotland Act 1706.

[48] Interpretation Act 1978, s 5 and Sch 1.

[49] Immigration Act 1971, s 1(3).

[50] Croatia, Turkey and the former Yugoslav Republic of Macedonia are 'candidate countries' for accession to the EU. Albania, Bosnia and Herzegovina, Serbia and Montenegro are all due to make political changes before applying to become 'candidate countries'. The EU is considering the position of Kosovo. See www.europa.eu.int for an up-to-date list.

[51] Immigration (European Economic Area) Regulations 2006, SI 2006/1003. See Appendix 2 of this book.

[52] See **3.89–3.94**.

[53] See **3.95–3.98**.

Box 2

The European Union (EU):

Member States:[54] Austria, Belgium, Cyprus, Denmark, Finland, France, Germany, Greece, Ireland, Italy, Luxembourg, Netherlands, Malta, Portugal, Spain, Sweden and the UK; and

Accession States acceding in 2004 ('A8 states'): Czech Republic, Estonia, Hungary, Latvia, Lithuania, Poland, Slovakia, Slovenia; and

Accession States acceding in 2007 ('A2 states): Bulgaria and Romania

The European Economic Area (EEA):

All EU States[55] plus Iceland, Liechtenstein and Norway.

Switzerland is not part of the EEA, but its nationals are treated as EEA nationals for these purposes.[56]

3.28   Obviously, the lists given in these boxes will fluctuate from time to time. The English Code, Annex 9 provides useful lists and web site addresses that will help advisers keep up to date.[57]

3.29   If a consideration of the provisions shows that the applicant, even if newly arrived in the UK, does not require leave to enter or remain in the UK, he or she will usually be 'eligible' *unless* rendered ineligible by falling within the second sub-category.[58] For these purposes, it is important to emphasise that a person, usually an EEA national, who does not require leave to enter but who does require leave to remain and does not have it, is a person subject to immigration control.[59] It is only a person who requires neither leave to enter nor leave to remain who is not subject to immigration control. Strangely, a person can be ineligible for an allocation of social housing even if he or she was

---

[54]   All Member States as at 30 April 2004, plus Cyprus and Malta, who both joined on 1 May 2004 along with the A8 states. Cyprus and Malta are not subject to the derogations that the A8 states are subject to.

[55]   The Channel Islands, Isle of Man and Gibraltar are not part of the EEA.

[56]   Immigration (European Economic Area) Regulations 2006, SI 2006/1003, reg 2.

[57]   Both Codes were published before 1 May 2004 and so do not include the 10 countries which joined in May 2004 or the two which joined in January 2007. See also Welsh Code, Annex 12 and English Homelessness Code, Annex 11 at Appendix 2 of this book. Up-to-date information can be obtained from www.europa.eu.int or http://ukba.homeoffice.gov.uk/eucitizens/.

[58]   See **3.61–3.136**.

[59]   *Abdi v Barnet London Borough Council, Ismail v Barnet London Borough Council* [2006] EWC Civ 383, [2006] HLR 23, CA.

born in the UK and has never left it, simply because he or she does require leave to enter or remain in the UK and does not have it.[60]

3.30 Everyone else is a 'person subject to immigration control' and is *not* eligible for assistance *unless* he or she falls into one of the classes prescribed by the Regulations.[61]

3.31 If there is any uncertainty about an applicant's immigration status, local housing authorities are advised to contact the UK Border Agency (UKBA).[62] The UKBA advises on an applicant's immigration status, but the decision on eligibility is for the local housing authority itself. Before making the inquiry, local housing authorities should inform the applicant that an inquiry will be made, giving the applicant an opportunity to withdraw the application for social housing, so that no further action will be taken and the UKBA will not be informed of the inquiry.[63] If the applicant is an asylum seeker, the application for help with accommodation will usually be referred to the UKBA for support under Immigration and Asylum Act 1999, Part 6.[64]

Sub-category one: those who are subject to immigration control

3.32 Anyone who requires leave to enter or remain in the UK is a 'person subject to immigration control' and will not be eligible for an allocation unless he or she falls within one of the classes prescribed as eligible in regulations made by the Secretary of State or the Welsh Assembly Government.[65]

3.33 The Secretary of State and the Welsh Assembly Government cannot designate as 'eligible' anyone who is excluded from entitlement to housing benefit by the Immigration and Asylum Act 1999, s 115.[66]

3.34 The Secretary of State and the Welsh Assembly Government have exercised their powers given by HA 1996, s 160A(3) to set out classes of persons subject to immigration control who are nevertheless eligible for an allocation of accommodation.

---

60 *Ehiabor v Kensington & Chelsea Royal London Borough Council* [2008] EWCA Civ 1074, [2008] All ER (D) 104 (May), CA.
61 Allocation of Housing and Homelessness (Eligibility) (England) Regulations 2006, SI 2006/1294, reg 4 as amended. Allocation of Housing (Wales) Regulations, SI 2003/239 (W36), reg 4.
62 At http://ukba.homeoffice.gov.uk.
63 English Code, para 4.17; Welsh Code para 3.11.
64 Formerly provided by the National Asylum Support Service (NASS).
65 HA 1996, s 160A(3).
66 HA 1996, s 160A(4). Immigration and Asylum Act 1999, s 115 prescribes that 'a person subject to immigration control' is not eligible for housing benefit unless he or she falls within one of the classes of people prescribed by the Secretary of State. Classes of persons subject to immigration control who are entitled to housing benefit are prescribed in the Social Security (Immigration and Asylum) Consequential Amendment Regulations 2000, SI 2000/636, Sch 1, Part 1 and the Housing Benefit Regulations 2006, SI 2006/213, reg 10(3B).

The English rules

Applications for an allocation made on or after 1 June 2006

3.35   The basic rule is that a 'person subject to immigration control' is *not eligible*. The exceptions to that basic rule are contained in classes set out in Regulations. Regulation 3 of the Allocation of Housing and Homelessness (Eligibility) (England) Regulations 2006[67] prescribes that the following classes of people from abroad are eligible even though they are subject to immigration control:

(1)   Class A:[68] a person recorded by the Secretary of State as a refugee and who has leave to enter or remain in the UK.

(2)   Class B:[69] a person who has—
    (a)   exceptional leave to enter or remain in the UK; and
    (b)   whose leave is not subject to conditions requiring him or her to maintain and accommodate himself or herself and any dependants without recourse to public funds.

(3)   Class C:[70] a person—
    (a)   who is habitually resident in the CTA; and
    (b)   who has current leave to enter or remain in the UK which is not subject to any limitation or condition; but
    (c)   is not someone who has—
        (i)   been given leave to enter or remain in the UK upon a written undertaking from a sponsor that he or she will be responsible for maintenance and accommodation; and
        (ii)   has been resident in the CTA for less than 5 years beginning on the date of entry or the date of the undertaking (whichever is the later date); and
        (iii)   whose sponsor is still alive.

(4)   Class D:[71] a person who has humanitarian protection granted under the Immigration Rules.

---

[67]   Allocation of Housing and Homelessness (Eligibility) (England) Regulations 2006, SI 2006/1294, reg 3, as amended; see Appendix 2.

[68]   SI 2006/1294, reg 3(a).

[69]   SI 2006/1294, reg 3(b).

[70]   SI 2006/1294, reg 3(c).

[71]   SI 2006/1294, reg 531)(d), as amended by Allocation of Housing and Homelessness (Miscellaneous Provisions) (England) Regulations 2006, SI 2006/2527, reg 2, for applications for an allocation of social housing made on or after 9 October 2006. For applications made before 9 October 2006, Class D contained 'a person who left the territory of Montserrat after 1 November 1995 because of the effect on that territory of a volcanic eruption.' For discussion of Class D prior to 9 October 2006, see **3.49–3.58**.

3.36 Guidance on Classes A, B and C is given in the English Code, paras 4.3, 4.14 and Annexes 4, 5, 6 and 8.[72]

3.37 A number of the Classes contain common terms that are themselves defined by the regulations or by case law. For the meaning of:

– 'Common Travel Area' (CTA), see **3.26**, Box 1;

– 'habitually resident', see **3.71–3.79;**

– UK, see **3.26**, Box 1.

3.38 Each class can now be examined in further detail.

Class A:[73] *Refugees*

3.39 If a former asylum seeker is granted refugee status by the Secretary of State, he or she will also have the 'leave to enter or remain in the UK' required for Class A purposes and will be eligible for homelessness assistance, welfare benefits and community care services and for an allocation of social housing according to the same criteria as those applicable to British citizens.

3.40 It is not unusual for someone to be granted refugee status and then apply for his or her family to come to the UK. The family enters the UK with the refugee acting as their sponsor. A refugee is entitled to such family reunion,[74] and so the usual rules regarding maintenance and accommodation (which would normally involve a condition of 'no recourse to public funds') do not apply to a refugee's family members. Thus, those family members will also be eligible persons, because they are entitled to 'refugee' status.[75]

Class B:[76] *Exceptional leave to enter or remain*

3.41 'Exceptional leave to enter or remain' was generally a status granted to asylum-seekers whose claim for full refugee status had not succeeded, but where the Home Office recognised that there were compelling humanitarian and/or compassionate circumstances that required that the applicant should be allowed to stay in the UK. From 1 April 2003, the Home Office has called leave granted in those circumstances 'humanitarian protection' or 'discretionary

---

[72] Class D is a new Class, prescribed by the Allocation of Housing and Homelessness (Miscellaneous Provisions) (England) Regulations 2006, SI 2006/2527 after the English Code was published in 2002.

[73] Allocation of Housing and Homelessness (Eligibility) (England) Regulations 2006, SI 2006/1294, reg 3(a); English Code, paras 4.3(d)(i), 4.14(i), Annexes 4, 6 and 8.

[74] *Immigration Rules*, HC 395, paras 352A–352F (23 May 1994), as amended, at http://www.ukba.homeoffice.gov.uk/policyandlaw/immigrationlaw/immigrationrules/part11/.

[75] *R (Jimaali) v Haringey London Borough Council* (2002) November *Legal Action*, p 24, Admin Ct.

[76] Allocation of Housing and Homelessness (Eligibility) (England) Regulations 2006, SI 2006/1294, reg 3(b); English Code, paras 4.3(d)(ii), 4.14, Annexes 4, 6 and 8.

leave'.[77] Viewed broadly, anyone who has been granted leave when the Secretary of State has recognised that he or she does not fully meet the requirements of the Immigration Rules has been treated 'exceptionally' and may be said to have been granted 'exceptional leave'.

3.42 People with exceptional leave to enter or remain will be eligible for an allocation unless that leave is subject to a condition requiring them to maintain and accommodate themselves, and their dependents, without recourse to public funds. The presence or absence of such a condition will be manifest from the document, or stamp, containing the grant of leave.

3.43 Subject to that exception, they will not only be entitled to an allocation of social housing but also homelessness assistance, welfare benefits and community care services.

3.44 Leave is normally, but not always, granted for a period of 3 years. If, after the end of that period, the leave is not renewed, the person will no longer be eligible for assistance, unless he or she falls within one of the other classes. However, once an applicant has been allocated a tenancy of social housing, that tenancy cannot be terminated on the basis that he or she is no longer eligible. The applicant will be entitled to remain in his or her tenancy or to apply for another allocation as an existing secure, introductory or assured tenant.[78]

Class C:[79] *A person with current leave to enter or remain in the UK with no condition or limitation and who is habitually resident in the CTA.*

3.45 The type of leave contemplated by this class is commonly referred to as 'indefinite leave to enter or remain' and cannot be granted subject to conditions.[80] Anyone granted indefinite leave will be eligible if he or she is also habitually resident in the CTA.[81]

3.46 If leave to enter or remain was granted on a written undertaking that a sponsor would be responsible for the applicant's maintenance and accommodation, the applicant will *not* be eligible under this class for an allocation for the 5 years running from:

- the date of his or her arrival in the UK, or

- the date the sponsorship undertaking was given,

---

[77] Letter from the Homelessness Directorate to Chief Executives and Housing Directors of English local housing authorities (ODPM, 25 March 2003, www.communities.gov.uk).

[78] *Akinbolu v Hackney London Borough Council* (1996) 29 HLR 259, CA; HA 1996, s 160A(6).

[79] Allocation of Housing and Homelessness (Eligibility) (England) Regulations 2006, SI 2006/1294, reg 3(c), English Code, paras 4.3(d)(iii), 4.14(iii) and Annexes 4, 6 and 8.

[80] Immigration Act 1971, s 3(1)(b) and (c).

[81] For the meaning of 'habitually resident' see **3.71–3.79**.

starting from whichever is the later event.

3.47 After those 5 years, or during the 5 years if the sponsor (or at least one of several sponsors) has died, an applicant will be eligible under this class (subject to satisfying the test of habitual residence).[82]

Class D:[83] *a person granted humanitarian protection under the immigration rules*

3.48 'Humanitarian protection' is granted to those people whose claims for asylum do not succeed, but who have international protection needs (ie they face a serious risk of the death penalty, unlawful killing, torture, inhuman or degrading treatment or punishment if removed from the UK). The status must be granted pursuant to the Immigration Rules.[84] People with humanitarian protection are entitled to family reunion in the same way as refugees.[85] This class was substituted by the Allocation of Housing and Homelessness (Miscellaneous Provisions) (England) Regulations 2006[86] and is in force for applications for an allocation of social housing made on or after 9 October 2006.[87]

Applications for an allocation made before 1 June 2006

Applications made between 20 April 2006 and 31 May 2006

3.49 For applications for an allocation made to English local housing authorities before 1 June 2006, the relevant Regulations are the Allocation of Housing (England) Regulations 2002.[88] Regulation 4 contained the classes of persons subject to immigration control who were, nevertheless, prescribed as eligible. The 2002 Regulations were amended by the Allocation of Housing and Homelessness (Amendment) (England) Regulations 2006,[89] with effect from

---

[82] See **3.71–3.79**.
[83] Allocation of Housing and Homelessness (Eligibility) (England) Regulations 2006, SI 2006/1294, reg 3(d), as amended by the Allocation of Housing and Homelessness (Miscellaneous Provisions) (England) Regulations 2006, SI 2006/2527 and in force for applications for an allocation of social housing made on or after 9 October 2006. There is no guidance in the English Code, as this Class was first introduced on 9 October 2006, after the Code was published.
[84] See *Immigration Rules, HC 395*, paras 339C–339H (23 May 1994 as amended), at http://www.ukba.homeoffice.gov.uk/policyandlaw/immigrationlaw/immigrationrules/part11/.
[85] *Immigration Rules, HC 395*, paras 352FA–352FI.
[86] SI 2006/2527.
[87] For applications made between 1 June 2006 and 8 October 2006, Class D contained 'a person who left the territory of Montserrat after 1 November 1995 because of the effect on that territory of a volcanic eruption' (Allocation of Housing and Homelessness (Eligibility) (England) Regulations 2006, SI 2006/1294, as originally enacted. This class of person is discussed in relation to the Welsh rules on eligibility for homelessness assistance (Homelessness (Wales) Regulations 2006, SI 2006/2646 (W 227), reg 3(1)(d)) at **12.91** and there is guidance on that old Class D at the English Homelessness Code, para 9.10(iv).
[88] SI 2002/3264.
[89] SI 2006/1093.

20 April 2006.[90] The amended reg 4 prescribed three classes of persons subject to immigration control who were, nevertheless, eligible for an allocation. Those three classes are Classes A, B and C and they are identical to Classes A–C in the current Regulations.[91]

Applications made before 20 April 2006

3.50 For applications for allocation of social housing made to English local housing authorities before 20 April 2006, there are two further classes of persons subject to immigration control who are, nevertheless, eligible. The two further classes are Classes D(i) and D(ii) in reg 4 of the Allocation of Housing (England) Regulations 2002.[92] They are:

- Class D(i): a person who is habitually resident in the CTA and who is a national of a state which has ratified the European Convention on Social and Medical Assistance (ECSMA) or the European Social Charter (ESC) and is lawfully present in the UK; and

- Class D(ii): a person who is habitually resident in the CTA and before 3 April 2000 was owed a duty by a local housing authority under Housing Act 1985, Part 3 or HA 1996, Part 7 which is extant, and who is a national of a state which is a signatory to ECSMA or ESC.

3.51 These classes were abolished by the Allocation of Housing and Homelessness (Amendment) (England) Regulations 2006[93] with effect from 20 April 2006. Any applicant who, on 20 April 2006, had made an application for an allocation and had not been notified that he or she was ineligible for an allocation, will be eligible if they fall within one of these classes.[94] The classes principally benefited EEA nationals who were not 'qualifying persons'[95] and were therefore excluded from eligibility under HA 1996, s 160A(5),[96] or were nationals of Croatia, Turkey, the former Yugoslav Republic of Macedonia, Romania or the Ukraine if they fulfilled the other conditions at Classes D(i) or D(ii).

3.52 For an applicant to fall within either of these classes, he or she must be habitually resident in the CTA.[97]

---

90 The amendment was intended to prevent EEA nationals who were not economically active and so did not enjoy EEA Treaty rights to reside from falling within classes of persons prescribed as eligible under HA 1996, s 160A(3) and thus overturn the effect of the Court of Appeal's decision in *Abdi v Barnet London Borough Council, Ismail v Barnet London Borough Council* [2006] EWCA Civ 283, [2006] HLR 23, CA.

91 For Class A, see **3.39–3.40**; for Class B, see **3.41–3.44**; for Class C, see **3.45–3.47**.

92 SI 2002/3264.

93 SI 2006/1093.

94 Allocation of Housing and Homelessness (England) Regulations 2006, SI 2006/1093, reg 2(2).

95 See **12.116** for 'qualifying persons'.

96 See **3.63–3.64**.

97 For 'habitually resident', see **3.71–3.79**. For the 'Common Travel Area', see Box 1.

Class D(i):[98] *a person who is a national of a country that has ratified ECSMA or ESC and who is lawfully present in the UK and habitually resident in the CTA*

3.53   To qualify as 'eligible' under this class, an applicant must be:

(1)   a national of one of the ratifying countries to the ECSMA or ESC; and

(2)   lawfully present in the UK; and

(3)   habitually resident[99] in the CTA.

Box 3

States which have *ratified* the ECSMA are: Belgium, Denmark, Estonia, France, Germany, Greece, Iceland, Ireland, Italy, Luxembourg, Malta, Netherlands, Norway, Portugal, Spain, Sweden, Turkey and the UK.[100] The same states have also *signed* the ECSMA.

States which have *ratified* the ESC are: Austria, Belgium, Croatia, Cyprus, the Czech Republic, Denmark, Finland, France, Germany, Greece, Hungary, Iceland, Ireland, Italy, Latvia, Luxembourg, Malta, Netherlands, Norway, Poland, Portugal, Slovakia, Spain, Sweden, Turkey, the former Yugoslav Republic of Macedonia and the UK.[101] These states plus Liechtenstein, Romania, Slovenia, Switzerland and the Ukraine have also *signed* the ESC.

3.54   A comparison with the list of members of the EEA[102] reveals that the beneficiaries of this class are nationals of Croatia, Turkey and the former Yugoslav Republic of Macedonia.

3.55   He or she must also be 'lawfully present in the UK',[103] which means that he or she must have leave to enter and remain in the UK, or not require it. Asylum seekers from ECSMA or ESC countries who have been given 'temporary admission', pending the determination of their claims for asylum, are considered to be 'lawfully present'.[104]

---

[98]   Allocation of Housing (England) Regulations 2002, SI 2002/3264, reg 4(d)(i). English Code, paras 4.3(e), 4.14(iv) and Annex 6.

[99]   See **3.71–3.79**.

[100]   For up to date lists, see http:www.conventions.coe.int.

[101]   For up-to-date lists, see http:www.conventions.coe.int.

[102]   See Box 2.

[103]   The UK comprises England, Wales, Scotland and Northern Ireland: Interpretation Act 1978, s 5 and Sch 1. See Box 1.

[104]   *Szoma v Secretary of State for the Department of Work and Pensions* [2005] UKHL 64, [2006] 1 AC 564, HL and *R (YA) v Secretary of State for Health* [2009] EWCA Civ 225, (2009) The Times, April 2, CA.

Class D(ii):[105] *a person who is a national of a country that has signed the ECSMA or ESC and before 3 April 2000 was owed a homelessness duty which is still extant and who is habitually resident in the CTA*

3.56 To qualify as eligible under this class, a person must be:

(1) a national of a state which has signed the ECSMA or ESC;[106] and

(2) have been owed a homelessness duty before 3 April 2000; and

(3) still be owed a homelessness duty; and

(4) be habitually resident in the CTA.

3.57 To fall within this class, an applicant must have been owed a homelessness duty before 3 April 2000 and that duty must not have come to an end. In other words, he or she must have both made an application for homelessness assistance and had that application accepted before 3 April 2000 and must still be continuing to receive homelessness assistance under that duty. The duty will be owed either under HA 1996, Part 7, or under its statutory predecessor (Housing Act 1985, Part 3). The only duty likely to be still extant would be the main housing duty under HA 1996, s 193 (or Housing Act 1985, s 65(2)).

3.58 There is no additional requirement that a person should be lawfully present in the UK in order to qualify for this class. Any national of a country ratifying or signing the ECSMA or ESC could potentially fall within this class, provided he or she fulfilled the other conditions.

The Welsh rules

3.59 Applications for an allocation made to Welsh local housing authorities are governed by the Allocation of Housing (Wales) Regulations 2003[107] and those Regulations apply to all applications made on or after 29 January 2003.

3.60 Regulation 4 of the Allocation of Housing (Wales) Regulations 2003[108] prescribes six classes of people who are subject to immigration control and nevertheless are eligible for an allocation. Classes A–C inclusive are identical to Classes A–C in the current English Regulations.[109] Classes D(i) and D(ii) are

---

[105] Allocation of Housing (England) Regulations 2002, SI 2002/3264, reg 4(d)(ii). Unfortunately, the English Code does not contain any guidance on this Class D(ii), confining itself to guidance on Class D(i).

[106] For states that have signed the ECSMA or ESC, see Box 3.

[107] SI 2003/239 (W 36).

[108] SI 2003/239 (W 36).

[109] For Class A, see **3.39–3.40**; For Class B, see **3.41–3.44**; For Class C, see **3.45–3.47**.

identical to Classes D(i) and D(ii) in the English Regulations prior to amendment on 20 April 2006.[110] Class D1[111]is identical to the English Class D[112].

Sub-category two: other 'persons from abroad' not subject to immigration control but prescribed as not eligible

3.61 Ordinarily, persons not subject to immigration control would be eligible for an allocation of social housing. However, the Secretary of State and the Welsh Assembly Government are permitted to make regulations treating some people who are not subject to immigration control as 'persons from abroad' and therefore not eligible for allocation.[113] Both have exercised these powers.

Who is, and who is not, a 'person from abroad'?

3.62 In short summary, persons who are not 'subject to immigration control' comprise:[114]

- British citizens;

- some Commonwealth citizens;

- EEA and Swiss nationals exercising certain treaty rights;

- family members of EEA or Swiss nationals exercising certain treaty rights; and

- certain people exempt from immigration control, such as diplomats, their family members and some military personnel.

Disqualifying those who are not 'persons subject to immigration control' but are nevertheless not eligible

3.63 In general, the effect of the exercise of the Regulation-making powers in both England and Wales has been to produce a situation in which British and Commonwealth citizens will only be eligible for an allocation of social housing if they satisfy the 'habitual residence'[115] test, *or* fall into one of the classes of people exempt from the test.[116]

---

110 For Class D(i), see **3.53–3.55**; for Class D(ii), see **3.56–3.58**.
111 Inserted by Allocation of Housing (Wales) Regulations 2006, SI 2006/2645 (W 226), reg 2 and in force for applications for an allocation of social housing made on or after 9 October 2006.
112 See **3.48**.
113 HA 1996, s 160A(5).
114 Immigration Act 1971, ss 1–3.
115 See **3.71–3.79**.
116 HA 1996, s 160A(5); Allocation of Housing and Homelessness (Eligibility) (England) Regulations 2006, SI 2006/1294, reg 4(1)(a) and (2); Allocation of Housing (Wales) Regulations 2003, SI 2003/239 (W 36), reg 5(1)(a) and (2).

3.64   For EEA nationals and/or their family members,[117] the situation is more complex. In summary:

- If they do not have any rights of residence pursuant to European Union law, they are 'persons subject to immigration control', and fall within HA 1996, s 160A(3) and the appropriate Regulations, ie the first sub-category of people who are not eligible.[118]

- In England, if their only right to reside is the initial 3-month right of residence or because of their status as jobseekers, they will not be eligible.[119]

- If they have a right of residence pursuant to European Union law, they will either have to satisfy the habitual residence[120] test, or fall into one of the classes of people exempt from that test so as to be eligible for an allocation of social housing.[121]

The various rights of residence available to EEA nationals and their family members are considered at **12.111–12.129**.

The English rules

Applications for an allocation made on or after 1 June 2006

3.65   In the Allocation of Housing and Homelessness (Eligibility) (England) Regulations 2006,[122] in force for applications made on or after 1 June 2006, the Secretary of State exercised the power to treat some people who are not subject to immigration control as 'persons from abroad'.[123] This means that some British citizens, nationals of EEA member states, and others who are exempt

---

[117]   The general rights of residence for EEA nationals and their family members are considered at **12.111–12.129**.

[118]   *Abdi v Barnet London Borough Council, Ismail v Barnet London Borough Council* [2006] EWCA Civ 383, [2006] HLR 23, CA. They are not likely to fall within any of the classes prescribed as eligible by either the English or the Welsh Regulations: Allocation of Housing and Homelessness (Eligibility) (England) Regulations 2006, SI 2006/1294, reg 3 (see **3.35–3.48**); and Allocation of Housing (Wales) Regulations 2003, SI 2003/239 (W 36), reg 5 (see **3.59–3.66**).

[119]   Allocation of Housing and Homelessness (Eligibility) (England) Regulations 2006, SI 2006/1294, reg 4(1)(b) and (c). In Wales, they are likely to be eligible if they are jobseekers and satisfy the habitual residence test: Allocation of Housing (Wales) Regulations 2003, SI 2003/239 (W 36), reg 5(1)(a). Those who are relying on the 3-month initial right of residence may find that they are unlikely to satisfy the habitual residence test. See **3.137–3.139**.

[120]   For 'habitual residence', see **3.71–3.79**.

[121]   Allocation of Housing and Homelessness (Eligibility) (England) Regulations 2006, SI 2006/1294, reg 4(1)(a) and (2). Allocation of Housing (Wales) Regulations 2003, SI 2003/239 (W 36), reg 5(1)(a) and (2).

[122]   SI 2006/1294.

[123]   For applications for an allocation of social housing made *before* 1 June 2006, the relevant provisions are in reg 5 of the Allocation of Housing (England) Regulations 2002, SI 2002/3264, as substituted by the Allocation of Housing and Homelessness (Amendment) (England) Regulations 2004, SI 2004/1235. See **3.123–3.126**.

from immigration control may nevertheless be denied an allocation on the grounds that they are 'not eligible'. The primary function of these provisions is to confine new allocations of social housing to the ordinary residents of the UK, ie those habitually resident here, and to EEA nationals exercising Treaty rights.

3.66 Allocation of Housing and Homelessness (Eligibility) (England) Regulations 2006, reg 4, establishes three classes of people who are to be treated as 'persons from abroad' and therefore *ineligible* for an allocation despite not being subject to immigration control.

3.67 The *first class*[124] comprises persons who are 'not habitually resident'[125] in the CTA.[126] But that test of habitual residence does not apply to:

- EEA nationals who are 'workers';[127] or

- EEA nationals who are self-employed;[128] or

- Accession State workers requiring registration ('A8 nationals');[129] or

- Accession State nationals subject to worker authorisation ('A2 nationals');[130] or

- family members of EEA nationals where the EEA national is a worker, a self-employed person, an Accession State worker requiring registration or an Accession State national subject to worker authorisation;[131] or

- EEA nationals who have certain permanent rights to reside in the UK;[132] or

- persons who left the territory of Montserrat after 1 November 1995 because of the effect on that territory of a volcanic eruption;[133] or

---

[124] Allocation of Housing and Homelessness (Eligibility) (England) Regulations 2006, SI 2006/1294, reg 4(1)(a).

[125] See **3.71–3.79**.

[126] See **3.26**, Box 1.

[127] Allocation of Housing and Homelessness (Eligibility) (England) Regulations 2006, SI 2006/1294, reg 4(2)(a). See **3.27** and Box 2 for list of EEA countries and **3.82–3.86** for 'worker'.

[128] SI 2006/1294, reg 4(2)(b). See **3.87–3.88**.

[129] SI 2006/1294, reg 4(2)(c)(i), substituted by Allocation of Housing and Homelessness (Eligibility) (England) (Amendment) (No 2) Regulations 2006, SI 2006/3340, reg 2. See **3.89–3.94**.

[130] SI 2006/1294, reg 4(2)(c)(ii), substituted by Allocation of Housing and Homelessness (Eligibility) (England) (Amendment) (No 2) Regulations 2006 SI 2006/3340, reg 2, in force from 1 January 2007. See **3.95–3.98**.

[131] SI 2006/1294, reg 4(2)(d). See **3.99–3.105**.

[132] SI 2006/1294, reg 4(2)(e). See **3.106–3.108**.

[133] SI 2006/1294, reg 4(2)(f). See **3.109**.

- persons who are in the UK as a result of having been deported, expelled or otherwise removed by compulsion of law from another country to the UK;[134] or

- between 25 July 2006 and 31 January 2007 only, people who left Lebanon on or after 12 July 2006 because of the armed conflict there;[135] or

- a person who arrived in Great Britain or after 28 February 2009 but before 18 March 2011 and who immediately before arriving in Great Britain had been resident in Zimbabwe and, before leaving Zimbabwe, had accepted an offer made by Her Majesty's Government to assist that person to settle in the UK.[136]

3.68 The *second class* comprises EEA nationals and their family members whose only right to reside in the UK is derived from their status as jobseekers, as family members of jobseekers or from their initial right to reside in the UK for a period not exceeding 3 months.[137]

3.69 The *third class* comprises EEA nationals and their family members whose only right to reside in the rest of the CTA (Channel Islands, Isle or Man or the Republic of Ireland)[138] is derived from their status as jobseekers, as family members of jobseekers, or from their initial right to reside in the UK for a period not exceeding 3 months.[139]

3.70 Each of these classes will be examined in turn.

The first class: not habitually resident[140]

3.71 'Habitual residence' is not a term of reference to someone's immigration status. A person may be a British citizen, but if he or she is not habitually resident in the CTA,[141] he or she will not be eligible. Nor is the term 'habitual residence' defined in either HA 1996 or the Regulations.[142] It is a question of fact for the local housing authority to decide. Happily, there is some guidance in the Code.[143]

---

[134] SI 2006/1294, reg 4(2)(g). See **3.110**.
[135] SI 2006/1294, reg 4(2)(h) inserted by Allocation of Housing and Homelessness (Eligibility) (England) (Amendment) Regulations 2006, SI 2006/2007, reg 2(5): see **3.111–3.112**.
[136] SI 2006/1294, reg 4(2)(i) inserted by the Allocation of Housing and Homelessness (Eligibility) (England) (Amendment) Regulations 2009, SI 2009/358; for applications made on or after 18 March 2009, see **3.113–3.115**.
[137] SI 2006/1294, reg 4(1)(b). See **3.116–3.120**.
[138] See Box 1 at **3.26**.
[139] Allocation of Housing and Homelessness (Eligibility) (England) Regulations 2006, SI 2006/1294, reg 4(1)(c). See **3.121–3.122**.
[140] SI 2006/1294, reg 4(1)(a).
[141] See Box 1 at **3.26**.
[142] SI 2006/1294.
[143] English Code, paras 4.4–4.10 and Annex 11. Note that the Code was published in 2002. More up-to-date guidance can be found at paras 9.3(i) and 9.15–9.18 and Annex 10 of the English Homelessness Code. See Appendix 2 of this book.

3.72 A person who is not habitually resident will also not be entitled to social security benefits. If the person is receiving social security benefits, it must follow that the Department for Work and Pensions (DWP) has determined that he or she is habitually resident.

3.73 There are two aspects required to be present in order to constitute habitual residence:

(1) a settled purpose of establishing residence in the CTA; and

(2) an appreciable period of such residence.

3.74 Whether each aspect is satisfied is a question of fact for the local housing authority to decide. Normally, if someone has lived in the CTA for 2 years continuously prior to his or her application for an allocation, he or she is likely to be considered to be habitually resident without further inquiry.[144]

3.75 Establishing a 'settled purpose' will obviously involve consideration of an applicant's subjective intentions and motivations. Someone in stable employment may be more likely to be able to establish his or her 'settled purpose' to be habitually resident than someone in transitory employment, or dependent on benefit. However, local housing authorities must be careful not to give too much weight to an applicant's lack of finances and not enough weight to other factors such as the applicant's nationality, ties with the UK, and future intentions.[145]

3.76 What constitutes an 'appreciable period of residence' likewise varies according to the circumstances of each individual's case. If a former British resident returns to the UK after living and working abroad, she or he may be habitually resident from the first day of his or her return.[146] When someone is coming to live in the UK for the first time, there must be an appreciable period of residence before habitual residence is obtained. To determine how long that period of residence should be, local housing authorities should consider all the circumstances, including:

- whether the person is seeking to bring any family members to the UK;

- whether he or she has brought his or her personal property and possessions to the UK;

- whether he or she has done everything necessary to establish a residence before coming;

---

[144] English Code, para 4.4.
[145] *Olokunboro v Croydon London Borough Council* (2003) February *Legal Action*, p 37, Croydon County Court.
[146] *Swaddling v Adjudication Officer* [1999] All ER (EC) 217, ECJ, and see CIS/1304/1997 and CJSA/5394/1998. English Code Annex 11, para 4.6.

- whether he or she has a right of abode; and

- what 'durable ties' there are with the CTA.[147]

3.77 Some EEA nationals, and their family members, are not exempted from the habitual residence test,[148] nor are they prescribed as 'ineligible' by virtue of falling within the second or third classes.[149] For those people to be eligible, they will have to satisfy the habitual residence test.

3.78 Types of EEA nationals who may be required to satisfy the habitual residence test include:

- an EEA national who has resided in the UK in accordance with the Immigration (European Economic Area) Regulations[150] for a continuous period of 5 years;[151] or

- a family member of an EEA national, the family member having resided in the UK in accordance with the Immigration (European Economic Area) Regulations for a continuous period of 5 years;[152] or

- a person who has resided in the UK for a continuous period of 5 years and was, at the end of that period, a family member of an EEA national who had retained the right of residence;[153] or

- potentially, a person who has a right to reside that falls outside the Immigration (European Economic Area) Regulations.[154]

3.79 Given the length of their residence, most of those people should not have any difficulty in satisfying the habitual residence test.

---

[147] *Nessa v Chief Adjudication Officer* [1999] 1 WLR 1937, HL. English Code, Annex 11.

[148] Allocation of Housing and Homelessness (Eligibility) (England) Regulations 2006, SI 2006/1294, reg 4(2): see **3.67** and **3.80–3.115**.

[149] Allocation of Housing and Homelessness (Eligibility) (England) Regulations 2006, SI 2006/1294, reg 4(1)(b) and (c): see **3.116–3.122**.

[150] SI 2006/1003. See Appendix 2 of this book.

[151] Entitled to a permanent right of residence by reg 15(1)(a) of the Immigration (European Economic Area) Regulations 2006, SI 2006/1003. See Appendix 2.

[152] Entitled to a permanent right of residence by reg 15(1)(b) of the Immigration (European Economic Area) Regulations 2006, SI 2006/1003. For 'family member', see **12.118–12.121**.

[153] Entitled to a permanent right of residence by reg 15(1)(f) of the Immigration (European Economic Area) Regulations 2006, SI 2006/1003. For 'family member', see **12.118–12.121**. For family member who has retained the right of residence, see reg 10 of the Immigration (European Economic Area) Regulations 2006, SI 2006/1003 and **12.121**.

[154] *Baumbast and R v Secretary of State for the Home Department (Case C-413/99)* [2002] ECR I-7091; *Teixeira v Lambeth London Borough Council and Secretary of State for the Home Department, European Court of Justice, C-4380/08, 23 February 2010*; and *Ibrahim v Harrow London Borough Council and Secretary of State for the Home Department, European Court of Justice, C-310/08, 23 February 2010*. See **12.125–12.129** for discussion.

Exemptions from the habitual residence test

3.80 As noted above,[155] the following people are eligible for assistance even if they are not habitually resident:

- an EEA national who is a 'worker';[156] or

- an EEA national who is self-employed;[157] or

- a person who is an Accession State worker requiring registration ('an A8 national');[158] or

- a person who is an Accession State national subject to worker authorisation ('an A2 national')[159] or

- a family member of an EEA national who is a worker, a self-employed person, an Accession State worker requiring registration or an Accession State national subject to worker authorisation;[160] or

- a person who has one of certain permanent rights to reside in the UK;[161] or

- a person who left the territory of Montserrat after 1 November 1995 because of the effect on that territory of a volcanic eruption;[162] or

- a person who is in the UK as a result of having been deported, expelled or otherwise removed by compulsion of law from another country to the UK;[163] or

- between 25 July 2006 and 31 January 2007 only, a person who left Lebanon on or after 12 July 2006 because of the armed conflict there;[164] or

---

[155] See **3.67**.
[156] Allocation of Housing and Homelessness (Eligibility) (England) Regulations 2006, SI 2006/1294, reg 4(2)(a). See paras **3.82–3.86**.
[157] SI 2006/1294, reg 4(2)(b). See **3.87–3.88**.
[158] SI 2006/1294, reg 4(2)(c)(i) substituted by Allocation of Housing and Homelessness (Eligibility) (England) (Amendment) (No 2) Regulations 2006, SI 2006/3340, reg 2. See **3.89–3.94**.
[159] SI 2006/1294, reg 4(2)(c)(ii) substituted by Allocation of Housing and Homelessness (Eligibility) (England) (Amendment) (No 2) Regulations 2006 SI 2006/3340, reg 2, in force from 1 January 2007. See **3.95–3.98**.
[160] SI 2006/1294, reg 4(2)(d). See **3.99–3.105**.
[161] SI 2006/1294, reg 4(2)(e). See **3.106–3.108**.
[162] SI 2006/1294, reg 4(2)(f). See **3.109**.
[163] SI 2006/1294, reg 4(2)(g). See **3.110**.
[164] SI 2006/1294, reg 4(2)(h), inserted by Allocation of Housing and Homelessness (Eligibility) (England) (Amendment) Regulations 2006, SI 2006/2007, reg 2(5). See **3.111–3.112**.

- a person who arrived in Great Britain on or after 28 February 2009 but before 18 March 2011 and who, immediately before arriving in Great Britain, had been resident in Zimbabwe and, before leaving Zimbabwe, had accepted an offer made by Her Majesty's Government to assist that person to settle in the UK.[165]

3.81 Most of these categories refer to those persons exercising rights of freedom of movement enjoyed under European Union law, and to the Immigration (European Economic Area) Regulations 2006,[166] which are the current regulations transposing European Union freedom of movement legislation into domestic law. Each of them will be considered in turn. See **12.110–12.129** for consideration of the different European Union 'rights to reside'.

EEA nationals who are workers[167]

3.82 In order to qualify as a 'worker' under this provision, the person must first be a national of an EEA Member State.[168] The term 'worker' is not defined in HA 1996 or the regulations and nor is it exhaustively defined in European Union legislation. The European Court of Justice has emphasised that a narrow approach should *not* be taken:

> '[I]t is settled case law that the concept of worker has a specific Community meaning and must not be interpreted narrowly. It must be defined in accordance with objective criteria which distinguish an employment relationship by reference to the rights and duties of the person concerned. In order to be treated as a worker, a person must pursue an activity which is genuine and effective, to the exclusion of activities on such a small scale as to be regarded as purely marginal and ancillary. The essential feature of an employment relationship is that for a certain period of time a person performs services for and under the direction of another person in return for which he receives remuneration. By contrast, neither the *sui generis* nature of the employment relationship under national law, nor the level of productivity of the person concerned, the origin of the funds from which the remuneration is paid or the limited amount of the remuneration can have any consequence in regard to whether the person is a worker for the purposes of Community law …'.[169]

---

[165] SI 2006/1294, reg 4(2)(i), inserted by the Allocation of Housing and Homelessness (Eligibility) (England) (Amendment) Regulations 2009, SI 2009/358, for applications made on or after 18 March 2009. See **3.113–3.115**.

[166] SI 2006/1003, in force from 30 April 2006. See Appendix 2 of this book.

[167] Allocation of Housing and Homelessness (Eligibility) (England) Regulations 2006, SI 2006/1294, reg 4(2)(a). There is no up-to-date guidance in the English Allocation Code. Up-to-date guidance is contained at English Homelessness Code, para 9.14(a), Annex 12, paras 15–19. See Appendix 2.

[168] See Box 2 at **3.27**.

[169] *Kurz Case C-188/00* [2002] ECR I-10691 at para 32.

3.83 A person will be a 'worker'[170] if he or she:

- is actually working in the UK, whether full or part-time (any genuine and effective work should count, so long as it is not so irregular and/or so limited that it is a purely marginal and ancillary activity);[171] or

- has worked in the UK (at any time and even for a short period) but has become temporarily incapable of work as a result of an illness or accident, or involuntarily unemployed in certain circumstances;[172] or

- has worked in the UK, but has become involuntarily unemployed and has embarked on vocational training;[173] or

- has voluntarily given up work in the UK to take up vocational training related to his or her previous job.[174]

3.84 Attempts to argue that people who have never worked in the UK are, nevertheless, 'workers' for the purpose of entitlement to jobseeker's allowance and Children Act assistance have failed.[175] A jobseeker who has never worked is not, therefore, a 'worker' and, in any event, is specifically excluded from eligibility because he or she would fall into the second or third classes of people who are not eligible.[176] Students and au pairs, working part-time, have been held by the Court of Appeal and the European Court of Justice not to be 'workers'.[177]

---

170 Immigration (European Economic Area) Regulations 2006, SI 2006/1003, reg 4(1)(a). 'Worker' is defined by Regulation (EEC) No 1612/68 of the Council of 15 October 1968 on freedom of movement for workers within the Community or Regulation (EEC) No 1251/70 of the Commission of 29 June 1970 on the right of workers to remain in the territory of a Member State after having been employed in that State. English Homelessness Code, Annex 12, paras 15–18.

171 *Levin 53/81* [1982] ECR 1035; *Kempf Case 139/85* [1986] ECR 1741; *Raulin Case C-357/89* [1992] ECR 1027.

172 *Scrivner Case 122/84* [1985] ECR 1027; Immigration (European Economic Area) Regulations 2006, SI 2006/1003, reg 6(2)(a) and (b). To be treated as a 'worker' if involuntarily unemployed, the person must be registered as a jobseeker and: (1) have been employed for a year or more before becoming unemployed; and (2) have been unemployed for no more than 6 months; or (3) provide evidence that he or she is seeking employment in the UK and has a genuine chance of being engaged. See English Homelessness Code, Annex 12, para 19(a) and (b).

173 *Lair Case 39/86* [1988] ECR 3161; *Raulin Case C-357/89* [1992] ECR 1027. Immigration (European Economic Area) Regulations 2006, SI 2006/1003, reg 6(2)(c). English Homelessness Code, Annex 12, para 19(c).

174 *Raulin Case C-357/89* [1992] ECR 1027. Immigration (European Economic Area) Regulations 2006, SI 2006/1003, reg 6(2)(d). English Homelessness Code, para 19(d), Annex 12.

175 *Collins v Secretary of State for Work and Pensions, C-138/02, 23 March 2004, ECJ; R (Conde) v Lambeth London Borough Council* [2005] EWHC 62 (Admin) [2005] HLR 29; and *Ali v SSHD* [2006] EWCA Civ 484, [2006] 3 CMLR 326, [2006] ELR 423, CA.

176 Allocation of Housing and Homelessness (Eligibility) (England) Regulations 2006, SI 2006/1294, regs 4(1)(b) and 4(1)(c). See **3.116–3.122**.

177 *Ozturk v Secretary of State for the Home Department* [2006] EWCA Civ 541, [2007] 1 WLR 508, CA; C-294/06, 24 January 2008, ECJ.

3.85 The decision as to whether an applicant is or is not a worker is a question of fact for the local housing authority. In *R (Mohamed) v Harrow London Borough Council*,[178] it was held that the local housing authority had not made any errors of law in concluding that a woman who had worked part-time for 3 months, finishing a year before her application for homelessness assistance, spoke little or no English, had two small children to look after and had not registered with an employment agency was not and had not retained the status of being a 'worker'. In *Barry v Southwark London Borough Council*,[179] the local housing authority was wrong to decide that an applicant was not a 'worker' during a 2-week period when he was employed by Group 4 Securicor for stewarding duties at the Wimbledon All England Tennis Championships. The work done was of economic value, there were PAYE deductions from his pay and the services provided by him to his employer were real and actual, and not merely marginal and ancillary.[180]

3.86 A8 and A2 nationals will not be 'workers' if they are Accession State workers requiring registration[181] or Accession State nationals subject to worker authorisation.[182] If they no longer fall into either of those classes (eg because they have been working for more than 12 months, or because they did not need to register as an Accession State worker), they are treated as all other EEA nationals who are workers.

EEA nationals who are self-employed persons[183]

3.87 A 'self-employed person' is defined as 'a person who establishes himself in order to pursue activity as a self-employed person in accordance with Article 43 of the Treaty establishing the European Community'.[184]

3.88 Article 43 refers to 'freedom of establishment' which is itself defined as 'the right to take up and pursue activities as self-employed persons and to set up and manage undertakings'.

Accession State workers requiring registration or 'A8 nationals'[185]

3.89 An 'Accession State worker requiring registration' is defined in the Accession (Immigration and Worker Registration) Regulations 2004,[186] as a

---

178   [2005] EWHC 3194 (Admin), [2006] HLR 18, Admin Ct.
179   [2008] EWCA Civ 1440, [2009] HLR 30, CA.
180   Arden LJ at [23].
181   See **3.89–3.94**.
182   See **3.95–3.98**.
183   Allocation of Housing and Homelessness (Eligibility) (England) Regulations 2006, SI 2006/1294, reg 4(2)(b). There is no guidance in the English Allocation Code. Up-to-date guidance can be found at English Homelessness Code, para 9.14(b) and Annex 12, paras 26–30.
184   Immigration (European Economic Area) Regulations 2006, SI 2006/1003, reg 4(1)(b). The Treaty referred to is the Treaty of Rome (1957).
185   Allocation of Housing and Homelessness (Eligibility) (England) Regulations 2006, SI 2006/1294, reg 4(2)(c), substituted by Allocation of Housing and Homelessness (Eligibility) (England) (Amendment) (No 2) Regulations 2006, SI 2006/3340, reg 2. There is no guidance in

national of one of the A8 countries[187] who is working in the UK at some time between 1 May 2004 and 30 April 2011. Once an Accession State worker requiring registration has legally worked for a period of 12 months without interruption, he or she is no longer an 'Accession State worker requiring registration' and is to be treated as any other EEA national who is a worker.

3.90 An 'Accession State worker requiring registration' is treated as a 'worker' while he or she is working for an authorised employer, but not otherwise.[188] An employer is 'an authorised employer' if:

- the worker has received a valid registration certificate authorising him or her to work for that employer; or

- the worker was legally working for the employer on 30 April 2004 and has not ceased working for that employer; or

- the worker is in his or her first month of employment with the employer and has applied for, but not yet received, a valid registration certificate; or

- the employer is employing certain seasonal agricultural workers.[189]

3.91 An Accession State worker requiring registration will have a registration card and/or a registration certificate.[190] An A8 national who is a jobseeker will not have any right of residence and will not be eligible for homelessness assistance.[191]

3.92 After 30 April 2011, nationals of A8 Member States are to be treated in the same way as other EEA nationals.[192]

3.93 It should be noted that not all nationals of the A8 Member States are 'Accession State workers requiring registration'. If a national of an A8 Member

---

the English Allocation Code. Up-to-date guidance can be found at English Homelessness Code, para 9.14(c) and Annex 10, paras 20–25 and Annex 13.

[186] SI 2004/1219, reg 2, as amended by reg 2 of the Accession (Immigration and Worker Registration) (Amendment) Regulations 2009, SI 2009/892.

[187] See Box 2 at **3.27**.

[188] SI 2004/1219, reg 5(2) as amended by reg 1 of the Immigration (European Economic Area) Regulations 2006, SI 2006/1003.

[189] SI 2004/1219, reg 7.

[190] SI 2004/1219, reg 8.

[191] SI 2004/1219, reg 4(2). He or she will be a 'person subject to immigration control' and therefore fall within the first sub-category of persons from abroad at HA 1996, s 160A(3). He or she is unlikely to fall within Classes A–E of the Allocation of Housing and Homelessness (Eligibility) (England) Regulations 2006, SI 2006/1294, reg 3(1) and therefore unlikely to be eligible. See **3.35–3.48**.

[192] SI 2004/1219, reg (1)(a) and (c), as substituted by Accession (Immigration and Worker Registration) (Amendment) Regulations, SI 2009/892, reg 2, extending the period beyond the original termination date of 30 April 2009.

State falls into one of the following categories, he or she will not be an 'Accession State worker requiring registration' and should be treated like any other EEA national:

- an A8 national who is self-employed, self-sufficient or a student;[193]

- a person who, on 30 April 2004, had leave to enter or remain in the UK under the Immigration Act 1971 and that leave was not subject to any conditions restricting his or her employment;[194]

- an Accession State worker requiring registration who has legally worked for a period of 12 months (before or after 30 April 2004) without interruption;[195]

- a person who is a dual national, and who is a national of the UK and of another EEA Member State (except for the A8 States) or Switzerland;[196]

- a person who is a diplomat, or a family member of a diplomat;[197]

- a person who is a 'posted worker';[198]

- a person who is a family member of an EEA national where the EEA national has a right to reside, unless the EEA national is an Accession State worker requiring registration, an Accession State national subject to worker authorisation, or a jobseeker from the A8 or A2 states.[199]

3.94 It follows that an A8 national who is self-employed will be exempt from the habitual residence test and eligible for an allocation of social housing.

---

[193] The derogation permitted by EU law in respect of workers from A8 and A2 countries only applies to 'workers' and 'jobseekers'. It does not apply to freedom of establishment of the self-employed or movement for any other purpose. This is reflected in Accession (Immigration and Worker Registration) Regulations 2004, SI 2004/1219, reg 2(1), which defines an 'Accession State worker requiring registration' as someone who is 'working in *the UK*' [emphasis added].

[194] Accession (Immigration and Worker Registration) Regulations 2004, SI 2004/1219, reg 2(2).

[195] SI 2004/1219, reg 2(3) and (4).

[196] SI 2004/1219, reg 2(5).

[197] SI 2004/1219, reg 2(5A).

[198] SI 2004/1219, reg 2(6)(a). A 'posted worker' is a worker who, for a limited period, is working in the territory of a different Member State from that where he or she normally works (Directive 96/71/EC, arts 1 and 3).

[199] SI 2004/1219, reg 2(6)(b). For 'family member', see **12.117–12.121**. For 'right to reside', see **12.111–12.129**. For 'Accession State national subject to worker authorisation', see **3.95–3.98**.

Accession State nationals subject to worker authorisation or 'A2 nationals'[200]

3.95 An 'Accession State national requiring worker authorisation' is defined in the Accession (Immigration and Worker Authorisation) Regulations[201] as a national of one of the A2 countries.[202]

3.96 An Accession State national subject to worker authorisation will be exempt from the habitual residence test and thus eligible for an allocation of social housing during such time as he or she holds an Accession Worker authorisation document and is working in accordance with the conditions set out in that document.[203] The document normally issued is a registration certificate.[204] An A2 national who is a jobseeker will not have any right of residence and will not be eligible for an allocation of social housing.

3.97 After 31 December 2011, A2 nationals are to be treated in the same way as other EEA nationals.[205]

3.98 Not all nationals of Bulgaria or Romania fall within the definition of 'an Accession State national subject to worker authorisation'. They should be treated in the same way as other EEA nationals if they fall into one of these categories:

- a person who, on 31 December 2006, had leave to enter or remain without any restriction on taking employment;[206] or

- a person who has legally (with leave to remain) worked in the UK without interruption for a period of 12 months;[207] or

- a person also holding nationality of another EEA Member State (other than Bulgaria or Romania) or British nationality;[208] or

- a spouse or civil partner of a UK national or of a person settled in the UK;[209] or

---

[200] SI 2006/1294, reg 4(2)(c)(ii), substituted by Allocation of Housing and Homelessness (Eligibility) (England) (Amendment) (No 2) Regulations 2006, SI 2006/3340, reg 2, in force from 1 January 2007.

[201] SI 2006/3317, reg 2(1).

[202] Bulgaria and Romania. See Box 2 at **3.27**.

[203] SI 2006/3317, reg 6(2).

[204] SI 2006/3317, reg 7.

[205] SI 2006/3317, reg 1(2)(c) and reg 6(1).

[206] SI 2006/3317, reg 2(2), as substituted by the Accession (Immigration & Worker Authorisation) (Amendment) Regulations 2007, SI 2007/475, reg 2(2).

[207] SI 2006/3317, reg 2(3) and (4). This is the case whether the 12-month period falls wholly before 31 December 2006, partly before and partly after 31 December 2006, or wholly after 31 December 2006.

[208] SI 2006/3317, reg 2(5).

[209] SI 2006/3317, reg 2(6).

- a diplomat or family member of a diplomat;[210] or

- a person who has a permanent right of residence pursuant to Immigration (European Economic Union) Regulations 2006, reg 15;[211] or

- a family member of an EEA national who has the right to reside in the UK, other than EEA nationals who are Accession State nationals subject to worker authorisation or are family members of such an Accession State national;[212] or

- a family member of an A2 national who has the right to reside in the UK by virtue of being a self-employed person, or a self-sufficient person or a student;[213] or

- a person who holds a registration certificate to the effect that he or she is a highly skilled person and has unconditional access to the labour market;[214] or

- a person who is in the UK as a student, who holds a registration certificate that includes a statement that he or she is a student who has access to the UK labour market, and who is working not more than 20 hours a week during term time,[215] or is working for no more than 4 months after the end of his or her course and who holds a registration certificate that includes a statement that he or she may work during that period;[216] or

- a 'posted worker'.[217]

Any national of Bulgaria or Romania who falls within one of these categories will fall to be treated as any other EEA national would be.

---

[210] SI 2006/3317, reg 2(6A).

[211] SI 2006/3317, reg 2(7). See **12.123–12.124**.

[212] SI 2006/3317, reg 2(8)(a), as substituted by the Accession (Immigration and Worker Authorisation) (Amendment) Regulations 2007, SI 2007/475, reg 2(2). For 'family member', see **12.117–12.121**. For 'right to reside', see **12.111–12.129**.

[213] SI 2006/3317, reg 2(8)(b), as substituted by the Accession (Immigration and Worker Authorisation) (Amendment) Regulations 2007, SI 2007/475, reg 2(2). For 'family member', see **12.117–12.121**. For 'right to reside', see **12.111–12.129**. For 'self-employed person', see **3.87–3.88**. For student, see **12.116**.

[214] SI 2006/3317, reg 2(9).

[215] He or she may work full-time during vacation (SI 2006/3317, reg 10A(b)).

[216] SI 2006/3317, reg 2(10), (10A) and (10B), as substituted by the Accession (Immigration and Worker Authorisation) (Amendment) Regulations 2007, SI 2007/475, reg 2(2).

[217] SI 2006/3317, reg 2(11) and (13)(a). A 'posted worker' is a worker who, for a limited period, is working in the territory of a different Member State from that where he or she normally works (Directive 96/71/EC, arts 1 and 3).

Family members of certain EEA nationals[218]

3.99 A family member of an EEA national (who is a worker, a self-employed person, an Accession State worker requiring registration, or an Accession State national subject to worker authorisation) is exempt from having to satisfy the habitual residence test.

3.100 The 'family member' need not be a worker, a self-employed person, an Accession State worker requiring registration or an Accession State national subject to worker authorisation. Indeed, he or she need not be economically active at all. Nor need he or she be an EEA national. So long as he or she is a 'family member' of an EEA national (who is a worker, a self-employed person, an Accession State worker requiring registration or an Accession State national subject to worker authorisation), he or she is exempt from the habitual residence test. He or she can apply for an allocation for social housing in his or her own right. There is no need for the EEA worker, self-employed person or Accession State worker requiring registration to be the applicant.

3.101 In some circumstances, there is not even any need for the EEA national to be part of the applicant's household in order for the applicant to be eligible as a 'family member'.[219]

3.102 'Family members' are defined at Immigration (European Economic Area) Regulations 2006, reg 7[220] as:

- the EEA national's spouse or civil partner;[221]

- any direct descendants of the EEA national, or of his or her spouse or civil partner, who are under 21, or who are dependent on the qualifying person, or his or her spouse or civil partner;[222]

---

[218] Allocation of Housing and Homelessness (Eligibility) (England) Regulations 2006, SI 2006/1294, reg 4(2)(d). There is no guidance in the English Allocation Code. Up-to-date guidance can be found at English Homelessness Code, para 9.14(d) and Annex 12, paras 43–50.

[219] For example, spouses and civil partners remain 'family members' until their marriage or partnership is legally terminated, whether or not they are actually cohabiting with the EEA national. See **12.117**.

[220] SI 2006/1003.

[221] Immigration (European Economic Area) Regulations 2006, SI 2006/1003, reg 7(1)(a). A 'spouse' means a person who is formally contracted to a legal marriage (*Netherlands v Reed 59/85* [1986] ECR 1283; *R v Secretary of State for the Home Department ex p Monro-Lopez* [2007] Imm AR 11, QBD; *Diatta v Land Berlin* [1986] 2 CMLR 164, ECJ). 'Civil partnership' is defined at Civil Partnership Act 2004, s 1. In both cases, the emphasis is on the legal condition, not on whether or not the parties continue to live together. A marriage or civil partnership only ends upon death, divorce, annulment, or dissolution of the civil partnership. A party to a marriage of convenience, or to a civil partnership of convenience, is excluded from the definition (SI 2006/1003, reg 2(1)).

[222] SI 2006/1003, reg 7(1)(b).

- any dependent direct relatives in the ascending line of the EEA national or his or her spouse or civil partner;[223] and

- any extended family member who has been issued with an EEA family permit, a registration certificate or residence card.[224]

There are special rules for students.[225]

3.103 'Family members' thus include dependent children, dependent parents, parents-in-law, and parents of a qualifying person's civil partner.[226] So long as adult children are 'dependent' on the qualifying person, their ages are irrelevant. Children who are not dependent on the qualifying person, but are nevertheless under 21 (an 18-year-old who is working, for example) also fall within the definition.

3.104 Cohabiting partners, whether of the same sex or different sex, do *not* fall within the definition of 'spouse' or 'civil partner'. For cohabiting partners to be 'family members', they must be:

- the partner of an EEA national; and

- in a 'durable relationship' with him or her; and

- have been issued with an EEA family permit, registration certificate or residence card.[227]

3.105 Other types of relationship could fall within the definition of 'extended family members'.[228] If an extended family member of an EEA national has been issued with an EEA family permit, a registration certificate or a residence card, he or she is to be treated as a 'family member' of an EEA national, so

---

[223] SI 2006/1003, reg 7(1)(c).

[224] SI 2006/1003, reg 7(1)(d). For 'extended family member' see fn 229.

[225] SI 2006/1003, reg 7(2) and (4).

[226] The inclusion of the word 'direct' in the Immigration (European Economic Area) Regulations 2006, SI 2006/1003 suggests that 'family members' cannot be grandchildren or grandparents.

[227] 'Partner' falls within the definition of 'extended family members' if the relationship is a 'durable relationship' (Immigration (European Economic Area) Regulations 2006, SI 2006/1003, reg 8(5)). 'Extended family members' are to be counted as 'family members' if they have been issued with an EEA family permit, registration certificate or residence card which has not ceased to be valid and has not been revoked (reg 7(1)(d) and (3)).

[228] 'Extended family members' are defined at reg 8 of the Immigration (European Economic Area) Regulations 2006, SI 2006/1003 and are either: (1) relatives of an EEA national, his or her spouse or civil partner, who are: (a) residing with the EEA national in an EEA state and are dependent upon the EEA national or a member of his or her household, or (b) on serious health grounds strictly require the personal care of the EEA national, his or her spouse or civil partner, or (c) would meet the requirements in the immigration rules for indefinite leave to enter or remain in the UK as a dependent relative of the EEA national; or (2) A cohabiting partner (same sex or different sex) of an EEA national if he or she can prove that he or she is in a 'durable relationship' with the EEA national.

long as he or she continues to fall within the definition of an 'extended family member' and so long as the documentation has not ceased to be valid or been revoked.[229]

EEA nationals and their family members who have certain permanent rights to reside in the UK[230]

3.106 'Permanent right of residence' is defined at reg 15 of the Immigration (European Economic Area) Regulations 2006.[231] This exemption from the habitual residence test only applies to three sub-classes of persons who are entitled to a permanent right of residence.

3.107 Those three sub-classes give permanent rights of residence to:

(1)   an EEA national who was a worker[232] or self-employed person[233] who has ceased activity;[234]

(2)   the family member[235] of such an EEA national;[236] and

(3)   a person who was:
  - the family member of an EEA national who was a worker or self-employed person; and
  - the EEA national has died; and
  - the family member had resided with the EEA national immediately before his or her death; and
  - either the EEA national had resided in the UK for at least 2 years immediately before his or her death; or
  - the death was the result of an accident at work or an occupational disease.[237]

---

[229]   Immigration (European Economic Area) Regulations 2006, SI 2006/1003, reg 7(4). Paragraph 9.14 of the English Homelessness Code suggests that extended family members who have been issued with an EEA family permit, registration certificate or residence card which has not ceased to be valid and has not been revoked will not fall within this exception. This does not seem to be a proper construction of the Regulations and is at odds with the guidance at English Homelessness Code, Annex 12, paras 15 and 43.

[230]   Allocation of Housing and Homelessness (Eligibility) (England) Regulations 2006, SI 2006/1294, reg 4(2)(e). There is no guidance in the English Allocation Code. Up-to-date guidance can be found at English Homelessness Code, Annex 12, paras 38–39.

[231]   SI 2006/1003. See **12.123–12.124**.

[232]   For 'worker', see **3.82–3.86**.

[233]   For 'self-employed person', see **3.87–3.88**.

[234]   Immigration (European Economic Area) Regulations 2006, SI 2006/1003, reg 15(1)(c). See **12.123**. 'Worker or self-employed person who has ceased activity' is defined at SI 2006/1003, reg 5. See Appendix 2.

[235]   For 'family member', see **12.117–12.121**.

[236]   SI 2006/1003, reg 15(1)(d). See **12.123–12.124**.

[237]   SI 2006/1003, reg 15(1)(e). See **12.123**.

3.108 There will be other EEA nationals who have a permanent right of residence that is not within these three specified sub-classes.[238] They will have to satisfy the habitual residence test in order to be eligible.[239]

People from Montserrat[240]

3.109 This group of people, who are eligible for an allocation even if they are not habitually resident, are persons who left the territory of Montserrat after 1 November 1995 because of the effect on that territory of a volcanic eruption. They will normally be British citizens or Commonwealth citizens.[241] Not all people leaving Montserrat are rendered eligible by this provision. It does not apply to those who left on or before 1 November 1995. Nor does it apply to those who left after that date for reasons unconnected with the volcanic eruption. The regulation emphasises the departure location, ie it covers those who were in Montserrat and left after 1 November 1995. It also emphasises the reason for departure: the effect of the volcanic eruption. The person's nationality is not relevant. Most of those displaced to the UK in consequence of the volcanic eruption will long since have become habitually resident and will not need to rely on this exception to that test.

People who are in the UK as a result of having been deported, expelled or otherwise removed by compulsion of law from another country to the UK[242]

3.110 This group of persons who are eligible even if not habitually resident is probably small. The inclusion of this class brings eligibility for an allocation of social housing into line with eligibility for housing benefit.

A person who left Lebanon on or after 12 July 2006 because of the armed conflict there[243]

3.111 This group of people, who are eligible even if not habitually resident, is self-explanatory. In similar terms to the provision exempting those fleeing the volcanic eruption in Montserrat, it refers to people who are British citizens, or have other rights to enter or remain in the UK, but have not been habitually resident in the CTA.[244] This provision exempts them from complying with the habitual residence test. To fall within this group:

---

238 See **12.125–12.129**.

239 Allocation of Housing and Homelessness (Eligibility) (England) Regulations 2006, SI 2006/1294, reg 4(1)(a). See **3.71–3.79** for 'habitual residence'.

240 SI 2006/1294, reg 4(2)(f). There is no guidance in the English Allocation Code. Up-to-date guidance can be found at English Homelessness Code, paras 9.19–9.20.

241 Obviously, to be eligible at all, he or she must not be a 'person subject to immigration control'. See **3.23–3.31** for who is and who is not a 'person subject to immigration control'.

242 SI 2006/1294, reg 4(2)(g). There is no guidance in the English Allocation Code. Up-to-date guidance can be found at English Homelessness Code, para 9.21.

243 SI 2006/1294, reg 4(2)(h), inserted by Allocation of Housing and Homelessness (Eligibility) (England) (Amendment) Regulations 2006, SI 2006/2007, reg 2(5) and in force from 4pm on 25 July 2006.

244 See **3.71–3.79** for 'habitual residence' and **3.26**, Box 1 for CTA.

- a person must have left Lebanon, not elsewhere;

- he or she must have left on or after 12 July 2006; and

- his or her reason for leaving Lebanon must have been 'because of the armed conflict there'.

3.112 This provision is only effective for 'the relevant period', which is defined as being between 4pm on 25 July 2006 and 31 January 2007.[245] After 31 January 2007, anyone who has fled Lebanon because of the armed conflict, and had not made his or her application for an allocation during the relevant period, would have to satisfy the habitual residence test.

People who arrived in Great Britain on or after 28 February 2009 but before 18 March 2011 and who immediately before arriving in Great Britain had been resident in Zimbabwe and, before leaving Zimbabwe, had accepted an offer made by Her Majesty's Government, to assist them to settle in the UK[246]

3.113 This exception applies to British citizens, who have left Zimbabwe and arrived in Great Britain between 28 February 2009 and 18 March 2011. They must have left as a result of having accepted an offer of assistance from the British government. The government intends to offer assistance only to British citizens and British nationals who have the right of abode in the UK. They will either be aged 70 or over, or will be vulnerable due to health and social care needs that mean that they are not able to look after themselves.[247]

3.114 Their spouses, partners and any dependants can accompany them, but whether they too will be offered assistance is to be decided on a case-by-case basis.

3.115 This exception applies only to applications for homelessness assistance made on or after 18 March 2009.[248]

---

[245] Allocation of Housing and Homelessness (Eligibility) (England) Regulations 2006, SI 2006/1294, reg 2(4), inserted by Allocation of Housing and Homelessness (Eligibility) (England) (Amendment) Regulations 2006, SI 2006/2007, reg 2(2).

[246] SI 2006/1294, reg 4(2)(i), inserted by the Allocation of Housing and Homelessness (Eligibility) (England) (Amendment) Regulations 2009, SI 2009/358.

[247] Explanatory Memorandum to the Allocation of Housing and Homelessness (Eligibility) (England) (Amendment) Regulations 2009, SI 2009/358, para 7.

[248] Allocation of Housing and Homelessness (Eligibility) (England) (Amendment) Regulations 2009, SI 2009/358, reg 1.

The second class of persons not subject to immigration control but nevertheless not eligible: EEA nationals with a right to reside in the UK by virtue of being jobseekers, family members of a jobseeker, or by exercising an initial right to reside[249]

3.116 Anyone who falls exclusively within this class cannot be eligible for housing allocation. The habitual residence test is not relevant. If an EEA national is:

(a)   a jobseeker,[250] or

(b)   a family member[251] of a jobseeker, or

(c)   only entitled to remain in the UK by virtue of the initial right to reside for 3 months,[252]

he or she cannot be eligible.

3.117 So, this second class operates to ensure that any EEA national, or family member of an EEA national, whose *only* right of residence in the UK is the initial 3-month right of residence is not eligible for an allocation of social housing.

3.118 It also excludes jobseekers from an allocation of social housing. EEA nationals who are 'jobseekers' are 'qualified persons'[253] and therefore are entitled to the extended right of residence.[254] A 'jobseeker' is defined as 'a person who enters the UK in order to seek employment and can provide evidence that he is seeking employment and has a genuine chance of being engaged'.[255] If the jobseeker had previously been employed, he or she may still be a 'worker' in certain circumstances and therefore potentially eligible for that reason.[256]

3.119 However, if a person's only claim to the extended right of residence is because of his or her status as a 'jobseeker', or as a family member of a jobseeker, he or she will not be eligible.

3.120 If a person has more than one right of residence, such as being both a jobseeker and being the family member of a worker or self-employed person,

---

[249]   Allocation of Housing and Homelessness (Eligibility) (England) Regulations 2006, SI 2006/1294, reg 4(1)(b). There is no guidance in the English Allocation Code. Up-to-date guidance can be found at English Homelessness Code, para 9.13(ii) and (iii), and Annex 12, paras 9–10, 12–14.
[250]   See **12.116**.
[251]   See **12.117–12.121**.
[252]   See **12.112–12.114**.
[253]   Immigration (European Economic Area) Regulations SI 2006/1003, reg 6(1)(a). See **12.116**.
[254]   See **12.115–12.122**.
[255]   Immigration (European Economic Area) Regulations 2006, SI 2006/1003, reg 6(1)(a) and (4).
[256]   See **3.83**.

then his or her right to reside is not 'only' derived from his or her status as a jobseeker and he or she will not fall within this second class of persons (not subject to immigration control) who are not eligible for an allocation of social housing.

The third class of persons not subject to immigration control but nevertheless not eligible: EEA nationals with a right to reside in the rest of the Common Travel Area by virtue of being jobseekers, family members of a jobseeker or exercising an initial right to reside[257]

3.121 For 'jobseeker' see **12.116**. For 'family member' see **12.117–12.121**. For 'initial right to reside' see **12.112–12.114**. For 'Common Travel Area' see **3.26**, Box 1.

3.122 This third class refers to people who have been residing in the Channel Islands, the Isle of Man or the Republic of Ireland. The rest of the CTA is dealt with by the second class.[258]

Applications for an allocation made before 1 June 2006

3.123 For applications for an allocation of social housing made to English local housing authorities before 1 June 2006, the Allocation of Housing (England) Regulations 2002, reg 5[259] contained the exercise of the Secretary of State's power to designate classes of persons who were not subject to immigration control as 'other persons from abroad' and therefore not eligible. Those Regulations were amended (and reg 5 substituted in its entirety) by the Allocation of Housing and Homelessness (Amendment) (England) Regulations 2004,[260] which came into force on 1 May 2004.

3.124 It is necessary, therefore, to consider the position for applications made between 1 May 2004 and 31 May 2006, and then to consider the position for applications made before 1 May 2004.

Applications made between 1 May 2004 and 31 May 2006

3.125 Regulation 5 of the Allocation of Housing (England) Regulations 2002[261] designated two classes of persons as not eligible for housing allocation despite the fact that they were not persons subject to immigration control.[262] Those were:

---

[257] Allocation of Housing and Homelessness (Eligibility) (England) Regulations 2006, SI 2006/1294, reg 4(1)(c). There is no guidance in the English Allocation Code. Up-to-date guidance can be found at English Homelessness Code, para 9.13(iv).

[258] See **3.116–3.120**.

[259] SI 2002/3264.

[260] SI 2004/1235, in force from 1 May 2004.

[261] SI 2002/3264, as amended.

[262] The Code was published in 2002 and therefore does not contain any guidance as to these classes, which were introduced in 2004.

(1)   Class E:[263] people not habitually resident in the Common Travel Area, subject to exemptions; and

(2)   Class F:[264] people whose right to reside in the Common Travel Area derived solely from their status as self-sufficient or retired persons.

Each of these Classes will be examined in turn.

Class E:[265] those who are not habitually resident in the CTA, with exemptions

3.126   For 'habitually resident' see **3.71–3.79**. For 'Common Travel Area' see Box 1 at **3.26**.

3.127   Those not subject to the habitual residence test are:

(1)   EEA nationals who are 'workers';[266]

(2)   Accession State workers requiring registration;[267]

(3)   EEA nationals who have the right to reside in the UK;[268] and

(4)   persons who had left the territory of Montserrat after 1 November 1995 because of the effect on that territory of a volcanic eruption.[269]

3.128   Three of these exemptions are replicated in the current Regulations:

•   For 'worker', see **3.82–3.86**.

•   For 'Accession State workers requiring registration', see **3.89–3.94**.

•   For 'persons who had left the territory of Montserrat', see **3.109**.

3.129   The 'right to reside' in the third exemption was the 'right to reside' enjoyed by 'qualified persons' and by 'family members' of qualified persons under the Immigration (European Economic Area) Regulations 2000.[270] If an

---

[263]   Allocation of Housing (England) Regulations 2002, SI 2002/3264 as amended, reg 5(1)(a).

[264]   SI 2002/3264 as amended, reg 5(1)(b).

[265]   SI 2002/3264 as amended, reg 5(1)(a).

[266]   SI 2002/3264 as amended, reg 5(2)(a).

[267]   SI 2002/3264 as amended, reg 5(2)(b).

[268]   SI 2002/3264 as amended, reg 5(2)(c).

[269]   SI 2002/3264 as amended, reg 5(2)(d).

[270]   For applications made between 30 April 2006 and 31 May 2006, the relevant definitions are at Immigration (European Economic Area) Regulations 2006, SI 2006/1003, reg 6 'qualified person', reg 7 'family member' and reg 14 'extended right of residence'. For applications made before 30 April 2006, the relevant definitions are at Immigration (European Economic Area) Regulations 2000 SI 2000/2326, reg 5 'qualified person', reg 6 'family members' and reg 14 'right to reside'. Note that the definitions in the two Regulations are slightly different.

EEA national was not a 'qualified person' and did not have the 'right to reside', then he or she was deemed not to be habitually resident.[271]

Class F:[272] *nationals of EEA Member States who have a right to reside in the CTA based solely on their status as self-sufficient or retired persons*

3.130 Class F comprises those EEA nationals whose right to reside was solely derived from European Union Council Directives 90/364/EEC or 90/365/EEC. Those Directives referred to nationals of EEA Member States who were self-sufficient or retired. There are no exceptions to Class F. Someone who falls within this class is ineligible, whether or not he or she is habitually resident.

3.131 Their right to reside must derive 'solely' from these Directives. If someone has a right to reside derived from other provisions, he or she will not fall within this class and (depending on the other provisions) may be eligible. Thus, a retired person who is also a family member[273] of an EEA national who is a 'qualifying person'[274] will have a right to reside derived both from his or her own status and also from the qualifying person's economic activity. He or she will therefore not fall within this class.

Applications made on or before 30 April 2004

3.132 The English rules applying to applications made on or before 30 April 2004 prescribed that people who were not habitually resident in the CTA[275] were 'persons from abroad' and therefore not eligible unless they fell within certain prescribed exemptions.[276]

3.133 Those exemptions were:

(1) 'workers' who are EEA nationals;

(2) people with a right to reside in the UK derived from the Immigration (European Economic Area) Regulations 2000;[277] and

(3) people who left the territory of Montserrat after 1 November 1995 because of the effect on that territory of a volcanic eruption.[278]

---

[271] Allocation of Housing (England) Regulations 2002 SI 2002/3264 as amended, reg 5(3).
[272] SI 2002/3264 as amended, reg 5(1)(b).
[273] See Immigration (European Economic Area) Regulations 2000, SI 2000/2326, reg 6 for definition.
[274] SI 2000/2326, reg 5.
[275] The UK, the Republic of Ireland, the Channel Islands and the Isle of Man. See Box 1.
[276] Allocation of Housing (England) Regulations 2002, SI 2002/3264, reg 5. See also English Code, paras 4.4–4.10. For discussion on 'habitual residence' see **3.71–3.79**.
[277] Immigration (European Economic Area) Regulations 2000, SI 2000/2326.
[278] See Allocation of Housing (England) Regulations 2002, SI 2002/3264, reg 5 (unamended). See also English Code, para 4.9.

3.134　These categories are all discussed earlier in this chapter or elsewhere in this book.

- For 'worker', see **3.82–3.86**.

- For 'a person with a right to reside', see **12.111–12.129**.

- For 'a person who left the territory of Montserrat', see **3.109**.

3.135　Two groups of people (who would not be eligible under the later rules) may therefore be eligible if their applications for an allocation were made on or before 30 April 2004:

- EEA nationals who were habitually resident at the time of their application; and

- EEA nationals whose right to reside derived solely from Council Directives (EEC) 90/364 or 90/365 (self-sufficient or retired people), whether or not they were habitually resident.

3.136　Only nationals of those states that were members of the EEA prior to 1 May 2004 could fall within these categories.

The Welsh rules

3.137　Applicants to Welsh local housing authorities who have come from abroad will find their applications determined under Allocation of Housing (Wales) Regulations 2003, reg 5.[279] These regulations apply to all applications made on or after 29 January 2003.[280]

3.138　The basic rule is that people who are not subject to immigration control but who are not habitually resident in the CTA are not eligible unless they are:

(1)　workers exercising European Economic Area Treaty right;[281]

---

[279] Allocation of Housing (Wales) Regulations 2003, SI 2003/239 (W 36) as amended by the Allocation of Housing and Homelessness (Eligibility) (Wales) Regulations 2009, SI 2009/393 (W 42), the latter in force for applications for an allocation of social housing made on or after 20 March 2009.

[280] As a result, the regulations in force in Wales do not reflect the extended rights given by the European Union Citizens' Rights Directive (Directive on the right of citizens of the Union and their family members to move and reside freely within the territory of the Member States, 2004/38/EC) or, indeed, the Civil Partnership Act 2004. It may be that an applicant to a Welsh local housing authority who would be eligible had he or she applied to an English local housing authority after 1 June 2006 can argue that the Directive is capable of direct effect, and he or she should be entitled to those extended rights.

[281] Allocation of Housing (Wales) Regulations 2003, SI 2003/239 (W 36), reg 5(a).

(2)   people with a right to reside in the UK pursuant to the Immigration (European Economic Area) Regulations 2000;[282] or

(3)   people who left the territory of Montserrat after 1 November 1995 because of the effect on that territory of a volcanic eruption;[283] or

(4)   a person who arrived in Great Britain between 28 February 2009 and 18 March 2011 and who before arriving had been resident in Zimbabwe and who had accepted an offer made by the UK government to settle in the UK.[284]

3.139   These groups have all been discussed earlier in this chapter or elsewhere in this book:

• For discussion of 'habitual residence', see **3.71–3.79**.

• For 'worker', see **3.82–3.86**.

• For 'a person with a right to reside', see **12.111–12.129**.[285]

• For 'a person who left the territory of Montserrat', see **3.109**.

• For 'a person who arrived in Great Britain between 28 February 2009 and 18 March 2001 from Zimbabwe and who had accepted an offer made by the UK government to settle in the UK', see **3.113–3.115**. A person falling within this last group will be exempt from the habitual residence test if he or she made an application for an allocation of social housing on or after 20 March 2009.

Summary of differences in eligibility as between English and Welsh local housing authorities

Overview

3.140   People considering making applications for an allocation of social housing may want to consider whether they should direct their applications towards English or Welsh local housing authorities, since the eligibility rules are governed by different Regulations depending on which country the local housing authority is in. Unlike HA 1996, Part 7 ('Homelessness'), there is no

---

[282]   SI 2003/239 (W 36), reg 5(b). Although this Order remains in the text of the Allocation of Housing (Wales) Regulations 2003, reg 5, it was repealed by the Immigration (European Economic Area) Regulations 2006, SI 2006/1003, reg 31 and Sch 3.

[283]   Allocation of Housing (Wales) Regulations 2003 (W 36), SI 2003/239, reg 5(c).

[284]   Allocation of Housing (Wales) Regulations 2003, SI 2003/239 (W 36), reg 5(d), inserted by the Allocation of Housing and Homelessness (Eligibility) (Wales) Regulations 2009, SI 2009/393 (W 42), reg 2 and in force for applications to Welsh local housing authorities made on or after 20 March 2009.

[285]   For applications made before 30 April 2006, the relevant 'right to reside' is in the Immigration (European Economic Area) Regulations 2000, SI 2000/2326.

procedure within HA 1996, Part 6, for any referral between local housing authorities.[286] As a result, an applicant should direct his or her application for an allocation of social housing towards the local housing authorities in whose district he or she would wish to live. There is nothing to prevent an applicant making applications to more than one local housing authority.

Applications to Welsh local housing authorities

3.141   The following applicants would be eligible for an allocation of social housing if they apply to Welsh local housing authorities, but would not be eligible if they apply to English local housing authorities:

- a person who is subject to immigration control and is habitually resident[287] in the CTA[288] and who either:
  - is a national of a state which has ratified the ECSMA or the ESC and is lawfully present in the UK,[289] or
  - before 3 April 2000 was owed a duty by a local housing authority under Housing Act 1985, Part 3, or HA 1996, Part 7, which is extant and is a national of a state which is a signatory to the ECSMA or ESC;[290] or

- a person who is not subject to immigration control and whose sole right of residence in the CTA is by virtue of being a jobseeker or of being a family member of a jobseeker will be exempt from the habitual residence test.[291]

Applications to English local housing authorities

3.142   The only group of persons who might be found to be eligible on application to an English local housing authority, but not on application to a Welsh local housing authority, are persons who are in the UK as a result of their deportation, expulsion or other removal by compulsion of law from another country to the UK. If a person falling within that group applies to an English local housing authority, he or she will be exempt from the habitual residence test.[292] If he or she applies to a Welsh local housing authority, the habitual residence test will be applied.

---

[286]   See Chapter 15.

[287]   See **3.71–3.79**.

[288]   See **3.26**, Box 1.

[289]   Class D(i). See Allocation of Housing (Wales) Regulations 2003, SI 2003/239 (W 36), reg 4. See **3.53–3.55**.

[290]   Class D(ii). See Allocation of Housing (Wales) Regulations 2003, SI 2003/239 (W 36) and **3.56–3.58**.

[291]   SI 2003/239 (W 36), reg 5. See **3.138**. Such a person would be exempt from the habitual residence test.

[292]   Allocation of Housing and Homelessness (Eligibility) (England) Regulations, SI 2006/1294, reg 6(2)(g).

THE SECOND CATEGORY: INELIGIBLE DUE TO UNACCEPTABLE BEHAVIOUR

Introduction

3.143 Sensible management of social housing would be wholly undermined if vacant properties had to be let to applicants whose recent past behaviour had amply demonstrated their continuing unsuitability to hold such tenancies. Indeed, in the absence of any control mechanism, a local housing authority might find that its allocation scheme required the immediate re-housing of an applicant who had only recently been evicted on conduct grounds by that very same local housing authority or by the Registered Social Landlord (RSL) to which the allocation scheme would require it to make a nomination.

3.144 From 1996 to 2003, the control mechanism was the ability of a local housing authority to exclude from its housing register those classes of applicant it chose to designate as 'non-qualifying persons'.[293] Not all local housing authorities chose to use this power, although some used suspension from the housing register as an unlawful alternative. Where it was used, it was often targeted at classes of applicants such as those owing arrears of rent or other debts to the local housing authority or those evicted for anti-social behaviour. Indeed, some local housing authorities adopted a plethora of excluded classes, some of dubious propriety.[294]

3.145 With the abolition of the need to keep housing registers in January 2003,[295] it became necessary to offer local housing authorities a substitute mechanism allowing them to control access to allocation schemes. Parliament decided to deprive local housing authorities of the power to exclude 'classes of persons'.[296] Instead, it gave them a power to exclude only particular individual applicants who could be identified as falling within a very narrowly drawn statutory definition. The remainder of this chapter is concerned with the operation of that provision.

The current control mechanism – an overview

3.146 A local housing authority now may, but is not required to, decide that an applicant is to be treated as ineligible for allocation as a result of his or her

---

[293] HA 1996, s 161(4) repealed by Homelessness Act 2002, Sch 2. See **1.18–1.19**.
[294] *Exclusions from the Housing Register* (Northern Housing Consortium, May 2000), www.northern-consortium.org.uk. Unhappily, research has shown that too many local housing authorities have continued to apply blanket exclusions. See 'Housing Allocation and Homelessness: A Special Report by the Local Government Ombudsman for Wales' (www.ombudsman-wales.gov.uk, February 2006); 'Exclusions in Tyne and Wear: an investigation by Shelter's NEHAC into why applicants are excluded from social rented housing' (Shelter, April 2006), at http://england.shelter.org.uk/files/docs/20824/Exclusions%20in%20Tyne%20and%20Wear.pdf; *Am I on the list? Exclusion from and reinclusion on social housing waiting lists* (Chartered Institute of Housing Cymru, May 2008); and **1.60–1.64**.
[295] HA 1996, s 162 repealed by Homelessness Act 2002, Sch 2.
[296] HA 1996, s 161(4) repealed by Homelessness Act 2002, Sch 2.

past unacceptable behaviour, or the behaviour of a member of his or her household. The wording of the statutory provision (HA 1996, s 160A) prevents local housing authorities from operating blanket exclusions, and requires them to consider the behaviour of each applicant, or a member of his or her household, individually.

3.147 A local housing authority's decision that an applicant is 'ineligible', and thus excluded from consideration for an allocation, requires consideration of two stages:

(1) Does the applicant meet certain statutory conditions?

(2) Will the local housing authority, in the exercise of its discretion, elect to treat the applicant as 'ineligible' as a result of the applicant fulfilling those conditions?[297]

3.148 As far as the *first stage* of the test for ineligibility on behaviour grounds is concerned, there are two statutory conditions:

(a) that the applicant, or a member of his or her household, has been guilty of past unacceptable behaviour of a specified standard (described in the rest of this chapter as Condition One);[298] and

(b) in the circumstances at the time when the application for allocation is considered, the applicant is unsuitable to be a tenant of the local housing authority by reason of that past behaviour (described in the rest of this chapter as Condition Two).[299]

At the *second stage* the local housing authority is deciding, in the exercise of an unfettered discretion, whether to in fact treat an applicant who satisfies both of the two statutory conditions as ineligible for its scheme.

3.149 The statutory conditions of the *first stage* are intended to provide a 'high test'. During the passage of the Homelessness Bill,[300] these provisions attracted concern, not just from the opposition during Parliamentary debate, but also from the Joint Select Committee on Human Rights. The government justified the new provisions as part of its:

> '... wider policy on tackling anti-social behaviour and ensuring that the relevant agencies have the means of dealing with it. The test ... is *a high test*, and will ensure that authorities will be able to decline only those applicants whose behaviour would genuinely render them unsuitable to be a tenant. This provision

---

[297] HA 1996, s 160A(7).
[298] HA 1996, s 160A(7)(a).
[299] HA 1996, s 160A(7)(b).
[300] Subsequently Homelessness Act 2002.

will enable housing authorities to protect the rights of their existing tenants and others to the peaceful enjoyment of their home and neighbourhood'[301] (emphasis added).

3.150 The government emphasised that the power to decide that an individual was ineligible for allocation was a discretionary power, that local housing authorities were not required to use it, and that it could only be used in a manner that was compatible with an applicant's Convention rights.[302] Even an applicant who met the first stage conditions may not be found ineligible in the exercise of the *second stage* discretion. The government referred to the safety net of accommodation available to those excluded from an allocation under the National Assistance Act 1948 and the Children Act 1989,[303] and noted that persons declared ineligible by virtue of their behaviour would still be eligible for housing benefit, and thus able to access private rented accommodation. In respect of the latter feature, matters have since moved on with the introduction of pilot schemes of housing benefit sanctions for tenants who lost their previous homes by reason of anti-social behaviour.[304]

3.151 The Joint Select Committee accepted that the government's argument was tenable. It remained concerned that those excluded from eligibility by their behaviour might suffer degrading treatment by reason of homelessness affecting their health and welfare, or suffer a failure of respect for their home and family life. Despite those concerns, the Joint Select Committee was satisfied that the provision was compatible with Convention rights.[305]

The statutory conditions

Condition One: guilty of unacceptable behaviour

3.152 The first condition is that the local housing authority must be satisfied that the applicant or a member of his household has been guilty of unacceptable behaviour serious enough to make him unsuitable to be a tenant of that authority.[306]

---

[301] DTLR memo to the Joint Select Committee on Human Rights, para 6.3, reproduced in the Appendix to the report of the Joint Committee dated 7 November 2001 and available at www.publications.parliament.uk/pa/jt200102/jtselect/jtrights/30/3005.htm.

[302] Rights under the European Convention of Human Rights set out in Human Rights Act 1998, Sch 1.

[303] See **20.15–20.48** and **20.55–20.82**.

[304] *Housing Benefit Guidance On Housing Benefit Anti-Social Behaviour Sanction For Local Authorities Participating in the Pilot Scheme*, http://research.dwp.gov.uk/housingbenefit/claims-processing/claims-guidance/docs/hb-guidance.pdf.

[305] The section has yet to generate any litigation claiming that it is incompatible with the provisions of Human Rights Act 1998, although it has been unsuccessfully contended that a decision that an applicant is not eligible for an allocation engages (and may infringe) the right to respect for a home protected by Human Rights Act 1998, Sch 1, art 8: *R (Dixon) v Wandsworth London Borough Council* [2007] EWHC 3075 (Admin) at [28]-[30] and *R (Dixon) v Wandsworth London Borough Council* [2008] EWCA Civ 595 at [11].

[306] HA 1996, s 160A(7)(a).

The statutory definition of 'unacceptable behaviour'

3.153 Parliament has particularly specified, in HA 1996, s 160A(8), what standard of behaviour is to be considered bad enough to meet the first condition for ineligibility. 'Unacceptable behaviour' is defined as only that behaviour, by the applicant or by a member of his or her household, which would, if the applicant were a secure tenant of the local housing authority, entitle it to a possession order on any ground in Housing Act 1985, Part 1, Sch 2 (other than Ground 8).[307]

3.154 This rather curious phrasing generates four important preliminary points.

(1) Literal or hypothetical approach

3.155 The test may arise for application either literally or hypothetically, in that the applicant may or may not have been a secure tenant of the local housing authority at the time of the relevant past misconduct. If the applicant, or a relevant member of his or her household, was at that time a secure tenant of the same local housing authority and a possession order was obtained, then the definition can be readily and literally applied. There will be a possession order in existence for the local housing authority to consider. But in many more circumstances the question will be being posed hypothetically. The local housing authority will be asking itself: 'What if the applicant had at that time been one of our secure tenants?' This hypothetical approach will be needed where the applicant was, at the relevant time:

- only an introductory or non-secure tenant of the same local housing authority; or

- a secure tenant of the same local housing authority who lost that tenancy otherwise than in response to a possession order;[308] or

- a secure or other tenant of any other local housing authority; or

- a tenant, of whatever type, of any other landlord; or

- a homeowner; or

- a guest, lodger, or any other form of occupier of a previous home.

3.156 Indeed, Condition Two of the statutory conditions (discussed later in this chapter) also contains an element that requires either a literal or a hypothetical approach, and that relates to the identity of the likely future

---

[307] HA 1996, s 160A(8).

[308] In *R (Dixon) v Wandsworth London Borough Council* [2007] EWHC 3075 (Admin) and *R (Dixon) v Wandsworth London Borough Council* [2008] EWCA Civ 595, the applicant's secure tenancy was lost when his co-joint tenant gave notice to quit.

landlord. If the likely future landlord is the local housing authority itself, a literal approach can be taken: 'Is the applicant "unsuitable" for one of our own tenancies?' But the ineligibility test is also available where a successful applicant could only expect to be nominated to a different landlord (an RSL or a different local housing authority).[309] In such a case, the test is one of suitability to be the local housing authority's tenant even though there is no prospect or possibility of such a tenancy.

(2) The meaning of 'entitle'

3.157 The second general point to emerge from the definition is the curious use of the word 'entitle' in the phrase 'would ... entitle the authority to a possession order ...'.[310] None of the relevant grounds for possession are mandatory grounds.[311] Instead, all of them require the court to find that 'it is reasonable to make the order' for possession.[312] Strictly speaking, it is impossible to say that any landlord is 'entitled' to possession where possession is sought on a discretionary ground that depends (for the grant of an order) on the exercise of discretion by the court. It has been left to the Codes of Guidance to spell out that the intention is that the definition will only catch behaviour so bad that a landlord could properly be said to be 'entitled' to an outright order for possession from the court.[313] This has led a judge to accept that 'the effect of the provisions is to require the local housing authority to be satisfied that a notional county court judge would probably make an outright order for possession in the circumstances of the case'.[314]

(3) The meaning of 'behaviour'

3.158 The statutory wording is concerned with the 'behaviour' of the applicant, or, where relevant, that of a member of his or her household. Indeed, the terminology used is 'guilty of unacceptable behaviour'. This would naturally be understood to require some past action or activity on that person's part. But in context it must, at least arguably, also include an applicant's omission, failure to act, passivity or inactivity in circumstances where there has been an expectation of action. Otherwise it would not embrace common cases of 'unacceptable behaviour' such as:

(1)   failing to pay rent or other charges; or

(2)   simple inactive non-compliance with obligations under a tenancy, eg failing to maintain the garden; or

---

309   Because the local housing authority may have disposed of all of its stock to one or several RSLs.

310   HA 1996, s 160A(8)(a).

311   See Housing Act 1985, Sch 2.

312   Under Housing Act 1985, s 84(2)(a). These grounds are therefore commonly referred to as 'discretionary grounds' for possession.

313   English Code, para 4.22(ii); Welsh Code, para 3.17(ii); and see **3.175–3.181**.

314   *R (Dixon) v Wandsworth London Borough Council* [2007] EWHC 3075 (Admin) at [17].

(3)   failing to control the actions of lodgers or visitors.

3.159 Such a wide construction would be consistent with the judicial approach to the term 'guilty of conduct causing or likely to cause a nuisance or annoyance' in a statutory ground for possession.[315] It is rather surprising that, in this context, parliamentary counsel did not adopt the now familiar rubric of 'deliberately does or fails to do anything' to be found in other provisions of HA 1996.[316] The Codes provide particular guidance as to how local housing authorities should approach unacceptable 'behaviour' in the context of mental illness.[317]

3.160 The statutory emphasis on the behaviour of the applicant (or a member of the applicant's household) was relied upon by the claimant in *R (McQ) v Bolton Metropolitan Borough Council*.[318] He had given up his former home for reasons associated with the anti-social behaviour of third parties with whom he had been involved. He argued that that conduct (being neither his conduct nor that of any member of his household) was irrelevant. The Administrative Court held that the claimant's former association with the third parties – members of a paramilitary organisation in Northern Ireland which had undertaken the anti-social conduct – itself constituted ample factual material to support the decision that *his own* behaviour would have notionally made out the statutory grounds for possession.

(4) Household membership

3.161 Plainly, the policy of the legislation, reflected in the wording used, is to avoid the control mechanism being circumvented by an application being made in the name of an innocent member of the household rather than by the actual perpetrator of the misconduct. Accordingly, local housing authorities may not only consider the applicant's own behaviour but also that of 'a member of his [or her] household'.[319] HA 1996, Part 6 contains no statutory definition of the term 'household'. It will therefore be for the local housing authority to decide which persons constitute the applicant's household for these purposes. The local housing authority's allocation scheme might set out how membership of a household will be ascertained or may be silent on the issue, leaving the decision to be made by officers on the facts of individual cases interpreting 'household' by reference 'to its ordinary, everyday usage'.[320]

3.162 HA 1996, Part 6 appears to be looking to the *present* household composition. So, an applicant with an unblemished past may find that he or

---

[315]   Housing Act 1985, Sch 2, Ground 2. See also *Kensington and Chelsea Royal London Borough Council v Simmonds* (1997) 29 HLR 507, CA.

[316]   Such as the test of intentional homelessness in HA 1996, s 191(1). See **14.30–14.77**.

[317]   English Code, para 4.25.

[318]   [2005] EWHC 1285 (Admin), (2005) August *Legal Action*, p 17, Admin Ct.

[319]   HA 1996, s 160A(7)(a).

[320]   *R (Ariemuguvbe) v Islington London Borough Council* [2009] EWHC 470 (Admin), (2009) April *Legal Action*, p 21 at [14], upheld on appeal in *R (Ariemuguvbe) v Islington London Borough Council* [2009] EWCA 1218, (2010) January *Legal Action*, p 35.

she is rendered ineligible by having formed a common household with a person who brings to that household past misconduct, either the new partner's own misconduct, or that of any other person. As will be seen, the innocent applicant is only saved from any adverse consequence of the new partner's past misconduct if that history is immaterial to the applicant's own present suitability to be a tenant.[321]

3.163 But the statutory provision also engages with the *past* composition of the applicant's household. HA 1996, Part 6, when defining unacceptable behaviour, does so in terms that include past 'behaviour of a member of his [or her] household'.[322] Given that the statutory language is taking attention back to past misbehaviour, it must be capable of being satisfied by the misconduct of a person who was at that time a member of the applicant's household but is no longer. This, it appears, preserves the control mechanism against the abuse that an applicant may have temporarily separated from a past member of his or her household to avoid the prospect of ineligibility through misconduct, with every intention of resuming residence together once a tenancy has been allocated. It does mean, however, that an innocent applicant, whose former miscreant household member has permanently departed, may nevertheless still be disqualified. Whilst a safeguard is provided by the requirement that the past misconduct must presently render the applicant unsuitable as a tenant (Condition Two – discussed below), that requirement may well be met, even where the perpetrator is long gone, if it is considered material that the applicant failed to bring to an earlier end the misconduct of that other.

Applying the statutory definition of 'unacceptable behaviour'

3.164 On detailed examination, the definition in HA 1996, s 160A(8) itself breaks down into three constituent questions, each of which the local housing authority needs to address in succession:

(1)   Is one, or are more than one, of the seven relevant grounds for possession made out by the circumstances of the past behaviour?

(2)   If so, would a court consider it reasonable to make an order for possession under Housing Act 1985, s 84 on the basis of that behaviour?

(3)   If so, would a court make an *outright* order for possession?

3.165 The applicant is only guilty of 'unacceptable behaviour' for the purposes of this statutory provision if the local housing authority is able to answer 'Yes' to all three questions. It can be readily envisaged that different local housing authorities may well give different answers to some or all of these questions, even when considering the same set of facts. Indeed, it might be thought common knowledge that a county court judge sitting at one court

---

[321]   See **3.183**.
[322]   HA 1996, s 160A(8)(b).

would certainly evict for a particular level of misconduct which, had the matter been tried before the county court judge at another court, would have resulted in dismissal or adjournment of the possession claim or the making of a postponed order for possession. Precisely because the making of a possession order does require a discretionary decision, the statutory definition is sensitive to such variables.[323]

3.166   The first step in applying the statutory definition is to be clear as to the wording of the relevant statutory grounds for possession. The current wording of Housing Act 1985, Sch 2, Part 1, Grounds 1–7, is given in Table A.

Table A
Grounds For Possession Under Housing Act 1985, Sch 2, Part 1

Ground 1	Rent lawfully due from the tenant has not been paid or an obligation of the tenancy has been broken or not performed.

Ground 2	The tenant or a person residing in or visiting the dwelling-house:
	 (1) has been guilty of conduct causing or likely to cause a nuisance or annoyance to a person residing, visiting or otherwise engaging in a lawful activity in the locality; or
	 (2) has been convicted of:
	     (i) using the dwelling-house or allowing it to be used for immoral or illegal purposes; or
	     (ii) an indictable offence committed in, or in the locality of, the dwelling house.[324]

---

[323] See **3.176**.

[324] 'Indictable' inserted by Serious Organised Crime and Police Act 2005, s 111 and Sch 7, in force from 1 January 2006 (Serious Organised Crime and Police Act 2005 (Commencement No 4 and Transitory Provision) Order 2005, SI 2005/3495, art 2(1)(m).)

Ground 2A	The dwelling-house was occupied (whether alone or with others) by a married couple, a couple who are civil partners of each other,[325] a couple living together as husband and wife or a couple living together as if they were civil partners[326] and:
	(a) one or both of the partners is a tenant of the dwelling-house;
	(b) one partner has left because of violence or threats of violence by the other towards:
	(i) that partner, or
	(ii) a member of the family of that partner who was residing with that partner immediately before the partner left; and
	(c) the court is satisfied that the partner who has left is unlikely to return.
Ground 3	The condition of the dwelling-house or of any of the common parts has deteriorated owing to acts of waste by, or the neglect or default of, the tenant or a person residing in the dwelling-house and, in the case of an act of waste by, or the neglect or default of, a person lodging with the tenant or a sub-tenant of his, the tenant has not taken such steps as he ought reasonably to have taken for the removal of the lodger or sub-tenant.
Ground 4	The condition of furniture provided by the landlord for use under the tenancy, or for use in the common parts, has deteriorated owing to ill-treatment by the tenant or a person residing in the dwelling-house and, in the case of ill-treatment by a person lodging with the tenant or a sub-tenant of his, the tenant has not taken such steps as he ought reasonably to have taken for the removal of the lodger or sub-tenant.
Ground 5	The tenant is the person, or one of the persons, to whom the tenancy was granted and the landlord was induced to grant the tenancy by a false statement made knowingly or recklessly by:
	(a) the tenant; or
	(b) a person acting at the tenant's instigation.

---

[325] Inserted by Civil Partnership Act 2004, s 81, s 263(2) and Sch 8, in force from 5 December 2005 (Civil Partnership Act 2004 (Commencement No 2) Order 2005, SI 2005/3175.
[326] Inserted by Civil Partnership Act 2004, s 81, s 263(2) and Sch 8, in force from 5 December 2005 (Civil Partnership Act 2004 (Commencement No 2) Order 2005, SI 2005/3175.

Ground 6	The tenancy was assigned to the tenant, or to a predecessor in title of his who is a member of his family and is residing in the dwelling-house, by an assignment made by virtue of s 92 (assignments by way of exchange) and a premium was paid either in connection with that assignment or the assignment which the tenant or predecessor himself made by virtue of that section. In this paragraph 'premium' means any fine or other like sum and any other pecuniary consideration in addition to rent.
Ground 7	The dwelling-house forms part of, or is within the curtilage of, a building which, or so much of it as is held by the landlord, is held mainly for purposes other than housing purposes and consists mainly of accommodation other than housing accommodation, and: (a) the dwelling-house was let to the tenant or a predecessor in title of his in consequence of the tenant or predecessor being in the employment of the landlord; or of – a local authority; – a new town corporation; – a housing action trust; – an urban development corporation; or – the governors of an aided school; and (b) the tenant or a person residing in the dwelling-house has been guilty of conduct such that, having regard to the purpose for which the building is used, it would not be right for him to continue in occupation of the dwelling-house.

3.167   In practice, behaviour that falls within either or both of Grounds 1 or 2[327] (arrears, breach of tenancy, and nuisance) is likely to be the most common form of 'unacceptable behaviour' considered by local housing authorities. But when considering the applicant's behaviour, or that of a member of his or her household, local housing authorities should take care to ensure that the behaviour would in fact have given rise to a ground for possession by satisfying the precise wording of the statute. For example, the only 'rent' that counts for Ground 1 purposes is 'rent lawfully due', and not unpaid instalments of overpaid housing benefit, or arrears owed by a previous tenant.[328] Likewise, nuisance behaviour or indictable offences committed *away* from the locality of the dwelling house do not fall within Ground 2.

---

[327]   Housing Act 1985, Sch 2.
[328]   *Tickner v Clifton* [1929] 1 KB 207, Div Ct.

3.168 However, if the applicant's behaviour, or that of a member of his or her household, demonstrably does fall within the precise words of one or more of the grounds for possession, the next question is whether it would have been reasonable for a court to make an order for possession. The question arises because all of the prescribed grounds are discretionary grounds upon which the landlord must be able to satisfy the court that 'it is reasonable to make' a possession order (of whatever type).[329] The test of reasonableness is a very broad one, and will depend on the individual circumstances of each case. The courts themselves are warned by judicial precedent against applying hard and fast rules.[330]

3.169 Where the behaviour consists of allowing 'rent arrears' to accrue, a court hearing possession proceedings would normally consider, on the question of reasonableness:

• the level of the arrears;

• the reason for the arrears accruing, including the degree of personal culpability for those arrears;

• any outstanding housing benefit issues;

• any offers to repay; and

• the tenant's, and his or her household's, personal circumstances.[331]

3.170 If relevant past behaviour was 'nuisance or annoyance', the court hearing a possession claim is required to consider:

• the effect that the nuisance or annoyance has had on persons other than the person against whom the order is sought;

• any continuing effect the nuisance or annoyance is likely to have on such persons;

• the effect that the nuisance or annoyance would be likely to have on such persons if the conduct is repeated.[332]

---

329   Housing Act 1985, s 84(2).

330   *Cresswell v Hodgson* [1951] 2 KB 92, CA and, more recently, *Whitehouse v Lee* [2009] EWCA Civ 375, CA.

331   *Woodspring District Council v Taylor* (1982) 4 HLR 95, CA; *Second WRVS v Blair* (1987) 19 HLR 104, CA; *Haringey London Borough Council v Stewart* (1991) 23 HLR 557, CA; *Lambeth London Borough Council v Thomas* (1998) 30 HLR 89, CA; and *Brent London Borough Council v Marks* (1999) 31 HLR 343, CA. See also Madge, McConnell, Gallagher and Luba *Defending Possession Proceedings* (Legal Action Group, 6th edn, 2006).

332   Housing Act 1985, s 85A, inserted by Anti-social Behaviour Act 2003, s 16 (with effect from 30 June 2004).

3.171 The court hearing a possession claim based on nuisance behaviour should also consider:

- the tenant's personal circumstances and those of his or her household;

- the landlord's obligation to its other tenants and to the neighbours;

- the degree of personal culpability of the tenant;

- any factors explaining or mitigating the behaviour (such as a medical condition or a disability);

- the degree of compliance since notices were served and/or proceedings issued;

- any assurances as to future conduct; and

- any other relevant circumstances.[333]

3.172 Where the behaviour in question consists of the commission of a serious criminal offence in the dwelling-house or in the locality of the dwelling-house, it would only be in exceptional circumstances that the court would consider that it is not reasonable to make an order for possession[334] (although, in such a case, a court should also consider the possibility that an order for possession, postponed on conditions, could succeed in controlling the tenant's behaviour).[335]

3.173 In *R (McQ) v Bolton Metropolitan Borough Council*,[336] the applicant argued that the local housing authority's decision on his application had failed to address the question of whether a judge would have found it 'reasonable' to make an order for possession (assuming that a ground for possession based on anti-social behaviour would have been made out). In refusing permission to

---

[333] *Cresswell v Hodgson* [1951] 2 KB 92, CA; *Woking Borough Council v Bistram* (1993) 27 HLR 1, CA; *Wandsworth London Borough Council v Hargreaves* (1994) 27 HLR 142, CA; *Kensington and Chelsea Royal London Borough Council v Simmonds* (1996) 29 HLR 507, CA; *West Kent Housing Association v Davies* (1998) 31 HLR 415, CA; *Camden London Borough Council v Gilsenan* (1999) 31 HLR 81 CA; *Croydon London Borough Council v Moody* (1999) 31 HLR 738, CA; *Portsmouth City Council v Bryant* (2000) 32 HLR 906, CA; *Newcastle upon Tyne City Council v Morrison* (2000) 32 HLR 891, CA; *Lambeth London Borough Council v Howard* [2001] EWCA Civ 468, (2001) 33 HLR 636, CA; *North Devon Housing Association v Brazier* [2003] EWHC 574, [2003] 35 HLR 59, QBD; *Manchester City Council v Higgins* [2005] EWCA Civ 1423, [2006] 1 All ER 841, CA; and *North Devon Homes v Batchelor* [2008] EWCA Civ 840, (2008) September *Legal Action*, p 23 are some of the reported cases on whether it would be reasonable to make a possession order in respect of nuisance or other anti-social behaviour. See also Madge et al *Defending Possession Proceedings* (Legal Action Group, 6th edn, 2006).
[334] *Bristol City Council v Mousah* (1997) 30 HLR 32, CA, but see also *North Devon Homes v Batchelor* [2008] EWCA Civ 840, (2008) September *Legal Action*, p 23.
[335] *Norwich City Council v Famuyiwa* [2004] EWCA Civ 1770, (2005) February *Legal Action*, p 34, CA.
[336] [2005] EWHC 1285 (Admin), (2005) August *Legal Action*, p 17, Admin Ct; and see **3.160**.

bring judicial review proceedings, the Administrative Court held that there was only one answer to the question of whether it would have been reasonable to make an order for possession on the facts of the applicant's case, which was that it would have been reasonable.

3.174 For guidance on the application of the reasonableness requirement as operated in relation to the other five relevant prescribed grounds of possession see the discussion in Madge, McConnell, Gallagher and Luba *Defending Possession Proceedings.*[337]

3.175 The final question for the local housing authority, in applying the 'unacceptable behaviour' limb of the ineligibility test, is whether the court did make (or, in the hypothetical cases, would have made) an outright or a suspended/postponed (conditional) order. HA 1996, Part 6 is silent as to whether suspended or postponed (conditional) possession orders fall within the statutory definition, which refers only to 'a possession order'.[338] However, both Codes of Guidance are very clear that only behaviour that would result in an outright order for possession falls within the statute.[339] During the Parliamentary debate on the then Homelessness Bill,[340] the opposition quoted figures for the number of possession actions brought by social landlords in 2000, showing that in 82% of possession cases the social landlord had believed that it was entitled to an outright order for possession, but the court decided that it was not.[341] In response, the Minister gave assurances that only behaviour justifying an outright, rather than a suspended or postponed (conditional), possession order would fall within this section:

> '... the authority would need to be satisfied that, if a possession order were granted, it would not be suspended by the court.'[342]

3.176 If an outright order was in fact granted in relation to the past misconduct, there is, perhaps, little difficulty with this element of the definition. But applying it to hypothetical cases[343] is probably the most difficult part of the local housing authority's decision-making on ineligibility for misbehaviour. Whether an order is made outright, or is suspended or postponed on terms, is a very broad discretionary decision for the court, taking into account all the circumstances as at the date of the decision.[344] It is not sufficient for the local housing authority to conclude that, on the facts as they have emerged, it would have requested that the court make an outright possession order. For the

---

[337] *Defending Possession Proceedings* (Legal Action Group, 6th edn, 2006).
[338] HA 1996, s 160A(8).
[339] English Code, para 4.22(ii); Welsh Code, para 3.17(ii).
[340] Subsequently the Homelessness Act 2002.
[341] *Hansard*, HL Deb, vol 629, ser 6, col CWH 48 (10 December 2001) (Baroness Maddock): 150,000 actions were started (the vast majority being for rent arrears); 65% resulted in an order being made; but only 18% resulted in an outright order for possession. For current figures see fn 348 below.
[342] *Hansard*, HL Deb, vol 629, ser 6, col CWH 51 (10 December 2001) (Lord Falconer).
[343] See **3.155–3.156**.
[344] Housing Act 1985, s 85(2).

applicant not to be eligible, the local housing authority must be able to conclude that a court *would* in all probability have actually made an outright possession order and *not* a suspended or postponed (conditional) possession order.

3.177 Examples of behaviour that may lead to only a suspended or postponed possession (conditional) order are given in the Codes:

• rent arrears resulting from factors beyond the applicant's control, such as delays in housing benefit, liability for a partner's debts, where the applicant was not in control of the household finances or was unaware of the accrual of arrears;[345]

• where allegations of nuisance are relatively minor, or the nuisance was caused by a member of the household who has since left, or the court would have been satisfied that a suspended or postponed (conditional) order would be sufficient to control the household's future behaviour.[346]

3.178 Local housing authorities frequently request that courts make outright possession orders, but they are far less successful in obtaining them.[347]

3.179 As far as *rent arrears* are concerned, day-to-day practice in the courts suggests that suspended or postponed (conditional) possession orders are made far more regularly than the Codes advise. Postponed (conditional) possession orders are not confined to cases of arrears that are the responsibility, but not the fault, of the tenant. In practice, postponed (conditional) possession orders are made where there are realistic offers by the tenant to repay the arrears, however the arrears accrued.[348]

3.180 In *nuisance cases*, postponed (conditional) possession orders have been approved by the Court of Appeal where the behaviour appears to have ceased, or where the court considers that a postponed (conditional) possession order should be a sufficient deterrent from future misconduct.[349] Often the principal considerations for the court are whether the tenant has some insight into the nuisance caused to his or her neighbours, and whether the court can accept the

---

345　English Code, para 4.22(ii); Welsh Code, para 3.17(ii).

346　Welsh Code, para 3.17(ii).

347　In 2008, social landlords commenced 104,165 claims for possession; 43,972 suspended possession orders were made and only 26,184 outright orders for possession. The latter will include claims by registered social landlords under mandatory grounds for possession (HA 1988, s 21, and Sch 2, Ground 8). Overall, outright possession orders were made in about a quarter of the claims for possession, including claims brought under mandatory grounds (Judicial Statistics 2008, Ministry of Justice, September 2009, Table 4.3).

348　*Lambeth London Borough Council v Henry* (1999) 32 HLR 874, CA; and *Taj v Ali (No 2)* (2001) 33 HLR 259, CA.

349　*Kensington and Chelsea Royal London Borough Council v Simmonds* (1996) 29 HLR 507, CA; *West Kent Housing Association v Davies* (1998) 31 HLR 415, CA; *Portsmouth City Council v Bryant* (2000) 32 HLR 906, CA; *Greenwich London Borough Council v Grogan* (2001) 33 HLR 12, CA; and *Gallagher v Castle Vale Housing Action Trust* [2001] EWCA Civ 944, (2001) 33 HLR 72, CA.

tenant's assurances as to future behaviour. The prescribed statutory criteria which apply in a nuisance case and may have driven the court to be satisfied that it was 'reasonable' to order possession do not expressly apply to the stage at which the court is deciding whether the order should be outright or postponed, but they are intended to remind the court that the focus is on the effect that nuisance and annoyance has on others, and it would be appropriate to consider them again at this stage.[350]

3.181 Two cases well illustrate the operation of this element of the statutory conditions for ineligibility on behaviour grounds:

(1)　In *R (Dixon) v Wandsworth London Borough Council*,[351] the applicant had a history of drug-related incidents at his former home. He accepted that a ground for possession would have been made out and that a judge would have found it reasonable to have made a possession order. However, he challenged the decision of the local housing authority – that he was not eligible for an allocation – on the grounds that his conduct would not have led to the making of an outright order, but only to a suspended or postponed (conditional) order. His claim failed. The judge was satisfied that, in reaching the decision that a county court would probably have granted an outright order, the reviewing officer had applied the correct test, had regard to the relevant considerations, made proper findings of fact (in a lengthy decision letter) and had not reached an irrational conclusion. The applicant's renewed application for permission to appeal was rejected by the Court of Appeal, which said:

> 'it was open to the authority to conclude that an outright order was likely to be made on the facts of this case. The applicant had a history of drug abuse for a period of ten years, during which time the flat was raided three times. The raid that resulted in this conviction had caused £1000 worth of damage to the flat itself, and each raid must have been very disturbing for the applicant's neighbours.'[352]

(2)　In *R (M) v Hackney London Borough Council*,[353] the applicant was an elderly council tenant living alone and seeking a transfer. He had a long history of convictions for sexual offences and in 2004 he had been made subject, by consent, to a sexual offences prevention order which recited activities relating to a teenage boy. The local housing authority decided that the events of 2004 were so serious that had possession been sought on the basis of them the court would have granted an outright order.

---

[350] Housing Act 1985, s 85A, added by Anti-Social Behaviour Act 2003, s 16(1) (with effect from 30 June 2004), *Lambeth London Borough Council v Debrah* [2007] EWCA Civ 1503, (2008) May *Legal Action*, p 44, CA. As to the more general question of whether a conditional or outright order would be made in a nuisance case see *Moat Housing Group-South Ltd v Harris & Hartless* [2005] EWCA 287, [2005] HLR 33, CA; and *Manchester City Council v Higgins* [2005] EWCA Civ 1423, [2006] 1 All ER 841, CA per Ward LJ at [29].

[351] [2007] EWHC Admin 3075.

[352] [2008] EWCA Civ 595, CA at [7].

[353] [2009] EWHC 2255 (Admin), (2009) May *Legal Action*, p 26.

Dismissing a claim for judicial review of that decision, the judge emphasised that the judgment as to whether an outright order would have been made was one for the housing authority not the reviewing court. He said:

'The Council took the view that the incident of 2004 constituted anti-social behaviour sufficient to justify an outright possession order. In considering that matter I have regard to two background factors. In *Hensley*[354] Gage LJ referred to the need for a council, as a provider of social housing, to make sure that its properties are properly managed and kept free from undesirable activity. It is in my view also necessary to underline the remarks in the judgment of Otton LJ, which I have quoted, that the judicial and administrative functions should not be elided.[355] Admittedly the remarks were in a somewhat different context. But the message to me is clear: it is not for me to allocate Hackney's housing.'

Condition Two: unsuitable to be a tenant

3.182 The second condition necessary to sustain a decision of ineligibility on behaviour grounds is that, at the time that the application for allocation falls to be considered, the applicant is still unsuitable to be a tenant of the local housing authority by reason of past behaviour.[356] It must be noted that the relevant date for applying this test is *not* the date that the application for allocation was made (which will be an earlier, and sometimes considerably earlier, date than the critical date, which is the date on which the local housing authority reaches a decision on eligibility or concludes a review of that decision). Although the test refers to suitability to be a tenant of the housing authority, it may fall to be applied even by a local housing authority that no longer has any housing stock that it could let to tenants.[357]

3.183 In determining whether past behaviour renders the applicant currently 'unsuitable', local housing authorities should consider whether the tenant's behaviour has improved, whether the circumstances that caused the behaviour have changed (eg in the case of nuisance behaviour that was caused by drug or alcohol problems whether the tenant has successfully resolved those problems), whether the member of the household who was responsible for the behaviour remains a member of the applicant's household, and whether it can accept any assurances from the applicant as to future behaviour.[358]

3.184 If the local housing authority has reason to believe that the past unacceptable behaviour was due to physical, mental or learning difficulties, it

---

[354] *Sandwell Metropolitan Borough Council v Hensley* [2007] EWCA Civ 1425, [2008] HLR 22, CA.
[355] Referring to the judgment of Otton LJ in *City of Bristol v Mousah* (1998) 30 HLR 32 at 40.
[356] HA 1996, s 160A(7)(b).
[357] See **3.156**.
[358] *Hansard*, HL Deb, vol 629, ser 6, col CWH 52, (10 December 2001), the Minister, Lord Falconer, referred to the circumstances as 'all the relevant matters before it. Those will include all the circumstances relevant to the particular applicant, whether health, dependants or other factors'.

should consider whether the applicant could now maintain a tenancy with appropriate care and support.[359] Local housing authorities cannot adopt a blanket approach of treating all applicants who were in the past guilty of nuisance behaviour, or were in substantial rent arrears, as ineligible.[360]

The exercise of the local housing authority's discretion

3.185 Even if the statutory conditions for ineligibility on the basis of past behaviour are made out, the local housing authority must go on to consider whether to exercise its discretion to treat the applicant as ineligible due to that unacceptable behaviour. The word used in the statute is 'may' and not 'shall', making it clear that the local housing authority has such a discretion.[361]

3.186 The local housing authority must take into account, in exercising this discretion, the applicant's particular circumstances, any health needs, any dependants and any other relevant factors.[362] The importance of the discretion is most acutely demonstrated in cases where the applicant meets the statutory conditions for ineligibility by reason of previous default in payment of rent and still has arrears outstanding. The local housing authority must be careful not to automatically de-bar such applicants but instead exercise a discretion on a case-by-case basis. It is essential to avoid loose language which suggests that a fixed rule rather than a discretion is being exercised, e g 'It is the policy of this Council not to make offers to applicants who owe property related debts'.[363]

3.187 The local housing authority, faced with a case meeting the statutory conditions, could nevertheless decide to accept the applicant as eligible for its allocation scheme, but give him or her no preference, or a reduced preference within that scheme (even if she or he would otherwise have been entitled to a

---

[359] English Code, para 4.25.
[360] English Code, para 4.22(iii); Welsh Code, para 3.17(iii). In *R (Onuegbu) v Hackney London Borough Council* [2005] EWHC 1277 (Admin), (2005) August *Legal Action*, p 17, Admin Ct, Hackney explained its operation of the eligibility test in relation to an existing tenant who had rent arrears. Hackney said that its scheme provided that it should assess the application for a transfer, allow the applicant onto its scheme and give the applicant the points to which he or she would be entitled. However, if the applicant then reached the top of the list, he or she would not be offered accommodation. Instead, the applicant would be by-passed, because of his or her rent arrears, and the accommodation offered to the next applicant on the list. It is hard to see how this approach complies with the statutory scheme. It appears to involve unlawful blanket exclusions, rather than individual consideration. There was no evidence that the unacceptable behaviour test was applied, or that the applicant was told of his right to a review of Hackney's decision. If, despite Hackney's use of the word 'eligibility', it was an attempt to apply the unacceptable behaviour test within the reasonable preference categories, or to prioritise good behaviour over bad behaviour, Hackney's policy did not spell that out in the terms of the statute.
[361] HA 1996, s 160A(7).
[362] English Code, para 4.23; Welsh Code, para 3.18.
[363] A passage from a decision letter cited in *R (Joseph) v Newham London Borough Council* [2008] EWHC 1637 (Admin). The claimant went on to succeed in the claim for judicial review because the property related debt on which the council was relying was an irrecoverable overpayment of housing benefit: *R (Joseph) v Newham London Borough Council* [2009] EWHC 2983 (Admin), Admin Ct.

statutory reasonable preference).[364] That is because, if the behaviour affects the applicant's suitability to be a tenant but does not meet the strict ineligibility test, it can still be taken into account when deciding what priority the applicant receives within the scheme. The Welsh Code reminds local housing authorities that they are not obliged to find that an applicant is ineligible on the grounds of unacceptable behaviour, but could instead give the applicant no preference.[365] However, the local housing authority cannot refuse to give any preference at all to an applicant in a category entitled to a reasonable preference except on the same specified grounds as the 'unacceptable behaviour' test of eligibility.[366]

3.188 The Welsh Code sets out detailed policy considerations for local housing authorities to take into account when they are deciding whether or not to treat applicants as ineligible on the grounds of unacceptable behaviour. Starting from the view that 'barriers to social housing should be minimised', the Welsh Code recommends that local housing authorities should:

- carefully consider their role as providers of social housing in order to meet housing need in their area;

- develop their own 'unacceptable behaviour' policies specifying the grounds when a person is likely to be thought ineligible;

- ensure that the procedures used are robust;

- try to keep exclusions to a minimum;

- work collaboratively with the police, probation services and other statutory agencies to share information; and

- monitor and evaluate their policies and practice.[367]

3.189 There has been no systematic national monitoring of the operation of the ineligibility provisions relating to behaviour. It is simply not known how many applicants have been held to fall within the statutory conditions and how many of those have gone on to be excluded from an allocation scheme in the exercise of a local housing authority's discretion. A recent, but limited, study[368] found that 'considerable staff member discretion is often used in determining appropriate treatment of applicants with rent arrears or believed previously responsible for anti-social behaviour. Whether actions taken are fully recorded and monitored is a question beyond the scope of this research.'[369]

---

[364] HA 1996, s 167(2B). English Code, para 4.26.
[365] Welsh Code, para 4.15.
[366] HA 1996, s 167(2A), (2B) and (2C). See also **4.102–4.108**.
[367] Welsh Code, paras 3.20–3.21.
[368] *Exploring local authority policy and practice on housing allocations* (CLG, July 2009).
[369] *Exploring local authority policy and practice on housing allocations* (CLG, July 2009), para 4.6.

WHEN TO DETERMINE ELIGIBILITY

3.190 Under HA 1996, Part 6, as enacted, the eligibility test operated as a control on the admission of an applicant to the local housing register. With the abolition in 2003 of the requirement to keep housing registers, the scheme now works by prohibiting the specific allocation of housing to ineligible applicants. This has led to the practice of testing eligibility twice in respect of any given applicant. First, the eligibility tests are operated when an applicant initially applies for consideration under the particular local allocation scheme. Second, assuming satisfaction of the tests at that stage, they are applied again later when the allocation of a specific property is being contemplated.

3.191 There are two obvious justifications for this double testing.[370] First, if an applicant is admitted for consideration under the local scheme, she or he will have a reasonable (or 'legitimate') expectation that the local housing authority has satisfied itself that he or she is entitled to be allocated property under that scheme.[371] So it is important that eligibility is tested on initial application. Second, there must be a further check just prior to the later prospective allocation of a specific property, because otherwise the local housing authority may mistakenly infringe the statutory injunction that it 'shall not allocate' to an ineligible person.[372] That may include a person who was initially eligible on application but is not eligible when a specific allocation is about to be made. It is therefore particularly important that when a person from abroad receives an initially favourable decision on eligibility, she or he is informed that any changes to his or her immigration status – or, indeed, changes to the complex statutory rules about eligibility and immigration status – could affect eligibility later for a particular allocation of property.[373]

RIGHT TO REVIEW

3.192 All applicants who have been found ineligible (whether on grounds of immigration status or of past misconduct) have the right to written notification of that decision and of the grounds for it.[374] They have the right to request a review of that decision, and to submit new information, as well as any representations, in support of that review.[375] The reviewer should reconsider afresh the whole of the information put before him or her, and consider the facts as at the date of the review decision.

3.193 The applicant is entitled to be informed of the reviewer's decision and the grounds for it. If the reviewer upholds the original decision, there is no mechanism to appeal to the county court and the only available legal challenge

---

[370] Specifically recommended by the Secretary of State in the English CBL Code 2008, para 3.10.
[371] English CBL Code, para 3.10.
[372] HA 1996, s 160A(1).
[373] English CBL Code, para 3.11.
[374] HA 1996, s 160A(9).
[375] HA 1996, s 167(4A)(d).

to the review decision is by judicial review, alleging an error of law in the review process, in the tests applied by the local housing authority in reaching its decision on review, or in the decision itself.[376] In *R (Dixon) v Wandsworth London Borough Council*[377] the applicant complained that the reviewing officer had failed to give the 'grounds' for the review decision because the notice of that decision (a lengthy document) gave insufficient reasons. The judge rejected that claim and was upheld by the Court of Appeal which said that 'the reasons were stated in sufficient detail to enable the applicant to know what conclusion the decision maker had reached on the principal important controversial issues.'[378] In another case, the local housing authority's correspondence relating to a decision on eligibility was described as 'opaque', but a challenge based on inadequate reasons was rejected as the claimant himself was well apprised of the issues being addressed.[379]

RENEWED APPLICATIONS

3.194 The decision reached by a local housing authority on an applicant's eligibility (whether on immigration-related grounds or behaviour-related grounds) does not bind any other local housing authority to reach the same decision. Disappointed applicants unable to overturn the adverse decision may be advised to apply elsewhere.

3.195 Alternatively, the applicant could make a further application to the same local housing authority. Plainly, a person who has been declared ineligible on immigration-related grounds will wish to apply again, as soon as his or her immigration status alters.

3.196 HA 1996, Part 6 expressly envisages that an applicant found to be ineligible on behaviour-related eligibility grounds may want to re-apply on the basis that she or he should no longer be treated as ineligible. It provides for the making of 'a fresh application' in such cases.[380] This is no doubt because the two statutory conditions for ineligibility in the behaviour category link:

(1)   past misconduct; and

(2)   present suitability to be a tenant.

3.197 Inevitably, that link will become weaker with the passage of time and with other changes in an applicant's circumstances. A further application need

---

[376]   Further information on reviews is given at **2.65–2.78**.
[377]   [2007] EWHC 3075 (Admin).
[378]   [2008] EWCA Civ 595 at [9].
[379]   *R (M) v London Borough of Hackney* [2009] EWHC 2255 (Admin), (2009) May *Legal Action*, p 26, Admin Ct.
[380]   HA 1996, s 160A(11).

only be 'fresh' in the sense that the circumstances of the application are not exactly the same as those which obtained when the previous application was determined.[381]

---

[381] *Tower Hamlets London Borough Council v Rikha Begum* [2005] EWCA Civ 340, [2005] HLR 34, CA, and *R (G) v Haringey London Borough Council* [2009] EWHC 2699 (Admin).

Chapter 4

ALLOCATION SCHEMES

INTRODUCTION

4.1 Each local housing authority is required by the Housing Act 1996 (HA 1996), Part 6 ('Allocation of Housing Accommodation') to have a scheme for the allocation of social housing.[1] Even if there were no statutory requirement, each local housing authority would, in practice, need to adopt arrangements for the selection of candidates for the grant of available secure or introductory tenancies in its own housing stock (if any) and for the nomination of applicants to local registered social landlords (RSLs). Without an allocation scheme, a local housing authority would not have the essential framework enabling it to determine the relative priorities between applicants for housing, nor a comprehensive statement of the procedure that should be followed when considering such applications and making allocations.[2]

4.2 This chapter discusses how these local allocation schemes must be framed (whether from the outset or by amendment) in order to comply with HA 1996, Part 6 and how they must work to enable a lawful assessment of each applicant's housing need. The process of actual allocation to those who have had their needs assessed is reviewed in the next chapter. To make sure that the rules described here are followed, HA 1996, Part 6 states that everything that counts as an 'allocation'[3] must be undertaken in accordance with the local allocation scheme or it will be unlawful.[4] As long as a local housing authority complies with the basic requirements set out in this chapter, it is allowed to exercise its own discretion in settling on a scheme for determining how it actually makes allocations and to whom.[5]

4.3 The allocation scheme is therefore the essential starting point for answering the question 'Will I be allocated a home?', whether that question is directed at a member of the local housing authority's staff or a local housing adviser. That is why the schemes must be publicly available for purchase and why each local housing authority must produce a free summary of its scheme.[6]

---

[1]   Housing Act 1996, s 167(1). Statutory guidance on allocation schemes is given by *Allocation of Accommodation: Code of Guidance for local housing authorities for England* (Office of the Deputy Prime Minister, November 2002) [English Code], Chapter 5; *Code of Guidance for local housing authorities on allocation of accommodation and homelessness for Wales* (National Assembly for Wales, April 2003) [Welsh Code], Chapter 4; *Allocation of Accommodation: Choice-based Lettings Code of Guidance for Local Housing Authorities* (Communities & Local Government [CLG], August 2008) [English CBL Code]; *Circular 04/2009* (CLG, April 2009) and by *Fair and flexible: statutory guidance on social housing allocations for local authorities in England* (CLG, December 2009) [English 2009 Code]. See Appendix 1 of this book for the English Codes and Circular and the accompanying CD-ROM for the Welsh Code.

[2]   As required by HA 1996, s 167(1).

[3]   For the definition see HA 1996, s 159(2); and see also the discussion at **1.24–1.26** of circumstances in which a person can become a tenant of social housing without an allocation.

[4]   HA 1996, s 167(8).

[5]   HA 1996, s 159(7) and s 167(6).

[6]   Further detail on access to information about local allocation schemes and individual applications is given at **2.7–2.24**.

ADOPTING OR AMENDING AN ALLOCATION SCHEME

Adopting a scheme

4.4   Most local housing authorities will have long since adopted an allocation scheme as first required by HA 1996, Part 6. But new local housing authorities are now being created in the present Government's drive to establish new unitary authorities for areas with multiple layers of local government. Where such a new unitary authority is being established, which will be a local housing authority for a district, it will need to formulate and adopt a new allocation scheme. There are two essential statutory pre-requisites before any new scheme can be adopted.

4.5   The first is that the local housing authority must undertake the impact assessments required under anti-discrimination legislation and by the local housing authority's own statements of equality policy.[7] Where the proposed scheme will involve choice based letting, the English CBL Code draws the attention of the local housing authority to seven pieces of legislation to which it will need to have regard when drawing up its draft.[8] Indeed, the latest guidance strongly recommends that all local housing authorities carry out an equality impact assessment of any *change* to allocation policies and, by inference therefore, that such an assessment is essential before any *new* scheme is adopted.[9]

4.6   The second requirement is one of limited consultation. Before an allocation scheme is adopted, the local housing authority is required to consult every RSL with which it has nomination arrangements. As part of that consultation, it must send those landlords a copy of the draft scheme and give them a reasonable opportunity to comment on the proposals.[10] 'A reasonable opportunity' is specified in the Welsh Code as being a minimum period of 12 weeks.[11]

4.7   These are, of course, the *minimum* statutory prerequisites. A local housing authority drawing up a scheme for the first time might well be expected to undertake a much wider range of measures before finally adopting its scheme. There is no *statutory* requirement to consult any other people or organisations before adopting a scheme, but much might usefully be gained by eliciting the views of local tenants' organisations, housing advice agencies and the like. The Codes advise that social services departments, health authorities,

---

7   See **4.129–4.132**.
8   English CBL Code, para 1.6. The seven are: the Race Relations Act 1976, the Disability Discrimination Act 1995, the Sex Discrimination Act 1975, the Equality Act (Sexual Orientation) Regulations 2007, SI 2007/1263, the Human Rights Act 1998, the Freedom of Information Act 2000 and the Data Protection Act 1998. The Code advises that this is *not* an exhaustive list.
9   English 2009 Code, para 21.
10   HA 1996, s 167(7).
11   Welsh Code, para 5.14. A similar provision originally appeared in the English Code, para 6.6.

Supporting People teams, Connexions Services, relevant voluntary sector organisations and other recognised referral bodies should be consulted.[12]

4.8　　Indeed, local housing authorities have recently been urged to 'engage with and involve the wider community before they produce their allocation scheme so that people are given the opportunity to contribute to the development of the allocation priorities'.[13]

4.9　　A local housing authority should take into account the findings and conclusions of its own homelessness review and strategy when settling upon (or amending) an allocation scheme and, conversely, the homelessness strategy should take into account the local allocation scheme.[14] HA 1996. Part 6 prescribes that the scheme must set out:

(1)　how the local housing authority will determine priorities between applicants; and

(2)　what procedures it will follow in allocating housing accommodation.[15] The degree of detail required in the finished scheme is considered later in this chapter.[16]

Amending the current local allocation scheme

4.10　　There is no statutory obligation on a local housing authority to keep the terms of its allocation scheme under review or to revise it regularly.[17] However, where as a result of a review of an existing scheme (or for any other reason) the local housing authority proposes to make any significant change to the local allocation scheme, two sets of statutory requirements are triggered. First, the local housing authority will again need to make an impact assessment in compliance with the requirements of anti-discrimination and equalities legislation.[18] Second, if an alteration is to be made which amounts to 'a major change of policy', the local housing authority is required to notify and consult with local RSLs with which it has nomination arrangements and give them a reasonable opportunity to comment on the proposed changes.[19] A minimum consultation period of 12 weeks is recommended.[20]

4.11　　The Welsh Code advises that 'a major change of policy' for these purposes would include any amendment affecting the relative priority of a large number of people being considered for an allocation of social housing, and any

---

12　　English 2009 Code, para 7; Welsh Code, para 5.13.
13　　English 2009 Code, para 44.
14　　English 2009 Code, para 54. See also Homelessness Act 2002, s 1(5).
15　　HA 1996, s 167(1).
16　　See **4.17–4.19**.
17　　In contrast to the requirements in relation to homelessness strategies set out in Homelessness Act 2002, ss 1–4. See **7.162–7.169**.
18　　See **4.129–4.132**.
19　　HA 1996, s 167(7).
20　　Welsh Code, para 5.14. A similar provision originally appeared in the English Code, para 6.6.

significant alteration to allocation procedures.[21] The English 2009 Code suggests that the broadest possible approach be taken to involving the local community in both development and variation of allocation schemes.[22] That can obviously best be secured by taking a wide view of what constitutes a 'major change of policy'.

4.12 The Court of Appeal in *R (A) v Lambeth London Borough Council*[23] was concerned with Lambeth's decision to change the proportions of allocations ('quotas') made available to different groups within its scheme, so that three of the seven groups would receive no allocations whatsoever. Arguably, this constituted 'a major change of policy', certainly as far as the applicants in those three groups were concerned. The prospects of any of them receiving an offer of an allocation had suddenly become 'zero'. The allocation scheme itself did not refer to the quotas of allocations that each group could expect, merely stating 'the effect of preference on each applicant Group is also reviewed, and targets changed if necessary'. The Court of Appeal, whilst holding that other aspects of the scheme were unlawful,[24] held that since the actual proportion of allocations between the different groups was not part of the published scheme, and there was no requirement for it to be published, a change in the proportion did not constitute 'a major change of policy' and there was no need to inform applicants. It follows that 'a major change of policy' must at least be a change relating to the information which is contained, or should be contained, in the published allocation scheme.

4.13 In recent years, the most commonly proposed 'major change of policy' has been to move from officer-led allocations towards applicant choice through the adoption of a choice based element in a current scheme or of a complete replacement choice based letting scheme.[25] Where that is the proposed alteration, the English CBL Code urges local housing authorities to go much further than the basic minimum statutory consultation requirements, and most particularly to consult 'existing tenants, applicants and residents'.[26] It advises that involving a wide range of groups will help local housing authorities to meet 'their race equality, disability and gender equality duties' in respect of the proposed change.[27] In the immediate future, all local housing authorities in England can be expected to be undertaking reviews of, and making possible amendments to, their current allocation schemes in the light of the latest statutory guidance[28] and the need to comply with the new national housing allocation standards coming into effect on 1 April 2010.[29]

---

[21]   Welsh Code, para 5.12. A similar provision originally appeared in the English Code, para 6.3.
[22]   English 2009 Code, paras 40–46.
[23]   *R (A) v Lambeth London Borough Council* [2002] EWCA Civ 1084, [2002] HLR 57, CA.
[24]   See **5.48**.
[25]   See **5.7–5.61**.
[26]   English CBL Code, paras 5.2–5.4.
[27]   English CBL Code, paras 1.7–1.13 and 5.3.
[28]   English 2009 Code, para 15.
[29]   See **1.66**.

4.14 If such an alteration is then made which reflects a 'major change of policy', the local housing authority must take such steps as it considers reasonable to bring the effects of the change to the attention of those likely to be affected by it.[30] Most obviously, that will be the pool of actual or prospective applicants and those likely to be advising them. Very little guidance is given in the Codes as to what steps might be considered reasonable. The English 2009 Code takes a generally expansive approach, encouraging the maximum possible community engagement and involvement.[31] The Welsh Code recommends that a major policy change will require 'each potential applicant to be informed personally by letter', leaving unanswered the question as to how a local housing authority can identify potential, as opposed to actual, applicants.[32]

4.15 Plainly those applicants already being dealt with under the current allocation scheme can be directly written to. However, potential applicants and other members of the public will have to be informed through the usual information mechanisms available to the local housing authority, such as publication on the website, notice in the local newspaper, informing housing advice agencies, etc. Given that existing tenants of social housing who are seeking transfers fall within the allocation scheme arrangements, and would therefore be likely to be affected, arguably the local housing authority should inform all social housing tenants and tenants' organisations in its district of any 'major change of policy' to be reflected in the revised allocation scheme.

4.16 One of the most difficult aspects of adopting extensive amendments to a local housing allocation scheme is the need to deal with those applicants who have already been considered and assessed under the old scheme. In the absence of any express provision to the contrary in the newly amended scheme, the assumption would be that the requirements of the amended scheme would apply immediately to all applicants. In September 2005 one London Borough Council changed its housing allocation scheme from having been points-based to using wholly new assessment bands in which priority operated by reference to registration date. The new scheme did not deal with how applicants registered on the old scheme would be dealt with under the new one. The Court of Appeal declined to fill that gap, holding that it was 'questionable' on what basis the local housing authority could give any applicant a registration date earlier than the date of the adoption of the new scheme – while also indicating that if any such provision was to be made in the future, it should be published.[33]

---

[30]   HA 1996, s 168(3).
[31]   English 2009 Code, paras 39–46.
[32]   Welsh Code, para 5.12.
[33]   *R (Faarah) v Southwark London Borough Council* [2008] EWCA Civ 807, [2009] HLR 12, CA.

ENSURING THAT THE SCHEME IS SUFFICIENTLY DETAILED

4.17   The scheme adopted by the local housing authority must not only set out how the local housing authority will prioritise *between* applicants[34] but additionally the *procedure* that it follows in allocating housing.[35] Where the local housing authority has adopted a choice based letting arrangement, the formal allocation scheme should set out the procedures and priorities as they apply not only to the initial consideration of an applicant's application but also how any bid made by the applicant for specific accommodation will be treated.[36]

4.18   Experience would suggest that there has been a failure to grasp the significance of the fact that, for these purposes, 'procedure' includes 'all aspects of the allocation process, including the persons or descriptions of persons by whom decisions are to be taken'.[37] Too many allocation schemes simply set out broad policy statements, unlawfully leaving the mechanics to be detailed in unpublished procedure manuals or staff training materials. In short, the statutory requirement is that the published scheme deals with both how allocations are made and why that is.

4.19   The courts have not taken an altogether consistent line as to how much detail on the prioritisation of applications or the procedures to be followed in processing them is required in a local allocation scheme. The range of approaches taken by the courts is illustrated by the examples already given in Chapter 2.[38]

DETERMINING PRIORITY FOR ALLOCATION

4.20   The primary function (and requirement) of a local allocation scheme is that it sets out the local housing authority's priorities in allocating housing accommodation. It represents the local housing authority's policy choices about discrimination between applicants – which applicants are to have more priority than others and, where priorities are broadly evenly matched, which applicant is to be preferred. The scheme needs to explain to those operating it or advising about it the circumstances in which Applicant A will have greater or lesser preference than Applicant B. Sadly, the piecemeal evolution of statutory guidance for local housing authorities in England has produced a situation in which the already difficult process of determining priorities within an

---

34   HA 1996, s 167(1).
35   HA 1996, s 167(1).
36   English CBL Code, para 3.7.
37   HA 1996, s 167(1).
38   See **2.18**.

allocation scheme is not made any easier. Such local housing authorities must now wade through three Codes and a Circular to glean the Secretary of State's guidance on the subject.

4.21 HA 1996, Part 6 leaves a local housing authority free to adopt its own locally agreed policies and principles, subject to the terms of HA 1996, Part 6 itself (and any regulations made by the Secretary of State or the Welsh Minister under HA 1996, Part 6).[39] Of course, although the whole process is one of discrimination about access to services, any unlawful discrimination is to be avoided.[40] The most significant constraint on the local housing authority's freedom to select particular applicants is the requirement that the scheme is framed to give a preference to those groups of applicants set out in HA 1996, Part 6. That requirement is considered below.[41]

Giving a 'reasonable preference'

4.22 In relation to prioritisation between applicants, HA 1996, Part 6 states that every local allocation scheme must secure a 'reasonable preference' for the groups of people specified in s 167(2).[42] Local housing authorities must draw up and operate schemes that broadly comply with the statutory list. That does not mean that the local allocation scheme must adopt precisely the same text as that given in HA 1996, Part 6. All that is required is that the local scheme does actually give a reasonable preference to applicants falling into one or more of the statutory groups. The statutory list contains five broad groups and each of the five groups is described and discussed in detail[43] after a consideration of what the concept of a 'reasonable' preference entails.

How much preference is 'reasonable'?

4.23 HA 1996, Part 6 does not accord *absolute* preference to those in the listed groups. Local housing authorities need give them only a *'reasonable* preference' in the allocation scheme.[44] The scheme must, in effect, be framed so as to ensure that applicants with reasonable preference are given a head start over those who do not have a reasonable preference.[45] Just how much preference is reasonable under a particular local scheme for each of the five groups is a

---

39   HA 1996 s 167(6). The functions exercisable by the Secretary of State in HA 1996 were transferred to the National Assembly for Wales when the National Assembly was set up in 1999 (Government of Wales Act 1998, s 22, Sch 3 and National Assembly for Wales (Transfer of Functions) Order 1999, SI 1999/672). The Government of Wales Act 2006, s 162 and Sch 3 transferred the National Assembly for Wales' functions to the relevant Welsh Ministers.

40   See **4.129–4.132**.

41   See **4.22** et seq.

42   HA 1996, s 167(3) permits the Secretary of State for Communities and Local Government and the Welsh Minister to specify further groups of people, or to amend or repeal the groups specified in the Act. Neither the Secretary of State nor the Welsh Minister has exercised these powers since HA 1996, s 167 was amended by Homelessness Act 2002.

43   See **4.39–4.86**.

44   HA 1996, s 167(2); emphasis added by the authors.

45   English 2009 Code, para 18.

matter for the exercise of local discretion. HA 1996, Part 6 does not require that people in the reasonable preference groups must be given preference in relation to every property which is let under the scheme. It is the scheme taken as a whole that must give a reasonable preference to the statutory groups. Accordingly, a scheme which enabled a mere 5% of its available properties to be open to bids from transfer applicants who were not in the reasonable preference categories did not fail to give those statutory priority groups a 'reasonable' preference overall.[46]

4.24 However, HA 1996, Part 6 prohibits local housing authorities from adopting a scheme which awards no *preference* at all to a person within one of the preference groups unless either:

(1) the local housing authority has decided that the applicant has been guilty of 'unacceptable behaviour' within the statutory definition of that term;[47] or

(2) the applicant is entitled to a preference solely because she or he is in one of the first two reasonable preference categories and that category is only satisfied because of the presence in the applicant's household of a 'restricted person'.[48]

4.25 Beyond the statutory list of reasonable preference groups, and, whilst local housing authorities are permitted a good deal of autonomy to decide the procedures and principles they wish to apply locally, HA 1996 steers them to some specific factors. Local housing authorities are, for example, permitted to give 'additional preference' to people with 'urgent housing needs' who fall within any of the reasonable preference categories,[49] and to take account of such an applicant's financial resources, his or her behaviour (good or bad), any local connection with a particular local housing authority's area, or any other matter.[50]

4.26 Provided that they comply with these broad statutory 'reasonable preference' categories, local housing authorities may thereafter decide for themselves on the principles for determining priorities in the local allocation scheme.[51] They will have to decide, for example, how to choose between applicants who fall into the different 'reasonable preference' categories when they come to allocate accommodation, and also how to organise people within each of those different groups according to their comparative need, or

---

46   *R (Ahmad) v Newham London Borough Council* [2009] UKHL 14, at [17]–[21], (2009) April *Legal Action*, p 21, HL.

47   HA 1996, s 167(2B) and (2C); see **4.101–4.108**.

48   HA 1996, s 167(2ZA). For more on the meaning of 'restricted person', see **4.109–4.110**.

49   HA 1996, s 167(2); see **4.87–4.90**.

50   HA 1996, s 167(2A); see **4.91–4.100**.

51   HA 1996, s 167(6).

according to some other locally adopted criteria. The scheme will also need to address the priority to be given to applicants who are not in the reasonable preference categories at all.

4.27 Prior to 2009 it was thought that local housing authorities had to have provision in their allocation schemes to enable them to make a *composite assessment* of the whole of each *applicant's* needs.[52] In addition, local housing authorities were expected to make a composite assessment of the whole of the applicant's *household's* needs, so that the needs of all of the members of the household were identified and taken into account.[53] This approach could be applied to all members of the applicant's household, whether they are eligible for an allocation in their own right or not. Schemes that did not reflect these principles were struck down by the courts.

4.28 However, in 2009 the House of Lords decided that the amendments made to HA 1996, Part 6 by the Homelessness Act 2002 had given local housing authorities even greater flexibility than had previously been thought and that it was *not* necessary for an allocation scheme to provide a mechanism for composite assessments or, put another way, for a scheme to accord priority by reference to the relative gravity of each applicant's housing needs.[54] While the statutory provisions[55] enabled such an approach to be adopted, they did not require it.[56] Indeed, the statutory flexibility given by the terms of HA 1996, Part 6 is such that it would be 'impossible to argue that an authority's allocation scheme is unlawful unless the basis on which it accords priority as between those applicants [in the reasonable preference categories] is irrational'.[57] It follows that, whether the cases decided on the pre-amendment terms of HA 1996, Part 6[58] had been rightly decided or not, they can no longer be relied upon. This decision of the House of Lords was strongly welcomed by the Secretary of State.[59]

4.29 Notwithstanding the degree of flexibility thus permitted, local housing authorities must actually identify the criteria for determining priorities within

---

[52]　*R v Islington London Borough Council ex p Reilly and Mannix* (1999) 31 HLR 651, QBD; *R (A) v Lambeth London Borough Council, R (Lindsay) v Lambeth London Borough Council* [2002] EWCA Civ 1084, [2002] HLR 57, CA; *R (Cali) v Waltham Forest London Borough Council* [2006] EWHC 302 (Admin), [2007] HLR 1 at [31], Admin Ct; and *R (Ahmad) v Newham London Borough Council* [2008] EWCA Civ 400, (2008) April *Legal Action*, p 40, CA (subsequently considered and overturned by the House of Lords): see **5.46–5.54**.

[53]　*R v Tower Hamlets London Borough Council ex p Uddin* (1999) 32 HLR 391, QBD.

[54]　*R (Ahmad) v Newham London Borough Council* [2009] UKHL 14, (2009) April *Legal Action*, p 21, HL; see **5.55–5.57**.

[55]　Particularly the closing sentence of HA 1996, s 167(2) read with the opening words of s 167(2A).

[56]　*R (Ahmad) v Newham London Borough Council* [2009] UKHL 14, at [14], (2009) April *Legal Action*, p 21, HL.

[57]　*R (Ahmad) v Newham London Borough Council* [2009] UKHL 14, at [49], (2009) April *Legal Action*, p 21, HL.

[58]　Most particularly those cases noted at fn 52 above.

[59]　English 2009 Code, para 15.

their allocation schemes.[60] A scheme which did not clearly identify and define the criteria for awarding a reasonable preference was held not to comply with the requirements of HA 1996, s 167(2).[61]

4.30 Once it has identified whether an applicant falls into one or more of the 'reasonable preference' categories, the local housing authority needs a method enabling it to rank applicants, both those falling within and those outside the preference categories, according to their different needs and any other relevant factors, including – if the scheme makes provision for it – the length of time that the applicant has been waiting for an offer. An allocation scheme could therefore be based on awarding points to applicants, or grouping applicants into bands. Either method should accord some preference to those in the 'reasonable preference' categories. In some allocation schemes, a combination of the two methods is used. The most straightforward scheme of allocation, strict date order for all applicants, simply cannot work in the modern statutory framework, which requires some classes of applicants to be given a reasonable preference over others.

4.31 In a *points-based scheme*, points could be awarded to reflect different categories of need, for example for medical and welfare needs, overcrowding, etc, and further points may reflect the length of time that an applicant has been waiting for accommodation after having been accepted onto the scheme. The English 2009 Code suggests that points-based systems can be complex, lacking in transparency and difficult to understand. Local housing authorities retaining such schemes are encouraged to consider simplifying them.[62]

4.32 If a *banding system* is adopted, applicants within each band may be prioritised by points and/or by date order, reflecting the degree of their need and/or their waiting time. The English 2009 Code strongly suggests this as a preferred model.[63]

4.33 Self-evidently, an allocation scheme that placed in the same band or group those applicants who were entitled to 'reasonable preference' and those who were not so entitled, and then treated them equally, would be unlawful.[64] A local housing authority must be able to distinguish between applicants who are entitled to the statutory 'reasonable preference' and those who are not.

4.34 An emphasis on prioritisation by combinations of 'reasonable preference' and the assessment of a particular household's 'need'[65] can produce bizarre results. An applicant could be ceaselessly moving, yo-yo fashion, up and

---

60   HA 1996, s 167(1) and (2A), English Code, para 5.9; Welsh Code, para 4.22.
61   *R (Cali) v Waltham Forest London Borough Council* [2006] EWHC 302 (Admin), [2007] HLR 1, CA at [31].
62   English 2009 Code, para 74.
63   English 2009 Code, paras 70–73.
64   English 2009 Code, para 81; and see *R (A) v Lambeth London Borough Council, R (Lindsay) v Lambeth London Borough Council* [2002] EWCA Civ 1084, [2002] HLR 57, CA.
65   HA 1996, s 167(2).

down the list of those eligible for an allocation as his or her own housing circumstances and needs change and as others apply for an allocation. For example, a household with no children may find itself almost at the top of the list of those awaiting a bed-sit or other small unit of accommodation, only to be taken towards the bottom of the list of those waiting for larger accommodation when a child arrives. On this basis, one local housing authority's scheme survived a challenge to its decision that, where the applicants' need had changed, so that they required a two-bedroom rather than a one-bedroom unit, they should be put at the bottom of the two-bedroom property list, and lose their points awarded for the time that they had waited on the one-bedroom property list.[66] Similarly, in any scheme based on housing need, a household provided with temporary accommodation under HA 1996, Part 7 ('Homelessness') may find that the prospects of securing an early allocation under HA 1996, Part 6 actually diminish if the household is moved to a higher standard of self-contained temporary accommodation. In one case considered by the Local Government Ombudsman, a homeless couple rejected temporary accommodation from the local housing authority precisely because its superior quality was such that they would fall into a lower priority category under the allocation scheme if they accepted it.[67]

4.35   In *R (Ahmad) v Newham London Borough Council*[68] the House of Lords was persuaded that a scheme based on banding together those applicants in *any* of the reasonable preference categories and then prioritising between them by reference to waiting-time had the merit of being 'quantifiable, transparent and hard to manipulate',[69] in contrast to schemes for the affording of relative priority by case-by-case assessment of housing need reflected by the awarding of points. That outcome coincided with the general tone of the Housing Green Paper[70] – which was the precursor to the 2003 amendments to HA 1996, Part 6[71] – and also chimed with the content of the latest statutory guidance in England on how schemes should best be drawn to accord preference while facilitating choice.[72]

4.36   There is one form of prioritisation not accorded by the statute, and which does not turn on 'need'. It arises where applicants have been given a 'legitimate expectation' that they will be allocated local housing authority

---

[66]   *R (El Yemlahi) v Lambeth London Borough Council* [2002] EWHC 1187 (Admin), Sullivan J holding that either scenario created injustice: if the applicants had been placed towards the top of the list for two-bedroom properties (reflecting their waiting time on the list for one-bedroom properties), those below the applicants who had a longer standing need for two-bedroom properties would rightly feel aggrieved.

[67]   *Complaint against Hounslow London Borough Council* (14 April 2009, No 07/A/14215), (2009) June *Legal Action*, p 34.

[68]   *R (Ahmad) v Newham London Borough Council* [2009] UKHL 14, (2009) April *Legal Action*, p 21, HL.

[69]   *R (Ahmad) v Newham London Borough Council* [2009] UKHL 14, at [52], (2009) April *Legal Action*, p 21, HL.

[70]   *Quality & Choice: A decent home for all* (DETR, April 2000), http://www.communities.gov.uk/archived/publications/housing/qualitychoice2.

[71]   By Homelessness Act 2002.

[72]   The English CBL Code.

tenancies, or nominated to an RSL.[73] The possibility of such an expectation being generated must be provided for in the scheme, so that the applicants receive points or are placed in a specific band in order to take account of those expectations.[74] A 'legitimate expectation' generally arises in this context where homeless applicants, who had been accepted as such under the Housing Act 1985, had also been told that they would be given a local housing authority or housing association tenancy in performance of the homelessness duty. It may also arise where a local housing authority has announced a policy giving carers the right to take over tenancies on the death of tenants for whom they were caring. The local housing authority must make provision for such an eventuality in its allocation scheme in order to achieve the recognition of that expectation.

4.37 As already indicated, once the local housing authority has adopted its scheme, it must comply with it. It is unlawful for a local housing authority to allocate accommodation otherwise than in accordance with the scheme.[75]

4.38 The rest of this chapter is concerned with how a local scheme must be framed to meet the statutory and other legal requirements.

The 'reasonable preference' groups

4.39 Five groups of people must be accorded a 'reasonable preference' in housing allocation schemes framed under HA 1996, Part 6. They are:

(1) people who are 'homeless', within the meaning of HA 1996, Part 7;

(2) people who are owed a particular statutory duty by any local housing authority under certain provisions of homelessness legislation;[76]

---

[73] The issue of 'legitimate expectation' arises where a person is, contrary to his or her expectations, deprived: '... of some benefit or advantage which either (i) he had in the past been permitted by the decision-maker to enjoy and which he can legitimately expect to be permitted to continue to do until there has been communicated to him some rational grounds for withdrawing it on which he has been given an opportunity to comment; or (ii) he has received assurance from the decision-maker that they will not be withdrawn without giving him first an opportunity of advancing reasons for contending that they should not be withdrawn': *Council of Civil Service Unions v Minister for the Civil Service* [1985] AC 374, HL, at 408, per Lord Diplock. See *R v North and East Devon Health Authority ex p Coughlan* [2001] QB 213, CA, and for a more recent discussion, *R (Bhatt Murphy (a firm)) v The Independent Assessor* [2008] EWCA Civ 755, CA.

[74] *R (Bibi and Al-Nashed) v Newham London Borough Council* [2001] EWCA Civ 495, (2001) 33 HLR 84, CA; *R (Ibrahim) v Redbridge London Borough Council* [2002] EWHC 2756 (Admin), (2003) February *Legal Action*, at p 35, Admin Ct; and *R (Bibi) v Newham London Borough Council* [2003] EWHC 1860 (Admin), (2003) September *Legal Action*, at p 28, Admin Ct.

[75] HA 1996, s 167(8), *R (Amirun Begum) v Tower Hamlets London Borough Council* [2002] EWHC (Admin) 633, (2003) 35 HLR 8.

[76] HA 1996, s 190(2), s 193(2) and s 195(2); Housing Act 1985, s 65(2) and s 68(2) and people who are occupying accommodation provided for them by any local housing authority under HA 1996, s 192(3). These sections define duties to homeless applicants in priority need (whether they became homeless intentionally or not), duties to applicants threatened with homelessness

(3)   people occupying insanitary or overcrowded housing or otherwise living in unsatisfactory housing conditions;

(4)   people who need to move on medical or welfare grounds, including grounds relating to a disability;[77] and

(5)   people who need to move to a particular locality in the district of the local housing authority, where failure to meet that need would cause hardship, to themselves or to others.[78]

The list may be extended or reduced by ministerial regulations without the need for primary legislation.[79] No such regulations have been made since that power was enacted, and, at the time of writing, there had been no move to give effect to the proposed extension of the reasonable preference categories in England, as had been suggested in a ministerial announcement made in December 2007.[80] Indeed, in a letter to local housing authorities sent with the consultation draft of what was to become the English 2009 Code the current Minister for Housing wrote that he did *not* propose to change or add to the categories.[81]

4.40   It must be noted that HA 1996, Part 6 does not require priority to be given to any particular applicant. All HA 1996 stipulates is that 'the scheme shall be framed' so that it gives reasonable preference to the statutory classes.[82] Each of the present five categories entitled to 'reasonable preference' requires detailed and careful consideration.

People who are 'homeless'[83]

4.41   'Homelessness' is defined in HA 1996, Part 7.[84] Under that definition, a person is homeless if he or she has no accommodation available for his or her occupation, in the UK or elsewhere, which he or she is entitled to occupy:

(1)   by virtue of an interest in the land; or

(2)   because of an order of a court; or

---

who have a priority need and are not intentionally threatened with homelessness, and the power to provide accommodation to unintentionally homeless applicants not in priority need.

77   HA 1996, s 167(2)(d) amended by Housing Act 2004, s 223, adding '(including grounds relating to a disability)' in force in England from 27 April 2005 (Housing Act 2004 (Commencement No 2) (England) Order 2005, SI 2005/1120) and yet to be brought into force in Wales.

78   HA 1996, s 167(2).

79   HA 1996, s 167(3).

80   See **1.65**.

81   John Healey MP, letter 31 July 2009.

82   HA 1996, s 167(2).

83   HA 1996, s 167(2)(a).

84   HA 1996, ss 175–177; see Chapter 11 of this book.

(3)   by an express or implied licence to occupy; or

(4)   by virtue of an enactment or rule of law giving him or her the right to remain in occupation; or

(5)   by reason of a restriction on the right of another person to obtain possession.[85]

4.42   A person who has somewhere to live is therefore 'homeless' *unless* he or she has at least one of these forms of entitlement to occupy – so a person living in a squat is 'homeless'.

4.43   A person is also homeless if he or she has a right to occupy accommodation but cannot secure entry to it, or it is not available, or it is not reasonable for him or her to continue to occupy it.[86] Accommodation is only regarded as 'available' if it is available to be occupied by all the members of the applicant's family who normally reside with him or her, and also by any other person who might reasonably be expected to reside with him or her.[87] Occupiers of caravans, mobile homes, and houseboats are homeless if they have no place where they are permitted both to place and to reside in their vehicle or vessel.[88]

4.44   To fall within the definition of 'homeless', an applicant need not actually have made an application for homelessness assistance to any local housing authority, let alone have received a decision on such an application. The assessment of whether the applicant is 'homeless' will need to be made by the local housing authority to which the application for an allocation has been directed.[89] A person who has already applied to a local housing authority as 'homeless' and has been provided with accommodation in compliance with that local housing authority's duty will obviously have ceased to be 'homeless' (and thus normally falls within the second reasonable preference category – category (2) – which specifically deals with those formerly homeless persons owed housing duties).[90] In one case it was conceded, rightly, that a person provided with interim accommodation by a local housing authority pending the determination of an application for homelessness assistance under HA 1996, Part 7 remained 'homeless' for the purposes of this provision while in that accommodation.[91]

4.45   To obtain a 'reasonable preference' under the 'homeless' category, applicants need not have a 'priority need', a concept relevant only to the

---

[85]   HA 1996, s 175(1).

[86]   HA 1996, s 175(2)(a) and (3).

[87]   HA 1996, s 176.

[88]   HA 1996, s 175(2)(b).

[89]   An applicant for accommodation who gives the local housing authority sufficient reason to believe that she or he may be homeless must also be dealt with under the homelessness provisions in HA 1996, Part 7. See **9.19–9.22**.

[90]   See **4.50–4.54**.

[91]   *R (Alam) v Tower Hamlets London Borough Council* [2009] EWHC 44 (Admin), (2009) March *Legal Action*, p 24, Admin Ct.

assessment of any HA 1996, Part 7 duty.[92] Nor is there any need for the local housing authority to consider whether or not applicants have become homeless intentionally.[93] All homeless people fall within this category[94] – even those who are not entitled to a housing duty under the provisions for homelessness assistance in HA 1996, Part 7 because, for example, they have no priority need.[95]

4.46 Precisely because homelessness duties provide a safety net to pick up and accommodate those who are in priority need and are unintentionally homeless, this first category of 'reasonable preference' works to ensure that all *other* homeless people secure a reasonable preference in allocation: those other homeless people being fit and healthy individuals, couples without children, the deliberately homeless, etc.

4.47 The policy behind HA 1996, Part 6 is therefore unashamedly to ensure that every allocation scheme is open to, and gives preference to, those who are homeless for any reason and in any circumstances. It is intended to 'include rough sleepers and all others who do not have a home, for whatever reason'.[96]

4.48 Indeed, in Wales, the statutory guidance goes further than a strict reading of HA 1996, Part 6 requires and suggests that local housing authorities define homelessness for these purposes as arising 'where a person lacks accommodation or where their tenure is not secure.'[97] This approach, unlike the statutory definition, includes persons who are threatened with homelessness and those who have no suitable alternative accommodation, whether they are leaving institutions, required to leave by family or friends or due to relationship breakdown, or facing a possession order.[98] When deciding whether or not a person is 'homeless' for these purposes, Welsh local housing authorities must have regard to the Welsh Code's more generous approach, although it is somewhat difficult to reconcile with the terms of HA 1996, Parts 6 or 7.[99]

---

[92] See Chapter 13.

[93] The English Code, para 5.8(a), now replaced by the broader guidance in the English 2009 Code, had specified that the category includes people who became homeless intentionally and those who are not in priority need. Welsh Code, para 4.8(i) is not so specific, simply referring to HA 1996, Part 7 for the meaning of 'homeless', but see the Welsh Code's broader definition of 'homeless' at **4.48** below. See Chapter 14 of this book for definition of 'becoming homeless intentionally'.

[94] Applicants who are 'threatened with homelessness' (defined in HA 1996, s 175(4)) will not fall within the category until they are actually homeless.

[95] *R (Alam) v Tower Hamlets London Borough Council* [2009] EWHC (Admin) 44, (2009) March *Legal Action*, p 24, Admin Ct.

[96] *Hansard,* HL Deb, vol 630, ser 6, col 1013 (15 January 2002), Lord Falconer.

[97] Welsh Code, para 8.10.

[98] Welsh Code, para 8.10, giving examples of people who are within 3 months of the end of their tenancies, are subject to possession proceedings, or are under the threat of eviction, as people whose tenure is not secure.

[99] Welsh Code, para 4.9. HA 1996, s 167(2)(a) provides that to get within the first category of 'reasonable preference' the person must be homeless 'within the meaning of Part 7'. The Welsh

4.49 A person in this first 'reasonable preference' category may also obtain 'additional preference' if his or her housing needs are 'urgent'[100] or if he or she also falls into another of the preference categories.[101] The remaining four categories deal with applicants who already have accommodation. A person who would otherwise qualify in this first 'reasonable preference' category will not in fact be entitled to receive it if the only reason they qualify is because regard has been had to a 'restricted person' in determining their application.[102] The remaining four categories deal with applicants who already have accommodation.

People who are owed certain homelessness duties[103]

4.50 This category encompasses applicants for an allocation who have already applied to a local housing authority as homeless and have received a decision that the local housing authority owes them a duty because:

(1) they are homeless and have a priority need, whether or not they became homeless intentionally;[104] or

(2) they are threatened with homelessness, have a priority need and did not become threatened with homelessness intentionally.[105]

4.51 Applicants who have been found to be homeless, but not to have a priority need, will only fall within this category if:

(1) they did not become homeless intentionally; and

(2) a local housing authority has decided to exercise its power to provide accommodation for them.[106]

4.52 By definition, these applicants must have made applications for homelessness assistance, and have received decisions that a duty of the prescribed type is owed to them. The duty need not be owed by the same local housing authority as the local housing authority to which the applicant is applying for an allocation. So an applicant who has applied as homeless to District A, and been placed by that local housing authority, pursuant to one of the prescribed duties, in District B might wish to apply for an allocation to the local housing authorities for both Districts A and B. He or she will have an entitlement to a 'reasonable preference' in both authorities' schemes.

Code can only work on the premise that those embraced by its terms would meet that standard because their present accommodation is not 'reasonable for them to continue to occupy' (HA 1996, s 175(3)).

[100] See **4.87–4.90**.
[101] See **4.85**.
[102] HA 1996, s 167(2ZA). For more on 'restricted person' see **4.109–4.110**.
[103] HA 1996, s 167(2)(b).
[104] Duty owed either under HA 1996, s 190(2) or s 193(2), or under Housing Act 1985, s 65(2).
[105] Duty owed under HA 1996, s 195(2) or Housing Act 1985, s 68(2).
[106] Under HA 1996, s 192(3).

4.53 It must be noted that the terms of this second category of 'reasonable preference' are very tightly drawn. They certainly do *not* cover all applicants who have already applied to a local housing authority as homeless, nor all of those who have benefited from a duty under HA 1996, Part 7 (the homelessness safety net). For example, the following applicants for a housing allocation would fall outside the second of the 'reasonable preference' categories because they are not owed one of the prescribed statutory homelessness duties:

- people provided with interim accommodation (pending a HA 1996, Part 7 decision);[107]

- people provided with accommodation pending a review of an unfavourable decision or pending an appeal;[108]

- people accommodated pending a local connection referral;[109]

- people who are not eligible for homelessness assistance;[110]

- people who are homeless, who are not in priority need and who became homeless intentionally;[111]

- people who are threatened with homelessness who are not in priority need;[112] and

- people who have become threatened with homelessness intentionally.[113]

Those persons may, depending on their circumstances, fit into the first category, or one or more of the third to fifth categories, of those entitled to a 'reasonable preference'.[114]

4.54 A person in this second 'reasonable preference' category may also obtain 'additional preference' if his or her housing needs are 'urgent'[115] or if he or she also falls into another of the preference categories.[116] A person who would otherwise qualify in this second 'reasonable preference' category will not in fact be entitled to receive it if the only reason they qualify is because regard has been had to a 'restricted person' in determining their application.[117]

---

107   HA 1996, s 188(1). They would still be 'homeless' and entitled to a reasonable preference under the first 'reasonable preference' category: *R (Alam) v Tower Hamlets London Borough Council* [2009] EWHC (Admin) 44, (2009) March *Legal Action*, p 24, Admin Ct.
108   HA 1996, ss 188(3) and 204(4).
109   HA 1996, s 200(1).
110   HA 1996, s 185.
111   HA 1996, s 190(3).
112   HA 1996, s 195(5).
113   HA 1996, s 195(5).
114   See **4.41–4.49** for the first category and **4.55–4.76** for the third to fifth categories.
115   HA 1996, s 167(2). See also **4.87–4.90**.
116   See **4.85**.
117   HA 1996, s 167(2ZA). For more on 'restricted person' see **4.109–4.110**.

People occupying insanitary or overcrowded housing or otherwise living in unsatisfactory housing conditions[118]

4.55 Nothing in HA 1996, Part 6 defines the three key adjectives in this 'reasonable preference' category: 'insanitary', 'overcrowded', and 'unsatisfactory'. Nor does HA 1996, Part 6 provide a direct link to the meanings that they have in other legislation, even other housing legislation.

4.56 This means that local housing authorities are largely free to develop, and incorporate into allocation schemes, their own policies to determine the circumstances in which an applicant would fall into this 'reasonable preference' category.

4.57 The law governing insanitary conditions, overcrowding, and unsatisfactory housing standards is scattered over a number of statutes. The Environmental Protection Act 1990, Part III is designed to address unhealthy premises. The rules on overcrowding are set out in the Housing Act 1985, Part 10. The law relating to hazardous housing is contained in the Housing Act 2004, Part 1. These statutory provisions should be taken into account by local housing authorities when drawing up their criteria for admission to this third 'reasonable preference' category. However, local housing authorities could, and many do, adopt a more generous approach than the statutory minimum standards when operating this category.[119] Many local housing authorities, for example, will have a broader definition of 'overcrowding' than the statutory definition.[120] Indeed, one judge has said:

> 'in my judgment, section 167(2)(c) need must include those who live in unsatisfactory housing conditions but need not necessarily statutorily be overcrowded.'[121]

4.58 As to the scope of 'unsatisfactory' housing conditions, the Codes of Guidance each provide a list of suggested criteria, which is said to be for illustrative purposes only, although many local housing authorities will adopt most, or all, of the criteria in their own list for assessment of unsatisfactory housing conditions.[122] The Codes emphasise that the list is not comprehensive or exhaustive and that there may, in particular, be *local* factors that a local housing authority would wish to acknowledge in the allocation scheme.

---

[118] HA 1996, s 167(2)(c).

[119] In defining 'overcrowding' in their allocation schemes, local housing authorities have been found to be adopting a wide variety of approaches: *Exploring local authority policy and practice on housing allocations* (CLG, July 2009), para 14.

[120] See Housing Act 1985, ss 325–326.

[121] *R (Ahmad) v Newham London Borough Council* [2007] EWHC 2332 (Admin), at [64], (2007) November *Legal Action*, p 38, Admin Ct, Blake J. This part of the decision was not subject to appeal.

[122] English Code, Annex 3; Welsh Code, Annex 3.

4.59 'Under-occupation' is included in the illustrative list[123] contained in the Codes. Local housing authorities are often keen to transfer their own tenants who want a smaller property, so as to free up the larger property for an allocation. Of course, where such a transfer is at the landlord's initiative, there is no 'allocation' at all and the allocation scheme does not apply.[124] Where the transfer request is made by the applicant, the inclusion of 'under-occupation' within this criterion (presumably as 'unsatisfactory' housing conditions) allows local housing authorities to give those tenants who are applying for transfers on those grounds a statutory 'reasonable preference'. In one case in which a local allocation scheme gave considerable preference to under-occupying applicants, none of the parties 'suggested that the very favourable treatment given to under-occupation transfers is unlawful'.[125] The possibility of enlarging the reasonable preference categories to explicitly refer to under-occupation was floated by the Minister for Housing in 2007, but in July 2009 the then Minister of Housing announced that it would not be pursued.[126]

4.60 Neither the statutory minimum definitions nor the illustrative lists contained in the Codes should inhibit advisers from assisting applicants to press for a local housing authority to treat them as within the third 'reasonable preference' category where circumstances suggest that the present home is 'overcrowded', 'insanitary' or otherwise 'unsatisfactory' on the broadest approach to that terminology. Advisers will need to consider the wording adopted in the particular local allocation scheme used to reflect this broad statutory category and do their best to bring their clients within that wording.

4.61 A person in this third 'reasonable preference' category may also obtain 'additional preference' if his or her housing needs are 'urgent'[127] or if he or she also falls into another of the 'reasonable preference' categories.[128]

People who need to move on medical or welfare grounds (including grounds relating to a disability)[129]

4.62 This fourth 'reasonable preference' category includes any applicant for accommodation whose health or welfare, or that of a member of his or her household, is impaired by remaining in the accommodation currently occupied, and thus there is a 'need to move' elsewhere. For obvious reasons, no 'reasonable preference' is to be accorded simply because an applicant wishes to

---

[123] English Code, Annex 3.

[124] See **1.24**. This may explain why under-occupation does *not* attract such high priority within allocation schemes as might otherwise have been expected: see *Exploring local authority policy and practice on housing allocations* (CLG, July 2009), para 16.

[125] *R (Ahmad) v Newham London Borough Council* [2009] UKHL 14, at [19], (2009) April *Legal Action*, p 21, HL; and see English 2009 Code, para 77.

[126] See **4.39**.

[127] See **4.87–4.90**.

[128] See **4.85**.

[129] HA 1996, s 167(2)(d) as amended.

move on welfare or medical grounds, for example to a warmer part of the country or to be nearer friends or relatives. The category is designed for those who 'need' to move.

4.63 Again, none of the terms 'medical grounds', 'welfare grounds' or 'grounds relating to a disability' is defined by HA 1996, Part 6. Nor are there any direct links made to the definition of these terms in any other statutes. In the first instance it is for local housing authorities to decide what the categories mean and to apply them when framing an allocation scheme.

4.64 The terms do not relate exclusively to the impact, on health or welfare, of the present accommodation alone, although any detrimental effect caused by the present accommodation would obviously fall within this test. As one judge put it:

> 'the relevant question is whether the current housing conditions are having an adverse effect on the medical condition of the claimant, which itself creates a particular need for her to move.'[130]

The detrimental effect on health or welfare could be caused by the location of the present accommodation as much as by the physical conditions of the present accommodation.

4.65 Thus, 'medical grounds' could relate to an adverse impact of the current accommodation on health (such as inaccessible washing and toilet facilities, or dampness having an effect on health) or there may be sound medical grounds for changing location, eg to relocate closer to a particular medical facility or to a carer, or to escape adverse environmental factors in the present location.

4.66 'Welfare grounds' would seem to refer to care and support needs or other social needs that do not require medical care or support. Examples given in the Codes are the needs of those leaving care or other vulnerable persons who need a stable base from which to build a secure life, and the needs of vulnerable people who are not able to find their own accommodation.[131]

4.67 Specialist advice is obviously helpful when assessing whether the applicant's health or welfare necessitates a move. The Codes recommend that the health or social care professional with direct knowledge of the applicant's condition is contacted by the local housing authority for an opinion on the applicant's health and its impact on the applicant's housing needs.[132] Such a person will usually be the applicant's GP, consultant or social worker. The local housing authority should not confine itself to an assessment by its own internal medical adviser without first seeking information from the applicant's own doctors or other relevant professionals. Even after a local housing authority's

---

[130] *R (Ghandali) v Ealing London Borough Council* [2006] EWHC 1859 (Admin), at [34], (2006) September *Legal Action*, p 14, Admin Ct, per Leveson J.
[131] English Code, para 5.14; Welsh Code, para 4.12.
[132] English Code, para 5.13; Welsh Code, para 4.11.

medical adviser has advised on the evidence available at that time, and the local housing authority has made a decision as to the applicant's entitlement to reasonable preference and priority, if there is then further medical evidence and social work opinion, and/or subsequent events, the medical adviser is under a duty to consider that new information properly. In a case where the medical adviser's advice was not based on a proper consideration of new evidence and events, the local housing authority's decision not to award the applicant any reasonable preference under this category was quashed and required to be reconsidered.[133] When the report from an independent or in-house medical adviser is obtained, the local housing authority should not rely on expressions of opinion or value judgments that it contains and which are beyond the remit of true medical advice.[134]

4.68 The additional words '(including grounds relating to a disability)' were added on 27 April 2005[135] so as to make it clear that those applicants whose need to move relates to a disability (but who are not ill or otherwise in 'medical' need) would fall within this 'reasonable preference' category.[136] Prior to the statutory amendment, the view that medical needs should be taken to include those needs relating to a disability was recommended by the Codes in any event.

4.69 It is plain from the additional wording that the 'disability' referred to is not restricted to a disability of the applicant; it could be the disability of any member of the applicant's household. Alternatively, the wording would be satisfied where a non-disabled applicant needs to move so as to be nearer to a disabled relative or some other disabled person. Local housing authorities may consider whether the applicant's needs would be better served by providing aids and adaptations to the current accommodation, enabling applicants to remain in their present homes.[137]

4.70 The Codes provide illustrative lists of different types of 'medical grounds' and 'welfare grounds'.[138] Those illustrations encompass the types of accommodation that may be needed (adapted, improved, sheltered or ground floor), the type of medical condition that might fall within this criterion (mental illness or disorder, physical or learning disability, chronic or progressive medical conditions), and other types of vulnerability (such as young people at risk, people with behavioural difficulties or those recovering from the effects of violence). The needs of those who provide care, as well as those who receive it, are included in the illustrative lists. The need to be near friends, relatives or medical facilities for medical reasons also appears. The Welsh Code, but not the

---

[133] *R (Ghandali) v Ealing London Borough Council* [2006] EWHC 1859 (Admin), (2006) September *Legal Action*, Admin Ct, p 14.

[134] *R (Bauer-Czarnomski) v Ealing London Borough Council* [2010] EWHC 130 (Admin).

[135] In England, not yet in force in Wales.

[136] HA 1996, s 167(2)(d) as amended by Housing Act 2004, s 223.

[137] English Code, para 5.15.

[138] English Code, Annex 3; Welsh Code, Annex 3.

English Code, includes recovery from alcohol or drug abuse as a type of 'medical ground' that could fall within this category.[139]

4.71 The Codes recommend that once accommodation is allocated to a person falling within this category, his or her support and care needs should be assessed and there should be liaison with social services, Supporting People and other agencies providing support.[140]

4.72 A person in this fourth 'reasonable preference' category may also obtain 'additional preference' if his or her housing needs are 'urgent',[141] or if he or she also falls into another of the 'reasonable preference' categories.[142]

People who need to move to a particular locality in the local housing authority's district where hardship would be caused if they did not move[143]

4.73 This is a relatively new 'reasonable preference' category introduced from January 2003.[144] The Codes suggest that people may fall within it if they need to move in order to give or receive care, to be able to access specialised medical treatment, or to take up particular education, employment or training opportunities in some particular locality.[145] The new category will also be suitable for victims of harassment or violence needing to move to safer areas. Some, but not all, of those examples would fall within 'medical or welfare grounds' in the fourth category, but those applicants who overlap are now entitled to be placed in both categories. Again, the emphasis is on 'need' to move, not a desire to move.

4.74 A particular locality should be identified, which must be within the district of the local housing authority to which application is made. Any need to move outside the district of the local housing authority in which the applicant presently resides requires either application to the other local housing authority in whose district the specific locality falls, or the use of any reciprocal agreements or nomination rights agreed between the two local housing authorities involved.

4.75 The need to move must be sufficiently great that 'hardship' would otherwise be caused, either to the applicant or to others. The HA 1996, Part 6 and the Codes do not define 'hardship', nor the degree of severity required for an applicant to fall within this category. The hardship that might be caused to *the applicant* if he or she is not moved may well be fairly self-evident: deterioration in health, inability to take up education, employment or training

---

139 Welsh Code, Annex 3.
140 English Code, para 5.15; Welsh Code, para 4.13.
141 See **4.87–4.90**.
142 See **4.85**.
143 HA 1996, s 167(2)(e).
144 Homelessness Act 2002, s 16(3).
145 English Code, para 5.16; Welsh Code, paras 4.14 and 4.74.

opportunities, etc. The hardship that might be caused to *others* includes situations where an applicant needs to move to a particular locality to provide care to a friend or relative already living in that locality. The category is not limited to personal hardship. It may include financial hardship, for example, so as to accord preference to an applicant of limited means who needs to move from a high rent to a low rent district.

4.76 A person in this fifth 'reasonable preference' category may also obtain 'additional preference' if his or her housing needs are 'urgent',[146] or if he or she also falls into another of the 'reasonable preference' categories.[147]

Assessment of the right 'reasonable preference' category

4.77 The local housing authority will usually want to take into account the whole of the applicant's needs and circumstances, and the needs and circumstances of those members of his or her household who are included in the applicant's application, to determine which, if any, of the 'reasonable preference' categories applies to the applicant.

4.78 But beyond identifying the relevant 'reasonable preference' categories, HA 1996, Part 6 does not dictate how preferences are to be determined. For example, where:

(1)   a single household spans two or more categories; or

(2)   there are several households in a particular 'reasonable preference' category, eligible for a particular allocation; or

(3)   there are two households, each in a different 'reasonable preference' category, eligible for a single allocation.

4.79 HA 1996, Part 6 expressly gives the local housing authority a considerable degree of flexibility in according 'additional preference' or in reducing the extent of the 'reasonable preference' that would otherwise be received.[148] It has fallen to the courts to spell out the limits (if any) on the ways in which an allocation scheme can be framed to enhance or reduce the reasonable preference to which a person in one of the statutory categories may otherwise be entitled.

4.80 Between 1996 and 2009 the courts took a fairly interventionist approach. Allocation schemes faced difficulty in the courts if they were too inflexible to respond to comparative needs, whether within categories, across categories, or where applicants fell within more than one category of 'reasonable preference'.

---

[146]   See **4.87–4.90**.
[147]   See **4.85**.
[148]   See **4.87–4.100**.

4.81 For example, once the whole of the relevant household's needs are assessed, it may transpire that it falls into more than one of the statutory categories. Until 2009 it was considered that the applicant's subsequent priority in the allocation scheme must reflect that fact. A scheme, whether it operated by bands, points or a combination of the two, had to be sufficiently flexible for the applicant's cumulative needs to be recognised and for circumstances spanning more than one reasonable preference category to be taken into account.[149] Even for those applicants within the same 'reasonable preference' category, there will be different 'housing needs' between them. Until 2009, it was thought that an allocation scheme must be capable of reflecting that fact. For example, an allocation scheme that only awarded medical points for the member of the applicant's household in most medical need, and which failed to recognise the medical needs of any other member of the same household was held to be unlawful.[150] An allocation scheme which did not recognise different needs of different members of the household was found to be unlawful and not saved by a discretion to award more points in exceptionally serious cases.[151] An allocation scheme which was entirely points-based and contained no discretion to award points for any other need not specified in the scheme was unlawful because it wholly fettered the local housing authority's discretion.[152]

4.82 Likewise, applying the pre-2009 approach, a scheme which gave existing secure tenants seeking a transfer an additional 100 points each, when not all of them were entitled to a reasonable preference, was held to be unlawful because it artificially raised the points threshold to the detriment of applicants who were not existing tenants and were entitled to a statutory preference.[153]

4.83 However, an argument that a local housing authority's allocation scheme was unlawful because it did not allocate points to reflect 'disability' failed when the points awarded for health needs were shown to have included needs arising from disabilities.[154]

4.84 'Need' for housing must, of course, be assessed objectively by the local housing authority. Schemes which rely upon applicants assessing their own needs have been held to be unlawful in that they run the risk of encouraging

---

[149] An allocation scheme which had no mechanism for identifying cumulative need and therefore could not award additional preference for cumulative need was held to be unlawful in *R (Cali) v Waltham Forest London Borough Council* [2006] EWHC 302 (Admin), [2007] HLR 1, Admin Ct.

[150] *R v Tower Hamlets London Borough Council ex p Uddin* (2000) 32 HLR 391, QBD; and *R (Vatansever) v Southwark London Borough Council* [2001] EWHC 546 (Admin), (2001) October *Legal Action*, p 14, Admin Ct.

[151] *R v Islington London Borough Council ex p Reilly and Mannix* (1999) 31 HLR 651, QBD.

[152] *R v Lambeth London Borough Council ex p Anderson* (2000) February *Legal Action*, at p 25, QBD.

[153] *R (Lin) v Barnet London Borough Council* [2006] EWHC 1041 (Admin), [2006] HLR 440, Admin Ct; Barnet London Borough Council successfully appealed to the Court of Appeal (*Lin v Barnet London Borough Council* [2007] EWCA Civ 132, [2007] HLR 30, CA) but not on that point.

[154] *R v Lewisham London Borough Council ex p Pinzon* (1999) 2 CCLR 152, QBD.

applicants to assess themselves as requiring unsuitable accommodation, in the hope of a shorter waiting period for undesirable accommodation.[155]

4.85 In 2009, the House of Lords identified that, beyond requiring a local allocation scheme to be framed so as to accord a reasonable priority to those in the 'reasonable preference' categories, HA 1996, Part 6 (as modified in 2003) left it largely to individual local housing authorities to determine how their schemes should deal with applicants in more than one reasonable preference category or how to prioritise between applicants in different categories.[156] A local housing authority could adopt a scheme which enabled it to make fine distinctions between different applicants and then prioritise accordingly, based on individual assessments. Alternatively, the scheme could take a broad brush approach gathering all (or almost all) reasonable preference category applicants into a single band or group and then prioritise between them by date of application or some other simple criterion. The House of Lords was clear that it was not for the courts to become embroiled in the details of prioritisation mechanisms in individual schemes. Subject only to the requirements of rationality and compliance with the terms of the statutory provisions, the arrangements for prioritisation within any particular scheme are a matter for local political judgment by a local housing authority. The English 2009 Code draws attention to the 'considerable flexibility' available to local housing authorities in the light of this interpretation of Part 6 by the House of Lords.[157]

4.86 Having rehearsed the importance of the relevant statutory categories for affording 'reasonable preference', this chapter will next consider how a local housing allocation scheme can:

(1) deal with need by awarding additional preference; and/or

(2) reduce preference despite need.

Additional preference

4.87 An allocation scheme *may* be framed so as to give 'additional preference' to particular descriptions of people who are already within the reasonable preference categories.[158] The scheme does not need to contain a provision for this form of enhanced priority. HA 1996, Part 6 simply gives a local housing authority a discretion to provide for 'additional preference'.[159] HA 1996, Part 6 itself neither defines that concept nor offers illustrations of it.

---

[155] *R (A) v Lambeth London Borough Council, R (Lindsay) v Lambeth London Borough Council* [2002] EWCA Civ 1084, [2002] HLR 57, CA and *R (Cali) v Waltham Forest London Borough Council* [2006] EWHC 302 (Admin), [2007] HLR 1.

[156] *R (Ahmad) v Newham London Borough Council* [2009] UKHL 14, (2009) April *Legal Action*, p 21, HL.

[157] English 2009 Code, para 57.

[158] HA 1996, s 167(2), last sentence.

[159] HA 1996, s 167(2).

4.88 Local housing authorities are advised by the Codes that they should consider whether they have a local need to exercise this discretion, taking into account their local circumstances, and presumably the particular circumstances of likely applicants.[160] The allocation scheme will be formulated as a result of that consideration and individual decisions made according to whatever terms the scheme adopted.

4.89 Examples of people who may be identified by a local housing authority in its allocation scheme as likely to be treated as having more urgent housing needs than other reasonable preference applicants include those who are owed homelessness duties as a result of violence or threats of violence and therefore need urgent re-housing, and those who need to move for urgent medical reasons. The Welsh Code gives the additional example of applicants who have reasonable prospects of an offer of accommodation within a relatively short period and who suddenly lose their existing homes as a result of a disaster. Both Codes are clear, however, that these are only examples.[161] The intention is that the local scheme should spell out the sorts of circumstances in which additional preference, and thus priority, will be given in respect of the most urgent housing needs. Thus, the House of Lords has upheld as lawful a scheme which made additional priority (beyond ordinary reasonable preference) available to only a small proportion of applicants and only on satisfaction of 'stringent' and 'very strict' criteria.[162]

4.90 In April 2009, the Secretary of State for Communities and Local Government issued statutory guidance to English local housing authorities identifying one very specific category of applicant who should be embraced by any allocation scheme which has been framed to give 'additional preference' to applicants who are in the 'reasonable preference' groups.[163] The new category is:

'any applicant who needs to move to suitable adapted accommodation because of a serious injury, medical condition or disability which he or she, or a member of their household, has sustained as a result of service in the Armed Forces.'

The ability to give effect to this guidance will depend on:

(1) whether the application has already attracted 'reasonable preference' status; and

(2) whether a particular local scheme has been framed to give additional preference in words sufficiently wide to embrace this new category.

---

[160] English 2009 Code, para 19; Welsh Code, para 4.20.

[161] English 2009 Code, para 19; Welsh Code, para 4.20.

[162] *R (Ahmad) v Newham London Borough Council* [2009] UKHL 14, at [54], (2009) April *Legal Action*, p 21, HL.

[163] *Communities & Local Government Circular 04/2009*, 9 April 2009 at http://www.communities. gov.uk/publications/housing/armedforcesallocations reproduced in Appendix 1 of this book.

Unhappily, in giving this guidance, the 2009 Circular makes reference to a now replaced provision of the main English Code[164] but has not itself been amended to take account of the broader guidance contained in the later English 2009 Code.[165]

Adding, or reducing, preference for other reasons

4.91 Beyond expressly enabling the local scheme to be framed so that additional preference can be given to some applicants who are already in the reasonable preference categories, HA 1996, Part 6 leaves local housing authorities free to frame their schemes in such manner as they wish to prioritise between applicants who are already within one or more of the 'reasonable preference' categories. Local housing authorities are entitled to give additional or reduced prioritisation for any reasons that they choose to set out in their allocation scheme. Enhancing priority by reference to the length of time an applicant has been waiting is an increasingly popular method,[166] but HA 1996, Part 6 directs local housing authorities towards three particular factors that they might wish to take into account in framing their schemes:

(1)   the financial resources available to an applicant or a member of his or her household to meet his or her own housing costs; and/or

(2)   any behaviour of the applicant or a member of his or her household which affects his or her suitability to be a tenant; and/or

(3)   any local connection[167] which exists between the applicant or a member of his or her household and the local housing authority's district.[168]

4.92 The 'financial resources' category permits local housing authorities to give a higher priority in the allocation scheme to applicants who cannot afford to pay a market rent or to take out a mortgage, and, as the other side of that coin, a lower priority to applicants who are in a better financial position. An on-line survey of local housing authority practice in two English regions found that household income (including, in some cases, equity/savings) was taken into account under the allocation policies of most authorities responding to the

---

[164]   English Code, para 5.18.
[165]   English 2009 Code, para 5.
[166]   The use of waiting time is described in the English 2009 Code as 'the simplest way' of determining priorities between those with a similar level of need: para 65. Its use as a criterion is suggested to have benefits of simplicity and transparency: para 66.
[167]   Within the meaning of HA 1996, s 199. For more on 'local connection' see Chapter 15.
[168]   HA 1996, s 167(2A). The Welsh Code refers to 'the applicant's' financial resources and/or local connection and only to members of the applicant's household in relation to behaviour (Welsh Code, para 4.22). However, HA 1996, Part 6 refers to 'a person' in respect of all three categories, and the authors of this book suggest that the proper interpretation is that 'a person' refers both to the applicant and to the members of the applicant's household. Any other interpretation would place undue emphasis on an issue irrelevant to the household's housing needs, ie the question of which household member was listed as 'applicant' on the application form.

survey. Troublingly, it also found that in rare cases authorities were using resources as a complete bar to allocation.[169] That goes substantially beyond what HA 1996, Part 6 permits.

4.93 The 'behaviour' category permits local housing authorities to include provision in an allocation scheme to reward good behaviour and penalise bad behaviour. During the debate in the House of Lords on this provision, the Minister, Lord Falconer, contrasted the examples of two applicants: one had

> '... a history of persistent but minor rent arrears not caused by any problems with housing benefit and another ... who has demonstrated that he is a model tenant.'[170]

The latter could be accorded priority over the former. The minor rent arrears example of relevant 'behaviour' has been carried into the statutory guidance with the additional example of 'low level anti-social behaviour'.[171] In *R (Osei) v Newham London Borough Council*[172] the local allocation scheme enabled the housing authority to take into account former tenant arrears as an aspect of 'behaviour' when prioritising between applicants who would otherwise qualify for urgent rehousing on domestic violence or other emergency grounds. The court held that such a provision would not be unlawful provided it was applied with a flexibility which took into account the personal circumstances of an applicant which might justify not taking into account that past behaviour in their particular case. In R (Joseph) v Newham London Borough Council[173] the allocation scheme enabled account to be taken of 'property-related debts' and gave the example of housing benefit overpayments. The court held that this did not permit the local housing authority to reduce preference where an overpayment had been outstanding so long that it could not be recovered by any legal process.

4.94 An example of good behaviour given in the English Code is where an applicant's actions have directly benefited other residents on his or her estate.[174]

4.95 The 'local connection' category enables discrimination in the allocation scheme in favour of local applicants. 'Local connection' is defined in HA 1996.[175] A local housing authority is entitled, should it so choose, to make provision in its scheme so as to give a higher priority to an applicant who has a local connection with its district (either personally or because a member of his or her household has a local connection). Local housing authorities are advised in both Codes that they should be careful, when using this provision, not to

---

[169] *Exploring local authority policy and practice on housing allocations* (CLG, July 2009), para 12.
[170] *Hansard,* HL Deb, vol 630, ser 6, col 1017 (15 January 2002), (Lord Falconer).
[171] English 2009 Code, para 67.
[172] *R (Osei) v Newham London Borough Council* [2010] EWHC 368 (Admin), (2010) March *Legal Action*, p 30, Admin Ct.
[173] [2009] EWHC 2983 (Admin).
[174] English 2009 Code, para 67.
[175] HA 1996, s 167(2A)(c) importing the definition used in HA 1996, s 199(1). For more on 'local connection' see Chapter 15.

discriminate against any ethnic group. Some local housing authorities have operated 'sons and daughters' policies whereby children of local residents are given priority over applicants who have moved into the area more recently. This provision for enhanced priority by reference to local connection permits local housing authorities to operate such policies, provided that they ensure that the local allocation scheme adopted is not contrary to the Race Relations Act 1976 and, more generally, does not run counter to other equal opportunities considerations[176].

4.96 Where the allocation scheme gives additional weighting based on local connection, it is likely to result in greater complexity, particularly if the scheme generally uses a banding system to confer priority and it is well recognised that a scheme which attaches particular priority to local connection could disadvantage some applicants. Nevertheless, allocation schemes frequently reflect local political priorities by providing for enhanced priority for local connection cases. The Secretary of State has indicated that, while there is nothing to prevent local housing authorities framing their allocation schemes to include local policy priorities such as this, they must ensure that these do not dominate the scheme, and that overall the scheme operates to give reasonable preference to people in the reasonable preference categories.[177] In *R (van Boolen) v Barking & Dagenham London Borough Council*[178] the council's policy was to take account of local connection when there was more than one bidder in the same high priority band shortlisted for a property under its choice based letting scheme. The bidder in that band with a local connection would normally be preferred to a bidder without such a connection. Although the practice had resulted in the claimant being repeatedly shortlisted, but never successful, her claim that the policy was unlawful was rejected.

4.97 The statutory definition of 'local connection' was enlarged for applications for homelessness assistance or for an allocation made to an English local housing authority on or after 1 December 2008.[179] The amendment provides that persons serving in the Armed Forces can establish a local connection with a district through residence or employment there, in the same way as civilians can.[180] The Secretary of State has advised that:

'Where housing authorities frame their allocation scheme to give greater priority to applicants with a local connection, the effect of the amendments ... will be:

(a) applicants who are serving in the Armed Forces and who are either employed or resident in the district will be able to establish a local connection with the district

(b) when considering applications from serving or former members of the Armed Forces, who are not currently employed or resident in the district, the

---

176　See **4.129–4.130**.

177　English 2009 Code, para 68.

178　*R (van Boolen) v Barking & Dagenham London Borough Council* [2009] EWHC 2196 (Admin).

179　Housing and Regeneration Act 2008, s 315. The enlarged definition applies to applications made to Welsh local housing authorities on or after 30 March 2009.

180　HA 1996, s 199(1), (2) and (3) as amended by Housing and Regeneration Act 2008, s 315.

local housing authority will need to consider whether they have a local connection through previous residence in the district as a result of a former posting in the area while serving in the Armed Forces.'[181]

Again, in giving this guidance, the 2009 Circular makes reference to a now replaced provision of the main English Code[182] but has not itself been amended to take account of the broader guidance contained in the later English 2009 Code.[183]

4.98 Local housing authorities are reminded by the Codes that the statutory factors are not exhaustive.[184] Within local housing allocation schemes, local housing authorities may give priority to, or downgrade, classes of applicant who are otherwise within the 'reasonable preference' categories for reasons not listed in HA 1996, Part 6 provided that they act fairly and in accordance with their policy as reflected in the published scheme. They are also reminded that each application has to be considered on its own merits.[185]

4.99 The scope of the statutory discretion to set priorities among those within the 'reasonable preference' categories is plainly wide enough to allow an allocation scheme, for example, to:

- give extra preference for length of time spent waiting; and

- reduce preference for those who have been offered an allocation but rejected it; and

- give additional priority to key workers.

The first of those is perhaps the most commonly adopted. The English 2009 Code suggests that differentiating between households with broadly similar needs by reference to waiting time is the 'simplest way' of prioritising between them and represents an approach which would be 'simple, transparent and easy to understand'.[186]

4.100 However, the bottom line is that (save in respect of the circumstances described at **4.101–4.110**) the effect of any reduction in priority must not be to eliminate all preference, with the result that a person in a 'reasonable preference' category is in practice getting *no* preference at all.

---

[181] CLG *Circular 04/2009*, para 12, available at http://www.communities.gov.uk/publications/housing/armedforcesallocations and reproduced in Appendix 1 of this book.
[182] English Code, para 5.23.
[183] English 2009 Code, para 5.
[184] For example, English 2009 Code, para 64.
[185] For example, Welsh Code, para 4.22.
[186] English 2009 Code, para 66.

Removing 'reasonable preference' altogether

4.101 An applicant who falls within one or more of the 'reasonable preference' categories may be deprived of that status and given no preference at all, but only if either:

(1)   the local housing authority decides that he or she has been guilty of 'unacceptable behaviour';[187] or

(2)   the applicant's household includes a 'restricted person' and the applicant's entitlement to a reasonable preference would not have arisen under the first or second of the statutory reasonable preference categories without the presence of that person.[188]

The 'unacceptable behaviour' test

4.102   A local housing authority may *only* treat an applicant otherwise entitled to a 'reasonable preference' as having no preference when it is satisfied that:

- the applicant, or a member of his or her household, has been guilty of unacceptable behaviour serious enough to make him or her unsuitable to be a tenant of the local housing authority; and

- at the time that the application is being considered and by reason of that behaviour, the applicant deserves not to be treated as a member of a group of people who are given 'reasonable preference'.[189]

4.103   The definition of 'unacceptable behaviour' is the same as that applied in determining eligibility for an allocation. That is to say:

'... behaviour of the person concerned which would (if he were a secure tenant of the authority) entitle the housing authority to a possession order under s 84 of the Housing Act 1985 on any ground mentioned in Part I of Schedule 2 to that Act (other than ground 8) or behaviour of a member of his household which would (if he were a person residing with a secure tenant of the authority) entitle the housing authority to such a possession order.'[190]

4.104   Before removing any 'reasonable preference' to which an applicant would otherwise be entitled, a local housing authority must therefore ask itself:

---

[187]   HA 1996, s 167(2B) and (2C).

[188]   HA 1996, s 167(2ZA) inserted by Housing and Regeneration Act 2008, Sch 15, para 2. Applicable to applications for homelessness assistance and for an allocation made on or after 2 March 2009: Housing and Regeneration Act 2008 (Commencement No 1 and Savings Provisions) Order 2009, SI 2009/415 (C 28), art 2.

[189]   HA 1996, s 167(2B) and (2C). See also English Code, paras 5.19–5.22; Welsh Code, paras 4.15–4.19.

[190]   HA 1996, s 167(2D) applying HA 1996, s 160(8). For a full discussion see **3.146–3.181**.

(1)   Would the applicant's behaviour, or that of a member of his or her household, have come within one of the grounds for possession?

(2)   Would the court have considered it reasonable to make an order for possession?

(3)   Would the order be an outright, not a suspended or postponed, possession order?

4.105   Only after it has considered those three questions and answered them all in the affirmative, may the local housing authority then decide whether, at the time that the application is being considered, the applicant deserves not to be given the preference to which she or he would otherwise be entitled. The key issue that the local housing authority should consider is whether there has been a change of circumstances since those events that led to the affirmative answers to the three questions identified above.[191]

4.106   If the local housing authority decides that an applicant should have his or her 'reasonable preference' removed on the grounds of 'unacceptable behaviour', it must notify the applicant in writing of the decision and the grounds for it. The applicant has the right to request a review of that decision and to be informed of the review decision and the grounds for it.[192] Any further challenge to the review decision would be by judicial review or by complaint, ultimately to the Local Government Ombudsman.

4.107   This provision, permitting the removal of preference, operates as an alternative to the power to treat an applicant as wholly ineligible for an allocation by reason of his or her unacceptable behaviour.[193] It may therefore be used in respect of an applicant where the local housing authority has considered his or her behaviour for the purposes of eligibility and concluded that he or she is eligible but nevertheless considers that the behaviour should deprive him or her of the 'reasonable preference' that would otherwise be accorded.

4.108   Even if an applicant, with a background of unreasonable behaviour, survives both the eligibility test and the removal of 'reasonable preference' test,

---

[191]   For a fuller discussion of the correct approach to this part of the statutory test, see **3.182–3.189**.

[192]   HA 1996, s 167(4A)(b) and (d). See also **2.65–2.83**.

[193]   Discussed at **3.143–3.189**. It may be that Hackney's policy that an applicant in rent arrears would be allowed onto its allocation scheme and entitled to points, but not receive an offer whilst the arrears continued was an attempt to apply this provision, rather than to hold the applicant ineligible: *R (Onuegbu) v Hackney London Borough Council* [2005] EWHC 1277 (Admin), (2005) August *Legal Action*, p 17, Admin Ct (and see note to **3.184**). *Hackney*'s interpretation, however, does not sit easily with the statutory provision. It does not allow for suspension but simply a removal of preference as against other applicants.

he or she may still be accorded a lower preference than others in similar circumstances by being given a lower priority than she or he would otherwise receive.[194]

The presence of a 'restricted person'

4.109 The second ground for removal of a reasonable preference arises where:[195]

(1) the reasonable preference is made out by satisfaction of the first or second categories for such a preference (homelessness or a specific duty owed to the homeless);[196] and

(2) the application would not have fallen within those categories without the local housing authority having had regard to a restricted person (within the meaning of HA 1996, Part 7).

If, and only if, *both* those conditions are fulfilled is the applicant deprived of the reasonable preference to which he or she would otherwise have been entitled. An applicant entitled to a reasonable preference under any of the third to fifth statutory categories retains that preference even if it has been triggered by the needs of a restricted person.[197] A 'restricted person' is defined at HA 1996, s 184(7).[198]

4.110 A homeless applicant who is owed the main housing duty under HA 1996, s 193(2)[199] because of the presence in his or her household of a 'restricted person' will also find that the main housing duty is modified so as to permit the local housing authority to bring the duty to an end by an offer of 'private accommodation'.[200] This provision, coupled with the lack of reasonable preference under the first and second categories, illustrates the policy intention that households with 'restricted persons' should be looking to the private rented sector, rather than to social housing, for their long-term accommodation needs.

---

[194] In exercise of the power at HA 1996, s 167(2A). See **4.93–4.94**.

[195] HA 1996, s 167(2ZA) inserted by Housing and Regeneration Act 2008, Sch 15, para 2. Applicable to applications for homelessness assistance and for an allocation made on or after 2 March 2009: Housing and Regeneration Act 2008 (Commencement No 1 and Savings Provisions) Order 2009, SI 2009/415 (C 28), art 2.

[196] HA 1996, s 167(2)(a) and (b). See **4.41–4.49** for the first category and **4.50–4.54** for the second category.

[197] HA 1996, s 167(2)(c), (d) and (e). See **4.55–4.61** for the third category, **4.62–4.72** for the fourth category and **4.73–4.76** for the fifth category.

[198] See **17.99**.

[199] See **17.21–17.27**.

[200] HA 1996, s193(7AA)–(7AD) inserted by Housing and Regeneration Act 2008, s 314 and Sch 15, para 5. See **17.102–17.108**.

PRIORITY FOR PARTICULAR TYPES OF ACCOMMODATION

4.111 An allocation scheme does not need to apply uniformly to the whole of a local housing authority's available housing stock, or to all the available nominations to RSLs. HA 1996, Part 6 provides that a scheme may, in effect, identify certain accommodation to be allocated:

(1) only to those who make specific applications for it; or

(2) only for a particular group or groups of applicants (whether or not in one of the statutory reasonable preference categories).[201]

4.112 By these means, HA 1996, Part 6 allows the local allocation scheme to be drawn so that, in respect of certain types of accommodation specified in the scheme, the normal 'reasonable preference' categories do not, in effect, apply. Care must be taken in framing these provisions in a scheme. These two special provisions are still subject to the over-arching requirement that the scheme must be framed to secure a reasonable preference to the statutory categories. The position remains that the scheme must be framed so as to ensure that, *overall*, reasonable preference is given to applicants who fall within the reasonable preference categories over those who do not.[202]

4.113 The function of the first special provision – that the scheme may provide for the allocation of particular accommodation to those who specifically apply for it – is 'to facilitate choice by providing for the adoption of "advertising schemes" whereby applicants can apply for particular properties which have been advertised as vacant by the housing authority'.[203] It is thus the lynch-pin for the concept of choice based lettings,[204] but it is a rather elliptically expressed way of achieving that object.

4.114 In local allocation schemes not generally based on choice based letting, the type of accommodation most likely to be specifically earmarked for those who make 'a specific application' for it[205] is what is commonly known as 'hard to let' housing in respect of which there is little point in operating the normal allocation scheme, because offers are likely to be refused.

4.115 The most likely type of accommodation earmarked to persons of a particular description under the second special provision[206] is the stock of purpose-built (or adapted) accommodation designed for use by the disabled and/or elderly. Inclusion of such a provision in an allocation scheme can ensure that the housing is available to those who most need it. The Secretary of State

---

[201] HA 1996, s 167(2E).
[202] English 2009 Code, paras 18 and 76.
[203] English CBL Code, para 2.5 (and see English Code, para 5.4).
[204] See **5.7–5.61**.
[205] HA 1996, s 167(2E)(a).
[206] HA 1996, s 167(2E)(b).

has specifically suggested that, where possible, priority be given any applicant who needs to move to suitable adapted accommodation because of a serious injury, medical condition or disability which he or she, or a member of their household, has sustained as a result of service in the Armed Forces.[207] More controversially, the power enables, for example, all ground floor accommodation to be earmarked only for applicants with mobility problems or with young children.

4.116 Use of the power can produce unusual results. For example, a local housing authority may have a surfeit of applicants for general accommodation who fall within one or more 'reasonable preference' categories, but its scheme may have excluded particular accommodation from the general pool and earmarked it for the elderly or disabled. If there is little demand for that earmarked accommodation, an elderly or disabled applicant could receive an offer almost immediately, even if his or her circumstances command no reasonable, or other, preference at all.

4.117 The Codes of Guidance contain recommendations as to which kinds of applicants may, within an allocation scheme compliant with the overall statutory framework, be given a certain preference or earmarked for certain properties. Specific attention is given to identifying particular types of housing for particular types of applicants and dealing with them by way of local lettings policies.

4.118 For example, the Codes suggest that local housing authorities may:

- wish to give sympathetic consideration to the housing needs of extended families;

- provide affordable accommodation within a reasonable travelling distance from work to essential workers who would otherwise not be able to afford to live in the communities that they serve; or

- attempt to lower or increase the child-adult density on particular estates by excluding certain properties from general allocation.[208]

4.119 The Codes further consider three specific forms of accommodation suitable for special treatment under these statutory powers:

- accommodation with linked support;

- accommodation particularly suited for agricultural workers; and

- accommodation subject to an application from a former tenant or other occupier of it.

---

[207] *CLG Circular 04/2009*, para 12, available at http://www.communities.gov.uk/publications/housing/armedforcesallocations and reproduced in Appendix 1 of this book.

[208] English 2009 Code, paras 26, 33 and 86; Welsh Code, paras 4.51–4.53.

Each of these three suggested categories requires careful consideration.

Accommodation with linked support

4.120 Certain applicants may not only seek accommodation but also have needs for support. Where an applicant's household includes a child who needs accommodation on medical and welfare grounds, local housing authorities are advised by the Codes to consult with social services about the appropriate level of priority, what support needs are present, and how those support needs will be met.[209] Where applicants for an allocation are cared for by people who do not live with them, local housing authorities are advised that the applicant will need a spare bedroom (for overnight stays).[210]

4.121 The Codes further suggest that single parents aged under 18, who are not living with their parents, should be offered semi-independent accommodation with support. A joint assessment of the applicant's housing, care and support needs should be undertaken by the housing and social services departments, provided that the applicant consents to the involvement of social services. It would be unusual for a young single parent to be given an independent tenancy, but arrangements should be made for the young parent to move on from supported accommodation as he or she reaches adulthood.[211] Local housing authorities should not be deterred by the legal problems associated with the granting of a tenancy to a minor: social services authorities may underwrite the tenancy agreement, and the tenancy itself can be treated as a trust for land (giving the minor the beneficial interest) and/or as a contract for a lease.[212]

4.122 The Codes also recommend that access to the allocation of such accommodation is available for rough sleepers and people at risk of sleeping rough. Many rough sleepers will also need support with other problems: mental health, alcohol or drug problems, and basic life skills. Local housing authorities should work with social services and Supporting People Teams to provide such support.[213] Where sex offenders are allocated accommodation, there should be joint working with the police, probation services, social services, health professionals and other bodies to manage any risk to the community.[214]

---

[209] English Code, paras 5.33–5.36; Welsh Code, paras 4.70–4.72.

[210] English Code, para 5.37; Welsh Code paras 4.73–4.74.

[211] English Code paras 5.38–5.48; Welsh Code, paras 4.75–4.85.

[212] English Code, para 5.49; Welsh Code, para 4.85, Annex 25; *Kingston upon Thames Royal London Borough Council v Prince* (1999) 31 HLR 794, CA; *Newham London Borough Council v Ria* [2004] EWCA Civ 41, [2004] All ER (D) 88 (Jan), CA and *Alexander-David v Hammersmith & Fulham London Borough Council* [2009] EWCA Civ 259, [2009] 2 FLR 329, CA.

[213] English Code, paras 5.50–5.51; Welsh Code, paras 4.86–4.87.

[214] See English Code, para 5.52; Welsh Code, paras 4.91–4.93. See too the discussion of *R (M) v Hackney London Borough Council* [2009] EWHC 2255 (Admin), (2009) May *Legal Action*, p 26, Admin Ct, at **3.181**.

Accommodation particularly suited for agricultural workers

4.123 Local housing authorities are required by the Rent (Agriculture) Act 1976 to use their best endeavours to provide accommodation for displaced agricultural workers where they are satisfied that the dwelling house from which the worker is displaced is needed to accommodate another agricultural worker, that the farmer cannot provide suitable alternative accommodation for the displaced worker and that the displaced worker needs to be rehoused in the interests of efficient agriculture.[215] Local housing authorities should include within their allocation schemes a policy statement in respect of the priority that will be accorded to displaced agricultural workers.[216]

Accommodation subject to an application from a former tenant or other occupier[217]

4.124 The exercise of these statutory powers to exclude or ring-fence certain accommodation from the general allocation provisions might be particularly apt where an applicant seeks the specific allocation of the property which he or she is already living in. For example, this might arise:

- where the applicant has married an existing tenant and they both seek the grant of a fresh tenancy into their joint names; or

- where the applicant is a former joint tenant and the joint tenancy has ended; or

- where the applicant is a relation of the previous tenant who has died without there being a right of succession; or

- where the applicant has otherwise occupied the particular property for a considerable time.

4.125 Unless the local housing authority has used this power to identify in its scheme the exclusion of accommodation in such cases from the general allocation provisions, it would be in difficulty in lawfully allocating the specific property to the applicant, given the entitlement of many others to a 'reasonable preference' in allocation. The position will be all the more acute where a scheme provides that 'all' allocations will be by way of choice based letting. A local housing authority will need to ensure that its scheme is framed sufficiently flexibly to take account of these particular cases.

4.126 For example, when a former joint tenancy has ended, a local housing authority may be asked to decide whether to grant a sole tenancy to the former joint tenant who remains in the property. One of the joint tenants may have terminated the former joint tenancy by service of a notice to quit on the

---

215   Rent (Agriculture) Act 1976, ss 27–28.
216   English Code, paras 5.53–5.55; Welsh Code, paras 4.94–4.96.
217   See **1.27** for an introduction to this topic.

landlord.[218] Local housing authorities should set out the circumstances in which they will exercise their discretion to grant new sole tenancies in these situations in their allocation schemes.[219] Of course, if the couple are married, have a civil partnership, or have children, the Family Court has jurisdiction to decide that a joint tenancy should be transferred to a sole tenancy in one of the partners' names and a transfer made following the court's decision is not subject to the allocation scheme.[220]

4.127 Again, when a secure tenant dies, and there is no entitlement to a statutory succession, local housing authorities may consider granting a tenancy to somebody who has been living with the tenant. To do so they must specifically provide for that scenario in their allocation schemes and set out the circumstances they will take into account in determining applications. The Codes recommend that local housing authorities consider granting tenancies where the applicant is a former household member who was living with the tenant for the year prior to the tenant's death, had been providing care for the tenant and/or has accepted responsibility for the tenant's dependants, and needs to live with them.[221]

4.128 Although not referred to in the Codes, an applicant for homelessness assistance who has been granted a non-secure tenancy of local housing authority accommodation under the main housing duty at HA 1996, s 193 could apply to his or her local housing authority for a secure tenancy of that very same property. The local housing authority could only allocate a secure tenancy if its allocation scheme made provision for such circumstances.[222]

AVOIDING DISCRIMINATION AND ENHANCING EQUALITY OF OPPORTUNITY IN ALLOCATION SCHEMES

4.129 All the Codes remind local housing authorities that their allocation schemes, and the detailed policies and procedures they contain, should not discriminate, directly or indirectly, on the grounds of race, ethnicity, sex,

---

[218] *Hammersmith and Fulham London Borough Council v Monk* [1992] 1 AC 478, HL.

[219] *R (Hussey) v Southwark London Borough Council* [2002] EWHC 1142 (Admin), [2002] All ER (D) 332 (May), Admin Ct and *R (Dixon) v Wandsworth London Borough Council* [2007] EWHC 3075 (Admin), (2008) February *Legal Action*, p 40, Admin Ct.

[220] Transfers made by virtue of Matrimonial Causes Act 1973, s 24; Matrimonial and Family Proceedings Act 1984, s 17(1); Children Act 1989, Sch 1 para 1; and Civil Partnership Act 2004, Part 2, Sch 5 are excluded from counting as allocations by HA 1996, s 160(2)(e) and (3)(d). See **1.24**.

[221] English Code, para 3.10; Welsh Code, para 4.7. See *R (Sleith) v Camden London Borough Council* [2003] EWHC 347 (Admin), (2003) May *Legal Action*, p 33, Admin Ct, in respect of which an application for permission to appeal was refused: *R (Sleith) v Camden London Borough Council* [2003] EWCA Civ 347, CA. For a more recent example of this scenario, see *R (Neville) v Wandsworth London Borough Council* [2009] EWHC 2405 (Admin), (2009) December *Legal Action*, p 17, Admin Ct.

[222] HA 1996, s 159(3).

disability or sexual orientation.[223] Local housing authorities are advised to ensure that they consult with a wide range of groups when drawing up their allocation schemes, and particularly with those who are currently under-represented in social housing. Translation of the scheme into different languages spoken in the local community is recommended.[224] The Welsh Code advises that local housing authorities should be sensitive to the housing needs of refugees, people with disabilities, older people, people with mental health problems, and lesbian, gay and bisexual people.[225]

4.130 The allocation scheme must not discriminate, directly or indirectly, on grounds of race, ethnicity, sex or disability[226] and must comply with the Commission for Racial Equality's *Code of Practice for Racial Equality in Housing* (there are separate versions of the Code for England, Scotland and Wales respectively).[227] That Code contains the following examples of potential racial discrimination relating to social housing allocation schemes (in the version for England):

> 'A council generally allocates the worst properties to homeless applicants, whereas tenants transferring to housing association accommodation receive better properties. Ethnic minority households are disproportionately represented among those whom the council has a duty to house because they are homeless. This policy would be unlawful direct discrimination, unless the council could show it to be a proportionate means of achieving a legitimate aim. It may also be unlawful under the Housing Act 1996' (Example 30).

> 'A housing association's allocation policy gives priority for lettings to tenants' sons and daughters. If the racial profile of tenants does not reflect the racial profile of people in need of housing in the association's catchment area, the policy could disadvantage prospective tenants from under-represented racial groups and could amount to unlawful indirect discrimination. It would therefore need to be carefully considered, and the justification for the policy tested against any possible discriminatory effects' (Example 31).

---

[223] Welsh Code, paras 4.59–4.66; English CBL Code, paras 1.6–1.11; and English 2009 Code, para 21. The Equality Bill being debated by Parliament at the time of writing will prohibit discrimination in the provision of services and disposal and management of premises on the grounds of disability, gender reassignment, pregnancy and maternity, race, religion or belief, sex or sexual orientation and, in the case of the provision of services, it also prohibits discrimination on the grounds of age, except to persons who have not reached the age of 18. The English 2009 Code, para 22 draws the attention of local housing authorities to the content of the Bill.

[224] Welsh Code, para 4.61. The guidance to the same effect in English Code, para 5.31 has been replaced by the broader guidance in English 2009 Code.

[225] Welsh Code, paras 4.63–4.69 and 4.88.

[226] Race Relations Act 1976; Sex Discrimination Act 1975; Disability Discrimination Act 1995; Welsh Code, para 4.60. The guidance to the same effect in English Code, para 5.28 has been replaced by the broader guidance in English 2009 Code.

[227] Welsh Code, para 4.60. The guidance to the same effect in English Code, para 5.30 has been replaced by the broader guidance in English 2009 Code. All the versions of the CRE's Code are available at http://www.equalityhumanrights.com/advice-and-guidance/information-for-advisers/codes-of-practice/.

'A local council (or housing association) fails to make sure that information about its lettings services reaches people from all racial groups; for example, by not advertising the service in outlets which it knows are preferred by ethnic minority residents. This could amount to indirect discrimination' (Example 35).

'A CRE inquiry into a major public sector landlord's "choice-based" lettings scheme found that:

- the city council had not done a race equality impact assessment of the scheme;
- it had not consulted affected groups and agencies in the community adequately;
- ethnic monitoring of applications and allocations was poor; and
- information about the new scheme was not available in relevant languages.

The CRE concluded that there had been contraventions of the duty to promote race equality, and that these failings should be rectified' (Example 38).

'Analysis of a council's housing allocations shows that people from certain racial groups are consistently offered inferior accommodation. This constitutes direct discrimination' (Example 39).

4.131 In relation to disability, the publication *Housing and the Disability Equality Duty: A guide to the Disability Equality Duty and Disability Discrimination Act 2005 for the social housing sector* from the former Disability Rights Commission offers considerable advice (and examples of good practice) on drawing-up allocation schemes.[228] The statutory guidance is *The Duty to Promote Disability Equality: Statutory Code of Practice England and Wales* and it also contains a number of examples of unlawful discrimination on the grounds of disability in the housing and social housing area.[229]

4.132 When considering any substantial variation of its housing allocation scheme, a local housing authority will probably first need to undertake an equality impact assessment[230] and should ensure that views of groups which are currently under-represented in social housing are taken into account in any consultation undertaken. Indeed, local housing authorities are encouraged to monitor the operation of their allocation schemes in order to identify and prevent discrimination and to review their schemes if particular groups are shown to be disadvantaged.

---

[228] *Housing and the Disability Equality Duty: A guide to the Disability Equality Duty and Disability Discrimination Act 2005 for the social housing sector* (DRC, 2006), pp 54–57.

[229] Disability Rights Commission, October 2006. The statutory guidance on gender discrimination is *Gender Equality Duty: Code of Practice for England and Wales* (Equal Opportunities Commission, November 2006). All of these Codes are at http://www.equalityhumanrights.com/advice-and-guidance/information-for-advisers/codes-of-practice/.

[230] Such as required by Race Relations Act 1976, s 71, as explained in *R (Kaur and Shah) v Ealing London Borough Council* [2008] EWHC 2062 (Admin), [2008] All ER (D) 08 Oct, Admin Ct. English 2009 Code para 21.

CHALLENGES TO ALLOCATION SCHEMES

4.133   Ordinarily, an applicant will only be concerned with whether his or her particular application has been correctly considered under the terms of the applicable local housing allocation scheme. In other words, whether the application has been allocated to the right band (in a banding scheme) or accorded the appropriate points (in a points-based scheme). Disputes about these and other case-specific matters can be dealt with by reviews, complaints and litigation.[231]

4.134   But, not infrequently, a particular applicant's case may demonstrate that there is – at least arguably – something wrong with the local allocation scheme more generally. In those circumstances the applicant may need to challenge the legality of the scheme or some part of it. That is normally done by proceedings for judicial review.[232]

4.135   For example, it might be suggested that:

• the scheme has failed to comply with some express statutory requirement of HA 1996, Part 6; or

• it has been adopted or varied without the requisite prior consultation;[233] or

• it fails to set out the local housing authority's policies on priority or procedures for allocation;[234] or

• it has been drafted without regard to the statutory Codes of Guidance – or is contrary to them (without explanation);[235] or

• the scheme is discriminatory in an unlawful respect.[236]

In short, a scheme must 'be lawfully and fairly operated, for example without unlawful discrimination'.[237]

4.136   Very exceptionally, it may be said that the whole or part of a scheme is irrational in the sense that no reasonable local housing authority could have framed its scheme in that way. Between 1996 and 2008 several schemes adopted under HA 1996, Part 6 were described in those terms by the courts. But in 2009

---

[231]   See **2.65–2.83** for general information about reviews, complaints and litigation and **3.192–3.193** for challenges to decisions about eligibility.

[232]   For a fuller description of judicial review principles and procedures, see **19.211–19.237**.

[233]   See **1.28**, **4.6** and **4.10**.

[234]   See **2.16–2.18**.

[235]   HA 1996, s 169(1).

[236]   See **4.129–4.132**.

[237]   *R (Ahmad) v Newham London Borough Council* [2009] UKHL 14, at [14], (2009) April *Legal Action*, p 21, HL.

the House of Lords emphasised just how difficult it would be to sustain such a criticism, given the very broad terms in which the statute is now framed since the amendments to HA 1996, Part 6 by the Homelessness Act 2002. As Lord Neuberger put it:

> 'once a housing allocation scheme complies with the requirements of section 167 and any other statutory requirements, the courts should be very slow to interfere on the ground of alleged irrationality.'[238]

Indeed, the judicially approved examples of schemes that might be irrational are extreme:

> 'one possibility might be a policy which ensured that small families had priority over large ones, or that people coming from outside the borough had priority over those living within it, or that people who had been waiting the shortest time had preference over those waiting the longest.'[239]

4.137 Where, in such a very exceptional case, a scheme or part of one is described as 'irrational', the relevant court will probably do no more than declare that to be the case and leave it to the local housing authority to work out how to revise or amend the scheme to address the particular problem:

> 'Castigating a scheme as irrational is of little help to anyone unless a rational alternative can be suggested. Sometimes it may be possible to do this. But where the question is one of overall policy, as opposed to individual entitlement, it is very unlikely that judges will have the tools available to make the choices which Parliament has required a housing authority to make.'[240]

However, shortly after setting out the high hurdle that would need to be surmounted to establish that an allocation scheme was in whole or in part irrational, the House of Lords itself declared unlawful an irrational provision in the allocation scheme adopted by the largest housing authority in England.[241]

---

[238] [2009] UKHL 14, HL, at [55].
[239] [2009] UKHL 14, HL, at [16].
[240] [2009] UKHL 14, HL, at [22].
[241] *Birmingham City Council v Ali* [2009] UKHL 36, [2009] 1 WLR 1506, HL.

Chapter 5

BEING ALLOCATED A PROPERTY

INTRODUCTION

5.1　Successfully establishing eligibility for allocation and securing considera-tion under a local housing authority's housing allocation scheme are only the first stages in obtaining a rented home from a social landlord. What the applicant will usually want is an early opportunity to consider an offer of a tenancy of a house or flat.

5.2　Most social landlords experience a regular turnover in their housing stock and need to make rapid and effective arrangements to re-let properties falling vacant (or, more unusually, to fill newly constructed or acquired property available for first letting), not least because rapid turnover maximises rental receipts. For local housing authorities, the question will be whether to re-let pursuant to an 'allocation' or by a letting which does not constitute an allocation.[1] For registered social landlords (RSLs), the question will be whether to make the property available for nomination of a tenant by the local housing authority (which would then count as an 'allocation' by that local housing authority), or whether to keep it as part of their own pool of properties for re-letting to their existing tenants or to those making applications directly to them.[2]

5.3　If the local housing authority has property which is to be re-let in circumstances which do *not* count as an allocation, for example, by offering the tenancy to an existing secure or introductory tenant whom the local housing authority has invited to move,[3] the local housing authority can make that re-letting free of the legal constraints of its ordinary allocation scheme. Alternatively, the property may be let on a tenancy which is not secure or introductory: for example, it may be used to provide temporary accommoda-tion to a homeless household.[4] Only local housing authority lettings to secure or introductory tenants are controlled by the allocation scheme requirements. Beyond those requirements a local housing authority's only duty is to select a tenant in the lawful exercise of its general discretion to manage its housing stock.[5]

5.4　If a property, whether owned by a local housing authority or an RSL, is to be re-let, in circumstances which do count as an 'allocation', that will trigger the operation of the local allocation scheme arrangements described in this book. To whom, and when, an actual offer of that accommodation will be made depends entirely on the detailed operation of the particular local allocation scheme. The allocation scheme is, however, only a process of

[1]　See **1.24–1.26** for a review of the circumstances in which a person may become a tenant of social housing without an allocation.

[2]　For a discussion of RSL lettings see Chapter 6.

[3]　Housing Act 1996, ss 159(5) and 160. See also **1.24–1.26** for circumstances which do not count as an 'allocation'.

[4]　Housing Act 1985, Sch 2, para 4.

[5]　Housing Act 1957, s 111 substituted by Housing Act 1985, s 21 (as discussed in *R v Canterbury City Council ex p Gillespie* (1987) 19 HLR 7, QBD).

selection or sifting among potential candidates for a tenancy, or nomination for a tenancy. Following the selection or nomination the actual offer and acceptance of the tenancy agreement (or 'grant' of a tenancy) is separate from the process of allocation and will take place after that process has completed.[6] It will be dictated by rules of contract and any relevant statutory controls on the ability of the local housing authority or RSL to let property.[7]

5.5 Essentially, in a true 'allocation' situation, prospective candidates for the particular tenancy will be identified through one of two routes:

(1) by self-selection, in the sense that candidates for the tenancy will put themselves forward or bid for the property in a choice based letting scheme; or

(2) by the local housing authority itself selecting a prospective tenant from among the applicants who fall to be considered under its allocation scheme.

5.6 Which route is available will depend upon whether the particular local housing authority has adopted a choice based letting element in its allocation scheme. As the government's target is that every local housing authority in England must be operating a choice based letting scheme by 2010, this chapter first considers those arrangements. The second part of the chapter covers the alternative – selection by the local housing authority. Finally, we review more general points affecting offers and refusals under both routes.

CHOICE BASED LETTINGS
The policy background

5.7 In 2000, the Labour Government issued Green and White Papers on Housing Policy, both entitled *Quality and Choice: A Decent Home for All*.[8] Those Papers emphasised that applicant 'choice' would be a feature of the new allocation regime to be brought in by what became the Homelessness Act 2002.

5.8 In anticipation of the amendments later made to the Housing Act 1996 (HA 1996), Part 6 ('Allocation of social housing') by the Homelessness Act 2002, the government and local housing authorities – and to an initially

---

[6] *Birmingham City Council v Qasim* [2009] EWCA Civ 1080, (2009) December *Legal Action*, p 16, CA.

[7] For example, the powers of local housing authorities to let or otherwise dispose of the housing they own are controlled by Housing Act 1985, Part 2.

[8] *Quality and Choice: A Decent Home for All* (Green Paper, DETR, April 2000), at http://www.communities.gov.uk/archived/publications/housing/qualitychoice2. *Quality and Choice: A Decent Home for All — the Way Forward for Housing* (White Paper, DETR, December 2000), at http://www.communities.gov.uk/archived/publications/housing/qualityand choice2.

more limited extent RSLs,[9] and combinations of local housing authorities and RSLs[10] – began exploring the prospects for implementation of allocation schemes based on applicant choice, ie choice based letting schemes. In 2001, the government funded 27 local housing authorities to conduct pilot schemes to test the scope for choice based lettings.[11] The pilots ended in March 2003, and the evaluation reports are available on the website of the Department for Communities and Local Government.[12] Most of the schemes established in the pilot period have continued to operate.

5.9 The 27 English local housing authorities that participated in the pilot scheme between April 2001 and March 2003 were, on the whole, positive about the experience. They found that the number of households registered for social housing had increased in almost all of the areas. Choice based letting was considered, both by local housing authorities and by the applicants, to be more transparent and the system itself more open and simpler to understand. The system required greater participation from applicants than previously, in that they were expected to monitor advertised properties and bid themselves. On the whole, applicants seemed to consider that the benefits were worth the extra effort. There was an overall reduction in the rates of refusal of offers.

5.10 The pilot schemes included areas of high and low demand for social housing. However, in none of those areas, even those of low demand, was a truly 'choice based' lettings scheme implemented. All of the schemes had a mechanism for prioritising candidate households who were entitled to reasonable preference under HA 1996, Part 6 (and, in particular, for prioritising homeless households), as a failure to do so would be unlawful. The methods used to prioritise varied. In some areas, particularly those where there was high demand for social housing, local housing authorities used banding systems to give those households with higher needs a higher priority. In areas of lower demand, local housing authorities were more likely to give points for waiting time, and to give households with higher needs priority cards, which provide a particular period in which to bid for properties.

---

9   Early RSL schemes are described in N Winn *The bIGPicture: Choice in Lettings* (Housing Corporation, September 2001) at http://www.housingcorp.gov.uk/server/show/conWebDoc. 1709.

10 Such as the scheme in Harborough described in T Brown et al *Allocate or let? Your Choice: Lessons from Harborough Home Search* (Chartered Institute of Housing, 2003) at http://www.cih.org/publications/pub228.htm; and *Implementing a choice-based lettings system for social housing tenants* (Joseph Rowntree Foundation, Findings, January 2003) at http://www.jrf.org.uk/publications/implementing-choice-based-lettings-system-social-housing-tenants.

11 See *How to Choose Choice: Lessons from the first year of the ODPM's CBLs Pilot Schemes* (Office of the Deputy Prime Minister, October 2002) at: http://www.communities.gov.uk/archived/publications/housing/howchoose.

12 *Piloting Choice-Based Lettings: An Evaluation* (ODPM, August 2004) at: http://www.communities.gov.uk/publications/housing/pilotingchoicebasedlettings; and *Applicants' Perspectives on Choice-Based Lettings* (ODPM, March 2004) at http://www.communities.gov.uk/archived/publications/housing/applicantsperspectives.

5.11 Properties were advertised in local newspapers, in council offices and on the internet. Local housing authorities were advised to identify and support those households who may have difficulty in understanding the system and in making their own bids unassisted. Local housing authorities found that there were fewer households with difficulties than they had expected. It was, however, noticeable, and concerning, that homeless households seemed to bid less frequently than other households. Whether this was because those households were more vulnerable and had more difficulty in accessing or understanding the system, or because they were less anxious to move from their temporary accommodation than were existing tenants waiting for transfers, was unclear.

5.12 Interestingly, the pilot schemes had not resulted in much movement around the country from areas of high demand to areas of low demand. But an early (and continuing) concern was the impact on members of black and minority ethnic (BME) communities in areas where choice based letting had been introduced. In October 2004 the government established an advisory group chaired by Lord Adebowale to explore how the new choice based letting schemes affected BME groups and to undertake a full Race Equality Impact Assessment of the policy.[13] Unpublished research for the Federation of Black Housing Organisations in 2004 showed that the proportion of BME tenants responding to suitable advertised properties was small.[14]

5.13 In 2005, Shelter issued a separate evaluation of the pilot schemes, based on direct contact with eight local housing authorities, information publicly available from others, and the experiences of their own housing advisers and clients.[15] Shelter confirmed that choice based letting was considered by both applicants and local housing authority staff as fairer and more transparent, the process was quicker and there were fewer refusals than under previous schemes. However, Shelter discovered 'a disturbing pattern' that homeless applicants were given less choice, and were compelled to bid more often or more quickly for properties than other applicants, resulting in an increasing concentration of previously homeless households in low-demand areas.[16] It was also concerned that most local housing authorities had not allocated extra resources to help vulnerable applicants with the bidding process. Shelter concluded by identifying the difficulties of providing choice, given the lack of social housing available, and warning:

> '... choice is a hollow concept when there is a chronic housing shortage ... given the current lack of available social housing, choice-based letting cannot realise its full potential.'

---

[13] ODPM *News Release 2004/0237*, 8 October 2004.
[14] 'Choice-based lettings threat to BMEs' (2004) *Inside Housing* 5, 12 November 2004 at http://www.insidehousing.co.uk/story.aspx?storycode=446675.
[15] *A Question of Choice: Good practice and issues in choice-based letting*, Shelter, June 2005, http://england.shelter.org.uk/shop/publications/good_practice/reports/a_question_of_choice.
[16] Principally through the use of time-limited priority cards; see **5.10** and **5.32**.

5.14 Based upon the perceived successes of the pilot scheme, and the general policy shift towards 'choice' in the provision of public services,[17] in 2005 the government set a target in its 5-year plan[18] for 25% of local housing authorities to adopt some form of choice based letting scheme by the end of 2005 and for all local housing authorities to be offering choice to applicants by 2010.[19]

5.15 There has been considerable progress towards that target. Housing Investment Programme returns from 2005 showed that 100 (out of 354) local housing authorities had adopted choice based letting schemes by the end of 2005 and that approximately a further 192 planned to do so by 2010.[20] Housing Strategy Statistical Appendix returns for 2007/8 showed that 47% of local housing authorities had implemented choice based letting and a further 49% had plans to do so.[21] By 1 April 2009 there were 217 local housing authorities participating in choice based letting schemes. That represents 61% of local housing authorities in England but masks wide regional variations. In London, 91% of local housing authorities had moved to choice based lettings compared to only 30% of authorities in the North-East.[22] By January 2010, the number of English local housing authorities with schemes in place or under development had reached 285.[23]

5.16 The Government has continued to commission and publish research on the operation of the individual choice based lettings schemes. A major study of 13 schemes, which had each been operating for over 18 months, was published in October 2006.[24] It found that:

---

[17] See House of Commons Public Administration Select Committee report, *Choice, Voice and Public Services*, Fourth Report of Session 2004–05, 10 March 2005 at http://www.publications. parliament.uk/pa/cm200405/cmselect/cmpubadm/49/4902.htm.

[18] *Sustainable Communities: Homes for All – A Five Year Plan* (ODPM, January 2005) at http://www.communities.gov.uk/archived/publications/corporate/homesforall; and *Sustainable Communities: Homes for All – A Strategy for Choice Based Lettings* (ODPM, June 2005) at *http://www.communities.gov.uk/publications/housing/sustainablecommunitieshomes*.

[19] A useful overview of how choice based lettings schemes work, and government policies and targets for their implementation, is given in *'Choice-Based Lettings: A Factsheet'* (ODPM, March 2005).

[20] The pilot arrangements and the subsequently established local choice based schemes have been monitored and analysed at the Centre for Comparative Housing Research (www.cchr.net), De Montfort University, in association with the Department for Communities and Local Government. A database of material that they have assembled is available at www.choicemoves.org.uk. See T Brown and N Yates *The Choice is yours!: Moving Forward on Choice-based lettings* (De Montfort University, November 2005) at http://www.choicemoves. org.uk/pp/gold/viewGold.asp?IDType=Page&ID=11629.

[21] Figures taken from: http://www.communities.gov.uk/housing/housingmanagementcare/choice basedlettings/.

[22] *Local Authority Housing Statistics, England, 2008-2009* (CLG, November 2009), p 8.

[23] CLG News Release, 20 January 2010, available at http://www.communities.gov.uk/news/ housing/1440887.

[24] *Monitoring the Longer Term Impact of Choice-based lettings* (CLG, October 2006) at http://www.communities.gov.uk/publications/housing/monitoringlonger summarised in Housing Research Summary No 231, CLG, 2006 at http://www.communities.gov.uk/publications/ housing/monitoringlonger.

- the significance of 'waiting time' as a factor in allocation had increased compared to pre-choice arrangements;

- the vast majority of lettings continued to go to high need applicants;

- many applicants saw bidding as a positive pro-active way of looking for a home, but some who had been bidding unsuccessfully over long periods expressed frustration with the systems and lack of confidence in their fairness;

- while most applicants understood the bidding system, many reported having less understanding of the rules by which bidders were ranked;[25]

- the schemes appeared to have improved rather than damaged the prospects of statutory homeless households;

- in most cases, there had been improvement in tenancy sustainment (measured by the proportion of tenancies lasting more than 12 months); and

- the additional costs of the schemes were more than offset by tenancy management savings (in faster re-lets and lower turnover).

5.17 For its part, the Department of Health has commissioned and published research on the experiences of the disabled in accessing choice based letting schemes[26] and associated guides for social landlords establishing such schemes[27] and for people with learning difficulties who try to use them.[28]

5.18 Perhaps the most comprehensive recent report on the operation of choice based schemes was that commissioned by Wirral Council from Heriot Watt University. It examined 26 such schemes operating across the country, although the conclusions and recommendations are primarily expressed by reference to the Wirral homes scheme.[29]

---

[25] A point later emphasised by the report's author, Professor Hal Pawson: see 'Choice ranking rules not always fully understood' (2007) *Inside Housing* 15, 7 September 2007.

[26] *Choice Based Lettings and People with Learning Disabilities* (DH, February 2008) at http://www.dhcarenetworks.org.uk/IndependentLivingChoices/Housing/Topics/browse/LearningDisabilities/?parent=992&child=3433.

[27] *Making Choice Based Lettings work for People with Learning Disabilities: A Guide for Choice-based lettings schemes and landlords* (DH, February 2008) at http://www.dhcarenetworks.org.uk/IndependentLivingChoices/Housing/Topics/type/resource/?cid=3433.

[28] *Choice Based Lettings: A guide to choosing a home through the council* (DH, February 2008), also at http://www.dhcarenetworks.org.uk/IndependentLivingChoices/Housing/Topics/type/resource/?cid=3433.

[29] H Pawson et al *Review of Wirralhomes Choice Based Lettings Service* (Incisive Minds Ltd, March 2008), available at www.wirral.gov.uk; and see 'Spoilt for choice' [2008] *Inside Housing* 23, 25 April 2008.

5.19　In addition to individual local housing authority schemes, a number of regional and sub-regional consortia of local housing authorities have also been set up, so that local housing authorities can make available a choice of properties offered by a range of landlords to their local applicants. Indeed, much of the emphasis in the modern statutory guidance issued by the Secretary of State to English local authorities is placed on the need to establish choice based schemes embracing a range of social housing providers across regions and sub-regions.[30] Applicants can access details of regional and sub-regional schemes through the internet, as well as through the local housing authority to which they have applied. The government has been stimulating their development since 2005/06 by providing substantial start-up funding.[31] The funding (nearly £7 million over 5 years) is specifically designed to support the development of new sub-regional and regional CBL schemes and to enable all local housing authorities to be part of a sub-regional or regional scheme by 2010.[32] The distribution of funds under what was said to be the fifth and *final* round from that Regional Choice Fund was announced on 20 January 2010.[33]

5.20　There has been less success in establishing a cross-regional (ie national) social housing allocation or mobility scheme. In 2006 a national service, 'Move UK', was being developed with the intention of providing information about social housing and job vacancies across the country. But that scheme never went fully live. Its unsuccessful launch and collapse saw the end, in its wake, of a successful scheme called 'HOMES' which had provided information allowing tenants of local housing authorities and RSLs to exchange properties with each other, and a mechanism by which local housing authorities could nominate applicants for housing in the districts of other local housing authorities. Sir George Young MP told a Parliamentary debate that the HOMES website had been 'the largest and most used public sector website in the UK, with 10 million hits a month and more than 800 new home swap registrations online every day'.[34] In response, the Housing Minister gave a depressing account of the difficulties the government had faced in establishing a national scheme since 1997.[35] However, in April 2008 the Housing Corporation approved funding for a feasibility study into a national mobility scheme,[36] a summary of moves towards a national scheme was published in December 2008,[37] and in June 2009

---

[30]　For references to the plethora of statutory guidance on housing allocation see the note to **5.27**.

[31]　*Choice Based Lettings Newsletter Issue 9* (ODPM, Winter 2005), at http://www.communities. gov.uk/archived/publications/housing/choicebasednews9.

[32]　Not all the start-up funding has actually resulted in the establishment of a regional or sub-regional scheme: see 'Providers begin to veer off choice-based lettings road' (27 July 2007) *Inside Housing* 13.

[33]　CLG News Release, 20 January 2010, available at http://www.communities.gov.uk/news/ housing/1440887.

[34]　*Hansard Debates*, 5 June 2007, col 230, at http://www.publications.parliament.uk/pa/ cm200607/cmhansrd/cm070605/debtext/70605-0017.htm#07060568000001.

[35]　*Hansard Debates*, 5 June 2007, col 234, at http://www.publications.parliament.uk/pa/ cm200607/cmhansrd/cm070605/debtext/70605-0018.htm.

[36]　*National mobility scheme study announced* (Housing Corporation Statement, 19/08, 10 March 2008), at http://www.housingcorp.gov.uk/server/show/ConWebDoc.13407/changeNav/431.

[37]　*Housing mobility schemes* (House of Commons Library, Standard Note: SN/SP/4696, December 2008), at http://www.parliament.uk/topics/Social-rented-housingArchive.htm#SN.

the government re-stated its intention to establish a scheme to enable social housing to be available on a nationwide basis.[38] The Housing Corporation funded research was published in November 2009. It showed that, of a representative sample of social housing tenants, 17% were keen to move and of those some 19% were interested in a move to a different English region.[39]

5.21 While the development of a national mobility scheme is stalled, the organisation Housingmoves helps social housing tenants aged over 55 and living in London to find alternative accommodation in other areas of England through the 'choice based mobility scheme'. It also runs the 'Seaside & Country Homes scheme' which is open to households living in local housing authority or RSL accommodation in London and where the eldest family member is 60 years of age or older.[40] In the North of England, the Northern Housing Consortium commissioned the provision of a choice based lettings framework capable of being adapted and adopted by member authorities across the region.[41] The Association of London Government ('London Councils') tried for several years to set up a pan-London scheme ('Capital Moves') but that project was abandoned in autumn 2008.[42]

5.22 All these various policy initiatives were developed against the background of, and within the framework of, the government's 5-year strategic plan for housing, which was published in January 2005 and was expressed (in relation to choice based letting) in the following terms:[43]

'**Improving choice**

5.18 Those who need help with their housing should have choice about where they live. We want to support people looking for homes to choose the option that is best for them, giving information on opportunities for shared ownership, low cost home ownership, and social rented housing. We want to end the situation in which social tenants have to accept the accommodation that is allocated to them on a "take it or leave it" basis. This benefits both tenants and landlords.

5.19 Considerable progress has already been made in encouraging local housing authorities to introduce "choice-based" lettings systems — a way of tenants having a greater say over where they live and a more transparent allocations

---

38 *Building Britain's Future*, June 2009, para 52 at http://www.number10.gov.uk/Page19835.
39 *Mobility Matters: Exploring mobility aspirations and options for social housing residents* (Broomleigh Housing Association, November 2009).
40 www.housingmoves.org/index.htm.
41 www.consortiumprocurement.org.uk/Page/ChoiceBasedLettings.aspx.
42 www.insidehousing.co.uk/story.aspx?storycode=6501086.
43 *Sustainable Communities: Homes for All* (ODPM, January 2005), at http://www.communities. gov.uk/archived/publications/corporate/homesforall. More recently, some have suggested that the initiatives on choice be expanded further, e g to enable an existing tenant to advertise his or her own home in the hope that a successful 'bid' for it will free the existing tenant to 'bid' for a different property he or she would prefer: see Dr T Leunig 'The Power of Choice' (28 November 2008) *Inside Housing* 23, at http://www.insidehousing.co.uk/story.aspx? story-code=6502070 and *The right to move: a new agenda for social housing tenants* (Policy Exchange, January 2009), at http://www.policyexchange.org.uk/publications/publication.cgi?id =103.

process. We want *all* local housing authorities to operate choice-based systems by 2010 and will support them in achieving this aim.

5.20 Housing markets do not follow local authority boundaries. We are therefore keen that choice-based lettings systems should operate sub-regionally or regionally.

5.21 To increase choice and opportunity further we want to make it as easy as possible for tenants to move between local authority, housing association and privately owned accommodation. We are therefore keen to encourage the extension of choice-based lettings to cover low cost home ownership options and properties for rent from private landlords, as well as social housing. We will work towards a nationwide system of choice by 2010.'

5.23 The extent to which the envisaged 'nationwide system of choice' can be delivered by the end of 2010 depends on both the available statutory framework and national and local policy priorities. It was, however, given a significant push in the summer of 2008 by the publication of *Allocation of Accommodation: Choice-based Lettings*[44] – a new code of statutory guidance issued by the Secretary of State to English local housing authorities under the powers given by HA 1996, s 162. The detail of that Code, and of further guidance issued in December 2009 is discussed in the relevant passages of this book. Both sets of guidance are reproduced in full in Appendix 1.

The statutory basis for choice based lettings

5.24 Despite all the emphasis on 'choice' in *policy* terms, there is no *statutory* obligation on local housing authorities to implement choice based letting schemes. HA 1996, Part 6 merely provides that applicants should be informed of any local policy on offering either:

(1) 'a choice of housing accommodation'; or

(2) 'the opportunity to express preferences' about what is to be allocated to them.

In either case that must be by way of a statement in the local housing allocation scheme.[45] Strictly speaking, this obligation could be met by a simple statement in the allocation scheme to the effect that there is *no* local policy on 'choice' or customer 'preferences'. At a minimum, however, local housing authorities could be expected to allow applicants an opportunity to express a preference for accommodation of a particular type or in a particular location. The statutory guidance sees a local policy on expression of preferences as an interim measure or as a second-best to a full-blown policy on choice.[46]

---

[44] 'The English CBL Code', reproduced in Appendix 1.
[45] HA 1996, s 167(1A).
[46] English CBL Code, para 2.4.

5.25 Not only is there no statutory duty positively to give effect to applicant choice or preference, but there is no duty to promote any such policy to prospective or actual applicants. HA 1996, Part 6 only requires that each 'homeless' applicant to whom the local housing authority has accepted a particular accommodation duty[47] must receive a copy of the statutorily required statement about choice or preference.[48] Absurdly, the same homeless person is not entitled to any choice in the selection of temporary accommodation provided in fulfilment of that homelessness duty.[49] Other applicants and members of the public can obtain their copies of the policy statement on 'choice' when they request a copy of the free published summary of the allocation scheme, or if they purchase – or otherwise obtain – a copy of the full local allocation scheme.[50]

5.26 In summary, therefore, HA 1996, Part 6 simply permits, but does not require, local housing authorities to contain within their allocation schemes provisions allowing applicants opportunities to state preferences or make choices. For those local housing authorities wishing to adopt choice based letting, HA 1996, Part 6 expressly enables local allocation schemes to include provision for the allocation of particular units of accommodation in response to specific applications for that accommodation.[51] This is the sole statutory basis for local housing authorities to implement 'choice' by means of enabling applicants to 'bid' for specific properties.

5.27 In this absence of any legislative compulsion, the direction of travel towards choice based letting is set out in the four relevant statutory Codes of Guidance on housing allocation.[52]

England

5.28 In England, local housing authorities are advised by the Codes that choice should be provided for applicants wherever possible.[53] The Secretary of State believes that:

---

47 A duty under HA 1996, s 193 or s 195. See Chapter 17 for a description of these and other duties to secure housing for the homeless.

48 HA 1996, s 193(3A) and s 195(3A).

49 *R (Khatun) v Newham London Borough Council* [2004] EWCA Civ 55, (2004) 36 HLR 29, CA.

50 HA 1996, s 168(1) and (2). See **2.13–2.18**.

51 HA 1996, s 167(2E), discussed further at **4.111–4.113**.

52 *Allocation of Accommodation: Code of Guidance for local housing authorities for England* (Office of the Deputy Prime Minister, November 2002) [English Code], Chapter 5; *Code of Guidance for local housing authorities on allocation of accommodation and homelessness for Wales* (National Assembly for Wales, April 2003) [Welsh Code], Chapter 4; *Allocation of Accommodation: Choice-based Lettings Code of Guidance for Local Housing Authorities* (CLG, August 2008) [English CBL Code] passim; and *Fair and flexible: statutory guidance on social housing allocations for local authorities in England* (CLG, December 2009) [English 2009 Code]. The three English Codes are reproduced in Appendix 1 and in the CR-ROM supplied. The Welsh Code is on the CD-ROM.

53 English CBL Code, para 2.4.

'... this is the best way to ensure sustainable tenancies and to build settled and stable communities, as tenants are more likely to meet their tenancy obligations, maintain the property in good condition and remain in situ for longer',

if they have exercised choice.[54]

5.29 English local housing authorities have previously been advised that if they do not offer a choice of accommodation, they should at least consider giving applicants the opportunity to express preferences about the location and type of accommodation to be allocated to them, and to try to take those preferences into account.[55] That earlier guidance has now been replaced by a more general statement that the Government believes that allocation schemes 'should provide for applicants to be given more of a say and a greater choice over the accommodation which they are allocated.'[56]

5.30 The more recent English Codes expressly recommend a simplified system of applicant prioritisation in place of a complex points-based approach.[57] In short, they promote bands as a simpler alternative than assessment by points – and the whole emphasis of the English CBL Code at Chapter 4 is on the former rather than the latter. Having canvassed the options of either:

(1) a 'banding' system, so that applicants are placed in different bands reflecting their different needs, and, within those bands, applicants are prioritised according to the length of time they have waited; or

(2) simply giving those applicants with the most urgent housing needs priority over others with less urgent needs,[58]

the statutory guidance describes the former as simpler for applicants to understand and simpler for housing authorities to operate than the old points systems.[59]

5.31 Where available properties are openly advertised, so that applicants can apply for particular properties, the advertising should state the level of priority or the waiting time required by the likely successful applicant. The thinking is that providing this information allows applicants to assess their chances of success, and so to refrain from bidding if they would have no prospect of being allocated the accommodation.[60]

---

[54] English CBL Code, para 2.8.
[55] English Code, para 5.6.
[56] English 2009 Code, para 24.
[57] English CBL Code and English 2009 Code.
[58] Whether by a simplified points system or by 'time limited priority cards' which would enable an applicant with the most urgent need to have priority over other applicants for a specified period.
[59] English 2009 Code, paras 70–74.
[60] English Code, para 5.57; Welsh Code, para 4.102.

5.32 Shelter's evaluation of the pilot scheme published in June 2005[61] was highly critical of time-limited priority cards for those in greatest need, arguing that the effect was to put pressure on those applicants to bid for unpopular properties. Shelter also identified at least two local housing authorities that refused to accept bids from homeless applicants for high-demand properties. Shelter recommended that, if time-limited priority cards were to be used, they should be valid for a long enough period of time (at least 6 months) to allow for a suitable range of properties to become available, and that the applicant's needs should be reviewed at the end of the period. Perhaps in response to that, or to other research reports, the Secretary of State now suggests that, rather than use time-limited priority cards, an alternative approach based on increasing the number of bands in a scheme would be simpler to understand and operate.[62]

5.33 The advice given in both the English Code and the English CBL Code was premised on the basis that, however it is constructed, the local choice based scheme should allow for identification of housing needs and recognise 'composite' or 'cumulative' needs – especially for applicants in the reasonable preference categories.[63] The English CBL Code promoted, as an appropriate mechanism to achieve that objective, a core banding scheme of at least four broad levels of priority, with the possibility of increased numbers of bands or 'mechanisms for differentiating between applicants in the same band' where that would be necessary to deal with complex cases.[64] The Secretary of State expressly recommended that local housing authorities adopt schemes which prioritise applicants according to housing need rather than primarily by reference to waiting time.[65]

5.34 However, that more prescriptive approach has been abandoned and the relevant passages of those two codes have been replaced. The English 2009 Code now encourages all local housing authorities to review their schemes to make them simpler to understand, more transparent in their operation and more responsive to local circumstances. They are invited to adopt much greater flexibility in structuring their schemes in order to reflect the Government's strategic view that schemes should be 'promoting greater choice for prospective and existing tenants' wherever possible.[66] The availability of a greater flexibility is said to have emerged as a result of developments in the case law on the interpretation of HA 1996, Part 6. Those developments are described[67] after an outline of the position in Wales.

---

61   *A Question of Choice: Good Practice and issues in choice-based letting* (Shelter, June 2005), at http://england.shelter.org.uk/shop/publications/good_practice/reports/a_question_of_choice. See also **5.13**.
62   English CBL Code, paras 4.29-4.32.
63   English CBL Code, paras 4.6 and 4.14.
64   English CBL Code, paras 4.15-4.19.
65   English CBL Code, para 4.48.
66   English 2009 Code, para 1.
67   See **5.46 – 5.57**.

Wales

5.35 The Welsh Code is more equivocal than the English Codes, making the point that the Assembly Government does not recommend any one system of allocation, and encouraging local housing authorities to determine housing need in, and strategic priorities for, their own areas, after consultation.[68]

5.36 The Welsh Code describes three different approaches:

(1) choice based lettings;

(2) needs-based schemes; and

(3) midway schemes.

5.37 It emphasises that any scheme will, in reality, include both an element of choice and also an attempt to meet need. The difference between the three approaches lies in the balance that each attempts to strike between choice and need.[69]

5.38 Within the phrase 'choice based letting', a number of different systems can be operated in Wales. Generally, under such schemes, available properties are advertised, and let only to those housing applicants who decide to apply for them. Alternatively, properties can be labelled as available for certain types of applicants. If more than one applicant applies, the local housing authority must select which applicant will be successful, either on the basis of greater need, or on the basis of length of time spent waiting. Time limited priority cards are recommended.[70]

5.39 'Needs-based schemes' generally make use of points in order to prioritise applicants with different needs. Vacant properties are not advertised but offered to the applicant with the greatest need for that type of property. Under a 'needs-based' scheme, the Welsh Code describes various options that can still maximise choice, such as:

(1) removing penalties for refusals;

(2) offering several properties at the same time to a selected list of applicants, and then allocating to the household with the greatest need from those who express an interest in a particular property; or

(3) providing an opportunity for preferences to be expressed.[71]

---

[68] Welsh Code, paras 4.24–4.27.
[69] Welsh Code, paras 4.24–4.44.
[70] Welsh Code, paras 4.30–4.32, 4.38.
[71] Welsh Code, paras 4.33–4.34, 4.39.

5.40 The Welsh Code uses the phrase 'mid-way scheme' to describe a process of both providing choice and allocating according to need. The most common model is to band applicants into groups reflecting their different levels of housing need: for example, 'emergency', 'high', 'medium' and 'low/no particular need'. Under that model, advertised vacant properties should be labelled to indicate which band is entitled to bid for each property. Where more than one household in the same band bids for a property, it should be allocated according to length of waiting time. If there is no interest from anyone in the band, it can then be advertised to lower bands of applicants.[72]

5.41 In general, the Welsh Code suggests that maintaining common housing lists, rather than separate lists for different groups of applicants, encouraging mobility between different areas and different types of tenure, providing good quality information, making the widest practicable range of options available to applicants and, above all, operating a simple and transparent system should be hallmarks of a system allowing applicants a choice (whether the overall approach of each local housing authority's allocation scheme is choice based, needs based or mid-way).[73]

5.42 Since issuing the Welsh Code, the Assembly Government has commissioned a project to review choice based allocation systems in use by social landlords in Wales. The project report identified some 11 choice based schemes which covered the whole of a social landlord's available stock.[74] The report describes the key features of those schemes, recording a shift away from 'time waiting' to 'housing need' as the main means of prioritising among applicants. It found that the weakest general feature of the schemes was the late provision of feedback on bid outcomes and patchy content of that feedback. In keeping with the theme of the Welsh Code, the report's recommendations are non-prescriptive as to the type of scheme a local housing authority should adopt.

5.43 In the light of that report, and of the most recent case law,[75] the Welsh Code may well require significant revision. That revision is likely to be set in train after publication of a new National Housing Strategy for Wales later in 2010.

The issue of balancing choice and need

5.44 It had been thought that the greatest difficulty in operating choice based schemes would arise in areas where demand most heavily outstripped supply. How, after all, could a local housing authority offer a realistic 'choice' if the statutory scheme requires a reasonable preference to be given to applicants in

---

[72] Welsh Code, paras 4.35–4.36.
[73] Welsh Code, paras 4.40–4.44.
[74] *A Review of Welsh Social Landlords' Approaches to Increasing Choice in Letting Accommodation* (Welsh Assembly Government, 2008), at http://cymru.gov.uk/topics/ housingandcommunity/research/housing/choiceletting/?lang=en.
[75] See **5.55 – 5.57**.

specified categories of housing need and there is not even enough housing available to meet the needs of those 'priority' applicants?[76]

5.45 When the English Code was published on 11 November 2002, it was accompanied by an undertaking by the then relevant Government department (ODPM) to issue further guidance on this question 'towards the end of' 2003.[77] Despite that commitment, it was not until August 2008 that the English CBL Code was issued to local housing authorities providing that guidance. In the light of subsequent developments in case law on the interpretation of HA 1996, Part 6, some of that Code has in turn been replaced by further guidance in the English 2009 Code. The unhappy consequence is that any local housing authority in England seeking to review or revise its allocation scheme to best address issues of 'choice' and 'need' must take account of all three Codes (and a statutory Circular). Those materials are all reproduced in Appendix 1. The prompt for the most recent guidance has, as indicated, come from developments in the case law and it is to these we now turn.

The courts' approach

1996–2009

5.46 In the first decade of operation of HA 1996, Part 6, the courts discerned the meeting of housing 'need' as the primary policy driver in the legislation[78] and, from 2000 onwards, had several opportunities to consider the application of that principle in the operation of choice based letting schemes adopted by particular local housing authorities.

5.47 An early attempt to implement a choice based lettings scheme, reconciling freedom of choice with providing reasonable preference to those groups falling within the statutory categories by the adoption of broad priority bands, was made by the London Borough of Lambeth.[79]

5.48 The Court of Appeal considered that attempt in the linked cases *R (A) v Lambeth London Borough Council, R (Lindsay) v Lambeth London Borough Council*[80] and concluded that Lambeth had been unsuccessful and had failed to give effect to the statutory scheme properly. Lambeth's bands, recognising different categories of needs, were organised in such a way that applicants who

---

[76] See R Latham 'Allocating Accommodation: reconciling choice and need', Parts 1 and 2 (2005) March *Legal Action* at p 16 and May *Legal Action* at p 15.

[77] 'Letter by Housing Policy Advisor ODPM to Directors of all local authorities in England' (ODPM, November 2002), at http://www.communities.gov.uk/housing/housingmanagement care/housingallocation/, reproduced in Appendix 1.

[78] See the discussion at **4.79–4.84**. Notwithstanding later developments in the case law, the Government's policy is still that 'overall, priority for social housing should go to those in greatest need': English 2009 Code, para 17.

[79] The Lambeth experiment with choice based letting is well-charted by Cowan and Marsh 'From Need to Choice' (2004) 67 MLR 3, p 478 at www.modernlawreview.co.uk.

[80] *R (A) v Lambeth London Borough Council, R (Lindsay) v Lambeth London Borough Council* [2002] EWCA Civ 1084, (2002) 34 HLR 57, CA.

did not fall within any of the reasonable preference categories could have the same priority as those who did. The Court of Appeal also criticised Lambeth's policy of allowing applicants to define their own needs, by specifying the size and location of accommodation they sought (and being encouraged to do so as widely and flexibly as possible), as haphazard and not capable of ensuring that the categories of applicants falling within the statutory 'reasonable preference' groups were given preference. The court expressed concern that applicants might under-estimate their own needs, in order to stand a greater chance of being allocated accommodation, but that some applicants, such as families with young children, would have fewer chances of being allocated accommodation as they would not find it possible to under-estimate their own needs. In reality, the main 'choice' offered by the Lambeth scheme was a freedom to opt for poorer quality or less satisfactory accommodation in the hope of an earlier offer. Having been declared unlawful in July 2002, it was replaced by a new allocation scheme in February 2004.

5.49   Surprisingly few cases then reached the courts in relation to choice based letting schemes after the introduction of the new allocation regime in January 2003.

5.50   In the London Borough of Newham, where a choice based scheme had been operating (with amendments) since September 2002, at least two early judicial review applications were launched. The first resulted in an undertaking to amend the scheme in June 2003.[81] The second was again settled on terms that the local housing authority further amend its allocation scheme.[82] Some of those amendments were later revoked by the local housing authority's Director of Housing, and others were incorporated into a scheme that reached its seventh revision before being upheld as lawful.[83]

5.51   In *R (Najha Al-Juboori) v Ealing London Borough Council*,[84] permission had been granted for a challenge to the local choice based allocation scheme in a judicial review claim. The trial was adjourned to enable other boroughs to join the proceedings. By the time it was restored, the claimant had been re-housed and the scheme amended.

5.52   In *R (Cali) v Waltham Forest London Borough Council*,[85] a choice based scheme containing a banding system was declared to be unlawful because it did not provide for the identification of a household's cumulative needs and so

---

[81]   *R (Nazma Begum) v Newham London Borough Council* CO/566/2003 (unreported) 26 June 2003.

[82]   *R (Heather Phillip) v Newham London Borough Council* CO/1731/2004 (unreported) 22 June 2004. See also 'Choice scheme revised after challenge' (2004) *Inside Housing*, 30 July, p 71, at http://www.insidehousing.co.uk/story.aspx?storycode=446065.

[83]   See **5.55–5.57**.

[84]   *R (Najha Al-Juboori) v Ealing London Borough Council* [2002] EWHC 2627 (Admin).

[85]   [2006] EWHC 302 (Admin), [2007] 39 HLR 1.

could not effectively offer additional preference.[86] Nor did it identify, within the published scheme, the criteria by which an applicant qualified for reasonable preference.

5.53　In *R (Lin & Hassan) v Barnet London Borough Council*,[87] a points-based scheme of choice based letting was held to be unlawful as its provision giving 100 points to its existing tenants, seeking transfers, artificially raised the points threshold (above which a bid might succeed) to the detriment of applicants who were not existing tenants and who were entitled to a statutory preference. That decision was not disturbed on an appeal pursued (for the most part unsuccessfully) by the claimants, who sought to establish that the choice based scheme gave insufficient opportunity to the homeless to secure long-term housing.[88]

5.54　The central problem identified by the litigation in this period was how to establish a system that was easy to operate and understand, gave priority to customer choice, but that also took account of the vast range of needs exhibited by applicants and ranked them in a way which gave effect to the perceived statutory purpose that those in the greatest need should be housed first.

2009 onwards

5.55　The legal landscape changed dramatically in March 2009 with the first House of Lords decision on a choice based letting scheme.[89] Newham had adopted a banding scheme with three bands:

(1)　applicants in reasonable preference categories;

(2)　transfer cases with no reasonable preference;

(3)　non-transfer applicants with no reasonable preferences.[90]

Unsurprisingly, the vast majority of advertised properties went to bidders from the first band. But within that band applicants were afforded relative priority as between one another, not by reference to housing need (in the sense of particular assessments of cumulative or composite need), but by date order. The applicant waiting longest among the highest banded bidders for a

---

[86]　See **4.77–4.85** and **4.91–4.100**.

[87]　[2006] EWHC 1041 (Admin), [2006] HLR 440. See **4.69**.

[88]　*R (Lin) v London Borough of Barnet* [2007] EWCA Civ 132, [2007] HLR 30, CA.

[89]　*R (Ahmad) v Newham London Borough Council* [2009] UKHL 14, (2009) April *Legal Action*, p 21, HL.

[90]　In common with the schemes of many other authorities, Newham's allocation scheme included a 'top slice' facility catering for a very small number of those in the most acute housing need to obtain a priority higher than the main bandings. Subsequently published research has shown that across local housing authorities which assess housing 'need' among applicants the proportion of the 'top banded' applicants was in most cases under 3% of all applicants: *Exploring local authority policy and practice on housing allocations* (CLG, July 2009), para 10.

particular property would be allocated it. In both the High Court and Court of Appeal the scheme was held unlawful.[91]

5.56 The House of Lords allowed the local housing authority's appeal. It decided that nothing in HA 1996, Part 6, as amended by the Homelessness Act 2002, *required* allocation to those in the greatest need, nor *required* a facility for cumulative or composite assessment of needs. A local housing authority such as Newham, where demand vastly outstripped supply, was entitled to adopt a simple banding scheme which met the statutory obligation to give a reasonable preference to the statutory categories but then prioritised amongst them by waiting time.

5.57 This dramatic change in the judicial perception of HA 1996, Part 6 (as amended) has given new impetus to simplified choice based banding schemes. For the reasons explained in Chapter 4, many fewer legal challenges to allocation schemes can now be expected. Indeed, in the light of the *Ahmad* decision, new guidance on housing allocation has been issued by the Secretary of State to English local housing authorities encouraging all those authorities, including authorities already operating choice based letting schemes, to review and revise their schemes to take advantage of perceived new flexibilities.[92] The guidance suggests that freedom from the previously understood *requirement* to take account of the cumulative needs of applicants provides the opportunity for more use of:

> 'the flexibilities local authorities have within the allocation legislation to meet local pressures by:
>
> - adopting local priorities alongside the statutory reasonable preference categories
> - taking into account other factors in prioritising applicants, including waiting time and local connection
> - operating local lettings policies.'[93]

In keeping with the national policy objectives in England, the new statutory guidance encourages development of choice based letting schemes that operate as simply and as transparently as possible with a strong endorsement of simplified banding arrangements.[94]

The effectiveness of choice

5.58 Despite the use of the name 'choice based letting' to describe the process, the ultimate allocation of any particular property by a local housing authority will lie with the local housing authority itself. Many individuals will have

---

[91] *R (Ahmad) v Newham London Borough Council* [2007] EWHC 2332 (Admin), (2007) November *Legal Action*, p 38, Admin Ct; and *R (Ahmad) v Newham London Borough Council* [2008] EWCA Civ 140, (2008) April *Legal Action*, p 38, CA.
[92] English 2009 Code, issued in December 2009.
[93] English 2009 Code, para 1.
[94] English 2009 Code, paras 54–86.

expressed their preference to be allocated a particular advertised vacancy – it will then be for the local housing authority to select one household from among them (or none of them).[95] Of course, the terms of the local allocation scheme may, and should, spell out precisely how the choice is to be made between them, and by whom. For example, the scheme might specify that the property is to be offered to the candidate with the highest banding, longest waiting time, greatest number of points, or whatever.[96] And the scheme may also specify who is to be considered next, if the highest bidder pulls out.

5.59 In this sense, 'choice based letting' is a misnomer. Almost all the schemes adopted are in reality choice based *applications* seeking that the bidder be considered for the particular property available for letting. It does not necessarily follow that the highest ranked bidder at the closing date *will* be allocated the property. For example, most schemes incorporate an element of re-assessment of shortlisted bidders to ensure that they are still eligible and have maintained their initially awarded degree of priority. That element of re-checking (or 'evaluating the bids') is specifically encouraged by the English CBL Code.[97] Indeed, the statutory guidance identifies the need for schemes to retain some form of override enabling the rejection of bids by applicants unsuitable for the particular property.[98]

5.60 In many avowedly 'choice based' schemes, not all the available property is advertised. Empty homes are often reserved for applicants entitled to what schemes may describe as 'direct lets' or 'direct offers'. In some schemes, advertised properties may be withdrawn to be offered outside the allocation scheme or to direct-let cases. In others, properties are offered subject to multiple qualifications as to the type of bid that will be considered. In yet others, bidding preferences expire if not used within a fixed period or on the refusal of offers. While the English CBL Code recognises and addresses each of these features,[99] the policy thrust remains that the maximum degree of choice should be available for the widest range of properties.

5.61 It has yet to be seen whether the courts will recognise any enforceable 'legitimate expectation' on the part of the candidate who would be due to receive the offer on the strict terms of the choice based allocation scheme.[100]

---

95   Or, where the property is owned by an RSL or a different local housing authority, to decide which applicant(s) to *nominate* to that landlord.

96   For example, in *R (van Boolen) v Barking and Dagenham London Borough Council* [2009] EWHC 2196 (Admin) the policy of the authority was to identify the bidders in the highest band and then to give further preference as between them to those applicants with a local connection.

97   English CBL Code, para 3.10.

98   English CBL Code, para 3.3.

99   English CBL Code, chapter 4, in significant parts replaced by the more general guidance in the English 2009 Code.

100 For a discussion of 'legitimate expectation' in an allocation context see *R v Brent London Borough Council ex p Jerke* CO/2069/97 (unreported) 8 May 1998, QBD and *R v Lambeth London Borough Council ex p Trabi* (1998) 30 HLR 975, QBD. See also **4.36** and the notes to that paragraph.

Could, for example, the local housing authority withdraw a property, advertised under the choice based scheme, and offer it to another applicant, or let it in circumstances that do not constitute an 'allocation' after the bid process had closed? What would be the legal effect of mistakenly overlooking the bidder with the highest priority under the scheme, and offering the property, inadvertently, to the next person in the queue of bidding candidates? These issues will no doubt be explored by the courts in the reasonably near future. Any individual applicant who believes that they have not been treated appropriately under a choice based scheme will need to obtain access to the courts very quickly if they are to prevent letting of a property for which they and others have bid. Unless an application for judicial review is launched very quickly and, if necessary, an injunction obtained to prevent the property being let, the disappointed applicant may well find that the claim has become academic[101] or at best is reduced to an attempt to prevent any future departure from the published arrangements.[102]

LOCAL HOUSING AUTHORITY LED ALLOCATION

5.62 If a local housing authority is not operating a choice based allocation scheme, all aspects of allocation decisions will be made by officers of the local housing authority applying principles set out in the local allocation scheme. Indeed, the scheme must identify the procedure for making actual allocation decisions, including the name or designation of the responsible officer(s).[103]

5.63 Planning for such allocations usually starts well before a specific property becomes available to offer. Once an applicant has been accepted onto the allocation scheme, and the preference to which he or she is entitled has been assessed and accorded, the local housing authority must decide what type of property the applicant should be offered, and whether there is any particular geographic area in which an allocation would or would not be appropriate.

5.64 The extent and circumstances of the applicant's household as assessed under the allocation scheme obviously determines the number of bedrooms that the applicant may expect to find in an allocated property.[104] An applicant, or a member of his or her household, may have a medical need for a ground floor property or an accessible bathroom, or an additional bathroom or toilet.

---

[101]   *R (Fidelis-Auma) v Octavia Housing and Care* [2009] EWHC 2263 (Admin), (2009) November *Legal Action*, p 25, Admin Ct.

[102]   *Birmingham City Council v Qasim* [2009] EWCA Civ 1080, (2009) December *Legal Action*, p 16, CA, at [39].

[103]   HA 1996, s 167(1).

[104]   *R v Lewisham London Borough Council ex p Pinzon* (1999) 2 CCLR 152, QBD. This may not be a straightforward task. In *R (Bibi) v Camden London Borough Council* [2004] EWHC 2527 (Admin), [2005] HLR 18, Admin Ct, the local housing authority offered a woman a one-bedroom property, overlooking the fact that she had a joint residence order in respect of her children with her former husband. It was required to reconsider the offer, taking into account that order, as well as the other demands on its housing stock and any potential under-occupancy of the property. For a discussion of 'household' in this context see **3.161**.

The Codes advise that applicants who receive support from a carer, who does not live with them, should have their need for a spare bedroom taken into account wherever possible.[105] In Wales, local housing authorities are reminded that elderly applicants who are awaiting an allocation of accommodation may desire to bring any pets with them, and the allocation should take account of that need.[106] When determining the extent and circumstances of the applicant's household, the local housing authority must take all of the members of the household into account, whether they were eligible for an allocation in their own right or not, unless the local allocation scheme otherwise provides. There is no statutory provision permitting local housing authorities to ignore the needs of members who would not have satisfied the eligibility test had they been the applicant. The matter is one to be determined by the terms of the local scheme.[107]

5.65 An applicant may need or prefer a property to be in a particular location, or there may be locations that the applicant cannot be placed in, if, for example, the applicant has left an area due to violence.

5.66 HA 1996, s 167(2E)(b) permits local housing authorities to target certain properties to certain groups of applicants.[108] Building on that provision, the English 2009 Code now gives extended guidance on the adoption and operation of 'local' lettings policies.[109]

5.67 Once a property of the requisite description in the appropriate area becomes available for letting, the local housing authority must decide from among the pool of available applicants which of them should first be offered it. This is the most sensitive aspect of allocation and the stage at which greatest transparency will be needed. How the actual selection is made is determined by the local scheme.

GENERAL POINTS

The offer of accommodation

5.68 Under either of the two routes described earlier in this chapter, a particular applicant will be identified to receive an offer of the tenancy of an available property. At that stage the strict 'allocation' process, which involves simple selection or nomination of a candidate, comes to an end.[110] The actual letting will normally be handled by housing management staff who will 'sign up' the new tenant by the offer and acceptance of a tenancy agreement.

---

[105] English Code, para 5.37; Welsh Code, paras 4.73–4.74.

[106] Welsh Code, para 4.68.

[107] See *R (Ariemuguvbe) v Islington London Borough Council* [2009] EWCA Civ 1218, (2010) January *Legal Action*, p 35, CA.

[108] See **4.111–4.128**.

[109] English 2009 Code, paras 84–92.

[110] *Birmingham City Council v Qasim* [2009] EWCA Civ 1080, (2009) December *Legal Action* p16, CA.

5.69 Once an offer of accommodation has been made, the Codes recommend that the applicant should be given 'a reasonable period' to consider whether to accept it.[111] 'Reasonable period' is not defined in HA 1996, Part 6, or the Codes. The applicant should be 'given sufficient time for careful consideration' and the length of time provided should depend on the individual circumstances of each applicant. Vulnerable applicants, or applicants who are unfamiliar with the property, are likely to need longer.[112] An applicant who is in hospital or in temporary accommodation such as a hostel or refuge may also need longer, as may those who are working or have childcare commitments.[113]

Types of tenancies to be offered

Sole or joint tenancy?

5.70 Where there are joint applicants, or a partner, friend or live-in carer is included as part of an applicant's household, local housing authorities are advised normally to grant joint tenancies so that either person would have the right to remain in the property if the other died. The Codes recommend that same-sex partners should be treated in the same way as heterosexual partners.[114] If prospective tenants ask to be granted a joint tenancy, and are refused, the local housing authority should give clear, written reasons for the refusal.[115] Couples with children may prefer to take a secure tenancy in the sole name of the adult likely to live longest (because there can be no succession to a *joint* secure tenancy – so the tenancy could only pass to a child on the death of a *sole* tenant parent).[116]

Fully secure or less secure?

5.71 An offer of accommodation made under the allocation scheme may be the offer of a secure, introductory or assured tenancy.[117] An assured shorthold tenancy is a form or type of assured tenancy and so assured shorthold tenancies may be offered by RSLs.[118] In practice, if an assured shorthold tenancy is offered as an allocation, it is intended to fulfil the same function as an introductory tenancy, ie that it should cease to be an assured shorthold tenancy, and become a fully assured tenancy, after a specified period. Guidance on housing management issued by the Tenant Services Authority (TSA) to all social landlords in England is likely to require from 1 April 2010 that they 'offer and issue the most secure form of tenure compatible with the purpose of the housing and the sustainability of the community'.[119]

---

[111] English Code, paras 3.11–3.12; Welsh Code, paras 4.49–4.50.
[112] English CBL Code, para 3.16.
[113] English Code, paras 3.11–3.12; Welsh Code, paras 4.49–4.50.
[114] See *Rodriguez v Minister of Housing of the Government of Gibraltar* [2009] UKPC 52.
[115] English Code, paras 3.7–3.8; Welsh Code, paras 4.5–4.6.
[116] Housing Act 1985, ss 87–89.
[117] HA 1996, s 159(2).
[118] HA 1996, s 230; Housing Act 1988, s 1 and ss 19A–20.
[119] See the draft 'Tenancy Standard', para 3: Tenure, in *A new regulatory framework for social housing in England: A statutory consultation* (TSA, November 2009).

Furnished or unfurnished?

5.72 The allocation scheme will govern selection or nomination for both furnished and unfurnished properties. Most local housing authority stock is let unfurnished, but a significant proportion of properties designed for the elderly or others with support needs will be partly or wholly furnished. The same general pattern is true of the RSL stock made available for nominations from local housing authorities.

5.73 An applicant cannot insist on the provision of (or removal of) furnishings. However, local housing authorities have very broad powers to furnish and fit out their properties and/or sell or hire furniture to tenants.[120] The economies of scale that can be achieved by a local housing authority in bulk buying furniture and selling it on to incoming tenants should not be underestimated. The golden rule must be that it is always open to an applicant to ask. A local housing authority which responded to a request with a pronouncement that it never provided furniture would be guilty of unlawfully fettering its discretion, and the relevant decision would be quashed in proceedings for judicial review. The question of whether furniture will be provided in lettings by RSLs will be subject to the terms of any relevant TSA guidance and/or the terms of the RSL's own governing instrument (for example, the Articles of Association).

Quality of accommodation offered

5.74 There is no minimum standard of accommodation that a property must achieve before a local housing authority or RSL offers a particular unit to an applicant under a local allocation scheme. Indeed, it may be precisely the least desirable properties that are most frequently on offer.

5.75 In contrast to the law relating to homelessness, there is no requirement that the offered property be 'suitable' or 'available for occupation'.[121] Advisers must be careful to ensure that this distinction between offers under HA 1996, Parts 6 and 7 is made clear to applicants.[122]

5.76 The principle in operation is 'caveat lessee' or 'let the prospective tenant beware'. It is for the prospective tenant to decide whether he or she wants to accept or reject what is offered, having carefully considered it. Accordingly, a tenant who accepts the property can later have no complaint in law if she or he subsequently finds that it is in a more noisy location or situation than expected,[123] or if there is a pungent smell which the tenant erroneously thought could be removed by cleaning.[124]

---

[120] Housing Act 1985, s 10.
[121] See Chapter 18 of this book for 'suitable' and Chapter 14 for the concept of 'available for occupation'.
[122] *Brent London Borough Council v Sharp* [2003] EWCA Civ 779, [2004] HLR 65, CA.
[123] *Southwark London Borough Council v Tanner and Mills* [2002] 32 HLR 148, HL.
[124] *Smith v Wrekin Housing Trust* [2004] EWCA Civ 1792, CA. In one case, the Local Government

5.77 There is no general legal rule that the properties of a public authority landlord or RSL must meet minimum standards at the date of letting.[125] The previous statutorily implied term that a property must be 'fit for human habitation' at the date of letting no longer has any practical application as a result of failure to up-rate the rent thresholds that govern its operation.[126] What is left is only the old common law rule that a property let furnished (which is itself unusual in social housing) must be fit for occupation at the date of letting.[127]

5.78 Of course, a new tenant who finds that the property is unsatisfactory for some reason may give it up, by notice to quit or surrender, if he or she has somewhere else to go, or could pursue a complaint about the allocation and/or apply for a transfer to more satisfactory accommodation under the allocation scheme.

Offers to transfer applicants[128]

5.79 Where the offer is made to an applicant who is already a tenant of the local housing authority or an RSL, two particular issues arise:

(1) getting the type of tenancy right; and

(2) determining the old tenancy.

5.80 If the transferring tenant is currently a secure or assured tenant (but not an assured shorthold tenant), whether under a sole or a joint tenancy, the new tenancy to be offered of any local housing authority property can only be a secure tenancy and not an introductory tenancy, even if the local housing authority normally only offers introductory tenancies to new tenants.[129] If the allocation process has resulted in a tenant being nominated to an RSL (not currently that tenant's landlord) and in an offer of a tenancy from the RSL, the tenancy may be offered as an assured tenancy or assured shorthold tenancy irrespective of the applicant's current form of tenancy. In practice, most RSLs will offer a full assured tenancy to an incoming tenant who has been the secure or assured tenant of another social landlord.

5.81 It will be important for the local housing authority or RSL to ensure that the successful applicant's current tenancy is brought to an end at, or

---

Ombudsman did find the local housing authority guilty of maladministration where it had allocated a property , which the Ombudsman described as 'so filthy it could not be lived in' to an applicant: *Complaint against Nottingham City Council* (2007) (05/C/2965), (2007) June *Legal Action*, p 37.

[125] *Siney v Dublin Corporation* [1980] IR 400.

[126] Landlord and Tenant Act 1985, s 8(1) and (4), only applicable to properties let on low rents (the threshold is now unrealistically low).

[127] See Luba, Prevatt and Forster *Repairs: Tenants Rights* (LAG, 4th edn, 2010), p 13.

[128] For the renewed emphasis on securing tenancy transfers through allocation schemes see English 2009 Code, paras 79–80.

[129] HA 1996, s 124(2).

immediately following, the commencement of the new tenancy. Unless (unusually) the tenancy is of the same property, the grant of the new tenancy does *not* automatically determine the old one. The old tenancy will need to be determined by a tenant's notice to quit or by a surrender, the latter being most safely achieved by deed. If the landlord and tenant have overlooked the need to determine the old tenancy before the new one commences, it will usually be possible for the old one to be immediately surrendered or subject to a notice to quit, with, perhaps, both parties agreeing to short notice.[130]

5.82 A common issue will be whether any arrears of rent extant on the old tenancy can be transferred to the new one. Although the parties can make an agreement as to how those arrears will be cleared, that agreement cannot be enforced in possession proceedings for the new tenancy in respect of those arrears, unless either:

(1) the parties have agreed that any payments made after the date of transfer will be first applied to meet the old debt, in which case arrears will accrue in the new tenancy unless the tenant makes double payment; or

(2) the parties have agreed that compliance with the arrears agreement will be a term of the new tenancy.[131]

Refusal of offers

5.83 No applicant can be compelled to accept an offer of accommodation made under an HA 1996, Part 6 allocation scheme. Where the offer has been made to a homeless applicant, however, the effect of a refusal may, in narrowly prescribed circumstances, operate to bring a homelessness duty to an end.[132]

5.84 In other cases, the effect (if any) of a refusal will be dealt with in the allocation scheme itself. An applicant who has rejected a property cannot properly be subject to some form of penalty or suspension under an allocation scheme unless a rule to that effect appears in the published scheme and has been properly applied.[133] Indeed, even if such a provision did appear in a published scheme, if the scheme itself was based on a needs-led priority system it would be difficult to impose any sanction unless the refusal itself evidenced a change in assessed need.

5.85 If the penalty provision for a refusal is legitimately included, the local housing authority must still ensure that its operation is considered on a

---

[130] See *Hackney London Borough Council v Snowden* (2001) 33 HLR 49, CA and *Ealing Family Housing Association v McKenzie* [2003] EWCA Civ 1602, [2004] HLR 21, CA.

[131] *Notting Hill Housing Trust v Jones* [1999] L&TR 397, CA.

[132] See the discussion in Chapter 17. In the English CBL Code, para 4.51 the Secretary of State encourages local housing authorities to offer homeless households a choice of Part 6 accommodation, wherever possible.

[133] *R v Wandsworth London Borough Council ex p Lawrie and Heshmati* (1997) 30 HLR 153, QBD.

case-by-case basis, having regard to the circumstances of each refusal.[134] Indeed, many allocation schemes make provision for 'appeals' against, or 'review' of offers, made under the scheme and a significant proportion of such challenges made are successful.[135]

---

[134] *R v Gateshead Metropolitan Borough Council ex p Lauder* (1996) 29 HLR 360, QBD and *R v Westminster City Council ex p Hussain* (1999) 31 HLR 645, QBD.

[135] In about half the areas where appeals had been heard in 2006/07 most such appeals had been upheld. The average 'appeal success rate' ('success' from an applicant perspective) was 40%: *Exploring local authority policy and practice on housing allocations* (CLG, July 2009), para 2.14.

Chapter 6

LETTINGS BY REGISTERED SOCIAL LANDLORDS

INTRODUCTION

6.1 More new lettings of social housing homes in England are now made by Registered Social Landlords[1] (RSLs) than by local housing authorities.[2] That position having become the norm since we prepared the first edition of this book, and, with further local housing authorities in the process of transferring ownership of their housing stock to RSLs, it has now become necessary to address the topic of RSL lettings in this new chapter.[3]

6.2 We embark upon that course with some trepidation at this time, given the changes currently under way in the arrangements by which housing associations and other social housing providers are registered and regulated, and given the very recent and continuing developments in case law on the legal status of RSLs. At the time of writing, the new arrangements for registration, supervision and regulation of RSLs in England,[4] set out in the Housing and Regeneration Act 2008, had been passed by Parliament but not yet fully commenced. The two new bodies set up by that Act to replace the former Housing Corporation in England – the Homes & Communities Agency (HCA) and the Tenant Services Authority (TSA) – had been established and were operating but were not yet invested with the full range of their new statutory powers. The TSA had embarked upon, but not concluded, a round of consultation covering, among many other matters, new standards in allocating social housing. The final round of statutory consultation was planned to conclude in February 2010. The projected date for commencement of all the new arrangements was scheduled for 1 April 2010. The Welsh Assembly Government is also proposing to introduce new regulatory arrangements for Wales from April 2010.[5]

6.3 In that state of flux, and although the commencement of the new statutory arrangements for control of RSL lettings in both England and Wales is therefore not far off, the text that follows outlines the *present* law, guidance

---

[1]   These are landlords of social housing other than local housing authorities (ie primarily, housing associations) registered with the Housing Corporation in England – now, the Tenant Services Authority – or with the relevant statutory authorities in Wales, pursuant to the registration scheme in Housing Act 1996 ('HA 1996'), Part 1.

[2]   In England in 2008/2009 there were 139,504 lettings by RSLs and only 112,980 by local housing authorities: *Table 750 General needs social lettings made by RSL and LA landlords, 2008/09, England: household type* (Communities and Local Government) at http://www.communities.gov.uk/housing/housingresearch/housingstatistics/housingstatisticsby/rentslettings/livetables/). In Wales, a new system of data collection on lettings of social housing is being established following the recent report *Who gets social housing in Wales?* – the final report of a project to investigate the desirability of collecting and analysing data on social housing lettings and sales in Wales (Community Housing Cymru, March 2009), http://www.chcymru.org.uk.

[3]   We are grateful, in particular, to Robert Latham (barrister) for his encouragement in this direction and for the pointers contained in his article, 'Allocating social housing: the registered social landlord context' (2008) October *Legal Action*, p 42.

[4]   Arrangements for regulation of the RSLs in Wales will remain governed by the arrangements for registration etc set out in the Housing Act 1996, Part 1.

[5]   See **6.89**.

and other related material. It refers extensively to statutory guidance issued by the Housing Corporation, albeit that that organisation closed down on 1 November 2008. This is because until April 2010 that guidance remains applicable (statutory responsibility for it having passed, in England, to the TSA). Likewise, for RSLs operating in Wales, the statutory guidance contained in the Welsh Assembly Government's *Regulatory Code for Housing Associations Registered in Wales*[6] will remain applicable until new regulatory arrangements are established later in 2010. A concluding section of this chapter looks to the future.[7]

OVERVIEW

6.4 The stock of social housing owned by RSLs (primarily housing associations) for rent in England now exceeds 2 million units. In Wales, there are a further 95,000 homes owned by RSLs.[8] That stock is gradually being increased with the development of new housing schemes and the acquisition of more properties through funding channelled to RSLs by the HCA and by the Welsh Assembly Government respectively. It will increase still further as more local housing authorities transfer their stock of council homes to existing or newly created RSLs. The RSL sector does not face the same prospect of diminution in the rented stock as local housing authorities face (particularly because of the restricted access to the 'right-to-buy' for sitting RSL tenants). The availability of new or newly converted stock for letting and the natural incidences of tenant mobility (and mortality) in the existing stock now combine to provide a greater number of opportunities for letting in the RSL sector than in the local housing authority sector. Against that background, the Secretary of State has advised that:

> 'Virtually all provision of new social housing is delivered through RSLs and, under the transfer programme, ownership of a significant proportion of housing authority stock is being transferred from housing authorities to RSLs, subject to tenants' agreement. This means that, increasingly, RSLs will become the main providers of social housing. Consequently, it is essential that housing authorities work closely with RSLs, as well as all other housing providers, in order to meet the housing needs in their district and ensure that the aims and objectives of their homelessness strategy are achieved.'[9]

6.5 However, there is (at least as yet) no equivalent in the RSL sector to the relatively strict and over-arching statutory control on allocations imposed on local housing authorities by HA 1996, Part 6. Each RSL will, within the terms of its own governing legal instrument, be free to let its available homes to such

---

[6] Published by the Welsh Assembly Government in March 2006, at http://wales.gov.uk/topics/housingandcommunity/housing/publications/regulatorycodehas?lang=en.

[7] See **6.83–6.90**.

[8] *The Housing Associations of Wales: Measuring the Impact* (Welsh Economy Research Unit, October 2008), at http://www.chcymru.org.uk/policy/weru.html.

[9] *English Homelessness Code of Guidance* (CLG, July 2006) (reproduced in Appendix 2 of this book), Annex 5, para 2.

applicants as it pleases (subject to the applicable constraints of the general law – eg as to the prohibition of certain forms of discrimination). There is no prohibition preventing an RSL from letting, for example, to a person who would not meet the statutory eligibility requirements[10] for local housing authority accommodation in the same district.

6.6   An RSL may – if it chooses – operate a transfer scheme enabling its existing tenants to seek alternative homes within its stock. Most RSLs take that course. For *non-transfer* applicants, it may operate an open list or direct applications system so that anyone who applies may be considered for a tenancy in its stock, and then order or organise that list in such manner as it chooses. It may, additionally or alternatively, make available some part or the majority of its stock to the local housing authority or other RSLs to make 'nominations' of prospective tenants – whom it may then accept or reject as it pleases. It may, if it chooses, advertise its available properties through a choice based letting scheme. That may be the RSL's own scheme, a scheme operated jointly with a local housing authority, or even a common scheme shared with other RSLs and local housing authorities.

6.7   Some of the largest RSLs are those created specifically to take the housing stock of particular local housing authorities in large scale voluntary transfers. Most local housing authorities engaging in such transfers took the opportunity, before transfer of their stock, to entrench the RSL's future arrangements for allocation of the transferred stock (and, in some cases, after-acquired stock) through contractual commitments. Those contractual obligations operate as a fetter on the freedom in letting that most other RSLs enjoy.

6.8   An RSL's responsibility in housing allocation may not necessarily be confined to the letting of *its own* stock. Several RSLs have commercially contracted to operate housing allocation services for local housing authorities. Those services are contracted out to them pursuant to the arrangements described in Chapter 21 of this book. Such an RSL may thus find itself directly allocating some of its own stock, managing allocation of council stock and also operating the local housing authority's system for nomination of prospective tenants to itself.[11] However, even in the case where functions are contracted out to a stock transfer RSL, and stock is allocated under a choice based letting scheme, local housing authorities are 'strongly advised' to remain active participants in allocation arrangements.[12]

---

[10]   Described in Chapter 3 of this book.
[11]   See **6.72–6.73**.
[12]   *Allocation of Accommodation: Choice Based Lettings Code of Guidance for Local Housing Authorities* ['English CBL Code'] (reproduced in Appendix 1 of this book), para 6.22.

DIRECT APPLICATIONS

Duty to maintain a lettings policy

6.9 Many, if not all, RSLs retain at least some of their available stock for letting by them to new applicants – those who have directly applied to that RSL for housing – or to their own current tenants who wish to move within that RSL's stock. Lettings to the latter category are dealt with separately later in this chapter.[13]

6.10 The RSL's governing body will have adopted a lettings policy relating to direct applications (and other lettings) and there will usually be a procedure guide or manual setting out the way in which housing staff are to implement the policy. In 2007/2008, 22.3% of RSL lets in England were made to direct applicants.[14]

6.11 As Chapters 1–5 of this book have explained, HA 1996, Part 6 requires local housing authorities, but not RSLs, to incorporate a statement of their policies for selection priorities and lettings procedures into a single local allocation scheme, copies of which must be available on request. A similar, but not precisely the same, statutory obligation is cast on RSLs by Housing Act 1985, s 106. That requires any 'landlord authority' (a term defined to embrace RSLs)[15] to maintain two sets of rules:

(1) the rules for determining *priority* as between applicants in the allocation of its housing accommodation;[16] and

(2) the rules which it has laid down governing the *procedure* to be followed in allocating its housing accommodation.[17]

An RSL is under a statutory duty to publish a summary of the first set of rules but not of the second.[18] Although any applicant can *ask* for a full copy of both sets of rules, there is no statutory duty to make them available at the RSL's offices. Copies need only be sent to the relevant statutory regulator and to any local housing authority in the area of which the RSL still has stock let on secure tenancies.[19] An applicant could inspect the rules, or take copies of them, at the office of any such local housing authority.[20]

---

[13] See **6.49–6.53**.
[14] Taken from 'Allocations by RSLs 2007/2008', reproduced at (2008) October *Legal Action*, p 43.
[15] Housing Act 1985, s 114.
[16] HA 1985, s 106(2)(a).
[17] HA 1985, s 106(2)(a).
[18] HA 1985, s 106(1)(a).
[19] HA 1985, s 106(3).
[20] HA 1985, s 106(4).

Guidance on contents of lettings policies

6.12 In England, the Housing Corporation ('the Corporation') exercised its statutory powers to give guidance to RSLs in relation to lettings policies, but the guidance (in contrast to the guidance given to local housing authorities by the Secretary of State under HA 1996, s 162) is modest and often expressed in very general terms. In its Regulatory Code and Guidance ('RCG')[21] the Corporation simply required that lettings policies be framed so as to be 'flexible, non-discriminatory and responsive to demand, while contributing to the need to be inclusive and the need to ensure sustainable communities'.[22] It has been suggested that this rubric represents an important shift of emphasis by the Corporation, enabling RSLs to use factors other than *housing need* when allocating accommodation, and allowing the use of local lettings and choice based lettings schemes.[23] In Wales, the statutory guidance issued to Welsh RSLs contains a 'key expectation' that each RSL should have a fair selection policy and should seek to achieve a balance in housing allocation between:

- the needs and preferences of applicants and transferees;

- the need to maximise social inclusion;

- the need to build stable communities; and

- the need to make best use of a publicly funded resource.[24]

6.13 The generality of the wording in all this guidance suggests, as already indicated, that, subject to the constraints of the general law (e g the prohibition of certain forms of discrimination), RSLs have a relatively free hand in the arrangements they make for direct applications and in the organisation of what will usually be a waiting list where demand exceeds supply.[25] However, it should not be assumed that demand will always exceed supply in the RSL sector. Many RSLs offer specialist or niche accommodation designed to meet particular needs, and others hold stock targeted at meeting the housing needs of particular groups. There may not always be sufficient applicants to meet the qualifying conditions for such accommodation.

---

[21]   *The Regulatory Code and Guidance* ('RCG') (Housing Corporation, August 2005), at http://www.housingcorp.gov.uk/server/show/nav.493, containing housing management guidance given under HA 1996, s 36.

[22]   RCG, para 3.6(a).

[23]   Adler and Handy *Housing Association Law and Practice* (4th edn, 2003), para 10-008.

[24]   Welsh Assembly Government's *Regulatory Code for Housing Associations Registered in Wales*, March 2006, Key expectation 1.3, http://wales.gov.uk/topics/housingandcommunity/housing/publications/regulatorycodehas?lang=en.

[25]   The Welsh Assembly Government has issued *Housing Association Circular 023/09* (February 2009) indicating that housing associations should take account of the *Code of Guidance for Local Authorities on Allocation of Accommodation and Homelessness* ['The Welsh Code'] (April 2003) when addressing key expectations in 1.3 of the *Regulatory Code*. The full text of the Welsh Code is contained in the CD-ROM supplied with this book.

6.14   In relation to the specific terms of particular RSLs' lettings policies, the Corporation's guidance requires only that they:

*   are responsive to local housing authority housing duties;

*   take account of the need to give reasonable priority to transfer applicants, including applicants from other associations;

*   are responsive to national, regional and local mobility and exchange schemes; and

*   are demonstrably fair and effectively controlled.[26]

6.15   Where the lettings policy includes circumstances in which some applicants will not be *eligible* for an allocation, the Corporation guidance expects that the process to be followed by the RSL staff in assessing eligibility for housing will form part of the written lettings policy itself and that:

(1)   to achieve consistency, procedures should be clearly written; and

(2)   to achieve demonstrable fairness, decisions should be clearly documented and monitored.[27]

6.16   The RCG frames the suggested test for exclusion from eligibility for past misconduct in terms not dissimilar to those adopted in HA 1996, Part 6, s 160A(7).[28] Applicants are to be excluded from consideration for housing only when their unacceptable behaviour is serious enough to make them unsuitable to be a tenant of the RSL and only in circumstances where the RSL itself will not be unlawfully discriminating by rejecting the application.[29] There is even more resonance with the statutory test contained in HA 1996, Part 6 in this passage from another Housing Corporation publication:

> 'Your application may not be considered in certain circumstances, for example if your previous behaviour is considered to be unacceptable and serious enough to make you unsuitable as a resident. You should be told about these rules when you apply.'[30]

6.17   Unsurprisingly, guidance expressed in such comparatively general terms has had to be supplemented by a series of Circulars particularly designed to

---

[26]   RCG, para 3.6(f).
[27]   Housing Corporation Circular 02/07 at http://www.housingcorp.gov.uk/server/show/ConWebDoc.11074.
[28]   See Chapter 3 of this book.
[29]   RCG, para 3.6(e).
[30]   *A charter for housing association applicants and residents* (Housing Corporation, April 2007), p 8, at http://www.housingcorp.gov.uk/server/show/conWebDoc.1564).

address instances of RSLs adopting restrictive policies. In April 2007, Circular 02/07,[31] the latest of that series, specifically dealt with three issues:

- the relevance of previous misconduct by applicants;

- local connection preferences; and

- local lettings policies.

6.18 The guidance on the first of those subjects (previous misconduct) is in two parts, dealing respectively with financial matters and anti-social behaviour. But it is underpinned by the general proposition that there should be no blanket rules applying in absolute terms to all applicants:

'Applicants should not be excluded automatically from housing if their circumstances "fit" a defined category. Every case must be judged on its merits and efforts made to resolve any possible ineligibility'.

6.19 In relation to *financial* matters, the guidance provides that:

- An applicant's rent arrears should not be an automatic barrier to access to an RSL letting. Where, in a particular case, an applicant is considered to be ineligible for housing because he or she owes rent for a previous tenancy, RSLs should actively encourage applicants to enter into agreements to pay their arrears. If such agreements are maintained for a reasonable period, the application should be re-activated.

- Debts arising from arrears of non-housing payments, such as council tax or hire purchase, should not have a bearing on eligibility for RSL lettings.

- If RSLs conduct checks on the credit status of applicants, that policy should be approved by the governing board, the applicant should be informed and should be shown a copy of the check without charge.

- Details of a household's financial position might help an RSL to identify vulnerability and to offer appropriate support, but should not have a bearing on eligibility.

- Applicants for housing should not be asked to provide a guarantor for rent, as a condition of a tenancy offer (save for when the tenancy is to be offered to a minor).

6.20 Where the previous misconduct has taken the form of *anti-social behaviour* (ASB), the guidance directs RSLs to a statutory definition of such

---

[31] *Tenancy management: Eligibility and evictions* (Housing Corporation, April 2007), at http://www.housingcorp.gov.uk/server/show/ConWebDoc.11074.

behaviour[32] and then stresses that any potential ineligibility for housing on the ground of the applicant's anti-social behaviour should be based on evidence of that behaviour. Such evidence might include the previous eviction of an applicant or a member of his or her household for ASB, or a previous injunction or Anti-Social Behaviour Order (ASBO) taken out against the applicant or a member of the household.

6.21 In an attempt to ensure that a 'mark of Cain'[33] scenario does not develop, the guidance suggests:

(1)   that previous tenancy enforcement action for ASB should not be taken into account if it occurred 2 or more years prior to the date of the making of an application for housing to the RSL and the tenant's household has conducted a tenancy satisfactorily in the intervening period;

(2)   that a RSL should not ask an applicant about 'spent' convictions; and

(3)   that a previous conviction is not an automatic barrier to access, especially for low-risk offenders.

6.22 The eligibility of an ex-offender should only be in question if there is reason to suppose that he or she is likely to pose a risk to his or her household, neighbours and/or the wider community. RSLs are reminded that they should be able to justify the exclusion of ex-offenders, by reference to accountable policies and procedures.[34]

6.23 However, the guidance recognises that some applicants are going to need help and support in maintaining a tenancy which the RSL may be unable to provide or arrange. In such circumstances, it suggests that an applicant may be excluded from the RSL's letting scheme if the applicant will be unable to meet the conditions of tenancy without additional support, and additionally that:

(1)   the RSL, despite every effort, is unable to ensure that appropriate support is available; or

(2)   the level of support required would seriously undermine the RSL's ability to support other residents in a scheme.

6.24 Precisely because RSLs operate free from the constraints imposed on local housing authorities by HA 1996, Part 6, they have been able to develop

---

[32]   'Conduct which is capable of causing nuisance or annoyance to any person and which directly or indirectly relates to or affects the housing management functions of a relevant landlord': Anti-social Behaviour Act 2003, s 13.

[33]   A term coined in this context in *Din v Wandsworth London Borough Council* (1981, unreported), CA, per Ackner LJ, quoted in *Lambert v Ealing London Borough Council* [1982] 1 WLR 550, CA, per Lord Denning, and referring to findings that applicants for homelessness assistance had become homeless intentionally with enduring adverse consequences.

[34]   Housing Corporation Circular 02/07.

and retain their own particular practices and procedures. It is not uncommon for RSL lettings policies to provide for the admission of applicants to the RSL's allocation scheme but then to permit their suspension from it on misconduct grounds (or, indeed, any grounds). The Housing Corporation guidance on suspension is that the meaning and purpose of any suspension period, during which an application for housing is held inactive, should be clearly defined and should last no longer than 2 years. As the guidance advises, the notion of 'suspension' implies that the applicant will be invited to apply to have his or her application re-activated at a specified time or for specified reasons.

6.25 The relevance of *local connection* as a criterion in allocation of RSL property is also separately addressed in the guidance. Circular 02/07 suggests that:

- housing need should normally override any special consideration of local connection; and

- no applicant should be excluded by an RSL because he or she does not have a local connection, except in the following specific circumstances:
    - on rural exception sites;[35]
    - where s 106 development agreements apply;[36]
    - if an offer of accommodation would conflict with the association's governing instrument; or
    - if a local lettings policy is in place.

6.26 The subject of such 'local lettings' policies is then also addressed by the statutory guidance in Circular 02/07. It provides that if an RSL has adopted such a policy as part of its overall letting arrangements, that policy should demonstrably and reasonably balance the competing demands of local housing authority nominations, and any other indicator of pressing housing need, against policies promoting balanced communities. The practical issues arising from RSLs operating local lettings policies are explored in a recent Homelessness Action Team discussion paper.[37]

6.27 Beyond this broad guidance about the outline of RSL lettings policies and procedures, it is for each RSL to set its own categories for prioritising applicants and its own arrangements for allocating particular properties. However, in keeping with the general policy emphasis on choice based letting,

---

[35] Areas designated by the Secretary of State or Welsh Assembly Government in relation to dwellings in which the right to acquire does not arise (HA 1996, s 17(1)(b)). See *Planning Policy Statement 3* (PPS3) Housing (CLG, November 2006), at http://www.communities.gov.uk/publications/planningandbuilding/pps3housing.

[36] Town and Country Planning Act 1990, s 106.

[37] Homelessness Action Team discussion paper, *Local lettings policies* (TSA, March 2009), at http://www.tenantservicesauthority.org/server/show/nav.00f004005002.

the Secretary of State has encouraged local housing authorities to negotiate with RSLs to make all their vacancies 'available through joint choice-based letting schemes'.[38]

Information about lettings policies and procedure

6.28 The starting point for any applicant considering a direct application to an RSL will be to obtain details of a particular RSL's letting scheme.[39] The advice given to applicants by the Housing Corporation is that:

'you can ask to see the details of the type of services your housing association will provide, who can apply and how they will consider your application. All housing associations must have these documents.'[40]

6.29 Although no applicant for an RSL direct letting has a statutory right to make such an application, or even to be informed of the outcome, the statutory guidance suggests at least some basic procedural requirements should be observed. In particular:

- a copy of the Housing Corporation's Charter for Applicants[41] should be provided to all applicants;[42]

- where appropriate, assistance in the allocation process should be provided;[43]

- rejected applicants should be referred to housing advice agencies;

- rejected applicants should have information about and access to an appeals process; and

- the appeal should be heard by adjudicators who were not involved in the original decision to reject the housing application.[44]

---

[38] English CBL Code, para 6.5.
[39] See **6.9–6.11**.
[40] *A charter for housing association applicants and residents* (Housing Corporation, April 2007), p 8, at http://www.housingcorp.gov.uk/server/show/conWebDoc.1564.
[41] *A charter for housing association applicants and residents* (Housing Corporation, April 2007), http://www.housingcorp.gov.uk/server/show/conWebDoc.1564.
[42] RCG, para 3.5b.
[43] *A charter for housing association applicants and residents* (Housing Corporation, April 2007), http://www.housingcorp.gov.uk/server/show/conWebDoc.1564 states 'You should be offered help to fill in forms if you need it. Housing associations should make sure that the forms and information can be understood by everyone. If you have difficulty with the forms and information and need assistance or need them in another language, you can ask the association for a translation or help in other ways.' This simply augments the general guidance given at RCG, para 3.5f that 'Vulnerable and marginalised residents are provided with appropriate responsive housing services. Support and care arrangements (including liaison with other agencies) are in place, where appropriate.'
[44] Circular 02/07.

6.30 A dissatisfied applicant has access to a range of opportunities to press matters beyond the suggested 'appeal', e g through complaints procedures, the Housing Ombudsman and the courts.[45]

NOMINATIONS BY LOCAL HOUSING AUTHORITIES

The legal basis

6.31 Most RSLs make available some proportion of their available lettings to applicants who are nominees of local housing authorities. Indeed, in England in 2007/2008, over 54% of RSL lettings were to local housing authority nominees.[46]

6.32 Arrangements made between the RSL and any particular local housing authority may provide for that local housing authority to nominate applicants for general consideration by an RSL, or for consideration for a particular property, or may involve the RSL providing details of its premises available for letting to be advertised as available to nominees under a local housing authority's choice based letting scheme. These locally agreed arrangements may be highly informal or, at the other extreme, may be set out in legally binding contractual agreements. The latter are more common in the cases of RSLs which have taken a large scale transfer of local housing authority stock.

6.33 From the perspective of the local housing authority, nominating an applicant to be an assured tenant of housing accommodation held by an RSL constitutes an 'allocation' of accommodation and is therefore governed by the local allocation scheme adopted by that particular local housing authority.[47] To count as an 'allocation', and therefore be governed by the allocation scheme, the nomination need not be for the tenancy of a specific property. The statutory concept of nomination covers nominations under any arrangements (whether legally enforceable or not) that require housing accommodation generally, or a specific proportion of stock, to be made available to the local housing authority nominees.[48] Of course, as in the case of the local housing authority's own stock, the letting will not constitute an 'allocation' by the local housing authority if the nominee is a local housing authority's secure or introductory tenant transferring to an RSL home not at his or her initiative but at the initiative of the local housing authority (e g as part of a clearance scheme or some other form of management-driven transfer).[49]

6.34 Save in those cases where the RSL has entered into a contractual commitment to take local housing authority nominations, there is no legal

---

45   See **6.74–6.82**.
46   Taken from 'Allocations by RSLs 2007/2008', reproduced at (2008) October *Legal Action*, p 43.
47   HA 1996, s 159(2)(c).
48   HA 1996, s 159(4).
49   HA 1996, s 159(5). See **1.24**.

obligation on an RSL to agree to take local housing authority nominations either generally or for specific properties.

Guidance to RSLs on co-operation

6.35 In the absence of any legal obligation, the matter of RSL participation in nomination arrangements is simply another issue covered by both the Housing Corporation's and the Welsh Assembly Government's statutory guidance to RSLs. The Housing Corporation's RCG very generally states that:

- when requested to do so by a local housing authority, and to such an extent as is reasonable in the circumstances, RSLs should provide a proportion of their stock to local authority housing nominations; and

- criteria should be adopted, following consultation with local housing authorities, for accepting or rejecting nominees.[50]

6.36 Somewhat fuller guidance is given in Housing Corporation Circular 02/03 *Local authority nominations*,[51] which set out the Corporation's requirements of RSLs in respect of nominations from local housing authorities. The 'minimum expectations' of the Corporation were that:

- each RSL reaches agreement with its local housing authority, where so requested and in so far as is reasonable, on the proportion of 'true voids' to be offered to nominees; the proportion should be reasonable in relation to the local housing authority's assessment of local housing need;

- in such circumstances the RSL must sign an effective nominations agreement with the local housing authority, setting out in detail how the nominations process will operate and in what circumstances nominations will be refused; and

- in areas where evidence of local housing need is reflected in local planning criteria for affordable housing provision, agreements should provide for 50% or more of 'true voids' be available for nominations (agreed percentages may be considerably higher in areas of housing stress).[52]

6.37 What appears at first impression to be a commitment to making available at least half of all available RSL lettings for local housing authority nominations, at least in areas of housing need, is seriously qualified by the very narrow definition of the term 'true voids'. For the purposes of the statutory guidance, these 'true voids' are empty RSL homes that are available to let but *exclude* a 'reasonable proportion of housing set aside to satisfy internal

---

50   RCG, para 3.6c and 3.6d.
51   Circular 02/03 (Housing Corporation, February 2003), at http://www.housingcorp.gov.uk/server/show/conWebDoc.2035.
52   Circular 02/03, para 4.1.

transfers, decants, mobility and move-on agreements'.[53] This terminology serves essentially to leave the proportion of the stock made available for nominations as a matter for the particular RSL to determine. In practice, across RSL stock in England as a whole, in excess of 50% of vacancies go to local housing authority nominees, with even higher proportions for lettings of larger RSL general needs units.[54]

6.38 In some circumstances RSLs, responding to co-operation duties[55] or acting pursuant to local partnership arrangements, may make very high proportions of their stock available for nominations and – in some cases – all of it. The statutory guidance reflects that option by giving RSLs the maximum possible flexibility. It provides that 'for the avoidance of doubt' RSLs may enter into arrangements with local housing authorities whereby *all* allocations are covered by a common allocations policy or *up to 100%* of true voids are offered to nominations for defined properties.[56] For their part, local housing authorities are advised to 'negotiate for the maximum number of lettings that will be required to enable them to discharge their housing functions and which would be reasonable for the RSL to deliver.'[57] Indeed, the Welsh Code contains robust and detailed guidance for local housing authorities in Wales (described as 'temporary' but still in force) setting out precisely how it is expected that RSLs will co-operate with local housing authorities, particularly in relation to nominations.[58]

Guidance to local housing authorities on co-operation with RSLs

6.39 Somewhat surprisingly, the statutory guidance issued to local housing authorities in England concerning housing allocation initially contained very little about nominations to RSLs, in contrast to (1) the content of the *English Homelessness Code of Guidance* which covered the subject fairly fully,[59] and (2) the ample non-statutory guidance.[60] That omission was addressed in August 2008 with the issue of *Allocation of Accommodation: Choice Based Lettings Code of Guidance for Local Housing Authorities*[61] (the 'English CBL Code'),[62] which contained a chapter[63] on the delivery of choice in partnership with RSLs

---

⁵³ Circular 02/03, para 3.
⁵⁴ For a full breakdown see *The use of nominations to RSLs by local authorities in Tackling Homelessness: Efficiencies in lettings functions* (Housing Corporation, November 2007), at http://www.housingcorp.gov.uk/server/show/ConWebDoc.12840.
⁵⁵ See **6.62–6.67**.
⁵⁶ Circular 02/03, para 4.3.
⁵⁷ *English Homelessness Code of Guidance*, Annex 5, para 13. See Appendix 2 of this book.
⁵⁸ Welsh Code, Annex 22.
⁵⁹ *English Homelessness Code of Guidance*, Annex 5, passim. See Appendix 2 of this book.
⁶⁰ See, for example, *Effective Co-operation in Tackling Homelessness: Nomination Agreements and Exclusion* produced jointly by Communities and Local Government (formerly the ODPM), the Housing Corporation, the National Housing Federation and the Local Government Association in November 2004, at http://www.communities.gov.uk/archived/publications/housing/effectivecooperation.
⁶¹ Department for Communities and Local Government ('CLG'), August 2008.
⁶² Reproduced in Appendix 1 of this book.
⁶³ English CBL Code, Chapter 6.

and specifically covered nomination agreements. Although the guidance it contains is directed at those local housing authorities which have adopted schemes of choice based lettings, the policy initiative designed to ensure that all local housing authorities have adopted such schemes by 2010 gives the guidance more general application. Indeed, those local housing authorities which have not yet embraced choice based letting are now subject to statutory guidance issued in very similar terms in December 2009: *Fair and flexible: statutory guidance on social housing allocations for local authorities in England*[64] ('the English 2009 Code').[65]

6.40 The English CBL Code and the English 2009 Code place considerable emphasis on negotiation between RSLs and local housing authorities followed by the adoption of nomination agreements rather than on loose informal nomination arrangements (although the guidance interchangeably uses the terms 'agreement' and 'protocol').[66] The English CBL Code envisages that these agreements (which are assumed to have been made in writing) will detail:

- the proportion of RSL lettings that will be made available;

- any criteria which the RSL has adopted, following consultation with the local housing authority, for accepting or rejecting nominees; and

- how any disputes about suitability and eligibility will be resolved.[67]

6.41 Local housing authorities are encouraged to monitor the outcome of nominations made pursuant to the nomination agreements closely and robustly, not least so as to be able to identify those nominations which are successful and those which fail. Such monitoring is described as 'crucial' so as to ensure that local housing authorities:

> 'can demonstrate that they are meeting their statutory obligations under Part 6, and in particular the requirement to give reasonable preference to persons in the categories set out in section 167(2).'[68]

In short, the local housing authority needs to be able to check that the RSL is accepting the broad range of nominations made and not itself picking and choosing from among nominated applicants.

6.42 Because most nominations will be made under the auspices of the local housing authority's own allocation scheme, it will be the local housing authority which has ultimate responsibility to the applicant for any difficulties. It may well be that an applicant seeks redress against that local housing

---

64 Reproduced in Appendix 1 of this book.
65 English 2009 Code, paras 93–100.
66 English CBL Code, paras 6.9 and 6.13.
67 English CBL Code, para 6.10. A good deal more detailed guidance is given in the Welsh Code, Annex 22.
68 English CBL Code, para 6.13.

authority. However, a 'nominated' applicant will also have access to avenues of redress against the RSL, where appropriate.[69]

'Failed' or 'problematic' nominations

6.43 A particular difficulty with the operation of nomination agreements, in practice, has been the rejection of nominated applicants by RSLs. This occurs most often where applicants have met the local housing authority's criteria (under the local allocation scheme) for nomination, but do not meet the particular RSL's letting criteria for the particular property (or, in some cases, for any letting by that RSL). These have been described as 'failed nominations'[70] or 'problematic nominations'.[71]

6.44 The two most common reasons for rejection of nominations are addressed in the statutory guidance from both government and the Housing Corporation. The first cause is information mismatching, ie the RSL and the local housing authority both hold information about the applicant, but the content differs. The English CBL Code emphasises that, for their part, local housing authorities should provide RSLs with details about nominated households that are 'clear comprehensive and up-to-date' and that in particular they should provide RSLs with any available information about vulnerability, support needs and arrangements for support.[72] The English 2009 Code recognises that failure to get this sort of information-sharing right could undermine a nomination process, but that getting it right will ensure that there are the best chances of new tenancies being sustained.[73] It goes on to draw the attention of local housing authorities to the Housing Corporation's recent guidance on information sharing.[74]

6.45 The second common reason for failed nominations is a mismatch between the criteria for nomination adopted by the local housing authority and the criteria for allocation, *after* nomination, adopted by the RSL. As already indicated, the statutory guidance in England from both the Housing Corporation[75] and the Secretary of State[76] is that all such criteria should be the subject of consultation and subsequent incorporation into the written nominations agreement between the RSL and the local housing authority. If

---

[69] See **6.74–6.82**.
[70] English CBL Code, para 6.14.
[71] D Cowan et al *Problematic Nominations* (School of Law, Bristol University, December 2007), at http://www.bris.ac.uk/law/research/centres-themes/nominations/index.html.
[72] English CBL Code, para 6.13. Where there is a support need, the Code expressly provides that: 'housing authorities should ensure, wherever possible, that adequate support packages are in place for applicants who need them before a nominee is expected to take up their tenancy'. For more on information-sharing, see **6.68–6.71**.
[73] English 2009 Code, para 98.
[74] English 2009 Code, para 100. The Corporation's guidance is contained in *Access to Housing: Information Sharing Protocol* (Housing Corporation, November 2007), at http://www.housingcorp.gov.uk/server/show/ConWebDoc.12842.
[75] RCG, para 3.6d.
[76] English 2009 Code, para 97.

rejection of nominations on these grounds occurs frequently, it may seriously impair a local housing authority's statutory obligations, e g to give a 'reasonable preference' to particular categories of its applicants.[77] To avoid these difficulties it is especially important that local housing authorities enter into robust, clear, and enforceable nomination agreements with those RSLs acquiring the whole or part of their stock of housing. The non-statutory ODPM guidance *Housing Allocation, Homelessness and Stock Transfer – A Guide to Key Issues*[78] sets out the policy and operational matters which the nomination agreement between a local housing authority and its transfer RSL should cover.

6.46 More recently, the Secretary of State, no doubt mindful of the difficulties occurring in practice, has advised local housing authorities in England that in negotiating nomination agreements 'housing authorities should try to ensure that criteria for rejecting nominees are kept to a minimum' and that 'this will be particularly important where the housing authority have transferred their housing stock'.[79] However, the language of this guidance is particularly unfortunate, as it suggests that attention is given to the matter not *before* but *after* a local housing authority has transferred its stock. The research that has been conducted on rejected nominations has shown that the phenomenon of large scale stock transfer has not resolved the frequency with which there are disputes between local housing authorities and RSLs over rejected nominations.[80]

6.47 The particular problems arising from inconsistent criteria are thrown into sharp focus when RSL accommodation available for local housing authority nominees is advertised through the local housing authority's choice based lettings scheme. The highest ranked bidder for that property will expect to be offered the tenancy if he or she meets the local housing authority's criteria and will not expect to be denied it for failure to meet the RSL's own criteria, e g because it has wider exclusion criteria than the local housing authority or because it gives particular emphasis to local connection or local lettings policies.[81] In an attempt to avoid such difficulties, the English CBL Code advises that:

> 'the exclusion policy of each participating RSL should be clearly set out in the published CBL scheme details. In addition, where this is feasible, the exclusion

---

77 The English CBL Code states, 'It is particularly important to monitor failed nominations to identify whether any particular applicants in the reasonable preference categories are being consistently denied access to accommodation for which they should be given priority' (para 6.14). For the meaning of 'reasonable preference', see Chapter 4 of this book.

78 ODPM, 2004, http://www.communities.gov.uk/publications/housing/housingallocationhome lessness.

79 English CBL Code, para 6.11 and English 2009 Code, para 97.

80 D Cowan et al *Problematic Nominations* (School of Law, Bristol University, December 2007), at http://www.bris.ac.uk/law/research/centres-themes/nominations/index.html.

81 As to 'legitimate expectation' in the housing allocation context see **4.36**.

criteria applied by an RSL should be stated in the advertisement of any relevant vacancy, so that applicants are clear about the basis on which the property is offered.'[82]

6.48 In parallel to all the emphasis in the statutory guidance on the negotiating position of local housing authorities in formulating nomination agreements, the Housing Corporation, for its part, reminded RSLs of the need to protect their own interests. Its guidance stated that, in order to preserve an RSL's independence, any nomination agreement must:

- reflect the RSL's objectives both as set out in its governing instrument and as agreed by the governing body;

- be approved by the governing body;

- be subject to regular and timely review; and

- run for such a term as will enable the parties to exit from it should circumstances or requirements change.[83]

This advice is mirrored in the *English Homelessness Code of Guidance* which reminds local housing authorities to:

'bear in mind that RSLs are required to retain their independence. They must honour their constitutional obligations under their diverse governing instruments, and will make the final decision on the allocation of their housing, within their regulatory framework.'[84]

CURRENT RSL TENANTS WHO WANT TO MOVE

6.49 All RSLs will have arrangements in place to accommodate receipt of, and subsequent determination of, requests from existing tenants to move to other homes within that RSL's stock, ie from tenants seeking a transfer. Indeed, in 2007/2008 some 11.8% of RSL lettings were to internal transfer applicants.[85]

6.50 Although the adoption of such arrangements might be thought in any event to represent sensible housing management, the matter has been the subject of statutory guidance to RSLs. They are directed to ensure that their written lettings policies not only 'take account of the need to give reasonable

---

82   English CBL Code, para 6.7.
83   Circular 02/03, para 4.2 at http://www.housingcorp.gov.uk/server/show/conWebDoc.2035.
84   At Annex 5, para 9 of the *English Homelessness Code of Guidance*; see Appendix 2 of this book.
85   Taken from 'Allocations by RSLs 2007/2008', reproduced at (2008) October *Legal Action*, p 43.

priority to transfer applicants', but also include arrangements for applications to be made to them from tenants of other RSLs.[86]

6.51 To ensure that there is sufficient stock available to facilitate internal transfer, the Housing Corporation Guidance on nomination agreements ensures (by the use of the term 'true voids'[87]) that sufficient stock is ring-fenced for transfer applicants, even where there is a 100% nomination agreement in place. This may enable an RSL to meet requests for transfers from applicants seeking a particular property who would not meet the criteria for allocation of that property if it was made available for allocation only through a nomination arrangement or a common allocation scheme.[88]

6.52 The precise detail of a particular RSL's internal transfer scheme is not regulated by any statutory parameters or guidance and RSLs have, essentially, a free rein. This is, of course, subject to the constraints of the general law (eg the need to avoid unlawful discrimination) and the requirement to act fairly and in accordance with the RSL's own published scheme. The RSL may even differentiate between the criteria it applies to transfer applicants and those applying to direct applicants. For example, Housing Corporation Circular 02/07 suggests that the RSL may take a stricter view of the effect of rent arrears on eligibility for allocation if the arrears are owed by its own tenant.[89]

6.53 The information generally provided by the RSL about its lettings arrangements[90] should be made available to transfer applicants. Complaints by, and redress for, dissatisfied transfer applicants are considered later in this Chapter.[91]

CO-OPERATION IN ORDER TO OFFER 'CHOICE'

Common housing registers

6.54 In line with the general policy shift towards consumer choice, RSLs are being increasingly encouraged to expose more of their available lettings to wider groups of prospective new tenants – where possible, through advertising and other mechanisms for choice based letting. The Housing Corporation's guidance gave such moves a broad green light by stating that 'for the avoidance of doubt' RSLs in England were free to enter into arrangements, including arrangements with their local housing authority partners, by which:

- housing is allocated to people from a common housing register; and/or

---

[86] RCG, para 3.6f.
[87] See **6.37**.
[88] See *R (Fidelis-Auma) v Octavia Housing & Care* [2009] EWHC 2263 (Admin), Admin Ct.
[89] Circular 02/07: *Tenancy Management: Eligibility and Evictions* (Housing Corporation, April 2007), at http://www.housingcorp.gov.uk/server/show/ConWebDoc.11074.
[90] See **6.9–6.11**.
[91] See **6.74–6.82**.

- lettings arise from a choice based lettings scheme;[92] and/or

- allocations are covered by a common allocations policy.[93]

6.55 A further considerable impetus was given in August 2008 by publication of the English CBL Code in which the Secretary of State recommended that all local housing authorities work with their local RSLs to provide 'joint choice based lettings schemes which extend to all or the majority' of local social housing vacancies.[94]

6.56 A 'common housing register' is defined in the English CBL Code as an arrangement under which a local housing authority and an RSL develop a single list or database of all applicants for housing allocation who have applied to either of them.[95] The intention is that, where the operation of such a register has been agreed, properties will actually thereafter be allocated to those on the common register under a jointly operated choice based 'common allocation scheme'. The Secretary of State considers that the adoption of common housing registers has advantages:

- for applicants (because a single application form and a single access point obviates the need to register separately);

- for local housing authorities (because the register provides a more reliable assessment of housing need in their districts, providing important information for the development of their housing strategy, and enabling the best use to be made of existing stock);[96] and

- more generally, because the process of negotiating and drawing up such registers can build trust between RSL and local housing authority partners.[97]

6.57 However, considerable care is needed in drawing up such schemes. In particular, it needs to be clear whether the register is simply a facility for joint storage of information or rather whether it is a means of enabling common criteria to be applied in assessing applications (eg to ascertain eligibility and priority). There is a significant distinction between the former, which are true common housing registers, and the latter, which are common allocations policies. As a recent report on the situation in Wales indicated:

'The presence of a common housing register in an authority area is not necessarily a requisite for a common allocations policy. 29% of respondents have common

---

[92] See further, Housing Corporation Good Practice Note 12 *Choice Based Lettings* (Housing Corporation, October 2005), at http://www.housingcorp.gov.uk/server/show/conWebDoc.5045.

[93] Circular 02/03, para 4.3, at http://www.housingcorp.gov.uk/server/show/conWebDoc.2035.

[94] English CBL Code, para 6.1 and English 2009 Code, para 99.

[95] English CBL Code, para 6.16.

[96] English CBL Code, para 6.17 and English 2009 Code, para 99.

[97] English 2009 Code, para 100.

registers but no common allocations policy. However, in the 3 authorities where a common allocations policy is in operation, 2 of the authorities also have a common register operating.'[98]

6.58 In England, in 2007/2008 over 10% of all RSL lettings were made through Common Housing Registers or Common Allocation Schemes.[99] A discussion paper, *Common Housing Registers*, published by the Homelessness Action Team in May 2009 contains a useful literature review and a consideration of topical issues concerning such registers.[100]

6.59 As already explained,[101] if an applicant on the common register is applying directly for an RSL property, the only eligibility criteria will be those adopted by the RSL. But if the applicant is going to be a local housing authority nominee for an RSL vacancy, the statutory eligibility criteria must be met. The Secretary of State has expressly reminded local housing authorities that applicants on a common housing register who wish to bid for local housing authority allocations (including RSL vacancies to which the local housing authority has nomination rights) will need to meet the HA 1996, s 160A eligibility criteria described in Chapter 3 of this book.[102]

6.60 These complications are thrown into even sharper relief when an RSL participates in a common registration scheme with more than one local housing authority or with a number of local housing authorities and other RSLs. Ambitious plans to amalgamate registers and allocations policies to produce common schemes, involving RSLs but run by a single central organisation exercising the delegated powers of all participants, have run into difficulties. The Secretary of State has advised that local housing authorities cannot use their general statutory powers of delegation to operate such common lettings schemes together with RSLs although 'it would be possible to include within such a scheme RSL vacancies to which a local authority had nomination rights'.[103]

6.61 Provided that there is no delegation to a central body, RSLs are encouraged to participate in *regional* choice based lettings schemes with other local housing authority and RSL partners. But the statutory guidance indicates that where RSL property is advertised through a joint choice based lettings scheme in which the RSL participates with local housing authorities which each have their own allocation scheme:

(1) the partners in the scheme should be clear as to which local housing authority is the nominating local housing authority; and

---

[98] Homelessness Strategy Working Group Report: *Housing Association Lettings* (Community Housing Cymru).
[99] Taken from 'Allocations by RSLs 2007/2008', reproduced at (2008) October *Legal Action*, p 43.
[100] Housing Action Team discussion paper: *Common Housing Registers* (TSA, May 2009), at http://www.tenantservicesauthority.org/server/show/nav.00f004005002.
[101] See **6.15–6.27**.
[102] English CBL Code, para 6.16.
[103] English CBL Code, para 7.8.

(2)   there should be clear information available for applicants as to which local housing authority's allocation scheme applies to that property (and therefore how priority will be determined).[104]

There is no equivalent modern statutory guidance for Welsh local housing authorities or RSLs. The Welsh Code has not been revised since its first issue in April 2003 and does not therefore reflect developments towards choice based letting over the past 7 years. The most recent statutory guidance for Welsh RSLs simply refers them back to the Welsh Code.[105]

Co-operation with local housing authorities

6.62   Much of what has already been written in this chapter has assumed a degree of partnership working between RSLs and local housing authorities as the two main providers of social housing.[106] But that assumption has a statutory underpinning. HA 1996, s 170 expressly addresses co-operation between RSLs and local housing authorities. It provides that on request from a local housing authority, an RSL shall co-operate 'to such extent as is reasonable in the circumstances' in offering accommodation to people with priority under the local housing authority's allocation scheme. It should be noted that this is not restricted to requiring co-operation in respect of offering homes to those in the statutory 'reasonable preference' categories. A local housing authority may also have identified other applicants in its scheme as having 'priority'.[107]

6.63   This duty to co-operate with a local housing authority to a reasonable extent mirrors the duty imposed on RSLs to co-operate in assisting a local housing authority in discharging its homelessness functions under HA 1996, s 213(1)(a).[108] Indeed, that duty is subjected to extended treatment in statutory guidance under the title *Co-operation between registered social landlords and housing authorities*[109] – much of which is directed not only to homelessness functions but also to housing allocations – and has been the subject of detailed research as to its effect in practice.[110]

---

[104]   English CBL Code, para 7.18.

[105]   *Housing Association Circular 023/09* (Welsh Assembly Government, February 2009).

[106]   See generally *A Framework for Partnership* (published jointly by the Local Government Association, the National Housing Federation and the Housing Corporation, 2006), at http://www.dhcarenetworks.org.uk/_library/Resources/ICN/A%20Framework%20for%20Partnership%20by%20LGA,%20Housing%20Corporation%20&%20NHF.pdf and, more recently, Homelessness Action Team discussion paper: *Developing Partnerships* (TSA, May 2009), at http://www.tenantservicesauthority.org/server/show/nav.13936.

[107]   See Chapter 4 of this book.

[108]   Discussed at **18.131–18.132**.

[109]   *English Homelessness Code of Guidance*, Annex 5 (CLG, July 2006); see Appendix 2 of this book.

[110]   *Tackling Homelessness: Efficiencies in lettings functions* (Housing Corporation, November 2007), http://www.housingcorp.gov.uk/server/show/ConWebDoc.12840.

6.64 The Housing Corporation dealt with these two duties together, requiring that:

> 'when requested to do so by the local authority and to such an extent as is reasonable in the circumstances, associations provide a proportion of their stock to local authority nominations and temporary accommodation to the homeless'.[111]

The Regulatory Code in Wales contains the 'key expectation' that RSLs should work in partnership with relevant local housing authorities on the allocation of housing.[112]

6.65 The statutory obligation to co-operate over housing allocation arises only 'on request'.[113] A generic request from a local housing authority might cause an RSL to offer nomination arrangements or to negotiate a common housing register or some other joint scheme with the requesting local housing authority. But the request may also be applicant specific. The local housing authority may, for example, owe a duty to accommodate a particular applicant needing accommodation of a particular type held by the RSL and may make a request accordingly. The duty to co-operate is, however, limited to 'such extent as is reasonable in the circumstances'. A reasonable response to such a request might include an invitation to the local housing authority to transfer a unit of its stock to the RSL or to accept a reciprocal nomination.

6.66 If an RSL does not co-operate in the face of a request from the local housing authority, the local housing authority could pursue the matter with the relevant regulator or through the courts (because the statutory duty is mandatory).[114] Alternatively, the individual (if there is one) who is the subject of the request could use the RSL's complaints procedure or pursue one of the other means of redress.[115]

6.67 Of course, there are a host of other functions in respect of which RSLs and local housing authorities should co-operate. The Housing Corporation expects RSLs to be able to demonstrate their co-operation with local housing authorities at least in:

(1) local homelessness reviews;

(2) in the formulation of local homelessness strategies; and

---

[111] RCG, para 3.6c.
[112] Welsh Assembly Government's *Regulatory Code for Housing Associations Registered in Wales*, Key Expectation 1.3.2, (National Assembly for Wales, March 2006), at http://wales.gov.uk/topics/housingandcommunity/housing/publications/regulatorycodehas?lang=en.
[113] HA 1996, s 170.
[114] HA 1996, s 170 says '*shall* co-operate' (emphasis added).
[115] See **6.74–6.82**.

(3)   in the delivery of local housing authorities' homelessness functions.[116]

Information sharing

6.68   Where RSLs and local housing authorities are working closely together over social housing allocation, there will inevitably be a need to share information. But information-sharing relating to the particulars of individual applicants requires very careful handling.

6.69   Those who have applied to a local housing authority for accommodation under HA 1996, Part 6 have the statutory assurance that even the simple fact that they have applied will not be shared with others (including RSLs) without their consent.[117] It will therefore be essential for the local housing authority to have the written consent of each and every applicant before sharing access to its information database with an RSL.

6.70   Those who have applied to RSLs may seek to rely on the assurances given in the Housing Corporation's Applicant's Charter that:

'Information your housing association holds about you must be kept safe and secure. It must be kept up to date and deleted when no longer required ... Housing associations can only pass on information about you to other people or organisations if you have consented or where the law permits them to do so.'[118]

6.71   Against this background, both the Housing Corporation and the government have produced publications designed to help local housing authorities and RSLs to resolve information-sharing issues.[119]

RSLs as local housing authority contractors

6.72   There is no reason why a local housing authority should not contract-out its HA 1996, Part 6 responsibilities for housing allocation to a local RSL. Indeed, many RSLs do act as such contractors, particularly following large-scale voluntary transfers of local housing authority stock.

6.73   Chapter 21 of this book deals more fully with both contracting-out and stock transfer. The report *Housing allocation, homelessness and stock transfer: A guide to key issues* contains advice for RSLs and local housing authorities on all three subjects – stock transfer, contracting-out and housing allocation

---

116   RCG, para 3.6b. For 'homelessness strategies' and 'homelessness reviews', see Chapter 7. For 'homelessness functions', see **21.20–21.24**.

117   HA 1996, s 166(3). See Chapter 2 of this book.

118   *A charter for housing association applicants and residents* (Housing Corporation, April 2007), at http://www.housingcorp.gov.uk/server/show/nav.546, p 20.

119   See, in particular, *Access to Housing: Information Sharing Protocol* (Housing Corporation, November 2007), at http://www.housingcorp.gov.uk/server/show/ConWebDoc.12842.

nominations – in a single publication, but this must now be read with some caution as it has not been revised since 2005.[120]

COMPLAINTS, APPEALS AND LEGAL CHALLENGES

6.74 Before deciding whether or how to dispute a decision made on an application for (or nomination for) an RSL housing allocation, an applicant should first obtain such details as she or he can about the particular RSL's housing allocation scheme.[121] At the same time, she or he should ask the RSL to provide the details of the particulars which she or he has given to the local housing authority about 'himself and his family' and which the RSL has recorded as being relevant to the application for accommodation. The applicant has the statutory right to have that information made available on request at all reasonable times and without charge.[122] Complying with the request will require disclosure of not only the application form but any details the RSL has subsequently obtained in its consideration of the application. Most simply, the applicant can ask for and will usually be provided with a copy of the application file. Armed with the file and the copy scheme, the applicant (or an adviser) will usually be able to identify, and draw to the RSL's attention, any simple error, missing material or other mishap that has occurred in considering the application.

6.75 In case any difficulty is not so easily resolved, every RSL was required by the Housing Corporation to have a complaints procedure open to use by the RSL's applicants and tenants. Indeed, the Corporation's *Charter* addressed to applicants states that those disappointed with the service that they have received should use the complaints procedure in the first instance and are entitled to receive a copy of the RSL's complaints procedure and help in utilising it. It states:

> 'All housing associations must have an effective complaints and compensation policy.
>
> You should be given information about how to complain, who to complain to and what is involved. This may be in your handbook or guidebook or in a leaflet that you can get from your housing association.
>
> The policy and procedure should be clear and easy to follow and should allow you to take your complaint to the people who manage the association at a senior level, including the governing body.'[123]

---

[120] *Housing allocation, homelessness and stock transfer: A guide to key issues* (CLG, 2005), available at http://www.communities.gov.uk/documents/housing/rtf/156843.rtf.

[121] See **6.28–6.30**.

[122] Housing Act 1985, s 106(5).

[123] *A charter for housing association applicants and residents* (Housing Corporation, November 2007), at http://www.housingcorp.gov.uk/server/show/conWebDoc.1564, p 22.

6.76 If the complaints procedure does not resolve the matter, an applicant with a continuing grievance concerning an RSL operating in England can press the complaint to the Housing Ombudsman Service.[124] The Ombudsman is established by statute[125] and provides a free and independent service. RSLs are expected to comply with his recommendations. The Ombudsman's case-load in relation to allocations and transfers complaints is set out in his Annual Report. The Annual Report for 2009 indicates that 9% of complaints related to housing allocation problems.[126] More detailed information is available through an online searchable digest of cases.[127] For example, in respect of allocation complaints against RSLs, the latest case in the digest deals with a failure to consider medical circumstances properly when a couple applied for a housing transfer.[128]

6.77 Complaints about RSLs operating in Wales can be directed to the Public Services Ombudsman for Wales.[129]

6.78 Although an RSL may operate a system of complaints handling, reviews of decisions or even 'appeals', there is strictly no right of appeal to the courts or tribunals from any decision of an RSL, of an RSL complaints officer, or of the Ombudsmen.

6.79 The Divisional Court and the Court of Appeal (by a majority) have decided that the decision of an RSL in relation to the allocation of social housing can be amenable to judicial review – at least to the extent that, in allocating its housing, the RSL might be described as undertaking a 'public function'.[130] The RSL in that case was refused leave to appeal to the new Supreme Court. Therefore, unless and until – in some other case – the Supreme Court overrules the decision of the Court of Appeal, a dissatisfied RSL applicant is now able to invoke the jurisdiction of the Administrative Court to review an RSL's decision-making on a housing allocation application (whether the applicant was seeking a transfer[131] or was a direct applicant or was a nominee or was simply an RSL tenant seeking a mutual exchange).[132] The grounds on which the court will interfere with such a decision are narrowly drawn and are described later in this book.[133]

6.80 The Divisional Court and the Court of Appeal (by a majority) have also decided that the act of an RSL in granting or terminating a tenancy of social

---

[124] At http://www.ihos.org.uk.
[125] Housing Act 1996, s 51 and Sch 2.
[126] See http://www.housing-ombudsman.org.uk/downloads/HOS_AR_09.pdf.
[127] See http://www.housemark.co.uk/hmkb2.nsf/CDHP?Openform.
[128] *Complaint reference 08007395 – Allocations*, 10 Aug 2009, at http://www.housemark.co.uk/hmkb2.nsf/9/9BF5CB600B4AE2628025762E003943C1?OpenDocument.
[129] See http://www.ombudsman-wales.org.uk/.
[130] *R (Weaver) v London & Quadrant Housing Trust* [2008] EWHC Admin 1377; [2009] 1 All ER 17, [2009] EWCA Civ 587, [2009] 4 All ER 865, CA.
[131] As in *R (Fidelis-Auma) v Octavia Housing & Care* [2009] EWHC 2263 (Admin).
[132] As in *R (McIntyre) v Gentoo Group Ltd* [2010] EWHC 5 (Admin).
[133] See Chapter 19.

housing is, where it is done pursuant to a function of a public nature, an act to which the requirements of the Human Rights Act 1998 ('HRA 1998') apply.[134] HRA 1998 prohibits a public authority from acting in a manner contrary to an individual's Convention rights as set out in the Articles reproduced in HRA 1998, Sch 1.[135] Although no Convention right gives an applicant a right to an RSL home, the Convention rights might assist an applicant who has been denied a proper hearing of an application or an appeal by an RSL (Art 6), who has been denied a transfer and thus is left in an unsatisfactory RSL home (Art 8) or who has been a victim of discrimination in consideration of his or her application (Art 14). Obviously, an applicant seeking to conduct a judicial review or to assert his or her Convention rights against an RSL should be referred for specialist legal advice.

6.81 Equally obviously, where the applicant considers that there has been unlawful discrimination or an infringement of human rights, the assistance of the Equality and Human Rights Commission can be sought.[136]

6.82 When it was the regulator for RSL housing, the Housing Corporation took little interest in complaints made directly by individuals and mainly referred them back to the RSL's own complaints procedures or to the Housing Ombudsman. But, from April 2010, the Tenant Services Authority will have statutory powers to intervene when it receives individual complaints. Specifically, it will be able to award compensation and require RSLs to provide other forms of redress.[137] Its procedures for dealing with matters raised directly by individual applicants will be in place by 1 April 2010.

THE FUTURE

6.83 As described in the introduction to this chapter, the arrangements for supervision, registration and regulation of RSLs in England have been re-drawn by provisions of the Housing and Regeneration Act 2008 ('HRA 2008'), not all of which are yet in force. At the date of writing the Housing Corporation had been wound up and its statutory functions in relation to RSLs, conferred by HA 1996, Part 1, were being exercised by the Tenant Services Authority (TSA).

6.84 From 1 April 2010 the TSA will cease to use the old Corporation's powers, as it will be invested by the HRA 2008 with a wide range of new powers and functions to regulate social housing provided by RSLs in England (and by local housing authorities).

---

[134] *R (Weaver) v London & Quadrant Housing Trust* [2008] EWHC Admin 1377; [2009] 1 All ER 17, [2009] EWCA Civ 587, [2009] 4 All ER 865, CA.

[135] HRA 1998, s 6(1).

[136] At http://www.equalityhumanrights.com/.

[137] Housing and Regeneration Act 2008, ss 236–242.

6.85   Among its new functions is the issue of national standards relating to housing allocation. The TSA will be able to set standards for registered providers of social housing as to the nature, extent and quality of accommodation, facilities or services provided by them in connection with social housing, and these standards may, in particular, require registered providers to comply with specified rules about criteria for allocating accommodation.[138]

6.86   Before adopting these new national standards, the TSA was required to undertake a round of statutory consultation with stakeholders and, ultimately, to secure the approval of the Secretary of State.

6.87   In early 2009 the TSA undertook an initial non-statutory consultative exercise with social housing tenants (called the 'National Conversation'). Based on the results of that consultation,[139] it published in June 2009 an initial indicator of what the draft of the national standards to be distributed for statutory consultation might contain.[140] In respect of housing allocation, the TSA there indicated that:

> 'the way tenants and potential tenants get social housing is a fundamental issue for our regulation. This national standard should make sure that there is a transparent, fair and consistent approach by landlords to allocating lettings to the homes they provide.'[141]

6.88   In November 2009 the TSA embarked on a statutory round of consultation. Its consultation draft of the new national standard for housing allocation has already been set out at the end of Chapter 1 of this book. The final version of the standard will be published in March 2010 and take effect from 1 April 2010.

6.89   For its part, the Welsh Assembly Government has undertaken a consultation exercise on its proposals for introducing a new regulatory system for RSLs in Wales from 2010/11.[142] The consultation exercise closed in July 2009 and further developments are likely to follow the adoption of a new Legislative Competence Order by the Welsh Assembly later in 2010. If adopted, the Order will enable the establishment of a wholly distinct system of social housing regulation in Wales, similar to the TSA in England.

---

[138]   HRA 2008, s 193(1) and (2)(a).

[139]   *National Conversation Phase one findings* (TSA, June 2009), at http://www. nationalconversation.co.uk/Your-feedback.aspx.

[140]   *Building a new regulatory framework: A discussion paper* (TSA, June 2009), at http://www.tenantservicesauthority.org/server/show/ConWebDoc.18499.

[141]   Ibid, para 4.103.

[142]   *Developing a modern regulatory framework for Housing Associations in Wales* (Welsh Assembly Government, April 2009), at http://cymru.gov.uk/consultations/housingcommunity/ regulatoryframework/;jsessionid=hTgHK7hRv2JYfWQFnM4dnrRw1hLp6v2FRG1pyJz35Yd fYJMvhfpW!392406782?lang=en&ts=4.

6.90 Given the breadth of these changes, the subject of RSL allocation of social housing will no doubt require considerable reconsideration in the next edition of this work.

PART II

HOMELESSNESS

Chapter 7

LOCAL HOUSING AUTHORITIES' HOMELESSNESS REVIEWS AND STRATEGIES

INTRODUCTION

7.1 This chapter and the following chapters of this book deal with 'Homelessness'. Like the legislation itself, this book's primary focus is on the individual applicant for assistance and the powers and duties of a local housing authority in dealing with the application. However, over recent years, increasing attention has been focused on the need to take a more strategic approach to the problem of homelessness beyond simply operating the safety net mechanism for individual applicants now contained in the Housing Act 1996 (HA 1996), Part 7. The steady rise, between 2001 and 2004, in the number of applications for homelessness assistance in all parts of the UK, and the consequent growth in the numbers of households in temporary accommodation, caused the focus of attention to shift towards methods of preventing homelessness and to dealing more effectively with it when it does arise. Central government began encouraging a more proactive rather than reactive approach to the issue of homelessness.

7.2 This chapter reviews the consequences of this modern emphasis. It considers, in turn, the development of 'homelessness strategies' at national, regional and local level. Most of the focus is upon the latter, particularly as a result of statutory duties imposed on local housing authorities to draw up their own local homelessness strategies.[1] Those duties are considered in particular detail. The next chapter deals specifically with homelessness prevention.

NATIONAL STRATEGIES

7.3 Policy-making at national level relating to homelessness is undertaken by central government for England, and by the devolved governments of Wales, Scotland and Northern Ireland.[2] The UK government has no single national strategy directed towards the prevention of homelessness or to tackling homelessness when it arises. A useful review of practice, and of policy, across the whole of the United Kingdom is contained in *Homelessness in the UK: Problems and Solutions*.[3]

7.4 However, the UK government has recognised homelessness as a factor in social exclusion, and thus includes tackling homelessness within the work of its Social Exclusion Task Force. The latest report of the Task Force contains a summary of the different homelessness strategies and actions undertaken by the four national governments.[4]

---

[1] Homelessness Act 2002, ss 1–4.

[2] See 'What has devolution done for the homeless' (2009) *Roof Magazine*, September/October, p 31.

[3] Fitzpatrick, Quilgars and Please (eds) (Chartered Institute of Housing, 2009).

[4] *Working Together – the UK National Action Plan on Social Inclusion 2006–2008* (Department for Work and Pensions, 2006), pp26–29, at http://www.dwp.gov.uk/publications/policy-publications/uk-national-report/archive/.

7.5   In the absence of a UK-wide strategy, we consider each of the four national strategic plans in turn.

England

7.6   Although a 5-year national strategy for addressing homelessness in England is currently in force, its development took some considerable time. Before considering its terms, it may be instructive briefly to review that history.

7.7   The former Department for Transport, Local Government and the Regions (DTLR) consulted on the development of a National Homelessness Strategy for England in 2001, but no national strategy emerged from that exercise.[5]

7.8   Between July 2004 and January 2005, the Parliamentary Select Committee on the work of the Office of the Deputy Prime Minister (ODPM)[6] carried out an Inquiry into the effectiveness of implementation of the Homelessness Act 2002. It heard evidence from ministers, civil servants, local housing authorities' representatives, charitable providers such as the Salvation Army and Shelter, and other housing campaigns. Its report was published in January 2005.[7] Its strong view was that the government should aim to eradicate homelessness, through increasing the stock of social housing, and that government action to reduce the number of homeless households in temporary accommodation had not been effective. It expressed concern that the tests of 'vulnerability' for the purposes of priority need[8] and 'becoming homeless intentionally'[9] were not being fairly or consistently applied by local housing authorities. It recommended that the government issue clear and authoritative guidance on the assessment of vulnerability and the test for becoming homelessness intentionally, and that social services authorities should be issued with guidance on accepting referrals of families who had been found to have become homeless intentionally. There was concern that many local housing authorities displayed a lack of strategic thinking when it came to dealing with the question of homelessness. Above all, the biggest problem in tackling homelessness was said to be the lack of supply of adequate housing, especially social rented housing.

7.9   In January 2005, the ODPM itself published a national 5-year housing strategy, *Sustainable Communities: Homes for All*,[10] and then followed it, in March 2005, with a strategy for tackling homelessness, *Sustainable*

---

5   *A national homelessness strategy: an invitation to comment* (DTLR, 21 September 2001).
6   Now the Communities and Local Government Parliamentary Select Committee.
7   Select Committee on Office of the Deputy Prime Minister 'Housing, Planning, Local Government and the Regions, Third report of session 2004–2005', at http://www.publications. parliament.uk/pa/cm200405/cmselect/cmodpm/61/6102.htm.
8   See **13.62–13.76**.
9   See Chapter 14 of this book.
10   ODPM, January 2005, at http://www.communities.gov.uk/archived/publications/corporate/ homesforall.

Communities: settled homes; changing lives.[11] More recently, a Housing Green Paper *Homes for the Future: more affordable, more sustainable* was published by the Department for Communities and Local Government (CLG) in July 2007.[12] These documents remain the foundations of the government's policy on homelessness for England.

7.10 The 'housing strategy' document emphasises the government's commitment to promoting home ownership. New houses are to be built for sale. Local housing authority and Registered Social Landlord (RSL) tenants are to be given opportunities to buy part of their homes. In the rented sector, there are to be more social rented homes (from RSLs) and choice based letting schemes are to be extended into the RSL sector so that there is a nationwide system of choice by 2010.[13] The quality of private rented accommodation is to be improved. There is emphasis on preventing homelessness through mediation schemes to resolve family disputes, or disputes between landlords and tenants. Rent deposit or rent guarantee schemes are to be available, so that people facing homelessness can be helped to find private rented accommodation. Local housing authorities will be encouraged to maintain approved lists of private landlords. The housing strategy also set an ambitious target: to halve the use of temporary accommodation for homeless households by 2010. The more recent Housing Green Paper contains plans to increase the supply of affordable housing, including homes provided by local housing authorities and RSLs.

7.11 The national 'homelessness strategy' develops the homelessness aspects of these national housing strategy commitments. Its specific aim is to halve the number of households living in temporary accommodation by 2010 and it identifies as methods to achieve this:

- prevention of homelessness;

- providing support for vulnerable people;

- tackling the wider causes and symptoms of homelessness;

- helping people move away from rough sleeping; and

- providing more settled homes.

7.12 Since the national homelessness strategy was published, the government has monitored progress principally through the release of quarterly statistics. Each English local housing authority makes a regular statistical return to central government on its performance of functions under HA 1996, Part 7.

---

[11]   ODPM, March 2005, at http://www.communities.gov.uk/publications/housing/sustainable communitiessettled2.

[12]   Department for Communities and Local Government, July 2007, at http://www.communities. gov.uk/publications/housing/homesforfuture.

[13]   See **5.7–5.23**.

The government then publishes quarterly Homelessness Statistics based on those returns.[14] The Housing Inspectorate of the Audit Commission also publishes inspections of local housing authority services. Those inspections use, as an assessment tool, a 'key line of inquiry' on homelessness and housing advice.[15] In March 2006, the CLG published an account of the progress made during the first year of the national homelessness strategy.[16] The Homelessness Code of Guidance for Local Authorities published in July 2006 reflects the national strategy's emphasis on prevention.[17]

7.13 Guidance on specific aspects of homelessness prevention,[18] and assistance towards specifically identified groups, has also been published. Briefings have been published on homelessness and domestic violence,[19] repeat homelessness,[20] the health needs of homeless people,[21] rough sleeping,[22] and tackling youth homelessness.[23]

7.14 The CLG announced in November 2006 that reducing youth homelessness was a particular priority. It set out a series of measures: a commitment to end the use of bed and breakfast for 16- and 17-year-olds by 2010, increased use of family mediation, and a supported lodgings development scheme to provide accommodation for young people.[24]

7.15 There is no statutory obligation on any English local housing authority to have regard to the government's national homelessness strategy, either in formulating its own homelessness strategy or when it comes to the performance of its homelessness functions. However, local housing authorities should ordinarily take government policy into account, and they are being given direct

---

14　At http://www.communities.gov.uk/housing/housingresearch/housingstatistics/housingstatistics by/homelessnessstatistics/.

15　See http://www.audit-commission.gov.uk/housing/housingkloe/kloe8.asp?CategoryID=english ^1628.

16　*Sustainable Communities: settled homes; changing lives – one year on* (CLG, March 2006), at http://www.communities.gov.uk/publications/housing/sustainablecommunitiessettled3.

17　*Homelessness Code of Guidance for Local Authorities* (Department for Communities and Local Government, Department for Education and Skills, Department of Health, July 2006) (English Code) at Appendix 2 of this book.

18　See Chapter 8.

19　ODPM, 'Policy Briefing No 2', September 2002, at http://www.communities.gov.uk/archived/ publications/housing/homelessnessstatisticsseptember.

20　ODPM, 'Policy Briefing No 6', January 2004, at http://www.communities.gov.uk/archived/ publications/housing/homelessnessstatisticsbriefing6.

21　ODPM, 'Policy Briefing No 7', April 2004, at http://www.communities.gov.uk/archived/ publications/housing/homelessnessstatisticsbriefing7.

22　CLG, 'Policy Briefing No 20', September 2007, at http://www.communities.gov.uk/ publications/housing/policybrief20; and *No One Left Out – Communities Ending Rough Sleeping* (CLG, November 2006), at http://www.communities.gov.uk/publications/housing/ roughsleepingstrategy.

23　CLG, 'Policy Briefing No 18', March 2007, at http://www.communities.gov.uk/publications/ housing/policybriefing18.

24　The CLG web-site has a dedicated section on youth homelessness at http://www.communities. gov.uk/youthhomelessness/.

encouragement to implement the CLG's target of halving the number of homeless households in temporary accommodation by 2010.

Wales

7.16 When the Welsh Assembly Government was formed in 1999, it made a commitment to set up a Homelessness Commission to advise the Assembly on how it should be tackling homelessness in Wales. Once established, the Commission undertook an intensive programme of activity over 7 months. Its report comprised a major review of the causes of homelessness, with 91 recommendations on how it should be addressed.[25]

7.17 The Welsh Assembly Government has since published three national homelessness strategies. The 2003 *National Homelessness Strategy*[26] was based on an overall strategic national housing policy document, *Better Homes for People in Wales – National Housing Strategy for Wales*.[27] The two strategies identified measures to:

- significantly reduce the numbers of long-term homeless households;

- eliminate the need for rough sleeping; and

- promote access to specialist housing advice where this was needed.

7.18 The application of homelessness legislation by local housing authorities in Wales has been reviewed several times since publication of these strategies.[28]

7.19 In June 2004 the Chartered Institute of Housing Cymru produced a policy briefing paper indicating how, if at all, the national policy initiatives were impacting on service delivery in terms of homelessness provision.[29]

7.20 In June 2005, the Welsh Assembly Government commissioned a general review of the housing and homelessness situation in Wales.[30] The report of that review emphasised prevention of homelessness. It analysed the number of applications for homelessness assistance and acceptances and concluded that

---

25 The Homelessness Commission report to the Minister for Finance, Local Government and Communities, August 2001.

26 Welsh Assembly Government, March 2003.

27 Welsh Assembly Government, July 2001, at http://new.wales.gov.uk/topics/housingand community/housing/strategy/publications/betterhomes/?lang=en.

28 See, for example, *Review of the Implementation of Homelessness Legislation, Housing Research Report 01/2004 and Housing Research Summary HRS 01/2004* (January 2004), at http://new.wales.gov.uk/topics/housingandcommunity/housing/homelessness/homelessnessresearch/implementlegislation/?lang=en.

29 *No Place like Home – homelessness in Wales* (Chartered Institute of Housing Cymru, June 2004), www.cih.org/cymru/policy/key1.htm.

30 Report to the Welsh Assembly Government, *Tackling Homelessness – Key issues for consideration by Welsh Local Authorities* (Tarki Technology Ltd, June 2005), at http://new.wales.gov.uk/topics/housingandcommunity/housing/publications/tacklinghomelessness?lang=.

more preventative work would reduce those numbers. Somewhat controversially, it suggested that too many applications for homelessness assistance were inappropriate, that some local housing authorities were failing to apply homelessness legislation, and therefore they were accepting that a main housing duty was owed to applicants who were not necessarily entitled to it.[31]

7.21 In November 2005, the Welsh Assembly Government published its second *National Homelessness Strategy for Wales (2006–2008)*.[32] It emphasised:

- prevention of homelessness;[33]

- co-operative working between different agencies and local housing authority departments;

- reducing the incidence of repeat homelessness; and

- improving the quality of temporary accommodation.

7.22 It set out specific targets to be achieved by April 2008:

- preventing homelessness among 50% of households who considered themselves at risk of homelessness, who approached or were referred to the local housing authority and for whom housing advice casework intervention could resolve their situation;

- reducing the number of homeless households found to be unintentionally homeless and in priority need by 20% from 2004/05 levels;

- reducing the numbers of households in bed and breakfast accommodation by 50% from 2004/05 levels; and

- reducing the average length of time spent in temporary accommodation by 20% from 2004/05 levels.

The Assembly Government also intended that targets should be set to reduce rough sleeping and repeat homelessness.

7.23 A few months after the publication of the *National Homelessness Strategy for 2006–2008*, the Public Services Ombudsman for Wales published in February 2006 an account of Welsh local housing authorities' practices:

---

[31]   For 'main housing duty' owed under HA 1996, s 193(2), see **17.21–17.110**.
[32]   *National Homelessness Strategy for Wales (2006–2008)* (Welsh Assembly Government, November 2005), at http://new.wales.gov.uk/topics/housingandcommunity/housing/public ations/homelessnesstrategy?lang=en.
[33]   Stopping short of some of the more controversial analysis in the June 2005 report.

Housing Allocations and Homelessness: A Special Report by the Local Government Ombudsman for Wales.[34] The Ombudsman summarised his findings:

> 'A significant number of the 22 Welsh local authorities have failed to introduce housing allocation and homelessness policies and procedures that implement in practice the relevant legislative requirements.'

7.24   According to the Public Services Ombudsman for Wales, too many local housing authorities were:

- refusing to accept applications for homelessness assistance;

- failing to conduct inquiries into homelessness applications;

- failing to issue decisions; and

- failing to inform homeless applicants (and applicants to their allocation schemes) of their statutory rights (see also **10.60** et seq).

Far from too many local housing authorities accepting a main housing duty for applicants who were not necessarily entitled to it, the opposite was more frequently the case.

7.25   A review of the National Housing Strategy, published in November 2006, found that, as far as the *National Homelessness Strategy 2006–2008* was concerned, it was 'somewhat premature to make an assessment of its efficacy', but there had been a decrease in the number of homelessness acceptances and a decrease in the use of temporary accommodation.[35]

7.26   In January 2007, the Wales Audit Office published *Tackling Homelessness in Wales: A Review of the Effectiveness of the National Homelessness Strategy.*[36] The Wales Audit Office found that:

- the number of households accepted by local housing authorities as being owed the main housing duty[37] fell between 2004 and 2006;

- there was a similar fall in the number of applications for homelessness assistance;

- there was a notable reduction in the number of 16- and 17-year-olds who were owed the main housing duty;

---

[34]   http://www.ombudsman-wales.org.uk/en/publications/?pID=76. See **8.14** and **8.52**.
[35]   *National Housing Strategy for Wales, a selective review* (Welsh Assembly Government Housing Directorate, November 2006).
[36]   Wales Audit Office, January 2007 at http://www.wao.gov.uk/reportsandpublications/1347.asp.
[37]   HA 1996, s 193(2). See **17.21–17.110**.

- further progress, particularly 'a more joined-up approach' was required on prevention of homelessness;

- many local prevention services, particularly advice services, were still at an early stage of development;

- the Supporting People programme can play an important part in helping to prevent homelessness, but it needs a more strategic structure;

- more accurate data and effective monitoring is required; and

- the supply of affordable accommodation is a prerequisite to preventing homelessness.

7.27 In July 2009, the Welsh Assembly Government published its *Ten Year Homelessness Plan for Wales 2009–2019*.[38] When the Plan was out for consultation, Shelter Cymru called for extra resources to be given to homelessness, which is likely to grow in the coming period, and for the Assembly Government to aim for an end to all homelessness by 2019.[39]

7.28 The *Ten Year Homelessness Plan for Wales 2009–2019* aims to reduce homelessness 'to a minimum' by 2019 and to eliminate rough sleeping altogether. It will achieve those goals by preventing homelessness wherever possible, and working across organisational and policy boundaries. The Plan requires prevention services to recognise 'the need for a holistic approach to break cycles of homelessness', so that housing advice services should be providing not only advice on homelessness, and on sustaining existing homes, but also referrals for employment, training, education, financial problems and debt, and health advice. The needs of veterans, young homeless people and care-leavers, former prisoners, those fleeing domestic abuse, asylum seekers and refugees are specifically addressed, as is rural homelessness.

7.29 Greater use of the private rented sector is contemplated. Housing support should try to reduce the number of private rented tenants who lose their homes, advice services should provide early and comprehensive information on accessing private rented accommodation, and local housing authorities should be working with the private rented sector as part of their work to tackle homelessness. Mortgage rescue schemes are to be encouraged, along with more advice available to consumers prior to their taking out mortgages. The Welsh Assembly Government wants to see improvements in regulation and its enforcement, so that courts only approve mortgage possession actions when lenders have explored all other options to prevent possession. It also wishes to see the development of a protocol between lenders and local housing authorities so that lenders would notify local housing

---

[38]   Available from the Welsh Assembly Government, at housingmanagement&homelessness branch@wales.gsi.gov.uk.

[39]   See http://www.sheltercymru.org.uk/shelter/policy/rdetail.asp?cat=6.

authority homelessness prevention teams of any possession proceedings, allowing the homelessness prevention teams to assist households.

7.30 The Plan concludes that the existing framework of HA 1996, Part 7 'does not allow everyone to receive the level of service that they need to ensure that their housing needs can be met'. It plans to review 'key areas of homelessness legislation and the duties placed on Local Authorities, especially around the area of priority need, intentionality, local connection and the discharge of duty into the private rented sector, consulting widely on specific proposals for amendments to the existing statutory framework'. Obviously responsibility for amending HA 1996, Part 7 itself lies with the UK Parliament in Westminster, but the Welsh Assembly Government has delegated powers to issue circulars, guidance and secondary legislation. It wishes to ensure that 'everyone can have access to the help that they need, to secure a home that meets their needs and provides a platform from which to address their aspirations'.

7.31 Individual Welsh local housing authorities should take into account both the *Ten Year Homelessness Plan* and the national housing policy document when formulating their own homelessness strategies.[40]

Northern Ireland

7.32 Since the restoration of the Northern Ireland Executive in May 2007, policy on housing, including homelessness, has been the responsibility of the Department for Social Development. Statutory responsibility for dealing with homeless people lies with the Northern Ireland Housing Executive. Supervision is conducted by the Northern Ireland Audit Office, which produced a report on service provision for the homeless in March 2002.[41] This was followed in June 2002 by the publication of the report of the Social Development Committee's Inquiry into Homelessness.[42] The Northern Ireland Housing Executive published its own Homelessness Strategy in September 2002.[43] That strategy remains the basis of the Northern Ireland Housing Executive's homelessness activities.

---

[40]   *Code of Guidance for local housing authorities on allocation of accommodation and homelessness for Wales* (National Assembly for Wales, April 2003) (Welsh Code), paras 6.1–6.3 and 8.9.

[41]   *Housing The Homeless* (NI Audit Office, 21 March 2002), at http://www.niauditoffice.gov.uk/ pubs/onereport.asp?arc=True&id=82&dm=0&dy=0.

[42]   *Second Report on the Inquiry into Housing in Northern Ireland* (Social Development Committee of the Northern Ireland Assembly, June 2002), at http://www.niassembly.gov.uk/social/reports/ report3-01r_main.htm.

[43]   *The Homelessness Strategy* (Northern Ireland Housing Executive, September 2002), at http://www.nihe.gov.uk/index/sp_home/strategies/independent_living-2/homelessness_strategy. htm. The website contains a reference to a 2005 Homelessness Strategy, which appears in fact to be the 2002 document.

7.33 In 2004 both the Department and the Executive were criticised by the House of Commons Public Accounts Committee for their delay in bringing forward that comprehensive strategy.[44]

7.34 In July 2007 and after a 3-year consultation period, the Department for Social Development published *Including the Homeless, a Strategy to promote the social inclusion of homeless people, and those at risk of becoming homeless, in Northern Ireland.*[45] This document places homelessness, and potential homelessness, as one of the causes of social exclusion and identifies the different statutory and voluntary agencies that can play their part in tackling the causes of homelessness. It also contains figures showing a dramatic increase between 1999 and 2006 in the numbers of people applying for homelessness assistance and in the numbers accepted as being owed the main housing duty.

7.35 The 2002 Homelessness Strategy is being reviewed. The Housing (Amendment) Bill (Northern Ireland) 2009, being debated by the Northern Ireland Assembly at the time of writing, will create a duty on the Northern Ireland Housing Executive to formulate and publish a homelessness strategy within 12 months of the legislation coming into force, and then no later than every 5 years thereafter.[46]

7.36 While these deliberations have been taking place, there has been an inexorable increase in homelessness applications in Northern Ireland.

Scotland

7.37 At national policy level, homelessness in Scotland is the responsibility of the Scottish Executive. Soon after devolution in 1999, the Executive established a Homelessness Task Force charged with mapping out a programme to address the issue of homelessness in Scotland.

7.38 The initial report of the Task Force (in April 2000) led in due course to the amendment of the statutory homelessness scheme in Scotland, until then contained in the Housing (Scotland) Act 1987, by the Housing (Scotland) Act 2001.

7.39 The final report of the Task Force, *Homelessness: an action plan for prevention and effective response,*[47] spelt out a 12-year action programme to eliminate and thereafter prevent homelessness in Scotland. The subsequent Homelessness etc (Scotland) Act 2003 contains radical statutory measures designed to implement the Task Force recommendations. These include the enlargement and eventual abolition of priority need categories, the abolition of

---

[44] *Housing the Homeless* (Public Accounts Committee 21st report of session 2003/04), at www.publications.parliament.uk/pa/cm200304/cmselect/cmpubacc/559/55902.htm.

[45] Department for Social Development, July 2007, at http://www.nihe.gov.uk/index/sp_home/strategies/independent_living-2/homelessness_strategy/objectives-4.htm.

[46] Housing (Amendment) Bill (Northern Ireland) 2009, s 1.

[47] February 2002, at www.scotland.gov.uk/library3/society/htff-00.asp.

the local connection referral arrangements, and an obligation to accommodate all the homeless (including the intentionally homeless). A Homelessness Monitoring Group was set up in May 2002 to monitor the implementation of the reports of the Homelessness Task Force. Its most recent report was published in March 2008.[48] In May 2004 the Executive issued a new Code of Guidance on Homelessness: *Guidance on legislation, policies and practices to prevent and resolve homelessness*.[49] The Code of Guidance was updated and re-published in May 2005: *Code of Guidance on homelessness*.[50] An addition to the Code of Guidance was published in June 2009: *Prevention of Homelessness Guidance*.[51]

7.40 The ambitious target of abolishing priority need by 2012 remains.

7.41 The statutory responsibility for providing homelessness services in Scotland falls upon the Scottish local authorities. Delivery of around a quarter of the Task Force recommendations will depend on their being adopted by the 32 local authorities and then incorporated into the homelessness strategies already prepared by them and submitted to the Executive.

7.42 The Executive's Minister has power to reject local strategies submitted by those local authorities.[52]

REGIONAL STRATEGIES

7.43 In England, steps have been taken towards the development of regional homelessness strategies. In 2003, Regional Housing Boards were established to develop strategic housing policy for the regions. That role passed to the eight English Regional Assemblies, plus the Mayor of London, in September 2006.

7.44 All of the Regional Assemblies have Regional Housing Strategies. Only the West Midlands Regional Assembly and the East of England Regional Assembly have published Regional Homelessness Strategies.[53]

7.45 In London, responsibility for housing and homelessness strategy was given to the Mayor in 2006. The London Boroughs retain the statutory obligation for the delivery of homelessness services under HA 1996, Part 7, and

---

48 *Helping Homeless People*, Homelessness Monitoring Group Report (Scottish Government, 2008), at http://www.scotland.gov.uk/Publications/2008/03/27142559/0.
49 No longer available on the Scottish Executive website.
50 Scottish Executive, May 2005, at http://www.scotland.gov.uk/Publications/2005/05/31133334/33388.
51 Scottish Executive, June 2009, at http://www.scotland.gov.uk/Publications/2009/06/08140713/0.
52 Housing (Scotland) Act 2001, s 1(6).
53 For the West Midlands Regional Homelessness Strategy see http://www.wmra.gov.uk/Housing/Regional_Homelessness_Strategy.aspx. For the East of England Regional Homelessness Strategy, see http://www.eera.gov.uk/News.asp?cat=-1&id=SXC7F4-A77FB1E9. The South West Regional Assembly has a South West Homelessness Delivery Group at http://www.southwesthousingbody.org.uk/nqcontent.cfm?a_id=3993&tt=swra.

must also publish their own homelessness strategies and reviews. In September 2007, the then Mayor of London published a draft housing strategy for consultation.[54] Five specific aims on homelessness were set out:

- borough homelessness strategies would be expected to demonstrate how targets will be achieved, and how the numbers of rough sleepers, and people waiting for 'move-on' accommodation would be rehoused

- borough homelessness strategies would be expected to focus on prevention where possible but not to seek to achieve government targets through gate-keeping;

- boroughs would be expected to make greater use of private rented homes to discharge their responsibilities, but only if the homes were offered on a long tenancy from an accredited landlord;

- support temporary to settled schemes, where they provide more settled homes, more affordable rents and social assets; and

- boroughs would be expected to sign up to cross-London protocols to improve the response to homeless people who move across borough boundaries.

The emphasis in the draft Housing Strategy 2007 was on increasing the supply of affordable housing.

7.46 Following the election of a new Mayor of London, a new draft housing strategy for London was published in May 2009. Consultation on the new draft concluded in August 2009. In respect of homelessness, the 2009 draft housing strategy states:

> 'The number of households in temporary accommodation should be halved by 2010 and rough sleeping should end by 2012. Good quality advice and information on housing, including housing options, should be available to all Londoners who need it.'[55]

LOCAL HOMELESSNESS STRATEGIES AND REVIEWS

Overview

7.47 The Homelessness Act 2002[56] introduced what amounts to a statutory duty on local housing authorities to formulate and publish local homelessness strategies. The relevant provisions of the Homelessness Act 2002 came into

---

[54] *Draft Housing Strategy* (Greater London Assembly, September 2007).
[55] *London Housing Strategy* (Greater London Authority, May 2009), at http://www.london.gov. uk/mayor/housing/strategy/index.jsp.
[56] HA 2002 (HA 2002), ss 1–4, see Appendix 2 of this book.

force on 31 July 2002 for English local housing authorities and 30 September 2002 for Welsh local housing authorities.

7.48 Local housing authorities were required to publish their first local homelessness strategy within a year, ie by 31 July 2003 for English local housing authorities and by 30 September 2003 for Welsh authorities. They are required to keep the local strategies under review, and modify them if necessary. At the very least, they must publish new strategies every 5 years,[57] unless they have been categorised as 'excellent', '4-star' or '3-star' English local authorities, in which case that duty has been disapplied by regulations.[58] This meant that all other local housing authorities had to publish new homelessness strategies by 31 July 2008 in England (30 September 2008 in Wales). A further round of new strategies will be needed in or before 2013.

7.49 The purpose of preparing a local strategy is to enable local housing authorities to have an accurate picture of the levels of homelessness in their district, and to set out the steps to be taken in order to tackle and prevent homelessness.

7.50 Of course, to devise an effective local strategy, the local housing authority must have access to the raw data on the extent of homelessness in its area and on the current prevention programmes and local initiatives to tackle it. The Homelessness Act 2002, therefore, requires every local housing authority to conduct a 'review' of such matters, in relation to its area, so that the design and content of the local strategy may be undertaken on the best possible information.[59]

7.51 In short, the *review* is meant to paint the picture on homelessness locally and the *strategy* is intended to set out how the problem is to be addressed.

7.52 The fundamental objectives underlying the requirement both for a review and for a strategy are:

(1) identifying action that can be taken to prevent homelessness;

(2) providing suitable services and accommodation for people who are, or may become homeless; and

(3) supporting people who are homeless or potentially homeless and those who were formerly homeless and need support, to prevent them becoming homeless again.[60]

---

57 HA 2002, s 1(3) and (4).
58 Local Authorities' Plans and Strategies (Disapplication) (England) Order 2005, SI 2005/157, art 3, as amended by the Local Authorities' Plans and Strategies (Disapplication) (England) (Amendment) Order 2009, SI 2009/714; English Code, para 1.42.
59 HA 2002, s 1(1)(a).
60 HA 2002, ss 2(2) and 3(1).

7.53 The Homelessness Act 2002 and the Codes of Guidance all emphasise a multi-agency approach, with co-operation between local housing authorities and social services authorities, and with consultation and joint working with other public authorities, voluntary organisations and individuals in the undertaking of the review and in the formulation of the strategy.[61]

7.54 The strategies, once produced, should not be filed away to gather dust. Both local housing authorities and the relevant social services authorities are required to take the contents of the local homelessness strategy into account when exercising other statutory functions, such as decisions on homelessness and allocation and the performance of social services duties owed to young people, families with children and other vulnerable people.[62] As this chapter indicates, the requirement to have regard to them in day-to-day work will enable strategies to be used as legal tools, where appropriate.

7.55 There is no statutory timetable for the undertaking, production or publication of the initial homelessness *review* (or any subsequent reviews). In practice, many local housing authorities published both their initial review and initial strategy documents together or, indeed, incorporated the homelessness review into the first local homelessness strategy. Since the strategy must be based on the findings in the review, it follows that a review should always be carried out first.

7.56 Because the statutory requirement to prepare a homelessness strategy was entirely novel when brought into force in 2003, considerable resources were deployed to assist local housing authorities with the task of formulating their first strategies. The government provided additional financial resources to assist local housing authorities in drawing up their local reviews and strategies.[63] Substantial written guidance was provided to local housing authorities. This included: *Homelessness Strategies: A Good Practice Handbook*[64] and *Preventing tomorrow's rough sleepers: a good practice handbook*,[65] and they were in turn followed by publication of the Homelessness Codes of Guidance providing more assistance.

7.57 Those representing special interest groups lobbied hard for particular consideration to be given to specific aspects of the homelessness issue. The UK

---

[61]   HA 2002, s 1(2) and s 3(2)–(4); English Code, paras 1.39–1.41, chapter 5 and Annexes 3, 5–6; Welsh Code, paras 8.13–8.26, and Annexes 17–18. For an example of guidance on joint working see *Joint working between Housing and Children's Services, Preventing homelessness and tackling its effect on children and young people* (Communities and Local Government and Department for Children, Schools and Families, May 2008), at http://www.communities.gov. uk/publications/housing/goodpracticeguide.

[62]   Homelessness Act 2002, s 1(5) and (6).

[63]   See, for example, the letter from Neil O'Connor, Head of Homelessness Team, ODPM Homelessness Directorate to all Local Housing Authorities, 14 March 2002.

[64]   Department for Transport, Local Government and the Regions, 13 March 2002, available from http://www.communities.gov.uk/archived/publications/housing/homelessnessstrategies.

[65]   ODPM, June 2001, at http://www.communities.gov.uk/archived/publications/housing/prevent ingtomorrowsrough. See also English Code, para 1.4 and Annex 1.

Coalition on Older Homelessness, for example, produced *Local Homelessness Strategies and Older People* in April 2003.[66] The group Health Action at Crisis published *A Checklist on Health for Local Authorities and PCTS working on their Homelessness Strategy* in February 2003.[67] Least well served (it would seem) were the interests of the gypsy and travelling community. The Local Government Association was subsequently to find that 62% of the initial round of strategies (2003–2008) made no reference to the needs of homeless travellers at all.[68]

7.58   At local level, the individual reviews and strategies are expected to take into account other local authority and national government plans and strategies relevant to addressing the causes of homelessness.[69] Joint working with social services departments or authorities (in the case of non-unitary authorities) is a statutory requirement,[70] and local housing authorities are encouraged to involve other public authorities, such as health authorities, the police, RSLs and private landlords, voluntary organisations and other organisations and individuals.[71]

7.59   By the end of 2003, every English and Welsh local housing authority had complied with the duty to conduct a review and had adopted and published a strategy, and most local housing authorities had repeated that exercise in 2008. Copies of those strategies are relatively easy to obtain. Many local housing authorities now maintain internet websites on which their reviews and strategies may be posted. Copies of most local housing authorities' reviews and strategies were helpfully gathered together and links to them published on the web at www.homelesspages.org.uk and by Homeless Link (www.homelesslink. org.uk).[72] Hard copies of local reviews and strategies are available from individual local housing authorities on request.[73]

7.60   A review of the content or methodology in the many hundreds of local housing authorities' published reviews and strategies is beyond the scope of this book. However, there have been several useful reviews of initial local homelessness strategies (2003–2008).

7.61   In January 2004, Shelter published *The Act in Action, an assessment of homelessness reviews and strategies*.[74] Shelter's conclusion was that:

---

66   See http://www.olderhomelessness.org.uk/documents/olderstrategy.pdf.

67   http://www.crisis.org.uk/publications_djhsearch.php?submitted=search&fullitem=157.

68   *Homelessness Strategies: A Survey of Local Authorities, Research Briefing 6.04* (Local Government Association, October 2004), and see now the English Code, para 1.5.

69   English Code, paras 1.3–1.4, and Annex 1; Welsh Code, para 8.9 and Annex 18.

70   HA 2002, s 1(2) and (6).

71   English Code, para 1.39 and chapter 5; Welsh Code, paras 8.19–8.20.

72   The page on homelessness strategies is at http://www.homeless.org.uk/policyandinfo/briefings/ strategies. Unfortunately it appears only to contain reviews and strategies published in 2003.

73   HA 2002, ss 2(3) and 3(9) and see **7.109–7.111** and **7.159–7.161**.

74   *The Act in Action, an assessment of homelessness reviews and strategies* (Shelter, January 2004).

'... compiling reviews and strategies appears to have produced positive outcomes beyond simply delivering an assessment of homelessness levels and patterns. In a broader sense, it has enabled authorities to identify gaps in their knowledge (even where these gaps are yet to be tackled), build stronger relationships with other departments and agencies and develop a multi-agency approach not just to homelessness, but also to wider issues.'

7.62 A more detailed national picture was given in *Homelessness strategies – a survey of local authorities* published by the Local Government Association (LGA).[75] It contained the troubling finding that only 52% of local housing authorities thought that the exercise of preparing a strategy would help to any extent in determining likely future levels of homelessness in their areas.

7.63 The government undertook that its Homelessness Directorate would assess the strategies drawn up, notwithstanding that there is no statutory role for ministerial interference with local strategies such as that contained in the scheme in Scotland.[76] In August 2003 it announced that each local housing authority was required to lodge a copy of its strategy with the Directorate. During the first half of 2004, Housing Quality Network Services carried out an evaluation of those strategies (and consulted a number of English local housing authorities). A summary of that evaluation was published (*Local Authorities' Homelessness Strategies: Evaluation and Good Practice*)[77] and local housing authorities were encouraged to refer to it in carrying out future local homelessness reviews and drawing up further local strategies.[78] The research considered both homelessness reviews and homelessness strategies.

7.64 Analysis of homelessness *reviews* revealed that:

- most local housing authorities worked well at understanding the causes of, and current levels of, homelessness but few estimated future levels of homelessness;

- the availability of data, particularly about the scale and causes of homelessness for those persons considered to be in 'non-priority groups', was acknowledged as a difficulty;

- the main causes of homelessness were:
  - parents/friends/relatives no longer willing or able to accommodate; or
  - violent relationship breakdown with a partner; or
  - the termination of an assured shorthold tenancy;

---

[75] *Homelessness Strategies: A Survey of Local Authorities, Research Briefing 6.04* (Local Government Association, October 2004).

[76] See **7.42**.

[77] *Local Authorities' Homelessness Strategies: Evaluation and Good Practice* (ODPM, 2003), at http://www.communities.gov.uk/publications/housing/localauthoritieshomelessness2.

[78] English Code, para 1.4.

- all local housing authorities provided some information about the current services available, and most had gone further and mapped advice services provided in other sectors, and accommodation provided by other organisations;

- nine out of ten local housing authorities included prevention of homelessness in their reviews, although some had not taken a wide enough view of prevention;

- four out of five local housing authorities considered all forms of homelessness, although one in five confined themselves to groups who would be in priority need;

- many local housing authorities missed particular client groups;

- the groups most frequently missed were single homeless people and/or rough sleepers, ex-services personnel, black and minority ethnic groups, former asylum seekers and gypsies or travellers;

- the key priority groups most often identified by local housing authorities for particular attention were:
  - young people;
  - women and their children who are victims of domestic violence; and
  - people with drug or alcohol problems;

- although many local housing authorities had consulted widely with other agencies and groups, the involvement of social services at a strategic level was considered disappointing and other statutory agencies such as the health and probation service were also hard to engage; and

- local housing authorities had generally found it difficult to engage with, and consult, homeless people and service users.

7.65 When it came to homelessness *strategies*, the evaluation concluded:

- the great majority of strategies were clearly based on findings from the homelessness reviews;

- consultation with service users or other agencies had resulted in a new emphasis on prevention or other new approaches in the strategies;

- local housing authorities had focused on tackling rough sleeping and the use of bed and breakfast accommodation, although a number had failed to identify solutions and a small number had increased, rather than decreased, their use of bed and breakfast accommodation;

- only two in five local housing authorities managed to address the issue of wider links with other agencies and only about half demonstrated corporate or wider commitment in their strategies;

- most local housing authorities included all forms of homelessness within their strategy, but a significant number confined themselves to statutorily homeless groups;

- some local housing authorities engaged with black and minority ethnic communities, but many neglected those issues;

- strategies contained a number of innovative ideas for prevention and support activities;

- district councils were less developed in partnership-working than unitary or metropolitan councils;

- a lack of action planning was a weak point in many strategies; and

- many local housing authorities had not identified resources necessary to implement the whole of their strategy.

7.66 The ODPM issued a policy briefing *Homelessness Strategies: Moving Forward* based on this evaluation.[79] The document recommended that local housing authorities bring forward plans for comprehensively reviewing their homelessness strategies. It suggested that they should be:

- ensuring greater involvement from the voluntary sector;

- engaging in more co-operation with other authorities, regions and agencies;

- working with Supporting People authorities; and

- taking a more multi-agency approach.

Much of the material in the Policy Briefing was taken forward into the content of the July 2006 edition of the English *Code of Guidance for Local Authorities*.

7.67 Since the Code, the CLG has published *Preventing Homelessness: A Strategy Check-list*,[80] which will have been used by local housing authorities in preparing their new strategies in 2008. There was no attempt by CLG to repeat in 2008–2009 its earlier exercise of calling in, for review and evaluation, the individual strategies of English local housing authorities.

---

[79] ODPM, November 2004, at http://www.communities.gov.uk/publications/housing/home lessnessstrategiesmoving.

[80] CLG, September 2006, at http://www.communities.gov.uk/publications/housing/preventing homelessness.

7.68 The remainder of this chapter will outline the detailed legal duties imposed on local housing authorities in relation to reviews and local homelessness strategies, the powers given to them, and the guidance that has been provided. All statutory references in this chapter, unlike the rest of this book, are to the Homelessness Act 2002 (and not to the Housing Act 1996) unless specifically stated.

7.69 To avoid confusion, it is necessary to emphasise that a local 'Homelessness Strategy' is not the same thing as a local 'Housing Strategy'. The latter is required by the terms of any direction made under the Local Government Act 2003 and is beyond the scope of this book. However, the English Code does suggest that the two strategies may be combined in one document where 'it is consistent to do so'.[81] Indeed, Annex 2 of the English Code lists no fewer than 25 other strategies and programmes that may address homelessness and with which the local homelessness strategy may need to interface.

A power or a duty to have local reviews and strategies?

7.70 Strictly speaking, HA 2002 gives power to local housing authorities to carry out homelessness reviews for their districts and to formulate and publish homelessness strategies based on the results of those reviews.[82]

7.71 However, HA 2002 also set out mandatory time-scales for the publication of the first local homelessness strategies and of further strategies thereafter. It thereby converted the *power* to formulate and publish the strategy into a *duty*.[83]

7.72 The intention is that strategies will follow the local homelessness review. Homelessness strategies are defined as being 'based on the results of that review'.[84] It follows that local housing authorities are under a *duty* both to conduct reviews and to formulate and publish strategies.

A power or a duty to have regard to the local strategy?

7.73 Once the strategy has been published, the local housing authority is under a *duty* to take its content into account when exercising its homelessness functions or, indeed, any of its other statutory functions.[85] The strategy should therefore inform, for example, a local housing authority's allocation policy as well as the decisions on any individual homelessness application.

---

81   English Code, para 1.2.
82   Homelessness Act 2002, s 1(1).
83   HA 2002, s 1(3) and (4).
84   HA 2002, s 1(1)(b).
85   HA 2002, s 1(5), further discussed at **7.174–7.176.**

7.74   In *R (Ho-Sang) v Lewisham London Borough Council*,[86] an applicant for homelessness assistance, who had not been provided with interim accommodation to which she was entitled, brought a test case challenging the local housing authority's routine and systematic practice of turning away applicants without providing interim accommodation. The judicial review claim cited the local housing authority's homelessness review, which had identified the provision of interim accommodation as being a major problem for the local housing authority, and attacked the homelessness strategy, which only made provision for 50 additional units of temporary accommodation. The local housing authority settled the judicial review claim by conceding that the strategy was inadequate and agreeing to take measures to acquire additional units for interim accommodation (in addition to accepting that it owed the claimant a duty to provide interim accommodation which it would perform).

Duty on social services to co-operate

7.75   In the case of non-unitary authorities, the social services authority is under a duty to give its local housing authority (or authorities) such assistance as the local housing authority (or authorities) may reasonably require with both the carrying out of the local review and the formulation of the homelessness strategy.[87] Examples of the types of assistance that might be required are given in the Homelessness Codes of Guidance for both England and Wales. They range through:

- providing information to the local housing authority, as part of the review process;

- providing financial assistance so as to prevent homelessness; and

- providing support with homeless persons' associated needs.[88]

7.76   Once the exercise has been completed and a local homelessness strategy has been drawn up, the social services authority is under a duty to take the homelessness strategy into account when carrying out its social services functions.[89]

7.77   In the case of unitary authorities, the same obligations apply to the social services department to provide assistance at the strategy design stage and to take account of the strategy in the performance of its own functions.[90]

---

[86]   *R (Ho-Sang) v Lewisham London Borough Council* (2004) CO/5652/03, (2004) July *Legal Action,* p 19, Admin Ct.

[87]   HA 2002, s 1(2).

[88]   English Code, paras 1.6–1.8 and 1.10 and chapters 5 and 13; Welsh Code, para 8.13 and Annex 17.

[89]   HA 2002, s 1(6).

[90]   English Code, para 1.6; Welsh Code, para 8.13.

Duty on registered social landlords to co-operate

7.78 RSLs are under a duty to co-operate with local housing authorities to assist them in performing their functions under HA 1996, Parts 6 and 7, if requested, and so far as is reasonable.[91]

7.79 They would normally expect to be consulted by local housing authorities before homelessness strategies are adopted or modified.[92]

7.80 The *Regulatory Code and Guidance for RSLs*, published by the Housing Corporation, requires RSLs to work with local housing authorities to enable them to perform their duties to the homeless.[93] Specifically, RSLs must be able to demonstrate their co-operation with local housing authorities in homelessness reviews, in formulating homelessness strategies and delivering homelessness functions. If requested, they should make a certain proportion of their stock available for local housing authority nominations and for temporary accommodation for the homeless.[94]

7.81 Both government and the Tenant Services Authority (TSA) (which has replaced the Housing Corporation) are encouraging RSLs to play a more active role in working with local housing authorities to prevent homelessness and to tackle it.[95] The English Code, Annex 5 contains a full account of the extent to which RSLs and local housing authorities are expected to co-operate in addressing homelessness. In early 2006, the Housing Corporation consulted on how to encourage RSLs to help develop local housing authority homelessness strategies. The results of the consultation were published in the then Housing Corporation's *Tackling Homelessness: the Housing Corporation Strategy*.[96] The strategy emphasised that RSLs must fulfil their statutory duty to work with local housing authorities to tackle homelessness and must entrench prevention of homelessness and tenancy sustainment in their work. The Homelessness Action Team established by the Housing Corporation in response to that strategy is now part of the Tenant Services Authority[97].

---

91   HA 1996, ss 170 and 213(1).
92   HA 2002, s 3(8).
93   *Housing Corporation Regulatory Code and Guidance*, August 2005, Principle 3.6, at http://www.housingcorp.gov.uk/server/show/nav.493.
94   HA 1996, s 160A(7)–(9); see **6.62–6.67**.
95   See, for example, *Effective Co-operation in Tackling Homelessness: Nominations and Exclusions* (ODPM, Housing Corporation, Local Government Association and National Housing Federation, November 2004), at http://www.housingcorp.gov.uk/server/show/conWebDoc.3540 and *Homelessness Prevention and Housing Associations – Contributing to Efficiency* (Housing Corporation and Chartered Institute of Housing, April 2006), at www.cih.org/policy/homelessnessbriefing.pdf.
96   Housing Corporation, November 2006 at http://www.housingcorp.gov.uk/server/show/Con WebDoc.9131.
97   See http://www.tenantservicesauthority.org/server/show/nav.13910.

LOCAL HOMELESSNESS REVIEWS[98]

7.82 Since the homelessness strategy must be based on the results of the homelessness review, the review must logically be carried out and concluded first (although in the first round of the exercise in 2003 many local housing authorities published both documents simultaneously, or published their review and strategy within the same document).

7.83 The review is an audit of the local scene in relation to homelessness. It is defined to mean a review of:

(1) the levels and likely future levels of homelessness in the local housing authority's district;[99]

(2) the activities which are carried out in the district for the purpose of preventing homelessness, securing accommodation for people who are or may be homeless, or providing support for those people or for formerly homeless people who need support to prevent them becoming homeless again;[100] and

(3) the resources available to the local housing authority, the social services authority, other public authorities, voluntary organisations and other persons in the district for carrying out these activities.[101]

Each of those aspects will be considered in turn.

What is meant by 'homelessness' for the purposes of conducting the review?

7.84 To be able to assess current and future levels of homelessness with any accuracy, the review must apply the relevant meaning of 'homelessness'. But there can be different interpretations of that concept. Does it mean the likely numbers of applicants to the local housing authority for HA 1996, Part 7 assistance? Or does it have a more practical interpretation, referring to the likely number of people who will be homeless, whether they seek the help of the local housing authority or not? Does it refer simply to literal street homelessness or does it also include those living in temporary or insecure accommodation?

7.85 The English Code advises local housing authorities that they should 'take account of *all* forms of homelessness within the meaning of [Part 7 of] the 1996 Act'.[102] English local housing authorities should not, therefore, consider

---

[98] HA 2002, s 2.
[99] HA 2002, s 2(1)(a).
[100] HA 2002, s 2(1)(b) and (2).
[101] HA 2002, s 2(1)(c).
[102] English Code, para 1.13.

only those applicants towards whom the main housing duty[103] has been accepted in the past, or would be accepted in the future. They should ensure that homeless people who do not have a priority need, or who are or have become or may become intentionally homeless, also fall within the scope of the review. The Codes specifically refer to 'people sleeping rough', as well as 'those who might be more difficult to identify'.[104] The review should therefore consider those who are likely, in future, to have no accommodation that they are entitled to occupy and also those who do have (or will have) accommodation that is not reasonable for them to continue to occupy.

7.86 The Welsh Code contains a different definition of homelessness drawn up by the Welsh Assembly Government –'where a person lacks accommodation or where their tenure is not secure' – and gives examples of the types of people, and the types of accommodation, that would fall within that definition.[105]

7.87 The Welsh approach is much wider than that contained in the English Code, drawing attention to the needs of those in insecure accommodation as well as those who are literally roofless. However, the statutory emphasis (on preventing homelessness, identifying those who might become homeless in the future, and providing support to those who are potentially homeless) should mean that, in practice, English and Welsh local housing authorities are considering the same groups of people when undertaking their reviews.

Current and future levels of homelessness in the local housing authority's district

7.88 The review will need to analyse data on local homelessness in the recent past, on current homelessness, and on likely future homelessness.

7.89 The local housing authority will have its own records and statistics of the number of homelessness applications it has received in the past, and the outcome of those applications. It will also regularly compile returns for the government's national statistics.[106] However, the review should not be confined to those records of past homelessness alone.

7.90 The local housing authority should take into account any information it possesses (or can find with reasonable diligence) on the local homelessness problem. That will include counts or estimates of the numbers of people sleeping rough and estimates of the numbers of people who are staying with family or friends on a temporary or insecure basis. The local housing authority

---

103   HA 1996, s 193. See **17.21–17.110**.
104   For a discussion on the definition of homelessness contained in HA 1996, ss 175–177, see Chapter 11 of this book. See further English Code, paras 1.13–1.18; Welsh Code, paras 8.10–8.12.
105   Welsh Code, para 8.10.
106   *Statutory Homelessness Quarterly Statistics* (Department for Communities and Local Government), at http://www.communities.gov.uk/housing/housingresearch/housingstatistics/housingstatisticsby/homelessnessstatistics/. See also **7.12**.

can also consider its own records of the numbers (and outcomes) of possession proceedings it has brought, and the records held by the local court and by local RSLs. Local advice agencies may hold records and statistics on the numbers of clients who seek homelessness or housing advice. Hospitals, prisons, the armed forces, and the National Offender Management Service[107] should all have records of people discharged from their various services who had nowhere to live. Social services departments or authorities should be asked for their records on homeless families with children, young people leaving care and children in need requiring accommodation. Local hostels and refuges should also be asked for records and statistics.[108] This should provide, in its totality, a fairly accurate picture of both past and current homelessness.

7.91 In order to predict *future* levels of homelessness in the district, the local housing authority will need to identify those groups of people most likely to be at risk of homelessness, the reasons why they might become homeless and the extent to which the supply of affordable accommodation locally is likely to increase or decrease.

7.92 The Codes suggest that young people estranged from their families or leaving care, vulnerable people leaving the armed forces or prison, people exposed to domestic or other violence, vulnerable people with mental health problems, age-related problems or ill health, people with drug and alcohol problems, people with debt problems, and former asylum seekers given permission to stay in the UK, are likely to be amongst those with a higher risk of homelessness.[109]

7.93 Drawing up a 'profile of those who have experienced homelessness' is recommended in the Codes.[110] Such a profile would consider:

- where the person became homeless;

- why;

- the tenure of accommodation from which he or she became homeless;

- his or her personal characteristics, such as ethnic background;

- any institutional or care background;

- age;

- employment or benefits history;

- any specific vulnerabilities;

---

107 Formerly the Probation Service.
108 English Code, para 1.14; Welsh Code, paras 8.64–8.70.
109 English Code, para 1.15; Welsh Code, para 8.78.
110 English Code, para 1.16; Welsh Code, paras 8.71–8.77.

- any health or drug needs;

- the overall composition of the household; and

- other elements.

7.94 Local factors that affect the future levels of homelessness should be considered, such as:

- the extent to which affordable accommodation is available;

- property prices;

- rent levels; and

- supply of accommodation in the private rented sector, from RSLs and from the local housing authority's own stock.

7.95 Broader factors such as:

- the extent of redevelopment and regeneration activity;

- unemployment;

- the strength of the local economy;

- the local population and projected trends in demography;

- the level of migration into and out of the district;

- the flow of itinerant populations such as gypsies, travellers and rough sleepers; and

- the numbers of people likely to be homeless on leaving the armed forces, the care system, prison, hospital or Home Office accommodation

are also relevant.[111]

7.96 The identification of the current and future levels of homelessness in the district is therefore a substantial task, involving social and economic mapping and projections. Bare statistics of current or recent applications for homelessness assistance will certainly not suffice.[112]

7.97 The government-commissioned evaluation of homelessness strategies in 2003 found that many local housing authorities had difficulties in assessing

---

[111] English Code, para 1.17; Welsh Code para 8.80.
[112] See Welsh Code, paras 8.84–8.87 for guidance on analysing issues.

future levels of homelessness. Local housing authorities that tackled the issue well had used: population trends; indicators of needs, demands and aspirations from Housing Needs Surveys; trends in homelessness data; and plans for prevention through, for example, advice to those leaving prison, hospital or care.[113]

Current activities being carried out

7.98　This is the second matter that HA 2002 requires to be considered within the local homelessness review.[114] The required review of activities currently being carried out should not be confined to the activity of the local housing authority's own homeless persons' department or officer(s).

7.99　The current 'activities' to be reviewed are defined as activities for the purposes of:

(1)　preventing homelessness in the local housing authority's district;

(2)　securing that accommodation is or will be available for people who are currently homeless or may become homeless; and

(3)　providing support for those people and for people who were formerly homeless and need support to prevent them becoming homeless again.[115]

7.100　The Codes recommend that the activities, and resources, of a wide range of public authorities and voluntary organisations be considered,[116] but local housing authorities should not confine themselves to those organisations referred to in the Code. They should be considering:

> '... the activities of *all* the various agencies and organisations, across all sectors, which are providing, or contributing to the provision of accommodation, support or relevant services in the district'[117]

including organisations not traditionally associated with housing support such as education or employment organisations, the Samaritans, the police, and faith groups.[118]

7.101　Activities for the prevention of homelessness, for securing accommodation and for providing support to homeless people (or those likely to become homeless) go much further than simply providing a roof over someone's head. They include the 'activities' of giving advice on the availability of benefits and

---

[113]　*Local Authorities' Homelessness Strategies: Evaluation and Good Practice* (ODPM Homelessness Research Summary, Number 1, 2004), at http://www.communities.gov.uk/publications/housing/localauthoritieshomelessness. See also **7.63–7.66**.
[114]　HA 2002, s 2(1)(b).
[115]　HA 2002, s 2(2).
[116]　See English Code, Annex 3; Welsh Code, Annex 18 for indicative lists.
[117]　English Code, para 1.19; Welsh Code, paras 8.81–8.83.
[118]　As set out in Annex 3 to the English Code.

employment, on debt management and on other financial issues. Local housing authorities and social services authorities have statutory powers to provide assistance in the form of rent deposits, rent guarantees and disabled facilities grants for adaptations. The exercise of those powers is a relevant activity. Local charities, or even local businesses, may provide limited financial assistance to the homeless and they too would be relevant 'activities'.[119] The local housing authority should also consider what other 'activities' are being carried out to provide support for the homeless and for those potentially homeless, including support with their other needs, such as health care, education, etc.

Resources currently available for such activities

7.102   This is the third matter that HA 2002 requires to be considered within the local homelessness review.[120] The local housing authority should obviously consider its own resources, and also those available to the social services authority, other public authorities, voluntary organisations and any other persons. Equally obviously, 'resources' in this context means far more than just the financial resources available to tackle local homelessness. The 2006 edition of the English Code places even more emphasis than earlier editions on the importance that government attaches to a move away from the historic local housing authority role as the potential provider of the resources (and, most particularly, homes) for relieving homelessness and into a more modern role of encouraging and facilitating provision by others. The focus has very much shifted from inviting attention to the resources that might be supplied by the local housing authority itself to those which may be marshalled from others in relation to homelessness. As elsewhere in the current Code, the primary emphasis is on those resources which may be directed to homelessness *prevention* in the first instance.[121]

7.103   When it comes to their own resources in relation to prevention, local housing authorities are advised to consider their own infrastructure (staff, administrative costs, etc) and also any resources available to them to provide rent guarantees, or other grants or loans to homeless people or to provide funds or other resources to other organisations working to support homeless people.[122] They should also consider the infrastructure resources available in other public authorities, including the local social services authorities, and, again, any ability those other authorities may have to contribute to the prevention of homelessness or give financial help to the homeless.

---

[119]   For example, some water companies have charitable funds available to relieve arrears of water charges, which could directly help prevent evictions due to arrears of rent.

[120]   HA 2002, s 2(1)(c).

[121]   See English Code, chapters 2–5, Annexes 2–7.

[122]   English Code, para 1.27; Welsh Code, para 8.82.

7.104 The infrastructure provided by voluntary organisations and RSLs should be considered, along with resources available from any other relevant organisations (including charitable organisations or philanthropic activities by private businesses).[123]

7.105 Physical resources available for securing accommodation to those actually homeless obviously include the local housing authority's own housing stock and that of RSLs and private landlords in the district.[124] The availability of hostel and refuge spaces should also be considered. In the English Code, Chapter 3 is directed entirely to the steps that might be taken to ensure a sufficient supply of accommodation locally.

7.106 The mechanisms available to increase the supply of accommodation should be taken into account. These include:

- securing affordable accommodation through planning conditions;

- future developments by RSLs;

- the resources made available by the government to the local housing authority; and

- the extent of new development, self-build homes, shared ownership schemes, etc.[125]

7.107 The local housing authority should consider what initiatives could increase the supply of affordable accommodation. Can the local housing authority increase the proportion of lettings made available by RSLs or that of affordable homes obtained through planning conditions, etc?

7.108 Local housing authorities are advised to take all available steps to identify the housing resources that might be available in their districts.[126] This includes taking the opportunity of filling any empty accommodation in the district.[127] Such a 'strategy for minimising empty homes' should be an integral part of the homelessness review and strategy and should include tackling any hard-to-let properties, bringing empty private sector properties back into use and encouraging landlords to let flats over shops. The local housing authority should consider what financial resources are available that could be used to encourage private homeowners to repair empty properties and make them available for letting. The new powers to take over and manage empty properties[128] should also be considered. 'Resources' for these purposes also includes the resources available to provide 'support' to homeless people, to

---

[123] English Code, para 1.27; Welsh Code para 8.80.
[124] English Code, para 1.27; Welsh Code, para 8.82.
[125] English Code, para 1.28 and chapter 3; Welsh Code, paras 8.91–8.92.
[126] English Code, para 1.28 and chapter 3; Welsh Code, paras 8.91–8.92.
[127] English Code, paras 3.24–3.26.
[128] Given by the Housing Act 2004, ss 132-138.

those likely to become homeless and to those formerly homeless people who need support to prevent them losing their accommodation.[129] This will embrace the availability of housing benefit and other welfare benefits locally, the provision of easily accessible advice, and accommodation with specific levels of support (for elderly people, or substance abusers, young parents, etc).[130] In keeping with the modern policy emphasis on sustainability of new homes for the homeless, the current English Code deals at length with the importance of reviewing resources available locally for 'support', and dedicates a chapter[131] to how support services may be identified and utilised.

Publication and inspection

7.109 Once the review is completed, the local housing authority is required to ensure that the results of the review can be inspected by any member of the public, free, at its principal office.[132]

7.110 It is also required to provide a copy of those results to any member of the public who requests one. The local housing authority may charge a reasonable fee for copying.[133]

7.111 In practice, many local housing authorities make the whole of their review (and strategy) available on their website. Local libraries may provide free internet access enabling these documents to be read online free of charge.

LOCAL HOMELESSNESS STRATEGIES[134]
Overview

7.112 Once the local housing authority has assembled the raw material and completed its review, it can begin to formulate its strategy (or to reconsider an earlier strategy).

7.113 The required content of the local homelessness strategy is defined in HA 2002.[135] The strategy to be formulated by the local housing authority must be a strategy for:

---

[129] HA 2002, s 2(2)(c).
[130] English Code, para 1.29 and chapter 4; Welsh Code, para 8.82.
[131] English Code, chapter 4.
[132] HA 2002, s 2(3)(a). Lewisham London Borough Council was found to have acted in breach of the Freedom of Information Act 2000 when it failed to provide, in response to a request, updated information on material originally published in its homelessness review (Information Commissioner's Office Decision Notice FS50092310, 7 August 2006, (2006) October *Legal Action*, p 25).
[133] HA 2002, s 2(3)(b). See also English Code, para 1.30; Welsh Code, para 8.30.
[134] HA 2002, s 3.
[135] HA 2002, s 3.

(1)   the prevention of homelessness in the local housing authority's district;[136]

(2)   the securing of suitable accommodation for those people in the local housing authority's district who are, or may become, homeless;[137] and

(3)   the provision of satisfactory services to those people in the local housing authority's district who are actually or potentially homeless, including those who used to be homeless and now need support in order to prevent them becoming homeless again.[138]

7.114   The strategy is based on the results of the homelessness review[139] and must identify specific objectives for the local housing authority and specific action as to how the local housing authority aims to achieve those objectives.[140]

7.115   A multi-agency approach[141] enables the local housing authority to identify specific objectives and action, not only for itself, but also for the local social services authority or department.[142] The local housing authority can also identify specific action to be taken by any of the other organisations involved, but only if each organisation agrees to that action being included in the strategy.[143]

7.116   As with the homelessness review,[144] the strategy, once completed, must be made available free for inspection and the public permitted to purchase copies.[145]

7.117   Importantly, both the local housing authority and the local social services authority are required to take the homelessness strategy into account when exercising their statutory functions.[146] Obviously, the local housing authority should take the strategy into account when making decisions on applications for homelessness assistance, or under its allocation scheme. It might also be argued that the local housing authority should take the strategy into account when exercising its housing management functions, for example, in considering whether or not to bring possession proceedings in respect of a property occupied by one of its own tenants.

7.118   The social services authority or department should take the local housing authority's homelessness strategy into account when exercising its functions under the Children Act 1989, so that assistance can be given to

---

[136]   HA 2002, s 3(1)(a).
[137]   HA 2002, s 3(1)(b).
[138]   HA 2002, s 3(1)(c).
[139]   HA 2002, s 1(1)(b).
[140]   HA 2002, s 3(2).
[141]   See **7.124–7.132**.
[142]   HA 2002, s 3(2)(a) and (b).
[143]   HA 2002, s 3(3) and (4).
[144]   See **7.109–7.111**.
[145]   HA 2002, s 3(9).
[146]   HA 2002, s 1(5) and (6).

homeless young people or to homeless families with children. The strategy should also be taken into account when the social services authority or department considers its obligations under community care legislation towards those with mental health needs, drug and alcohol abuse problems, the disabled, and ill or elderly people.[147]

Identification of objectives for the strategy

7.119 The Welsh Code identifies some broad objectives not specified in the statute. It advises that homelessness strategies:

> '... should aim to ensure that there is no need for anyone to become or remain homeless due to a lack of accessible, appropriate and co-ordinated services.'[148]

7.120 There should be 'clear principles' on which strategies will be based. Nine principles are set out that should be included in any strategy.[149] These principles underline the emphasis on prevention of homelessness, tailoring services to meet individual needs, ensuring that services are accessible to a wide variety of homeless people and that the views of homeless people are reflected.

7.121 The Welsh Code further advises that homeless people should be provided with choices, and helped to express their needs and preferences about the type and location of accommodation offered to them.[150] The strategy should be sensitive to the particular difficulties facing homeless people from disadvantaged groups. The needs of ethnic minority groups, lesbian, gay and bisexual people, women, people with disabilities and older homeless people should be particularly addressed.[151] It also recommends that progress on the objectives should be monitored by the use of performance indicators.[152] Examples of the types of specific action that might be taken by other organisations are set out at Annex 17 of the Welsh Code.

7.122 The English Code gives examples of the types of specific objectives and actions that might be included in a homelessness strategy for the local housing authority and the social services authority or department.[153] Annex 6 of the English Code contains examples of the types of specific action that might be expected to be taken by other authorities or organisations.

7.123 Obviously, the strategy must be drawn with relevant consideration of the local housing authority's wider responsibilities in relation to equality and diversity issues. Sadly, in the English Code the advice given on importance of the interface between these issues and the discharge of homelessness functions

---

[147] See Chapter 20 of this book for an outline of some of those powers and duties under which a local authority can provide accommodation.

[148] Welsh Code, para 8.31.

[149] Welsh Code, para 8.32.

[150] Welsh Code, para 8.35.

[151] Welsh Code, para 8.63.

[152] Welsh Code, para 8.37.

[153] English Code, Annex 4.

(including the drawing-up of the strategy) has been set out only in the Introduction,[154] where it is likely to be overlooked.

Consultation and the multi-agency approach

7.124　The local housing authority is required to consult before adopting a homelessness strategy or modifying it.[155] HA 2002 gives the local housing authority a very broad discretion as to which organisations it should consult, being such public or local authorities, voluntary organisations or other persons as it considers appropriate. The English Code offers a list of those with whom an English local housing authority may wish to consult.[156]

7.125　Social services authorities are required to co-operate with the local housing authority to the extent that the local housing authority may reasonably require.[157] Examples of joint working between the local housing authority and social services include joint assessments of homeless families with children, or young applicants for homelessness assistance,[158] as well as the provision of hostels, support services, family reconciliation schemes, mental health support and drug and alcohol support by social services.[159]

7.126　HA 2002 insists upon a multi-agency approach, reaching far beyond the local housing authority or even other public authorities. The local housing authority is required to consider whether any of the objectives can be achieved through joint action with the social services authority or department, with other public authorities, with voluntary organisations or with other people whose activities might contribute to their achievement.[160] The strategy should then identify which of those organisations will take what specific action, either individually or in association with other organisations.[161] The strategy should only identify specific action to be taken by other public authorities if those other authorities or organisations consent to their inclusion.[162]

7.127　The other organisations that should be consulted over the contents of the homelessness strategy, and the extent to which the actions within the strategy can be performed by them, fall into two categories:

(1)　public authorities (other than the local housing authority and social services authority) which have functions that are capable of contributing

---

[154]　English Code, Introduction, paras 7–13.
[155]　HA 2002, s 3(8).
[156]　English Code, para 1.41 and Annex 3.
[157]　HA 2002, s 1(2).
[158]　English Code, para 5.6.
[159]　See English Code, para 5.6 and Annex 6; Welsh Code, para 8.13.
[160]　HA 2002, s 3(5) and (3).
[161]　HA 2002, s 3(3).
[162]　HA 2002, s 3(4).

to the achievement of the objectives of preventing homelessness, securing sufficient accommodation, and securing the satisfactory provision of support;[163] and

(2)   any voluntary organisation or other person whose activities are capable of contributing to the achievement of the objectives.[164]

7.128   Examples of such public authorities, voluntary organisations and other people are listed in the Annexes to the Codes.[165]

7.129   Public authorities whose functions may contribute to the objectives of the homelessness strategy include the health authority and other health organisations, the police, the National Offender Management Service[166], the Benefits Agency, the Home Office, the armed forces, education and employment programmes, etc.

7.130   The voluntary organisations and 'other persons' mentioned in the legislation would obviously include housing advice agencies and citizens' advice bureaux, local RSLs, private landlords and their representative forums. Casting the net wider, youth action groups, refuges, faith groups, victim support groups, refugee organisations, local businesses and the Samaritans are also suggested. Local housing authorities are advised, in the English Code, to consider 'all the organisations and persons working to prevent and alleviate homelessness in the district', public, private and voluntary.[167] In particular, local housing authorities should be entering into 'constructive partnerships' with local RSLs.[168]

7.131   Examples of joint working include multi-agency forums to share information and ideas, and clear protocols and agreements about the referral of clients between services and agencies, so that homeless people are not shuttled between different organisations.[169]

7.132   The government-commissioned evaluation of the initial local housing authority homelessness strategies[170] noted that the involvement of social services at a strategic level tended to be disappointing, and that other statutory agencies, such as health and probation services, were also hard to engage. When those other agencies did play a part, they provided helpful input.

---

[163]   HA 2002, s 3(3)(a).
[164]   HA 2002, s 3(3)(b).
[165]   English Code, Annex 3; Welsh Code, Annex 18.
[166]   Formerly the Probation Service.
[167]   English Code, para 1.39.
[168]   English Code, para 1.36, and Annex 5; Welsh Code, para 8.19.
[169]   English Code, para 1.39, and chapter 5; Welsh Code, Annex 17.
[170]   *Local Authorities' Homelessness Strategies: Evaluation and Good Practice* (ODPM, 2004), at http://www.communities.gov.uk/publications/housing/localauthoritieshomelessness2. See also **7.63–7.66**.

Consulting the homeless

7.133   There is no specific requirement in HA 2002 to consult the former or current users of the local housing authority's services, homeless people, or people who have been or might become homeless. However, the broad discretion given to local housing authorities to consult 'such ... voluntary organisations or other persons as they consider appropriate'[171] certainly permits them to consult both representative forums for the homeless and individual homeless people themselves. The English Code suggests that local housing authorities should consult service users and homeless people.[172] The Welsh Code describes the views of homeless people as 'crucial in developing a successful strategy' and recommends that they should be consulted on their own views of their situation, their needs, their experiences of services, what services work, what barriers there are and what suggestions they have for improvements.[173] The Welsh Assembly Government's *National Homelessness Strategy*, published in 2003 re-iterated that advice:

> 'Responses to homelessness should reflect the views of homeless people, who
> should be encouraged to contribute to the development of appropriate services,
> and enabled to take more control in meeting their own needs.'[174]

7.134   The Welsh Assembly Government has applied that advice to all public services, advising in *Consulting with Homeless People* that homeless people should be, and want to be, consulted over all areas of the public services that they use, including the homelessness service.[175]

7.135   Many local housing authorities have taken the opportunity to consult homeless people in their district. Shelter's review of homelessness strategies noted:

> '... consultation with users has enabled authorities to identify and distinguish
> between the needs of different groups and plan for services which meet their
> particular needs, rather than providing a "blanket" approach to the problem of
> homelessness. Importantly, they have identified the need to adopt a proactive
> approach to tackling homelessness.'[176]

---

[171]   HA 2002, s 3(8).

[172]   English Code, para 1.41 and Annex 3.

[173]   Welsh Code, paras 8.88–8.89, 8.93 and Annex 18.

[174]   *National Homelessness Strategy* (Welsh Assembly Government, March 2003). The more recent *Ten Year Homelessness Plan for Wales* (Welsh Assembly Government, July 2009) does not contain any specific recommendations on drawing up homelessness reviews and strategies, or on consulting homeless people.

[175]   *Consulting with Homeless People* (National Assembly for Wales, August 2004), at http://new.wales.gov.uk/topics/housingandcommunity/housing/publications/consultingwithhomeless?lang=en.

[176]   *The Act in action: an assessment of homelessness reviews and strategies* (Shelter, January 2004), at http://england.shelter.org.uk/shop/publications/reports/research/act_in_action. See also **7.61**.

7.136 The government-commissioned evaluation of initial strategies noted that, in general, local housing authorities found it difficult to engage with homeless people and users of homelessness services. Local housing authorities said to have addressed this problem creatively had gone to speak to homeless people on the street, or gone into hostels or day centres to talk with them.[177]

The three matters the strategy must address

7.137 As already indicated,[178] the legislation requires a local homelessness strategy to address three essential matters: prevention; provision of accommodation; and support.

7.138 Following consideration and evaluation of the first homelessness strategies published in 2003 in England, the opportunity was taken in the 2006 edition of the English Code to expand substantially the advice previously given by government on the content of the strategies. Each of the three essential matters has been addressed with a whole chapter of the new guidance in chapters 2, 3 and 4 of the Code respectively. This material was intended significantly to influence the content of the new strategies that English local housing authorities were required to publish by the summer of 2008.

7.139 The very detailed guidance on the first matter – 'preventing homelessness' – reflects modern policy considerations that are reviewed in a separate chapter of this book.[179]

7.140 Each of the three essential components of a local homelessness strategy is considered in the following paragraphs.

(1) Prevention of homelessness[180]

7.141 This is the first of the three matters that HA 2002 requires the strategy to address.[181] Any strategy to prevent homelessness will obviously include ensuring that general advice and information on homelessness, housing benefit, occupiers' rights, etc is available, and is both comprehensive and effective.[182] The local housing authority has a statutory obligation to ensure that free advice and information on homelessness assistance is available to any person in its district.[183]

---

[177] *Local Authorities' Homelessness Strategies: Evaluation and Good Practice* (ODPM Homelessness Research Summary, Number 1, 2004), at http://www.communities.gov.uk/publications/housing/localauthoritieshomelessness2. See also **7.63–7.66**.
[178] See **7.113**.
[179] See Chapter 8 of this book.
[180] English Code, chapter 2; Welsh Code, paras 8.46–8.50.
[181] See **7.113**.
[182] English Code, chapter 2; Welsh Code para 8.47.
[183] Housing Act 1996, s 182(1).

7.142 The Codes advise local housing authorities to take into account the good practice on homelessness prevention published by the government in *Homelessness Strategies – A Good Practice Handbook*[184] and *Preventing tomorrow's rough sleepers – A Good Practice Handbook*.[185] But surprisingly little emphasis is given to the comprehensive government publication on the subject: *Homelessness Prevention: A guide to good practice*.[186]

7.143 In broad terms, the Codes advise that strategies should recognise the needs of certain groups of people who may be reluctant to contact statutory agencies, such as young people or drug or alcohol abusers, and consider funding voluntary agencies to provide homelessness prevention advice for those groups.

7.144 In order to contribute to homelessness prevention by minimising the number of evictions for rent arrears, the local housing authority itself should aim to have an effective arrears collection policy and should ask local RSLs to ensure that their arrears policies take into account the homelessness strategy's aims.[187] The objective is that all local social landlords should facilitate access to financial and housing advice. The local housing authority is advised to ensure that its housing benefit service is efficient. The Department of Work and Pensions should be asked by local housing authorities to ensure speedy access to severe hardship payments, social fund loans, and the like. The social services authority should be asked by the local housing authority to exercise its functions under the Children Act 1989 to give children, or families with children, financial assistance with deposits, rent payments in advance, and/or rent guarantees. Tenants in financial difficulties should be enabled to obtain local advice to help them manage their finances or negotiate with any creditors.

7.145 The extended guidance in the Codes (and, in particular, chapter 2 of the English Code) offers local housing authorities a range of advice on homelessness prevention initiatives. For example:

- a significant number of applications for homelessness assistance are made by people who have been asked to leave by their parents, relatives or friends.[188] Action to reduce those numbers can include: ensuring that the accommodation provided to the applicant's family is suitable at the outset for the needs of all members of the household; operating mediation and reconciliation services;[189] and providing social services' support for young people;

---

[184]   DTLR, March 2002, at http://www.communities.gov.uk/archived/publications/housing/homelessnessstrategies.

[185]   Rough Sleepers Unit, 2001, at http://www.communities.gov.uk/archived/publications/housing/preventingtomorrowsrough. See also English Code, paras 1.4 and 5.8.

[186]   CLG, June 2006, at http://www.communities.gov.uk/publications/housing/homelessness prevention.

[187]   English Code, para 2.23 and Annex 5, para 13.

[188]   Homelessness statistics in England for 2009 (CLG), at www.communities.gov.uk showed 37% of applicants as coming from this group.

[189]   But see *Robinson v Hammersmith & Fulham London Borough Council* [2006] EWCA Civ 1122,

- mediation schemes can also help with neighbour disputes that might otherwise lead to one of them leaving his or her home and making an application for homelessness assistance; and

- adaptations can ensure that people with disabilities remain in their own homes, rather than having to apply for social services or other accommodation.

7.146 The government-commissioned evaluation of homelessness strategies published in 2003 recommended a number of 'good practice ideas' on prevention.[190] They included:[191]

- refocusing the housing allocation arrangements to reflect the main causes of homelessness, so that an assessment of potential homelessness could be undertaken when someone applies for an ordinary housing allocation;

- improving housing advice services so that there are systems to identify a housing problem and provide advice to prevent homelessness, before an application for homelessness assistance is made;

- mediation schemes to prevent the loss of homes resulting from exclusion by parents, relatives or friends;

- family reconciliation work;

- working with private landlords to develop accreditation schemes;

- improving housing benefit systems so that the payment of housing benefit is speeded up;

- tackling domestic violence and trying to prevent repeat applications for homelessness assistance from victims of domestic violence;

- identifying the triggers for repeat homelessness;

- addressing homelessness for ex-prisoners (by work with prison advice services);

- addressing the needs of vulnerable tenants at risk from crack dealers;

[2007] HLR 7, CA, holding that mediation should not be used to delay inquiries and thus deprive a homeless applicant of a benefit he or she would otherwise have been entitled to. See **8.44, 8.49, 10.61–10.62** and **13.112–13.117**.

[190] Later contained in *Homelessness Prevention: A Guide to Good Practice* (CLG, June 2006), at http://www.communities.gov.uk/publications/housing/homelessnessprevention.

[191] *Local Authorities' Homelessness Strategies: Evaluation and Good Practice* (ODPM, 2004), at http://www.communities.gov.uk/publications/housing/localauthoritieshomelessness2. See also **7.63–7.66**.

- reviewing the rent arrears policies of local RSLs; and

- providing floating support.

7.147 These, and all other relevant local opportunities to prevent homelessness, should be considered and addressed in each local housing authority's homelessness strategy.

(2) Securing that sufficient accommodation is (and will be) available for people who are (or may become) homeless[192]

7.148 This is the second statutory objective of the local homelessness strategy. Its fulfilment is, of course, primarily the responsibility of the local housing authority itself, but RSLs and private landlords should be working with the local housing authority to ensure that the supply of affordable and suitable accommodation is maximised.[193]

7.149 While both Codes of Guidance outline the ways in which accommodation can be secured by local housing authorities in order to meet statutory obligations towards particular homeless applicants for homelessness assistance, the English Code places special emphasis on the role of the local homelessness strategy in enabling a local housing authority to meet likely demand for alternative homes. Chapter 3 of the English Code provides guidance, not only as to how the strategy should address the need to secure an increased supply of new housing (through the distribution of financial aid and by planning measures), but also guidance as to the steps that can be taken to maximise the use of existing housing stock, including:

- maximising use of the private rented sector;

- making best use of existing social housing;

- exercising powers over empty privately-owned property; and

- using Housing Renewal policies and the Disabled Facilities Grant to maximise use of existing dwellings.

7.150 The Welsh Code advises that local housing authorities should aim to minimise the need for people who are owed a duty under HA 1996, Part 7 to spend time in temporary accommodation and, in particular, to avoid the use of bed and breakfast for families with children.[194] Social services authorities should aim to provide supported accommodation for homeless 16- and

---

[192] English Code, chapter 3; Welsh Code, paras 8.51–8.54.

[193] English Code, chapter 3; Welsh Code, para 8.51.

[194] Welsh Code, para 8.52. Avoiding the use of bed and breakfast for families with children (England) and anyone who has a priority need (Wales) is now a statutory requirement; see **16.74–16.75** and **18.93–18.113**.

17-year-olds who need a supported environment.[195] The local housing authority should ensure that there is access to women's refuges, night stop shelters and supported accommodation provided by voluntary organisations for those who need it.

7.151 Both Codes advise local housing authorities to consider the extent to which they can increase the supply of affordable accommodation to homeless, or potentially homeless, people. Examples include:

- bidding for government resources;

- attracting private investment;

- maximising the amount of private rented accommodation available;

- using planning powers to increase the amount of affordable social or private housing;

- using their nomination agreements with RSLs;[196] and

- using their own allocation schemes to provide for homeless people.[197]

7.152 The government-commissioned evaluation of the initial homelessness strategies published in 2003 noted that, in practice, the proportion of lettings by RSLs to homeless households (via the local housing authority) is not always at a significant level.[198]

7.153 The Welsh Code advises that pets may be important to some homeless people, particularly the elderly or those who have slept rough, and that local housing authorities should give careful consideration to being able to provide accommodation that permits homeless people to retain their pets.[199]

7.154 Commenting on this second statutory objective, one judge has said:

'Local authorities such as the defendant may reasonably say that, given the reduction in its housing stock and the pressure of numbers of those seeking accommodation, it is well nigh impossible at present to achieve what is set out in [Homelessness Act 2002] s 3(1)(b). However, it is important to note that Parliament has clearly placed an understandable emphasis upon the need for authorities to take measures to try to avoid homelessness.'[200]

---

[195] See the English Code, Annex 4.
[196] See **6.31–6.48**.
[197] English Code para 1.22; Welsh Code, para 8.51.
[198] *Local Authorities' Homelessness Strategies: Evaluation and Good Practice,* (ODPM, November 2004), at http://www.communities.gov.uk/publications/housing/localauthoritieshomelessness2, para 3.175. See **7.63–7.66**.
[199] Welsh Code, para 4.68.
[200] *R (Aweys) v Birmingham City Council* [2007] EWHC 52 (Admin), [2007] HLR 27, Admin Ct, at [12], per Collins J. The case subsequently reached the House of Lords, but not on this point.

(3) Providing support for people who are (or were, or may be) homeless[201]

7.155   The 'support' envisaged under this third category of matters that must be embraced by the homelessness strategy falls into two sub-categories:

(1)   ongoing support for those who already are, or may soon become, homeless; and

(2)   help for formerly homeless people who need support to stay in their new homes.

7.156   People in the *first* sub-category have a greater need for support than the provision of bare advice or minimal services to prevent homelessness. For these purposes, 'support' can include help with a homeless person's drug or alcohol addiction, or mental health problems. Rough sleepers and those in temporary accommodation should be able to have access to primary health care, to employment opportunities and to education.

7.157   The objectives, and the activities to be carried out, in relation to the *second* sub-category are very similar to those within the prevention of homelessness objective.[202] Obviously, advice should be available, both from the statutory sector and the voluntary sector, to enable occupiers – particularly formerly homeless occupiers – to stay in their homes. Sources of financial and other assistance should be identified and made available.

7.158   Both Codes emphasise joint working with the Supporting People teams established by local authorities.[203]

Publication and inspection

7.159   Once the strategy has been completed, the local housing authority is required to make a copy available at its principal office for inspection at all reasonable hours, free, by any member of the public.[204] It must also provide a copy of the strategy to any member of the public who requests one, and can charge a reasonable fee for doing so.[205] These statutory provisions mirror the general requirement on local authorities under the Freedom of Information Act 2000 to provide such information.[206]

7.160   Since the local housing authority and the local social services authority are both required to take the homelessness strategy into account in the exercise

---

[201]   English Code, chapter 4; Welsh Code, paras 8.55–8.70.
[202]   See **7.141–7.147**.
[203]   English Code, para 4.5; Welsh Code, paras 8.55–8.59.
[204]   HA 2002, s 3(9)(a). See also English Code, para 1.43; Welsh Code, para 8.102.
[205]   HA 2002, s 3(9)(b). See also English Code, para 1.43; Welsh Code, para 8.102.
[206]   In force from 1 January 2005.

of their functions,[207] it should be expected that the strategy will be readily available to housing and social services staff making decisions related to homelessness or to homeless people.

7.161 In practice, many local housing authorities publish the strategy on their websites.

New strategies

7.162 English local housing authorities were required to have published their first statutory homelessness strategies by 31 July 2003 and Welsh local housing authorities by 30 September 2003.[208] By the end of 2003 all local housing authorities had a first strategy in place.

7.163 But homelessness presents a changing landscape. Local housing authorities can keep up to date with the changing local picture by regularly undertaking the homelessness review function.[209] The power to conduct a statutory homelessness review can be exercised at any time.

7.164 Changing circumstances locally, whether identified by a statutory review or otherwise, may require the local homelessness strategy to be re-visited. There is, accordingly, a general statutory duty to keep the strategy under review and a statutory power to modify it from time to time.[210] Local housing authorities may therefore publish modified strategies at any time. Some anticipated that their initial strategies would stand for 3 or more years before requiring reconsideration; others have revisited their strategies earlier than that.

7.165 Before producing a revised or replacement strategy, the local housing authority may conduct another homelessness review and, in any event, must consult those public and local authorities, voluntary organisations and members of the public whom it considers appropriate to be consulted.[211]

7.166 Any modified or replacement strategy must be made available to the public in the same way as the initial strategy.[212]

7.167 The Codes advise that local housing authorities might consider modifying their strategies at various key stages: after they have transferred their housing stock to RSLs; after establishing an ALMO, when new data on homelessness has become available; or when there have been significant changes in the levels or causes of homelessness locally or in homelessness legislation.[213]

---

[207] HA 2002, s 1(5) and (6).
[208] 12 months after the HA 2002 was implemented.
[209] See **7.82–7.111**.
[210] HA 2002, s 3(6).
[211] HA 2002, s 3(8).
[212] See **7.159–7.161**.
[213] English Code, para 1.44; Welsh Code, paras 8.94–8.99.

7.168 At a minimum, a new strategy must be published within 5 years of the publication of the last strategy, although that obligation does not apply to English local housing authorities designated as 'excellent', '4-star' or '3-star'.[214] In effect, therefore, most local housing authorities had updated and published their homelessness strategy by July 2008. Again, before a new strategy is adopted, the appropriate organisations should be consulted. Once the new strategy is adopted, it must be published and made available to members of the public.

7.169 The obligation to keep a homelessness strategy under review and to consult upon necessary modifications to it was considered in *R (Calgin) v Enfield London Borough Council*.[215] The local housing authority had adopted a homelessness strategy in October 2003, but in spring 2004 it adopted a policy for out-of-borough placements of some homeless households without modifying the strategy or consulting upon its modification. In a challenge brought by judicial review, it was contended that this rendered both the strategy and the policy unlawful. The court found that, at the time of adoption of the strategy, an earlier version of the out-of-borough policy had been in place and the strategy had made reference to households placed out of the borough. The new policy was being applied only to a small proportion (1%) of homeless households. In those circumstances, it was held that there had been no unlawfulness in the failure to modify the strategy or consult upon proposed modification. The judge said:

> 'Furthermore it cannot be the case that every variation of each specific policy relating to the homeless and directed to implementing the strategy has to be made the subject of a formal amendment to the strategy document. The time and cost would take valuable resources away from front line services. I accept that in theory the adoption of a major new homelessness policy could involve such a shift from the strategy that a reasonable authority would need to reflect it in a modified strategy and go through the consultation mechanism laid down in the Act.'[216]

Who should draw up the strategies and reviews?

7.170 As already emphasised, the drawing up of the local homelessness strategy and homelessness review is a key task for the local housing authority. These documents will inform all decisions taken by local housing authority officers under HA 1996, Part 7, and will also set out the local housing authority's policy commitments, the extent to which it works in partnership

---

[214] HA 2002, s 1(4); Local Authorities' Plans and Strategies (Disapplication) (England) Order 2005, SI 2005/157, art 3, as amended by the Local Authorities' Plans and Strategies (Disapplication) (England) (Amendment) Order 2009, SI 2009/714; and English Code, para 1.42. The Welsh Code recommends commencing a fundamental review no later than 4 years after the adoption of the strategy: Welsh Code, para 8.100.

[215] [2005] EWHC 1716 (Admin), [2006] HLR 4, Admin Ct.

[216] *R (Calgin) v Enfield London Borough Council* [2005] EWHC 1716 (Admin), [2006] HLR 4, Admin Ct, at [50] per Elias J.

with RSLs, other statutory agencies, voluntarily organisations, and what present and future users of the homelessness service can expect from that service.

7.171 Elsewhere in this book, we discuss the extent to which local housing authorities are permitted to contract out any of the activities that they carry out under HA 1996, Parts 6 and 7.[217] The Local Authorities (Contracting Out of Allocation of Housing and Homelessness Functions) Order 1996[218] only applies to activities carried out under HA 1996, Parts 6 and 7, and not to activities carried out under HA 2002, ss 1–4.

7.172 By HA 2002, s 1, a local housing authority is under a 'duty' to formulate a homelessness strategy, and that homelessness strategy must be informed by the raw data contained in the homelessness review.[219] There are similar duties imposed by HA 2002 on a local housing authority to arrange for its homelessness strategy and its homelessness review to be available for inspection at all reasonable hours, and to provide a copy of those documents on request on payment of a reasonable charge.[220] Any failure to draw up a homelessness strategy would be a breach of the local housing authority's duty.

7.173 It follows, therefore, that the task of formulating the homelessness review and strategy cannot be contracted out. It might be appropriate for a local housing authority to seek assistance in the formulation of those documents from other organisations, such as staff working for RSLs, etc. However, the final content of the homelessness review and strategy should be the local housing authority's decision.

USING THE STRATEGIES AND REVIEWS

7.174 The local homelessness *review* document will contain essential data on the local homelessness (and prevention of homelessness) scene. It will therefore be an invaluable source of data for those providing, or planning to provide, housing-related services in a local housing authority's district. It will also help the local housing authority itself in dealing with the exercise of judgment in individual homelessness cases. For example, in assessing whether a person is 'homeless' or 'has become homeless intentionally' a local housing authority may (for limited purposes) have regard to 'general circumstances prevailing in relation to housing in the district'.[221] The local homelessness review should provide an up-to-date snapshot of those 'general circumstances' for easy reference by officers and advisers alike.

---

[217] See Chapter 21.
[218] SI 1996/3205. See Appendix 1 of this book.
[219] See **7.112–7.114**.
[220] HA 2002, ss 2(3) and 3(9).
[221] HA 1996, s 177(2). See **11.94–11.95** and **14.118–14.120**.

7.175 The local homelessness *strategy* document is an essential additional ingredient in the local housing authority's own work in dealing with individual applications for homelessness assistance and/or housing allocation. For this reason, the strategy document will not contain bland statements of policy objectives, but rather 'action plans' with targets and arrangements for monitoring and evaluation of their attainment.[222] The requirement on local housing authorities to 'take their homelessness strategy into account' makes the strategy document, in effect, a local mini-Code of Guidance.[223] Failure to take the strategy into account where it contains material relevant to a particular decision would potentially render that decision unlawful (for failure to have regard to a relevant consideration). The strategy should certainly help officers who are making decisions about the exercise of discretionary powers (for example, whether to accommodate a non-priority unintentionally homeless applicant) to make decisions which fit with local strategic objectives.[224]

7.176 Both documents will, of course, be relied upon by advisers assisting the homeless. They may well contain material which can be referred to when making representations on behalf of a particular applicant or in making a complaint under the local housing authority's complaints procedure. It might be expected that the Local Government Ombudsman will ask to see copies of the current strategy when investigating homelessness complaints. Indeed, as has already been demonstrated, the review and strategy may well provide material which can be deployed (on both sides) in litigation concerning an individual applicant for homelessness assistance or a local housing authority's policies and procedures on services for the homeless.[225]

---

[222] See, for example, English Code, para 1.40.

[223] HA 2002, s 1(5).

[224] See *R (Seabrook) v Brighton & Hove CC* (2005) CO/5670/2004, (2005) March *Legal Action*, p 23, Admin Ct.

[225] See *R (Ho-Sang) v Lewisham London Borough Council* (2004) CO/5652/03, (2004) July *Legal Action*, p 19, Admin Ct, as an example of such an approach in practice. See also **7.74**.

Chapter 8

HOMELESSNESS PREVENTION

INTRODUCTION

8.1   Since publication of *More than a Roof*[1] in 2002 and of the Welsh Code of Guidance in 2003,[2] the policy of both the central government department overseeing homelessness functions of local housing authorities in England, and of the Welsh Assembly Government, has been to promote work on the prevention of homelessness.

8.2   The policy of 'prevention' has been embraced so enthusiastically by some local housing authorities that it has led to criticism that the true agenda is the prevention of homelessness *applications* rather than of homelessness itself and to accusations of 'gate-keeping'. However, the Department for Communities and Local Government (CLG) hopes that it has found the balance between assisting people to remain in their homes, or to find new homes without an intervening period of homelessness, on the one hand, and ensuring that homeless people and potentially homeless people secure the rights given to them in Housing Act 1996 (HA 1996), Part 7, on the other. Its June 2006 publication *Homelessness Prevention: a good practice guide*[3] was intended to help local housing authorities get that balance right. CLG subsequently published an evaluation of prevention practices by English local housing authorities in December 2007: *Evaluating Homelessness Prevention.*[4]

HISTORY OF PREVENTION POLICY

8.3   In *More than a Roof*, the then Department of Transport and Local Government (DTLR) emphasised the complex reasons why people may become homeless:

> 'Housing supply is important in preventing homelessness but there are "people" factors in addition to "place" factors that must feature more in the way Government and its partners work. Homelessness is as much a manifestation of social exclusion as it is of housing market failures.'[5]

8.4   *More than a Roof* noted that homelessness should not be considered as a condition only experienced by those people recognised as statutorily homeless, ie those who make applications for homelessness assistance under HA 1996, Part 7, and who are accepted as having a priority need and as being not intentionally homeless. Nor are the non-statutorily homeless to be confined to the visible category of 'rough sleepers'. The report suggested that research, and

---

[1]   *More than a Roof: a Report into Tackling Homelessness* (DTLR, March 2002).
[2]   *Code of Guidance for Local Authorities on Allocation of Accommodation and Homelessness* (Welsh Assembly Government, April 2003), chapter 10 (see the Welsh Code on CD-ROM).
[3]   CLG, June 2006, at http://www.communities.gov.uk/publications/housing/homelessness prevention.
[4]   Pawson, Netto, Jones, Wager, Fancy and Lomax (CLG, December 2007), at http://www.communities.gov.uk/publications/housing/preventhomelessness.
[5]   *More than a Roof: a Report into Tacking Homelessness* (DTLR, March 2002), chapter 2.

the compilation of statistics about the causes of homelessness, was required. The basic categories used at that time in data recording the causes of homelessness, such as 'excluded by family or friends' or 'loss of assured shorthold tenancy', were to be broken down into more detail. In particular, vulnerable people leaving institutions (such as prison, hospital or care), and young people leaving home were recognised as people who might need positive help with finding homes, if homelessness was to be prevented.

8.5   Local housing authorities were encouraged to adopt a partnership and 'joined-up government' approach, working with other statutory services, particularly social services, and with the voluntary sector and other institutions, to tackle the causes of homelessness and the supply of accommodation. Emphasis was laid on helping people to remain in their present homes, or to accomplish a smooth transition between the loss of one home and the acquisition of another. Local housing authorities were to consider strategies to help tenants, particularly those in financial difficulties, sustain their tenancies. Housing benefit services should be improved. Local housing authorities were encouraged to consider landlord-tenant mediation schemes, in the hope of ameliorating any conflicts that could otherwise lead to a tenant's eviction. Homeowners facing mortgage arrears could be given financial help. Increased information and advice services for both tenants and homeowners were recommended.

8.6   *More than a Roof* realistically acknowledged that the causes of homelessness are much wider than the lack of housing supply (although the decline in the number of homes in the social housing sector was acknowledged as one of the reasons). Poverty, unemployment, drug addiction, and mental health problems were all among the complex causes of homelessness. 'Joined-up government', partnership approaches and the DTLR's (then) new scheme of 'Supporting People'[6] could help by providing medical services, support with addiction, education, training and employment schemes.

8.7   The DTLR recommended a twin-track approach of increasing the supply of social housing ('affordable housing', principally through the then Housing Corporation funding of Registered Social Landlords (RSLs)) and the increased use of the private rented sector. Rent deposit schemes were to be encouraged, as were 'accredited landlord' schemes.

8.8   Many of the recommendations in *More than a Roof* were already part of the Homelessness Bill 2002, making its way through Parliament at the time. The categories of vulnerable people who had a priority need were extended in the Homelessness (Priority Need for Accommodation) (England) Order 2002.[7] The new Homelessness Act 2002 obliged local housing authorities to draw up

---

[6]   See www.spkweb.org.uk/.

[7]   SI 2002/2051, applicable to English local housing authorities (reproduced at Appendix 2). The Welsh Assembly Government had passed the Homeless Persons (Priority Need) (Wales) Order 2001, SI 2001/607 (W 30) over a year earlier on 27 February 2001 (reproduced at Appendix 3). See **13.106–13.171**.

homelessness reviews and strategies, carrying out the statistical analysis recommended by *More than a Roof* and working with other agencies, statutory and voluntary, to deliver advice and information, and services for 'preventing homelessness in their district'.[8] By the end of 2002, prevention was firmly on the agenda.

8.9   The Welsh Assembly Government published *The prevention of homelessness: an advice note* in August 2004.[9] The document was aimed at the voluntary sector, not at local housing authorities. Drawing on research from elsewhere in the United Kingdom, and from the United States, Germany and Australia, it stressed the importance of early intervention in order to prevent homelessness. It identified six particularly vulnerable groups of people who would benefit from advice tailored to their needs:

- young people;

- households at risk of homelessness through anti-social behaviour;

- those suffering from mental health problems;

- ex-offenders;

- long-term homeless people; and

- drug users.

The main recommendations were:

- increased use of rent in advance and deposit schemes to access the private rented sector;

- offering mediation between families, neighbours, and landlords and tenants; and

- providing long-term support to assist vulnerable people to maintain tenancies.

8.10   In England, the government's national housing strategy, *Sustainable Communities: Homes for All*[10] and its national homelessness strategy, *Sustainable Communities: Settled Homes; Changing Lives*,[11] both published in early 2005, emphasised:

---

8   Homelessness Act 2002, ss 1–4; see **7.46–7.173**.

9   See   http://new.wales.gov.uk/topics/housingandcommunity/housing/publications/preventhome less?lang=en.

10   ODPM, January 2005, at http://www.communities.gov.uk/archived/general-content/housing/ homesforall2005/; see **7.9–7.10**.

11   ODPM, March 2005, at http://www.communities.gov.uk/publications/housing/sustainable communitiessettled2; see **7.9–7.15**.

- an increase in use of the private rented sector;

- financial assistance for tenants;

- mediation schemes between landlord and tenant or, more commonly, family mediation schemes; and

- identification of possible homelessness at an early stage, so as to allow for intervention to prevent homelessness.

They also set an ambitious target: to halve the then number of homeless households in temporary accommodation by 2010.

8.11 These policy statements were underscored in April 2005 by the announcement of two Best Value Performance Indicators relevant to homelessness prevention: *BV 213 Housing Advice*, intended to measure the effectiveness of housing advice in preventing homelessness; and *BV 214 Repeat Homelessness*, intended to monitor the proportion of households accepted as statutorily homeless who are repeat applicants, having been accepted as statutorily homeless by the same local housing authorities within the preceding 2 years. A third BVPI, *BV 225 Actions Against Domestic Violence*, was intended to assess the overall provision and effectiveness of local housing authority services designed to help victims of domestic violence and prevent further domestic violence. BVPIs were replaced by 'national indicators' in April 2008. National Indicator (NI) 156 requires local housing authorities to maintain data on the number of households in their districts living in temporary accommodation.[12]

8.12 Between September and November 2005, the then Office of the Deputy Prime Minister (ODPM)[13] carried out a survey of all English local housing authorities to assess the progress of their work on prevention. Its findings were published in December 2005 in the ODPM's 13th Policy Briefing, *Homelessness Prevention.*[14] All but one local housing authority ran at least one prevention scheme, most having a range available. The most popular schemes were rent deposit or bond schemes, so that potentially homeless households could be helped to obtain private sector rented accommodation. Mediation schemes were also commonly offered. Other methods of homelessness prevention included providing advice and assistance for money and debt problems, mediating between landlord and tenant and offering existing temporary accommodation to homeless households as an allocation under HA 1996,

---

[12] *National Indicators for Local Authorities and Local Authority Partnerships: Handbook of Definitions* (CLG, April 2008), at www.communities.gov.uk/publications/housing/sustainablecommunitiessettled2.

[13] The government department responsible for housing and homelessness in England between 2003 and 2006.

[14] ODPM Policy Briefing No 13 *Homelessness Prevention*, December 2005, now at http://www.communities.gov.uk/publications/housing/surveyenglish.

Part 6, or as a qualifying offer of an assured shorthold tenancy.[15] Choice based lettings, allowing potentially homeless households to bid for and be allocated properties in the social housing sector before they became homeless, also helped reduce the number of homeless acceptances. Local housing authorities were reported to be enthusiastic about prevention, partly because they anticipated budget savings if they reduced the number of households in temporary accommodation.

8.13 The responses of local housing authorities suggested that not all offers of help to prospectively homeless households were enthusiastically received. For example, offers to pay rent deposits were being refused because households found that they could not afford high private sector rents, even with help, or because properties were not available. Offers to assist with family mediation were even more commonly refused. The local housing authorities surveyed displayed a degree of cynicism about the reasons for refusal: a determination to obtain social housing was seen as one of the reasons.

8.14 Some critical reports of local housing authority practice on prevention have emerged, notably the Welsh Public Services Ombudsman's report *Housing Allocations and Homelessness: A Special Report by the Local Government Ombudsman for Wales*.[16] The Public Services Ombudsman found that too many local housing authorities were refusing to accept applications for homelessness assistance, failing to conduct inquiries or issue decisions and failing to inform homeless applicants (and applicants to their allocation schemes) of their statutory rights. The findings were particularly ironic, given that a report just 6 months earlier had castigated some Welsh local housing authorities for permitting too many homelessness acceptances (by recognition of the main housing duty) and for not implementing the prevention agenda.[17] Since the publication of the *Special Report*, the Public Services Ombudsman has found both Cardiff City Council and Conwy County Borough Council guilty of maladministration for failing to recognise the trigger for homelessness applications.[18]

8.15 The Welsh Assembly Government's *Ten Year Homelessness Plan for 2009–2019*[19] has 'preventing homelessness' as its first strategic aim, to achieve the overall goals of reducing homelessness to a minimum in 2019 and

---

[15] See **17.92–17.97**.

[16] February 2006, at http://www.ombudsman-wales.org.uk/en/publications/?pID=76. See **7.23–7.24**.

[17] See *Report to the Welsh Assembly Government on Tackling Homelessness – Key issues for consideration by Welsh Local Authorities* (Tarki Technology Ltd, June 2005), at http://new.wales.gov.uk/topics/housingandcommunity/housing/publications/tacklinghomelessness?lang=en. See **7.20**.

[18] 'Public Services Ombudsman for Wales investigation into Cardiff CC 200600749, 16 April 2008' (2008) June *Legal Action*, p 32, and 'Public Services Ombudsman for Wales investigation into Conwy CBC 200702044, 11 December 2008' (2009) April *Legal Action*, p 22. See **8.52** and **9.51**.

[19] Welsh Assembly Government, July 2009, at http://new.wales.gov.uk/topics/housingandcommunity/housing/publications/homelessnessplan/?lang=en. See also **7.27–7.31**.

eliminating rough sleeping. It encourages housing advice and early intervention, before an existing home has been lost. In the private rented sector, local housing authorities should work with private landlords so that those landlords might be encouraged to let to people traditionally seen as vulnerable and 'high risk'. Housing benefits payments should be made quickly, accurately and promptly. There should be more financial and debt advice available. In the social housing sector, there should be more help to assist tenants to sustain their tenancy and possession should only be pursued as a last resort.

8.16 The Welsh Assembly Government wants there to be comprehensive advice and assistance available to consumers before they purchase their homes and enter into mortgage commitments. It also wants to see improvements in regulation and enforcement, so that the courts only approve possession actions when lenders have explored all other options, to explore the possibility of regulation for private sale and leaseback schemes, and to develop a protocol between lenders and local housing authorities so that lenders would notify local housing authorities' homelessness prevention teams, presumably in advance of any possession claim being issued.

8.17 The emphasis on the Plan on 'prevention' makes no specific reference to the concerns raised by the Public Services Ombudsman for Wales.

8.18 Investigation reports from the English Local Government Ombudsmen added to the general concern that, in their enthusiasm for preventing homelessness, local housing authorities might not be allowing homeless people, or, more often, potentially homeless people to make applications for assistance under HA 1996, Part 7.[20] In other words, they were not applying the statutory test at HA 1996, s 183(1):

> 'the following provisions of this Part apply where a person applies to a local housing authority for accommodation, or for assistance in obtaining accommodation, and the authority have reason to believe that he is or may be homeless or threatened with homelessness.'[21]

8.19 The English government department was sufficiently concerned at reports of bad practice for the then Minister for Housing to write to all English local housing authorities on 12 April 2006 reminding them that reductions in homelessness numbers were to be achieved through more effective help, but not through 'a gate-keeping approach that discourages people from applying for housing assistance'.[22]

---

[20]   For example, 'LGO reports Blackpool Borough Council 03/C/373 and London Borough of Barnet 04/A/9817', at www.lgo.org.uk.

[21]   See **9.50–9.53**.

[22]   Minister for Housing and Planning 'Letter to Chief Housing Officers, English local housing authorities', 12 April 2006; see Appendix 2 of this book.

CURRENT GUIDANCE

8.20 In June 2006, the CLG published *Homelessness prevention, a guide to good practice*,[23] bringing together all the various policy initiatives and guidance since *More than a Roof*. The advice was then supplemented by chapter 2 and Annex 7 to the new English Homelessness Code of Guidance published in July 2006.[24] The CLG has also published guidance on specific aspects of prevention: *Prevention of Homelessness – the role of health and social* care,[25] and *Joint Working between Housing and Children's Services, preventing homelessness and tackling its effects on children and young people.*[26] An evaluation of local housing authorities' prevention activities was published in December 2007: *Evaluating Homelessness Prevention.*[27]

8.21 In response to the recession, the CLG introduced a 'mortgage rescue' scheme for use by English local housing authorities in January 2009.[28] People who have a priority need[29] and whose household earns less than £60,000 a year may apply to their local housing authorities for help. The help comes in the form of a shared equity loan, whereby an RSL pays a proportion of the mortgage in return for a share of the equity, or an outright purchase by an RSL on terms that the homeowner continues to occupy the property as a tenant.[30] It has also provided additional money in the 2009 budget to help families at risk of homelessness through repossession or eviction.[31] A *Short Guide from Regional Resource Teams to Local Authorities on how to Prevent Homelessness due to Mortgage and Landlord Repossession* was published in April 2009.[32]

---

23 CLG, June 2006, at http://www.communities.gov.uk/publications/housing/homelessness prevention.
24 *Homelessness Code of Guidance for Local Authorities* (Department for Communities and Local Government, Department for Education and Skills, Department of Health, July 2006) (English Code) at Appendix 2 of this book.
25 CLG, Department of Health and the Housing Learning and Improvement Network, May 2007, at http://www.dhcarenetworks.org.uk/IndependentLivingChoices/Housing/Topics/browse/Homelessness/index.cfm?parent=980&child=1985.
26 CLG and Department for Children, Schools and Families, May 2008, at http://www.communities.gov.uk/publications/housing/goodpracticeguide.
27 Pawson, Netto, Jones, Wager, Fancy and Lomax (CLG, December 2007), at http://www.communities.gov.uk/publications/housing/preventhomelessness.
28 See http://www.direct.gov.uk/en/HomeAndCommunity/Keepingyourhomeevictionsandhome lessness/Mortgagesandrepossessions/DG_174005.
29 See Chapter 13 of this book.
30 By the end of June 2009, 1,321 households had approached English local housing authorities and been assessed as eligible for help under this scheme. Only 14 had progressed as far as to receive and accept an offer from an RSL. Other households were waiting for the RSL to decide whether to make an offer, or the threat of possession had been resolved by advising and assisting the households. See http://www.communities.gov.uk/publications/corporate/statistics/mortgagerescuestatistic.
31 See http://www.communities.gov.uk/housing/homelessness/tacklingpreventing/.
32 And is, surprisingly, only available on the web at http://www.solihull.gov.uk/akssolihull/images/att19880.pdf.

8.22 The Welsh Assembly Government funds a similar mortgage rescue scheme for Welsh homeowners in difficulties.[33] A scheme for the whole of the UK, 'Homeowners Mortgage Support', involves the government encouraging lenders to delay some of the monthly interest payments due on a mortgage.[34]

8.23 The CLG also encourages local housing authorities to work closely with private landlords, and particularly to give incentives to private landlords to rent properties to low income households.

8.24 For RSLs, the Tenant Services Authority (TSA) has a Homelessness Action Team[35] which publishes the Homelessness Toolkit, a template Homelessness Action Plan and monthly Homelessness Action Team Updates. RSLs are encouraged to work in partnership with local housing authorities to prevent homelessness and to take steps themselves to identify possible homelessness and try to prevent it.

Homelessness Prevention: a guide to good practice

8.25 The non-statutory Good Practice Guidance[36] defines homelessness prevention as 'activities that enable a household to remain in their current home, where appropriate, or that provide options to enable a planned and timely move and help to sustain independent living'.[37]

8.26 The approach is consistent with *More than a Roof* and subsequent policy documents. The financial as well as the social cost of homelessness is emphasised,[38] as is increased use of the private sector and offering 'choice' in housing options, principally by encouraging geographical mobility.

8.27 The Good Practice Guidance reviews the activities undertaken by local housing authorities with the aim of homelessness prevention. The six most common prevention practices are:

- provision of housing advice;

- rent deposit schemes;

- family mediation;

- domestic violence victim support;

33 See http://new.wales.gov.uk/topics/housingandcommunity/housing/private/buyingandselling/mortgagerescue/?lang=en.
34 See http://www.direct.gov.uk/en/HomeAndCommunity/Keepingyourhomeevictionsandhomelessness/Mortgagesandrepossessions/DG_177639.
35 At http://www.tenantservicesauthority.org/server/show/nav.13910.
36 *Homeless Prevention: a guide to good practice* (CLG, June 2006), at http://www.communities.gov.uk/publications/housing/homelessnessprevention.
37 *Homelessness prevention*, para 2.2.
38 *Homelessness prevention*, appendix 3: 'The wider costs of homelessness'.

- assistance for ex-offenders; and

- tenancy sustainment services.

8.28   The Guidance concentrates on the same areas and is couched in fairly familiar terms: recommending rent deposits and rent guarantees schemes; home visits and mediation; keeping records; liaison with local private sector and voluntary sector landlords. For a solution to constitute 'prevention', it must be 'durable for at least six months'.[39]

8.29   It criticises local housing authorities for focusing prevention schemes mainly on households judged potentially in priority need, in other words those more likely to be entitled to statutory assistance. It emphasises that prevention services should be offered irrespective of any potential priority need.[40] Prevention is not solely intended to reduce the number of households being accepted as statutorily homeless.

8.30   The involvement of the private rented sector is stressed, along with the need to lower applicants' expectations. A 'housing options interview' is recommended in order to avoid 'any initial assumption that a social rented tenancy is necessarily the most appropriate solution'.[41]

8.31   Early intervention is seen as good practice: interviewing a potentially homeless person at an early stage and exploring all the options to retain a tenancy, or obtain another one. The appraisal of current housing circumstances should provide enough information 'to assess whether there is reason to believe the applicant is homeless or threatened with homelessness – and therefore eligible for a formal homelessness assessment',[42] so emphasising the importance of not using prevention to avoid the statutory homelessness procedure. Housing advice and assessment could include home visits, particularly where young people have been asked to leave by family or friends. Local housing authorities should consider targeting their homelessness prevention services, so as to best address the main causes of homelessness locally. Maintaining records of each approach to a local housing authority is key to ensuring that prevention services are being delivered.

8.32   Local housing authorities should work with private landlords, and encourage them to contact local housing authorities to help resolve problems that would otherwise lead to eviction.[43] It remains to be seen how many private landlords will be willing to co-operate, when they have the legal ability to evict a tenant with those problems and to re-let the property to a tenant potentially less problematic (eg one who is not dependent on housing benefit, or one more

---

[39]   *Homelessness prevention,* para 2.39.
[40]   Somewhat ironically, the CLG later fashioned its mortgage rescue scheme entirely by reference to priority need; see **8.21**.
[41]   *Homelessness prevention,* para 2.10.
[42]   *Homelessness prevention,* para 2.12.
[43]   *Homelessness prevention,* chapter 3.

likely to pay his or her rent on time). Advice and assistance should also be made available to vulnerable people who need help with navigating choice based lettings systems.[44]

8.33 A chapter is devoted to financial assistance[45] and another to sustaining tenancies.[46] Rent deposit and grant schemes should be used as a lever to persuade landlords to offer assured shorthold tenancies for longer than the usual 6-month fixed term. Applicants who have been assessed as being owed one of the duties under HA 1996, Part 7 could be offered rent deposits and assured shorthold tenancies rather than waiting for an offer of a secure or assured tenancy under HA 1996, Part 6.[47] Private landlords should be approached to agree that rents will be set at no higher than housing benefit limits, and consideration should be given to making discretionary housing benefit payments available where there is a shortfall between rent and housing benefit limits.

8.34 Three chapters deal with particular prevention work with beneficiaries of some of the newer categories of priority need: young people; victims of domestic violence; and ex-offenders.[48]

8.35 When it comes to young people facing homelessness, family mediation schemes are recommended.[49] The Guidance warns local housing authorities to be alert to collusive arrangements, whilst also ensuring that they respond appropriately to the genuinely homeless young person. The warning against collusive arrangements runs the very real risk that young people are turned away by local housing authorities, are offered family mediation schemes but nothing else, or are found to have become homeless intentionally (because they refused mediation, or where the mediation is unsuccessful).[50]

8.36 Victims of domestic violence should be given assistance to remain in their homes where possible.[51] It is to be hoped that this does not result in local housing authorities insisting that a person who complains of domestic violence

---

44 See the criticisms by Shelter in *A Question of Choice: Good practice and issues in choice-based letting* (Shelter, June 2005), at http://england.shelter.org.uk/shop/publications/good_practice/reports/a_question_of_choice. And see **5.13**.
45 *Homelessness prevention*, chapter 4.
46 *Homelessness prevention*, chapter 8.
47 A 'qualifying offer' under HA 1996, s 193(7B). See **17.92–17.97**.
48 Homelessness (Priority Need for Accommodation) (England) Order 2002, SI 2002/2051, arts 3, 4, 5(e) and 6. See **13.107–13.143**, **13.165–13.171** and **13.158–13.164** and Appendix 2 of this book. Homeless Persons (Priority Need) (Wales) Order 2001, SI 2001/607 (W 30), arts 3, 4, 5 and 7. See **13.172–13.184**, **13.185–13.190** and **13.196–13.202** and Appendix 3 of this book.
49 *Homelessness prevention*, chapter 5.
50 See *Robinson v Hammersmith & Fulham London Borough Council* [2006] EWCA Civ 1122, [2007] HLR 7, CA, where the Court of Appeal said that, while 'reconciliation and mediation are obviously to be encouraged, indeed more than to be encouraged', 'it cannot be right that an authority can persuade a family into mediation while a child is 17 and then use the time that the mediation would take to deprive the child of a right that it would have had without mediation', per Waller LJ at [39] and [41]. See **8.44**, **8.49**, **10.61–10.62** and **13.112–13.117**.
51 *Homelessness prevention*, chapter 6.

should be required to take legal remedies to exclude the abuser.[52] Those who leave their homes should be supported to move to independent or settled housing quickly, so as to minimise disruption of benefits, schooling and employment.

8.37 Homelessness prevention schemes operating from prison should be expanded, so as to plan for a prisoner's release.[53] Difficulties include the loss of the prisoner's tenancy during the sentence of imprisonment, the loss of family support and the frequent moves between prisons, as well as the vulnerable nature of the ex-offenders themselves. Saving existing tenancies by working to maximise housing benefit and tackle rent arrears is emphasised, along with making applications for new accommodation from prison, before a prisoner's release date. In reality, many prisoners who lose their accommodation whilst in prison, and then make applications as homeless, are likely to be found intentionally homeless.[54] Unfortunately, this Guidance does not discourage local housing authorities from that practice.

8.38 As the Guidance warns, homelessness has both a social cost[55] and a direct financial cost for each local housing authority.[56] The challenge for local housing authorities is to ensure that their understandable eagerness to avoid both types of costs does not lead them to turn a blind eye when they are approached by someone whom they have 'reason to believe ... may be homeless or threatened with homelessness',[57] and who is therefore entitled to make an application for homelessness assistance and have it determined under HA 1996, Part 7.

Prevention in the English Code of Guidance

8.39 The high-point of the new emphasis on prevention was achieved with publication in July 2006 of the current edition of the English Homelessness Code of Guidance. The previous edition had dealt with 'prevention' relatively briefly, but the current edition devotes a substantial chapter (Chapter 2) to the subject, together with a very full annex (Annex 7) almost exclusively directed to homelessness prevention as applied to tackling the most common causes of homelessness. The content of the Code reflects the issues discussed at **8.25–8.38**.

---

52   Such a practice is contrary to the provisions of HA 1996, s 175(3) and s 177(1), which require local housing authorities only to ask whether it is probable that continued occupation would lead to violence or threats of violence that are likely to be carried out (*Bond v Leicester City Council* [2001] EWCA Civ 1544, [2002] 34 HLR 6, CA); see **11.78–11.88**.

53   *Homelessness prevention,* chapter 7.

54   *Stewart v Lambeth London Borough Council* [2002] EWCA Civ 753, [2002] 34 HLR 40, CA. See **14.217–14.218**.

55   *Homelessness prevention,* appendix 3.

56   *Homelessness prevention,* paras 2.49–2.62.

57   Section 183(1). See **9.8–9.71**.

Prevention in the Welsh Code of Guidance

8.40   The Welsh Code of Guidance, published in 2003, has a specific chapter (chapter 10) on the prevention of homelessness. It addresses common problems that lead to people losing their homes, and how those can be prevented. Eviction 'should only be sought as a last resort, particularly by social landords'. Advice is given on monitoring and reducing rent arrears, so as to reduce possession claims in the social housing sector. In the private rented sector, the Code suggests that local housing authorities are notified in advance of possession claims, so as to allow them to help resolve financial problems, or to provide advice and assistance so that the occupier can remain in their own home, or be helped to find another home. Financial help and advice and assistance may also be available to owner-occupiers facing repossession, although the advice in those paragraphs is out-of-date and reference should be made to the current Mortgage Rescue Scheme operated by the Welsh Assembly Government and the UK-wide Homeowners' Mortgage Support.[58] Other paragraphs deal with advice tailored to certain groups identified as being most at risk of homelessness: armed forces personnel; people with mental health illness or disability; those with substance misuse problems; young people aged between 16 and 25; those experiencing domestic disputes, violence or harassment; hospital patients and prisoners; and people affected by redevelopment or otherwise displaced.

EVALUATING HOMELESSNESS PREVENTION

CLG evaluation

8.41   In December 2007, research commissioned by the CLG was published: *Evaluating Homelessness Prevention*.[59] The research had studied local housing authorities' homelessness prevention activities launched as a result of their homelessness strategies. It found that homelessness prevention work was increasing amongst local housing authorities. To be effective, prevention should be pro-active rather than reactive and aim at resolving applicants' housing problems. The most widely adopted methods of homelessness prevention were:

- enhanced housing advice;

- rent deposit and similar schemes to increase access to private tenancies;

- family mediation schemes;

- domestic violence victim support; and

- help sustaining tenancies.

---

[58]   See **8.20–8.22**.
[59]   Pawson, Netto, Jones, Wager, Fancy and Lomax (CLG, December 2007), at http://www.communities.gov.uk/publications/housing/preventhomelessness.

8.42 The intended beneficiaries of homelessness prevention work included those people who did not have a priority need, as well as those who were likely to be assessed as being homeless and having a priority need. However, the sharp drop in the numbers of homeless applicants who were found to be owed the main housing duty[60] showed that those who did have a priority need were also likely to receive prevention assistance. Prevention was cost-effective, particularly where households who had a priority need were concerned, and also particularly for Greater London local housing authorities (because there were substantial savings in the cost of temporary accommodation). Monitoring of outcomes had been patchy, but, in so far as they could be assessed, the outcomes appeared to have resulted in savings, in that the operating costs were less than the costs of temporary accommodation and administration that would otherwise have been incurred. It is, unfortunately, noticeable that the measure of what is a positive outcome is based on whether or not it is cost-effective, rather than it whether it leads to a secure and affordable roof over a person's head.

8.43 The authors of the report were aware of the criticisms made by housing advisers, and occasionally reiterated in the courts, that homelessness prevention activities can amount to 'gatekeeping' and to an unlawful delay or postponement of inquiries under HA 1996, Part 7. They recommended that local housing authorities should review their procedures and practices to ensure that they are complying with their obligations under HA 1996, Part 7.

8.44 As far as particular areas of homelessness prevention are concerned, enhanced and pro-active housing advice is thought to be cost-effective for those people who would otherwise have made an application for homelessness assistance under HA 1996, Part 7, and be owed the main housing duty. The cost-effectiveness of housing advice to a household that is unlikely to be owed the main housing duty is less clear-cut. Rent deposits and other schemes assisting people to find private tenancies are said to be 'highly cost-effective'. Family mediation schemes are more problematic. The operation of one family mediation scheme was subjected to criticism in *Robinson v Hammersmith & Fulham London Borough Council*.[61] Family mediation can be effective in reconciling relationships. Mediation, where young people are expected by default to participate, needs to be implemented sensitively, in particular where encouraging an applicant to return to his or her former home could place him or her at risk of violence or abuse. For applicants leaving domestic violence, sanctuary schemes had proved effective in preventing homelessness, provided it was recognised that they were not appropriate in every case. Housing advice provided in prison to offenders approaching release was considered effective. There remains a lack of suitable post-release supported and mainstream accommodation for prisoners, and only a few ex-prisoners are likely to be classed as 'vulnerable' and therefore have a priority need.[62] Support to

---

[60]   HA 1996, s 193(2). See **17.21–17.110**.
[61]   [2006] EWCA Civ 1122, [2007] HLR 7, CA. See **8.49**, **10.61–10.62** and **13.112–13.117**.
[62]   The requirement that ex-offenders must also be 'vulnerable' in order to have a priority need

vulnerable tenants to help retain their existing tenancies can be potentially important, but there is insufficient monitoring to be able to assess what works and what does not.

8.45 The authors conclude that, since the number of applicants for homelessness assistance who are found to be owed the main housing duty has declined substantially since 2003, homelessness prevention is a success, even taking into account the economic stability between 2003 and 2006 and other factors that may influence the numbers of applicants for homelessness assistance. Their principal recommendation is that the outcomes of homelessness prevention should be more carefully monitored, so that their effectiveness can be better assessed.

Other commentators on homelessness prevention

8.46 Shelter has published concerns at the use of prevention, whilst supporting the principle of prevention of homelessness. In its *Policy Briefing: Homelessness Prevention*,[63] it comments:

'the current policy framework around homelessness prevention contains certain ambiguities and tensions that must be resolved if suitable prevention is to be achieved. These tensions centre around the relationship between homelessness prevention policy and the statutory safety net provided by homelessness legislation.'

It recommends:

'applicants who are entitled to accommodation as a result of a duty being owed to them under HA 1996, Part 7, should be free to decide to accept that accommodation in addition to any other options being offered to them under homelessness prevention services.'

8.47 Shelter criticises *Homelessness Prevention: A Guide to Good Practice*[64] as suggesting a two-stage process for households that are homeless and likely to be owed the main housing duty, so that options and prevention are considered first, with the homelessness duty acting as a 'safeguard'. The target to halve the number of households living in temporary accommodation by 2010, combined with the shortage of social rented housing, has created a strong incentive for local housing authorities to pursue homelessness prevention as a means of reducing the number of homelessness acceptances. Shelter urges local housing authorities to review their practices. It is concerned that some of the prevention options only provide a short-term response to long-term housing problems.

---

applies to applicants to English local housing authorities only (see **13.158–13.164**) and not to applicants to Welsh local housing authorities (see **13.196–13.202**).

63   Shelter, August 2007, at http://england.shelter.org.uk/professional_resources/policy_library/ policy_library_folder/homelessness_prevention.
64   CLG, June 2006, at http://www.communities.gov.uk/publications/housing/homelessness prevention.

The causes of homelessness – including changes in the legal ability of landlords to obtain possession orders – should be tackled.

8.48 Alongside this general briefing, Shelter has published briefings on particular aspects of homelessness prevention schemes: *Homelessness prevention and the private rented sector*,[65] *Homelessness prevention and sanctuary schemes*,[66] and *Homelessness prevention and mediation*,[67] and its own Good Practice Guide: *Homelessness: Early Identification and Prevention – A Good Practice Guide*.[68]

Prevention in the courts

8.49 The Court of Appeal first considered a local housing authority's use of prevention – in the particular case, family mediation – alongside its statutory duty to an applicant for homelessness assistance under HA 1996, Part 7, in *Robinson v Hammersmith & Fulham London Borough Council*.[69] A homeless 17-year-old girl, approaching her eighteenth birthday, had applied to the local housing authority for homelessness assistance, having been excluded from the family home by her mother. The local housing authority accepted the application, but postponed making its inquiries into whether or not she was homeless, and whether it owed her a duty,[70] while it attempted to set up mediation between the girl and her mother. The Court of Appeal held that it was not legitimate to use mediation to postpone either the making of inquiries or the taking of a decision. Mediation may be used in order to *perform* any duty that is owed to the applicant under HA 1996, Part 7, but not to prevent the duty arising in the first place.[71]

8.50 A more general practice came under scrutiny in *R (Aweys) v Birmingham City Council*.[72] Birmingham City Council operated a policy whereby someone who indicated that he or she might be homeless was required to go through a

---

[65]   Shelter, August 2007, at http://england.shelter.org.uk/professional_resources/policy_library/policy_library_folder/homelessness_prevention_and_the_private_rented_sector.

[66]   Shelter, August 2007, at http://england.shelter.org.uk/professional_resources/policy_library/policy_library_folder/homelessness_prevention_and_sanctuary_schemes.

[67]   Shelter, August 2007, at http://england.shelter.org.uk/professional_resources/policy_library/policy_library_folder/homelessness_prevention_and_mediation.

[68]   Shelter, June 2007, at http://england.shelter.org.uk/professional_resources/policy_library/policy_library_folder/good_practice_guide_homelessness_early_identification_and_prevention.

[69]   [2006] EWCA Civ 1122, [2007] HLR 7, CA.

[70]   See **10.61–10.62**.

[71]   If, for example, the mediation had achieved reconciliation between mother and daughter, the local housing authority could have performed any duty owed to the daughter to accommodate her by securing that accommodation from the mother, or by providing advice and assistance that had secured that the mother's accommodation was available to the daughter (HA 1996, s 206(1)(b) and c)). See **8.53** and **17.28**.

[72]   [2007] EWHC 52 (Admin), [2007] HLR 27, Admin Ct. Birmingham subsequently appealed to the Court of Appeal and to the House of Lords, whose decision, in the name of *Ali & others v Birmingham City Council* is at [2009] UKHL 36, [2009] 1 WLR 1506, HL. The appeal was not against the first-instance judge's findings in relation to the Home Options Interview.

Home Options Interview so that the local housing authority could consider whether homelessness could be prevented or alternative accommodation provided.[73]

8.51 The Administrative Court judge said:

> 'the Home Options Scheme ... cannot lawfully be used to defer consideration of a homeless application. All steps taken to avoid homelessness are of course laudable. But any such steps must be taken in parallel to the carrying out of the duty under Pt VII.'[74]

Ombudsmen reports

8.52 The Ombudsmen for both England and Wales have made the same point. The Local Government Ombudsmen for England have said that alternatives to using the homelessness legislation may be considered by local housing authorities but 'should not be used to set aside the rights and duties conferred by law'.[75] As already noted,[76] the Public Services Ombudsman for Wales has found both Cardiff City Council[77] and Conwy County Borough Council guilty of maladministration for operating schemes similar to that operated in Birmingham, whereby those approaching the councils for homelessness assistance were seen first by housing advisers and were only in some cases referred for a homelessness assessment. In the Conwy County Borough Council investigation, the Ombudsman said:

> '[I]t is possible that the failure to recognise the trigger for homelessness inquiries occurs because emphasis is placed on the council's prevention of homelessness work to such an extent that homelessness inquiries are deferred ... The advice and written information ... could be perceived as seeking to actively dissuade [the complainant and her partner] from seeking assistance from the council with their housing, persuading them instead to look in the private rented sector.'[78]

---

[73] Cardiff County Council operated a similar 'housing *advice*' scheme. The Public Services Ombudsman for Wales found that operation of the scheme had caused undue delay to Mr F, who was homeless or threatened with homelessness and had a priority need. There had been undue delay in addressing his housing problems, a failure to carry out inquiries and a failure to offer temporary accommodation whilst those inquiries were carried out. The Ombudsman recommended that the Council should apologise to Mr F, pay him £1,500, and introduce improved procedural guidance and training for its staff (Public Services Ombudsman for Wales Investigation 200600749, 16 April 2008, at http://www.ombudsman-wales.org.uk/en/investigation-reports-public-interest/?pID=163, (2008) June *Legal Action*, p 32).

[74] *R (Aweys) v Birmingham City Council* [2007] EWHC 52 (Admin), [2007] HLR 27 at [25] per Collins J.

[75] Complaint E8, 04/C/18012, Local Government Ombudsman, Annual Digest of Cases 2006/07, at http://www.lgo.org.uk/publications/digest-of-cases/.

[76] See **8.14**.

[77] Public Services Ombudsman for Wales investigation into Cardiff City Council 200600749, (2008) June *Legal Action*, p 32. See footnote 73.

[78] Public Services Ombudsman for Wales investigation into Conwy County Borough Council 200702044, 11 December 2008, para 67; (2009) April *Legal Action*, p 22, and http://www.ombudsman-wales.org.uk/en/investigation-reports-public-interest/?pID=203.

APPLYING PREVENTION POLICY TO HA 1996, PART 7 DUTIES

8.53 These comments from the Ombudsmen succinctly set out how prevention measures can and cannot lawfully be used in tandem with local housing authorities' statutory duties towards applicants for homelessness assistance under HA 1996, Part 7. Prevention can be used at any stage, but should not be used to avoid or escape the obligations that local housing authorities owe to applicants for homelessness assistance who appear to be, or may be, homeless or threatened with homelessness.[79] Prevention may be used at any time *before* a person in contact with a local housing authority appears to be, or may be, homeless. As soon as that statutory threshold is achieved, prevention can be used at the same time as the obligations under HA 1996, Part 7 are performed. Those obligations are to make inquiries,[80] notify the applicant of a decision,[81] and provide interim accommodation, if appropriate.[82] The local housing authority cannot refuse to undertake these obligations whilst it provides prevention advice and assistance. If, as a result of advice and assistance provided whilst the local housing authority is carrying out its inquiries, the applicant finds his or her own suitable accommodation before the inquiries are concluded, the local housing authority will be entitled to find that the applicant is not homeless and no duty is owed.[83] If the applicant is still homeless (and eligible for assistance), however, a duty will be owed to the applicant, and the local housing authority must perform that duty.

8.54 At that stage, the local housing authority may use the various forms of advice and assistance normally provided under prevention activities in order to perform the duty that it owes to the applicant. Advice may result in the applicant accepting a qualified offer of an assured shorthold tenancy, for example.[84] However, the local housing authority cannot refuse to perform, or delay performing, any duty that it owes to the applicant whilst it requires the applicant to participate in its prevention schemes.

---

[79]   HA 1996, s 183(1). See **9.8–9.53**.
[80]   HA 1996, s 184(1). See **10.1–10.59**.
[81]   HA 1996, s 184(3). See **10.60–10.81**.
[82]   HA 1996, s 188(1). See **9.53** and **16.11–16.24**.
[83]   See **11.1–11.117** for definition of 'homeless' and Chapter 17 of this book for duties owed.
[84]   See **17.92–17.97**.

Chapter 9

ADVISORY SERVICES AND APPLICATIONS FOR HOMELESSNESS ASSISTANCE

INTRODUCTION

9.1   Anyone seeking assistance with homelessness from a local housing authority must take the initiative and approach that local housing authority or its contracted provider of homelessness services. There is no legal duty on local housing authorities in England and Wales to seek out homeless people within their districts in order to offer their services to them. That is as true for those who are 'vulnerable' in housing terms[1] as it is for all the homeless.

9.2   As this chapter explains, at the point of first contact, a local housing authority has twin responsibilities:

- to ensure that an advice and information service is available locally for those who want help in preventing or dealing with their homelessness; and

- to receive applications made to it for accommodation (or for assistance in obtaining accommodation).

9.3   This chapter outlines the statutory requirements relating to advice and information before reviewing the considerable body of law on the treatment of applications.

ADVICE AND INFORMATION

9.4   Each local housing authority must make arrangements so that free advice and information about homelessness and the prevention of homelessness is available to everyone in its district.[2] Beyond that bald requirement, Housing Act 1996 (HA 1996), Part 7, does not specify where, or in what form, or even in what language(s), the free advice and information is to be provided. It is certainly intended that the arrangements should provide 'wide ranging and comprehensive' advice and information.[3] Indeed, the availability of such 'comprehensive' or 'wide-ranging' advice is intended to play an 'important part' in delivering the local housing authority's locally adopted Homelessness Strategy.[4] But beyond that, it is a matter for each local housing authority to determine the format and content of its advice and information arrangements.

9.5   The scope of the advice and information provided should obviously include an outline of what different housing options might be available in the particular district. The advice and information should also try to address some

---

[1]   See Chapter 13.

[2]   Housing Act 1996, s 179(1).

[3]   *Homelessness Code of Guidance for Local Authorities* (Department for Communities and Local Government, Department for Education and Skills, Department of Health, July 2006) (English Code), para 2.10; *Code of Guidance for local housing authorities on allocation of accommodation and homelessness for Wales* (National Assembly for Wales, April 2003) (Welsh Code), para 9.2 and paras 9.9–9.12.

[4]   English Code, para 2.9; Welsh Code, para 9.1 and see **7.112–7.143**.

of the common reasons why people may become homeless (such as financial difficulties, delays with housing benefit payments, etc). If advice or information is provided before someone becomes homeless, it is intended that it be specifically targeted to help that person keep his or her home and thus prevent homelessness.[5] The English and Welsh Codes go so far as to suggest that local housing authorities might provide an advocacy service for people facing the loss of their homes as part of the advice service.[6] It is also suggested that advice services should be able to refer people to more specialised advice provision, such as debt counselling, family mediation or counselling services, or for advice on drug or alcohol abuse.[7]

9.6   The advice and information service may either be provided by the local housing authority itself, or the local housing authority may fund or otherwise support other organisations to enable them to provide the advice and information.[8] Whoever provides it, the advice should be available and accessible to everyone in the local housing authority's district, free of charge and of a high standard.[9] The Welsh Code recommends that it should be 'impartial'.[10] The English Code suggests that 'an independent advisory service may help to avoid conflicts of interest'.[11] The English Code identifies, by way of illustration, more than a dozen issues which could be covered by advice on *prevention* of homelessness.[12] The Welsh Code includes a useful chapter on various common problems that can cause homelessness (such as rent or mortgage arrears or anti-social behaviour) and identifies some of the groups most likely to become homeless. It also provides guidance as to the type of advice that might be needed in order to prevent homelessness in common scenarios.[13]

9.7   The English Code, reflecting the policy emphasis on 'prevention', repeats some of its guidance on appropriate forms of advice and assistance as part of prevention in its chapter on 'Applications, inquiries, decisions and notifications'.[14] It is important, however, as the Code acknowledges, that, while local housing authorities may 'suggest alternative solutions in cases of potential homelessness', they 'must not avoid their obligations under Part 7 (especially the duty to make inquiries ...)'.[15]

---

[5]   English Code, paras 2.11–2.15. See Chapter 8 of this book.

[6]   English Code, para 2.12; Welsh Code, para 9.10.

[7]   English Code, para 2.14; Welsh Code, paras 9.1–9.2 and 9.8–9.12.

[8]   HA 1996, s 179(2)–(3).

[9]   English Code, paras 2.9 and 2.17–2.20; Welsh Code, paras 9.3–9.17.

[10]   Welsh Code, para 9.9.

[11]   English Code, para 2.18.

[12]   English Code, para 2.12. See **8.25–8.39** and Chapter 9 of this book.

[13]   Welsh Code, paras 10.1–10.37.

[14]   English Code, chapter 6. See Chapter 8 of this book.

[15]   English Code, para 6.4. A point subsequently made by Collins J in *R (Aweys) v Birmingham City Council* [2007] EWHC 52 (Admin), [2007] HLR 27, Admin Ct at [17]. See **8.50–8.51** of this book. The case was later considered by the Court of Appeal and the House of Lords (*Ali & others v Birmingham City Council* [2009] UKHL 36, [2009] 1 WLR 1506, HL) but not in relation to that specific point. See also Local Government Ombudsman decision 04/C/18012 (Annual Digest of Cases 2006–2007 at http://www.lgo.org.uk/publications/digest-of-cases/) and

APPLICATIONS

Where can an application be made?

9.8   Local housing authorities are obliged to have arrangements in place so that anyone who wants to make an application for homelessness assistance can do so.[16] In practice, that means that there must be, at the very least, a locally accessible contact point where an applicant can make an application. Usually this will be an office of the local housing authority where applications can be made face to face and, if necessary, in private.[17] Where necessary, and particularly in urban areas, there must also be an emergency 24-hour service enabling applications to be made and received day or night.[18] Local housing authorities should publicise the opening hours, address and telephone number of the homelessness service and the 24-hour emergency contact details, translate the information into any 'main languages' in their district, and ensure that interpreters are accessible for less frequently spoken languages.[19] They should ensure that emergency services, such as the police and social services, have details of the opening hours and contact numbers.[20] An application need not be directed to any particular department of the local housing authority.[21] A letter giving details of an applicant's homelessness and containing a request for accommodation which is sent, for example, to the local housing authority's own housing or social services department should be sufficient to trigger the duty to make inquiries.

9.9   A local housing authority's practice of requiring an applicant for homelessness assistance to go through a 'home options interview' before the local housing authority accepted that the applicant had made an application and triggered duties under HA 1996, Part 7, was conceded, by the local housing authority, to be unlawful after the applicant had brought a challenge in judicial review[22]. The judge said:

> 'the Home Options Scheme … cannot lawfully be used to defer consideration of a homeless application. All steps taken to avoid homelessness are of course laudable. But any such steps must be taken in parallel to the carrying out of the duty under Part [7].'[23]

---

decisions of the Public Services Ombudsman for Wales regarding Cardiff City Council 20060749 at (2008) June *Legal Action*, p 32 and Conwy CBC 200702044 at (2009) April *Legal Action*, p 22, both discussed at **8.52**. See also **10.1–10.59**.

16   HA 1996, s 183(1).

17   English Code, para 6.9.

18   *R v Camden London Borough Council ex p Gillan* (1988) 21 HLR 114, QBD.

19   English Code, para 6.10.

20   English Code, paras 6.8 and 6.9; Welsh Code, paras 12.1–12.2 and 12.14–12.16.

21   English Code, para 6.6; Welsh Code, para 12.2.

22   *R (Aweys) v Birmingham City Council* [2007] EWHC 52 (Admin), [2007] HLR 27, Admin Ct. The case was later considered by the House of Lords under the name of *Ali v Birmingham City Council* [2009] UKHL 36, HL, but not in relation to that specific point.

23   *R (Aweys) v Birmingham City Council* [2007] EWHC 52 (Admin), [2007] HLR 27, Admin Ct at [17] per Collins J. See also decisions of the Public Services Ombudsman for Wales regarding

Applications made to other organisations

9.10 If the local housing authority has contracted out its homelessness services, applications may need to be directed to, or referred to, that contractor.[24] No doubt the contractor will be anxious to demonstrate that its arrangements for receiving applications are at least as wide-ranging and flexible as the arrangements the local housing authority itself would have made.

9.11 Local housing authorities may choose to contract out the delivery of housing advice and information, or, indeed, the administration of part or all of their mainstream homelessness services. If they do, they remain responsible for the acts or omissions of the contractor in the exercise of the local housing authorities' advice and homelessness functions.[25] They cannot contract out:

- their strategic functions of drawing up homelessness strategies and reviews;

- their duty to ensure that housing advice and assistance is provided free to any person in their district;

- their power to fund voluntary organisations concerned with homelessness; or

- their duty to co-operate with other local housing authorities.[26]

9.12 Nor, it would seem, can they contract out of their responsibilities for decisions made on applications for homelessness assistance, the performance of any duties owed and the exercise of any powers.[27]

To which local housing authority can the application be made?

9.13 There are several hundred local housing authorities in England and Wales. People seeking accommodation or assistance in obtaining accommodation can apply to any local housing authority they choose, as they need not fulfil any residence requirement or other preliminary condition.[28] Indeed, applications can be made consecutively or concurrently to several local housing authorities.[29] As it is not necessary to make an application in person, applications can be directed to widely dispersed local housing authorities.

Cardiff City Council (20060749) (2008) June *Legal Action*, p 32, and Conwy CBC (200702044, (2009) April *Legal Action*, p 22. See also **8.49–8.54**.

[24] See **21.14–21.39**.

[25] Local Authorities (Contracting Out of Allocation of Housing and Homelessness Functions) Order 1996, SI 1996/3205, at Appendix 1 of this book. See also English Code, chapter 21; Welsh Code, Annex 21; and **21.1–21.2**.

[26] HA 1996, s 179(2) and (3), s 180(1) and s 213. See **21.36**.

[27] See **21.1** and **21.20–21.23**.

[28] *R v Slough Borough Council ex p Ealing London Borough Council* [1981] QB 801, CA.

[29] See **9.39–9.45**.

9.14 The statutory scheme is obviously based on the premise that the applicant will apply to the local housing authority for the area in which he or she wishes to be accommodated. Not surprisingly, therefore, if the local housing authority to which the application is made decides to accept and perform the main housing duty by providing accommodation in its area, the applicant has no redress against that decision, even if he or she would have preferred to have been referred to a different local housing authority for it to perform that duty.[30]

9.15 It is notorious that local housing authorities have different approaches to the strictness with which they apply homelessness legislation. In areas of acute housing shortage, applicants must expect the law to be tightly applied. In areas where there is a surplus of housing accommodation available, applicants may find that their applications receive very little scrutiny and promptly result in the acceptance of the main housing duty.

9.16 Those considering making applications could therefore often benefit from early advice as to the appropriate local housing authority to approach with an application. If their home local housing authority takes a very strict approach to applications, they may be better advised to apply to a more generous local housing authority in the hope that the duty to accommodate them will be promptly accepted and then referred back to their home area.[31]

9.17 Indeed, the adoption of different rules governing priority need[32] and eligibility[33] and different Codes of Guidance for England and Wales[34] may mean that the same applicant will be differently treated if the application is made to a local housing authority in one country rather than the other.

9.18 There is no eligibility condition or geographic connection required to make an application. The local housing authority cannot therefore turn away homeless applicants who appear to have just arrived in the UK from overseas, nor those who seem to have no local connection with its district (even if they have an obvious and current connection with the district of another local housing authority). The proper course, if an applicant does not appear to have a local connection with the local housing authority's district, is for the local housing authority to make the usual inquiries into:

(1) whether the applicant is 'eligible' for services under HA 1996, Part 7; and

(2) if so, whether any duty is owed under HA 1996, Part 7 to the applicant.[35]

---

30   *Hackney London Borough Council v Sareen* [2003] EWCA Civ 351, (2003) 35 HLR 54, CA.
31   Under the 'local connection' provisions described in Chapter 15.
32   See **13.106–13.171** (England) and **13.172–13.202** (Wales).
33   See **12.94–12.196** and **12.198–12.200** (England) and **12.97–12.76** (Wales).
34   English Code at Appendix 2 of this book; Welsh Code on CD-ROM.
35   HA 1996, s 184(1). See Chapter 10 of this book.

The scope of those latter inquiries may (but does not need to) include considering whether the applicant has a local connection with the local housing authority and, if not, whether he or she has a local connection elsewhere.[36]

Form in which the application is made

9.19 Whenever a person approaches a local housing authority for accommodation, or for assistance in obtaining accommodation, and the local housing authority has reason to believe that she or he may be homeless or threatened with homelessness, then he or she has made a homelessness application.[37]

9.20 Although it may be convenient for a local housing authority to have its own application form for applicants to complete, there is no legal requirement that an application should be in writing or in any specified form.[38] An application could perfectly properly be made in person, by letter, fax, telephone, or even by email. So long as the communication seeks accommodation or assistance in obtaining accommodation and sets out an account that gives the local housing authority reason to believe that the person might be homeless or threatened with homelessness, it constitutes an application. As the Codes make clear, there is absolutely no requirement on applicants to specify that they are seeking services under HA 1996, Part 7.[39] Obviously, there is room for possible disagreement as to whether what is said in the course of a conversation constitutes an application. In *R v Cherwell District Council ex p Howkins*,[40] the applicant's solicitor telephoned the local housing authority shortly after it had evicted the applicant (who had been a council tenant) for rent arrears. The judge was quite satisfied that an application for homelessness assistance did not need to be in writing. He said that:

'... in order to be treated as an application it seems to me that an oral conversation has to be conducted in such a way that it is clear that it amounts to an application.'

9.21 On the facts, the conversation had simply been an inquiry by the solicitor as to whether the local housing authority was going to offer temporary accommodation and was not itself an application for any accommodation.

9.22 Once an application meeting the above (fairly minimal) requirements is received, the local housing authority cannot ignore it until the applicant has

---

[36]   HA 1996, s 184(2). For further discussion of local connection see **15.40–15.110**.
[37]   HA 1996, s 183.
[38]   *R v Chiltern District Council ex p Roberts* (1990) 23 HLR 387, QBD; *R (Aweys) v Birmingham City Council* [2007] EWHC 52 (Admin), [2007] HLR 27, Admin Ct at [8] per Collins J. The case was later considered by the House of Lords under the name of *Ali v Birmingham City Council* [2009] UKHL 36, [2009] 1 WLR 1506, HL, but not in relation to that specific point. See English Code, para 6.6.
[39]   English Code, para 6.6; Welsh Code, para 12.2.
[40]   *R v Cherwell District Council ex p Howkins* (unreported) 14 May 1984, QBD.

completed the local housing authority's standard application form. It must act upon the application and start to make inquiries.

'Actual' and 'deemed' applications

9.23 The regime for homelessness assistance does not recognise the concept of an implied, constructive or deemed homelessness application. The only application which counts, and triggers the duty to make inquiries, is one actually made.

9.24 This can be a source of frustration for a local housing authority that is seeking to free itself from responsibility for particularly problematic tenants. It is not at all uncommon for tenants, in both the social housing and the private rented sectors, who are facing eviction for rent arrears or persistent anti-social behaviour, to be forewarned that the local housing authority will not accept a responsibility for rehousing them once evicted. If the tenant potentially has a priority need, and chooses to refrain from making a homelessness application until the moment of eviction (or very shortly beforehand), it is likely that the local housing authority will have to provide further accommodation, at least initially (while inquiries are made into the application[41]) and thereafter yet more temporary accommodation (even if the finding is of intentional homelessness).[42]

9.25 For this reason, some local housing authorities have in the past tried to explore a concept of an implied or deemed application made well before the eviction, allowing them to undertake inquiries while the tenants are still in their homes (and awaiting the bailiffs) and thus reducing any temporary accommodation responsibility to an absolute minimum. However, it seems that (very properly) this device has been abandoned.

Who can make an application?

9.26 Anyone can make a request for accommodation or for assistance in obtaining accommodation. If that person does not appear to be homeless or threatened with homelessness, he or she will be entitled to housing advice, free of charge, but the local housing authority will owe no further duty.[43] If the person appears to be homeless or to be threatened with homelessness, the local housing authority must treat the request as an application for homelessness and start to make inquiries.[44]

9.27 There is no eligibility condition or geographic connection required to make an application. The local housing authority cannot therefore turn away homeless applicants who appear to have just arrived in the UK from overseas,

---

41   HA 1996, s 188(1). See **16.11–16.24**.
42   HA 1996, s 190(2)(a). See **17.11–17.13** and **17.21–17.118**.
43   HA 1996, s 179(1).
44   English Code, para 6.12; Welsh Code, para 12.4.

nor those who seem to have no local connection with its district (even if they have an obvious and current connection with the district of another local housing authority).[45]

9.28 A person must have *legal capacity* in order to make an application for homeless assistance. Accordingly, those who lack mental capacity cannot apply.[46] It is for the local housing authority, in the first instance, to decide whether the applicant has the mental capacity to make an application.[47] There is no right of statutory review or appeal if the application is refused on the basis of lack of capacity. The obvious practical route to achieving a reversal of the local housing authority's decision would be the submission of clear medical evidence that the applicant did have capacity. If the local housing authority persisted in its refusal to accept the application, proceedings for judicial review would need to be brought.[48]

9.29 There is no minimum *age* for applicants (although the Codes wrongly suggest that all applicants must be 'adults').[49] In the absence of a statutory minimum age, the House of Lords has, in dealing with an application made by a 4-year old, held that applications from 'dependent' children should not be considered.[50] There is no statutory definition of that term.[51] It follows that an application may be made by any child who is no longer 'dependent'. As the House of Lords recognised:

> 'There will obviously be the case from time to time when a child leaves home under the age of 16 and ceases to be dependent on the parents or those with whom he or she was living.'[52]

9.30 Such an individual can make his or her own application. Applicants need not show a history of independence from their parents or others. Plainly, the very first step that an applicant may have taken to demonstrate that he or she is no longer 'dependent' might be making the application.

9.31 There are occasionally applications made by non-dependent young people under the age of 16,[53] but applications by those aged 16 or 17 are more common. Since 31 July 2002 in England,[54] most 16- and 17-year-olds have been designated as being in priority need.[55] As a result there has been an increase in

---

45   See Chapter 15 of this book.
46   *R v Oldham Metropolitan Borough Council ex p Garlick, R v London Borough of Tower Hamlets ex p Begum* [1993] AC 509, HL.
47   [1993] AC 509 HL at 520, per Lord Griffiths.
48   See **19.211–19.237**.
49   English Code, para 6.6; Welsh Code, para 12.2.
50   *R v Oldham Metropolitan Borough Council ex p Garlick* [1993] AC 509, HL.
51   The guidance given on it by the Codes is discussed at **13.36**.
52   [1993] AC 509, HL at 517, per Lord Griffiths.
53   *Kelly v Monklands District Council* (1985) SLT 169, OH.
54   1 March 2001 in Wales.
55   See **13.107–13.136** (England) and **13.175** (Wales).

applications from non-adults in that age group.[56] Guidance suggests that local housing authorities should have arrangements in place so that, when homeless applications are received from 16- or 17-year-olds, assessments of their housing, care and support needs are carried out jointly with social services.[57] Obviously, unless the local housing authority is a unitary authority, the consent of the young person will be required before his or her details are disclosed to the social services department of a different authority.

Joint applications

9.32 The law does not recognise an application for accommodation, or for assistance in obtaining accommodation, made by a couple, a family or a household. Applications are made by individuals. HA 1996, Part 7 refers to 'a person' making the application.[58] One judge has said:

> 'I am quite unable to conclude that an application for housing as a homeless person falls to be treated as being made by a family unit. It is, and must be, an application at the instance of an individual. Of course, if that individual is residing with others in a family, that will affect the accommodation he requires, and whether he has priority need, but it does not alter the fact that the application is the application of an individual.'[59]

9.33 Of course, there is nothing to prevent more than one individual in the same household from making applications. Indeed, several applicants from a single household may apply at the same time to the same local housing authority and even on the same application form. This is particularly common where there are two adult heads of household and both choose to apply.

9.34 There is some helpful judicial guidance on how to deal with such jointly made applications:

> 'It seems to me that where the application which is made to the authority is, as here, a joint application, it is a joint application which the authority must determine. If there is no request by one of two joint applicants for his or her case to be treated separately, there is no obligation upon the authority to deal with the application as being other than a joint application. However, in considering the

---

[56] Homelessness (Priority Need for Accommodation) (England) Order 2002, SI 2002/2051, reg 3; Homeless Persons (Priority Need) (Wales) Order 2001, SI 2001/607 (W 30), reg 4. Until 2002, around 3–4,000 applicants in England each year were accepted as homeless and having priority need due to their vulnerability as young people. The number rose to 11,050 in 2003/04 and then fell to 4,070 in 2008/09: www.communities.gov.uk/housing/housingresearch/housingstatistics/ housingstatisticsby/homelessnessstatistics/livetables/.

[57] English Code, para 6.19 and paras 12.1–12.17; Welsh Code, para 12.10. *See R (M) v Hammersmith & Fulham London Borough Council* [2008] UKHL 14, [2008] 1 WLR 535, HL, and *R (G) v Southwark London Borough Council* [2009] UKHL 26, [2009] 1 WLR 2399, HL. See **13.126–13.130**.

[58] HA 1996, s 183(1).

[59] *MacLeod (aka Hynds) v Midlothian District Council* (1986) SLT 54, (1985) November SCOLAG 163, per Lord Ross.

joint application there may be an obligation on the housing authority to consider the separate circumstances of the individuals who are making the joint application.'[60]

9.35 In practice, this enables local housing authorities to proceed on the basis that there is an identity of interest between the joint applicants unless and until material before the local housing authority indicates that separate consideration of each application is required. Such material could be a disagreement between the joint applicants in the course of interviews with the local housing authority or might be implied from the giving of mutually inconsistent accounts. The safer course must ordinarily be to treat even joint applicants with a degree of separate consideration.

9.36 This sense, in which even supposed joint applications are simply two applications contained in one single form, was emphasised in *Lewis v Brent London Borough Council*.[61] Mr and Mrs Lewis had applied together for homelessness assistance to the local housing authority, but Mrs Lewis was unable to rely on her husband's circumstances in an appeal against a decision that she was intentionally homeless. Although they had made a joint application, he was not a party to the appeal and so his – more favourable – circumstances could not be raised by her.

9.37 Where more than one individual in a household *could* apply, it may be sensible for one rather than the other to make the application. For example, one may be eligible for HA 1996, Part 7 services and the other not; or one may be more likely to be found to have become homeless intentionally. There may even be an advantage in applicants in similar circumstances making consecutive applications in order to obtain not only the possibility of a second, and more favourable decision, but also to obtain at least a further period in interim accommodation whilst the second application is considered.

9.38 Where the application by one adult member of the household results in the acceptance of the main housing duty, accommodation will be provided for the whole household.[62] What happens, however, if the applying adult rejects that offer and the other household members then make further applications? This occurred in *R v Camden London Borough Council ex p Hersi*.[63] In that case, the new applicant was a 19-year-old daughter of the first applicant, her own mother; after the mother had rejected an offer of accommodation, the local housing authority refused to accept the daughter's application. The Court of Appeal described the daughter as having 'no standing' to apply for homelessness assistance for the whole family (although the reasoning seems to suggest that this was because the younger children of the household were dependent on their mother and not on her). However, in that case Camden

---

[60] *R v Wandsworth London Borough Council ex p Lord* (unreported) 8 July 1985, QBD per Woolf J.
[61] [2005] EWCA Civ 605, (2005) July *Legal Action*, p 29, CA.
[62] See **17.26**.
[63] *R v Camden London Borough Council ex p Hersi* (2001) 33 HLR 577, CA.

accepted (correctly) that had the new application been from another adult member of the household on whom the children *were* dependent, inquiries into that application would need to have been made.

Multiple applications

9.39　There is nothing to prevent someone applying simultaneously to more than one local housing authority. If this happens, each local housing authority will be obliged to carry out its own inquiries, potentially resulting in a wasteful duplication of effort. The Codes suggest that the receiving local housing authorities should agree amongst themselves which one will be responsible for carrying out inquiries.[64] Presumably this is on the basis that the local housing authority which does undertake the inquiries does so both on its own behalf and as agent for (or delegate of) the others.[65] Each local housing authority should then make its own assessment of the results of the inquiries and reach its own decision. It seems implicit in this suggested arrangement, however, that in practice the applicant will withdraw all other applications as soon as one of the local housing authorities recognises that the main housing duty is owed.

Consecutive applications

9.40　As already stated, there is nothing to prevent an applicant applying first to one local housing authority and then to another. When an applicant has previously applied to one local housing authority (the first local housing authority), the second or subsequent local housing authority (in the course of making inquiries into the second or subsequent application) is free to contact the first local housing authority and request information on the application made and on that local housing authority's decision (if any) on that application. The first local housing authority is under a duty to co-operate with any such request.[66]

9.41　The second local housing authority, however, must not rely solely on the first local housing authority's decision in reaching its own decision on the application made to it, although it may take it into account. Nor may it merely adopt the earlier local housing authority's decision. It must make its own independent inquiries and reach an independent decision on the application it has received.[67]

9.42　It may well be that the second local housing authority reaches a different decision from the first local housing authority. For example, it may decide that the applicant *is* owed a main housing duty because he or she is eligible, in priority need and unintentionally homeless even if the first local housing authority had decided all (or any) of those matters against the applicant.

64　English Code, para 6.7; Welsh Code, para 12.3.
65　As permitted by Local Government Act 1972, s 101(1)(b).
66　HA 1996, s 213. See also, English Code, para 6.20; Welsh Code, para 12.5.
67　English Code, para 6.7; Welsh Code, para 12.3.

9.43 The second local housing authority may also decide that the main housing duty is to be referred to the first local housing authority on the grounds that the applicant has no local connection with the second local housing authority but does have a connection with the first local housing authority.[68] This can result in the first local housing authority being obliged to receive back and accommodate an applicant to whom it had recently notified an adverse decision.

9.44 A dispute resolution mechanism exists where there is a disagreement between two local housing authorities as to which of them the applicant has a local connection with. However, that mechanism does not apply in cases where there is no dispute over the local connection conditions, but the local housing authority to whom the applicant has been referred does not agree with the referring local housing authority's decision that a duty to accommodate is owed to the applicant. In those circumstances, the first local housing authority cannot refuse to accept the referral unless it can successfully demonstrate, in the usual way, that the local connection conditions are not satisfied.[69]

9.45 If the first local housing authority believes that the second local housing authority has incorrectly reached a decision that the main duty is owed to the applicant, it cannot simply refuse the referral of the duty and wait for the applicant or the second local housing authority to bring legal proceedings.[70] Instead, it must take the initiative and bring judicial review proceedings to demonstrate that the decision-making by the second local housing authority was unlawful. Obviously, the second local housing authority must apply the law correctly when making its inquiries and reaching its decision. If it has not done so, the first local housing authority will succeed in having the decision overturned. In *R v Newham London Borough Council ex p Tower Hamlets London Borough Council*,[71] the Court of Appeal held that Newham had been entitled to accept an application from someone whom Tower Hamlets had previously found to have become homeless intentionally. Newham would have been, had it applied the law correctly, entitled to refer the applicant back to Tower Hamlets under the local connection provisions. However, Newham made an error of law when considering whether the applicant had become homeless intentionally, in that it took into account its own local housing conditions rather than those of Tower Hamlets. Tower Hamlets succeeded in having the Newham decision, and consequently the referral, set aside.

---

68   For a discussion of local connection see **15.40–15.110**.
69   *R v Slough Borough Council ex p Ealing London Borough Council* [1981] QB 801, CA; *R (Bantamagbari) v Westminster City Council and Southwark London Borough Council* [2003] EWHC 1350 (Admin), [2003] All ER (D) 163 (May), Admin Ct.
70   *R (Bantamagbari) v City of Westminster and Southwark London Borough Council* [2003] EWHC 1350 (Admin), [2003] All ER (D) 163 (May), Admin Ct.
71   *R v Newham London Borough Council ex p London Borough of Tower Hamlets* [1991] 1 WLR 1032, CA.

Applications from owners and tenants

9.46   It is not necessary for someone to be physically without a roof over his or her head in order to make an application for accommodation (or for assistance in obtaining accommodation) which requires consideration under HA 1996 Part 7. An applicant cannot be treated as having accommodation unless it is accommodation which it would be reasonable for him or her to continue to occupy.[72] Such an applicant may be a freehold owner, long leaseholder or a tenant who gives the local housing authority some reason to believe that it is no longer reasonable for him or her to continue occupying the present accommodation. The concept of reasonable continued occupation is discussed in detail elsewhere,[73] but obvious examples of those who may be homeless include owners or tenants who cannot afford their accommodation or experience gross overcrowding or other adverse physical conditions.

9.47   Local housing authorities need particular sensitivity to this type of application where an applicant is an existing tenant of a local housing authority. Local housing authorities should be aware that an application for alternative accommodation from one of their existing tenants might, in reality, be an application for homelessness assistance if the tenant is saying that it is not reasonable for him or her to continue to occupy the existing home. Generally, a local housing authority is entitled to presume that an application for a transfer from one of its existing tenants is exactly that – an application for a transfer – rather than an application under HA 1996, Part 7.[74] However, where, from the circumstances of the application, it is clear that the tenant is saying that it is not reasonable for him or her to continue in occupation, the local housing authority would be in breach of its statutory duty to make inquiries if it treated the application as a simple application for a transfer rather than as an application for HA 1996, Part 7 assistance.[75] An obvious example, where a tenant apparently seeking a transfer is in fact asserting that his or her existing accommodation is not reasonable to continue to occupy, is where the tenant is complaining that he or she has to be transferred because of violence or harassment.[76] It is not necessary for the applicant to spell out that the application should be considered under HA 1996, Part 7.[77]

---

[72]   HA 1996, s 175(3).

[73]   See **11.72–11.117**.

[74]   *R v Lambeth London Borough Council ex p Pattinson* (1996) 28 HLR 214, QBD.

[75]   *R v Islington London Borough Council ex p B* (1998) 30 HLR 706, QBD. See also *R v Sefton Metropolitan Borough Council ex p Healiss* (1995) 27 HLR 34, QBD, and Local Government Ombudsman Investigations 91/A/2474 (Tower Hamlets London Borough Council) and 99/A/03731 (Hounslow London Borough Council). See also Commissioner for Complaints Northern Ireland Housing Executive, where a tenant whose accommodation was unsuitable because of his disability wrote asking to be assessed as homeless, and no inquiries were made promptly (200700491: (2009) April *Legal Action*, p 22.

[76]   Local Government Ombudsman Report 99/A/03731 (Hounslow London Borough Council).

[77]   *R (Aweys) v Birmingham City Council* [2007] EWHC 52 (Admin), [2007] HLR 27, Admin Ct. The case was later considered by the House of Lords under the name of *Ali v Birmingham City Council,* [2009] UKHL 36, [2009] 1 WLR 1506, HL, but not in relation to that specific point.

9.48   Local housing authorities must take exactly the same approach with applications from those who are not existing local housing authority tenants but who apply for accommodation under the local housing authority's ordinary allocation scheme. An applicant for long-term council accommodation (or for nomination to an RSL) who writes, on his or her application form seeking permanent re-housing, that the application must be considered urgently because the present home is grossly overcrowded, unfit for occupation, or is for some other reason no longer suitable to occupy, must likewise be the subject of inquiries under HA 1996, Part 7.[78] Self-evidently that information is sufficient to give the local housing authority reason to believe that the applicant may be homeless. The applicant does not need to spell out that he or she is applying for consideration under both HA 1996, Part 6[79] and Part 7.

Warnings

9.49   It is a criminal offence for an applicant to make a false statement in order to induce the local housing authority to believe that he or she is entitled to accommodation or assistance with homelessness. It is also a criminal offence for the applicant to withhold information reasonably required by the local housing authority, or to fail to notify the local housing authority of any change of facts material to his or her case.[80] Local housing authorities are obliged to explain this duty, and what it means, to each applicant, in ordinary language, and are encouraged to explain it in a sensitive way, in order to avoid intimidating applicants.[81]

A local housing authority's immediate duties

9.50   As soon as a local housing authority has reason to believe that a person who has made an application may be homeless or threatened with homelessness, it is obliged to make inquiries into whether the person is eligible for assistance and, if so, whether any duty is owed to him or her under the homelessness provisions.[82] The duty to make inquiries cannot be postponed.

9.51   There have been a number of findings of maladministration by the Local Government Ombudsmen against local housing authorities which, instead of considering whether applicants were homeless or might be threatened with homelessness, refused to make inquiries, or told applicants that they would not be helped (thereby pre-judging the result of inquiries), or told them that they should make their own accommodation arrangements.[83] The Local

---

In these seven linked cases, tenants were accepted to be homeless because their tenancies were so overcrowded that it was not reasonable for them, and all the members of their households, to continue to occupy. See **11.105–11.107.**

[78]   Conwy CBC (200702044), (2009) April *Legal Action*, p 22. See also **8.52.**
[79]   See **2.30–2.40.**
[80]   HA 1996, s 214. See also English Code, para 6.11; Welsh Code, para 12.5.
[81]   English Code, para 6.11; Welsh Code, para 12.5.
[82]   HA 1996, ss 183 and 184(1).
[83]   Investigations 518/L/85 (Boston Borough Council), 88/B/1216 (East Lindsay Borough Council), 88/B/1795 (Cheltenham Borough Council), 89/B/076 (Broxbourne Borough

Government Ombudsmen have indicated that it is essential to good administration that all applicants receive equal treatment, and that their applications are given fair consideration and are properly investigated before decisions are reached.[84] The Public Services Ombudsman for Wales has taken the same approach.[85]

9.52 Given this absolute duty, it is essential that local housing authority staff in direct contact with the public are well trained and can recognise and receive applications and ensure that inquiries are put in hand. Far too often, applicants are wrongly turned away by busy or inexperienced reception staff. It is not unknown for applicants to be told:

- 'you need to apply to a different local housing authority'; or

- 'we do not take homelessness applications from our own tenants'; or

- 'we only help the priority homeless here'.

All of these responses to an application, and any other similar statements, are wrong in law.

The local housing authority's first decision: interim accommodation

9.53 The very first issue that a local housing authority must consider is whether it has reason to believe that an applicant *may* be homeless, eligible for assistance and have a priority need. If the local housing authority does have reason to believe that the applicant *may* fall into all of these categories and the application for homelessness assistance cannot be inquired into and concluded on the spot, it *must* provide accommodation for the applicant and his or her household pending notification of a decision.[86] That duty cannot be postponed.[87] The threshold trigger is very low: the local housing authority need only have 'reason to believe' that the applicant 'may be' homeless, eligible for

---

Council), 04/C/373 (Blackpool Borough Council), 04/C/18012, (Nottingham City Council), 04/A/09817 (Barnet London Borough Council); and see Commissioner for Complaints Northern Ireland Housing Executive 200700491 (2009) April *Legal Action*, p 22.

[84] Local Government Ombudsman Investigation 88/B/1795 (Cheltenham Borough Council).

[85] Cardiff City Council (20060749), (2008) June *Legal Action*, p 32, and Conwy CBC (200702044), (2009) April *Legal Action*, p 22. See also **8.52**.

[86] HA 1996, s 188(1). See also English Code, para 6.5; Welsh Code, para 12.11; and see Chapter 14.

[87] In *R (Ho-Sang) v Lewisham London Borough Council* (2004) CO 5562/03, (2004) July *Legal Action*, p 19, Admin Ct, the local housing authority conceded that it was in breach of its statutory duty by not immediately providing accommodation in those circumstances. In Investigation 03/A/15819 (Waltham Forest London Borough Council), the local housing authority was very severely criticised by the Local Government Ombudsman and ordered to pay compensation and legal costs, where it had failed to provide accommodation to a vulnerable single man who was forced to sleep rough as a result.

assistance and 'may' have a priority need.[88] The English Code reminds local housing authorities that 'having reason to believe' is a lower test than 'being satisfied'.[89] If in doubt, interim accommodation should be provided.

Repeat applications

9.54 There is no bar on someone who has made an earlier application for homelessness assistance, and had that application determined by the local housing authority, from re-applying to the same local housing authority for accommodation (or assistance in obtaining accommodation) at any later time.[90] The local housing authority must accept the application if there is reason to believe the applicant may be homeless or threatened with homelessness.

9.55 Nothing in the legislation cuts down the right to make such repeat applications. Indeed, HA 1996, Part 7 specifically states that even a person whose previous application resulted in the local housing authority owing him or her the main housing duty can make a fresh application when that duty ends.[91]

9.56 In these circumstances it has been left to the courts to work out sensible limits to protect local housing authorities from having to investigate fully what are essentially repetitive applications. The broad rule established by the courts is that a local housing authority is entitled to preface any inquiries into a repeat application by simply considering whether the factual circumstances have relevantly changed since the previous application.

9.57 If there has been no factual change, the local housing authority is entitled to refuse to entertain the application and to rely on its previous decision (including any previous decision that the local housing authority's duty to the applicant had been discharged). If, however, there has been such a change of circumstances, the local housing authority can no longer rely on its previous decision and must make inquiries into the application in the usual way.[92] In *R v Harrow London Borough Council ex p Fahia*,[93] the House of Lords held that there were no administrative short cuts enabling a local housing authority to avoid the duty to make at least that level of inquiries into a repeat application.

88 *R (Aweys) v Birmingham City Council* [2007] EWHC 52 (Admin), [2007] HLR 27, Admin Ct, at [8]–[9] per Collins J. See also *R (Kelly & Mehari) v Birmingham City Council* [2009] EWHC 3240 (Admin), (2010) January *Legal Action*, p 35, Admin Ct. See **16.11–16.24**.
89 English Code, para 6.5.
90 English Code, para 6.27; Welsh Code, para 15.13.
91 HA 1996, s 193(9).
92 *R v Harrow London Borough Council ex p Fahia* [1998] 1 WLR 1396, HL.
93 (1998) 30 HLR 1124, HL.

9.58 The Court of Appeal applied this approach in *Begum v Tower Hamlets London Borough Council*.[94] Unless a repeat application discloses no new facts on the application form, or any new facts that are disclosed are merely fanciful or trivial, the local housing authority must accept the application, make its enquiries, comply with any other statutory duties that might arise (such as securing accommodation) and notify its decision in accordance with HA 1996, Part 7. The English Code reflects this approach.[95]

9.59 Prior to the decision in *Begum v Tower Hamlets London Borough Council*,[96] most local housing authorities were only prepared to accept repeat applications if there had been a 'material change of circumstances'. There was also a practice of asking repeat applicants if they had obtained and occupied settled accommodation since their earlier applications. The former approach was overruled by *Begum v Tower Hamlets London Borough Council*,[97] and the latter practice is no longer appropriate. Intervening settled accommodation should be treated as one of those changes in the factual circumstances which would require a local housing authority to accept and determine a fresh application.

Factual changes

9.60 In *R v London Borough of Harrow ex p Fahia*,[98] the applicant had occupied guest house accommodation originally provided by the local housing authority while it was making inquiries into her first application. After the local housing authority had decided that she had become intentionally homeless, she had been permitted by the guest house manager to stay on there. She claimed housing benefit in order to pay the rent. Over a year later, she was asked to leave the guest house and applied again to the local housing authority. The local housing authority's refusal to accept her application was quashed. The local housing authority had failed to address itself to whether the loss of the non-settled accommodation was a new or supervening event causing a new incidence of homelessness.

9.61 In *Begum v Tower Hamlets London Borough Council*,[99] the presence of two additional adults in the applicant's accommodation, rendering it overcrowded, was a material change of circumstances sufficient for the local housing authority to have to accept a further application.[100]

---

94   [2005] EWCA Civ 340, [2005] HLR 34, CA.
95   English Code, para 6.27. The Welsh Code, para 5.13, was published before the Court of Appeal's decision in *Begum v Tower Hamlets London Borough Council* [2005] EWCA Civ 340, [2005] HLR 34, CA, and so should not be relied upon as reflecting the current legal position.
96   [2005] EWCA Civ 340, [2005] HLR 34, CA.
97   [2005] EWCA Civ 340, [2005] HLR 34, CA.
98   *R v London Borough of Harrow ex p Fahia* [1998] 1 WLR 1396, HL.
99   [2005] EWCA Civ 340, [2005] HLR 34, CA.
100   See **11.105–11.107**.

9.62 There has been very little case law since the Court of Appeal's decision in *Begum v Tower Hamlets London Borough Council*.[101] Case law decided under the old test of material change of circumstances had held that events that *might* have been sufficient to require a local housing authority to entertain a second application included:

- the breakdown of the applicant's marriage;[102]

- the award of Disability Living Allowance for night-time supervision (so that an applicant who originally needed one bedroom later needed two-bedroom accommodation);[103]

- a threat of possession proceedings combined with overcrowded accommodation;[104] and

- where a medical report showed that an applicant's health was poor and deteriorating and contained additional material relevant to the original decision that the applicant had become homeless intentionally (a case said to be unusual on its facts).[105]

9.63 Changes of circumstances which, on their facts, the courts found, under the old test, were *not* sufficient to give rise to a duty to entertain a second application included:

- the illness and death of a friend who had been providing unsettled accommodation;[106]

- pregnancy of the applicant;[107]

- the failure of an arrangement made by a prisoner for his sister to pay the rent during his sentence;[108] and

---

[101] [2005] EWCA Civ 340, [2005] HLR 34, CA. In *R (Daie) v Camden London Borough Council* [2006] EWHC 452 (Admin), (2006) May *Legal Action*, p 34, Admin Ct, permission was given for an applicant to bring judicial review proceedings where the local housing authority had refused to accept a second application saying that there had been no 'material change of circumstances'. By the time that the judicial review claim came to a full hearing, the local housing authority had not only accepted the second application but had also concluded that the applicant was owed the main housing duty.

[102] *R v Basingstoke and Deane Borough Council ex p Bassett* (1983) 10 HLR 125, QBD.

[103] *Ali v Camden London Borough Council* (1998) October *Legal Action*, p 22, Central London County Court.

[104] *R (Jeylani) v Waltham Forest London Borough Council* [2002] EWHC 487 (Admin), (2002) May *Legal Action*, p 30, Admin Ct.

[105] *R (Van der Stolk) v Camden London Borough Council* [2002] EWHC 1621 (Admin), (2002) July *Legal Action*, p 26, Admin Ct.

[106] *R v Brighton Borough Council ex p Harvey* (1997) 30 HLR 670, QBD.

[107] *R v Hackney London Borough Council ex p Ajayi* (1997) 30 HLR 473, QBD.

[108] *Stewart v Lambeth London Borough Council* [2002] EWCA Civ 753, [2002] HLR 40, CA.

- disrepair to the applicant's home.[109]

Many of these would now constitute changed factual circumstances requiring the local housing authority to entertain a new application under the modern approach.

9.64 Particular issues may arise where the first application results in the local housing authority accepting a duty to accommodate the applicant, but the applicant refuses the accommodation offered (or the local connection referral then made) and then later makes a repeat application. In general, a local housing authority is entitled to rely on the ending of its duty following a refusal of accommodation.[110] However, if, after the refusal of accommodation (and ending of duty), the factual circumstances have changed, the local housing authority can no longer rely on its earlier ending of duty. That was the case in *Begum v Tower Hamlets London Borough Council*,[111] where a homeless applicant unreasonably refused an offer of accommodation. She spent a year in unsettled accommodation, returned to her former home and re-applied to the local housing authority when overcrowding there worsened. The Court of Appeal held that the local housing authority was not entitled to rely on its earlier ending of duty and had to accept the further application in the light of the changed factual situation.

Abandoned and withdrawn applications

9.65 Having made an application, an individual may decide not to proceed with it or otherwise be unable to proceed with it. Although this must be commonplace, there is no statutory process for the deemed abandonment or withdrawal of applications. In the absence of such provision, local housing authorities will want to make sensible practical arrangements.

9.66 For example, if the applicant dies before a decision is reached on the application, the local housing authority can simply substitute (with that person's consent) another member of the late applicant's household as applicant.[112]

9.67 Likewise, each local housing authority will have its own procedures and policies for allowing applicants to withdraw their own applications.[113]

9.68 More controversial is the question as to whether there are circumstances in which the local housing authority may itself treat an application as withdrawn. The Codes recommend that local housing authorities may wish to consider an application as 'closed' where there has been no contact from the applicant for 3 months or longer and that any further approach after that time

---

109   *R (Campbell) v Enfield London Borough Council* [2001] EWHC 357 (Admin).
110   *R v Westminster City Council ex p Chambers* (1982) 6 HLR 24, QBD. See **17.109–17.110**.
111   [2005] EWCA Civ 340, [2005] HLR 34, CA.
112   As was done in *R v Camden London Borough Council ex p Hersi* (2001) 33 HLR 577, CA.
113   English Code, para 6.27; Welsh Code, para 12.31.

may be treated as a fresh application. If the applicant renews contact during the 3 months, the suggestion is that the local housing authority should resume its original inquiries, and consider all relevant matters, including whether there are any relevant changes of circumstances that affect those inquiries.[114]

9.69 That guidance is somewhat at variance with HA 1996, Part 7. The legislation recognises that contact will be lost with at least some applicants, because it makes special provision for notice of decision on applications to be retained for later collection at the local housing authority's offices.[115] This would suggest that the proper course is for every application to result in a decision even if the decision is that, on the material available to the local housing authority, it is not satisfied that the applicant is homeless or threatened with homelessness. This has the additional advantage of enabling a local housing authority to maintain comprehensive statistics for decisions on all applications (and the time it takes to reach them) for the purpose of demonstrating compliance with performance standards.

Challenges to refusals to accept applications

9.70 If a local housing authority refuses to accept an application for homelessness assistance (and therefore declines to undertake inquiries into it) there is no right to any statutory review of that decision, or appeal against it. The applicant could lodge a complaint through the local housing authority's complaints procedure, but if a swifter remedy is needed, the applicant should apply for a judicial review[116] and ask for a mandatory order requiring the local housing authority to accept the application and comply with its consequent statutory duties. Judicial review is also the proper course if the applicant is dissatisfied with a local housing authority's decision that it need not accept an application because it is a repeat application and there is no relevant change of facts.[117]

9.71 If the judicial review challenge results in the local housing authority being required to entertain and inquire into the application, then a decision must be reached on it by the local housing authority and notified with reasons. The applicant will then be entitled to seek a review of that decision (and, if necessary, appeal) in the usual way.[118]

---

[114] English Code, para 6.27; Welsh Code, para 12.31.
[115] HA 1996, ss 184(6) and 203(8).
[116] See **19.211–19.237**.
[117] See **9.54–9.64**.
[118] See **19.8–19.210**.

Chapter 10

INQUIRIES AND DECISIONS

INQUIRIES INTO APPLICATIONS

10.1 Once a local housing authority has reason to believe that a person who has made an application for accommodation (or for assistance in obtaining accommodation) may be homeless or threatened with homelessness, it *must* make inquiries sufficient to enable it to answer three questions:

(1)   whether the applicant is 'eligible' for assistance;

(2)   if so, whether any duty under the Housing Act 1996 (HA 1996) Part 7 is owed to the applicant; and

(3)   if so, what duty is owed.[1]

10.2 Separately, the local housing authority has a power, but not a duty, to make inquiries into whether the applicant has a local connection with its district and, if not, whether he or she has a local connection elsewhere.[2] This is an entirely discretionary line of inquiry for the local housing authority; it can choose whether or not to make inquiries into local connection, but if it chooses not to do so, the applicant has no right to a review of that negative decision.[3]

10.3 The trigger for the making of inquiries into the applicant's eligibility and whether any duty is owed to him or her is extremely low.[4] Any information that causes the local housing authority to have reason to believe that the applicant *may* be homeless or threatened with homelessness is sufficient. An applicant does not need to be applying explicitly for homelessness assistance.

10.4 The scope of the compulsory inquiries may appear to be quite limited. For example, although local housing authorities must inquire into an application to see whether any duty is owed under HA 1996, Part 7, there does not appear to be any obligation to inquire into the application to see whether the applicant could be the beneficiary of the exercise of any *power* that the provisions of HA 1996, Part 7 confer on the local housing authority (eg the power to accommodate the non-priority unintentionally homeless).[5] Likewise, inquiries only need be made to determine 'whether' a duty is owed and, therefore, inquiries need not necessarily be made as to the way in which it is appropriate to perform the duty.

10.5 In practice these artificial statutory constraints are ignored. It is good administration for a local housing authority to direct inquiries not only to the

---

[1]   Housing Act 1996, s 184(1).
[2]   HA 1996, s 184(2).
[3]   *Hackney London Borough Council v Sareen* [2003] EWCA Civ 351, (2003) 35 HLR 54, CA.
[4]   See *R (Aweys) v Birmingham City Council* [2007] EWHC 52 (Admin), [2007] HLR 27, Admin Ct at [8] per Collins J; and see **9.50–9.53**.
[5]   See **17.14–17.15**.

prescribed matters but also to broader questions, such as whether it should exercise its relevant powers and as to how it might best discharge any duties it finds it owes the applicant.

10.6 In addition, the legal obligation is to inquire into the possible application of *every* relevant duty under HA 1996, Part 7 regarding the applicant's circumstances. That would include, for example, whether the duty to protect the applicant's possessions had been triggered.[6] This minimum requirement should not be overlooked.

10.7 Considerable guidance as to how these inquiries should be carried out is provided in each of the Codes.[7]

The sequence of inquiries

10.8 The process of making inquiries may be undertaken in stages, thus reflecting the statutory scheme. For example, the first statutory inquiry is as to whether the applicant is 'eligible'.[8] If the local housing authority decides that an applicant is not eligible for assistance, it is not required to make any further inquiries. It would be a waste of time and effort if the local housing authority had to embark on detailed inquiries into other matters (eg whether the applicant had become homeless intentionally), because no duty is owed to an applicant who is ineligible for assistance, beyond the duty to notify the applicant of the reasons for that decision. Treating eligibility as a discrete first issue may therefore lead to a saving of resources. However, if the applicant may be eligible but the question of eligibility cannot be inquired into and resolved immediately, at least some preliminary further inquiries will be necessary in order for the local housing authority to determine whether the applicant may also be homeless and may have priority need and thus be the subject of a duty to provide interim accommodation.[9]

10.9 If the local housing authority decides as a result of its inquiries that an applicant is eligible for assistance, it must then inquire into whether it owes him or her a duty under HA 1996, Part 7. In order to resolve that general question, it must first inquire into and decide whether the applicant is homeless or threatened with homelessness. If the applicant is neither homeless nor threatened with homelessness, no further duty will be owed under HA 1996, Part 7. No further inquiries need be made and the applicant will be notified accordingly that no duty is owed and provided with the reasons for that decision.

---

6   HA 1996, s 211. See **17.163–17.184**.
7   *Homelessness Code of Guidance for local authorities* (Communities and Local Government, Department for Education and Skills, Department of Health, July 2006) (English Code), paras 6.1–6.20; *Code of Guidance for local housing authorities on allocation of accommodation and homelessness for Wales* (National Assembly for Wales, April 2003) (Welsh Code), paras 12.4–12.10.
8   HA 1996, s 184(1)(a). See Chapter 12 of this book.
9   HA 1996, s 188(1). English Code, para 6.16; Welsh Code, para 12.11. See also **16.11–16.24**.

10.10 If the applicant is both eligible for assistance and homeless (or threatened with homelessness), the local housing authority will owe the applicant at least some duty under HA 1996, Part 7. The question then arises as to which duty is owed. In order to answer that question, the local housing authority must inquire into and determine two further issues:

(1)   whether the applicant has a priority need; and

(2)   whether the applicant became homeless intentionally, or became threatened with homelessness intentionally.[10]

10.11 Both of those issues must be the subject of inquiry by the local housing authority in order to determine what duty is owed to the applicant. This requirement to inquire into both matters represents something of a departure from local housing authority practice prior to the Homelessness Act 2002. Before the amendments made by that Act, it was common for local housing authorities to 'slice up'[11] the making of inquiries and to stop if it became plain that the applicant had no priority need for accommodation. Inquiries into intentional homelessness are among the most difficult and time-consuming to make. They were to be avoided, if possible, and there was no point in making them if the applicant had no priority need. This practice had been approved by the courts.[12]

10.12 The new approach requires both matters to be the subject of inquiries in all cases where homelessness, or threatened homelessness, and eligibility are established, and irrespective of any finding that the applicant does not have priority need.[13] To this extent, the old practice of ceasing to make inquiries once an applicant had been found not to have a priority need has gone.[14]

10.13 If the local housing authority decides to exercise its discretionary power to inquire into whether an applicant has a local connection, care must be taken in deciding when to make such inquiries. If the applicant is owed anything short of the main housing duty, such inquiries will have been a waste of time and effort (because local connection is only of relevance if the main housing duty is owed).[15] On the other hand, a local housing authority may want to inquire into local connection at the same time as making its other inquiries, where there is a real prospect that the main housing duty might be found to be

---

[10]   HA 1996, s 184(1)(b).

[11]   *Crawley Borough Council v B* (2000) 32 HLR 636, CA per Buxton LJ.

[12]   *Crawley Borough Council v B* (2000) 32 HLR 636, CA.

[13]   English Code, para 6.12; Welsh Code, Annex 26.

[14]   Although the Court of Appeal has held that there was no error of law where a local housing authority decided that an applicant did not have a priority need and did not make any decision as to whether she had become homeless intentionally: *Gaskin v Norwich City Council* [2007] EWCA Civ 1239, (2008) January *Legal Action*, p 38, CA.

[15]   HA 1996, s 198(1). See also English Code, para 6.14; Welsh Code, para 16.9. See **15.140–15.110**.

owed – thus allowing the local housing authority to make a referral of the main housing duty to a different local housing authority as soon as it has been identified that the duty is owed.

10.14 If the main housing duty[16] is owed (or the equivalent duty is owed to an applicant who is threatened with homelessness),[17] the local housing authority must consider whether that duty is only owed as a result of the presence in the applicant's household of a restricted person.[18] It follows that the local housing authority need only make inquiries into whether the applicant's household contains a restricted person if it has already accepted that the main housing duty is owed to the applicant. It also follows that, if the main housing duty would be owed whether or not the applicant's household included a restricted person, there is no obligation to make inquiries into the presence of the restricted person.[19]

Burden of proof

10.15 The burden of making inquiries rests on the local housing authority. It is for the local housing authority to make the inquiries necessary to 'satisfy' itself whether the applicant is 'eligible' and then, if satisfied that she or he is eligible, to make the inquiries necessary to satisfy itself whether any duty is owed under HA 1996, Part 7.[20]

10.16 It is not for the applicant to 'prove' his or her case.[21] This point has been reiterated in case law and in successive editions of the Codes.[22] The applicant can obviously be asked, or invited, to co-operate with the inquiries and to provide information, but an application cannot be rejected simply because the applicant has not provided some document or other material considered necessary to prove part of his or her case. It follows that the local housing authority cannot suspend inquiries or transfer its responsibilities onto the applicant by such practices as refusing to make a decision unless the applicant obtains a letter from a person with whom he or she recently resided, or a medical report, or a copy of a police or accident report.[23]

10.17 The correct approach was summarised in *R v Gravesham Borough Council ex p Winchester*.[24] The burden lies on local housing authorities to make

---

16   HA 1996, s 193(2). See **17.21–17.110**.
17   HA 1996, s 195(2). See **17.119–17.125**.
18   HA 1996, s 184(3A). See **10.37–10.38** for definition of restricted person. In force for applications made on or after 2 March 2009.
19   See **17.98–17.101**.
20   HA 1996, s 184(1).
21   *R v Woodspring Borough Council ex p Walters* (1984) 16 HLR 73, QBD.
22   English Code, para 6.15; Welsh Code, para 12.5.
23   See Local Government Ombudsman decision D7 (Annual Digest of Cases 2005–2006, at http://www.lgo.org.uk/publications/digest-of-cases/), where a local housing authority was criticised for failing to make any inquiries until the applicant had completed and returned a medical self-assessment form.
24   *R v Gravesham Borough Council ex p Winchester* (1986) 18 HLR 207, QBD.

appropriate inquiries in a caring and sympathetic way. Such inquiries should be pursued rigorously and fairly, but there is no duty to conduct 'CID type inquiries'. Applicants should be given an opportunity to explain matters which local housing authorities consider may weigh substantially against them.[25]

10.18 Very infrequently, an applicant will simply make an application and then refuse to co-operate in the conduct of inquiries, or refuse to provide any but the barest details of himself or herself, or of his or her circumstances. This is not a position that any applicant who was sensibly advised would take, and, if adopted, might suggest that there were issues relating to the applicant's capacity to conduct his or her affairs.[26]

10.19 At the end of the inquiries there is unlikely to be any remaining doubt or uncertainty as to whether an applicant is 'eligible', or over most of the decisions as to what duties, if any, are owed. The local housing authority will be able to determine whether it is satisfied that the applicant is 'eligible', 'homeless', and has a 'priority need'. However, the burden of proof may be decisive where the issue is 'intentional homelessness'. On that matter the legal question is whether the local housing authority is *not* satisfied that the applicant became homeless, or threatened with homelessness, intentionally.[27] Accordingly, on that question, if there is doubt or uncertainty, the issue must be resolved in the applicant's favour.

Scope of inquiries

10.20 The legal obligation on the local housing authority is to make 'such inquiries as are necessary'.[28] But who decides which inquiries are 'necessary'? The courts have repeatedly indicated that it is for the local housing authority to decide what inquiries it considers 'necessary' to undertake. A local housing authority will only err in law if it has failed to make an inquiry that no reasonable local housing authority would have regarded as unnecessary.[29]

10.21 The local housing authority must ensure that it has, in the course of its inquiries, taken all of the applicant's circumstances into account and come to an overall, or composite, view. Whilst inquiries into different aspects, such as medical factors, may be made by different officers of the local housing authority, the final decision should be taken by an officer who has all of the information available.[30]

---

25   See **10.23–10.33**.
26   *AB v Leicester City Council* [2009] EWCA Civ 192, CA.
27   HA 1996, s 193(1); and see **14.14–14.19**.
28   HA 1996, s 184(1), as explained in *R v Kensington and Chelsea Royal London Borough Council ex p Bayani* (1990) 22 HLR 406, CA.
29   See *R v Nottingham City Council ex p Costello* (1989) 21 HLR 301, QBD; *R v Kensington and Chelsea Royal London Borough Council ex p Bayani* (1990) 22 HLR 406, CA; and *Cramp v Hastings Borough Council* [2005] EWCA Civ 1005, [2005] HLR 48, CA.
30   *R v Lewisham London Borough Council ex p Dolan* (1993) 25 HLR 68, QBD.

10.22 Local housing authorities are required by statute to take into account the guidance contained in the Codes of Guidance and any other guidance that the Secretary of State (or the Welsh Assembly Government) issues. For this purpose, local housing authorities need to be able to refer to the current version of the relevant Codes.[31]

Interviewing the applicant

10.23 A local housing authority is obviously obliged to give the applicant the opportunity to explain his or her circumstances fully. In particular, matters that could lead to a decision against the applicant's interests must be put to him or her for comment before the decision is made.[32] One county court judge has decided that, where an applicant's credibility is at issue, he or she should be personally interviewed by the officer making the relevant decision, not by another officer.[33] However, the Court of Appeal would be unlikely to hold that *every* applicant must be interviewed, but also very likely to find that, in some circumstances, an interview would be essential.[34] The Codes are premised on there being at least an initial interview on the day of application.[35]

10.24 Generally, the local housing authority will interview the applicant face to face, although there is no reason why the local housing authority should not put questions to the applicant by letter.[36] There is no statutory requirement that the applicant must be interviewed or offered an interview. Whether the applicant should be interviewed is a matter for the local housing authority to decide.[37]

10.25 The Welsh Code reminds local housing authorities that they should ensure that there is free access to competent interpreters for applicants for whom English is not their first language.[38] An English local housing authority was severely criticised by the Local Government Ombudsman for failing to use

---

[31] HA 1996, s 182. See also *R v Newham London Borough Council ex p Bones* (1993) 25 HLR 357, QBD, where a decision based on an out-of-date edition of the Code was quashed.

[32] English Code, para 6.15; Welsh Code, para 12.6. See also *R v Wyre Borough Council ex p Joyce* (1983) 11 HLR 73, QBD and *R v Dacorum Borough Council ex p Brown* (1989) 21 HLR 405, QBD.

[33] *N v Allerdale Borough Council* (2008) October *Legal Action*, p 38, Carlisle County Court.

[34] *Burr v Hastings Borough Council* [2008] EWCA Civ 1217, (2009) January *Legal Action*, p 27, CA.

[35] English Code, para 616; Welsh Code para 12.22.

[36] In *Rowley v Rugby Borough Council* [2007] EWCA Civ 483, [2007] HLR 40, CA, a local housing authority had not made an error of law when it asked the applicant to confirm what it understood to be her version of events on a tear-off slip, and then relied upon that confirmation.

[37] *Tetteh v Kingston upon Thames London Borough Council* [2004] EWCA Civ 1775, [2005] HLR 21, CA at [26].

[38] Welsh Code, para 12.6.

interpreters in all the interviews with an applicant.[39] In another case, an applicant with impaired hearing was not provided with sufficient assistance during the inquiries.[40]

10.26 The local housing authority's inquiries and, in particular, any interview of the applicant should be conducted in a 'caring and sympathetic way'.[41] It is for the local housing authority to decide how it conducts any interview, how long it lasts and what questions are asked. An error of law will only be made if the style of questioning has the effect of inhibiting the applicant from putting forward his or her case or facts which might assist the application.[42]

10.27 The local housing authority is not required to accept what the applicant says at face value.[43] If the applicant's response raises a relevant matter of fact that the local housing authority is not prepared simply to accept, the local housing authority must investigate it.[44] If there is any doubt, and the matter cannot be resolved by further reasonable inquiries, the question should be resolved in the applicant's favour.[45]

10.28 Where a local housing authority is minded to disbelieve an applicant's account, it should put to the applicant the matters that cause concern.[46]

10.29 Statements from third parties containing material contrary to the applicant's case should be put to the applicant for comment before the local housing authority decides whether or not it accepts those statements. Usually this can be achieved by simply showing the applicant the statements. Guidance in the situation which arises where it is important not to disclose the identity of the third party is given in *R v Poole Borough Council ex p Cooper*.[47] It may be that the applicant is able to provide reasons why the adverse information from the third party cannot be relied upon.[48] Adverse medical evidence, whether

---

39   Local Government Investigation 03/A/15819 (2005) (Waltham Forest London Borough Council).
40   As a result, the decision on the homelessness applications took 15 months, which the Local Government Ombudsman found to be unreasonable delay. The Council paid the applicant £750 for its failure to provide an interpreter and textphone facility and the Ombudsman recommended that the Council should pay the applicant an additional £500 for the inconvenience and uncertainty of living in nightly-let accommodation for 2 years longer than necessary (Redbridge London Borough Council 07/A/03275). See also **10.34–10.36** on delay in notifying decisions.
41   *R v Gravesham Borough Council ex p Winchester* (1986) 18 HLR 207, QBD.
42   *R v Tower Hamlets London Borough Council ex p Khatun (Shafia)* (1996) 27 HLR 465, CA.
43   *R v Kensington & Chelsea Royal London Borough Council ex p Cunha* (1989) 21 HLR 16, QBD.
44   See *R v Tower Hamlets London Borough Council ex p Bibi* (1991) 23 HLR 500, QBD; *R v Northampton Borough Council ex p Clarkson* (1992) 24 HLR 529, QBD; *R v Newham London Borough Council ex p Bones* (1993) 25 HLR 357, QBD; *R v Kensington & Chelsea Royal London Borough Council ex p Silchenstedt* (1996) 29 HLR 728, QBD; and *Forbes v Lambeth London Borough Council* (2000) July *Legal Action*, p 30, Lambeth County Court.
45   *R v Gravesham Borough Council ex p Winchester* (1986) 18 HLR 207, QBD.
46   *R v Hackney London Borough Council ex p Decordova* (1994) 27 HLR 108, QBD.
47   (1994) 27 HLR 605, QBD.
48   See *R v Ealing London Borough Council ex p Chanter* (1992) December *Legal Action*, p 22, QBD, where the applicant's sister had informed the local housing authority that the applicant

from the local housing authority's own medical adviser or the applicant's doctor(s), should also be put to the applicant for comment before a decision is reached.[49]

10.30 If the local housing authority is relying on certain factual information in relation to the applicant's case which conflicts with the applicant's own account, that information should be put to the applicant for comment.[50]

10.31 The local housing authority is entitled to rely upon the applicant's own statement. However, if there is ambiguity or subsequent contradiction of that statement by the applicant, the local housing authority should give the applicant an opportunity to challenge its interpretation of his or her earlier statement.[51]

10.32 It is not for the applicant to volunteer matters that may or may not be relevant. It is for the local housing authority, through interview and other inquiries, to identify those relevant matters and then make the necessary inquiries into them.[52]

10.33 Where an interview would not yield more information than is already known to the local housing authority, an interview will not be a necessary part of the duty to make inquiries.[53]

Timescale

10.34 There is no time limit prescribed by HA 1996, Part 7 for the completion of inquiries. The Codes work on the premise that the obligation to inquire is triggered as soon as the applicant gives the local housing authority reason to believe that he or she may be homeless, or threatened with homelessness. They encourage local housing authorities to carry out their inquiries 'as quickly as possible'.[54] They suggest that local housing authorities should aim to complete their inquiries and notify the applicant of their decision within 33 working

---

had left accommodation voluntarily but, had the statement been put to the applicant, she would have told the local housing authority of long-standing hostility between herself and her sister.

49   *R v Newham London Borough Council ex p Lumley* (2001) 33 HLR 11, QBD, and *Begum (Amirun) v Tower Hamlets London Borough Council* [2002] EWHC 633, (2003) 35 HLR 8, QBD. A careful distinction should be drawn between adverse medical evidence and adverse medical opinion. See **10.48–10.58** for a fuller discussion on the proper conduct of medical inquiries.

50   See *Lane and Ginda v Islington London Borough Council* (2001) April *Legal Action*, p 21, Clerkenwell County Court, where the local housing authority's failure to put information as to the frequency of lift breakdown to the applicant before deciding that accommodation offered was 'suitable' resulted in the decision being quashed.

51   *Robinson v Brent London Borough Council* (1999) 31 HLR 1015, CA.

52   *R v Tower Hamlets London Borough Council ex p Ullah* (1992) 24 HLR 680, QBD.

53   *Kacar v Enfield London Borough Council* (2001) 33 HLR 64, CA.

54   English Code, para 6.16; Welsh Code, paras 12.22–12.23.

days, counted from the date on which the application was received.[55] Local housing authorities are advised that they should carry out an interview and preliminary assessment on the day that the application is received.[56]

10.35 It is unlawful for a local housing authority to postpone the taking of a decision on the conclusion of inquiries (or to extend the inquiry process artificially) simply in order to avoid a duty. Most commonly, this might arise where a 17-year-old makes an application for homelessness assistance shortly before his or her eighteenth birthday.[57]

10.36 If the local housing authority simply fails to progress or complete its inquiries, or fails to notify the decision to the applicant, the applicant is left in a limbo situation. As no decision has been notified, the applicant does not have the right to request a review of it. Instead, an applicant would need to bring judicial review proceedings for a mandatory order requiring the local housing authority to complete its inquiries and notify its decision by a specified date.[58] Alternatively, the applicant could complain through the local housing authority's complaints procedure and ultimately to the Local Government Ombudsmen who can recommend that inquiries be concluded and/or that the applicant should be compensated for delays which amount to maladministration.[59]

---

[55] English Code, para 6.16, adding that 'in many cases it should be possible for authorities to complete the inquiries significantly earlier'; Welsh Code, para 12.22 gives a further 3 working days in which to notify the applicant.

[56] English Code, para 6.16; Welsh Code, para 12.22.

[57] *Robinson v Hammersmith & Fulham London Borough Council* [2006] EWCA Civ 1122, [2007] HLR 7, CA. While 17-year-olds have a priority need by virtue of their age, that is not the position with 18-year-olds: Homelessness (Priority Need for Accommodation) (England) Order 2002, SI 2002/2051, art 3 and Homeless Persons (Priority Need) (Wales) Order 2001, SI 2001/607 (W 30), art 4 and see **10.61–10.62** and **13.112–13.117**.

[58] In *R v Lambeth London Borough Council ex p Weir* [2001] EWHC 121 (Admin), (2001) June *Legal Action*, p 26, Admin Ct, the local housing authority was required to notify the applicant within 14 days after a 20-month delay; in *R v Brent London Borough Council ex p Miyanger* (1996) 29 HLR 628, QBD, the local housing authority was required to make a decision within 28 days and notify the applicant within a further 3 days, after the local housing authority had failed to comply with an agreement made 3 months earlier that a decision would be made. See **17.217**.

[59] Local Government Ombudsman reports: 99/C/4261, where £750 was paid for a period over 300 days to determine an application; 99/B/3040, where a 5-month period was held to be excessive and £1,750 was paid in compensation; D7 2005–2006, where £2,000 compensation was paid; and *Report on an investigation into complaints numbers 07/B/01138 and 07/B/05232 against the London Borough of Lambeth* (LGO, 30 June 2008), (2008) September *Legal Action*, p 25, where £500 was paid for delay causing uncertainty and anxiety, but no serious disadvantage. The Commissioner for Complaints investigating the Northern Ireland Housing Executive recommended £4,000 for a delay of a year ((200700491), (2009) April *Legal Action*, p 22). See **19.241–19.245**.

The special rules for restricted persons

10.37 Where the applicant's household includes a 'restricted person',[60] there may be additional inquiries to be made and additional notification duties.[61]

10.38 A 'restricted person' is defined as a person:

- who is not eligible for assistance under HA 1996, Part 7;[62] and

- who is subject to immigration control within the meaning of the Asylum and Immigration Act 1996;[63] and either

- does not have leave to enter or remain in the UK; or

- whose leave to enter or remain in the UK is subject to a condition to maintain and accommodate himself or herself, and any dependant, without recourse to public funds.[64]

It follows that British nationals, some Commonwealth nationals and most EEA nationals and their family members cannot be restricted persons.[65]

PARTICULAR SITUATIONS

Violence or harassment

10.39 The Codes recommend that inquiries into cases where violence is alleged 'will need careful handling'. Local housing authorities are advised that it is essential that their inquiries do not provoke further violence and are warned against approaching the alleged perpetrator. Information may be sought from friends, relatives, social services, or the police.[66]

10.40 If the violence alleged is *domestic* violence, local housing authorities are reminded that the applicant 'may be in considerable distress'. The interview should be conducted by an officer who is trained to deal with domestic violence allegations, and the applicant should have the option of requesting an officer of the same sex as him or her.[67] Local housing authorities are advised that applicants alleging domestic violence may not be able to produce independent evidence of the violence. Whilst a local housing authority may seek corroboration, it should not reject the applicant's account merely because there

---

60   HA 1996, s 184(7). See **10.38**.
61   HA 1996, s 184(3A). See **10.14**.
62   See Chapter 12 of this book.
63   See **12.53–12.59**.
64   HA 1996, s 184(7).
65   See **12.54**.
66   English Code, para 6.17; Welsh Code, para 12.9.
67   English Code, para 6.17; Welsh Code, para 12.9.

is no evidence of complaints to the police or other agencies.[68] Local housing authorities are reminded that the test to be applied is not whether violence occurred in the past but whether it is probable that there will be violence (or threats of violence that are likely to be carried out) if the applicant continues to occupy his or her home.[69]

10.41 A local housing authority must investigate accounts of violence or harassment given by the applicant when it is making its inquiries into whether accommodation is or was reasonable for the applicant to continue to occupy.[70] A local housing authority cannot refuse to investigate these accounts merely because the applicant had failed to raise them at an earlier stage.[71]

10.42 If the local housing authority is considering disbelieving an applicant because of contradictions or inconsistencies in his or her account, or because of information derived from other sources, those contradictions or inconsistencies should be put to the applicant for explanation.[72]

Financial problems

10.43 If accommodation has been lost as a result of the applicant accruing rent or mortgage arrears, the local housing authority will need to make inquiries into the applicant's financial affairs. Those same issues may also be relevant to the question of whether accommodation currently occupied by the applicant is reasonable for him or her to continue to occupy.[73]

10.44 The local housing authority should examine why an applicant had fallen into arrears and give him or her an opportunity to explain the cause of the arrears, their extent and any arrangements made to repay them.[74] The local housing authority should investigate whether an applicant knew about the availability of housing benefit, whether housing benefit was claimed and if not, why not.[75] In a case where the applicants had not disputed the landlord's claim to possession on the grounds that they were in arrears, but had subsequently argued that the contractual rent was lower than that put forward to the court and therefore they were not in arrears, the local housing authority was not

---

[68] *Hawa Abdilah Ali v Newham London Borough Council* (2000) November *Legal Action*, p 23, Bow County Court. English Code, paras 6.19 and 8.22.

[69] English Code, paras 6.17–6.18 and 8.18–8.25; Welsh Code, paras 12.9, 13.23 and 14.52. See also *Bond v Leicester City Council* [2001] EWCA Civ 1544, (2002) 34 HLR 6, CA. See further **11.78–11.88**.

[70] *R v Northampton Borough Council ex p Clarkson* (1992) 24 HLR 529, QBD, where the local housing authority's decision that an applicant had become homeless intentionally was quashed, as it had failed to make inquiries into her account that her brother had sexually harassed her at the accommodation.

[71] *R v Hackney London Borough Council ex p Decordova* (1994) 27 HLR 108, QBD.

[72] *R v Camden London Borough Council ex p Mohammed* (1997) 30 HLR 315, QBD.

[73] Homelessness (Suitability of Accommodation) Order 1996, SI 1996/3204. See **11.97** and **14.164–14.171**.

[74] *R v Wyre Borough Council ex p Joyce* (1983) 11 HLR 73, QBD.

[75] *R v Tower Hamlets London Borough Council ex p Saber* (1992) 24 HLR 611, QBD.

obliged to make inquiries into the actual level of the contractual rent. The court would not have made a possession order if the contractual rent had been the amount stated by the applicants.[76]

10.45 If an applicant gave up his or her accommodation due to financial pressure, the local housing authority must determine the extent of that pressure, eg what debts may have been owed by the applicant and what the arrangements for repayment were. If loans were taken out to support a business venture, it is relevant to inquire into what the applicant knew or ought to have known about the business's prospects.[77] The local housing authority must consider fully whether or not an applicant could have afforded to have remained in accommodation, but need not engage in detailed arithmetical calculations or verification of itemised expenses.[78]

Acquiescence

10.46 In general, if a couple has lost accommodation as a result of the deliberate act or omission of one of them (eg by the one who was the tenant or owner accruing rent or mortgage arrears or engaging in nuisance behaviour), the local housing authority is entitled to assume that the other one acquiesced in that behaviour.[79] However, if there is any suggestion to the contrary, the local housing authority must investigate whether there was such acquiescence in that particular case.[80] Whilst the English Code states 'the applicant will need to demonstrate that he or she was not involved in the acts or omissions that led to homelessness, and did not have control over them'[81] – a reversal of the burden of proof – this is over-stating the lawful approach which can be found in the judgment of Woolf J in *R v North Devon District Council ex p Lewis*:[82]

> 'it would be perfectly proper in the ordinary case for the housing authority to look at the family as a whole and assume, in the absence of material which indicates to the contrary, where the conduct of one member of the family was such that he should be regarded as having become homeless intentionally, that was conduct to which the other members of the family were a party.'[83]

---

76   *Green v Croydon London Borough Council* [2007] EWCA Civ 1367, [2008] HLR 28, CA.
77   *R v Exeter City Council ex p Tranckle* (1993) 26 HLR 244, QBD.
78   *R v Brent London Borough Council ex p Grossett* (1994) 28 HLR 9, CA; and *Bernard v Enfield London Borough Council* [2001] EWCA Civ 1831, (2002) 34 HLR 46, CA. English local housing authorities should have regard to the Secretary of State's *Supplementary Guidance on Intentional Homelessness* (CLG, August 2009): see Appendix 2.
79   *R v North Devon District Council ex p Lewis* [1981] 1 WLR 328, QBD.
80   *R v Eastleigh Borough Council ex p Beattie (No 2)* (1984) 17 HLR 168, QBD. See **14.78–14.82**.
81   English Code, para 11.5. The reversal of the burden of proof is not reproduced in the Welsh Code.
82   [1981] 1 WLR 328, QBD.
83   *R v North Devon District Council ex parte Lewis* [1981] 1 WLR 328, QBD at 333.

10.47 Where there is material that indicates that the applicant did not acquiesce in the action that rendered the household homeless intentionally, that material must be considered.[84]

Medical conditions

10.48 Local housing authorities may need to make inquiries into an applicant's medical condition in order to decide whether he or she has a priority need,[85] whether previous accommodation was reasonable for the applicant to continue to occupy,[86] or whether accommodation currently occupied is suitable for the applicant's needs.[87]

10.49 Where a medical issue is raised by an applicant, the local housing authority should obtain medical evidence.[88] A local housing authority can obtain the opinion of its own medical adviser, but any decision on the facts and the overall assessment should be made by the local housing authority and not delegated to the medical adviser.[89]

10.50 The medical adviser must act fairly in obtaining any relevant information from the applicant's own doctors and in coming to an opinion. Depending on the circumstances, the applicant's medical records should be considered and it may even be necessary to examine the applicant personally or to discuss the applicant's case with his or her own doctors.[90]

10.51 If the applicant complains that he or she is anxious or depressed, it may be appropriate to obtain specialist psychiatric evidence.[91]

---

[84] *R v West Dorset District Council ex parte Phillips* (1984) 17 HLR 336, QBD; and *N v Allerdale Borough Council* (2008) October *Legal Action*, p 38, Carlisle County Court.

[85] See **13.62–13.99**.

[86] See **11.72–11.117** and **14.108–14.126**.

[87] See Chapter 18 of this book.

[88] *Osmani v Camden London Borough Council* [2004] EWCA Civ 1706, [2005] HLR 22, CA.

[89] *R v Lambeth London Borough Council ex p Walters* (1994) 26 HLR 170, QBD; *Osmani v Camden London Borough Council* [2004] EWCA Civ 1706, [2005] HLR 22, CA; *Cramp v Hastings Borough Council* [2005] EWCA Civ 1005, [2005] HLR 48, CA; and *Shala v Birmingham City Council* [2007] EWCA Civ 624, [2008] HLR 8, CA.

[90] *R v Lambeth London Borough Council ex p Walters* (1994) 26 HLR 170, QBD; and *Shala v Birmingham City Council* [2007] EWCA Civ 624, [2008] HLR 8, CA. Whether or not a personal examination is required will depend on the particular facts. See *Khelassi v Brent London Borough Council* [2006] EWCA Civ 1825, (2007) February *Legal Action*, p 31, CA (where there had been a personal medical examination); *Shala v Birmingham City Council* [2007] EWCA Civ 624, [2008] HLR 8, CA (where the local housing authority was reminded to bear in mind that its medical adviser had not examined the applicant); *Wandsworth London Borough Council v Allison* [2008] EWCA Civ 354, (2008) June *Legal Action*, p 33, CA (where a pesonal examination was not necessary); and *R (Bauer-Czarnomski) v Ealing London Borough Council* [2010] EWHC Admin 130, Admin Ct.

[91] *R v Brent London Borough Council ex p McManus* (1993) 25 HLR 643, QBD. But see *Wells v Tower Hamlets London Borough Council* [2006] EWCA Civ 755, (2006) September *Legal Action*, p 14, CA, where the local housing authority was entitled to rely on the opinion of its own medical adviser, a GP, who had accepted (but provided a 'gloss' to) the opinion expressed by the applicant's treating psychiatrist.

10.52 If there are differences of opinion between the local housing authority's medical advisers and the medical opinion put forward on behalf of the applicant, the local housing authority should request an explanation for those differences.[92] The local housing authority should also take into account differences in medical expertise when trying to reconcile conflicting medical opinion.[93]

10.53 An adverse medical opinion, including one from the applicant's own doctor(s), should normally be put to the applicant for comment.[94] So too should any medical advice that raises new issues or contentious points.[95]

10.54 Where a local housing authority's policy was to 'encourage persons who have any knowledge of an applicant's medical or social history to attend' the decision-making panel, and the applicant's doctor had expressed a wish to attend, the local housing authority was severely criticised by the Local Government Ombudsman for failing to invite the doctor.[96]

10.55 The final decision (for example, as to whether or not an applicant is vulnerable) is for the local housing authority, not for the medical adviser, but normally the medical adviser should be asked to address the relevant statutory test (such as vulnerability).[97]

10.56 Where the local housing authority has to make decisions on both medical and non-medical aspects, it cannot treat the two aspects entirely separately. It must come to an overall, or composite, assessment of the applicant's circumstances.[98]

---

[92]   *R v Kensington & Chelsea Royal London Borough Council ex p Assiter* (1996), (1996) September *Legal Action*, p 13, QBD.

[93]   *Yemlahi v Lambeth London Borough Council* (2000) August *Legal Action*, p 26, Wandsworth County Court; *Khelassi v Brent London Borough Council* [2006] EWCA Civ 1825, (2007) February *Legal Action*, p 31, CA; and *Shala v Birmingham City Council* [2007] EWCA Civ 624, [2008] HLR 8, CA.

[94]   *R v Newham London Borough Council ex p Lumley* (2001) 33 HLR 11, QBD; *Yemlahi v Lambeth London Borough Council* (2000) August *Legal Action*, p 26, Wandsworth County Court; and *R (Amirun Begum) v Tower Hamlets London Borough Council* [2002] EWHC 633 (Admin), (2003) 35 HLR 8, QBD. But see *Wells v Tower Hamlets London Borough Council* [2006] EWCA Civ 755, (2006) September *Legal Action*, p 14, CA, where the applicant's medical evidence had been accepted and the local housing authority's medical adviser had added 'a gloss'. In those circumstances, there was no obligation to put the medical adviser's comments to the applicant.

[95]   *Hall v Wandsworth London Borough Council* [2004] EWCA Civ 1740, [2005] HLR 23, CA.

[96]   Local Government Ombudsman Investigation 03/A/15819 (Waltham Forest London Borough Council).

[97]   *Sicilia v Waltham Forest London Borough Council* (2002) December *Legal Action*, p 21, Bow County Court; *Ryde v Enfield London Borough Council* [2005] EWCA Civ 1281, (2006) January *Legal Action*, p 32, CA. See also, in the context of an application for an alocation of social housing, *R (Bauer-Czarnomski) v Ealing London Borough Council* [2010] EWHC Admin 130, Admin Ct, where the medical adviser did overstep the remit.

[98]   *R v Lewisham London Borough Council ex p Dolan* (1993) 25 HLR 68, QBD; and *Crossley v City of Westminster* [2006] EWCA Civ 140, [2006] HLR 26, CA.

10.57 When the local housing authority is assessing whether an applicant is 'vulnerable', and care, health or other support needs are identified in the course of that assessment, the local housing authority should liaise with social services and health authorities, where appropriate, as part of its inquiries.[99] It may be necessary to obtain an assessment from the relevant specialist authority.[100]

10.58 The Court of Appeal has considered the issue of the use, by local housing authorities, of medical advisers.[101] It has held:

> 'It is entirely right that local authority officers, themselves without any medical expertise, should not be expected to make their own critical evaluation of applicants' medical evidence and should have access to specialist advice about it. What would not be acceptable is seeking out advisers to support a refusal of priority need housing wherever possible.'[102]

It reminded local housing authorities that it is not the medical advisers but the local housing authorities that have the task of determining whether an applicant has a priority need (or any other medically related question). It is appropriate for medical advisers to be asked to address the specific issue which the local housing authority has to decide, and to furnish material within their professional competence which addresses that issue.[103] It also reminded local housing authorities that, unless their medical adviser has personally examined the applicant, his or her opinion cannot be considered expert evidence of the applicant's condition.[104]

Overcrowded accommodation

10.59 If an applicant claims that his or her present or previous accommodation is or was overcrowded, and therefore not reasonable for him or her to continue to occupy, the local housing authority must make inquiries to determine whether the accommodation is or was overcrowded and, if so, to what extent.[105] Where there is a dispute as to the size, space or arrangement of

---

[99]   English Code, para 10.17.

[100] Welsh Code, para 12.10.

[101] *Shala v Birmingham City Council* [2007] EWCA Civ 624, [2008] HLR 8, CA.

[102] *Shala v Birmingham City Council* [2007] EWCA Civ 624, [2008] HLR 8, CA at [19] per Sedley LJ.

[103] Or, as a later Court of Appeal decision put it, to comment 'on the medical evidence in order to enable the local authority to understand the medical issues and to evaluate for itself the evidence before it as to [the applicant's] medical condition'. In those circumstances 'it would plainly not have been appropriate for [the local housing authority's medical adviser] to examine' the applicant. *Wandsworth London Borough Council v Allison* [2008] EWCA Civ 354, (2008) June *Legal Action*, p 33, CA.

[104] *Shala v Birmingham City Council* [2007] EWCA Civ 624, [2008] HLR 8, CA at [19]–[22] per Sedley LJ. An attempt to argue that the particular medical adviser's organisation was 'biased in favour of their paymasters' received short shrift from the Court of Appeal in *Harper v Oxford City Council* [2007] EWCA Civ 1169, (2008) January *Legal Action*, p 37, CA.

[105] *R v Tower Hamlets London Borough Council ex p Bibi* (1991) 23 HLR 500, QBD. See **11.105–11.107**.

the accommodation, inquiries should be made so that the local housing authority can make its own decision on the disputed issues.[106]

DECISIONS ON APPLICATIONS

10.60 Once the local housing authority has completed its inquiries into an application, it is required to notify the applicant of its decision.[107] *Every* application therefore results in notification of a decision.[108] The requirements as to the content of the decision notice are given in HA 1996, s 184, so that the colloquialism 'a section 184 notice' or 'section 184 letter' is commonly used to refer to a local housing authority's notification of a decision on an application. There is no question of applicants being given the result informally in lieu of a written notification. Every applicant, even if she or he is found to be not eligible or not homeless, is entitled to a written decision. Even those successful in their application obtain a written record of that success[109].

10.61 There is one circumstance in which it might be important to distinguish between the date on which the decision was actually made and the date when it was put in writing and 'notified' to the applicant. The local housing authority is under an obligation, when making its decision, to consider the facts and the law in existence at the date of the decision. If either the facts or the law change in an interval between the actual making of the decision and putting it in writing, it will be the facts and law that existed at the date of the actual making of the decision that are relevant, not those existing at the date of the written notification.

10.62 In one case, the local housing authority concluded, on the day before an applicant's eighteenth birthday, that she did not have a priority need. The decision was actually put in writing on the following day. The Court of Appeal held that the decision was made on the day before the birthday, and therefore, applying the facts and law at that date, the local housing authority should have concluded that the applicant had a priority need by reason of her age.[110]

10.63 However, time limits attaching to rights to request a review (and subsequently appeal) run from the date when the written decision is 'notified' to

---

[106] *R v Kensington & Chelsea Royal London Borough Council ex p Silchenstedt* (1997) 29 HLR 728, QBD.

[107] HA 1996, s 184(3). The Codes recommend that inquiries should be completed as quickly as possible and that applicants are notified within 33 working days: English Code, para 6.16; Welsh Code, paras 12.2–2.23. See **10.34–10.36**.

[108] English Code, paras 6.21–6.25; Welsh Code, paras 12.24–12.30.

[109] The Local Government Ombudsman found maladministration when a local housing authority failed to notify the applicant of the decision on his application for homelessness assistance (Local Government Ombudsmen Digest of Cases 2005–2006, D7, at http://www.lgo.org.uk/publications/digest-of-cases/).

[110] *Robinson v Hammersmith & Fulham London Borough Council* [2006] EWCA Civ 1122, [2007] HLR 7, CA. See **13.112–13.117**.

the applicant. This is likely to be a date different from, and later than, either the actual date of the decision, or the date of the written decision.[111]

10.64 There is no statutory time limit within which the decision reached on the application must be notified.[112] HA 1996, Part 7 assumes that notice of the decision will be given by local housing authorities 'on completing their inquiries', which suggests immediately.[113] However, and rather more practically, previous editions of the Code have suggested that written notifications be produced within 3 working days of the completion of inquiries. The present English Code reproduces the statutory formula: notification of a decision must be given 'when a housing authority has completed its inquiries'.[114]

10.65 The decision must be put in writing.[115] If any issue has been decided against the applicant's interests, the local housing authority must not only notify that decision but also inform the applicant in writing of the reasons for its decision.[116] The duty to give reasons applies to all decisions that the local housing authority is obliged to make on an application (decisions as to whether the applicant is 'eligible', whether a duty is owed, and, if so, what duty) and to any decision that it chooses to make as to whether the applicant has a local connection.[117] However, to make sense in practice, this obligation is interpreted to mean that any adverse finding on any issue decided in the course of working out what duty is owed must be explained by reasons. Therefore, it is not sufficient for a local housing authority simply to notify a positive decision that the duty owed is the limited duty in HA 1996, s 190. It must explain, with reasons, why the applicant is not owed the highest duty set out in HA 1996, s 193.[118]

---

[111] Notification refers to receipt of the decision by the applicant, not the date on the letter: see **19.57**.

[112] See **10.60**.

[113] HA 1996, s 184(3).

[114] English Code, para 6.21. The Welsh Code, para 12.23 suggests 3 working days from completion of inquiries. A decision which was reached 11 months after the applicant had been interviewed and where the applicant's circumstances had changed during those 11 months was held to be 'manifestly' flawed, and the special procedure under Allocation of Housing and Homelessness (Review Procedures) Regulations 1999, SI 1999/71, reg 8(2) should have been implemented: *Lambeth London Borough Council v Johnston* [2008] EWCA Civ 690, [2009] HLR 10, CA. See **19.84–19.93** for reg 8(2). See also *Report on an investigation into complaints numbers 07/B/01138 and 07/B/05232 against the London Borough of Lambeth* (LGO, 30 June 2008), (2008) September *Legal Action*, p 25, where £500 was paid for delay causing uncertainty and anxiety, but no serious disadvantage. The Commissioner for Complaints investigating the Northern Ireland Housing Executive recommended £4,000 for a delay of a year ((200700491), (2009) April *Legal Action*, p 22).

[115] HA 1996, s 184(6).

[116] HA 1996, s 184(3).

[117] HA 1996, s 184(4); where a local housing authority found that an applicant did not have a priority need, but failed to make any decision as to whether or not he was homeless, the Local Government Ombudsman said that the decision was defective: Local Government Ombudsman Investigation 03/A/15819 (Waltham Forest London Borough Council, Annual Digest of Cases 2005/06, at http://www.lgo.org.uk/publications/digest-of-cases/).

[118] As to the detail required to be given see **10.68–10.74**.

10.66 The decision is limited to whether or not the statutory criteria are met and, as a result of those findings, what duty (if any) is owed to the applicant. The decision cannot impose further requirements on an applicant or suggest that a duty is conditional upon the applicant doing something, such as surrendering an existing tenancy.[119]

10.67 Whether the decision notified by the local housing authority is favourable or unfavourable, the notification letter must inform the applicant of his or her right to request a review and also of the 21-day period within which any request for a review must be made.[120] The Codes advise local housing authorities that the decision letter should also notify applicants about the local housing authority's procedure for conducting reviews.[121]

Reasons

10.68 The Codes recommend that the reasons for the decision are explained clearly and fully and that any assistance that can be made available to the applicant is also clearly set out. If the applicant has difficulty in understanding the decision, the local housing authority should consider arranging for a member of staff to explain the decision in person.[122]

10.69 The reasons given must be proper, intelligible and adequate and relate to the substantive issues raised by the applicant.[123] An applicant is entitled to reasons so that he or she can understand, clearly, why he or she has not succeeded and can properly assess any prospects of challenging that decision.[124] In addition, adequate reasons serve to indicate that:

'... the decision-maker has gone through the right process of thinking in arriving at its conclusion.'[125]

10.70 Merely reciting the relevant legal formula set out in HA 1996, Part 7, and stating that the applicant does not meet it, will not amount to giving adequate and sufficient reasons.[126] For example, where a local housing authority is satisfied that an applicant has become homeless intentionally, the decision letter should state:

---

[119] *R (Hammia) v Wandsworth London Borough Council* [2005] EWHC 1127 (Admin), [2005] HLR 45, Admin Ct. However, conditions may attach to the duty to protect the applicant's possessions: see **17.163–17.184**.

[120] HA 1996, s 184(5).

[121] English Code, para 6.22; Welsh Code, paras 12.24–12.25.

[122] English Code, para 6.23; Welsh Code, para 12.28.

[123] *Re Poyser and Mills' Arbitration* [1964] 2 QB 467, QBD; *Westminster City Council v Great Portland Estates plc* [1985] AC 661, HL; and *South Bucks District Council v Porter (No 2)* [2004] UKHL 33, [2004] 1 WLR 1953, HL.

[124] *R v Croydon London Borough Council ex p Graham* (1993) 26 HLR 286, CA; *R v Camden London Borough Council ex p Mohammed* (1998) 30 HLR 315, QBD; and *Shire v Birmingham City Council* (2003) March *Legal Action*, p 30, Birmingham County Court.

[125] *R v Newham London Borough Council ex p Qureshi* (1998) March *Legal Action*, p 14, QBD.

[126] *R v Camden London Borough Council ex p Adair* (1996) 29 HLR 236, QBD; and *R v Islington London Borough Council ex p Trail* (1993) Times, 27 May, QBD.

(1)   when the local housing authority considers that the applicant became homeless;

(2)   why he or she become homeless;

(3)   whether the accommodatoin lost was 'available' for the applicant's occupation;[127] and and

(4)   why it would have been be reasonable for the applicant to have continued to occupy the accommodation.[128]

10.71   The deliberate act or omission of the applicant which is said to have caused the intentional homelessness should be identified, even though the findings can be expressed simply and briefly.[129] Where the central issue is whether it would have been reasonable for the applicant to have continued to occupy the previous accommodation, the decision letter should state what factors were considered in deciding that it would have been reasonable to continue to occupy and specifically address the reasons given by the applicant for leaving.[130]

10.72   Where there are medical issues, the decision letter should give reasons for rejecting any medical opinions.[131]

10.73   Where there were contradictory factual accounts put before the local housing authority, and it prefers one account to another, the decision letter should explain that that was the case, and why a particular account was preferred.[132]

10.74   If a decision letter fails to refer to part of the applicant's case, the inference will be that the local housing authority has failed to have regard to that matter.[133]

---

[127]   HA 1996, s 175(1). See **11.15–11.31**.

[128]   *R v Gloucester City Council, ex p Miles* (1985) 17 HLR 292, CA.

[129]   *R v Hillingdon London Borough Council ex p H* (1988) 20 HLR 554, QBD.

[130]   *R v Tower Hamlets London Borough Council ex p Monaf* (1988) 20 HLR 529, CA; and *R v Tower Hamlets London Borough Council ex p Ojo* (1991) 23 HLR 488, QBD.

[131]   *R v Kensington and Chelsea Royal London Borough Council ex p Campbell* (1995) 28 HLR 160, QBD. In *Al-Kabi v Southwark London Borough Council* (2008) March *Legal Action*, p 21, Lambeth County Court, a decision letter was found to be defective for its failure to mention the medical evidence at all, and no reasons were given for the local housing authority's decision to reject the undisputed medical evidence.

[132]   *R v Wandsworth London Borough Council ex p Dodia* (1997) 30 HLR 562, QBD.

[133]   *R (Jeylani)v Waltham Forest London Borough Council* [2002] EWHC 487 (Admin), (2002) May *Legal Action*, p 30, Admin Ct.

The special rules for restricted persons

10.75 There is an additional notification duty falling on local housing authorities where the applicant's household includes a restricted person.[134]

10.76 This additional notification duty only arises if:

- the local housing authority decides that the applicant is owed the main housing duty[135] or the equivalent duty where the applicant is threatened with homelessness;[136] and

- that duty is only owed to the applicant because of the presence of the restricted person in the applicant's household.[137]

10.77 If those two conditions are met, the local housing authority must:

- inform the applicant that the decision that he or she is owed the main housing duty (or equivalent duty) was reached having regard to the restricted person in the applicant's household;

- include the name of the restricted person;

- explain why the person is a restricted person; and

- explain the effect of the modification to the main housing duty, or equivalent duty, as a result of HA 1996, s 193(7AD) or s 195(4A).[138]

10.78 It should be noted that the additional notification duty does not apply in all cases where the applicant's household includes a restricted person. If the main housing duty, or equivalent duty where the applicant is threatened with homelessness, is not owed, the notification duty does not apply. Nor does it apply if the main housing duty (or equivalent duty) would have arisen despite the presence in the applicant's household of a restricted person.[139]

Insufficient reasons

10.79 A properly notified decision should give sufficient reasons for the applicant to understand why she or he has been unsuccessful on an issue and to enable the applicant to assess whether to make, and how best to frame, an application for review.

---

[134] HA 1996, s 184(3A) and (7), inserted by Housing and Regeneration Act 2008, s 314 and Sch 15. For 'restricted person', see **10.37–10.38**. This provision applies to applications to both English and Welsh local housing authorities made on or after 2 March 2009.

[135] HA 1996, s 193(2). See **17.21–17.110**.

[136] HA 1996, s 195(2). See **17.119–17.131**.

[137] HA 1996, s 184(3A).

[138] HA 1996, s 184(3A). For the modification to the main housing duty, and equivalent duty, as a result of HA 1996, s 193(7AD) and s 195(4A), see **17.98–17.108** and **17.126–17.131**.

[139] See **7.98**.

10.80 If the applicant considers that the reasoning given is insufficient to explain the decision, she or he could simply ignore the deficiency and apply for a review.[140] If the reasons given in a subsequent review decision are sufficient, the failure to comply with the requirement to give reasons in the initial decision will generally be cured by the reasons in the review decision (but not always).[141]

10.81 However, where the paucity of reasons in the initial decision means that the applicant cannot make a properly informed assessment as to whether to request a review, or how best to frame a review request, there will be a real need to secure the proper reasons. In the first instance the applicant might simply ask the local housing authority to give, or to supplement, its reasons. If the local housing authority's response does not provide adequate reasons, then the applicant may want to seek a judicial review and a declaration that the obligation to give reasons has not been complied with, in breach of the legal requirement. The courts will be slow to intervene unless it is clear that the deficiency in the reasons is such as to render any attempt to use the statutory mechanism unfair because the applicant simply does not know what was found against him or her, and what the case is that needs to be met.[142] As a fall-back, to protect against the eventuality that the court may find the reasons adequate, the applicant may want to lodge a formal request for a review within the 21-day time limit and invite the local housing authority to hold the conclusion of the review until the outcome of the judicial review proceedings.

The effect of a section 184 decision

10.82 When a local housing authority has concluded its inquiries and notified the applicant as to whether he or she is owed a duty and, if so, what duty, then (unless the applicant requests a review of the decision) that is normally the end of the matter. If the notification is that a duty is owed, the local housing authority then has to ensure that the duty is performed. The duty cannot be postponed or made conditional upon the applicant complying with certain requirements.[143]

10.83 Once the local housing authority has complied with the relevant statutory duty to provide accommodation or provide advice and assistance, then it has performed its duty. If the duty towards the applicant is the main HA 1996, s 193 duty to provide accommodation, it only comes to an end if one or more of the events set out at HA 1996, s 193(5)–(7F) inclusive occur.[144]

---

[140] See **19.8–19.140**.

[141] *Simpson v Brent London Borough Council* (2000) November *Legal Action*, p 23, Willesden County Court; and *R (Lynch) v Lambeth London Borough Council* [2006] EWHC 2737 (Admin), [2007] HLR 15, Admin Ct.

[142] *R v Camden London Borough Council ex p Mohammed* (1998) 30 HLR 315, QBD.

[143] *R (Hammia) v Wandsworth London Borough Council* [2005] EWHC 1127 (Admin), [2005] HLR 45, Admin Ct.

[144] See **17.38–17.108**.

10.84 Once the local housing authority has accepted a duty towards the applicant, it cannot subsequently reconsider its decision if the applicant's circumstances change (if, for example, he or she ceases to have a priority need).[145] If the HA 1996, s 184 decision has been obtained by the applicant's fraud or deception, or is the result of a fundamental mistake over the facts prevailing at the date of the decision, the local housing authority may revisit and re-open its decision.[146]

DECISIONS PENDING THE OUTCOME OF AN APPLICATION

10.85 Not every decision made by a local housing authority in the course of dealing with an application must be notified to the applicant in writing, let alone with reasons given. In the course of dealing with an application for homelessness assistance, the local housing authority may well take a number of decisions of importance to the applicant. For example:

(1) whether to provide interim accommodation pending a decision on the application;

(2) what accommodation to provide;

(3) whether to withdraw the interim accommodation, perhaps because the applicant has rejected it;

(4) whether to conduct an interview in the course of inquiries;

(5) which matters to inquire into;

(6) whether to explore local connection issues;

and many more.

10.86 None of these decisions need be put in writing by the local housing authority. None of them give rise to an opportunity for a statutory review. If a local housing authority is asked for a written notification and/or reasons for one of these decisions, it may provide them. On any challenge to the relevant decision (in proceedings brought by judicial review) it would be helpful to the

---

[145] *R v Brent London Borough Council ex p Sadiq* (2001) 33 HLR 47, QBD, unless the duty is that owed under HA 1996, s 193(2) and the change of circumstances is one of the events set out at HA 1996, s 193(6). See **17.59–17.77**.

[146] *R v Southwark London Borough Council ex p Dagou* (1995) 28 HLR 72, QBD; *Crawley Borough Council v B* (2000) 32 HLR 636, CA; and *Porteous v West Dorset District Council* [2004] EWCA Civ 244, [2004] HLR 30, CA. For a discussion of the limited circumstances in which s 184 decisions might be withdrawn unilaterally by a local housing authority, see Ian Loveland 'Homelessness reviews: when can local authorities withdraw s 184 decisions?' (2007) March *Legal Action*, p 20.

local housing authority to be able to point to a contemporaneous written explanation to the applicant as to why it had reached the decision under challenge.

INQUIRIES AND DECISIONS AFTER THE INITIAL APPLICATION HAS BEEN DETERMINED

10.87　The decision notified to the applicant on the conclusion of inquiries into his or her application is unlikely to be the last important decision that has to be made by the local housing authority, particularly where the initial decision is that the applicant *is* owed a duty under HA 1996, Part 7.

10.88　Very commonly, having made the initial decision on the application, the local housing authority will have to make a whole series of subsequent decisions in its dealings with the applicant. Even in the relatively simple case, that of a priority need applicant who has been found to have become homeless intentionally, the decision on the application will only be that there is a duty owed under HA 1996, Part 7, and that that duty is the duty contained in HA 1996, s 190 (in summary, to assess housing needs and to provide assistance and short-term accommodation).[147] But later, having conducted the assessment required by HA 1996, s 190(4), the local housing authority must decide exactly what assistance to provide and for how long accommodation should be provided. It must decide which members of the household to accommodate and where to accommodate them. And so on.

10.89　While HA 1996, s 184 gives helpful direction about the content and terms of written decisions on the initial application, HA 1996, Part 7 has little guidance to offer about such subsequent matters which will be the subject of significant decision-making.

10.90　A few specific decisions made after determination of the initial application *are* subject to notification requirements. These include:

(1)　a decision to refer an application to another local housing authority under the local connection provisions (because the local housing authority making the referral owes the main housing duty and believes that the conditions for referral may be met);[148]

(2)　a decision that the conditions for referral of an application to another local housing authority are actually met;[149]

---

[147] See **17.111–17.118**.

[148] HA 1996, s 184(4): a decision which must be notified with reasons. See **15.125–15.129**.

[149] HA 1996, s 200(2): a decision which must be notified with reasons. See **15.130–15.133**.

(3) a decision that the local housing authority regards its duty under HA 1996, s 193 as ended by operation of HA 1996, s 193(5), (6), (7) or (7B).[150]

10.91 Beyond that, the question of how and when local housing authorities conduct inquiries into post-application matters and how, if at all, they must notify decisions on those matters are not directly answered by HA 1996, Part 7.

10.92 It is probably safe to suggest that the proper inference to be drawn from the structure of the statutory provisions on the 'right to request a review'[151] is that, at least in respect of the decisions that are potentially subject to a right of review, the local housing authority must notify (ie put in writing) those decisions.

10.93 For example, the first potentially reviewable decision is a decision as to whether an applicant is 'eligible' for assistance.[152] Where that decision has been made on the initial application, no difficulty arises. The decision must have been the subject of inquiries and must be notified in writing with reasons.[153]

10.94 But the question of eligibility can fall for consideration again at a later stage. There may be a question as to whether an applicant who was found to be eligible on the initial application and was owed the main HA 1996, s 193 duty has since ceased to be eligible, with the effect that that duty has ended.[154] HA 1996, Part 7 imposes no express obligation on a local housing authority to inquire into the applicant's possibly changed circumstances in relation to eligibility, nor any duty to reach a new decision, nor to notify a new decision – let alone with reasons.

10.95 However, the structure of HA 1996, s 202 suggests that all reviewable decisions will have been notified in writing.[155] So, if the proper reading of HA 1996, s 202(1)(a) is that it applies to a decision that an applicant has *ceased* to be eligible, the inference is that that decision must be notified in writing. Although there is no express obligation to give reasons for the decision, it makes good administrative sense for reasons to be given, so that both the applicant and any subsequent reviewing officer can understand why the new decision was made.

10.96 Two further decisions which frequently fall to be made by local housing authorities, *after* the notified HA 1996, s 184 decision on the original application, are:

---

[150] HA 1996, s 193: a decision which is not required to be notified with reasons, but carries a right to request a review under HA 1996, s 202(1)(b) (*Warsame v Hounslow London Borough Council* (2002) 32 HLR 335, CA). See **17.38–17.108**.

[151] HA 1996, s 202(1). See **19.8–19.127**.

[152] HA 1996, s 202(1)(a). See also Chapter 12 and **19.13**.

[153] HA 1996, s 184 (1) and (3).

[154] HA 1996, s 193(6)(a). See **17.59–17.61**.

[155] See, in particular, HA 1996, s 202(3). See **19.36–19.38** and **19.56–19.62**.

(1)   whether accommodation offered to an applicant in performance of a HA 1996, Part 7 duty is 'suitable';[156] and

(2)   whether the circumstances triggering an end of a duty owed to an applicant are made out.[157]

10.97   The decision as to suitability is not specifically required to be notified in writing, nor is it the subject of any obligation to give reasons. Nor, indeed, is there any express obligation on the local housing authority to make inquiries into the issue of suitability (although, because it is a public authority, it must have regard to all relevant considerations and otherwise comply with the ordinary principles of administrative law). However, where the issue of suitability relates to anything other than HA 1996, s 188 interim accommodation, the applicant has a right to request a review of the local housing authority's assessment of suitability.[158] So again, the necessary inference is that the local housing authority is required to give a written notification of the decision on 'suitability'. Although there is no express obligation to give reasons for the decision, it makes good administrative sense for reasons to be given so that both the applicant (and any subsequent reviewing officer) can understand why the decision has been made.

10.98   The same inference applies to any decision that the duty owed to the applicant has come to an end. The Court of Appeal has decided that a local housing authority's decision that 'has the effect of causing the duty to cease to exist' is a decision which is capable of statutory review.[159] Accordingly, the necessary inference must be that the decision in respect of which there is a right to review is one that must be notified in writing. But again, there is no express obligation on the local housing authority to conduct any inquiries leading up to its decision, nor is there any duty to give reasons for the decision. So, although there is no express obligation to give reasons for the decision, it makes good administrative sense for reasons to be given so that both the applicant (and any subsequent reviewing officer) can understand why the new decision has been made.

10.99   This still leaves a large number of decisions which will be made by a local housing authority in the course of its dealings with an applicant which are not the subject of any express requirement:

(1)   to make inquiries;

(2)   to notify the decision in writing; or

(3)   to give reasons.

---

[156]   See Chapter 18 of this book.
[157]   See **17.38–17.108**.
[158]   HA 1996, s 202(1)(f). See **19.27–19.35**.
[159]   *Warsame v Hounslow London Borough Council* (2000) 32 HLR 335, CA.

10.100 Those are the decisions in relation to which there is no explicit statutory requirement under HA 1996, s 184 or elsewhere,[160] and no right to a statutory review.[161] Accordingly, these decisions are subject only to the normal constraints of good administration and administrative law. An applicant aggrieved by any such decision could use the complaints procedure, complain to the Local Government Ombudsmen and/or bring proceedings for judicial review. These options are explored in Chapter 19.[162]

---

[160] See **10.1**.
[161] See **19.12–19.35**.
[162] See **19.238–19.240** and **19.241–19.245**.

Chapter 11

HOMELESS OR THREATENED WITH HOMELESSNESS

INTRODUCTION

11.1 The main statutory duties set out in Part 7 of the Housing Act 1996 (HA 1996) are owed only to those whom a local housing authority is satisfied are either 'homeless' or 'threatened with homelessness'. Each of those terms is very tightly defined by HA 1996, Part 7, so that there is no room for alternative terminology, such as 'rooflessness', or for more colloquial approaches such as whether someone has 'a place to sleep' or 'a home of their own'. As this chapter demonstrates, the tightness of the legal definitions can produce some surprising results: even the owner of a mansion could, in certain circumstances, be 'homeless' for the purposes of HA 1996, Part 7.

DEFINITION OF 'HOMELESS'

Overview

11.2 The legal definition of 'homeless' is contained in three inter-related sections of HA 1996, Part 7.[1] Taken together, these sections provide that a person is homeless if he or she:

(1) has no accommodation physically available for him or her to occupy in the UK or elsewhere;[2] or

(2) has no accommodation available which he or she is legally entitled to occupy;[3] or

(3) has accommodation which is available and which he or she is entitled to occupy, but cannot secure entry to that accommodation;[4] or

(4) has accommodation available, which he or she is entitled to occupy, but that accommodation consists of a moveable structure and there is no place where the applicant is entitled or permitted both to place and reside in it;[5] or

(5) has accommodation available, which he or she is entitled to occupy and entry can be secured to it, but that accommodation is not reasonable to continue to occupy.[6]

11.3 In practice, the easiest way to apply the statutory definition is to start from the presumption that everyone is homeless. Then to ask whether, on the facts, *all* of the following conditions are satisfied:

---

[1] Housing Act 1996, ss 175–178.
[2] HA 1996, s 175(1).
[3] HA 1996, s 175(1)(a)–(c).
[4] HA 1996, s 175(2)(a).
[5] HA 1996, s 175(2)(b).
[6] HA 1996, s 175(3).

(1) there is 'accommodation';[7] and

(2) it is 'available' for the applicant's occupation;[8] and

(3) the applicant has some right to occupy it;[9] and

(4) the applicant can physically enter it;[10] and

(5) it would be reasonable for the applicant to continue to occupy it.[11]

11.4 Only if *all* of those conditions are fulfilled can the applicant be said not to be 'homeless'. There is an extra condition which must be satisfied if the relevant accommodation is 'a moveable structure'.[12]

11.5 In the following paragraphs each of these conditions, which form the component parts of the statutory definition of 'homeless', are examined in turn.

The meaning of 'accommodation'

11.6 The question is not 'Does the applicant have an "address"?'[13] or 'Does he or she have somewhere to stay?' but rather 'Does the applicant have "accommodation"?'.

11.7 HA 1996, Part 7 gives no definition of this term. The standard dictionary definitions refer to 'lodgings or premises'.[14] In practice, ordinary English usage tends to refer to 'accommodation' as shelter with a degree of permanence.

11.8 It is for the local housing authority to decide whether what it is considering is 'accommodation'. Houses or flats (or parts of them) are not the only units that the local housing authority can regard as falling within the meaning of 'accommodation'. In *R v Hillingdon London Borough Council ex p Puhlhofer*,[15] the courts upheld a local housing authority's decision that a modest hotel room in a bed and breakfast guest house occupied by a husband and wife and their two children (later described as a 'single cramped and squalid bedroom')[16] was 'accommodation'.

---

7   See **11.6–11.14**.
8   See **11.15–11.31**.
9   See **11.32–11.64**.
10 See **11.65–11.66**.
11 See **11.72–11.117**.
12 Discussed at **11.67–11.71**.
13 *Tickner v Mole Valley District Council* [1980] LAG Bull 187, CA.
14 For example, in the *Shorter Oxford English Dictionary*.
15 *R v Hillingdon London Borough Council ex p Puhlhofer* [1986] AC 484, HL.
16 *R v Brent London Borough Council ex p Awua* [1996] 1 AC 55, HL at 68B–D per Lord Hoffmann.

11.9 This does not mean that anything pressed into service for sleeping in can constitute 'accommodation'. Examples not constituting 'accommodation' canvassed in the case law include 'Diogenes' barrel'[17] and 'a potting shed'.[18] It would be hard to describe a cardboard box in a shop doorway, a factory where a homeless worker was allowed to sleep overnight, or a car used to sleep in as 'accommodation'. Even though a prison cell is physically capable of accommodating a prisoner, it cannot be treated as 'accommodation' for the purposes of the definition of 'homeless'.[19]

11.10 From 1982 until 2008, the approach of the courts was that *crisis accommodation* should not fall within the definition of 'accommodation' for these purposes. This approach was based on a 1982 decision that women's refuges did not fall within the definition.[20] The approach was reviewed, and held to be wrong, by the Court of Appeal in 2008 in *Moran v Manchester City Council, Richards v Ipswich Borough Council*.[21] The House of Lords subsequently considered an appeal in that case and decided that women's refuges were not reasonable for women to continue to occupy indefinitely. As a result, the House of Lords held that there was no need to consider, in reaching its own decision in that case, whether other refuges and hostels, or other forms of shelter such as prison cells or hospital wards, were 'accommodation' or not.[22]

11.11 For policy reasons, accommodation provided by a local housing authority under the interim duty to accommodate,[23] or under its power to provide accommodation pending review[24] or pending appeal,[25] is not 'accommodation' for the purposes of the statutory definition. An applicant is still homeless even if occupying such interim accommodation.[26]

---

17   *R v Hillingdon London Borough Council ex p Puhlhofer* [1986] AC 484, HL at 517 per Lord Brightman, also referred to in *R v Newham London Borough Council ex p Ojuri (No 2)* (1999) 31 HLR 452, QBD by Collins J. In *Moran v Manchester City Council, Richards v Ipswich Borough Council* [2008] EWCA Civ 378, [2008] HLR 39, CA at [28] Wilson LJ described Lord Brightman's reference to Diogenes' barrel as a phrase 'which, with respect, was neatly apt but has since become hackneyed by repetition'.

18   *R v Hillingdon London Borough Council ex p Puhlhofer* [1986] AC 484, HL at 491 per Ackner LJ (giving judgment in the Court of Appeal).

19   *Stewart v London Borough of Lambeth* [2002] EWCA Civ 753, [2002] HLR 40, CA and *R (B) v Southwark London Borough Council* [2003] EWHC 1678 (Admin), (2004) 36 HLR 3, Admin Ct.

20   *R v Ealing London Borough Council ex p Sidhu* (1982) 2 HLR 41, QBD, applying *Williams v Cynon Valley Borough Council* [1980] LAG Bull 16.

21   [2008] EWCA Civ 378, [2008] HLR 39, CA.

22   *Ali & others v Birmingham City Council, Moran v Manchester City Council* [2009] UKHL 36, [2009] 1 WLR 1506, HL at [52] and [56] per Baroness Hale.

23   HA 1996, s 188(1). See **16.10–16.18**.

24   HA 1996, s 188(3). See **16.19–16.28**.

25   HA 1996, s 204(4). See **16.29–16.33**.

26   *R (Alam) v Tower Hamlets London Borough Council* [2009] EWHC 44, (2009) March *Legal Action*, p 24. In *Ali & others v Birmingham City Council, Moran v Manchester City Council* [2009] UKHL 36, [2009] 1 WLR 1506, HL, Manchester City Council accepted that an applicant remained homeless while occupying interim accommodation provided under HA 1996, s 188(1): see Baroness Hale at [55].

11.12 But some circumstances can generate real issues as to whether the subject matter is 'accommodation'. For example, is a tent or a beach hut that a family has been forced to occupy for several weeks 'accommodation'?

11.13 These issues on the meaning of 'accommodation' are brought into sharper focus by the globalisation of the definition of homelessness. Until 1996 the question was whether the applicant had 'accommodation' in England, Scotland or Wales. Now the question is whether the applicant has 'accommodation' in the United Kingdom (bringing Northern Ireland within scope)[27] or 'elsewhere', ie anywhere in the world.[28] As a result, the question 'Is it "accommodation"?' must now be applied to a wider range of forms of habitation.

11.14 If the local housing authority has decided that the applicant has 'accommodation', the next inquiry is whether it is 'available for his occupation'.[29]

The meaning of 'available for occupation'

11.15 The local housing authority must consider first whether the accommodation is factually 'available'. If so, the second consideration is whether the accommodation is 'available for' the applicant's occupation and for the occupation of all members of the applicant's household as defined by HA 1996, s 176.

The factual test

11.16 The factual question is the most straightforward: is the particular accommodation 'available' to the applicant as a matter of fact? HA 1996, Part 7 specifically deals with situations where admission to the accommodation is physically barred so that the applicant cannot secure entry to it.[30] But factual 'availability' can embrace broader issues, especially given that the accommodation under consideration might be anywhere in the world. In *Begum v Tower Hamlets London Borough Council*,[31] the accommodation being considered was a room in the applicant's father-in-law's house in Bangladesh. The court was satisfied that if the applicant had said to the local housing authority that she could not get to Bangladesh (eg because of her lack of means) or could not enter that country (eg because of her immigration status) the local housing authority would have had to decide whether the accommodation was in fact 'available' to her:

---

27   See Chapter 12, Box 1.
28   HA 1996, s 175(1).
29   HA 1996, s 175(1).
30   HA 1996, s 175(2)(a); see **11.65–11.66**.
31   *Begum v Tower Hamlets London Borough Council* (2000) 32 HLR 445, CA.

'To hold that it is available to her because it is legally and physically hers to occupy, without regard to the question of whether she has any way of getting there, is not only to take leave of reality; it is to drain the word "available" of any meaning.'[32]

11.17 So, if there is perfectly good accommodation that the applicant has the right to occupy, but it is not in fact 'available', the applicant is homeless. Those granted refugee status in the UK because they cannot return to their countries of origin may have perfectly good homes in those countries but would be 'homeless' here because their accommodation is not 'available'. Likewise, the issue of whether accommodation is 'available' is raised where:

(1) a person leaves his or her home in search of work, travels to the other end of the country and expends all his or her resources looking for work, leaving him or her unable to return home;

(2) a person is the subject of a banning order under anti-terrorism legislation preventing him or her from returning to a country (or a part of this country) in which his or her home is situated; or

(3) a person is prohibited by a court order (such as an injunction, closure notice, closure order, or bail conditions) from entering the premises or geographic area in which his or her home is situated.[33]

11.18 In each of these cases, although the applicant would have accommodation which he or she is legally entitled to occupy, the accommodation would not be 'available' for his or her occupation.

The special statutory definition

11.19 If there is accommodation factually available to the applicant, the next question is whether the special statutory definition of 'available' is met.[34] Accommodation only counts as available if it is available for occupation not only by the applicant, but also by those people who normally reside with the applicant as members of his or her family, and also by any other person who might reasonably be expected to reside with the applicant.[35]

---

[32]   *Begum v Tower Hamlets London Borough Council* (2000) 32 HLR 445, CA at 464 per Sedley LJ. It should be noted that the majority of the Court of Appeal in *Begum v Tower Hamlets London Borough Council* said that the issue of whether or not accommodation was reasonable for an applicant to occupy was not relevant where the applicant was not actually occupying the accommodation. That has now been held to be wrong by the Court of Appeal in *Waltham Forest London Borough Council v Maloba* [2008] EWCA Civ 1281, [2008] HLR 26, CA. See **11.73**.

[33]   First two examples cited in *Begum v Tower Hamlets London Borough Council* (2000) 32 HLR 445, CA at 464 per Sedley LJ.

[34]   HA 1996, s 176.

[35]   HA 1996, s 176.

11.20 In effect, this means that accommodation will only be considered available if it is available for both the applicant and all of the other members of his or her household to occupy. The purpose of the provision is clear: a person is to be considered homeless *unless* there is accommodation sufficient in its factual and legal capacity to accommodate the applicant's entire household. So the local housing authority first needs to establish the extent of the relevant household and then consider whether there is accommodation available for all those persons to occupy together.

Members of the applicant's household

11.21 Two different groups of people could fall within the applicant's household for these purposes:

(1) Group One – those who normally reside with the applicant as a member of the applicant's family.[36]

(2) Group Two – any other persons who might reasonably be expected to reside with the applicant.[37]

Group One: 'normally resides with him as a member of his family'[38]

11.22 To fall within Group One a person must fulfil two conditions:

• he or she must normally reside with the applicant; and

• must do so as a member of the applicant's family.

11.23 There is no additional condition that it would be 'reasonable' for that person to reside with the applicant.[39] The local housing authority may or may not think it reasonable for the applicant to be normally residing, as part of one family unit, with a host of relatives, in-laws, or even friends and others. But the local housing authority's opinion is irrelevant. The conditions raise simple factual questions for decision – who is living with the applicant and why – not issues of judgment.

11.24 To fall within the first condition, it is necessary that the person concerned 'resides with' the applicant. Someone who is simply a regular visitor to the applicant's home will not fall within the definition.[40] A very short period of temporary residence with the applicant is also unlikely to suffice, because the

---

[36] HA 1996, s 176(a).

[37] HA 1996, s 176(b).

[38] HA 1996, s 176(a).

[39] *R v Newham London Borough Council ex p Khan and Hussain* (2001) 33 HLR 269, QBD, where the local housing authority's decision that two adult sisters, who both occupied accommodation together along with their husbands and children, did not normally reside together was held to be irrational.

[40] See further discussion of 'resides with' at **13.44–13.47**.

person must 'normally' reside with the applicant. Finally, there is no requirement that the person who normally lives with the applicant is literally doing so at the time of the application for homelessness assistance.[41] Children will still 'normally reside' with their mother even if she fled the family home in fear of domestic violence a few days earlier. An elderly frail person unable to return from hospital to his or her normal home will 'normally reside with' those with whom he or she was living before going into hospital.

11.25 The second condition is that the person normally resides with the applicant 'as a member of his [or her] family'.[42] This term is not defined in HA 1996, Part 7. Indeed, a definition of 'family' would not help, as the test is whether the person lived with the applicant 'as' a member of the applicant's family. The question is not whether the other person *is* a member of the applicant's family.

11.26 Limited help is to be found in the Codes of Guidance, not least because the English and Welsh Codes have slightly different approaches.

11.27 According to the English Code,[43] '[t]he phrase "as a member of his [or her] family" will include those with close blood or marital relationships and cohabiting partners (including same sex partners)'. In the Welsh Code, 'as a member of his [or her] family' is given a broader treatment and the Code advises that the phrase be taken to include foster children, housekeepers, companions and carers as well as those falling within the English Code's definition of relationships through blood, marriage or cohabitation.[44] The approach taken in the Welsh Code more accurately reflects the statutory language. To paraphrase, the correct legal question is 'Does this person normally live with the applicant *as* a member of the applicant's family?' That person may or may not actually *be* a member of the applicant's family.

Group Two: 'any other person who might reasonably be expected to reside with him'[45]

11.28 The second group who may qualify for these purposes as members of the applicant's household (Group Two) contains three potential sub-groups. These comprise:

(1) any member of the applicant's family not normally residing with him or her, but who might reasonably be expected to reside with the applicant.

---

41 This is recognised by the English Code at para 8.6.

42 HA 1996, s 176(a).

43 *Homelessness Code of Guidance for local authorities* (Communities and Local Government, Department for Education and Skills, Department of Health, July 2006) (English Code), paras 8.5–8.6, at Appendix 2 of this book.

44 *Code of Guidance for local housing authorities on allocation of accommodation and homelessness for Wales* (National Assembly for Wales, April 2003) (Welsh Code), para 13.3.

45 HA 1996, s 176(b).

For example, a dependent child who has been living with his or her mother but who is, by arrangement between the separated parents, to begin living with his or her father (the applicant) will fall within this category.[46] As the Codes helpfully emphasise, the question of who the child is to reside with is nowadays more likely to be dealt with by parental agreement than by court order.[47] Another example would be a young married couple who have to live apart, with their respective parents, because they have nowhere they can live together.[48] It must be remembered that one expressed purpose of the legislation is 'bringing families together'.[49]

(2) someone already normally residing with the applicant (but not as a member of his or her family) who might reasonably be expected to continue to reside with the applicant.

This might be a lodger, nanny, paid housekeeper, au pair, friend of the family or anyone else who has been living with the applicant but not 'as' a family member. Obviously the fact that the person is already actually residing with the applicant will be a powerful factor when the local housing authority decides whether it is reasonable for him or her to continue to live with the applicant.

(3) someone who is not a member of the applicant's family and does not normally live with the applicant but who might reasonably be expected to reside with the applicant.

This sub-group will embrace those who wish to live with the applicant but do not currently do so. The classic examples are the prospective carer or live-in companion who wishes to live with and look after the applicant. But the classic example can sometimes cause a local housing authority to believe that the relevant question is whether the applicant needs a companion or carer. That is not the correct approach.[50] The question is simple: 'Is it reasonable to expect this person to reside with the applicant?'

11.29 The English Code gives two further examples of those who will fall within the second group of household members (Group Two):

• foster children;[51] and

• companions for elderly or disabled applicants.

---

[46] For further examples where the person is a dependent child see **13.48–13.61**.

[47] English Code, para 8.6; Welsh Code, para 13.4. See *Holmes-Moorhouse v Richmond upon Thames Royal London Borough Council* [2009] UKHL 7, [2009] 1 WLR 413, HL for a discussion on 'reside with' in the context of the priority need test. See **13.56**.

[48] As was the case in *R v Westminster City Council ex p Chambers* [1982] 6 HLR 24, QBD.

[49] *Din v Wandsworth London Borough Council* [1983] 1 AC 657, HL at 663, per Lord Wilberforce.

[50] *R v Hackney London Borough Council ex p Tonnicodi* (1998) 30 HLR 916, QBD.

[51] Although the correct approach in the authors' view should be that existing foster children would fall within Group One, and prospective foster children within Group Two.

The Code advises that they might reasonably be expected to reside with an applicant.[52] A full-time live-in carer has been held to fall within this category.[53]

Application of the special statutory definition

11.30 Once the local housing authority has identified the total number of people forming the applicant's household (ie the composite of Groups One and Two), it can return to the central task of determining whether the applicant is 'homeless'. The relevant question posed by HA 1996, Part 7 is then whether the accommodation under consideration is available not just for occupation by the applicant but also for occupation by all the members of the applicant's household.[54]

11.31 This is essentially a factual issue about practical and legal availability. If the only accommodation available to a male applicant is a shared room with four other men in a men-only lodging house, he will be homeless if his household now includes a female (for example, a woman he has just married or a wife with whom he has been reunited)[55] and he does not have other accommodation into which he can move. Likewise, if a husband and wife have a home together, but the husband is prevented from returning to it by some legal restriction (such as a court order obtained by a third party) the wife will be 'homeless' on her application to the local housing authority, because her home is no longer available to a member of her family with whom she normally resides.

The meaning of 'entitled to occupy'

11.32 Assuming that the local housing authority is satisfied that there is accommodation[56] available to the applicant and his or her household,[57] the next question is whether the applicant has some sort of right or legal entitlement to occupy the accommodation.[58]

11.33 An applicant will have a relevant entitlement to occupy accommodation only if he or she has the right to occupy by reason of one of the following:

- a legal interest in it;[59] or

---

52 English Code, para 8.5. The Welsh Code advises that housekeepers, companions or carers would fall within Group One as people who normally reside with the applicant as a member of his or her family: Welsh Code, para 13.3.
53 *R v Kensington and Chelsea Royal London Borough Council ex p Kassam* (1994) 26 HLR 455, QBD, and *R v Hackney London Borough Council ex p Tonnicodi* (1998) 30 HLR 916, QBD.
54 HA 1996, s 176.
55 As was the case in *R v Hillingdon London Borough Council ex p Islam* [1983] 1 AC 688, HL.
56 See **11.6–11.14**.
57 See **11.15–11.31**.
58 HA 1996, s 175(1).
59 HA 1996, s 175(1)(a).

- the benefit of an order of a court that he or she is entitled to occupy it;[60] or

- an express or implied licence to occupy it;[61] or

- some legal protection preventing the applicant from being evicted from it.[62]

11.34 If an applicant rids himself or herself of the right to occupy (eg by selling owned property or by assigning or ending a lease or tenancy), then he or she will be homeless but is likely to be found to have become homeless intentionally.[63]

11.35 Each of the relevant forms of right to occupy requires close consideration.

'... an interest in it'[64]

11.36 This first alternative is satisfied if the applicant has a legal interest in the accommodation. That might be freehold or leasehold ownership or a tenancy. Unless the applicant enjoys some other right to occupy the accommodation, he or she will become homeless when the legal interest is brought to an end. For example, a joint tenant's legal interest will end on the expiry of a notice to quit given by the other joint tenant.[65]

11.37 However, a legal interest only counts for these purposes if, by virtue of it, the applicant is entitled to occupy the accommodation. It is not sufficient for the local housing authority to establish that the applicant owns the accommodation. He or she may have let or sub-let it to others who are, as a result, the people entitled to occupy it, whereas the applicant is not. The local housing authority could not, in those circumstances, avoid finding that the applicant is homeless by advising him or her to repossess the property let out to tenants. The applicant is 'homeless' now.

'... an order of a court'[66]

11.38 A person may be entitled to occupy accommodation under an order of a court, if, for example, he or she has the protection of a court order granting him or her the right to occupy in family proceedings, or (more unusually) a

---

60   HA 1996, s 175(1)(a).
61   HA 1996, s 175(1)(b).
62   HA 1996, s 175(1)(c).
63   *R v Wandsworth London Borough Council ex p Oteng* (1994) 26 HLR 413, CA. See Chapter 14.
64   HA 1996, s 175(1)(a).
65   *Fletcher v Brent London Borough Council* [2006] EWCA Civ 960, [2007] HLR 12, CA.
66   HA 1996, s 175(1)(a).

court has made a declaration that the person has a beneficial interest in the land carrying a right to immediate occupation.[67]

'... *express or implied licence to occupy*'[68]

11.39 A licence is simply permission to occupy. The person giving the permission is a licensor; the person given the permission is the licensee. An express licence arises when permission to occupy is explicitly given verbally or in writing. An implied licence exists when permission to occupy has never been expressly granted but can simply be inferred or assumed (for example, very few parents expressly say to their young children 'you can live with me' – such permission is to be inferred).

11.40 Sometimes, the permission will have been granted in return for the payment of money or provision of services. More often, the licence will be a bare licence, the simple grant of permission to occupy without any money or services paid in return. Examples of licensees given in the Codes are lodgers, employees who have service occupancies (ie accommodation that they occupy in order to do their jobs) and those living with relatives.[69] Precisely because 'licence' simply means 'permission' it can be used to apply to accommodation anywhere in the world without the need to refer to the property laws of the relevant country.

11.41 The task for the local housing authority is to identify whether the applicant 'has' (present tense) an express or implied licence to occupy the relevant accommodation.[70] This means that a licence that an applicant did have in the past, or could get in the future, is quite irrelevant to the question of whether he or she is homeless now. Even if the local housing authority can identify accommodation that the applicant has recently occupied under a licence (which has ended), and where a further licence is being offered, the applicant will still be 'homeless'. So, where a former live-in housekeeper, having lost her employment and the licence to occupy accommodation, had been offered re-employment and a further licence, she was still homeless at the date of her application.[71] Likewise, an applicant who has a licence to occupy a night shelter for one night only is homeless during the day, even if he or she could secure another licence for another night in the same shelter.[72]

11.42 If an applicant occupies accommodation under an express or an implied licence, she or he will normally be entitled to 4 weeks' written notice to

---

[67] Family Law Act 1996, ss 30–39; Trusts of Land and Appointment of Trustees Act 1996, s 12.
[68] HA 1996, s 175(1)(b).
[69] English Code, paras 8.7(ii) and 8.8(ii); Welsh Code, para 13.5.
[70] HA 1996, s 175(1)(b).
[71] *R v Kensington and Chelsea Royal London Borough Council ex p Minton* (1988) 20 HLR 648, QBD.
[72] *R v Waveney District Council ex p Bowers* [1983] QB 238, CA. The decision that the applicant was homeless in these circumstances was made at first instance by Stephen Brown J (as he then was) and was not subject to appeal to the Court of Appeal. The first instance decision is at (1982) The Times, May 25.

end that licence.[73] If the legal requirement of 4 weeks' notice does not apply,[74] the notice period will be whatever is stated in any written licence agreement. If there is no such agreement, the licence can be ended by reasonable notice, which can be given verbally. In certain circumstances 'you've got 10 minutes to leave my house' could be sufficient reasonable notice to end a licence. Obviously, during any notice period, the licence will still be in place.

11.43 Once the licence has ended (ie any fixed term, or notice period, has expired), the former licensee will be a trespasser in the accommodation. Some ex-licensees will be protected by the Protection from Eviction Act 1977 from eviction without a court order and will therefore not be immediately homeless (because there is a restriction on the former licensor recovering possession).[75]

11.44 For those licensees who are *not* protected by the Protection from Eviction Act 1977,[76] homelessness will arise immediately the licence ends, even if they do not actually move out. In such cases, the Codes correctly advise local housing authorities that if the licence has been determined, but the occupier remains in occupation as a trespasser, the occupier will be homeless.[77] The Codes give, as examples, the termination of licences to those who have been living with friends or relatives, in hostels or hospitals, or former employees occupying premises under a service occupancy whose contracts of employment have ended.[78] Each of those examples is outside the protection of the Protection from Eviction Act 1977.

11.45 The Court of Appeal has held that, where a secure tenant leaves his or her accommodation, and the landlord subsequently terminates the tenancy by service of a notice to quit, but has refrained from taking possession proceedings, the former tenant becomes a licensee during the 'period of grace' before proceedings are brought.[79] This is a difficult decision to construe. If the tenant was occupying his or her accommodation at the date of expiry of the notice to quit, then the notice would not have determined the tenancy and the tenant would have continued to enjoy security of tenure.[80] If, on the other hand, the tenant had not been occupying his or her accommodation at that

---

73 Protection from Eviction Act 1977, s 5.
74 There are a wide range of circumstances in which it will not, such as where the licensee shares accommodation with the licensor. See *R v Hammersmith & Fulham London Borough Council ex p O'Sullivan* [1991] EGCS 110, QBD.
75 See **11.58–11.64** and **11.98–11.99**.
76 Protection from Eviction Act 1977, s 3A defines licences and tenancies which are excluded from protection.
77 English Code, para 8.8; Welsh Code, para 13.6. See also *R v Surrey Heath Borough Council ex p Li* (1984) 16 HLR 79, QBD, where the local housing authority's advice to a former licensee asked to leave service accommodation – that s/he could remain in occupation until a possession order was obtained – was held to be wrong, and a decision that the applicant was not homeless was quashed.
78 English Code, para 8.8; Welsh Code, para 13.6.
79 *Porteous v West Dorset District Council* [2004] EWCA Civ 244, [2004] HLR 30, CA.
80 Housing Act 1985, ss 81–82 for secure tenancies; Housing Act 1988, ss 1 and 5 for assured tenancies.

date,[81] then he or she was not a residential occupier and was not entitled to the protection offered by the Protection from Eviction Act 1977. In effect, this former tenant was being offered a chance to return to the accommodation, even though the previous tenancy had been terminated and she did not enjoy the protection of the Protection from Eviction Act 1977. It is hard to see how that chance can be construed as a licence.

11.46 Various Local Government Ombudsman investigations have found maladministration where applicants who did not enjoy protection under the Protection from Eviction Act 1977 were wrongly told that they were not homeless until possession orders were obtained against them.[82]

11.47 One of the most common causes of homelessness is the termination of a licence to occupy the home of a friend or relative with whom the applicant has been staying. Many such applicants apply to local housing authorities reporting simply that they have been 'asked to leave'. Quite properly, the English Code recommends that where someone reports being asked to leave accommodation by family or friends: 'the housing authority will need to consider carefully whether the applicant's licence to occupy has in fact been revoked' (so that the applicant is 'homeless') or whether, instead, the request to leave is merely a warning of an intention to terminate the licence at some future date (in which case the applicant may not be homeless, although he or she may be threatened with homelessness).[83]

11.48 Beyond that, the English Code offers a confusing mix of advice on best practice in such cases. It warns that there may be collusion in order to assist the applicant to obtain housing from the local housing authority. Or there may be genuine difficulties between the guest and host that could be resolved with help. It suggests that local housing authorities should consider providing support, arranging family mediation services, or assisting the applicant to find alternative accommodation. Local housing authorities are reminded that they should be sensitive to the possibility that applicants may be at risk of violence or abuse if they return home.[84] But all this guidance leaves unasked and unanswered the important central question: whether the permission to occupy (ie the licence) has been ended or not ended.

11.49 All too often the resolution of that simple question is deferred by (quite improperly) requiring the friend or relative, who has already told the applicant to leave, to confirm it in writing or by suggesting that a home visit at some later date will be necessary. As indicated above, save in those cases covered by the

---

81 As was the case in *Porteous v West Dorset District Council* [2004] EWCA Civ 244, [2004] HLR 30, CA.

82 See eg Local Government Ombudsman Investigation 90/A/1038 (Ealing London Borough Council), where the local housing authority was invited to repay to the complainants the legal costs that they had been ordered to pay to their resident landlord by the court in the possession proceedings, having been wrongly told by the local housing authority that they should await a court order.

83 English Code, para 8.9; not reproduced in the Welsh Code.

84 English Code, paras 8.9–8.12.

Protection from Eviction Act 1977, there is no need for notice terminating a licence to be given in writing.[85] If the licence has been terminated, the applicant has no home to visit. Worse still, applicants are sometimes told that the local housing authority will not even entertain applications for homelessness assistance without the applicants themselves producing a letter from their former hosts requiring them to leave. This practice is, of course, an unlawful attempt to reverse the burden imposed on the local housing authority to undertake the inquiries itself.[86]

11.50 Sadly, it is often young people asked to leave their parental home (frequently in sudden and traumatic circumstances), who find it most difficult to achieve prompt decisions as to whether they are 'homeless' because their licence has been determined. A person who has been told 'Get out now and never set your foot in this house again' is pretty plainly 'homeless'.

11.51 The English Code contains specific guidance on dealing with 16- and 17-year-olds in this situation.[87] The Secretary of State's view is that generally it is in their best interests to remain in the family home, unless they would be at risk of violence or abuse. The Code warns that turbulent relationships between a 16- or 17-year-old and his or her family are not unusual. There may be temporary disagreements or estrangements, but not always a genuine intention to exclude the child from the family home. Local housing authorities are advised to consider the possibility of family reconciliation, or of the 16- or 17-year-old residing with a member of the wider family. They are advised to be particularly alive to the possibility of collusion when assessing applications from 16- and 17-year-olds.[88] Again, such general guidance can blur the real question: whether the licence to occupy has been ended or not. If it has, the young person is 'homeless'.

11.52 The guidance was considered by the House of Lords in *R (M) v Hammersmith & Fulham London Borough Council*.[89] Giving the leading judgment, Baroness Hale considered the guidance in the English Code. She noted the 'risk of collusion and fabrication' but added that 'any mediation or reconciliation will need careful brokering and housing authorities may wish to seek the assistance of social services in all such cases'.[90]

11.53 The Court of Appeal has considered the position of a 17-year-old, approaching her eighteenth birthday, who made an application for homelessness assistance having been asked to leave the family home by her

---

85   See **11.44**.
86   See **10.15–10.19**. *R v Woodspring District Council ex p Walters* (1984) 16 HLR 73, QBD is one example, albeit not concerning applicants living with friends or relatives.
87   English Code, paras 8.9–8.13 and paras 12.7–12.11; not reproduced in the Welsh Code.
88   English Code, paras 8.9 and 12.10–12.11.
89   [2008] UKHL 14, [2008] 1 WLR 535, HL.
90   *R (M) v Hammersmith & Fulham London Borough Council* [2008] UKHL 14, [2008] 1 WLR 535, HL at [26] and [27], quoting English Code, paras 12.9 and 12.11. See also *R (G) v Southwark London Borough Council* [2009] UKHL 26, [2009] 1 WLR 2399, HL.

mother.[91] The local housing authority delayed making its decision until the day before her eighteenth birthday and then, unlawfully, decided that she did not have a priority need.[92] The Court of Appeal acknowledged that 'an authority is entitled to have time to check the genuineness of the decision to exclude the child, and indeed the reasons given by the child for being excluded, for example where there may have been collusion'.[93] However, 'it cannot be right that an authority can persuade a family into mediation while a child is 17 and then use the time that the mediation would take to deprive the child of a right that it would have had without mediation.'[94] If the child genuinely has had his or her licence withdrawn, he or she will be homeless.

11.54   In such circumstances it is suggested that the better interpretation of the guidance in the English Code is that local housing authorities should accept that the applicant is homeless and then perform their statutory duty to secure accommodation for the homeless person by achieving a 'reconciliation' under which the applicant can in future live either with his or her parents or with members of the wider family.[95]

'... enactment or rule of law'[96]

11.55   Even if an applicant does not have any legal interest in, or licence to occupy, his or her accommodation, she or he may nevertheless be entitled to live there under an 'enactment' or 'rule of law' permitting his or her occupation or preventing another person from obtaining possession.[97] Such occupation is treated for the purposes of HA 1996, Part 7 as though it was under a right to occupy and may prevent the applicant from being homeless.

11.56   An 'enactment' in this context would normally mean an Act of Parliament. But in HA 1996, Part 7 it is defined to include 'an enactment comprised in subordinate legislation (within the meaning of the Interpretation Act 1978)'.[98] This wide definition brings in orders, rules, regulations, by-laws, schemes, warrants and other instruments made under any Act of Parliament.[99] So, if any of those give a right to occupy, or inhibit someone else from recovering possession, the applicant may not be homeless.

---

[91]   *Robinson v Hammersmith & Fulham London Borough Council* [2006] EWCA Civ 1122, [2007] HLR 7, CA.

[92]   See **13.107–13.117**.

[93]   *Robinson v Hammersmith & Fulham London Borough Council* [2006] EWCA Civ 1122, [2007] HLR 7, CA at [39] per Waller LJ.

[94]   *Robinson v Hammersmith & Fulham London Borough Council* [2006] EWCA Civ 1122, [2007] HLR 7, CA at [41] per Waller LJ.

[95]   English Code, para 12.7. *Robinson v Hammersmith & Fulham London Borough Council* [2006] EWCA Civ 1122, [2007] HLR 7, CA at [41] per Waller LJ. See **13.110** and **13.117**.

[96]   HA 1996, s 175(1)(c).

[97]   HA 1996, s 175(1)(c).

[98]   HA 1996, s 230.

[99]   Interpretation Act 1978, s 21.

11.57 A 'rule of law' is not defined in HA 1996, Part 7. In contrast to 'enactment', it probably means a judge-made rule of common law, eg the rule that a licence to occupy may not normally be ended without giving reasonable notice.

11.58 Some Acts of Parliament expressly provide that individuals who are otherwise without rights may remain in possession. The classic example is the Rent Act 1977. Statutory tenants, whose contractual tenancies have ended, enjoy a personal right under the Rent Act 1977 not to be evicted without a court order, and thus fall within this category.[100] The Codes specifically refer to Rent Act statutory tenants because the personal right to remain is created by statute.[101] A statutory tenant remains under the protection of the Rent Act 1977 and the Protection from Eviction Act 1977 not just until a possession order has been obtained against him or her, but until the point of actual eviction by court bailiffs.[102]

11.59 Other Acts of Parliament provide that tenancies cannot be ended without landlords obtaining possession orders. This is the case for both secure and assured tenants.[103] Even where former tenants remain in occupation as trespassers, they are not 'homeless', because a different form of enactment, the procedural rules of court, restricts them from being ousted other than by a bailiff's warrant. They do not lose the benefit of that enactment until the bailiffs actually turn them out.[104]

11.60 Anyone who is occupying premises where a possession order has been obtained but has not yet been executed will fall within this category and will not become 'homeless' until actually evicted by the bailiffs.[105]

11.61 It is not possible to set out in this text details of all the primary and secondary legislation giving rights to remain in occupation of accommodation or restricting the rights of others to recover possession. Spouses, heterosexual cohabitants and same-sex partners (who have registered a civil partnership or

---

[100] Rent Act 1977, s 2.

[101] English Code, para 8.7(iii); Welsh Code, para 13.5.

[102] *Haniff v Robinson* [1993] QB 419, CA.

[103] Housing Act 1985, Part 4 governs secure tenants; Housing Act 1988, Part 1 governs assured tenants.

[104] There are complex provisions, which are beyond the scope of this text, governing when tenancies end on or after the making of a possession order. All assured tenants remain tenants until any possession order is executed against them (*Knowsley Housing Trust v White* [2008] UKHL 70, [2009] HLR 17, HL). From 20 May 2009, secure tenants are in the same position (Housing Act 1985, s 82 as amended by Housing and Regeneration Act 2008, s 299 and Sch 11). There were certain 'tolerated trespassers' who had originally been secure tenants until they were subject to outright or suspended possession orders made before 20 May 2009. Most of them became holders of 'replacement tenancies' on 20 May 2009 (Housing and Regeneration Act 2008, Sch 11, Part 2).

[105] *R (Sacupima) v Newham London Borough Council* (2001) 33 HLR 2, CA; if the possession order is to be executed within 28 days, the applicant will be threatened with homelessness.

are living together as if they were civil partners) may have rights to remain in their homes under the Family Law Act 1996.[106]

11.62 It must not be assumed that all residential occupiers have the benefit of enactments or rules of law enabling them to remain in occupation or restricting others from recovering possession. True trespassers – squatters who have entered property without authority – have no such rights and are 'homeless' throughout.

11.63 Even in relation to former tenants and licensees, the Protection from Eviction Act 1977 is not comprehensive. There are very many occupiers who are excepted from its protection and will become 'homeless' as soon as their tenancies or licences end. That is precisely because there is no legal right to remain, nor any restriction on their eviction. A comprehensive list of those excluded from the Protection from Eviction Act 1977 is found at s 3A of that Act. It includes those living with resident landlords, occupying holiday lets or subject to licences granted not for money or money's worth.[107]

11.64 There are many people – owners, tenants, former tenants and former licensees – who have no defence to an inevitable possession order, but who do have the benefit of the protection of an enactment or rule of law preventing their eviction. They will not be automatically 'homeless' in that they have accommodation that they are entitled to occupy.[108] However, if the mortgage lender, landlord, former landlord or former licensor is taking steps to obtain a possession order, it may not be reasonable for them to continue in occupation and they may nevertheless be 'homeless'.[109]

Can the applicant secure entry to the accommodation?

11.65 Even if 'accommodation'[110] is 'available'[111] which the applicant is 'entitled to occupy',[112] he or she will still be homeless if he or she is physically barred from entering the property.[113] The examples given in the Codes are where an occupier has been illegally evicted, or comes home to find his or her accommodation occupied by squatters.[114] But those examples are far from exhaustive. The property may be cut off temporarily by floodwaters or sealed behind a police barrier. An emergency may have rendered it temporarily

---

[106] The Civil Partnership Act 2004 introduced registration of civil partnerships for same-sex couples, in force from 5 December 2005.
[107] Protection from Eviction Act 1977, s 3A.
[108] Protection from Eviction Act 1977, s 3; HA 1996, s 175(1)(c).
[109] English Code, paras 8.14 and 8.30–8.32a; Welsh Code, para 13.14. See **11.98–11.99**.
[110] See **11.6–11.14**.
[111] See **11.15–11.31**.
[112] See **11.32–11.64**.
[113] HA 1996, s 175(2).
[114] English Code, para 8.16; Welsh Code, para 13.9. See also *Nipa Begum v Tower Hamlets London Borough Council* (2000) 32 HLR 445, CA.

impossible to enter the property. Whatever the cause, if the applicant physically cannot enter (and has no other accommodation meeting the legal definition) he or she is 'homeless'.

11.66 Even though practical or legal remedies to gain entry at some later stage will usually be available to the applicant, he or she remains homeless until entry can be secured. Local housing authorities cannot, therefore, decide that the applicant is not homeless because he or she has not yet exhausted all legal and practical remedies to secure entry (although they can, of course, give advice on the remedies available). To put it in the language of the English Code:

> '... although legal remedies may be available to the applicant to regain possession of the accommodation, housing authorities cannot refuse to assist while he or she is actually homeless.'[115]

The special rule for mobile homes

11.67 A local housing authority may find that an applicant has 'accommodation' in the form of a moveable structure (eg a mobile home or towing caravan), or in the form of a vehicle or vessel designed for, or adapted for, human habitation. The latter category includes not only purpose built caravanettes and houseboats but also adapted or converted buses, lorries, vans and boats.

11.68 An applicant who has a right to occupy such accommodation, which is available to him or her, will be homeless unless he or she has a place where he or she is permitted or entitled both to place it and to reside in it. Simply having a place to put or park the mobile home is not enough. The applicant must also be entitled to live in it at that location.

11.69 Typically, a mobile home occupier has a licence to station and live in his or her home on a particular plot or to tie up and live in his or her boat at a particular mooring. The English Code advises that, where an applicant has an itinerant lifestyle, the site or mooring need not be permanent in order to avoid homelessness.[116] But it is quite common for those with mobile homes to have no permission to stay anywhere. Such travellers would obviously be 'homeless', however comfortable their mobile accommodation.

11.70 A person who has a licence to bring his or her mobile home onto a particular piece of land to live in it has an entitlement or permission to 'place it and to reside in it' and would therefore not be homeless.[117] So, a houseboat owner with permission to use and live in the houseboat on a particular waterway is not homeless.[118] If the licence then expires, but no proceedings are brought and he or she continues to occupy the land (or water), she or he may or

---

[115] English Code, para 8.16.
[116] English Code, para 8.17.
[117] HA 1996, s 175(2)(b).
[118] *R v Hillingdon London Borough Council ex p Bax* (1992) December *Legal Action*, p 21, QBD.

may not be homeless, depending upon whether it can be inferred from the landowners' inaction that the permission is continuing.[119] If an occupier is required to leave a site, but has another site to go to, he or she will not be homeless.[120] If, on the other hand, an occupier is required to leave and has no alternative provision in place, he or she will be homeless. An occupier who is camping unlawfully, and never had the right or permission to occupy the land, is homeless throughout.[121]

11.71 Local Government Ombudsman investigations have found maladministration where caravan-dwellers were subject to imminent eviction proceedings but the local housing authorities refused to accept them as homeless.[122]

Is the accommodation reasonable for the applicant to occupy?

11.72 If the applicant has 'accommodation'[123] which is 'available',[124] which he or she is 'entitled to occupy',[125] and to which entry can be secured,[126] that would, before 1986, have been sufficient to demonstrate that he or she was not homeless. But that approach could and did produce absurd results. It paid no attention to the quality, condition or appropriateness of the accommodation for the applicant and his or her family. The narrowness of the definition was amply demonstrated by the finding in the *Puhlhofer*[127] case that a family of four occupying a small squalid single room in a guest house was not homeless. As a direct response to that decision, in 1986, Parliament enlarged the definition of 'homeless' so that, as well as fulfilling all other parts of the statutory definition, the accommodation in question also had to be 'reasonable' for the applicant to continue to occupy.[128]

11.73 The words 'continue to occupy' refer to Parliament's intention to deal specifically with accommodation that an applicant already 'has', and is therefore occupying, rather than accommodation that the applicant has left.[129] The Court of Appeal has held that the words 'continue to occupy' mean that the question of reasonableness of occupation is relevant to any accommodation that is 'available' to the applicant, whether or not she or he is actually occupying it.[130]

---

119   *R (O'Donoghue) v Brighton and Hove City Council* [2003] EWHC (Admin) 129, (2003) April *Legal Action*, p 27, Admin Ct and [2003] EWCA Civ 459, (2003) May *Legal Action*, p 35, CA.
120   *R v Chiltern District Council ex p Roberts* (1991) 23 HLR 387, QBD.
121   *Higgs v Brighton and Hove City Council* [2003] EWCA Civ 895, [2004] HLR 2, CA.
122   For example, Local Government Ombudsman Investigations 518/L/85 (Boston Borough Council) and 88/B/1216 (East Lindsey District Council).
123   See **11.6–11.14**.
124   See **11.15–11.31**.
125   See **11.32–11.64**.
126   See **11.65–11.71**.
127   *R v Hillingdon London Borough Council ex p Puhlhofer* [1986] AC 484, HL.
128   HA 1996, s 175(3), previously inserted into Housing Act 1985, s 58(2A) by Housing and Planning Act 1986, s 14(2).
129   *R v Brent London Borough Council ex p Awua* [1996] 1 AC 55, HL at 67 per Lord Hoffmann.
130   *Waltham Forest London Borough Council v Maloba* [2007] EWCA Civ 1271, [2008] HLR

11.74 The words 'continue to occupy' look to occupation over time and suggest an element of looking to the future. This means that accommodation could be considered not to be reasonable to continue to occupy, even though the occupiers could get by in it for a little while longer.[131]

11.75 The words ' . . . shall not be treated as having accommodation unless it is accommodation which would be reasonable for him to continue to occupy' used in HA 1996, s 175(3) might suggest that a local housing authority had to probe, with the applicant, every conceivable aspect of the existing property to establish whether or not it was reasonable to occupy. That would be unworkable. A local housing authority must always consider whether or not the accommodation is affordable for the applicant, as it is required to do so by ministerial order.[132] A local housing authority must also make inquiries into any other material before it that might lead it to conclude that the accommodation would not be reasonable.

11.76 Once a finding has been made that accommodation is not reasonable for an applicant to continue to occupy, the applicant is homeless and, if the other statutory criteria are met, the main housing duty will be owed. The local housing authority cannot impose any additional conditions, such as requiring the applicant to terminate his or her tenancy, before performing the duty.[133]

11.77 There are two distinct circumstances in which accommodation will not be reasonable for the applicant to continue to occupy:

(1) where the circumstances are such that HA 1996, Part 7 *deems* the accommodation to be unreasonable to continue to occupy;[134] or

(2) where the circumstances are such that, *as a matter of fact*, the accommodation is not reasonable to continue to occupy.[135]

Deemed unreasonableness

11.78 If it is 'probable' that continued occupation of the accommodation will lead to 'domestic violence or other violence' against the applicant or against a member of the applicant's household,[136] the accommodation is deemed by HA 1996, Part 7 not to be reasonable for the applicant to continue to occupy and

---

26, CA, which considered the dicta in *Begum v Tower Hamlets London Borough Council* (2000) 32 HLR 445, CA and held that *Begum* was wrongly decided on this point.

[131] *Ali & others v Birmingham City Council, Moran v Manchester City Council* [2009] UKHL 36, [2009] 1 WLR 1506, HL at [36]–[39], per Baroness Hale.

[132] Homelessness (Suitability of Accommodation) Order 1996, SI 1996/3204; see **11.97**.

[133] *R (Hammia) v Wandsworth London Borough Council* [2005] EWHC 1127 (Admin) [2005] HLR 45, Admin Ct. See **10.66**.

[134] See **11.78–11.88**.

[135] See **11.89–11.117**.

[136] HA 1996, s 177(1)(a) and (b). For this purpose household membership is to be ascertained in the way described at **11.19–11.31**.

the applicant is homeless.[137] The local housing authority's inquiries are simply confined to finding the facts necessary to answer the question of whether such violence is probable.

11.79 This is currently the only circumstance in which accommodation is deemed to be unreasonable to continue to occupy. There is provision within HA 1996, Part 7 for the Secretary of State (or the Welsh Assembly Government) to specify by order other circumstances in which accommodation should be regarded, as a matter of law, as not reasonable for the applicant to continue to occupy.[138] This power has not yet been exercised.

11.80 For the purposes of the deeming provision, 'violence' means 'violence from another person; or threats of violence from another person which are likely to be carried out'.[139] Although HA 1996, Part 7 refers to 'threats' of violence, this can include a single threat of violence.[140] It is 'domestic violence' if the violence or threats of violence come from 'a person who is associated with the victim'.[141]

11.81 The modern approach is to understand 'violence' as a very broad concept. The English Code records the Secretary of State's opinion that 'the term "violence" should not be given a restrictive meaning' and that:

> '"domestic violence" should be understood to include threatening behaviour, violence or abuse (psychological, physical, sexual, financial or emotional) between persons who are, or have been, intimate partners, family members or members of the same household, regardless of gender or sexuality.'[142]

However, the Court of Appeal has held that the Secretary of State's guidance is wrong and that 'violence' should be given a narrow interpretation, requiring physical contact.[143] Subject to any contrary decision by the UK Supreme Court, it is the Court of Appeal's decision that is determinative.

11.82 'A person who is associated with the victim' is exhaustively defined in HA 1996, Part 7.[144] If the relationship between the perpetrator and the victim does not fall within the statutory definition, the violence cannot be domestic violence (but will be 'other violence'). The Codes reiterate that the question of whether the violence is 'domestic' or not turns on the relationship between the

---

[137] HA 1996, s 177(1).
[138] HA 1996, s 177(3)(a).
[139] HA 1996, s 177(1A).
[140] Interpretation Act 1978, s 6(c): '... unless the contrary intention appears ... words in the singular include the plural and words in the plural include the singular'.
[141] HA 1996, s 177(1A).
[142] English Code, para 8.21.
[143] *Yemshaw v Hounslow London Borough Council* (unreported) 15 December 2009, CA (extempore judgment not yet reported at the date of this book going to print), and relying on *Danesh v Kensington & Chelsea Royal London Borough* [2006] EWCA Civ 1404, [2007] 1 WLR 69, CA; see **15.103**.
[144] HA 1996, s 178(1)–(3).

perpetrator and the victim; not on where the violence took place.[145] The statutory definition of 'associated person' is very widely drawn, so as to include both existing and former spouses or civil partners, heterosexual and same-sex cohabitants, any person who has lived in the same household as the victim, any blood relation or relation by marriage, cohabitation or civil partnership, and any person who shares the parentage of, or parental responsibility for, a child with the victim (including adoptive parents in their relationship to natural parents).[146]

11.83 Before the implementation of the Homelessness Act 2002, only 'domestic' violence led to it being deemed that it would not be reasonable for an applicant to continue to occupy accommodation. Since the amendment made by the Homelessness Act 2002, which inserted 'or other violence' into the deeming section, it is no longer necessary for local housing authorities to distinguish between domestic or other violence for the purposes of taking a decision on whether an applicant is homeless.[147] Where it is probable that continued occupation of the accommodation will lead to violence or threats of violence that are likely to be carried out against the applicant or a member of his or her household, that accommodation cannot be reasonable for the applicant to continue to occupy, whoever the violence (or threat of it) comes from. However, the distinction between 'domestic' violence and 'other violence' remains relevant if a local housing authority is considering a referral under the local connection provisions.[148]

11.84 The test is not whether there has been violence in the past, or whether violence will definitely occur in the future. The question for the local housing authority is whether it is 'probable' that continued occupation of the accommodation would lead either to violence, or to threats of violence which are likely to be carried out. The Court of Appeal set aside a local housing authority's decision that an applicant was not homeless because she could have invoked legal remedies in order to prevent a recurrence of domestic violence. The local housing authority had asked itself the wrong question and had taken into account wider considerations (including whether the applicant had acted reasonably) rather than confining itself to the probability of her being subject to violence or threats of violence likely to be carried out if she remained in her accommodation.[149] 'Probable' means 'more likely than not'. 'Likely' in the context of 'threats of violence' includes 'a real or serious possibility'. If, therefore, it is more likely than not that an applicant's continued occupation of

---

[145] English Code, paras 8.19–8.25; Welsh Code, paras 13.16–13.25.

[146] Civil Partnership Act 2004, s 81 and Sch 8, para 61 amended HA 1996, s 178 to include references to civil partnerships and same-sex couples living together as though they were civil partners, in force from 5 December 2005. Para 8.20 of the English Code contains an up-to-date list, but wrongly omits relatives of a civil partner or former civil partner (para 8.20(e)). The list at para 13.18 of the Welsh Code was published prior to the Civil Partnership Act 2004, and so is out of date.

[147] Homelessness Act 2002, s 10. During its passage the Minister specifically referred to racial violence as falling within this provision (*Hansard*, SC, 10 July 2001, Sally Keeble MP).

[148] See **15.94–15.106**.

[149] *Bond v Leicester City Council* [2002] EWCA Civ 1544, [2002] HLR 6, CA.

his or her home will lead to violence, or to threats of violence where there is a real or serious possibility that those threats will be carried out, the applicant will be homeless.

11.85 Local housing authorities are entitled to advise applicants about any legal or practical remedies (obtaining injunctions, improving security, etc) but should make it clear to applicants that they are not under any obligation to use these remedies.[150] The safety of the applicant and his or her household must be the primary consideration at all stages.[151] Local housing authorities are also advised that the fact that violence has not yet occurred does not mean that it is not likely to occur; and that (particularly in cases of domestic violence) they should not necessarily expect direct evidence of violence to be available from the applicant.[152]

11.86 The definition of 'violence 'and 'threats of violence' as coming 'from another person' means that the risk of self-harm from continued occupation of accommodation does not put an applicant into this deemed unreasonableness category (although any risk of self-harm may be relevant to the broader test of whether the accommodation is reasonable to continue to occupy, as a matter of fact).

11.87 The local housing authority cannot take into account, when determining whether an applicant falls within this deemed unreasonableness category, general housing circumstances prevailing in its district. The local housing authority can only consider the applicant's individual circumstances and that of his or her household.

11.88 Where there is harassment falling short of actual violence, or threats of violence that are likely to be carried out, the accommodation will not be deemed to be unreasonable for the applicant and members of his or her household to continue to occupy, but may be as a matter of fact unreasonable for them to continue to occupy.[153]

Factual unreasonableness

11.89 As a matter of fact, accommodation may not be reasonable for an applicant to continue to occupy. This is a much broader question for the local housing authority to determine than the relatively narrow deemed unreasonableness category. It is always required to consider whether or not the accommodation is 'affordable' for the applicant.[154] It should also take into account any other relevant matters, including all those raised by the applicant. In making its decision as to whether or not the accommodation is reasonable

---

[150] English Code, paras 18.23–18.24; Welsh Code, para 13.22.
[151] English Code, para 8.24.
[152] English Code, paras 6.17 and 8.22; Welsh Code, paras 13.23–13.24.
[153] See **11.113**.
[154] HA 1996, s 177(3)(b); Homelessness (Suitability of Accommodation) Order 1996, SI 1996/3204.

for the applicant to continue to occupy, the local housing authority may, but is not obliged to, have regard to the general housing circumstances prevailing in its district.[155]

11.90 The phrase 'reasonable to continue to occupy' is also used as part of the definition of intentional homelessness.[156] Case law and guidance relating to that part of the definition of intentional homelessness applies to the interpretation of the same phrase in relation to homelessness.

11.91 'There is no simple test of reasonableness'.[157] Each case will require an individual assessment involving consideration of the applicant's circumstances and (if the local housing authority elects to have regard to them) the general housing conditions in the district.

11.92 As already noted, a local housing authority must always consider whether the applicant can afford to occupy the accommodation, and should then also consider any other relevant issues, whether raised directly by the applicant or becoming apparent during the local housing authority's inquiries. Examples of matters that might be relevant are given in the Codes, but the scope of the local housing authority's inquiries is not confined to those examples.[158] Any matter that appears to be relevant must be considered. The question of reasonableness is not limited to the characteristics of the accommodation alone; it can include other factors such as whether the applicant has access to employment or to welfare benefits in the place (or country) where the accommodation is located.[159]

11.93 The Court of Appeal has set out a useful list of indicative factors that might be taken into account when considering whether any accommodation is reasonable to continue to occupy.[160] The House of Lords allowed an appeal in that case against the Court of Appeal's decision that women's refuges were accommodation that might be reasonable to continue to occupy, but did not specifically overrule the list.[161] Those factors are:

'•   the size, type and quality of the accommodation made available to the woman, including the extent of her need to share its facilities;
•   the terms of the agreement by which it is made available to her;
•   her ability to afford it;
•   the appropriateness of its location for her and her child (if any);
•   the extent of its facilities for her child;

---

[155]   HA 1996, s 177(2).
[156]   Discussed at **14.108–14.126**.
[157]   English Code, para 8.18; Welsh Code, para 13.13.
[158]   English Code, paras 8.26–8.34; Welsh Code, paras 13.11–13.15.
[159]   *R v Hammersmith and Fulham London Borough Council ex p Duro-Rama* (1983) 9 HLR 71, QBD, and *R v Gravesham Borough Council ex p Winchester* (1986) 18 HLR 207, QBD.
[160]   *Moran v Manchester City Council* [2008] EWCA Civ 378, [2008] HLR 39, CA.
[161]   *Ali & others v Birmingham City Council, Moran v Manchester City Council* [2009] UKHL 36, [2009] 1 WLR 1506, HL.

- its appropriateness for her and her child in the light of any particular characteristics (including as to health) which each may have;
- the length of time for which they have already occupied it;
- the state of their physical and emotional health while in occupation of it; and
- the length of time for which, unless accepted as homeless, they might expect to continue to occupy it'.[162]

General circumstances prevailing in relation to housing in the local housing authority's district

11.94 The local housing authority may, but is not obliged to, take into account 'the general circumstances prevailing in relation to housing in the district of the local housing authority to whom [the applicant] has applied'.[163] The Codes give two examples of when such a comparison might be appropriate: where the application is based on the physical condition of the property, or on overcrowding.[164] Other circumstances that local housing authorities have lawfully taken into account include the demands for housing in the local housing authority's area,[165] its capacity to absorb homeless families,[166] the shortage of supply,[167] and conflicts of lifestyle in multi-occupied homes.[168] A reasonably up-to-date picture of general housing conditions in a local housing authority's district will be available from the local housing authority's own local homelessness review.[169]

11.95 It is the local housing authority that is in the best position to assess the seriousness of the general conditions relating to housing in its area, and the extent to which an applicant's complaints might take his or her case out of the norm and makes it unreasonable to continue in occupation.[170] It follows that applicants who apply to hard-pressed local housing authorities will find that satisfying the local housing authority that accommodation is not reasonable for them to continue to occupy is a harder task than if they had applied to local housing authorities with more accommodation available.[171]

---

[162] *Moran v Manchester City Council* [2008] EWCA Civ 378, [2008] HLR 39, CA at [49] per Wilson LJ.

[163] HA 1996, s 177(2).

[164] English Code, paras 8.26–8.28; Welsh Code paras 13.12–13.13. See **11.100–11.104** for physical conditions and **11.105–11.107** for overcrowding.

[165] *Noh v Hammersmith & Fulham London Borough Council* [2001] EWCA Civ 905, [2002] HLR 54, CA.

[166] *Noh v Hammersmith & Fulham London Borough Council* [2001] EWCA Civ 905, [2002] HLR 54, CA.

[167] *R v Kensington & Chelsea Royal London Borough Council ex p Moncada* (1997) 29 HLR 289, QBD.

[168] *R v Brent London Borough Council ex p Yusuf* (1997) 29 HLR 48, QBD; *R v Brent London Borough Council ex p Bariise* (1999) 31 HLR 50, CA.

[169] See **7.82–7.111**.

[170] *R v Brent London Borough Council ex p Bariise* (1999) 31 HLR 50, CA.

[171] See *Harouki v Kensington & Chelsea Royal London Borough Council* [2007] EWCA Civ 1000, [2008] HLR 16, CA for one such example.

11.96 The following paragraphs deal with the more common situations in which questions arise about factual reasonableness to continue to occupy.

Affordability

11.97 Accommodation is not reasonable for an applicant to continue to occupy if the cost of paying for it would deprive the applicant of the means to provide for 'the ordinary necessities of life'.[172] What constitutes 'the ordinary necessities of life' is a question of fact and can vary according to each applicant's needs.[173] The local housing authority is required to consider the whole of the applicant's financial resources as against the cost of the accommodation, any child support or other payments that the applicant is required to make, and all the applicant's other reasonable living expenses.[174]

Imminent or actual possession proceedings

11.98 Where an applicant is entitled to occupy rented accommodation, because no possession order has yet been obtained, but possession proceedings are imminent or have been started, the local housing authority should consider whether in those circumstances it is reasonable for the applicant to continue to occupy until the possession order has been obtained, and executed. Factors that the local housing authority should take into account include: the general cost to the local housing authority of accepting the applicant as 'homeless' at that stage; the position of the tenant; the position of the landlord; the likelihood that the landlord will actually proceed (or continue with) the possession claim; and the burden on the courts of unnecessary proceedings where there is no defence to a claim for possession; as well as the general housing circumstances prevailing in the local housing authority's district.[175] The Codes suggest that it is unlikely to be reasonable for an assured shorthold tenant (who has received a proper statutory notice)[176] to continue to occupy where the local housing authority is satisfied that the landlord intends to seek possession and where there would be no defence to a possession claim.[177] This guidance would also apply to other tenants or licensees faced with imminent possession proceedings to which they have no defence and who would therefore become liable to pay the costs of those proceedings.[178]

---

[172] *R v Wandsworth London Borough Council ex p Hawthorne* [1994] 1 WLR 1442, CA, and *R v Brent London Borough Council ex p Baruwa* (1997) 29 HLR 915, CA. See English Code, para 8.29; Welsh Code, para 13.13.

[173] *R v Hillingdon London Borough Council ex p Tinn* (1988) 20 HLR 305, QBD.

[174] Homelessness (Suitability of Accommodation) Order 1996, SI 1996/3204, reg 2.

[175] English Code, paras 8.32–8.32a; Welsh Code, paras 13.14–13.15.

[176] Complying with Housing Act 1988, s 21.

[177] English Code, para 8.32, which adds a caveat that dis-applies the advice where the local housing authority is taking steps to persuade the landlord to withdraw the notice or to allow the tenant to continue to occupy the accommodation for a reasonable period; Welsh Code, para 13.15.

[178] Such as introductory tenants, demoted tenants, non-secure tenants, occupiers whose former tenancies were determined by notices to quit, and other common-law tenants.

11.99 Case law has stressed that 'it is undesirable that a tenant, or an ex-tenant, in those circumstances should be required to hang on till the bitter end and require a court order'.[179] However, the decision as to the imminence of possession proceedings, and whether or not an applicant would have a defence, is a question of fact for the local housing authority.[180]

Physical conditions

11.100 The English Code suggests that the local housing authority can ask itself:

> '... whether the condition of the property was so bad in comparison with other accommodation in the district that it would not be reasonable to expect someone to continue to live there.'[181]

11.101 The Welsh Code repeats that proposed test, but also refers to the question of whether the property is unfit for human habituation and draws attention not only to the needs of disabled people, but also the needs of the elderly and people with HIV/AIDS.[182]

11.102 The English Code also refers to 'the physical characteristics of the accommodation' being reasonable for the particular applicant (eg a wheelchair user) to continue to occupy.[183]

11.103 Whether or not a property has adequate fire prevention and escape facilities, in comparison with other properties in the local housing authority's district, is a relevant consideration.[184] A vandalised property was, on the facts of a particular case, found to be not reasonable for the applicant to continue to occupy.[185] A damp beach chalet, which a pregnant applicant had been told would be unsafe for her baby, was held not to be reasonable to continue to occupy, given the clear medical advice.[186]

---

[179] *R v Croydon London Borough Council ex p Jarvis* (1994) 26 HLR 194, QBD at 205 per Collins J.

[180] *R v Bradford Metropolitan Borough Council ex p Parveen* (1996) 28 HLR 681, QBD. See also *Goddard v Torridge District Council* (1982) January *Legal Action*, p 9; *R v Portsmouth City Council ex p Knight* (1983) 10 HLR 115, QBD; and *R v Surrey Heath Borough Council ex p Li* (1984) 16 HLR 69, QBD. In *Khadija Ali v Bristol City Council* (2007) October *Legal Action*, p 26, Bristol County Court, the review decision was defective because there was no reference to the guidance in the Code, or explanation of the reviewing officer's decision to depart from it.

[181] English Code, para 8.27.

[182] Welsh Code, para 13.13.

[183] English Code, para 8.34.

[184] *R v Kensington and Chelsea Royal London Borough Council ex p Ben-El-Mabrouk* (1995) 27 HLR 564, CA, and *R v Haringey London Borough Council ex p Flynn* (1995), (1995) June *Legal Action*, p 21, QBD.

[185] *City of Gloucester v Miles* (1985) 17 HLR 292, CA.

[186] *R v Medina Borough Council ex p Dee* (1992) 24 HLR 562, QBD. See also *Bavi v Waltham Forest London Borough Council* [2009] EWCA Civ 551, (2009) August *Legal Action*, p 37, CA, where the local housing authority had properly considered all the relevant defects, including rising dampness, and found that the applicant was not homeless.

11.104 Local housing authorities are entitled to compare the physical conditions of the applicant's accommodation with the general physical conditions of housing in their districts.[187]

Overcrowding

11.105 When considering the question of overcrowding, local housing authorities should consider all the different aspects of the statutory overcrowding test at Housing Act 1985, ss 324–326.[188] They must not limit themselves to whether the property is statutorily overcrowded, although that can be a key or contributing factor to their decision on reasonableness.[189] They should also consider any overcrowding that does not amount to statutory overcrowding, any medical needs and any other matters.[190] The extent to which the accommodation may be a 'hazard', as defined by Housing Act 2004,[191] and the severity of that hazard, should also be relevant.[192]

11.106 Even when accommodation is statutorily overcrowded, a local housing authority may be entitled to find that it is reasonable to continue to occupy, taking into account the general housing circumstances prevailing in its district.[193] However, a decision that an overcrowded property was reasonable to continue to occupy because the overcrowding was a result of the increasing size of the applicant's family was quashed. It was a value judgment that had no place in the statutory scheme. The reason for the overcrowding is simply not relevant to whether or not the property is reasonable to continue to occupy.[194] A local housing authority is entitled to compare the degree of overcrowding with the general housing circumstances prevailing in its district,[195] but it should ensure that it addresses the particular degree of overcrowding experienced by the applicant. Merely asserting the general prevalence of overcrowding in the

---

[187] HA 1996, s 177(2). For examples, see *R v Brent London Borough Council ex parte Yusuf* (1997) 29 HLR 48, QBD; *R v Brent London Borough Council ex p Bariise* (1999) 31 HLR 50, CA; *R (Lynch) v Lambeth London Borough Council* [2006] EWHC 2737 (Admin), [2007] HLR 15, Admin Ct. See **11.94–11.95**.

[188] *Elrify v Westminster City Council* [2007] EWCA Civ 332, [2007] HLR 36, CA.

[189] English Code, para 8.28 and Annex 16; Welsh Code, para 13.13.

[190] *R v Westminster City Council ex p Alouat* (1989) 21 HLR 477, QBD.

[191] Housing Act 2004, ss 1–2.

[192] *Khadija Ali v Bristol City Council* (2007) October *Legal Action*, p 26, Bristol County Court.

[193] *Harouki v Kensington & Chelsea Royal London Borough Council* [2007] EWCA Civ 1000, [2008] HLR 16, CA, where an applicant was statutorily overcrowded and thus committing an offence (Housing Act 1985, s 327). It should be noted that the extent to which the accommodation might constitute a 'hazard' within the meaning of the Housing Act 2004 was not considered.

[194] *R v Eastleigh Borough Council ex p Beattie (No 1)* (1983) 10 HLR 134, QBD; *R v Eastleigh Borough Council ex p Beattie (No 2)* (1985) 17 HLR 168, QBD; and *R v Tower Hamlets London Borough Council ex p Hoque* (1993) The Times, July 20, QBD.

[195] *R v Tower Hamlets London Borough Council ex p Monaf* (1988) 20 HLR 529, CA; *R v Tower Hamlets London Borough Council ex p Ojo* (1991) 23 HLR 488, QBD; *R v Tower Hamlets London Borough Council ex p Uddin* (1993) June *Legal Action*, p 15, QBD; *Osei v Southwark London Borough Council* [2007] EWCA Civ 787, [2008] HLR 15, CA; and *Harouki v Kensington & Chelsea Royal London Borough Council* [2007] EWCA Civ 1000, [2008] HLR 16, CA.

district without evidence showing the numbers of households experiencing a similar degree of overcrowding to that experienced by the applicant is not sufficient.[196]

11.107 Local housing authorities are entitled to compare the degree of overcrowding in the applicant's accommodation with the general degree of overcrowding in their districts.[197]

Relationship breakdown

11.108 A local housing authority's decision that it was reasonable for an ex-husband to occupy his former matrimonial home with his ex-wife and her new boyfriend, given the general housing circumstances prevailing in its district, was held not to contain errors of law. Although it was undesirable for a divorced couple to have to live together, the local housing authority was entitled to take into account the shortage of accommodation in its district.[198]

Types of accommodation

11.109 Short-term crisis-type accommodation, such as women's refuges, direct access hostels and night shelters, should not be considered accommodation that it is reasonable to continue to occupy in the medium and long term (assuming that such facilities are capable of constituting 'accommodation' at all).[199]

11.110 The House of Lords has held that women's refuges, in particular, should not be considered reasonable to continue to occupy indefinitely. Baroness Hale said:

> '... a refuge is not simply crisis intervention for a few nights. It is a safe haven in which to find peace and support. But it is not a place to live. There are rules which are necessary for the protection of residents but make it impossible to live a normal family life. It is a place to gather one's strength and one's thoughts and to decide what to do with one's life.'[200]

---

[196] *Mohamoud v Greenwich London Borough Council* (2003) January *Legal Action*, p 23, Woolwich County Court; *Khadija Ali v Bristol City Council* (2007) October *Legal Action*, p 26, Bristol County Court.

[197] HA 1996, s 177(2). See **11.94–11.95.**

[198] *R v Kensington and Chelsea Royal London Borough Council ex p Moncada* (1997) 29 HLR 289, QBD.

[199] English Code, para 8.34; Welsh Code, para 13.13. The House of Lords, when considering the special position of women's refuges in *Ali & others v Birmingham City Council, Moran v Manchester City Council* [2009] UKHL 36, [2009] 1 WLR 1506, HL, held that since refuges were not reasonable for women to continue to occupy indefinitely, they did not need to decide whether refuges were 'accommodation' within the meaning of HA 1996, s 175. See also **11.10–11.12.**

[200] *Ali & others v Birmingham City Council, Moran v Manchester City Council* [2009] UKHL 36, [2009] 1 WLR 1506, HL at [43].

Tenure

11.111 Accommodation need not be subject to any security of tenure for it to be accommodation which is available to the applicant and reasonable for him or her to continue to occupy. The mere fact that accommodation is temporary will not, in itself, render accommodation not reasonable to continue to occupy.[201] If accommodation is so precarious that the occupier is likely to have to leave within 28 days, then the applicant will in any event be threatened with homelessness.[202]

Former members of the armed forces

11.112 Former members of the armed forces, who were provided with accommodation during their service, are likely to lose that accommodation upon discharge. The Ministry of Defence will usually issue a Certificate of Cessation of Entitlement to Occupy Service Living Accommodation, which contains a date on which entitlement to occupy service quarters will end. The English Code recommends that local housing authorities should accept the date in the Certificate as being the date upon which an applicant becomes homeless, and should not insist upon the Ministry of Defence obtaining possession orders.[203] It adds that the 6-month notice period before the date of cessation in the certificate can be used to ensure that service personnel receive advice on housing options available to them. Obviously, if by the date of cessation the advice has not succeeded in providing alternative accommodation, the applicant will be homeless (having been threatened with homelessness in the preceding 28 days) and entitled to have his or her application for homelessness assistance determined in accordance with HA 1996, Part 7.

Harassment falling short of violence

11.113 Where there is harassment falling short of actual violence, or threats of violence that are likely to be carried out, the English Code recommends that local housing authorities should 'consider carefully' the question of whether or not it would be reasonable for the applicant and his or her household to continue to occupy. Examples of verbal abuse, damage to property or the risk of intimidation of witnesses in criminal proceedings are given.[204]

Accommodation overseas

11.114 Where the applicant has accommodation available to him or her overseas,[205] the question of whether it is reasonable to occupy the accommodation requires consideration of all relevant matters, including the affordability of the accommodation, its physical condition, etc. The local

---

[201] *R v Brent London Borough Council ex p Awua* [1996] AC 55, HL.
[202] HA 1996, s 175(4); see **11.118–11.121**.
[203] English Code, para 8.33 and Annexes 14 and 15; Welsh Code, Annex 19.
[204] English Code, para 8.34.
[205] See **11.16–11.17**.

housing authority should not limit itself to the issue of the accommodation's size and facilities. Any risk of violence to the applicant, the location of the accommodation, the applicant's personal circumstances, financial circumstances and employment prospects are also relevant.[206]

11.115 When considering the location, physical characteristics, etc, of the accommodation abroad, the local housing authority is entitled to take into account the general circumstances prevailing in relation to housing in its own district. The comparison is not with general housing circumstances in the area in which the accommodation is located.[207]

Other circumstances

11.116 It is impossible to set out and examine all of the many factors that may cause accommodation to be, or to have become, unreasonable for an applicant to continue to occupy. That is precisely why the local housing authority will have to examine carefully any matter raised by the applicant. Applicants may advance highly subjective reasons for not wanting to continue in occupation of a particular property.[208] The question for the local housing authority is not 'Would it be reasonable for this applicant to leave this property?' but rather 'Would it be reasonable for the applicant to continue in occupation?' Even when faced with what might seem to be compelling personal objections to the applicant continuing to occupy accommodation, a local housing authority may be able to point to more general housing conditions in its area to demonstrate that it would be reasonable for the applicant to stay on.

Reasonable for whom?

11.117 When a local housing authority is considering whether accommodation is 'available' for the applicant, HA 1996, Part 7 requires it to consider availability for all others in the applicant's household.[209] In contrast, when considering the reasonableness of continued occupation, the focus is only on the reasonableness of *the applicant* continuing in occupation, and not on

---

[206]   *R v Hammersmith & Fulham London Borough Council ex p Duro-Rama* (1983) 9 HLR 71, QBD; *R v Camden London Borough Council ex p Aranda* (1998) 30 HLR 76, CA; *R v Kensington & Chelsea Royal London Borough Council ex p Bayani* (1990) 22 HLR 406, CA; *R v Newham London Borough Council ex p Ajayi* (1996) 28 HLR 25, QBD; and *Waltham Forest London Borough Council v Maloba* [2007] EWCA Civ 1291, [2008] HLR 26, CA, where a decision that it was reasonable for a family to occupy accommodation in Uganda when the husband had lived in the UK for 10 years and had acquired British citizenship was held to be a decision that no reasonable local housing authority would have come to on those particular facts.

[207]   *R v Tower Hamlets London Borough Council ex p Monaf* (1988) 20 HLR 529, CA; *R v Newham London Borough Council ex p Tower Hamlets London Borough Council* [1991] 1 WLR 1032, (1991) 23 HLR 62, CA; and *Osei v Southwark London Borough Council* [2007] EWCA Civ 787, [2008] HLR 15, CA.

[208]   In *R v Nottingham City Council ex p Costello* (1989) 21 HLR 301, QBD, the issue was whether the accommodation was troubled by poltergeists (either actually or in the applicant's belief) and therefore not reasonable to continue to occupy.

[209]   See **11.19–11.31**.

whether or not it is reasonable for his or her *household* to continue in occupation. HA 1996, Part 7 expressly addresses the others in the household for the purposes of deemed unreasonableness (violence or threats of violence),[210] but not otherwise. However, this does not mean that, in cases not involving violence, the circumstances of the applicant's household can be ignored. An applicant may very commonly assert that the factor causing the accommodation to be no longer reasonable for his or her occupation is the medical or other situation of a different member of their household. The local housing authority must make enquiries sufficient to determine whether, in view of those matters, the accommodation is not reasonable for the applicant to continue to occupy.

THREATENED WITH HOMELESSNESS

11.118 If it is likely that an applicant will become homeless (within the extended definition explained in this chapter) within 28 days, that person is 'threatened with homelessness'.[211] In practice, many homeless applicants are likely to be threatened with homelessness rather than being actually homeless when they first make their application to a local housing authority for accommodation or assistance in obtaining accommodation. The Codes advise that local housing authorities should not wait for homelessness to be imminent before providing assistance.[212]

11.119 Where a local housing authority has reason to believe that an applicant 'may be threatened with homelessness', it is subject to the duty to accept the application and make inquiries.[213] If, upon concluding its inquiries, the local housing authority decides that the applicant is threatened with homelessness and that it has a duty towards him or her, that duty may either be:

(1) to take reasonable steps to secure that accommodation does not cease to be available for his or her occupation;[214] or

(2) to provide advice and assistance to help the applicant secure that accommodation does not cease to be available for his or her occupation.[215]

11.120 The English Code emphasises that advice and assistance might succeed in preventing homelessness.[216] This recommendation muddles two distinct occasions when advice and assistance might be provided. When it is

---

[210] HA 1996, s 177(1).
[211] HA 1996, s 175(4).
[212] English Code, para 8.3; Welsh Code, para 13.2.
[213] HA 1996, s 184(1). *R v Newham London Borough Council ex p Khan & Hussain* (2001) 33 HLR 269, QBD. See also **10.3**.
[214] HA 1996, s 195(2) and (9).
[215] HA 1996, s 195(5).
[216] English Code, para 8.3.

provided at an early stage, *before* a local housing authority might have reason to believe that an applicant may be homeless or threatened with homelessness, it is provided as part of the policy aim of homelessness prevention.[217] When advice and assistance is provided *during* the 28 days before the date on which the applicant is to be homeless, it is provided in performance of the local housing authority's duty to take reasonable steps to secure that the accommodation does not cease to be available, or to help the applicant secure that accommodation does not cease to be available.[218] If the advice and assistance does not succeed in retaining the accommodation for the applicant, he or she will become homeless and entitled to performance of one of the statutory duties owed to applicants who are found to be homeless.[219]

11.121 There is obviously a wide range of circumstances in which an applicant may face the prospect of homelessness within 28 days. One of the more common arises where an applicant has been informed that a court has issued a warrant for his or her eviction and there are fewer than 28 days left before the date scheduled for execution of the warrant.[220] If an applicant in these circumstances is not homeless, he or she will be threatened with homelessness.

---

[217] See **8.53–8.54**.
[218] HA 1996, s 195(2), (5) and (9).
[219] HA 1996, ss 190, 192, 193 and 200.
[220] *R (Sacupima) v Newham London Borough Council* (2001) 33 HLR 2, CA.

Chapter 12

ELIGIBILITY FOR ASSISTANCE

INTRODUCTION

12.1 Not everyone qualifies for help from a local housing authority under the homelessness provisions. There is an 'eligibility' test and, because of that, one of the first inquiries that a local housing authority must make of an applicant for assistance is whether he or she is eligible to obtain any help at all.[1]

12.2 As this chapter will demonstrate, 'eligibility' normally (but not exclusively) depends on the immigration status of the person seeking assistance. For this reason, both those who advise the homeless, and the staff who receive and determine their applications, need a familiarity with the homelessness eligibility rules set out here, and also with the basic rules of UK immigration control.[2] Self-evidently, a system which discriminates between potential service-users on the basis of nationality may lay itself open to a complaint of discrimination. Not surprisingly, the impact of the anti-discrimination provisions of the European Convention on Human Rights, Art 14 on the eligibility test has already been explored in the courts.[3]

12.3 The normal rule is that anyone is able to apply for help to any local housing authority, whatever his or her connection with the district of that particular local housing authority (or even if he or she has no connection with the UK at all). When the homelessness safety net was first brought into law by the Housing (Homeless Persons) Act 1977, it contained no eligibility test at all. Anyone from anywhere could apply.[4] It was left to the courts to identify the first ineligible categories: those who had entered the country unlawfully and those who, having entered lawfully, remained unlawfully in the UK.[5]

12.4 But nowadays the modern statutory regime contains sophisticated exclusion provisions. The general rule, that homelessness assistance is available to all, is preserved. However, the Housing Act 1996 (HA 1996), Part 7, at ss 185 and 186, provides for the exclusion of specific categories of applicants. As a result, eligibility is defined in the negative. A person is *not excluded* from homelessness assistance *unless* caught by the provisions of either HA 1996, s 185 or s 186.[6]

12.5 The largest excluded group comprises those rendered ineligible by HA 1996, s 185, which contains two categories of 'persons from abroad'. They are:

(1) 'persons subject to immigration control'; and

---

[1] Housing Act 1996, s 184(1)(a).
[2] Immigration law is beyond the scope of this book. Standard texts include MacDonald and Toal *MacDonald's Immigration Law and Practice* (Butterworths Law, 7th edn, 2009) and Seddon *Immigration, Nationality and Refugee Law Handbook* (JCWI, 2nd edn, 2006).
[3] *R (Morris) v Westminster City Council* [2005] EWCA Civ 1184, [2006] HLR 8, CA.
[4] *R v Hillingdon London Borough Council ex p Streeting* [1980] 1 WLR 1430, CA.
[5] See *R v Hillingdon London Borough Council ex p Streeting* [1980] 1 WLR 1430, CA at 1434, per Lord Denning MR.
[6] HA 1996, s 183(2).

(2)   'other persons from abroad'.

12.6   Anyone falling within the first category will be excluded from homelessness assistance, *unless* he or she is within one of the classes of persons prescribed as eligible by Regulation.[7] Anyone falling within the second category will be excluded from homelessness assistance if he or she is not habitually resident,[8] unless he or she falls within one of the groups of people prescribed as exempt from the habitual residence test,[9] or falls within the two other classes of people[10] prescribed as excluded within the Regulations.[11]

12.7   The classes of people prescribed as exempt from the overall exclusory provisions are different depending on whether an applicant has applied for homelessness assistance to an English local housing authority or to a Welsh local housing authority. In England, the current relevant Regulations apply to applications for homelessness assistance made on or after 1 June 2006.[12] In Wales, the current Regulations apply to applications made on or after 9 October 2006.[13] For applications to English local housing authorities made *before* 1 June 2006 (England) or 9 October 2006 (Wales), the relevant Regulations are considered in Chapter 3.[14]

12.8   The law relating to the eligibility of EEA nationals is particularly complex and requires understanding not only of the Regulations made under HA 1996, s 185(2) and (3), but also of the immigration status of EEA nationals and their family members. We therefore consider the various rights of residence available to EEA nationals and their family members later in this chapter.[15]

12.9   In this chapter, we review the two categories of persons from abroad as defined by HA 1996, s 185 as follows:

•   the meaning of the phrase 'subject to immigration control';[16]

•   'persons subject to immigration control':
     –   the English exemptions to the overall exclusionary rule;[17]

---

[7]   HA 1996, s 185(2); the relevant Regulations are the Allocation of Housing and Homelessness (Eligibility) (England) Regulations 2006, SI 2006/1294 (as amended), reg 5; and the Homelessness (Wales) Regulations 2006, SI 2006/2646 (W 227) (as amended), reg 5. See **12.60–12.86** (England) and **12.87–12.102** (Wales).
[8]   See **12.136–12.141**.
[9]   See **12.145–12.178** (England) and **12.190–12.192** (Wales).
[10]   See **12.179–12.186** (England) and **12.193** (Wales).
[11]   HA 1996, s 185(3); Allocation of Housing and Homelessness (Eligibility) (England) Regulations 2006, SI 2006/1294 (as amended), reg 6; and the Homelessness (Wales) Regulations 2006, SI 2006/2646 (W 227) (as amended), reg 6.
[12]   Allocation of Housing and Homelessness (Eligibility) (England) Regulations 2006, SI 2006/1294, regs 5 and 6, as amended.
[13]   Homelessness (Wales) Regulation 2006, SI 2006/2646 (W 227), reg 5.
[14]   See **3.49–3.58** and **3.123–3.136** (England) and **3.59–3.60** and **3.137–3.139** (Wales).
[15]   See **12.106–12.129**.
[16]   See **12.53–12.59**.
[17]   See **12.60–12.86**.

– the Welsh exemptions to the overall exclusionary rule;[18]

• 'other persons from abroad':[19]
  – rights to reside for EEA nationals and their family members;[20]
  – the English classes of people from abroad prescribed as excluded from homelessness assistance;[21]
  – the English exemptions to the prescribed exclusionary rules;[22]
  – the Welsh classes of people from abroad prescribed as excluded from homelessness assistance;[23]
  – the Welsh exemptions to those prescribed exclusionary rules.[24]

12.10 The other provision, HA 1996, s 186, catches the ever-diminishing number of pre-April 2000 asylum seekers who are eligible for homelessness assistance.[25] It will be repealed when the last of those cases passes through the asylum system.[26] It contains additional exclusions from assistance for those asylum-seekers who are eligible.[27] It is dealt with separately towards the end of this chapter.[28]

12.11 The Isles of Scilly have their own separate eligibility criteria, also dealt with at the end of this chapter.[29]

Ineligible for what?

12.12 Those who are 'not eligible' are excluded from almost all the forms of assistance available under HA 1996, Part 7. This is because HA 1996, Part 7 defines 'assistance' to mean:

> '... the benefit of any functions under the following provisions of this Part relating to accommodation or assistance in obtaining accommodation.'[30]

12.13 Someone who is not eligible will not be entitled to the benefit of any of the duties or powers set out from HA 1996, s 188 onwards. However, he or she

---

[18] See **12.87–12.102**.
[19] See **12.103–12.193**.
[20] See **12.106–12.129**.
[21] See **12.130–12.134** and **12.179–12.186**.
[22] See **12.145–12.178**.
[23] See **12.187–12.189** and **12.193**.
[24] See **12.190–12.192**.
[25] See **12.75–12.86** (England) and **12.88–12.89** (Wales).
[26] See Immigration and Asylum Act 1999, ss 117(5), 169(3) and Sch 16.
[27] HA 1996, s 185(2); Allocation of Housing and Homelessness (Eligibility) (England) Regulations, SI 2006/1294, reg 5(1)(e), Classes E(i)–(iii) (see **12.75–12.86**); and Homelessness (Wales) Regulations 2006, SI 2006/2646 (W 227), reg 3(1)(f): Class F(i)–(ii), (g): Class G(i)–(iii), (h): Class H(i)–(ii) (see **12.88–12.89**).
[28] See **12.201–12.204**.
[29] See **12.205–12.206**.
[30] HA 1996, s 183(2).

will still be able to obtain advice and information about homelessness (and about the prevention of homelessness) from the local housing authority, free of charge.[31]

12.14 This very wide definition of the exclusion from assistance under HA 1996, Part 7 makes it all the more important that the provisions of HA 1996, ss 185 and 186 (and the Regulations made under them) are looked at very carefully to ensure that only those whom HA 1996 deems 'not eligible' are in fact excluded.

Going in and out of eligibility

12.15 Because eligibility is linked to immigration status, which can change, it is possible for an applicant's eligibility also to change.

12.16 The *first crucial date* for determining eligibility is the date on which the local housing authority reaches its decision as to whether the applicant is 'eligible'.[32] If there is then a review of that decision, the critical date becomes the date of the review decision.[33] It would be maladministration and unlawful for a local housing authority deliberately to delay its inquiries in the hope that an applicant's eligibility might change,[34] although it may be sensible in particular circumstances to delay a determination of eligibility if a decision of the immigration authorities is a matter of hours or days away.

12.17 If, at the first crucial date, the applicant is 'eligible', then the appropriate service under HA 1996, Part 7 must be provided. That may even be the main housing duty owed under HA 1996, s 193(2).[35] If, subsequently, the applicant's immigration status changes such that he or she becomes 'not eligible', that does not mean that all services or, more importantly, accommodation can simply be withdrawn.

12.18 If the applicant has been provided with only short-term accommodation (for example, a person who has been found to have become homeless intentionally),[36] the loss of eligibility is irrelevant. Likewise, if the homeless

---

31 HA 1996, ss 179(1) and 183(3). See Chapter 8 and **9.4–9.7**.

32 Unless the applicant has applied for homelessness assistance before 1 June 2006 (English local housing authorities) or 9 October 2006 (Welsh local housing authorities), in which case transitional provisions state that his or her eligibility will be determined by the relevant Regulations in force at the date of his or her application (Allocation of Housing and Homelessness (Eligibility) (England) Regulations 2006, SI 2006/1294, reg 8; and Homelessness (Wales) Regulations 2006, SI 2006/2646 (W 227), reg 5). See **3.49–3.58**, **3.123–3.136** (England) and **3.59–3.60** and **3.137–3.139** (Wales) for the Regulations in force prior to those dates in relation to applications for an allocation of social housing.

33 *Ealing London Borough Council v Surdonja* [2001] QB 97, CA; and *Mohammed v Hammersmith and Fulham London Borough Council* [2001] UKHL 57, [2002] 1 AC 547, HL.

34 *Robinson v Hammersmith & Fulham London Borough Council* [2006] EWCA Civ 1122, [2007] HLR 7, CA.

35 See **17.21–17.108**.

36 HA 1996, s 190(2)(a). See **17.111–17.118**.

applicant has passed through HA 1996, Part 7 into longer-term social housing allocated under HA 1996, Part 6, the change in eligibility is irrelevant to his or her status as a tenant.[37]

12.19 However, there is one circumstance in which a change in eligibility is very important. If the applicant has the benefit of the HA 1996, s 193(2) main housing duty, that duty comes to an end at the point at which he or she ceases to be eligible.[38] The date when he or she ceases to be eligible is therefore the *second crucial date*. On the strict wording of HA 1996, s 193(6)(a), it would appear that the duty automatically ceases. However, normally a decision that the applicant is no longer eligible should be notified to the applicant in the usual way (providing reasons and notifying him or her of the right to a review).[39]

12.20 Even if an applicant who is owed the main housing duty becomes ineligible on a change in his or her immigration status, this does not mean that he or she is instantly put out onto the streets. The expectation is that public authorities will behave reasonably which (in this context) means that accommodation provision should at least be continued for such time as gives the applicant a fair chance to find somewhere else to live.[40]

12.21 Where an ineligible applicant (or an applicant who becomes ineligible) has children under the age of 18 (or is himself or herself a child), the local housing authority should make arrangements to refer the applicant's case to the relevant children's authority, so that social services can consider the exercise of their statutory duties and powers to protect children.[41]

12.22 Any applicant who is found to be ineligible for homelessness assistance (whether on his or her initial application or subsequently while occupying accommodation provided under the main housing duty at HA 1996, s 193(2))

---

[37]   HA 1996, s 160A(6). See also **3.2**. Once a person has been granted a secure or assured tenancy, that tenancy does not come to an end, nor is the landlord entitled to apply for possession, simply because he or she has become ineligible for a grant of a secure or assured tenancy. The landlord can only obtain possession under the grounds for possession at Housing Act 1985, Sch 2 (secure tenants), or Housing Act 1988, Sch 2, (assured tenants), or if the tenant loses his or her security of tenure (*Akinbolu v Hackney London Borough Council* (1997) 29 HLR 259, CA).

[38]   HA 1996, s 193(6)(a). See **17.59–17.61**.

[39]   HA 1996, s 184(3) and (5), discussed at **10.60–10.84**. See *Tower Hamlets London Borough Council v Deugi* [2006] EWCA Civ 159, [2006] HLR 28, CA at [33], where May LJ doubted whether a loss of eligibility required a decision under HA 1996, s 193(6)(a), since the local housing authority had no discretion, but recognised that there may be a dispute over the decision that eligibility has been lost.

[40]   *R v Secretary of State for the Environment ex p Shelter and the Refugee Council* [1997] COD 49, QBD; and *R v Newham London Borough Council ex p Ojuri (No 5)* (1999) 31 HLR 631, QBD.

[41]   HA 1996, s 213A; see *R (Badu) v Lambeth London Borough Council* [2005] EWCA Civ 1184, [2006] HLR 8, CA, and see Chapter 20 for the range of statutory powers and duties available to social services authorities.

may re-apply for homelessness assistance if his or her circumstances change such that he or she may have become eligible.[42]

Whose eligibility?

12.23 The eligibility test is primarily directed to working out whether the 'applicant' is eligible for, or excluded from, homelessness services. If the applicant is found not to be eligible, that will (subject to any review or appeal) be an end to his or her attempt to obtain homelessness services, even if other members of his or her household are plainly eligible for such services. The proper course in that situation is for the other household member(s) to apply to the local housing authority on behalf of the household.[43]

Disregard of ineligible members of the household

Overview

12.24 Even if an applicant is eligible for assistance, not all of the members of his or her household will necessarily also be eligible. HA 1996 provides, at s 185(4), that any member of the applicant's household who is not eligible for assistance must be disregarded when the local housing authority is considering whether the applicant is homeless or threatened with homelessness, or whether the applicant has a priority need.[44]

12.25 HA 1996, s 185(4) was declared incompatible with the European Convention on Human Rights (ECHR) in 2005 by the Court of Appeal.[45] The reason was because its wording at that date provided for a difference in treatment between applicants on the grounds of national origin or on a combination of one or more of nationality, immigration control, settled residence or social welfare, and that difference in treatment could prevent the applicant and his or her child from being able to enjoy their right to respect for their home and family life (Art 8) and was therefore discriminatory (Art 14). The court found that the difference in treatment was not justified. However, until the government took action to remedy the incompatibility, local housing authorities were required to continue to operate HA 1996, s 185(4).[46]

---

[42] Local housing authorities must accept fresh applications where there are 'new facts' that are not merely fanciful or trivial (*Begum v Tower Hamlets London Borough Council* [2005] EWCA Civ 340, [2005] HLR 34, CA): see English Code, para 6.27; and see **9.54–9.64**. Applicants who cease to be owed the main housing duty at HA 1996, s 193(2) may make a fresh application (HA 1996, s 193(9)): see **17.109–17.110**.

[43] Any accommodation duty owed to the new applicant may extend to accommodating everyone else who falls within the definition of 'household' at HA 1996, s 176 (see **11.21–11.29**).

[44] HA 1996, s 185(4).

[45] *R (Morris) v Westminster City Council* [2005] EWCA 1184, [2006] HLR 8, CA

[46] Human Rights Act 1998, s 4(6)(a).

The new rules

Retaining the disregard where the applicant is a person subject to immigration control

12.26   For applications to local housing authorities made on or after 2 March 2009,[47] this disregard of non-eligible household members *only* applies where the eligible *applicant* is:

- a person subject to immigration control;[48] and

- is eligible as a result of falling within one of the classes of people prescribed as eligible by Regulation;[49] and

- is not a national of an EEA state or of Switzerland.[50]

12.27   If the applicant falls within that statutory test, any ineligible members of his or her household must be disregarded when the local housing authority is considering whether the applicant is homeless or threatened with homelessness, or whether the applicant has a priority need.[51] So, when a local housing authority is considering whether, for example, overcrowded accommodation is reasonable for the applicant and his or her household to continue to occupy for the purpose of deciding whether the applicant is homeless or threatened with homelessness, ineligible members of the household cannot be considered. Even more importantly, if an applicant's children or other family members are all persons from abroad and ineligible for assistance, they cannot provide the applicant with a priority need.[52]

12.28   It does not follow, however, that those members of an applicant's household who are not eligible are to be disregarded for all purposes. When it comes to the discharge of the local housing authority's duty by the provision of suitable accommodation, that accommodation must be suitable for the needs of the applicant and his or her household, even if the household includes persons who are not eligible for assistance.

12.29   In addition, local authorities have a range of other statutory duties and powers under which they may provide accommodation, particularly where

---

[47]   The date applies to applications to both English and Welsh local housing authorities (Housing and Regeneration Act 2008, s 314 and Sch 15).

[48]   See **12.53–12.59**.

[49]   For applications to English local housing authorities, the classes are Classes A–E at Allocation of Housing and Homelessness (Eligibility) (England) 2006, SI 2006/1294 (as amended), reg 5(1): see **12.61–12.86**. For applications to Welsh local housing authorities, the classes are Classes A–J at Homelessness (Wales) Regulations 2006, SI 2006/2646 (W 227), reg 3(1): see **12.87–12.107**.

[50]   HA 1996, s 184(5).

[51]   HA 1996, s 185(4), as amended by Housing and Regeneration Act 2008, s 314 and Sch 15, para 4.

[52]   *R (Morris) v Westminster City Council* [2005] EWCA 1184, [2006] HLR 8, CA.

there are dependent children.[53] If a household is caught by HA 1996, s 185(4), and none of any dependent children or other vulnerable members are eligible and so cannot confer a priority need, local authorities may consider using those other statutory duties and powers in order to provide accommodation. But they may not do so simply with the object of circumventing the restriction in HA 1996, s 185(4).[54]

Disregard abolished where the applicant is not a person subject to immigration control

12.30 The disregard of ineligible household members no longer applies if the applicant is not a person subject to immigration control.[55] The applicant will be entitled to have the whole of his or her household assessed for the purposes of determining whether he or she is homeless and whether he or she has a priority need, irrespective of the immigration status of the people in his or her household.

12.31 However, if there are ineligible members of an applicant's household in those circumstances, the ineligible members are to be known as 'restricted persons' and, in some circumstances, the main housing duty owed to the applicant may be modified as a result of that person's presence in the household.[56]

12.32 A 'restricted person' is defined as a person:

- who is not eligible for assistance under HA 1996, Part 7; and

- who is subject to immigration control within the meaning of the Asylum and Immigration Act 1996;[57] and

- either does not have leave to enter or remain in the UK;[58] or

- whose leave to enter or remain in the UK is subject to a condition to maintain and accommodate himself or herself, and any dependants, without recourse to public funds.[59]

12.33 If the applicant is owed the main housing duty,[60] or the equivalent duty owed to those threatened with homelessness,[61] and that duty is only owed to the

---

53 See Chapter 20 generally, and **20.55–20.82** for Children Act duties.
54 *R (Badu) v Lambeth London Borough Council* [2005] EWCA Civ 1184, [2006] HLR 8, CA; and see Chapter 20 for the range of statutory powers and duties available to local authorities.
55 HA 1996, s 185(4) and (5), as amended and inserted by Housing and Regeneration Act 2008, s 314 and Sch 15, para 4. See **12.26**.
56 HA 1996, s 184(7), inserted by Housing and Regeneration Act 2008, s 314 and Sch 15, para 3.
57 See **12.53–12.59**.
58 See **12.58**.
59 HA 1996, s 184(7), inserted by Housing and Regeneration Act 2008, s 314 and Sch 15, para 3.
60 HA 1996, s 193(2). See **17.21–17.110**.
61 HA 1996, s 195(2). See **17.119–17.131**.

applicant because of the presence in his or her household of a restricted person, the local housing authority has additional notification duties.[62] It must notify the applicant that the main housing duty, or equivalent duty, is owed on the basis of the restricted person's presence in the applicant's household, must name the restricted person, must explain why that person is a restricted person, and must explain the effects of the modifications to the main housing duty or equivalent duty.

12.34 In those circumstances, the applicant's case becomes known as 'a restricted case'[63] or a 'restricted threatened homelessness case'.[64]

12.35 The mere presence of a restricted person in an applicant's household is not sufficient for the applicant's case to become a restricted case. The applicant's case *only* becomes a restricted case if the presence of the restricted person has either:

- caused the applicant to become homeless or threatened with homelessness;[65] or

- caused the applicant to have a priority need.

12.36 If the applicant would have been homeless or threatened with homelessness, and/or had a priority need, whether or not he or she had the restricted person in his or her household, his or her case will not be a restricted case.

12.37 For restricted cases, the main housing duty[66] is modified in two respects:

- there is no obligation on the local housing authority to give the applicant a copy of its statement of the policy in its allocation scheme as to choice;[67] and

- the local housing authority is required, so far as is reasonably practicable, to start to bring the main housing duty to an end by arranging for the

---

62 HA 1996, s 184(3A), inserted by Housing and Regeneration Act 2008, s 314 and Sch 15, para 3.

63 HA 1996, s 193(3B), inserted by Housing and Regeneration Act 2008, s 314 and Sch 15, para 5.

64 HA 1996, s 195(4B), inserted by Housing and Regeneration Act 2008, s 314 and Sch 15, para 6.

65 If, for example, the restricted person or persons has brought the level of overcrowding in the applicant's household to such an extent that it is not reasonable for the applicant to continue to occupy (HA 1996, s 175(3)): see **11.103–11.107**. Or where the applicant is homeless because accommodation is not available for the occupation of the applicant and the restricted person. (HA 1996, s 176): see **11.15–11.31**.

66 HA 1996, s 193(2). See **17.21–17.110**.

67 HA 1996, s 193(3A), as amended by Housing and Regeneration Act 2008, s 314 and Sch 15, para 5. This is because the applicant will not be entitled to reasonable preference in a local housing authority's allocation scheme as a result of being owed the main housing duty (HA 1996, s 167(2ZA), inserted by Housing and Regeneration Act 2008, s 314 and Sch 15, para 1. See **4.49** and **4.54**.

applicant to be made a 'private accommodation offer', defined as an assured shorthold tenancy made available by a private landlord for a fixed term of at least 12 months.[68]

12.38 The offer of private accommodation must be suitable for the needs of the applicant and his or her household.[69] If the applicant accepts or refuses the offer, the duty can come to an end.[70] The applicant has the right to request a review of any decision by the local housing authority that the private accommodation was suitable for him or her, and his or her household.[71]

12.39 Where the applicant is threatened with homelessness, and the duty owed to him or her is the duty to take reasonable steps to secure that accommodation does not cease to be available,[72] that duty is similarly modified in a restricted case.[73]

Working out whether the applicant is 'eligible'

12.40 To work out whether either of the two statutory exclusion provisions (HA 1996, ss 185 and 186) apply, it is first necessary to know something of the nationality and immigration status of the applicant. Inquiries need to be made sensitively and without applying any form of discriminatory approach as between different applicants.[74]

12.41 Detailed discussion of an applicant's immigration status is outside the scope of this book, but very helpful guidance in this complex area is provided at chapter 9 and Annexes 8–13 inclusive of the *Homelessness Code of Guidance for local authorities* (England) and chapter 11 and Annexes 4–15 inclusive of the *Code of Guidance for local housing authorities on allocation of accommodation and homelessness for Wales*.[75] It should be remembered, however, that:

---

[68] HA 1996, s 193(7AA)–(7AD), inserted by Housing and Regeneration Act 2008, s 314 and Sch 15, para 5. See **17.98–17.108**.

[69] See Chapter 18.

[70] HA 1996, s 193(7AA)–(7AD), inserted by Housing and Regeneration Act 2008, s 314 and Sch 15, para 5.

[71] HA 1996, s 202(1)(g), inserted by Housing and Regeneration Act 2008, s 314 and Sch 15, para 7.

[72] HA 1996, s 195(2). See **17.119–17.131**.

[73] HA 1996, s 195(3A), (4) and (4A–4B), inserted by Housing and Regeneration Act 2008, s 314 and Sch 15, para 6.

[74] *Homelessness Code of Guidance for local authorities* (Communities and Local Government, Department for Education and Skills, Department of Health, July 2006) (English Code), para 9.2: see Appendix 2 of this book. *Code of Guidance for local housing authorities on allocation of accommodation and homelessness for Wales* (National Assembly for Wales, April 2003) (Welsh Code), para 11.2: see CD-ROM.

[75] It should be noted that the Welsh Code refers to classes of people prescribed as eligible and ineligible under the old Homelessness (Wales) Regulations 2000, SI 2000/1079 (W 72), reg 2. Many of the classes are, however, the same as under the current Regulations. Where the class of persons is the same as that in the previous Regulations, we refer to the relevant guidance in

- for English local housing authorities, the guidance was published in July 2006 and does not take account of amendments to the Regulations since then;[76] and

- for Welsh local housing authorities, the guidance was published in April 2003, and the Regulations governing eligibility at that time have since been repealed and new Regulations have been made.[77]

12.42 The resolution of any uncertainty about an applicant's immigration or asylum status, or the relevant dates (eg of entry into the UK or application for asylum) may require the help of the UK Border Agency (UKBA).[78] Local housing authorities are advised to contact the UKBA if there is any uncertainty arising from an application, and to inform the applicant that an inquiry will be made before doing so. This allows the applicant an opportunity to withdraw his or her application for homelessness assistance if she or he does not want such an inquiry to be made.[79]

12.43 The UKBA is required to provide local housing authorities, on request, with information about whether a person falls within any particular statutory category (eg within Immigration and Asylum Act 1999, s 115)[80] or any other information required to enable local housing authorities to determine whether applicants are eligible for assistance.[81] Most requests for information are made, and the responses to them given, by telephone. Having regard to the complexity of the subject matter and the importance of accuracy, it may be sensible for a local housing authority receiving complex information from UKBA (particularly if it is going to be used to make or support an adverse eligibility decision) to ask that UKBA provide the information in writing.[82] The UKBA

---

the Welsh Code. For classes of people who are now prescribed as eligible or ineligible in the current Welsh Regulations and are not referred to in the Welsh Code, we give the reference to the English Code, if applicable.

[76] Specifically, the English Code does not deal with: the amendments to the disregard at HA 1996, s 185(4) and (5) (see **12.16–12.29**), 'restricted persons' (see **12.31**), 'restricted cases' (see **12.32–12.34**), the concept of EEA rights of residence not contained in domestic Regulations (see **12.125–12.129**), the position of A2 nationals (see **12.160–12.163**), the exemptions from the habitual residence for certain people leaving Lebanon (see **12.175–12.176**), and for certain people leaving Zimbabwe (see **12.177–12.178**).

[77] The current Regulations are the Homelessness (Wales) Regulations 2006, SI 2006/2646 (W 227), as amended: see **12.49–12.50**. Where the current Regulations are identical to the previous Regulations, we make reference to the relevant guidance in the Welsh Code.

[78] Both Codes refer to the Home Office Immigration and Nationality Directorate (IND). The UKBA replaced the IND in April 2008. See http://ukba.homeoffice.gov.uk/.

[79] English Code, para 9.9; Welsh Code, para 11.8.

[80] Which excludes 'persons subject to immigration control' from housing benefit and is referred to at HA 1996, s 185(2A).

[81] HA 1996, s 187(1) and (2).

[82] Contact details for the former Immigration and Nationality Directorate are given in English Code, Annex 8; Welsh Code, Annex 13. The contact details for the UKBA are at the same postal address: Lunar House, Croydon, CR9 2BY, but it is not known whether the same fax number given in the Annexes applies. Contact details for the UKBA can also be found at http://www.bia.homeoffice.gov.uk/contact/.

need not provide written confirmation unless the request itself is in writing.[83] A local housing authority is entitled to rely on the UKBA's view of an applicant's current immigration status, and need not make inquiries as to, for example, the possible outcome of a pending appeal.[84] The UKBA may advise on an applicant's immigration status, but the decision on eligibility is for the local housing authority itself.

12.44 If the UKBA does provide information to a local housing authority, it is then under a continuing obligation to notify that local housing authority, in writing, if there are any subsequent applications, decisions or other changes of circumstance affecting the particular applicant's status.[85] This continuing obligation is obviously of crucial importance if the applicant's immigration status is under review (or awaiting an initial decision or subject to an appeal) when the local housing authority makes its first request for information.

THE PRIMARY EXCLUSION PROVISION: HOUSING ACT 1996, SECTION 185

Overview

12.45 The governing provision for the main excluded group is HA 1996, s 185(1).[86] It provides that 'a person from abroad who is ineligible for housing assistance' is not eligible for assistance from a local housing authority under the homelessness provisions in HA 1996, Part 7. Working out who is, and who is not, caught by that term is therefore crucial in deciding whether homelessness services can be provided.

12.46 There are two categories of 'persons from abroad' for the purposes of HA 1996, s 185:

(1) those subject to immigration control –
   - they are *not eligible* for assistance
   - *unless* they fall within a class prescribed as 'eligible' in regulations made by the Secretary of State or the Welsh Assembly Government;[87]

(2) those not subject to immigration control but who are nevertheless prescribed by regulations as being 'persons from abroad' –

---

83 HA 1996, s 187(2).
84 *Burns v Southwark London Borough Council* [2004] EWHC 1901 (Admin), [2004] All ER (D) 328 (Jul).
85 HA 1996, s 187(3). From the wording, it appears that the UKBA is obliged to notify these changes of circumstances in writing, whether or not the information originally provided was provided in writing or verbally.
86 *R (Morris) v Westminster City Council* [2005] EWCA Civ 1184, [2006] HLR 8, CA, at [13] and [14] per Sedley LJ.
87 HA 1996, s 185(2).

- they are *not eligible* if they are not habitually resident in the Common Travel Area *unless* they are prescribed as exempt from the habitual residence test, or

- they are *not eligible* if they are prescribed as ineligible because of their particular rights of residence under European Union law.[88]

12.47 As is apparent from the terms of these provisions, the general rule is that people from abroad are excluded. But the Secretary of State and the Welsh Assembly Government[89] each have the power to make regulations exempting some people from abroad from that exclusory rule.[90] They each also have the power to make regulations excluding people who would otherwise be eligible. Each of these powers has been exercised several times in both England and Wales.

12.48 For England, the Secretary of State has made the Allocation of Housing and Homelessness (Eligibility) (England) Regulations 2006,[91] which apply to all applications for homelessness assistance to local housing authorities in England made on or after 1 June 2006.[92] Those Regulations have since been made amended by:

- the Allocation of Housing and Homelessness (Eligibility) (England) (Amendment) Regulations 2006;[93] and

- the Allocation of Housing and Homelessness (Eligibility) (England) (Miscellaneous Provisions) Regulations 2006;[94] and

---

88   HA 1996, s 185(3).

89   This power was exercisable by the National Assembly for Wales until 25 May 2007. On that day (which was the day of the appointment of the First Minister after the May 2007 elections to the National Assembly for Wales) functions previously exercised by the National Assembly for Wales were transferred to the Welsh Assembly Government (Government of Wales Act 2006, s 161 and Sch 11, para 30).

90   They cannot designate as eligible any person who is excluded from entitlement to housing benefit by the Immigration and Asylum Act 1999, s 115 (HA 1996, s 185(2A)). Immigration and Asylum Act 1999, s 115 prescribes that 'a person subject to immigration control' is not eligible for housing benefit unless he or she falls within one of the classes of people prescribed by the Secretary of State. Classes of persons subject to immigration control who are entitled to housing benefit are prescribed in the Social Security (Immigration and Asylum) Consequential Amendment Regulations 2000, SI 2000/636, reg 2 and Sch 1, Part 1 and the Housing Benefit Regulations 2006, SI 2006/213, reg 10(3B).

91   SI 2006/1294. See Appendix 2 of this book.

92   Any applications for homelessness assistance made before 1 June 2006 to English local housing authorities are determined according to the Homelessness (England) Regulations 2000, SI 2000/701, amended by Allocation of Housing and Homelessness (Amendment) (England) Regulations 2004, SI 2004/1235, and further amended by the Allocation of Housing and Homelessness (Amendment) (England) Regulations 2006, SI 2006/1093. See **3.49–3.58** and **3.123–3.136** for a discussion of those Regulations in relation to an application for an allocation.

93   SI 2006/2007, in force for applications to English local housing authorities made on or after 25 July 2006.

94   SI 2006/2527, in force for applications to English local housing authorities made on or after 9 October 2006.

- the Allocation of Housing and Homelessness (Eligibility) (England) (Amendment No 2) Regulations 2006;[95] and

- the Allocation of Housing and Homelessness (Eligibility) (England) (Amendment) Regulations 2009.[96]

Appendix 2 of this book contains the text of the Allocation of Housing and Homelessness (Eligibility) (England) Regulations 2006,[97] as amended by all of the above Regulations.

12.49 In Wales, the National Assembly for Wales[98] made the Homelessness (Wales) Regulations 2006,[99] which apply to all applications for homelessness assistance to Welsh local housing authorities made on or after 9 October 2006.[100]

12.50 The Welsh Regulations have been amended by:

- the Employment and Support Allowance (Consequential Provisions) (No 3) Regulations 2008, para 31;[101] and

- the Allocation of Housing and Homelessness (Eligibility) (Wales) Regulations 2009.[102]

Appendix 3 of this book contains the text of the Homelessness (Wales) Regulations 2006,[103] as amended by both these Regulations.

12.51 The Regulations in both England and Wales set out classes of persons who are subject to immigration control but are prescribed as nevertheless eligible. They also set out classes of persons who are not subject to immigration control, but are nevertheless ineligible.

12.52 Each of the two categories of persons from abroad (those subject to immigration control and those not subject to such control) needs careful examination. But first it is necessary to work out which category an applicant is within. That depends on whether or not the applicant is 'subject to immigration control'.

---

[95] SI 2006/3340, in force for applications to English local housing authorities made on or after 1 January 2007.
[96] SI 2009/358, in force for applications to English local housing authorities made on or after 18 March 2009.
[97] SI 2006/1294.
[98] Its functions were acquired by the Welsh Assembly Government on 25 May 2007. See fn 89.
[99] SI 2006/2646 (W 227).
[100] For the relevant regulations in Wales before 9 October 2006, see **3.59–3.60** and **3.137–3.139**.
[101] SI 2008/1879, in force for applications to Welsh local housing authorities on or after 27 October 2008.
[102] SI 2009/393 (W 42), in force for applications to Welsh local housing authorities on or after 20 March 2009.
[103] SI 2006/2646 (W 227).

Meaning of 'subject to immigration control'

12.53 The starting point is the special meaning of 'subject to immigration control'. It means 'a person who is subject to immigration control within the meaning of the Asylum and Immigration Act 1996'.[104] The Asylum and Immigration Act 1996 itself states:

> '... "person subject to immigration control" means a person who under the 1971 Act requires leave to enter or remain in the United Kingdom (whether or not such leave has been given).'[105]

12.54 Tracing that route back to the Immigration Act 1971[106] reveals that:

• British citizens;

• Commonwealth citizens with the right of abode;

• European Economic Area ('EEA') nationals and Swiss nationals exercising certain Treaty rights[107] (see Box 2 at **12.56**);

• family members and some extended family members of those EEA and Swiss nationals exercising certain Treaty rights;[108] and

• certain people who are exempt from immigration control under the Immigration Acts (diplomats and their family members based in the UK, and some military personnel)

do *not* require leave to enter or remain in the UK and therefore cannot be 'persons subject to immigration control'.[109] Those applicants will be eligible *unless* they fall within the second category of persons prescribed as being 'persons from abroad' and not eligible.[110]

---

104   HA 1996, s 185(2).

105   Asylum and Immigration Act 1996, s 13(2).

106   Immigration Act 1971, ss 1–3.

107   Immigration Act 1988, s 7; Immigration (European Economic Area) Regulations 2006, SI 2006/1003, regs 13–15. From 1 June 2002, Swiss nationals have had the same rights to freedom of movement and social security within the EEA as EEA nationals: and so Swiss nationals fall within the definition of EEA nationals at Immigration (European Economic Area) Regulations 2006, SI 2006/1003, reg 2. All references to 'EEA nationals' in this book include Swiss nationals.

108   Immigration (European Economic Area) Regulations 2006, SI 2006/1003, regs 7 and 8, in force from 30 April 2006.

109   English Code, paras 9.7–9.8. If an EEA national is not a 'qualifying person', he or she does not have the right to remain without leave, and is therefore a 'person subject to immigration control' and would fall within HA 1996, s 185(2) (*Abdi v Barnet London Borough Council, Ismail v Barnet London Borough Council* [2006] EWCA Civ 383, [2006] HLR 23, CA).

110   HA 1996, s 185(3) and Allocation of Housing and Homelessness (Eligibility) (England) Regulations 2006, SI 2006/1294, reg 6, or Homelessness (Wales) Regulations 2006, SI 2006/2646 (W 227), reg 4. See **12.103–12.186** for the position in England and **12.187–12.193** for the position in Wales.

12.55 The legal definition of the term 'the United Kingdom' and its related parts is given in Box 1.

Box 1

Key Geographic Terms:

England: counties established by Local Government Act 1972, s 1, Greater London area and the Isles of Scilly.[111]

Great Britain: England, Wales, and Scotland.[112]

United Kingdom: England, Wales, Scotland and Northern Ireland.[113]

Common Travel Area (CTA): England, Wales, Scotland, Northern Ireland, Republic of Ireland, Isle of Man, and the Channel Islands.[114]

12.56 Box 2 shows which countries are members of the European Union (EU) and/or members of the wider European Economic Area (EEA).[115] For these purposes, nationals of Iceland, Liechtenstein, Norway, and Switzerland have the same rights to enter or reside as nationals of most of the EU Member States.[116] Rights for nationals of the eight 2004 Accession States ('A8 states')[117] and for nationals of Bulgaria and Romania ('the A2 states')[118] are slightly different from those enjoyed by nationals of other EEA states. We refer throughout this chapter to nationals of EEA Member States, by which we mean all the EU Member States, including the A8 and A2 states, plus the three additional EEA Member States and Switzerland.

---

[111] Interpretation Act 1978, s 5 and Sch 1.
[112] Union of Scotland Act 1706.
[113] Interpretation Act 1978, s 5 and Sch 1.
[114] Immigration Act 1971, s 1(3).
[115] Croatia, Turkey and the former Yugoslav Republic of Macedonia are 'candidate countries' for accession to the EU. Albania, Bosnia and Herzegovina, Serbia and Montenegro are all due to make political changes before applying to become 'candidate countries'. The EU is considering the position of Kosovo. See www.europa.eu.int for an up-to-date list.
[116] Immigration (European Economic Area) Regulations 2006, SI 2006/1003. See Appendix 2 of this book.
[117] See **12.154–12.159**.
[118] See **12.160–12.163**.

Box 2

The European Union (EU):

Member States:[119] Austria, Belgium, Cyprus, Denmark, Finland, France, Germany, Greece, Ireland, Italy, Luxembourg, Netherlands, Malta, Portugal, Spain, Sweden and the UK; and

Accession States acceding in 2004 ('A8 states'): Czech Republic, Estonia, Hungary, Latvia, Lithuania, Poland, Slovakia, Slovenia; and

Accession States acceding in 2007 ('A2 states): Bulgaria and Romania

The European Economic Area (EEA):

All EU States[120] plus Iceland, Liechtenstein and Norway.

Switzerland is not part of the EEA, but its nationals are treated as EEA nationals for these purposes.[121]

12.57 Obviously, the lists given in these boxes will fluctuate from time to time. Annex 11 of the *Homelessness Code of Guidance* (England) provides useful lists and web site addresses that will help advisers keep up to date.[122]

12.58 If a consideration of these provisions shows that the applicant is *not* 'subject to immigration control', because she or he does not require leave to enter or remain in the UK, he or she will usually be 'eligible' *unless* rendered ineligible by falling within the second category. For these purposes, it is important to emphasise that a person, usually an EEA national, who does not require leave to enter but who does require leave to remain and does not have it, is a person subject to immigration control.[123] It is only a person who requires neither leave to enter nor leave to remain who is not subject to immigration control. Strangely, a person can be ineligible for homelessness assistance even if

---

[119] All Member States as at 30 April 2004, plus Cyprus and Malta, who both joined on 1 May 2004 along with the A8 states. Cyprus and Malta are not subject to the derogations that the A8 states are subject to.

[120] The Channel Islands, Isle of Man and Gibraltar are not part of the EEA.

[121] Immigration (European Economic Area) Regulations 2006, SI 2006/1003, reg 2.

[122] English Code, Annex 11 does not include any reference to the A2 countries, which acceded in 2007. See also Welsh Code, Annex 12, which was published in 2003 and does not include Member States who acceded in 2004 or 2007. Up-to-date information can be obtained from www.europa.eu.int or http://ukba.homeoffice.gov.uk/eucitizens/.

[123] *Abdi v Barnet London Borough Council, Ismail v Barnet London Borough Council* [2006] EWCA Civ 383, [2006] HLR 23, CA.

he or she was born in the UK and has never left it, simply because he or she does require leave to enter or remain in the UK and does not have it.[124]

12.59 Everyone else is a 'person subject to immigration control' and is *not* eligible for assistance *unless* he or she falls into one of the classes prescribed by Allocation of Housing and Homelessness (Eligibility) (England) Regulations 2006, reg 5 or by Homelessness (Wales) Regulations 2006, reg 3.[125]

Category One: those who are subject to immigration control

12.60 The starting point is that:

'... a person who is subject to immigration control within the meaning of the Asylum and Immigration Act 1996 is not eligible for housing assistance unless he is of a class prescribed by regulations made by the Secretary of State.'[126]

The English rules

The basic rule

12.61 The basic rule is that 'a person subject to immigration control' is *not eligible*. The exceptions to that basic rule are contained in classes set out in Regulations. Regulation 5 of the Allocation of Housing and Homelessness (Eligibility) (England) Regulations 2006[127] prescribes that the following classes of persons from abroad are eligible even though they are subject to immigration control:

(1) Class A:[128] a person recorded by the Secretary of State as a refugee and who has leave to enter or remain in the UK.

(2) Class B:[129] a person who has:
   (a) exceptional leave to enter or remain in the UK granted outside of the provisions of the Immigration Rules; and
   (b) whose leave is not subject to conditions requiring him or her to maintain and accommodate himself or herself and any dependants without recourse to public funds.

(3) Class C:[130] a person who:
   (a) is habitually resident in the CTA;[131] and

---

[124] *Ehiabor v Kensington & Chelsea Royal London Borough Council* [2008] EWCA Civ 1074, [2008] All ER (D) 104 (May), CA.

[125] SI 2006/1294; SI 2006/2646 (W 227).

[126] HA 1996, s 185(2).

[127] SI 2006/1294. See Appendix 2 of this book.

[128] SI 2006/1294, reg 5(1)(a). See **12.65–12.67**.

[129] SI 2006/1294, reg 5(1)(b). See **12.68–12.70**.

[130] SI 2006/1294, reg 5(1)(c). See **12.71–12.73**.

[131] See Box 1 at **12.55**.

    (b)   has current leave to enter or remain in the UK which is not subject to any limitation or condition; but

    (c)   is not a person who:

        (i)   has been given leave to enter or remain in the UK upon a written undertaking from a sponsor that he or she will be responsible for maintenance and accommodation; and

        (ii) has been resident in the CTA for less than 5 years beginning on the date of entry or the date of the undertaking (whichever is the later date); and

        (iii) whose sponsor is still alive.

(4)   Class D:[132] a person who has humanitarian protection granted under the Immigration Rules.

(5)   Class E:[133] a person who is an asylum-seeker[134] whose claim for asylum is recorded by the Secretary of State as having been made before 3 April 2000 and in one of the following circumstances:

    (i)   on arrival in the UK from a country outside the CTA;[135] or

    (ii) within 3 months from the day on which the Secretary of State made a declaration of upheaval and where the applicant was in Great Britain[136] on the date of the declaration;[137] or

    (iii) on or before 4 February 1996 by an applicant who was on 4 February 1996 entitled to housing benefit under reg 7A of the Housing Benefit (General) Regulations 1987.[138]

12.62 Guidance on the scope of each of these classes is given in the English Code at paras 9.10–9.12.[139] These classes are individually considered at **12.65–12.86**.

12.63 A number of the classes contain terms that are defined by the regulations or by case law. For the meaning of:

- 'asylum seeker' see **12.75–12.80**;

- 'Common Travel Area (CTA)' see Box 1 at **12.55**;

---

[132] SI 2006/1294, reg 5(1)(d), as amended by Allocation of Housing and Homelessness (Miscellaneous Provisions) (England) Regulations 2006, SI 2006/2527, reg 2, for applications for homelessness assistance made on or after 9 October 2006. See **12.74**. For applications made before 9 October 2006, Class D contained 'a person who left the territory of Montserrat after 1 November 1995 because of the effect on that territory of a volcanic eruption'. For discussion of Class D prior to 9 October 2006, see **12.91–12.93**.

[133] SI 2006/1294, reg 5(1)(e). See **12.75–12.86**.

[134] See **12.75–12.80**.

[135] See **12.81**.

[136] See Box 1 at **12.55**.

[137] Two declarations of upheaval have been issued: Zaire (on 16 May 1997) and Sierra Leone (on 1 July 1997). See **12.82–12.84**.

[138] SI 1987/1971. See **12.85–12.86**.

[139] Note that the guidance at para 9.10(iv) on Class D is out of date and refers to the former Class D (English Code, para 9.10(iv)).

- 'habitually resident' see **12.136–12.141**.

12.64 Even if an applicant is eligible under any of these five classes, any members of his or her household who are not eligible are to be disregarded for the purposes of deciding whether the applicant is homeless and whether he or she has a priority need.[140]

Exemptions from the basic rule

Class A: refugees[141]

12.65 If a former asylum seeker has been granted refugee status by the Secretary of State, he or she will also have the 'leave to enter or remain in the UK' required for Class A purposes and will be eligible for homelessness assistance, welfare benefits, community care services and for an allocation of social housing according to the same criteria as those applicable to British citizens.

12.66 It is not unusual for someone to be granted refugee status and then to apply for his or her family to come to the UK. The family enters the UK with the refugee acting as their sponsor. A refugee is entitled to such family reunion,[142] and so the usual rules regarding maintenance and accommodation (which would normally involve a condition of 'no recourse to public funds') do not apply to a refugee's family members. Thus, those family members will also be eligible for homelessness assistance because they are entitled to 'refugee' status.[143]

12.67 Once a former asylum-seeker is granted refugee status, any accommodation which was provided by the UKBA[144] under Immigration and Asylum Act 1999, Part 6 will be withdrawn. If the asylum-seeker was occupying accommodation provided by the UKBA under Immigration and Asylum Act 1999, s 95 (the main duty to provide support to asylum-seekers), he or she will have a local connection with the local housing authority in whose district the UKBA accommodation was situated.[145] This does not preclude the former asylum-seeker from establishing a local connection, or several local connections, elsewhere, whether by residence, family associations, employment or special circumstances. He or she might then have a local connection with more than one local housing authority.

---

[140] HA 1996, s 185(4) in its original form and as amended by Housing and Regeneration Act 2008, s 314 and Sch 15, para 4. See **12.24–12.29**.

[141] Allocation of Housing and Homelessness (Eligibility) (England) Regulations 2006, SI 2006/1294, reg 5(1)(a). English Code, para 9.10(i).

[142] See *Immigration Rules*, HC 395 (23 May 1994 as amended), paras 352A–352F at http://www.ukba.homeoffice.gov.uk/policyandlaw/immigrationlaw/immigrationrules/part11/.

[143] *R (Jimaali) v Haringey London Borough Council* (2002) November *Legal Action*, p 24, Admin Ct.

[144] Formerly the National Asylum Support Service or 'NASS'.

[145] HA 1996, s 199(6), as amended. See **15.84–15.90**.

Class B: exceptional leave to enter or remain[146]

12.68 'Exceptional leave to enter or remain' was generally a status granted to asylum-seekers whose claim for full refugee status had not succeeded but where the Home Office recognised that there were compelling humanitarian and/or compassionate circumstances that required that the applicant should be allowed to stay in the UK. From 1 April 2003, the Home Office has called leave granted in those circumstances 'humanitarian protection' or 'discretionary leave'.[147] Viewed broadly, anyone who was granted leave to enter or remain when the Secretary of State has recognised that he or she does not fully meet the requirements of the Immigration Rules has been treated 'exceptionally' and may be said to have been granted 'exceptional leave'.

12.69 People with exceptional leave to enter or remain will be eligible for homelessness assistance unless that leave is subject to a condition requiring them to maintain and accommodate themselves (and their dependants) without recourse to public funds. The presence or absence of such a condition will be manifest from the document (or stamp) containing the grant of leave itself.

12.70 Unless they fall within the prohibition of 'no recourse to public funds', they will not only be entitled to homelessness assistance but also to welfare benefits and community care services, and can apply for an allocation of social housing.

Class C: a person with current leave to enter or remain in the UK with no condition or limitation and who is habitually resident in the Common Travel Area[148]

12.71 The type of leave contemplated by this class is commonly referred to as 'indefinite leave to enter or remain' and cannot be granted subject to conditions.[149] Anyone granted indefinite leave to enter or remain will be eligible if he or she is also habitually resident in the CTA.[150]

12.72 If leave to enter or remain has been granted on the basis of a written undertaking that a sponsor would be responsible for the applicant's maintenance and accommodation, the applicant will *not* be eligible for homeless assistance under Class C for 5 years running from:

- the date of his or her arrival in the UK; or

---

[146] Allocation of Housing and Homelessness (Eligibility) (England) Regulations 2006, SI 2006/1294, reg 5(1)(b). English Code, para 9.10(ii).
[147] Letter from the Homelessness Directorate (Office of the Deputy Prime Minister) to Chief Executives and Housing Directors of English local housing authorities, dated 25 March 2003.
[148] Allocation of Housing and Homelessness (Eligibility) (England) Regulations 2006, SI 2006/1294, reg 5(1)(c). English Code, para 9.10(iii).
[149] Immigration Act 1971, s 3(1)(b) and (c).
[150] For the meaning of 'habitually resident', see **12.136–12.141**. For the 'Common Travel Area', see Box 1 at **12.55**.

• the date the sponsorship undertaking was given;

starting from whichever is the later event.[151]

12.73 After those 5 years, or if the sponsor (or at least one of several sponsors) dies within the 5 years,[152] an applicant will be eligible under this class (subject to satisfying the test of habitual residence).[153]

Class D: a person granted humanitarian protection under the Immigration Rules[154]

12.74 'Humanitarian protection' is granted to those people whose claims for asylum do not succeed, but who have international protection needs (ie they face a serious risk of the death penalty, unlawful killing, torture, inhuman or degrading treatment or punishment if removed from the UK). The status must be granted pursuant to the Immigration Rules.[155] People with humanitarian protection are entitled to family reunion in the same way as refugees.[156]

Class E: asylum-seekers (in three specific circumstances)[157]

12.75 An 'asylum-seeker' is defined in the Regulations as:

'... a person who is at least 18 years old, who is in the UK, and who has made a claim for asylum.'[158]

12.76 A person ceases to be an asylum-seeker 'when his claim for asylum is recorded by the Secretary of State as having been decided (other than on appeal) or abandoned',[159] unless he or she continues to be eligible for housing benefit.[160]

12.77 A 'claim for asylum' is defined as:

---

[151] SI 2006/1294, reg 5(1)(c)(ii).

[152] SI 2006/1294, reg 5(1)(c)(iii).

[153] See **12.136–12.141**.

[154] Allocation of Housing and Homelessness (Eligibility) (England) Regulations 2006, SI 2006/1294, reg (1)(d), as amended by Allocation of Housing and Homelessness (Miscellaneous Provisions) (England) Regulations 2006, SI 2006/2527, reg 3(2). Paragraph 9. 10(iv) of the English Code is out of date and deals with the former Class D applying to applications made before 9 October 2006. There is reference at English Code, para 9.10(ii) to humanitarian protection. See **12.91–12.93** for Class D prior to 9 October 2006.

[155] See *Immigration Rules*, HC 395, paras 339C–339H (23 May 1994, as amended), at http://www.ukba.homeoffice.gov.uk/policyandlaw/immigrationlaw/immigrationrules/part11/.

[156] *Immigration Rules*, HC 395, paras 352FA–352FI. See **12.77–12.78**.

[157] Allocation of Housing and Homelessness (Eligibility) (England) Regulations 2006, SI 2006/1294, reg 5(1)(e). English Code, paras 9.11–9.12 and Annex 9.

[158] SI 2006/1294, reg 5(2)(a).

[159] SI 2006/1294, reg 5(2)(d).

[160] SI 2006/1294, reg 5(3).

'... a claim that it would be contrary to the UK's obligations under the Refugee Convention for the claimant to be removed from, or required to leave the UK.'[161]

12.78 The date of a claim for asylum is the date on which it was recorded by the Secretary of State.[162] To fall within Class E, that date must be *before 3 April 2000*. There will be very few people now falling within any of the three parts of Class E. For these few asylum-seekers, there are additional exclusionary rules for those who do fall within Class E made at HA 1996, s 186.[163]

12.79 'Asylum-seekers' who fall into the three different variants of Class E described below must be adult asylum seekers who made their claims for asylum before 3 April 2000 and are still waiting for determination of their applications. All other adult asylum seekers will be the responsibility of the UKBA providing support under Immigration and Asylum Act 1999, Part 6. Asylum seekers who are children will be the responsibility of children's authorities.[164]

12.80 Asylum-seekers who are eligible for homelessness assistance as a result of falling within Class E are also eligible for welfare benefits.[165]

Class E(i): claims for asylum made on arrival[166]

12.81 Class E(i) is concerned with those who made an asylum claim 'on arrival' in the UK. The Home Office may have made a decision, when the asylum-seeker first came to its attention, as to whether he or she claimed 'on arrival'. The Home Office has a duty to inform a local housing authority of its decision on that question or any change in that decision.[167]

Class E(ii): claims for asylum made within 3 months of a relevant declaration of upheaval[168]

12.82 The claim for asylum must have been made *after* the declaration of upheaval and have been recorded by the Secretary of State as made within 3 months of it. Any person who claims asylum within that period, but who had already made a prior claim for asylum in the UK will not fall within this class.

---

[161] SI 2006/1294, reg 5(2)(b). The scope would normally include claims for leave to remain based on Art 3 of the European Convention on Human Rights.

[162] SI 2006/1294, reg 5(1)(e).

[163] See **12.201–12.204**.

[164] See **20.73–20.76**.

[165] Because the provision excluding asylum-seekers from certain welfare benefits at Immigration and Asylum Act 1999, s 115 does not apply to those people who sought asylum before 3 April 2000 and whose claims have not yet been determined.

[166] Allocation of Housing and Homelessness (Eligibility) (England) Regulations 2006, SI 2006/1294, reg 5(1)(e)(i). English Code, Annex 9, para 7(i).

[167] HA 1996, s 187. English Code, Annex 9, para 11.

[168] Allocation of Housing and Homelessness (Eligibility) (England) Regulations 2006, SI 2006/1294, reg 5(1)(e)(ii). English Code, Annex 9, para 7(ii).

12.83 Two declarations of upheaval have been made by the Secretary of State: Zaire (16 May 1997) and Sierra Leone (1 July 1997). Nationals of Zaire/the Congo must have claimed asylum between 16 May 1997 and 15 August 1997 and nationals of Sierra Leone between 1 July 1997 and 30 September 1997 to fall within this class. Accordingly, the class only currently operates to assist those who sought asylum from those two countries over 12 years ago and who still await final decisions on their claims.

12.84 Note that the individual must have been in 'Great Britain'[169] when the declaration was made. The terms of the class will not be satisfied if on that date he or she was in Northern Ireland or elsewhere in the CTA.[170]

Class E(iii): an asylum-seeker who claimed asylum on or before 4 February 1996 and who was entitled to benefit on 4 February 1996[171]

12.85 This class is largely self-explanatory. For the purposes of this class, the 'benefit' to which the person was entitled must have been Housing Benefit payable under the Housing Benefit (General) Regulations 1987 until 2006 and since then under the Housing Benefit Regulations 2006.[172] The individual must still be an asylum-seeker,[173] ie a person still awaiting final determination of his or her claim for asylum.

12.86 If a person who is subject to immigration control is *not* within any of the Classes A–E described above, and made his or her application for homelessness assistance on or after 1 June 2006, he or she is *not* 'eligible' for homelessness assistance.

The Welsh rules

The basic rule

12.87 The National Assembly for Wales has exercised its power to prescribe classes of people who are subject to immigration control, but are nevertheless eligible, by the Homelessness (Wales) Regulations 2006, as amended.[174] These Regulations apply to applications for homelessness assistance made to Welsh

---

[169] 'Great Britain' is defined as England, Scotland and Wales: Union with Scotland Act 1706; see Box 1 at **12.55**.

[170] See Box 1 at **12.55**.

[171] Allocation of Housing and Homelessness (Eligibility) (England) Regulations 2006, SI 2006/1294, reg 5(1)(e)(iii). English Code, Annex 9, para 7(iii).

[172] SI 1987/1971, reg 7A.The current housing benefit regulations are Housing Benefit Regulations 2006, SI 2006/213, in force from 6 March 2006.

[173] As defined at Allocation of Housing and Homelessness (Eligibility) (England) Regulations 2006, SI 2006/1294, reg 5(2)(a). See **12.75–12.80**.

[174] SI 2006/2646 (W 227), reg 3. The National Assembly for Wales' functions to make regulations under HA 1996, Parts 6 and 7, were transferred to the Welsh Assembly Government on 25 May 2007 (see fn 89). See **12.50** for a list of the amendments to the Homelessness (Wales) Regulation 2006, SI 2006/2646 (W 227).

local housing authorities on or after 9 October 2006.[175] It should be noted that the guidance in the Welsh Code refers to the earlier Regulations in force in 2003.[176]

Exemptions to the basic rule

12.88 Regulation 3 of the Homelessness (Wales) Regulations 2006[177] prescribes that the following classes of persons from abroad are eligible, even though they are subject to immigration control:

(1)   Class A:[178] a person recorded by the Secretary of State as a refugee within the definition in Art 1 of the Refugee Convention.

(2)   Class B:[179] a person:
   (a)   who has been granted by the Secretary of State exceptional leave to remain in the UK outside the provisions of the Immigration Rules; and
   (b)   whose leave is not subject to a condition requiring that person to maintain and accommodate himself or herself and any dependants, without recourse to public funds.

(3)   Class C:[180] a person who:
   (a)   is habitually resident in the CTA;[181] and
   (b)   has current leave to enter or remain in the UK which is not subject to any limitation or condition; but
   (c)   is not a person who:
      (i)   has been given leave to enter or remain in the UK upon a written undertaking from a sponsor that he or she will be responsible for maintenance and accommodation; and
      (ii)   has been resident in the CTA for less than 5 years beginning on the date of entry or the date of undertaking (whichever is the later date); and
      (iii) whose sponsor is still alive.

(4)   Class D:[182] a person who left the territory of Montserrat after 1 November 1995 because of the effect on that territory of a volcanic eruption.

---

[175]   Homelessness (Wales) Regulations 2006, SI 2006/2646 (W 227), as amended, reg 5. For the position for applications made before 9 October 2006, see **3.59–3.60**.

[176]   See paras 11.1–11.11 and Annexes 4–11, 13 and 15 of the Welsh Code. All the six classes discussed at para 11.9 of the Welsh Code remain eligible under the current Regulations. Classes D, F, G, and J are new classes and there is no guidance about them in the Welsh Code. Where appropriate, reference has been made to guidance on those classes in the English Code.

[177]   SI 2006/2646 (W 227).

[178]   SI 2006/2646 (W 227), reg 3(1)(a). See Welsh Code, para 11.9(i). See **12.65–12.67**.

[179]   SI 2006/2646 (W 227), reg 3(1)(b). See Welsh Code, para 11.9(ii). See **12.68–12.70**.

[180]   SI 2006/2646 (W 227), reg 3(1)(c). See Welsh Code, para 11.9(iii). See **12.71–12.73**.

[181]   See Box 1 at **12.55**.

[182]   SI 2006/2646 (W 227), reg 3(1)(d). See English Code, para 9.10(iv). See **12.91–12.93**.

(5)   Class E:[183] a person who is habitually resident[184] in the CTA[185] and who is either:

    (a)   a national of a state which has ratified the European Convention on Social and Medical Assistance ('ECSMA') or the European Social Charter ('ESC') and is lawfully present in the UK;[186] or

    (b)   before 3 April 2000 was owed a duty by a local housing authority under Housing Act 1985, Part 3, or HA 1996, Part 7, which is extant and who is a national of a state which is a signatory to the ECSMA or to the ESC.[187]

(6)   Class F:[188] a person who is an asylum-seeker and who made a claim for asylum which is recorded by the Secretary of State as having been made on his or her arrival in the UK from a country outside the CTA and which has not been recorded by the Secretary of State as having been either decided (other than on appeal) or abandoned.

(7)   Class G:[189] a person who is an asylum-seeker and who was in Great Britain when the Secretary of State made a declaration of upheaval in respect of his or her country, who made a claim for asylum which is recorded by the Secretary of State as having been made within a period of 3 months from the day on which that declaration was made and whose claim for asylum has not been recorded by the Secretary of State as having been either decided (other than on appeal) or abandoned.

(8)   Class H:[190] a person who is an asylum-seeker and who made a relevant claim for asylum on or before 4 February 1996 and was, on that date, entitled to housing benefit under Housing Benefit (General) Regulations 1987, reg 7A.[191]

(9)   Class I:[192] a person who is on income-based jobseeker's allowance or income support (with certain exceptions).

(10)   Class J:[193] a person who has humanitarian protection granted under the Immigration Rules.

12.89   Several of these classes are identical to those prescribed as eligible under the English Regulations and are discussed at **12.61–12.86**.

---

[183]   SI 2006/2646 (W 227), reg 3(1)(e). See Welsh Code, paras 11.9(iv) and (v). See **12.94–12.99**.
[184]   See **12.136–12.141**.
[185]   See Box 1 at **12.55**.
[186]   See **12.94–12.96**.
[187]   See **12.97–12.99**.
[188]   SI 2006/2646 (W 227), reg 3(1)(f). See English Code, paras 9.11–9.12; Welsh Code, para 11.11 and Annex 10. See **12.75–12.81**.
[189]   SI 2006/2646 (W 227), reg 3(1)(g). See English Code, Annex 9, para 7(ii). See **12.82–12.84**.
[190]   SI 2006/2646 (W 227), reg 3(1)(h). See English Code, Annex 9, para 7(iii). See **12.85–12.86**.
[191]   SI 1987/1971.
[192]   SI 2006/2646 (W 227), reg 3(1)(i). See Welsh Code, para 11.9(vi). See **12.100–12.102**.
[193]   SI 2006/2646 (W 227), reg 3(1)(j). See **12.74**.

– 　For Class A, see **12.65–12.67**.

– 　For Class B, see **12.68–12.70**.

– 　For Class C, see **12.71–12.73**.

– 　For Class F, see **12.75–12.81**.

– 　For Class G, see **12.82–12.84**.

– 　For Class H, see **12.85–12.86**.

– 　For Class J, see **12.74**.

– 　Classes D, Ei, Eii and I are considered in turn.

12.90　For an applicant who is eligible because he or she falls within one of these classes, members of his or her household who are not eligible are to be disregarded for the purposes of deciding whether the applicant is homeless and whether he or she has a priority need.[194]

Class D:[195] *a person who left the territory of Montserrat after 1 November 1995 because of the effect on that territory of a volcanic eruption*

12.91　This class refers to persons who are subject to immigration control and who left Montserrat for this identified reason. A British citizen, or other person who is not 'subject to immigration control',[196] and who had left Montserrat for this identified reason would fall within HA 1996, s 185(3) and be treated as an 'other person from abroad'.[197] He or she will normally be exempt from the habitual residence test.[198]

12.92　Note that not all those leaving Montserrat are rendered eligible by this class. It does not apply to those who left on or before 1 November 1995, nor to those who left after that date for reasons unconnected with the volcanic eruption. The Regulation emphasises the *location* of the departure: those who were living in Montserrat and left after 1 November 1995. It also emphasises the *reason* for departure: because of the effect of the volcanic eruption.

12.93　A person falling within this class does not need to be habitually resident in the CTA. Nor is his or her nationality relevant.

---

[194]　HA 1996, s 185(4), in its original form and as amended by Housing and Regeneration Act 2008, s 314, and Sch 15, para 4, in force for applications to local housing authorities made on or after 2 March 2009. See **12.24–12.29**.

[195]　SI 2006/2646 (W 227), reg 3(1)(d). See English Code, para 9.10(iv).

[196]　See **12.53–12.59**. British citizens, certain Commonwealth citizens, EEA nationals exercising EU Treaty rights and their family members are not subject to immigration control.

[197]　See **12.104**.

[198]　SI 2006/2646 (W 227), reg 4(2)(d). See **12.173**.

Class Ei:[199] *a person who is habitually resident in the CTA and who is a national of a state which has ratified the ECSMA or the ESC and is lawfully present in the UK*

12.94   To qualify as eligible under this class, an applicant must be:

- a national of one of the ratifying countries to the ECSMA or ESC;[200] and

- lawfully present in the UK;[201] and

- habitually resident in the CTA.[202]

For 'habitually resident', see **12.136–12.141**.

Box 3

> States which have *ratified* the ECSMA are: Belgium, Denmark, Estonia, France, Germany, Greece, Iceland, Ireland, Italy, Luxembourg, Malta, Netherlands, Norway, Portugal, Spain, Sweden, Turkey and the UK.[203] The same states have also *signed* the ECSMA.
>
> States which have *ratified* the ESC are: Austria, Belgium, Croatia, Cyprus, the Czech Republic, Denmark, Finland, France, Germany, Greece, Hungary, Iceland, Ireland, Italy, Latvia, Luxembourg, Malta, Netherlands, Norway, Poland, Portugal, Slovakia, Spain, Sweden, Turkey, the former Yugoslav Republic of Macedonia and the UK.[204] These states plus Liechtenstein, Romania, Slovenia, Switzerland and the Ukraine have also *signed* the ESC.

12.95   A comparison with the list of members of the EEA[205] reveals that the beneficiaries of this class are nationals of Croatia, Turkey and the former Yugoslav Republic of Macedonia.

12.96   A person falling within this class must also be 'lawfully present in the UK'. This means that he or she must have leave to enter or remain in the UK, or not require it. Asylum-seekers from ECSMA or ESC countries who have been given 'temporary admission', pending the determination of their claims for asylum, are considered to be 'lawfully present'.[206]

---

[199]   SI 2006/2646 (W 227), reg 3(1)(e)(i); Welsh Code, para 11.9(iv).
[200]   See Box 3.
[201]   See Box 1 at **12.55**.
[202]   See Box 1 at **12.55**.
[203]   For up to date lists, see http:www.conventions.coe.int.
[204]   For up-to-date lists, see http:www.conventions.coe.int.
[205]   See Box 2 at **12.56**.
[206]   *Szoma v Secretary of State for the Department of Work and Pensions* [2005] UKHL 64, [2006] 1 AC 546, HL; and *R (YA) v Secretary of State for Health* [2009] EWCA Civ 225, [2010] 1 WLR 279, CA.

***Class Eii:*[207]** *a person who is habitually resident in the CTA and who before 3 April 2000 was owed a duty by a housing authority under Housing Act 1985, Part 3, or HA 1996, Part 7, which is extant, and who is a national of a state which is a signatory to the ECSMA or the ESC*

12.97   To qualify as eligible under this class, an applicant must be:

- habitually resident in the CTA;[208] and

- a national of a state which has signed the ECSMA or ESC;[209] and

- have been owed a homelessness duty before 3 April 2000;[210] and

- still be owed a homelessness duty.[211]

For 'habitually resident', see **12.136–12.141**. For states that have signed the ECSMA or ESC, see Box 3 at **12.94**.

12.98   To fall within this class, an applicant must have been owed a homelessness duty before 3 April 2000 and that duty must not have come to an end. In other words, he or she must have both made an application for homelessness assistance and had that application accepted before 3 April 2000, and must still be continuing to receive homelessness assistance under that duty. The duty will be owed either under HA 1996, Part 7 or under its statutory predecessor (Housing Act 1985, Part 3). The only duty likely to be still extant would be the main duty under HA 1996, s 193(2) (or Housing Act 1985, s 65(2)).

12.99   There is no additional requirement that a person should be lawfully present in the UK in order to qualify for this class. Any national of a country signing the ECSMA or ESC can fall within this class, provided he or she fulfils the other conditions.

***Class I:*[212]** *a person who is on an income-based jobseeker's allowance or in receipt of income support (with certain exceptions)*

12.100   The benefit received must be *income-based jobseeker's allowance* (rather than contribution-based jobseeker's allowance) or *income support*.[213]

---

[207] SI 2006/2646 (W 227), reg 3(1)(e)(ii); Welsh Code, para 11.9(v).
[208] See Box 1 at **12.55**.
[209] See Box 3 at **12.94**.
[210] See **12.98**.
[211] See **12.98**.
[212] SI 2006/2646 (W 227), reg 3(1)(b); Welsh Code, para 11.9(vi).
[213] For entitlement to these benefits, see *Welfare Benefits and Tax Credits Handbook 2009/10* (Child Poverty Action Group, 11th edn, 2009).

12.101 If the applicant is receiving benefit only because he or she has limited leave to enter or remain in the UK, given in accordance with the Immigration Rules, and remittances from abroad have been disrupted so that he or she is temporarily without funds, he or she will not be eligible under this class.[214] A person who has been granted leave to enter or remain in the UK exceptionally for the purposes of the provision of means of subsistence,[215] and is only receiving benefit as a result, will also not be eligible.[216]

12.102 This class benefits some EEA nationals, who do not have a right to reside[217] and are therefore 'persons subject to immigration control',[218] provided that they are receiving the appropriate benefit.

Category Two: other 'persons from abroad'

Overview

12.103 Ordinarily, persons not subject to immigration control would be eligible for homelessness assistance. However, the Secretary of State and Welsh Assembly Government are permitted to make regulations treating some people who are not subject to immigration control as 'persons from abroad' and therefore ineligible for homelessness assistance. Both have exercised these powers.

Who is, and who is not, a 'person from abroad'?

12.104 In short summary, persons who are not 'subject to immigration control' comprise:[219]

- British citizens;

- some Commonwealth citizens;

- EEA and Swiss nationals exercising certain Treaty rights;

- family members of EEA or Swiss nationals exercising certain Treaty rights; and

- certain people exempt from immigration control such as diplomats, their family members and some military personnel.

---

[214] SI 2006/2646 (W 227), reg 3(1)(b)(i).
[215] Displaced Persons (Temporary Protection) Regulations 2006, SI 2006/1379, reg 3.
[216] SI 2006/2646 (W 227), reg 3(1)(b)(ii).
[217] See **12.58** and **12.110–12.129**.
[218] *Abdi v Barnet London Borough Council, Ismail v Barnet London Borough Council* [2006] EWCA Civ 383, [2006] HLR 23, CA.
[219] Immigration Act 1971, ss 1–3.

Disqualifying those who are not 'persons subject to immigration control'

12.105 In general, the effect of the exercise of the regulation-making powers in both England and Wales has been to produce a situation in which British and Commonwealth citizens will only be eligible for homelessness assistance if they satisfy the 'habitual residence' test, or fall into one of the classes of people exempt from the test.[220]

12.106 For EEA nationals and/or their family members, the situation is more complex. In summary:

- if they do not have any rights of residence pursuant to European Union law, they are 'persons subject to immigration control, and fall within the first category of ineligible persons at HA 1996, s 185(2) and the appropriate Regulations;[221]

- in England, if their only right to reside is the initial 3-month right of residence or because of their status as jobseekers, they will not be eligible;[222]

- if they have a right of residence pursuant to European Union law, they will either have to satisfy the habitual residence test, or fall into one of the classes of people exempt from that test so as to be eligible for homelessness assistance.[223]

For 'habitual residence', see **12.136–12.141**.

12.107 It is therefore necessary to consider general rights of residence for EEA nationals and their family members[224] before turning to the relevant homelessness rules for English and Welsh local housing authorities.[225]

12.108 In addition, EEA nationals and their family members may be subject to the restrictions on the provision of accommodation pending review of an initially adverse decision and accommodation pending appeal.[226]

---

[220] HA 1996, s 185(3); Allocation of Housing and Homelessness (Eligibility) (England) Regulations 2006, SI 2006/1294, reg 6(1)(a) and (2); Homelessness (Wales) Regulations 2006, SI 2006/2646 (W 227), reg 4(1)(a) and (2).

[221] *Abdi v Barnet London Borough Council, Ismail v Barnet London Borough Council* [2006] EWCA Civ 383, [2006] HLR 23, CA. See **12.58** and **12.60–12.86**.

[222] Allocation of Housing and Homelessness (Eligibility) (England) Regulations 2006 SI 2006/1294, reg 6(1)(b) and c). See **12.179–12.186**. In Wales, they are likely to be eligible (Homelessness (Wales) Regulations 2006, SI 2006/2646 (W 277), reg 4(1)(a)), but may find that they become ineligible when the 3-month initial right of residence ends. See **12.187–12.193**.

[223] Allocation of Housing and Homelessness (Eligibility) (England) Regulations 2006, SI 2006/1294, reg 6(1)(a) and (2). Homelessness (Wales) Regulations 2006, SI 2006/2646 (W 227), reg 4(1)(a) and (2).

[224] See **12.117–12.121**.

[225] For the English rules, see **12.130–12.186**. For the Welsh rules, see **12.187–12.193**.

[226] Nationality, Immigration and Asylum Act 2002, s 54 and Sch 3, para 5. See **16.35** and **16.41**.

12.109 If an applicant is eligible under these provisions, any ineligible members of his or her household will be taken into account for the purposes of deciding whether the applicant is homeless and whether he or she has a priority need for applications made for homelessness assistance on or after 2 March 2009.[227] However, if the applicant's household contains a 'restricted person',[228] and it is the presence of that restricted person that has resulted in the local housing authority accepting that a main housing duty[229] (or equivalent duty to applicants threatened with homelessness)[230] is owed, the local housing authority must notify the applicant to that effect,[231] and special modifications apply to the main housing duty (or the equivalent duty to applicants threatened with homelessness).[232]

European Union rights of residence

12.110 The principal rights of residence are the three conferred in domestic law by the Immigration (European Economic Area) Regulations 2006, regs 13–15.[233] Those Regulations are derived from the European Citizens' Directive.[234] Prior to the making of the Citizens' Directive, the European Court of Justice held that European Union Treaties and Regulations can confer rights to residence directly, whether or not those rights are specifically found in domestic law.[235] There is an unresolved issue as to whether that still remains the case since the making of the Citizens' Directive.[236]

The rights of residence in the Immigration (European Economic Area) Regulations 2006[237]

12.111 These Regulations confer three rights of residence:

- an initial right of residence;[238]

---

227 HA 1996, s 185(4) and (5), inserted by Housing and Regeneration Act 2008, Sch 15, para 4.
228 Defined at HA 1996, s 184(7), inserted by Housing and Regeneration Act 2008, Sch 15, para 3. See **12.32**.
229 HA 1996, s 193(2). See **17.21–17.110**.
230 HA 1996, s 195(2). See **17.119–17.131**.
231 HA 1996, s 184(3A), inserted by Housing and Regeneration Act 2008, s 314 and Sch 15, para 3. See **10.37–10.38** and **10.75–10.78**.
232 See **17.98–17.118** and **17.126–17.131**.
233 SI 2006/1003.
234 Directive 2004/38/EC.
235 *Baumbast & R v Secretary of State for the Home Department* [2002] ECR I-7091, ECJ.
236 See **12.125–12.129**. The Court of Appeal has referred to the European Court of Justice (ECJ) the issue of whether a primary carer of school-age children of an EEA national who is no longer a 'qualifying person' has a right of residence derived from European Union Treaties and Regulations that is not specifically recognised in the Immigration (European Economic Area) Regulations 2006, SI 2006/1003 (*Ibrahim v Harrow London Borough Council* [2008] EWCA Civ 386, [2009] HLR 2, CA; *Teixeira v Lambeth London Borough Council* [2008] EWCA Civ 1088, [2009] HLR 9, CA). The case has been heard by the ECJ and judgment is awaited.
237 SI 2006/1003.
238 SI 2006/1003, reg 13. See **12.112–12.114**.

- an extended right of residence;[239] and

- a permanent right of residence.[240]

Each will be examined in turn.

The 'initial right of residence'[241]

12.112 Regulation 13 of the Immigration (European Economic Area) Regulations 2006[242] gives all EEA nationals and their family members[243] an initial right of residence in the UK for a period not exceeding 3 months, upon condition that each person has a valid national identity card or passport.

12.113 There is an exception where the Secretary of State has decided that a person's removal is justified for the purposes of public policy, public security or public health, or where the person has become an unreasonable burden on the social assistance system of the UK.[244]

12.114 Any person whose sole right of residence in the CTA[245] is as a result of this initial right of residence will not be eligible for homelessness assistance in England.[246] In Wales, a person whose sole right of residence is as a result of the initial right of residence would be eligible if the habitual residence test is also satisfied.[247] In practice, it seems unlikely that such a person would be habitually resident.[248]

The 'extended right of residence'[249]

12.115 'Qualified persons' and their family members are entitled to an 'extended right of residence' in the UK for so long as they remain qualified persons and/or family members of qualified persons.

---

[239] SI 2006/1003, reg 14. See **12.115–12.122**.
[240] SI 2006/1003, reg 15. See **12.123–12.124**.
[241] SI 2006/1003, reg 13.
[242] SI 2006/1003.
[243] Defined at SI 2006/1003, reg 7. See **12.117–12.121**.
[244] SI 2006/1003, reg 13(3)(a) and (b).
[245] See Box 1 at **12.55**.
[246] Allocation of Housing and Homelessness (Eligibility) (England) Regulations 2006, SI 2006/1294, reg 6(1)(b) and (c).
[247] See **12.136–12.141** for 'habitual residence'. Homelessness (Wales) Regulations 2006, SI 2006/2646 (W 277), reg 4(1)(a); see **12.187–12.192**.
[248] In any event, once the initial 3 months have expired, if there is no further right of residence, the person will not be treated as habitually resident and will no longer be eligible (Homelessness (Wales) Regulations 2006, SI 2006/2646 (W 277), reg 4(3)). Any outstanding homelessness duties will come to an end (HA 1996, s 193(6)(a)). See **17.59–17.61**.
[249] SI 2006/1003, reg 14.

12.116 'Qualified person' is defined at reg 6 of the Immigration (European Economic Area) Regulations 2006[250] as being a person who is an EEA national and, in the UK, is:

- a job-seeker;[251] or

- a worker;[252] or

- a self-employed person;[253] or

- a self-sufficient person;[254] or

- a student.[255]

12.117 'Family members' are defined at reg 7 of the Immigration (European Economic Area) Regulations 2006[256] as:

- the EEA national's spouse or civil partner;[257]

- any direct descendants of the EEA national, or of his or her spouse or civil partner, who are under 21, or who are dependent on the qualifying person, or his or her spouse or civil partner;[258]

- any dependent direct relatives in the ascending line of the EEA national or his or her spouse or civil partner;[259] and

- any extended family member who has been issued with an EEA family permit, a registration certificate or residence card.[260]

There are special rules for students.[261]

---

[250] SI 2006/1003.
[251] Defined at SI 2006/1003, reg 6(4).
[252] Defined at SI 2006/1003, regs 4(1)(a) and 6(2). See **12.147–12.151**.
[253] Defined at SI 2006/1003, regs 4(1)(b) and 6(3). See **12.152–12.153**.
[254] Defined at SI 2006/1003, reg 4(1)(c).
[255] Defined at SI 2006/1003, reg 4(1)(d).
[256] SI 2006/1003.
[257] Immigration (European Economic Area) Regulations, SI 2006/1003, reg 7(1)(a). A 'spouse' means a person who is formally contracted to a legal marriage (*Netherlands v Reed 59/85* [1986] ECR 1283, ECJ; *R v Secretary of State for the Home Department ex p Monro-Lopez* [1007] Imm AR 11, QBD; and *Diatta v Land Berlin* [1986] 2 CMLR 164, ECJ). 'Civil partnership' is defined at Civil Partnership Act 2004, s 1. In both cases, the emphasis is on the legal condition, not on whether or not the parties continue to live together. A marriage or civil partnership only ends upon death, divorce, annulment, or dissolution of the civil partnership. A party to a marriage of convenience, or to a civil partnership of convenience, is excluded from the definition (Immigration (European Economic Area) Regulations 2006, SI 2006/1003, reg 2(1)).
[258] Immigration (European Economic Area) Regulations, SI 2006/1003, reg 7(1)(b).
[259] SI 2006/1003, reg 7(1)(c).
[260] SI2006/10033, reg 7(1)(d). For 'extended family member', see **12.119–12.120** and fn 263.
[261] SI 2006/1003, reg 7(2) and (4).

12.118 'Family members' thus include dependent children, dependent parents, parents-in-law, and parents of a qualifying person's civil partner.[262] So long as adult children are 'dependent' on the qualifying person, their ages are irrelevant. Children who are not dependent on the qualifying person, but are nevertheless under 21 (for example, an 18-year-old who is working) also fall within the definition.

12.119 Cohabiting partners, whether of the same sex or different sex, do *not* fall within the definition of 'spouse' or 'civil partner'. For cohabiting partners to be 'family members', they must be:

• the partner of an EEA national; and

• in a 'durable relationship' with him or her; and

• have been issued with an EEA family permit, registration certificate or residence card.[263]

12.120 Other types of relationship could fall within the definition of 'extended family members'.[264] If an extended family member of an EEA national has been issued with an EEA family permit, a registration certificate or a residence card, he or she is to be treated as a 'family member' of an EEA national for so long as he or she continues to fall within the definition of an 'extended family member' and so long as the documentation has not ceased to be valid or been revoked.[265]

12.121 A person who was a family member of a qualified person may have 'retained the right of residence'[266] if the qualified person has subsequently died.

---

[262] The inclusion of the word 'direct' in the Immigration (European Economic Area) Regulations, SI 2006/1003 suggests that 'family members' cannot be grandchildren or grandparents.

[263] 'Partner' falls within the definition of 'extended family members' if the relationship is a 'durable relationship' (Immigration (European Economic Area) Regulations 2006, SI 2006/1003, reg 8(5)). 'Extended family members' are to be counted as 'family members' if they have been issued with an EEA family permit, registration certificate or residence card which has not ceased to be valid and has not been revoked (SI 2006/1003, reg 7(1)(d) and (3)).

[264] 'Extended family members' are defined at reg 8 of the Immigration (European Economic Area) Regulations 2006, SI 2006/1003 and are either: (1) relatives of an EEA national, his or her spouse or civil partner, who are: (a) residing with the EEA national in an EEA state and are dependent upon the EEA national or a member of his or her household; or (b) on serious health grounds strictly require the personal care of the EEA national, his or her spouse or civil partner; or (c) would meet the requirements in the immigration rules for indefinite leave to enter or remain in the UK as a dependent relative of the EEA national; or (2) a cohabiting partner (same sex or different sex) of an EEA national if he or she can prove that he or she is in a 'durable relationship' with the EEA national.

[265] Immigration (European Economic Area) Regulations 2006, SI 2006/1003, reg 7(4). Para 9.14 of the English Code suggests that extended family members who have been issued with an EEA family permit, registration certificate or residence card which has not ceased to be valid and has not been revoked will not fall within this exception. This does not seem to be a proper construction of the Regulations and is at odds with the guidance at Annex 12, paras 43 and 15 of the English Code.

[266] SI 2006/1003, reg 10.

Similarly, if a person was a spouse or civil partner of a qualified person, and they have divorced or terminated the civil partnership, he or she may have 'retained the right of residence'. If that is the case, the surviving person (or former spouse or civil person) may be entitled to the extended right of residence, even though he or she is not a qualifying person.[267]

12.122 Applying the categories of 'qualified persons' and their 'family members' to eligibility for homelessness assistance, in summary:

- if a person has an extended right of residence solely as a result of being a job-seeker, or a family member of a job-seeker, he or she will not be eligible in England,[268] but will be eligible in Wales if he or she satisfies the habitual residence test;[269]

- a person who is a worker will be exempt from the habitual residence test in both England and Wales;[270]

- self-employed persons are exempt from the habitual residence test in England[271] and will have to satisfy it in Wales;[272]

- family members of workers and self-employed persons are exempt from the habitual residence test in England[273] and will have to satisfy it in Wales;[274]

- self-sufficient persons and students and their family members will be eligible if they satisfy the habitual residence test.[275]

---

[267] SI 2006/1003, reg 14(3).

[268] Allocation of Housing and Homelessness (Eligibility) (England) Regulations 2006, SI 2006/1294, reg 6(1)(b) and (c). See **12.179–12.186**.

[269] Homelessness (Wales) Regulations 2006, SI 2006/2646 (W 277), reg 4(1)(a). See **12.187–12.192**.

[270] Allocation of Housing and Homelessness (Eligibility) (England) Regulations 2006, SI 2006/1294, reg 6(1)(a) and (2)(a) (see **12.147–12.151**); Homelessness (Wales) Regulations 2006, SI 2006/2646 (W 277), reg 4(1)(a) and (2)(a) (see **12.190**).

[271] Allocation of Housing and Homelessness (Eligibility) (England) Regulations 2006, SI 2006/1294, reg 6(1)(a) and (2)(b). See **12.152–12.153**.

[272] Homelessness (Wales) Regulations 2006, SI 2006/2646 (W 277), reg 4(1)(a). See **12.187–12.192**.

[273] Allocation of Housing and Homelessness (Eligibility) (England) Regulations 2006, SI 2006/1294, reg 6(1)(a) and (2)(d). See **12.164–12.167**.

[274] Homelessness (Wales) Regulations 2006, SI 2006/2646 (W 277), reg 4(1)(a). See **12.187–12.192**.

[275] Allocation of Housing and Homelessness (Eligibility) (England) Regulations 2006, SI 2006/1294, reg 6(1)(a): see **12.136–12.141**; Homelessness (Wales) Regulations 2006, SI 2006/2646 (W 277), reg 4(1)(a): see **12.187–12.192**. However, note that the definitions of each category require that self-sufficient people and students have sufficient resources not to become a burden on the social assistance system on the UK during the period of residence (SI 2006/1003, reg 4(1)(c) and (d)) and so any person who required homelessness assistance may not fall within these definitions.

The 'permanent right of residence'[276]

12.123 The permanent right of residence is defined by Immigration (European Economic Union) Regulations 2006, reg 15(1).[277] There are six categories of people who can acquire 'permanent rights of residence':

(1)   an EEA national who has resided in the UK in accordance with the Regulations for a continuous period of 5 years;[278]

(2)   a family member of an EEA national who is not himself or herself an EEA national but who has resided in the UK with the EEA national in accordance with the Regulations for a continuous period of 5 years;[279]

(3)   a worker or self-employed person who has ceased activity;[280]

(4)   a family member of a worker or self-employed person who has ceased activity;[281]

(5)   a person who was the family member of a worker or self-employed person where:
   (a)   the worker or self-employed person has died, and
   (b)   the family member resided with him or her immediately before his or her death, and
   (c)   the worker or self-employed person had resided continuously in the UK for at least the 2 years immediately before his or her death, or the death was the result of an accident at work or an occupational disease;[282]

(6)   a person who:
   (a)   has resided in the UK in accordance with the Regulations for a continuous period of 5 years, and
   (b)   was, at the end of that period, a family member who has retained the right of residence.[283]

For 'family member', see **12.117–12.121**.

12.124 Applying these categories of people to the rules governing eligibility for homelessness assistance in *England*, in summary:

---

276   SI 2006/1003, reg 15(1).
277   SI 2006/1003.
278   SI 2006/1003, reg 15(1)(a).
279   SI 2006/1003, reg 15(1)(b).
280   SI 2006/1003, reg 15(1)(c). Note that 'worker or self-employed person who has ceased activity' is defined at SI 2006/1003, reg 5.
281   SI 2006/1003, reg 15(1)(d).
282   SI 2006/1003, reg 15(1)(e).
283   SI 2006/1003, reg 15(1)(f). For 'a family member who has retained the right of residence'. See **12.121**.

- the third, fourth and fifth categories are exempt from the habitual residence test;[284] and

- the first, second and sixth categories would have to satisfy the habitual residence test.[285]

In *Wales*, any person who has a permanent right of residence would have to satisfy the habitual residence test.[286] Given their length of residence, any of these people would normally be expected to satisfy that test.

Rights of residence not contained in the Immigration (European Economic Area) Regulations

12.125 The scope of European Union law continues to expand and, unlike domestic courts, the European Court of Justice (ECJ) is purposive in its approach. The detail is beyond the scope of this book. In brief, the ECJ has held that certain scenarios fall within rights of residence based on EU Treaties, even though those rights may not be specifically contained in either domestic Regulations[287] or even in the EU Directive which the domestic Regulations transpose.

12.126 One scenario concerns primary carers of children who have been installed in a Member State while their parents are exercising Treaty rights there, and who are in educational courses in the host Member State. In *Baumbast & R v Secretary of State for Home Department*,[288] the ECJ held that, where a child's parent is no longer exercising Treaty rights as a worker, the child and his or her primary carer each derive a right of residence from the child's right to enter into or complete his or her education. The parents might have divorced, or one of them might have left the UK. The nationality of the primary carer is irrelevant. What matters is that the child had been admitted to an educational course, and that one of the child's parents is a worker or former worker.

12.127 Following the *Baumbast* decision, the European Union legislature enacted the Citizens' Rights Directive,[289] which has been transposed, in large part, in domestic law by the Immigration (European Economic Area) Regulations 2006.[290] The Directive and the Regulations provide for a right of residence embracing the *Baumbast* scenario by encompassing it within the

---

[284] Allocation of Housing and Homelessness (Eligibility) (England) Regulations 2006, SI 2006/1294, reg 6(1)(a) and (2)(d): see **12.168–12.172**.

[285] SI 2006/1294, reg 6(1)(a). See **12.136–12.141**.

[286] Homelessness (Wales) Regulations 2006, SI 2006/2646 (W 227), reg 4(1)(a). See **12.187–12.192**.

[287] Currently the Immigration (European Economic Area) Regulations 2006, SI 2006/1003.

[288] [2002] ECR I-7091, ECJ.

[289] The Directive on the right of citizens of the Union and their family members to move and reside freely within the territory of the Member States, 2004/38/EC.

[290] SI 2006/1003.

definition of 'family member who has retained the right of residence'[291] so that those falling within the definition acquire the extended right of residence.[292] Such a right of residence is lawful residence in itself and, further, may count as 'residing' in the UK for the purposes of the acquisition of a permanent right of residence.[293] Where children of a qualified person[294] exercising his or her EU Treaty rights to reside in the UK (or children who are the direct descendants of the spouse or civil partner of a qualified person) have been attending an educational course in the UK, and the qualified person subsequently ceases to be a qualified person on ceasing to reside in the UK, or dies, where the children continue to attend an educational course, they will retain a right of residence. In this scenario, the parent with actual custody of those children will also retain a right of residence, whether or not he or she is a national of an EEA Member State.[295]

12.128 A right of residence may also be derived from Art 12 of Regulation (EEC) 1612/68[296] without reference to the Citizens' Rights Directive for the primary carer of a child. This applies where the child has been installed in a Member State at a time when one of his or her parents was exercising rights as an EEA worker and the child has been admitted to an educational course in that State. The child has a right to enter into and complete his or her education in the host Member State, and both the child and his or her primary carer derive a right of residence from this in order to render the child's education right effective. This derived right of residence under Art 12 applies even where it is the former worker who is also the primary carer. The derived right of residence is not conditional on the EEA national parent having been a worker on the date on which the child started in education. The parent's right of residence, as the child's primary carer, ends when the child reaches the age of 18, unless the child continues to need the presence and care of that parent in order to be able to pursue and complete his or her education.[297] The parent's right of residence is not conditional on him or her being self-sufficient.[298]

12.129 There remain rights of residence, such as in the scenario considered above, that are not specifically recognised in the Immigration (European Economic Area) Regulations 2006.[299] Such rights may potentially arise under a variety of provisions including, additionally, Arts 21 and 56 of the Treaty on

---

[291] Directive 2004/38/EC, Arts 12 and 13; Immigration (European Economic Area) Regulations 2006, SI 2006/1003, reg 10(3), (4) and (5). See **12.121**.

[292] SI 2006/1003, reg 14(3). See **12.115–12.121**.

[293] SI 2006/1003, reg 15(1)(f). See **12.123**.

[294] See **12.116**.

[295] SI 2006/1003, reg 10(3) and (4). See **12.121**.

[296] Regulation on Freedom of Movement for Workers within the Community 1612/68 (EEC).

[297] *Teixeira v Lambeth London Borough Council and Secretary of State for the Home Department*, European Court of Justice, C-4380/08, 23 February 2010.

[298] *Ibrahim v Harrow London Borough Council and Secretary of State for the Home Department*, European Court of Justice, C-310/08, 23 February 2010.

[299] SI 2006/1003.

the Functioning of the European Union.[300] Whether anyone having such a right of residence would be further required to satisfy the habitual residence test in order to be eligible for homelessness assistance may depend, among other things, on whether he or she derives a right from having been formerly economically active in the UK.[301]

The English rules

The basic rule

12.130 In the Allocation of Housing and Homelessness (Eligibility) (England) Regulations 2006,[302] in force for applications for homelessness assistance made on or after 1 June 2006, the Secretary of State has exercised the power to treat some people who are not subject to immigration control as 'persons from abroad'.[303] This means that some British citizens, nationals of EEA Member States, and others who are exempt from immigration control may nevertheless be denied homelessness assistance on the grounds that they are 'not eligible'. The primary function of these provisions is to confine homelessness assistance to the ordinary residents of the UK, ie those habitually resident here, and to EEA nationals exercising Treaty rights.

12.131 Allocation of Housing and Homelessness (Eligibility) (England) Regulations 2006, reg 6 establishes three classes of people who are to be treated as 'persons from abroad' and therefore *ineligible* for housing assistance despite not being subject to immigration control.

12.132 The *first class*[304] comprises persons who are 'not habitually resident'[305] in the CTA.[306] But that test of habitual residence does *not* apply to

- EEA nationals who are 'workers';[307] or

- EEA nationals who are self-employed;[308] or

---

[300] Article 21 on the right of EU citizens to move and reside as EU citiziens; Art 56 on the freedom to provide and receive services.

[301] Allocation of Housing and Homelessness (England) Regulations 2006, SI 2006/1294, reg 6(1)(a); Homelessness (Wales) Regulations 2006, SI 2006/2646 (W 277), reg 4(1)(a). See **12.136–12.141** for 'habitual residence'.

[302] SI 2006/1294, as amended.

[303] For applications for homelessness assistance made *before* 1 June 2006, the relevant provisions are in reg 4 of the Homelessness (England) Regulations 2000, SI 2000/701, as substituted by the Allocation of Housing and Homelessness (Amendment) (England) Regulations 2004, SI 2004/1235. See **3.123–3.136**.

[304] Allocation of Housing and Homelessness (Eligibility) (England) Regulations 2006, SI 2006/1294, reg 6(1)(a).

[305] See **12.136–12.141**.

[306] See Box 1 at **12.55**.

[307] Allocation of Housing and Homelessness (Eligibility) (England) Regulations 2006, SI 2006/1294, reg 6(2)(a). See Boxes 2 at **12.56** for list of EEA countries, and **12.147–12.151** for 'worker'.

[308] SI 2006/1294, reg 6(2)(b). See **12.152–12.153**.

- Accession State workers requiring registration ('A8 nationals');[309] or

- Accession State nationals subject to worker authorisation ('A2 nationals');[310] or

- family members of EEA nationals where those EEA nationals are workers, self-employed, Accession State workers requiring registration or Accession State nationals subject to worker authorisation;[311] or

- EEA nationals who have certain permanent rights to reside in the UK;[312] or

- persons who left the territory of Montserrat after 1 November 1995 because of the effect on that territory of a volcanic eruption;[313] or

- persons who are in the UK as a result of having been deported, expelled or otherwise removed by compulsion of law from another country to the UK;[314] or

- between 25 July 2006 and 31 January 2007 only, people who left Lebanon on or after 12 July 2006 because of the armed conflict there;[315] or

- a person who arrived in Great Britain or after 28 February 2009 but before 18 March 2011 and who immediately before arriving in Great Britain had been resident in Zimbabwe and, before leaving Zimbabwe, had accepted an offer made by Her Majesty's Government to assist that person to settle in the UK.[316]

12.133 The *second class* comprises EEA nationals and their family members whose only right to reside in the UK is derived from their status as job-seekers, as family members of job-seekers, or from their initial right to reside in the UK for a period not exceeding 3 months.[317]

12.134 The *third class* comprises EEA nationals and their family members whose only right to reside in the rest of the CTA (Channel Islands, Isle of Man

---

[309] SI 2006/1294, reg 6(2)(c)(i), substituted by Allocation of Housing and Homelessness (Eligibility) (England) (Amendment) (No 2) Regulations 2006, SI 2006/3340, reg 27. See **12.154–12.159**.

[310] SI 2006/1294, reg 6(2)(c)(ii), substituted by SI 2006/3340, reg 2, in force from 1 January 2007. See **12.160–12.163**.

[311] SI 2006/1294, reg 6(2)(d). See **12.164–12.167**.

[312] SI 2006/1294, reg 6(2)(e). See **12.168–12.172**.

[313] SI 2006/1294, reg 6(2)(f). See **12.173**.

[314] SI 2006/1294, reg 6(2)(g). See **12.174**.

[315] SI 2006/1294, reg 6(2)(h), inserted by Allocation of Housing and Homelessness (Eligibility) (England) (Amendment) Regulations 2006, SI 2006/2007, reg 2(8). See **12.175–12.176**.

[316] SI 2006/1294, reg 6(2)(i), inserted by the Allocation of Housing and Homelessness (Eligibility) (England) (Amendment) Regulations 2009, SI 2009/358, for applications made on or after 18 March 2009. See **12.177–12.178**.

[317] SI 2006/1294, reg 6(1)(b). See **12.179–12.184**.

or the Republic of Ireland) is derived from their status as job-seekers, as family members of job-seekers, or from their initial right to reside in the UK for a period not exceeding 3 months.[318]

12.135 Each of the three classes will be examined in turn.

The first class: not habitually resident[319]

12.136 'Habitual residence' is not a term of reference to someone's immigration status. A person may be a British citizen, but if he or she is not habitually resident in the CTA,[320] he or she will not be eligible. Nor is the term 'habitual residence' defined in either HA 1996 or in the Regulations.[321] It is a question of fact for the local housing authority to decide. Happily, there is useful guidance in the Codes.[322]

12.137 A person who is not habitually resident will also not be entitled to social security benefits. If the person is receiving social security benefits, it must follow that the Department for Work and Pensions (DWP) has determined that he or she is habitually resident.

12.138 There are two aspects required to be present in order to constitute habitual residence:

(1) a settled purpose of establishing residence in the CTA; and

(2) an appreciable period of such residence.

12.139 Whether each aspect is satisfied is a question of fact for the local housing authority to decide. Normally, if someone has lived in the CTA for 2 years continuously prior to his or her application for homelessness assistance, he or she should be considered to be habitually resident without further inquiry.[323]

12.140 Establishing a 'settled purpose' will obviously involve consideration of an applicant's subjective intentions and motivations. Someone in stable employment may be more likely to be able to establish his or her 'settled purpose' to be habitually resident than someone in transitory employment, or dependent on benefit. However, local housing authorities must be careful not

---

[318] SI 2006/1294, reg 6(1)(c). See **12.185–12.186**.
[319] SI 2006/1294, reg 6(1)(a).
[320] See Box 1 at **12.55**.
[321] SI 2006/1294.
[322] English Code, paras 9.3(i) and 9.15–9.18 and Annex 10.
[323] English Code, para 9.16.

to give too much weight to an applicant's lack of finances and not enough weight to other factors such as the applicant's nationality, ties with the UK, and future intentions.[324]

12.141 What constitutes an 'appreciable period of residence' likewise varies according to the circumstances of each individual's case. If a former British resident returns to the UK after living and working abroad, she or he may be habitually resident from the first day of his or her return.[325] When someone is coming to live in the UK for the first time, there must be an appreciable period of residence before habitual residence is obtained. To determine how long that period of residence should be in any particular case, local housing authorities should consider all the circumstances, including:

- whether the person is seeking to bring any family members to the CTA;

- whether he or she has brought his or her personal property and possessions to the CTA;

- whether he or she has done everything necessary to establish a residence before coming;

- whether he or she has a right of abode; and

- what 'durable ties' there are with the CTA.[326]

12.142 Some EEA nationals, and their family members, are not exempted from the habitual residence test,[327] nor are they prescribed as 'ineligible' by virtue of falling within the second or third classes.[328] For those people to be eligible, they will have to satisfy the habitual residence test.

12.143 Types of EEA nationals who may be required to satisfy the habitual residence test include:

- an EEA national who has resided in the UK in accordance with the Immigration (European Economic Area) Regulations[329] for a continuous period of 5 years;[330] or

---

[324] *Olokunboro v Croydon London Borough Council* (2003) February *Legal Action*, p 37, Croydon County Court.

[325] *Swaddling v Adjudication Officer* [1999] All ER (EC) 217 ECJ; and see CIS/1304/1997 and CJSA/5394/1998. English Code, para 9.17 and Annex 10, paras 7–8.

[326] *Nessa v Chief Adjudication Officer* [1999] 1 WLR 1937, HL. English Code, Annex 10, paras 9–20.

[327] Allocation of Housing and Homelessness (Eligibility) (England) Regulations 2006, SI 2006/1294, reg 6(2). See **12.145**.

[328] SI 2006/1294, reg 6(1)(b) and (c). See **12.179–12.186**.

[329] SI 2006/1003. See Appendix 2 of this book.

[330] Entitled to a permanent right of residence by reg 15(1)(a) of the Immigration (European Economic Area) Regulations 2006, SI 2006/1003. See **12.123**(1).

- a person who is not an EEA national but is a family member of an EEA national, the family member having resided in the UK in accordance with the Immigration (European Economic Area) Regulations for a continuous period of 5 years;[331] or

- a person who has resided in the UK for a continuous period of 5 years and was, at the end of that period, a family member of an EEA national who had retained the right of residence;[332] or

- potentially, a person who has a right to reside that falls outside the Immigration (European Economic Area) Regulations.[333]

12.144 Given the length of their residence, few of those people should have any difficulty in satisfying the habitual residence test.

Exemptions from the habitual residence test

12.145 As noted above,[334] the following people are eligible for assistance even if they are *not habitually resident*:

- an EEA national who is a 'worker';[335] or

- an EEA national who is self-employed;[336] or

- a person who is an Accession State worker requiring registration ('an A8 national');[337] or

---

[331] Entitled to a permanent right of residence by reg 15(1)(b) of the Immigration (European Economic Area) Regulations 2006, SI 2006/1003. See **12.123**(2). For 'family member', see **12.117–12.121**.

[332] Entitled to a permanent right of residence by reg 15(1)(f) of the Immigration (European Economic Area) Regulations 2006, SI 2006/1003. See **12.123**(6). For 'family member', see **12.117–12.121**. For family member who has retained the right of residence, see Immigration (European Economic Area) Regulations 2006, SI 2006/1003, reg 10 and **12.121**.

[333] *Baumbast & R v Secretary of State for the Home Department (Case C-413/99)* [2002] ECR 1-7091. Whether or not such a right exists has been considered by the ECJ as a result of references to it by the Court of Appeal in *Ibrahim v Harrow London Borough Council* [2008] EWCA Civ 386, [2009] HLR 2, CA and *Teixeira v Lambeth London Borough Council* [2008] EWCA Civ 1088, [2009] HLR 9, CA. Judgment is awaited at the time of writing. See **12.125–12.129** for discussion.

[334] See **12.132**.

[335] Allocation of Housing and Homelessness (Eligibility) (England) Regulations 2006, SI 2006/1294, reg 6(2)(a). See **12.147–12.151**.

[336] SI 2006/1294, reg 6(2)(b). See **12.152–12.153**.

[337] SI 2006/1294, reg 6(2)(c)(i), substituted by Allocation of Housing and Homelessness (Eligibility) (England) (Amendment) (No 2) Regulations 2006, SI 2006/3340, reg 2. See **12.154–12.159**.

- a person who is an Accession State national subject to worker authorisation ('an A2 national');[338] or

- a family member of an EEA national who is a worker, a self-employed person, an Accession State worker requiring registration or an Accession State national subject to worker authorisation;[339] or

- a person who has one of certain permanent rights to reside in the UK;[340] or

- a person who left the territory of Montserrat after 1 November 1995 because of the effect on that territory of a volcanic eruption;[341] or

- a person who is in the UK as a result of having been deported, expelled or otherwise removed by compulsion of law from another country to the UK;[342] or

- between 25 July 2006 and 31 January 2007 only, a person who left Lebanon on or after 12 July 2006 because of the armed conflict there;[343] or

- a person who arrived in Great Britain on or after 28 February 2009 but before 18 March 2011 and who immediately before arriving in Great Britain had been resident in Zimbabwe and, before leaving Zimbabwe, had accepted an offer made by Her Majesty's Government to assist that person to settle in the UK.[344]

12.146 Most of these categories refer to those persons exercising rights of freedom of movement enjoyed under European Union law and contained in the Immigration (European Economic Area) Regulations 2006,[345] which are the current regulations transposing European Union freedom of movement legislation into domestic law. Each of them will be considered in turn. See **12.110–12.129** for consideration of the different European Union 'rights to reside'.

---

[338] SI 2006/1294, reg 6(2)(c)(ii), substituted by Allocation of Housing and Homelessness (Eligibility) (England) (Amendment) (No 2) Regulations 2006, SI 2006/3340, reg 2(4), in force from 1 January 2007. See **12.160–12.163**.

[339] SI 2006/1294, reg 6(2)(d). See **12.164–12.167**.

[340] SI 2006/1294, reg 6(2)(e). See **12.168–12.172**.

[341] SI 2006/1294, reg 6(2)(f). See **12.173**.

[342] SI 2006/1294, reg 6(2)(g). See **12.174**.

[343] SI 2006/1294, reg 6(2)(h), inserted by Allocation of Housing and Homelessness (Eligibility) (England) (Amendment) Regulations 2006, SI 2006/2007, reg 2(8). See **12.175–12.176**.

[344] SI 2006/1294, reg 6(2)(i), inserted by Allocation of Housing and Homelessness (Eligibility) (England) (Amendment) Regulations 2009, SI 2009/358, for applications made on or after 18 March 2009. See **12.177–12.178**.

[345] SI 2006/1003, in force from 30 April 2006.

EEA nationals who are workers[346]

12.147 In order to qualify as a 'worker' under this provision, the person must first be a national of an EEA Member State.[347] The term 'worker' is not defined in HA 1996 or regulations and nor is it exhaustively defined in European Union legislation. The European Court of Justice has emphasised that a narrow approach should *not* be taken:

'[I]t is settled case law that the concept of worker has a specific Community meaning and must not be interpreted narrowly. It must be defined in accordance with objective criteria which distinguish an employment relationship by reference to the rights and duties of the person concerned. In order to be treated as a worker, a person must pursue an activity which is genuine and effective, to the exclusion of activities on such a small scale as to be regarded as purely marginal and ancillary. The essential feature of an employment relationship is that for a certain period of time a person performs services for and under the direction of another person in return for which he receives remuneration. By contrast, neither the *sui generis* nature of the employment relationship under national law, nor the level of productivity of the person concerned, the origin of the funds from which the remuneration is paid or the limited amount of the remuneration can have any consequence in regard to whether the person is a worker for the purposes of Community law ...'[348]

12.148 A person will be a 'worker'[349] if he or she:

- is actually working in the UK, whether full- or part-time. Any genuine and effective work should count, so long as it is not so irregular and/or so limited that it is a purely marginal and ancillary activity;[350] or

- has worked in the UK (at any time and even for a short period) but has become temporarily incapable of work as a result of an illness or accident, or involuntarily unemployed in certain circumstances;[351] or

---

[346] Allocation of Housing and Homelessness (Eligibility) (England) Regulations 2006, SI 2006/1294, reg 6(2)(a). English Code, para 9.14(a), and Annex 12, paras 15–19.

[347] See Box 2 at **12.56**.

[348] *Kurz* [2002] ECR I-10691, para 32.

[349] Immigration (European Economic Area) Regulations 2006, SI 2006/1003, reg 4(a). 'Worker' is defined by Regulation (EEC) No 1612/68 of the Council of 15 October 1968 on freedom of movement for workers within the Community, or Regulation (EEC) No 1251/70 of the Commission of 29 June 1970 on the right of workers to remain in the territory of a Member State after having been employed in that State. English Code, Annex 12, paras 15–18.

[350] *Levin 53/81* [1982] ECR 1035; *Kempf Case 139/85* [1986] ECR 1741; *Raulin Case C-357/89* [1992] ECR 1027.

[351] *Scrivner Case 122/84* [1985] ECR 1027: Immigration (European Economic Area) Regulations 2006, SI 2006/1003, reg 6(2)(a) and (b). To be treated as a 'worker' if involuntarily unemployed, the person must be registered as a job-seeker and: (1) have been employed for a year or more before becoming unemployed; and (2) have been unemployed for no more than 6 months; or (3) provide evidence that he or she is seeking employment in the UK and has a genuine chance of being engaged. See English Code, Annex 12, paras 19(a) and (b).

- has worked in the UK, but has become involuntarily unemployed and has embarked on vocational training;[352] or

- has voluntarily given up work in the UK to take up vocational training related to his or her previous job.[353]

12.149 Attempts to argue that people who have never worked in the UK are, nevertheless, 'workers' for the purpose of entitlement to job-seeker's allowance and Children Act assistance have failed.[354] A job-seeker who has never worked is not, therefore a 'worker' and, in any event, is specifically excluded from eligibility because he or she would fall into the second or third classes of people who are not eligible.[355] Students and au pairs, working part-time, have been held by the Court of Appeal and the European Court of Justice to be 'workers'.[356]

12.150 The question, as to whether an applicant is or is not a worker, is a question of fact for the local housing authority. In *R (Mohamed) v Harrow London Borough Council*,[357] it was held that the local housing authority had not made any errors of law in concluding that a woman who had worked part-time for 3 months, finishing a year before her application for homelessness assistance, spoke little or no English, had two small children to look after and had not registered with an employment agency was not and had not retained the status of being a 'worker'. In *Barry v Southwark London Borough Council*,[358] the local housing authority was wrong to decide that an applicant was not a 'worker' during a 2-week period when he was employed by Group 4 Securicor for stewarding duties at the Wimbledon All England Tennis Championships. The work done was of economic value, there were PAYE deductions from his pay and the services provided by him to his employer were real and actual, and not merely marginal and ancillary.[359]

12.151 A8 and A2 nationals will not be 'workers' if they are Accession State workers requiring registration[360] or Accession State nationals subject to worker authorisation.[361] If they no longer fall into either of those classes, for example

---

[352] *Lair Case 39/86* [1988] ECR 3161; and *Raulin Case C-357/89* [1992] ECR 1027. Immigration (European Economic Area) Regulations 2006, SI 2006/1003, reg 6(2)(c). English Code, Annex 12, para 19(c).

[353] *Raulin Case C-357/89* [1992] ECR 1027. Immigration (European Economic Area) Regulations 2006, SI 2006/1003, reg 6(2)(d). English Code, Annex 12, para 19(d).

[354] *Collins v Secretary of State for Work and Pensions, C-138/02 ECJ, 23 March 2004*; *R (Conde) v Lambeth London Borough Council* [2005] EWHC 62 (Admin) [2005] HLR 29; and *Ali v SSHD* [2006] EWCA Civ 484, [2006] 3 CMLR 326, [2006] ELR 423, CA.

[355] Allocation of Housing and Homelessness (Eligibility) (England) Regulations 2006, SI 2006/1294, reg 6(1)(b) and (c). See **12.179–12.186**.

[356] *Ozturk v Secretary of State for the Home Department* [2006] EWCA Civ 541, [2007] 1 WLR 508, CA; C-294/06, judgment 24 January 2008, ECJ.

[357] [2005] EWHC 3194 (Admin), [2006] HLR 18.

[358] [2008] EWCA Civ 1440, [2009] HLR 30, CA.

[359] Arden LJ at [23].

[360] See **12.154–12.159**.

[361] See **12.160–12.163**.

because they have been working for more than 12 months, or because they did not need to register as an Accession State worker, they are treated as all other EEA nationals who are workers.

EEA nationals who are self-employed persons[362]

12.152 A 'self-employed person' is defined as 'a person who establishes himself in order to pursue activity as a self-employed person in accordance with Article 43 of the Treaty establishing the European Community'.[363]

12.153 Article 43 refers to 'freedom of establishment', which is itself defined as 'the right to take up and pursue activities as self-employed persons and to set up and manage undertakings'.

'Accession State workers requiring registration' or 'A8 nationals'[364]

12.154 An 'Accession State worker requiring registration' is defined in the Accession (Immigration and Worker Registration) Regulations 2004[365] as a national of one of the A8 countries[366] who works in the UK at some time between 1 May 2004 and 30 April 2011. Once an Accession State worker requiring registration has legally worked for a period of 12 months without interruption, he or she is no longer an 'Accession State worker requiring registration', and is to be treated as any other EEA national who is a worker.

12.155 An 'Accession State worker requiring registration' is treated as a 'worker' while he or she is working for an authorised employer, but not otherwise.[367] An employer is 'an authorised employer' if:

- the worker has received a valid registration certificate authorising him or her to work for that employer; or

- the worker was legally working for the employer on 30 April 2004 and has not ceased working for that employer; or

- the worker is in his or her first month of employment with the employer and has applied for, but not yet received, a valid registration certificate; or

---

[362] Allocation of Housing and Homelessness (Eligibility) (England) Regulations 2006, SI 2006/1294, reg 6(2)(b). See English Code, para 9.14(b) and Annex 12, paras 26–30.
[363] Immigration (European Economic Area) Regulations 2006, SI 2006/1003, reg 4(1)(b). The Treaty referred to is the Treaty of Rome (1957).
[364] Allocation of Housing and Homelessness (Eligibility) (England) Regulations 2006, SI 2006/1294, reg 6(2)(c)(i), substituted by Allocation of Housing and Homelessness (Eligibility) (England) (Amendment) (No 2) Regulations 2006, SI 2006/3340, reg 2(4). See English Code, para 9.14(c), Annex 10, paras 20–25 and Annex 13.
[365] SI 2004/1219, reg 2(1), as amended by reg 2 of the Accession (Immigration and Worker Registration) (Amendment) Regulations 2009, SI 2009/892.
[366] See Box 2 at **12.56**.
[367] SI 2004/1219, reg 5(2) as amended by reg 1 of the Immigration (European Economic Area) Regulations 2006, SI 2006/1003.

- the employer is employing certain seasonal agricultural workers.[368]

12.156　An Accession State worker requiring registration will have a registration card and/or a registration certificate.[369] An A8 national who is a job-seeker will not have any right of residence and will not be eligible for homelessness assistance.[370]

12.157　After 30 April 2011, nationals of A8 Member States are to be treated in the same way as other EEA nationals.[371]

12.158　It should be noted that not all nationals of the A8 Member States are 'Accession State workers requiring registration'. If a national of an A8 Member State falls into one of the following categories, he or she will not be an 'Accession State worker requiring registration' and should be treated like any other EEA national:

- an A8 national who is self-employed, self-sufficient or a student;[372]

- a person who, on 30 April 2004, had leave to enter or remain in the UK under the Immigration Act 1971 and that leave was not subject to any conditions restricting his or her employment;[373]

- an Accession State worker requiring registration who has legally worked for a period of 12 months (before or after 30 April 2004) without interruption;[374]

- a person who is a dual national, and who is a national of the UK and of another EEA Member State (except for the A8 states) or Switzerland;[375]

- a person who is a diplomat, or a family member of a diplomat;[376]

---

[368]　SI 2004/1219, reg 7.

[369]　SI 2004/1219, reg 8.

[370]　SI 2004/1219, reg 4(2). He or she will be a 'person subject to immigration control' and therefore fall within the first category of persons from abroad at HA 1996, s 185(2). He or she is unlikely to fall within Classes A–E of Allocation of Housing and Homelessness (Eligibility) (England) Regulations 2006, SI 2006/1294, reg 5(1) and therefore unlikely to be eligible. See **12.58** and **12.61**.

[371]　SI 2004/1219, reg 1(2)(c) as substituted by Accession (Immigration and Worker Registration) (Amendment) Regulations 2009, SI 2009/892, reg 2, extending the period beyond the original termination date of 30 April 2009.

[372]　The derogation permitted by EU law in respect of workers from A8 and A2 countries only applies to 'workers' and 'jobseekers'. It does not apply to freedom of establishment of the self-employed or movement for any other purpose. This is reflected in Accession (Immigration and Worker Registration) Regulations 2004, SI 2004/1219, reg 2(1), which defines an 'Accession State worker requiring registration' as someone who is 'working in the UK'.

[373]　Accession (Immigration and Worker Registration) Regulations 2004, SI 2004/1219, reg 2(2).

[374]　SI 2004/1219, reg 2(3) and (4).

[375]　SI 2004/1219, reg 2(5).

[376]　SI 2004/1219, reg 2(5A).

- a person who is a 'posted worker';[377]

- a person who is a family member of an EEA national where the EEA national has a right to reside, unless the EEA national is an Accession State worker requiring registration, an Accession State national subject to worker authorisation or a job-seeker from the A8 or A2 states.[378]

12.159 It follows that an A8 national who is self-employed will be exempt from the habitual residence test and eligible for homelessness assistance.[379]

'Accession State nationals subject to worker authorisation' or 'A2 nationals'[380]

12.160 An 'Accession State national requiring worker authorisation' is defined in the Accession (Immigration and Worker Authorisation) Regulations[381] as a national of one of the A2 countries.[382]

12.161 An Accession State national subject to worker authorisation will be exempt from the habitual residence test and thus eligible for homelessness assistance during such time as he or she holds an Accession Worker authorisation document and is working in accordance with the conditions set out in that document.[383] The document normally issued is a registration certificate.[384] An A2 national who is a job-seeker will not have any right of residence and will not be eligible for homelessness assistance.[385]

12.162 After 31 December 2011, A2 nationals are to be treated in the same way as other EEA nationals.[386]

---

[377] SI 2004/1219, reg 2(6)(a). A 'posted worker' is a worker who, for a limited period, is working in the territory of a different Member State from that where he or she normally works (Directive 96/71/EC, Arts 1 and 3).

[378] SI 2004/1219, reg 2(6)(b). For 'family member', see **12.117–12.121**. For 'right to reside', see **12.110–12.129**. For 'Accession State national subject to worker authorisation', see **12.160–12.163**.

[379] Allocation of Housing and Homelessness (Eligibility) (England) Regulations 2006, SI 2006/1294, reg 6(1)(a) and (2)(b). See **12.145**.

[380] SI 2006/1294, reg 6(2)(c)(ii), substituted by Allocation of Housing and Homelessness (Eligibility) (England) (Amendment) (No 2) Regulations 2006, SI 2006/3340, reg 2(4), in force from 1 January 2007.

[381] SI 2006/3317, reg 2(1).

[382] Bulgaria and Romania. See Box 2 at **12.56**.

[383] SI 2006/3317, reg 6(2).

[384] SI 2006/3317, reg 7.

[385] SI 2006/3317, reg 6(2). He or she will be a 'person subject to immigration control' and therefore fall within the first category of persons from abroad at HA 1996, s 185(2). See **12.58**. He or she is unlikely to fall within Classes A–E of Allocation of Housing and Homelessness (Eligibility) (England) Regulations 2006, SI 2006/1294, reg 5(1) and therefore unlikely to be eligible. See **12.61**.

[386] SI 2006/3317, reg 1(2)(c) and reg 6(1).

12.163   Not all nationals of Bulgaria or Romania fall within the definition of 'an Accession State national subject to worker authorisation'. They should be treated in the same way as other EEA nationals if they fall into one of these categories:

- a person who, on 31 December 2006, had leave to enter or remain without any restriction on taking employment;[387] or

- a person who has legally (with leave to remain) worked in the UK without interruption for a period of 12 months;[388] or

- a person also holding nationality of another EEA Member State (other than Bulgaria or Romania) or British nationality;[389] or

- a spouse or civil partner of a UK national or of a person settled in the UK;[390] or

- a diplomat or family member of a diplomat;[391] or

- a person who has a permanent right of residence pursuant to Immigration (European Economic Area) Regulations 2006, reg 15;[392] or

- a family member of an EEA national who has the right to reside in the UK, other than EEA nationals who are Accession State nationals subject to worker authorisation or are family members of such an Accession State national;[393] or

- a family member of an A2 national who has the right to reside in the UK by virtue of being a self-employed person, or a self-sufficient person or a student;[394] or

---

[387]   SI 2006/3317, reg 2(2), as substituted by the Accession (Immigration and Worker Authorisation) (Amendment) Regulations 2007, SI 2007/475, reg 2(2).

[388]   SI 2006/3317, reg 2(3) and (4). This is the case whether the 12-month period falls wholly before 31 December 2006, partly before and partly after 31 December 2006, or wholly after 31 December 2006.

[389]   SI 2006/3317, reg 2(5).

[390]   SI 2006/3317, reg 2(6).

[391]   SI 2006/3317, reg 2(6A).

[392]   SI 2006/3317, reg 2(7). See **12.123–12.124**.

[393]   SI 2006/3317, reg 2(8)(a), as substituted by the Accession (Immigration and Worker Authorisation) (Amendment) Regulations 2007, SI 2007/475, reg 2(2). For 'family member', see **12.117–12.121**. For 'right to reside', see **12.110–12.129**.

[394]   SI 2006/3317, reg 2(8)(b), as substituted by the Accession (Immigration and Worker Authorisation) (Amendment) Regulations 2007, SI 2007/475, reg 2(2). For 'family member', see **12.117–12.121**. For 'right to reside', see **12.110–12.129**. For 'self-employed person', see **12.152–12.153**. For 'student', see **12.116**.

- a person who holds a registration certificate to the effect that he or she is a highly skilled person and has unconditional access to the labour market;[395] or

- a person who is in the UK as a student, who holds a registration certificate that includes a statement that he or she is a student who has access to the UK labour market, and who is working not more than 20 hours a week during term time,[396] or is working for no more than 4 months after the end of his or her course and who holds a registration certificate that includes a statement that he or she may work during that period;[397] or

- a 'posted worker'.[398]

Any national of Bulgaria or Romania who falls within one of these categories will fall to be treated as any other EEA national would be.

Family members of certain EEA nationals[399]

12.164 A family member of an EEA national (who is a worker, a self-employed person, an Accession State worker requiring registration or an Accession State national subject to worker authorisation) is exempt from having to satisfy the habitual residence test.

12.165 The 'family member' need not be a worker, a self-employed person, an Accession State worker requiring registration or an Accession State national subject to worker authorisation. Indeed, he or she need not be economically active at all. Nor need he or she be an EEA national. So long as he or she is a 'family member' of an EEA national (who is a worker, a self-employed person, an Accession State worker requiring registration or an Accession State national subject to worker authorisation), he or she is exempt from the habitual residence test. He or she can apply for homelessness assistance in his or her own right. There is no need for the EEA worker, self-employed person, Accession State worker requiring registration or Accession State national subject to worker authorisation to be the applicant.

---

[395] SI 2006/3317, reg 2(9).

[396] He or she may work full-time during vacation (SI 2006/3317, reg 10A(b)).

[397] SI 2006/3317, reg 2(10), (10A) and (10B), as substituted by the Accession (Immigration and Worker Authorisation) (Amendment) Regulations 2007, SI 2007/475, reg 2(2).

[398] SI 2006/3317, reg 2(11) and (13)(a). A 'posted worker' is a worker who, for a limited period, is working in the territory of a different Member State from that where he or she normally works (Directive 96/71/EC, Arts 1 and 3).

[399] Allocation of Housing and Homelessness (Eligibility) (England) Regulations 2006, SI 2006/1294, reg 6(2)(d). See English Code, para 9.14(d) and Annex 12, paras 43–50.

12.166 In some circumstances, there is not even any need for the EEA national to be part of the applicant's household in order for the applicant to be eligible as a 'family member'.[400]

12.167 For 'family member', see **12.117–12.121**.

EEA nationals and their family members who have certain permanent rights to reside in the UK[401]

12.168 'Permanent right of residence' is defined at Immigration (European Economic Area) Regulations 2006, reg 15(1).[402] This exemption from the habitual residence test only applies to three sub-classes of persons who are entitled to a permanent right of residence.

12.169 Those three sub-classes give permanent rights of residence to:

(1) an EEA national who was a worker or self-employed person who has ceased activity;[403]

(2) the family member of such an EEA national;[404] and

(3) a person who was:
- the family member of an EEA national who was a worker or self-employed person; and
- the EEA national has died; and
- the family member had resided with the EEA national immediately before his or her death; and
- either the EEA national had resided in the UK for at least 2 years immediately before his or her death; or
- the death was the result of an accident at work or an occupational disease.[405]

12.170 'Worker or self-employed person who has ceased activity' is defined at Immigration (European Economic Area) Regulations 2006, reg 5.[406]

12.171 For 'family member', see **12.117–12.121**. For 'worker', see **12.147–12. 151**. For 'self-employed person' see **12.152–12.153**.

---

[400] For example, spouses and civil partners remain 'family members' until their marriage or partnership is legally terminated, whether or not they are actually cohabiting with the EEA national. See fn 256.

[401] Allocation of Housing and Homelessness (Eligibility) (England) Regulations 2006, SI 2006/1294, reg 6(2)(e). English Code, Annex 12, paras 38–39.

[402] SI 2006/1003. See **12.123–12.124**.

[403] Immigration (European Economic Area) Regulations 2006, SI 2006/1003, reg 15(1)(c). See **12.123**(3).

[404] SI 2006/1003, reg 15(1)(d). See **12.123**(4).

[405] SI 2006/1003, reg 15(1)(e). See **12.123**(5).

[406] SI 2006/1003.

12.172 There will be other EEA nationals who have a permanent right of residence that is not within these three specified sub-classes.⁴⁰⁷ They will have to satisfy the habitual residence test in order to be eligible.⁴⁰⁸

*People from Montserrat*⁴⁰⁹

12.173 This group of persons who are eligible even if they are not habitually resident are persons who left the territory of Montserrat after 1 November 1995 because of the effect on that territory of a volcanic eruption. They will normally be British citizens or Commonwealth citizens.⁴¹⁰ Not all people leaving Montserrat are rendered eligible by this provision. It does not apply to those who left on or before 1 November 1995. Nor does it apply to those who left after that date for reasons unconnected with the volcanic eruption. The regulation emphasises the departure location, ie it covers those who were in Montserrat and left after 1 November 1995. It also emphasises the reason for departure: the effect of the volcanic eruption. Most of those displaced to the UK in consequence of the volcanic eruption will long since have become habitually resident and will not need to rely on this exception to that test.

*People who are in the UK as a result of having been deported, expelled or otherwise removed by compulsion of law from another country to the UK*⁴¹¹

12.174 This group of persons, who are eligible even if not habitually resident, is probably small. The inclusion of this group brings eligibility for homelessness assistance into line with eligibility for housing benefit.

*People who left Lebanon on or after 12 July 2006 because of the armed conflict there*⁴¹²

12.175 This group of people, who are eligible even if not habitually resident, is self-explanatory. In similar terms to the provision exempting those fleeing the volcanic eruption in Montserrat, it refers to people who are British citizens, or have other rights to enter or remain in the UK, but who have not been habitually resident in the CTA.⁴¹³ This provision exempts them from complying with the habitual residence test. To fall within this group:

- a person must have left Lebanon, not elsewhere;

- he or she must have left on or after 12 July 2006; and

---

⁴⁰⁷ See **12.125–12.129**.

⁴⁰⁸ Allocation of Housing and Homelessness (Eligibility) (England) Regulations 2006, SI 2006/1294, reg 6(1)(a). See **12.136–12.141**.

⁴⁰⁹ SI 2006/1294, reg 6(2)(f). English Code, paras 9.19–9.20.

⁴¹⁰ Obviously, to be eligible at all, he or she must not be a 'person subject to immigration control'. See **12.53–12.59** for who is and who is not a 'person subject to immigration control'.

⁴¹¹ SI 2006/1294, reg 6(2)(g). English Code, para 9.21.

⁴¹² SI 2006/1294, reg 6(2)(h), inserted by Allocation of Housing and Homelessness (Eligibility) (England) (Amendment) Regulations 2006, SI 2006/2007, reg 2(8) and in force from 4pm on 25 July 2006.

⁴¹³ See Box 1 at **12.55**.

- his or her reason for leaving Lebanon must have been 'because of the armed conflict there'.

12.176 This provision is only effective for 'the relevant period', which is defined as being between 4pm on 25 July 2006 and 31 January 2007.[414] After 31 January 2007, anyone who had fled Lebanon because of the armed conflict, and had not made his or her application for homelessness assistance during the relevant period, would have to satisfy the habitual residence test.

People who arrived in Great Britain on or after 28 February 2009 but before 18 March 2011 and who immediately before arriving in Great Britain had been resident in Zimbabwe and, before leaving Zimbabwe, had accepted an offer made by Her Majesty's Government, to assist them to settle in the UK[415]

12.177 This exception applies to British citizens, who have left Zimbabwe and arrived in Great Britain between 28 February 2009 and 18 March 2011. They must have left as a result of having accepted an offer of assistance from the British government. The government intends to offer assistance only to British citizens and British nationals who have the right of abode in the UK. They will either be aged 70 or over, or will be vulnerable due to health and social care needs that mean that they are not able to look after themselves.[416] Their spouses, partners and any dependants can accompany them, but whether they too will be offered assistance is to be decided on a case-by-case basis.

12.178 This exception applies only to applications for homelessness assistance made on or after 18 March 2009.[417]

The second class of persons not subject to immigration control but nevertheless not eligible: EEA nationals with a right to reside in the UK by virtue of being job-seekers, family members of a job-seeker, or by exercising an initial right to reside[418]

12.179 Anyone who falls exclusively within this class cannot be eligible for homelessness assistance. The habitual residence test is not relevant. If an EEA national is:

---

[414] Allocation of Housing and Homelessness (Eligibility) (England) Regulations 2006, SI 2006/1294, reg 2(4), inserted by Allocation of Housing and Homelessness (Eligibility) (England) (Amendment) Regulations 2006, SI 2006/2007, reg 2(2).

[415] SI 2006/1294, reg 6(2)(i), inserted by the Allocation of Housing and Homelessness (Eligibility) (England) (Amendment) Regulations 2009, SI 2009/358.

[416] Explanatory Memorandum to the Allocation of Housing and Homelessness (Eligibility) (England) (Amendment) Regulations 2009, SI 2009/358, para 7.

[417] Allocation of Housing and Homelessness (Eligibility) (England) (Amendment) Regulations 2009, SI 2009/358, reg 1.

[418] Allocation of Housing and Homelessness (Eligibility) (England) Regulations 2006, SI 2006/1294, reg 6(1)(b). English Code, para 9.13(ii) and (iii), Annex 12, paras 9–10 and 12–14.

(a)   a job-seeker;[419] or

(b)   a family member[420] of a job-seeker; or

(c)   only entitled to remain in the UK by virtue of the initial right to reside for 3 months;[421]

he or she cannot be eligible.

12.180   So, this second class operates to ensure that any EEA national, or family member of an EEA national, whose *only* right of residence in the UK is the initial 3-month right of residence is not eligible for homelessness assistance.

12.181   It also excludes job-seekers from homelessness assistance. EEA nationals who are 'job-seekers' are 'qualified persons'[422] and therefore are entitled to the extended right of residence.[423] A 'job-seeker' is defined as 'a person who enters the UK in order to seek employment and can provide evidence that he is seeking employment and has a genuine chance of being engaged'.[424] If a job-seeker had previously been employed, he or she may still be a 'worker' in certain circumstances and is potentially eligible because of the 'worker' status.[425]

12.182   However, if a person's *only* claim to the extended right of residence is because of his or her status as a 'job-seeker', or as a family member of a job-seeker, he or she will not be eligible.

12.183   For 'family member' see **12.117–12.121**. For 'initial right of residence', see **12.112–12.114**.

12.184   If a person has more than one right of residence, such as being both a job-seeker and being the family member of a worker or self-employed person, then his or her right to reside is not 'only' derived from his or her status as a job-seeker and he or she will not fall within this second class of persons (not subject to immigration control) who are not eligible for homelessness assistance.

---

[419]   See **12.181**.
[420]   See **12.117–12.121**.
[421]   See **12.112–12.114**.
[422]   Immigration (European Economic Area) Regulations, SI 2006/1003, reg 6(1)(a).
[423]   See **12.115–12.122**.
[424]   Immigration (European Economic Area) Regulations 2006, SI 2006/1003, reg 6(1)(a) and (4). See English Code, Annex 12, paras 12–14.
[425]   SI 2006/1003, reg 6(2)(b). See **12.147–12.151**.

The third class of persons not subject to immigration control but nevertheless not eligible: EEA nationals with a right to reside in the rest of the Common Travel Area by virtue of being job-seekers, family members of a job-seeker or exercising an initial right to reside[426]

12.185

– For 'job-seeker', see **12.181**.

– For 'family member', see **12.117–12.121**.

– For 'initial right to reside', see **12.112–12.114**.

– For 'Common Travel Area' see Box 1 at **12.55**.

12.186 This third class refers to people who have been residing in the Channel Islands, the Isle of Man or the Republic of Ireland. The rest of the CTA is dealt with by the second class.[427]

The Welsh rules

The basic rules

12.187 The National Assembly for Wales[428] has exercised its power to prescribe other classes of persons from abroad who are not persons subject to immigration control but are to be treated as ineligible by the Homelessness (Wales) Regulations 2006.[429] These Regulations apply to applications for homelessness assistance made to Welsh local housing authorities on or after 9 October 2006.[430] It should be noted that the guidance in the Welsh Code still refers to the regulations in force in 2003.[431]

12.188 Regulation 4 of the Homelessness (Wales) Regulations 2006[432] designates two classes of people as not eligible for homelessness assistance, even though they are not persons subject to immigration control. They are:

---

[426] Allocation of Housing and Homelessness (Eligibility) (England) Regulations 2006, SI 2006/1294, reg 6(1)(c). English Code, para 9.13(iv).

[427] See **12.179–12.184**.

[428] The National Assembly for Wales' power to make regulations under HA 1996, Part 7, was transferred to the Welsh Assembly Government on 25 May 2007 (Government of Wales Act 2006, s 161 and Sch 11, para 30). See fn 89.

[429] SI 2006/2646 (W 227), reg 3.

[430] Homelessness (Wales) Regulations 2006, SI 2006/2646 (W 227), reg 5. For the position for applications made before 9 October 2006, See **3.137–3.139**.

[431] See Welsh Code. paras 11.1–11.11 and Annexes 4–11, 13 and 15. However, all the six classes discussed at para 11.9 remain eligible under the current Regulations. Classes D, F, G, and J are new classes and there is no guidance in the Welsh Code. Where appropriate, reference has been made to guidance on those classes in the English Code.

[432] SI 2006/2646 (W 227).

- people not habitually resident in the CTA, subject to exemptions;[433] and

- people whose right to reside in the CTA is derived solely from their status as self-sufficient or retired persons.[434]

The first class of persons not subject to immigration control but nevertheless not eligible: not habitually resident[435]

12.189 For 'habitually resident', see **12.136–12.141**. For 'Common Travel Area', see Box 1 at **12.55**.

Exemptions from the habitual residence test[436]

12.190 Five groups of persons from abroad are not required to satisfy the habitual residence. They are:

- EEA nationals who are workers;[437] and

- Accession State workers requiring registration ('A8 nationals');[438] and

- EEA nationals who have the right to reside in the UK;[439] and

- persons who left the territory of Montserrat after 1 November 1995 because of the effect on that territory of a volcanic eruption; and

- for applications made on or after 20 March 2009, persons who arrived in Great Britain on or after 28 February 2009 but before 18 March 2011 and who, immediately before arriving in Great Britain, had been resident in Zimbabwe and before leaving Zimbabwe had accepted an offer made by Her Majesty's Government to assist that person to settle in the UK.[440]

12.191 Four of these exemptions are discussed in relation to the English Regulations. For 'worker', see **12.147–12.151**. For 'Accession State worker requiring registration', see **12.154–12.159**. For 'person who left the territory of Montserrat', see **12.173**. For 'persons who left Zimbabwe', see **12.177–12.178**.

---

433   SI 2006/2646 (W 227), reg 4(1)(a). See **12.136–12.141** for habitual residence and **12.190–12.192** for exemptions.
434   SI 2006/2646 (W 227), reg 4(1)(b). See **12.110–12.129** for 'right to reside' and Box 1 at **12.55** for 'CTA'.
435   SI 2006/2646 (W 227), reg 4(1)(a).
436   SI 2006/2646 (W 227), reg 4(2).
437   SI 2006/2646 (W 227), reg 4(2)(a). For 'worker' see **12.147–12.151**.
438   SI 2006/2646 (W 227), reg 4(2)(b). Note that the Regulations have not been amended to include Accession State nationals subject to worker authorisation. For 'Accession State worker requiring registration' see **12.154–12.159**.
439   SI 2006/2646 (W 227), reg 4(2)(c). For 'right to reside', see **12.110–12.129**.
440   SI 2006/2646 (W 227), reg 4(2)(d), as inserted by Allocation of Housing and Homelessness (Eligibility) (Wales) Regulations 2009, SI 2009/393 (W 42), reg 3. For 'persons who left Zimbabwe', see **12.177–12.178**.

12.192   The third group of people are exempt from the habitual residence test if they apply to Welsh local housing authorities, but are not exempt if they are apply to English local housing authorities. They are EEA nationals and family members of EEA nationals who have the right to reside in the UK. The rights of EEA nationals and their family members to reside are discussed at **12.110–12.129**. Note that if a person does not have a 'right to reside', he or she will not be treated as habitually resident.[441] If the 'right to reside' enjoyed by the EEA national is derived solely from his or her status as a self-sufficient or retired person, he or she will not be eligible (because he or she falls into the second class of people from abroad prescribed as not eligible).[442]

The second class of persons not subject to immigration control but nevertheless not eligible: people whose right to reside in the CTA is derived solely from their status as self-sufficient or retired persons[443]

12.193   The second class of persons who are not eligible for homelessness assistance, even though they are not persons subject to immigration control, comprises those EEA nationals, and their family members, whose right to reside is derived solely from European Union Council Directives 90/364/EEC or 90/365/EEC.[444] These Directives refer to nationals of EEA Member States who are self-sufficient or retired. There are no exceptions to this class. Anyone who falls within this class will be ineligible whether or not he or she is habitually resident.

SUMMARY OF DIFFERENCES IN ELIGIBILITY AS BETWEEN ENGLISH AND WELSH LOCAL HOUSING AUTHORITIES

Overview

12.194   Since any person is entitled to make an application for homelessness assistance to any local housing authority in England or Wales without having any geographical connection to that local housing authority, applicants and their advisers might consider whether they should direct their applications to a local housing authority in the country where they will be found to be eligible under HA 1996, s 185 and the different Regulations made under this section.

12.195   If the applicant has no local connection with the local housing authority to which he or she applied, and is found to be eligible for assistance, to be homeless, to have a priority need and not to have become homeless intentionally, the local housing authority would be entitled to consider whether the applicant should be referred to another local housing authority under the

---

[441]   SI 2006/2646 (W 227), reg 4(3).
[442]   SI 2006/2646 (W 227), reg 4(1)(b). See **12.193**.
[443]   SI 2006/2646 (W 227), reg 4(1)(b).
[444]   SI 2006/2646 (W 277), reg 4(1)(b).

conditions for referral at HA 1996, s 198(2) or (4).[445] It may be, therefore, that an applicant who is eligible under the Welsh Regulations and who directs his or her application to a Welsh local housing authority, and who has no local connection with the Welsh local housing authority but does have a local connection with an English local housing authority, will find that he or she is referred to the English local housing authority for performance of the main housing duty at HA 1996, s 193(2). The English local housing authority will be required to perform the main housing duty, and secure accommodation for the applicant and his or her household, even though the applicant would not have been eligible for homelessness assistance if he or she had applied directly to the English local housing authority. The same analysis applies where an applicant who is not eligible under the Welsh Regulations directs his or her application for homelessness assistance to an English local housing authority.

12.196 Of course, if a duty other than the main housing duty[446] is owed to the applicant, the conditions for referral do not apply and that duty must be performed by the local housing authority to which the applicant applied. In addition, there is no obligation on a local housing authority to consider whether the conditions for referral are made out, and an applicant cannot insist on being referred under the conditions for referral.[447]

Applications to Welsh local housing authorities

12.197 The following applicants would be eligible for homelessness assistance if they apply to Welsh local housing authorities, but would not be eligible if they apply to English local housing authorities:

- a person subject to immigration control who left the territory of Montserrat after 1 November 1995 because of the effect on that territory of a volcanic eruption;[448]

- a person subject to immigration control who is habitually resident in the CTA and who is either:
  - a national of a state which has ratified the ECSMA or the ESC and is lawfully present in the UK;[449] or
  - before 3 April 2000 was owed a duty by a local housing authority under Housing Act 1985, Part 3, or HA 1996, Part 7, which is extant and who is a national of a state which is a signatory to the ECSMA or ESC;[450]

---

[445] See Chapter 15.
[446] Such as the duty to secure accommodation in the short term to applicants who have a priority need but have become homeless intentionally (HA 1996, s 190(2)(a): see **17.111–17.118**) or the duty to provide advice and assistance to the applicant (HA 1996, ss 190(2)(b) and 192(2): see **17.132–17.144**).
[447] *Hackney London Borough Council v Sareen* [2003] EWCA Civ 351, [2003] HLR 54, CA.
[448] Homelessness (Wales) Regulations 2006, SI 2006/2646 (W 227), reg 3(1)(d). See **12.91–12.93**.
[449] SI 2006/2646 (W 227), reg 3(1)(e)(i). See **12.94–12.96**.
[450] SI 2006/2646 (W 227), reg 3(1)(e)(ii). See **12.97–12.99**.

- a person who is subject to immigration control and who is on income-based jobseeker's allowance or income support (with certain exceptions);[451]

- a person who is not subject to immigration control and whose sole right of residence in the CTA[452] is by virtue of being a job-seeker[453] or of being a family member[454] of a job-seeker and who is habitually resident in the CTA.[455]

Applications to English local housing authorities

12.198 Applicants who are persons subject to immigration control will find that there are no classes of people who are prescribed as eligible for homelessness assistance from English local housing authorities who are not also prescribed as eligible for homelessness assistance from Welsh local housing authorities. There is therefore no benefit in directing an application specifically to an English rather than a Welsh local housing authority on issues of eligibility.

12.199 However, applicants who are not persons subject to immigration control but may have difficulty in satisfying the habitual residence test could consider applying to English local housing authorities if they fall within the following exemptions to the habitual residence test:

- an Accession State national subject to worker authorisation ('an A2 national');[456] or

- a person who is in the UK as a result of having been deported, expelled or otherwise removed by compulsion of law from another country to the UK.[457]

---

451 SI 2006/2646 (W 227), reg 3(1)(i). See **12.100–12.102**.
452 See Box 1 at **12.55**.
453 See **12.181**.
454 See **12.117–12.121**.
455 There is no prescription for this group of people in the Homelessness (Wales) Regulations 2006, SI 2006/2646. It follows that a person will be eligible if he or she satisfies the habitual residence test (SI 2006/2646, reg 4(1)(a)). See **12.187–12.193**. The same could apply to a person whose sole right of residence in the UK is by virtue of exercising an initial right to reside (see **12.112–12.114**), but such a person would be unlikely to satisfy the habitual residence test.
456 Allocation of Housing and Homelessness (Eligibility) (England) Regulations 2006, SI 2006/1294, reg 6(2)(c)(ii), substituted by Allocation of Housing and Homelessness (Eligibility) (England) (Amendment) (No 2) Regulations 2006, SI 2006/3340, reg 2(4), in force from 1 January 2007; see **12.160–12.163**.
457 Allocation of Housing and Homelessness (Eligibility) (England) Regulations 2006, SI 2006/1294, reg 6(2)(g). See **12.174**.

12.200 These exemptions do not feature in the Welsh Regulations and so, if an application for homelessness assistance was made to a Welsh local housing authority, the habitual residence test would have to be applied.[458]

THE SECONDARY EXCLUSION PROVISION: HOUSING ACT 1996, SECTION 186

Who does this apply to?

12.201 This exclusory provision is addressed to asylum-seekers who are eligible for assistance applying the provisions of HA 1996, s 185. Those asylum seekers must have claimed asylum on any date up to and including 2 April 2000 and also fall within any of Classes E(i), (ii) or (iii),[459] described above. Particular guidance relating to such asylum-seekers is given at paras 9.11–9.12 and Annex 9 of the English Code.[460] Even if they do fall within any of Classes E(i), (ii) or (iii), HA 1996, s 186 applies an additional test of eligibility for homelessness assistance.

Additional test of eligibility for homelessness assistance

12.202 Any pre-3 April 2000 asylum-seeker who is in fact eligible for homelessness assistance (by virtue of falling within one of the Classes) will not be eligible if he or she has 'any accommodation in the United Kingdom, however temporary, available for his or her occupation'.[461] That accommodation must be accommodation which (save for its temporary nature) would otherwise be reasonable for the asylum-seeker to continue to occupy.[462]

Modification of main housing duty

12.203 If a homeless asylum-seeker is eligible for assistance, and the local housing authority decides that it owes the main housing duty to provide accommodation for him or her,[463] that duty may be performed by the local housing authority by referring the applicant to another local housing authority, without regard to the asylum-seeker's preference as to whether and where he or she is referred.[464] Whether or not the asylum-seeker is referred under these provisions, his or her preference as to the locality of any accommodation

---

[458] Homelessness (Wales) Regulations 2006, SI 2006/2646 (W 227), reg 4(1)(a).
[459] Allocation of Housing and Homelessness (Eligibility) (England) Regulations 2006, SI 2006/1294, reg 5. See **12.75–12.86**. The relevant classes are F, G, and H of reg 3 of the Homelessness (England) Regulations 2000, SI 2000/701, for applications to Welsh local housing authorities and for applications to English local housing authorities made before 1 June 2006.
[460] Welsh Code, Annex 10.
[461] HA 1996, s 186(1).
[462] *Lismane v Hammersmith and Fulham London Borough Council* (1998) 31 HLR 427, CA.
[463] HA 1996, s 193(2).
[464] HA 1996, s 198(4A) and (4B), added by Homelessness (Asylum Seekers) (Interim Period) (England) Order 1999, SI 1999/3126, reg 3.

provided in the performance of the local housing authority's duty is not to be taken into account by the local housing authority.[465] In addition, the fact that accommodation is to be temporary pending the determination of the claim for asylum is relevant to determining the suitability of the accommodation to be provided.[466]

12.204 These provisions are designed to mirror the dispersal scheme for asylum-seekers falling under the UKBA arrangements for accommodation.[467] They are inserted into HA 1996, Part 7 by Ministerial order.[468] There is power for the Secretary of State to repeal all of these provisions. That power has not yet been exercised and, presumably, will only be exercised when there are no longer any 'eligible' asylum seekers entitled to homelessness assistance.[469]

ISLES OF SCILLY

12.205 The Isles of Scilly are administratively part of England,[470] but special measures have been taken to protect the very limited stock of social housing on those islands. HA 1996[471] enables the Secretary of State to make an Order adapting HA 1996, Part 7 in its application to the Isles of Scilly and that power has been used to make special provisions governing eligibility for applicants applying for homelessness assistance there.[472]

12.206 The Order amends HA 1996, ss 183–218, to provide that a person is not eligible for homelessness assistance from the authorities in the Isles of Scilly unless he or she has been resident in the district of the Isles of Scilly for a total period of 2 years and 6 months during the period of 3 years immediately prior to the application.[473] If an applicant is eligible, by virtue of having resided in the Isles of Scilly for that period, he or she is also deemed to have a local connection with the Isles of Scilly.[474]

---

[465] HA 1996, s 210(1A), added by SI 1999/3126, reg 6.
[466] HA 1996, s 206(1A), added by SI 1999/3126, reg 4.
[467] Guidance is at English Code, para 9.12 and Annex 9, para 6, and Welsh Code, Annex 11.
[468] Homelessness (Asylum Seekers) (Interim Period) (England) Order 1999, SI 1999/3126, inserting ss 198(4A), (4B), 206(1A), 208(1A) and 210(1A) into HA 1996.
[469] Immigration and Asylum Act 1999, s 117(5); Homelessness (Asylum Seekers) (Interim Period) (England) Order 1999, SI 1999/3126, reg 7.
[470] Interpretation Act 1978, s 5 and Sch 1.
[471] HA 1996, s 225(1).
[472] Homelessness (Isles of Scilly) Order 1997, SI 1997/797.
[473] SI 1997/797, reg 2(2).
[474] SI 1997/797, reg 2(3). See also **15.188–15.191**.

Chapter 13
PRIORITY NEED

INTRODUCTION

13.1 Once a local housing authority has decided that someone is homeless or threatened with homelessness, and is eligible for assistance, it owes that person a duty. The next question is: What duty does it owe?[1] In order to answer that, the local housing authority must decide whether the applicant has a 'priority need' for accommodation. That involves the local housing authority applying the tight statutory definition of the term,[2] not making a value judgment.

13.2 The local housing authority should initially consider whether the applicant has a priority need in his or her own right. If not, it should ask whether any person who resides, or might reasonably be expected to reside, with the applicant falls into one of the priority need categories which would confer a priority need on the applicant.

Why it matters

13.3 If the applicant *does not* have a priority need for accommodation, the local housing authority's duty is to assess his or her housing needs and then to provide him or her with advice and assistance in any attempts he or she may make to obtain accommodation to meet those needs.[3] Additionally, if an applicant without priority need has not become homeless intentionally, the local housing authority has a power (but not a duty) to provide accommodation for the applicant and his or her household.[4] Where the non-priority need applicant has not become 'threatened with' homelessness intentionally, there is a parallel power to take reasonable steps to secure that accommodation does not cease to be available for his or her occupation.[5]

13.4 If the applicant *does* have a priority need, he or she will be entitled to accommodation together with his or her household. If that applicant has become homeless intentionally, the accommodation will only be provided for such period as the local housing authority considers will give him or her a reasonable opportunity of securing accommodation.[6] If the applicant has not become homeless intentionally, accommodation must be provided until the duty is discharged by the occurrence of one of the events listed at Housing Act 1996 (HA 1996), s 193.[7] Similar duties are owed to applicants who are

---

[1]   Housing Act 1996, s 184(1)(b).
[2]   See **13.14–13.19**.
[3]   HA 1996, ss 190(3), (4), 192(2) and (4). See **17.132–17.144**.
[4]   HA 1996, s 192(3). See **17.145–17.152**.
[5]   HA 1996, s 195(9). See **17.145**.
[6]   HA 1996, s 190(2)(a). See **17.111–17.118**.
[7]   HA 1996, s 193(2), (3) and (5)–(7F). See **17.49–17.97**.

'threatened with' homelessness and have a priority need.[8] Again, the extent of the duty owed turns on whether the applicant has become threatened with homelessness intentionally.[9]

When it matters

13.5 There are four stages in the handling of a homelessness application at which the question of 'priority need' may be significant.

At the application stage

13.6 At the outset of an application for homelessness assistance, the local housing authority must take a preliminary view about priority need. If the local housing authority has reason to believe that the applicant may have a priority need and may also be homeless and eligible, it *must* provide interim accommodation while it works out what duty under HA 1996, Part 7 (if any) the applicant is owed.[10] The threshold for the provision of interim accommodation is very low; any 'reason to believe' that an applicant may have a priority need is sufficient. There have been findings of maladministration against local housing authorities which turned away applicants, telling them to obtain medical evidence, and, as a result, failed to discharge their duty to provide interim accommodation.[11]

13.7 On receiving an application, the local housing authority is under a duty to make all necessary inquiries into whether or not the applicant actually has a priority need. That burden rests on the local housing authority; it is not for the applicant to have to prove his or her case. The local housing authority should make its inquiries as quickly as possible and aim to complete them and notify the applicant of the outcome within 33 working days.[12]

The decision stage

13.8 The local housing authority is *not*, at this stage, concerned with whether the applicant had a priority need at the date of *application*, but rather with whether she or he has a priority need at the date of the *decision* as to what HA 1996, Part 7 duty is owed (if any). If there has been a change of circumstances

---

[8]   HA 1996, s 195(2) and (5)(b). See **17.111–17.118**.
[9]   For more on the concepts of becoming homeless (or becoming threatened with homelessness) intentionally, see Chapter 14.
[10]   HA 1996, s 188(1). See also *Homelessness Code of Guidance for local authorities* (Communities and Local Government, Department for Education and Skills, Department of Health, July 2006), (English Code), chapter 7 and para 10.3, at Appendix 2 of this book. *Code of Guidance for local housing authorities on allocation of accommodation and homelessness for Wales* (National Assembly for Wales, April 2003), (Welsh Code), para 12.11, on CD-ROM. The interim duty is more fully discussed at **16.11-16.24**.
[11]   Local Government Ombudsman Investigations 89/A/2825 (Tunbridge Wells Borough Council); 90/A/2032 (Ealing Borough Council); 90/C/2893 (Kingston upon Hull City Council); and 06/B/7896 (Eastleigh Borough Council).
[12]   English Code, para 6.16; Welsh Code, para 12.22. See **10.34–10.36**.

between the making of the application and the date of the decision, the local housing authority must take that change into account. In one case, which reached the Court of Appeal, the applicant had had a priority need at the date of application and for the following 6 days, but not at the date of the decision.[13]

13.9　The question for the local housing authority is whether, at the date of its decision (or, if a review has been requested, at the date of the review decision) the applicant has a priority need.[14] The local housing authority must not improperly delay making its decision (or concluding its review) in order to see whether the applicant might meanwhile lose an apparent priority need.[15] It is not at all unusual for an applicant to have one form of priority need at the date of application (eg pregnancy) and another at the date of decision or review (eg dependent children).

The stage after decision

13.10　Once the local housing authority has reached a decision that the applicant has a priority need and has established the duty it therefore owes to the applicant, that duty will not be displaced by any later change in the applicant's priority need (unless a review has been sought and the change takes place between the original decision and conclusion of the review). The scheme of HA 1996, Part 7 does not permit a concluded duty to be re-opened simply because priority need has been lost. Once a duty has been accepted, the duty continues until it is discharged.[16]

13.11　However, the manner in which the local housing authority's duty to the applicant is performed may be affected if priority need is lost. An obvious example would be where the applicant is provided with temporary four-bedroom accommodation because four dependent children residing with him or her confer a priority need. If those children all leave, the local housing authority will be entitled to perform its duty by providing smaller accommodation.

On a new application

13.12　If the applicant has been owed the main housing duty[17] and that duty ends, the applicant may apply again.[18] It is quite irrelevant that the applicant had a priority need on his or her earlier application. What is important is whether she or he may have a priority need at the date of the new application.

13　*R v Kensington and Chelsea Royal London Borough Council ex p Amarfio* (1995) 27 HLR 543, CA.
14　*Mohammed v Hammersmith and Fulham London Borough Council* [2001] UKHL 57, [2002] 1 AC 547, HL.
15　*Robinson v Hammersmith & Fulham London Borough Council* [2006] EWCA Civ 1122, [2007] HLR 7, CA.
16　*R v Brent London Borough Council ex p Sadiq* (2001) 33 HLR 47, QBD. English Code, para 10.4; Welsh Code, para 14.5.
17　HA 1996, s 193(2). See **17.21–17.110**.
18　HA 1996, s 193(9). See **9.54–9.64** and **17.109–17.110**.

13.13 If the applicant was not owed the main duty on the initial application (because she or he had no priority need) but has now applied again, it will be critically important whether she or he has since acquired a priority need. Subsequently acquiring a priority need may constitute a change of the factual position so that the local housing authority is required to entertain and inquire into the new application.[19]

THE STATUTORY SCHEME

13.14 The concept and definition of 'priority need' was first given statutory expression in the Housing (Homeless Persons) Act 1977 and is now found in very similar (but not precisely the same) terms in HA 1996, s 189(1). The statute sets out four different categories. If the applicant falls into any one of the four categories, he or she has a priority need.

13.15 Those categories are:

- a pregnant woman or a person with whom she resides or might reasonably be expected to reside;[20]

- a person with whom dependent children reside or might reasonably be expected to reside;[21]

- a person who is vulnerable as a result of old age, mental illness or mental handicap or physical disability or other special reason, or with whom such a person resides or might reasonably be expected to reside;[22] and

- a person who is homeless or threatened with homelessness as a result of an emergency such as flood, fire or other disaster.[23]

Each of these four categories is examined in more detail at **13.25–13.105**.

13.16 The Secretary of State and the Welsh Assembly Government[24] are given power under HA 1996, Part 7, to specify further categories of priority need and to amend or repeal any part of the four statutory categories.[25] For more than 20 years, the statutory categories remained unchanged. In recent years, however, further categories have been added by both the Secretary of State and the National Assembly.

---

19   *R (Van der Stolk) v Camden London Borough Council* [2002] EWHC 1261 (Admin), (2002) July *Legal Action*, p 26, Admin Ct.
20   HA 1996, s 189(1)(a). See **13.26–13.29**.
21   HA 1996, s 189(1)(b). See **13.30–13.61**.
22   HA 1996, s 189(1)(c). See **13.62–13.99**.
23   HA 1996 s 189(1)(d). See **13.100–13.105**.
24   The power was exercised by the National Assembly for Wales until 25 May 2007, when it was transferred to the Welsh Assembly Government (Government of Wales Act 2006, s 161 and Sch 11, para 30).
25   HA 1996, s 189(2).

13.17 In *England*, the Homelessness (Priority Need for Accommodation) (England) Order 2002,[26] made by the Secretary of State, came into force from 31 July 2002. It applies to applications made to English local housing authorities that are determined (at the initial decision or on review) on or after 31 July 2002. It adds six *additional* categories to those at HA 1996, s 189(1). In summary they cover:

(1)   most children aged 16 or 17;[27]

(2)   young people under 21, who have been looked after, accommodated or fostered, but are not students in full-time education;[28]

(3)   those over 21 who are vulnerable as a result of having been looked after, accommodated or fostered;[29]

(4)   people who are vulnerable as a result of having served in the armed forces;[30]

(5)   people who are vulnerable as a result of having been imprisoned;[31]

(6)   people who are vulnerable as a result of ceasing to occupy accommodation because of actual or threatened violence.[32]

Each of these six categories is examined in more detail at **13.106–13.171**.

13.18 In *Wales*, the Homeless Persons (Priority Need) (Wales) Order 2001,[33] made by the National Assembly for Wales, came into force on 1 March 2001. It applies to applications made to Welsh local housing authorities if the decision (or review decision) is made on or after 1 March 2001. It adds six *additional* categories to those in HA 1996, s 189(1). In summary, these are:

(1)   young people aged 18, 19 or 20 who have been looked after, accommodated or fostered;[34]

(2)   young people aged 18, 19 or 20 who are at particular risk of sexual or financial exploitation;[35]

(3)   16- and 17-year-olds;[36]

---

26   SI 2002/2051. See Appendix 2.
27   SI 2002/2051, art 3. See **13.107–13.136**.
28   SI 2002/2051, art 4. See **13.137–13.143**.
29   SI 2002/2051, art 5(1). See **13.148–13.152**.
30   SI 2002/2051, art 5(2). See **13.153–13.157**.
31   SI 2002/2051, art 5(3). See **13.158–13.164**.
32   SI 2002/2051, art 6. See **13.165–13.171**.
33   SI 2001/607 (W 30). See Appendix 3.
34   SI 2001/607, art 3(1)(a) and (b). See **13.177–13.180**.
35   SI 2001/607, art 3(1)(a) and (c). See **13.181–13.184**.
36   SI 2001/607, art 4. See **13.175**.

(4) anyone who has been subject to domestic violence, or is at risk of domestic violence;[37]

(5) a person who is homeless after leaving the armed forces;[38] and

(6) a former prisoner who is homeless after being released from custody.[39]

Each of these categories is examined in more detail at **13.172–13.202**.

13.19 Each Code of Guidance has a separate chapter giving guidance on the priority need categories applicable to local housing authorities in the two countries.[40]

How do the categories work?

13.20 An applicant may acquire a priority need in one of two ways. The statutory categories make the available routes clear.

13.21 In some cases, the applicant will only acquire a priority need if he or she personally meets the qualifying conditions. For example, if priority need arises from homelessness caused by an emergency, it must be the applicant who has been personally rendered homeless by the emergency.

13.22 In other cases, the applicant may acquire priority need as a result of another person's circumstances. When it comes to pregnancy or the main statutory category of vulnerability, the applicant will be in priority need either if he or she personally is in that condition or if it applies to any person with whom the applicant resides or might reasonably be expected to reside.

13.23 If the applicant is a person subject to immigration control[41] who is eligible for assistance[42] and is not a British or EEA national, and if the applicant has (or may have) a priority need only because a person with whom he or she resides, or might reasonably be expected to reside, is pregnant, vulnerable or a dependent child, that person must be 'eligible' for assistance.[43] Otherwise the person is invisible, for the purposes of assessing priority need, to the local housing authority.[44] If the applicant has a priority need only because

---

[37] SI 2001/607, art 5. See **13.185–13.190**.
[38] SI 2001/607, art 6. See **13.191–13.195**.
[39] SI 2001/607, art 7. See **13.196–13.202**.
[40] English Code, chapter 10; Welsh Code, chapter 14.
[41] See **12.53–12.59**.
[42] By virtue of falling within one of Classes A–E at reg 5 of the Allocation of Housing and Homelessness (Eligibility) (England) Regulations 2006, SI 2006/1294 (see **12.61–12.86**), or within one of Classes A–J at reg 3 of the Homelessness (Wales) Regulations 2006, SI 2006/2646 (W 227); see **12.87–12.102**.
[43] HA 1996, s 185(4) and (5); *Kaya v Haringey London Borough Council* [2001] EWCA Civ 677, [2002] HLR 1, CA.
[44] HA 1996, s 185(4) and (5). See **12.26–12.29**.

of the presence in his or her household of a 'restricted person',[45] and the applicant is entitled to the main housing duty,[46] that duty will be modified.[47]

13.24 Both the English and Welsh Priority Need Orders set out additional categories which refer only to an applicant's own personal circumstances. They do not contain any mechanism whereby a member of the applicant's household who falls within one of those priority need categories could confer priority need upon the applicant.[48] In that situation, the proper course is for the application to be made by any person who does fall within any of those categories. Any housing duty he or she is owed will be met by accommodation being provided to all members of his or her household (including non-priority members).[49] For example, if a childless couple is considering making an application for homelessness assistance, and one of the two is vulnerable as a result of having been in care, having served in the armed forces, or having been imprisoned, it is that person who should be the applicant.

THE STATUTORY CATEGORIES IN HOUSING ACT 1996, SECTION 189(1)

13.25 These categories apply to applicants to both English and Welsh local housing authorities.

Pregnancy[50]

13.26 It is a question of fact whether an applicant, or someone who resides with or might reasonably be expected to reside with the applicant, is pregnant at the date of the local housing authority's decision.[51] The length of the pregnancy is not an issue. Nor is the age of the pregnant woman.

13.27 It is for the local housing authority to undertake such sensitive inquiries as it considers necessary to satisfy itself whether a woman is pregnant. It is not for the applicant to prove pregnancy in any particular way (or at all).

---

[45] As defined at HA 1996, s 184(7); see **12.37**.
[46] At HA 1996, s 193(2), or the equivalent main duty owed to those threatened with homelessness at HA 1996, s 195(2); see **17.21–17.110** and **17.119–17.131**.
[47] See **12.30–12.39**.
[48] Although the Welsh Code recommends that applicants should be treated as having a priority need if a member of their household falls within one of the categories in the Welsh Order: Welsh Code, para 14.2.
[49] See *R (Ogbeni) v Tower Hamlets London Borough Council* [2008] EWHC 2444 (Admin), (2008) October *Legal Action*, p 37, Admin Ct, where a 17-year-old applicant had a priority need and was entitled to the main housing duty. The local housing authority was required to secure accommodation for both himself and his aunt, who had normally resided with him as a member of his family.
[50] HA 1996, s 189(1)(a).
[51] English Code, para 10.5; Welsh Code, para 14.9.

Obviously, as the Codes advise,[52] the normal confirmation of pregnancy issued by a GP or midwife should be accepted as sufficient evidence of pregnancy.

13.28 If the pregnant woman is not herself the applicant, the applicant will have a priority need if he or she resides with the pregnant woman or might reasonably be expected to reside with her. This would include the non-pregnant partner in a couple who had not previously lived together, but who now, in the light of the pregnancy, intend to do so. In those circumstances, it is for the local housing authority to determine whether such a couple might reasonably be expected to reside together, although it might be thought manifestly reasonable if the partner is the father of the expected child. Self-evidently, both same sex and different sex couples can fall within this statutory definition.

13.29 If the pregnancy ends *before* the decision is made, there will be no priority need under this category, although local housing authorities are advised to consider whether the woman is vulnerable for some other special reason where there has been a miscarriage or termination.[53] Conversely, if the pregnancy ends *after* the decision has been made, the local housing authority will continue to owe its acknowledged duty towards the applicant, whether or not a child has been born. The safeguard for the local housing authority is the obligation on the applicant to notify any relevant change of circumstance occurring during the assessment process.[54]

Dependent children[55]

13.30 Dependent children cannot be applicants for homelessness assistance in their own right.[56] Where an application is made which involves dependent children, the question for the local housing authority is, therefore, whether the applicant is someone with whom dependent children reside or with whom they might reasonably be expected to reside.

13.31 That question itself breaks down into several parts:

(1) Is there a 'child' or 'children'?

(2) Is that child, or are those children, 'dependent'?

(3) Does the dependent child, or do the dependent children, reside with the applicant?

(4) If not, might that child or those children be reasonably expected to reside with the applicant?

---

52   English Code, para 10.5; Welsh Code, para 14.9.
53   English Code, para 10.5; Welsh Code, para 14.9.
54   HA 1996, s 214(2).
55   HA 1996, s 189(1)(b).
56   *R v Oldham Metropolitan Borough Council ex p Garlick* [1993] AC 509, HL.

13.32 Advice on this priority need category is set out in the English Code, paras 10.6–10.11 and in the Welsh Code, paras 14.6–14.8.

13.33 It is no part of the statutory requirement that the dependent children are the applicant's children. The Codes make this plain: 'dependent children need not necessarily be the applicant's own children'.[57] Confusingly, the Codes also refer to the category as comprising those applicants who '*have* one or more dependent children who normally live with them or who might reasonably be expected to live with them'.[58] The word 'have' in that sentence must refer to the sense that the children physically live with the applicant, rather than to their parentage.

'Children'

13.34 HA 1996, Part 7 does not specify an age at which a child ceases to be a 'child' for the purposes of this priority need category; so there is no statutory maximum age. The critical distinction is not the child's age, but the date at which the child (of whatever age) ceases to be 'dependent'.[59]

13.35 One judge has expressed the view that the word 'child' should be construed in a narrower rather than a broader sense. He suggested that:

'... "children" cannot be taken to refer to children of any age but to those who have not, or perhaps have only just, attained their majority.'[60]

13.36 The Codes of Guidance refer to the phrase 'dependent children' as embracing 'all children under 16', and also:

'... all children aged 16–18 who are in, or are about to begin, full-time education or training or who for other reasons are unable to support themselves and who live at home.'[61]

This wording suggests that adults aged 18 can be 'children' for the purposes of HA 1996, Part 7.

13.37 In *Miah v Newham London Borough Council*,[62] the Court of Appeal was dealing with a 'child' of 18. It refused the local housing authority permission to appeal against a decision that she was a dependent child. The court accepted that, applying the guidance in the Code, the words could include children of any age up to the child's nineteenth birthday and would therefore include someone in his or her eighteenth year.

---

[57] English Code, para 10.8; Welsh Code, para 14.6.
[58] English Code, para 10.6; Welsh Code, para 14.6 (emphasis added).
[59] See **13.41–13.43**.
[60] *R v Kensington and Chelsea Royal London Borough Council ex p Amarfio* (1995) 27 HLR 543, CA at 545, per Nourse LJ.
[61] English Code, para 10.7; Welsh Code, para 14.6.
[62] *Miah v Newham London Borough Council* [2001] EWCA Civ 487, (2001) June *Legal Action*, p 25, CA.

13.38 The fact that the Codes offer no guidance concerning those who have reached their nineteenth birthday does not mean that a person of 19 or older could not be a dependent child.

13.39 The Codes suggest that there must be something in the nature of a parent/child relationship between the child and the applicant, which, they suggest, could include adoptive, foster or step relationships.[63] However, nothing in HA 1996, Part 7 requires a relationship of this nature or any form of relationship between the applicant and the dependent child.

13.40 It would be an extreme use of language to suggest that a person who had married could simultaneously be a 'dependent child' for the purposes of this priority need provision. The Court of Appeal has decided that a 17-year-old wife was not a 'dependent child' and, as a result, her husband did not fall within this priority need category.[64] The better course, now, would be for the 16- or 17-year-old wife to be the applicant, as she would have a priority need under the Priority Need Orders[65] and the husband would be accommodated with her in discharge of the local housing authority's duty to her.

Dependent

13.41 The term 'dependent' is also not defined in HA 1996, Part 7. While it obviously includes financial dependence, local housing authorities are reminded by both the Codes and the case law that children aged 16 or over may be financially independent, but not yet mature enough to live independently from their parents. They will therefore still be 'dependent' for these purposes.[66]

13.42 HA 1996, Part 7 does not say that the dependent child must be dependent on the applicant. On the face of it, the statutory language could be satisfied if a dependent child is living with the applicant, even if the child is wholly dependent on another. An example would be two brothers who live together, the eldest being in full-time employment, and the younger being financially supported by his parents who are abroad but send money. In such a case, the older brother would have a priority need, even though his brother was not financially dependent on him or her. The point is probably academic since, in this and any other similar examples, the younger brother would be likely to have some emotional dependence on his older brother.

13.43 The English Code advises that 'there must be actual dependence on the applicant' although the dependence need not be wholly or exclusively on the

---

63 English Code, para 10.8; Welsh Code, para 14.6.
64 *Hackney London Borough Council v Ekinci* [2001] EWCA Civ 776, (2002) 34 HLR 2, CA.
65 Homelessness (Priority Need for Accommodation) (England) Order 2002, SI 2002/2051, reg 3 (see **13.107–13.136**) and Homeless Persons (Priority Need) (Wales) Order 2001, SI 2001/607 (W 30), reg 4 (see **13.175**).
66 English Code, para 10.7; Welsh Code, para 14.6; and *R v Kensington and Chelsea Royal London Borough Council ex p Amarfio* (1995) 27 HLR 543, CA.

applicant, suggesting that a child may be dependent upon more than one person.[67] This wording, which was not in the previous edition and is not in the Welsh Code, reflects the statutory language originally used in the Housing (Homeless Persons) Act 1977, when the category was defined as 'if he has dependent children who are residing with him or who might reasonably be expected to reside with him'.[68] Indeed, in 1996, a judge decided that this language did require that there be at least some dependency by the child on the applicant.[69] However, that decision does not, strictly speaking, apply to the definition in HA 1996, Part 7, and there is nothing in the case law on HA 1996, Part 7 to suggest that this priority need category can only be met if the child is dependent on the applicant, rather than upon someone else.

'Resides with' the applicant

13.44 The next question for the local housing authority is whether the dependent child actually resides with the applicant. This is a straightforward question of fact and the question of whether or not the children 'might reasonably be expected' to reside with him or her does not arise.[70]

13.45 The word 'reside' would not normally be used to describe a situation in which one person is visiting another, or even staying with them for a short time, such as for a holiday. The Codes of Guidance go, perhaps, too far in suggesting that there must be:

> '... some degree of permanence or regularity, rather than a temporary arrangement whereby the children are merely staying with the applicant for a limited period.'[71]

13.46 Certainly, the English Code is wrong to suggest that the test is whether applicants have children who *'normally* live with them'.[72] Where HA 1996 intends to address a concept of normally living together, it uses the term

---

67 English Code, para 10.6.
68 Housing (Homeless Persons) Act 1977, s 2(1)(a).
69 *R v Westminster City Council ex p Bishop* (1997) 29 HLR 546, QBD at 551–554. The decision is complicated, because the language considered by the judge was not that in the Housing (Homeless Persons) Act 1977 but instead that in the Housing Act 1985, where the relevant category was said to be 'with whom dependent children reside' – removing 'he has'. However, the Housing Act 1985 was a consolidating Act and so the judge held that the language used was not intended to change the original statutory meaning. HA 1996, which reproduces the language of the Housing Act 1985 (and not the language of the Housing (Homeless Persons) Act 1977) is not a consolidating Act, but replaces the legislative scheme in the Housing Act 1985. The language of HA 1996 is not, therefore, subject to the same construction and can be considered afresh.
70 *R v Hillingdon London Borough Council ex p Islam* [1983] 1 AC 688, HL (a decision on priority need at first instance and that aspect of the judgment not subject to appeal); *R v Lambeth London Borough Council ex p Ly* (1986) 19 HLR 51, QBD; and *R v Lambeth London Borough Council ex p Bodunrin* (1992) 24 HLR 647, QBD.
71 English Code, para 10.6; Welsh Code, para 14.6.
72 English Code, para 10.6 (emphasis added).

'normally resides with him'.[73] In the case of this priority need category, the simple question is: 'With whom do the children reside?' – not 'With whom do they normally reside?'

13.47 Children who are temporarily away from the applicant on holiday or for other temporary purposes would ordinarily be said to 'reside with' the applicant during their absence, not with the person with whom they are staying.[74]

'Reasonably expected to reside' with the applicant

13.48 Even if no dependent child is actually residing with him or her, an applicant will have priority need if at least one dependent child might reasonably be expected to reside with him or her.[75] This covers the situation where the applicant and the dependent child (or children) are not currently living together but might reasonably be expected to live together in future. It will come into play where, for example, children are temporarily in the care of social services or staying with relatives, but would return to live with their parents if the parents obtain accommodation.

13.49 Where children are in the care of a social services authority (whether voluntarily or under the terms of a care order) and are not currently living with the applicant, local housing authorities are advised that liaison with the social services authority[76] is essential and that there should be joint consideration before the local housing authority reaches its decision.[77]

13.50 The correct approach to the question of whether it is reasonable to expect a person who does not currently live with the applicant to live with him or her is more fully discussed in Chapter 11.[78]

Separated parents and dependent children

13.51 Most of the difficult decisions on the 'dependent children' priority need category arise where the application is made by one of two parents who are separated. The local housing authority will have to consider three questions:

(1) Is there a child who is dependent ('dependency')?

(2) If so, does the child reside with the applicant ('residence')?

---

73 HA 1996, s 176(a). See **11.21–11.29**.
74 *Halonen v Westminster City Council* (1997) September *Legal Action*, p 19, Central London County Court, and *R v Lewisham London Borough Council ex p Creppy* (1992) 24 HLR 121, CA.
75 HA 1996, s 189(1)(b).
76 Or social services department, in the case of a unitary authority.
77 English Code, para 10.11; Welsh Code, para 14.8.
78 See **11.28–11.29**.

(3)   If not, is the child reasonably expected to reside with the applicant in the future ('future residence')?[79]

Dependency

13.52   As already indicated above, HA 1996, Part 7 itself does not require that the child be dependent on the applicant.[80] However, in cases where parents are separated, the expectation will be that the child is at least to some extent dependent on the parent who is applying. Where a local housing authority found on the facts of a particular case that a child was exclusively dependent upon his mother (who received both child benefit and income support for the child) and not the father (who was the applicant), the father's challenge to that decision was dismissed.[81] However, the question for the local housing authority is not whether the child is wholly and exclusively dependent upon the applicant, or upon its other parent,[82] but simply whether the child is dependent. The question of dependency has been described as 'fact-sensitive to a very large degree'.[83]

Residence and co-residence

13.53   When considering whether the child resides with the applicant, the local housing authority should consider all the circumstances, including whether or not a court order has been made in respect of where the child should reside.

Residence orders

13.54   Where a residence order in favour of one of the parents has been made, the Codes advise that the local housing authority should normally follow the provisions of the order and treat the child as residing with the person identified in the order.[84]

13.55   Nowadays, it is not unusual for family courts to make shared residence orders, either after a contested hearing between the parents, or by consent.[85] Shared residence orders can be made even when the child does not divide his or her time equally between the parents.[86] This is recognised in the current version of the English Code, which no longer advises that it is exceptional for a child to reside with both parents.[87]

---

[79]   *R v Port Talbot Borough Council ex p McCarthy* (1990) 23 HLR 207, CA.
[80]   See **13.41–13.43**.
[81]   *R v Westminster City Council ex p Bishop* (1997) 29 HLR 546, QBD and see n 65 above.
[82]   *R v Lambeth London Borough Council ex p Vagliviello* (1991) 22 HLR 392, CA.
[83]   *McGrath v Camden LBC* [2007] EWCA Civ 1269, (2008) January *Legal Action*, p 37, CA.
[84]   English Code, para 10.9; Welsh Code, para 14.7.
[85]   Children Act 1989, s 8. As recognised by the House of Lords in *Holmes-Moorhouse v Richmond upon Thames Royal London Borough Council* [2009] UKHL 7, [2009] 1 WLR 413, HL at [7], per Lord Hoffmann.
[86]   See *D v D* [2000] EWCA Civ 3009, [2001] 1 FLR 495, CA.
[87]   English Code, para 10.10. The 2002 Code contained similar advice at para 8.10 (Homelessness Code of Guidance for Local Authorities (England) (Department of Health and Office of the

13.56 The relationship between a residence order made in the family courts and the decision that a local housing authority must take was considered by the House of Lords in *Holmes-Moorhouse v Richmond upon Thames Royal London Borough Council*.[88] In that case, the Court of Appeal had held that once a family court had decided in contested proceedings that residence should be shared, and made an order to that effect, the local housing authority could not deny that the children might reasonably be expected to live with the father (who was applying for homelessness assistance) as well as with their mother. The House of Lords overturned the Court of Appeal's decision. It held that when the local housing authority is deciding whether dependent children might reasonably be expected to reside with a homeless parent, the local housing authority is entitled to take into account the fact that housing is a scarce resource, and to have regard to the social purposes of HA 1996, Part 7, to the claims of other homeless applicants and the scale of the local housing authority's own responsibilities. The question for the local housing authority is whether it is reasonably to be expected, in the context of a scheme for housing the homeless, that children who already had a home with one parent should also be able to reside with their other parent. The existence of a shared residence order is relevant, but not a determinative factor. It added that the paramount consideration for family courts, when deciding issues about the upbringing of a child, is the child's welfare under Children Act 1989. A local housing authority should not intervene in family proceedings to argue against a court making a shared residence order, but the family court should not make a shared residence order unless it appears reasonably likely that both parties will have accommodation in which the children can reside.

Informal arrangements

13.57 Where no court order has been obtained, the local housing authority cannot just refuse to consider the question of a child's residence until the court makes such an order.[89] The local housing authority must consider all the present circumstances of the case. It is looking to see whether the child resides with the applicant; it is not enough that the child visits the applicant. A court order or parental agreement for staying contact does not make the visiting child resident or co-resident with the applicant, because 'staying access does not equal residence'[90] and 'the staying access will not amount to residence with their father'.[91]

Deputy Prime Minister), July 2002) but concluded 'it would only be in very exceptional cases though that a child might be considered to reside with both parents'. This last sentence is omitted from the current guidance at para 10.10 of the English Code. In *Holmes-Moorhouse v Richmond upon Thames Royal London Borough Council* [2009] UKHL 7, [2009] 1 WLR 413, HL at [11], Lord Hoffmann described the paragraph in the 2002 Code as 'muddling in its reasoning' and saying little as to what considerations the local housing authority should take into account.

88   [2009] UKHL 7, [2009] 1 WLR 413, HL.
89   *R v Ealing London Borough Council ex p Sidhu* (1982) 2 HLR 45, QBD.
90   *R v Port Talbot Borough Council ex p McCarthy* (1991) 23 HLR 207, CA at 210, per Butler-Sloss LJ.
91   *R v Port Talbot Borough Council ex p McCarthy* (1991) 23 HLR 207, CA at 211, per Dillon LJ.

13.58 A child need not live full-time with the applicant in order to 'reside' with him or her. The child may divide his or her time between the two parents. However, there should be 'some regularity' to the arrangement.[92] The possibility that the child may be residing with both of his or her separated parents was previously described by the courts as 'unlikely to be the normal arrangement'[93], as 'a remote possibility', or 'a very rare case'.[94] However, the current edition of the English Code reflects a more modern and flexible approach: 'housing authorities should remember that where parents separate, it will often be in the best interests of the child to maintain a relationship with both parents'.[95]

13.59 Local housing authorities which have considered where a child's 'main' residence is, or which parent has a 'greater' responsibility, have been held to be wrong in law.[96] But where a local housing authority applied the correct test ('Does the child reside with the applicant?'), its decision that an applicant's children did not reside with him (even though they spent 3 or 4 nights each week with him) was not wrong in law.[97]

13.60 It is often very difficult to say whether a child is residing with an applicant (as distinct from visiting), and a sensitive home visit by an officer can provide the local housing authority with much useful information. But even when the facts are established, two officers of the same local housing authority (and, indeed, of different local housing authorities) can legitimately reach different conclusions. For example, in one case[98] a visiting officer found the child with the applicant at his flat and the presence of 'many personal effects, toothbrush and paste, clothing and food' belonging to the child. The visiting officer concluded that this (together with assertions by both the separated parents that the child was residing with the applicant) established that the child was therefore living with the applicant. Her recommendation was reversed by her superior, who took a different view of the facts. The case amply demonstrates why, in this context, an initial adverse decision could usefully be subject to the review procedure[99] in almost all cases. If the initial adverse decision is upheld on review, it may be sensible to apply to a different local housing authority with the prospect of receiving a more favourable decision.

---

[92]   English Code, para 10.10; Welsh Code, para 14.7.
[93]   *R v Port Talbot Borough Council ex p McCarthy* (1991) 23 HLR 207, CA at 210, per Butler-Sloss LJ.
[94]   *R v Lambeth London Borough Council ex p Vaglivello* (1990) 22 HLR 392, CA at 397, per Purchas LJ.
[95]   English Code, para 10.10. See also *Holmes-Moorhouse v Richmond upon Thames Royal London Borough Council* [2009] UKHL 7, [2009] 1 WLR 413 HL, at **13.56**.
[96]   *R v Kingswood Borough Council ex p Smith-Morse* [1995] 2 FLR 137, QBD, and *R v Leeds City Council ex p Collier* (1998), (1998) June *Legal Action*, p 14, QBD.
[97]   *R v Oxford City Council ex p Doyle* (1998) 30 HLR 506, QBD.
[98]   *R v Westminster City Council ex p Bishop* (1997) 29 HLR 546, QBD.
[99]   Described at **19.8–19.140**.

Future residence

13.61 If the child is not currently residing with the applicant, the local housing authority should consider whether it is reasonable to expect the child to reside with him or her in the future. It may be that there is a genuine arrangement between the separated parents that the child should reside with the applicant once the applicant has suitable accommodation. Again, this is a question of fact for the local housing authority. Its decision letter should show that it has separately considered the questions:

(1)   Is the child now residing with the applicant?

(2)   If not, is it reasonable to expect the child to reside with the applicant in the future?[100]

Vulnerability[101]

13.62 To meet this category of priority need the relevant person (the applicant or a person with whom the applicant resides or might reasonably be expected to reside) must:

(1)   be currently 'vulnerable'; and

(2)   be vulnerable by reason of one of the prescribed statutory matters.

'Vulnerable'

13.63 The term 'vulnerable' is not defined in HA 1996, Part 7. It has been judicially defined by the Court of Appeal in *R v Camden London Borough Council ex p Pereira*.[102] That definition has been repeatedly followed and applied in later cases, and that definition is reproduced in the current Codes.[103] A person is 'vulnerable' if he or she is less able to fend for himself or herself than an ordinary homeless person and so will suffer injury or detriment in circumstances in which the ordinary homeless person would not.

13.64 In its very earliest form, the judicial definition of 'vulnerable' in 1982 was:

---

[100]   For an illustration of a judicial challenge prompted by the failure to distinguish these two questions see *R v Port Talbot Borough Council ex p McCarthy* (1997) 23 HLR 207, CA. See *Holmes-Moorhouse v Richmond upon Thames Royal London Borough Council* [2009] UKHL 7, [2009] 1 WLR 413, HL, discussed at **13.56**.

[101]   HA 1996, s 189(1)(c).

[102]   *R v Camden London Borough Council ex p Pereira* (1999) 31 HLR 317, CA, reconciling the earlier and somewhat contradictory authorities of *R v Waveney District Council ex p Bowers* [1982] 3 WLR 661, CA; *R v Lambeth London Borough Council ex p Carroll* (1987) 20 HLR 142, QBD; and *R v Westminster City Council ex p Ortiz* (1993) 27 HLR 364, CA.

[103]   English Code, para 10.13; Welsh Code, para 14.11.

'... less able to fend for oneself so that injury or detriment would result when a less vulnerable man would be able to cope without harmful effects.'[104]

13.65 The most recent authoritative guidance from the Court of Appeal is contained in the judgment of Auld LJ in *Osmani v Camden London Borough Council*.[105] In *Osmani*, the judicial meaning of 'vulnerable' was put in this way:

'the test is a single one of a homeless person's less than normal ability to fend for himself such that he will suffer more harm than would an ordinary homeless person – a 'composite' assessment'.[106]

13.66 Other important points from the same judgment are:

(1) The test as formulated by the judiciary is not a statutory formulation but a judicial guide.

(2) The test has to be applied in its broad and immediate statutory context, that context being the priorities between different homeless persons within a scheme of social welfare conferring benefits at public expense to those identified as entitled to priority.

(3) Decisions on identifying those priorities, weighed in the context of local housing authorities' own local burdens and finite resources, are likely to be highly judgmental and it is local housing authorities, not judges, who are best placed to make those decisions.

(4) Local housing authorities should take care to apply the test on the assumption that the applicant has become, or will become, street homeless, not on any ability to fend for him or herself while still housed.

(5) In this respect, regard should be had to the particular debilitating effects of depressive disorders and the fragility of those suffering from them if suddenly deprived of the prop of their own home.

(6) Although local housing authorities should look for, and pay close regard to, medical evidence, it is for the local housing authority to determine whether an applicant is vulnerable.

(7) Reasons should be given for a decision, and those reasons should be sufficient to enable an applicant to form a view on whether to challenge it

---

[104] *R v Waveney District Council ex p Bowers* [1982] 3 WLR 661, CA at 122, per Donaldson MR, Waller and Griffiths LJJ.
[105] [2004] EWCA Civ 1706, [2005] HLR 22, CA at [38], per Auld LJ.
[106] *Osmani v Camden London Borough Council* [2004] EWCA Civ 1706, [2005] HLR 22, CA at [38.6], per Auld LJ.

on a point of law. But decision letters should not be treated as if they were statutes. When looking for reasoning in a letter, it should be read as a whole to get its full sense.[107]

13.67 The previous edition of the English Code suggested that the definition is also met if it is 'likely' that the person would suffer such injury or detriment.[108] But the Court of Appeal has held that there is no element of likelihood in the definition of vulnerability.[109] The current editions of each Code refer to 'would suffer' rather than 'likely to'.[110]

13.68 The material sense in which the person must be less well able to 'fend' for himself or herself is in coping with his or her actual (or threatened) homelessness.[111] It had previously been suggested that being 'able to fend' for himself or herself was a general reference to ability to find or keep accommodation, or to the ability to deal with being homeless.[112] In other words, the relevant 'vulnerability' was thought to be 'vulnerability loosely in housing terms or in the context of housing'[113] and therefore to mean 'vulnerable in the context of a need for housing accommodation'.[114] However, since the decision in the leading 'vulnerability' case of *Pereira* (in which all the earlier judgments were considered and explained or overruled), the test has

---

[107] *Osmani v Camden London Borough Council* [2004] EWCA Civ 1706, [2005] HLR 22, CA at [38.7], per Auld LJ, confirmed in *Bellouti v Wandsworth London Borough Council* [2005] EWCA Civ 602, [2005] HLR 46, CA. See also *Frempomah v Haringey London Borough Council (Shelter Housing Law Update June 2006)*, Edmonton County Court, where the local housing authority had found 'scarcely any homeless people are on the streets'. This was the wrong test, as Haringey had not considered what would happen if the applicant were street homeless. See also *Dostenko v Westminster City Council* [2007] EWCA Civ 1325, (2008) February *Legal Action*, p 40, CA, where the applicant was actually street homeless while his request for a review was being considered. He appealed on the ground that the reviewing officer had not taken into account the effects on him of being street homeless. The appeal was dismissed in part because the reviewing officer had not been told that he was street homeless and permission to bring a second appeal was refused by the Court of Appeal. The Court of Appeal commented that, if there had been a significant deterioration in his ability to cope, he might have been better advised to make a fresh application. See also *Littlejohn v City of Westminster Council* [2007] EWCA Civ 1652, (2008) October *Legal Action*, p 37, CA, where Rix LJ, although dismissing the applicant's application for permission to bring a second appeal, said 'It may be that a proven ability to obtain accommodation will not prevent an applicant from being found to be vulnerable within the statutory guidelines, if his obtaining of accommodation proves to be illusory because of an inability to maintain that accommodation'.

[108] *Homelessness Code of Guidance for Local Authorities (England)* (Department of Health and Office of the Deputy Prime Minister, July 2002), para 8.13.

[109] *Griffin v City of Westminster* [2004] EWCA Civ 108, [2004] HLR 32, CA.

[110] English Code, para 10.13; Welsh Code, para 14.11.

[111] *R v Camden London Borough Council ex p Pereira* (1998) 31 HLR 317, CA at 330, per Hobhouse LJ.

[112] *R v Lambeth London Borough Council ex p Carroll* (1988) 20 HLR 142, QBD.

[113] *R v Bath City Council ex p Sangermano* (1984) 17 HLR 94, QBD at 97, per Hodgson J, followed with approval in *R v Wandsworth London Borough Council ex p Banbury* (1986) 19 HLR 76, QBD at 78, by Russell J and in *R v Reigate and Banstead District Council ex p Di Domenico* (1988) 20 HLR 153, QBD at 154, per Mann J.

[114] *R v Kensington and Chelsea Royal London Borough Council ex p Kihara* (1997) 29 HLR 147, CA at 158, per Neill LJ.

been narrowed in its application by reference to its strict statutory context of homelessness or threatened homelessness:

> 'It must appear that his inability to fend for himself whilst homeless [or threatened with homelessness] will result in injury or detriment to him which would not be suffered by an ordinary homeless person who was able to cope.'[115]

Obviously, that test will be satisfied by a person whose circumstances are such that he or she is not able to obtain housing unaided and is thus unable to deal with homelessness in the ordinary way.[116] There need not be actual injury or detriment. An increase in the risk of injury or other harm is itself a 'detriment'. 'Injury or detriment' can include physical injury, a deterioration of a person's mental condition, or the risk of self-harm.[117]

13.69   The difficult exercise required in applying the *Pereira* test has been summed up by one judge who referred to two important and in part conflicting interests:

> 'One is the need of local housing authorities to husband their resources and to ensure that only those genuinely entitled are treated as in priority need. The other is the catastrophic consequences of a failure to house someone whose vulnerability will make them unable to cope with homelessness – a legal test which itself makes the dubious assumption that homelessness is something fit people can always cope with.'[118]

Making inquiries into whether a person is vulnerable[119]

13.70   Whether a person is 'vulnerable' is a question of fact and degree for the local housing authority to determine. It is not a question that can be delegated to a doctor, nurse, consultant or anyone else.[120]

13.71   A local housing authority will usually need to make inquiries into the applicant's medical condition in order to determine vulnerability. The local

---

115   *R v Camden London Borough Council ex p Pereira* (1998) 31 HLR 317, CA at 330, per Hobhouse LJ. Note that there is no requirement on local housing authorities to identify precisely the attributes of the normal homeless person with whom the applicant is being compared (*Tetteh v Kingston upon Thames Royal London Borough Council* [2004] EWCA 1775, [2005] HLR 21, CA).

116   *R v Camden London Borough Council ex p Pereira* (1998) 31 HLR 317, CA at 330, per Hobhouse LJ.

117   *Griffin v City of Westminster Council* [2004] EWCA Civ 108, CA, [2004] HLR 32, CA; *Gentle v Wandsworth London Borough Council* [2005] EWCA Civ 1377, (2006) January *Legal Action*, p 32, CA; and *Khelassi v Brent London Borough Council* [2006] EWCA Civ 1825, CA.

118   *Shala v Birmingham City Council* [2007] EWCA Civ 624, [2008] HLR 8, CA at [24], per Sedley LJ.

119   See also **10.48–10.58**.

120   *R v Lambeth London Borough Council ex p Walters* (1994) 26 HLR 170, QBD; *Osmani v Camden London Borough Council* [2004] EWCA Civ 1706, [2005] HLR 22, CA; and *Cramp v Hastings Borough Council* [2005] EWCA Civ 1005, [2005] HLR 48, CA.

housing authority should take account of any medical opinion it receives and may seek its own medical adviser's view. Indeed,

'... where the applicant claims to be vulnerable for medical reasons or where on making proper inquiries it is apparent to the authorities that such is his claim, it is both proper and necessary ... to take and consider a medical opinion, unless the applicant's condition renders him so obviously vulnerable that that is not necessary.'[121]

13.72 Very often the medical evidence will be helpful in identifying the physical disability, mental handicap or mental illness, but less useful on whether the applicant satisfies the definition of 'vulnerable'. That is a question for a local housing authority, not a doctor. If a view is expressed by a medical expert, that is merely one consideration which may influence the local housing authority's own conclusion, but it is certainly not bound by it.[122] Likewise, the local housing authority's own medical adviser may express a view on 'vulnerability', but the local housing authority should not merely rubber-stamp that view.[123] Where there is competing medical evidence, the evaluation of it is a matter for the local housing authority.[124]

13.73 In keeping with the general burden on the making of inquiries,[125] it is for the local housing authority to make all necessary inquiries into the person's medical condition, not for the applicant to produce medical evidence. The applicant may, however, be expected to give written consent to the local housing authority's medical advisers to seek medical information or inspect medical records. The local housing authority is under a duty to act fairly in its gathering of, and use of, medical information. That includes a requirement to put adverse medical opinions to the applicant for comment before an initial decision is reached.[126]

13.74 There has been some judicial consideration of the role of medical advisers to local housing authorities. A local housing authority is entitled to obtain its own expert opinion, but care has to be taken not to appear to be using professional medical advisers simply to provide or shore up reasons for a

---

[121] *R v Lambeth London Borough Council ex p Carroll* (1988) 20 HLR 142, QBD at 150, per Webster J.

[122] *Chowdhoury v Newham London Borough Council* [2004] EWCA Civ 8, (2004) March *Legal Action*, p 25, CA; *Cramp v Hastings Borough Council* [2005] EWCA Civ 1005, [2005] HLR 48, CA; and *R (Bauer-Czarnomski) v Ealing London Borough Council* [2010] EWHC Admin 130, Admin Ct.

[123] *R v Wandsworth London Borough Council ex p Banbury* (1987) 19 HLR 76, QBD; and *R v Lambeth London Borough Council ex p Carroll* (1988) 20 HLR 142, QBD.

[124] *Mehmet v Wandsworth London Borough Council* [2004] EWCA Civ 1560, (2005) January *Legal Action*, p 28, CA.

[125] See **10.15–10.19**.

[126] *Yemlahi v Lambeth London Borough Council* (2000) August *Legal Action*, p 26, Wandsworth County Court; and *Thorne v Winchester City Council* (2000), (2000) April *Legal Action*, p 32, CA. There is no requirement that the applicant should always have 'the last word' in respect of medical advice (*Bellouti v Wandsworth London Borough Council* [2005] EWCA Civ 602, [2005] HLR 46, CA).

negative decision.[127] Where there is a conflict between medical opinions, the local housing authority must bear in mind the qualifications of the experts.[128] The local housing authority's medical adviser has the function of enabling the local housing authority to understand the medical issues and to evaluate for itself the expert evidence from the applicant's medical advisers. In the absence of an examination of the patient, the authority's medical adviser's advice cannot itself constitute expert evidence of an applicant's condition. The local housing authority must take any absence of a personal examination of the applicant into account. If a medical adviser has not personally examined the applicant, he or she could consider discussing the applicant's condition with his or her treating doctors.[129]

13.75 It is for the local housing authority to decide what inquiries are necessary and what weight to give to the various pieces of medical evidence.[130] A local housing authority's decision is only susceptible to challenge for failure to make all necessary inquiries if no reasonable local housing authority would have failed to regard certain additional inquiries as necessary.[131] Inquiries by local housing authorities in these 'medical' cases are further considered at **10.48–10.58**.

13.76 Once the local housing authority is satisfied that there is 'vulnerability', the next step is for it to decide on the cause. For there to be priority need, it must decide whether the vulnerability has arisen as a result of one of the specified statutory causes[132] or, in the case of applications to English local housing authorities, one of the additional causes set out in the Priority Need Order.[133] If the relevant person is vulnerable, but the cause of the vulnerability cannot be put into one of the specified categories, the relevant person may still be vulnerable for some 'other special reason'.[134]

---

[127] *Hall v Wandsworth London Borough Council, Carter v Wandsworth London Borough Council* [2004] EWCA Civ 1740, [2005] HLR 23, CA; *Shala v Birmingham City Council* [2007] EWCA Civ 624, [2008] HLR 8, CA.

[128] *R v Newham London Borough Council ex p Lumley* (2001) 33 HLR 11, QBD; *Khelassi v Brent London Borough Council* [2006] EWCA Civ 1825, CA; and *Shala v Birmingham City Council* [2007] EWCA Civ 624, [2008] HLR 8, CA. All of those cases concerned medical evidence from a psychiatrist which had been evaluated by a GP advising the local housing authority.

[129] *Shala v Birmingham City Council* [2007] EWCA Civ 624, [2008] HLR 8, CA at [23], per Sedley LJ. The Court of Appeal made these comments in relation to the use of medical advisers from the organisation, Nowmedical, which is regularly used by local housing authorities. However, the Court of Appeal refused permission to bring a second appeal where the applicant was arguing that advice from Nowmedical should not be relied upon by local housing authorities in any circumstances (*Harper v Oxford City Council* [2007] EWCA Civ 1169, (2008) January *Legal Action*, p 37, CA).

[130] *Wandsworth London Borough Council v Allison* [2008] EWCA Civ 354, (2008) June *Legal Action*, p 33, CA.

[131] *Cramp v Hastings Borough Council* [2005] EWCA Civ 1005, [2005] HLR 48, CA; and see **10.15–10.33**.

[132] HA 1996, s 189(1)(c). See **13.77**.

[133] SI 2002/2051. See **13.77**.

[134] HA 1996, s 189(1)(c). See **13.90–13.99**.

The statutory matters

13.77 A range of potential causes of vulnerability are set out in HA 1996, Part 7, and in the English Priority Need Order,[135] including 'old age', 'physical disability' and many others. But a person does not accrue priority need simply by achieving 'old age' or by reason of having a 'physical disability', etc. Neither being 100 years old nor having lost a limb (or even two) automatically qualifies the relevant person as having priority need. The specified statutory causes are relevant only in that they could give rise to a vulnerability that counts for priority need purposes. The test is not whether an applicant, or a member of his or her household, falls within the ambit of one of these causes, but whether he or she is vulnerable and, if so, whether the vulnerability is the result of one of the specified reasons (or the result of some 'other special reason'). The full list (for both England and Wales) is:

(1) old age;[136]

(2) mental illness;[137]

(3) mental handicap;[138]

(4) physical disability;[139] or

(5) other special reason.[140]

For applications to English local housing authorities only,[141] the list also includes:

(6) having been looked after, accommodated or fostered;[142]

(7) having been in the armed forces;[143]

(8) having been imprisoned;[144] or

(9) having been driven from home by actual or threatened violence.[145]

13.78 The vulnerability need not be *wholly* the result of one of the specified matters listed above. Many vulnerable individuals will have been rendered

---

135 SI 2002/2051.
136 See **13.79–13.80**.
137 See **13.81–13.85**.
138 See **13.81–13.85**.
139 See **13.86–13.89**.
140 See **13.90–13.99**.
141 See **13.106** and **13.144–13.147**.
142 See **13.148–13.152**.
143 See **13.153–13.157**.
144 See **13.158–13.164**.
145 See **13.165–13.171**.

vulnerable by several causes or by a combination of factors. Some causal factors may be in the list, others not. The statutory test is satisfied if at least one of the listed matters contributes to the vulnerability. So, in one case,[146] the court considered that a man who had been reduced to a state of vulnerability by alcoholism would not normally, by that reason alone, have qualified. But he had suffered a severe head injury a year prior to his application and the medical advice was that this had caused 'some persistent disability made worse by his drinking habits'. The court said that whether the brain injury was described as a 'mental handicap' or 'other special reason', it was 'another important factor' in the applicant's current vulnerability and made the 'whole difference' so as to bring him into the priority need category. In another, a man who had an addiction to hard drugs, partly as a result of having spent most of his childhood in care, might be 'vulnerable' as a result of the combination of difficulties he suffered from.[147]

Old age

13.79 'Old age' is not defined in HA 1996, Part 7. The Codes advise that applications concerning people aged over 60 should be 'considered carefully', and that local housing authorities should not assume that people over 60 will be automatically vulnerable nor, conversely, that people younger than 60 are ruled out of vulnerability on the basis of 'old age'. The Codes recommend that each case should be considered on its individual circumstances.[148] Such guidance is of little practical value and local housing authorities are left to determine for themselves whether a person aged 54 or 58 (or whatever age) can be said to be 'old' for these purposes.

13.80 Earlier editions of the Codes had suggested particular ages but this only produced unhelpful rigidity. For example, an early Code suggested that men reaching 65 should be accepted. 'Taken literally this would mean that a healthy man of 64 would not be vulnerable while the same man at 65 would be'.[149] Not surprisingly, therefore, there is no specific guidance offered by the current Codes, nor by any reported cases, as to what constitutes 'old age'.

Mental illness or (mental) handicap

13.81 The statutory term 'mental illness or handicap' plainly includes a wide range of disabilities. Mental illness and mental handicap are, however, two very different things. The reference to 'handicap' in this context embraces what, in somewhat dated language, has been described as 'subnormality or severe subnormality'[150] or, in more modern language, could be described as 'learning disability'.[151] In determining whether there is such illness or handicap

---

[146] *R v Waveney District Council ex p Bowers* [1983] QB 238, CA.
[147] *Crossley v City of Westminster* [2006] EWCA Civ 140, [2006] HLR 26, CA.
[148] English Code, para 10.15; Welsh Code, para 14.12.
[149] *R v Waveney District Council ex p Bowers* [1983] QB 238, CA at 245, per Waller LJ.
[150] *R v Bath City Council ex p Sangermano* (1984) 17 HLR 94, QBD at 101, per Hodgson J.
[151] English Code, para 10.16; Welsh Code, para 14.13.

contributing to current vulnerability, local housing authorities should have regard to any available medical opinion and to any advice available from a social services authority or department. They should consider the nature and extent of the illness or handicap, and the relationship between the illness or handicap and the individual's ability to deal with the obvious difficulties associated with being homeless.

13.82 Those discharged from psychiatric hospitals or from hostels for people with mental health problems are likely to be vulnerable.[152] Although health authorities are supposed to make appropriate pre-discharge arrangements,[153] if the applicant is actually vulnerable, the fact that such arrangements should have been (or could have been) made is irrelevant.

13.83 Local housing authorities should clearly distinguish in the decision letter dealing with this category of priority need between any mental illness and any mental handicap.[154]

13.84 Where there is more than one mental condition, the local housing authority must consider the cumulative impact of the various conditions on the applicant, as well as any physical disability or other conditions that cumulatively might render the applicant vulnerable.[155]

13.85 A wide range of conditions has been explored in the case law as potentially or actually falling within the terms 'mental illness' and 'handicap'. These include:

(1) accidental brain injury;[156]

(2) subnormal intelligence (without any psychiatric disturbance or psychiatric history);[157]

(3) depression;[158]

(4) epilepsy;[159]

---

[152] English Code, paras 10.16–10.17; Welsh Code, paras 14.13–14.14.
[153] English Code, para 10.17; Welsh Code, para 14.14; Mental Health Act 1983, s 117. See **20.49–20.54**.
[154] *R v Bath City Council ex p Sangermano* (1985) 17 HLR 94, QBD.
[155] *Crossley v Westminster City Council* [2006] EWCA Civ 140, [2006] HLR 26, CA.
[156] *R v Waveney District Council ex p Bowers* [1983] QB 238, CA; and *R v Lambeth London Borough Council ex p Carroll* (1988) 20 HLR 142, QBD.
[157] *R v Bath City Council ex p Sangermano* (1985) 17 HLR 94, QBD.
[158] *Griffin v City of Westminster Council* [2004] EWCA Civ 108, [2004] HLR 32 CA; *Chowdhoury v Newham London Borough Council* [2004] EWCA Civ 08, (2004) March *Legal Action*, p 25, CA; *Hall v Wandsworth London Borough Council* [2004] EWCA Civ 1740, [2005] HLR 23, CA; *Osmani v Camden London Borough Council* [2004] EWCA Civ 1706, [2005] HLR 22, CA; and *Shala v Birmingham City Council* [2007] EWCA Civ 624, [2008] HLR 8, CA.
[159] *R v Wandsworth London Borough Council ex p Banbury* (1986) 19 HLR 76, QBD; and *R v Reigate and Banstead District Council ex p Di Domenico* (1988) 20 HLR 153, QBD.

(5)   persecutory delusion disorder and lack of insight;[160]

(6)   severe poly-drug dependence syndrome;[161] and

(7)   post-traumatic stress disorder.[162]

Physical disability

13.86   Physical disabilities that have an adverse impact on an applicant's ability to fend for him or herself when homeless may be readily discernible, but the Codes advise that medical or social services advice should be sought wherever necessary.[163]

13.87   There is no requirement that any particular degree of disability is present, nor that it is of any particular duration. The phrase 'substantial disability' is not part of the statutory rubric.[164] Nor does HA 1996, Part 7 require a significant or permanent disability. The question is simply whether the relevant person is vulnerable wholly or partly by reason of his or her current physical disability.[165]

13.88   Where there is more than one physical disability, the local housing authority must consider the cumulative impact of the various conditions on the applicant, as well as any other conditions, such as mental illness or handicap, that cumulatively might render the applicant vulnerable.[166]

13.89   It is to be noted that HA 1996, Part 7 does not specifically deal with vulnerability arising through physical illness. Plainly a person suffering from, for example, influenza may be rendered 'vulnerable' in the relevant sense. But unless the local housing authority is prepared to accept the fact of physical illness as some 'other special reason',[167] vulnerability caused by it will not

---

[160]   *R v Greenwich London Borough Council ex p Dukic* (1996) 29 HLR 87, QBD.

[161]   *R v Camden London Borough Council ex p Pereira* (1999) 31 HLR 317, CA.

[162]   *Shala v Birmingham City Council* [2007] EWCA Civ 624, [2008] HLR 8, CA; and *Sesay v Islington London Borough Council*(2009) September *Legal Action*, p 25, Clerkenwell & Shoreditch County Court.

[163]   English Code, paras 10.16 and 10.18; Welsh Code, para 14.15.

[164]   *R v Lambeth London Borough Council ex p Carroll* (1988) 20 HLR 142, QBD at 145, per Webster J.

[165]   In *Wandsworth London Borough Council v Brown* [2005] EWCA Civ 907, the Court of Appeal refused permission to appeal against a first-instance judge's order varying the local housing authority's decision from one of no priority need to a decision that the applicant had a priority need. The applicant suffered from 'extreme sciatica, back pain, asthma, severe psoriasis and dermatitis and narcolepsy' and an 'extreme combination of a variety of very different ailments', which made the case unusual and one in which there could be only one conclusion – that he was vulnerable.

[166]   *Crossley v Westminster City Council* [2006] EWCA Civ 140, [2006] HLR 26, CA.

[167]   See **13.90–13.99**.

attract a finding of 'priority need'. On the other hand (as the Codes recognise), there will be circumstances in which acute long-term illness itself amounts to disability.[168]

Other special reason

13.90 If a person is vulnerable, but not by reason of any of the factors specified in HA 1996, Part 7, or the Priority Need Order, the question is whether he or she is vulnerable by reason of some 'other special reason' or reasons.[169] This term is not defined in HA 1996, Part 7, or in the Codes. It is a free-standing category, and is not limited to physical or mental factors.

13.91 In *R v Kensington and Chelsea Royal London Borough Council ex p Kihara*,[170] the Court of Appeal held that 'special' means that the difficulties faced must be of an unusual degree of gravity. Asylum-seekers who were homeless, had no right to receive welfare benefits, had no income or capital, no family or friends, no opportunity to work and, in some cases, spoke no English were plainly in priority need for some 'other special reason'.[171]

13.92 There are no set or pre-determined groups of people who would fall within this category. Local housing authorities should keep an open mind, and consider the whole of an applicant's circumstances.[172]

13.93 Whilst reminding local housing authorities of the need to consider the relevant individual's circumstances, the Codes do give a number of examples of people whose circumstances might amount to their being vulnerable for an 'other special reason'. A number of cases have also come before the courts.

13.94 Groups of people who may be vulnerable due to an 'other special reason' can include those who are chronically sick, including people with HIV/AIDS-related illnesses. Local housing authorities should take into account not only physical symptoms, but also common social attitudes towards some of these illnesses.[173]

13.95 Young people who do not fall within any other category of priority need may also be vulnerable, and local housing authorities should consider the degree of support available to a young person, along with the cost and practicalities of finding and maintaining a home for the first time. Young people who were forced to leave the parental home, or who left it because of

---

[168] English Code, para 10.18; Welsh Code, para 14.15 (referring to 'chronic illness').

[169] HA 1996, s 189(1)(c).

[170] (1997) 29 HLR 147, CA.

[171] Since 3 April 2000, most asylum seekers who are destitute are not eligible for homelessness assistance (see further **12.75–12.86** and **12.88–12.89** for eligible asylum-seekers) and receive support and accommodation from the Home Office.

[172] English Code, paras 10.30–10.35; Welsh Code, paras 14.16–14.24.

[173] English Code, para 10.32; Welsh Code, para 14.18.

violence or sexual abuse, are particularly likely to be vulnerable.[174] In Wales, former care-leavers aged 21 or over who are vulnerable might fall within this category.[175] In England, former care-leavers who are vulnerable as a result of having been looked after, accommodated or fostered have a priority need under the Priority Need Order.[176]

13.96 People who flee their homes as a result of harassment that falls short of actual violence or threats of violence may be vulnerable for an 'other special reason'. Witnesses who may be at risk of intimidation could also fall within this category.[177]

13.97 Former asylum-seekers may fall within this category if they are vulnerable. Their experience of persecution in their country of origin and/or severe hardship in reaching the UK would be relevant, and local housing authorities should be sensitive to the fact that former asylum-seekers may be reluctant to discuss some of their experiences.[178]

13.98 In Wales, local housing authorities are advised to consider whether rough sleepers may be vulnerable as a result of multiple needs, including mental health or substance misuse problems.[179]

13.99 Drug or alcohol addiction and the risk of relapsing could fall within this category if the relevant person is vulnerable as a result of it.[180] In *R v Waveney District Council ex p Bowers*,[181] the Court of Appeal held that self-induced alcoholism would not normally result in a finding of 'vulnerability'. This was described as a 'grey area' in *Crossley v City of Westminster*.[182] Giving the judgment of the court, Sedley LJ said: 'drug addiction by itself, for all its personal and social consequences, cannot amount

---

174 English Code, para 10.33; Welsh Code, para 14.19. See also the Scottish cases of *Kelly v Monklands District Council 1985 SLT 165, OH*; and *Wilson v Nithsdale District Council 1992 SLT 1131, OH*.

175 Welsh Code, para 14.29.

176 SI 2002/2051, art 5(1). See **13.148–13.152**.

177 English Code, para 10.34; Welsh Code, para 14.22. The Welsh Code also refers to people fleeing their homes as a result of violence that is not domestic violence; they would need to be vulnerable for an 'other special reason' in order to have a priority need.

178 English Code, para 10.35. See *Al-Oumian v Brent London Borough Council*(1999) June *Legal Action*, p 24, Willesden County Court; *Al-Kabi v Southwark London Borough Council* (2008) March *Legal Action*, p 21, Lambeth County Court; and *Sesay v Islington London Borough Council* (2008) September *Legal Action*, p 25, Clerkenwell & Shoreditch County Court. In *Shala v Birmingham City Council* [2007] EWCA Civ 624, [2008] HLR 8, CA the applicant suffered from depression and post-traumatic stress disorder as a result of her experiences as an Albanian Kosovan in the 1990s.

179 Welsh Code, paras 14.23–14.24.

180 *R v Camden London Borough Council ex p Pereira* (1999) 31 HLR 317, CA; *R v Westminster City Council ex p Ortiz* (1993) 27 HLR 364, CA; *Hoolaghan v Motherwell District Council 1997 CLY 6114, OH*; *Tetteh v Kingston Royal London Borough Council* [2004] EWCA Civ 1775, [2005] HLR 21, CA; and *Ryde v Enfield London Borough Council* [2005] EWCA Civ 1281, (2005) January *Legal Action*, p 32, CA.

181 [1983] QB 238, CA.

182 [2006] EWCA Civ 140, [2006] HLR 26, CA.

to a special reason for vulnerability which is capable of being addressed by housing'.[183] The local housing authority should, however, consider whether there are other factors, including the possibility of relapse into drug addiction if the applicant is on the streets, particular harm suffered as a result of the addiction, or the lack of family support available, which would render the applicant 'vulnerable' for an 'other special reason'. In *Crossley*, the applicant's combination of problems – he had spent his childhood from the age of 3 in care, he had developed his addiction to heroin at the age of 13, he had been sleeping rough from the age of 17, with short spells in hostels and in prison, he was chronically depressed and suffered from asthma and hepatitis C – were described as 'stark facts' pointing to a decision that he was vulnerable.[184]

Homeless 'as a result of an emergency'[185]

13.100 Any applicant (the only relevant person under this category) will have a priority need if currently homeless (or threatened with homelessness) as a 'result of an emergency such as a flood, fire or other disaster'.[186]

There are therefore two questions for the local housing authority:

(1) Is the applicant's present or threatened homelessness 'as a result of' an emergency?

(2) If so, was the emergency a 'flood, fire or other disaster'?

Cause and effect

13.101 The 'emergency' must cause the actual or prospective loss of accommodation and therefore the current or threatened homelessness.[187] The category is intended to deal with sudden emergencies rather than the loss of accommodation that has been anticipated for some time.[188] If the person is already 'homeless', in the technical sense used in HA 1996, Part 7,[189] before the emergency occurs, then the homelessness did not result from the emergency. For example, in one case, a caravan-dweller suddenly lost his caravan. But the

---

183 [2006] EWCA Civ 140, [2006] HLR 26 at [30].

184 Another case involving multiple problems, including drug misuse, was *Payne v Kingston upon Thames Royal London Borough Council* (2008) March *Legal Action*, p 21, Central London Civil Justice Centre, where a decision that a single woman, who had been a victim of abuse and domestic violence, and had a history of mental health problems and of drug misuse, was not vulnerable was quashed

185 HA 1996, s 189(1)(d).

186 English Code, para 10.42; Welsh Code, para 14.25.

187 In *Sadiq v Hackney London Borough Council* [2007] EWCA Civ 1507, (2008) April *Legal Action*, p 34, CA, a local housing authority's decision that the applicant had become homeless as a result of the withdrawal of accommodation provided to him as an asylum-seeker, rather than as a result of his losing his home in Darfur, was not wrong in law. He was not therefore homeless as a result of an emergency.

188 *R v Walsall Metropolitan Borough Council ex p Price* [1996] CLY 3068, QBD; and *R v Camden London Borough Council ex p Wait* (1986) 18 HLR 434, QBD.

189 See **11.2–11.117**.

caravan had been on a site where he had not had permission to station it or occupy it. So he had been homeless when the loss of the caravan occurred. Whilst the sudden loss of his home was 'an emergency', it did not cause his homelessness.[190]

13.102 On the other hand, if a person loses his or her home as the result of an emergency, it is irrelevant (to the question of priority need) that he or she might have been made homeless anyway at a later date.[191] So, a person who is in no other sense in 'priority need' will be within this category if made homeless by an emergency (such as a fire) even if that occurs just before an imminent eviction from his or her accommodation for massive rent or mortgage arrears.

What type of emergency?

13.103 The emergency must have some physical nature, such as a flood, fire or some similar event. But the flood or fire or other disaster need not have been naturally caused. The person made homeless by flooding from a burst communal water tank is as much in priority need as the person made homeless by reason of sea or river flooding. The person made homeless by an arsonist or by a fire caused by faulty electric wiring is as much in priority need as the victim made homeless by a forest fire or lightning strike. Homelessness caused by a sudden gas leak or explosion is likewise the result of an emergency. A person whose mobile home is stolen from its lawful pitch, site or mooring is also within this provision.[192]

13.104 On the other hand, homelessness resulting from the enforcement of a demolition order is not the result of an emergency.[193] Likewise, an unlawful eviction (where the locks were changed and the applicant's belongings placed outside) did not constitute some 'other disaster' falling within the term 'emergency'.[194]

13.105 The volcanic eruptions in Montserrat are an obvious example of an 'emergency' that falls within this subsection, and people fleeing from the eruption which caused the loss of their home will have a priority need.[195] Where a person resides in any building which has been made subject to an order of the magistrates court under the GLC (General Powers) Act 1984, s 37 (Removal of occupants of dangerous buildings in outer London) or s 38 (Removal of occupants of buildings in vicinity of dangerous structures, etc), he or she is deemed to have a priority need by virtue of an emergency.[196]

---

190 *Higgs v Brighton and Hove City Council* [2003] EWCA Civ 895, [2004] HLR 2, CA.
191 *R v Camden London Borough Council ex p Wait* (1986) 18 HLR 434, QBD.
192 *Higgs v Brighton and Hove City Council* [2003] EWCA Civ 895, [2004] HLR 2, CA.
193 *Noble v South Herefordshire District Council* (1985) 17 HLR 80, CA.
194 *R v Bristol City Council ex p Bradic* (1995) 27 HLR 584, CA.
195 *Telesford v Ealing London Borough Council* (2000) August *Legal Action*, p 26, Brentford County Court. English Code, para 10.42; Welsh Code, para 14.25.
196 GLC (General Powers) Act 1984, s 39.

ADDITIONAL CATEGORIES IN ENGLAND: THE PRIORITY NEED ORDER

13.106   The Homelessness (Priority Need for Accommodation) (England) Order 2002[197] came into force on 31 July 2002. It applies to all decisions, or review decisions, made on or after 31 July 2002 by English local housing authorities, irrespective of when the initial homelessness application was made. Under the Order, there are six extra categories of people who have a priority need in addition to the four categories set out in HA 1996, Part 7 itself.[198] These additional categories only operate to confer priority need on the applicant personally.

People aged 16 or 17[199]

13.107   Young people, who are aged 16 or 17, have a priority need simply by virtue of their age.[200] There is no additional requirement that they be 'vulnerable' or fall into any of the other priority need categories of HA 1996, Part 7, or the Order. There are only two exceptions specified in the Order:

(1)   'relevant' children; or

(2)   children who ought to be being accommodated by a social services authority which owes them duties under the Children Act 1989, s 20.

13.108   In dealing with a homelessness application from such a young person, local housing authorities should consider whether the applicant:

(a)   is aged 16 or 17; and then

(b)   whether she or he:
   (i)   falls within the definition of 'a relevant child'; or
   (ii)   is owed a duty pursuant to the Children Act 1989, s 20.

Age

13.109   In most cases, the child's age is unlikely to be in any doubt. If there is doubt, a local housing authority will have to make its own decision on the child's age, relying on the applicant's appearance, family and educational background and any ethnic or cultural considerations.[201]

---

[197]   SI 2002/2051. See Appendix 2.
[198]   SI 2002/2051, arts 3–6.
[199]   SI 2002/2051, art 3.
[200]   English Code, paras 10.36–10.39 and chapter 12.
[201]   *R (B) v Merton London Borough Council* [2003] EWHC 1689 (Admin), [2003] 4 All ER 295. In the context of the provision of accommodation under Children Act 1989, s 20, the Supreme Court has held that if a child disagrees with a social services' authority's assessment of his or her age, the child can bring judicial review proceedings and, unlike most claims in judicial review, ask the court to review the evidence available and make its own decision as to what age

13.110 The local housing authority must decide whether the child is 16 or 17 at the date of its initial decision or review decision, rather than at the date of application.

13.111 What should happen when a 17-year-old, approaching his or her eighteenth birthday, makes an application for homelessness assistance? The Local Government Ombudsman has found maladministration where local housing authorities have refused to help 17-year-olds who were attempting to make applications for homelessness assistance.[202]

13.112 The Court of Appeal considered these circumstances in *Robinson v Hammersmith & Fulham London Borough Council*.[203]

13.113 First, the making of the decisions on the application for homelessness assistance should not be postponed. The local housing authority's duty is to make its inquiries 'as quickly as possible'.[204] The issue of the applicant's priority need is a very straightforward question of fact, which would not normally take much time to determine. The Court of Appeal said:

> 'in the case of a 17-year-old child, it would not ... be lawful for a local authority to postpone the taking of a decision even for a short period on the basis that by postponing that decision the child will have reached the age of 18 before the decision is taken.'[205]

13.114 Second, a local housing authority cannot find that a young person approaching his or her eighteenth birthday does not have a priority need because he or she is 'so nearly 18 that the difference between 18 and 17 should be ignored'.[206] If, at the date of the decision, the young person is, as a matter of fact, 17 (even if the following day is his or her eighteenth birthday), he or she has a priority need.

---

he or she is (*R (A) v Croydon London Borough Council, R (M) v Lambeth London Borough Council* [2009] UKSC 8, [2009] 1 WLR 2557, SC). It remains to be seen how this decision might fit into the review and appeal provisions of HA 1996, Part 7 (see Chapter 19).

[202] For one example see Local Government Ombudsman Investigation No 04/C/18995 (South Tyneside Council), where £2,000 compensation was recommended after the local housing authority failed to give a 17-year-old a homeless application form to complete or provide him with any interim accommodation. He returned after 2 months, by which time he had turned 18 and no longer had a priority need.

[203] [2006] EWCA Civ 1122, [2007] HLR 7, CA.

[204] English Code, para 6.16; Welsh Code, para 12.22.

[205] *Robinson v Hammersmith & Fulham London Borough Council* [2006] EWCA Civ 1122, [2007] HLR 7, CA at [38], per Waller LJ. See also *R (MM) v Lewisham London Borough Council* [2009] EWHC 416 (Admin), (2009) April *Legal Action*, p 23, Admin Ct, where the local housing authority simply failed to make a decision on an application from a 17-year-old for over 4 months. The Administrative Court judge said, 'I would urge the defendant to take action to ensure that ... steps are taken to ensure that the imminence of a child attaining 18 years is not taken as a basis for failing to take action and ... there is due and proper contact between its housing authority and its social services authority'.

[206] *Robinson v Hammersmith & Fulham London Borough Council* [2006] EWCA Civ 1122, [2007] HLR 7, CA at [29], per Waller LJ.

13.115 Third, where the young person requests a review of any negative decision, but turns 18 before the review is concluded, it is not lawful for the local housing authority simply to state that, at the date of the review decision, the young person does not have a priority need:

> 'if the original decision was unlawful ... the review decision should have so held and made a decision that would have restored to the appellant the rights she would have had if the decision had been lawful.'[207]

13.116 It may be that the local housing authority has a genuinely difficult issue to make inquiries into, for example: whether or not the young person is homeless from his or her parents' accommodation, or whether, in fact, the family home is still available to the young person and reasonable for him or her to continue to occupy.[208] The English Code recommends that local housing authorities consider the possibility of collusion (in order to obtain homelessness assistance) between the parents and child,[209] and that they should also explore the possibility of mediation and/or reconciliation. Pursuing those avenues might delay the decision on an application until after the young person's eighteenth birthday. The Court of Appeal has held that a local housing authority is entitled:

> 'to have time to check the genuineness of the decision to exclude the child, and indeed the reasons given by the child for being excluded, for example where there may have been collusion.'[210]

However:

> 'if an authority are of the view that a child genuinely has no place to go unless a mediation can sort matters out, and a mediation cannot take place without depriving the child of a right it would otherwise have had, then in my view the authority has to take the view that its full duty must be performed, and use mediation in order to fulfil that duty.'[211]

13.117 As the last extract makes clear, if the local housing authority accepts that a main housing duty is owed to the 17-year-old, it can still use its mediation service to attempt to persuade the parent to welcome the child back, and, if successful, it will have performed the main housing duty by ensuring that the accommodation is provided at the parental home.[212]

---

[207] *Robinson v Hammersmith & Fulham London Borough Council* [2006] EWCA Civ 1122, [2007] HLR 7, CA at [32], per Waller LJ.

[208] See **11.2–11.71** and **11.72–11.117**.

[209] English Code, paras 8.12 and 12.10–12.11.

[210] *Robinson v Hammersmith & Fulham London Borough Council* [2006] EWCA Civ 1122, [2007] HLR 7, CA at [39], per Waller LJ.

[211] *Robinson v Hammersmith & Fulham London Borough Council* [2006] EWCA Civ 1122, [2007] HLR 7, CA at [41], per Waller LJ.

[212] HA 1996, s 206(1)(b) or (c); see **17.12**.

The exceptions

13.118 Both of the exceptions to this category are designed to ensure that young people to whom social services have owed duties in the past, or do owe a present duty to accommodate by virtue of Children Act 1989, s 20, should be the responsibility of social services. This is because young people in those circumstances are likely to have needs over and above the simple need for a roof over their heads, and those needs are best met by social services.[213]

Relevant child

13.119 'A relevant child' is defined by the Children Act 1989, s 23A(2) as any child, aged 16 or 17, who was formerly being looked after by any local authority for a prescribed period of time while of a prescribed age, but who is no longer being looked after.[214] This exception, as described in the English Code,[215] is satisfied only if:

(1)   the child is 16 or 17; and

(2)   the child was 'looked after'[216] by a social services authority:
    (a)   for at least 13 weeks,
    (b)   after the age of 14; and

(3)   has been looked after while he or she was 16 or 17; and

(4)   is no longer being looked after.

13.120 As the Code itself foreshadows,[217] each of these elements is subject to close technical definition in the Children Act 1989 (as amended) and in the Children (Leaving Care) (England) Regulations 2001.[218] If the terms of the exception appear to be satisfied, the local housing authority should obviously refer to the precise terms of the Children Act 1989 and the Regulations to confirm the actual position. Although the Code recommends that any uncertainty as to whether this exception applies should lead to social services being contacted,[219] the decision as to whether the child meets the technical definition of 'relevant child' is for the local housing authority to make and not for social services to decide.

---

213   *R (M) v Hammersmith & Fulham London Borough Council* [2008] UKHL 14, [2008] 1 WLR 535, HL at [31] per Baroness Hale. See also *R (G) v Southwark London Borough Council* [2009] UKHL 26, [2009] 1 WLR 2399, HL.

214   Children Act 1989, Sch 2, para 19B; Children (Leaving Care) (England) Regulations 2001, SI 2001/2874.

215   English Code, paras 10.37–10.39.

216   See **13.138**.

217   English Code, para 10.37.

218   SI 2001/2874.

219   English Code, para 10.39.

Children owed duties under the Children Act 1989, section 20

13.121 A 16- or 17-year-old does not have automatic priority need if she or he is a person to whom a social services authority 'owe a duty to provide accommodation' under the Children Act 1989, s 20.[220] Note that the exception only applies if the duty 'is' owed (that is currently owed). That the duty was owed in the past or might be owed in the future is irrelevant. A social services authority is not obliged to notify a decision that it owes a young person the duty under Children Act 1989, s 20 in writing, so there is unlikely to be a convenient short-cut for inquiries by simply requesting sight of such a document.

13.122 Children owed duties under the Children Act 1989, s 20 are those children who appear to the social services authority to require accommodation either:

(1) because they are 16 or over and their welfare is otherwise likely to be seriously prejudiced; or

(2) because they have no parents or other people who are able to provide accommodation for them.

13.123 Where a child has been provided with accommodation by social services, there may be some doubt as to whether that accommodation was provided under the duty at Children Act 1989, s 20, or the power at Children Act 1989, s 17.[221] The courts have held that where accommodation has been provided as a result of a young person falling within the test at Children Act, s 20, the local authority cannot side-step its responsibility by recording or arguing that it was in fact acting under the Children Act 1989, s 17 power or some other legislation.[222] Equally, the social services authority cannot side-step its responsibility by telling a child aged 16 or 17 who falls within the criteria at s 20 of the Children Act 1989 to make an application for homelessness assistance.[223]

Social services' duties towards relevant children and 'looked after' children

13.124 The thrust of the amendments made to the Children Act 1989 by the Children (Leaving Care) Act 2000 is that social services authorities should be

---

[220] SI 2001/2051, art 3(2).

[221] See **20.55–20.72** for Children Act 1989, s 17; and **20.73–20.78** for Children Act 1989, s 20.

[222] *Southwark London Borough Council v D* [2007] EWCA Civ 182, (2007) 10 CCLR 280, CA; *R (H) v Wandsworth London Borough Council, R (Barhanu) v Hackney London Borough Council, R (B) v Islington London Borough Council* [2007] EWHC 1082 (Admin), (2007) 10 CCLR 441; and *R (L) v Nottinghamshire County Council* [2007] EWHC 2364 (Admin).

[223] *R (G) v Southwark London Borough Council* [2009] UKHL 26, [2009] 1 WLR 2399, HL; and *R (MM) v Lewisham London Borough Council* [2009] EWHC 416 (Admin), (2009) April *Legal Action*, p 23, Admin Ct.

responsible for meeting the accommodation and other needs of young people who have been in, but are no longer in, the care system (at least until they reach 18), or who have been 'looked after' under Children Act 1989, s 20. To accord such 16- and 17-year-olds priority need would shift the responsibility for accommodating young people on to local housing authorities when social services should be arranging accommodation.[224]

13.125 Where a child is a relevant child, or is accommodated under Children Act 1989, s 20, he or she then becomes a 'looked after' child. The social services authority is then responsible for safeguarding and promoting the child's welfare, including his or her educational achievement,[225] and for maintaining the child in other respects apart from providing accommodation.[226] In addition, if the 'looked after' 16- or 17-year-old has been looked after by the social services authority for a total of 13 weeks or more at any time since the age of 14, he or she is entitled to services under the Children (Leaving Care) Act 2000. Those services include an assessment of the child's future needs, preparation of a detailed pathway plan for him or her, and a personal adviser.[227] The services continue until the child is 21, or has completed his or her education or training.[228] It is precisely because of these obligations of social services towards 16- and 17-year-olds that the exceptions to this priority need category have been made.

Joint working between housing and social services

13.126 In cases of uncertainty, the Code recommends that social services be contacted to help ascertain whether the applicant is a relevant child or a child owed a Children Act 1989, s 20 duty.[229] The House of Lords has taken a stronger view and held that, when a 16- or 17-year-old presents himself or herself to the housing department as homeless, the housing department must make a referral to the social services department as part of its ongoing inquiries into whether or not the young person has a priority need, or is a relevant child or is owed a Children Act 1989, s 20 duty. The social services department should then carry out its own assessment in accordance with its responsibilities under the Children Act 1989.[230] It is precisely because 'relevant children' and children entitled to a Children Act 1989, s 20 duty have needs over and above the simple need for a roof over their heads that the Priority Need Order clearly contemplates that social services should take the long term responsibility.[231]

---

224 *R (G) v Southwark London Borough Council* [2009] UKHL 26, [2009] 1 WLR 2399, HL.
225 Children Act 1989, s 22(3) and (3A).
226 Children Act 1989, s 23(1)(b).
227 Children Act 1989, s 23B.
228 Children Act 1989, s 23C(7).
229 English Code, para 10.39.
230 *R (M) v Hammersmith & Fulham London Borough Council* [2008] UKHL 14, [2008] 1 WLR 535, HL at [29], per Baroness Hale. See **20.73–20.78** for social services' responsibilities.
231 *R (M) v Hammersmith & Fulham London Borough Council* [2008] UKHL 14, [2008] 1 WLR 535, HL at [31], per Baroness Hale. See also *R (G) v Southwark London Borough Council* [2009] UKHL 26, [2009] 1 WLR 2399, HL.

13.127 Government guidance emphasises the need for a joint approach, underpinned by a joint protocol, to prevent 16- and 17-year-olds in crisis from being passed between housing and social services departments unnecessarily.[232] There is no statutory mechanism available to resolve such disagreements between different local authorities, or between different departments of a unitary authority. In the first instance, the local housing authority will need to provide accommodation pending its own decision (because the young person 'may' have priority need).[233] This is important to ensure that the young person is not 'passed from pillar to post'.[234] If it reaches a decision that the young person is owed a Children Act 1989, s 20 duty and that decision is disputed on review (or appeal) by the applicant, perhaps with social services support, the case for the exercise of the discretionary power to accommodate pending review (or appeal) would seem compelling.[235]

13.128 A 16- or 17-year old applicant who falls within (or is likely to fall within) either of these exceptions may consider directing an application (or a further application) to a local housing authority in Wales.[236] As indicated,[237] there is no parallel to either of these exceptions to priority need status for a 16- or 17-year-old in the Welsh Order.[238] He or she will automatically be found to have a priority need by a Welsh local housing authority.

13.129 Even if a homeless 16- or 17-year-old is the responsibility of social services, the local housing authority's duty does not simply end as a result of the acceptance of the referral. If the local housing authority's inquiries have reached the stage of considering 'priority need', that process must be formally completed. A local housing authority must therefore go on to consider whether the applicant may have a priority need under one of the other categories of priority need (pregnancy, vulnerability, etc). The process must always conclude with a reasoned written decision.[239]

13.130 Local housing authorities are advised to work with social services authorities in dealing with applications from 16- and 17-year-olds and to conduct joint assessments of children falling within this category.[240] However,

---

[232] *Joint Working between Housing and Children's Services: Preventing homelessness and tackling its effects on children and young people* (Communities and Local Government, Department for Children, School and Families, May 2008) at http://www.communities.gov.uk/publications/housing/goodpracticeguide.

[233] HA 1996, s 188(1). English Code, para 10.39. *R (M) v Hammersmith & Fulham London Borough Council* [2008] UKHL 14, [2008] 1 WLR 535, HL at [15], per Baroness Hale. See **16.11–16.24.**

[234] *R (M) v Hammersmith & Fulham London Borough Council* [2008] UKHL 14, [2008] 1 WLR 535, HL at [31], per Baroness Hale.

[235] HA 1996, s 188(3) and s 204(4). See **16.25–16.36** for accommodation pending review and **16.37–16.42** for accommodation pending appeal.

[236] If he or she prefers to be accommodated pursuant to a homelessness duty rather than a social services duty.

[237] See **13.175.**

[238] SI 2001/607.

[239] HA 1996, s 184(3).

[240] English Code, para 10.39.

it is always ultimately for the local housing authority to decide for itself whether the applicant does or does not have 'priority need' under this part of the Order and/or under any one of the four categories in HA 1996.

Responsibilities to 16- and 17-year-old applicants

13.131 The fact that most 16- and 17-year-olds now have priority need (without having to show any vulnerability) has led to concerns that local housing authorities will have an additional burden in accommodating such people when they are teenagers and then in the longer term. But, as the Code rightly indicates, there are at least three reasons why that burden should not be as great as feared.[241]

13.132 First, even if the young applicant is homeless and in priority need, she or he may have become homeless intentionally.[242] The Code reminds local housing authorities to be alive to the specific possibility of 'collusion' when dealing with young applicants aged 16 or 17 who may have been party to arrangements with their parents under which they were excluded from the parental home.[243]

13.133 Secondly, there is always the possibility of discharging any duty owed to the applicant by securing accommodation provided by another 'person' instead of by the local housing authority itself.[244] That 'other person' might be a parent, relative or friend. The Code encourages local housing authorities specifically to consider reconciliation with those who have previously provided the teenager with accommodation and to draw on the help of social services.[245] This should not be taken as a recommendation that a decision on the application might be deferred and the duty to provide interim accommodation[246] extended while these possibilities are explored. The local housing authority is really considering at this stage *how* its duty will be performed. It should have already notified the applicant of its decision on what duty is owed, and should have replaced the interim accommodation with accommodation provided under the main housing duty (if applicable).[247]

---

[241] English Code, paras 12.7–12.11.
[242] See Chapter 14. See *Denton v Southwark London Borough Council* [2007] EWCA Civ 623, [2008] HLR 11, CA, which concerned a homeless 21-year-old who had been excluded by his mother, and *White v Southwark London Borough Council* [2008] EWCA Civ 792, (2008) October *Legal Action*, p 37, CA, where the court held that children as young as 13 might be considered to have acted deliberately and thus made themselves intentionally homeless. See **14.20–14.145**.
[243] English Code, paras 12.10–12.11.
[244] HA 1996, s 206(1)(b). See **17.12**.
[245] English Code, paras 12.8–12.9.
[246] HA 1996, s 188(1). See **10.60–10.64** and **16.11–16.24**.
[247] See *Robinson v Hammersmith & Fulham London Borough Council* [2006] EWCA Civ 1122, [2007] HLR 7, CA.

13.134 Thirdly, many homeless 16- and 17-year-olds are likely to have needs over and above the simple need for a roof over their heads, and thus fall within the responsibility of social services pursuant to s 20 of the Children Act 1989.[248]

13.135 Recognising the particular vulnerability of young people falling within this category, the Code advises that bed and breakfast is unlikely to be suitable for them.[249] Recent non-statutory government guidance has gone further and advises:

> 'no 16 or 17 year old should be placed in Bed and Breakfast (B&B) accommodation by Housing Services or Children's Services, except in an emergency, where B&B accommodation is the only available alternative to rooflessness.'[250]

A broader view of the category

13.136 Although the provision in the English Priority Need Order only confers priority need on an applicant who is 16 or 17, the benefits are not restricted to single people. A young childless and homeless couple will find themselves owed the main housing duty if the application is made by one of them who is 16 or 17 years old (provided that the applicant is not found to have become homeless intentionally). So, for example, an 18-year-old living at home with his parents and wishing to establish a home with a 16-year-old partner who has been turned out by her parents can, on his partner's application as homeless, expect that they will be accommodated together.[251] Furthermore, a working teenager aged 16 or 17 living as part of a household made homeless can secure the benefits of the main housing duty for the whole family by making the application in his or her name.[252] The head of the household in the latter example could not achieve the same result, where the teenager is the only child at home, because the teenager is not 'dependent'.

---

[248] *R (M) v Hammersmith & Fulham London Borough Council* [2008] UKHL 14, [2008] 1 WLR 535, HL, at [31], per Baroness Hale. For one example, see *LGO Complaint against Waltham Forest London Borough Council* 08 016 986, 21 October 2009, at (2010) February *Legal Action*, p 34.

[249] English Code, para 12.14

[250] *Joint Working between Housing and Children's Services: Preventing homelessness and tackling its effects on children and young people* (Communities and Local Government, Department for Children, School and Families, May 2008) at http://www.communities.gov.uk/publications/housing/goodpracticeguide, chapter 3.

[251] Had these provisions been in force, the wife in *Kaya v Haringey London Borough Council* [2001] EWCA Civ 677, [2002] HLR 1, CA, could have made a homeless application herself and would have been in priority need, thereby securing accommodation for herself and her husband.

[252] As happened in *R (Ogbeni) v Tower Hamlets London Borough Council* [2008] EWHC 2444 (Admin), (2008) *Legal Action* October, p 37, Admin Ct, where a 17-year-old applicant had a priority need and normally resided with his aunt, who was a member of his family. Accommodation had to be provided for both the applicant and his aunt.

Young people under 21[253]

13.137 Despite the apparent breadth of this category, the detail indicates that only a very small number of applicants have priority need by virtue of this provision.[254] Under it, an applicant now aged 18, 19 or 20 who was 'looked after, accommodated or fostered' at any time between the ages of 16 and 18 will have a priority need unless he or she is 'a relevant student'. In non-technical language, the criteria are likely to be fulfilled by recent care leavers who are not yet 21. If the applicant falls within this priority need category, he or she does not also need to be 'vulnerable' or fall into any other category.

13.138 The term 'looked after, accommodated or fostered'[255] takes its meaning from the Children Act 1989, s 24(2), which itself has been completely substituted by the Children (Leaving Care) Act 2000. The current definition is accurately set out in the English Code.[256] Recent case law has provided some additional guidance on the 'looked after' element in that definition.[257]

13.139 As long as the applicant was 'looked after, accommodated or fostered' at some stage when he or she was 16, 17 or 18 years old, the criteria will be met. No minimum period of time during which he or she was 'looked after, accommodated or fostered' is prescribed.

13.140 These former care leavers will be owed by social services the Children (Leaving Care) Act 2000 duties of support, a pathway plan, and a personal adviser.[258] Again, government guidance emphasises joint working between the housing and social services department, and a continuing need for support.[259]

The exception to this category

13.141 The exception[260] applies where the applicant is a 'relevant student'.[261] That term is only met by a person:

(a)   who is a care leaver; and

(b)   to whom s 24B(3) of the Children Act 1989 applies; and

---

[253]   Homelessness (Priority Need for Accommodation) (England) Order 2002, SI 2002/2051, art 4.
[254]   English Code, paras 10.40–10.41.
[255]   SI 2002/2051, art 1(3).
[256]   English Code, para 10.40.
[257]   *R (Berhe) v Hillingdon London Borough Council and Secretary of State for Education and Skills* [2003] EWHC 2075 (Admin), [2003] All ER (D) 01 Sep.
[258]   Children Act 1989, ss 23A–23E
[259]   *Joint Working between Housing and Children's Services: Preventing homelessness and tackling its effects on children and young people* (Communities and Local Government, Department for Children, School and Families, May 2008), at http://www.communities.gov.uk/publications/housing/goodpracticeguide, chapter 4.
[260]   Disqualifying 18-, 19- or 20-year-olds who have been 'looked after, accommodated or fostered' from securing priority need by this route.
[261]   SI 2002/2051, art 1(3). See English Code, para 10.40.

(c)   who is in full time higher or further education; and

(d)   whose term time accommodation is unavailable during vacation.

13.142 Social services authorities continue to have duties to provide accommodation to those young people who meet these very specific conditions, and for that reason they are not accorded priority need under this provision.[262]

13.143 Applicants who fall within the very narrow exception of 'relevant student' cannot simply be turned away to the social services authority which should be accommodating them. If the local housing authority's inquiries have reached the stage of considering 'priority need', that process must be formally completed. The local housing authority must therefore go on to consider whether the applicant may have a priority need under one of the other categories of priority need (pregnancy, vulnerability, etc). The process must always conclude with a reasoned written decision.[263]

Vulnerability: institutional backgrounds

13.144 People applying to English local housing authorities who are 'vulnerable' as a result of:

- having been 'looked after, accommodated or fostered'[264] (and who are aged 21 or over and not 'relevant students');[265] or

- having been a member of Her Majesty's regular naval, military or air forces; or

- having served a custodial sentence, been committed for contempt of court or other kindred offences, or having been remanded in custody,

all have a priority need.[266] Each sub-category is described in more detail in the following paragraphs.

13.145 To qualify, the applicant must be 'vulnerable' within the *Pereira* test.[267] So, simply having been in the military, in care, or in prison is not enough. The applicant must be vulnerable, and that vulnerability must be the result, in whole or in part, of having been in care, in custody or in the military.

13.146 The provisions do not require any immediate link between the end of military service, imprisonment or care and the application for homelessness assistance. They direct attention to the present vulnerability of the applicant.

---

[262]   Children Act 1989, s 24B(5); Children (Leaving Care) Act 2000.
[263]   HA 1996, s 184(3). See Chapter 10.
[264]   See **13.119**.
[265]   See **13.141**.
[266]   SI 2002/2051, art 5.
[267]   See **13.63–13.69**.

Although a person may be particularly vulnerable when first released, discharged, or at the point of leaving care, that may not be the only time at which he or she experiences relevant vulnerability. The provisions of the Order[268] will be met by any current vulnerability that is the result of the experience of a period in care, in the military or in prison, even if that period ended many months or years earlier.

13.147 Unlike the category of 'vulnerable' persons set out in HA 1996, Part 7,[269] this category of priority need can only be satisfied if the applicant personally is vulnerable for these reasons. A member of the applicant's household who is vulnerable as a result of one of these reasons does not confer priority need on the applicant. Obviously, in those circumstances, it would make sense for the vulnerable individual to apply in his or her own right for accommodation for the household.

Former care leavers aged 21 or over[270]

13.148 The local housing authority must address the following questions:

(1)   Is the person aged 21 or over?

(2)   Was he or she formerly looked after, accommodated or fostered?

(3)   Is he or she a relevant student?

(4)   Is he or she vulnerable?

(5)   Is that vulnerability *as a result of* having been looked after, accommodated or fostered?[271]

13.149 The meanings of 'looked after, accommodated or fostered' and 'relevant student' are defined in the Priority Need Order.[272] If the applicant is a 'relevant student',[273] he or she cannot qualify under this category.

13.150 Unlike the category of care leavers aged 18, 19 and 20,[274] there is no requirement, for those aged 21 or over, that their period in care should have been at any particular age. The effects of a traumatic period in care (at any age) may only manifest themselves later in life.

13.151 The first three questions are therefore simple questions of fact for the local housing authority to determine.

---

[268]   SI 2002/2051.
[269]   HA 1996, s 189(1)(c).
[270]   SI 2002/2051, art 5(1).
[271]   English Code, paras 10.19–10.20.
[272]   SI 2002/2051, art 1(3).
[273]   See **13.141**.
[274]   See **13.137–13.140**.

13.152 By contrast, determining:

(1) whether the applicant is vulnerable; and

(2) whether that vulnerability is *as a result of* having been 'looked after, accommodated or fostered'

require much more difficult judgments. The Code recommends that local housing authorities consider:

(1) the length of time that the applicant was 'looked after, accommodated or fostered';

(2) the reasons why the applicant was looked after, accommodated or fostered;

(3) the length of time since that ended;

(4) whether the applicant has been able to obtain or maintain accommodation since then; and

(5) whether the applicant has existing support networks, particularly family, friends or a mentor.[275]

A person who is vulnerable as a result of having been a member of the armed forces[276]

13.153 The questions for the local housing authority are:

(1) Was the applicant a member of the armed forces?

(2) Is he or she vulnerable?

(3) Is that vulnerability *as a result of* having been a member of the armed forces?[277]

13.154 The first question is a very straightforward question of fact, although military service is very broadly defined. The Order[278] refers to membership of 'Her Majesty's regular naval, military or air forces' without linking back to the much more technical definition used in HA 1996, Part 7.[279] The Code suggests that this definition includes a person who has been released following detention

---

[275] English Code, para 10.20.
[276] SI 2002/2051, art 5(2).
[277] English Code, paras 10.21–10.23.
[278] SI 2002/2051.
[279] HA 1996, s 199(4). See **15.58**.

in a military correctional training centre.[280] It is difficult to see how the words could be met by a person who has been in anything other than the British armed services.

13.155   The next question is whether a person is 'vulnerable' according to the ordinary *Pereira* test.[281]

13.156   The final question is whether the applicant is vulnerable *as a result of* time spent in the armed forces. Local housing authorities are advised to consider:

(1)   the length of time spent in the forces (they should not assume that vulnerability cannot occur after even a short period of time);

(2)   the type of service that the applicant was engaged in (those on active service might find it more difficult to cope with civilian life);

(3)   whether the applicant spent any time in a military hospital (possibly an indicator of a serious health problem or of post-traumatic stress);

(4)   whether the Forces' medical and welfare advisers judged the individual to be particularly vulnerable and issued a Medical History Release Form;

(5)   the length of time since discharge; and

(6)   whether the applicant has any existing support networks, particularly family or friends.[282]

13.157   Some applicants (who have served for a long period or who have been medically discharged) ought to have been offered assistance with resettlement by the armed forces.[283] This does not mean that they are to be turned away by the local housing authority or redirected to their former unit. In any event, such assistance from the armed forces is directed to the point of discharge, not to any later need for accommodation. The Welsh Priority Need Order[284] does not contain the additional requirement of vulnerability.[285] Former members of the armed forces who may not be vulnerable might consider directing an application (or a further application) to a local housing authority in Wales.

---

[280]   English Code, para 10.21.
[281]   See **13.63–13.69**.
[282]   English Code, para 10.23.
[283]   English Code, para 10.22.
[284]   SI 2001/607 (W 30).
[285]   SI 2001/607 (W 30), art 6. See **13.191–13.195**.

Former prisoners who are vulnerable[286]

13.158 The questions for the local housing authority in dealing with an applicant who may fall within this category follow the same pattern as described for the previous two categories:

(1) Is he or she vulnerable?

(2) If so, is the vulnerability *as a result of* having served a custodial sentence, having been committed for contempt of court (or other kindred offences), or having been remanded in custody?[287]

13.159 The term 'custodial sentence' is defined to include:

- a sentence of imprisonment for those aged 21 or over;

- a sentence of detention for those aged under 18;

- a sentence of detention for public protection for those under 18 who commit serious offences;

- a sentence of detention for those under 18 who commit certain violent or sexual offences;

- a sentence of custody for life for persons under 21;

- a sentence of detention in a young offender institution for those aged between 18 and 21; and

- a detention and training order.[288]

13.160 Being 'committed for contempt of court' refers to punishment under the inherent jurisdiction of the court to commit,[289] and 'other kindred offences' refers to committals under the court's statutory powers. Being 'remanded in custody' refers to being remanded by an order of the court, being remanded or committed to local authority accommodation, or being remanded, admitted or removed to hospital under the sentences available under the Mental Health Act 1983.[290]

---

[286] SI 2002/2051, art 5(3).

[287] English Code, paras 10.24–10.27.

[288] Powers of Criminal Courts (Sentencing) Act 2000, s 76; the references to sentence of custody for life and sentences of detention in a young offender institution are due to be repealed by the Criminal Justice and Court Services Act 2000, but no date for their repeal has yet been appointed (Criminal Justice and Court Services Act 2000, s 80(1)).

[289] County Court Act 1984, s 118.

[290] Referred to in the Order as being defined by the Powers of Criminal Courts (Sentencing) Act 2000, s 88. That section has been repealed and the definition is now found at Criminal Justice Act 2003, s 242(2) and Mental Health Act 1983, ss 35, 36, 38 or 48.

13.161 The Code recommends that, in determining 'vulnerability', and whether it is the result of imprisonment or custody, local housing authorities should consider:

(1) the length of time served (it should not be assumed that vulnerability could not occur as a result of a short period of imprisonment);

(2) whether the applicant is receiving supervision from a criminal justice agency and any advice received from those agencies;

(3) the length of time since release;

(4) the extent to which the applicant has been able to obtain and maintain accommodation during that time; and

(5) whether the applicant has existing support networks, particularly family or friends, and how much of a positive influence those networks are likely to be.[291]

13.162 In one county court decision, the judge found that the local housing authority had been wrong to reject the opinion of a prison officer that the applicant was institutionalised, and had also been wrong to find that the applicant had a history of managing to secure housing when, in fact, his only accommodation in recent years had been insecure accommodation with a friend and he had previously been recalled to prison because he had not managed to secure housing.[292]

13.163 Former prisoners who have a priority need for this reason may still be found intentionally homeless by the local housing authority if their homelessness arose as a result of their deliberate acts or omissions (which led them to prison and to lose their previous accommodation).[293] The Code reminds local housing authorities not to adopt a blanket policy of assuming that former prisoners who are homeless will have become homeless intentionally (or, indeed, always have become homeless unintentionally).[294] The Welsh Priority Need Order[295] does not contain the additional requirement of vulnerability.[296] Former prisoners who may not be vulnerable might consider directing an application (or a further application) to a local housing authority in Wales.

---

291 English Code, para 10.25.
292 *Kelly v City of Westminster Council* (2008) December *Legal Action*, p 27, Central London County Court.
293 *R v Hounslow London Borough Council ex p R* (1997) 29 HLR 939, QBD; and *Stewart v Lambeth London Borough Council* [2002] EWCA Civ 753, [2002] HLR 40, CA.
294 English Code, para 10.27.
295 SI 2001/607 (W 30).
296 SI 2001/607 (W 30), art 7. See **13.196–13.202**.

13.164 Some of the problems faced by ex-offenders in trying to find accommodation on their release from prison are discussed in the Citizens' Advice Bureau publication, *Locked Out*.[297]

Persons who are vulnerable as a result of fleeing violence or threats of violence[298]

13.165 The questions for the local housing authority when dealing with an applicant who may fall within this category are:

(1) Did the person cease to occupy accommodation as a result of violence from another person or threats of violence from another person which were likely to be carried out?

(2) Is the person vulnerable?

(3) Is that vulnerability *as a result of* having ceased to occupy accommodation because of violence from another person or threats of violence from another person which were likely to be carried out?[299]

13.166 Although this category was intended primarily to benefit people without children who had been subject to domestic violence, its terms include people fleeing accommodation as a result of any type of violence (except self-inflicted harm). The Code refers to all forms of violence, including racially motivated violence.[300] A recent decision of the Court of Appeal has held that the definition of 'violence' in HA 1996, Part 7 should be given a narrow interpretation, requiring physical contact.[301]

13.167 The Code recommends that:

- the safety of the applicant and ensuring his or her confidentiality are of paramount concern;

- inquiries should not be made of the perpetrator; and

- the correct approach is to consider:

  '... the probability of violence, and not actions which the applicant could take (such as injunctions against the perpetrators).'[302]

---

[297] *Locked Out* (Citizens' Advice Bureau, March 2007), at http://www.citizensadvice.org.uk/locked_out.
[298] SI 2002/2051, art 6.
[299] English Code, paras 10.28–10.29.
[300] English Code, para 10.28.
[301] *Yemshaw v Hounslow London Borough Council* (unreported) 15 December 2009, CA (extempore judgment not yet reported at the date of this book going to print), and relying on *Danesh v Kensington & Chelsea Royal London Borough* [2006] EWCA Civ 1404, [2007] 1 WLR 69, CA. See **11.81** and **15.103**.
[302] English Code, para 10.28.

13.168   This reflects the approach taken in relation to the question whether it would be reasonable for the applicant to continue to occupy accommodation in which violence is being experienced or threatened.[303]

13.169   In considering whether an applicant is vulnerable for this reason, local housing authorities are advised to take into account:

(a)   the nature of the violence or threats (whether a single but significant incident or a number of incidents over an extended period of time which have a cumulative effect);

(b)   the impact and likely effects of the violence or threats on the applicant's physical and mental health and well-being; and

(c)   whether the applicant has any existing support networks, particularly by way of family or friends.[304]

13.170   Considering an applicant who claimed to have left his home because of threats of violence,[305] a county court judge held that the local housing authority should consider the following:

- Did the applicant leave his or her house due to threats?

- Were those threats likely to be carried out?

- Was he or she vulnerable?

In relation to the third question, the judge held that a person who is subject to threats of violence, and who is street homeless, is less likely to be able to protect himself or herself.[306]

13.171   To qualify under this category the applicant must have actually left accommodation and have left it because of the violence or threatened violence. This need not be, but is very likely to have been, the accommodation he or she most recently occupied. Accordingly, the category will only apply infrequently to an applicant who is threatened with homelessness rather than actually homeless.

---

[303]   See **11.778–11.88**.
[304]   English Code, para 10.29.
[305]   Not domestic violence.
[306]   *Logan v Havering London Borough Council*, (2007) May *Legal Action*, p 31, Romford County Court.

ADDITIONAL CATEGORIES IN WALES: THE WELSH PRIORITY NEED ORDER

13.172 The Homeless Persons (Priority Need) (Wales) Order 2001[307] came into force on 1 March 2001 and applies to all decisions, or reviews of decisions, made after that date by local housing authorities in Wales, irrespective of the date on which the homelessness application was first made.

13.173 It adds six additional categories of priority need to the four contained in HA 1996. Unlike the English Order, there is no reference in the Welsh Order to any new category which turns on an applicant being 'vulnerable'. If an applicant's circumstances mean that he or she falls within one of the categories, he or she will have a priority need.

13.174 The wording of the Order states that a person falling into one of the categories will have a priority need, suggesting that he or she must actually be the applicant. The Code, however, advises that the categories should also apply to members of the applicant's household, so that if one of them falls within any of the categories, the applicant will have a priority need.[308] This probably goes further than the Order permits. To avoid any difficulty, it would be sensible for the application to be made by the individual who personally falls within the relevant category in the Order.

People aged 16 or 17[309]

13.175 This category embraces all 16- and 17-year-olds. In contrast to the situation under the English Order,[310] there are no exceptions to this category.[311] There is certainly no requirement that the applicant be vulnerable or separated from his or her parents. It is simply being aged 16 or 17 that gives rise to the priority need.[312]

People aged 18, 19 or 20[313]

13.176 Two specific groups within this age range are accorded priority need status by the Order: care leavers and those at risk of 'exploitation'. Both concepts are further refined.

13.177 If a person:

- is aged 18 or over, but under 21; and

---

[307] SI 2001/607 (W 30). See Appendix 3.
[308] Welsh Code, para 14.2.
[309] SI 2001/607, art 4.
[310] SI 2002/2051, art 3.
[311] See **13.107–13.136** and Welsh Code, paras 14.36–14.40.
[312] See **13.111–13.117** on the duties owed when a 17-year-old, approaching his or her eighteenth birthday, makes an application for homelessness assistance.
[313] SI 2001/607, art 3.

- he or she was 'looked after, accommodated or fostered'; or

- is at particular risk of sexual or financial exploitation,

then he or she will have a priority need.

13.178 The definition of 'looked after, accommodated or fostered' is given in the Order[314] and is very broad. Although the shorthand commonly used for this rubric is 'care leaver', there is no requirement that the applicant has been in care. For example, the definition is met if the applicant has at some time in the past been 'privately fostered'.[315]

13.179 There is no minimum period of time during which the person must have been looked after, accommodated or fostered in order to qualify. Nor is there any specified age at which the applicant must have been looked after, fostered or accommodated.

13.180 Any young person (now aged 18, 19 or 20), who was 'looked after, accommodated or fostered' at any point in his or her life, for any period, will fall within this category.[316]

13.181 The second or alternative route to qualification under this provision is met by an 18-, 19- or 20-year-old who 'is at particular risk of sexual or financial exploitation'.

13.182 The Welsh Code advises that the risks that young people may be subject to include:

- being at risk of sexual abuse; or

- being at risk due to their sexual orientation; or

- being at risk of prostitution; or

- suffering from a learning disability; or

- being at risk of misuse of power or exercise of control by another person; or

- being at risk of financial extortion; or

- on a low income (ie an income falling substantially below their needs), and vulnerable due to a lack of alternative financial means (excluding students in further education).

---

[314] SI 2001/607, art 3(2).

[315] SI 2001/607, art 3(2)(e).

[316] Welsh Code, para 14.28: 'anytime, *however short*, during their childhood in care' (emphasis in original).

13.183 The Code advises that it is not good practice for local housing authorities always to expect evidence of actual or threatened sexual or financial exploitation.[317]

13.184 Note that the applicant must be at 'particular' risk for the terms of the Order to be satisfied, not merely subject to the general risk of sexual or financial exploitation that any young person may face. Presumably this additional criterion will be satisfied by some personal characteristic of the applicant (eg drug or alcohol dependency) or perhaps some special feature of his or her local area (eg prevalent street prostitution).

A person fleeing domestic violence or threatened domestic violence[318]

13.185 This category is satisfied if an applicant:

- has been subject to domestic violence; or

- is at risk of domestic violence; or

- is at risk of domestic violence if he or she returns home; and

- is without dependent children.

13.186 Unlike the equivalent category in the English Order,[319] there is no need for the applicant to be vulnerable as a result of having fled accommodation in order to qualify in this category.

13.187 The other important distinction from the English Order is that only 'domestic' violence (presumably as defined in HA 1996, s 177(1))[320] rather than any other violence will result in a person falling into this category. A recent decision of the Court of Appeal has held that the definition of 'violence' in HA 1996, Part 7 should be given a narrow interpretation, requiring physical contact.[321]

13.188 Although the description above this category (as given in the Order itself) refers to a person 'fleeing' domestic violence, that is not part of the words used in the relevant article in the order. It therefore embraces victims of actual or threatened domestic violence who have not yet left home. This enables an

---

[317] Welsh Code, paras 14.33–14.35. See the Scottish cases of *Kelly v Monklands District Council 1985 SLT 165, OH*, and *Wilson v Nithsdale District Council 1992 SLT 1131, OH*.

[318] SI 2001/607, art 5.

[319] SI 2002/2051, art 6. See **13.165–13.171**.

[320] See **11.78–11.88**. It must be noted however that the Welsh Order itself does not define 'domestic violence', nor does it refer expressly to the definition in HA 1996.

[321] *Yemshaw v Hounslow London Borough Council* (unreported) 15 December 2009, CA (extempore judgment not yet reported at the date of this book going to print), and relying on *Danesh v Kensington & Chelsea Royal London Borough* [2006] EWCA Civ 1404, [2007] 1 WLR 69, CA. See **11.81** and **15.103**.

applicant to apply for accommodation and quickly be accepted as homeless, in priority need and unintentionally homeless, whilst still at home. She or he will therefore be able take the benefit of the main housing duty without first having to be provided with interim accommodation.

13.189 This category only applies to people without dependent children. Those who do have dependent children will have a priority need under the relevant category contained in HA 1996, Part 7.[322]

13.190 The Welsh Code advises that 'domestic violence' can occur in same-sex relationships as well as in heterosexual relationships.[323] Guidance on the sympathetic and careful nature of the inquiries to be carried out is given in the Welsh Code at paras 14.41–14.52.

A person homeless after leaving the armed forces of the Crown[324]

13.191 This category is met by any applicant who is a former member of the armed forces and:

(1)   is homeless; and

(2)   has been homeless since leaving the armed forces.

13.192 Unlike the English equivalent category,[325] there is no requirement that the applicant be 'vulnerable', whether by reason of service in the forces or otherwise.

13.193 Only service in the 'regular armed forces of the Crown' satisfies the condition for this category. The definition of 'armed forces' used is the technical one adopted in HA 1996.[326]

13.194 The emphasis is on a continuing chain of homelessness since discharge. The Code recommends that homelessness should be treated as lack of 'suitable permanent accommodation', ie not having had a tenancy or having been permanently settled with family or friends.

13.195 The length of time since discharge is not in point; the issue is whether the applicant has remained homeless since he or she was discharged.[327]

---

[322]   See **13.30–13.61**.
[323]   Welsh Code, para 14.43. Since 5 December 2005, violence from same-sex partners falls under the definition of 'domestic violence' at HA 1996, s 177(1), (1A) and s 178, as amended by the Civil Partnership Act 2004.
[324]   SI 2001/607, art 6.
[325]   SI 2002/2051, art 5(2). See **13.153–13.157**.
[326]   HA 1996, s 199(4); SI 2001/607, art 6(2). See **15.58**.
[327]   Welsh Code, paras 14.53–14.57.

Former prisoners who have been homeless since being released from custody[328]

13.196 To qualify under this category the applicant must:

(1)   be a former prisoner; and

(2)   be homeless; and

(3)   have been homeless since leaving custody; and

(4)   have a local connection with the local housing authority's area.

13.197 Again, unlike the English equivalent,[329] there is no requirement that the former prisoner be 'vulnerable'.

13.198 A 'prisoner' is defined as 'any person for the time being detained in lawful custody as the result of a requirement imposed by a court that he or she be detained'.[330] That includes time spent on remand, in a young offender's institution or in prison, whether as a result of a conviction or not.[331]

13.199 The inclusion of a 'local connection' requirement reflects a concern later expressed during the passage of the Homelessness Act 2002 through Parliament, when MPs representing constituencies containing sizeable prisons were anxious that their local housing authorities should not suddenly receive a host of applications from former prisoners. The solution in England was to restrict the extension of priority need to those former prisoners who were 'vulnerable' as a result of their imprisonment. The solution in Wales was to require that former prisoners must have a local connection with the local housing authority to which they apply in order to obtain the benefit of this priority need category.

13.200 Local connection to an area cannot be acquired by residence as a result of lawful detention in that area.[332] A former prisoner would, therefore, not acquire a local connection in the area where his or her prison was situated, unless he or she had acquired a local connection with that area for a reason other than residence, eg by employment (either before or after the period of imprisonment).[333]

13.201 The wording leaves open the question of what happens if a prisoner has no local connection with any area, but otherwise falls within this category. Any local housing authority to which he or she chooses to apply must accept

---

[328]   SI 2001/607, art 7.
[329]   SI 2002/2051, art 5(3). See **13.158–13.164**.
[330]   SI 2001/607, art 7(2).
[331]   Welsh Code, para 14.62.
[332]   HA 1996, s 199(3)(b). See **15.59**.
[333]   See **15.64–15.69**.

his or her application.[334] However, on a literal reading of this article,[335] a prisoner who has been homeless since release but has no local connection with any local housing authority will not be able to acquire a priority need under this category if he or she has directed his or her application for homelessness assistance to a Welsh local housing authority.

13.202 In contrast to the English Code, the Welsh Code specifically advises local housing authorities that the actions of former prisoners that led to their imprisonment should not also lead to their being considered intentionally homeless unless the offence committed was a direct breach of the tenancy agreement, leading to repossession of the prisoner's previous tenancy. Otherwise, finding former prisoners intentionally homeless 'would doubly penalise the offender and undermine the purpose of the Order, which is to assist the resettlement of ex-offenders'.[336]

---

[334] HA 1996, s 198(2). See **15.17–15.18**.
[335] SI 2001/607, art 7.
[336] Welsh Code, paras 14.64–14.65.

Chapter 14

BECOMING HOMELESS INTENTIONALLY

INTRODUCTION

14.1 Once a local housing authority has determined that an applicant is homeless (or is threatened with homelessness), and that she or he is eligible for assistance, a duty under the Housing Act 1996 (HA 1996), Part 7 is owed to the applicant. In order to decide which precise duty is owed, the local housing authority must decide whether the applicant has a priority need[1] and whether she or he has become homeless (or has become threatened with homelessness) intentionally.

14.2 Because different duties arise depending upon the answers, the local housing authority must answer both of those two questions. Traditionally, if local housing authorities had decided that the applicant had no priority need, they felt it unnecessary to consider whether or not an applicant had become homeless intentionally (or had become threatened with homelessness intentionally). But now that there is a power available to the local housing authority to provide accommodation for people who do not have a priority need and who did not become homeless (or threatened with homelessness) intentionally, both questions must be asked and answered.[2]

14.3 For the first 20 years of statutory homelessness provision in the UK (1977–1997), the decision as to whether or not the homelessness of a priority need applicant had come about 'intentionally' was pivotal. Those who had not become homeless intentionally were treated as entitled to a permanent home. Those who had become homeless intentionally would merely be given temporary accommodation and then only for a very short period. Disputes about whether an applicant had become homeless 'intentionally' accordingly dominated the work of housing advisers and homelessness officers, and formed the bulk of the reported court cases on the statutory provisions. To have been found to have become 'homeless intentionally' was to be given what one judge described as the 'mark of Cain'.[3]

14.4 Much has changed since the early days of homelessness law. First, a decision of the House of Lords in 1996 exploded the myth that those applicants who had become homeless unintentionally were entitled to be provided with permanent homes under the statutory homelessness provisions.[4] Second, the new statutory framework of HA 1996 made it clear that the highest duty owed to any applicant would be met by the provision of temporary

---

[1]   See Chapter 13.

[2]   Housing Act 1996, s 192(3). In *Gaskin v Norwich City Council* [2007] EWCA Civ 1239, (2008) January *Legal Action*, p 38, CA, the local housing authority had reached a decision that the applicant did not have a priority need without considering the issue of whether she had become homeless intentionally. In subsequent proceedings, after it had found that she did have a priority need but had become homeless intentionally, that earlier approach was not criticised by the courts.

[3]   *Din v Wandsworth London Borough Council* (unreported) 23 June 1981, CA, per Ackner LJ, quoted in *Lambert v Ealing London Borough Council* [1982] 1 WLR 550, CA at 557, per Lord Denning MR.

[4]   *R v Brent London Borough Council ex p Awua* [1996] AC 55, HL.

accommodation only.[5] Third, changes to the arrangements for allocation of social housing (most recently made by the Homelessness Act 2002) have required local housing authorities to give a preference to all homeless people, including those who have become homeless intentionally.[6] Fourth, a deepening crisis in the availability of decent affordable housing on the open market in many areas has made the search for alternative homes by those who become homeless intentionally all the more difficult. That last factor, coupled with the new obligation on a local housing authority to assess the housing needs of those applicants it finds have become homeless intentionally,[7] has ensured that ever longer periods of temporary accommodation provision must be made for those applicants. In short, the gap should have significantly narrowed between the duties owed to those in priority need who have become homeless intentionally, and those who did not become homeless intentionally. Statistics show, however, that the proportion of applicants for homelessness assistance found to have become homeless intentionally has been steadily rising since the implementation of HA 1996 in 1997.[8]

14.5 These changes have not rendered the question of 'becoming homeless intentionally' (or 'becoming threatened with homelessness intentionally') altogether academic. As any list of the different powers and duties in HA 1996, Part 7 indicates,[9] much still turns on whether actual (or threatened) homelessness was (or is) intentional. The English Code explains the policy reasoning behind the different duties owed to those applicants found to have become homeless intentionally and those found not to have become homeless intentionally:

'This recognises the general expectation that, wherever possible, people should take responsibility for their own accommodation needs and ensure that they do not behave in a way which might lead to the loss of their accommodation.'[10]

14.6 However, even an adverse finding that actual or threatened homelessness has been brought about 'intentionally' is simply the result of one local housing authority having applied a complex statutory test and its own judgment to the facts of the application. Two equally reasonable local housing authorities may quite lawfully reach different conclusions on the same statutory test and the

---

[5]   HA 1996, s 193(2). See **17.21–17.110**.
[6]   HA 1996, s 167(2)(a) and (b). See **4.41–4.54**.
[7]   HA 1996, s 190(4). See **17.136–17.137**.
[8]   *Quarterly Homelessness Statistics from Communities and Local Government* at (http://www.communities.gov.uk/housing/housingresearch/housingstatistics/housingstatisticsby/homelessnessstatistics/livetables/). 'Table 637: Decisions taken by local authorities under the Housing Act 1996 on applications by eligible households' shows that the number of decisions where the applicant had a priority need and had become homeless intentionally had been 3% each year. From 2003, the proportion started rising to the current high of 8% for 2008–2009. No figures are shown for those applicants found not to have a priority need and to have become homeless intentionally.
[9]   See **17.9**.
[10] *Homelessness Code of Guidance for local authorities* (Communities and Local Government, Department for Education and Skills, Department of Health, July 2006) (English Code), para 11.3, at Appendix 2 of this book.

same set of facts. This means that there are often reasonable prospects for an applicant, who has been found to have become homeless intentionally by one local housing authority, to apply to another local housing authority and find that a different conclusion will be reached.[11]

14.7 Likewise, it is important to appreciate that the adverse finding is one that is applicable only so long as the particular actual or threatened homelessness lasts. First, a person who is found to have become threatened with homelessness intentionally may apply again once actually homeless, in the hope that there may be a different finding about why he or she became homeless. Second, a person who is found to have become homeless intentionally may render that finding irrelevant to any future incidence of homelessness by obtaining settled accommodation. This limited life of a finding of becoming homeless (or threatened with becoming homeless) intentionally means that a fresh application can always be made to a local housing authority for assistance under HA 1996, Part 7, unless the facts are precisely the same on the new application as upon the occasion of the last application.[12] Obviously, to save repeating what may have been extensive recent investigations on a previous application, the local housing authority is entitled initially to rely on its original finding that the applicant had become homeless intentionally and to confine its inquiries to whether there has been any intervening settled accommodation or other factual change since the earlier finding.

THE DIFFERENT DUTIES

14.8 An applicant who is homeless but is *not found to have become homeless intentionally* and who does have a *priority need* is owed the highest duty under HA 1996, Part 7 (sometimes referred to as the 'main housing duty'). That duty requires the local housing authority 'to secure that accommodation is available for occupation by the applicant'.[13]

14.9 In contrast, an applicant who became homeless *intentionally* and who has a *priority need* will be owed lesser duties:

'... to secure that accommodation is available for his occupation for such period as they consider will give him a reasonable opportunity of securing accommodation'[14]

and to

---

11   See **9.39–9.45**.
12   *R v Harrow London Borough Council ex p Fahia* (1996) 30 HLR 1124, HL; and *Begum v Tower Hamlets London Borough Council* [2005] EWCA Civ 340, [2005] HLR 34, CA. See **9.54–9.64**.
13   HA 1996, s 193(2). See **17.21–17.110**.
14   HA 1996, s 190(2)(a). English Code, para 11.4. See **17.111–17.118**.

'... provide him with (or secure that he is provided with) advice and assistance in any attempts he may make to secure that accommodation becomes available for his occupation.'[15]

There is also a duty to assess the applicant's housing needs.[16]

14.10 An applicant who does *not* have a *priority need* and who became homeless *intentionally* is owed a limited duty, which is that the local housing authority:

'... shall provide him with (or secure that he is provided with) advice and assistance in any attempts he may make to secure that accommodation becomes available for his occupation.'[17]

There is also a duty to assess the applicant's housing needs.[18]

14.11 If an applicant is 'threatened with homelessness', there is a similar range of duties, depending upon whether or not he or she has a priority need and whether he or she has become threatened with homelessness intentionally.[19]

14.12 Further discussion as to the extent of these various duties, and the methods of performing them, is provided at Chapter 17.

14.13 In this chapter, we consider the test used to determine whether or not someone has become homeless (or threatened with homelessness) intentionally, and then outline some of the common scenarios in which an applicant may or may not be found to have become homeless (or threatened with homelessness) intentionally. Because the circumstances of 'threatened with homelessness' and actual homelessness are treated differently in HA 1996, Part 7, the remainder of this chapter deals separately with, first, 'becoming homeless intentionally'[20] and then with 'becoming threatened with homelessness intentionally'.[21]

MAKING INQUIRIES INTO 'BECOMING HOMELESS INTENTIONALLY'

14.14 A local housing authority must conduct such inquiries into an application as will enable it to determine what duty under HA 1996, Part 7 (if any) is owed.[22] Where the local housing authority is satisfied that an applicant is both eligible and homeless (or threatened with homelessness), it must then

---

15 HA 1996, s 190(2)(b). English Code, para 11.4. See **17.132–17.144**.
16 HA 1996, s 190(4). English Code, para 11.4. See **17.132–17.144**.
17 HA 1996, s 190(3). English Code, para 11.4. See **17.132–17.144**.
18 HA 1996, s 190(4). English Code, para 11.4. See **17.132–17.144**.
19 HA 1996, s 195(2) and (5). See **17.119–17.125** and **17.132–17.144**.
20 See **14.14–14.145**.
21 See **14.146–14.156**.
22 HA 1996, s 184(1)(b).

make such further enquires as will enable it to determine whether that particular applicant has become homeless or threatened with homelessness 'intentionally'.

14.15 Obviously, an individual and applicant-centred approach to the question is required. Local housing authorities should not adopt general policies which seek to predetermine that particular classes of applicant (eg tenants of the local housing authority who were evicted for arrears of rent or anti-social behaviour) will or will not be found to have become homeless intentionally.[23] Local housing authorities should make all necessary inquiries about each particular application and reach a decision in the light of those inquiries. If there is doubt about the matter at the conclusion of initial inquiries, then either inquiries should continue until the matter is free of doubt, or the benefit of the doubt should be given to the applicant and he or she should be found not to have become homeless (or threatened with homelessness) 'intentionally'.[24] If it is not possible for the local housing authority to satisfy itself that the applicant became homeless intentionally, because the events it is inquiring into occurred some years earlier and the facts are unclear, the applicant should be considered not to have become homeless intentionally.[25]

14.16 Any decision that an applicant has become homeless or threatened with homelessness intentionally should be accompanied by clear reasons for that finding, even though the formal decision being notified to the applicant is only the decision as to what precise HA 1996 Part 7 duty the applicant is owed.[26]

14.17 The burden of making the inquiries rests with the local housing authority. It is not for the applicant to have to prove his or her case, and satisfy the local housing authority that she or he did not become homeless intentionally. This was reinforced by the Court of Appeal in *O'Connor v Kensington and Chelsea Royal London Borough Council*,[27] where it was held that a local housing authority, when considering the question of whether the applicant had become homeless intentionally, should consider whether the applicant had been unaware of a relevant fact in good faith, regardless of whether this latter point had been raised by the applicant. A later Court of Appeal decision refined the point, adding that the decision-maker need not consider matters that were not raised by the applicant, unless those matters were within 'the circumstances of obviousness'.[28]

---

[23]   English Code, para 11.6; *Code of Guidance for local housing authorities on allocation of accommodation and homelessness for Wales* (National Assembly for Wales, April 2003) (Welsh Code), para 15.1. See CD-ROM.

[24]   *R v Thurrock Borough Council ex p Williams* (1981) 1 HLR 128, QBD, and see **10.15–10.19**.

[25]   English Code, para 11.6; Welsh Code, para 15.1.

[26]   English Code, paras 11.5–11.6; Welsh Code, para 15.1; *Southall v West Wiltshire District Council* (2002) October *Legal Action*, p 31, Swindon County Court.

[27]   *O'Connor v Kensington and Chelsea Royal London Borough Council,* [2004] EWCA Civ 394, [2004] HLR 37, CA at [37], per Sedley LJ and at [54], per Waller LJ.

[28]   *Aw-Aden v Birmingham City Council* [2005] EWCA Civ 1834, (2006) July *Legal Action*, p 29, CA, per Maurice Kay LJ at [12].

14.18 The English Code suggests that there is one exception to the general rule: if an applicant is seeking to establish that he or she did not acquiesce in the deliberate actions of another member of his of her household (who has already been found to have caused the homelessness of the household), the burden is on the applicant to raise and demonstrate a lack of acquiescence in those actions.[29] This is probably putting the test too high: the proper approach is that acquiescence may be assumed by the local housing authority 'in the absence of material which indicates to the contrary.'[30] Where there is any material that indicates that the applicant may not have acquiesced, the local housing authority must make inquiries in the usual way.[31]

14.19 If, during its inquiries, the local housing authority has reason to believe that an applicant whose household includes children under 18 might be found to have become homeless intentionally, it is under a duty to ask the applicant to give consent for his or her circumstances to be referred to the social services authority, and then (if consent is given) to make that referral.[32] This will enable social services to begin planning what assistance it might provide for the household if the local housing authority's final conclusion is that the applicant did become homeless intentionally. The local housing authority is obliged to follow up the referral by advising the social services authority of the decision that it actually reaches on the application for homelessness assistance.[33]

THE STATUTORY MEANING

Overview

14.20 In the homelessness provisions of HA 1996, Part 7, the word 'intentionally' is not given its ordinary or dictionary meaning, but is accorded a very tightly prescribed statutory meaning. Most obviously this is because, in the ordinary use of language, an applicant's homelessness is very often brought about, not by an intentional act of the applicant, but rather by the intentional act of another party (such as a landlord, parent or court bailiff) who has deliberately ejected the applicant. Moreover, it is something of a contradiction to suggest that an applicant has become homeless intentionally, since the whole point of the applicant making an application for homelessness assistance is to avoid or end his or her state of homelessness.

14.21 As Lord Denning MR observed, in one of the earliest homelessness cases:

---

[29] English Code, para 11.5; the reversal of the burden of proof in acquiescence cases is not reproduced in the Welsh Code. See **10.46–10.47** and **14.78–14.82**.

[30] *R v North Devon District Council ex parte Lewis* [1981] 1 WLR 328 at 333, per Woolf J.

[31] *R v West Dorset District Council ex parte Phillips* (1985) 17 HLR 336, QBD; and *N v Allerdale Borough Council* (2008) October *Legal Action*, p 38, Carlisle County Court.

[32] HA 1996, s 213A(1). English Code, para 11.29; and see Chapter 15; Welsh Code, para 15.12. See **17.155–17.162**.

[33] HA 1996, s 213A(2) and (3).

'Many people would have thought that [the applicant's] conduct, however deplorable, was not 'deliberate' in the sense required by ... [the Act]. She did not deliberately do anything to get herself turned out.'[34]

Similarly, Lord Lowry said:

'No one really becomes homeless or threatened with homelessness intentionally; the word is a convenient label to describe the result of acting or failing to act as described in [the Act].'[35]

The statutory definition of 'becoming homeless intentionally' is that:

'... a person becomes homeless intentionally if he deliberately does or fails to do anything in consequence of which he ceases to occupy accommodation which is available for his occupation and which it would have been reasonable for him to continue to occupy'.[36]

14.22 This complex composite definition has been described as part of a statutory 'semantic nightmare'.[37]

14.23 Because each and every element of the composite must be in place before a local housing authority can be satisfied that an applicant 'became homeless intentionally', initial expectations (when the phrase was first enacted) were that it would only be satisfied infrequently. The first edition of the *Code of Guidance* in 1978 indicated that the number of applicants falling foul of it was 'expected to be small'.[38]

14.24 The statutory formulation is most practically approached by treating it as having five elements. To ensure that they are all in place, the local housing authority needs to address five questions in the course of its inquiries and decision-making. The necessary premise for the questions is that the applicant is currently homeless (ignoring, of course, any interim accommodation that the local housing authority may have provided), so that all the attention is directed to the past:

(1) Was there a deliberate act or omission (which does not include an act or omission in good faith by a person unaware of a material fact)?[39]

(2) Was that a deliberate act or omission by the applicant?[40]

---

[34] *R v Slough Borough Council ex p Ealing London Borough Council* [1981] 1 QB 801, CA at 809.
[35] *Din v Wandsworth London Borough Council* [1983] 1 AC 657, HL at 679, referring to Housing (Homeless Persons) Act 1977, s 17, containing the same definition of 'becoming homeless intentionally' as at HA 1996, s 191(1).
[36] HA 1996, s 191(1).
[37] *Roughead v Falkirk District Council 1979 SCOLAG 188*, per Sheriff Sinclair.
[38] *Code of Guidance* (Department of Environment, 1978), para 2.19.
[39] See **14.30–14.77**.
[40] See **14.78–14.82**.

(3)   Was it as a consequence of that deliberate act or omission that the applicant ceased to occupy accommodation?[41]

(4)   Was that accommodation available for the applicant's occupation and for occupation by members of the applicant's family who normally resided with the applicant and by persons with whom the applicant might reasonably have been expected to reside?[42]

(5)   Would it have been reasonable for the applicant to have continued to occupy the accommodation?[43]

14.25 If the local housing authority's answer to each of these five questions is 'Yes', then the applicant will have 'become homeless intentionally'. If the answer to *any* of them is 'No', the applicant cannot have become homeless intentionally.

14.26 'Becoming threatened with homelessness intentionally' is also defined in HA 1996, Part 7, in similar but not identical terms.[44]

14.27 There is, in addition, a category of applicants who are deemed to have become homeless intentionally and to whom the five-question approach is not to be applied. An applicant is 'treated as' becoming homeless intentionally if:

(1)   he or she has (in the past) entered into an arrangement to give up accommodation; and

(2)   it was accommodation which it would have been reasonable to continue to occupy; and

(3)   the purpose of the arrangement was to trigger entitlement to help under HA 1996, Part 7; and

(4)   there is no other good reason why the applicant is homeless.[45]

14.28 This deeming provision is obviously designed to prevent collusive arrangements, but in practice is hardly ever used. Not only are the conditions tightly drawn, but they only deem the 'person' who 'enters into' the arrangement as having become homeless intentionally.[46] Its effect can therefore be avoided by a different member of the homeless household making the

---

41   See **14.83–14.101**.
42   See **14.102–14.107**.
43   See **14.108–14.126**.
44   HA 1996, s 196(1) and (2); and discussed further at **14.146–14.155**.
45   HA 1996, s 191(3). See also English Code, paras 11.8 and 11.28; Welsh Code, para 15.3. See **14.156–14.162**.
46   HA 1996, s 191(3)(a).

application for homelessness assistance.[47] There is a similar deeming provision in the definition of 'becoming threatened with homelessness intentionally'.[48]

14.29 The following paragraphs address, in turn, each of the five elements of the composite statutory definition of 'becoming homeless intentionally'.

Was there a deliberate act or omission?

A deliberate act or omission

14.30 The first step in the statutory definition is that the applicant 'deliberately does or fails to do anything' which results in his or her loss of accommodation.[49] There is no definition of 'deliberate act' or 'deliberate omission' in HA 1996, Part 7.[50] Instead, HA 1996, Part 7 stipulates that some acts or omissions are not to be treated as deliberate, by providing that:

> '... an act or omission in good faith on the part of a person who was unaware of any relevant fact shall not be treated as deliberate.'[51]

14.31 So the word 'deliberate' in this setting must connote a free election to act (or fail to act) in a particular way by a person in possession of all the relevant facts. As one English judge has put it:

> 'I am satisfied from a consideration of the whole of the section ... that "deliberately" is used in the ordinary sense of the word and is not to be narrowly construed. In particular the provisions of [the] subsection ... indicate that "deliberately" means "after a consideration of all the relevant facts".'[52]

14.32 The most obvious example of an act 'deliberately' done arises where an applicant has surrendered or given notice on his or her tenancy, or sold his or her house, and made no provision for future accommodation.[53] The most obvious example of a 'deliberate' omission would be failure to pay housing costs notwithstanding having the means and opportunity to pay them.

14.33 The English Code of Guidance introduces the notions of 'force' and 'fault':

---

[47] Discussed further at **14.162**.

[48] HA 1996, s 196(3). See **14.162**.

[49] HA 1996, s 191(1).

[50] The dictionary definition of 'deliberate' is 'intentional', which, in the context of HA 1996, s 191, seems to take one round in circles (*Shorter Oxford English Dictionary*, 1993).

[51] HA 1996, s 191(2).

[52] *Devenport v Salford City Council* (1983) 8 HLR 54, CA, per Waller LJ.

[53] See *Dyson v Kerrier District Council* [1980] 1 WLR 1205, CA (a case in which the applicant gave up long-term accommodation for a precarious winter let), or, more recently, *F v Birmingham City Council* [2006] EWC Civ 1427, [2007] HLR 18, CA, where a tenant gave up her secure tenancy for unaffordable private rented accommodation

'... an act or omission should not generally be treated as deliberate, even where deliberately carried out, if it was forced upon the applicant through no fault of their own.'[54]

14.34 Adopting the approach in this guidance and adding a non-statutory gloss to HA 1996, Part 7 itself, a non-deliberate act could therefore occur either when:

(1) someone was forced to do something; or

(2) someone may have chosen to act in a particular way, but did so in ignorance of all the relevant facts.[55]

14.35 An example of the former would arise where the applicant had deliberately vacated accommodation, but did so because remaining there would lead to him or her experiencing further violence from a neighbour. Similarly, an applicant's choice to spend his or her last available money to buy food for hungry children rather than paying the rent is not, for the purposes of the legislation, 'deliberate'.[56] On the latter set of facts, a local housing authority argued:

> 'a person does or fails to do something "deliberately" if he makes a considered choice between two courses of action or inaction, either of which he is able to take. Thus, if he makes a considered decision to apply the only money he has in his pocket in maintaining his children instead of paying it to his landlord, he deliberately fails to pay the rent'.[57]

14.36 This submission was rejected. The Court of Appeal said:

> 'The purpose of ... the ... Act is to house the homeless. Admittedly it is no part of that purpose to house those whose homelessness has been brought upon them by their own fault. But equally it is no part of it to refuse housing to those whose homelessness has been brought upon them without fault on their part, for example by disability, sickness, poverty or even a simple inability to make ends meet.'[58]

---

[54] English Code, para 11.16; there is no equivalent in the Welsh Code.

[55] The important question of an applicant's mental capacity at the time of the act or omission in this context is discussed at **14.54–14.58**.

[56] As happened in *R v Wandsworth London Borough Council ex p Hawthorne* (1995) 27 HLR 59, CA. See also *Adekunkle v Islington London Borough Council* (2009) November *Legal Action*, Mayor's and City of London County Court, where the local housing authority had decided that the applicant's choice to sell her house in the face of serious financial difficulties was 'a conscious and deliberate decision' which fell within the definition of 'deliberate act'. The judge said that view was 'mistaken and wrong' in the circumstances where a person's conscious decision is taken 'in a situation where there is no realistic alternative'.

[57] *R v Wandsworth London Borough Council ex p Hawthorne* (1995) 27 HLR 59, CA at 63.

[58] *R v Wandsworth London Borough Council ex p Hawthorne* (1995) 27 HLR 59, CA at 63, per Nourse LJ.

Unaware of a relevant fact

14.37   The proviso dealing with ignorance of material facts can be difficult to operate in practice. First, the local housing authority must identify whether the fact of which the applicant was ignorant was 'relevant'. Second, assuming that there was ignorance of a relevant fact, it must ask whether the applicant acted 'in good faith'.[59]

14.38   As one judge has observed, the proviso is:

> '... not without its difficulties. It is to be noted that the test is not the reasonableness of the applicant's actions, but whether they were taken in ignorance. This may seem unjust. A person who takes the trouble to find out all the relevant facts, but makes a reasonable but mistaken judgment, cannot apparently claim the benefit of the section; a person who makes no enquiries at all and therefore acts in ignorance, may be able to do so. The omission of a test of reasonableness has been criticised in the courts (see for example *R v Tower Hamlets London Borough Council, ex p Rouf*)[60] but the section remains unamended.'[61]

14.39   In using the words 'any relevant fact', Parliament has indicated that it intended a wide construction to be given to that phrase.[62] But 'relevant' to what? A person may have deliberately given up his or her existing home in the mistaken belief that there would be accommodation (or employment capable of funding accommodation) in a place to which he or she then moved. If that person was factually wrong about the availability of other accommodation (or employment) can that render the giving up of the original home not a 'deliberate' act?

14.40   In one case, a young woman gave up her home overseas to come to the UK in the mistaken belief that her family would accommodate her here. In another, a businessman gave up his home in the UK to move abroad in the mistaken belief that he would be pursuing a sound business venture overseas capable of financing alternative accommodation there. Both were ignorant of the true facts, but were these facts 'relevant' to the giving up of their homes? In both cases, the judges decided that they were 'relevant facts' that were capable of triggering the application of the proviso to what was otherwise manifestly the deliberate giving-up of their homes.[63]

14.41   Subsequently, the courts have drawn a distinction between 'matters of hope' and relevant facts.[64] In the case of a scientist who gave up

---

59   HA 1996, s 191(2).

60   *R v Tower Hamlets London Borough Council, ex p Rouf* (1991) 23 HLR 460, CA.

61   *R v Westminster City Council ex p Obeid* (1996) 29 HLR 389, QBD at 394, per Carnwath J.

62   *R v Hammersmith and Fulham London Borough Council ex p Lusi* (1991) 23 HLR 260, QBD at 269, per Roch J.

63   *R v Wandsworth London Borough Council ex p Rose* (1983) 11 HLR 105, QBD, and *R v Hammersmith and Fulham London Borough Council ex p Lusi* (1991) 23 HLR 260, QBD.

64   See the analysis of relevant case law in *Aw-Aden v Birmingham City Council* [2005] EWCA Civ 1834, (2006) July *Legal Action*, p 29, CA.

accommodation in Belgium to come to Birmingham, the Court of Appeal described his prospects of finding suitable employment as resting on 'little more than a wing and a prayer'.[65] The question of good faith simply did not arise, because the scientist's over-optimism did not constitute a relevant fact.[66]

14.42 Note that what the individual has been ignorant of must have been a 'fact', and not the legal consequences of that fact. For example, an applicant who decides not to pay his or her housing costs, in the mistaken belief that this (and the consequent eviction) will not prejudice any subsequent application for homelessness assistance, has not acted in ignorance of any fact but rather in ignorance of the legal consequences of the deliberate omission to pay.[67] A secure tenant who leaves her home in fear of threats of violence cannot be said to have been unaware of the 'fact' that her security of tenure would be lost in her absence. That is not a fact but 'a legal result of the factual departure which she made'.[68] Likewise, it has been suggested that ignorance of legal rights is not ignorance of a 'fact'.[69] The English Code contains some confusing advice regarding the scenario of a former tenant who left his or her home in response to a valid notice from the landlord where the former tenant was genuinely unaware that he or she had a legal right to remain until a possession order (and even execution of the subsequent warrant). This scenario is described as 'a general example of an act made in good faith' even though the tenant had 'the belief that they had no legal right to continue to occupy the accommodation', which suggests an ignorance of the legal position.[70] More obviously, if, as a matter of fact, an applicant had to do something by a particular date to retain his or her home and did not understand that there was such a deadline, the applicant's failure to act will not have been deliberate, as it was in ignorance of a relevant 'fact'.[71]

14.43 These two problem issues of 'relevant' and 'fact' come together in the situation in which an applicant leaves accommodation (A) to move to other accommodation (B) in the erroneous belief that he or she will be able to afford accommodation (B) or that the availability of benefits or employment will

---

[65] *Aw-Aden v Birmingham City Council* [2005] EWCA Civ 1834, (2006) July *Legal Action*, p 29, CA, per Maurice Kay LJ, at [11].

[66] Similarly, in *F v Birmingham City Council* [2006] EWCA Civ 1427, [2007] HLR 18, CA, where a young woman had 'closed her eyes to the obvious', in that case that housing benefit would not be available for the whole of the contractual rent, there was no relevant fact and thus the issue of whether she had acted in good faith did not arise for consideration.

[67] *R v Eastleigh Borough Council ex p Beattie (No 2)* (1984) 17 HLR 168, QBD.

[68] *R v Croydon London Borough Council ex p Toth* (1987) 20 HLR 576, CA at 582, per O'Connor LJ.

[69] *Brown v Hamilton District Council 1983 SLT 397*, per Lord Fraser and *R v Harrow London Borough Council ex p Weingold* (unreported) 24 August 1992, QBD.

[70] English Code, para 11.25; see **14.50** for an interpretation relating to ignorance of material facts rather than law.

[71] *R v Christchurch Borough Council ex p Conway* (1987) 19 HLR 238, QBD. In *Abdullahi v Brent London Borough Council* [2007] EWCA Civ 885, (2007) October *Legal Action*, p 26, CA, a woman's ignorance of her responsibility to pay the shortfall between her contractual rent and housing benefit was held to be a relevant fact and the issue of whether she had acted in good faith should have been considered by the local housing authority.

make property (B) affordable. If that all turns out to be wrong, can the applicant be said to have moved from (A) in ignorance of a relevant fact?[72] In *R v Westminster City Council ex p Obeid*, Carnwath J said:

> '... an applicant's appreciation of the prospects of future housing or future employment can be treated as "awareness of a relevant fact" for the purposes of the subsection, provided it is sufficiently specific (that is related to specific employment or specific housing opportunities) and provided it is based on some genuine investigation and not mere "aspiration". Although that interpretation may not accord with what one would normally understand by a reference in a statute to a "relevant fact", it is an interpretation by which I am bound. It is perhaps justified by the general intent of the Act, to ensure that those who find themselves under the extreme pressures of homelessness should not be penalised except for decisions made with their eyes fully open.'[73]

This formulation was approved by the Court of Appeal in *Aw-Aden v Birmingham City Council*[74] and in *Ugiagbe v Southwark London Borough Council*.[75]

Good faith

14.44 'Good faith' is a phrase introducing similar complexity.[76] HA 1996, Part 7 couples lack of awareness and 'good faith'. The test on lack of awareness is subjective: 'Was *the applicant* unaware of any relevant fact?' rather than 'would a reasonable person have been unaware of that fact?'[77] Then, if there was lack of awareness, the applicant must additionally have acted in 'good faith' for the act not to be considered 'deliberate' for the purposes of the definition of intentional homelessness.

14.45 A mistake of judgment may constitute an act in good faith, but not those instances based on 'wilful ignorance'[78] nor those based on 'mere aspiration'.[79] As the Court of Appeal put it in one case:

---

[72] This was precisely the scenario in *F v Birmingham City Council* [2006] EWCA Civ 1427, [2007] HLR 18, CA, where a tenant gave up her secure tenancy in the belief that housing benefit would be available for the whole of the contractual rent on a private rented tenancy. She had 'closed her eyes to the obvious' and so the issue of whether she had acted in good faith did not arise. There is a helpful synopsis of the issue of 'relevant fact' in the judgment of May LJ at [17].

[73] *R v Westminster City Council ex p Obeid* (1996) 29 HLR 389, QBD, at 398.

[74] [2005] EWCA Civ 1834, (2006) July *Legal* Action, p 29, CA, per Maurice Kay LJ, at [11]. See **14.41**.

[75] [2009] EWCA Civ 31, (2009) April *Legal Action*, p 22, CA, per Lloyd LJ, at [20].

[76] HA 1996, s 191(2).

[77] *O'Connor v Kensington and Chelsea Royal London Borough Council* [2004] EWCA Civ 394, [2004] HLR 37, CA at [30] and [34], per Sedley LJ.

[78] *O'Connor v Kensington and Chelsea Royal London Borough Council* [2004] EWCA Civ 394, [2004] HLR 37, CA at [30] per Sedley LJ.

[79] *R v Westminster City Council ex p Obeid* (1996) 29 HLR 389, QBD at 397, per Carnwath J.

'... the statutory dividing line ... comes not at the point where the applicant's ignorance of a relevant fact was due to his own unreasonable conduct, but at the point where, for example, by shutting his eyes to the obvious he can be said not to have acted in good faith.'[80]

14.46 If there is dishonesty, the act or omission cannot have been made in good faith.[81] Lloyd LJ has said in the Court of Appeal:

'the use of the phrase "good faith" carries a connotation of some kind of impropriety, or some element of misuse or abuse of the legislation. It is aimed at protecting local housing authorities from finding that they owe the full duty under Part 7 of the 1996 Act to a person who, despite some relevant ignorance, ought to be regarded as intentionally homeless ... Dishonesty is the most obvious kind of conduct which it would catch, and wilful blindness in the Nelsonian sense comes close to that.'[82]

14.47 'Foolish or imprudent' or unreasonable behaviour is not sufficient to put a person into the category of not acting in good faith.[83]

14.48 In *R v Westminster City Council ex p N-Dormadingar*,[84] the court set out the following principles to be considered by local housing authorities in relation to 'unaware of a relevant fact' and 'good faith':

(1) the applicant must show that he or she was unaware of some relevant fact existing at the date that the accommodation was given up;

(2) whether or not the applicant made any inquiries into the existence of that relevant fact is relevant to determining the applicant's awareness (or not) of its existence;

(3) a fact is relevant where, had the applicant been aware of it, he or she would have taken it into account in deciding whether to give up the accommodation;[85]

(4) the fact must be sufficiently clear and definite for its existence to be objectively determined; and

(5) an applicant's lack of foresight in the future, or a deficiency in the applicant's foresight into the future, is not unawareness of an existing fact.

---

[80] *O'Connor v Kensington and Chelsea Royal London Borough Council* [2004] EWCA Civ 394, [2004] HLR 37, CA at [34], per Sedley LJ.

[81] English Code, para 11.26; *R v Barnet London Borough Council ex p Rughooputh* (1993) 25 HLR 607, CA.

[82] *Ugiagbe v Southwark London Borough Council* [2009] EWCA Civ 31, [2009] HLR, CA at [27], per Lloyd LJ.

[83] *Ugiagbe v Southwark London Borough Council* [2009] EWCA Civ 31, [2009] HLR, CA at [26], per Lloyd LJ.

[84] *R v Westminster City Council ex p N-Dormadingar* (1997) Times, 20 November, QBD.

[85] See **14.37–14.43**.

14.49 Both Codes give examples of acts or omissions that could be made in good faith:[86]

(1)   a person accrues rent arrears, unaware that he or she may be entitled to housing or other social security benefits;

(2)   an owner-occupier, faced with foreclosure or possession proceedings to which there is no defence, sells or surrenders the property before a possession order is obtained;

(3)   a tenant faced with possession proceedings to which there is no defence surrenders the property to the landlord.

14.50 The latter two examples could be analysed as ignorance of the legal right to remain in the property. In relation to the last example, both Codes advise that the ignorance might be of 'the general pressure on the authority for housing' – a matter of fact rather than law.[87]

14.51 Note that the adverb 'deliberately' governs only the act or omission itself, not the outcome, or consequences, of the act or omission. The question is not: 'Has the applicant deliberately become homeless?' but rather: 'Has the applicant deliberately done something, or failed to do something, as a result of which he or she is now homeless?'[88]

14.52 Whilst each case must be considered on its own facts, the Codes and the courts have considered a number of different scenarios that provide some useful guidance.[89] Each is examined below.

Acts or omissions not generally considered deliberate

14.53 The Codes of Guidance suggest several circumstances in which acts or omissions of applicants 'should not' be considered to be 'deliberate'.[90]

(1)   Incapacity

14.54 The Codes advise that where the local housing authority has reason to believe that an applicant was incapable of managing his or her affairs, for example by reason of age, mental illness or disability, his or her act or failure to act at that time should not be considered to have been 'deliberate'.[91] The formulation in the English Code suggests that both the very old and the very young might be considered incapable as a result of their age.[92] Applying this

---

86   English Code, para 11.27; Welsh Code, para 15.9.
87   English Code, para 11.27(iii); Welsh Code, para 15.9(iii).
88   *Devenport v Salford City Council* (1983) 8 HLR 54, CA.
89   English Code, paras 11.16–11.20; Welsh Code, paras 15.4–15.7.
90   English Code, para 11.17; Welsh Code, para 15.5 prefers 'may not be considered deliberate'.
91   English Code, para 11.17(ii); Welsh Code, para 15.5(i).
92   Earlier editions of the English Code referred to 'old age' rather than 'age', an approach still

approach, if the applicant was incapable at the date when the act or omission was committed, he or she will not have become homeless intentionally.

14.55 Even if the applicant appears (at the date of his or her application) to be capable, he or she may have been temporarily incapable at the date that he or she committed the act or omission.

14.56 Although the phrasing in the Code appears to reflect part of the priority need test for 'vulnerability',[93] it does not follow, just because an applicant has been found to be vulnerable (and thereby to have a priority need) at the date of the application for homelessness assistance, that he or she was incapable at the time when the accommodation was lost.[94]

(2)   Limited capacity and/or frailty

14.57 Even if the applicant is generally capable of managing his or her own affairs and had a measure of capacity at the relevant time, both Codes advise local housing authorities to consider whether the particular act or omission leading to the loss of accommodation was 'the result of limited mental capacity; or a temporary aberration or aberrations caused by mental illness or frailty'.[95]

14.58 The English Code advises that a temporary aberration or aberrations may have been caused by an assessed substance abuse problem and that, in those circumstances, an act or omission should not be considered as deliberate.[96]

(3)   Lacking foresight or prudence

14.59 The act or omission may have been imprudent or have been a result of lack of foresight. If the applicant acted in good faith, it will not generally be considered that such act or omission was deliberate.[97]

---

contained in the Welsh Code. This guidance should not be taken as meaning that young people and children cannot be found to have become homeless intentionally even when their deliberate acts were committed when they were children. See *Denton v Southwark London Borough Council* [2007] EWCA Civ 623, [2008] HLR 161, CA, where the Court of Appeal upheld a finding that a 21-year-old had become homeless intentionally, and *White v Southwark London Borough Council* [2008] EWC A Civ 792, (2008) October *Legal Action* , p 37, where the Court of Appeal said that actions of children as young as 13 might be 'deliberate acts'. See **14.197–14.201**.

[93]   HA 1996, s 189(1)(c); see **13.62–13.69**.

[94]   *R v Wirral Metropolitan Borough Council ex p Bell* (1995) 27 HLR 234, QBD.

[95]   English Code, para 11.17(iii); Welsh Code, para 15.5(ii); *Hijazi v Kensington and Chelsea Royal London Borough Council* [2003] EWCA Civ 692, [2003] HLR 72, CA.

[96]   See *Kendall v City of Westminster Council* (2009) November *Legal Action*, Central London County Court. However, a drug abuser who rendered himself incapable of breaking his addiction has been found to have 'deliberately' spent his available money on drugs rather than accommodation, and thereby caused his own homelessness.

[97]   English Code, para 11.17(v); Welsh Code, para 15.6(i).

(4) Financial difficulties beyond the applicant's control

14.60 The Codes give examples of a tenant not paying the rent as a result of housing benefit delays, or financial difficulties which were beyond the applicant's control.[98] Where the applicant was genuinely unable to keep up rent (or mortgage) payments, even after claiming benefits, and there was no further financial help available, giving up possession of the home would not generally be considered deliberate.[99] However, in those circumstances, the local housing authority is entitled to consider why the arrears accrued and the applicant's ability to meet the commitment to pay housing costs at the time that it was taken on.[100] That is because the 'act' of the applicant, which may have ultimately caused his or her homelessness, could have been the taking out of an impossible rent or mortgage commitment in the first place.

(5) Under duress

14.61 The English Code advises that an act or omission made when the applicant was under duress should not generally be considered deliberate.[101] There is no further explanation. An example would presumably be someone subjected to domestic violence who is required by his or her partner to give up any legal interest in the home.

(6) Fleeing violence

14.62 The Codes advise that where an applicant fled his or her home because of violence (or threats of violence likely to be carried out), but failed to pursue all legal remedies against the perpetrator, neither the act of leaving nor the omission to use remedies should be considered 'deliberate'.[102]

14.63 However, the result may be different where the applicant's own misbehaviour had led to the violence or threats of violence.[103]

(7) Serving a prison sentence

14.64 The Welsh Code gives an example of a prisoner who has just served a sentence (and presumably lost his or her accommodation during the term of

---

[98] English Code, para 11.17(i); Welsh Code, para 15.6(ii), which does not refer to housing benefit delays but to real financial difficulties. See **14.164–14.173**.

[99] English Code, para 11.18; Welsh Code, para 15.6(ii). For a recent example, see *Adekunkle v Islington London Borough Council* (2009) November *Legal Action*, Mayor's and City of London County Court.

[100] English Code, para 11.19; Welsh Code, para 15.6(ii). See *William v Wandsworth London Borough Council* [2006] EWCA Civ 535, [2006] HLR 42, CA.

[101] English Code, para 11.17(iv).

[102] English Code para 11.23; Welsh Code, para 15.6(iii), which mentions the circumstances where legal remedies were not pursued because of a 'well-grounded fear of reprisal'. See **14.187–14.196**.

[103] English Code, para 11.20(vi); Welsh Code, para 15.7(v); *R v Hammersmith and Fulham London Borough Council ex p P* (1990) 22 HLR 21, QBD. See **14.195–14.196**.

imprisonment) for offences which were not in themselves breaches of his or her tenancy agreement.[104] This reflects the Welsh Assembly Government's view that 'the actions that caused the person to be imprisoned ... should not be considered as grounds for regarding him or her as intentionally homeless',[105] unless the offence which resulted in the sentence of imprisonment was a direct breach of the prisoner's tenancy agreement.

14.65 In England, the tendency has been to treat the criminal act as having been 'deliberate', but then to focus on whether it was causative of the homelessness.[106]

Activities that may be regarded as 'deliberate'

14.66 The Codes of Guidance suggest a number of circumstances in which acts or omissions of applicants 'may be regarded as deliberate'.[107]

(1) Voluntary sale or voluntary non-payment of housing costs

14.67 If an applicant has chosen to sell his or her home where there was no risk of losing it, that action will generally be treated as having been 'deliberate'. The question of whether any resultant homelessness was intentional will turn on other aspects of the statutory definition, eg whether it would have been reasonable to have continued in occupation of that home.[108]

14.68 Where a home has been lost for failure to meet liabilities for housing costs and where any rent or mortgage arrears accrued as a result of a 'wilful and persistent refusal to pay', the omission to pay will generally be treated as having been 'deliberate'.[109] The Codes' emphasis on persistent and wilful default underscores the obvious point that non-payment caused by lack of funds will not be deliberate.[110] 'Wilful default' in making payment, however, is sufficient to establish a deliberate omission.[111]

(2) Neglecting affairs

14.69 An omission may be regarded as deliberate where 'someone could be said to have significantly neglected his or her affairs having disregarded sound advice from qualified persons'.[112] Into the scope of this example would fall an

---

[104] Welsh Code, para 15.6(iv). See **14.217–14.218**.

[105] Welsh Code, para 14.64.

[106] English Code, para 11.14. See **14.217–14.218**.

[107] English Code, para 11.20; Welsh Code, para 15.7.

[108] See **14.108–14.126**.

[109] English Code, para 11.20(ii); Welsh Code, para 15.7(i). For example, see *William v Wandsworth London Borough Council* [2006] EWCA Civ 535, [2006] HLR 42, CA and *Watchman v Ipswich Borough Council* [2007] EWCA Civ 348, [2007] HLR 33, CA. See **14.164–14.173**.

[110] See **14.164–14.173**.

[111] *R v Wyre Borough Council ex p Joyce* (1983) 11 HLR 73, QBD, discussed further at **14.72**.

[112] English Code, para 11.20(iii); Welsh Code, para 15.7(ii).

applicant who temporarily left accommodation without making arrangements for the rent to be paid in his or her absence.[113]

(3)   Giving up a home

14.70   The Codes advise that 'voluntary surrender of adequate accommodation in this country or abroad which it would have been reasonable for the applicant to continue to occupy' may be regarded as a deliberate act.[114] Again, whether the applicant is likely to be found to have become homeless intentionally will turn on other parts of the statutory definition and, in particular, on whether it would have been reasonable to have continued occupying the accommodation given up.[115]

(4)   Eviction for anti-social behaviour

14.71   The Codes suggest that 'where someone is evicted because of anti-social behaviour, nuisance to neighbours, harassment, etc', that behaviour may be treated as having been deliberate.[116] The nuisance or anti-social behaviour that brings about the eviction will often be the deliberate 'act' of the applicant. In other cases, the applicant's deliberate 'omission' may have been his or her failure to control or remove the perpetrator of the nuisance, thus constituting his or her acquiescence in the perpetrator's nuisance behaviour.[117] In such cases a local housing authority is entitled to consider the behaviour of the family as a whole and to come to a decision that the applicant had either acquiesced in, or failed to prevent, the nuisance behaviour which had resulted in the family's eviction.[118] A tenant subject to a possession order on the grounds of waste to the property or deterioration of the furniture may also be considered to have committed a deliberate act (damage) or omission (failure to maintain).[119]

14.72   Local housing authorities need not restrict their application of this guidance to cases where tenants enjoying security of tenure have been subject to possession orders under one or more of the 'fault' grounds for possession.[120] If a private landlord refuses to renew an assured shorthold tenancy, and subsequently obtains a possession order under the Housing Act 1988, s 21, the local housing authority is entitled to consider the reason for the landlord seeking possession. If it was due to the fault of the tenant, or members of the

---

113   *R v Wycombe District Council ex p Mahsood* (1988) 20 HLR 683, QBD.
114   English Code, para 11.20(iv); Welsh Code, para 15.7(iii). See **14.174–14.180**.
115   For an unusual example involving joint owners see *Bellamy v Hounslow London Borough Council* [2006] EWCA Civ 535, [2006] HLR 42, CA. See **14.81** and **14.108–14.126**.
116   English Code, para 11.20(v); Welsh Code, para 15.7(iv). See **14.195–14.196**.
117   *Devenport v Salford City Council* (1983) 8 HLR 54, CA, and *R v Swansea City Council ex p John* (1982) 9 HLR 56, QBD. See **14.78–14.82**.
118   *R v East Hertfordshire District Council ex p Bannon* (1986) 18 HLR 515, QBD.
119   *R v Sevenoaks District Council ex p Reynolds* (1990) 22 HLR 250, CA.
120   Housing Act 1988, Sch 2, Part 1 and Housing Act 1985, Sch 2.

tenant's household, the loss of accommodation may be found to have been caused by the deliberate act of, or omission by, the tenant.[121]

(5) Inflicting violence

14.73 Perpetrators of 'violence or threats of violence', as defined by HA 1996, Part 7,[122] who are evicted because of their behaviour, may be considered to have committed a deliberate act.[123] Such an eviction may arise from the landlord applying for possession on one or more of the grounds that specifically relate to nuisance, criminal convictions or domestic violence,[124] or as a result of the victim of domestic violence either:

(1) obtaining an occupation order in family court proceedings requiring the perpetrator to leave;[125] or

(2) bringing the tenancy to an end by notice.

(6) Giving up tied accommodation

14.74 Where an applicant has been living in tied accommodation and leaves his or her job, thereby losing the accommodation, the local housing authority may well find that there has been a 'deliberate' act.[126] The Codes remind local housing authorities that they should go on to consider the other elements of the statutory definition, in particular whether it would have been reasonable for the employee to have continued in the employment and/or reasonable to have continued to occupy the accommodation. If the applicant has been dismissed, the local housing authority should make inquiries to ascertain whether the acts or omissions leading to the applicant's dismissal were the applicant's 'deliberate' acts or omissions. The English Code recommends that former members of the armed forces, who are required to vacate service quarters as a result of giving notice to leave the service, should not be considered to have become homeless intentionally.[127]

Summary of 'deliberate act or omission'

14.75 In summary, a deliberate act or omission is one that:

- is freely made;

- by a person (the applicant) in possession of all the relevant facts;

---

[121] *R v Rochester upon Medway City Council ex p Williams* (1994) 26 HLR 588, QBD, and *R v Nottingham City Council ex p Edwards* (1999) 31 HLR 33, QBD.

[122] See HA 1996, s 177(1) and (1A) and s 178. See **11.78–11.88**.

[123] English Code, para 11.20(vi)); the Welsh Code, para 15.7(v). See **14.195–14.196**.

[124] Housing Act 1985, Sch 2, Grounds 2 and 2A; Housing Act 1988, Sch 2, Grounds 14 and 14A.

[125] Family Law Act 1996, s 33.

[126] English Code, para 11.20(vii)); Welsh Code, para 15.7(vi); *R v Kyle and Carrick District Council ex p Speck 1993 GWD 1566, OH.*

[127] English Code, para 11.15.

- who is not forced to act (or fail to act); and

- who is not unaware of a relevant fact.

14.76 If the applicant was unaware of a relevant fact, his or her act will not be considered deliberate if he or she acted in good faith, ie he or she was genuinely ignorant of that relevant fact and that ignorance was not based on an unrealistic degree of optimism, a shutting of the eyes to the obvious, or on dishonesty.

14.77 Even if the local housing authority finds that this limb of the test is satisfied, it cannot find that the applicant has become homeless intentionally unless the other four limbs are also made out.

Was the deliberate act or omission *by the applicant?*

14.78 Each applicant is entitled to individual consideration of his or her application. This means that even where one member of a household has been found to have become homeless intentionally, an application from another member must still be individually considered. For this reason it is inappropriate to use the term 'intentionally homeless family'. An applicant can only be found to have become homeless intentionally if it was his or her deliberate act or omission that caused the homelessness.[128] Local housing authorities should therefore consider whether the particular applicant acted deliberately or deliberately failed to act and, if not, whether the applicant had acquiesced in the deliberate act or omission of another that led to the loss of accommodation. In this sense, acquiescence can be a deliberate failure to prevent another from acting or failing to act in a particular way.

14.79 Where an applicant's case is that he or she did not acquiesce in the deliberate act or omission of another member of the household (that has led to the loss of accommodation), the English Code suggests that the burden of proof rests on the applicant.[129] That slightly overstates the position and is not repeated in the specific part of the Code dealing with the 'Whose conduct?' issue.[130] Perhaps a more accurate way of summarising the relevant law would be that there is a presumption (or a local housing authority is entitled to make an assumption or draw an inference), in the absence of any material indicating the contrary, that where one member of the household's conduct has been such that she or he would be regarded as having deliberately acted or failed to act in such a way as to cause the homelessness, the other household members were party to that conduct.[131] However, once there are positive assertions by an applicant (or some other evidence) that there was no acquiescence, such as one partner asserting that he or she had always protested at the other partner's

---

[128] English Code, para 11.9; Welsh Code, para 15.11; *R v North Devon District Council ex p Lewis* [1981] 1 WLR 328, QBD, and *City of Gloucester v Miles* (1985) 17 HLR 292, CA.

[129] English Code, para 11.5; not reproduced in the Welsh Code.

[130] English Code, para 11.9; Welsh Code, para 15.11.

[131] *R v North Devon District Council ex p Lewis* [1981] 1 WLR 328, QBD.

failure to pay the rent or mortgage, the local housing authority must abandon any presumption, assumption or inference and inquire into the issue fully.[132]

14.80 The case law is replete with examples of everyday situations in which the question has arisen as to whether the applicant has acquiesced in the conduct of another household member. This includes situations in which the other household member has:

- failed to pay the rent in circumstances where both partners were involved in managing the household's finances;[133] or

- terminated a joint tenancy;[134] or

- given up his or her job (to which tied accommodation was linked);[135] or

- changed jobs (from one to which future re-housing was linked to another with no promise of re-housing);[136] or

- misspent the money earmarked for housing costs (whether on drink, drugs or gambling);[137] or

- caused nuisance or annoyance to others;[138] or

---

[132] *R v West Dorset District Council ex p Phillips* (1985) 17 HLR 336, QBD; *R v Eastleigh Borough Council ex p Beattie (No 2)* (1984) 17 HLR 168, QBD; *R v East Northamptonshire Borough Council ex p Spruce* (1988) 20 HLR 508, QBD; *R v Thanet District Council ex p Groves* (1990) 22 HLR 223, QBD; *Quinton v East Hertfordshire District Council* (2003) April *Legal Action*, p 27, Luton County Court; and *N v Allerdale Borough Council* (2008) October *Legal Action*, p 38, Carlisle County Court.

[133] *R v Barnet London Borough Council ex p O'Connor* (1990) 22 HLR 486, QBD; and *R v Nottingham City Council ex p Caine* (1996) 28 HLR 374, CA, where, in both cases, the local housing authority was entitled to find acquiescence.

[134] *R v Penwith District Council ex p Trevena* (1984) 17 HLR 526, QBD, where a decision that the former joint tenant remaining in occupation had acquiesced was held to be one that no reasonable local housing authority would have come to.

[135] *R v North Devon DC ex p Lewis* [1981] 1 WLR 328, QBD, where it was held that, on the evidence, the local housing authority was entitled to find acquiescence.

[136] *R v Mole Valley DC ex p Burton* (1989) 20 HLR 479, QBD, where the decision that the applicant had acquiesced in that behaviour was quashed. She had known of the behaviour but had also acted in good faith in believing his assurances that they would qualify for council housing.

[137] *R v West Dorset DC ex p Phillips* (1984) 17 HLR 336, QBD, where a decision that the wife had acquiesced (when she had informed the local housing authority that she did not know about the non-payment and had always said that the husband's drinking would lead to trouble) was quashed.

[138] *Smith v Bristol City Council* [1981] LAG Bull 287, CA; *Devenport v Salford City Council* (1983) 8 HLR 54, CA, where there was acquiescence; *R v Swansea City Council ex p John* (1982) 9 HLR 56, QBD, where a finding that the wife had acquiesced by failing to remove her husband who had caused nuisance was upheld; *R v East Hertfordshire District Council ex p Bannon* (1986) 18 HLR 515, QBD, where a finding that the conduct of the whole of the family was to blame and therefore the applicant had acquiesced was upheld; and *N v Allerdale*

- as head of the household, taken the family from secure to insecure accommodation;[139] or

- withheld the rent in the mistaken belief that there was an entitlement to do so on account of disrepair;[140] or

- re-mortgaged the home to such an extent that the debt became unmanageable.[141]

14.81 In summary, the deliberate act or omission must have been by the applicant. In cases where the deliberate act or omission was by another member of the applicant's household, a local housing authority is entitled to presume that the applicant acquiesced in that conduct unless there is an assertion, or evidence, that the applicant did not acquiesce. Where there is an assertion, or evidence, that the applicant did not acquiesce, the local housing authority must then make full inquiries into the issue.[142]

14.82 Even if the local housing authority finds that this limb of the test is satisfied, it cannot find that the applicant has become homeless intentionally unless the other four limbs are also made out.

Was it as a consequence of that deliberate act or omission that the applicant ceased to occupy accommodation?

14.83 This requires consideration of two elements:

(1) Has there been any cessation of occupation at all?

(2) If so, did the deliberate act or omission cause the cessation of occupation?

Only if both are answered affirmatively will this limb of the statutory definition be made out.

Borough Council (2008) October *Legal Action*, p 38, Carlisle County Court, where the local housing authority's inquiries into whether a mother had acquiesced in her son's anti-social behaviour were inadequate.

[139] *R v Tower Hamlets London Borough Council ex p Khatun (Asma)* (1993) 27 HLR 344, CA, where the wife was found to have acquiesced by having been content to leave the decisions to her husband.

[140] *R v Nottingham City Council ex p Caine* (1995) 28 HLR 374, CA, where the decision that the applicant had acquiesced was upheld, as she must have known of the non-payment.

[141] *R v Barnet London Borough Council ex p O'Connor* (1990) 22 HLR 486, QBD, where the decision that the wife had acquiesced was upheld – she had said that she left financial matters to her husband, but had signed two mortgage applications on which she had made false representations.

[142] In the unusual case of *Bellamy v Hounslow London Borough Council* [2006] EWCA Civ 535, [2006] HLR 42, CA, the applicant's case was that she was not aware that she, as a legal joint owner of her home with her mother, had a power to object to a sale. The local housing authority did not believe the applicant and the Court of Appeal held that the local housing authority had been entitled not to believe her.

Has there been any cessation of occupation at all?

14.84 The deliberate act or omission must have had the consequence that the applicant 'ceases to occupy' accommodation.[143] Accordingly, the applicant must have actually occupied the accommodation the loss of which was caused by his or her deliberate act or omission.[144] There need not have been continuous occupation at all times, but the accommodation must at least have been at the disposal of the applicant and available for his or her occupation at the time it was given up.[145]

14.85 The accommodation the applicant has ceased to occupy may have been anywhere in the world; local housing authorities are not restricted to considering accommodation the applicant has occupied in the UK.[146]

14.86 It follows that decisions by applicants:

(1) to rid themselves of accommodation that they have not occupied; or

(2) not to accept accommodation offered to them to occupy,

cannot result in findings that they have become homeless intentionally. In *R v Wandsworth London Borough Council ex p Oteng*,[147] the applicant left a home that she shared with her two sisters and, over 2 years later, she transferred her interest in the property to her mother. The local housing authority decided that she had become homeless intentionally as a result of voluntarily transferring her interest. The Court of Appeal rejected that approach. The transfer of interest had not caused the applicant to cease to occupy the accommodation – that had occurred 2 years earlier.[148]

14.87 Applying the correct approach, homeless applicants in temporary accommodation provided under HA 1996, Part 7 who refuse offers of

---

[143] HA 1996, s 191(1).

[144] *R v Westminster City Council, ex p Chambers* (1982) 6 HLR 24, QBD, and *Din v Wandsworth London Borough Council* [1983] 1 AC 657, HL.

[145] See the unusual facts of *R v Westminster City Council ex p Khan* (1991) 23 HLR 230, QBD, where the applicant had not actually occupied the accommodation, but it was held to have been at her disposal and available for her occupation; and see *Lee-Lawrence v Penwith District Council* [2006] EWCA Civ 1672, (2006) July *Legal Action*, p 29, CA, where holding the keys to a house provided on a tenancy and claiming housing benefit in order to pay the charges was held to be sufficient evidence to uphold a finding of occupation for the purposes of HA 1996, s 191(1).

[146] English Code, para 11.10.

[147] *R v Wandsworth London Borough Council ex p Oteng* (1994) 26 HLR 413, CA. See also *R v Westminster City Council ex p De Souza* (1997) 29 HLR 649, QBD.

[148] In *Quaid v Westminster City Council* (2008) February *Legal Action*, p 41, Central London County Court, the applicant had committed offences while he was street homeless. He subsequently acquired a place at a Salvation Army hostel. He was convicted of those offences, sent to prison and lost the hostel place. The local housing authority found that he had become homeless intentionally as a result of the offences committed. The decision was varied to a decision that he had not become homeless intentionally. The commission of offences had not caused the loss of the hostel place.

accommodation cannot become homeless intentionally from the accommodation that they refuse, as they have never occupied it (although they may be found to have become homeless intentionally from temporary accommodation lost as a result of their refusal of other accommodation).[149] However, in such cases, local housing authorities should consider whether it was the refusal that caused the loss of the temporary accommodation, or whether there was some other reason for its loss.[150]

Did the act or omission cause the cessation of occupation?

Identifying the operative causes of the loss of accommodation

14.88 In most situations, there will be a number of events that, taken together, caused the applicant to cease to occupy the accommodation. Some of those events may not be the direct causes of the loss of the accommodation, but may have started off the chain of events that led to the loss of accommodation.

14.89 HA 1996, Part 7 uses the word 'anything' to refer to what has been done (or failed to be done).[151] However, the subject of enquiry is not every act or omission in which the applicant engaged at the time she or he became homeless, or in the lead-up to that time. HA 1996, Part 7 is concerned only with the doing of (or failure to do) something 'in consequence of which' the applicant ceased to occupy his or her accommodation.

14.90 It is necessary, therefore, to identify the operative causes of the loss of accommodation, and then to consider whether any of those operative causes was the applicant's deliberate act or omission.[152] Such an operative cause can be doing (or failing to do) 'anything'.[153] If just one of the operative causes was the applicant's deliberate act or omission, that will be sufficient for the applicant to fall within this limb of the definition of having become homeless intentionally.[154]

14.91 Various judges have commented on the difficulties involved in establishing the cause or causes of the loss of accommodation. In *R v Hackney London Borough Council ex p Ajayi*,[155] Dyson J said:

> 'Questions of causation are notoriously difficult and, in my judgment, the Court should be slow to intervene to strike down the decisions of administrative bodies on such questions and should do so only in clear cases. I cannot accept that the effective cause should always be regarded in these cases as the chronologically

---

149   For example, *R v Brent London Borough Council ex p Awua* [1996] AC 55, HL.
150   *Sonde v Newham London Borough Council* (1999) June *Legal Action*, p 24, Bow County Court. See **14.219–14.220**.
151   HA 1996, s 191(1).
152   See **14.164–14.220**.
153   HA 1996, s 191(1).
154   *O'Connor v Kensington and Chelsea Royal London Borough Council* [2004] EWCA Civ 394, [2004] HLR 37, CA.
155   (1997) 30 HLR 473, QBD.

immediate or proximate cause. In some cases, the cause closest in point of time will be regarded as the effective cause ... In others, the cause closest in time will be not so regarded.'[156]

14.92 In *O'Connor v Kensington and Chelsea Royal London Borough Council*[157] the applicant's father was terminally ill and the whole family travelled to Ireland to his bedside, starting off a chain of events that eventually resulted in the loss of their accommodation in London. The father's illness was not an act or omission of the applicants and, although the decision to travel to Ireland was the applicants' act:

> '... nobody but a logician would say that it was in consequence of the family's going to Ireland to see a sick relative that they lost their accommodation.'[158]

The 'reasonable likelihood' test

14.93 A loss of accommodation must have occurred as a consequence of the applicant's deliberate act or omission. This does not mean that there needs to be any direct link between the nature of the act done (or the omission) and the occupation of accommodation. An applicant, who deliberately gambles at a casino and loses every resource he or she has, has done an act (the gambling) that is in itself entirely unrelated to the accommodation subsequently lost for failure to pay housing costs. A convicted international drug dealer who, while in prison, has his or her house confiscated and sold as a proceed of crime, has done an act (criminal drug dealing) wholly unrelated to the former home. The issue, however, is not whether the loss of the home was the intended consequence of the deliberate act or omission but whether it is *a* consequence.

14.94 This is not to say that acts or omissions wholly removed from any connection at all with the eventual loss of accommodation can always be counted if they, as a matter of fact, did 'cause' that loss. Without any sensible restraint on the plain words, absurd decisions might be made, eg that a father who chastised his son too harshly for the liking of the mother (who then excluded the father from her home) had lost his accommodation in consequence of the deliberate act of chastisement.[159] The courts have, accordingly, striven to identify a narrower basis on which the link between the act and its consequences must be made out rather than a simple test of strict causation. Through the case law a test of 'reasonable likelihood' has emerged.[160] The question to be posed is: 'Was the loss of the accommodation the reasonably likely result of what the applicant did?' Rather more straightforwardly, one judge has suggested that the correct approach is:

---

[156] *R v Hackney London Borough Council ex p Ajayi* (1997) 30 HLR 473, QBD at 479, per Dyson J, subsequently approved by the Court of Appeal in *William v Wandsworth London Borough Council* [2006] EWCA Civ 535, [2006] HLR 42, CA and in *Watchman v Ipswich Borough Council* ([2007] EWCA Civ 348, [2007] HLR 33, CA.
[157] [2004] EWCA Civ 394, [2004] HLR 37, CA.
[158] [2004] EWCA Civ 394, [2004] HLR 37, CA at [27] per Sedley LJ.
[159] *R v Westminster City Council ex p Reid* (1994) 26 HLR 690, QBD.
[160] *R v Hounslow London Borough Council ex p R* (1997) 29 HLR 939, QBD.

- to look at what the applicant did;

- find that the ultimate result was loss of accommodation; and

- then to ask 'if the fair-minded bystander could say to himself, "He asked for it".'[161]

14.95 This approach of 'reasonable likelihood' has been approved by the Court of Appeal[162] and is to be preferred to a test of whether the act done was too 'remote' from the resultant loss of accommodation.[163]

14.96 The most recent formulation of the correct approach by the Court of Appeal is:

> 'What is called for, then, in a case where there are potentially multiple causes of an applicant's homelessness, is a careful judgment on the particular facts looking to see whether homelessness is shown to have been a likely consequence of the applicant's deliberate act, bearing in mind that it is the applicant's own responsibility for his homelessness that the statute is looking for. The precise question to be asked and answered of course relates to the time when the applicant in fact became homeless: that is the result of their Lordships' decision in *Din*.'[164]

14.97 Applying this approach, former prisoners, who are homeless on their release, face being found to have become homeless intentionally if the reasonably likely result of their deliberate acts in committing criminal offences, viewed objectively, was a sentence of imprisonment resulting in the loss of their accommodation.[165]

Intervening events

14.98 The causative link between the deliberate act or omission and the actual loss of accommodation must be in place throughout. An act or omission of a third party that actually causes the loss of accommodation will break that link. For example, an applicant may be on the brink of having his or her home repossessed for non-payment of rent or a mortgage, but if, on the eve of eviction, the house is burnt down by a third party, the homelessness cannot

---

[161] *Robinson v Torbay District Council* [1982] 1 All ER 726, QBD at 731, per HHJ Goodall.

[162] *Devenport v Salford City Council* (1983) 8 HLR 54, CA; *R v Westminster City Council ex p Reid* (1994) 26 HLR 691, CA; *Stewart v Lambeth London Borough Council* [2002] EWCA Civ 753, [2002] HLR 40, CA; and, most recently, *Watchman v Ipswich Borough Council* [2007] EWCA Civ 348, [2007] HLR 33, CA.

[163] *R v Thanet District Council ex p Reeve* (1981) 6 HLR 31, QBD.

[164] *Watchman v Ipswich Borough Council* [2007] EWCA Civ 348, [2007] HLR 33, CA at [22], per Laws LJ.

[165] *R v Hounslow London Borough Council ex p R* (1997) 29 HLR 939, QBD; *Minchin v Sheffield City Council* (2000) Times, 26 August, CA, and *Stewart v Lambeth London Borough Council* [2002] EWCA Civ 753, (2002) 34 HLR 40, CA. The Welsh Code, however, advises Welsh local housing authorities against findings of intentional homelessness in such circumstances, unless the acts, which led to the applicant's imprisonment, were also breaches of his or her tenancy: Welsh Code, para 15.6(iv). See **14.217–14.218**.

have been intentional, as it was not a consequence of the applicant's omission to pay. In *Gloucester City Council v Miles*,[166] the applicant left her home, but (because she did not give up her tenancy) she was not homeless. Finding her gone, her husband vandalised the home, rendering it uninhabitable; his act rendered her homeless. As Stephenson LJ put it:

'The relevant questions – when, how and why did she become homeless – admit of only one answer: on vandalisation of her home.'[167]

14.99 Again, loss of accommodation by prisoners can provide classic examples of the operation of these provisions. Many prisoners will find difficulty in paying rent for their homes whilst they are in custody. Rent arrears and consequent loss of the tenancy may be inevitable. But if the landlord wrongfully repossesses without a court order, it will be that illegal eviction that actually causes the homelessness and the prisoner cannot become homeless intentionally.[168] If the prisoner asks a third party to pay the rent and that third party fails to pay, that may, depending on the facts, result in a decision that the prisoner became homeless intentionally (because the prisoner has failed to make an effective arrangement),[169] or in a decision that the prisoner became homeless unintentionally (where a proper and genuine arrangement is frustrated by the third party stealing the prisoner's money rather than paying the rent).

14.100 In summary, the deliberate act or omission by the applicant must have caused him or her actually to cease to occupy accommodation. An applicant's decision to rid himself or herself of accommodation that he or she was not occupying, or to refuse an offer of accommodation, cannot fall within this limb of the test. In deciding whether the deliberate act or omission caused the cessation of occupation, the local housing authority must identify:

- the operative causes of the loss of accommodation; and

- whether any one of those operative causes was the deliberate act or omission by the applicant; and

- whether the cessation of accommodation was the reasonably likely result of the act or omission; and

---

[166] *Gloucester City Council v Miles* (1985) 17 HLR 292, CA.
[167] (1985) 17 HLR 292, CA, at 304. See also *Bolah v Croydon London Borough Council* (2008) February *Legal Action*, p 40, Central London County Court, where the applicant was homeless as a result of the expiry of her landlord's lease, not as a result of having withdrawn an application for homeless assistance made to another local housing authority. See also *Black v Wandsworth London Borough Council* (2008) February *Legal Action*, p 41, Lambeth County Court.
[168] *Wilkins v Barnet London Borough Council* (1998) December *Legal Action*, p 27, Watford County Court.
[169] *Stewart v Lambeth London Borough Council* [2002] EWCA Civ 753, [2002] HLR 40, CA.

- that there was no intervening event by a third party causing the loss of accommodation.

14.101   Even if the local housing authority finds that this limb of the test is satisfied, it cannot find that the applicant has become homeless intentionally unless the other four limbs are also made out.

Was the accommodation available for the applicant?

14.102   If the applicant deliberately did (or failed to do) something in consequence of which he or she ceased to occupy accommodation, the next question for consideration is whether the accommodation lost was accommodation that was available for his or her occupation.

14.103   In HA 1996, Part 7 the phrase 'available for his occupation' has a special meaning. The statutory definition relates both to the physical availability of the accommodation and to the nature and extent of the applicant's right to occupy it.[170] The same definition is used in determining whether an applicant is 'homeless'. The detail has already been explored in Chapter 11. The following paragraphs contain only a brief summary.

14.104   The accommodation must have been available for occupation by the applicant and by any person who normally resided with the applicant as a member of the applicant's family, and also available for occupation by any person who might reasonably have been expected to reside with the applicant at the date it was lost.[171]

14.105   The importance of this provision is to disapply a finding that the applicant has become homeless intentionally when what the applicant has lost was accommodation that could not actually accommodate his or her household. Frequently, it is applied to split or separated households that have no accommodation in which they can live together. For example:

- A head of household who left his or her home country and took up a hostel room for a single person in the UK will not become homeless intentionally when he or she is later asked to leave that hostel once the family arrives (because the single person's hostel was not accommodation 'available' to the family).[172]

- Two young people living in their respective parental homes may develop a relationship and have a child. If neither set of parents will accommodate

---

[170]   HA 1996, s 175(1) and s 176. See also English Code, paras 8.5–8.17; Welsh Code, paras 13.3–13.10. See further **11.6–11.117**.

[171]   See HA 1996, s 176 for the definition of the applicant's household. *R v Wimborne Borough Council ex p Curtis* (1986) 18 HLR 79, QBD; *R v Hammersmith and Fulham London Borough Council ex p O'Sullivan* [1991] EGCS 110, QBD; and *R v Peterborough City Council ex p Carr* (1990) 22 HLR 206, QBD. See also **11.19–11.31**.

[172]   *R v Westminster City Council ex p Ali* (1983) 11 HLR 83, QBD.

their child's partner, neither of the two will become homeless intentionally when the parental home is lost (eg on ejection following a family dispute) because neither partner had accommodation 'available' to accommodate the other.[173]

14.106 In summary, the accommodation must have been actually available both for the applicant and any person who normally resided with him or her as a member of his or her family and for any person who might reasonably have been expected to reside with him or her at the date it was lost.

14.107 Even if the local housing authority finds that this limb of the test is satisfied, it cannot find that the applicant has become homeless intentionally unless the other four limbs are also made out.

Would it have been reasonable for the applicant to have continued to occupy the accommodation?

14.108 To reach this stage in the application of the 'becoming homeless intentionally' test, the local housing authority must have satisfied itself that it was by his or her own deliberate act (or failure to act) that the applicant ceased to occupy available accommodation. The last issue to be settled is whether it would (at the point at which the deliberate act was done) have been reasonable for the applicant to have remained in occupation. It cannot be over-emphasised that the question is not 'Was it reasonable for the applicant to leave?' but rather 'Was it reasonable for the applicant to have continued in occupation?'

14.109 This reasonableness aspect of the test is the parallel of the part of the definition of 'homelessness' which uses exactly the same rubric.[174] Cases decided on whether an applicant is homeless or not homeless, having regard to the reasonableness of continued occupation, are therefore equally relevant to decisions as to whether a person became homelessness intentionally.

14.110 The question of whether accommodation was 'reasonable to continue to occupy' involves consideration of all the circumstances at the time of the applicant's deliberate act or omission, and is not limited to the physical quality of the accommodation that the applicant has ceased to occupy.[175]

---

[173] *R v Peterborough City Council ex p Carr* (1990) 22 HLR 206, QBD.

[174] HA 1996, s 175(3). See also English Code, paras 8.18–8.32; Welsh Code, paras 13.11–13.25. See further **11.72–11.117**.

[175] *R v Broxbourne Borough Council ex p Willmoth* (1989) 22 HLR 118, CA. See *Moran v Manchester City Council, Richards v Ipswich Borough Council* [2008] EWCA Civ 378 at [49]–[50] per Wilson LJ. The case went to the House of Lords, which decided the discrete issue that women's refuges could not be accommodation that was reasonable for an applicant and her household to continue to occupy: *Ali & others v Birmingham City Council, Moran v Manchester City Council* [2009] UKHL 36, [2009] 1 WLR 1506, HL. However, their Lordships did not specifically overrule the list of general considerations set out by Wilson LJ at [49]. See **11.93**.

14.111 When considering whether accommodation was reasonable for the applicant to continue to occupy, a local housing authority is directed by HA 1996, Part 7 only to the reasonableness of *the applicant* remaining in occupation. But the local housing authority must also consider whether it was reasonable for other members of the applicant's household to continue to occupy as an element in determining whether accommodation was 'available' for occupation by the whole family unit.[176] If there is an issue as to whether the accommodation lost would not have been reasonable for other persons in the household to continue to occupy, the local housing authority must resolve that issue. In *R v Westminster City Council ex p Bishop* the local housing authority and the court were satisfied that it would have been reasonable for the applicant herself to have remained in occupation of the former home, but the issue of whether it would have been reasonable for her dependent daughter to have remained had not been properly considered by the local housing authority.[177] Rose LJ said:

> '... accommodation can only be regarded as available for an applicant's occupation if both she and those members of her family who normally live with her can reasonably be expected to occupy it. Accordingly, although I accept that the question of reasonableness of continued occupation within [s 191(1)] has to be looked at in relation to the applicant herself, if, in the present case, it was reasonable for her daughter to leave, it could not, in my view, be said that it was reasonable for the applicant to have remained alone. The daughter's position was, therefore, as it seems to me, of great significance.'[178]

14.112 Accordingly, the English Code advises that, as part of determining whether it was reasonable to have continued to occupy, a local housing authority will find it 'necessary' to consider the circumstances of both the applicant 'and the household' in each case.[179]

14.113 There is an important distinction, prescribed by HA 1996, Part 7, between the test of 'reasonable to continue to occupy' to be applied where an applicant has ceased to occupy accommodation because of *violence* (or threats of violence that are likely to be carried out) and all other cases. As a matter of law, accommodation where, had the applicant continued to occupy it, it was probable that she or he (or a member of his or her household) would have been subject to violence or to threats of violence that were likely to be carried out, cannot be reasonable for the applicant to have continued to occupy.[180]

14.114 In all other cases, including cases of harassment that fall short of violence (or threats of violence that are likely to be carried out), the local

---

[176] See **11.19–11.31**.

[177] *R v Westminster City Council ex p Bishop* (1993) 25 HLR 459, CA.

[178] *R v Westminster City Council ex p Bishop* (1993) 25 HLR 459, CA at 465.

[179] English Code, para 11.22.

[180] HA 1996, s 177(1). *Bond v Leicester City Council* [2001] EWCA Civ 1544, (2002) 34 HLR 6, CA. English Code, para 11.13; there is no equivalent in the Welsh Code, but para 15.6(iii) relates fleeing domestic violence to a non-deliberate act or omission. See **11.78–11.88** and **14.187–14.190**.

housing authority should consider all the circumstances in determining whether it would have been reasonable for the applicant to have continued in occupation. Those circumstances could include:

- the availability or otherwise of alternative remedies to tackle the problem that drove the applicant to leave;

- the possibility of it being reasonable for the applicant to have continued to occupy the accommodation for at least the period it would have taken to arrange alternative accommodation; and

- any other relevant matters.

14.115 The local housing authority is specifically required by regulations to consider whether the accommodation that the applicant has ceased to occupy was *affordable* for him or her.[181] A local housing authority that fails to consider affordability when determining whether or not accommodation had been reasonable for the applicant to continue to occupy will find its decision quashed.[182] Obviously, whether or not accommodation was 'affordable' will be a critical factor where accommodation has been lost by reason of mortgage default or rent arrears.

14.116 In the specific case of women's refuges, the House of Lords has held that it would not be reasonable for a woman to continue to occupy a refuge indefinitely. Even if she is asked to leave the refuge because of her own deliberate act, therefore, she should not be found to have become homeless intentionally.[183]

14.117 On the face of it, the question whether it was reasonable for a particular applicant to have continued in occupation is directed to the specific circumstances of that applicant. However, HA 1996, Part 7 allows a local housing authority to inject a comparative element by comparing the situation that faced the applicant with the *general circumstances in relation to housing* in its area. A local housing authority, when determining whether it was reasonable for the applicant to have continued in occupation, is permitted (but not required) to have regard to general housing circumstances in its area.[184] This element of comparison is also a feature of the definition of being 'homeless'.[185]

14.118 Where the accommodation that the applicant has lost was not within the local housing authority's district, and particularly if the accommodation was outside the UK, the question for the local housing authority is not:

---

[181] Homelessness (Suitability of Accommodation) Order 1996, SI 1996/3204. See Appendix 2. See **18.45–18.46**.
[182] *Odunsi v Brent London Borough Council* [1999] 6 CLD 348, Willesden County Court.
[183] *Ali & others v Birmingham City Council, Moran v Manchester City Council* [2009] UKHL 36, [2009] 1 WLR 1506, HL.
[184] HA 1996, s 177(2).
[185] See **11.94–11.95**.

'... was the accommodation reasonable to continue to occupy given general housing circumstances prevailing in the area where the accommodation was situated?'

but rather:

'... was the accommodation reasonable to continue to occupy given the general housing circumstances prevailing in our own area?'

14.119	The reasonableness of continued occupation of accommodation that was given up (eg in Bangladesh) has to be balanced against the general housing circumstances in the area of the English or Welsh local housing authority to which the applicant has applied.[186] That balancing exercise should include the prospects available to the applicant in the accommodation that he or she has ceased to occupy, including employment prospects, the availability of welfare benefits, the applicant's financial position, and the space and arrangement (and any overcrowding) of the accommodation lost.[187] Strict application of this test could mean that an applicant who gives up accommodation in an area of acute housing need would be best advised to direct an application for homelessness assistance to an area where the general circumstances in relation to housing were much better, in the hope of then being referred back to the first area.[188]

14.120	Where the local housing authority has elected to take general housing circumstances prevailing in its district into account, the courts will be loath to interfere with its assessment of those circumstances. It is the local housing authority that is in the best position to judge the seriousness of any housing crisis in its district and to determine whether the applicant's particular complaints about his or her previous accommodation took him or her out of the norm of difficult housing circumstances in the district.[189]

14.121	For their part, applicants must be careful not to jump the gun. The question for the local housing authority is: 'Was the accommodation reasonable for the applicant and members of his or her household to continue to occupy at the date of the applicant's deliberate act or omission?', not at some date in the future.[190] So an applicant who faces the prospect, perhaps in the relatively near future, that the accommodation may become unreasonable to continue to occupy, would perhaps be best advised to wait until he or she is within 28 days of that situation crystallising and then make an application on the basis that he or she has become threatened with homelessness unintentionally.

---

[186]	*R v Tower Hamlets London Borough Council ex p Monaf* (1988) 20 HLR 529, CA, and *De Falco v Crawley Borough Council* [1980] QB 460, CA.

[187]	*R v Tower Hamlets London Borough Council ex p Ojo* (1991) 23 HLR 488, QBD, and *Osei v Southwark London Borough Council* [2007] EWCA Civ 787, [2008] HLR 15, CA.

[188]	However, judicially developed control measures in relation to the law on referral of applications (see **15.20**) have made it somewhat more difficult for applicants to expect referral back to the first area by this route.

[189]	*R v Brent London Borough Council ex p Bariise* (1999) 31 HLR 50, CA.

[190]	*Din v Wandsworth London Borough Council* [1983] 1 AC 657, HL.

14.122 Although the statutory formula appears to suggest that the relevant date, when considering whether it was 'reasonable for him to continue to occupy', is the date when the applicant ceases to be in occupation of the accommodation, the better view is that the test should be applied as at the date of any earlier act or omission (if any) that caused the accommodation to be lost. For example, as at the date of actual eviction, the defaulting mortgage borrower may have faced such a level of repayments as to make it impossible to say that it would be reasonable to have continued in occupation. Nevertheless, the applicant may have become homeless intentionally if it would have been reasonable to have continued in occupation at the date when the property was unwisely remortgaged or the borrowing was increased so that the level of instalments became unmanageable.[191]

14.123 The question whether it would have been reasonable for the applicant to continue in occupation of particular accommodation should be considered in light of all the facts that occurred *before* the applicant's deliberate act or omission which led to the loss of the accommodation. The local housing authority must ignore later deliberate acts or omissions when deciding whether it was reasonable for the applicant to continue in occupation.[192]

14.124 In summary, for an applicant to have become homeless intentionally, the accommodation that he or she was occupying, and lost, must have been reasonable for him or her to continue to occupy. The accommodation must also have been reasonable for anyone who normally resides with the applicant as a member of his or her family and for any other person who might reasonably be expected to reside with the applicant to continue to occupy. Accommodation cannot be reasonable for an applicant to continue to occupy if it was probable that continued occupation would have led to violence (or to threats of violence that were likely to be carried out) against the applicant or a member of his or her household. In all other cases, the local housing authority has to make a decision as to whether or not the accommodation was factually reasonable for the applicant and his or her household to continue to occupy, taking account, if it chooses, of the general housing circumstances prevailing in its area.

14.125 The relevant date, when considering whether it was reasonable for the applicant to continue to occupy accommodation, should be the date of the deliberate act or omission that caused the loss of accommodation.[193]

14.126 Even if the local housing authority finds that this limb of the test is satisfied, it cannot find that the applicant has become homeless intentionally unless the other four limbs are also made out.

---

[191] In *Bellamy v Hounslow London Borough Council* [2006] EWCA Civ 535, CA, [2006] HLR 42, CA, the Court of Appeal held that it would have been reasonable for a joint legal owner to remain in the property whilst she contested any application for sale that her co-owner might make.

[192] *Denton v Southwark London Borough Council* [2007] EWCA Civ 623, [2008] HLR 161, CA.

[193] See **14.88–14.101**.

Breaking the chain of causation

14.127 The test for 'becoming homeless intentionally', as set out by HA 1996, Part 7, appears to be satisfied where a local housing authority has found that the applicant satisfies all five limbs:

(1) there was a deliberate act or omission (which does not include an act or omission in good faith by a person unaware of a material fact);[194] and

(2) that deliberate act or omission was committed by the applicant;[195] and

(3) the applicant ceased to occupy accommodation as a consequence of that deliberate act or omission;[196] and

(4) that accommodation was available for the applicant's occupation and for occupation by members of the applicant's household;[197] and

(5) it would have been reasonable for the applicant and for all members of his or her household to have continued to occupy the accommodation.[198]

14.128 However, the courts, in interpreting HA 1996, Part 7, have posed an additional question to be addressed before an applicant can be found to have become homeless intentionally.

Is the deliberate act (or omission), and the cessation of occupation it caused, an operative cause of the present homelessness?

14.129 As we have just seen, the exercise of determining whether a person became homeless intentionally for the purpose of the statutory definition involves travelling back in time to consider the point at which (at the latest) that person ceased to occupy accommodation as a result of his or her own deliberate act or failure to act. But this begs the question 'How far back?' Many applicants will at some point in their lives have given up accommodation it would have been reasonable to continue to occupy (not least on leaving the parental home on achieving adulthood). If local housing authorities were free to run backwards indefinitely when applying the statutory test, significant numbers of applicants could be found to have deliberately given up occupation of some accommodation during their lifetimes and investigations would be extensive and expensive.

---

[194] See **14.30–14.77**.
[195] See **14.78–14.82**.
[196] See **14.83–14.101**.
[197] See **14.102–14.106**. The applicant's household is defined at HA 1996, s 176. See **11.19–11.31**.
[198] See **14.108–14.126**.

Settled accommodation

14.130 The Codes advise that local housing authorities should consider only the current incidence of homelessness to examine whether it is the result of a past deliberate act or omission. They suggest, adopting an approach developed from the case law, that local housing authorities look back only to 'the last period of settled accommodation' and examine why the applicant left that.[199] In their earlier versions, the Codes had suggested that attention be focused on the 'most immediate cause' of present homelessness 'rather than events that may have taken place previously', but that approach was subsequently considered too narrow.

14.131 The current formulation correctly echoes the approach taken by the courts. They have decided that past intentional homelessness can be expunged by the subsequent acquisition of 'settled' accommodation. The phrase was first coined by Ackner LJ in *Din v Wandsworth London Borough Council*.[200] He said:

> 'To remove his self-imposed disqualification, he must therefore have achieved what can be loosely described as "a settled residence", as opposed to what from the outset is known ... to be only temporary accommodation. What amounts to "a settled residence" is a question of fact and degree depending upon the circumstances of each individual case.'

14.132 Consequently, where housing was lost in circumstances meeting the statutory definition of becoming homeless intentionally, a local housing authority's inquiries can be limited to determining those circumstances and then to whether there has been any such settled accommodation since that loss of accommodation. The local housing authority is entitled to ignore the acquisition and loss of temporary or insecure accommodation (even if occupation of such accommodation brought the applicant's state of homelessness to an end for a time) and may track back to the loss of the last settled accommodation. That loss, looking at the whole history, may be the real reason for the present homelessness.[201]

14.133 Not surprisingly, a whole body of case law has developed as to the circumstances in which accommodation is to be treated as 'settled' for the purpose of applying this test. While the matter is one primarily for the local housing authority itself to determine on the facts of the particular application, it should take a careful and measured approach. In the words of a current Justice of the Supreme Court:

---

[199] English Code, paras 11.11–11.12; Welsh Code, para 15.4.

[200] *Din v Wandsworth London Borough Council* (unreported) 23 June 1981, CA, quoted by Lord Denning MR in *Lambert v Ealing London Borough Council* [1982] 1 WLR 550, CA at 557.

[201] In accordance with the principle that it is not for the applicant to prove his or her case (see **10.15–10.19** and **14.14–14.19**), the local housing authority must consider whether the facts as disclosed by the applicant amount to there being intervening settled accommodation, whether or not the applicant has specifically raised the point (*Black v Wandsworth London Borough Council* (2008) February *Legal Action*, p 41, Lambeth County Court).

'Given the grave difficulty of securing settled accommodation, and given too that the clear legislative objective underlying the concept of intentionality – to discourage people from needlessly leaving their accommodation and becoming homeless – is surely sufficiently achieved without too protracted a period of consequential disqualification from re-housing, it is much to be hoped that housing authorities will in general interpret benevolently the character of accommodation secured by applicants after a finding of intentionality, namely as to whether or not it is settled.'[202]

14.134　The case law has thrown up many helpful illustrations as to what some authorities have respectively considered unsettled and settled accommodation for these purposes.

Not usually treated as 'settled' accommodation:

14.135

- Holiday lets.[203]

- Out of season (or winter) lettings.[204]

- Bed and breakfast or other short-term hostel style accommodation.[205]

- Tied accommodation linked to short fixed-term employment.[206]

- A temporary stay with relatives.[207]

- Decrepit caravans.[208]

- Lodging in a council house.[209]

- Accommodation in another country in breach of immigration laws.[210]

- Moving in temporarily with a cohabitant.[211]

---

[202]　*R v Merton London Borough Council ex p Ruffle* (1988) 21 HLR 361, QBD at 366–367, per Simon Brown J (as he then was).

[203]　*Lambert v Ealing London Borough Council* [1982] 1 WLR 550, CA.

[204]　*Dyson v Kerrier District Council* [1980] 1 WLR 1205, CA.

[205]　*R v Harrow London Borough Council ex p Holland, R v Rushcliffe District Council ex p Summerson* (1992) 25 HLR 577, QBD.

[206]　*R v Dacorum District Council ex p Wright* (unreported) 16 October 1991, QBD.

[207]　*De Falco v Crawley Borough Council* [1980] QB 460, CA.

[208]　*Davis v Kingston Royal London Borough Council* (1981) Times 28 March, CA.

[209]　*R v Merton London Borough Council ex p Ruffle* (1988) 21 HLR 361, QBD, and *Mazzaccherini v Argyll and Bute District Council* (1987) SCLR 475.

[210]　*R v Croydon London Borough Council ex p Easom* (1992) 25 HLR 262, QBD.

[211]　*R v Purbeck District Council ex p Cadney* (1986) 17 HLR 534, QBD.

- An insecure, statutorily overcrowded and unaffordable assured shorthold tenancy.[212]

- Precarious occupation, whether as a bare licensee or as an unlawful sub-tenant.[213]

- Occupation in a caravan on a site without permission.[214]

- A non-secure tenancy provided in performance of the main housing duty.[215]

Usually treated as settled accommodation:

14.136

- Freehold or leasehold ownership.

- A tenancy enjoying security of tenure.

- An indefinite licence or permission to occupy.

- Returning to long-term occupation of the parental home.[216]

- Indefinite stay with friends or relatives.[217]

- Tied accommodation as a long-term employee.

14.137 The most difficult application of the test of 'settled' accommodation arises where an applicant who had been found to have become homeless intentionally has subsequently obtained a tenancy with a private sector landlord. Since February 1997, any such letting will have been on an assured shorthold tenancy (AST) involving hardly any security of tenure. The Court of Appeal has rejected the proposition that because an AST is the normal or default tenancy it must always count as 'settled'.[218] The true question for the local housing authority is whether, having regard to the circumstances and terms of its creation, the AST can properly be treated as having provided 'settled' accommodation for the applicant.

---

212 *Mohamed v Westminster City Council* [2005] EWCA Civ 796, [2005] HLR 47, CA.
213 *Gilby v Westminster City Council* [2007] EWCA Civ 604, [2008] HLR 7, CA.
214 *Stewart v Kingston upon Thames RLBC* [2007] EWCA Civ 565, [2007] HLR 42, CA.
215 *Ali v Haringey London Borough Council* [2008] EWCA Civ 132, (2008) April *Legal Action*, p 34, CA. For 'main housing duty' see **17.21–17.110**.
216 *Robson v Kyle and Carrick District Council* (1994) SCLR 259.
217 *Krishnan v Hillingdon London Borough Council* (1981) SCOLAG January 1981, p 137, and *Black v Wandsworth London Borough Council* (2008) February *Legal Action*, p 41, Lambeth County Court.
218 *Knight v Vale Royal District Council* [2003] EWCA Civ 1258, [2004] HLR 9, CA.

14.138 The material consideration is (generally) the position at the commencement of the new accommodation, 'since if the causal link is broken at that point nothing that happens thereafter will mend it'.[219] Of course, the reverse is also true. An arrangement may not have been 'settled' at the outset, but may become so at a later stage (e g when an originally short-term tenancy is renewed for an extended term) and it is at that stage that the causal link from previous intentional homelessness may be severed.

14.139 Properly understood, the application of the 'settled' accommodation test is all about cause and effect. The search is for a causal link between past deliberate loss of accommodation and the present homelessness. The local housing authority is really asking itself whether the earlier intentional act is causative of the present homelessness. It will usually conclude that it is, unless there has been some intermediate 'settled' accommodation.

Other events breaking the causal link

14.140 However, there may potentially be other circumstances in which the causal chain between present unintentional homelessness and past intentional homelessness may be broken. While it is well established that the obtaining of settled accommodation is sufficient to break the causal link between an earlier intentional homelessness and the immediate homelessness in question, there has been some doubt whether that was the only way in which the causal link could be severed.[220]

14.141 Precisely when, and in what circumstances, such a situation might arise has been canvassed twice in recent years in the House of Lords.

14.142 In *R v Brent London Borough Council ex p Awua*,[221] Lord Hoffman reached no concluded view. He said the jurisprudence concerning 'settled' accommodation:

> '... is well-established (it was approved by this House in *Din*'s case) and nothing I have said is intended to cast any doubt upon it, although I would wish to reserve the question of whether the occupation of a settled residence is the sole and exclusive method by which the causal link can be broken.'[222]

---

[219] *R v Westminster City Council ex p Obeid* (1996) 29 HLR, 389, QBD at 400 per Carnwath J.

[220] In *R v Basingstoke and Deane District Council ex p Bassett* (1983) 10 HLR 125, QBD, the applicant and her husband gave up secure accommodation to go and stay with her husband's relations. The marriage then broke down, she left her in-laws' house and became homeless. She had not had any intervening settled accommodation and the local housing authority considered that she had therefore become homeless intentionally. Taylor J held that the final homelessness resulted from the breakdown of the marriage, not from the decision to give up the settled accommodation.

[221] *R v Brent London Borough Council ex p Awua* [1996] AC 55, HL.

[222] *R v Brent London Borough Council ex p Awua* [1996] AC 55, per Lord Hoffmann.

14.143   In *R v Harrow London Borough Council ex p Fahia*,[223] both the first-instance judge and the Court of Appeal held that the chain of causation could be broken in ways other than by obtaining intervening settled accommodation. They held that the local housing authority had misdirected itself in looking only to the question whether Mrs Fahia had obtained settled accommodation. Harrow petitioned for leave to appeal to resolve this 'doubtful point of law', but later conceded that the chain of causation could be broken by means other than the obtaining of intervening settled accommodation. The Law Lords were invited, despite this concession, to decide the point, but considered:

'.... it would not be right to do so. The point may be one of some importance to local authorities generally and your Lordships should decline to express any view, one way or the other, on the point.'[224]

14.144   So this area of law remains in a state of flux, but for the time being the position must be (in keeping with the Court of Appeal's decision in *Fahia*) that acquisition of settled accommodation is *not* necessarily the only way of breaking the causal chain between past intentional homelessness and the present incident of homelessness.

14.145   Both aspects of the causation issue can arise where an applicant had given up accommodation in the UK in order to emigrate, and then later returns to the UK.[225] On the assumption that the statutory definition of 'becoming homeless intentionally' was met upon giving up the accommodation in the UK, the local housing authority must go on to ask whether that is the cause of the applicant's present homelessness. This will involve considering both whether the accommodation overseas was 'settled' and (if it was not) whether there was an intervening event, such as the applicant's marriage breaking up[226] or the overseas accommodation becoming otherwise unreasonable to continue to occupy, that caused the present homelessness.[227]

BECOMING THREATENED WITH HOMELESSNESS INTENTIONALLY

14.146   The wording in the statutory definition of 'becoming threatened with homelessness intentionally' is similar to, but not quite the same as, the definition of 'becoming intentionally homeless'.[228] After all, the applicant will

---

[223]   *R v Harrow London Borough Council ex p Fahia* [1998] 1 WLR 1396, HL.

[224]   *R v Harrow London Borough Council ex p Fahia* [1998] 1 WLR 1396, HL at 1129, per Lord Browne-Wilkinson.

[225]   See **14.213–14.216**.

[226]   The example cited by the English Code, para 11.12. See *Blackstock v Birmingham City Council* (2008) March *Legal Action*, p 22, Birmingham County Court.

[227]   *R v Basingstoke and Deane Borough Council ex p Bassett* (1983) 10 HLR 125, QBD, and *R v Harrow London Borough Council ex p Louis* (1997) June *Legal Action*, p 23, QBD.

[228]   HA 1996, s 196.

still be in occupation of accommodation and much will turn on an early decision as to whether the threatened homelessness is intentional. If the decision is adverse to the applicant who is threatened with homelessness, she or he will receive only advice and assistance to avoid actual homelessness.[229] If the decision is that the applicant has not become threatened with homelessness intentionally, the local housing authority has the power (and, if the applicant has a priority need, will be obliged) to take steps to prevent actual homelessness.[230]

14.147 HA 1996, Part 7 provides that a person becomes threatened with homelessness intentionally if he or she has committed a deliberate act or omission the 'likely result of which' is that he or she will be forced to leave accommodation, but he or she has not yet had to leave.[231]

14.148 In order for the local housing authority to find that an applicant has become threatened with homelessness intentionally, it must also find that the accommodation is available for his or her occupation and that it would be reasonable for him or her to continue to occupy the accommodation. If the applicant has acted in good faith, but in ignorance of a relevant fact, he or she has not become threatened with homelessness intentionally, because the act or failure to act will not be treated as having been deliberate.[232]

14.149 Several features of the main definition of 'becoming threatened with homelessness intentionally' are in precisely the same terms as those used to define 'becoming homeless intentionally'. The following components are discussed in detail above in relation to 'becoming homeless intentionally':

- 'deliberate' act or failure to act;[233]

- accommodation 'available for his occupation';[234] and

- 'reasonable for him to continue to occupy'.[235]

14.150 The missing element, loss of accommodation 'in consequence of' the act or failure to act, is replaced by a test of reasonable likelihood ('the likely result of which'), which in fact mirrors the approach taken by the courts in construing the term used in the definition of becoming homeless intentionally.[236]

---

[229] HA 1996, s 195(5). See **17.132–17.144**.
[230] HA 1996, s 195(2), (9). See **17.119–17.131**.
[231] HA 1996, s 196(1).
[232] HA 1996, s 196(2).
[233] See **14.30–14.77**.
[234] See **14.102–14.107**.
[235] See **14.108–14.126**.
[236] See **14.93–14.97**.

14.151 As with 'becoming homeless intentionally', there is a separate provision dealing with collusive arrangements.[237] If the applicant has:

- entered into an arrangement under which he or she is required to cease to occupy accommodation; and

- the purpose of that arrangement is to enable him or her to receive homelessness assistance; and

- there is no other good reason why he or she is threatened with homelessness;

he or she has become threatened with homelessness intentionally.[238]

14.152 There is very little developed case law on becoming threatened with homelessness intentionally. This is perhaps because local housing authorities often find that they have insufficient time to conclude their inquiries before the applicant actually becomes homeless. The local housing authority can only reach a decision on the question within the very tight period of 28 days between the applicant first becoming 'threatened with homelessness' and the homelessness then crystallising.[239]

14.153 A local housing authority cannot find that an applicant has become homeless intentionally unless he or she has actually become homeless and, likewise, cannot find an applicant to have become threatened with homelessness intentionally until he or she is actually threatened with homelessness, ie is within 28 days of becoming homeless.[240]

14.154 This shortage of cases has enabled the courts to avoid grappling with the problems of language and logic that arise where the applicant is facing homelessness from accommodation that would not constitute 'settled' accommodation and has previously been found to have become homeless intentionally. For example, an applicant who has previously been found to have become homeless intentionally may be within 28 days of actual homelessness as a result of his or her current landlord obtaining an order for possession to bring to an end an assured shorthold tenancy which both landlord and tenant understood would only last 6 months. It is exceptionally difficult to bring that scenario within the strict definition of 'becoming threatened with homelessness intentionally'. To do so would require a decision that the previous act that caused the applicant to become homeless intentionally was the act 'the likely result' of which was that the current accommodation would be lost. The

---

[237] See **14.156–14.162**.
[238] HA 1996, s 196(3).
[239] HA 1996, s 175(4). See **11.118–11.121**.
[240] *R v Rugby Borough Council ex p Hunt* (1992) 26 HLR 1, QBD.

attempt by Brightman LJ to square this particular circle[241] has been described as 'distinctly odd'.[242] and has attracted adverse judicial comment.[243]

14.155　The better view is perhaps that the causal connection approach cannot properly work to link past intentional homelessness to present intentional threatened homelessness. If that is right, an applicant, who would be likely, if homeless, to be found to have become homeless intentionally because she or he has not acquired settled accommodation since previous intentional homelessness, would do well to apply as soon as she or he is threatened with homelessness from current unsettled accommodation and to press for an early decision.

ENTERING INTO AN ARRANGEMENT TO CEASE TO OCCUPY ACCOMMODATION

14.156　Until 1997, an applicant could only be considered to have become homeless intentionally by falling foul of the five-part statutory definition considered above. However, HA 1996, Part 7 introduced a wholly new and separate class of intentional homelessness. If the statutory requirements of the new category are met, then the applicant is deemed to have become homeless intentionally without consideration of the longstanding five-part definition.

14.157　Under the new provisions, if a local housing authority decides that an applicant has entered into an arrangement by which he or she was required to leave accommodation, and that the purpose of that arrangement was to enable the applicant to receive homelessness assistance, he or she will have become homeless intentionally.[244]

14.158　The essential elements are that:

(1)　the applicant is homeless; and

(2)　he or she had previously entered into an arrangement under which she or he would be required to leave accommodation; and

(3)　the accommodation to which that arrangement applied would have been reasonable to continue to occupy; and

(4)　the purpose of the arrangement was to enable the applicant to become entitled to HA 1996, Part 7 assistance; and

---

[241]　*Dyson v Kerrier District Council* [1980] 1 WLR 1205, CA.
[242]　D Hoath *Homelessness* (Sweet & Maxwell, 1983), p 114.
[243]　*Din v Wandsworth London Borough Council* [1983] 1 AC 657, HL at 678–679, per Lord Lowry.
[244]　HA 1996, s 191(3).

(5)   there is no other good reason for the applicant's present homelessness.[245]

14.159   The Codes advise that particular care should be taken when local housing authorities assess applications from 16- or 17-year-olds in respect of this new definition.[246]

14.160   The provision is obviously directed to preventing collusion to bring about homelessness that would result in HA 1996, Part 7 duties. Collusion could occur in informal arrangements, between friends or relations, or in the more formal relationship between landlord and tenant. Even if there has been collusion, the applicant will not have become homeless intentionally if the accommodation given up was not reasonable for the applicant to continue to occupy.[247] If the applicant was staying with friends or relatives, the relationship may have broken down to such an extent that the accommodation has become unreasonable to continue to occupy.

14.161   The Codes advise that an 'other good reason' why an applicant may be homeless might include overcrowding, or an obvious breakdown in relations between the applicant and his or her host.[248] In those circumstances, an applicant will not be caught by this test.

14.162   Local housing authorities must be satisfied that collusion exists and should not rely on hearsay or unfounded suspicions if they are to find that the applicant became homeless intentionally under this provision. As already noted,[249] the provision is hardly ever used in practice by local housing authorities to sustain a decision that the applicant became homeless intentionally, and it can be avoided altogether by ensuring that the application for homelessness assistance is made by someone other than the person who entered into the arrangement. As already indicated, there is an equivalent provision to prevent collusion by those who are threatened with homelessness.[250]

COMMON SCENARIOS

14.163   The remainder of this chapter seeks to apply the above analysis of the statutory definitions of 'becoming homeless intentionally' and 'becoming threatened with homelessness intentionally' to common factual circumstances in which local housing authorities may be called upon to apply those tests.

---

[245]   HA 1996, s 191(3).
[246]   English Code, para 11.28; Welsh Code, para 15.10. See **13.107–13.136** and **13.175**.
[247]   See **14.108–14.126**.
[248]   English Code, para 11.28; Welsh Code, para 15.10.
[249]   See **14.28**.
[250]   See **14.151**.

Rent or mortgage arrears

14.164 The local housing authority will need to consider why it was that the applicant accrued the rent or mortgage arrears that caused the loss of accommodation.[251] If the applicant had simply refused to pay the rent or mortgage payments and had spent the money elsewhere, that would constitute a deliberate act (spending it) or omission (to pay it towards housing costs) necessary to satisfy the first part of the definition of becoming homeless intentionally.[252]

14.165 But the enquiry cannot stop there, because, if the accommodation was unaffordable for the applicant, in that he or she could not afford the housing costs as well as meet the ordinary necessities of life, the property would not be reasonable for the applicant and the members of his or her household to continue to occupy.[253] What constitute 'the ordinary necessities of life' may vary according to the individual circumstances of each applicant and is a question of fact for the local housing authority to decide, having regard to the matters set out in a statutory order.[254]

14.166 Of course, the two elements of (1) a deliberate act and (2) the reasonableness of continued occupation may overlap. That is particularly likely where the deliberate act of the applicant has itself arguably rendered the accommodation unaffordable. The local housing authority is entitled to consider the applicant's financial position both when he or she first obtained the accommodation, and throughout the occupation of that property. So, for example, if the applicant had been able to afford the mortgage for the accommodation when it was first acquired, but had later taken on an additional loan that became unaffordable, that decision to extend the lending or remortgage the property could properly be described as a deliberate act which, eventually, led to the loss of accommodation.[255] Equally, if the applicant's financial difficulties occurred as a result of his or her raising a secured loan to finance an unsuccessful business venture (which led to inability to meet repayments), the local housing authority would be entitled to consider the prospects of that venture as they appeared at the time that the mortgage

---

[251] Or, in the case of an applicant threatened with homelessness, why the applicant might have accrued the arrears which are threatening to cause the loss of accommodation.

[252] See *William v Wandsworth London Borough Council* [2006] EWCA Civ 535, [2006] HLR 42, CA.

[253] Homelessness (Suitability of Accommodation) Order, SI 1996/3204. English Code, paras 8.29 and 11.17–11.19; Welsh Code, paras 13.13(i) and 15.6(ii). See also *R v Hillingdon London Borough Council ex p Tinn* (1988) 20 HLR 305, QBD; *R v Wandsworth London Borough Council ex p Hawthorne* [1994] 1 WLR 1442, CA; *R v Brent London Borough Council ex p Baruwa* (1997) 29 HLR 915, CA; *Saunders v Hammersmith and Fulham London Borough Council* [1999] 6 CLD 347, West London County Court; and *Bernard v Enfield London Borough Council* [2001] EWCA Civ 1831, (2002) 34 HLR 46, CA. For affordability in relation to suitability, see **18.45–18.46**.

[254] Homelessness (Suitability of Accommodation) Order, SI 1996/3204.

[255] *R v Barnet London Borough Council ex p Rughooputh* (1993) 25 HLR 607, CA; and *R v Wandsworth London Borough Council ex p Onwudiwe* (1993) 26 HLR 302, CA.

was taken out.[256] If the applicant genuinely believed that the business venture would be sound, he or she will have acted in good faith in taking out a mortgage to finance it. However, if that judgment involved an unrealistic degree of optimism or any dishonesty, he or she will not have acted in good faith.[257] Two recent Court of Appeal decisions have upheld local housing authorities' decisions that the taking out of a mortgage that was unaffordable was a deliberate act which subsequently rendered the applicants homeless and therefore they had become homeless intentionally.[258]

14.167 If an applicant was receiving welfare benefits to help with the accommodation costs, the local housing authority should not simply assume that the housing costs were therefore affordable, but should still look at all the circumstances. Even if the applicant failed to use his or her available welfare benefits to pay his or her rent or mortgage, the property might still be unaffordable in any event due to the shortfall between the benefit received and the contractual rent or mortgage payments.[259]

14.168 If the applicant failed to apply for benefit to which he or she would have been entitled, that would generally be considered to have been a deliberate omission. However, if he or she was genuinely unaware of his or her entitlement to benefit, he or she may not have been guilty of deliberate omission if she or he acted in good faith.[260]

14.169 The English Code advises that non-payment of rent due to housing benefit delays which were beyond the applicant's control should not generally be considered deliberate.[261] This guidance must refer to situations where a landlord is entitled to a mandatory order of possession, either based on rent arrears[262] or as a result of a notice requiring possession,[263] and the court had

---

[256] *R v Exeter City Council ex p Tranckle* (1994) 26 HLR 244, CA; and *R v Warrington Borough Council ex p Bryant* (2000) October *Legal Action*, p 24, QBD.

[257] English Code, para 11.26. See also *R v Hammersmith and Fulham London Borough Council ex p Lusi* (1991) 23 HLR 260, QBD.

[258] *William v Wandsworth London Borough Council* [2006] EWCA Civ 535, [2006] HLR 42, CA; and *Watchman v Ipswich Borough Council* [2007] EWCA Civ 348, [2007] HLR 33, CA.

[259] *R v Shrewsbury and Atcham Borough Council ex p Griffiths* (1993) 25 HLR 613, QBD; *R v Brent London Borough Council ex p Grossett* (1996) 28 HLR 9, CA; *Ahmed v Westminster City Council* (1999)June *Legal Action*, p 24, Central London County Court; and *Odunsi v Brent London Borough Council* [1999] CLY 3063, Willesden County Court.

[260] *R v Tower Hamlets London Borough Council ex p Saber* (1992) 24 HLR 611, QBD; and *R v Westminster City Council ex p Moozary-Oraky* (1993) 26 HLR 213, QBD. Note that in *F v Birmingham City Council* [2006] EWCA Civ 1427, [2007] HLR 18, CA, a tenant had 'closed her eyes to the obvious' when she gave up a secure tenancy for a private rented tenancy in ignorance of the fact that housing benefit would not cover the whole of the contractual rent and therefore the issue of good faith did not arise. In different circumstances, in *Abdullahi v Brent London Borough Council* [2007] EWCA Civ 885, (2007) October *Legal Action*, p 26, CA, an assured tenant's ignorance of the shortfall between contractual rent and housing benefit was a relevant fact which required consideration of whether she had acted in good faith. For 'relevant fact', see **14.37–14.43**. For 'good faith', see **14.44–14.52**.

[261] English Code, para 11.17(i).

[262] Housing Act 1988, Sch 2, Ground 8.

[263] Housing Act 1988, s 21.

no discretion to adjourn or refuse a possession order, even though the arrears might be due to be paid by a late determination of housing benefit entitlement.[264]

14.170 Occupiers in financial difficulties would do well to approach the local housing authority for help at an early stage. They certainly cannot assume that, if they leave the accommodation because of financial difficulties, they will not be found to have become homeless intentionally. If they have left, the local housing authority will consider whether leaving the accommodation was the only option available to them, ie whether or not it would have been reasonable to have continued in occupation at the date when they left. If the applicant is still in the accommodation, the local housing authority can at least decide the issue of whether he or she has become threatened with homelessness intentionally while the family is in occupation. In *R v Leeds City Council ex p Adamiec*,[265] the applicant considered that he could no longer afford his mortgage and contracted to sell his home. The local housing authority decided that he had become threatened with homelessness intentionally. His finances at the date he contracted to sell were not such that his accommodation was unaffordable. The decision was upheld, but the judge noted that:

> '... [W]ere he not to get work in a month or two, and if he were to be threatened with repossession, it would almost certainly at that stage have been unreasonable to expect him not to sell his home. But that stage had not yet been reached.'[266]

14.171 The local housing authority is, accordingly, entitled to consider how desperate the applicant's financial position was and whether, for example, his or her creditors were actually threatening to recover loans or obtain possession of the accommodation or not.[267] The correct approach has been crisply stated in this way:

> 'As a matter of common sense, it seems to me that it cannot be reasonable for a person to continue to occupy accommodation when they can no longer discharge their fiscal obligations in relation to that accommodation, that is to say, pay the rent and make the mortgage repayments, without so straining their resources as to deprive themselves of the ordinary necessities of life, such as food, clothing, heat, transport and so forth.'[268]

---

[264] In *Houghton v Sheffield City Council* [2006] EWCA Civ 1799, (2007) March *Legal Action*, p 18, CA, the applicant was found to have become homeless intentionally even though, at the date the possession order had been made against him, he had reduced his rent arrears from £1,000 to £7. A first-instance judge found that the local housing authority's decision was perverse, and that he had not become homeless intentionally, and the Court of Appeal refused the local housing authority permission to bring a second appeal. For applicants who are homeless as a result of possession orders, see **14.174–14.180**.

[265] (1992) 24 HLR 138, QBD.

[266] (1992) 24 HLR 138, QBD at 153, per Webster J.

[267] *R v Tower Hamlets London Borough Council ex p Ullah* (1992) 24 HLR 680, QBD; and *R v Westminster City Council ex p Ali* (1997) 29 HLR 580, QBD.

[268] *R v Hillingdon London Borough Council ex p Tinn* (1988) 20 HLR 305, QBD at 308, per Kennedy J. See, more recently, *Adekunle v Islington London Borough Council* (2009) November *Legal Action*, Mayor's and City of London County Court.

14.172 A local housing authority is entitled to presume that, where one partner in a household accrued rent or mortgage arrears, the other partner acquiesced in that behaviour.[269] If, however, the applicant asserts that he or she did not acquiesce and puts forward some relevant material, the local housing authority must make inquiries into that assertion.[270] Where the applicant has been actively involved in the family finances, the local housing authority may be entitled to find that he or she acquiesced in a decision not to pay the rent or mortgage arrears, or to over-extend the family budget.[271]

14.173 Decisions as to whether or not the applicant could have afforded to pay both the housing costs and the ordinary necessities of life apply equally to accommodation that has been lost outside the UK. If an applicant gives up accommodation overseas in order to migrate to the UK for economic reasons, the question for the local housing authority is whether or not the applicant could have afforded to pay his or her housing costs and the ordinary necessities of life in the overseas accommodation. If not, the accommodation will not have been reasonable for the applicant and members of his or her household to have continued to occupy.[272]

Tenants facing possession proceedings

14.174 Most landlords cannot lawfully obtain possession of tenanted premises without obtaining an order for possession.[273] The legal proceedings may not be the tenant's fault, there may be no defence and the tenant may be anxious to leave before a court hearing, not least to avoid liability for court costs. If the tenant chooses to leave, that may be a perfectly reasonable thing to do, but there may still be a finding that he or she became homeless intentionally if it would have been reasonable to have remained in occupation.[274]

14.175 If the application for homelessness assistance is made while the tenant is still in occupation, it is for the local housing authority to decide whether or

---

269 See the discussion on acquiescence at **14.78–14.82**.

270 *R v Wyre Borough Council ex p Joyce* (1983) 11 HLR 73, QBD; *R v West Dorset District Council ex p Phillips* (1985) 17 HLR 336, QBD; *R v Eastleigh Borough Council ex p Beattie (No 2)* (1985) 17 HLR 168 QBD; *R v East Northamptonshire Borough Council* (1988) 20 HLR 508, QBD; *R v Thanet District Council ex p Groves* (1990) 22 HLR 223, QBD; and *Quinton v East Hertfordshire District Council* (2003) April *Legal Action*, p 27, Luton County Court.

271 *R v Barnet London Borough Council ex p O'Connor* (1990) 22 HLR 486, QBD; and *R v Nottingham City Council ex p Caine* (1996) 28 HLR 374, CA.

272 *R v Islington London Borough Council ex p Bibi* (1996) 29 HLR 498, QBD.

273 Protection from Eviction Act 1977.

274 In *Ugiagbe v Southwark London Borough Council* [2009] EWCA Civ 31, [2009] HLR 35, CA, an assured shorthold tenant left the premises before the landlord served a Housing Act 1988, s 21 notice or started possession proceedings. Having been told by the landlord to leave, she sought advice from a council advice centre which told her to go to the Homeless Persons Unit who would put her into temporary accommodation. The advice centre did not tell her that she had the right to remain in the property until the landlord obtained a possession order. Had she gone to the Homeless Persons Unit, she would have been advised accordingly. The Court of Appeal found that she was ignorant of a relevant fact (her security of tenure) and that her failure to obtain that advice had been in good faith.

not it would be reasonable for the tenant in those circumstances to continue to occupy the accommodation until a possession order had been obtained and/or executed. The Codes advise that the local housing authority should take into account:

- the general cost to the local housing authority;

- the positions of the tenant and the landlord;

- the likelihood that the landlord will actually proceed;

- the burden on the courts of unnecessary proceedings where there is no defence to a possession claim; and

- general housing circumstances (if they wish to do so).[275]

14.176 Both Codes advise that:

- where an assured shorthold tenant has received a proper Housing Act 1988, s 21 notice;[276] and

- the local housing authority is satisfied that the landlord intends to seek possession; and

- it is satisfied that there would be no defence to a claim for a possession order,

it is unlikely to be reasonable for the applicant to continue to occupy the accommodation beyond the date given in the s 21 notice.[277]

14.177 Local housing authorities should consider any other application from a tenant facing possession proceedings on its own facts.

14.178 It follows from the guidance regarding assured shorthold tenants that other tenants who have been served with notices terminating their tenancies or requiring them to give possession, who would face possession proceedings to which they would have no defence, are also unlikely to be considered to be occupying accommodation that is reasonable to continue to occupy. The crucial issue is, of course, the intention of the landlord to bring possession proceedings once the notice has expired.

14.179 The local housing authority is entitled to take into account the general housing conditions prevailing in its district when considering whether or not it would be reasonable for the tenant to remain in occupation pending any

---

[275] English Code, para 8.31; Welsh Code, para 13.14.

[276] Housing Act 1988, s 21.

[277] English Code, para 8.32; Welsh Code, para 13.15. See also *R v Newham London Borough Council ex p Ugbo* (1993) 26 HLR 263, QBD.

inevitable possession proceedings.[278] However, a tenant who surrenders accommodation rather than waiting for inevitable possession proceedings may be acting in ignorance of a material fact (ie the general housing circumstances prevailing in the district), and such an act could not have been done 'deliberately' if done in good faith.[279]

14.180 Of course, the local housing authority is also entitled to take into account the landlord's reasons for requiring possession.[280]

Loss of accommodation as a result of a possession order

14.181 As already referred to above,[281] most owner-occupiers and tenants of rented accommodation are entitled not to be evicted unless a possession order has been made against them. In one sense, occupiers who leave or are evicted from property as a result of a possession order cannot be said to have become homeless intentionally. They have been required to leave against their wishes.

14.182 However, applying the 'operative cause'[282] and 'reasonable likelihood'[283] tests described above, local housing authorities are entitled to consider the reasons for the bringing of possession proceedings.[284] Possession proceedings themselves fall into three categories:

- claims for possession where the reason is said to be some fault by the tenant;

- claims for possession where there is no obligation on the landlord to show fault; and

- claims for possession brought by lenders.

14.183 The Court of Appeal has declined an invitation to hold that a local housing authority is always obliged to accept what is said on the face of a possession order (such as the correct figures for the arrears).[285] However, it would be unusual for a local housing authority to come to a different decision from the facts as determined by the judge and recorded on the face of the order. There may, however, be a number of matters that were not raised before or considered by a judge hearing the possession claim, that could be relevant to the question of whether the occupier has become homeless intentionally.

---

[278] HA 1996, s 177(2).
[279] English Code, paras 11.25 and 11.27(iii); Welsh Code, para 15.9(iii).
[280] See **14.181–14.186**.
[281] See **14.174**.
[282] See **14.88–14.92**.
[283] See **14.93–14.97**.
[284] *Devenport v Salford City Council* (1988) 8 HLR 54, CA; and *Bratton v Croydon London Borough Council* [2002] EWCA Civ 1494, (2002) December *Legal Action*, p 22, CA.
[285] *Green v Croydon London Borough Council* [2007] EWCA Civ 1367, (2008) *Legal Action*, p 41, CA.

14.184 Where the claim for possession is brought by a landlord who alleges fault on the part of a secure or assured tenant,[286] the court hearing the claim for possession will determine whether there has been fault, so as to entitle the landlord to possession, and will normally consider whether it is reasonable to make an order for possession and whether the order should be postponed on terms.[287] A tenant evicted as a result of one of these 'fault-based' grounds for possession is likely to find that the local housing authority finds that he or she has become homeless intentionally for the same reason that the court decided to make a possession order. Common scenarios include where the tenant has accrued rent arrears or has been found responsible for nuisance behaviour.[288] Normally, in these fault-based claims for possession, the tenant will have had the opportunity to put everything that is relevant to a decision as to whether he or she had become homeless intentionally to the judge hearing the possession claim, and so it would be unusual for there to be additional relevant facts to be put before the local housing authority.

14.185 Where the possession claim has been brought without any need for the landlord to show that the tenant is at fault, such as possession proceedings brought under Housing Act 1988, s 21 against assured shorthold tenants, or proceedings by local housing authorities against introductory, demoted or non-secure tenants, then very little information will have been put before the judge. The local housing authority is entitled to consider the reasons for the landlord's decision to bring (and continue) possession proceedings and, of course, must hear the tenant's side of the story. If those reasons are because of the fault of the tenant, he or she may have become homeless intentionally, even though the possession claim was not brought on any of the fault-based grounds.[289]

14.186 Where the occupier is evicted as a result of mortgage foreclosure proceedings, the reason for the bringing of the proceedings will have been the

---

[286]	Under Housing Act 1985, Sch 2, Part 1 (secure tenants) or Housing Act 1988, Sch 2, Grounds 8, 10, 11, 12, 13, 14, 15, or 17 (assured tenants).

[287]	The exception is Housing Act 1988, Sch 2, Ground 8, where the landlord is entitled to possession if the ground is made out.

[288]	For cases concerning rent arrears, see *R v Wandsworth London Borough Council ex p Hawthorne* [1994] 1 WLR 1442, CA; *R v Brent London Borough Council ex p Baruwa* (1997) 29 HLR 915, CA; and *R v Newham London Borough Council ex p Campbell* (1994) 26 HLR 183, QBD (where the real cause of homelessness was not the reason for the making of the possession order). For cases concerning nuisance behaviour see *Devenport v Salford City Council* (1983) 8 HLR 54, CA; *R v Swansea City Council ex p John* (1983) 9 HLR 56, QBD (where the tenant had acquiesced in her partner's nuisance behaviour and so had become homeless intentionally); *Griffiths v St Helens MBC* [2004] 142 Housing Aid Update, St Helens County Court, noted at Madge & Sephton *Housing Law Casebook* (LAG, 4th edn, 2008), T24.4 (where the tenant had tried to stop her children's misconduct and had not become homeless intentionally) and *Walcot v Lambeth London Borough Council* [2006] EWCA Civ 809, (2006) September *Legal Action*, p 14, CA.

[289]	*Bratton v Croydon London Borough Council* [2002] EWCA Civ 1494, (2002) December *Legal Action*, p 22, CA. See *Houghton v Sheffield City Council* [2006] EWCA Civ 1799, (2007) March *Legal Action*, p 18, where a local housing authority was wrong to find that a tenant who had reduced arrears from £1,000 to £7, but was still subject to a possession order, had become homeless intentionally.

occupier having accrued arrears under the mortgage, and the local housing authority will be entitled to consider the reasons for those arrears and for the decision to take out the mortgage in the first place.[290]

Leaving accommodation because of violence/threats of violence/harassment

Violence/threats of violence

14.187 As a matter of law, if the local housing authority finds that it is probable that, if the applicant continues to occupy his or her accommodation, he or she or a member of his or her household will be subject to violence or threats of violence that are likely to be carried out, the accommodation cannot be reasonable for the applicant and members of his or her household to continue to occupy.[291] The applicant is already 'homeless' and may therefore leave without a finding that he or she has become homeless intentionally.

14.188 For these purposes, 'violence' and 'threats of violence' can include sexual or physical abuse from another member of the family[292] or any other form of actual or threatened violence. The Court of Appeal has held that 'violence' should be given a narrow interpretation, requiring physical contact.[293]

14.189 A failure to pursue legal remedies against the perpetrator because of fears of reprisal, or because the applicant was unaware of the remedies available, should not generally be considered a deliberate act or omission if the applicant was acting in good faith.[294]

14.190 Where a woman leaves her accommodation because of domestic violence, and goes to a women's refuge, the refuge will not be reasonable to continue to occupy indefinitely.[295] Consequently, the local housing authority should look back to the reasons why the woman left her accommodation, and whether it was due to violence, or threats of violence that were likely to have been carried out if she continued in occupation, as defined at HA 1996, s 177(1).

---

[290] See **14.164–14.173**.

[291] HA 1996, s 177(1). See also English Code, paras 8.19–8.25, 11.13, 11.23; Welsh Code, paras 13.16–13.25 and 15.6(iii). *Bond v Leicester City Council* [2001] EWCA Civ 1544, (2002) 34 HLR 6, CA. See **11.78–11.88**.

[292] *R v Northampton Borough Council ex p Clarkson* (1992) 24 HLR 529, QBD.

[293] *Yemshaw v Hounslow London Borough Council* (unreported) 15 December 2009, CA (extempore judgment not yet reported at the date of this book going to print), and relying on *Danesh v Kensington & Chelsea Royal London Borough* [2006] EWCA Civ 1404, [2007] 1 WLR 69, CA; see **15.103**.

[294] English Code, para 11.23; Welsh Code, para 15.6(iii).

[295] *Ali & others v Birmingham City Council, Moran v Manchester City Council* [2009] UKHL 36, [2009] 1 WLR 1506, HL.

Harassment not amounting to violence/threats of violence

14.191 If the applicant says that he or she left accommodation due to harassment, on a scale that does not amount to violence or threats of violence that are likely to be carried out, the local housing authority should determine whether, in all the circumstances, including (if it chooses) taking into account general housing conditions in its district, the accommodation was reasonable for the applicant to continue to occupy.[296] Many of the cases that considered this point were decided before the enactment of the current statutory formula, 'reasonable for him to continue to occupy' in respect of violence or threats of violence that were likely to be carried out.[297] Those cases now only apply to a lower level of harassment: one that does not amount to violence or threats of violence that are likely to be carried out.

14.192 When considering non-violent harassment cases, local housing authorities are entitled to consider whether or not the applicant could have arranged to move away (eg by arranging a sale or through a transfer), and the extent to which it might be reasonable for the applicant to have continued to occupy the accommodation whilst that move was arranged.[298] Similarly, local housing authorities are entitled to consider whether it would have been reasonable for the applicant to have continued to occupy the accommodation with police protection rather than to have simply left.[299]

14.193 Once an applicant has raised the issues of violence, threats of violence and/or lower-level harassment, the local housing authority has a duty to make all necessary inquiries of all agencies that have been involved.[300] The burden rests on the local housing authority and not on the applicant.[301] The local housing authority must make a finding of fact as to whether or not it accepts the applicant's account of events.[302] If significant matters are to be held against the applicant, they should first be put to him or her for comment.[303] Having made that finding of fact, the local housing authority should then consider whether it is probable that continued occupation of the accommodation would have led to violence or threats of violence against the applicant. If it was probable, the accommodation was not reasonable to continue to occupy and the applicant cannot have become homeless intentionally. If violence or threats of violence were not probable, the local housing authority should consider

---

[296] English Code, para 8.34.

[297] HA 1996, ss 175(3), 177(1). See **11.78–11.88**.

[298] *R v Hillingdon London Borough Council ex p H* (1988) 20 HLR 554, QBD, and *R v Newham London Borough Council ex p McIlroy* (1991) 23 HLR 570, QBD.

[299] *R v Croydon London Borough Council ex p Toth* (1988) 20 HLR 576, CA.

[300] *Hawa Abdilah Ali v Newham London Borough Council* (2000) November *Legal Action*, p 23, Bow County Court.

[301] *R v Barnet London Borough Council ex p Babalola* (1995) 28 HLR 196, QBD.

[302] *R v Newham London Borough Council ex p Bones* (1993) 25 HLR 357, QBD. See *Eren v Haringey London Borough Council* [2007] EWCA Civ 1796, (2007) June *Legal Action*, p 38, CA, and *Rodrigues v Barking & Dagenham London Borough Council* [2008] EWCA Civ 271, (2008) June *Legal Action*, p 33, CA, for examples of cases where the local housing authority did not believe the applicant.

[303] *R v Brent London Borough Council ex p McManus* (1995) 25 HLR 643, QBD.

whether, in all the circumstances, it was reasonable for the applicant to continue to occupy the accommodation. If the applicant's account is accepted, the local housing authority should give proper, adequate and intelligible reasons if it concludes that the accommodation was, in any event, reasonable for the applicant to continue to occupy.[304]

14.194 The question for the local housing authority is whether it was reasonable for the applicant *and* all other members of his or her household to continue to occupy the accommodation.[305] If the violence, threat of violence or harassment was directed against a member of the household, rather than the applicant, the accommodation will still not be reasonable for the applicant to continue to occupy.[306]

14.195 Where the applicant has actually been responsible for violence, threats of violence, harassment or nuisance behaviour and has lost his or her home as a result, he or she will generally be considered to have committed a deliberate act leading to the loss of accommodation.[307] An applicant who has not directly participated in nuisance behaviour carried out by another household member may have acquiesced if he or she failed to take any steps to prevent the behaviour.[308]

14.196 However, if the accommodation has been lost for any other reason, not related to the applicant's deliberate act, even though the applicant has also been guilty of violent behaviour, he or she will not have become homeless intentionally.[309] If the applicant's own behaviour has led to the harassment, that behaviour can constitute a deliberate act, and he or she could be found to have become homeless intentionally.[310]

Exclusion by friends or relatives

14.197 Where people are living with friends or relatives, but are not themselves the tenant or owner of the accommodation, they are usually bare licensees or tenants with no statutory protection.[311] Their host will be entitled to require them to leave, provided that the licence or tenancy is terminated upon reasonable notice, which might be as little as 24 hours.

---

[304] *R v Westminster City Council ex p Ermakov* [1996] 2 All ER 302, CA.

[305] See **11.19–11.31** and **11.78–11.88**.

[306] *R v Westminster City Council ex p Bishop* (1993) 25 HLR 459, CA.

[307] English Code, para 11.20(vi); Welsh Code, para 15.7(v). See also *Devenport v Salford City Council* (1983) 8 HLR 54, CA, and *R v Swansea City Council ex p John* (1983) 9 HLR 56, QBD.

[308] See **14.78–14.82**.

[309] *R v Westminster City Council ex p Reid* (1994) 26 HLR 690, QBD; *R v Leeds City Council ex p Collier* (1998) June *Legal Action*, p 14, QBD; and *Demirtas v Islington London Borough Council* (2003) April *Legal Action*, p 27, Mayor's and City of London County Court.

[310] *R v Hammersmith and Fulham London Borough Council ex p P* (1990) 22 HLR 21, QBD.

[311] Protection from Eviction Act 1977, s 3.

14.198 The local housing authority is entitled in these cases to consider the reasons for the host's decision to exclude. It is not unusual for guests in these circumstances to have been staying with their hosts in overcrowded accommodation and for the accommodation therefore not to have been reasonable for the guests to continue to occupy.[312]

14.199 It might, however, have been the applicant's own conduct that led to the decision to exclude him or her from accommodation that would otherwise have been reasonable for him or her to continue to occupy. In *Denton v Southwark London Borough Council*,[313] the Court of Appeal held that a 21-year-old had become homeless intentionally after his mother had excluded him because of his unreasonable conduct. Arden LJ said:

> 'it is essential when people live together, that they show appropriate respect for each other's needs and follow any requests that one reasonably makes to the other. This is not a case where the mother was laying down inappropriate rules.'[314]

The situation would be different if the mother's rules had been unreasonable.[315]

14.200 If accommodation has become unreasonable to continue to occupy as a result of the applicant's deliberate act or omission, the fact that it was unreasonable when the applicant lost the accommodation should be disregarded.[316]

14.201 Perpetrators of domestic violence who are excluded from, or lose, their family home as a result of that violence could be found to have become homeless intentionally.[317]

Unsatisfactory accommodation

14.202 When considering the accommodation from which the applicant became (or is about to become) homeless, a local housing authority should consider the property's physical conditions and any overcrowding when deciding whether the accommodation was reasonable for the applicant (and members of his or her household) to have continued to occupy.[318]

---

[312] See **14.108–14.126** for 'reasonable to continue to occupy' and **14.202–14.207** for unsatisfactory accommodation.

[313] [2007] EWCA Civ 623, [2008] HLR 161, CA.

[314] *Denton v Southwark London Borough Council* [2007] EWCA Civ 623, [2008] HLR 161, CA at [21], per Arden LJ.

[315] In *White v Southwark London Borough Council* [2008] EWCA Civ 792, (2008) October *Legal Action*, p 37, CA, the Court of Appeal said that actions of children as young as 13 might be 'deliberate acts' and could be considered, even if the applicant was currently an independent young person. See also *Hassan v Brent London Borough Council* [2008] EWCA Civ 1385, (2009) February *Legal Action*, p 32, CA.

[316] *Denton v Southwark London Borough Council* [2007] EWCA Civ 623, [2008] HLR 161, CA.

[317] English Code, para 11.20(v); Welsh Code, para 15.7(v).

[318] English Code, para 8.34; Welsh Code, paras 13.13(ii) and (iii).

14.203 Local housing authorities are entitled to take into account (if they choose) the general housing conditions prevailing in their district when considering the question of reasonableness of continued occupation.[319] This is the case whether the relevant accommodation is in the local housing authority's own district, elsewhere in the UK, or outside the UK.[320] The local housing authority should not rely on assertions as to the general level of overcrowding or unfitness in its district, but should address itself to the particular degree of overcrowding or unfitness experienced by the applicant.[321]

14.204 Overcrowding which may render accommodation unreasonable for continued occupation is not restricted to statutory overcrowding.[322] If there are any medical needs arising as a result of the overcrowding or the physical condition of the property, they are relevant to the question of whether it would have been reasonable to continue to occupy.

14.205 Even when taking into account general housing conditions in its district, a local housing authority would normally be wrong to conclude that it would have been reasonable for a husband, wife and four children to have continued to occupy one room.[323] However, a local housing authority's decision that it would be reasonable, taking into account the shortage of accommodation in its district, for a separated husband to continue to occupy the same accommodation as his wife and her new boyfriend was not wrong in law.[324]

14.206 It is not appropriate for a local housing authority to conclude that the applicant has become homeless intentionally where the accommodation had become overcrowded (and is no longer reasonable to continue to occupy) as a result of the applicant's deliberate acts in having more children, or otherwise expanding his or her family.[325]

14.207 Other issues arising on the question of whether accommodation might not have been reasonable to have continued to occupy include the adequacy of

---

[319] HA 1996, s 177(2), *R v Brent London Borough Council ex p Bariise* (1999) 31 HLR 50, CA.

[320] *R v Tower Hamlets London Borough Council ex p Monaf* (1988) 20 HLR 529, CA; *R v Tower Hamlets London Borough Council ex p Ojo* (1991) 23 HLR 488, QBD; *R v Tower Hamlets London Borough Council ex p Bibi* (1991) 23 HLR 500, QBD; and *Osei v Southwark LBC* [2007] EWCA Civ 787, [2008] HLR 15, CA.

[321] *Mohamoud v Greenwich London Borough Council* (2003) January *Legal Action*, p 23, Woolwich County Court.

[322] *R v Westminster City Council ex p Alouat* (1989) 21 HLR 477, QBD.

[323] *R v Hillingdon London Borough Council ex p Islam* [1983] 1 AC 688, HL, although the opposite conclusion was not wrong in law in *R v Tower Hamlets London Borough Council ex p Uddin* (1993) June *Legal Action*, p 15, QBD. See also *R v Harrow London Borough Council ex p Louis* (1997) June *Legal Action*, p 23, QBD; and *R v Kensington and Chelsea Royal London Borough Council ex p Silchenstedt* (1997) 29 HLR 728, QBD.

[324] *R v Kensington and Chelsea Royal London Borough Council ex p Moncada* (1996) 29 HLR 289, QBD.

[325] *R v Eastleigh Borough Council ex p Beattie (No 1)* (1984) 10 HLR 134, QBD; and *R v Tower Hamlets London Borough Council ex p Hoque* (1993) Times 20 July, QBD.

fire prevention and escape facilities to the property and/or whether the accommodation was fit for human habitation.[326]

Medical needs

14.208 An applicant's medical needs can render the accommodation the applicant has left unreasonable to have continued to occupy.

14.209 Where medical issues are raised in relation to whether or not accommodation was reasonable to continue to occupy, the local housing authority is under a duty to inquire into them.[327] The local housing authority must consider the medical needs of the applicant and of all members of his or her household, together with any other factors which may, cumulatively, have resulted in the accommodation having been unreasonable to continue to occupy.[328]

14.210 If the applicant leaves accommodation that he or she anticipates will in the future become unreasonable to continue to occupy (such as where a pregnant applicant has been told that the property will not be suitable for her baby), he or she may still have become homeless intentionally if, at the particular time when the applicant left, the property was then reasonable to continue to occupy at least for some further period.[329]

14.211 The location of the accommodation and its effect on the applicant's state of health, or the health of members of his or her household, can be relevant and can render accommodation not reasonable for continued occupation, although in making its assessment the local housing authority would be entitled to take into account general housing conditions in its own area.[330]

14.212 The question for the local housing authority is not whether an applicant's medical needs, or those of his or her family members, would be better served elsewhere, but whether their medical needs rendered the accommodation unreasonable to continue to occupy at the date when the applicant left it.[331]

---

326 *R v Kensington and Chelsea Royal London Borough Council ex p Ben-El-Mabrouk* (1995) 27 HLR 564, CA; and *R v Haringey London Borough Council ex p Flynn* (1995) June *Legal Action*, p 21, QBD.

327 *R v Wycombe District Council ex p Homes* (1990) 22 HLR 150, QBD.

328 *R v Westminster City Council ex p Bishop* (1993) 25 HLR 459, CA.

329 *R v Brent London Borough Council ex p Yusuf* (1997) 29 HLR 48, QBD; but see also *R v Medina District Council ex p Dee* (1992) 24 HLR 562, QBD.

330 *R v Waltham Forest London Borough Council ex p Green* (1997) December *Legal Action*, p 15, QBD.

331 *R v Wandsworth London Borough Council ex p Nimako-Boateng* (1984) 11 HLR 95, QBD.

Employment and other social or economic prospects

14.213 The opportunities for employment (and any other financial prospects) that were available to the applicant at the accommodation may need to be taken into account in determining whether it would have been reasonable for him or her to have continued to occupy it.[332] Relevant matters may include employment prospects, any available capital or savings, debts, the availability of social security benefits and any other means of support, as well as the extent to which the applicant was socially isolated and any affect on his or her health as a result.[333]

14.214 Frequently, cases on this point will relate either to applicants migrating to the UK from elsewhere in the world for economic reasons, or to UK residents deciding to emigrate and then returning to the UK, again for economic reasons. The question for the local housing authority is not whether it was reasonable for the applicant to seek to live in (or return to) the UK, but rather whether it would have been reasonable to have continued to occupy the accommodation overseas. Local housing authorities should avoid decisions containing such phrases as 'you brought your family to the UK without making reasonable provision for their accommodation', as they suggest that the wrong issue is being addressed. The true focus of inquiry is whether it would have been reasonable for the applicant and his or her household to have remained in their accommodation overseas. The issue for the local housing authority is not why the applicant has left a particular country to come to the UK, but why he or she has left the particular accommodation in that country.[334]

14.215 Where the applicant raises the issue of the lack of employment prospects if he or she had continued to occupy his or her previous accommodation, the local housing authority is bound to make inquiries into that issue to see whether it would in fact have been reasonable for the applicant to have remained in occupation.[335]

14.216 If the applicant has lost tied accommodation as a result of his or her employment having come to an end, the local housing authority is entitled to consider whether his or her deliberate act or omission (in resigning or on being

---

[332] *R v Kensington and Chelsea Royal London Borough Council ex p Bayani* (1990) 22 HLR 406, CA.

[333] *R v Hammersmith and Fulham London Borough Council ex p Duro-Rama* (1983) 9 HLR 71, QBD; *R v Kensington and Chelsea Royal London Borough Council ex p Cunha* (1989) 21 HLR 16, QBD; *R v Camden London Borough Council ex p Aranda* (1997) 30 HLR 76, CA; *R v Camden London Borough Council ex p Cosmo* (1997) 30 HLR 817, QBD; *R v Wandsworth London Borough Council ex p Dodia* (1998) 30 HLR 562, QBD; *Kacar v Enfield London Borough Council* (2001) 33 HLR 5, CA; *Mohammed v Waltham Forest London Borough Council* (2002) October *Legal Action*, p 30, Bow County Court (permission to appeal refused by CA at [2002] EWCA Civ 1241, (2002) December *Legal Action*, p 22); and *Aw-Aden v Birmingham City Council* [2005] EWCA 1834, (2006) July *Legal Action*, p 29, CA.

[334] *R v Westminster City Council ex p Guilarte* (1994) June *Legal Action*, p 13, QBD.

[335] *Bowen v Lambeth London Borough Council* (1999) December *Legal Action*, p 22, Lambeth County Court; and *R v Westminster City Council ex p Augustin* (1993) 25 HLR 281, CA.

dismissed for misconduct) led to the loss of employment and hence the loss of accommodation.[336] Even if it finds such a deliberate act or omission, it must of course go on to consider whether the accommodation was available to the applicant and reasonable for him or her to have continued to occupy.

Ex-prisoners

14.217 The courts have held that the commission of a criminal offence, where the reasonably likely result is that the applicant will be sent to prison, can constitute a deliberate act as a consequence of which the applicant's accommodation may be lost. As a result, local housing authorities are entitled to find that a prisoner who loses his or her accommodation during the period of imprisonment because of inability to keep up payments for an unoccupied home has become homeless intentionally.[337] This conclusion was held not be wrong in law even in the case of a prisoner who made arrangements with his sister that she would pay the rent and a contribution to the arrears (required under a suspended possession order) during his sentence, when she then failed to honour the agreement.[338]

14.218 The Welsh Code advises that applicants who have just served a prison sentence and who find themselves homeless on release should not be considered to have become homeless intentionally unless the offences were themselves breaches of their previous tenancy agreements.[339]

Accommodation withdrawn by a local housing authority on completion of its homeless duty

14.219 Accommodation provided by the local housing authority while it is making inquiries,[340] or under the various short-term accommodation duties[341] or powers,[342] is unlikely to be settled accommodation and so unlikely to be relevant to any question of having become homeless intentionally.

---

[336] English Code, para 11.20(vii); Welsh Code, para 15.7(vi). See also *R v Kyle and Carrick District Council ex p Speck 1993 GWD 1566, OH.*

[337] *R v Hounslow London Borough Council ex p R* (1997) 29 HLR 939, QBD; and *Minchin v Sheffield City Council* (2000) Times, 26 April, CA. In *Minchin v Sheffield City Council,* the fact that the applicant had moved house after the commission of offences was irrelevant to her subsequently being found to have become homeless intentionally. In *Quaid v Westminster City Council* (2008) February *Legal Action*, p 41, Central London County Court, the applicant had not become homeless intentionally because he had committed offences when street homeless. It was not reasonably likely at the time that he had committed the offences that he would lose accommodation acquired after the offences had been committed. See also English Code, para 11.14.

[338] *Stewart v Lambeth London Borough Council* [2002] EWCA Civ 753, [2002] 34 HLR 40, CA.

[339] Welsh Code, paras 14.64, 15.6(iv).

[340] HA 1996, s 188(1). See **16.11–16.24.**

[341] HA 1996, s 190(2)(a) (see **17.111–17.118**) and s 200(1) (see **15.136–15.139**).

[342] HA 1996, s 188(3) (see **16.26–16.36**), s 192(3) (see **17.145–17.152**), s 200(5) (see **16.43–16.50**) and s 204(4) (see **16.37–16.42**).

14.220 However, where an applicant loses accommodation provided under the main housing duty,[343] the question arises whether that accommodation was lost as a result of the deliberate act or omission of the applicant.[344]

14.221 In the landmark case of *R v Brent London Borough Council ex p Awua*,[345] the House of Lords held that there was no requirement that the accommodation lost by a person who had become homeless intentionally should have been settled accommodation. As a result, Ms Awua had become homeless intentionally because she had lost her accommodation temporarily provided to her under the main housing duty as a result of her having refused an offer of accommodation.[346]

---

[343] HA 1996, s 193. See **17.21–17.110** for the main housing duty and for the ending of that duty.

[344] HA 1996, s 193(9) permits the applicant to make a fresh application to the local housing authority. For circumstances in which that application will be accepted, see **9.54–9.64** and **17.109–17.110**. Acceptance of the application, however, does not prevent a local housing authority from determining that the applicant has become homeless intentionally.

[345] [1996] AC 55, (1995) 27 HLR 453, HL.

[346] See, more recently, *Amanuel v Southwark London Borough Council* [2007] EWCA Civ 854, (2007) September *Legal Action*, p 18, CA; and *Ali v Haringey London Borough Council* [2008] EWCA Civ 132, (2008) April *Legal Action*, p 34, CA. Care must be taken to identify the reason for the loss of the accommodation; see *Bolah v Croydon London Borough Council* (2008) February *Legal Action*, p 40, Lambeth County Court. In *Keita v Southwark London Borough Council* [2008] EWCA Civ 963, (2008) October *Legal Action*, p 38, CA, the accommodation lost had not been provided under homelessness duties, but was terminated by the landlord charity after the applicant had refused an offer of accommodation.

Chapter 15

REFERRAL BETWEEN DIFFERENT LOCAL HOUSING AUTHORITIES

INTRODUCTION

15.1 The referral provisions in the Housing Act 1996 (HA 1996), Part 7 ensure that responsibility for accommodating those who are homeless is spread fairly between local housing authorities. Without a coherent set of rules governing which local housing authority owes a housing duty, homeless applicants would end up in the same position as their predecessors under the Poor Laws, when:

> '... each parish was responsible for the relief of those who were poor and unable to work. When a poor man moved from one parish to another, the question arose: which parish was responsible? The disputes, Blackstone tells us, "created an infinity of expensive lawsuits between contending neighbourhoods, concerning those settlements and removals".'[1]

15.2 In order to avoid intractable disputes (including 'expensive lawsuits'), HA 1996, Part 7 lays out the conditions under which local housing authorities can transfer responsibility for applicants by referring them to other local housing authorities. The conditions *only* apply to those applicants whom the first-approached local housing authority has already decided are homeless, are eligible for assistance, have a priority need and have not become homeless intentionally. Unless those applicants were referred, the main HA 1996, s 193(2) duty would be owed to them.[2] The referral provisions do not apply to applicants who have been found to be threatened with homelessness, or not to have a priority need, or to have become homeless intentionally.

15.3 In very broad terms, there are two sets of circumstances in which a local housing authority can refer a homeless applicant to another local housing authority. These are:

(1) where the applicant and his or her household have no connection with the area to which application for homelessness assistance has been made but do have a connection with another area to which they can safely be returned;[3] or

(2) where the applicant has been recently placed in the local housing authority's area by another local housing authority under its homelessness functions, but has become homeless again.[4]

15.4 However, the second condition now only applies to referrals between English local housing authorities and, possibly, from English local housing authorities to Welsh local housing authorities.[5]

---

[1]   *R v Slough Borough Council ex p Ealing London Borough Council* [1981] QB 801, CA at 808, per Lord Denning.

[2]   HA 1996, s 198(1).

[3]   HA 1996, s 198(2) and (2A). See **15.40–15.110**.

[4]   HA 1996, s 198(4). See **15.111–15.124**.

[5]   This is because the prescribed period was first contained in the Homelessness (England)

15.5 If the statutory conditions are satisfied, responsibility for a homeless applicant can be transferred from one local housing authority to another.

15.6 Several judges have remarked on the parallels with the Poor Laws:

'... it is all very reminiscent of the operation of the Poor Law of the nineteenth century and before, all dressed up in modern language.'[6]

'Given the pressures on many housing authorities, the natural tendency would be to try to export the homeless whenever possible. Moving the needy beyond the parish boundary has a long history.'[7]

15.7 Local housing authorities are not required to use these provisions. They are free to accept all those who apply to them. So, although they have power to make inquiries into an applicant's connection with another district if they wish, there is no obligation upon them to do so.[8]

15.8 However, if local housing authorities do choose to make those inquiries, the tests that they must apply to determine whether a referral can be made are strictly defined at HA 1996 s 198(2) and (2A) or (4).[9] If the conditions are not met, no referral to another local housing authority can be made and the first-approached local housing authority must perform its HA 1996, s 193(2) duty towards the applicant. If the local housing authority decides that the conditions are met, it retains a discretion, even at that stage, as to whether or not to make a referral. There is no obligation to do so.

15.9 Accordingly, there are potentially three decisions for a local housing authority to make in relation to each applicant:

Regulations 2000, SI 2000/701, reg 6, which was applied to Wales by the Homelessness (Wales) Regulations 2000, SI 2000/1079, reg 2. The Homelessness (Wales) Regulations 2000, SI 2000/1079, were revoked in their entirety from 9 October 2006 by the Homelessness (Wales) Regulations 2006, SI 2006/2646 (W 227), reg 6. The Homelessness (Wales) Regulations 2006, SI 2006/2646 (W 227) do not contain a prescribed period. In the absence of any prescribed period, Welsh local housing authorities cannot operate HA 1996, s 198(4), except for applications for homelessness assistance made before 9 October 2006. The prescribed period to be operated by English local housing authorities is at reg 3 of the Allocation of Housing and Homelessness (Miscellaneous Provisions) (England) Regulations 2006 (SI 2006/2527), at Appendix 2 of this book. See **15.112**.

[6]   *R v Hammersmith and Fulham London Borough Council ex p O'Brien* (1985) 17 HLR 471, QBD at 474, per Glidewell J.

[7]   *R v Slough Borough Council ex p Khan* (1996) 27 HLR 492, QBD at 496, per Toulson J (then Mr Roger Toulson QC).

[8]   HA 1996, s 184(2). *Homelessness Code of Guidance for local authorities* (Communities and Local Government, Department for Education and Skills, Department of Health, July 2006) (English Code), paras 18.2–18.5, at Appendix 2 of this book. *Code of Guidance for local housing authorities on allocation of accommodation and homelessness for Wales* (National Assembly for Wales, April 2003) (Welsh Code), para 20.1: see CD-ROM.

[9]   The inquiry into HA 1996, s 198(4) conditions is for English local housing authorities only. Or, in the special and increasingly rare case of eligible asylum seekers, by HA 1996, s 198(4A), (4B). See **15.167–15.172**.

(1) whether or not to make inquiries into the question of any local connection at all; if so,

(2) whether the conditions for referral as defined at either HA 1996, s 198(2) and (2A) or (4) are met; and, if so,

(3) whether or not to notify another local housing authority of its opinion that the conditions are met.

15.10 Given that the conditions for referral only apply to those applicants who would otherwise be owed a HA 1996, s 193(2) main housing duty by the local housing authority making the referral, the applicants affected have a right to be accommodated throughout the decision-making process. The duty to accommodate falls first on the first-approached local housing authority, and then on the local housing authority to which the referral is made.[10]

15.11 Applicants are most likely to seek assistance from the local housing authority for the district in which they want to live and so would be expected to dispute a decision to refer them to another local housing authority. It is therefore no surprise that applicants are entitled to request reviews of several of the decisions involved in the referral process. They may request reviews of any decision that they should be referred to another local housing authority, any decision that the conditions for referral are made out, and any decision as to the duties owed to them as a result.[11] Obviously, if any of those review decisions contain an error of law, the applicants may appeal to the county court.[12]

15.12 In order to avoid homeless applicants being caught in 'a game of battledore and shuttlecock – with the homeless the shuttlecock and the housing authorities wielding the battledore',[13] local housing authorities are obliged to accept a referral if the conditions for referral are met. If the local housing authority, which has been asked to accept a referral, disputes whether the conditions are met, a referee can be appointed. Those arrangements are described in detail in the English Code, Annex 18.[14] The local housing authorities involved are then bound by the referee's decision. However, the applicant still has the right to request a review of the referee's decision (and subsequently to appeal to the county court on a point of law).[15]

---

10 HA 1996, s 200. See **15.136–15.139**.
11 HA 1996, s 202(1)(c), (d) and (e). See **19.16–19.26**.
12 HA 1996, s 204(1).
13 *R v Slough Borough Council ex p Ealing London Borough Council* [1981] QB 801, CA at 808, per Lord Denning.
14 Welsh Code, Annex 20 contains the version of the Local Authorities' Agreement in existence at the date of publication of the Welsh Code (2003). The Local Authorities' Agreement has since been updated and Annex 18 of the English Code contains the current version. Annex 18 of the English Code thus applies to both English and Welsh authorities. Readers are advised not to refer to Annex 20 of the Welsh Code.
15 HA 1996, s 202(1)(d). See **15.153–15.166** and **19.23–19.25**.

15.13 There are special additional rules permitting local housing authorities to refer certain asylum-seekers (those who are eligible for homelessness assistance and to whom a HA 1996, s 193(2) main housing duty would otherwise be owed) to another local housing authority that has agreed to accept the referral.[16] There is a discussion of those rules later in this chapter. In practice, however, it is unlikely that many referrals are now made under these rules, as they only apply to asylum-seekers who had applied as homeless before 3 April 2000. Several years on, it is unlikely that there are many outstanding decisions to be made on those applications.[17]

15.14 There are also additional rules concerning former asylum-seekers who occupied accommodation provided by the Home Office (formerly National Asylum Support Service or NASS) in Scotland and subsequently made applications for homelessness assistance to English or Welsh local housing authorities. In those cases, English and Welsh local housing authorities are not subject to the main housing duty at HA 1996, s 193(2), but instead may provide accommodation for a limited period and provide advice and assistance to help the applicant apply to a Scottish local authority, or make other arrangements for accommodation.[18] These rules are discussed towards the end of this chapter.

15.15 Throughout this chapter, we use the statutory terms of 'notifying local housing authority' and 'notified local housing authority' to indicate respectively the local housing authority first receiving the application for homelessness assistance and subsequently making the referral (the 'notifying local housing authority'), and the local housing authority receiving the referral (the 'notified local housing authority').

15.16 The chapter concludes with a review of the circumstances in which applicants may be accommodated outside the district in which they sought to be housed but without the local housing authority invoking any referral procedure.

THE RIGHT TO MAKE AN APPLICATION FOR HOMELESSNESS ASSISTANCE TO ANY LOCAL HOUSING AUTHORITY

15.17 Any homeless person is free to apply to any local housing authority in England, Wales or Scotland (or to the Housing Executive in Northern Ireland) for assistance with accommodation. There is no prior condition that the applicant must apply to the local housing authority for any particular district. There is no filter that prevents an applicant who has no connection with a

---

[16] HA 1996, s 198(4A) and (4B). See **15.167–15.172**.

[17] See **12.75–12.86** and **12.88–12.89** for eligible asylum-seekers.

[18] Asylum and Immigration (Treatment of Claimants etc) Act 2004, s 11(2) and (3) in force from 4 January 2005. See **15.173–15.180**.

particular local housing authority from applying to that local housing authority. Once the application for homelessness assistance has been made, and there is reason to believe that the applicant may be homeless or threatened with homelessness, the local housing authority must conduct inquiries and make its decision as to whether or not the applicant is eligible and, if so, whether a duty and (if so) what duty, is owed to the applicant under HA 1996, Part 7.[19] Any local housing authority that tells an applicant that he or she has applied to the wrong local housing authority, that he or she cannot apply to that particular local housing authority, or that no inquiries will be made because he or she does not appear to have a connection with its district, is acting unlawfully.[20]

15.18 Because well-informed applicants may shop around between different local housing authorities,[21] it must be emphasised that the conditions for referral under the referral provisions only apply to applicants to whom the notifying local housing authority would otherwise owe a HA 1996, s 193(2) main housing duty (ie those who are homeless, eligible for assistance, have a priority need, and did not become homeless intentionally). No other applicants can be referred. Applicants who:

- are threatened with homelessness; or

- do not have a priority need; or

- have become homeless intentionally,

remain the responsibility of the local housing authority to which they have applied, and the limited duties owed to those applicants must be performed by that local housing authority. Put another way, the duties to provide:

- interim accommodation pending inquiries,[22]

- help for those who became homeless intentionally,[23]

- assistance to those threatened with homelessness,[24]

- protection for an applicant's property,[25] and

- any other assistance under HA 1996, Part 7 (except the main housing duty in s 193(2)),

---

19 HA 1996, s 184(1) and (3).
20 *R v Slough Borough Council ex p Ealing London Borough Council* [1981] QB 801, CA; and *R v Tower Hamlets London Borough Council ex p Camden London Borough Council* (1988) 21 HLR 197, QBD.
21 Where an applicant for homelessness assistance has made an earlier, or a simultaneous, application to a different local housing authority, see **9.39–9.45**.
22 HA 1996, s 188(1). See **16.11–16.24**.
23 HA 1996, s 190. See **17.111–17.118** and **17.132–17.144**.
24 HA 1996, s 195. See **17.119–17.131** and **17.132–17.144**.
25 HA 1996, s 211. See **17.163–17.184**.

cannot be transferred using the referral provisions.[26]

DISCRETIONARY POWER TO MAKE INQUIRIES INTO THE CONDITIONS FOR REFERRAL

Introduction

15.19 As soon as a local housing authority has 'reason to believe' that an applicant for assistance under HA 1996, Part 7 may be homeless or threatened with homelessness, it must make inquiries to satisfy itself whether the applicant is eligible and whether any duty, and if so what duty, is owed to the applicant.[27] It *may* also make inquiries into whether the applicant has a 'local connection' with the district of any other local housing authority in England, Wales or Scotland (which is one of the requirements enabling a referral to be made).[28] However, there is no obligation to make those latter inquiries. Even if the applicant self-evidently has no connection with the local housing authority to which he or she has applied, and has an obvious connection with another local housing authority, the first local housing authority can choose not to make inquiries into that connection.

15.20 Applicants cannot insist that the local housing authority to which they apply makes inquiries into their local connection. If the local housing authority decides not to make those inquiries, the applicant has no right to request a review of that decision, as it is not a decision that falls within one of the categories of decisions capable of review.[29] Any legal challenge could only be brought by judicial review.[30] Although many local housing authorities, anxious to reduce pressure on their resources, will jump at the possibility of referring an applicant to another local housing authority, local housing authorities are also entitled to assume that an applicant has applied to the local housing authority in whose district he or she would want to be housed.[31]

15.21 If an applicant does find that he or she has made an application for homelessness assistance to the wrong local housing authority, and is then disappointed that it decides not to make inquiries into his or her local connection elsewhere, there are three alternative courses of action available.

15.22 First, he or she could withdraw the first application and apply afresh to the local housing authority in whose district he or she wants to live.[32] That

---

26   English Code, para 18.3; Welsh Code, para 20.1.
27   HA 1996, s 184(1). See **10.1–10.36** and **15.44–15.46**.
28   HA 1996, s 184(2). See **10.2** and **10.13**.
29   HA 1996, s 202(1); see *Hackney London Borough Council v Sareen* [2003] EWCA Civ 351, [2003] HLR 54, CA.
30   See **19.211–19.237**.
31   *Hackney London Borough Council v Sareen* [2003] EWCA Civ 351, [2003] HLR 54, CA at [42], per Auld LJ.
32   English Code, para 6.26; Welsh Code, para 12.31. See **9.64–9.69**.

would only be possible before the first local housing authority had notified the applicant of its decision on the first application.[33]

15.23 Second, the applicant could seek to persuade the first local housing authority that he or she should be provided with accommodation in the district of the local housing authority where he or she wishes to live. The first local housing authority could facilitate that by arranging for a private landlord to offer the applicant an assured shorthold tenancy there;[34] by nominating the applicant to the second local housing authority under its housing allocation scheme;[35] or by nomination to a registered social landlord (RSL) in that district.[36]

15.24 Third, the applicant could (if still homeless or threatened with homelessness) promptly apply direct to the local housing authority in whose district he or she wishes to live, while leaving the first application pending.

What inquiries can the local housing authority make?

15.25 If the local housing authority does choose to make inquiries into the applicant's local connection, the results of those inquiries will only become relevant once the local housing authority has determined what duty, if any, it owes the applicant and, even then, only if the decision it has made is that it would otherwise owe the main housing duty under HA 1996, s 193(2).

15.26 Given that the conditions for referral only apply to those applicants to whom the local housing authority would owe a main HA 1996, s 193(2) duty, it may make practical sense for a local housing authority not to make inquiries into any local connection until it has completed the remainder of its inquiries and made decisions upon them. If an applicant appears to have become homeless intentionally or not to have a priority need, there is no point devoting additional resources to making wasteful inquiries into the question of local connection.

15.27 The local housing authority may only make inquiries into whether the applicant has a local connection with the district of any other local housing authority in England, Wales or Scotland.[37] A local connection with a local

---

33   Otherwise the applicant runs the risk of refusing, or becoming homeless intentionally from, an offer of suitable HA 1996, s 193 accommodation, and thus a finding that the duty towards him or her has ended. See **17.32–17.37**, **17.49–17.58** and **17.62–17.65**.

34   Either under HA 1996, s 193(2) (see **17.21–17.110**) or under s 193(7B). See **17.92–17.97**.

35   HA 1996, s 159(2)(b)

36   HA 1996, s 159(2)(c); see *R (W) v Sheffield City Council* [2005] EWHC 720 (Admin), where Mr W, who had been referred by Westminster to Sheffield, sought to persuade Sheffield that its duty to provide suitable accommodation for him could only be performed by arranging for accommodation in Westminster. See also para 6.4 of the Local Authorities' Agreement at Annex 18 of the English Code, which recommends that local housing authorities should consider their ability to nominate in order to avoid 'causing undue disruption'. And see Chapter 6 and **15.212–15.216**.

37   HA 1996, s 184(2).

housing authority elsewhere is not relevant.[38] In particular, a connection with other parts of the UK (eg Northern Ireland)[39] would not trigger the referral provisions in HA 1996, s 198.

15.28 Curiously, HA 1996, Part 7 limits the subject matter of the discretionary inquiries to whether the applicant himself or herself has a connection elsewhere.[40] A local housing authority which confined its inquiries only to that question would find it impossible to determine whether the conditions for referral to another local housing authority were in fact satisfied or not. As the remainder of this chapter indicates, the referral conditions are detailed and complex and go well beyond the question of whether the applicant personally has a local connection with the district of another local housing authority. The local housing authority which receives an application for homelessness assistance, and wishes to pursue the possibility of referring it, will also need to know whether:

(1)   the applicant or any member of his or her household has a local connection with its own area;[41] and whether

(2)   any other member of the applicant's household has a local connection with another local housing authority's area;[42] and whether

(3)   the applicant (or any member of his or her household) would be at risk of actual or threatened violence if returned to another area;[43] and whether

(4)   (for English local housing authorities only) the applicant was placed in its area by another local housing authority acting under the homelessness provisions of HA 1996, Part 7.[44]

15.29 Self-evidently, inquiries into those matters would go well beyond the scope of those expressly mentioned in HA 1996, s 184(2), and so the local housing authority will rely entirely upon the applicant and others voluntarily responding to its inquiries.

15.30 Accordingly, where the local housing authority has received an application for homelessness assistance, has opted to make inquiries into the matter and has discovered that the applicant has a local connection elsewhere,

---

38   *R v Westminster City Council ex p Esmail* (1989) June *Legal Action*, p 25, QBD.
39   See Box 1 at **12.55**.
40   HA 1996, s 184(2).
41   HA 1996, s 198(2)(a).
42   HA 1996, s 198(2)(b).
43   HA 1996, s 198(2)(c).
44   HA 1996, s 198(4).

it cannot simply assume that all the other ingredients of the conditions for a referral are made out. It must go on to explore whether the other conditions for referral are satisfied.[45]

THE CONDITIONS FOR REFERRAL

Introduction

15.31 The preliminary condition for *any* referral is that the local housing authority in receipt of the application for homelessness assistance is satisfied that it would itself owe the applicant the main housing duty.[46]

15.32 Beyond that, the detailed conditions for referral are set out in HA 1996, s 198. There are two separate and alternative tranches of conditions for referral contained in the statute. The second set of conditions for referral now applies only to referrals between English local housing authorities and, possibly, to referrals by English local housing authorities to Welsh local housing authorities.[47]

15.33 The *first* set of 'conditions for referral' is found in HA 1996, s 198(2) and (2A). These are that:

(1) neither the applicant nor any person who might reasonably be expected to reside with the applicant has a local connection with the district of the local housing authority to whom the application for homelessness assistance was made; and

(2) either the applicant or a person who might reasonably be expected to reside with the applicant has a local connection with the district of another local housing authority in England, Wales or Scotland; and

(3) neither the applicant nor any person who might reasonably be expected to reside with the applicant will run the risk of domestic violence in that other district; and

(4) neither the applicant nor any person who might reasonably be expected to reside with the applicant has suffered violence in the district of that other local housing authority; or,

---

[45] *R v Slough Borough Council ex p Khan* (1995) 27 HLR 492, QBD; and *R v Greenwich London Borough Council ex p Patterson* (1994) 26 HLR 159, CA.

[46] HA 1996, ss 193(1) and 198(1).

[47] This is because there is a period prescribed for English local housing authorities (Allocation of Housing and Homelessness (Miscellaneous Provisions) (England) Regulations 2006, SI 2006/2527, reg 3). The Homelessness (Wales) Regulations 2006, SI 2006/2646 (W 227) do not contain a prescribed period. In the absence of any prescribed period, Welsh local housing authorities cannot operate HA 1996, s 198(4), except for applications for homelessness assistance made before 9 October 2006. See **15.111–15.124**.

(5)   if violence has been suffered, it is not probable that a return to that district will lead to further violence of a similar kind against that person.[48]

15.34   This set of conditions requires additional consideration of the concepts of 'local connection',[49] 'violence',[50] and 'domestic violence'.[51] It also requires a determination by the local housing authority as to those persons with whom the applicant 'might reasonably be expected to reside' – a phrase that is not confined to those with whom the applicant is, or has been, living immediately prior to the application for homelessness assistance.[52]

15.35   The *second* set of 'conditions for referral' is to be found in HA 1996, s 198(4). It now applies to English local housing authorities only.

15.36   The conditions are that:

(1)   the applicant was placed in accommodation in the district of the local housing authority to which he or she has applied (authority A) by another local housing authority (authority B); and

(2)   that placement was made in pursuance of authority B's functions under HA 1996, Part 7; and

(3)   the application for homelessness assistance to authority A is made within a prescribed period.

15.37   For *English* local housing authorities, the prescribed period is the total of 5 years plus the period between the date of the applicant's application for homelessness assistance to authority A and the date when the applicant was placed in authority B.[53]

15.38   If this second set of conditions is met, the applicant can be referred by authority A to authority B. There is no additional requirement on authority A to consider whether the applicant ever had a local connection with authority B or has, more recently, acquired a local connection with its district. Nor is there any requirement to consider whether the applicant or any member of his or her household would be subject to domestic or other violence in the district of authority B.

---

[48]   HA 1996, s 198(2A).
[49]   Defined at HA 1996, s 199. See **15.40–15.90**.
[50]   Defined at HA 1996, s 198(3). See **15.94–15.97** and **15.102–15.106**.
[51]   Defined at HA 1996, s 198(3). See **15.98–15.101**.
[52]   See HA 1996, s 176 and **11.19–11.31**.
[53]   Allocation of Housing and Homelessness (Miscellaneous Provisions) (England) Regulations 2006, SI 2006/2527, reg 3, for applications to local housing authorities made on or after 9 October 2006. The prescribed period was the same for applications made up to and including 31 May 2006 (Homelessness (England) Regulations 2000, SI 2007/701, reg 6). For applications made between 1 June 2006 and 8 October 2006, the position is unclear, since there was no prescribed period.

15.39   Each set of conditions for referral is now separately considered.

The first set of conditions for referral – 'local connection'

Overview

15.40   The lynchpin of the first set of referral conditions is the concept of 'local connection'. That phrase is not itself defined by HA 1996, Part 7. The legislation simply limits the relevant methods by which a local connection can be acquired to one or more of the circumstances specified at HA 1996, s 199. The circumstances are that:

(1)   the person is, or was in the past, normally resident in a district and his or her residence there is, or was, of his or her own choice;[54] or

(2)   the person is employed in the district;[55] or

(3)   the person has a connection with the district through family associations;[56] or

(4)   the person has a connection with the district through special circumstances;[57] or

(5)   the person was provided with accommodation in the district (in England or Wales) under s 95 of the Immigration and Asylum Act 1999 (dispersal of asylum-seekers).[58]

15.41   Each of the above circumstances will be examined in turn in this chapter.

15.42   When considering whether the circumstances sufficient to establish a 'local connection' are made out, a local housing authority must have regard to both HA 1996, Part 7 and the relevant Code of Guidance. In addition, local housing authorities have also agreed and adopted additional guidance as to the interpretation of some of these statutory provisions.[59] The House of Lords has

---

[54]   HA 1996, s 199(1)(a). See **15.52–15.63**.
[55]   HA 1996, s 199(1)(b). See **15.63–15.69**.
[56]   HA 1996, s 199(1)(c). See **15.70–15.77**.
[57]   HA 1996, s 199(1)(d). See **15.78–15.83**.
[58]   HA 1996, s 199(6), added by Asylum and Immigration (Treatment of Claimants, etc) Act 2004, s 11(1) and in force from 4 January 2005. See **15.84–15.90**.
[59]   Guidelines for Local Authorities and Referees agreed by Association of London Government (ALG), Convention of Scottish Local Authorities (CoSLA), Local Government Association (LGA), Welsh Local Government Association (WLGA), reproduced at English Code, Annex 18. The Agreement as it appears at Annex 18 of the English Code is the current version and applies to both English and Welsh local housing authorities. The version at Annex 20 of the Welsh Code is out of date.

confirmed that local housing authorities are entitled to consider that additional guidance when making their decisions.[60] As Chadwick LJ put it:

> 'It is desirable that the notified authority – who is being asked to assume the burden of providing accommodation for the applicant in the place of the notifying authority – should be able to accept the view of the notifying authority both that the applicant has no local connection with the district of the notifying authority and that the applicant does have a local connection with their own district. Ready agreement is unlikely to be achieved on those two points unless both the notifying authority and the notified authority are able to approach the question from a common basis. It is the need for that common basis which, as it seems to me, provides the imperative for all authorities to apply the guidelines "generally to all applications which come before them".'[61]

15.43 If they do take the guidance into consideration, local housing authorities must still ensure that they consider the applicant's individual circumstances, particularly any exceptional circumstances, before reaching a decision.[62]

15.44 If they embark on inquiries into local connection at all, local housing authorities should consider each of the five circumstances in which an applicant, or a member of his or her household, may acquire a local connection.[63] It is not sufficient merely to establish that a local connection has been acquired by the applicant with the district of another local housing authority through one of the specified categories. The local housing authority must go on to consider what other local connections the applicant or his or her household members may have. Consideration of all the categories might reveal that the applicant, or a member of his or her household, has a local connection with the very local housing authority to which he or she applied.[64] If that is the case, the conditions for referral will not be met. Alternatively, it might be the case that the applicant or a member of his or her household has a local connection with more than one local housing authority (other than that to which he or she applied), in which case the conditions for referral are met, but the relative strengths of the connections[65] and the applicant's preference[66] are relevant when deciding which local housing authority should be notified by the local housing authority to whom the applicant has applied.[67]

15.45 The House of Lords has held in *Mohammed v Hammersmith and Fulham London Borough Council*[68] that the relevant date for determining whether an applicant has a local connection, and with which local housing

---

60   *R v Eastleigh Borough Council ex p Betts* [1983] 2 AC 613, HL at 627, per Lord Brightman.
61   *Ozbek v Ipswich Borough Council* [2006] EWCA Civ 534, [2006] HLR 41, CA at [39] per Chadwick LJ.
62   *R v Harrow London Borough Council ex p Carter* (1992) 26 HLR 32, QBD.
63   *R v Slough Borough Council ex p Khan* (1995) 27 HLR 492, QBD.
64   English Code, para 18.13; Welsh Code, para 20.9.
65   See **15.128**.
66   English Code, para 18.14; Welsh Code, para 20.10.
67   English Code, Annex 18, para 4.11.
68   [2001] UKHL 57, [2002] 1 AC 547, HL.

authority, is the date of the decision that the local housing authority (or local housing authorities jointly, or a referee) makes on the question or (if a review is requested) the date of the review decision. Although in that case, the House of Lords was concerned with the definition of 'normally resident', the principle must apply to any of the other statutory circumstances that fall to be considered. So, if an applicant acquires a family association or becomes employed in a local housing authority's district after his or her application for homelessness assistance but before the date of decision, or even the review decision, the question of local connection must be considered on the facts at that later date, not as at the date of application. More commonly, of course, the applicant might have been 'resident' in the local housing authority's district for long enough since applying to have established a local connection[69] by the time of the initial decision or review, even though the period of residence in the district prior to the application for homelessness assistance had not been long enough to establish such a local connection.[70]

15.46 It is possible for a person not to have any local connection with any local housing authority in England, Wales or Scotland. The example given in the Welsh Code is where a person has 'had an unsettled way of life for many years'.[71] Former prisoners, former long-term hospital residents, former servicemen or servicewomen, etc, may likewise not have any local connection with any district at all. Neither would someone newly arrived in the UK, with no prior period of residence in England, Wales or Scotland, who was not employed and who had no family associations here. If there is no local connection anywhere, the conditions for referral are not met and the applicant remains the responsibility of the local housing authority to which he or she applied.[72]

15.47 Three additional points about local connection must be made before the individual ingredients are considered further.

15.48 First, HA 1996, Part 7 does not exhaustively define 'local connection'. Most obviously, a person may have a local connection with an area but it may arise from circumstances falling outside the prescribed list of circumstances. If that is the case, that connection would not fall within the definition of 'local connection' for the purposes of HA 1996, Part 7. For example, the connection a person has with an area because it was the place of his or her birth would be immaterial: 'A local connection not founded upon any of the four stated factors is irrelevant'.[73]

15.49 There is another sense in which the subsection does not exhaustively define 'local connection'. A 'local connection' with a district is something more

---

69   Under HA 1996, s 199(1)(a).
70   For example, *Fetaj v Lambeth London Borough Council* (2002) September *Legal Action*, p 31, Lambeth County Court.
71   Welsh Code, para 20.13.
72   English Code, para 18.22; Welsh Code, para 20.13.
73   *R v Eastleigh Borough Council ex p Betts* [1983] 2 AC 613, HL per Lord Brightman.

than simply *a* connection by residence, employment, etc. While one of the five prescribed circumstances is a necessary pre-condition for a local connection, it is not sufficient alone to establish a local connection. For example, a person may have employment in an area, but it may be of only a transient or very part-time nature. A person may have 'family associations' with an area because his or her parents live there, but might be estranged from their parents and not have seen or spoken to them for years. What is required is that the connection by a person (by having been 'normally resident', 'employed', or having 'family associations' in an area) is of sufficient quality to amount to a present 'local connection'. As the House of Lords has put it, a local connection is a connection which has been built up or established so as to have become 'a connection in real terms'.[74]

15.50 Second, different local connections may be of different comparative strengths. For example, a person might be said to have a stronger local connection with the place in which she or he lives than with the place where she or he works. If the applicant (or anyone who might reasonably be expected to live with him or her) has *any* local connection (based on one or more of the five statutory circumstances) with the local housing authority to which an application for homelessness assistance has been made, the strength of that local connection is irrelevant. The conditions for referral will not be made out and the referral provisions cannot be used, even if the applicant has a much stronger local connection with another local housing authority.[75] But where there is no local connection with the district of the local housing authority applied to, but local connections with two or more other districts, the respective strengths of the local connections elsewhere, along with the applicant's preference, will be a factor for the first local housing authority in determining to which other local housing authority it should direct the referral.[76]

15.51 Third, the relevant local connection is with the 'district' of a local housing authority. That must mean with any part of the geographical area of that authority. So, a person who lives (and has always lived) just inside the boundaries of Borough A will have a local connection with that borough even if, in practice, most of his or her time is spent in neighbouring Borough B (for shopping, education, recreation or leisure purposes). None of the interesting questions which might arise in relation to local connection when district boundaries are moved (eg by implementation of recommendations of the Boundary Commission) have yet been considered by the courts.

---

74 *R v Eastleigh Borough Council ex p Betts* [1983] 2 AC 613, HL per Lord Brightman.
75 English Code, para 18.13; Welsh Code, para 20.9.
76 English Code, para 18.14 and Annex 18 para 4.11.

The relevant statutory circumstances

(1) Normal residence of his or her own choice[77]

15.52 A person must have been 'normally resident' in a district in order to acquire a local connection with that district by having lived there. 'Normal residence' is to be understood as meaning 'the place where at the relevant time the person in fact resides'.[78] There is no need for the place to be a permanent home, or even to be the place where a person most wants to be living.

> 'So long as that place where he eats and sleeps is voluntarily accepted by him, the reason why he is there rather than somewhere else does not prevent that place from being his normal residence. He may not like it, he may prefer some other place, but that place is for the relevant time the place where he normally resides. If a person, having no other accommodation, takes his few belongings and moves into a barn for a period to work on a farm that is where during that period he is normally resident, however much he might prefer some more permanent or better accommodation. In a sense it is "shelter" but it is also where he resides.'[79]

15.53 Applying this approach, even occupation of interim accommodation, provided under a local housing authority's homelessness duties, constitutes 'normal residence'. Likewise, occupation of accommodation provided under community care or other duties will be accommodation in which the applicant normally resides.

15.54 The assessment that has to be made in a 'residence' case:

> '... is not whether the homeless person is now or was in the past normally resident in the area of the notifying authority, but whether the applicant has now a local connection with either area based upon the fact that he is now or was in the past normally resident in that area.'[80]

15.55 The Local Authorities' Agreement[81] suggests that a working definition of normal residence sufficient to establish a 'local connection' should be residence for at least 6 months in an area during the previous 12 months, or for not less than 3 years during the previous 5-year period.[82] Local housing authorities may apply that working definition, although each case must be considered on its own particular facts.[83]

15.56 The concept of normal residence being 'of his own choice' was considered by the House of Lords in *Al-Ameri v Kensington and Chelsea Royal*

---

77 HA 1996, s 199(1)(a).
78 *Mohamed v Hammersmith and Fulham London Borough Council* [2001] UKHL 57, [2002] 1 AC 547, HL at [17], per Lord Slynn.
79 *Mohamed v Hammersmith and Fulham London Borough Council* [2001] UKHL 57, [2002] 1 AC 547, HL at [17], per Lord Slynn.
80 *R v Eastleigh Borough Council ex p Betts* [1983] 2 AC 613, HL, per Lord Brightman.
81 See **15.42**.
82 English Code, Annex 18, para 4.1(i).
83 *R v Eastleigh Borough Council ex p Betts* [1983] 2 AC 613, HL.

London Borough Council.[84] It decided that 'choice' in this context refers to a person's choice to go and live in a particular district. The district must have been selected by the individual, rather than by some other person (for example, by an official or a Secretary of State). The particular situation in *Al-Ameri* (asylum-seekers occupying accommodation provided under the then National Asylum Support Service (NASS) scheme) has since been specifically addressed by legislation.[85] However, the general definition of 'his own choice' remains. The House of Lords decision confirmed, for example, that children moved from one district to another by their parents would not have been resident in the new district 'of their own choice'.[86]

15.57 This freedom of choice aspect cannot be extrapolated too far. A person who moves from one area to another as a consequence of his or her employer relocating might be said to be simply falling in line with a choice made by another, and the point could be made with even more force about the employee's partner. However, in reality, the employee has chosen to move rather than to resign and the employee's partner has chosen to follow. Their residence is, accordingly, of their 'own choice'. Much more acute difficulties arise with the 'own choice' concept when an applicant to the local housing authority for District A has become resident in District A as a result of having been placed there by District B in pursuance of its statutory duties to accommodate the applicant. In one sense this was not residence of the applicant's 'own choice'. On the other hand, the applicant was not obliged to accept the accommodation in District A as offered by District B.[87]

Exceptions to normal residence of his or her own choice

Military service

15.58 Prior to 1 December 2008, people who were serving in the armed forces of the Crown, and people who might reasonably be expected to reside with them, were not considered as normally resident in a district of their own choice (HA 1996, s 199(3)(a)). This exception was repealed by s 315 of the Housing and Regeneration Act 2008 and does not apply to applications for homelessness assistance made to English local housing authorities on or after 1 December 2008,[88] nor to applications for homelessness assistance made to Welsh local housing authorities on or after 30 March 2009.[89]

---

84   *Al-Ameri v Kensington and Chelsea Royal London Borough Council* [2004] UKHL 4, [2004] 2 AC 159, HL.
85   HA 1996, s 199(6) and (7) as amended. See **15.84–15.90**.
86   See also English Code, Annex 18, para 4.1(iii); Welsh Code, Annex 20, para 4.1(iii).
87   This problem is side-stepped for English local housing authorities by the second set of referral conditions available to District A when this scenario arises (HA 1996, s 198(4)). See also **15.111–15.124**.
88   Housing and Regeneration Act 2008 (Commencement No 2 and Transitional, Saving and Transitory Provisions) Order 2008, SI 3068/2008, art 4(10).
89   Housing and Regeneration Act 2008 (Commencement No 1) (Wales) Order 2009, SI 773/2009 (W 65) (C 48).

Detention

15.59 Residence in a district is not 'of his own choice' if it occurs because a person is detained under the authority of an Act of Parliament.[90] This refers to any form of detention authorised by statute and therefore embraces detentions, for example, as a result of having been remanded in custody,[91] having been given a custodial sentence,[92] or being detained under the Mental Health Act 1983.[93] Periods of residence in a district prior to detention are not excluded and can count towards normal residence for the purposes of HA 1996, Part 7.[94] This exception encompasses spouses or other family members of detainees, who come to reside in the district in order to be close to their detained relative. Therefore, the person who moves from District A to District B to be near her partner, who is detained in District B, cannot acquire a local connection with District B unless either:

(1) a connection other than through normal residence is available (eg she becomes employed in District B); or

(2) there is a period of fresh residence (eg if she remained in District B after her partner was released, or after she had ended the relationship but chose to remain in the district).

Other exceptions

15.60 The Secretary of State has the power to specify circumstances in which residence in a district is not to be treated as being of a person's own choice.[95] To date, the Secretary of State has not exercised that power.

15.61 Previous editions of the Local Authorities' Agreement,[96] recommended that local housing authorities also treat time spent in hospital or time spent in an institution in which households are accepted only for a limited period (eg mother and baby homes, refuges, rehabilitation centres) as exceptions for the purposes of determining local connection.[97] These examples, not repeated in the current edition,[98] illustrate the point that having normal residence of one's own choice in an area is not sufficient. Such residence must have the character, additionally, of establishing a 'local connection' with a local housing authority's district. The examples given were of normal residence of choice which *may* be thought, as a general rule, not to be of sufficient character to establish a local connection.

---

90   HA 1996, s 199(3)(b).
91   Criminal Justice Act 2003, s 242(2).
92   Powers of Criminal Courts (Sentencing) Act 2000, s 76.
93   Mental Health Act 1983, ss 2–3.
94   English Code, para 18.16; Welsh Code, para 20.12.
95   HA 1996, s 199(5)(b).
96   Still at Annex 20 of the Welsh Code.
97   Welsh Code, Annex 20, para 4.3(iv) and (v).
98   At English Code, Annex 18.

Asylum-seekers

15.62 Asylum-seekers who have lived in accommodation provided by the Home Office under s 95 of the Immigration and Asylum Act 1999 (formerly known as 'NASS accommodation') do not reside in that district of their own choice.[99] However, asylum-seekers who occupied accommodation provided under IAA 1999, s 95 (the main duty to provide accommodation and support) are deemed to have a local connection with the local housing authority in whose district that accommodation is situated.[100] This deeming provision does not apply to asylum-seekers who only occupied accommodation provided under IAA 1999, s 98 (temporary support) or s 4 (hard cases support),[101] nor to asylum-seekers who were provided with accommodation by local authorities under the Asylum Seekers (Interim Provisions) Regulations 1999.[102]

15.63 Scottish law provides that residence in accommodation provided under the IAA 1999, s 95 cannot constitute residence 'of his own choice', and so asylum seekers dispersed to Scotland by the Home Office do not, as a matter of law, acquire a local connection with a Scottish local housing authority under this provision.[103]

(2) Employment[104]

15.64 An applicant, or a member of his or her household, who is employed in a district may acquire a local connection with that district by virtue of that employment. The Codes suggest that the person must actually work in the district, in the sense of being physically present, for the employment to establish a local connection, and so it would not be sufficient, as in the case of a peripatetic employee, for the employer's head office to be located there.[105]

---

[99] *Al-Ameri v Kensington and Chelsea Royal London Borough Council* [2004] UKHL 4, [2004] 2 AC 159, HL.

[100] By HA 1996, s 199(6). English Code, paras 18.17–18.19. See **15.84–15.90**.

[101] Although, since hard cases support is provided to asylum-seekers whose claims for asylum have been rejected, it would be unusual for there subsequently to be such a change of circumstances that he or she became eligible for assistance. See **12.75–12.86** and **12.88–12.89** for eligible asylum-seekers.

[102] SI 1999/3056; in the latter case, reg 6(2) is identical to Immigration and Asylum Act 1999, s 95, so that an asylum-seeker's preference as to the location of accommodation is not to be taken into account by local housing authorities. It follows, therefore, that asylum-seekers residing in accommodation provided under those Regulations are not resident in that district of their own choice; see *Ciftci v Haringey London Borough Council* (2004) January *Legal Action*, p 32, Central London County Court.

[103] Housing (Scotland) Act 1987, s 27 as amended by Homelessness etc (Scotland) Act 2003, s 7. As a result, there are lesser duties imposed on English and Welsh local housing authorities who receive applications for homelessness assistance from asylum seekers previously dispersed to Scotland (see **15.173–15.180**). English Code, paras 18.20–18.21.

[104] HA 1996, s 199(1)(b).

[105] English Code, para 18.10; Welsh Code, para 20.7(ii), although this is a difficult approach to apply to employment that is mobile, such as a mobile tradesperson working in a number of local housing authority districts in a metropolitan area, or a pilot spending more time in the air than in the airport where he or she is based.

15.65 Both HA 1996, Part 7 and the Codes use the present tense ('is employed').[106] The question is therefore whether the applicant, or a member of his or her household, is employed in the relevant district at the date of the initial decision or review decision.[107] However, the simple fact of such current employment will not necessarily establish a local connection in itself. To build up and establish a local connection there will usually need to have been 'a period of employment',[108] although neither HA 1996, Part 7 nor the Codes suggest any particular period of employment. If the person's connection with an area is through past employment that will count, if at all, only if it amounts to 'special circumstances'.[109]

15.66 Further, the Local Authorities' Agreement suggests that, if it is to found a local connection, employment should not be of a casual nature. It then suggests that employers be asked for confirmation of both the fact of employment and its non-casual nature.[110] This inquiry is obviously unnecessary if the applicant can produce a written statement of the terms and conditions of employment or a fixed-term contract.

15.67 Employment can be full-time or part-time and include both paid and unpaid employment.[111] For example, an unpaid pastor in a church has been held to have a local connection with a district by virtue of that employment.[112]

15.68 Prior to 1 December 2008, people who were serving in the armed forces of the Crown were not considered as employed in a district (HA 1996, s 199(2)). This exception has been repealed by s 315 of the Housing and Regeneration Act 2008 and will not apply to applications for homelessness assistance made to English local housing authorities on or after 1 December 2008,[113] and nor to applications for homelessness assistance made to Welsh local housing authorities on or after 30 March 2009.[114]

15.69 There is provision for the Secretary of State to specify other circumstances in which a person is not to be treated as employed in a district, but this power has not been exercised.[115]

---

106 HA 1996, s 199(1)(b).
107 *R v Ealing London Borough Council ex p Fox* (1998) Times, 9 March, QBD.
108 *Betts v Eastleigh Borough Council* [1983] 2 AC 613, HL at 627, per Lord Brightman.
109 HA 1996, s 199(1)(d). See also **15.78–15.83**.
110 English Code, Annex 18, para 4.1(ii).
111 *R v Ealing London Borough Council ex p Fox* (1998) Times, 9 March, QBD.
112 *Sarac v Camden London Borough Council* (2002) June *Legal Action*, p 28, Central London County Court.
113 Housing and Regeneration Act 2008 (Commencement No 2 and Transitional, Saving and Transitory Provisions) Order 2008, SI 3068/2008, art 4(10).
114 Housing and Regeneration Act 2008 (Commencement No 1) (Wales) Order 2009, SI 773/2009 (W 65) (C 48).
115 HA 1996, s 199(5)(a).

(3)   Family associations[116]

15.70 An applicant, or a member of his or her household, may have a local connection with a district if he or she has family associations with that district. 'Family associations' are not defined in HA 1996, Part 7. The Local Authorities' Agreement suggests that the phrase should 'normally' be understood to refer to 'parents, adult children or brothers and sisters' and that only in 'exceptional circumstances' should the place of residence of other relatives be taken into account.[117] In the past, this approach received a measure of judicial support:

> 'In my opinion family associations do not extend beyond parents, adult children or brothers and sisters. First cousins once removed (or cousins of any description) cannot provide the necessary connection.'[118]

15.71 In *R v Hammersmith and Fulham London Borough Council ex p Avdic*, it had been conceded that a first cousin once removed did not amount to a 'family association'. In a later case, *R v Ealing London Borough Council ex p Fox*, that expression of judicial opinion was directly followed and a local housing authority's decision that an uncle did not constitute a sufficiently close relative to establish a 'family association' was held not to be wrong in law.[119]

15.72 However, the better and more recent view, which has also received some support from the Court of Appeal, is that the question falls to be decided having regard to the fact-specific characteristics of the individual case:

> '... the starting point is the position of the applicant and his household and, in having regard to both "family association" and "special circumstances", while we do not discourage general rules such as are to be found in the Local Authority Agreement, we note that Parliament left those broad phrases undefined and to be judged as a matter of fact and degree in every case. For instance, the actual closeness of the family association may count for more than the precise degree of consanguinity.'[120]

15.73 In *Ozbek v Ipswich Borough Council*,[121] the Court of Appeal specifically rejected a submission that that only near relatives could found the basis for a local connection because of 'family associations'. Considering the judicial observations in *R v Hammersmith & Fulham London Borough Council*

---

[116] HA 1996, s 199(1)(c).

[117] English Code, Annex 18, para 4.1(iii).

[118] *R v Hammersmith and Fulham London Borough Council ex p Avdic* (1996) 28 HLR 897, QBD at 899, per Tucker J, confirmed on appeal at (1998) 30 HLR 1, CA.

[119] (1998) Times, 9 March, QBD.

[120] *Surdonja v Ealing London Borough Council* (2000) 32 HLR 481, CA at 489, per Henry LJ. Recent cases have stressed the importance of the local housing authority's role in fact-finding (*Bellis v Woking Borough Council* [2005] EWCA Civ 1671, (2006) February *Legal Action*, p 31, CA, where there was no error of law in the local housing authority's rejection of contact with a separated father as 'family association').

[121] [2006] EWCA Civ 534, [2006] HLR 41, CA.

ex p Avdic,[122] Chadwick LJ said that those observations were not authority for the proposition that only near relatives (parents, siblings, children) could provide a 'family association' and said that the relevant question is:

> 'whether, in the particular circumstances of the individual case, the bond between the applicant and one or more members of the extended family was of such a nature that it would be appropriate to regard those members of the extended family as "near relatives" in the sense in which that concept is recognised in the Referral Guidelines.'[123]

Sedley LJ said that, if the judge in *Avdic* had meant to confine 'family association' to near relatives, he was wrong and his judgment should not be followed in that regard. He gave examples of relatives whose presence might found a 'family association' as 'grandparents or uncles and aunts by whom the applicant had been brought up' and emphasised that 'the character of the family association must be at least as relevant – probably more relevant – than the degree of consanguinity'.[124]

15.74 Accordingly, the family relationship does not have to be one of blood or marriage. For example, an unmarried step-parent has been held to be a sufficiently close relative to provide a family association.[125]

15.75 The current edition of the English Code shows that the Secretary of State takes a similar view:

> 'the Secretary of State considers that [family associations] may extend beyond parents, adult children, or siblings. They may include association with other family members such as step-parents, grandparents, grandchildren, aunts or uncles provided that there are sufficiently close links in the form of frequent contact, commitment or dependency. Family associations may also extend to unmarried couples, provided that the relationship is sufficiently enduring, and to same sex couples.'[126]

Local housing authorities, certainly in England, are therefore advised against applying the guidelines in the Local Authorities' Agreement rigidly.[127]

15.76 The Local Authorities' Agreement recommends that, in order to give rise to a local connection, the family members relied upon as 'family associations' should have been resident in the district for a period of at least

---

[122] (1996) 28 HLR 897, QBD; see **15.71**.
[123] *Ozbek v Ipswich Borough Council* [2006] EWCA Civ 534, [2006] HLR 41, CA at [43]–[44] and [49], per Chadwick LJ.
[124] *Ozbek v Ipswich Borough Council* [2006] EWCA Civ 534, [2006] HLR 41, CA at [64], per Sedley LJ.
[125] *Munting v Hammersmith and Fulham London Borough Council* (1998) March *Legal Action*, p 15, West London County Court.
[126] English Code, para 18.10.
[127] Local housing authorities in Wales, even though not subject to the same guidance, should certainly ensure that they apply the Court of Appeal's approach in *Ozbek v Ipswich Borough Council* [2006] EWCA Civ 534, [2006] HLR 41, CA.

5 years at the date of application for homelessness assistance.[128] But no rule to this effect is contained in the statutory scheme, and the individual circumstances of a particular case might indicate that a shorter period of residence by a relation is sufficient. Local housing authorities need to guard against the temptation simply to apply the 5-year yardstick to every case.[129] This is particularly so in the cases of refugees or other recent arrivals to the UK, where local housing authorities should bear in mind that the relatives may not have had 5 years in which to build up a residence period in any district in the UK.[130]

15.77 The 'family associations' variant of local connection is an acknowledgment of 'the continuity of support that family associations can give'.[131] Accordingly, a local housing authority should not be relying on it in order to identify a connection with an area other than one where the applicant positively wants to live. The applicant must indicate a wish to be near those members of his or her family for a local connection to be acquired through 'family associations'. As the Local Authorities' Agreement sensibly acknowledges, a referral should not be made under 'family associations' if the applicant objects to being referred to a district in which other members of his or her family live.[132]

(4)   Special circumstances[133]

15.78 A person may have a local connection with a particular district if his or her connection with it arises because of 'special circumstances'.[134] Unsurprisingly, these are not defined in HA 1996, Part 7. The deliberately wide term embraces 'all special circumstances which can contribute to such a socially beneficial "local connection"' with an area.[135]

---

[128]   English Code, Annex 18, para 4.1(iii).
[129]   See *R v Harrow London Borough Council ex p Carter* (1992) 26 HLR 32, QBD at 37, where the applicant's sister had lived in the Harrow area for only 4 years. Roger Henderson QC, sitting as a deputy High Court judge, said: 'It will be seen that that clause of the agreement, if applied rigidly, would mean that a family association would not normally arise if a homeless person's sister had been resident in Harrow for less than five years, but the agreement would not preclude this abnormally. Thus, to say without more ado that Mrs Carter had no local connection with Harrow because her sister had lived in Harrow for between four and five years would have been erroneous (a) because the agreement is no more than a guideline, (b) because the agreement did not so provide and (c) because, in Mrs Carter's predicament with four small children, any form of sisterly support might well make a significant difference in coping with her parental responsibilities.'
[130]   *Ozbek v Ipswich Borough Council* [2006] EWCA Civ 534 [2006] HLR 41, (2006) June *Legal Action*, p 36, CA, at [46], per Chadwick LJ and at [65], per Sedley LJ.
[131]   *Surdonja v Ealing London Borough Council* (2000) 32 HLR 481, CA at 485, per Henry LJ.
[132]   English Code Annex 18, para 4.1(iii).
[133]   HA 1996, s 199(1)(d).
[134]   HA 1996, s 199(1)(d).
[135]   *Surdonja v Ealing London Borough Council* (2000) 32 HLR 481, CA at 485, per Henry LJ.

15.79 The Codes give as an example 'the need to be near special medical or support services which are available only in a particular district'.[136]

15.80 The Local Authorities' Agreement suggests that this category 'may be particularly relevant in dealing with people who have been in prison or in hospital' and gives an example of a person seeking to return to an area where he or she was brought up or lived for a considerable length of time.[137]

15.81 Absent a statutory definition, and with only limited guidance given by the Codes and the Local Authorities' Agreement, it is no surprise to find that a wide range of circumstances have been advanced (often unsuccessfully) as being sufficiently 'special' for these purposes. These include:

- the need to visit a particular mosque and attend a particular school;[138]

- medical advice that an applicant needed to live in a warmer area;[139]

- residence (not for a sufficient period to constitute normal residence under HA 1996, s 199(1)(a)), first with the man with whom the applicant believed that she was going to live and, secondly, in a woman's refuge;[140]

- the need to remain in the London area to receive medical treatment (the local housing authority was entitled to take the view that the medical treatment required was also available in the notified local housing authority's district);[141]

- the applicant's need for care and assistance would not be met in the notified local housing authority's district;[142]

- the applicant's traumatic experiences before fleeing as a refugee, the existence of an ethnic minority community of same-language speakers in the local housing authority's district, and enrolment at a local college;[143]

---

[136] English Code, para 18.10; Welsh Code, para 20.7(iv).

[137] English Code, Annex 18, para 4.1(iv).

[138] *R v Westminster City Council ex p Benniche* (1996) 29 HLR 230, CA, where the local housing authority's decision of 'no special circumstances' on the facts was not wrong in law.

[139] *R v East Devon District Council ex p Robb* (1997) 30 HLR 922, QBD, where the local housing authority was wrong in law not to have considered this as a potentially special circumstance.

[140] *R v Southwark London Borough Council ex p Hughes* (1998) 30 HLR 1082, QBD, where the local housing authority was wrong in law not to have considered this as a potentially special circumstance.

[141] *R v Hammersmith and Fulham London Borough Council ex p Avdic* (1998) 30 HLR 1, CA, where the local housing authority's decision of no special circumstances on the facts was not wrong in law.

[142] *Connor v Brighton and Hove Council* [1998] EWCA Civ 1396, (1999) August *Legal Action*, p 29, CA, where the local housing authority's decision of no special circumstances on the facts was not wrong in law.

[143] *R v Kensington and Chelsea Royal London Borough Council ex p Bishop* (unreported) 11 February 1983, QBD.

- the fact that the applicant's children had special educational needs and were making rapid progress at a particular local school;[144]

- a fear of leaving the area by reason of the risk of violence that might be experienced elsewhere;[145]

- membership of a church community around which the applicant's social life revolved;[146] and

- 14 years previous residence in the area in which the applicants' children had attended school and in which the family still had friends.[147]

15.82 The generally strict line taken by the courts (rejecting most of the above cases) reflects the fact that Parliament has left it to local housing authorities to determine whether there are sufficiently 'special' circumstances to amount to a local connection. However, a local housing authority must not gloss the statutory language by seeking some extra-special or particularly pressing 'special circumstances'. For example, a local housing authority considering an application based on a 'special circumstances' connection was held to have misdirected itself by looking for 'an essential compassionate, social or support need' to be in a particular area.[148]

15.83 Local housing authorities are advised in the Local Authorities' Agreement that, if they are referring on the basis that an applicant has no local connection with their area, but does have a local connection with another area under this category, they should only do so with the prior consent of the notified local housing authority.[149]

(5) Deemed 'local connection' for some former asylum-seekers[150]

15.84 By virtue of amendments made to HA 1996, Part 7 in 2005, a 'local connection' is deemed to have been acquired by a person with the district of any local housing authority in England or Wales in which he or she, while an asylum-seeker, was provided with accommodation under s 95 of the

---

[144] *R v Harrow London Borough Council ex p Carter* (1992) 26 HLR 32, QBD, where the local housing authority should have considered those circumstances.

[145] *R v Islington London Borough Council ex p Adigun* (1986) 20 HLR 600, QBD, where the local housing authority's decision of no special circumstances on the facts was not wrong in law.

[146] *R v White Horse District Council ex p Smith and Hay* (1984) 17 HLR 160, QBD, where the local housing authority's decision of no special circumstances on the facts was not wrong in law. See also *R (Gebremarium) v Westminster City Council* [2009] EWHC 2254 (Admin), (2009) November *Legal Action*, p 26, Admin Ct.

[147] *R v Waltham Forest London Borough Council ex p Koutsoudis* (unreported) 1 September 1986, QBD.

[148] *Surdonja v Ealing London Borough Council* (2000) 32 HLR 481, CA at 494, per Henry LJ.

[149] English Code, Annex 18, para 4.2.

[150] HA 1996, s 199(6) as so added and in force from 4 January 2005.

Immigration and Asylum Act 1999. The accommodation could have been provided 'at any time', ie before or after this provision for deemed local connection was enacted.[151]

15.85 The effect of this deeming provision is that former asylum-seekers, who previously occupied accommodation provided by the Home Office, will acquire a local connection with the local housing authority in whose district the Home Office accommodation was situated.[152]

15.86 Since HA 1996, s 199(6) specifies 'at any time', a former asylum-seeker will retain a local connection with that district for ever. Even if the Home Office accommodation came to an end some considerable time before the applicant's subsequent application for homelessness assistance, and even if the applicant had since then moved around the country and acquired a local connection with other local housing authorities, he or she will retain a local connection with that original district. It appears that the local connection cannot be lost, although it becomes of less importance if the former asylum-seeker is able to establish a local connection with another local housing authority (for example, by employment) and makes the application for homelessness assistance there.[153]

15.87 The lifetime acquisition of deemed local connection applies not just to the asylum-seeker, but also, it would seem, to every member of his or her household who had been 'provided with' Home Office accommodation in that area. Applying that deemed local connection to a homeless applicant's household means that any member of the applicant's household who had, in the past, been provided with Home Office accommodation, whether in his or her own right or as part of the household of an asylum-seeker, therefore acquires a local connection.[154] Nor does there appear to be any minimum period during which the asylum-seeker must occupy the Home Office accommodation for it to trigger a deemed local connection.[155]

---

[151] HA 1996, s 199(6), as amended and in force from 4 January 2005.

[152] As was the case in *Ozbek v Ipswich Borough Council* [2006] EWCA Civ 534, [2006] HLR 41, CA, where the applicant had a local connection with Portsmouth, having lived in NASS accommodation there for just under 3 months. In *Danesh v Kensington & Chelsea Royal London Borough Council* [2006] EWCA Civ 1404, [2007] HLR 17, CA, the applicant had spent 14 months in Home Office accommodation. See also *R (Gebremarium) v Westminster City Council* [2009] EWHC 2254 (Admin), (2009) November *Legal Action*, p 26, Admin Ct.

[153] English Code, para 18.19.

[154] Thus, for example, a former asylum-seeker, or the child of a former asylum-seeker, who marries a British citizen and moves into that British citizen's household has a deemed local connection with the district in which the NASS accommodation was provided. If there is no other local connection held by the applicant or any members of his or her household with the district of a different local housing authority, the conditions for referral will be met (HA 1996, s 198(2)).

[155] So, if a person moves into Home Office accommodation in District A on a Monday (having lived in District B for the previous 9 months), is accorded refugee status on the Tuesday, and that accommodation burns down on the Wednesday, he or she will have a local connection with District A, and his or her application for homelessness assistance made on Thursday to District A could not be referred to District B or anywhere else.

15.88 There are two statutory qualifications to the deemed local connection triggered by occupation of Home Office accommodation. First, the deemed local connection is only acquired with the district in which the *last* accommodation provided by the Home Office was situated. If the asylum-seeker was moved around by the Home Office, it is only the last accommodation that can be considered as giving rise to the deemed local connection.[156] Second, accommodation provided by the Home Office in an accommodation centre[157] cannot constitute accommodation by which an applicant acquires a deemed local connection.[158]

15.89 The deemed local connection category specifically refers to accommodation which was provided under s 95 of the Immigration and Asylum Act 1999. That is the main statutory power available to the Secretary of State to provide accommodation to asylum-seekers. It does not refer to other temporary accommodation, including accommodation provided under IAA 1999, s 98,[159] or to hard cases support,[160] or to accommodation provided by local authorities.[161] Former asylum-seekers who were accommodated only under one of these latter provisions, therefore, will not have acquired a deemed local connection.

15.90 The deemed local connection provisions are only part of homelessness legislation for *England and Wales* – there is no such deeming in Scotland. Instead, Home Office accommodation provided under s 95 of the Immigration and Asylum Act 1999 in Scotland is specifically not capable of giving rise to a local connection by virtue of normal residence because it is not 'residence of his own choice'.[162] Asylum-seekers who occupied Home Office accommodation in Scotland do not, therefore, acquire a local connection with the local authority in Scotland for the area in which that accommodation is situated, by virtue of such residence alone. Instead, the main housing duty under HA 1996, s 193(2) to provide accommodation (if owed by an English local housing authority to a former resident of Home Office accommodation in Scotland) is modified by s 11(2) and (3) of the Asylum and Immigration (Treatment of Claimants etc) Act 2004 so that former asylum-seekers are provided with accommodation for a period, giving him or her a reasonable opportunity of securing accommodation, and are given advice and assistance either to apply to a Scottish local authority as homeless or to find his or her own accommodation.[163] These rules are discussed later in this chapter.[164]

---

[156] HA 1996, s 199(7)(a) as amended; English Code, para 18.18(a).
[157] Nationality, Immigration and Asylum Act 2002, s 22; English Code, para 18.18(b). Plans to build accommodation centres have now been abandoned by the government.
[158] HA 1996, s 199(7)(b), as amended.
[159] Immigration and Asylum Act 1999, s 98. See *Berhane v Lambeth London Borough Council* [2007] EWHC 2702, (2008) March *Legal Action*, p 21, QBD.
[160] Immigration and Asylum Act 1999, s 4.
[161] SI 1999/3056.
[162] Housing (Scotland) Act 1987, s 27, as amended.
[163] Asylum and Immigration (Treatment of Claimants etc) Act 2004, s 11(2) and (3), in force from 4 January 2005; English Code, paras 18.20–18.21.
[164] See **15.173–15.180**.

Who acquires a local connection?

15.91 A relevant local connection may have been acquired (or deemed to have been acquired) by the applicant or by any person who might reasonably be expected to reside with the applicant.[165]

15.92 Any local housing authority choosing to investigate the question of local connection must obviously, therefore, make inquiries into any potential local connection that any of the people who might reasonably be expected to reside with the applicant might have, either with its own district or any other district in England, Wales or Scotland.

15.93 The extent of any local connection enjoyed by any other member of the household (if that local connection is different from any enjoyed by the applicant) could be relevant in various scenarios. For example:

(1) The applicant has no local connection with the local housing authority to which she or he has applied and does have a local connection with another local housing authority, but a member of his or her household has a local connection with the local housing authority to which the application has been made: the conditions for referral are not met and the applicant cannot be referred.

(2) Neither the applicant nor any member of his or her household has a local connection with the local housing authority to which she or has applied, the applicant has a local connection with another local housing authority and a member of the applicant's household has a local connection with a different local housing authority: the conditions for referral are met, but the local housing authority dealing with the application has a discretion as to which local housing authority it will refer the applicant to (if it decides to make any referral).[166]

(3) The applicant has a connection with the local housing authority applied to, but a member of the household has a stronger connection with the district of another local housing authority: if the applicant has a local connection with the district to which application has been made, there can be no referral – the connection of the other household member(s) is irrelevant.

Risk of domestic or other violence[167]

15.94 Even if the applicant is owed the HA 1996, s 193(2) main housing duty and he or she, or a member of his or her household:

---

[165] HA 1996, s 198(2). See also English Code, para 18.7, and Annex 18, para 4.1. The question of whether it is reasonable to expect a person to reside with the applicant arises both in relation to homelessness and priority need and is discussed at **11.19–11.31, 13.48–13.50** and **13.61**.

[166] See **15.128**.

[167] HA 1996, s 198(2)(c), (2A) and (3).

(1) does not have a local connection with the district of the local housing authority to which the application is made; and

(2) does have a local connection with the district of another local housing authority in England, Scotland or Wales,

the local housing authority in receipt of the application, and which has opted to consider local connection questions, must then inquire into whether or not:

(a) the applicant, or any member of his or her household, would run the risk of domestic violence in that other local housing authority's district; and

(b) the applicant, or any member of his or her household, had suffered violence in the district of that other local housing authority and it is probable that there would be further violence of a similar kind if he or she returned to that district.

15.95 The local housing authority is obliged to make inquiries itself into the risk of violence or domestic violence; it is not sufficient for it to wait for the applicant to volunteer any relevant information.[168]

15.96 The wording of the statutory provisions puts victims of domestic violence in a slightly different position from victims of other violence.

15.97 'Violence' is defined as 'violence from another person or threats of violence from another person which are likely to be carried out'.[169]

Domestic violence

15.98 Violence is 'domestic violence' if it is from a person who is associated with the victim.[170] The phrase 'a person who is associated with the victim' is defined at HA 1996, s 178 and includes:

• spouses and former spouses;

• civil partners and former civil partners;

• cohabitants and former cohabitants (heterosexual or same-sex);

• people who live or used to live in the same household;

• relatives;

---

[168] *R v Greenwich London Borough Council ex p Patterson* (1994) 26 HLR 159, CA.
[169] HA 1996, s 198(3). The definition is the same as that applying to the definition of homelessness at HA 1996, s 177(1). See **11.78–11.88**.
[170] HA 1996, s 198(3).

- people who have agreed to marry each other or to enter into a civil partnership; and

- people who share the parentage of, or parental responsibility for, a child (including the relationship between natural and adoptive parents).[171]

15.99 The definition also includes adoptive and natural parents of a child, step-relatives, grandparents and grandchildren, siblings, uncles, aunts, nieces and nephews, and in-laws or former in-laws (including relatives of a civil partner or former civil partner).[172]

15.100 If the issue of domestic violence is the subject of inquiries, the test is whether the applicant, or a member of the applicant's household, will run the risk of domestic violence in the district of the local housing authority intended to be notified.[173] It follows, therefore, that that person need not actually have been subject in the past to actual or threatened domestic violence there. Obviously, if there has been domestic violence, the relevant question to ask is whether it will recur. However, even where there has been no domestic violence in the past, if there is information that leads to the conclusion that the person would be at risk of violence, or threats of violence which are likely to be carried out, from an associated person, the conditions for referral are not made out.[174]

15.101 The English Code contains a very broad definition of 'violence', including 'domestic violence' and local housing authorities are advised not to interpret the test restrictively.[175] The Court of Appeal has held that the Secretary of State's guidance is wrong and that 'violence' should be given a narrow interpretation, requiring physical contact.[176] Subject to any contrary decision by the UK Supreme Court, it is the Court of Appeal's decision that is determinative.

Other violence

15.102 If there is no *domestic* violence, the test is slightly different (although the Codes of Guidance do not draw attention to, or give guidance upon, the

---

[171] Civil Partnership Act 2004, s 81 and Sch 8, para 61 amend s 178 to include references to civil partnerships and same-sex couples living together as though they were civil partners, in force from 5 December 2005.

[172] HA 1996, s 178(1), (2), (3). See also **11.82**.

[173] HA 1996, s 198(2)(c).

[174] For example, the applicant may have fled the family home in District A as a result of domestic violence experienced there. One of the perpetrators of the violence may have moved to District B, while the other remained in District A. On an application to District C, the applicant cannot be referred to either District A or District B if as a matter of fact he or she would now run the risk of domestic violence in either district.

[175] English Code, paras 8.21 and 18.23–18.25. See **11.81** and **15.103**.

[176] *Yemshaw v Hounslow London Borough Council* (unreported) 15 December 2009, CA (extempore judgment not yet reported at the date of this book going to print), and relying on *Danesh v Kensington & Chelsea Royal London Borough* [2006] EWCA Civ 1404, [2007] 1 WLR 69, CA; see **15.103**.

difference). There must have been 'violence', as defined by HA 1996,[177] suffered in the district of the local housing authority likely to be notified, and it must be probable that the return to that district will lead to further violence of a similar kind.[178] The past violence may have been carried out by any person, not being a person associated with the victim.

15.103   In *Danesh v Kensington & Chelsea Royal London Borough Council*,[179] the Court of Appeal held that 'violence' in HA 1996, s 198(3) means 'physical violence' and the word 'violence' on its own 'does not include threats of violence or acts or gestures, which lead someone to fear physical violence'.[180] It follows that there are three questions for the local housing authority:

(a)   Has there been physical 'violence'?

(b)   Have there been threats of violence that are likely to be carried out?

(c)   If the answer to either of the above questions is 'yes', is it 'probable' that the victim's return to the notified local housing authority's district will lead to 'further violence of a similar kind' against the same victim?

Probable' means 'more likely than not'.[181]

15.104   The local housing authority is entitled to take the applicant's perceptions, fears or concerns into account, but it is for the local housing authority to decide the facts, in order to answer these three questions objectively.[182]

15.105   It follows that if there is a probability of violence, other than domestic violence, which is of a different kind to that previously experienced, the test will not be made out. Similarly, if any violence in the future were to be directed against another member of the household, the test will not be made out. Although there would be no statutory bar on a local housing authority referring a victim back to an area in which a different kind of non-domestic violence was likely to be suffered by another member of the household, it might be expected that a local housing authority would exercise its discretion *not* to refer in those circumstances.

15.106   The factual decisions as to:

(1)   whether there is a risk of domestic violence; or

---

177   HA 1996, s 198(3). See **15.97**.
178   HA 1996, s 198(2A).
179   [2006] EWCA Civ 1404, [2007] HLR 17, CA.
180   *Danesh v Kensington & Chelsea RLBC* [2006] EWCA Civ 1404, [2007] HLR 17, CA at [14], per Neuberger LJ.
181   *Bond v Leicester City Council* [2001] EWCA Civ 1544, [2002] HLR 6, CA.
182   *Danesh v Kensington & Chelsea Royal London Borough Council* [2006] EWCA Civ 1404, [2007] HLR 17, CA at [26], per Neuberger LJ.

(2)   whether other violence occurred in the past; and

(3)   whether it is probable that there will be further violence of a similar kind in future,

are for the local housing authority to make, and its decisions will be upheld by the courts, provided that it lawfully applies the correct statutory tests.[183]

Conditions for referral by reason of local connection – a summary

15.107   Only if:

- the applicant is eligible, did not become homeless intentionally and has a priority need; and

- neither the applicant, nor any member of his or her household, has a local connection with the district of the local housing authority to which he or she has applied; and

- either the applicant, or a member of his or her household, has a local connection with the district of another English, Welsh or Scottish local housing authority; and

- there is no risk of domestic violence to the applicant or any member of his or her household in the district of the other local housing authority; and

- neither the applicant, nor any member of his or her household, had suffered violence or threats of violence that were likely to be carried out in the other local housing authority's district; and

- if either the applicant, or a member of his or her household, had suffered violence in the other local housing authority's district, it is not probable that there will be further violence of a similar kind against that person,

are the conditions for referral under the local connection route made out.

15.108   It follows that there can be no referral if:

- the applicant or a member of his or her household has a local connection with the local housing authority to which the application was made – the conditions for referral are not met; or

---

[183]   *R v Islington London Borough Council ex p Adigun* (1988) 20 HLR 600, QBD; *Danesh v Kensington & Chelsea Royal London Borough Council* [2006] EWCA Civ 1404, [2007] HLR 17, CA.

- there is no local connection with any local housing authority in England, Wales or Scotland – the conditions for referral are not met and the applicant remains the responsibility of the original local housing authority; or

- the applicant is ineligible, or only threatened with homelessness, or does not have a priority need, or became homeless intentionally.

15.109 Where the conditions for referral are met, and there is a local connection with *two or more* different local housing authorities (not including the local housing authority which received the application), the original local housing authority has a discretion as to which of the other local housing authorities it should refer the applicant (if any). When considering that discretion, it should take into account the applicant's own preference, as well as the relative strengths of the different local connections.[184]

15.110 Even if all the conditions for a referral are made out, the local housing authority is under no obligation to refer and has an unqualified discretion as to whether or not to refer.[185]

The second set of conditions for referral – out of district placements

Introduction

15.111 The second circumstance in which the conditions for referral are met is much more self-contained and has nothing to do with the statutory definition of 'local connection'.[186] It arises where an applicant has previously been placed by another local housing authority in the district of the local housing authority to which a new application for homelessness assistance is being made.

15.112 Its purpose is to underscore the statutory presumption that homeless households should be accommodated in the district to which they first apply by ensuring that a local housing authority cannot relieve itself of some future responsibility by placing the applicant outside its own district.[187] It was enacted in 1996 to meet the phenomenon of increasing numbers of local housing authorities placing their homeless households in other local housing authorities' districts. These conditions for referral no longer apply to Welsh local housing authorities considering any applications for homelessness assistance made on or after 9 October 2006. This is because the conditions for referral depend upon operation of a 'prescribed' period and no such period has been prescribed in Wales.[188]

---

[184] English Code, para 18.14, and Annex 18, para 4.12; Welsh Code, para 20.10.
[185] See **15.125–15.129**.
[186] See **15.40–15.110**.
[187] HA 1996, s 208(1); see **15.205–15.211** and **18.49–18.58**.
[188] HA 1996, s 198(4). The prescribed period for Welsh local housing authorities was the same as for English local housing authorities. It was to be found in the Homelessness (England)

15.113 The Local Authorities' Agreement refers to the second set of conditions for referral as 'for Welsh authorities only'.[189] This is out of date and should be read as 'for English authorities only'.[190]

15.114 The Codes and the Agreement are silent on what should happen if an English local housing authority wishes to refer under these conditions to a Welsh local housing authority, or indeed vice versa.[191]

15.115 This second set of conditions for referral does not apply in Scotland and cannot be used by an English or Welsh local housing authority to refer an applicant to a Scottish local authority.[192]

The second set of conditions

15.116 The conditions for a referral will be met where:

(1) the applicant had been placed in the district of the local housing authority to which he or she has now applied (authority A) by another local housing authority (authority B) in performance of any of authority B's homelessness functions; and

(2) the current application is made within a prescribed period running from the date of the application for homelessness assistance to authority B; and

(3) the duty owed by authority A would be the main homelessness duty owed to an eligible, homeless person who has a priority need and did not become homeless intentionally.[193]

Regulations 2000, SI 2000/701, reg 6, applied to Wales by the Homelessness (Wales) Regulations 2000, SI 2000/1079 (W 72), reg 2. The Homelessness (Wales) Regulations 2006, SI 2006/2646 (W 227), reg 6, revoked the Homelessness (Wales) Regulations 2000 and therefore the application of the prescribed period. There is no prescribed period in the Homelessness (Wales) Regulations 2006, SI 2006/2646 (W 227).

[189] English Code, Annex 18, paras 3.2(d) and 4.4.

[190] The Local Authorities' Agreement at Annex 18 of the English Code reflects the law as it was between 1 June 2006 and 8 October 2006 and indeed described in the first edition of this book. During that period, there was no prescribed period for English local housing authorities (because the Homelessness (England) Regulations 2000, SI 2000/701 had been revoked by the Allocation of Housing and Homelessness (Eligibility) (England) Regulations 2006, SI 2006/1294, reg 7 and Schedule without any new period being prescribed). The Allocation of Housing and Homelessness (Miscellaneous Provisions) (England) Regulations 2006, SI 2006/2527 prescribed a period to be applied by English local housing authorities with effect from 9 October 2006. There was, however, a prescribed period for Welsh local housing authorities because the Homelessness (Wales) Regulations 2000, SI 2000/1079 (W 72) remained in force until revoked by the Homelessness (Wales) Regulations 2006, SI 2006/2646 (W 227) with effect from 9 October 2006.

[191] See **15.182–15.188**.

[192] Because HA 1996, s 198(4) only applies to local housing authorities in England and Wales and Housing (Scotland) Act 1987, s 33 (the Scottish equivalent to HA 1996, s 198) does not contain an equivalent provision to HA 1996, s 198(4). See Local Authorities' Agreement, English Code, Annex 18, para 3.3; Welsh Code, Annex 20, para 3.4.

[193] HA 1996, s 198(4).

15.117 The currently prescribed period is 5 years *plus* any period between the date of the applicant's original application to authority B and the date of being placed in the accommodation in authority A's district.[194] This aggregate period is then applied running backwards from the date of the application to authority A (not from the date of authority A's decision on that application).[195] The advice on the duration of the prescribed period in the Codes of Guidance and the Local Authorities' Agreement is slightly imprecise.[196] The better approach is to use the precise formula as given in the regulation.[197]

15.118 This set of conditions for referral applies regardless of which of authority B's statutory homelessness functions it was carrying out when it provided the accommodation. Throughout the whole of the prescribed period, authority B retains responsibility for that applicant. A local housing authority which moves a homeless household over a series of districts (eg interim accommodation in District A, followed by short-term temporary accommodation in District C, and then longer term temporary accommodation in District D) will find that it is triggering a new prescribed period of responsibility on each move.

15.119 This second set of conditions for referral may be satisfied whether the applicant has become homeless from the accommodation actually provided by authority B or from some other accommodation in authority A's district. An applicant provided with accommodation in authority A's district by authority B may have found his or her own accommodation in authority A's district. However, if he or she becomes homeless again and applies to authority A within the prescribed period, the conditions for referral will be met and authority A may refer him or her back to authority B.

15.120 It has already been noted that the statutory scope of initial inquiries that a local housing authority undertakes on an application for homelessness assistance has not been expressly expanded to include the information required to make out this second set of conditions for referral.[198] Certainly there is no obligation on an applicant to volunteer (without being asked) the fact that he or she came into the local housing authority's district on placement by another local housing authority.

15.121 It must be emphasised that the conditions stipulated are conditions for formal referral. Authority A cannot merely turn the applicant away to apply for

---

[194] Allocation of Housing and Homelessness (Miscellaneous Provisions) Regulations 2006, SI 2006//2527, reg 3. English Code, Annex 18, para 3.2(d).

[195] So, if the applicant applied to local housing authority B on 3 June 2003 and was placed in the district of local housing authority A on 3 January 2004 (6 months later) the prescribed period would not have expired until 3 January 2009 (5 years and 6 months in all). If he or she applied to authority A on 30 August 2008, the conditions for referral to authority B will be met, even if authority A's decision is taken several weeks or months later. If he or she applied to authority A on 1 September 2009, the conditions for referral will not be met.

[196] English Code, Annex 18, para 3.2(d).

[197] SI 2006/2527, reg 3

[198] See **15.28**.

himself or herself at authority B. The referral can only be made after authority A has satisfied itself, on completion of inquiries into eligibility, homelessness, priority need and intentionality, that it would otherwise owe the applicant a main housing duty (at HA 1996, s 193(2)). The duty to provide interim accommodation pending those inquiries,[199] to provide accommodation to those found to have become homeless intentionally,[200] or to provide advice and assistance[201] remains on authority A.

15.122   Since this second set of conditions for referral is separate from the conditions governing a local connection referral under the first set of conditions, it must follow that there is no strict need for authority A to consider whether the applicant might be at risk of domestic or other violence if he or she is referred back to authority B. However, authority A retains a discretion whether or not to refer,[202] once it has decided that the conditions are met, and any risk of violence would be relevant to the exercise of that discretion.

15.123   It must also follow that, even if the applicant has acquired a local connection with the district of authority A, by residence, employment, family association or special circumstances, the second set of conditions for referral is still met. Although, if the applicant has a local connection with authority A, particularly if he or she is employed in that district or has family associations, this should be a relevant consideration when authority A is deciding whether or not to exercise its discretion to refer.

15.124   The second set of conditions for referral is only met if the applicant to authority A was also the applicant to authority B. They do not apply to people with whom the applicant resides or might reasonably be expected to reside. This suggests that, if the placement in the district of authority A was as a result of authority B's duty owed to one member of the household, another member of the household could apply to authority A and the second set of conditions for referral would not be made out.

THE DECISION WHETHER OR NOT TO REFER

15.125   Once a local housing authority has decided that the conditions for referral are met, either as a result of local connection or because of a previous, placement under HA 1996, Part 7 by another local housing authority, it must then decide whether or not to notify the other local housing authority of its opinion.[203] A local housing authority that failed properly to consider its discretion whether to refer, having determined that the conditions for referral were met, would have erred in law.[204] However, given the shortfall between

---

[199]   HA 1996, s 188(1). See **16.11–16.24**.
[200]   HA 1996, s 190(2)(a). See **17.111–17.118**.
[201]   HA 1996, s 190(3) and 192(2). See **17.132–17.144**.
[202]   See **15.125–15.129**.
[203]   HA 1996, s 198(1).
[204]   *R v East Devon District Council ex p Robb* (1997) 30 HLR 922, QBD.

housing supply and demand in many areas, there is nothing to prevent a local housing authority from adopting a general policy that it will normally refer an applicant in respect of whom the conditions are fulfilled, provided that it ensures that it considers any particular circumstances of an individual case that would suggest that a departure from the general policy should be made.[205]

15.126 Obviously, the applicant's personal circumstances (including any risk of violence that does not fall within any of the statutory criteria prohibiting referral) are relevant to the local housing authority's decision whether or not to notify.[206] There will be other cases in which the conditions for a referral are only tenuously met and where, for that reason and perhaps others, it would not be right to use the power to refer. In those and other cases the local housing authority will want to consider 'whether it is in the public interest' to accept the main housing duty or make a referral, taking into account the public expenditure involved, whether a referral involves disruption to an applicant's employment or education, etc.[207] In a case involving former asylum-seekers, who had a local connection by reason of having occupied accommodation provided by the Home Office, the notifying local housing authority was entitled to take into account the burden on its own resources and the giving of effect to Parliament's policy of dispersal of asylum-seekers. Absence of family or friends in the district of the notified local housing authority was not a sufficient reason for the notifying local housing authority to decide against making a referral.[208]

15.127 In addition, when considering a referral, local housing authorities may take into account, where it is relevant, the general housing circumstances prevailing in the district of the local housing authority potentially to be notified, particularly in cases where the applicant had made a previous application to that local housing authority and the two local housing authorities had come to different conclusions as to the nature of the homelessness duty owed to the applicant.[209]

15.128 Where the applicant or a member of his or her household has a local connection with more than one local housing authority (other than the local housing authority to which the application has been made), the notifying local housing authority is advised by the Local Authorities' Agreement to weigh up all the relevant factors in deciding which local housing authority to notify. The relevant factors include the applicant's own preference, and the relative strength of any residential local connection in relation to connections established by employment, family associations or special circumstances.[210]

---

[205] English Code, para 18.5.

[206] *R v Harrow London Borough Council ex p Carter* (1994) 26 HLR 32, QBD.

[207] Local Authorities' Agreement, English Code, Annex 18, para 3.4.

[208] *Ozbek v Ipswich Borough Council* [2006] EWCA Civ 534, [2006] HLR 41, CA at [61], per Chadwick LJ; see **15.73–15.77**.

[209] Local Authorities' Agreement, English Code, Annex 18, para 3.4. *R v Newham London Borough Council ex p Tower Hamlets London Borough Council* [1991] 1 WLR 1032, CA.

[210] English Code, para 18.14 and Annex 18, para 4.11.

15.129 There is no requirement on any local housing authority to notify another local housing authority of an application for homelessness assistance, even where it has decided that the conditions for referral are met. Local housing authorities are free to accept all those to whom they owe the main housing duty under HA 1996, s 193(2) duty, regardless of whether either set of the conditions for referral is met.[211]

DUTIES TO INFORM ABOUT REFERRAL

Notification to the applicant[212]

15.130 Where any question of referring to another local housing authority arises, the local housing authority which received the application must notify the applicant of its decision-making on two occasions:[213]

(1) 'the first notification': when it has decided that the conditions for referral are met, and that it intends to notify another local housing authority of that opinion;[214] and

(2) 'the second notification': when it has later been decided (by the two local housing authorities agreeing, or by a referee) that the conditions for referral are or are not met.[215]

15.131 Each notification to the applicant must inform him or her that he or she has a right to request a review of the decision and of the 21-day period in which a review must be requested.[216] At all times, there is a duty on one of the local housing authorities to accommodate the applicant, but which local housing authority is subject to that duty varies according to the progress of the notification.[217]

15.132 The *first* notification duty enables a local housing authority, in effect, to give the applicant a 'minded to refer' notification so that all the issues can be explored with the applicant before another local housing authority is troubled with what might transpire to be an inappropriate or impermissible referral. Alternatively, if the question of referral appears straightforward, it permits one local housing authority to give notice of referral to another straight away, whilst simultaneously also notifying the applicant that this has been done.

15.133 Once the *second* notification has been given to the applicant, the notifying local housing authority is no longer under a duty to provide

---

[211] English Code, para 18.4.
[212] See also **10.90**.
[213] See English Code, paras 18.26–18.30; Welsh Code, paras 20.16–20.19.
[214] HA 1996, s 200(1).
[215] HA 1996, s 200(2).
[216] HA 1996, ss 184(4) and 200.
[217] See also **15.136–15.140**.

accommodation for the applicant.[218] The notified authority becomes subject to the HA 1996, s 193(2) main housing duty.[219] The notifying local housing authority may continue to accommodate pending any review or appeal.[220]

Notification procedures between local housing authorities

15.134 Once the notifying local housing authority has formed the opinion that the conditions for referral are met and decided that a referral should be made, it is advised first to contact the local housing authority which it intends to notify by telephone and then confirm the notification in writing.[221] A pro-forma written notification is provided in the Local Authorities' Agreement.[222] Each local housing authority is expected to have a nominated officer to deal with such notifications as are received. Unless there is likely to be a dispute between the local housing authorities, the notified local housing authority should immediately start to make appropriate arrangements to provide accommodation and not wait for the written confirmation to arrive.[223] If it does accept responsibility (or is found by a referee to be responsible), the notified local housing authority should reimburse the notifying local housing authority for the cost of the accommodation it has provided to the applicant, unless there has been undue delay in making the referral.[224]

15.135 The notified local housing authority should reply to the notifying local housing authority (confirming whether or not it accepts responsibility) within 10 days of receiving the written confirmation of notification.[225]

DUTIES TO PROVIDE ACCOMMODATION

15.136 Once the first notification[226] has been given to the applicant, the notifying local housing authority's duty to provide interim accommodation for the applicant comes to an end.[227] In its place, a duty to provide accommodation under HA 1996, s 200(1) arises on the notifying local housing authority and runs until the second notification has been given.[228]

---

[218] HA 1996, s 200(1) and (5); English Code, para 18.27; Welsh Code, para 20.17.

[219] HA 1996, s 200(4).

[220] HA 1996, s 200(5); English Code, para 18.29; Welsh Code, para 20.18. See *R (Gebremarium) v Westminster City Council* [2009] EWHC 2254 (Admin), (2009) November *Legal Action*, p 26, Admin Ct, where the Administrative Court refused permission to seek a judicial review against Westminster's decision not to provide accommodation under HA 1996, s 200(5) pending a s 202 review of its decision to refer the claimant to Cardiff. See also **16.43–16.50**.

[221] English Code, Annex 18, para 6.1.

[222] English Code, Annex 18.

[223] English Code, Annex 18, para 6.1.

[224] English Code, Annex 18, para 7.3.

[225] English Code, Annex 18, para 6.5.

[226] See also **15.130** and **15.132**.

[227] HA 1996, s 188(1) and (3).

[228] See **16.46–16.50** for further details on the nature and extent of this duty.

15.137 Once the second notification[229] has been given to the applicant, the duty to provide accommodation passes to the notified local housing authority.[230] If the applicant requests a review of that notification,[231] the notifying local housing authority has a power, but not a duty, to provide accommodation pending the determination of the review (and a similar power to provide accommodation pending the determination of any appeal against that review decision). The notified local housing authority, meanwhile, owes the HA 1996, s 193(2) main housing duty to provide accommodation for the applicant.[232]

15.138 The Local Authorities' Agreement recommends that local housing authorities 'should try to avoid causing undue disruption to the applicant' and consider reciprocal arrangements so as to avoid having to move a household.[233]

15.139 If, after the first notification, it is decided that the conditions for referral are *not* met, the notifying local housing authority's duty to the applicant becomes the main housing duty owed under HA 1996, s 193(2).[234]

DISPUTES BETWEEN LOCAL HOUSING AUTHORITIES

15.140 Where the notified local housing authority disagrees with the opinion of the notifying local housing authority, as to whether the conditions for a referral are made out, there is a special procedure for resolution of the dispute.[235]

15.141 However, the notified local housing authority may have a more fundamental disagreement with the referral. It may disagree with one or more of the notifying local housing authority's earlier decisions: that the applicant is homeless, eligible for assistance, has a priority need and did not become homeless intentionally. In other words, it may dispute the proposition that the applicant is owed the HA 1996, s 193(2) main housing duty at all. The sense of grievance may be particularly strong when the notified local housing authority had previously accepted an application by the very same applicant, but had decided that the main housing duty was not owed (perhaps because the notified local housing authority had decided that the applicant had become homeless intentionally). The prospect of the applicant then applying to a different local housing authority, with which he or she has no local connection, and that local housing authority inquiring into the same facts, but coming to a different conclusion and then referring the performance of the main housing duty back to the original local housing authority is not one that the original local housing

---

[229] See **15.130** and **15.133**.
[230] HA 1996, s 200(4).
[231] See also **19.23–19.25**.
[232] See also **17.21–17.110**.
[233] English Code, Annex 18, para 6.4; see **15.212–15.216**.
[234] HA 1996, s 200(3).
[235] See **15.146–15.152**.

authority would find attractive. Although this may seem harsh to the notified local housing authority, an essential premise is that the notifying local housing authority has investigated all the circumstances 'with the same degree of care and thoroughness ... as it would for any other case'.[236]

15.142 The courts have made it very clear that, once a local housing authority has determined that the main housing duty is owed, and has notified another local housing authority that the conditions for referral are met, the notified local housing authority cannot re-open or go behind the inquiries and decisions made by the notifying authority as to the existence of the main housing duty.[237]

15.143 If it remains dissatisfied, the notified local housing authority can challenge, through judicial review, the lawfulness of the inquiries made by the notifying local housing authority before it came to its decision that the main housing duty was owed, or the legality of the decision itself. In *R v Tower Hamlets London Borough Council ex p Camden London Borough Council*,[238] the notifying local housing authority (Camden) should have made inquiries of the notified local housing authority (Tower Hamlets) and considered Tower Hamlets' reasons for finding that the applicant had become homeless intentionally, before making its own decision that a main housing duty was owed. In *R v Newham London Borough Council ex p Tower Hamlets London Borough Council*,[239] Newham notified Tower Hamlets of its intention to refer an applicant whom Tower Hamlets had previously found to have become homeless intentionally. Tower Hamlets successfully challenged the lawfulness of Newham's inquiries into the question of intentionality.

15.144 Similarly, if the applicant applied to the notifying local housing authority after refusing an offer of accommodation from the notified local housing authority (and the notified local housing authority had decided that its duty to the applicant had come to an end), the notifying local housing authority could be challenged for failing to conclude that there had been no fresh incidence of homelessness.[240] If the notified local housing authority disputes, but does not challenge in the courts, the lawfulness of the notifying local housing authority's decision that a main housing duty would be owed, it cannot simply refuse to accept the referral. Nor can it seek to raise the matter as part of the procedures for resolving disputes over whether the conditions for referral are satisfied. It is bound by the notifying local housing authority's decision unless that decision is withdrawn or is successfully challenged, and quashed, in judicial review proceedings.[241] An applicant should never be required to bring his or her own legal proceedings to compel a local housing authority to act on a referral.

---

[236] Local Authorities' Agreement, English Code, Annex 18, para 6.3.

[237] *R v Slough Borough Council ex p Ealing London Borough Council* [1981] QB 801, CA.

[238] (1989) 21 HLR 197, QBD.

[239] [1991] 1 WLR 1032, CA.

[240] *R v Hammersmith and Fulham London Borough Council ex p O'Brien* (1985) 17 HLR 471, QBD.

[241] *R (Bantamagbari) v Westminster City Council* [2003] EWHC 1350 (Admin), (2003) July *Legal*

15.145 The notified local housing authority can, however, perfectly properly dispute the notifying local housing authority's opinion that the conditions for referral are met. The following paragraphs explain the procedure involved.

Determining disputes about whether the conditions for referral are met

15.146 The arrangements for resolving disputes between local housing authorities as to whether either of the two sets of conditions for referral is met have been negotiated and agreed between the organisations representing English, Welsh and Scottish local authorities and have been approved by the Secretary of State.[242]

15.147 If the notified local housing authority wishes to challenge the referral, in the sense of contending that the conditions for referral are not made out, it must state its written reasons in full within 10 days of receiving the referral notification.[243] On receipt of that response, the notifying local housing authority may accept the notified local housing authority's position and withdraw the referral.

15.148 However, if there is no agreement between the two local housing authorities, the question of whether the conditions for referral are met should be decided by a referee. The referee should be appointed within 21 days of notification to the notified local housing authority of the referral.[244] The local housing authorities agree to be bound by the referee's decision. The two local housing authorities may themselves find and appoint an agreed referee, but if they cannot agree on the identity of the referee, one will be appointed by the chairperson of their appropriate local government organisation.[245] The request for a referee to be appointed should be jointly made, or can be made by the notifying local housing authority alone if the notified local housing authority has failed to agree to accept the referral within 6 weeks of the referral having been made.[246]

15.149 The referee, once appointed, invites both local housing authorities to submit representations within 14 working days. Each local housing authority will have the opportunity to consider the other's representations, and to comment in writing on those representations within a further 10 working days. If the representations are insufficient, the referee can invite further representations on any issue that he or she considers necessary. Although the

---

Action, p 27, Admin Ct; and *R (Enfield London Borough Council) v Broxbourne Borough Council* [2004] EWHC 1053 (Admin), (2004) May *Legal Action*, p 26, Admin Ct.

[242] Homelessness (Decisions on Referrals) Order 1998, SI 1998/1578, made under the Secretary of State's powers at HA 1996, s 198(5) and approving the Guidelines for Local Authorities and Referees Agreement at English Code, Annex 18.

[243] English Code, Annex 18, para 10.2.

[244] English Code, Annex 18, para 10.3.

[245] There is a small panel of referees established by the local authority organisations to perform this function. The list of panel members is maintained by the Local Government Association.

[246] English Code, Annex 18, paras 10.6–10.7.

applicant is not a party to this particular aspect of the dispute, he or she should be sent the local housing authorities' representations. It is up to the referee whether the applicant should be invited to comment, or to make written representations. The referee may choose to hold an oral hearing and the Local Authorities' Agreement advises that an oral hearing might be necessary or more convenient where the applicant is illiterate, where English is not his or her first language, or where further information is necessary for the issues to be resolved.[247]

15.150 The referee's decision must be given in writing. The Local Authorities' Agreement recommends that the decision should be reached 'as quickly as possible' and normally within one month from receipt of both the local housing authorities' written representations.[248] The decision should record the issues, the referee's findings of fact, the decision and the reasons for the decision. Copies should be sent to both local housing authorities and the appropriate local government organisation. The notifying local housing authority should inform the applicant of the decision.[249] One judge described the aims of the procedure:

> 'the legislature intended that these matters should be disposed of within a particular specified time frame and "as quickly as possible" and "promptly". It is also obvious from the terms of that guidance that it is, as one would expect, contemplated by the legislature that the relevant applicant should be kept informed of what is going on, to a reasonable extent.'[250]

15.151 The applicant may then request a review of the referee's decision, in which case a reviewer will have to be appointed by agreement between the two local housing authorities; this would commonly be another referee from the panel maintained by the local authority associations.[251]

15.152 The written decisions of the referees are collected by the local government associations and distributed among other members of the panel of referees (no doubt to encourage consistency of decision-making). They are not officially published. By the end of 2004 only some 120 decisions had been made by referees since the inception of the scheme in 1977. The great bulk had been made in the early years and over the past decade no more than a handful of disputes has been resolved by referees each year.[252]

---

247 English Code, Annex 18, paras 13.1–14.3.
248 English Code, Annex 18, para 13.5.
249 English Code, Annex 18, paras 15.1 and 17.1–17.2.
250 *Berhane v Lambeth London Borough Council* [2007] EWHC 2702, (2008) March *Legal Action*, p 21, QBD, at [36] per Eady J.
251 Allocation of Housing and Homelessness (Review Procedures) Regulations 1999, SI 1999/71, reg 7. See also **19.25**, **19.77–19.78** and **19.119**.
252 In November 1980 the then London Boroughs Association produced an indexed Digest covering decisions 1–25. A supplement in May 1982 added decisions 26–43. A second update in December 1986 added and indexed decisions up to No 60. However, production of the Digest ceased with the issue of a final supplement in 1993 (which added decisions up to and including No 89 to the text).

CHALLENGES BY THE APPLICANT

15.153 The applicant has the right to request the review of a number of the decisions that a local housing authority may make in connection with referral procedures, including:

(1) any decision made by the local housing authority to which the applicant applied, to notify another local housing authority;[253]

(2) any decision reached, by agreement between the two local housing authorities or by a referee's decision, that the conditions for referral are met;[254] and

(3) any decision[255] by either of the two local housing authorities as to which of them is subject to the HA 1996, s 193(2) main housing duty.[256]

15.154 Those rights, read together with the requirements of notification to the applicant,[257] have the effect that, during the referral process, the applicant could substantively challenge decisions to make a referral on two occasions and on a number of issues. The applicant has, in effect, the right to request a review in relation to a local connection referral, *of the notifying local housing authority's decision* that:

(1) the applicant, or a member of his or her household, has no local connection with it; or

(2) the applicant, or a member of his or her household, has a local connection with the district of another local housing authority; or

(3) the applicant, or a member of his or her household, will not run the risk of domestic violence in the district of the other local housing authority; or

(4) the applicant, or a member of his or her household, has not suffered violence in the district of the other local housing authority; or

(5) the applicant, or a member of his or her household, has suffered violence, but it is not probable that any return to the other local housing authority's district will lead to further violence of a similar kind against the victim; or

(6) the other local housing authority should be notified of the local housing authority's decision that the conditions for referral are met.

---

[253] HA 1996, s 202(1)(c). See **19.16–19.22**.
[254] HA 1996, s 202(1)(d). See **19.23–19.25**.
[255] Under HA 1996, s 200(3) or (4).
[256] HA 1996, s 202(1)(e). Now redundant: see **19.26**.
[257] See **15.130–15.133**.

15.155 In addition, the applicant has the right to request a review, following a referral, *of both local housing authorities' decisions*, or *of a referee's decision*, that:

(1) the applicant, or a member of his or her household, has no local connection with the local housing authority to which he or she applied; or

(2) the applicant, or a member of his or her household, has a local connection with the district of another local housing authority; or

(3) the applicant, or a member of his or her household, will not run the risk of domestic violence in the district of the other local housing authority; or

(4) the applicant or a member of his or her household, has not suffered violence in the other local housing authority's district; or

(5) the applicant, or a member of his or her household, has suffered violence, but it is not probable that any return to the other local housing authority's district will lead to further violence of a similar kind against the victim.

15.156 For applicants to English local housing authorities,[258] in relation to an out-district placement referral, the applicant has the right to request a review of any decision *by the notifying local housing authority* (authority A) that:

(1) the applicant was, on a previous application to authority B, placed in the district of authority A in performance of authority B's homelessness functions; or

(2) that the previous application to authority B was made within the prescribed period of the application to authority A; or

(3) that authority A should notify authority B of its decision that these conditions for referral are met.

15.157 In addition, the applicant has the right to request a review, following a referral, of *both local housing authorities' decisions*, or *of a referee's decision*, that:[259]

(1) the applicant was on a previous application to authority B placed in the district of authority A in performance of authority B's homelessness functions; or

(2) that previous application was within the prescribed period.

---

[258] And Welsh local housing authorities dealing with applications made before 9 October 2006 only. See **15.112**.

[259] Or Welsh local housing authorities dealing with applications made before 9 October 2006 only. See **15.112**.

15.158 However, there is *no* statutory right to request a review of any of the other decisions involved in the process, including:

(a) a decision, by the local housing authority to which he or she has applied, to make or not to make inquiries into local connection;[260]

(b) a decision by the local housing authority that the conditions of referral are met, but that another local housing authority should not be notified of the application;[261] and

(c) a decision by the notifying local housing authority not to exercise its power to provide accommodation pending determination of a request for a review of the decision made by the two local housing authorities jointly or by the referee.[262]

15.159 Challenges to those decisions can only be brought by judicial review.[263]

15.160 The procedure for requesting a review of any decision by the notifying local housing authority is the same as for any other request for a review, and the reviewer will be appointed by the notifying local housing authority in the usual way.[264] The trigger for a request for a review is notification to the applicant of one of the decisions above.[265]

15.161 If the request is to review a decision made as to whether the conditions for referral are met, the decision will have been made either by agreement between the notifying and notified local housing authorities, or by a referee. In either case, the request should be made to the notifying local housing authority.[266]

15.162 If the decision was one made by agreement between the two local housing authorities, then the review must be undertaken by them jointly.[267] Presumably this will mean an arrangement for a joint committee or a joint panel of officers.

---

[260] HA 1996, s 184(2); *Hackney London Borough Council v Sareen* [2003] EWCA Civ 351, [2003] HLR 54, CA. See **15.19–15.30**.

[261] HA 1996, s 198(1). See **15.125–15.129**.

[262] HA 1996, s 200(5). See *R (Gebremarium) v Westminster City Council* [2009] EWHC 2254 (Admin), (2009) November *Legal Action*, p 26, Admin Ct for an example of an unsuccessful challenge in judicial review to Westminster's decision not to exercise its HA 1996, s 200(5) power pending a review of its decision to refer her to Cardiff. See also **15.133**.

[263] See **19.211–19.237**.

[264] See **19.50–19.62**.

[265] *Berhane v Lambeth London Borough Council* [2007] EWHC 2702, (2008) March *Legal Action*, p 21, QBD. See **15.154–15.157**.

[266] Allocation of Housing and Homelessness (Review Procedures) Regulations 1999, SI 1999/71, reg 6(1)(b).

[267] SI 1999/71, reg 1(2)(b)(i).

15.163 If a referee made the decision, then the reviewer should be a person jointly appointed by the local housing authorities within 5 working days from the day on which the review request was received by the notifying local housing authority.[268] This appointee could be anyone to whom both local housing authorities are prepared to entrust the review process.[269] If an appointment is not agreed within that time frame, the notifying local housing authority (which has received the review request) has a further 5 working days to ask the chair of the Local Government Association (LGA)[270] to appoint another referee.[271] The chair of the LGA must then appoint a referee within a further 7 days[272] from among the membership of a panel appointed by the LGA.[273] That person then undertakes the review. Although this may appear to be a very tight time frame,[274] the membership of the panel comprises only a handful of referees, one of whom is already eliminated because he or she took the decision.[275] Whether appointed by the local housing authorities or by the LGA, the reviewer will in this chapter be referred to as to the 'appointed' reviewer.[276]

15.164 Once the appointed reviewer has been appointed, the local housing authorities should supply the reasons for the decision under review, together with information and evidence in support. The appointed reviewer will inform the applicant of the procedure to be followed during the review process and that he or she may make written representations. The request for a review and representations made by the applicant should be sent to the local housing authorities and they should be invited to respond. If there is thought to be a deficiency or irregularity in the original decision, further written or oral representations should be invited.[277]

15.165 If the appointed reviewer is a person appointed by agreement between the two local housing authorities, the review decision must be notified to the applicant within 10 weeks from the date of the request for the review.[278] If the appointed reviewer was appointed from a panel, the period is 12 weeks for notification to the applicant, and the review decision will be notified to the

---

268 SI 1999/71, reg 7(1).
269 English Code, Annex 18, para 20.2; Welsh Code, para 21.16.
270 Or Convention of Scottish Local Authorities, if the notified authority is in Scotland.
271 Allocation of Housing and Homelessness (Review Procedures) Regulations 1999, SI 1999/71, reg 7(2); English Code, Annex 18, para 20.2.
272 English Code, Annex 18, para 20.2; Welsh Code, para 21.16; it is unclear from the Regulations whether the LGA has 7 working days or 7 non-working days. The Codes both refer to the 5-day period as 'working days' and to the 7-day period simply as 'seven days', which suggests that the Regulations mean 7 working days, including non-working days.
273 Allocation of Housing and Homelessness (Review Procedures) Regulations 1999, SI 1999/71, reg 7(2)(b) and (3).
274 SI 1999/71, reg 7(7) defines 'working day'.
275 SI 1999/71, reg 7(6).
276 SI 1999/71, reg 7 refers to the reviewer appointed in these circumstances as 'the appointed person'.
277 SI 1999/71, regs 6(3), 7(4), (5), 8(1) and (2); and see **19.84–19.96**.
278 SI 1999/71, reg 9(1)(b).

local housing authorities one week prior to notification to the applicant, in order to give the local housing authorities concerned time to notify a review decision within the 12-week period.[279]

15.166 Once the review has been determined, and the decision on review notified to the applicant, the applicant may appeal to the county court against the review decision. The exercise of this right is entirely separate from any dispute that may be going on between the two local housing authorities. In one case, the county court judge's decision to adjourn the appeal whilst the notifying and notified local housing authorities sought to resolve their dispute was criticised by an appeal judge because it 'denies the appellant effective access to the court, where there is, or is likely to be, undue delay on the part of the relevant respondent.'[280]

SPECIAL RULES FOR ASYLUM-SEEKERS AND FORMER ASYLUM-SEEKERS

The referral of eligible asylum-seekers

15.167 There are special provisions for the referral of any asylum-seekers to whom a main housing duty under HA 1996, s 193(2) would otherwise be owed by a local housing authority.[281] They depend on voluntary arrangements made between local housing authorities.

15.168 These special conditions for referral can be met, where asylum-seekers are concerned, where the local housing authority to whom the application was made has a written agreement with another local housing authority that the case should be referred, and neither the applicant nor any person who might reasonably be expected to reside with him or her will run the risk of domestic violence in the district of the other local housing authority.[282] When reaching that agreement, neither of the local housing authorities need have regard to the applicant's preference as to the location of the accommodation, or to what local connection the applicant or any member of his or her household may have with any local housing authority.[283]

15.169 When handling applications made by asylum-seekers owed the main housing duty under HA 1996, s 193(2), local housing authorities are required to have regard to the desirability, in general, of securing accommodation in areas

---

[279] SI 1999/71, reg 9(1)(c) and (3). The Local Authorities' Agreement does not refer to the 12-week period for disputes between English local housing authorities (English Code, Annex 18, paras 9.1–9.6), but the Regulation is still in force.

[280] *Berhane v Lambeth London Borough Council* [2007] EWHC 2702, (2008) March *Legal Action*, p 21, QBD, at [43] per Eady J.

[281] Welsh Code, Annex 11 for guidance. See **12.75–12.86** and **12.88–12.89** for eligible asylum-seekers.

[282] HA 1996, s 198(4A), added by Homelessness (Asylum Seekers) (Interim Period) (England) Order 1999, SI 1999/3126, reg 3. See **15.94–15.101** for test of 'domestic violence'.

[283] HA 1996, s 198(4B), as added by SI 1999/3126, reg 3.

in which there is a ready supply of accommodation.[284] There is no general presumption against out-of-borough placements where there is a written agreement between two local housing authorities that the notifying local housing authority may provide accommodation for asylum-seekers in the notified local housing authority's district.[285] When determining whether or not accommodation is suitable for the needs of the asylum-seeker and his or her household, the fact that the accommodation is to be provided temporarily, pending the determination of the claim for asylum, must be taken into account. The asylum-seeker's preference as to location cannot be taken into account.[286]

15.170 There are diminishing numbers of asylum-seekers who are eligible for homelessness assistance and therefore to whom these special provisions can be applied. No asylum-seeker whose claim for asylum was made on or after 3 April 2000 can be eligible for HA 1996, Part 7 assistance. Those asylum-seekers who are eligible are likely to have applied as homeless before 3 April 2000, and any decision that the conditions for referral were met under these provisions is likely to have been made some considerable time ago.[287]

15.171 The special rules are intended to mirror the dispersal provisions for asylum-seekers contained in Immigration and Asylum Act 1999 and implemented by the Home Office. They will be repealed whenever HA 1996, s 186 is repealed.[288] There is provision to repeal s 186 by statutory instrument; that power has not yet been exercised but, no doubt, will be when there are no longer any eligible asylum-seekers receiving homelessness assistance.[289]

15.172 The accommodation provided to asylum-seekers must be suitable for the needs of the applicant and of his or her household.[290] Suitability is to be assessed taking into account the temporary nature of the accommodation to be provided, but the accommodation must still be suitable. This is not a charter to provide sub-standard accommodation to asylum-seekers.

The power to assist former asylum-seekers who occupied Home Office accommodation in Scotland

15.173 Former asylum-seekers who leave accommodation in Scotland provided by the Home Office under Immigration and Asylum Act 1999, s 95 and then apply as homeless to local housing authorities in England or Wales will not normally have a local connection with the district of the Scottish local authority (unless by reason of employment, family associations, or some other special circumstance).

---

[284] HA 1996, 206(1A), added by SI 1999/3126, reg 4.
[285] HA 1996, s 208(1A), added by SI 1999/3126, reg 5. See **18.49–18.58**.
[286] HA 1996, s 210(1A), added by SI 1999/3126, reg 6.
[287] See **12.75–12.86** and **12.88–12.89**.
[288] SI 1999/3126, reg 7.
[289] Immigration and Asylum Act 1999, ss 117(5), 169(3) and Sch 16.
[290] *R v Kensington & Chelsea Royal London Borough Council ex p Korneva* (1997629 HLR 709, CA.

15.174 If such former asylum-seekers do not have a local connection with any other local housing authority in England or Wales, they would ordinarily be owed the HA 1996, s 193(2) main housing duty by the English or Welsh local housing authority to which they applied. However, legislation passed in 2004 provides that where English or Welsh local housing authorities would otherwise have a HA 1996, s 193(2) main housing duty towards those former asylum-seekers, the duty does not apply.[291]

15.175 Instead, the English or Welsh local housing authority has a power (but no duty):

- to provide accommodation for the former asylum-seeker for a period that would give him or her a reasonable opportunity of obtaining accommodation; and

- to provide advice and assistance with any attempts he or she may make to obtain his or her own accommodation.[292]

15.176 The idea is that the former asylum-seeker will either obtain his or her own accommodation in England or Wales, with assistance from the local housing authority (if the local housing authority chooses to provide it), or will return to Scotland and make an application for homelessness assistance to a Scottish local authority.[293] Indeed, the English Code specifically suggests that the local housing authority consider:

> 'providing such advice and assistance as would enable the applicant to make an application for housing to the Scottish authority in the district where the section 95 accommodation was last provided, or to another Scottish authority of the applicant's choice'.[294]

Since, under Scottish law, the former asylum-seeker will most likely have no local connection with any authority in England, Wales or Scotland, any Scottish local authority will be subject to the main housing duty. There is no need for the former asylum-seeker to apply to the specific Scottish local authority in whose district he or she had been accommodated by the Home Office.[295]

---

[291] Asylum and Immigration (Treatment of Claimants etc) Act 2004, s 11(2) and (3), in force from 4 January 2005.

[292] Asylum and Immigration (Treatment of Claimants etc) Act 2004, s 11(3)(b), in force from 4 January 2005.

[293] Since an application for homelessness assistance can be made in any manner and should not require completion of the local housing authority's standard form, the former asylum-seeker could be assisted to make an application to any Scottish local authority in writing, by fax, or even by email. There should be no need to leave any accommodation provided by the English or Welsh local housing authority until the Scottish local authority has notified the applicant that the application for homelessness assistance has been received and that suitable accommodation will be provided.

[294] English Code, para 18.21.

[295] English Code, para 18.21.

15.177 The extraordinary effect of this provision is to put a former asylum-seeker who was dispersed to Scotland by the Home Office but has become homeless unintentionally from Home Office accommodation and wishes to apply for accommodation to an English or Welsh local housing authority in a worse position than a person who has become homeless intentionally. At least an applicant who has become homeless intentionally (who also had a priority need) would be owed a temporary accommodation *duty* by the local housing authority to which he or she had applied.[296] Moreover, the English or Welsh local housing authority is permitted no discretion. If the conditions are made out, no duty is owed to the former asylum-seeker.

15.178 Any decision by the local housing authority that such an applicant is caught by these provisions and not owed the main housing duty under HA 1996, s 193(2) would be a decision as to 'what duty (if any) is owed'. The applicant would have a right to request a review of that decision under HA 1996, s 202(1)(b).

15.179 The powers given to English and Welsh local housing authorities under the Asylum and Immigration (Treatment of Claimants etc) Act 2004 (whether or not to provide accommodation and/or whether or not to provide advice and assistance) are discretionary powers and carry no statutory right to request a review. If a local housing authority decided not to exercise these powers, any challenge could only be brought on a point of law in judicial review proceedings.

15.180 An applicant who had been provided with accommodation under the English or Welsh local housing authority's interim duty would be entitled to reasonable notice of the termination of that accommodation.[297]

CROSS-BORDER REFERRALS

15.181 All the countries of the UK[298] operate statutory homelessness schemes. This book is concerned only with the detailed scheme for England and Wales found in HA 1996, Part 7. But cross-border referrals may arise between English and Welsh local housing authorities and when English or Welsh local housing authorities make referrals to, or are asked to receive referrals from, other countries in the UK.

---

[296] HA 1996, s 190(2)(a). See **17.111–17.118**.
[297] HA 1996, s 188(1); *R v Newham London Borough Council ex p Ojuri (No 3)* (1999) 31 HLR 631, QBD.
[298] England, Wales, Scotland and Northern Ireland. See Interpretation Act 1978, s 5 and Sch 1; and see Box 1 at **12.55**.

Referrals within England and Wales

15.182 The referral arrangements in HA 1996, Part 7 govern all formal referrals between local housing authorities in England or Wales. They apply to referrals between:

• a Welsh local housing authority and one or more other Welsh local housing authorities;

• an English local housing authority and one or more other English local housing authorities;

• an English local housing authority and one or more Welsh local housing authorities; and

• a Welsh local housing authority and one or more English local housing authorities.

15.183 Since devolution, the Welsh Assembly Government has had its own powers to make secondary legislation[299] and to issue its own homelessness guidance.[300] It has exercised these powers in relation to the homelessness provisions. There is a separate Code of Guidance in Wales and the regulations made by the Welsh Assembly Government do not mirror precisely those made by English ministers. The net result is a potential for disparity between the treatment of an application for homelessness assistance by a Welsh local housing authority as compared to that by an English local housing authority. An applicant to a Welsh local housing authority might well be accepted as having priority need in circumstances in which no priority need would be found by an English local housing authority (because of the different wording of the two Priority Need Orders).[301] The result may be that an applicant is found to be owed the main housing duty by a Welsh local housing authority when no such duty would be found by an English local housing authority (and indeed may have been positively rejected on a previous application to an English local housing authority).[302]

15.184 These nuances cannot, however, make any difference to the application of the first set of referral conditions discussed in this chapter.[303] For example, if a Welsh local housing authority finds that it owes the main duty to an applicant who has no local connection with its district but who does have a local

---

[299] Orders and Regulations. The power was originally exercisable by the National Assembly for Wales and transferred to the Welsh Assembly Government effective from 25 May 2007.

[300] Government of Wales Act 1998 and Government of Wales Act 2006, s 161 and Sch 11, para 30.

[301] See **13.106–13.171** (English Priority Need Order), and **13.172–13.202** (Welsh Priority Need Order).

[302] There are also different legislative provisions in England and Wales governing eligibility (see Chapter 12 of this book) and different guidance on decisions about whether or not an applicant has become homeless intentionally (see Chapter 14 of this book).

[303] See **15.40–15.110**.

connection with an English local housing authority (and would run no risk of violence by returning there), it may make a referral. No doubt, in exercising its discretion whether to refer,[304] it might wish to take into account that, on the same facts, the notified local housing authority might not have owed the main housing duty at all.

15.185 However, as this chapter has described, an applicant to an English local housing authority who was placed in that authority's district by another local housing authority in performance of its homelessness functions could be referred back to the first local housing authority under the second set of conditions for referral.[305] This is no longer the case for applications to Welsh local housing authorities.

15.186 Where the two local housing authorities involved are both English local housing authorities, then the conditions for referral can be operated without difficulty. However, what happens in the following circumstances:

(1) Where an applicant to a Welsh local housing authority has previously been placed in that local housing authority's district, within the prescribed period by an English local housing authority, in pursuance of its homelessness functions?

(2) Where an applicant applies to an English local housing authority, having previously been placed in its district by a Welsh local housing authority?

15.187 There is nothing in HA 1996, Part 7, the Regulations, either of the Codes or the Local Authorities' Agreement that sheds any light on these cross-border problems. The authors' view is that it would certainly be difficult for an English local housing authority, in the first scenario, to attempt to apply the conditions for referral at HA 1996, s 198(4). It remains to be seen whether an English local housing authority in the second scenario could attempt to apply those conditions to refer to a Welsh local housing authority.

Referrals to the Isles of Scilly

15.188 The Isles of Scilly are administratively part of England,[306] but special measures have been taken to protect the very limited stock of social housing on those islands. HA 1996[307] enables the Secretary of State to make an order adapting HA 1996, Part 7 in its application to the Isles of Scilly, and that power has been used.[308] So, for example, there are special provisions governing eligibility for applicants applying there.[309]

---

[304] See **15.125–15.129**.
[305] See **15.111–15.124**.
[306] Interpretation Act 1978, s 5 and Sch 1.
[307] HA 1996, s 225(1).
[308] Homelessness (Isles of Scilly) Order 1997, SI 1997/797.
[309] Discussed at **12.205–12.206**.

15.189 To prevent these eligibility rules being circumvented by an application directed initially to a local housing authority elsewhere, modifications have been made by Order to arrangements for referral by other local housing authorities to the Isles of Scilly Council.

15.190 If a homeless applicant applies to a local housing authority elsewhere in England or in Wales and the conditions for a local connection referral to the Council of the Isles of Scilly would otherwise be met, they are displaced by other rules. The intended effect of the Order[310] is that the applicant will only have a local connection with the Isles of Scilly if she or he has resided in the district of the Isles of Scilly Council for 2 years and 6 months during the 3 years prior to the date that the latest application for homelessness assistance is made. If that period of residence is established, there is deemed local connection in place of the normal local connection provisions.[311]

15.191 It is recognised that the Isles of Scilly may need to accommodate some of its homeless applicants on the mainland. As a result, English local housing authorities can refer back to the islands if the second set of conditions for a referral is made out.[312] This is because the power to modify HA 1996[313] has not been used in relation to this set of conditions.

Referrals to Scotland

15.192 The provisions of HA 1996, Part 7 enable English and Welsh local housing authorities to make referrals to local authorities in Scotland in just the same way as they might make a referral to another local housing authority in England or Wales. The Local Authorities' Agreement[314] was drawn up in co-operation with the Confederation of Scottish Local Authorities (CoSLA) and applies in the same way to referrals to local authorities in Scotland as it would to any other referral.

15.193 The Local Authorities' Agreement provides that, where there is a cross-border dispute, the relevant law to be applied is that relevant to the location of the notified local housing authority.[315] This only applies to the issue of whether or not the conditions for referral are or are not made out, and not to any other disagreements that the notified local housing authority may have with the decision of the notifying local housing authority.[316]

15.194 The only procedural difference is that if the notified local authority (in Scotland) does not accept that the conditions for referral are made out and is

---

[310] Which is not well drafted.
[311] HA 1996, s 199(1).
[312] And Welsh local housing authorities for applications made before 1 June 2006. See **15.111–15.124**.
[313] HA 1996, s 225(2).
[314] See **15.42**.
[315] Local Authorities' Agreement, English Code, Annex 18, para 11.4; Welsh Code, Annex 20, para 9.4.
[316] See **15.140–15.152**.

unable to agree with the notifying local housing authority (in England and Wales) on the identity of a referee to resolve the dispute, then it is CoSLA which appoints a referee in default of such agreement.[317] The adjudication will then be governed by the procedural rules in the Homelessness (Decisions on Referrals) (Scotland) Order 1998.[318]

15.195 If the conditions for a referral are not made out, an English or Welsh local housing authority may nevertheless invite a local authority in Scotland to assist in the discharge of HA 1996, Part 7 functions. The local authority in Scotland would be bound to co-operate with that request to such extent as was reasonable in the particular circumstances.[319]

Referrals from Scotland

15.196 The capacity of a local authority in Scotland to refer an application for homelessness assistance to a local housing authority in England or Wales will primarily be regulated by the law of Scotland (which is beyond the scope of this book). It must be noted, however, that there are several differences in the operation of homelessness provisions, including those relating to referrals, as between Scotland and England and Wales. For example:

- applicants in Scotland have no statutory right to seek a review of a decision to refer them to a local housing authority in England or Wales;

- the second set of conditions for a statutory referral (reference back to a local housing authority which placed the applicant in the present local housing authority's area)[320] does not extend to Scotland; and

- the new deemed local connection for residents of Home Office accommodation[321] is not part of the law of Scotland.

15.197 However, if a Scottish local authority (applying the law of Scotland) forms the opinion that the conditions for a referral to a local housing authority in England or Wales are met, it may notify the English or Welsh local housing authority to that effect. If the notified local housing authority accepts that the conditions for a referral are satisfied, then the application is referred in the normal way. If the English or Welsh local housing authority does not accept that the necessary conditions are satisfied, a referee will be appointed by

---

[317] Local Authorities' Agreement, English Code, Annex 18, para 10.6.

[318] Homelessness (Decisions on Referrals) (Scotland) Order 1998, SI 1998/1603.

[319] HA 1996, s 213(1).

[320] HA 1996, s 198(4). See **15.111–15.124**.

[321] HA 1996, s 199(6) and (7), added by Asylum and Immigration (Treatment of Claimants etc) Act 2004, s 11(1), in force from 4 January 2005.

agreement or in default by the Local Government Association.[322] The adjudication will then be governed by the procedural rules in the Homelessness (Decisions on Referrals) Order.[323]

15.198 If the conditions for a referral are not made out, a local authority in Scotland may nevertheless invite a local housing authority in England or Wales to assist in the discharge of its homelessness duties. The English or Welsh local housing authority would be bound to co-operate with that request to such extent as was reasonable in the particular circumstances.[324]

15.199 The Homelessness etc (Scotland) Act 2003 contains powers under which ministers of the Scottish Executive may effectively abolish the referral powers of Scottish local authorities so that responsibility for a homeless person in Scotland will remain with the local authority to which an applicant first applies.[325] The powers have yet to be used.

Northern Ireland

15.200 Northern Ireland has its own self-contained legislative scheme for homelessness.[326] No doubt because there is a single authority dealing with applications for homelessness assistance in Northern Ireland (the Housing Executive), there are no 'local connection' or other referral provisions in the scheme. There is no power for the Executive to refer an application to a local housing authority in England, Scotland or Wales. Likewise, there is no power to make a referral in the other direction. Any referral could therefore only be through informal, co-operative arrangements.[327]

The Isle of Man

15.201 The Isle of Man has its own separate jurisdiction and, indeed, a self-contained legislative scheme defining the right of residence.[328] Any person who is not entitled to reside under that scheme commits a criminal offence by residence on the island. There are no legislative powers permitting referrals from the Isle of Man to English or Welsh local housing authorities or vice versa. Any referral could only, therefore, be informal through co-operative mechanisms, and the Isle of Man would be unlikely to co-operate unless the applicant had the right to reside under its statutes.

---

[322] Local Authorities' Agreement, English Code, Annex 18, para 10.3; Welsh Code, Annex 20, para 8.8.
[323] SI 1998/1603. See Local Authorities' Agreement, English Code, Annex 18, para 11.4; Welsh Code, Annex 20, para 9.4.
[324] HA 1996, s 213.
[325] Homelessness (Scotland) Act 2003, s 8.
[326] Housing (Northern Ireland) Order 1988, SI 1988/1990, as amended.
[327] See **15.212–15.216**.
[328] Residence Act 2001, s 9.

INFORMAL REFERRALS

15.202 This chapter has been primarily concerned with the formal mechanisms by which a local housing authority can refer a successful homelessness applicant to another local housing authority to be accommodated in another local housing authority's district. Where those provisions do not apply, the normal rule is that the local housing authority that has accepted the application must accommodate the applicant in its own area.[329]

15.203 But there is a wide range of circumstances beyond those covered by the formal referral arrangements when the provision of accommodation in the area of another local housing authority may be appropriate. For example:

- the applicant may not be safe (in that there is a risk of domestic or other violence) in the district of the local housing authority which has accepted his or her application and with which she or he may enjoy a local connection;[330] or

- the applicant may have other compelling reasons (eg relating to health or education or the need to be near a carer) for asking that local housing authority to provide accommodation in another local housing authority's district; or

- the local housing authority may simply be unable to provide any accommodation which is suitable for the applicant in its own district; or

- the local housing authority may have sought to make a referral under the formal provisions, and then been satisfied by the notified local housing authority's response that the conditions for referral were not made out, yet the applicant may still wish to be accommodated in the other local housing authority's area.

15.204 The following paragraphs explore the extent to which there is scope under HA 1996, Part 7 for a local housing authority to provide accommodation in another local housing authority's district outside the tailor-made referral provisions.

Unilateral placements in another district

15.205 Strictly, a local housing authority which has accepted a responsibility to accommodate an applicant, but finds that it is not 'reasonably practicable' to accommodate that applicant in its own district, can provide accommodation in

---

[329] HA 1996, s 208(1).
[330] English Code, para 16.7; Welsh Code, para 18.9.

the district of another local housing authority (provided that it is suitable), and may do so without any prior reference to that other local housing authority at all.[331]

15.206 A local housing authority might be tempted to do precisely that when it comes to its most needy and vulnerable applicants, so that the burden of meeting their special needs (for example, in relation to education or social services) falls on another district.[332] So as to meet this point directly, the Codes advise that these households should be given priority for placement *within* the district of the local housing authority to which they have applied rather than being placed in another district.[333]

15.207 Where an 'out of district'[334] placement is made, HA 1996, Part 7 requires the placing local housing authority to give notice of any such placement to the other local housing authority.[335] Notice is not required in advance but must be given within 14 days of the provision of accommodation in the notified local housing authority's district.[336]

15.208 HA 1996, Part 7 sets out the formal requirements of the notice (name of applicant, address of the accommodation, etc) including the provision of the date on which accommodation was provided to the applicant.[337]

15.209 The duty to notify an 'out of district' placement applies whenever a local housing authority is discharging any accommodation duty owed under HA 1996, Part 7 by securing accommodation in another district, whether the accommodation being provided is provided by a social or private sector landlord or anyone else. Thus, it is not confined to placement of those owed the main housing duty under HA 1996, s 193(2). It applies whenever accommodation is being provided, whether it is on an interim basis pending a decision on an application,[338] as part of the assistance required to be given to a priority need homeless household where the applicant has become homeless intentionally,[339] in performance of the main housing duty[340] or of any other HA 1996, Part 7 accommodation duty. Experience suggests that, particularly in relation to the first category where there can be a reasonably rapid turnover of households, the notification duty is honoured in the breach.

---

[331] HA 1996, s 208(1). When considering whether it is 'reasonably practicable' to provide accommodation in its own district, a local housing authority is entitled to have regard to any financial savings that might be achieved by out of borough placements, and to any differences in the quality of accommodation available within its district or out of borough (*R (Calgin) v Enfield London Borough Council* [2005] EWHC 1716 (Admin), [2006] HLR 4, Admin Ct).

[332] See the comments of Latham LJ in *R v Newham London Borough Council ex p Sacupima* (2001) 33 HLR 2, CA at [31].

[333] English Code, para 16.7; Welsh Code, para 18.13.

[334] English Code, paras 16.8–16.9; Welsh Code, paras 18.9–18.14.

[335] HA 1996, s 208(2). See also English Code, para 16.8; Welsh Code, para 18.10.

[336] HA 1996, s 208(4).

[337] HA 1996, s 208(3).

[338] HA 1996, s 188(1). See **16.11–16.24**.

[339] HA 1996, s 190(2)(a). See **17.111–17.118**.

[340] HA 1996, s 193(2). See **17.21–17.110**.

15.210   The simple dispatch of a notice is not sufficient to relieve the placing local housing authority of any responsibility for the homeless household. The Codes remind placing local housing authorities to consider the particular needs of a household being accommodated out of the area and advise that households who need social services support or need to maintain links with specialist medical services, special schools or other essential services within the authority's district should be given priority for accommodation within that district.[341]

15.211   Where a household is placed in a different district from the district of the local housing authority to which it applied, it might be prudent for that household to apply for long-term social housing under *both* local housing authorities' allocation schemes.

Placements by co-operation between local housing authorities

15.212   HA 1996, Part 7, the Codes and the Local Authorities' Agreement are all replete with references to the need for local housing authorities to co-operate with one another in their dealings with homeless applicants. Obviously, it is particularly important for local housing authorities to co-operate where a homeless household is being re-located from the district of the local housing authority to which it applied to another local housing authority's district.

15.213   The legislation facilitates that necessary co-operation in two ways. First, HA 1996, Part 7 requires any local housing authority receiving a request for assistance in discharging HA 1996, Part 7 functions from another local housing authority, to give such assistance as is reasonable in the circumstances.[342] Second, HA 1996, Part 7 enables a local housing authority to perform its housing functions by securing accommodation for the applicant from 'some other person' than the local housing authority itself.[343] That 'other person' might be a different local housing authority.

15.214   The most frequent instance of local housing authorities co-operating occurs when authorities with surplus accommodation make that stock available to other local housing authorities. These arrangements are particularly encouraged by the Codes.[344] Increasingly sophisticated schemes have been developed to match homeless applicants who apply to high demand areas with accommodation in lower demand areas (even though they may have previously had no connection with those areas).[345] Most of those schemes work on the premise that the applicant is willing to take up the opportunity of a home elsewhere.

---

[341]   English Code, para 16.9; Welsh Code, para 18.13.
[342]   HA 1996, s 213(1). See also English Code, para 16.29; Welsh Code, para 18.35.
[343]   HA 1996, s 206(1)(b).
[344]   English Code, paras 5.1–5.11 and 16.29; Welsh Code, para 18.35.
[345]   See, e g the LAWN scheme operated by a number of London and South East local housing

15.215   What is not permissible is for the local housing authority (to which an applicant has applied) to use the mere existence or activation of these co-operative arrangements as a purported performance of its own duties.[346] However, where a local housing authority has satisfied itself that another local housing authority is prepared to accommodate the applicant and that the accommodation to be provided for the applicant will be suitable, the main housing duty owed to an applicant can be performed upon the other local housing authority accepting that it would accommodate him or her.[347]

15.216   The second common form of co-operative out-of-district placements is a reciprocal arrangement, whereby one local housing authority agrees to accommodate an applicant who has applied as homeless elsewhere, and, in response, can place one of its homeless applicants in the transferring local housing authority's district. The Codes advise local housing authorities that this form of co-operation is particularly appropriate where an applicant has 'special housing needs' which can better be met in one area than another, or where the applicant needs be placed elsewhere to avoid the risk of violence in the area of the local housing authority to which he or she applied.[348] The Local Authorities' Agreement also promotes such reciprocal arrangements where, for one reason or another, a strict application of the formal referral rules would not result in a successful referral.[349]

---

authorities in partnership with local housing authorities in the Midlands, North of England, Scotland and elsewhere: www.lawnmoves.org.uk.

[346]   See *R v Bromley London Borough Council ex p Cafun* (2001) January *Legal Action*, p 27, Admin Ct, where Bromley had told the applicant that Greenwich, its neighbouring borough, would accommodate her. The court held that simple activation of the co-operative arrangements between the two boroughs was not enough. Bromley had to ensure that accommodation suitable for that particular applicant was actually going to be provided by Greenwich before its duty could be said to have been performed. Had *Bromley* satisfied itself that was the case, placing her in Greenwich would potentially have been lawful and its duty would have been discharged.

[347]   *R v Bristol City Council ex p Browne* [1979] 1 WLR 1437, QBD.

[348]   English Code, para 16.29. The Welsh Code, para 18.35 advises that such co-operative agreements 'will only be appropriate in exceptional circumstances' and gives the example of applicants at risk of violence or serious harassment.

[349]   For example, where the only ground for a local connection with the notified local housing authority would be 'special circumstances' or where a local connection is made out with the notifying local housing authority but the applicant does not wish to live in that local housing authority's area: English Code, Annex 18, paras 4.2 and 6.4.

Chapter 16

INTERIM ACCOMMODATION – DUTIES AND POWERS

INTRODUCTION

16.1   In the course of the consideration of any Housing Act 1996 (HA 1996) Part 7 application for accommodation (made by a person who has given reason to believe that he or she may be homeless or threatened with homelessness) there will be periods of time when it is not clear what duty (if any) will ultimately be owed to the applicant. That is most obviously the case between the date of the application and the date when the first decision on it is made. But it may also be true at later stages, eg pending a review or appeal, or where a referral to another local housing authority is under way. HA 1996, Part 7 requires that in some circumstances the local housing authority *must* secure accommodation during those 'interim' periods. In other circumstances, local housing authorities are given *powers* to secure accommodation during those periods. This chapter examines those duties and powers; it refers throughout to 'interim accommodation' to describe the accommodation secured during any of those periods.

THE DUTIES AND POWERS IN OUTLINE

16.2   If a local housing authority has reason to believe that an applicant may be homeless, eligible for assistance and have a priority need, it is under an absolute duty to secure accommodation for the applicant, and members of his or her household, pending its decision as to whether it owes any other duty to the applicant under HA 1996, Part 7.[1]

16.3   Even if the local housing authority has reason to believe that it may eventually refer the applicant to another local housing authority under the provisions described in Chapter 15, it must secure accommodation pending notification of that decision.[2] The initial 'interim' duty is therefore owed to those who have no connection at all with the area of the local housing authority to which they have applied, as well as to those who do have such a local connection.

16.4   The duty ends automatically when the local housing authority's decision is notified to the applicant.[3] If the applicant later requests a statutory review of one of the local housing authority's decisions (if the decision is capable of review),[4] the local housing authority has a power, but not a duty, to secure accommodation pending the outcome of the review.[5]

16.5   There is a similar power, but no duty, to secure accommodation pending the determination of an appeal to the county court.[6]

---

[1]   Housing Act 1996, s 188(1). See **16.11–16.24**.
[2]   HA 1996, s 188(2). See **15.17–15.18**.
[3]   HA 1996, s 188(3). See also **16.20–16.23**.
[4]   See **19.12–19.35**.
[5]   HA 1996, s 188(3). See also **16.24–16.36**.
[6]   HA 1996, s 204(4). See also **16.37–16.42**.

16.6 Powers and duties to secure interim accommodation may also be triggered by a decision to refer an application, made by someone who would otherwise be owed the main housing duty, to a different local housing authority. If, following a decision to refer the applicant to another local housing authority under the conditions for referrals,[7] the applicant requests a review (and/or subsequently brings an appeal against that review decision), the notifying local housing authority has a power, but no duty, to continue to secure accommodation pending the review (and/or the appeal).[8] Even if the decision to refer to another local housing authority is not challenged by the applicant, the notifying local housing authority is under a duty to secure accommodation until the applicant has been notified that the notified local housing authority accepts that the conditions for referral are fulfilled or any dispute between the local housing authorities is finally resolved.[9]

16.7 The Codes provide guidance on the interim duties to accommodate,[10] and on how and when local housing authorities should exercise their powers to secure interim accommodation.[11]

16.8 Where a local housing authority owes a duty to secure interim accommodation (or exercises a power to secure it), powers and duties to safeguard the applicant's furniture and other possessions may be triggered. Property protection is dealt with separately in Chapter 17.[12]

16.9 An applicant who is occupying interim accommodation is still 'homeless' within the statutory definition at HA 1996, ss 175–177.[13] He or she is therefore entitled to a reasonable preference within a local housing authority's allocation scheme under HA 1996, s 167(2)(a).[14]

16.10 Each of the duties and powers to secure interim accommodation is now considered in turn, followed by a review of common issues which apply to all forms of provision (as to the quality, size, location, cost, etc) of interim accommodation. The chapter concludes with guidance on:

- the enforcement of duties;[15]

---

[7] As described in Chapter 15.
[8] HA 1996, ss 200(5) and 204(4). See **16.43–16.50**.
[9] HA 1996, s 200(1)–(4). See **15.136–15.139**.
[10] *Homelessness Code of Guidance for local authorities* (Communities and Local Government, Department for Education and Skills, Department of Health, July 2006) (English Code), chapter 7. *Code of Guidance for local housing authorities on allocation of accommodation and homelessness for Wales* (National Assembly for Wales, April 2003) (Welsh Code), para 12.11.
[11] English Code, chapter 15; Welsh Code, paras 21.20–21.24 and 21.33–21.37.
[12] See **17.163–17.184**.
[13] *R (Alam) v Tower Hamlets London Borough Council* [2009] EWHC 44 (Admin), (2009) March *Legal Action*, p 24, Admin Ct. See Chapter 11 for statutory definition of 'homeless'.
[14] See **4.41–4.49**.
[15] See **16.89**.

- challenges to refusals to exercise powers;[16] and

- the limited availability of compensation.[17]

THE DUTIES AND POWERS IN DETAIL
The initial duty to secure interim accommodation

16.11   The initial duty to secure interim accommodation[18] is triggered when the local housing authority has 'reason to believe' that an applicant may be 'homeless',[19] 'eligible for assistance',[20] and may have a 'priority need'.[21] This is a very low threshold.[22] The governing word is 'may', which must be understood to apply to all the elements of the statutory formula. So the threshold is met when a local housing authority has reason to believe that an applicant:

- 'may' be homeless; and also

- 'may' be eligible; and also

- 'may' have a priority need.

16.12   These are some of the issues that the local housing authority will be making inquiries into, in due course, in order to determine what duty (if any) is ultimately owed to the applicant under HA 1996, Part 7.

16.13   Four additional points should be noted.

---

[16]   See **16.90–16.113**.
[17]   See **16.114–16.118**.
[18]   HA 1996, s 188(1).
[19]   See Chapter 11.
[20]   See Chapter 12.
[21]   See Chapter 13.
[22]   See *R (Kelly & Mehari) v Birmingham City Council* [2009] EWHC 3240 (Admin), (2010) January *Legal Action*, p 35, Admin Ct, and English Code, para 7.3. See **16.18**. See also the Local Government Ombudsman's decision against Haringey London Borough Council (06/A/12508, 30 June 2008, (2008) August *Legal Action*, p 42), where maladministration was found, as the local housing authority failed to secure HA 1996, s 188(1) interim accommodation at all to a woman with her baby. Haringey had not recorded the significant decision that it had 'reason to believe' that the applicant may be homeless, and that should have immediately triggered the requirement that interim accommodation be secured. It was 'good practice' for a council to apply the low threshold of whether it has reason to believe that a person may be homeless for the purposes of both HA 1996, s 184 and s 188(1). The Local Government Ombudsman's decision against Hounslow London Borough Council (07/A/14216, (2009) June *Legal Action*, p 34) found maladministration for a failure to secure interim accommodation for 2 months after the application had been made. The Council was recommended to pay the applicants £500 compensation for the distress and confusion caused. See **16.114–16.118**.

16.14 First, no interim accommodation duty is owed to an applicant who may be simply 'threatened with' homelessness. There is not even a power to secure interim accommodation for such an applicant.

16.15 Second, the question whether the initial duty is owed may arise not only when the initial application is made, but also at any stage before the local housing authority's decision on the application has been notified to the applicant. For example, where a local housing authority is making its inquiries into an application made by an applicant who appears to be threatened with homelessness, it is not under a duty to secure interim accommodation.[23] However, if, before the local housing authority has concluded its inquiries and notified the applicant of its decision, the situation changes and the local housing authority has reason to believe that the applicant may actually be homeless (and there is also reason to believe that the applicant may be eligible and may have a priority need) the duty to secure interim accommodation is immediately triggered. Similarly, if an applicant who appears to be homeless but has not previously been considered potentially to have a priority need suddenly acquires what appears to be a priority need,[24] the duty would be triggered.

16.16 Third, the initial duty arises irrespective of any local connection the applicant may have with any other local housing authority.[25]

16.17 Fourth, the initial duty to secure interim accommodation is not a duty capable of being referred to another local housing authority under the conditions for referral described in Chapter 15.

16.18 If the local housing authority does have reason to believe that the applicant may be homeless, may be eligible and may have a priority need, the duty to secure initial interim accommodation is an absolute one. The local housing authority must secure that accommodation is available; it cannot postpone that duty, which is triggered as soon as the requisite 'reason to believe' is present. One local housing authority's application form contained the following instruction to its officers: 'unless the applicant and family are at risk of harm, they should be advised to return to the homeless address whereby a visiting officer will attend the property'. As a result of that instruction, the local housing authority failed to engage with the criteria at HA 1996, s 188(1) and failed to provide accommodation to applicants for homelessness assistance whom it had reason to believe may be homeless, may be eligible and may have a priority need. A judge said:

> 'The approach of the Council to their obligations under Section 188 at the very least lacks legal coherence and a proper consideration of the relevant Section 188

---

23   HA 1996, s 184(1).
24   For example, the discovery of a pregnancy.
25   HA 1996, s 188(2).

criteria. So far as the Council are concerned that failure had and, insofar as that practice continues, continues to have, the effect of avoiding their obligations under Section 188.'[26]

16.19 If the local housing authority refuses to secure initial interim accommodation when the statutory conditions are fulfilled or, before the duty ends, withdraws any accommodation secured, it is in breach of its statutory duty. The applicant is entitled to bring judicial review proceedings for a mandatory order that accommodation be secured immediately.[27]

16.20 The duty to secure accommodation under the initial interim duty ends when the local housing authority's decision on the applicant's application (whether the applicant is 'eligible' and, if so, what duty if any is owed to him or her) is notified to the applicant.[28] The initial interim duty does not end when the decision is taken. It ends only when that decision is 'notified to' the applicant in writing. The decision may acknowledge that a further duty is owed to the applicant, or that no duty is owed. The initial accommodation duty ends whatever the content of the decision.

16.21 Where the local housing authority decides that it owes the applicant a duty to secure accommodation, the notification letter ought sensibly to spell out how that accommodation duty is going to be met from the moment of notification, because the interim duty to accommodate has ceased from the moment that the applicant receives the letter. Much confusion is caused by notifications which accept the main housing duty (under HA 1996, s 193(2)) but do not spell out how it is going to be performed from that day forward.

16.22 If the decision is adverse, the applicant might exercise his or her right to a review. This cannot keep the initial interim accommodation duty running. Any further accommodation secured by the local housing authority will either be the result of any limited accommodation duty owed to the applicant as notified in the decision letter,[29] or will be the result of the local housing authority exercising its power to secure accommodation pending review.

16.23 The fact that the initial interim accommodation duty is brought to an end by notification of the decision does not mean that the accommodation that has been secured will be instantly withdrawn. The local housing authority may secure the same accommodation for the applicant in performance of any other accommodation duty it owes. If there is no further accommodation duty owed, and the local housing authority is not willing to exercise its power to continue

---

[26]   *R (Kelly & Mehari) v Birmingham City Council* [2009] EWHC 3240 (Admin), (2010) January *Legal Action*, p 35, Admin Ct, at [40], per Hickinbottom J.

[27]   See **16.89**.

[28]   HA 1996, s 188(3).

[29]   For example, the duty to secure accommodation owed to a person found to have become homeless intentionally under HA 1996, s 190(2)(a). See **17.111–17.118**.

to secure accommodation pending review (or is not asked to exercise this power), the actual termination of the accommodation arrangement is discussed under 'Termination'.[30]

16.24 Any failure by the local housing authority to comply with its statutory duty will be an error of law and is challengeable by judicial review proceedings.[31]

Power to accommodate pending a statutory review[32]

16.25 Some of the decisions made by a local housing authority on an application under HA 1996 Part 7 carry a right to a statutory review.[33] If the applicant requests a review of such a decision, the local housing authority has a power, but not a duty, to secure accommodation until the review has been concluded.[34]

16.26 That power can be exercised irrespective of the nature of the decision which is being reviewed (provided it is a decision which may be subject to statutory review) and regardless of whether the applicant has previously been secured with any accommodation (interim or otherwise) by the local housing authority.

16.27 The local housing authority is not required automatically to consider the exercise of the power every time it receives a request for review. An applicant who wants interim accommodation, pending a decision on the review, should ask for it. There is no need for the request to be made in writing or on any particular form.

16.28 Once a request has been made, a local housing authority that refuses even to consider, or simply fails to consider, the exercise of its power would be acting unlawfully and may be vulnerable to a judicial review challenge.[35] Likewise, a local housing authority which decided never to exercise the discretionary power to accommodate pending review would be unlawfully fettering that discretion.

16.29 Busy local housing authorities, receiving large numbers of requests for reviews, may receive almost as many requests for accommodation pending decisions on those reviews. Although each such application must be given individual consideration, local housing authorities may draw up and apply policies governing the circumstances when they will exercise their power to secure such accommodation. Local housing authorities that adopt policies

---

30 See **16.80–16.84**. Issues relating to the cost, quality, location or terms of the occupation of the accommodation secured under the initial interim duty are discussed at **16.51–16.75**.
31 See **16.89** and **19.211–19.237**.
32 HA 1996, s 188(3).
33 HA 1996, s 202(1) provides an exhaustive list. See also **19.8–19.35**.
34 HA 1996, ss 188(3) and 195(8).
35 For challenges to a refusal to exercise the power, see **16.790–16.113**.

restricting the provision of discretionary accommodation pending review to 'exceptional circumstances' are not necessarily acting unlawfully. But any such policy must be flexible enough to ensure that individual consideration is given to the circumstances of each applicant requesting accommodation pending review.[36]

16.30 It is not unlawful for the decision-maker who made the original HA 1996, s 184(1) decision also to make the decision as to whether or not accommodation will be secured pending a statutory review.[37]

16.31 When a local housing authority considers the individual circumstances of each applicant, it must take into account:

- the strength of the applicant's case on review;

- whether any new material, information or argument has been raised since the initial decision was made;

- the personal circumstances of the applicant;

- the consequences for the applicant if accommodation is not secured; and

- any other relevant considerations.[38]

The task of taking into account these various factors is often referred to as the '*Mohammed* balancing exercise' (after the name of the case in which the factors were set out).[39]

16.32 Where a local housing authority has been provided with new information (in the sense that it was not available when the initial decision was made), the officer considering the request for interim accommodation pending review should consider the extent to which that material affects the strength of the applicant's case on review.[40] In deciding whether to exercise its power to secure accommodation pending review, a local housing authority is also entitled to take into account the demands on its resources involved in securing interim accommodation, the scarcity of accommodation and the demand for accommodation from other homeless applicants (provided that it does also consider the applicant's individual circumstances).[41]

---

[36] English Code, paras 15.12–15.20; Welsh Code, paras 21.20–21.24 provide guidance.
[37] *R (Abdi) v Lambeth London Borough Council* [2007] EWHC 1681 (Admin), [2008] HLR 5, Admin Ct.
[38] *R v Camden London Borough Council ex p Mohammed* (1998) 30 HLR 315, QBD and *R v Newham London Borough Council ex p Lumley* (2001) 33 HLR 11, QBD.
[39] *R v Camden London Borough Council ex p Mohammed* (1998) 30 HLR 315, QBD.
[40] *R v Newham London Borough Council ex p Lumley* (2001) 33 HLR 11, QBD.
[41] *R (Cole) v Enfield London Borough Council* [2003] EWHC 1454 (Admin), (2003) August *Legal Action*, p 32, Admin Ct. For an example of a local housing authority correctly applying the '*Mohammed* factors', see *R (Lusamba) v Islington London borough Council* [2008] EWHC 1149 (Admin), (2008) July *Legal Action*, p 22, Admin Ct.

16.33 In *R (Paul-Coker) v Southwark London Borough Council*,[42] the local housing authority had decided that the applicant was not eligible because she was not habitually resident.[43] She requested accommodation pending a review and her solicitors made a number of representations, both in relation to her personal circumstances and by providing new information that could have an effect on the review decision. The Administrative Court held that 'there was a complete absence of any explanation or reasoning in the decision letter dealing with these various important aspects of the case' and that the local housing authority, whilst referring to the *Mohammed* balancing exercise, had actually only paid 'lip-service' to it.[44]

16.34 This decision reminds local housing authorities that 'lip-service' is not good enough. They must actually consider the representations made in support of the request for accommodation and consider them in relation to the *Mohammed* factors.

16.35 The benefit of the power to secure accommodation pending a statutory review, and pending an appeal to the county court, is not available to nationals of other European Economic Area (EEA) states, refugees given refugee status by other states (including EEA states), former asylum-seekers who have failed to co-operate with removal directions, people who are unlawfully present in the UK, or to failed asylum-seekers with dependent children, unless the local housing authority decides that securing accommodation is necessary in order to prevent breach of the applicant's rights under the European Convention on Human Rights or under European Union law.[45] If accommodation is requested for former asylum-seekers who have failed to co-operate with removal directions, those who are unlawfully present in the UK, or for certain failed asylum-seekers with dependent children, local housing authorities are required to inform the Home Office.[46]

16.36 Any refusal to secure accommodation under this power can only be challenged if there is an error of law. Challenges are brought by judicial review proceedings.[47]

---

[42] [2006] EWHC 497 (Admin), [2006] HLR 32, Admin Ct.

[43] See **12.136–12.141**.

[44] *R (Paul-Coker) v Southwark London Borough Council* [2006] EWHC 497 (Admin), [2006] HLR 32, Admin Ct, at [49], per Forbes J.

[45] Nationality Immigration and Asylum Act 2002, Sch 3, para 3; see **16.41**, **20.46–20.48** and **20.65–20.72**, and English Code, para 15.3. See also *R (Mohammed) v Harrow London Borough Council* [2005] EWHC 3194 (Admin), [2006] HLR 18, Admin Ct, where the local housing authority's decision that accommodation was not 'necessary' to avoid a breach of European Union rights, as the claimant was not a worker or work-seeker and therefore not exercising those rights, contained no error of law.

[46] Nationality Immigration Asylum Act 2002, Sch 3, para 14; English Code, para 9.24. It is unlikely that any of those classes of people would be eligible for assistance. See Chapter 12.

[47] See **16.90–16.98** and **19.211–19.237**.

Power to secure accommodation pending an appeal to the county court[48]

16.37　Review decisions (and original decisions which can be subject to a statutory review) can be appealed to the county court.[49] The fact that an applicant might lodge or has lodged an appeal does not impose a duty on the local housing authority to accommodate the applicant pending the hearing of that appeal. Sadly, in many areas appeals cannot be heard for some weeks or months after they are lodged.

16.38　However, there is a discretionary power available for the local housing authority to secure interim accommodation at two stages:

(1)　during the 21-day period between notification of the review decision and the normal deadline for issue of a county court appeal;[50] and/or

(2)　pending the determination of the appeal itself, once made.[51]

The power can *only* be used where the local housing authority has already either:[52]

(a)　owed one of the following duties to the applicant:
    (i)　the duty to secure initial interim accommodation;[53] or
    (ii)　the duty to secure accommodation for a reasonable period to an applicant found to have become homeless intentionally;[54] or
    (iii)　the duty to secure accommodation pending referral under the 'conditions for referral' provisions;[55] or

(b)　had (whether it exercised it or not) power to accommodate the applicant pending a review of a decision that, although in priority need, the applicant had become threatened with homelessness intentionally.[56]

16.39　The common thread running through the above list is that the applicant either has, or the local housing authority initially had reason to believe that he or she might have, a priority need. Where the local housing authority has not been subject to any of those duties or that power, there is no power under HA 1996, Part 7 for a local housing authority to secure accommodation pending appeal. Where the power is available, an applicant may invite the local housing authority to exercise it while an appeal is being considered, prepared, or later, once the appeal has been lodged.

---

[48]　HA 1996, s 204(4).
[49]　HA 1996, s 204(1). See **19.141–19.210**.
[50]　HA 1996, s 204(4)(a).
[51]　HA 1996, s 204(4)(b).
[52]　HA 1996, s 204(4).
[53]　HA 1996, s 188(1). See **16.11–16.24**.
[54]　HA 1996, s 190(2). See **17.111–17.118**.
[55]　HA 1996, s 200. See **15.136–15.139**.
[56]　HA 1996, s 195(8).

16.40 When considering whether or not to exercise a power to accommodate, pending appeal to the county court, a local housing authority should carry out the same balancing exercise as it is required to undertake when considering a request for accommodation pending review.[57] It should consider all the relevant circumstances, and any new information, material or argument. It is required to consider the applicant's grounds of appeal, as part of its consideration of the merits of the case, but would not normally be expected to refer to any of the grounds of appeal in its decision letter, unless there is some important and striking ground which requires specific comment.[58] In addition, it will need to consider the applicant's personal and household circumstances, along with the terms of any general policy governing its discretion (if any), and the resources available.[59]

16.41 This power to secure accommodation pending appeal to the county court is not available to nationals of other EEA states, refugees given refugee status by other EEA states, former asylum-seekers who have failed to co-operate with removal directions, people who are unlawfully present in the UK, or failed asylum-seekers with dependent children, unless the local housing authority considers it necessary in order to prevent a breach of rights under the European Convention on Human Rights or European Union law.[60]

16.42 Challenges to a local housing authority's refusal to secure accommodation pending the determination of the HA 1996, s 204 appeal are brought by a separate appeal, also on a point of law, to the county court under HA 1996, s 204A.[61]

Powers and duties to secure interim accommodation to applicants referred under the conditions for referral provisions

16.43 Whichever local housing authority an applicant applies to, if that local housing authority has reason to believe that the applicant may be homeless, eligible for assistance, and have a priority need, the duty to secure initial interim accommodation is triggered.[62] Interim accommodation must be

---

[57] See **16.29–16.34**.
[58] *Lewis v Havering London Borough Council* [2006] EWCA Civ 1793, [2007] HLR 20, CA.
[59] English Code, paras 15.21–15.24; Welsh Code, paras 14.87–14.101 and 21.33–21.36. For the possibility of challenging a refusal to accommodate pending appeal, see **16.99–16.113** and **19.191–19.200**.
[60] Nationality Immigration and Asylum Act 2002, s 54 and Sch 3, paras 1 and 3, in force from 8 January 2003; see **16.235** above, **20.46–20.48** and **20.65–20.72**, and English Code, para 15.3. If accommodation is requested by a former asylum-seeker who has failed to co-operate with removal directions, anyone unlawfully present in the UK or a failed asylum-seeker with dependent children, the local housing authority is under an obligation to inform the Home Office (Nationality, Immigration and Asylum Act 2002, Sch 3, para 14; English Code, para 9.24). In practice, there are very few people who might be eligible who would also fall within one of those three categories (see Chapter 12).
[61] See **16.99–16.113** and **19.191–19.200**.
[62] See **16.11–16.24**.

secured, irrespective of whether or not the applicant appears to have a local connection with the local housing authority.[63] That duty continues while it carries out its inquiries.

16.44 If the local housing authority's conclusion upon those inquiries is that the applicant:

(1)   is homeless; and

(2)   is eligible; and

(3)   has a priority need; and

(4)   did not become homeless intentionally,

it would normally be subject to the main housing duty.[64] But if it considers that the conditions for referral of that duty to another local housing authority are made out, it may notify the other local housing authority that it holds that opinion.[65] The notifying local housing authority ('the first local housing authority') must notify the applicant that it has notified, or intends to notify, another local housing authority ('the second local housing authority') of its opinion.[66]

16.45 The effect of these two notices is:

(a)   to bring to an end the initial interim duty to accommodate;[67] and

(b)   to defer the triggering of the HA 1996, s 193(2) main housing duty until the conditions for referral issue is resolved.[68]

16.46 HA 1996, Part 7, therefore, creates a further interim duty on the first local housing authority so that it is required to continue to accommodate the applicant.[69] That further interim duty, which has been triggered by a notice given to the applicant by the first local housing authority, ends only when the applicant receives a further notice from the first local housing authority. That further notice will contain the final decision (reached by agreement between the notified and notifying authorities) that the conditions of referral are, or are not, met. If there is a dispute between the two local housing authorities, the first local housing authority remains under the duty to secure interim accommodation until the dispute is resolved.

---

63   HA 1996, s 188(2).
64   HA 1996, s 193(2). See **17.21–17.108**.
65   HA 1996, s 198(1). See **15.125–15.129**.
66   HA 1996, s 184(4). See **15.130–15.133**.
67   By the notification to the applicant under HA 1996, ss 184(4) and 200(1).
68   HA 1996, s 200(1).
69   HA 1996, s 200(1). See English Code, paras 18.26–18.30; Welsh Code, paras 20.16–20.19.

16.47 If the applicant is notified of a decision that the conditions for referral are *not* met, then the interim duty falls away and is replaced by the main housing duty owed by the first local housing authority.[70]

16.48 If, however, the applicant is notified that both local housing authorities agree (or it has been determined by arbitration) that the conditions for referral *are* met, then the interim duty to accommodate on the first local housing authority comes to an end. The second local housing authority is then subject to a duty to secure accommodation for the applicant under the main housing duty at HA 1996, s 193(2).[71]

16.49 If the applicant requests a review of the decision to refer, and asks to remain in accommodation secured by the first local housing authority while the review is considered, the first local housing authority has no further duty but does have a discretionary power to continue to secure accommodation pending review and pending appeal to the county court.[72] The refusal to exercise that power cannot be subjected to a statutory review or an appeal to the courts. Any challenge would have to be by way of judicial review.[73]

16.50 Obviously, when the first local housing authority considers whether or not to exercise its discretion to secure interim accommodation in these circumstances, one of the factors that it will take into account is the fact that there is an existing duty on the second local housing authority to secure accommodation and that therefore, if the applicant is willing to take it up, he or she will no longer be homeless.

GENERAL ISSUES ABOUT INTERIM ACCOMMODATION

Interim accommodation for whom?

16.51 Where a local housing authority owes an interim accommodation duty, or exercises a power to secure interim accommodation, the accommodation secured must be 'available' for the applicant's occupation. This means not only 'available' in the practical sense (that the applicant must be able to get to it), but also in the technical sense of 'available' as accommodation both for the applicant and for members of his or her household.[74] In short, the accommodation secured must be capable of providing for:

---

[70]   HA 1996, s 200(3).
[71]   HA 1996, s 200(4).
[72]   HA 1996, ss 200(5) and 204(4).
[73]   An example of an unsuccessful application for permission to bring judicial review proceedings to challenge a local housing authority's decision not to secure accommodation pending review of a decision that the applicant should be referred to another local housing authority can be found at *R (Gebremarium) v Westminster City Council* [2009] EWHC 2254 (Admin), (2009) November *Legal Action*, p 26, Admin Ct.
[74]   HA 1996, s 176. This technical meaning of 'available' is fully discussed at **11.15–11.31**.

(1)   the applicant; and

(2)   those who normally live with the applicant as members of his or her family; and

(3)   any others with whom it is reasonable to expect him or her to reside.[75]

16.52 Therefore, the interim accommodation duty (or exercise of power) cannot be performed by securing separate units of interim accommodation in different buildings (e g rooms in two hotels some distance apart) for the same household. It could possibly be performed by securing adjoining or adjacent units of accommodation (such as separate rooms in the same building or two neighbouring houses).[76]

Suitable interim accommodation

16.53 Where the local housing authority falls under a duty to secure interim accommodation, or exercises a power to secure such accommodation, the accommodation actually secured must be 'suitable' for the applicant (a requirement additional to its being 'available' for his and her household).[77]

16.54 Whether or not the accommodation is 'suitable' is primarily a matter for the local housing authority, but consideration of suitability must focus on whether the accommodation is suitable for the particular applicant.[78] Factors relevant to that decision include:

(1)   the space and arrangement of the accommodation;

(2)   health and safety considerations;

(3)   the affordability of the accommodation;[79]

(4)   the location of it;

(5)   the applicant's medical and physical needs and those of his or her household;

(6)   other social considerations;

(7)   any risk of violence or racial harassment;

(8)   the need for security and a secret location for those fleeing domestic violence, including single-sex accommodation where necessary; and

---

[75]   HA 1996, s 176. See **11.19–11.31**.
[76]   *R v Ealing London Borough Council ex p Surdonja* (1998) 31 HLR 686, QBD.
[77]   HA 1996, ss 206 and 210. See also English Code, para 7.5; Welsh Code para 12.11.
[78]   The wording is 'suitable for a person': HA 1996, s 210(1).
[79]   Homelessness (Suitability of Accommodation) Order 1996, SI 1996/3204. See Appendix 2.

(9)   any other circumstances that may be relevant in a particular case.[80]

16.55   The fact that accommodation is being secured for an 'interim' period only is relevant to the local housing authority's decision as to whether or not it is suitable. Accommodation that would not be suitable in the long term may be suitable in the short term.[81] Obviously, the urgency of securing the accommodation is a relevant consideration. Whilst local housing authorities are entitled to maintain policies as to the way in which they will secure the provision of interim accommodation, they are still required to consider, in each and every case, whether the accommodation is in fact suitable for the individual needs of the applicant. There is a minimum standard of suitability below which the accommodation must not fall, regardless of the urgency of the situation and any shortage of resources experienced by the local housing authority.[82]

16.56   If the accommodation is unsuitable, the local housing authority is in breach of its duty. The duty to secure suitable interim accommodation is enforceable by judicial review. The applicant could apply for a mandatory order requiring the local housing authority to secure suitable accommodation forthwith. The local housing authority cannot rely on shortage of available accommodation or lack of resources as a defence to its failure to secure suitable accommodation. However, the courts have stressed that judicial review is a discretionary remedy, even where a local housing authority is in breach of its statutory duty. Applicants and their advisers should not be too quick to rush to court where a local housing authority is doing all that it reasonably can to meet its duty and the applicant is not physically homeless.[83]

Location of interim accommodation

16.57   The location of interim accommodation is obviously relevant to the question of whether or not it is suitable. Applicants may need accommodation to be in a particular area or district in order to be able to take their children to school, to get to work or to college, to ensure that their children have contact with any non-resident parent, or just to keep in touch with family and friends.[84] Likewise, there may be a need to be near a particular medical facility. Clearly, the length of time that the applicant may expect to be in interim accommodation is also relevant to the question of whether the location of the accommodation renders it unsuitable.

---

80   English Code, paras 17.1–17.8; Welsh Code, chapter 19.
81   English Code, para 17.7.
82   *R v Newham London Borough Council ex p Ojuri (No 2)* (1998) 31 HLR 452, QBD, and *R v Newham London Borough Council ex p Sacupima* [2001] 1 WLR 563, (2001) 33 HLR 2, CA.
83   *R v Newham London Borough Council ex p Sacupima* [2001] 1 WLR 563, (2001) 33 HLR 2, CA. See English Code, para 7.5.
84   See *R v Newham London Borough Council ex p Ojuri (No 2)* (1998) 31 HLR 452, QBD; *R v Newham London Borough Council ex p Sacupima* (2001) 33 HLR 2, CA; and *R (Yumsak) v Enfield London Borough Council* [2002] EWHC 280 (Admin), (2003) 35 HLR 1, Admin Ct, for examples of all these difficulties.

16.58   Local housing authorities are required by HA 1996, Part 7 to secure interim accommodation in their own districts, so far as that is reasonably practicable.[85] If a local housing authority does accommodate homeless applicants outside its own district (because there is no reasonably practicable way of accommodating them in its own district), it is required formally to notify the local housing authority for the district in which the applicant has been placed.[86] This duty to notify applies even to the most minimal period of interim accommodation. The notification must be in writing and contain certain information prescribed by HA 1996, s 208(3). It must be given within 14 days from the accommodation being made available to the applicant. It is therefore an additional administrative deterrent to making placements out-of-district.

16.59   The Codes recommend that households who need social services support or have links with other essential services such as specialist medical services or special schools should be given priority for accommodation within the local housing authority's own district.[87]

16.60   Even when the conditions for placement outside local housing authorities' own districts are legitimately fulfilled, local housing authorities are not relieved of their continuing duties under HA 1996, Part 7 simply by placing applicants outside their own districts. The applicants continue to be the responsibility of the local housing authority to which they applied. However, if a local housing authority decides that it no longer owes a duty to secure interim accommodation for the applicant, and the applicant then needs help from social services, that help will be available from the social services department of the local housing authority for the district where he or she was actually residing in the interim accommodation.[88]

Type of interim accommodation

16.61   A local housing authority which is subject to a duty to secure interim accommodation (or is using its powers to secure such accommodation) is not

---

85   HA 1996, s 208(1): this provision was not in the Housing (Homeless Persons) Act 1977 or the Housing Act 1985, but was introduced in HA 1996, Part 7 to bring an end to the phenomenon of local housing authorities routinely placing applicants in other local housing authorities' districts, either because there was no accommodation available within a local housing authority's own district or, more commonly, simply because accommodation in other districts could be secured more cheaply. In *R (Calgin) v Enfield London Borough Council* ([2005] EWHC 1716 (Admin), [2006] HLR 4, Admin Ct, the Administrative Court held that, when considering whether it is 'reasonably practicable' to secure accommodation in its own district, a local housing authority is entitled to have regard to any financial savings that might be achieved by out-of-borough placements.

86   See **15.205–15.211, 18.50–18.52**; HA 1996, s 208(2)–(4); English Code, paras 16.7–16.9; Welsh Code, paras 18.9–18.14.

87   English Code, para 16.9; Welsh Code, para 18.13.

88   *R (Stewart) v Hammersmith and Fulham London Borough Council, Wandsworth London Borough Council and Lambeth London Borough Council* [2001] EWHC 709 (Admin), (2001) 4 CCLR 466, Admin Ct.

obliged to provide the applicant with council housing.[89] It may secure accommodation in any of the three ways open to it in performing any housing function under HA 1996, Part 7.[90] The three ways are explored in more detail in Chapter 18[91] but are, in summary:

(1) by providing accommodation itself;

(2) by arranging for someone else to secure accommodation; or

(3) by giving the applicant such advice and assistance as secures that accommodation is made available by someone else.

16.62 If the local housing authority is securing interim accommodation itself (option (1)), such accommodation would most likely be a place in a council-run hostel, a tenancy of a short-life council property, or some other non-secure council housing.[92]

16.63 If interim accommodation is being secured under options (2) or (3), it will often be in a hotel or hostel run privately or by a voluntary organisation, or a letting on a short-term tenancy from a private landlord or housing association. In the latter case, applicants are often offered what purport to be assured shorthold tenancies, although, as a matter of law, they cannot be any form of assured tenancy at all, not even an assured shorthold tenancy, unless the landlord notifies the applicant that the tenancy is to be regarded as an assured or assured shorthold tenancy.[93]

16.64 Generally, these arrangements for interim accommodation are unlikely to be subject to the Protection from Eviction Act 1977 and so can be terminated by the landlord upon reasonable notice.[94]

16.65 The various different ways in which the accommodation functions can be met are explored in more detail in Chapter 18, but there are two arrangements which are particularly common ways of securing interim accommodation. They are the arrangements commonly referred to as 'homeless at home' and 'bed and breakfast'.

'Homeless at home'

16.66 Many applications under HA 1996, Part 7 are made by individuals who have been asked to leave the homes of friends or relatives with whom they have

---

[89] Indeed, the English Code contains guidance that it would not generally be appropriate for social housing to be used as temporary accommodation (English Code, paras 16.6 and 16.12).

[90] HA 1996, s 206(1).

[91] See **18.7–18.9**.

[92] Under Housing Act 1985, Sch 1, para 4, none of those would amount to the grant of a secure tenancy or licence. See English Code, paras 16.11–16.14; Welsh Code, paras 18.15–18.19.

[93] HA 1996, s 209(2). English Code, paras 16.15–16.16; Welsh Code, paras 18.20–18.21.

[94] *Desnousse v Newham London Borough Council* [2006] EWCA Civ 547, [2006] HLR 38, CA; English Code, para 7.11.

been staying. An applicant who indicates that he or she has been asked to leave such accommodation plainly gives a local housing authority 'reason to believe' that he or she 'may' be homeless. If there is reason to believe that he or she may also be eligible and may have a priority need, then the duty to secure interim accommodation is triggered.[95]

16.67   In that situation the local housing authority may consider performing its interim duty by arranging[96] for the friend or relative to provide further accommodation, at least until it concludes its inquiries and notifies its decision to the applicant. Often friends or relatives are prepared to do this, on the assumption (which is not always correct) that this will only be for a matter of days. From the applicant's perspective, remaining there may be more attractive than other forms of interim accommodation that the local housing authority might provide. For obvious reasons, this common form of performance of the interim accommodation duty is called 'homeless at home'.

16.68   The arrangement is not altogether easy to square with the scheme of HA 1996, Part 7, not least because the readiness of the friend/relative to accommodate may suggest that there was no homelessness or threat of homelessness in the first place (or that the original request to leave was part of an arrangement to take advantage of HA 1996, Part 7).[97]

16.69   However, in practice these issues are overlooked. 'Homeless at home' has been a feature of the provision of interim accommodation for homeless applicants for over 20 years. Furthermore, even though local housing authorities make substantial savings by performing their duty in this way, rather than by paying for alternative forms of accommodation, it is very rare for a local housing authority to offer or pay anything to friends or relatives for providing this service.

16.70   It is important that the 'homeless at home' arrangement is made in the correct way. The accommodation must be 'secured' by the local housing authority.[98] It is not sufficient for an applicant to be told 'go back and see if they will let you stay until we make our decision'. It is for the local housing authority to ensure that accommodation is available, not for the applicant to take a chance that it might be.

16.71   Plainly, the local housing authority must also make sufficient investigations to satisfy itself that the 'homeless at home' arrangement can secure 'suitable' accommodation for the applicant.[99]

16.72   A driving force behind the popularity of 'homeless at home' has been the applicant's fear that the only alternative interim arrangement will be bed

---

[95]   HA 1996, s 188(1). See also **16.11–16.24**.
[96]   Under options (2) or (3) at **16.61**.
[97]   See **11.2–11.117**.
[98]   HA 1996, ss 188(1) and 206(1).
[99]   See Chapter 18.

and breakfast accommodation. With that form of provision effectively outlawed for applicants with family commitments, the future of 'homeless at home' may be thought uncertain.[100]

16.73 Where an applicant has made his or her application for homelessness assistance on the basis that he or she has accommodation available, but that accommodation is not reasonable for him or her to continue to occupy,[101] it may still be suitable for the purposes of securing interim accommodation. That is because the local housing authority is required to consider whether the accommodation is not reasonable to continue to occupy over time, even though the applicant could remain there in the short term.[102] However, if the accommodation is not reasonable for the applicant to continue to occupy for one more night, then it will not be suitable accommodation and the local housing authority should secure an alternative form of accommodation in performance of its interim duty.

'Bed and breakfast' and other 'shared accommodation'

16.74 Local housing authorities are advised against using bed and breakfast accommodation for the provision of interim accommodation to any homeless applicant, except on the rare occasions when it may be the most appropriate option for that particular applicant.[103]

16.75 In both England and Wales, there are now statutory instruments that deem bed and breakfast accommodation and, in the case of Wales, other shared accommodation, not to be suitable accommodation for certain applicants and with certain exceptions. Suitability of bed and breakfast accommodation is discussed in Chapter 18.[104]

Rejection of the accommodation (explicit or implied)

16.76 Where interim accommodation is secured for an applicant (whether under a power or a duty) the applicant is, of course, under no obligation to accept it. In particular, an applicant offered initial interim accommodation may (on receiving the details of it) prefer to make other arrangements pending the local housing authority's decision on his or her application. That will bring the local housing authority's initial interim accommodation duty to an end (unless it is revived by any change of circumstances), because it is not obliged to hold open accommodation that the applicant has rejected. Importantly, however, the duty to inquire into the application is *not* brought to an end by the rejection of

---

[100] Homelessness (Suitability of Accommodation) (England) Order 2003, SI 2003/3326 (see **18.99–18.104**) and Homelessness (Suitability of Accommodation) (Wales) Order 2006, SI 2006/650 (W 71) (see **18.105–18.113**).

[101] HA 1996, ss 175 and 176; see **11.72–11.117**.

[102] *Ali & others v Birmingham City Council, Moran v Manchester City Council* [2009] UKHL 36, [2009] 1 WLR 1506, HL.

[103] English Code, paras 7.6, 16.28 and 17.24–17.38; Welsh Code, paras 18.41–18.44.

[104] See **18.93–18.113**.

interim accommodation. Indeed, the outcome of those inquiries might well be affected by the results of the applicant's own attempts to meet interim accommodation needs. If he or she finds anything other than crisis accommodation,[105] then he or she will not be 'homeless' at the date of decision. On the other hand, detriment to the applicant resulting from a failure to secure anything other than crisis accommodation may help demonstrate that an applicant is 'vulnerable' and for that reason has a priority need.[106]

16.77 Local housing authorities must ensure that the applicant has actually rejected the accommodation before deciding that their initial accommodation duty has come to an end. One local housing authority was subject to judicial review proceedings when it refused to secure further accommodation, insisting that the applicant had rejected the accommodation, after the applicant had arrived at the accommodation a day late.[107]

16.78 Having taken up occupation of the interim accommodation, the applicant may, of course, subsequently reject it. Again, that will release the local housing authority from the accommodation duty. Rejection may be express or implied. For example, the applicant could simply walk out (and not return). Or the applicant's conduct might manifest a rejection of the accommodation, if, for example, the applicant flouts the terms on which the accommodation is available or, in extreme cases, damages or destroys the accommodation. Where the local housing authority is minded to treat the applicant's behaviour as an implied rejection, it should normally give the applicant a warning and an opportunity to provide an explanation for his or her conduct.[108] Particular sensitivity is needed when the applicant is in poor mental health (a phenomenon that is not infrequent, given the stressful nature of homelessness).

16.79 An applicant who rejects initial interim accommodation before having taken up occupation of it will not, for that reason, have become homeless intentionally.[109]

Termination of the accommodation

16.80 Once a duty to secure interim accommodation has ended, or a local housing authority decides that it will no longer exercise a power to secure interim accommodation, the applicant's legal right to occupation of the accommodation may need to be brought to an end.

---

[105] See **11.2–11.117**.
[106] See **13.62–13.99**.
[107] *R (Carstens) v Basildon District Council* (2006) CO/923/2006, (2007) September *Legal Action*, p 18, Admin Ct.
[108] *R v Kensington and Chelsea Royal London Borough Council ex p Kujtim* [1999] 4 All ER 161, (2000) 32 HLR 579, CA.
[109] See **14.83–14.101**.

16.81   The length of any notice period that the applicant is entitled to receive if he or she is required to leave the interim accommodation depends first on the terms of the licence or tenancy under which she or he has been occupying it. She or he cannot be excluded on shorter notice than is provided for in that tenancy or licence agreement.

16.82   However, almost by definition, any agreement for occupation of 'interim' accommodation will provide for quite short notice. Ordinarily, whatever the agreement itself says, those tenancies and licences that fall within the scope of the Protection from Eviction Act 1977 can only be terminated by the landlord on at least 4 weeks' written notice and the landlord will require a possession order from the court before he or she is entitled to obtain possession. But much of the accommodation secured as interim accommodation is provided under licences excluded from that protection.[110] In particular, a licence to occupy a local authority hostel is excluded from protection,[111] and so all the local housing authority or its manager need do is give the applicant reasonable notice to leave.[112]

16.83   Even in respect of the types of accommodation which might otherwise ordinarily fall within the scope of the Protection from Eviction Act 1977 (such as self-contained accommodation), the courts have not been inclined to apply the provisions of the Protection from Eviction Act 1977 to interim accommodation which is occupied under a licence. The approach taken has been that it is incompatible with a scheme for interim accommodation that the occupier should be entitled to 4 weeks' notice and then to the benefit of the further inevitable delay while possession is obtained through the courts.[113] However, the courts have so far left unanswered the question of whether interim accommodation occupied under a tenancy should be subject to the Protection from Eviction Act 1977.[114] After all, if Parliament had intended to exclude interim accommodation from the benefit of the Protection from Eviction Act 1977, it could easily have done so by amending that Act when it introduced HA 1996, Part 7.

16.84   Even if there is no minimum notice required and no need to obtain a possession order, this does not mean that the local housing authority can simply eject applicants accommodated on an interim basis. Local housing authorities must act reasonably, as any public authority would. The obligation to behave reasonably requires that the applicant be given at least some opportunity to find some other accommodation before the interim

---

[110]   Protection from Eviction Act 1977, s 3A lists exclusions.
[111]   Protection from Eviction Act 1977, s 3A(8).
[112]   *Minister of Health v Bellotti* [1944] 1 KB 298, CA.
[113]   *Mohammed v Manek and Kensington and Chelsea Royal London Borough Council* (1995) 27 HLR 439, CA; *Gibson v Paddington Churches Housing Association* (2003) November *Legal Action*, p 16, Central London County Court; and *Desnousse v Newham London Borough Council* [2006] EWCA Civ 547, [2006] HLR 38, CA.
[114]   *Desnousse v Newham London Borough Council* [2006] EWCA Civ 547, [2006] HLR 38, CA, at [69], per Lloyd LJ.

accommodation is withdrawn.[115] Reasonable notice in those circumstances should obviously be more than 24 hours[116] and periods of 6 or 7 days have also been held to be too short to constitute reasonable notice.[117] In a case in which the right to occupy interim accommodation was ended by new legislation, a judge suggested that the reasonable notice ought to be at least the period the local housing authority would have given to a person found to have become homeless intentionally.[118]

ENFORCEMENT OF DUTIES (AND CHALLENGES TO REFUSALS TO EXERCISE POWERS) TO SECURE INTERIM ACCOMMODATION

16.85 None of the decisions that a local housing authority might make in relation to its powers or duties to secure 'interim' accommodation can be subject to the statutory review procedure. None of the following decisions about the provision of interim accommodation, which may be among the most critical to be made concerning an applicant, are covered by the statutory review procedure:

(1)   a decision that no duty is owed;

(2)   a decision that a power will not be exercised;

(3)   a decision as to how a duty will be performed or a power exercised;

(4)   a decision as to which members of the applicant's household will be accommodated under the duty or the exercise of the power; and

(5)   a decision as to whether the interim accommodation is suitable.

16.86 There is no statutory obligation to notify the applicant of these decisions (in writing or otherwise), nor is there a statutory obligation to give reasons for those decisions.[119]

16.87 Although these decisions, if disputed, could be the subject of a formal complaint to the local housing authority under its complaints procedure and

---

[115]   *R v Secretary of State for the Environment ex p Shelter* [1997] COD 49, QBD, applied in *R v Newham London Borough Council ex p Ojuri (No 3)* (1999) 31 HLR 631, QBD. English Code, paras 7.10–7.12.

[116]   *R v Newham London Borough Council ex p Ojuri (No 3)* (1999) 31 HLR 631, QBD.

[117]   *R v Newham London Borough Council ex p Pembele* (1999) January *Legal Action*, p 27, QBD; *R v Westminster City Council ex p Abdulkadir* (1999) August *Legal Action*, p 29, QBD, although in *R v Newham London Borough Council ex p Lumley* (2001) 33 HLR 11, QBD, it was said obiter that 6 clear days' notice would not be unreasonable for a young single man.

[118]   *R v Secretary of State for the Environment ex p Shelter* [1997] COD 49, QBD, per Carnwath J.

[119]   It is obviously good administrative practice for decisions to be recorded in writing and, where appropriate, to be explained by written reasons.

(ultimately) to the Local Government Ombudsman,[120] the applicant will usually need the urgent provision of accommodation, and this can only be obtained (if at all) by a legal challenge to the decision.

16.88 Any challenge to the suitability of accommodation secured under any of these duties or powers to secure interim accommodation can only be brought by judicial review.[121] There is no right to request a statutory review of the suitability of interim accommodation and no appeal to the county court on such an issue.

Refusal to comply with a statutory duty

16.89 When the local housing authority is failing to comply with its acknowledged statutory duty, the position is relatively straightforward. Although the applicant cannot sue in the ordinary way for damages and for an injunction to compel the local housing authority to perform its duty,[122] he or she is not left without recourse to the courts. If the local housing authority fails to secure interim accommodation when it is under a duty to do so, the appropriate procedure is to bring a claim for judicial review,[123] including an application for both an interim and final mandatory order requiring the local housing authority to comply with its statutory duty.

Refusal to exercise power to secure accommodation pending review

16.90 Where a local housing authority has:

- failed to consider a request for accommodation pending review; or

- refused to secure accommodation pending a review; or

- decided to secure accommodation for a limited period only; or

- decided to withdraw accommodation that had been secured pending the review, before the notification of the review decision,

the appropriate avenue for the applicant to challenge any of these decisions is to bring a claim by way of judicial review. In order to succeed, the applicant must show that the local housing authority's decision (or failure to make one) was wrong in law.

16.91 Challenges to local housing authorities' decisions not to exercise a discretionary power are generally much more difficult for the applicant than challenges for breach of statutory duty. The courts can be particularly reluctant

---

[120] See **19.238–19.245**.
[121] See **19.211–19.237**.
[122] *O'Rourke v Camden London Borough Council* [1998] AC 188, HL.
[123] The procedure is explained at **19.213–19.219**.

to intervene where Parliament has left local housing authorities free of duties and enjoying a discretion to exercise (or not exercise) powers.

16.92 The principles that a local housing authority must consider when deciding whether or not to secure accommodation pending review are set out in *R v Camden London Borough Council ex p Mohammed*.[124]

16.93 On applying for permission to bring a claim by way of judicial review, the applicant can also apply for an interim injunction requiring the local housing authority to secure accommodation pending the determination of the judicial review proceedings. The test that the Administrative Court will apply in considering whether or not to make an interim injunction is two-fold:

- the merits of the claim for judicial review; and

- the balance of convenience.[125]

The onus is on the applicant to show a strong prima facie case, where he or she is applying for an interim injunction.[126]

16.94 In cases of emergency, where the applicant is or is about to be street homeless, an application for an interim injunction can be made out of hours and over the telephone to a duty judge. In *R (Lawer) v Restormel Borough Council*,[127] the applicant's legal representatives were reminded of the importance of their duty, in those situations, to make full and frank disclosure of all the relevant documents to the judge, that applications in these circumstances are exceptional, and that there should always have been compliance with the pre-action protocol in judicial review claims and service on the local housing authority's legal department.[128]

16.95 In practice, if the Administrative Court judge considers that the claim for judicial review has merit, the balance of convenience is likely to be in favour of making an interim injunction, since otherwise the applicant would be homeless.

16.96 Many judicial review claims against refusals to secure interim accommodation are disposed of at the time of, or shortly after, consideration of whether or not permission should be granted to bring the claim. If permission is refused, unless there is to be an appeal, that is the end of the matter for the applicant. If permission is granted, and an interim injunction made requiring

---

[124]	*R v Camden London Borough Council ex p Mohammed* (1998) 30 HLR 315, QBD. See also **16.31**, and English Code, paras 15.12–15.20; Welsh Code, paras 21.20–21.24.
[125]	*American Cyanamid Co v Ethicon Ltd* [1975] AC 396, HL; and *R v Kensington & Chelsea Royal London Borough Council ex parte Hammell* [1989] 1 QB 518, CA.
[126]	*R (Omatoyo) v City of Westminster Council* [2006] EWHC 2572 (Admin), (2006) December *Legal Action*, p 21, Admin Ct.
[127]	[2007] EWHC 2299 (Admin), [2008] HLR 20, Admin Ct.
[128]	See **19.220–19.225**.

the local housing authority to accommodate the applicant until the judicial review claim has been determined,[129] many local housing authorities will then agree to accommodate pending review. Even if there is no agreement, it is not unusual for the review decision to be notified to the applicant before the judicial review claim has been finally heard, and so the claim for judicial review becomes academic.

16.97 If the judicial review claim does proceed to a full hearing, the claim might be dismissed (if there is no error of law). If the claim succeeds, and the Administrative Court decides that the local housing authority did make an error of law in one or more of its decisions, it can set the decision aside (a 'quashing order'). The local housing authority will either have to reconsider its decision or the Administrative Court may make a mandatory order requiring the local housing authority to secure accommodation until the review decision has been notified to the applicant.

16.98 The *Paul-Coker*[130] case is an example of the Administrative Court deciding that a local housing authority, when it referred to the criteria involved in the *Mohammed* balancing-exercise, was in fact paying 'lip-service' to them. The refusal to exercise the power to secure accommodation in that case was unlawful.

Refusal to exercise a power to secure accommodation pending appeal

16.99 If the local housing authority refuses to secure accommodation pending appeal (or if it decides to secure accommodation for a limited period only), there is no right to a statutory review of that decision. Instead, the applicant has the right to appeal against that refusal. The appeal lies to the county court on a point of law.[131] To distinguish this appeal from the main or substantive appeal (usually brought against the review decision of the local housing authority) it is described in the paragraphs that follow as the 'accommodation appeal'.

16.100 The principles that a local housing authority must consider when deciding whether or not to secure accommodation pending appeal are set out in *R v Camden London Borough Council ex p Mohammed*.[132]

---

[129] Permission is granted where there is a reasonably arguable case. An interim mandatory injunction requires a strong prima facie case. The fact that permission has been granted, whilst not determinative, is certainly a relevant factor when the court considers whether an interim injunction should continue (*R (Omatoyo) v City of Westminster Council* [2006] EWHC 2572 (Admin), (2006) December *Legal Action*, p 21, Admin Ct).

[130] *R (Paul-Coker) v Southwark London Borough Council* [2006] EWHC 497 (Admin), [2006] HLR 32, Admin Ct; and see **16.33–16.34**.

[131] HA 1996, s 204A(2). See **19.191–19.200**.

[132] *R v Camden London Borough Council ex p Mohammed* (1998) 30 HLR 315, QBD. See also **16.31**, and English Code, paras 15.21–15.24; Welsh Code, paras 21.25–21.32.

16.101   The accommodation appeal may be against:

(1)   the refusal to accommodate at all pending appeal; or

(2)   a decision to exercise the power to accommodate only for a limited period; or

(3)   a decision to withdraw accommodation that had been secured pending appeal.[133]

16.102   There is no appeal on the facts. The applicant must show that the local housing authority's refusal, decision or withdrawal was wrong in law. The court will adopt the principles applied generally in judicial review claims when it considers the lawfulness of the local housing authority's decision-making.[134]

16.103   Prior to 30 September 2002, challenges to refusals to secure accommodation pending appeal were brought by way of judicial review.[135] The Court of Appeal had held that if the guidance given in *R v Camden London Borough Council ex p Mohammed*[136] had been followed by a local housing authority, when considering whether or not to secure accommodation pending appeal, challenges to the exercise of that discretion were likely to be futile, and applications for judicial review should only be brought in exceptional cases. The appropriate step for an applicant without accommodation was to seek to expedite the hearing of his or her substantive appeal, rather than challenge the refusal to accommodate pending appeal.[137]

16.104   The Court of Appeal has taken the same approach now that challenges to refusals are brought by way of a county court appeal rather than by way of judicial review.[138] If the local housing authority has properly directed itself in accordance with the *Mohammed* principles,[139] the court will not intervene. The county court hearing an accommodation appeal should not embark on a consideration of the merits of the main or main or substantive appeal.

---

[133]   HA 1996, s 204A(2).

[134]   HA 1996, s 204A(4)(b). See **19.151–19.157**.

[135]   *Ali v Westminster City Council* [1999] 1 WLR 384, (1999) 31 HLR 349, CA.

[136]   *R v Camden London Borough Council ex p Mohammed* (1998) 30 HLR 315, QBD. See also **16.31**.

[137]   *R v Brighton and Hove Borough Council ex p Nacion* (1999) 31 HLR 1095, CA.

[138]   *Francis v Kensington and Chelsea Royal London Borough Council* [2003] EWCA Civ 443, [2003] 35 HLR 50, CA; and *Brookes v Croydon London Borough Council* [2004] EWCA Civ 439, (2004) June *Legal Action*, p 31, CA.

[139]   *R v Camden London Borough Council ex p Mohammed* (1998) 30 HLR 315, QBD. See also **16.31**.

16.105 If the local housing authority has not properly directed itself, then the court will quash the decision and will consider whether it should exercise its power to order the local housing authority to secure accommodation pending appeal.[140]

16.106 This decision, in *Francis v Kensington & Chelsea Royal London Borough Council*,[141] begs the question as to what 'properly directed itself' means. Certainly, where a local housing authority fails to consider, at all, a request for accommodation pending appeal, it cannot be said to have properly considered the right factors, and must therefore have erred in law. Conversely, where a local housing authority has set out the *Mohammed* factors and carefully considered each of those, along with any other points raised by the applicant, then the decision is unlikely to be wrong in law.

16.107 In practice, the decision in *Francis* means that accommodation appeals may now be rarely brought, but in the rare cares in which they may justifiably be brought they may well succeed.[142]

16.108 If the accommodation appeal succeeds, the court may quash the decision appealed against. At that point, the court may either refer the matter back to the local housing authority for re-consideration of the request for accommodation pending appeal, or it may make an order requiring the local housing authority to secure accommodation. It can only make the latter order if it is satisfied that:

'... failure to exercise the section 204(4) power in accordance with the order would substantially prejudice the applicant's ability to pursue the main appeal.'[143]

16.109 This is a strikingly different test from that governing the local housing authority's own exercise of discretion. The determinative factor for the court can only be the ability of the applicant to pursue his or her main or substantive appeal with or without the provision of accommodation. Whilst an applicant's other personal circumstances may be relevant, they cannot be determinative.

16.110 An order to accommodate made by the court cannot extend beyond the conclusion of the main appeal. In other words, the county court has no jurisdiction to order the provision of accommodation pending any further appeal beyond the county court.

16.111 Accommodation appeals, like main or substantive appeals, can only be heard by a circuit judge.[144]

---

[140] See also **19.200**.
[141] [2003] EWCA Civ 443, [2003] 35 HLR 50, CA.
[142] As did *Onyaebor v Newham London Borough Council* (2004) May *Legal Action*, p 27, Bow County Court.
[143] HA 1996, s 204A(6).
[144] CPR 1998, Pt 2, PD2B, para 9.

16.112   Applications for interim orders, requiring the provision of accommodation pending determination of the accommodation appeal, can be made before the full accommodation appeal is heard. A judge hearing an interlocutory application will have to decide:

(1)   whether there is an arguable error of law in the decision being appealed against; and, if so,

(2)   whether, arguably, the ability of the applicant to pursue his or her main appeal would be substantially prejudiced if accommodation were not secured.

16.113   An interim order can only be made if the judge takes the view that both of those points are arguable by the applicant, and that the balance of convenience favours the making of an interim order.[145]

Compensation claims

16.114   Where a local housing authority wrongly fails to secure interim accommodation, in breach of its statutory duty so to do, the applicant cannot sue for compensation for loss, in the normal way, in respect of that breach of statutory duty[146] nor can he or she recover damages for that breach as an ancillary remedy in a claim by way of judicial review.[147] Nor can the applicant recover damages for any breach of the right to respect for his or her home[148] because, by definition, she or he has, at this point, no home to 'respect'. The right of 'respect for his home' does not encompass a right to a home.[149] There may be a legal right to compensation[150] if the breach of duty reduces the applicant to circumstances amounting to inhuman or degrading treatment,[151] or infringes his or her right to respect for private or family life.[152]

16.115   The absence of a general right to compensation in these circumstances makes it even more important that the applicant promptly obtains a mandatory order in judicial review proceedings requiring the local housing authority to perform its duty. Normally, any financial or other loss caused in the period before an order is obtained could only be recovered through a complaint under

---

[145]   HA 1996, s 204(4)(a).

[146]   *O'Rourke v Camden London Borough Council* [1998] AC 188, HL.

[147]   *R v Ealing London Borough Council ex p Parkinson* (1997) 29 HLR 179, QBD, per Laws J.

[148]   Protected by Art 8 of the European Convention on Human Rights: Human Rights Act 1998, Sch 1.

[149]   *O'Rourke v UK (Application 39022/97)* (unreported) 26 June 2001, ECHR.

[150]   Human Rights Act 1998, s 8(2).

[151]   Under Art 3 of the European Convention on Human Rights: Human Rights Act 1998, Sch 1; see **20.91–20.96**; *O'Rourke v UK (Application 39022/97)* (unreported) 26 June 2001, ECHR.

[152]   Under Art 8 of the European Convention on Human Rights. See *R (B) v Southwark London Borough Council (No 2)* (2004) January *Legal Action*, p 32, in which the local housing authority settled for £3,000 a claim for compensation where the failure to secure interim accommodation caused the applicant to stay in prison unnecessarily for an additional weekend.

the local housing authority's own complaints procedure (or thereafter by further complaint to the Local Government Ombudsman).[153]

16.116 Even where an applicant is secured with interim accommodation, the local housing authority will be in breach of its statutory duties if the accommodation is not 'suitable'. Again, the normal rule is that the applicant cannot sue for recompense.[154] However, where the standard of accommodation is so unsuitable that it infringes an applicant's right to respect for his or her home, family or private life, damages could be awarded for breach of the European Convention on Human Rights, Art 8(1).[155] Where the evidence shows that the conditions of the accommodation do infringe an applicant's rights under Art 8(1), the burden rests on the local housing authority to show that the interference with those rights was justified and proportionate under Art 8(2).[156]

16.117 Precisely because Art 8(1) does not provide a right to a home,[157] merely the right to respect for the applicant's existing home, any claims brought under it are likely to relate to the interference, as a result of the condition of the accommodation, with the applicant's right to respect for his or her family or private life.[158] For example, placing a London family in interim accommodation in Birmingham, when the child needed to retain contact with her father in London, was found to be contrary to the family's right to respect for their family life.[159] On the other hand, a claim for damages for 29 weeks spent in grossly overcrowded and unsuitable accommodation did not succeed as the applicant was not deprived of her home, she was not separated from her children and the health problems caused by the unsuitable accommodation were not so grave as to constitute an interference with her private life.[160] Damages were awarded for breach of the applicant's right to respect for her family and private life where a wheelchair-bound woman was restricted to a single room in unsuitable temporary accommodation for over 2 years.[161] However, where an elderly woman had been effectively confined to her

---

[153] See **19.238–19.245**. For an example of the Local Government Ombudsman finding maladministration where a local housing authority had failed to secure accommodation for a family, in breach of its interim duty at HA 1996, s 188(1), see Complaint against Eastleigh Borough Council 06/B/07896, (2007) November *Legal Action*, p 38, where £3,000 compensation was awarded.

[154] *R v Ealing London Borough Council ex p Parkinson* (1997) 29 HLR 179, QBD.

[155] Human Rights Act 1998, s 8, Sch 1; *R (Bernard) v Enfield London Borough Council* [2002] EWHC 2282 (Admin), (2003) 35 HLR 27, Admin Ct.

[156] *R (Yumsak) v Enfield London Borough Council* [2002] EWHC 280 (Admin), [2003] HLR 1, Admin Ct.

[157] See **16.114** and **20.97–20.99**.

[158] *R (Morris) v Newham London Borough Council* [2002] EWHC 1262 (Admin), (2002) July *Legal Action*, p 27, Admin Ct.

[159] *R (Yumsak) v Enfield London Borough Council* [2002] EWHC 280 (Admin), [2003] HLR 1, Admin Ct.

[160] *R (Morris) v Newham London Borough Council* [2002] EWHC 1262 (Admin), (2002) July *Legal Action*, p 27, Admin Ct.

[161] *R (Bernard) v Enfield London Borough Council* [2002] EWHC 2282 (Admin), (2003) 35 HLR 27, Admin Ct.

bedroom as a result of the steepness of the stairs in the family's temporary accommodation, and had missed the family interaction that took place principally in the kitchen, the local housing authority was held not to have interfered with her right to respect for her family life. It had secured accommodation, made offers of alternative accommodation that had been rejected, and had provided practical help. The obligations under ECHR imposed on the local housing authority did not extend to creating a set of circumstances in which all major impediments to the full enjoyment of family life were removed.[162]

16.118 Alternatively, complaint could be made to the Local Government Ombudsman that the local housing authority has been guilty of maladministration. Indeed, any awards of compensation for interference with an applicant's rights under Art 8(1) of the European Convention on Human Rights are likely to be assessed by reference to the sums recommended as compensation for maladministration by the Local Government Ombudsman in other cases.[163]

---

[162] *Anufrijeva v Southwark London Borough Council* [2003] EWCA Civ 1406, CA, [2004] 1 All ER 833, CA.
[163] *R (Bernard) v Enfield London Borough Council* [2002] EWHC 2282 (Admin), (2003) 35 HLR 27, Admin Ct. See **19.241–19.245**.

Chapter 17

DUTIES AND POWERS TO ASSIST THE HOMELESS

INTRODUCTION

17.1 The Housing Act 1996 (HA 1996) Part 7 ('Homelessness') places a wide range of duties on a local housing authority when it receives an application for homelessness assistance; it also supplies the local housing authority with additional powers. The full portfolio of *duties* extends from a simple duty to notify a decision at one end of the spectrum to an obligation to accommodate the applicant (until he or she can find a home of his or her own) at the other. The range of discretionary *powers* extends from care of personal possessions to provision of a temporary home.

17.2 Other chapters in this book have already examined the powers and duties relating to:

- homelessness reviews and strategies (Chapter 7);

- decisions and notifications (Chapter 10); and

- provision of interim accommodation (Chapter 16).

17.3 This chapter explores the remaining powers and duties, focusing on the most important of all the duties – the 'main housing duty' to accommodate the applicant.[1]

Notification to the applicant

17.4 The applicant will know which *duty* is owed to him or her from the notification letter issued once the local housing authority has completed its inquiries and decided 'whether any duty, and if so what duty, is owed to' the applicant under HA 1996, Part 7.[2]

17.5 Although there is no express requirement to consider whether to exercise a *power*, nor an obligation to notify any decision on the exercise of that power, it might be expected that local housing authorities would consider the relevant powers in HA 1996, Part 7 and, at least if requested, explain their decisions on whether or not to exercise them.

17.6 If the applicant is a 'restricted case',[3] or 'restricted threatened homelessness case',[4] because of the presence in his or her household of a 'restricted person'[5], the local housing authority has special notification duties.[6]

---

1   Housing Act 1996, s 193(2). See **17.21–17.110**.
2   HA 1996, s 184(1). See **10.60–10.84**.
3   HA 1996, s 193(3B), inserted by Housing and Regeneration Act 2008, Sch 15, para 5, in force for applications made on or after 2 March 2009. See **12.31**.
4   HA 1996, s 195(4B), inserted by Housing and Regeneration Act 2008, Sch 15, para 6, in force for applications made on or after 2 March 2009. See **12.33**.
5   HA 1996, s 184(7), inserted by Housing and Regeneration Act 2008, Sch 15, para 3, in force for applications made on or after 2 March 2009. See **10.37–10.38** and **12.30–12.39**.

Overview of duties and powers

17.7   Every applicant is owed at least one duty: the duty that the local housing authority must notify a decision on his or her application.[7]

17.8   Beyond notification of the decision, no further duty under HA 1996, Part 7 is owed to an applicant who is ineligible for assistance[8], or to one who is neither homeless nor threatened with homelessness.[9] There is no duty to give advice and assistance to those applicants, but they may receive advice from the local housing authority's homelessness advice service.[10] They may also benefit from the power to take care of their possessions.[11]

17.9   The duties owed to the other classes of applicant (generally the vast bulk of applicants) depend on whether they became homeless intentionally or unintentionally (or became threatened with homelessness intentionally or unintentionally),[12] and on whether or not they have a priority need.[13] For ease of reference the main duties and powers listed below have been divided up by reference to the key findings on the questions of intentionality and priority need:

Applicants who have not become homeless intentionally

- In priority need:
  - the 'main housing duty' to secure accommodation;[14] or
  - if referred to another local housing authority:[15]
    - an *interim duty* to secure accommodation until the applicant is notified that the conditions for referral have been met;[16]
    - a *duty* to secure accommodation if conditions for referral are not met;[17]
    - a *power* to secure accommodation if the conditions for referral are met and the applicant requests a review,[18] or
  - if the applicant is a 'restricted case', modifications to the main housing duty.[19]

---

[6]   HA 1996, s 184(3A), inserted by Housing and Regeneration Act 2008, Sch 15, para 3, in force for applications made on or after 2 March 2009. See **10.75–10.84**.
[7]   HA 1996, s 184(1) and (3). See **10.1** and **10.60–10.84**.
[8]   See Chapter 12.
[9]   See Chapter 11.
[10]   HA 1996, s 179. See **9.4–9.7**.
[11]   HA 1996, s 211(3). See **17.171**.
[12]   See Chapter 14.
[13]   See Chapter 13.
[14]   HA 1996, s 193(2). See **17.21–17.110**.
[15]   See Chapter 15.
[16]   HA 1996, s 200(1) and see **15.136–15.140** and **16.43–16.50**.
[17]   HA 1996, s 200(3) and s 193(2).
[18]   HA 1996, s 200(5), and see **16.43–16.50**.
[19]   HA 1996, s 193(3A), (7AA)–(7AD) inclusive, inserted by Housing and Regeneration Act 2008, Sch 15, para 5, in force from 2 March 2009. See **17.98–17.108**.

- Not in priority need:
  - – a *duty* to provide advice and assistance;[20] and
  - – a *power* to secure accommodation.[21]

Applicants who have become homeless intentionally

- In priority need:
  - – a *duty* to provide advice and assistance;[22] and
  - – a *duty* to secure accommodation for such period as will give the applicant a reasonable period to obtain accommodation for him or herself.[23]

- Not in priority need:
  - – a *duty* to provide advice and assistance.[24]

Applicants who have not become threatened with homelessness intentionally

- In priority need:
  - – a *duty* to take reasonable steps to ensure that accommodation does not cease to be available;[25] and
  - – a *duty* to secure accommodation if the previous accommodation ceases to be available;[26]
  - – if the applicant is a 'restricted threatened homelessness case', modifications to the duty to secure accommodation if the previous accommodation ceases to be available.[27]

- Not in priority need:
  - – a *duty* to provide advice and assistance;[28] and
  - – a *power* to take reasonable steps to ensure that accommodation does not cease to be available.[29]

Applicants who have become threatened with homelessness intentionally

- In priority need:
  - – a *duty* to provide advice and assistance.[30]

- Not in priority need:

---

20 HA 1996, s 192(2); see **17.132–17.144**.
21 HA 1996, s 192(3); see **17.145–17.152**.
22 HA 1996, s 190(2)(b); see **17.132–17.144**.
23 HA 1996, s 190(2)(a); see **17.111–17.118**.
24 HA 1996, s 190(3); see **17.132–17.144**.
25 HA 1996, s 195(2); see **17.119–17.131**.
26 HA 1996, s 193(2); see **17.121–17.110**.
27 HA 1996, s 195(3A), (4A)–(4B) inclusive, inserted by Housing and Regeneration Act 2008, Sch 15, para 6, in force from 2 March 2009. See **17.126–17.131**.
28 HA 1996, s 195(5); see **17.132–17.145**.
29 HA 1996, s 195(9); see **17.145–17.151**.
30 HA 1996, s 195(5); see **17.132–17.145**.

– a *duty* to provide advice and assistance.[31]

17.10 These duties and powers are summarised in both the English and Welsh Codes and those summaries are accompanied by considerable statutory guidance.[32]

Duties and powers to secure accommodation

17.11 A number of duties (and powers) by which local housing authorities are obliged to (or may) 'secure' accommodation for an applicant are set out in HA 1996, Part 7. The duties and powers to secure accommodation of an 'interim' nature are described in Chapter 16. In this chapter, the focus is on those accommodation duties and powers triggered by the local housing authority's decision on an application for homelessness assistance.

17.12 To save endless repetition, each time HA 1996, Part 7 deals with a different accommodation duty or power, it describes the performance of those duties or powers as being the performance of a 'housing function'.[33] It then sets out some common characteristics which apply to each housing function. These are:

(1)   a requirement that accommodation secured be 'suitable';[34]

(2)   a requirement that accommodation be 'available' not only for the applicant but also for others in his or her household;[35]

(3)   three different methods by which the duty or power can be performed:
        (a)   provision of the local housing authority's own housing;[36] or
        (b)   housing from some other person;[37] or
        (c)   advice and assistance that secures housing;[38]

(4)   a power to impose reasonable charges for accommodation;[39]

(5)   a presumption that accommodation will be secured in the local housing authority's own district;[40] and

---

[31]   HA 1996, s 195(5); see **17.132–17.145**.
[32]   *Homelessness Code of Guidance for local authorities* (Communities and Local Government, Department for Education and Skills, Department of Health, July 2006), (English Code), chapter 14. *Code of Guidance for local housing authorities on allocation of accommodation and homelessness for Wales* (National Assembly for Wales, April 2003), (Welsh Code), paras 16.1–16.14.
[33]   HA 1996, s 205.
[34]   HA 1996, ss 206(1) and 210. See Chapter 16.
[35]   HA 1996, s 176, and see the discussion at **11.19–11.31**.
[36]   HA 1996, s 206(1)(a).
[37]   HA 1996, s 206(1)(b).
[38]   HA 1996, s 206(1)(c).
[39]   HA 1996, s 206(2). See **17.14–17.18**.
[40]   HA 1996, s 208(1); see **15.205–15.211** and **16.58–16.60**.

(6)   modifications to security of tenure provisions, which might otherwise apply to such accommodation.[41]

In 'restricted cases',[42] there are additional modifications to the main housing duty.[43]

17.13   Local housing authorities are also required to give a statement of their policy on 'choice' in their allocation scheme to most applicants who are owed the main housing duty.[44]

Charging for accommodation

17.14   The local housing authority can secure accommodation free of charge. More usually it will require the applicant to pay whatever amount the local housing authority considers he or she can reasonably afford. The local housing authority has power to require the applicant to pay 'such reasonable charges as they may determine' in respect of the accommodation secured, by itself or by another person.[45] Where the local housing authority is itself paying for the accommodation,[46] it can require the applicant to pay 'such reasonable amount' towards the cost as it may determine.[47]

17.15   The local housing authority's performance of its duty to secure accommodation is not contingent upon the applicant paying any charges imposed.[48] Obviously, if an unpaid charge leads to loss of the accommodation, this may give rise to a further incidence of homelessness.

17.16   What is a 'reasonable' charge or amount will vary according to the type, nature and extent of the accommodation and the personal circumstances of the applicant.[49] Indeed, local housing authorities are required to consider 'affordability' as a function of 'suitability' whenever they secure accommodation.[50] Plainly, it would not be reasonable to impose a level of charges that pushed the applicant below subsistence levels of income.[51] Somewhat surprisingly, beyond a reminder to local housing authorities that

---

[41]   HA 1996, s 209; and see also Housing Act 1985, Sch 1, para 4.

[42]   HA 1996, s 193(3B), inserted by Housing and Regeneration Act 2008, Sch 15, para 5, in force for applications made on or after 2 March 2009. See **12.30–12.39**.

[43]   HA 1996, s 193(3A) and (7AA)–(7AD). See **17.98–17.110**.

[44]   HA 1996, s 193(3A). The exception is for 'restricted cases': see **17.103** and for 'restricted threatened homelessness cases' see **17.130**.

[45]   HA 1996, s 206(2)(a).

[46]   For example, where it is paying rent for accommodation that it is leasing from a private owner.

[47]   HA 1996, s 206(2)(b).

[48]   *R v Tower Hamlets London Borough Council ex p Khalique* (1994) 26 HLR 517, QBD, at 523.

[49]   In *R (Best) v Oxford City Council* [2009] EWHC 608 (Admin), (2009) May *Legal Action*, p 27, Admin Ct, it appears that the applicant argued that she could not afford to pay the charges because she was not entitled to housing benefit, but that the local housing authority did not agree and had decided that she had the resources to pay.

[50]   Homelessness (Suitability of Accommodation) Order 1996, SI 1996/3204. See **18.45–18.46** and Appendix 2

[51]   *R v Argyll and Bute District Council* (1986) SCOLAG 100, Sh Ct.

they should not place applicants in accommodation where the costs are such that they cannot afford the basic essentials, or would have to resort to welfare benefits, the Codes fail to provide any further guidance.[52]

17.17   There is no right to a statutory review of the amount charged by the local housing authority unless:

(1)   it could be said that the level of charging rendered the accommodation 'unsuitable'; and

(2)   the accommodation is being secured under one of the duties which carry a right to a review of its suitability.[53]

17.18   Otherwise, the amount of the charge can be disputed through the local housing authority's complaints procedure or (where an error of law is alleged) by a challenge by way of judicial review.[54]

Terms on which accommodation is secured

17.19   Beyond the requirement of suitability and the power to impose charges, HA 1996, Part 7 does not prescribe the terms on which the accommodation must be secured. These will be a matter of agreement (at least notionally) between the accommodation provider, which may be the local housing authority itself, and the applicant. If the terms offered are standard terms, then the provisions of the Unfair Terms in Consumer Contracts Regulations[55] are likely to apply.[56]

17.20   Because the local housing authority securing the accommodation is a public authority, it must fix any terms of occupation bearing in mind the applicant's rights to respect for his or her private and family life.[57]

---

52   English Code, paras 17.39–17.40; Welsh Code, paras 18.6–18.7 and 19.10.
53   HA 1996, s 202(1)(f) gives a right to request a review of the suitability of accommodation secured under HA 1996, ss 190(2), 193(2) and 195, or any offer of HA 1996, Part 6 accommodation (see **19.27** and **19.32**). HA 1996, s 202(1)(f) gives the same right for 'restricted cases' and 'restricted threatened homelessness cases' in relation to any offer of private accommodation. See **19.33–19.35**.
54   For complaints see **19.238–19.245** and for judicial review, see **19.211–19.237**.
55   Unfair Terms in Consumer Contracts Regulations 1999, SI 1999/2083. For an example of a review by the Office of Fair Trading (OFT) of the fairness (or otherwise) of the standard terms of a non-secure tenancy supplied to a homeless family, see OFT Press Release 163/05 (30 August 2005) at http://www.oft.gov.uk/news/press/2005/163-05.
56   *R (Khatun) v Newham London Borough Council* [2004] EWCA Civ 55, [2004] HLR 29, CA.
57   Human Rights Act 1998, Sch 1, art 8; *Orejudos v Kensington and Chelsea Royal London Borough Council* [2003] EWCA Civ 1967, [2004] HLR 23, CA.

THE 'MAIN HOUSING DUTY': TO SECURE ACCOMMODATION

The main housing duty in outline

17.21 The highest duty to secure accommodation that can be owed under HA 1996, Part 7[58] is often colloquially called the 'full housing duty', but HA 1996, Part 7 refers to it as the 'main housing duty'.[59] We use the statutory language to refer to the duty throughout this chapter and this book.

17.22 When the statutory homelessness provisions were first introduced, the Codes and the courts treated this main housing duty as requiring the provision of what was then called 'permanent accommodation', which was understood to mean a periodic tenancy of local housing authority property.

17.23 In 1996 the House of Lords decided that the wrong approach had been taken over the course of the previous two decades, and that the duty could be discharged by the simple provision of accommodation for such period as the local housing authority considered was suitable.[60] HA 1996, Part 7, as originally enacted, brought a new approach, under which the main housing duty became a duty to accommodate temporarily for a minimum of 2 years, with a statutory discretion to extend that period. That remained the law for over 5 years.

17.24 Now, as amended by the Homelessness Act 2002, the main housing duty is a duty to accommodate indefinitely. The duty can only come to an end by the happening of events specifically prescribed by HA 1996, s 193(5)–(7F) inclusive.[61]

17.25 The 'main housing duty' is owed to applicants who are homeless,[62] eligible for assistance,[63] have a priority need,[64] did not become homeless intentionally,[65] and whom the local housing authority does not intend to refer to another local housing authority under the conditions for referral.[66]

17.26 The duty is 'to secure that accommodation is available for occupation by the applicant' and by his or her household (ie by all other persons who normally reside with the applicant as a member of his or her family, or who might reasonably be expected to reside with the applicant).[67]

---

[58] HA 1996, s 193(2).
[59] Used in this sense in HA 1996, s 200(3).
[60] *R v Brent London Borough Council ex p Awua* [1996] 1 AC 55, HL.
[61] See **17.40** and **17.49–17.110**.
[62] See Chapter 11.
[63] See Chapter 12.
[64] See Chapter 13.
[65] See Chapter 14.
[66] See Chapter 15.
[67] HA 1996, s 176. This extension of the duty to the other household members is considered at **11.19–11.31**. See *R (Ogbeni) v Tower Hamlets London Borough Council* [2008] EWHC 2444

17.27 Although the duty is not limited to any particular minimum or maximum period, and in that sense can be owed indefinitely, it is important to emphasise that the duty owed is simply to secure 'accommodation' for the time being. It is not a duty to provide a lasting home. HA 1996, Part 7 is a safety net statutory scheme designed to resolve or prevent homelessness. The 'main housing duty' is the highest form of safety net. Under that duty, accommodation is secured until the applicant is able, with any appropriate assistance, to resolve his or her longer term housing needs. If that longer term need is most likely to be met by the provision of a tenancy of social housing, the applicant will need the assistance of HA 1996, Part 6 (Allocation of Housing Accommodation) described in Chapters 1–6 of this book.

What sort of accommodation?

17.28 Like all other accommodation secured under HA 1996, Part 7, what is secured under the 'main housing duty' must meet prescribed statutory requirements.[68] The accommodation secured must be 'suitable'[69] for the needs of the applicant and of his or her household.[70] So far as is reasonably practicable, it should be secured within the local housing authority's own district.[71] The local housing authority may provide its own accommodation, provide suitable accommodation from some other person, or give advice and assistance so as to obtain suitable accommodation for the applicant from some other person.[72]

17.29 No particular security of tenure is required or conferred. If the accommodation has been secured from a private landlord or Registered Social Landlord ('RSL'), it will usually be offered by that landlord on an assured shorthold tenancy. Accommodation secured from the local housing authority's own stock will be let on non-secure, non-introductory tenancies, unless the local housing authority notifies an applicant that the tenancy is to be a secure tenancy.[73]

17.30 An offer of accommodation which was not suitable for the applicant at the date it fell to be accepted could operate as an offer of suitable

---

(Admin), (2008) October *Legal Action*, p 37, Admin Ct, where the local housing authority was wrong to refuse to secure accommodation to a 17-year-old applicant and to his aunt, who normally resided with him as a member of his family.

68 See **17.12**.

69 See Chapter 18.

70 HA 1996, ss 206 and 210.

71 HA 1996, s 208(1); see **15.205–15.211** and **16.58–16.60**.

72 HA 1996, s 206(1).

73 Housing Act 1985, Sch 1, para 4. See English Code, para 16.13; Welsh Code, para 18.17. In *Westminster City Council v Boraliu* [2007] EWCA Civ 1339, [2007] All ER (D) 34 (Nov), CA the Court of Appeal held that HA 1985, Sch 1, para 4 applied to all tenancies granted by local housing authorities in performance of their housing functions under HA 1996, Part 7, whether the property occupied was local housing authority stock, or had been leased from another landlord by the local housing authority.

accommodation if it is accompanied with certain, binding and enforceable assurances about the works to be carried out before it is occupied to render it suitable.[74]

17.31 The concept of 'suitability' and its application to such matters as the location, affordability and size of accommodation secured under the main duty, is discussed in Chapter 18.

When does the duty start?

17.32 The main housing duty is triggered as soon as the local housing authority is satisfied that all four components required to activate the duty (eligibility, homelessness, priority need and lack of intentional homelessness) are in place.

17.33 The commencement of the duty is not dependent on notification being given to the applicant, but is owed as soon as the local housing authority is 'satisfied' that the four components are in place. That may be some hours or days before the formal written notification is delivered. The only circumstance in which such satisfaction does not trigger the main housing duty is if the local housing authority refers the homeless person's application to another local housing authority under the conditions for referral.[75]

17.34 The duty is an unqualified one and, once the four components are in place, its performance cannot be deferred. A local housing authority must secure accommodation, and it must be suitable, from the date the duty is first owed. The local housing authority cannot avoid the immediate performance of the duty by reference to the other demands on its housing services or its available stock.[76] The whole point of the safety net duty is that it kicks in immediately once its components are met.

17.35 If the local housing authority fails to secure suitable accommodation, the applicant can apply for a mandatory order in judicial review proceedings requiring the local housing authority to comply with its duty.[77] The courts have warned that applicants and their advisers should act reasonably before they start judicial review proceedings:

> 'where it is shown that a local housing authority has been doing all that it could, the court would not make an order to force it to do the impossible. Its duty was to secure the availability of suitable accommodation within a reasonable period of

---

[74] *Boreh v Ealing London Borough Council* [2008] EWCA Civ 1176, [2009] HLR 22, CA.

[75] That action would cause a different accommodation duty to trigger under HA 1996, s 200(1). See **15.136–15.139**.

[76] *Codona v Mid-Bedfordshire District Council* [2004] EWCA Civ 925, [2005] HLR 1, CA, at [36], per Auld LJ.

[77] See **19.230**.

time, the reasonableness of that period depending on the circumstances of each case and on what accommodation was available.'[78]

17.36 If the breach of duty is technical or minor, and the local housing authority can demonstrate it has done its best to comply with the duty, permission to bring a judicial review claim may be refused.[79]

17.37 When the local housing authority becomes subject to the duty, it must give the applicant a copy of its statement on its policy within its allocation scheme on offering applicants a choice of accommodation and on the opportunity to express preferences about the accommodation to be allocated.[80] This should encourage the applicant to make an application, if he or she has not already done so, for an allocation of accommodation under HA 1996, Part 6.[81]

How can the duty come to an end?

17.38 Once the local housing authority is under a main housing duty to secure accommodation for the applicant, that duty can only end if one or more of the events set out in HA 1996, s 193(5)–(7F) occurs.[82] The list of those events is exhaustive, so if there is a change of circumstances not featuring among the events specified, the duty is not brought to an end.[83] For example, where an applicant who had a priority need and was entitled to the main housing duty had a change of circumstances such that he no longer had a priority need, the local housing authority still had a duty towards him, because such a change is not among the listed events.[84]

17.39 Of course, if the local housing authority discovers that its decision that the main housing duty is owed was obtained as a result of fraud, or made under a fundamental mistake of fact, it may re-open that decision and, on further inquiries, may decide that it does not owe the main housing duty after all.[85]

---

[78] *Codona v Mid-Bedfordshire District Council* [2004] EWCA Civ 925, [2005] HLR 1, CA, at [38], per Auld LJ, approved by the House of Lords in *Ali & others v Birmingham City Council, Moran v Manchester City Council* [2009] UKHL 36, [2009] 1 WLR 1506, HL, at [3]–[4], per Lord Hope.

[79] *R v Newham London Borough Council ex p Sacupima* (2000) 33 HLR 2, CA, at [17].

[80] HA 1996, ss 193(3A) and 167(1A). See Chapter 5. This duty is not owed to 'restricted cases' and to 'restricted threatened homelessness cases' (see **17.102** and **17.126**).

[81] See Chapters 1–6.

[82] HA 1996, s 193(5)–(7F).

[83] *R v Hackney London Borough Council ex p K* (1997) 30 HLR 760, CA.

[84] *R v Brent London Borough Council ex p Sadiq* (2001) 33 HLR 525, QBD.

[85] *Porteous v West Dorset District Council* [2004] EWCA Civ 244, [2004] HLR 30, CA.

17.40   The events that can cause the duty to end are:

(1)   the refusal by an applicant of suitable accommodation secured in performance of the main housing duty;[86]

(2)   the applicant ceasing to be eligible for assistance;[87]

(3)   the applicant becoming homeless intentionally from his or her main housing duty accommodation;[88]

(4)   the applicant accepting an offer of a tenancy made under HA 1996, Part 6;[89]

(5)   the applicant accepting an offer of an assured, but not an assured shorthold, tenancy from a private landlord, including a registered social landlord (RSL);[90]

(6)   the applicant voluntarily ceasing to occupy his or her main housing duty accommodation as his or her only or principal home;[91]

(7)   the applicant refusing a final offer of suitable accommodation made under HA 1996, Part 6;[92]

(8)   the applicant accepting a qualifying offer of an assured shorthold tenancy from a private landlord, including from an RSL.[93]

17.41   From this list it is clear that the duty may end when the applicant *refuses* an offer of suitable accommodation made either under HA 1996, Part 6 or under the main housing duty itself. If, unusually, an offer of accommodation is made outside of the provisions of HA 1996, Part 6 or of the main housing duty, an applicant would be free to refuse it without fear that the main housing duty would end.

17.42   Since the consequence of refusal of a final offer made under HA 1996, Part 6, or any offer made under the main housing duty, is to bring the main housing duty to an end, applicants contemplating refusing an offer of accommodation, and their advisers, should first ensure that they are very clear whether the offer is made under either of these two provisions or not.

---

86   HA 1996, s 193(5). See **17.49–17.58**.
87   HA 1996, s 193(6)(a). See **17.59–17.61**.
88   HA 1996, s 193(6)(b). See **17.62–17.63**.
89   HA 1996, s 193(6)(c). See **17.66–17.73**.
90   HA 1996, s 193(6)(cc). See **17.74–17.77**.
91   HA 1996, s 193(6)(d). See **17.64–17.65**.
92   HA 1996, s 193(7)–(7A). See **17.78–17.91**.
93   HA 1996, s 193(7B)–(7E). See **17.92–17.97**.

Decisions and challenges about the ending of the main housing duty

17.43 There is a common misconception that it is for the local housing authority to decide whether or not the main housing duty has ended. In fact, HA 1996, Part 7 simply prescribes that, on the happening of one of the events listed above, the local housing authority 'shall cease to be subject to the duty'.[94] In other words, the main housing duty ends automatically and without any need for a freestanding decision to that effect by the local housing authority. In consequence, there is no obligation on a local housing authority to 'notify' any such decision to the applicant (subject to an exception at HA 1996, s 193(5)).[95]

17.44 However, many of the events which terminate the main housing duty are dependent upon the local housing authority being 'satisfied' that a particular situation has come about (eg that accommodation refused by the applicant was suitable).[96] Most local housing authorities will notify the applicant of their conclusions and indicate that, as a result, they consider that the main housing duty has ended. These are colloquially called 'discharge of duty' letters.

17.45 A decision made by a local housing authority that events have occurred that bring to an end its main housing duty towards the applicant has been held to constitute a decision as to 'what duty (if any) is owed to him'. The applicant therefore has a right to request a review of the decision to treat the main housing duty as at an end.[97]

17.46 Quite apart from this general right to a statutory review of any decision that events have occurred which bring the main housing duty to an end, the applicant also has a separate freestanding right to request a review of any decision that accommodation offered in performance of the main housing duty or as a final offer under HA 1996, Part 6 is suitable.[98] If an applicant receives an offer of accommodation under the main housing duty or as a final offer under HA 1996, Part 6, and he or she believes that the accommodation is not suitable, there is the right both to request a review of the decision that the property is suitable, and to accept the property in any event.[99] This must always be the sensible course of action for an applicant to take. Otherwise, she or he may lose the suitability review and find that the offer has meanwhile been withdrawn.[100]

---

[94] HA 1996, s 193(5), (6), (7) and (7B).
[95] See **17.49**.
[96] HA 1996, s 193(5) and (7).
[97] HA 1996, s 202(1)(b). *Warsame v Hounslow London Borough Council* (2000) 32 HLR 335, CA.
[98] HA 1996, s 202(1)(f). See **19.27–19.32**.
[99] HA 1996, s 202(1A).
[100] The Court of Appeal has made it clear that, once an offer of accommodation has been refused and the local housing authority has decided that its duty has come to an end, there is no obligation on the local housing authority to keep the accommodation available for the applicant while a review is being carried out (*Osseilly v Westminster City Council* [2007] EWCA Civ 1108, [2008] HLR 18, CA).

17.47 Where the local housing authority has decided to end its duty because the applicant has refused an offer of suitable accommodation,[101] and the applicant then requests a review of that decision (as he or she is entitled to do), the scope of the review will be different from the scope of reviews of other decisions. The normal rule for reviews is that the reviewing officer should consider all the facts, law and circumstances at the date of the review decision.[102] The Court of Appeal has considered whether the normal rule should apply to cases involving refusals of offers. In *Osseilly v Westminster City Council*,[103] it held that there was no obligation on the local housing authority to keep open the offer of accommodation until the review had been determined. In *Omar v Westminster City Council*,[104] the Court of Appeal considered the position where, at the date of refusal, the accommodation was unsuitable, but subsequent events had rendered it suitable by the date of the review decision. The Court of Appeal held that:

'the correct question for the reviewer is whether the council were right, as at the date of that original decision; and for that purpose what they should be examining is the facts that existed as of that date, albeit they may discover what facts existed as at that date, between the date of that original decision and the date of review.'[105]

17.48 A third decision of the Court of Appeal concerned accommodation which, at the date when the applicant was required to accept it, was not suitable but there were works proposed that would render it suitable. In *Boreh v Ealing London Borough Council*,[106] the Court of Appeal held that there would only be an offer of suitable accommodation in those circumstances if the offer were accompanied with certain, binding and enforceable assurances about what work would be carried out after acceptance and before occupation.[107] A reviewing officer should not take into account the works subsequently carried out if they had not been contained in such assurances.

---

[101] The accommodation might have been offered under the main housing duty and the decision to discharge duty made under HA 1996, s 193(5): see **17.49–17.58**. Or the accommodation may have been a final offer of HA 1996, Part 6 accommodation and the decision to discharge duty made under HA 1996, s 193(7): see **17.78–17.91**.

[102] *Mohammed v Hammersmith & Fulham London Borough Council* [2001] UKHL 57, [2002] 1 AC 547, HL; and *Crawley Borough Council v B* (2000) 32 HLR 636, CA. See **18.176–18.179** and **19.102–19.109**.

[103] [2007] EWCA Civ 1108, [2008] HLR 18, CA.

[104] [2008] EWCA Civ 421, [2008] HLR 36, CA.

[105] *Omar v Westminster City Council* [2008] EWCA Civ 421, [2008] HLR 36, CA, at [32], per Waller LJ.

[106] [2008] EWCA Civ 1176, [2009] HLR 22, CA.

[107] The Court of Appeal in *Boreh v Ealing London Borough Council* [2008] EWCA Civ 1176, [2009] HLR 22, CA, did not specify that the assurances must be to the effect that the works must be carried out before the accommodation is to be occupied. However, it must follow that if the accommodation before works were carried out was not suitable for occupation by the applicant, then the works must be carried out before occupation commences.

The eight events that may cause the main housing duty to end

(1) Refusal of main housing duty accommodation[108]

17.49   For the main housing duty to end for this reason, HA 1996, s 193(5) prescribes a number of fairly strict conditions which must all be fulfilled. These conditions are that:

(1)   the accommodation has been offered in performance of the main housing duty; and

(2)   the local housing authority is satisfied that it is 'suitable' accommodation; and

(3)   the applicant has been informed of the consequences of refusal of the offer; and

(4)   the applicant has been informed of the right to seek a review of the suitability of the offered accommodation; and

(5)   the applicant refuses the offer; and

(6)   the local housing authority notifies the applicant that it regards the main housing duty as having ended as a result of the refusal.[109]

17.50   Where a fixed-term assured shorthold tenancy is being offered in performance of the main housing duty, the Court of Appeal has held that the local housing authority should explain in the offer letter that:

> 'the authority acknowledges the accommodation would be temporary if the private landlord lawfully exercises his right to recover possession after the end of the fixed term and that, if that happens and assuming that the applicant's circumstances have not materially changed, the authority accepts that it would again become obliged to perform its duty under the section to secure that accommodation is available for occupation by the applicant.'[110]

17.51   The conditions potentially trigger two sets of rights to request a review:

(a)   a review of the decision as to suitability;[111] and

(b)   a review of the decision that the duty is regarded as ended.[112]

---

[108]   HA 1996, s 193(5).

[109]   HA 1996, s 193(5). See English Code, para 14.17(v); Welsh Code, para 16.5(i).

[110]   *Griffiths v St Helens Council* [2006] EWCA Civ 160, [2006] HLR 29, CA, at [42], per May LJ.

[111]   HA 1996, s 202(1)(f). See **19.27–19.32**.

[112]   HA 1996, s 202(1)(b). See **19.14–19.15**. For the specific considerations where an offer has been refused, see **17.47–17.48** and **18.176–18.179**.

This reflects the fact that the applicant will have received two letters. The first letter offered the accommodation on the basis that it was suitable, outlined the right to seek a review of suitability, and warned of the consequences of refusal. The second, following a refusal, notified the applicant of the fact that the local housing authority considered that the main housing duty had ended. Because an applicant can request a review whilst simultaneously accepting the accommodation (and thus preserve his or her position), it should become less common for the second letter to be sent.[113] Indeed, the Codes go further than HA 1996, s 193(5) and advise that the applicant should be specifically told that he or she will be able both to accept and to seek a review in an even earlier letter – the letter notifying the applicant of the local housing authority's decision under HA 1996, s 184.[114] In *Ali v Birmingham City Council*,[115] the Court of Appeal held that '"inform" in this statute is ... to be construed as requiring information to be conveyed in understandable English' and that 'notify' requires the giving of a notice which imports a degree of formality.[116]

17.52   A decision by the local housing authority that its main housing duty has come to an end as a result of this provision could arise at any time during the performance of the HA 1996, s 193(2) main housing duty. So, where an applicant who is offered a move from unsuitable accommodation secured under HA 1996, s 193(2) to suitable accommodation and refuses to move, he or she may find that the main housing duty has come to an end.[117]

17.53   The key issue for the applicant is likely to be the suitability or otherwise of the accommodation offered.[118] It may be that accommodation offered was not suitable at the date when it fell to be accepted, eg if it was not wheelchair-accessible. If accompanied by certain, binding and enforceable assurances about the work to be carried out after acceptance but before occupation, the accommodation may be suitable and a refusal of the offer may result in the ending of the main housing duty under this provision.[119] However, where no such assurance had been given by the date for acceptance, it will not have been an offer of suitable accommodation.

17.54   The expectation is that, following receipt of the offer of main housing duty accommodation, the applicant should have a reasonable opportunity to consider the offer and inspect the accommodation. This reflects best practice as set out in the Codes.[120] Circumstances might compel the local housing authority to require an immediate acceptance or rejection of the offer, even if

---

[113]   HA 1996, s 202(1A), added by Homelessness Act 2002, s 8 (in force from 26 February 2002) and overturning the effect of *Alghile v Westminster City Council* [2001] EWCA Civ 363, (2001) 33 HLR 627, CA.

[114]   English Code, para 19.3; Welsh Code, para 21.2.

[115]   [2009] EWCA Civ 1279, CA.

[116]   *Ali v Birmingham City Council* [2009] EWCA Civ 1279 at [39], per Sir Anthony May.

[117]   *Muse v Brent London Borough Council* [2008] EWCA Civ 1447, (2009) February *Legal Action*, p 32, CA.

[118]   See Chapter 18.

[119]   *Boreh v Ealing London Borough Council* [2008] EWCA Civ 1176, [2009] HLR 22, CA.

[120]   English Code, para 14.22; Welsh Code, para 16.19.

the applicant has not had the opportunity to see it or consider it. The safeguards, if the local housing authority insists on an immediate acceptance or rejection, are that:

(1)   the local housing authority must have satisfied itself that the accommodation is suitable; and

(2)   it must have notified the applicant of the right to a review; and

(3)   the applicant can both accept and seek a review.

17.55   The Court of Appeal has held that these safeguards are sufficiently compliant with the statutory scheme, and that there is no separate right for applicants to view, and comment on, the accommodation before being required to accept or reject it.[121]

17.56   The English Code, published after the Court of Appeal's decision, contains a recommendation from the Secretary of State that applicants should be:

> 'given the chance to view accommodation before being required to decide whether they accept or refuse an offer, and before being required to sign any written agreement relating to the accommodation.'[122]

17.57   This suggests that – certainly for English local housing authorities – they should normally give the applicant an opportunity to view the accommodation, even though they are not strictly required to under HA 1996, s 193(5).

17.58   The key ingredient to the ending of the duty under this first route is that the applicant has *refused* the accommodation offered. The statutory wording is that the applicant 'refuses' an offer – not simply fails to accept it. This must mean something more than that the applicant has not replied to the making of an offer. The local housing authority must be able to identify something that amounts to unequivocal rejection following receipt of the offer.[123]

(2)   Because the applicant ceases to be eligible[124]

17.59   When an applicant ceases to be eligible for homelessness assistance, the main housing duty ends. Eligibility is primarily determined by immigration status,[125] so the trigger to the ending of the main housing duty in these circumstances will normally be a change in that status.[126]

---

[121]   *R (Khatun) v Newham London Borough Council* [2004] EWCA 55, [2004] HLR 29, CA.

[122]   English Code, para 14.18.

[123]   *R v Haringey London Borough Council ex p Muslu* (2001) February *Legal Action*, p 29, QBD.

[124]   HA 1996, s 193(6)(a). English Code, para 14.17(vi); Welsh Code, para 16.20(i).

[125]   See Chapter 12.

[126]   As happened in *Tower Hamlets London Borough Council v Deugi* [2006] EWCA Civ 159, [2006]

17.60 HA 1996, s 193(6)(a) makes it clear that the issue is whether *the applicant* has ceased to be eligible. The main housing duty does not end if it is some other member of the applicant's household who ceases to be eligible for assistance, even if it is the very household member whose presence conferred priority need on the applicant in the first place. In those circumstances, the main housing duty will continue.

17.61 There is some debate as to whether or not a local housing authority needs to make a decision that the main housing duty has ended because the applicant is no longer eligible, since the issue is not a matter of discretion.[127] It is recognised, however, that the question of whether the applicant has ceased to be eligible may be disputed, and in those circumstances it would seem right for there to be a decision by the local housing authority, which can then be the subject of a request for a statutory review.[128] Alternatively, where the sequence of events has caused the applicant to make a new application for homelessness assistance,[129] a decision – again subject to a right to seek a review – may be taken on the new application and the question of the applicant's eligibility determined through that process

(3) Because the applicant becomes homeless intentionally from the main housing duty accommodation[130]

17.62 The local housing authority should apply the definition of intentional homelessness contained in HA 1996, Part 7[131] in this context to determine whether the applicant has become homeless intentionally from the main housing duty accommodation.[132] In *Orejudos v Kensington and Chelsea Royal London Borough Council*[133] the applicant was absent, despite warnings, on ten different occasions (over a period of more than a year) from hostel accommodation and, in breach of the conditions of his occupancy, had failed to give reasons in advance for absence.[134] The local housing authority terminated his booking, decided that he had become homeless intentionally and concluded that its duty toward him had ended. That decision was upheld on review, on appeal to the county court and on a further appeal to the Court of Appeal. Similarly, where an applicant lost her main housing duty accommodation because she did not pay the rent, and the local housing authority rejected her argument that she did not have the resources to pay for

---

HLR 28, CA, where the applicant had originally been eligible as a result of being the primary carer of a dependent child who was in full-time education (see **12.125–12.129**). She ceased to be eligible when the child left full-time education.

127 See the comments by May LJ in *Tower Hamlets London Borough Council v Deugi* [2006] EWCA Civ 159, [2006] HLR 28, CA, at [33].

128 HA 1996, s 202(1)(b). See **19.14–19.15**.

129 HA 1996, s 193(9). See **17.109–17.110**.

130 HA 1996, s 193(6)(b).

131 HA 1996, s 191. See English Code, para 14.17(vii); Welsh Code, para 16.20(ii).

132 For the appropriate application of that definition see Chapter 14.

133 [2003] EWCA Civ 1967, [2004] HLR 23, CA.

134 *Orejudos v Kensington and Chelsea Royal London Borough Council* [2003] EWCA Civ 1967, [2004] HLR 23, CA.

the accommodation, she had become homeless intentionally from the main housing duty accommodation.[135] It is, of course, a necessary pre-requisite that the applicant has actually been rendered homeless by termination of any rights to occupy the main housing duty accommodation. The duty does not end simply because the applicant has become threatened with homelessness intentionally.

17.63 The applicant has a right to request that the local housing authority reviews its decision that the main housing duty has ended for this reason.[136] Alternatively, where the sequence of events has caused the applicant to re-apply as homeless,[137] a decision, again subject to a right to seek a review, may be taken on the new application and the question of whether he or she had become homeless intentionally can be determined through that process.[138]

(4) Because the applicant voluntarily ceases to occupy the main housing duty accommodation[139]

17.64 The main housing duty will come to an end where the applicant voluntarily ceases to occupy as his or her only or principal home the accommodation made available under the main housing duty. The test to be applied is the same as that used for determining whether a tenant of social housing still enjoys security of tenure.[140] The test is not met, and the main housing duty will not have ended, merely because the applicant has been staying somewhere else temporarily.[141] Additionally, if the applicant has ceased to occupy, he or she must have done so 'voluntarily'. This requirement is especially important where the applicant has been accommodated because she or he is vulnerable as a result of mental illness.[142] Its presence corresponds to the requirement in the definition of 'becoming homeless intentionally' that the applicant's actions must have been 'deliberate'.[143]

---

135 *R (Best) v Oxford City Council* [2009] EWHC 608 (Admin), (2009) May *Legal Action*, p 27, Admin Ct.

136 HA 1996, s 202(1)(b). See **19.14–19.15**.

137 HA 1996, s 193(9). See **17.109–17.110**.

138 In one case, an applicant argued that once his main housing duty accommodation ended under this provision, the local housing authority should secure him with accommodation for such period as would give him a reasonable opportunity to secure his own accommodation under HA 1996, s 190(2)(a) (see **17.111–17.118**). By the time the appeal was heard, the applicant had been accommodated by friends and relatives for 6 months and the appeal was dismissed by the county court judge on the basis that it had become academic and futile. The Court of Appeal refused permission to appeal on the grounds that the decision had been justified on the facts, but reserved for another occasion whether a different result might be required in 'a starker case': *Newman v Croydon London Borough Council* [2008] EWCA Civ 1591, (2009) *Legal Action*, p 22, CA.

139 HA 1996, s 193(6)(d). See English Code, para 14.17(viii); Welsh Code, para 16.20(iii).

140 Housing Act 1985, s 81 (secure tenants) and Housing Act 1988, s 1 (assured tenants).

141 *Crawley Borough Council v Sawyer* (1987) 20 HLR 98, CA.

142 As was the case in *R v Kensington and Chelsea Royal London Borough Council ex p Kujtim* (1999) 32 HLR 579, CA.

143 HA 1996, s 191(1). See **14.30–14.77**.

17.65 The applicant has a right to request that the local housing authority reviews its decision that the main housing duty has ended for this reason.[144] Alternatively, where the sequence of events has caused the applicant to make a new application for homelessness assistance,[145] a decision, again subject to a right to seek a review, may be taken on the new application and the question as to whether he or she had voluntarily ceased to occupy the main housing duty accommodation can be determined through that process.

(5) By acceptance of a HA 1996, Part 6 offer[146]

17.66 An applicant owed the main housing duty will normally have applied to the same local housing authority for an allocation of a social housing tenancy under the provisions of HA 1996, Part 6 ('Allocation of housing accommodation'). He or she will have been given details of how to express a preference for particular accommodation (under the local housing authority's allocation scheme) when the local housing authority notified the applicant that it had accepted a main housing duty towards him or her.[147]

17.67 Because all homeless persons (including those owed the main housing duty) are entitled to a reasonable preference in an allocation scheme,[148] an offer under HA 1996, Part 6 could be made quite quickly. In some circumstances, a HA 1996, Part 6 offer could be made immediately upon the main housing duty being triggered.[149] If that offer is accepted, then it may not be necessary to secure any accommodation under the main housing duty at all.

17.68 Where the applicant has been secured with local housing authority or RSL accommodation under the main housing duty, the subsequent offer under HA 1996, Part 6 might be of a tenancy of the very same property. If that offer is accepted, the local housing authority or RSL will notify the applicant of his or her new tenancy status.[150]

17.69 Prior to the changes made by the Homelessness Act 2002, most local housing authorities made only a single offer of HA 1996, Part 6 accommodation to applicants owed the main housing duty. The modern expectation, however, is that a series of offers will be made, with the applicant being free to accept any of them. Likewise, she or he may reject all of them (save the final offer) without any effect on the continuance of the main housing duty. Alternatively, the applicant might be free to bid for properties, under a choice based lettings scheme,[151] without any penalties or risks to his or her

---

144   HA 1996, s 202(1)(b). See **19.14–19.15**.
145   HA 1996, s 193(9). See **17.109–17.110**.
146   HA 1996, s 193(6)(c). See English Code, para 14.17(i); Welsh Code, para 16.15(ii).
147   HA 1996, ss 167(1A) and 193(3A).
148   See **4.44–4.54**.
149   English Code, paras 3.22 and 14.15; Welsh Code, para 16.14.
150   English Code, paras 16.12–16.13; Welsh Code, para 18.17.
151   See Chapter 5.

temporary accommodation. The current framework was specifically introduced so that those owed the main housing duty would have:

'... a reasonable period in which they can exercise the same degree of customer choice of settled accommodation as is available to other people with urgent housing needs waiting on the housing register'.[152]

Precisely for this reason, there is no requirement in HA 1996, Part 7 that *all* the HA 1996, Part 6 offers made to an applicant should be of 'suitable' accommodation or that any reasons are required to be given by the applicant for refusal of those offers. There is no right to a statutory review of offers that are *not* expressed to be 'final' offers.

17.70 An applicant who accepts an offer, only to find subsequently that it is unsuitable, will simply apply for a transfer to alternative accommodation in the ordinary way.[153]

17.71 However, when a 'final' offer is made under HA 1996, Part 6, there is not the same flexibility. If a local housing authority's policy is to make one offer only to its HA 1996, Part 6 applicants, then the only offer made to someone owed the main HA 1996, Part 7 housing duty will be 'a final offer', and there may be consequences if the applicant refuses it.[154]

17.72 If the HA 1996, Part 6 offer which the applicant accepts is the 'final offer', he or she has the right also to request a review of the suitability of the offer.[155]

17.73 The local housing authority cannot make a 'final' offer of HA 1996, Part 6 accommodation without first being satisfied that the accommodation is suitable for the applicant and his or her household and that it is reasonable for the applicant to accept the offer.[156]

(6) By acceptance of an offer of an assured tenancy[157]

17.74 The main housing duty will end if the applicant accepts an assured tenancy offered by a private landlord (including by an RSL). In this context, assured tenancy does not include an assured shorthold tenancy.[158]

17.75 The offer will have been made other than as a result of a nomination under the local housing authority's allocation scheme (HA 1996, Part 6).[159]

---

[152] 'Quality and Choice: A Decent Home for All' (DETR Green Paper, April 2000), para 9.43.
[153] See **2.51–2.52**.
[154] HA 1996, s 193(7). See **17.78–17.91**.
[155] HA 1996, s 202(1A), as added. See **19.27–19.32** and **19.39–19.47**.
[156] HA 1996, s 193(7F). See English Code, paras 14.21–14.22; Welsh Code, paras 16.18–16.19.
[157] HA 1996, s 193(6)(cc). See English Code, para 14.17(ii); Welsh Code, para 16.15(iv).
[158] HA 1996, s 193(6)(cc).
[159] Because the acceptance of HA 1996, Part 6 offers is dealt with separately in HA 1996, s 193(6)(c).

Such an offer may have been elicited from a private sector landlord by a local housing authority seeking homes for its homeless households. Or it may have come from an RSL to which the applicant had applied directly for a tenancy.[160]

17.76 An offer of an assured tenancy, made separately from the HA 1996, Part 6 process, may be refused by the applicant with no adverse consequences upon the main housing duty, unless the accommodation is subsequently re-offered to him or her as a final HA 1996, Part 6 offer.[161]

17.77 The applicant has a right to request that the local housing authority reviews its decision that the duty has ended for this reason.[162] However, since the main housing duty only ends as a result of the voluntary acceptance by the applicant of accommodation, it would seem unlikely that the applicant would want to challenge such a decision.

(7) By refusal of a final offer made under HA 1996, Part 6[163]

17.78 Where the applicant refuses an offer of accommodation made under HA 1996, Part 6, the main housing duty will end if the following requirements are all fulfilled:

(1) the applicant was offered accommodation under HA 1996, Part 6;[164] and

(2) the offer was made in writing;[165] and

(3) the offer stated that it was a 'final offer for the purposes of section 193(7)';[166] and

(4) the local housing authority had satisfied itself that the accommodation was 'suitable' for the applicant;[167] and

(5) the local housing authority had satisfied itself that it would be 'reasonable' for the applicant to accept the offer;[168] and

(6) the applicant had been informed of the possible consequences of refusal;[169] and

---

[160] English Code, Annex 5, paras 8–12; Welsh Code, Annex 22, para 3.1. See Chapter 6.
[161] See **17.78–17.91**.
[162] HA 1996, s 202(1)(b). See **19.14–19.15**.
[163] HA 1996, s 193(7). See English Code, para 14.17(iv); Welsh Code, para 16.15(iii).
[164] HA 1996, s 193(7).
[165] HA 1996, s 193(7A).
[166] HA 1996, s 193(7A).
[167] HA 1996, s 193(7F)(a).
[168] HA 1996, s 193(7F)(a). See English Code, paras 14.21–14.22; Welsh Code, paras 16.18–16.19.
[169] HA 1996, s 193(7).

(7)   the applicant had been told of the right to request a review of the suitability of the accommodation;[170] and

(8)   the offer was refused.[171]

17.79   This possible avenue to the ending of the main housing duty only applies to a 'final offer' of HA 1996, Part 6 accommodation. That language reflects the policy objective that the applicant should have had an opportunity to receive more than one offer or make more than one bid for HA 1996, Part 6 accommodation (if that would be the norm under the particular local housing authority's HA 1996, Part 6 allocation scheme).[172]

Notification of final offer

17.80   The applicant will know whether or not the offer is a 'final offer' because the written notification must not only state that it is, but must also state that it is being treated as such for the purposes of the specific subsection in HA 1996, Part 7.[173] Meeting all of these different requirements, which enable the local housing authority to bring the main housing duty to an end under this route, requires careful organisation by the allocation staff and the homelessness staff.[174]

17.81   The formula for the ending of the main housing duty by refusal of a final offer of accommodation offered under HA 1996, Part 6 potentially triggers two sets of rights to request a review:

(1)   a right to request a review of the decision as to suitability;[175] and

(2)   a right to request a review of the decision that the duty is regarded as ended.[176]

17.82   This reflects the fact that the applicant will have received two letters. The first will have offered the accommodation on the basis that it was a final offer, outlined the right to seek a review of suitability, and warned of the

---

[170]   HA 1996, s 193(7).

[171]   HA 1996, s 193(7).

[172]   See Chapter 5.

[173]   The letter need not contain the exact words in HA 1996, s 193(7), provided that it conveys every matter of substance required at s 193(7) (*Omar v Birmingham City Council* [2007] EWCA Civ 610, [2007] HLR 43, CA). There was an obiter comment in *Omar* at [31] and [34] per May LJ that, if the Court of Appeal was wrong and the offer was not a 'final offer' for the purposes of s 193(7), it could be an offer of main housing duty accommodation, and the applicant's rejection of accommodation could therefore lead to the local housing authority deciding that its duty had ended under HA 1996, s 193(5). This obiter comment has not been considered by any other courts.

[174]   Particularly so where these functions are separately managed within the particular local housing authority.

[175]   HA 1996, s 202(1)(f). See **19.27–19.39**.

[176]   HA 1996, s 202(1)(b). See **19.14–19.15**. For the specific considerations where an offer has been refused, see **17.47–17.48** and **18.176–18.179**.

consequences of refusal. The second, following a refusal, will have notified the applicant that the local housing authority considers the main housing duty as having ended.

17.83 Because an applicant can both request a review whilst also simultaneously accepting the accommodation (and thus preserve his or her position), it should become less common for the stage to be reached at which the second letter comes to be sent.[177]

17.84 Indeed, the Codes go further than HA 1996, Part 7 in requiring that the applicant should be specifically told that he or she can both accept and seek a review in the letter in which the applicant is notified of the local housing authority's decision on his or her application.[178] This should ensure that offers are almost always accepted, even if a review is to be pursued.

Suitable accommodation

17.85 Before the offer is put to the applicant, the local housing authority must only satisfy itself that the accommodation offered is suitable. The question of suitability of accommodation is considered in Chapter 18.

Reasonable for the applicant to accept the offer

17.86 The local housing authority must also be satisfied that it is reasonable for the applicant to accept the offer.[179] This requires the local housing authority to think ahead and consider what the circumstances are likely to be when the applicant receives the offer. For example, the local housing authority must consider the contractual or other obligations (such as to notice) that the applicant may owe in respect of his or her existing accommodation. The local housing authority should consider whether the applicant will be able to bring those obligations to an end before he or she is required to take up the offered accommodation.[180] There may be a host of other reasons why it may not be reasonable to expect an applicant to take up even a final offer of suitable accommodation made under HA 1996, Part 6. HA 1996, Part 7:

> '... makes it clear that the question whether it was reasonable for an applicant to accept accommodation is distinct from the question whether the accommodation was suitable. There may be circumstances in which it is reasonable to refuse to accept accommodation which is suitable.'[181]

---

[177] HA 1996, s 202(1A). See **19.39–19.47**.
[178] English Code, para 19.3; Welsh Code, para 21.2.
[179] HA 1996, s 193(7F). See English Code, paras 14.21–14.22; Welsh Code, paras 16.18–16.19.
[180] HA 1996, s 193(8).
[181] *Warsame v Hounslow London Borough Council* (2000) 32 HLR 335, CA, at 339, per Chadwick LJ.

17.87 The Court of Appeal held in *Slater v Lewisham London Borough Council*[182] that there are two elements: (1) the suitability of the accommodation and (2) whether or not it would have been reasonable to accept the offer, and the local housing authority must consider and be satisfied in respect of each of those elements. In considering how the local housing authority should test the question of whether or not it would have been reasonable to accept the offer, the Court of Appeal held that an approach centred on the specific attributes of the applicant was required:

> 'the decision-maker must have regard to all the personal characteristics of the applicant, her needs, her hopes and her fears and then taking account of those individual aspects, the subjective factors, ask whether it is reasonable, an objective test for the applicant to accept. The test is whether a right-thinking local housing authority would conclude that it was reasonable that *this applicant* should have accepted the offer of *this* accommodation.'[183]

17.88 Given the potential consequences of refusal, applicants must be allowed a reasonable period in which to consider offers of HA 1996, Part 6 accommodation. There is no set reasonable period. The appropriate length of time depends on the applicant's circumstances. Local housing authorities should take into account:

- that applicants should have a longer period in which to consider offers made under HA 1996, Part 6 than the period they have in which to consider offers of temporary accommodation;

- that applicants may wish to seek advice; and

- that applicants may not be familiar with the property offered.

17.89 If the applicant is in hospital or temporarily absent, the local housing authority should take that into account.[184]

17.90 For English local housing authorities, the Secretary of State recommends that applicants should be given the opportunity to view the accommodation before deciding whether to accept or reject it.[185]

Refusal of offer

17.91 The key ingredient for ending the duty in these circumstances is that the applicant has *refused* the HA 1996, Part 6 accommodation offered. The wording in HA 1996, s 193(7) is that the applicant 'refuses' a final offer. It is not

---

[182] [2006] EWCA Civ 394, [2006] HLR 37, CA.

[183] *Slater v Lewisham London Borough Council* [2006] EWCA Civ 394, [2006] HLR 37, CA, at [34], per Ward LJ. This approach was followed and applied by the Court of Appeal in *Ahmed v Leicester City Council* [2007] EWCA Civ 843, [2008] HLR 6, CA. See also *Ahad v Tower Hamlets London Borough Council* [2008] EWCA Civ 606, (2008) July *Legal Action*, p 22, CA.

[184] English Code, para 14.22; Welsh Code, para 16.19.

[185] English Code, para 14.18. See **17.54**.

sufficient that there has been a simple failure to accept it. This must mean something more than that the applicant has failed to respond to an offer made to him or her. The local housing authority must be able to identify something that amounts to unequivocal rejection following receipt of the offer.[186]

(8) By acceptance of a qualifying offer of an assured shorthold tenancy[187]

17.92 The main housing duty ends if an applicant accepts a qualifying offer of an assured shorthold tenancy from a private landlord, including from an RSL, of accommodation which is available or will be made available to him or her to occupy.[188]

17.93 The offer must be of accommodation that the local housing authority has already satisfied itself is suitable for the needs of the applicant and his or her household. The local housing authority must also be satisfied before the offer is made that it is reasonable for the applicant to accept the offer.[189]

17.94 However, even though the accommodation must be suitable and reasonable to accept, the applicant is free to *refuse* a qualifying offer of an assured shorthold tenancy made under these provisions without fear of any consequences.[190]

17.95 The offer here envisaged is not one made by the local housing authority itself, but by an accommodation provider. A 'qualifying offer' is defined as:

(1) an offer made with the approval of the local housing authority, in pursuance of arrangements made between the local housing authority and the landlord, with a view to ending the local housing authority's main housing duty;

(2) of a fixed term tenancy (although there is no minimum period); and

(3) accompanied by a written statement informing the applicant of the length of the fixed term and explaining in ordinary language that there is no obligation to accept, but that the main housing duty will end if the offer is accepted.[191]

---

[186] *R v Haringey London Borough Council ex p Muslu* (2001) February *Legal Action*, p 29, QBD.

[187] HA 1996, s 193(7B).

[188] HA 1996, s 193(7B). See English Code, paras 14.17(iii), 14.19–14.20; Welsh Code, paras 16.15(v)–16.17.

[189] HA 1996, s 193(7F)(b).

[190] HA 1996, s 193(7C). If the offer of an assured shorthold tenancy is being made in performance of the main housing duty, instead of being a qualifying offer designed to end the main housing duty, and is suitable, refusal of the offer will bring the duty to an end under HA 1996, s 193(5). See **17.49–17.58**.

[191] HA 1996, s 193(7D).

17.96 The applicant must sign acknowledging that he or she has understood that statement.[192]

17.97 These procedures, described as 'elaborate' by one Court of Appeal judge:

> 'are there to recognise that, on the one hand, assured shorthold tenancies from private landlords have their disadvantages ... but that, on the other hand, some homeless applicants may reasonably prefer to accept the offer of such a tenancy, rather than remain in temporary accommodation for a long time until they may be offered secure accommodation under Part 6.'[193]

The applicant has a right to request that the local housing authority reviews its decision that the main housing duty has ended for this reason.[194] However, since the main housing duty only ends as a result of the voluntary acceptance by the applicant of accommodation, it would seem unlikely that the applicant would want to challenge such a decision.

The special rules for 'restricted cases'[195]

The definition of 'restricted case'

17.98 An applicant is a 'restricted case' where:

- the applicant is eligible;[196] and

- the applicant's household contains a 'restricted person';[197] and

- it is the presence in the household of the restricted person that has led to the main housing duty having been accepted.[198]

17.99 A 'restricted person'[199] is defined as a person:

- who is not eligible for assistance under HA 1996, Part 7;[200] and

---

[192] HA 1996, s 193(7E).

[193] May LJ in *Griffiths v St Helens Council* [2006] EWCA Civ 160, [2006] HLR 29, CA, at [36].

[194] HA 1996, s 202(1)(b). See **19.14–19.15**.

[195] HA 1996, s 193(3B), inserted by Housing and Regeneration Act 2008, Sch 15, para 5, in force for applications made on or after 2 March 2009.

[196] See Chapter 12.

[197] HA 1996, s 184(7), inserted by Housing and Regeneration Act 2008, Sch 15, para 3, in force for applications made on or after 2 March 2009.

[198] HA 1996, s 193(3B), inserted by Housing and Regeneration Act 2008, Sch 15, para 5, in force for applications made on or after 2 March 2009.

[199] HA 1996, s 184(7), inserted by Housing and Regeneration Act 2008, Sch 15, para 3, in force for applications made on or after 2 March 2009.

[200] See Chapter 12.

- is subject to immigration control within the meaning of the Asylum and Immigration Act 1996;[201] and

- either does not have leave to enter or remain in the UK; or

- whose leave to enter or remain in the UK is subject to a condition to maintain and accommodate himself, and any dependents, without recourse to public funds.

17.100 Importantly, a restricted case only arises where the applicant's entitlement to the main housing duty is *solely* because of the presence in the applicant's household of a restricted person. For example, if it were the presence of the restricted person that resulted in the applicant becoming homeless, or having a priority need, the applicant's case would be a restricted case. However, if the applicant would be entitled to the main housing duty regardless of the presence of the restricted person (if, for example, the applicant himself or herself had a priority need, or there were other members of the applicant's household whose presence entitled the applicant to a priority need), the applicant's case would not be a restricted case.

17.101 The applicant will know whether his or her case is a 'restricted case', because the local housing authority is required to notify him or her that the main housing duty is owed because of the presence in his or her household of a restricted person.[202] The applicant will have the right to request a review of any decision that he or she is a 'restricted case'.[203]

The modifications to the main housing duty

17.102 In a restricted case, the main housing duty is modified in two ways:

- by removing the requirement to give the applicant a copy of the local housing authority's statement on 'choice' in its allocation scheme;[204] and

- by allowing the local housing authority to bring the main housing duty to an end by an offer of 'private accommodation'.[205]

Removing the requirement to give the applicant a copy of the policy on 'choice'

17.103 HA 1996, s 193(3A) is modified so that applicants who are 'restricted cases' need not be given a copy of the local housing authority's statement on

---

[201] See **12.53–12.59**.

[202] HA 1996, s 184(3A), inserted by Housing and Regeneration Act 2008, Sch 15, para 2, in force for applications made on or after 2 March 2009. See **10.75–10.78**.

[203] Such a decision would be a decision as to 'what duty (if any)' is owed to the applicant and therefore carries a right to request a review at HA 1996, s 202(1)(b). See **19.14–19.15**.

[204] HA 1996, s 193(3A), amended by Housing and Regeneration Act 2008, Sch 15, para 5, in force for applications made on or after 2 March 2009. See **17.13** and **17.103**.

[205] HA 1996, s 193(7AA)–(7AD), inserted by Housing and Regeneration Act 2008, Sch 15, para 5, in force for applications made on or after 2 March 2009. See **17.104–17.108**.

'choice' in its allocation scheme. This is presumably because the applicant is not entitled to reasonable preference as a result of being owed the main housing duty.[206] It should be remembered, however, that the applicant may still be entitled to any reasonable preference other than those arising as a result of the applicant being homeless or being owed the main housing duty.[207]

An offer of 'private accommodation'

17.104 The main housing duty is modified so that the duty comes to an end if the applicant accepts or refuses an offer of 'private accommodation.[208]

17.105 An offer is an offer of 'private accommodation' if:

- it is an offer of an assured shorthold tenancy made by a private landlord; and

- it is made with the approval of the local housing authority in pursuance of arrangements made by the local housing authority with the landlord with a view to bringing the main housing duty to an end; and

- it is a fixed term tenancy for a period of at least 12 months.[209]

17.106 For the duty to come to an end, the applicant must have been informed of:

- the possible consequences of refusal of the offer; and

- that he or she has the right to request a review of the suitability of the accommodation.[210]

17.107 The private accommodation offer should not be approved by the local housing authority unless it is satisfied:

- that the accommodation is suitable for the needs of the applicant and his or her household; and

- that it is reasonable for the applicant to accept the offer.[211]

---

[206] HA 1996, s 167(2ZA), inserted by Housing and Regeneration Act 2008, Sch 15, para 2, in force for applications made on or after 2 March 2009.

[207] HA 1996, s 167(2)(c), (d) or (e). See **4.55–4.76**.

[208] HA 1996, s 193(7AA)–(7AD), inserted by Housing and Regeneration Act 2008, Sch 15, para 5, in force for applications made on or after 2 March 2009.

[209] HA 1996, s 193(7AC), inserted by Housing and Regeneration Act 2008, Sch 15, para 5, in force for applications made on or after 2 March 2009.

[210] HA 1996, s 193(7AB), inserted by Housing and Regeneration Act 2008, Sch 15, para 5, in force for applications made on or after 2 March 2009.

[211] HA 1996, s 193(7F), amended by Housing and Regeneration Act 2008, Sch 15, para 5, in force for applications made on or after 2 March 2009.

17.108   The applicant has the right to request a review of the suitability of the offer.[212] He or she may accept the offer whilst simultaneously requesting a review of the suitability.[213] For this reason, it is vital that the fixed-term agreement includes a break clause allowing the applicant to give notice ending the tenancy, so that the applicant can do so if his or her request for a review succeeds and the local housing authority decides that the accommodation is not suitable.

Re-applying after the main housing duty ends

17.109   An applicant in respect of whom the main housing duty has ended is free to make a new application for homelessness assistance to the same local housing authority, or any other authority, at any time.[214]

17.110   However, any local housing authority will be entitled to rely on the termination of the earlier duty towards the applicant, and will not come under a new duty to secure accommodation or provide other assistance unless there has been a fresh incidence of homelessness between the end of the last duty and the new application.[215] A fresh incidence arises where there are new facts put forward on the new application.[216]

DUTY TO SECURE ACCOMMODATION FOR A PERIOD THAT WILL GIVE THE APPLICANT A REASONABLE OPPORTUNITY OF SECURING HIS OR HER OWN ACCOMMODATION[217]

17.111   This duty is owed to an applicant whom the local housing authority is satisfied is homeless and has a priority need but whom it is also satisfied became homeless intentionally. The duty is triggered as soon as those conditions are fulfilled, although the local housing authority will provide written notification to the applicant indicating that this is the duty that it owes to him or her.[218] The duty owed by the local housing authority is to secure

---

[212]   HA 1996, s 202(1)(g), inserted by Housing and Regeneration Act 2008, Sch 15, para 7, in force for applications made on or after 2 March 2009.

[213]   HA 1996, s202(1A), as amended by Housing and Regeneration Act 2008, Sch 15, para 7, in force for applications made on or after 2 March 2009.

[214]   HA 1996, s 193(9).

[215]   *R v Westminster City Council ex p Chambers* (1982) 6 HLR 24, QBD.

[216]   *R v Harrow London Borough Council ex p Fahia* [1998] 1 WLR 1396, HL; and *Begum v Tower Hamlets London Borough Council* [2005] EWCA Civ 340, [2005] HLR 34, CA. See also **9.54–9.64**.

[217]   HA 1996, s 190(2)(a). See English Code, paras 14.27–14.29; Welsh Code, paras 16.37–16.40.

[218]   HA 1996, s 184(3). See **10.60**. Where a local housing authority had rejected the contention that it owed a limited duty to accommodate an applicant whom it had found to have become homeless intentionally, it was ordered to pay the costs of the applicant's judicial review claim. The prospect of the local housing authority losing the judicial review was 'towards the obvious end of the spectrum': per Walker J in *R (Dumbaya) v Lewisham London Borough Council* [2008] EWHC 1852 (Admin), (2008) September *Legal Action*, p 25, Admin Ct.

accommodation 'for such period as they consider will give him a reasonable opportunity of securing accommodation for his occupation'.[219] The accommodation secured for this period must meet all the usual requirements.[220] The local housing authority also has a duty to provide advice and assistance in the applicant's search for his or her own accommodation.[221]

17.112 The applicant owed these duties is likely to have been secured with interim accommodation pending the decision on his or her application. In that situation, the usual course will be for the local housing authority to continue the provision of that same accommodation for whatever further period it has decided will satisfy its duty. If it has not previously secured accommodation, it must do so for that same period.

17.113 Local housing authorities, having strategic responsibility for housing in their areas, are uniquely well placed to determine what sort of period an applicant will require in order to have a 'reasonable opportunity' of finding housing in their areas. The duty is not to secure accommodation for as long as it actually takes for the applicant to find his or her own housing. It is instead to secure accommodation for the period that the local housing authority considers will give the applicant a 'reasonable opportunity' to find and secure accommodation for himself or herself.

17.114 Plainly the period required will be longer in areas of housing shortage. In an inner London borough, for example, a period of 14 days for an applicant who had a family to have such a 'reasonable opportunity' was considered by the courts to be unlawfully short and a period of months might be expected The Administrative Court has also found that an initial decision to give a single parent of three children 6 or 7 days' accommodation could not be considered reasonable, but that there was no error of law in the local housing authority's subsequent decision not to extend the period beyond 28 days.[222]

17.115 The Codes advise that each case should be considered on its merits.[223] The Codes encourage local housing authorities, when fixing the period, to take

---

[219] HA 1996, s 190(2)(a).

[220] Described at **17.12**.

[221] See English Code, paras 14.27–14.29; Welsh Code, paras 16.37–16.40. And see **17.132–17.145**.

[222] *R (Nipyo) v Croydon London Borough Council* [2008] EWHC 847 (Admin), [2008] HLR 37, Admin Ct. In another case, the judge decided that any accommodation secured under HA 1996, s 190(2)(a) would have been for a maximum period of 3 months (*Newman v Croydon London Borough Council* [2008] EWCA Civ 1176, (2009) *Legal Action*, p 22, CA). In an application for permission to bring a judicial review claim, a judge decided that he should grant an interim injunction requiring the local housing authority to continue to secure accommodation to the applicant, where the evidence was that within a week the claimant would be able to clear previous arrears, secure housing benefit and with the help of a bond scheme, secure a private sector tenancy (*R (Anwar) v Manchester City Council* [2009] EWHC 2876 (Admin), (2010) January *Legal Action*, p 36, Admin Ct).

[223] English Code, para 14.28; Welsh Code, para 16.39. The Welsh Code, and earlier editions of the English Code, refer to a 28-day period. In the current edition of the English Code, this period has been replaced by 'a few weeks', reflecting the approach of determining what is reasonable

into account local housing circumstances and the supply of accommodation in the district, as well as the applicant's resources, his or her ability to fund rent in advance and pay a deposit for a private sector tenancy, and any other relevant circumstances. Perhaps the most relevant material that might help to assess the period that the applicant will require will come from the personal assessment of his or her housing needs.[224] Indeed, it is difficult to see how, save in the most straightforward case, the local housing authority could fix the period (except perhaps on a provisional basis) until the assessment had been completed.

17.116 The Court of Appeal has held that, when considering what period would give the applicant a 'reasonable opportunity', the local housing authority should consider what is reasonable from an applicant's standpoint, having regard to his or her circumstances and in the context of accommodation potentially available. Considerations peculiar to the local housing authority, such as the extent of its resources and the other demands on its resources, are not to be taken into account when determining the length of the period.[225]

17.117 If the applicant wants to challenge the local housing authority's decision as to the length of the period that it considers will give him or her 'a reasonable opportunity' of securing his or her own accommodation, she or he can only challenge by way of judicial review. This is because it is a dispute over the way in which the local housing authority is performing its duty, not over what duty, if any, is owed to the applicant, and so the statutory right to request a review is not available.[226]

17.118 Accommodation secured under this statutory duty is unlikely to be protected by the Protection from Eviction Act 1977. It can therefore be terminated on reasonable notice, but with no obligation on the landlord to obtain a possession order.[227]

---

from the applicant's standpoint rather than using a fixed or normal period (*R (Conville) v Richmond upon Thames London Borough Council* [2006] EWCA Civ 718, [2006] HLR 45, CA).
[224] HA 1996, s 190(4). See **17.136–17.137**.
[225] *R (Conville) v Richmond upon Thames London Borough Council* [2006] EWCA Civ 718, [2006] HLR 45, CA.
[226] *R (Conville) v Richmond upon Thames London Borough Council* [2006] EWCA Civ 718, [2006] HLR 45, CA. For judicial review, see **19.211–19.237**.
[227] Protection from Eviction Act 1977, s 3. See **16.80–16.84**. *Desnousse v Newham London Borough Council* [2006] EWCA Civ 547, [2006] HLR 38, CA, but note that this case was concerned with accommodation occupied under a licence, not a tenancy, and left open the question of whether the position might be different if the accommodation is let under a tenancy (per Lloyd LJ at [69]).

DUTY TO TAKE REASONABLE STEPS TO SECURE THAT ACCOMMODATION DOES NOT CEASE TO BE AVAILABLE[228]

17.119 If a local housing authority is satisfied that an applicant is threatened with homelessness unintentionally, and also has a priority need, its duty is to take reasonable steps to secure that accommodation does not cease to be available for the occupation of the applicant and his or her household.[229] The applicant will be informed that this is the duty that he or she is owed in the notification of the decision on his or her application.[230]

17.120 In these circumstances, the local housing authority will normally invite the applicant to apply for an allocation of accommodation under HA 1996, Part 6 (if he or she had not already done so). HA 1996, Part 7 requires that the local housing authority must also give the applicant a copy of its statement of policy on choice within the allocation scheme and of any policy allowing the applicant to express a preference within that scheme.[231]

17.121 In performing its duty under HA 1996, Part 7, the local housing authority will usually first consider what can be done to keep the applicant in the accommodation in which he or she is threatened with homelessness.

17.122 The Codes suggest that the local housing authority should consider:

- the possibility of constructive negotiations with the applicant's landlord (if the applicant is living in the private rented sector and facing repossession);

- the scope for mediation (if the applicant has been asked to leave accommodation provided by family or friends);

- providing support to the household so as to ease any pressures that may have led to a request that the applicant should leave the accommodation; and

- providing assistance with any specific problems that can be addressed, such as housing benefit delays.[232]

---

[228] HA 1996, s 195(2).

[229] HA 1996, s 195(2). See English Code, paras 14.6–14.9; Welsh Code, paras 16.23–16.24 for guidance.

[230] HA 1996, s 184(3). See **10.60**.

[231] HA 1996, s 195(3A). Unless the applicant's case is a 'restricted threatened homelessness case': HA 1996, s 195(4B), inserted by Housing and Regeneration Act 2008, Sch 15, para 6, in force for applications made on or after 2 March 2009. See **17.98–17.108**.

[232] English Code, para 14.7; Welsh Code, para 16.23.

17.123   The local housing authority's homelessness review and strategy should be consulted for the specific help that should be available in the district for those facing the prospect of homelessness and who are trying to retain their homes.[233]

17.124   If the local housing authority is unable to ensure the retention of the accommodation in which the applicant is threatened with homelessness, the local housing authority will then itself be under a duty to secure accommodation for the applicant and the members of his or her household.[234] That duty must be performed in accordance with the requirements that attach to all of the housing functions under HA 1996, Part 7.[235]

17.125   The duty contains no time limit and so could be owed indefinitely; it is brought to an end only in circumstances which would (as necessarily modified) bring the main housing duty to an end.[236]

The special rules for 'restricted threatened homelessness cases'[237]

17.126   A 'restricted threatened homelessness case' is defined as a case where the duty under this provision would not have arisen without the presence in the applicant's household of a restricted person.[238]

17.127   A restricted threatened homelessness case only arises where the applicant's entitlement to the duty is *solely* because of the presence in the applicant's household of a restricted person. For example, if it were the presence of the restricted person that resulted in the applicant becoming threatened with homeless, or having a priority need, the applicant's case would be a restricted case. However, if the applicant would be entitled to the duty regardless of the presence of the restricted person (if, for example, the applicant himself or herself had a priority need, or there were other members of the applicant's household whose presence entitled the applicant to a priority need), the applicant's case would not be a restricted threatened homelessness case.

17.128   The applicant will know whether or not his case is a 'restricted threatened homelessness case', because the local housing authority is required to notify him or her that the duty is owed because of the presence in his or her

---

[233]   See Chapter 8.
[234]   HA 1996, s 195(4).
[235]   See **17.12**.
[236]   HA 1996, s 195(4). Those circumstances are reviewed at **17.40** and **17.49–17.108**.
[237]   HA 1996, s 195(4B), inserted by Housing and Regeneration Act 2008, Sch 15, para 6, in force for applications made on or after 2 March 2009.
[238]   HA 1996, s 195(4B), inserted by Housing and Regeneration Act 2008, Sch 15, para 6, in force for applications made on or after 2 March 2009. 'Restricted person' is defined at HA 1996, s 184(7); and see **17.98–17.99**.

household of a restricted person.[239] The applicant will have the right to request a review of any decision that he or she is a 'restricted threatened homelessness case'.[240]

The modifications to the duty

17.129   In a restricted threatened homelessness case, the duty is modified in two ways:

- by removing the requirement to give the applicant a copy of the local housing authority's statement on 'choice' in its allocation scheme;[241] and

- by allowing the local housing authority to bring the duty to an end by an offer of 'private accommodation'.[242]

Removing the requirement to give the applicant a copy of the policy on 'choice'

17.130   HA 1996, s 195(3A) is modified so that applicants who are 'restricted threatened homelessness cases' need not be given a copy of the local housing authority's statement on 'choice' in its allocation scheme. This is presumably because the applicant is not entitled to reasonable preference as a result of being owed the duty.[243] It should be remembered, however, that the applicant may still be entitled to any reasonable preference other than those arising as a result of the applicant being homeless or being owed this duty or the main housing duty.[244]

An offer of 'private accommodation'[245]

17.131   If the local housing authority is unable to ensure the retention of the accommodation in which the applicant is threatened with homelessness, the local housing authority may bring the duty to an end by making the applicant an offer of 'private accommodation'.[246]

---

[239]   HA 1996, s 184(3A), inserted by Housing and Regeneration Act 2008, Sch 15, para 2, in force for applications made on or after 2 March 2009. See **10.75–10.78**.

[240]   Such a decision would be a decision as to 'what duty (if any)' is owed to the applicant and therefore carries a right to request a review at HA 1996, s 202(1)(b). See **19.14–19.15**.

[241]   HA 1996, s 195(3A) as amended by Housing and Regeneration Act 2008, Sch 15, para 6, in force for applications made on or after 2 March 2009. See **17.13**.

[242]   HA 1996, s 195(4A), inserted by Housing and Regeneration Act 2008, Sch 15, para 6, in force for applications made on or after 2 March 2009 and applying HA 1996, s 193(7AA)–(7AD) to restricted threatened homelessness cases.

[243]   HA 1996, s 167(2ZA), inserted by Housing and Regeneration Act 2008, Sch 15, para 2, in force for applications made on or after 2 March 2009.

[244]   HA 1996, s 167(2)(c), (d) or (e). See **4.55–4.76**.

[245]   HA 1996, s 195(4A)–(4B), inserted by Housing and Regeneration Act 2008, Sch 15, para 6, in force for applications made on or after 2 March 2009.

[246]   HA 1996, s 195(4A)–(4B), see **17.104–17.108**.

DUTY TO PROVIDE ADVICE AND ASSISTANCE

17.132 For more than two decades the duty to provide advice and assistance was a much-neglected aspect of the regime of powers and duties now to be found in HA 1996, Part 7. However, it has been transformed by the Homelessness Act 2002 and, most particularly, by the innovative requirement that 'the applicant's housing needs' should be assessed in every case in which the duty is owed, leading to person-specific advice and assistance, tailor-made for the individual applicant.

17.133 Duties to provide advice and assistance are owed to applicants who:

(1) became homeless unintentionally and do not have a priority need;[247] or

(2) became homeless intentionally, whether they have a priority need or not;[248] or

(3) became threatened with homelessness unintentionally and do not have a priority need;[249] or

(4) became threatened with homelessness intentionally, whether they have a priority need or not.[250]

17.134 The duty owed to an applicant in either of the first two categories is to provide:

> '... advice and assistance in any attempts he may make to secure that accommodation becomes available for his occupation.'[251]

17.135 The duty in respect of the second two categories of applicant is to provide advice and assistance with:

> '... any attempts he may make to secure that accommodation does not cease to be available for his occupation.'[252]

17.136 Before the advice and assistance is provided under these duties, the particular applicant's housing needs must be assessed so that the advice and assistance can be tailored to meet the applicant's individual needs.[253] The

---

[247] HA 1996, s 192(2).
[248] HA 1996, s 190(2)(b) and (3).
[249] HA 1996, s 195(5)(a).
[250] HA 1996, s 195(5)(b).
[251] HA 1996, ss 190(2) and 192(2)(b).
[252] HA 1996, s 195(5).
[253] HA 1996, ss 190(4), 192(4) and 195(6). See English Code, paras 14.4 and 14.29; Welsh Code, paras 16.25–16.36 for guidance. Surprisingly the current edition of the English Code contains *less* guidance on the duty to provide advice and assistance than previous editions did. It cross-references to the advice provided as part of the local housing authority's duty to ensure that a free advice and information service is provided under HA 1996, s 179. The latter service

quality and extent of the assessment will therefore be crucial in order to formulate properly the advice and assistance necessary to help the applicant best.

17.137 The scope of the assessment of the applicant's housing needs (for the future) is wider than the scope of the inquiries the local housing authority will have already made under HA 1996, Part 7 (which essentially look to the past and present). Local housing authorities should identify any factors making it difficult for the applicant to obtain accommodation, such as poverty, outstanding debts, health problems, disabilities, whether or not English (or Welsh) is the applicant's first language, and so on. They should take account of the factors that originally led to the applicant's homelessness (or threatened homelessness) and consider his or her ability to obtain and maintain accommodation. They should consider the type of accommodation (including size, location, affordability and any special needs) that would be appropriate for the applicant.[254]

17.138 The advice and assistance actually provided must include information about the likely availability of the type of accommodation appropriate to the applicant's housing needs in the local housing authority's district, including in particular the location and sources of that type of accommodation.[255] Gone are the days when all that applicants would receive under this duty was a general list of local estate or letting agents or hostels. If applicants are referred to local landlords or letting agencies under this duty nowadays, the local housing authority must have satisfied itself that those landlords or agencies will be in a position to supply the sort of accommodation required by the applicant.

17.139 If the applicant cannot afford to provide a deposit, or to pay rent in advance, in order to obtain private rented accommodation, the local housing authority should consider offering a rent guarantee. Local housing authorities may provide deposits and/or guarantees themselves.[256] Local housing authorities' power to pay deposits is derived from Local Government Act 1988, s 24 and requires consent from the Secretary of State.[257] Consent C permits local housing authorities to provide private landlords or RSLs with financial assistance for the purposes of carrying out their homelessness functions under HA 1996, Part 7 or the Homelessness Act 2002. Local housing authorities might also consider paying the costs of drawing up leases, making small one-off grants to landlords to encourage them to let to households owed homelessness duties, paying indemnities to guarantee tenancy obligations, and making discretionary housing payments to meet any shortfall between the rent and the

---

is, of course, provided under a different statutory duty available to anyone, not just applicants for homelessness assistance, and, crucially, does not contain the important requirement to assess an applicant's housing needs before providing advice and assistance. See **9.4–9.7**.

[254] English Code, para 14.4; Welsh Code, paras 16.31–16.36.

[255] HA 1996, ss 190(5), 192(5) and 195(7).

[256] English Code, paras 14.29 and 16.20; Welsh Code, paras 16.34–16.35. The statutory power is at Local Government Act 1988, ss 24–25.

[257] The General Housing Consents 2005 Consent C at www.communities.gov.uk/publications/housing/generalhousing.

amount of housing benefit payable. When deciding whether or not to provide such financial assistance, local housing authorities must act reasonably and in accordance with their duties towards all their tax and rent payers.[258]

17.140 The advice and assistance provided to an applicant who needs to acquire his or her own accommodation should include:

- details of how to apply for accommodation from local RSLs;

- details of the local housing authority's allocation scheme under HA 1996, Part 6, and of the right to apply for an allocation; and

- details of available assistance for those who would have difficulty in making an application to the allocation scheme without assistance.[259]

17.141 The local housing authority can arrange for the required advice and assistance to be provided by someone else (for example, by an independent housing advice agency) but first it must have carried out the assessment of the applicant's housing need itself, unless that function has been contracted out.[260] Only on completion of the assessment will it know which agency can provide the assistance appropriate to meet the applicant's particular housing needs.

17.142 There is *no* right to request a review of:

- any failure by the local housing authority to assess the applicant's needs;

- the conduct or results of the assessment;

- the content of the advice provided;

- the scope or quality of the assistance provided; or

- any other aspect of the local housing authority's performance of this duty.

17.143 If there is a claim by the applicant that:

- the local housing authority has failed to comply with its statutory duty to provide advice and assistance, or

- that it has failed to carry out an assessment,

the appropriate procedure is to bring judicial review proceedings seeking a mandatory order requiring the local housing authority to perform its duty.[261]

---

[258] English Code, para 16.20; Welsh Code, paras 16.34–16.35.
[259] English Code, paras 2.9–2.15, 14.4 and 14.29; Welsh Code, para 16.36.
[260] See **21.14–21.29**.
[261] See **19.211–19.237**.

17.144 If the applicant seeks to challenge the local housing authority's assessment of his or her housing needs, or the decision as to the type of advice and assistance that will be provided, the appropriate procedure is by seeking a quashing order in proceedings for judicial review.

POWERS TO SECURE ACCOMMODATION[262]

17.145 By way of a recent supplement to the portfolio of accommodation duties in HA 1996, Part 7, local housing authorities now have a power to secure accommodation for the applicant's occupation if the applicant did not become homeless intentionally and does not have a priority need.[263] The power is therefore targeted at the single homeless and at childless couples (not otherwise falling into the priority need categories). There is no maximum or minimum limit on the period for which such accommodation can be secured. If the power is exercised, then the normal requirements for the performance of any housing function apply.[264] There is a parallel power to take reasonable steps to secure that accommodation does not cease to be available for applicants who are unintentionally threatened with homelessness and do not have a priority need.[265]

17.146 An applicant who is the beneficiary of one of these powers will also have had the benefit of an assessment of housing need and the provision of advice and assistance.[266] Indeed, if accommodation is secured under these powers, the duty to provide advice and assistance (in any attempt that the applicant may make to obtain accommodation for him or herself) remains. So, if the accommodation is only secured for a temporary period,[267] advice and assistance must be directed to meeting the applicant's housing needs once the accommodation is withdrawn.

17.147 If local housing authorities use their own stock in order to secure the accommodation, any tenancies granted under those powers cannot be secure or introductory tenancies.[268]

17.148 When considering whether or not to use these powers, a local housing authority must take into account other demands on its housing stock (in particular the legitimate expectation of applicants to the allocation scheme that

---

[262] HA 1996, s 192(3), added by Homelessness Act 2002, s 5 (in force from 31 July 2002 (England) or 30 September 2002 (Wales)). See also English Code, paras 15.5–15.11; Welsh Code, paras 18.48–18.50 for guidance.

[263] HA 1996, s 192(3), as added.

[264] See **17.12**.

[265] HA 1996, s 195(9).

[266] HA 1996, s 192(2) and (4).

[267] The Codes recommend that this power should be exercised to secure accommodation 'for a limited period only ... as part of a managed programme of accommodation': English Code, para 15.10; Welsh Code, para 18.50.

[268] Secure and introductory tenancies can only be allocated in accordance with the provisions of HA 1996, Part 6; see Chapter 1. English Code, para 15.6; Welsh Code, para 18.49.

its own stock will be allocated according to the provisions of that scheme), together with the need to secure accommodation to other homeless persons as a result of its duties under HA 1996, Part 7. The powers are, as a result, most likely to be exercised where the supply of the appropriate type of accommodation matches or exceeds local demand.

17.149 The English Code suggests that accommodation might be secured under the powers to homeless key workers who do not have a priority need, particularly where it would be in the interests of the local community for accommodation to be provided for key workers to live in the local housing authority's district.[269] Recruiting workers to perform key public sector services (eg in hospitals, schools, fire services, or the police) is obviously an easier task if accommodation close by can be provided. The power can be used to secure short-term accommodation in the local housing authority's district for key workers to occupy as part of a managed programme to allow the applicants to obtain more settled accommodation in due course.

17.150 The English Code also suggests that local housing authorities should consider exercising their powers so as to comply with the European Convention on Human Rights and in circumstances where, if an available power was not exercised, they might be acting in a way incompatible with an applicant's Convention rights.[270] The expectation is therefore that the power could be used to secure accommodation where the applicant would normally have a priority need except that the member of his or her household who would confer the priority need is not eligible for assistance,[271] or where the applicant would be at risk of suffering inhuman or degrading treatment if accommodation was not secured.[272]

17.151 If accommodation is secured under these powers, it should be explained to the applicant that the accommodation is not secured for the long term and that the local housing authority and the applicant are expected to work together to obtain more settled long-term accommodation. If the accommodation is subsequently withdrawn from the applicant, reasonable notice of termination should be given.

17.152 There is no right to request a review of any refusal to exercise these powers in the applicant's favour, or of the local housing authority's decision as to the period for which the power will be exercised. Any challenge can only be brought by way of judicial review.

---

[269] English Code, para 15.9.

[270] English Code, para 15.8.

[271] HA 1996, s 185(4) as amended; *R (Morris) v Westminster City Council* [2005] EWCA 1184, [2006] HLR 8, CA. A refusal to exercise the power in favour of an applicant who had an ineligible young dependent child was not considered unlawful in *R (Bangura) v Southwark London Borough Council* [2007] EWHC 1681 (Admin), (2007) September *Legal Action*, p 18, Admin Ct. See **12.24–12.29**.

[272] See *R (Limbuela) v Secretary of State for the Home Department* [2005] UKHL 66, [2006] 1 AC 396, HL, and **20.91–20.96**.

WHEN THE DUTIES AND POWERS EXPIRE

17.153 Nothing in HA 1996, Part 7 addresses the factual situation that arises when the period for which accommodation has been secured, whether under a power or duty, comes to an end. Normally there is no further statutory duty to accommodate under HA 1996, Part 7 when those duties end.[273] If a review or appeal is being pursued, the local housing authority may have a discretion to accommodate,[274] but otherwise there will be no continuing statutory obligation.

17.154 However, even when a duty or power has expired, it does not follow that the applicant will be instantly on the streets. A local housing authority, like any other public body, must behave reasonably and so ensure that the applicant has had sufficient warning of the termination of accommodation to make alternative arrangements.[275] It must, of course, give whatever notice is required to bring the existing tenancy or licence to an end, and in some circumstances will need to apply for an order for possession.[276]

ADDITIONAL DUTIES AND POWERS

Duties to applicants whose household includes a person under 18

17.155 Special provision is made in HA 1996, Part 7 for situations in which it appears to a local housing authority that it will be unlikely to owe the main housing duty to a family with dependent children. The objective is to ensure that in those cases, where HA 1996, Part 7 will not provide the necessary safety net of the main housing duty, the alternative safety net of provision for children (under the Children Act 1989) is ready to be used by the time the local housing authority reaches its negative decision.

17.156 Where the applicant's household[277] includes a person under the age of 18, and the local housing authority has reason to believe that the applicant:

(1) may not be eligible for assistance; or

---

[273] Although it may be that the ending of main housing duty accommodation should be followed by a more limited duty, for example if the applicant is found to have become homeless intentionally. See *Newman v Croydon London Borough Council* [2008] EWCA Civ 1591, (2009) *Legal Action*, p 22, CA, where the Court of Appeal refused permission to appeal on the grounds that the decision had been justified on the facts, but reserved for another occasion whether a different result might be required in 'a starker case'.

[274] See **16.24–16.42**.

[275] *R v Secretary of State for the Environment ex p Shelter and the Refugee Council* [1997] COD 49, QBD, and *R v Newham London Borough Council ex p Ojuri (No 5)* (1999) 31 HLR 631, QBD.

[276] These issues (and in particular the question of what reasonable notice must be given) are explored further at **16.80–16.84**.

[277] In this context, the word 'household' is used to mean those persons who normally reside with the applicant as a member of his or her family, and any other persons who might reasonably be expected to reside with the applicant; see HA 1996, s 176 and **11.19–11.31**.

(2)   may have become homeless intentionally; or

(3)   may have become threatened with homelessness intentionally,

the local housing authority must ask the applicant to consent to the referral of the essential facts of his or her case to the local social services department or authority.[278] The local housing authority should not wait until its actual decision is made on the application under HA 1996, Part 7, but must obtain consent when the threshold conditions are met, which will usually be almost immediately after the application for homelessness assistance has been made.

17.157 This obligation is not triggered where the application is received from a lone applicant who is under 18, because such cases are covered by different liaison arrangements.[279]

17.158 Once the consent has been given, the essential facts and details of the application and of the subsequent HA 1996, Part 7 decision must be communicated to the social services authority.[280] This early notification obligation applies to unitary authorities (thus requiring notification between departments) as well as to separate local housing and social services authorities.[281] Social services should be alerted as quickly as possible, so as to have an opportunity to consider the case and plan their response well before the local housing authority has concluded its inquiries and reached any negative HA 1996, Part 7 decision.

17.159 If the applicant does not give his or her consent, the local housing authority may still disclose information about an application to the social services department if it has reason to believe that a child is, or may be, at risk of significant harm.[282]

17.160 HA 1996, Part 7 contains a provision designed to ensure that the local housing authority cannot simply wash its hands of the applicant and pass responsibility to social services. In the case of an applicant whose household includes a person under 18 and whom the local housing authority has decided:

•   is ineligible for assistance; or

•   has become homeless intentionally; or

•   has become threatened with homelessness intentionally,

---

[278] HA 1996, s 213A(2).

[279] See **13.107–13.136** and **13.175**. See also *R (M) v Hammersmith & Fulham London Borough Council* [2008] UKHL 14, [2008] 1 WLR 535, HL, and *R (G) v Southwark London Borough Council* [2009] UKHL 26, [2009] 1 WLR, 2399, HL.

[280] HA 1996, s 213A(1) and (2). See also English Code, chapter 13; Welsh Code, chapter 17 for guidance.

[281] HA 1996, s 213A(3).

[282] HA 1996, s 213A(4). See also English Code, para 13.7; Welsh Code, para 17.4.

the social services authority can call upon the local housing authority to provide such advice and assistance as is reasonable in the circumstances to help with the exercise of any social services functions under Part 3 of the Children Act 1989.[283] In this way it is intended that there should be a seamless scheme of social welfare provision for the most vulnerable families. In a Parliamentary debate initiated by a former housing minister, the Government spelt out its understanding that the scheme should work in this way.[284]

17.161 Any disagreement between the local housing authority and the social services authority should be resolved by discussion and negotiation and not by litigation.[285]

17.162 The assistance that the applicant can expect to receive from social services under the Children Act 1989 is outlined in Chapter 20.[286]

Duties and powers to protect the applicant's property

Introduction

17.163 The provisions of HA 1996, Part 7 recognise that a safety net scheme of assistance for the homeless will not be comprehensive if all it achieves is shelter for the people involved. Most applicants who are actually homeless or threatened with homelessness will also have at least a few personal possessions that need safeguarding, ranging from a single bag containing a change of clothes at one extreme to a full house of furniture, personal possessions and pets at the other. HA 1996, Part 7 imposes duties, and provides powers, for the safeguarding of these possessions.[287]

When duties are owed

17.164 A duty is owed to certain applicants[288] where the local housing authority has reason to believe that:

(1) there is a danger of loss of, or damage to, any of the applicant's personal property; and

(2) the danger arises because the applicant is unable to protect or deal with that property; and

(3) no other suitable arrangements have been or are being made.[289]

---

[283] HA 1996, s 213A(5) and (6).
[284] *Hansard*, HC Deb, vol 417, ser 6, cols 1092–1098 (6 February 2004).
[285] *R v Northavon District Council ex p Smith* [1994] 2 AC 402, HL, at 410 per Lord Templeman.
[286] See **20.55–20.82**.
[287] HA 1996, ss 211–212.
[288] Identified at HA 1996, s 211(2). See **17.166**.
[289] HA 1996, s 211(1). See English Code, chapter 20; Welsh Code, paras 16.47–16.53 for guidance.

17.165 'Danger' in this context means a genuine or real danger, that is something more than a possible danger, a slight risk or remote possibility of injury. It denotes a 'likelihood of harm'.[290] The duty will not therefore be triggered simply because property was left behind in a secure locked flat which was regularly visited by the applicant or by others on his or her behalf, giving rise to no greater risk of burglary than that experienced by a householder who is temporarily away from home.[291] Of course, the situation would be entirely different if the flat were insecure with 'a front door opened and banging in the wind', or the property was 'left in the gutter' after an eviction.[292]

17.166   If the local housing authority is or has been subject to:

(1)   an interim duty to accommodate; or

(2)   any of the accommodation duties towards people found to be homeless or threatened with homelessness; or

(3)   any of the accommodation duties towards applicants whose cases are being considered for referral,

it owes an applicant the duty to take reasonable steps to prevent the loss of property or prevent or mitigate any damage to it.[293]

17.167   Even if no such duty is or was owed to an applicant,[294] the local housing authority has a power to take any steps it considers reasonable in order to protect personal property.[295]

17.168   The local housing authority should therefore start by asking and answering the following questions:

(1)   Is there a danger of loss or damage?

(2)   Is that because the applicant is unable to protect or deal with his or her possessions?

(3)   Is that because no other suitable arrangements have been made or are being made?

17.169   The local housing authority is only under the duty imposed by HA 1996, Part 7, if all of the questions are answered positively.

---

290   *Deadman v Southwark London Borough Council* (2001) 33 HLR 75, CA, at [20], per Ward LJ. See English Code, para 20.6.
291   (2001) 33 HLR 75, CA at [21], per Ward LJ.
292   (2001) 33 HLR 75, CA, at [25], per Ward LJ.
293   HA 1996, s 211(2).
294   Because he or she has been found not to be homeless or threatened with homelessness, or not to be eligible for assistance, and was never secured with interim accommodation.
295   HA 1996, s 211(3).

17.170 If the applicant seeks to challenge a local housing authority's decision that all or any of the questions are to be answered 'No', the only challenge would lie in a claim by judicial review on the basis that the local housing authority's decision was wrong in law.[296]

17.171 If the answer to all three questions is 'Yes', then the next question for the local housing authority is whether it owes or has owed the applicant any of the duties identified at **17.166**. If it has done, even if that duty has since ended, it remains under a duty to take reasonable steps to prevent any loss of, or damage to, the property. If the local housing authority never owed the applicant any of those duties, it may still choose to take reasonable steps to prevent loss or damage.

The extent of the duty to prevent loss or damage

17.172 The local housing authority can deal with the personal property in any way that is reasonably necessary in order to prevent or mitigate loss or damage to it. This includes storing the property itself, or arranging for it to be stored by some other person.[297] If the applicant's previous home is not to be occupied immediately, the local housing authority may be able to arrange for the personal property to remain there if it can be adequately protected.[298]

17.173 The local housing authority has the right to impose conditions before it will take any steps to deal with personal property. These conditions can include levying reasonable charges and specifying in what circumstances the local housing authority may dispose of the property (usually upon reasonable notice to the applicant or if the applicant loses touch with the local housing authority and cannot be traced).[299]

17.174 In order to perform the duty and protect the property, the local housing authority is entitled to enter the applicant's usual or last place of residence at all reasonable times.[300]

Which possessions must be protected?

17.175 The powers and duties are concerned with the 'personal property' of the applicant. This is enlarged by HA 1996, Part 7 to embrace the 'personal property of any person who might reasonably be expected to reside with him'.[301] That terminology echoes wording used elsewhere in HA 1996,

---

[296] *Deadman v Southwark London Borough Council* (2001) 33 HLR 75, CA. There is no right to request a statutory review in respect of any of the functions of the local housing authority that relate to the protection of possessions.

[297] HA 1996, s 212(1).

[298] English Code, para 20.7; Welsh Code, para 16.49.

[299] HA 1996, s 211(4). English Code, para 20.10; Welsh Code, para 16.51.

[300] HA 1996, s 212(1)(a).

[301] HA 1996, s 211(5).

Part 7.[302] It does not automatically include all those with whom an applicant has been residing, but it is wide enough to include others with whom an applicant proposes to reside.

17.176 The term 'personal property' is not defined in HA 1996, Part 7. Given the wide variety of ways in which individuals accumulate possessions, the range will be enormous. In *R v Chiltern District Council ex p Roberts*,[303] the applicants were travelling showmen and the question arose as to whether their fairground equipment constituted their 'personal property'. Although, in the event, the case did not turn on the point, the judge said of 'personal property':

> 'I am inclined to the view that it would not extend to equipment used by an applicant in his business, at any rate where the business is conducted other than at the relevant accommodation ... The adjective "personal" is used to distinguish not only from real property, but from property used for commercial purposes, particularly if used elsewhere.'[304]

17.177 Nowadays, local housing authorities will want to avoid too restrictive a definition of personal property. Otherwise, they may run the risk of breaching the obligation on public authorities to take positive measures to prevent individuals losing their possessions contrary to the European Convention on Human Rights, Art 1, First Protocol.[305]

17.178 The most controversial issues in day-to-day practice arise where the personal possessions include pets. No local housing authority would deny that a goldfish bowl was 'personal property' – so, no less, the goldfish inside it. The safeguard for a local housing authority faced with a menagerie of cats, dogs and other pets is the power to impose, in advance, a condition that the applicant pays a reasonable charge for the action it takes.[306] Obviously, for applicants on a low income, the amount that is 'a reasonable charge' for them to pay may not meet the full cost to the local housing authority. But even the poorest applicant will have been paying something to feed the pets and so could be expected to pay a weekly charge equivalent to that amount so as to contribute to kennelling or other fees. Local housing authorities troubled by the need to arrange kennelling for a few dogs should sympathise with Harlow District Council, which faced the prospect of dealing with a homeless applicant with 56 cats.[307]

The ending of the duty

17.179 In most cases the duty to protect possessions will end at the same time as the most common form of the termination of the main housing duty, ie with

---

[302] See **11.19–11.31**.
[303] (1990) 23 HLR 387, QBD.
[304] *R v Chiltern District Council ex p Roberts* (1990) 23 HLR 387, QBD, at 396, per Pill J.
[305] Human Rights Act 1998, Sch 1.
[306] HA 1996, s 211(4)(a).
[307] *Harlow District Council v Sewell* [2000] JHL D29.

the applicant's move to a longer-term home. But this is not necessarily so. In one case the main housing duty ended by the applicant becoming homeless intentionally from his accommodation secured under HA 1996, Part 7. The duty to protect his possessions did not cease, and the local housing authority which had wrongly disposed of his personal possessions later agreed to pay £6,000 compensation and waive its storage charges.[308]

17.180 If the applicant requests that his or her property is moved to a particular address (whether it is the applicant's new long-term home or anywhere else), and the local housing authority agrees, the duty will have ended once the property has been moved. The authority must inform the applicant that this will be the case before it agrees to move the property.[309]

17.181 Otherwise, the duty ceases if the local housing authority no longer has reason to believe that there is a threat of loss of, or damage to, the applicant's property. For example, there may have been a change of circumstances in that the applicant has found accommodation or has become able to afford to pay private storage charges.

17.182 Once the duty has ended, the local housing authority retains a power to continue to store any property previously in storage, upon the same or modified conditions.[310]

17.183 If the local housing authority is no longer under the duty, and no longer intends to exercise the power, to store the property, it must notify the applicant of that fact. The notification must include the reasons for the decision that the duty no longer applies.[311]

17.184 Once the local housing authority has accepted a duty, then it is under a private law obligation to the applicant as bailee of his or her goods until the duty is discharged and the goods are collected.[312] If property is damaged or destroyed, the applicant would be entitled to bring a private law action for damages for breach of that duty, conversion and/or trespass to goods. The local housing authority may have a defence available if it can show that it took all reasonable steps to prevent the loss or damage, or if the loss or damage was not reasonably foreseeable.

FAILURE TO COMPLY WITH ANY STATUTORY DUTY

17.185 If the local housing authority fails to comply with any of the duties owed to the applicant discussed in this chapter, the appropriate remedy is a

---

[308] LGO Complaint against Sutton London Borough Council 03/B/6452, 9 December 2004, (2005) April *Legal Action*, p 30.
[309] HA 1996, s 212(2); English Code, para 20.12; Welsh Code, para 16.50.
[310] HA 1996, s 212(3).
[311] HA 1996, s 212(4).
[312] *Mitchell v Ealing London Borough Council* [1979] QB 1, QBD.

claim for a mandatory order in judicial review proceedings, requiring it to comply with its duty. Each of the different duties is absolute and cannot be deferred (unless specifically qualified in HA 1996, Part 7) once the statutory components or trigger factors are in place. However, as already indicated, no court will enforce the duty where a local housing authority has not been acting unreasonably in its attempts to perform its duties as quickly as possible.[313]

17.186   There is no common law or statutory provision that gives the applicant a right to financial compensation (damages) if the local housing authority fails to comply with any of these duties,[314] unless the failure constitutes breach of the applicant's rights under the European Convention on Human Rights.[315] If that is the case, damages under the Human Rights Act 1998, s 8 may be awarded.[316]

17.187   The applicant may prefer to seek recompense through the complaints scheme of the local housing authority and thereafter by complaint to the Local Government Ombudsman.[317]

17.188   An applicant might have a legitimate expectation that the duty owed to him or her is to be performed in a particular way, such as where the local housing authority had stated to the applicant that the duty would be performed by the provision of a certain type of accommodation (e g a permanent home or council tenancy). Where an applicant has a legitimate expectation that the duty towards him or her will be performed in a certain way, the Administrative Court in judicial review proceedings may intervene to uphold that legitimate expectation.[318] It will be for the local housing authority (subject to the supervision of the court) to decide how that expectation should be honoured. For example, the local housing authority may agree or the court may order that the applicant's points within the allocation scheme should include a number of points for legitimate expectation.[319]

---

[313]   *R v Newham London Borough Council ex p Mashuda Begum* (2000) 32 HLR 808, QBD.

[314]   *R v Ealing London Borough Council ex p Parkinson* (1995) 29 HLR 179, QBD, unless the local housing authority fails to prevent loss or damage to property, having accepted a duty under HA 1996, s 211.

[315]   HRA 1998, Sch 1, right to respect for the applicant's home, family and private life and correspondence.

[316]   See **20.88–20.99**.

[317]   See **19.238–19.245**.

[318]   For judicial review, see **19.211–19.237**.

[319]   *R (Bibi and Al-Nashed) v Newham London Borough Council* [2001] EWCA Civ 607, (2001) 33 HLR 955, CA; *R (Ibrahim) v Redbridge London Borough Council* [2002] EWHC 2756 (Admin), (2003) February *Legal Action*, p 35, Admin Ct; and *R (Bibi) v Newham London Borough Council* [2003] EWHC 1860 (Admin), (2003) September *Legal Action*, p 28, Admin Ct. See also **4.36**.

Chapter 18

SUITABILITY OF ACCOMMODATION

INTRODUCTION

18.1 There are three distinct stages at which, in applying the homelessness provisions of the Housing Act 1996 (HA 1996), Part 7, the question of the 'suitability' of accommodation may arise:

(1) in the provision of interim accommodation (pending an initial decision, a review decision, an appeal decision, or the outcome of a local connection referral);[1]

(2) in the provision of accommodation in performance of a housing duty owed under HA 1996, Part 7, or pursuant to a power to accommodate given by it;[2] or

(3) in the making of offers of accommodation where those offers are relied upon to release the local housing authority from duties owed under HA 1996, Part 7.[3]

This chapter is concerned with 'suitability' at the two latter stages.[4]

'Suitable' accommodation for whom?

18.2 Any accommodation secured by a local housing authority in performance of its duties or the exercise of its powers under HA 1996, Part 7, or offered with a view to achieving a release from its duties, must be 'suitable'. But suitable for whom?

18.3 The focus throughout HA 1996, Part 7 is on the 'applicant'.[5] Accommodation secured for the applicant must be 'available' for him or her. 'Available' is given a special meaning, ensuring that accommodation is 'available' not only for the applicant, but also for all those people who might loosely be included in his or her household.[6] There is no precise mirroring of this expanded approach, beyond the needs of the individual applicant, in the treatment of 'suitability'.

18.4 When dealing with 'suitability', HA 1996, Part 7 refers to suitability for 'a person' rather than for 'the applicant'.[7] From this, one can infer that the

---

[1]   For 'suitability' in this context see **16.53–16.56**.
[2]   See Chapter 17.
[3]   See **17.49–17.58, 17.71–17.91, 17.92–17.97** and **17.104–17.100**.
[4]   See for general guidance *Homelessness Code of Guidance for local authorities* (Department for Communities and Local Government, Department for Education and Skills, Department of Health, July 2006) (English Code), chapters 16–17. *Code of Guidance for local housing authorities on allocation of accommodation and homelessness for Wales* (National Assembly for Wales, April 2003) (Welsh Code), chapters 18–19.
[5]   See HA 1996, s 193(2) for one example.
[6]   As defined at HA 1996, s 176. See **11.19–11.31**. See *R (Ogbeni) v Tower Hamlets London Borough Council* [2008] EWHC 2444 (Admin), (2008) October *Legal Action*, p 37, Admin Ct.
[7]   HA 1996, s 210(1).

determination of suitability requires regard not only for the individual needs of the applicant, but also for the needs of all those other persons who are members of the applicant's family who normally reside with him or her and of anyone else who might reasonably be expected to reside with him or her.[8] This is certainly the approach taken in the Codes of Guidance, which, when dealing with suitability, specifically direct attention not only to the applicant but also to others in his or her family or household.[9]

18.5 In one of the leading modern cases on 'suitability', the Court of Appeal proceeded on the uncontested assumption that the accommodation:

> '... has to be suitable for the particular homeless person *and his or her family*. There is no doubt that the question of whether or not the accommodation is suitable requires an assessment of all the qualities of the accommodation in the light of the needs and requirements of the homeless person *and his or her family*.'[10]

18.6 'Family' was there used by the court in the sense of the household for whom accommodation must be made available.[11]

'Suitable' accommodation from whom?

18.7 When performing a duty (or exercising a power) to secure accommodation, a local housing authority need not provide the particular accommodation itself. HA 1996, Part 7 enables the securing of accommodation to be achieved in any one of three ways. These are:[12]

(1) by the local housing authority itself providing the accommodation.[13] This might be, for example, by providing council-owned housing, a place in a council-run hostel or supported housing scheme, or accommodation that the local housing authority has itself rented from a private owner;[14] or

---

8   HA 1996, ss 176, 206 and 210.

9   English Code, para 16.3; Welsh Code, paras 18.3, 19.7 and 19.11 (all referring to 'household'). In *R (McCammon-Mckenzie) v Southwark London Borough Council* [2004] EWHC 612 (Admin), [2004] All ER (D) 174 (Mar), Admin Ct, accommodation was not suitable for the applicant because her 16-year old son could not occupy it with her (and had been taken into care by social services as a result).

10   *R v Newham London Borough Council ex p Sacupima* (2001) 33 HLR 2, CA, at [28], per Latham LJ (emphasis added). More recently, the Court of Appeal referred to 'suitability': 'having regard to the circumstances of the occupant and his or her resident family' (*Codona v Mid-Bedfordshire District Council* [2004] EWCA Civ 925, [2005] HLR 1, CA, at [46], per Auld LJ). The House of Lords in *Ali & others v Birmingham City Council, Moran v Manchester City Council* [2009] UKHL 36, [2009] 1 WLR 1506, HL also referred to 'homeless families' rather than to 'applicants'

11   *R v Newham London Borough Council ex p Sacupima* (2001) 33 HLR 2, CA, at [32].

12   HA 1996, s 206(1).

13   HA 1996, s 206(1)(a).

14   English Code, paras 16.11–16.16; Welsh Code, paras 18.15–18.21.

(2) by obtaining accommodation for the applicant from some other person.[15] The other person may be a private landlord, a Registered Social Landlord ('RSL'), another local housing authority, a social services authority, a voluntary organisation or anyone else;[16] or

(3) by giving the applicant such advice and assistance that she or he is able to obtain accommodation from another person.[17] This would include helping an applicant to purchase accommodation from another person using her or his own funds.[18]

18.8 It is the local housing authority, and not the applicant, that chooses which of the three options will be used. For some local housing authorities (those which have transferred all their housing stock and other accommodation to new owners), only the latter two options will be available.

18.9 Where the local housing authority is relying on an offer of 'suitable' accommodation to release it from the duty under HA 1996, Part 7 that it already owes, that offer may be of local housing authority accommodation (its own or obtained from another local housing authority), of RSL property and, in some circumstances, of an assured shorthold tenancy from a private landlord.[19]

Suitability in general

18.10 In determining whether accommodation is 'suitable', local housing authorities must consider the applicant and his or her household's particular individual needs. A general assessment of what accommodation may be suitable could be made in advance (for example, that a unit of accommodation of a particular size or type is likely to be required). However, the question posed by HA 1996, Part 7 is whether the specific property secured for, or offered to, the applicant is 'suitable'.[20] Accordingly, local housing authorities cannot adopt blanket policies prescribing that certain types of accommodation will be suitable in certain circumstances.[21] If the applicant raises a reason why the accommodation that has been secured or offered is not suitable, the local housing authority must consider that particular reason. It cannot restrict itself to general considerations of whether the accommodation would be suitable for the average or ordinary applicant.[22]

18.11 The duty to secure suitable accommodation is a continuing one. If an applicant's circumstances change, so that the accommodation secured in

---

[15] HA 1996, s 206(1)(b).
[16] English Code, paras 16.17–16.31; Welsh Code, paras 18.22–18.36.
[17] HA 1996, s 206(1)(c)
[18] English Code, paras 16.32–16.36; Welsh Code, paras 18.37–18.39.
[19] See **18.123–18.135**.
[20] *R v Lambeth London Borough Council ex p Touhey* (1999) 32 HLR 707, QBD, at 716, 723 and 727, per Richards J.
[21] English Code, para 17.4; Welsh Code, para 19.7.
[22] *R v Brent London Borough Council ex p Omar* (1991) 23 HLR 446, QBD.

performance of a power or duty ceases to be suitable, the local housing authority has a duty to secure other, suitable accommodation.[23]

The bottom line

18.12   Where accommodation is being secured under HA 1996, Part 7, it must be 'suitable'. That represents a statutory bottom line. As later parts of this chapter demonstrate, 'suitability' is a flexible concept – what may be suitable for a few nights may not be suitable for a longer period.[24] But there is always an irreducible minimum standard below which accommodation must not fall:

> 'Although financial constraints and limited housing stock are matters that can be taken into account in determining suitability, there is a minimum and one must look at the needs and circumstances of the particular family and decide what is suitable for them, and there will be a line to be drawn below which the standard of accommodation cannot fall. If the accommodation falls below that line, and is accommodation which no reasonable local authority could consider to be suitable to the needs of the applicant, then the decision will be struck down, and an appeal to the resources argument will be of no avail.'[25]

18.13   The courts recognise that, from time to time, local housing authorities may find it simply impossible to secure 'suitable' accommodation. Strictly, the local housing authority concerned will be immediately in breach of an acknowledged statutory duty. On any legal challenge it will need compelling evidence in order to avoid the making of a mandatory order.[26] After all, if there is no accommodation reasonable for the applicant to occupy, he or she will still be 'homeless'.[27]

18.14   In *Codona v Mid-Bedfordshire District Council*,[28] Auld LJ, giving the leading judgment, surveyed the case law and held that there are three aspects of the issue of whether or not accommodation is 'suitable':

---

23   *R (Zaher) v Westminster City Council* [2003] EWHC 101 Admin, [2003] All ER (D) 253 (Jan), Admin Ct; and *R v Newham London Borough Council ex p Mashuda Begum* (1999) 32 HLR 808, QBD. English Code, para 17.8. An applicant in this situation, faced with a move from unsuitable accommodation to accommodation that the local housing authority has secured for him or her and has decided is suitable, will be at risk of the local housing authority deciding that its main housing duty has come to an end under HA 1996, s 193(5), if he or she refuses the offer of suitable accommodation (*Muse v Brent London Borough Council* [2008] EWCA Civ 1447, (2009) February *Legal Action*, p 32, CA). For the ending of the main housing duty under HA 1996, s 193(5), see **17.49–17.58**.

24   English Code, para 17.7.

25   *R v Newham London Borough Council ex p Sacupima* (2001) 33 HLR 2, CA, approving the first-instance decision of Dyson J, who had quoted Collins J in *R v Newham London Borough Council ex p Ojuri (No 3)* (1998) 31 HLR 452, QBD.

26   See *R v Lambeth London Borough Council ex p Touhey* (2000) 32 HLR 707, QBD.

27   HA 1996, s 175(3). See **11.72–11.117**.

28   [2004] EWCA Civ 925, [2005] HLR 1, CA.

'(1) suitability to a *Wednesbury* minimum level of suitability in the nature, location and standard of condition of the accommodation having regard to the circumstances of the applicant and his or her resident family, including the duration of their likely occupation of it;

(2) the absolute nature of the duty which, though coupled with an elastic concept of suitability taking account of financial constraints and limited availability of accommodation, is not so elastic as to permit an offer below the *Wednesbury* minimum standard (or … outside the margin of appreciation); and

(3) special consideration, in the regulatory provision for and in decision-making in individual cases, for the housing needs of particularly vulnerable applicants such as traditional gypsies with a view, so far as practicable and when considered with all the other circumstances, to facilitating their traditional way of life.'[29]

18.15 Where the applicant for homelessness assistance is applying on the basis that, although he or she has accommodation that is available for him or her, the accommodation is not reasonable to continue to occupy,[30] the accommodation might still be suitable for the applicant to occupy.[31] This is because the local housing authority will have to ask, and answer, two separate questions:

(1) Is the accommodation reasonable for the applicant to continue to occupy for as long as he or she would have to do unless the local housing authority takes action? If the answer is 'No', the applicant will be homeless.

(2) If the applicant is entitled to the main housing duty, is the accommodation suitable for him or her to occupy for the period during which the applicant can expect to live there until he or she receives an HA 1996, Part 6 offer or other accommodation?[32]

18.16 If the accommodation is not reasonable for the applicant to continue to occupy for one more night, then it will also not be suitable accommodation.[33]

Disputes over 'suitability'

Avenues for challenge

18.17 Although all accommodation secured under HA 1996, Part 7 must be 'suitable', not every decision about suitability is amenable to the statutory review procedure.[34]

---

[29] At [46].
[30] HA 1996, ss 175 and 176; see **11.72–11.117**.
[31] *Ali & others v Birmingham City Council, Moran v Manchester City Council* [2009] UKHL 36, [2009] 1 WLR 1506, HL.
[32] *Ali & others v Birmingham City Council, Moran v Manchester City Council* [2009] UKHL 36, [2009] 1 WLR 1506, HL, at [46]–[48], per Baroness Hale.
[33] *Ali & others v Birmingham City Council, Moran v Manchester City Council* [2009] UKHL 36, [2009] 1 WLR 1506, HL, at [47], per Baroness Hale.
[34] HA 1996, s 202(1). See **18.162–18.179** and **19.27–19.32** for a full description of that procedure.

18.18   The applicant has the right to request a review of a decision by the local housing authority that accommodation offered to him or her is suitable if:

(1)   the accommodation has been secured in 'discharge of their duty'; and

(2)   that duty is the duty owed under HA 1996, ss 190–193 or s 195 or s 196; or

(3)   the offer relied upon is made under a local housing authority's allocation scheme adopted under HA 1996, Part 6 and is intended to bring to an end the main housing duty in HA 1996, Part 7[35]; or

(4)   in 'restricted cases',[36] the offer is an offer of private accommodation[37] intended to bring the duty to an end.[38]

18.19   It is plain, therefore, that there is no right to a statutory review of the suitability of accommodation offered in the exercise of a power.[39] Presumably, this is a statutory representation of the maxim 'beggars can't be choosers'.

18.20   Even if the offer is made under a duty to accommodate, it must be under one of the specifically prescribed duties for there to be a right to a statutory review.

18.21   If the offer is made in order to release the local housing authority from the main housing duty, the offer must be the 'final' offer of accommodation offered under HA 1996, Part 6 in order to attract the right to a review.[40]

18.22   If a review on suitability is available and has been requested by the applicant, but is either unsuccessful or has not been determined by the local housing authority, the applicant can appeal to the county court on a point of law.[41]

18.23   'Suitability' decisions that do not fall within the scope of the statutory review scheme will need to be challenged by way of judicial review proceedings or under the local housing authority's complaints procedure.[42]

18.24   If the local housing authority and the applicant are agreed that accommodation which has been offered or secured is *not* suitable, the appropriate procedure in order to obtain suitable accommodation is for the applicant to bring judicial review proceedings for a mandatory order requiring

---

[35]   HA 1996, s 202(1)(f). See **19.27–19.32**.

[36]   As defined at HA 1996, ss 184(3A), 193(3B) and 195(4B). See **12.30–12.39** and **17.98–17.101**.

[37]   As defined at HA 1996, s 193(7A)–(7AD). See **17.104–17.108, 17.126–17.128** and **17.131**.

[38]   HA 1996, s 202(1)(g). See **19.33–19.35**.

[39]   For example, under HA 1996, s 192(3) or s 195(9). Any challenge would have to be brought by way of judicial review.

[40]   So any earlier offer under HA 1996, Part 6 or any offer of an assured tenancy outside Part 6 would not attract the right to a review. See **17.66–17.91**.

[41]   HA 1996, s 204(1). See **19.141–19.210**.

[42]   See **19.211–19.237** and **19.238–19.245**.

the local housing authority to secure such suitable accommodation. That remedy is discretionary. The High Court could refuse permission to seek judicial review if the breach of statutory duty was not particularly significant and of short duration,[43] or could refuse to make a mandatory order if the local housing authority demonstrated that it was doing all that it could to secure suitable accommodation.[44] But if there is plain and continuing failure and no clear evidence that everything possible is being done, the High Court should grant a mandatory order.[45]

Grounds for challenge

18.25 The question of whether or not accommodation is 'suitable' is a factual one for the local housing authority to answer. It is not for the applicant, the applicant's adviser, or for a judge to determine.

18.26 Any applicant wishing to challenge the decision in the courts, and to argue that no reasonable local housing authority would have found that the accommodation was suitable for his or her needs, has a high hurdle to overcome.[46]

18.27 A challenge may have a better prospect of success if it attacks the local housing authority's procedure in reaching its decision, or alleges a failure to consider a specific point raised, or a failure to have regard to a matter which ought to have been taken into account.

FACTORS THAT THE LOCAL HOUSING AUTHORITY MUST TAKE INTO ACCOUNT

18.28 As a matter of law, when it is determining whether particular accommodation is 'suitable', the local housing authority is required to consider five matters:

(1) the provisions of the Housing Act 1985 relating to slum clearance and overcrowding;[47]

(2) the provisions of Parts 1–4 of the Housing Act 2004 relating to housing conditions, houses in multiple occupation and licensing of accommodation;[48]

---

43 *R v Newham London Borough Council ex p Sacupima* (2001) 33 HLR 2, CA, at [17].
44 *R v Lambeth London Borough Council ex p Touhey* (2000) 32 HLR 707, QBD.
45 *R v Newham London Borough Council ex p Mashuda Begum* (2000) 32 HLR 808, QBD; and *R (McCammon-Mckenzie) v Southwark London Borough Council* [2004] EWHC 612 (Admin), [2004] All ER (D) 174 (Mar), Admin Ct.
46 *R v Haringey London Borough Council ex p Karaman* (1996) 29 HLR 366, QBD.
47 HA 1996, s 210(1); Housing Act 1985, Parts 9 and 10. See **18.35–18.37**.
48 HA 1985, s 210(1); Housing Act 2004 Parts 1–4. See **18.38–18.44**.

(3)　the affordability of the accommodation;[49]

(4)　the guidance given in the Codes of Guidance;[50] and

(5)　the relevant content (if any) of its own homelessness strategy.[51]

18.29　English local housing authorities should also be aware that bed and breakfast accommodation made available under their duties to secure accommodation is deemed not to be suitable for applicants with family commitments, unless no other accommodation is available (and even then for at most only a 6-week period).[52]

18.30　Welsh local housing authorities are required to take into account four other matters when deciding whether accommodation is suitable for a person in priority need[53] where the accommodation is secured under a statutory duty. Those are:

(a)　the specific health needs of the person;

(b)　the proximity and accessibility of social services;

(c)　the proximity and accessibility of the support of the family or other support services; and

(d)　any disability of the person.[54]

18.31　Welsh local housing authorities are prohibited from using bed and breakfast accommodation and other shared accommodation for all applicants who have a priority need except for very tightly defined periods of no more than 2 or 6 weeks (depending on the standard of the accommodation).[55]

18.32　The local housing authority's file notes, if not the terms of any letter written to the applicant, should demonstrate that these mandatory factors have been considered in respect of each unit of accommodation offered or secured. The presence of these factors in the statutory scheme ensures that a local

---

49　HA 1996, s 210(2); Homelessness (Suitability of Accommodation) Order 1996, SI 1996/3204. See **18.45–18.46** and Appendix 2.

50　English Code, chapter 17; Welsh Code, chapter 19.

51　Homelessness Act 2002, s 1(5). See **7.73–7.74**.

52　Homelessness (Suitability of Accommodation) (England) Order 2003, SI 2003/3326. See **18.93–18.113** and Appendix 2.

53　All applicants who are beneficiaries of any of the statutory duties to secure accommodation will have, or the local housing authority will have reason to believe that they may have, a priority need.

54　Homelessness (Suitability of Accommodation) (Wales) Order 2006, SI 2006/650 (W 71), art 3, in force from 3 April 2006. See **18.47–18.48** and Appendix 3.

55　Homelessness (Suitability of Accommodation) (Wales) Order 2006, SI 2006/650 (W 71), See **18.105–18.113**.

housing authority cannot rely on accommodation offered unless it has informed itself, at least, of the physical attributes of the specific accommodation and its cost.

18.33 Beyond the mandatory matters, however, numerous judicial decisions – most recently reviewed and applied by the Court of Appeal in *Codona v Mid-Bedfordshire District Council*[56] – have confirmed that 'suitability' has 'a broad meaning'.

> 'It must, as a matter of common-sense encompass considerations of the range, nature and location of accommodation as well as of its standard of condition and the likely duration of the applicant's occupancy of it. Standards of the condition of property are clearly important.'[57]

18.34 In the rest of this chapter, we consider first the three mandatory matters set out at **18.28**(1)–(3) above; second, the additional statutory factors for Welsh local housing authorities; and then the broader range of matters relevant to 'suitability'.

Slum clearance and overcrowding

18.35 The provisions of the Housing Act 1985 direct local housing authorities to take action where dwelling houses in their districts are in such condition as to require demolition or clearance or are statutorily overcrowded.[58]

18.36 These strategic responsibilities would be wholly undermined if homeless households were to be placed in such poor or overcrowded premises at the initiative of the very same local housing authority. For that reason, the local housing authority is required by HA 1996, Part 7 to 'have regard to' those statutory provisions addressing such housing conditions when considering what would be 'suitable' accommodation.[59]

18.37 HA 1996, Part 7 does not expressly say that accommodation which fails to meet statutory minimum standards or would be statutorily overcrowded is never suitable. It follows, therefore, that a local housing authority could determine that the state of the accommodation contravenes the statutory standards, but that it is still suitable, although it would seem that the local housing authority would need some compelling reasons for such a determination. The Welsh Code advises that any accommodation that is not fit for human habitation cannot be suitable, but accommodation that is statutorily overcrowded may be suitable, with the burden falling on the local housing authority to show that it is.[60]

---

56   [2004] EWCA Civ 925, [2005] HLR 1, CA.
57   Auld LJ at [34].
58   Housing Act 1985, Parts 9 and 10. See English Code, Annex 16 for the definition of statutory overcrowding.
59   HA 1996, s 210(1).
60   Welsh Code, paras 19.3–19.6. English Code, para 17.16 is more circumspect.

Housing conditions, houses in multiple occupation and licensing of accommodation

18.38 The Housing Act 2004 amended the statutory rubric of the mandatory considerations on the question of 'suitability' with effect from 6 April 2006 in England (16 June 2006 in Wales). From that date, local housing authorities should have regard to 'slum clearance and overcrowding and Parts 1 to 4 of the Housing Act'.[61] The following paragraphs provide only a summary outline of the scope of Parts 1–4 of the Housing Act 2004 to which the amended text now draws attention.[62]

18.39 Part 1 of the Housing Act 2004[63] contains duties and powers enabling local housing authorities to inspect the condition of residential premises in their areas and to assess them for hazards. A 'hazard' is a risk of harm to the health of an actual or potential occupier deriving from a deficiency in the dwelling or neighbouring land. Where there are hazards identified as 'Category One' hazards, the local housing authority will be under a duty to take enforcement action. Where there are 'Category Two' hazards, the local housing authority has a power, not a duty, to require remedial action. The hazards relate to physiological requirements (damp and mould growth, excess cold or heat, pollutants), psychological requirements (relating to space, security, light and noise), protection against infection and protection against accident. The assessment of hazards is a complex process, including an assessment of the likelihood of an occurrence, the risk to health and safety of an actual or potential occupant, and the spread of possible harms.[64]

18.40 Neither the Housing Act 2004, nor the amended HA 1996, s 210, provide that accommodation will be, as a matter of law, unsuitable if it constitutes a Category One or Category Two hazard. However, the English Code contains a recommendation from the Secretary of State that, as a minimum, local housing authorities should ensure that accommodation secured under HA 1996, Part 7 duties is free of Category One hazards.[65] This should not be read as guidance that 'suitable accommodation' can contain Category Two hazards. The local housing authority should still explicitly consider the condition of the building and the risk to health and safety when deciding whether it is suitable.

18.41 Part 2[66] of the Housing Act 2004 requires that houses in multiple occupation (HMOs), which include privately owned bed and breakfast and

---

61   HA 1996, s 210(1), amended by Housing Act 2004, s 265 and Sch 15, para 43 with effect from 6 April 2006 (England) and 16 June 2006 (Wales): Housing Act 2004 (Commencement No 5 and Transitional Provisions and Savings) (England) Order 2006, SI 2006/1060, arts 1(1), (3)(c) and 2(1)(d); and Housing Act 2004 (Commencement No 3 and Transitional Provisions and Savings (Wales) Order 2006, SI 2006/1535, arts 1(2)(c) and 2(b).

62   A useful summary is given at paras 17.10–17.23 of the English Code.

63   Housing Act 2004, ss 1–54

64   English Code, paras 17.10–17.15.

65   English Code, para 17.15.

66   Housing Act 2004, ss 55–78.

hostel accommodation, should be licensed by local housing authorities. For a licence to be granted, the local housing authority must be satisfied that the house is reasonably suitable for occupation by a specified number of persons or households, that the proposed licence holder and manager are both fit and proper persons and that the proposed management arrangements are satisfactory.[67]

18.42 Local housing authorities also have a discretionary power, in Part 3[68] of the Housing Act 2004, to designate areas in their districts as areas where there will be a requirement for the licensing of all privately rented housing.[69]

18.43 Where a local housing authority decides that there is no reasonable prospect of being able to grant a licence for a property under Parts 2 or 3 of the Housing Act 2004, Part 4[70] of Housing Act 2004 obliges the local housing authority to make a management order, taking over the management of the property. The local housing authority may also make management orders in respect of HMOs which do not fall within Parts 2 or 3 of the Housing Act 2004 and so do not require licences. Management orders may also be made where the local housing authority believes that they are necessary for the health and safety of the occupiers of the property, or of others in the vicinity. Local housing authorities can make interim management orders (for a maximum period of 12 months) and final management orders (maximum period 5 years).

18.44 There is nothing in the statutory scheme (HA 1996 and Housing Act 2004, Parts 2–4) explicitly providing that a house in multiple occupation which does not comply with these provisions is not 'suitable' accommodation. It would be difficult to describe a dwelling for which the owner does not have the requisite licence, or where he or she is in breach of the licence conditions, as 'suitable'. The English Code of Guidance directs local housing authorities to consider these provisions in particular when considering the suitability of bed and breakfast accommodation.[71]

Affordability

18.45 The local housing authority is directed, by specific statutory order, to consider the applicant's financial resources (including any available social security benefits), and the total costs of the accommodation, in determining whether particular accommodation would be 'suitable'.[72]

18.46 The Codes suggest that accommodation will not be suitable if the applicant's net income, after payment of housing costs, would be significantly less than Income Support or Jobseekers Allowance levels. Nor will it be suitable

---

67   English Code, paras 17.18–17.22.
68   Housing Act 2004, ss 79–100.
69   English Code, para 17.23.
70   Housing Act 2004, ss 101–147.
71   English Code, para 17.38; see **18.93–18.98**.
72   Homelessness (Suitability of Accommodation) Order 1996, SI 1996/3204, at Appendix 2.

if the applicant would not be able to afford basic essentials such as food, clothing, heating, or transport as well as the costs of the accommodation. Applicants who are in low-paid employment should not be placed in accommodation where they could only meet the housing costs by resorting to claiming benefit. If there is likely to be a substantial shortfall between housing benefit and the contractual rent, which the applicant would have to find from his or her own resources, accommodation will not be suitable.[73]

Additional statutory factors for Welsh local housing authorities[74]

18.47   Welsh local housing authorities are additionally directed to consider:

(a)   the specific health needs of the person;

(b)   the proximity and accessibility of social services;

(c)   the proximity and accessibility of the support of the family or other support services; and

(d)   any disability of the person,[75]

when determining whether or not accommodation is suitable for the needs of any person who has a priority need. In practice, this will mean all applicants for homelessness assistance for whom a duty to secure accommodation has been accepted. These additional matters clearly reflect a concern that applicants who need specific support should be secured with accommodation that enables their support to be maintained. The suggestion is that accommodation should be located within a reasonable travelling distance of such services or networks as:

• hospitals, if the applicant or members of his or her household regularly attend hospitals;

• social services, if support for health needs or children is being provided;

• family, friends or carers; or

• other facilities used by people with disabilities such as day centres etc.

---

[73]   English Code, paras 17.39–17.40; Welsh Code, paras 19.9–19.10.

[74]   Homelessness (Suitability of Accommodation) Wales Order 2006, SI 2006/650 (W 71). The Welsh Assembly Government has published guidance: *Homelessness (Suitability of Accommodation) Wales Order 2006 Summary* (Welsh Assembly Government, March 2006), at http://new.wales.gov.uk/topics/housingandcommunity/housing/publications/ suitabilityaccom?lang=en, both at Appendix 3.

[75]   Homelessness (Suitability of Accommodation) (Wales) Order 2006, SI 2006/650 (W 71), art 3, in force from 3 April 2006.

18.48 These additional considerations apply to accommodation secured under any of the HA 1996, Part 7 *duties*, but not to accommodation secured under HA 1996, Part 7 *powers*.[76]

PARTICULAR ASPECTS OF 'SUITABILITY'

Location

18.49 The location of the accommodation secured or offered is always relevant to the decision as to whether or not it is suitable.[77]

18.50 Local housing authorities are under a duty to secure accommodation for applicants in their own districts, so far as is reasonably practicable.[78] It will not be 'reasonably practicable' for accommodation to be secured locally where the applicant or a member of his or her household would be at risk of violence if housed in the local housing authority's own district.[79]

18.51 If, exceptionally, suitable accommodation is secured by a local housing authority outside its own district, it must give written notice to the local housing authority for the district where the accommodation is situated, because it is that local housing authority that will have to provide other, non-housing services such as social services, education, health care, etc.[80]

18.52 Normally, accommodation will be secured in the local housing authority's own area and the issue of location will focus on location within the local housing authority's boundaries. The Codes recommend that local housing authorities should avoid placing people in isolated accommodation, and that, wherever possible, they should be placed in accommodation as close as possible to where they were previously living. The need to travel to places of employment and/or education is also relevant. Care should be taken to minimise disruption to any young person's education.[81]

---

[76] Homelessness (Suitability of Accommodation) (Wales) Order 2006, SI 2006/650 (W 71), art 1(5).

[77] English Code, paras 17.4 and 17.41; Welsh Code, para 19.11. See also *R v Newham London Borough Council ex p Sacupima* (2001) 33 HLR 2, CA; *Codona v Mid-Bedfordshire District Council* [2004] EWCA Civ 925, [2005] HLR 1, CA.

[78] HA 1996, s 208(1). They are entitled to conclude that cheaper accommodation outside of their district would render the provision of more expensive accommodation within their district not 'reasonably practical': *R (Calgin) v Enfield London Borough Council* [2005] EWHC 1716 (Admin), [2006] HLR 4, Admin Ct. In deciding whether out of borough accommodation should be offered, the local housing authority should consider whether there is suitable accommodation available within the borough: *Sevine v Enfield London Borough Council* (2009) January *Legal Action*, p 27, Central London County Court.

[79] English Code, paras 16.7 and 17.6.

[80] HA 1996, s 208(2)–(4). See **15.205–15.211**.

[81] English Code, para 17.41; Welsh Code, paras 18.9–18.14, 19.11.

18.53 The additional statutory matters to be considered by Welsh local housing authorities specifically refer to the proximity and accessibility of various support services and, therefore, by implication to the location of the accommodation.[82]

18.54 The applicant's need for family or other support in a particular area is relevant to the question of suitability,[83] as are any particular cultural considerations such as the need to be near particular shops or community centres. When considering the applicant's needs to be located in a particular area, however, the local housing authority can also take into account the length of time that accommodation is to be secured for. The shorter the period of time, the more the applicant could be expected to endure a certain degree of disruption to normal arrangements.[84]

18.55 The risk of the applicant suffering harassment or violence, and any particular vulnerability of the applicant and his or her household, in certain geographic areas is also relevant to the question of whether the location of the accommodation is suitable.[85] Where accommodation situated on an estate renowned for racist attacks was offered to an Asian family, the local housing authority had to have regard to the incidence of racist attacks and racial harassment, as well to evidence showing a general under-reporting of racist attacks in making its assessment of 'suitability'.[86]

18.56 Where the applicant alleges risk of violence, the local housing authority should consider the actual degree of risk to the applicant, the frequency of visits made by the perpetrator to the area, and any risk from friends or relatives of the perpetrator.[87]

---

[82] Homelessness (Suitability of Accommodation) (Wales) Order 2006, SI 2006/650 (W 71), art 3. See **18.47–18.48**.

[83] *Mohamud v Haringey London Borough Council* (2000) November *Legal Action*, p 23, Edmonton County Court; and see Homelessness (Suitability of Accommodation) (Wales) Order, SI 2006/650 (W 71), art 3(c) directing Welsh local housing authorities specifically to consider the proximity and accessibility of the support of family or other support services; see **18.47**. In *Abdullah v Westminster City Council* [2007] EWCA Civ 1566, (2007) November *Legal Action*, p 38, CA, the reviewing officer found that the applicant 'would not be unable to cope' in accommodation outside the local housing authority's district and away from her social support network. The reviewing officer's decision was not wrong in law.

[84] *R v Westminster City Council ex p Abo-Ragheed CO/4020/2000* (unreported) 27 November 2000, QBD.

[85] *R v Islington London Borough Council ex p Okocha* (1997) 30 HLR 191, QBD.

[86] *R v Tower Hamlets London Borough Council ex p Subhan* (1992) 24 HLR 541, QBD; see also *Villaruel v Richmond upon Thames* (2003) March *Legal Action*, p 31, Brentford County Court.

[87] *R v Southwark London Borough Council ex p Solomon* (1994) 26 HLR 693, QBD; *R v Hackney London Borough Council ex p Decordova* (1995) 27 HLR 108, QBD; and *R v Haringey London Borough Council ex p Karaman* (1997) 29 HLR 366, QBD.

18.57 The risk of violence in a particular location to an applicant who had given or was to give evidence in a murder trial has been held to be a relevant consideration on the question of 'suitability'.[88]

18.58 The English Code recommends that applicants who have suffered domestic violence may need to have 'gender-specific' accommodation, whose location is kept a secret and which has security measures and appropriate staffing.[89]

Duration of likely occupation

18.59 If the accommodation offered is a final offer of accommodation under HA 1996, Part 6 (relied upon to release the local housing authority from the main housing duty), it would not necessarily be unreasonable for the local housing authority, when considering 'suitability', to expect the applicant to change schools, doctors, etc, although each case has to be considered on its individual facts.[90] However, it could be far more disruptive for an applicant offered accommodation under HA 1996, Part 7 to have to make those changes, as he or she would only be occupying the accommodation until the duty under HA 1996, Part 7 ended.

18.60 The duration of expected occupation is relevant to whether or not accommodation is suitable:

> 'What is suitable for occupation in the short term may not be suitable for occupation in the medium term, and what is suitable for occupation in the medium term may not be suitable for occupation in the longer term.'[91]

Space and arrangement

18.61 The English Code provides that space and arrangement of the accommodation are 'key factors' in determining its suitability.[92] But that, like the judicial pronouncement from which it is drawn,[93] is not intended to suggest to the local housing authority that it must do anything other than consider *all* relevant matters.

18.62 Particular issues in relation to space and arrangement of accommodation can arise where there are children in the household, or elderly or disabled persons.[94] Accommodation which is not suitable and requires adaptations

---

88   *R v Lambeth London Borough Council ex p Woodburne* (1997) 29 HLR 836, QBD; and see *R v Islington London Borough Council ex p B* (1997) 30 HLR 706, QBD.

89   English Code, para 17.6.

90   *R v South Holland District Council ex p Baxter* (1998) 30 HLR 1069, QBD; and *Williams v Birmingham City Council* [2007] EWCA Civ 691, [2008] HLR 4, CA.

91   *Ali & others v Birmingham City Council, Moran v Manchester City Council* [2009] UKHL 36, [2009] 1 WLR 1506, HL, at [47] per Baroness Hale.

92   English Code, para 17.4; not in the Welsh Code.

93   *R v Brent London Borough Council ex p Awua* [1996] AC 55, HL, at 72, per Lord Hoffmann.

94   English Code, para 17.5.

could be an offer of suitable accommodation (for the purpose of determining whether a refusal would bring the main housing duty to an end under HA 1996, s 193(5) or (7))[95] if the offer is accompanied with certain, binding and enforceable assurances as to the adaptations to be carried out before it is to be occupied in order to render the accommodation suitable.[96]

18.63 Where there are children, issues such as insecure door and window locks, access to a dangerous balcony, and inoperative fire doors will be relevant. They could produce a genuine risk to the health or safety of a child, and the local housing authority would be under a duty to consider those matters.[97]

18.64 Where the applicant, or any member of his or her household, is disabled, then the accessibility of the accommodation itself is relevant, as is the internal layout in terms of the provision of accessible bathroom and toilet facilities.[98]

18.65 In one case a local housing authority offered a five-bedroom house with one combined bathroom and toilet to an applicant to occupy with her husband, her ten children and two other family members. The applicant said that this accommodation could not be suitable as it would involve 14 people sharing one toilet. Rejecting that claim, the judge said that, when determining what is suitable accommodation, the local housing authority is entitled to take account of any general shortage of accommodation available to it in its district and the nature of the accommodation actually available to it.[99]

Standard of accommodation

18.66 Although the courts have recognised a minimum standard of suitability below which accommodation must not fall,[100] once that threshold is met it is for the local housing authority to determine the standard of the accommodation offered or secured. It must be remembered that even the 'main housing duty' under HA 1996, s 193(2) is only a safety net provision of temporary accommodation until the applicant's longer term housing needs are resolved. It would be wrong to raise expectations that this short-term accommodation will be of a high standard.

18.67 A local housing authority is entitled to have regard to the 'realities' in terms of the accommodation it can offer in areas of high demand where, therefore, 'a high standard of suitability cannot be obtained'.[101] The statutory

---

95   See **17.49–17.58** and **17.78–17.91**.
96   *Boreh v Ealing London Borough Council* [2008] EWCA Civ 1176, [2009] HLR 22, CA.
97   *R v Newham London Borough Council ex p Gentle* (1993) 26 HLR 466, QBD.
98   *R (Amirun Begum) v Tower Hamlets London Borough Council* [2002] EWHC 633 (Admin), (2003) 35 HLR 8, Admin Ct; and *Boreh v Ealing London Borough Council* [2008] EWCA Civ 1176, [2009] HLR 22, CA.
99   *R v Camden London Borough Council ex p Jibril* (1997) 29 HLR 785, QBD.
100   See **18.12–18.16**.
101   *R v Brent London Borough Council ex p Omar* (1991) 23 HLR 446, QBD, at 459 per Henry J.

references to 'slum clearance' and 'overcrowding' as mandatory considerations[102] indicate 'a relatively modest minimum standard that is relevant to the determination of suitability'.[103]

18.68 Obviously, once the applicant has taken up occupation of the accommodation, he or she can rely on the express or implied provisions of the tenancy agreement to secure any necessary repairs. Disrepair, and any other problems with the standard of the property (eg lack of soundproofing), can also be addressed by inviting the local Environmental Health Officer to inspect the accommodation.

18.69 Where the accommodation is offered under the allocation arrangements adopted under HA 1996, Part 6 (normally of long-term housing accommodation), a higher standard might be expected before the offer was to be considered 'suitable'.

Medical needs

18.70 The medical needs of the applicant and his or her household are clearly relevant to the question of suitability. When considering the suitability of accommodation offered to an applicant who has raised both medical and non-medical reasons as to why it might not be suitable, the local housing authority must take an overall or composite view of the applicant's needs.[104]

18.71 Where an applicant suffering from post-traumatic stress disorder rejected an offer of accommodation situated on the twenty-seventh floor, the local housing authority was under a duty to consider the medical evidence properly.[105] Where an applicant produced evidence that she had suffered a violent sexual assault on a housing estate, the local housing authority was under a duty to consider that evidence when deciding whether the offer of accommodation on an estate was suitable.[106] A local housing authority's decision that a property on the third or fourth floor, with no access by lift, was suitable for a single parent who suffered from back problems and who had two young children was quashed because it had failed to have proper or adequate regard to the medical evidence.[107] It was not wrong in law for a local housing

---

[102] See **18.35–18.37**. The Local Government Ombudsman found maladministration when an applicant was told to accept accommodation that was 'filthy' and in such a state as to be 'stomach turning'. The local housing authority paid the applicant £2,450 on the Ombudsman's recommendation in recognition of the distress caused (LGO complaint against Nottingham City Council 05/C/02965).

[103] *R v Camden London Borough Council ex p Jibril* (1997) 29 HLR 785, QBD, at 792 per Stephen Richards sitting as a deputy High Court judge.

[104] *R v Lewisham London Borough Council ex p Dolan* (1993) 25 HLR 68, QBD.

[105] *R v Kensington and Chelsea Royal London Borough Council ex p Campbell* (1996) 28 HLR 160, QBD.

[106] *R v Islington London Borough Council ex p Thomas* (1997) 30 HLR 111, QBD, although, once the local housing authority had considered the medical evidence and decided that the offer was suitable, its decision was upheld.

[107] *R v Haringey London Borough Council ex p Sampaio* (1999) 31 HLR 1, QBD.

authority to have offered a maisonette with thirteen internal steps to an applicant who suffered chronic back pain, even though there was medical evidence that climbing stairs would aggravate her back pain.[108]

18.72 Welsh local housing authorities are specifically directed to consider the health needs of the applicant, and any disability, along with proximity and accessibility of support services, when making a decision on the suitability of accommodation.[109]

Terms and tenure

18.73 The provisions of HA 1996, Part 7 do not require accommodation to be secured or offered on any particular terms, for any particular period, or with any security of tenure, in order for it to be 'suitable'.[110] However, if the accommodation is being offered on 'standard terms' set by the accommodation provider, those terms must be 'fair'.[111]

18.74 If the accommodation is self-contained premises, occupation is likely to be under a tenancy rather than on a licence. But even then the fairly minimal protection of the Protection from Eviction Act 1977 may not be available in respect of accommodation secured under HA 1996, Part 7.[112]

18.75 Although local housing authority accommodation can be secured under HA 1996, Part 7, it cannot be made available on a secure or introductory tenancy.[113] Likewise, accommodation rented by the local housing authority from a private owner and sub-let to the occupier will not be offered under a secure or introductory tenancy.[114] The occupier will simply be a bare contractual tenant.

18.76 Accommodation obtained from a private landlord or an RSL to fulfil any interim duties will not be offered on an assured tenancy. So applicants will normally occupy their accommodation under, at best, assured shorthold tenancies.[115] An assured shorthold tenancy offered in performance of the main

---

[108] *Abdi v Wandsworth London Borough Council* [2006] EWCA Civ 1099, (2006) October *Legal Action*, p 26, CA.

[109] Homelessness (Suitability of Accommodation) (Wales) Order 2006, SI 2006/650 (W 71), art 3. See **18.47–18.48**.

[110] Save that it must be affordable; see **18.45–18.46**.

[111] In that they must not contravene the Unfair Terms in Consumer Contracts Regulations 1999, SI 1999/2083: *R (Khatun) v Newham London Borough Council* [2004] EWCA Civ 55, [2004] HLR 29, CA.

[112] See the discussion at **16.80–16.85**.

[113] Housing Act 1985, Sch 1, para 4. English Code, para 16.13; Welsh Code, para 18.17. See *Westminster City Council v Boraliu* [2007] EWCA Civ 1339, [2008] HLR 42, CA.

[114] Housing Act 1985, Sch 1, para 6. English Code, paras 16.15–16.16; Welsh Code, paras 18.20–18.21.

[115] HA 1996, s 209. English Code, paras 16.21–16.22; Welsh Code, paras 18.27–18.28.

housing duty at HA 1996, s 193(2) was held by the Court of Appeal in principle to constitute an offer of suitable accommodation.[116]

18.77 The absence of any particular requirement for a minimum term, or for any security or stability, might enable a local housing authority to perform its duties under HA 1996, Part 7 by moving an applicant through a succession of very short-term placements. However, each unit of accommodation must itself be suitable. Furthermore, the very fact that the accommodation offered is yet another short-term placement, with minimum stability for the applicant, could, depending on the particular circumstances, render the accommodation 'not suitable'.

18.78 In a landmark case decided under the homelessness provisions of Part 3 of the Housing Act 1985,[117] the House of Lords held that a local housing authority was not required to provide permanent accommodation in performing its duty to applicants for homelessness assistance. Lord Hoffmann said:

> '[T]here is no reason why temporary accommodation should ipso facto be unsuitable. If the tenure is so precarious that the person is likely to have to leave within 28 days without any alternative accommodation being available, then he remains threatened with homelessness and the council has not discharged its duty. Otherwise, it seems to me that the term for which the accommodation is provided is a matter for the council to decide. Provided that the decision is not *Wednesbury* unreasonable ... I do not think that the courts should lay down requirements as to security of tenure.'[118]

18.79 Following on from that decision, the Court of Appeal held that a local housing authority could perform its duty to secure 'suitable' accommodation by arranging for assured shorthold tenancies for applicants.[119] Evans LJ considered that the tenure of the accommodation secured could be relevant to the local housing authority's decision as to whether or not the accommodation was 'suitable' and held:

> '[T]he House of Lords' ruling that there is no requirement of permanence does not lead to the conclusion that there is no temporal requirement whatever. In my judgment the question of tenure is not left to the unfettered discretion of the [local housing] authority: its decision must be proportionate to the relevant circumstances of the particular case. These include, in my judgment, both the needs of the applicant and the situation in the local housing market.'[120]

---

[116] *Griffiths v St Helens Council* [2006] EWCA Civ 160, [2006] HLR 29, CA.

[117] *R v Brent London Borough Council ex p Awua* [1996] AC 55, HL. Prior to this decision, it had been widely assumed that the duty at s 65(2) of the Housing Act 1985 to secure suitable accommodation for applicants required local housing authorities to grant secure tenancies from their own stock.

[118] *R v Brent London Borough Council ex p Awua* [1996] AC 55, HL, at 72, per Lord Hoffmann.

[119] *R v Wandsworth London Borough Council ex p Mansoor & Wingrove* (1996) 29 HLR 801, CA.

[120] *R v Wandsworth London Borough Council ex p Mansoor & Wingrove* (1996) 29 HLR 801, CA, at 811, per Evans LJ, followed and quoted with approval by Laws J (as he then was) when considering the duty under Housing Act 1985, s 65(2) in *R v Lambeth London Borough Council*

18.80   These cases were considering the duty to secure suitable accommodation under s 65(2) of the Housing Act 1985. Since the coming into force of HA 1996, accommodation offered under HA 1996, Part 6 with a view to releasing the local housing authority from the main housing duty will usually be offered on an assured, introductory or secure tenancy.[121]

18.81   More recently, the Court of Appeal has considered the distinction between local housing authorities offering assured shorthold tenancies as 'qualifying offers' (so bringing the main housing duty to an end if accepted by the applicant)[122] and offering them in performance of the main housing duty at HA 1996, s 193(2).[123] Considering 'qualifying offers', May LJ said:

> 'The elaborate provisions for a qualifying offer of an assured shorthold tenancy from a private landlord in sub-section (7B) are there to recognise that, on the one hand, assured shorthold tenancies from private landlords have their disadvantages – the rent is not controlled and the tenure is technically insecure – but, on the other hand, some homeless applicants may reasonably prefer to accept the offer of such a tenancy rather than remain in temporary accommodation for a long time until they may be offered secure accommodation under Part 6. Some homeless applicants may therefore be prepared to accept an offer of an assured shorthold tenancy from a private landlord as the permanent accommodation which in practice it is often capable of being. But they must only do so with their eyes fully open, and the local housing authority must be satisfied that it is reasonable for the applicant to accept the offer. Applicants are entitled to reject the offer. But if they do accept it, the local housing authority's duty ceases.'[124]

18.82   When an assured shorthold tenancy is offered in performance of the main housing duty, it:

> 'may be technically insecure, but may in practice extend for a number of years. If the applicant accepts the offer and the accommodation subsequently ceases to be available, the authority's duty will have to be performed again, assuming that the applicant's circumstances have not otherwise relevantly changed.'[125]

18.83   Where an applicant has been given an assurance that she or he would be given a secure tenancy, that assurance can constitute a legitimate expectation.[126] The local housing authority is then under a duty, when considering what accommodation is suitable for the needs of the applicant and his or her household, to take into account the applicant's legitimate expectation to be given a secure tenancy. That does not amount to a duty to give the applicant automatic priority above other applicants on the local housing

---

     ex p Ekpo-Wedderman (1998) 31 HLR 498, QBD; and by Richards J in *R v Lambeth London Borough Council ex p Touhey* (1999) 32 HLR 707, QBD.

[121]   HA 1996, s 193(7). See **17.74–17.91**.

[122]   HA 1996, s 193(7B)–(7D). See **17.91–17.97**.

[123]   *Griffiths v St Helens Council* [2006] EWCA Civ 160, [2006] HLR 29, CA.

[124]   *Griffiths v St Helens Council* [2006] EWCA Civ 160, [2006] HLR 29, CA at [36].

[125]   *Griffiths v St Helens Council* [2006] EWCA Civ 160, [2006] HLR 29, CA at [38].

[126]   Where such assurances have been given, they were usually given to applicants under Housing Act 1985, Part III: the previous homelessness provisions. See **4.36**.

authority's allocation scheme, but it does require it to adopt some method, such as the provision of additional points, to reflect that legitimate expectation.[127]

The applicant's views

18.84 The decision on suitability is for the local housing authority to make. HA 1996, Part 7 does not prescribe any specific inquiries to be undertaken before a local housing authority can determine whether particular accommodation will be suitable for a specific applicant. It need only ensure that it has had regard to the five prescribed matters it is required to consider in every case,[128] and to any other matters relevant to the circumstances of a particular case.

18.85 It may, if it wishes, invite the applicant's views on any general issues affecting the suitability of accommodation for him or her, or on a specific proposed offer or provision of accommodation. Indeed, the English Code contains advice from the Secretary of State that applicants should be given a chance to view the accommodation before being required to accept or refuse it.[129] This advice was published after the Court of Appeal's decision in *R (Khatun) v Newham London Borough Council*,[130] which held that there was no such obligation, and can therefore be taken as suggesting that viewing the accommodation is, at the very least, good practice.

18.86 However, a local housing authority may decide that the applicant's views as to suitability can be sufficiently aired at the review stage.[131]

Other considerations

18.87 Where a basement property on a large housing estate reminded the applicant, who was a refugee, of the prison in which she had been confined and tortured, the court quashed the local housing authority's decision that the accommodation was suitable, holding that this was an exceptional case.[132]

18.88 Where accommodation that was originally suitable was occupied by squatters before the applicant had been able to move in, it was held to be no longer suitable.[133] A local housing authority's decision, however, that squatted

---

[127] *R (Bibi and Al-Nashed) v Newham London Borough Council* [2001] EWCA Civ 607, (2001) 33 HLR 955, CA; *R (Ibrahim) v Redbridge London Borough Council* [2002] EWHC 2756 (Admin), (2003) February *Legal Action*, p 35, Admin Ct; and *R (Bibi) v Newham London Borough Council* [2003] EWHC 1860 (Admin), (2003) September *Legal Action*, p 28, Admin Ct. And see **4.36**.

[128] See **18.28–18.48**.

[129] English Code, para 14.18.

[130] [2004] EWCA Civ 55, [2005] HLR 29, CA.

[131] *R (Khatun) v Newham London Borough Council* [2004] EWCA Civ 55, [2005] HLR 29, CA.

[132] *R v Brent London Borough Council ex p Omar* (1991) 23 HLR 446, QBD.

[133] *R v Lambeth London Borough Council ex p Campbell* (1994) 26 HLR 618, QBD.

accommodation would be suitable once it had been repossessed and refurbished was held not to contain errors of law.[134]

18.89 Where an applicant had a cultural aversion to conventional bricks and mortar accommodation (having lived as a traveller all her life), an offer of conventional housing was held to be unsuitable for her needs. The local housing authority had failed to accord sufficient respect to her rights under the European Convention on Human Rights, Art 8(1).[135] However, if no sites or pitches are available, the local housing authority is not in breach of its statutory duty, nor of the applicant's rights under the Convention by making an offer of conventional accommodation unless that accommodation falls below the *Wednesbury* minimum standards of suitability.[136]

18.90 The English Code recommends that local housing authorities should be 'sensitive' to the importance of pets to some applicants, particularly elderly people and/or rough sleepers, when considering the suitability of accommodation offered.[137] If pets cannot be accommodated with the applicant, separate provision to kennel or otherwise look after them would fall under a local housing authority's duty to protect the applicant's property.[138]

TYPES OF ACCOMMODATION THAT MAY BE 'SUITABLE'

18.91 The Codes offer considerable guidance as to the types of accommodation that might be used by a local housing authority seeking to perform duties owed under HA 1996, Part 7 to secure 'suitable' accommodation.

18.92 The following review deals first with the forms of accommodation least likely to be suitable and progresses to accommodation more likely to be suitable.

Bed and breakfast accommodation

Generally

18.93 In general, bed and breakfast accommodation should only be regarded as suitable accommodation for any applicant when emergency accommodation

---

[134] *R v Ealing London Borough Council ex p Denny* (1995) 27 HLR 424, QBD.
[135] *R (Price) v Carmarthenshire County Council* [2003] EWHC 42 (Admin), (2003) March *Legal Action*, p 30, Admin Ct.
[136] English Code, para 16.38, and *Codona v Mid-Bedfordshire District Council* [2004] EWCA Civ 925, [2005] HLR 1, CA. See **18.12–18.16**.
[137] English Code, para 17.42.
[138] See **17.163–17.184**.

is required at very short notice, and there is simply no better accommodation available. It should only be used as a last resort and for the shortest period possible.[139]

18.94 Bed and breakfast accommodation allocated to a family with six children, in a hostel where the other residents were single men with histories of drug abuse, psychiatric illness and violent behaviour, was held not to be suitable for the family's needs.[140] In a case where the applicant had occupied bed and breakfast accommodation for over 18 months, in circumstances where her 16-year old son could not live there and had been taken into care, the Administrative Court held that 'the time has now come when the claimant cannot expect to return to hostel accommodation'.[141]

18.95 Relevant considerations on whether or not bed and breakfast accommodation may be suitable include:

(1) the length of time that the applicant and his or her household are expected to occupy it;

(2) the efforts made by the local housing authority to find other suitable accommodation;

(3) the degree of likelihood of suitable accommodation becoming available in the near future; and

(4) any other factors affecting the individual applicant.

18.96 However, lack of resources available to the local housing authority is not a relevant consideration.[142]

18.97 Where bed and breakfast accommodation has been secured, local housing authorities should ensure that the accommodation is of a good standard. Bed and breakfast accommodation will normally be provided in a building which falls within the definition of a house in multiple occupation. Minimum standards are set out in the Code of Guidance.[143]

18.98 If bed and breakfast accommodation has been secured under the local housing authority's duty to secure suitable interim accommodation,[144] and the local housing authority subsequently accepts a main housing duty,[145] it must

---

[139] English Code, paras 17.24–17.35; Welsh Code, paras 18.41–18.44.
[140] *Driver v Purbeck District Council* (1999) 10 CLD 407, Bournemouth County Court.
[141] *R (McCammon-Mckenzie) v Southwark London Borough Council* [2004] EWHC 612 (Admin), [2004] All ER (D) 174 (Mar), Admin Ct, at [15], per Keith J.
[142] *R (Khan) v Newham London Borough Council* [2001] EWHC (Admin) 589, (2001) October *Legal Action*, p 16, Admin Ct.
[143] English Code, paras 17.35–17.38 and Annex 17. See **18.38–18.45**.
[144] HA 1996, s 188(1). See **16.11–16.24**.
[145] HA 1996, s 193(2). See **17.21–17.110**.

consider anew whether or not the bed and breakfast accommodation is suitable for the needs of the applicant and his or her household with reference to that new duty.[146]

The special rules in England

18.99 For English local housing authorities, from 1 April 2004, bed and breakfast accommodation has been deemed to be unsuitable for applicants with family commitments.[147] It can only be used at all where 'no accommodation other than bed and breakfast is available[148] and for no longer than a total period of 6 weeks.[149] The 6-week period does not include any periods of occupation before the rules came into force on 1 April 2004. Where an applicant has been referred from one local housing authority to another under the conditions of referral,[150] any period spent in accommodation secured by the notifying local housing authority will be disregarded when calculating the total period of occupation. The Code of Guidance advises that, even if these two conditions are satisfied, bed and breakfast accommodation should only be used 'as a last resort'.[151]

18.100 It follows that a local housing authority is required to satisfy itself that no other accommodation is available. The Code of Guidance is unclear how an English local housing authority can demonstrate that 'no other accommoda- tion' can be secured for the applicant in order to be able to justify its use of bed and breakfast. It simply advises that, in making the determination that no other accommodation can be secured, local housing authorities should take account of the cost to the local housing authority in securing accommodation, its affordability and location. A local housing authority is not under an obligation to include accommodation which is to be allocated under its allocation scheme when considering whether there is any alternative accommodation.[152] This suggests that a local housing authority could decide to secure bed and breakfast accommodation even though an empty council home or a stay at a five-star hotel might be technically 'available'. The authors, with respect, doubt the correctness of this particular guidance. We suggest that, for a local housing authority to demonstrate that no other accommodation was available, it must show that it has done more than merely check with its usual providers of short-term accommodation. It should have considered all possible means of providing accommodation other than bed and breakfast, including considering whether it has any empty properties that could be made available, making inquiries of all potential providers, both in its own district and any

---

[146] *R (Chowdhury) v Newham London Borough Council* (2002) November *Legal Action*, p 24, Admin Ct (permission hearing); and *R (Cano) v Kensington and Chelsea Royal London Borough Council* [2002] EWHC 436 (Admin), (2002) December *Legal Action*, p 22, Admin Ct.

[147] Homelessness (Suitability of Accommodation) (England) Order 2003, SI 2003/3326.

[148] SI 2003/3326, art 4(1)(a). English Code, paras 17.25–17.29.

[149] SI 2006/3326, art 4(1)(b)

[150] See Chapter 15.

[151] English Code, para 17.26

[152] English Code, para 17.30.

other districts where it would be suitable for the applicant and his or her household to be located for the expected duration.

18.101 It should also be noted that the obligation is a continuing one throughout the 6-week period. It may be that no accommodation other than bed and breakfast is available for the first night after the local housing authority has come under a duty to secure accommodation, and so bed and breakfast accommodation will not be deemed to be unsuitable. That does not mean, however, that the local housing authority is then relieved of its obligation to consider whether any other accommodation is available after the first night. It cannot simply leave the applicant and his or her household in the bed and breakfast accommodation for a total period of 6 weeks.[153]

18.102 'Applicants with family commitments' are defined as applicants who are pregnant, or with whom a pregnant woman resides or might reasonably be expected to reside, or applicants with whom dependent children reside or might reasonably be expected to reside.[154]

18.103 'Bed and breakfast accommodation' is defined as accommodation which is not separate, self-contained premises and where a toilet, personal washing facilities or cooking facilities are shared between more than one household.[155] It does not include accommodation owned or managed by a local housing authority, an RSL or a voluntary organisation, and so use of bed and breakfast establishments owned by any of those organisations is not, as a matter of law, deemed unsuitable (although it may still be unsuitable for the particular needs of a specific applicant).[156]

18.104 This prohibition on the use of bed and breakfast by English local housing authorities does not apply where accommodation is being secured in the exercise of a power, eg the power to accommodate pending a review or appeal.[157]

The special rules in Wales

18.105 The special rules applying to the determination of 'suitable' by Welsh local housing authorities came into force in stages, concluding on 2 April 2008.[158] The Welsh legislation deals with use of bed and breakfast

153 The 6-week period 'does not allow the temporarily accommodating council to sit back – it must make all efforts to find suitable accommodation' said Collins J in *R (Nagaye) v Bristol City Council* (2005) CO/3477/2005, (2005) August *Legal Action*, p 19, Admin Ct (consideration of permission).
154 SI 2003/3326, art 2. English Code, para 17.26.
155 SI 2003/3326, art 2. English Code, para 17.27.
156 SI 2003/3326, art 2.
157 SI 2003/3326, art 1(2). See **16.24–16.50** and **17.145–17.152**.
158 Homelessness (Suitability of Accommodation) (Wales) Order 2006, SI 2006/650 (W 71), art 1.

accommodation and, separately, other 'shared accommodation'. Statutory guidance has been issued by the Welsh Assembly Government.[159]

18.106 'Bed and breakfast accommodation' has the same statutory definition in Wales as it does in England.[160] The Welsh Order requires that 'bed and breakfast accommodation' must meet one of two standards – the 'basic' and the 'higher' standard – in order to be 'suitable'.

18.107 'Basic standard' is defined as accommodation that meets all the prescribed statutory requirements and has a manager who has been deemed by the local housing authority to be a fit and proper person with the ability to manage bed and breakfast accommodation.[161] 'Higher standard' is basic standard accommodation which also complies with various additional standards relating to minimum amounts of space, adequate heating, facilities for storing and cooking food, exclusive washing and toilet facilities, lockable entrance doors and a common room.[162]

18.108 There is also an additional category of 'small Bed and Breakfast accommodation', defined as bed and breakfast accommodation where the manager resides on the premises and there are fewer than seven bedrooms available for letting.[163]

18.109 As in England, the legislation applies only to accommodation secured under HA 1996 *duties*, not powers.[164] Periods of occupation before the relevant provisions of the legislation came into force are to be disregarded when calculating the total period of occupation.[165] If an applicant is referred from one local housing authority to another under the conditions of referral,[166] the period spent in accommodation secured by the notifying local housing authority will be disregarded when calculating the total period of occupation.[167]

The rules since 7 April 2008

18.110 Since 7 April 2008, bed and breakfast accommodation has not been regarded as suitable for any applicant who has a priority need unless it is occupied for no more than 2 weeks (basic standard) or 6 weeks (higher

---

[159] SI 2006/650; *Homelessness (Suitability of Accommodation) Wales Order 2006 Summary* (Welsh Assembly Government, March 2006) at http://new.wales.gov.uk/docrepos/40382/sjr/housing/homelessness/suitabilityaccom?lang=en.
[160] SI 2006/650, art 2; and see **18.103**.
[161] SI 2006/650, art 2.
[162] SI 2006/650, art 2 and Schedule.
[163] SI 2006/650, art 2.
[164] See **18.104**.
[165] Homelessness (Suitability of Accommodation) (Wales) Order 2006, SI 2006/650 (W 71), arts 6(4)(a) and 9(4)(a).
[166] See Chapter 15.
[167] Homelessness (Suitability of Accommodation) (Wales) Order 2006 SI 2006/650 (W 71), arts 6(4)(b) and 9(4)(b).

standard).[168] If an offer of suitable alternative accommodation has been made during those periods and the person has chosen to remain in his or her bed and breakfast accommodation, higher standard small bed and breakfast accommodation can be considered suitable for an indefinite period.[169] In the case of basic standard small bed and breakfast accommodation, two offers of suitable alternative accommodation must be made and refused for it to be considered suitable indefinitely.[170]

18.111 The Welsh Order also effectively outlaws use of 'shared accommodation', which it defines as accommodation which is not separate, self-contained premises and where a toilet, personal washing facilities or cooking facilities are shared between more than one household, provided that it is not an institution registered under the Care Standards Act 2000.[171] Unlike 'bed and breakfast accommodation', 'shared accommodation' can be owned or managed by local housing authorities, RSLs or voluntary organisations.

18.112 Since 7 April 2008, 'shared accommodation' has not been regarded as suitable for an applicant who has a priority need unless it meets the higher standard.[172] Basic standard shared accommodation may be regarded as suitable for a period of no more than 2 weeks, or for a 6-week period if during the initial 2-week period an offer of suitable alternative accommodation has been made but the person has chosen to remain in the basic standard shared accommodation.[173]

18.113 If the 'shared accommodation' is owned or managed by a local authority or by an RSL and was being used on 7 April 2008 for accommodation under HA 1996, Part 7, this provision will not apply until 4 April 2011.[174]

Hostels

18.114 The Codes recommend that hostels may secure suitable accommodation for applicants who would benefit from a supported environment. However, they warn against an automatic assumption that hostels will be the most appropriate form of accommodation for all vulnerable people. Those for whom it is more likely to be suitable are those experiencing a temporary crisis, so that hostel accommodation provides an opportunity for them to take stock and then move on to live independently, or those whose need for a supported environment has been identified by a social services authority or department in a community care assessment.[175]

---

[168] SI 2006/650, arts 7 and 9.
[169] SI 2006/650, art 9(d) and (e).
[170] SI 2006/650, art 9(c) and (d).
[171] SI 2006/650, art 2.
[172] SI 2006/650, art 8.
[173] SI 2006/650, art 9(f) and (g).
[174] SI 2006/650, art 10.
[175] English Code, paras 16.25–16.26; Welsh Code, paras 18.19 and 18.30–18.32.

18.115   The hostels referred to in the Code are not the night shelter variety that simply secure accommodation overnight, leaving the applicant homeless again the next day.[176]

18.116   Some hostels, if privately run, will fall within the English or Welsh definitions of 'bed and breakfast' accommodation.[177] Since 7 April 2008, privately run hostels in Wales have been likely to fall within the definition of 'shared accommodation'.[178]

18.117   Hostels are also likely to fall within the definition of houses in multiple occupation and be subject to Parts 1–4 of the Housing Act 2004.[179]

Lodgings

18.118   Some young applicants, particularly those who are vulnerable, may benefit from lodgings rather than hostel or self-contained accommodation. Generally, such lodgings would be offered by landlords who provide a service for young people with support needs.[180]

Women's refuges

18.119   Women's refuges should generally be considered as emergency accommodation only and not be used to perform accommodation duties under HA 1996, Part 7.[181] Whether or not a particular refuge is suitable for a particular woman and her household will depend on the particular characteristics of the refuge and the applicant. The Codes of Guidance remind local housing authorities that using women's refuges to secure accommodation for female homeless applicants (and their children, if any) takes up bed space that would otherwise be available for the emergency occupation of women fleeing domestic violence. Where local housing authorities are able to persuade refuge organisers to make places available for applicants to whom HA 1996, Part 7 duties are owed, those places should be used for the minimum period possible.[182]

Mobile homes

18.120   Mobile homes are unlikely to be suitable for families with children, for the elderly, or for disabled applicants. Generally, if used at all, they should be

---

176   *R v Waveney District Council ex p Bowers* [1983] QB 238, CA.
177   For bed and breakfast accommodation generally, see **18.93–18.98**. For the English rules, see **18.99–18.104**. For the Welsh rules, see **18.105–18.113**.
178   See **18.111**.
179   See **18.38–18.44**.
180   English Code, para 16.24; Welsh Code, para 18.29.
181   See **11.109–11.110**.
182   English Code, para 16.27; Welsh Code, para 18.33.

used for emergency accommodation, when the local housing authority has not had an opportunity to arrange anything else. Holiday caravans should not be regarded as suitable at all.[183]

18.121 If the applicant normally occupies moveable accommodation and is homeless because she or he has no place at which to place the moveable home and reside in it,[184] the local housing authority is not required to provide a site or berth itself, but should consider whether sites, berths or pitches are reasonably available.[185] These may be its own sites, sites provided by other local housing authorities (in which case provision can be made by arrangement with the appropriate local housing authority), or private sites on which the local housing authority has been able to persuade the owner to receive the applicant and his or her home.[186]

18.122 Where an applicant has a strong cultural aversion to living in bricks-and-mortar accommodation, the only accommodation that would be suitable for his or her needs would be the provision of mobile or caravan accommodation, or a site on which to put the caravan or other mobile accommodation.[187]

Accommodation leased from a private landlord

18.123 Local housing authorities are able to lease accommodation from private owners, and then let it themselves to applicants who are owed a housing duty. This option, known as 'private sector leasing', is recommended in the Codes as a far preferable alternative to bed and breakfast accommodation.[188] Although the applicant becomes a tenant of the local housing authority, this is not an introductory or secure tenancy.[189]

18.124 In accordance with the Communities and Local Government's target of reducing the use of temporary accommodation,[190] the English Code encourages local housing authorities to plan ahead to when their leases of private rented accommodation are likely to expire, and then consider negotiating with the private owner to see if he or she would be willing to make an offer of the same accommodation directly to the applicant occupying it. If the owner made such an offer, it could be a 'qualifying offer' and, if accepted

---

[183] English Code, para 16.30; Welsh Code, para 18.36.
[184] HA 1996, s 175(2)(b). See **11.67–11.71**.
[185] English Code, para 16.37; Welsh Code, para 18.40.
[186] HA 1996, s 206(1)(a)–(c).
[187] *R (Price) v Carmarthenshire County Council* [2003] EWHC 42 (Admin), (2003) March *Legal Action*, p 31, Admin Ct; and see *Codona v Mid-Bedfordshire District Council* [2004] EWCA Civ 925, [2005] HLR 1, CA and English Code, para 16.38. However note that 'if there is no prospect of a suitable site for the time being, there may be no alternative solution' (English Code, para 16.38). See **18.142–18.152**.
[188] English Code, paras 16.15–16.16; Welsh Code, 18.20–18.21.
[189] Housing Act 1985, Sch 1, para 6. *Westminster City Council v Boraliu* [2007] EWCA Civ 1339, [2008] HLR 42, CA. See **18.125**.
[190] See **8.10**.

by the applicant, could bring the main housing duty to an end.[191] The Code advises that the 'household should not be pressured to accept offers of accommodation that would bring the homelessness duty to an end.'[192]

Local housing authority properties

18.125 Local housing authorities can use their own stock to secure accommodation under their HA 1996, Part 7 duty.[193] Tenancies granted by local housing authorities in performance of their own homelessness duties will not be secure or introductory tenancies.[194] The English Code advises against the use of social housing for temporary accommodation, except for short periods.[195]

Accommodation provided by other local housing authorities or social landlords

18.126 Local housing authorities may request other local housing authorities and other social landlords to assist them in the performance of their duties by providing accommodation for applicants who are owed housing duties. If requested, those bodies must co-operate and render assistance so far as is reasonable in the circumstances.[196] Other local housing authorities and social landlords could therefore assist either by providing temporary accommodation to meet a duty owed under HA 1996, Part 7, or by agreeing to accept a nomination made under the local housing authority's allocation scheme, thus enabling the local housing authority which owes the HA 1996, Part 7 duty to make the applicant an offer of HA 1996, Part 6 accommodation, so as to release it from its HA 1996, Part 7 duties.

18.127 A local housing authority cannot normally discharge its responsibility to secure 'suitable' accommodation by leaving the identification of the actual unit of accommodation to another local housing authority or social housing landlord. The decision about 'suitability' remains with the local housing authority which owes the HA 1996, Part 7 duty, so it must be able to assess the suitability of a specific property.[197]

---

[191] English Code, paras 16.39–16.43. A 'qualifying offer' must comply with the requirements of HA 1996, s 193(7B)–(7F) inclusive, and the applicant is free to refuse it without the main housing duty coming to an end. See **17.92–17.97**.

[192] English Code, para 16.41. Such pressure would be entirely inappropriate since HA 1996, s 193(7B)–(7F) makes it clear that an applicant owed the main housing duty is free to reject a qualifying offer without risk of the main housing duty coming to an end. See **17.94**.

[193] HA 1996, s 206(1)(a). See also English Code, paras 16.12–16.13; Welsh Code, paras 18.15–18.18.

[194] Housing Act 1985, Sch 1, para 4. See English Code, para 16.13.

[195] English Code, para 16.12; Welsh Code, para 18.16.

[196] HA 1996, s 213. See also English Code, paras 16.23 and 16.29; Welsh Code, 18.35.

[197] *R (Cafun) v Bromley London Borough Council* [2000] All ER (D) 1425, Admin Ct.

18.128 If temporary accommodation is obtained from another local housing authority, the housing duty owed towards the applicant remains with the first local housing authority to which the applicant applied.

18.129 These voluntary arrangements are different from the arrangements for the referral of an applicant under the conditions for referral.[198] The Codes advise that accommodation secured under such voluntary, and often reciprocal, arrangements is particularly appropriate for the needs of applicants who might be at risk of violence or serious harassment in the area of the local housing authority to which they applied.[199]

Accommodation provided by registered social landlords or private sector landlords

18.130 As already noted,[200] local housing authorities can discharge their duty to secure accommodation by ensuring that suitable accommodation is obtained from another person.[201] That might be a private landlord or an RSL such as a housing association.

18.131 RSLs are required by HA 1996, s 213(1)(a) and by Housing Corporation guidance to co-operate with local housing authorities in the carrying out of those local housing authorities' homelessness duties, if requested to and so far as is reasonable in the circumstances.[202]

18.132 Where nomination arrangements have been set up, an offer of an assured, or an assured shorthold, tenancy from an RSL could be made under the local housing authority's allocation scheme, and would therefore be capable of amounting to a final offer of accommodation made under HA 1996, Part 6, sufficient to release the local housing authority from the main housing duty.

18.133 Private landlords can also make accommodation available to help the local housing authority meet duties owed under HA 1996, Part 7. The Court of Appeal has held that assured shorthold tenancies can be secured under the local housing authority's main housing duty at HA 1996, s 193(2), provided that, if the accommodation subsequently ceases to be available and the

---

[198] See Chapter 15 generally and particularly **15.212–15.216**.

[199] English Code, para 16.29; Welsh Code, para 18.35.

[200] See **18.17**.

[201] HA 1996, s 206(1)(b).

[202] HA 1996, s 213. See also English Code, paras 16.18–16.22 and Annex 5; Welsh Code, paras 18.23–18.24. See also Housing Corporation Regulatory Code, August 2005, para 3.6, at http://www.housingcorp.gov.uk/server/show/conWebDoc.3832. We refer to Housing Corporation guidance here and elsewhere, even though that body was closed down on 1 November 2008, because its guidance remains applicable (statutory responsibility for regulation of English RSLs having passed to the Tenant Services Authority) and, in Wales, the Welsh Assembly Government's *Regulatory Code for Housing Associations Registered in Wales* will remain applicable until new regulatory arrangements are established later in 2010. See **6.1–6.3**.

applicant's circumstances have not changed, the local housing authority acknowledges that its main housing duty will have to be performed again.[203]

18.134 It is not unusual for there to be confusion as to the identity of the landlord in these circumstances. Accommodation is often secured under tripartite arrangements between a property owner, a local housing authority and an applicant.[204] That accommodation could either have been leased by the local housing authority from the private landlord,[205] or the local housing authority arranged for the applicant to be granted a tenancy by the property owner. The identity of the landlord is therefore a question of fact.[206]

18.135 Tenancies granted by private landlords cannot be provided under HA 1996, Part 6. But that is no reason to prevent a local housing authority from identifying accommodation that might be available from the private rented sector for the applicant. If an applicant accepts a qualifying offer of an assured shorthold tenancy from a private landlord, the local housing authority's main housing duty will end.[207] Where a rent deposit and/or rent in advance is required by the landlord, local housing authorities are empowered to pay these sums on the applicant's behalf. They may also pay 'finders' fees' to encourage lettings to homeless households. Discretionary housing payments can be used to make up any shortfall between housing benefit payable and the contractual rent.[208]

PARTICULAR APPLICANTS AND THEIR NEEDS

18.136 Precisely because the question of 'suitability' requires a person-centred approach, considerable statutory guidance is offered for those cases in which the provision of accommodation will need to be handled with particular sensitivity.

18.137 The Codes identify that some applicants may need support from social services to assist them to maintain the accommodation which is to be secured. Local housing authorities should therefore consider whether an applicant has support needs and, if so, make arrangements for effective links with other agencies (eg the Supporting People team, social services, and the health

---

[203] *Griffiths v St Helens Council* [2006] EWCA Civ 160, [2006] HLR 29, CA.

[204] *Apczynski v Hounslow London Borough Council* [2006] EWCA Civ 1833, (2007) April *Legal Action*, p 21, CA, at [6] per Neuberger LJ. In that case, the applicant occupied a room in a hotel owned by a private company, having been booked into the hotel by the local housing authority in performance of its housing duty owed to the applicant. He brought a claim against the local housing authority for damages for disrepair to the room. His claim was dismissed because the local housing authority was not his landlord.

[205] See **18.123–18.124**.

[206] *Apczynski v Hounslow London Borough Council* [2006] EWCA Civ 1833, (2007) April *Legal Action*, p 21, CA.

[207] HA 1996, s 193(7B)–(7F). This is suggested at English Code, paras 16.39–16.43. See **17.92–17.97**.

[208] English Code, para 16.20; Welsh Code, paras 18.22–18.26.

authority) so that a joint assessment of the applicant's housing needs can be carried out. The assessment should include consideration of what settled accommodation would be suitable for the needs of the applicant.[209]

Young people

18.138 Providing 'suitable' accommodation for young people can superficially seem difficult because of the rule that minors (persons aged under 18) cannot be the legal owners of an interest in land, which includes a tenancy. But they can be beneficial owners under a trust, and a tenancy granted to a young person takes effect as the grant of that tenancy on trust for the young person.[210] The Codes recommend that social services departments are asked to underwrite the tenancy and thus guarantee the rent in order to avoid a landlord's concern that he or she may not be able to recover rent from a minor.[211] This advice was described as 'not particularly informative' by the Court of Appeal in a case which discussed the legal framework surrounding the attempt to grant a tenancy to a minor (*Alexander-David v Hammersmith & Fulham London Borough Council*).[212] The Court of Appeal held that, where a local housing authority purports to grant a tenancy to a minor, and the terms and conditions of that tenancy contain no reference to the tenant being a minor, the local housing authority holds the land in trust for the minor. As a result, it was a breach of that trust for the local housing authority to purport to serve a notice to quit on the minor, and the notice to quit was not effective to terminate the tenancy. To overcome these difficulties, the Court of Appeal suggested that licences to occupy accommodation where the minor does not have exclusive possession of that accommodation should normally be granted. Alternatively, the authors suggest, a tenancy could contain a declaration of trust appointing another person as the legal owner and trustee of the land.

18.139 Some homeless young people may need help with managing tenancies or with household budgeting.[213] Close liaison with social services and the local Supporting People team is recommended as essential. Other young people may benefit from supported accommodation before they are sufficiently independent to manage a tenancy, although local housing authorities are reminded that they must consider each applicant's individual circumstances and not just assume that supported accommodation will be suitable for all young people. Generally, if the minor is also a parent, semi-independent accommodation with support is recommended. If the young parent is aged less than 16, she or he should always be referred to social services for an assessment of his or her care needs.[214]

---

[209] English Code, chapter 4, particularly paras 4.16–4.18, and para 16.4; Welsh Code, para 18.4.
[210] *Kingston upon Thames London Borough Council v Prince* (1999) 31 HLR 794, CA.
[211] English Code, para 16.31; Welsh Code, para 18.45 and Annex 25.
[212] [2009] EWCA Civ 259, [2009] HLR 39, CA, per Sullivan LJ at [13].
[213] English Code, paras 4.11 and 12.12–12.17.
[214] English Code, paras 12.15–12.17.

18.140 In *R (M) v Hammersmith & Fulham London Borough Council*,[215] the House of Lords held that housing authorities should always refer young people, aged less than 18 years, for an assessment by social services. The expectation is that, unless the minor's need for accommodation is relatively short-term, the responsibility for providing accommodation should be met by social services under Children Act 1989, s 20, and so the minor will receive not just accommodation but also the additional assistance to help and support her in the transition to independent adult living. The House of Lords stressed joint working between housing and social services departments. The referral to social services does not avoid the housing department's duty to secure accommodation to the young person while social services carry out an assessment and consider whether the young person is a child in need pursuant to Children Act 1989, s 20.[216] This emphasis on joint working between housing and social services' departments and authorities was reiterated by the House of Lords in *R (G) v Southwark London Borough Council*, where the social services' department was criticised for referring a homeless 17-year-old to the housing department, to make an application for homelessness assistance, rather than assessing the child's needs under the Children Act 1989.

Families with children

18.141 When offering or securing accommodation for families with children, local housing authorities are advised to ensure that all babies and young children in temporary accommodation have the opportunity to receive health and developmental checks from health visitors or other health professionals.[217]

Gypsies and travellers

18.142 Local housing authorities are advised to consider the needs and lifestyles of applicants who are gypsies and travellers when considering how to secure suitable accommodation. Where an applicant has a 'cultural aversion to the prospect of "bricks and mortar" accommodation', local housing authorities are advised that sites, or pitches, should be provided.[218] It is for the local housing authority to determine whether a particular applicant has 'a cultural aversion'.

18.143 In determining whether there is a 'cultural aversion', local housing authorities should:

> 'carefully ... examine a gypsy's claim for such special consideration and, if satisfied that it is genuine, whether in all the circumstances of the case, it should

---

[215] [2008] UKHL 14, [2008] 1 WLR 535, HL.

[216] See **13.107–13.136** and **13.175**.

[217] English Code, paras 4.16–4.18 and 16.10.

[218] *R (Price) v Carmarthenshire County Council* [2003] EWHC 42 (Admin), (2003) March *Legal Action*, p 31, Admin Ct, and see *Codona v Mid-Bedfordshire District Council* [2004] EWCA Civ 925, [2005] HLR 1, CA. English Code, para 16.38. See **18.120–18.123**.

attempt to meet it, and, if so, how. Those circumstances should, of course, include the likely duration of occupation in respect of which an offer is to be made.'[219]

18.144 In particular, they should consider:

(1) whether the applicant and his or her family lived in a caravan; and

(2) whether they subscribe to a gypsy culture; and

(3) whether they are itinerant or nomadic for a substantial part of the year; and

(4) whether itinerancy is linked to their livelihood; and

(5) whether they subscribe to the relevant features of the gypsy life.[220]

18.145 The English Code adds, drawing on decisions of the European Court of Human Rights,[221] that local housing authorities must also take into account their obligations to act consistently with the Human Rights Act 1998, and in particular the applicant's right to respect for his or her private and family life, and his or her home.[222]

18.146 Local housing authorities will have to address whether or not sites are available on four different occasions:

(1) in determining whether or not they have 'reason to believe' that an applicant may be homeless, in that there is no place where the applicant is entitled or permitted to place and live in his or her mobile home or caravan – if so, and if they also have 'reason to believe' that an applicant may be eligible and may have a priority need, they have a duty to secure suitable interim accommodation pending notification of their decision;[223]

(2) in determining whether or not the applicant is actually homeless according to the statutory test;[224]

(3) in determining, if a main housing duty is owed to the applicant, what suitable accommodation could be offered to the applicant in performance of the main housing duty[225]; and

---

[219] *Codona v Mid-Bedfordshire District Council* [2004] EWCA Civ 925, [2005] HLR 1, CA, at [49], per Auld LJ.

[220] *Codona v Mid-Bedfordshire District Council* [2004] EWCA Civ 925, [2005] HLR 1, CA, at [49]–[51], per Auld LJ.

[221] *Connors v United Kingdom* [2004] HLR 52, ECHR.

[222] English Code, para 16.38, referring to Art 8 of the European Convention on Human Rights and the Human Rights Act 1998, Sch 1.

[223] HA 1996, s 188(1). See **16.11–16.24**.

[224] HA 1996, s 175(2)(b). See Chapter 11 in general and in particular **11.67–11.71**.

[225] HA 1996, s 193(2).

(4)   in determining whether the main housing duty has come to an end.[226]

18.147   If, during any part of this process, a place on an acceptable permanent site becomes available, is suitable for the applicant's needs, and has been secured for him or her to occupy, the applicant will no longer be 'homeless', as there will be somewhere where he or she is entitled or permitted to park his or her mobile home or caravan and to live in it. If this occurs while the applicant is occupying interim accommodation under HA 1996, s 188(1), the local housing authority will be able to notify him or her that he or she is no longer homeless, and no further duty is owed.

18.148   If no permanent site is available, the local housing authority's duty is to secure 'suitable' accommodation. The starting point is that, if the applicant is accepted as having a cultural aversion to bricks and mortar, a temporary site should be found, so that, at least, 'suitable' accommodation has been secured under either the interim accommodation duty or the main housing duty.

18.149   But, given the shortage of permanent and temporary sites for travellers, what if no site is available?

18.150   The Code of Appeal has held that:

> 'where land is not available, or cannot readily be made available, on which a gypsy applicant can station his or her caravan, it is open to a local authority to provide other accommodation of the conventional bricks and mortar kind, providing that it satisfies the *Wednesbury* minimum line of suitability.'[227]

18.151   The English Code reflects this advice.[228] It follows that 'bricks and mortar' can be provided in performance of the interim duty to secure accommodation pending inquiries,[229] and of the main housing duty,[230] only if no site is available and the conventional accommodation is suitable in all other aspects.

18.152   Although not fitting entirely happily with the statutory scheme in HA 1996, Part 7, in practice if a site were then to be offered to, and accepted by, the applicant, the understanding would be that the main housing duty had come to an end.[231]

---

226   HA 1996, s 193(5)–(7F). See **17.38–17.108**.
227   *Codona v Mid-Bedfordshire District Council* [2004] EWCA Civ 925, [2005] HLR 1, CA, at [47], per Auld LJ. Followed and applied in *Lee v Rhondda Cynon Taf CBC* [2008] EWCA Civ 1013, (2008) November *Legal Action*, p 20, CA.
228   English Code, para 16.38.
229   HA 1996, s 188(1). See **16.11–16.24**.
230   HA 1996, s 193(2). See **17.21–17.110**.
231   The provision of a suitable site would render the applicant no longer 'homeless'. This is not one of the events that can bring the main housing duty at HA 1996, s 193(2) to an end (HA 1996, s 193(5)–(7F)). However, assuming that the applicant moves from the HA 1996, s 193

Asylum-seekers

18.153 A very small number of asylum-seekers are eligible for assistance under HA 1996, Part 7 while they remain asylum-seekers.[232] The vast majority of homeless asylum-seekers qualify instead for assistance from the Home Office.[233] For those who are within the scope of HA 1996, Part 7 and have applied to English local housing authorities, Part 7 applies with considerable modifications.[234] The provisions include additional considerations when the local housing authority is assessing the suitability of accommodation provided to asylum-seekers.[235]

Standard of accommodation

18.154 In determining whether accommodation provided to an asylum-seeker is suitable, the local housing authority must have regard to the fact that the accommodation is to be only temporary pending the determination of the asylum claim.[236]

Location

18.155 In performing its duty to accommodate an asylum-seeker, the local housing authority is required to have regard to the desirability of securing accommodation in areas in which there is a ready supply of accommodation.[237] The local housing authority may not take into account the applicant's preference regarding the location of the accommodation.[238] Subject to those two considerations, the accommodation secured for an asylum-seeker and his or her household must still be suitable for their needs.[239]

18.156 In order to implement a dispersal scheme similar to the one operated by the Home Office, the local housing authority may enter into a written

---

accommodation to the site, he or she would 'voluntarily cease[s] to occupy as his only or principal home the accommodation made available' (s 193(6)(d)), and the main housing duty would come to an end. See **17.64–17.65**.

[232] See **12.55–12.66** and **12.88–12.89**. English Code, para 17.43; Welsh Code, paras 19.13–19.15.
[233] Immigration and Asylum Act 1999, Part VI.
[234] The modifications are made by the Homelessness (Asylum-Seekers) (Interim Period) (England) Order 1999, SI 1999/3126. That order inserts a range of provisions which only apply to applicants who are asylum-seekers and are designed to mirror the dispersal provisions under Immigration and Asylum Act 1999, Part VI.
[235] The order sets up two mechanisms by which English local housing authorities can disperse asylum-seekers. The modifications to the assessment of 'suitability' are described in this chapter. Local connection provisions are also modified, so that asylum-seekers can be referred to other local housing authorities regardless of whether or not they have any local connection with that other local housing authority. See **15.167–15.172**.
[236] HA 1996, s 210(1A).
[237] HA 1996, s 206(1A).
[238] HA 1996, s 210(1A).
[239] *R v Kensington and Chelsea Royal London Borough Council ex p Korneva* (1997) 29 HLR 709, CA.

agreement with another local housing authority to ensure that accommodation is available for asylum-seekers in the other local housing authority's district.[240]

18.157 The requirement to ensure that accommodation is secured in the local housing authority's own district, so far as is reasonably practicable, does not apply in these circumstances.[241]

ADVICE AND ASSISTANCE WHICH SECURES ACCOMMODATION

18.158 As already noted,[242] as an alternative to providing accommodation (or arranging for someone else to secure accommodation), a local housing authority may discharge its duty to secure that suitable accommodation is available for the applicant and his or her household by:

> '... giving him such advice and assistance as will secure that suitable accommodation is available from some other person.'[243]

18.159 This is different from the distinct duties under HA 1996, Part 7 to provide advice and assistance to applicants who have no priority need, have become homeless intentionally, or are threatened with homelessness.[244]

18.160 If the advice and assistance provided under HA 1996, s 206(1)(c) enables the applicant to succeed in obtaining suitable accommodation, the local housing authority's HA 1996, Part 7 duty to him or her will have been performed. If suitable accommodation is not obtained, the local housing authority remains under that duty to secure accommodation for the applicant.

18.161 The Codes suggest, as examples of this method of performing the duty, the provision of advice on the financing of house purchases, advice on shared ownership schemes, financial assistance with rent deposits, or practical advice and assistance to obtain accommodation already identified by the applicants themselves.[245] So, if it is known that suitable accommodation is available to an applicant in a particular place, the duty may be performed by the provision of the information and assistance they need to get to that place (which might even be in another country).[246]

---

[240] See **15.168**.
[241] HA 1996, s 208(1A).
[242] See **18.7**(3).
[243] HA 1996, s 206(1)(c).
[244] HA 1996, ss 190(2)(b) and (3), 192(2) and 195(5). See **17.132–17.144**.
[245] English Code, paras 16.32–16.36; Welsh Code, 18.37–18.39.
[246] *R v Bristol City Council ex p Browne* [1979] 1 WLR 1437, DC.

SUITABILITY: DECISIONS AND CHALLENGES

Decisions

18.162 Save in the exceptional cases mentioned at **18.18**, there is no strict requirement for a local housing authority to notify its decision that it considers particular accommodation secured in performance of a duty owed under HA 1996, Part 7 (or under an HA 1996, Part 7 power) to be 'suitable' for the applicant. Nor is there any duty to provide reasons for such a decision.[247]

18.163 Usually, however, such a decision will be notified in writing if:

(1) an applicant is being told that accommodation initially secured under an interim duty is subsequently being treated as suitable accommodation secured in performance of a different accommodation duty (if an applicant remains in the same accommodation during different stages of the local housing authority's handling of his or her application under HA 1996, Part 7), since the local housing authority is under a duty at each stage to consider whether the accommodation is suitable for an applicant's needs;[248] or

(2) if the applicant has raised a concern or complaint about the accommodation secured or offered; or

(3) if there is some other reason why it makes good administrative practice to give such a notice.

18.164 If such notice is given, it would be good practice for the applicant to be advised of any right to review and the time limit within which that right should be exercised.

Statutory reviews

18.165 As already noted,[249] the applicant has the right to request a statutory review of the local housing authority's decision that accommodation offered to him or her under HA 1996, ss 190(2), 193, 195 or 196 is suitable. Additionally, the applicant may seek a review of the 'suitability' of a final offer of accommodation made under HA 1996, Part 6 where that is being relied upon to bring a main housing duty to an end.[250] Applicants who are restricted cases[251] (or are restricted threatened homelessness cases)[252] can request a review of the suitability of any accommodation offered to them as a private accommodation

---

[247] See **10.96–10.98**.
[248] *R v Lambeth London Borough Council ex p Touhey* (2000) 32 HLR 707, QBD.
[249] See **18.18**.
[250] HA 1996, s 202(1)(f). See **19.27–19.32**.
[251] HA 1996, s 193(3B). See **17.98–17.101**.
[252] HA 1996, s 195(4B). See **17.126–17.128**.

offer.[253] The Codes note that asking for a review of suitability of accommodation does not bring the main housing duty to an end.[254]

Informal reviews

18.166 Informally, an applicant can, at any time, request that the local housing authority reconsider its decision that the accommodation secured under HA 1996, Part 7 is suitable. An applicant might need to take that step if accommodation that was originally suitable for the applicant when first occupied has become unsuitable as a result of a change in the applicant's circumstances.[255]

Offers which end duties

18.167 Three types of offer of 'suitable' accommodation raise special issues. They are the offers which can, if refused, bring to an end the main housing duty owed under HA 1996, Part 7. They are:

(1)   an offer of suitable accommodation in performance of the main housing duty;[256] or

(2)   a final offer of suitable accommodation made through the allocation arrangements in HA 1996, Part 6;[257] or

(3)   for 'restricted cases'[258] and 'restricted threatened homelessness cases'[259] only, a 'private accommodation offer'.[260]

18.168 Because these offers are of crucial importance, they are subject to special preconditions before they operate to bring the main housing duty to an end.[261]

18.169   They also, exceptionally, confer on the applicant the right to request a review of the suitability of the accommodation whilst simultaneously accepting

---

253   HA 1996, s 202(1)(g). For 'private accommodation offer', see HA 1996, s 193(7AA)–(7AD) and **17.104–17.108**.

254   See English Code, para 17.45; Welsh Code, para 19.12.

255   *R v Southwark London Borough Council ex p Campisi* (1999) 31 HLR 560, CA; and *R v Newham London Borough Council ex p Mashuda Begum* (1999) 32 HLR 808, QBD. In *Muse v Brent London Borough Council* [2008] EWCA Civ 1447, (2009) February *Legal Action*, p 32, CA, the applicant refused to move from main housing duty accommodation which had become unsuitable to new accommodation offered to her which the local housing authority had decided was suitable for her and her household. As a result, the local housing authority's main housing duty to her came to an end under HA 1996, s 193(5) (see **17.49–17.58**).

256   HA 1996, s 193(5). See **17.49–17.50**.

257   HA 1996, s 193(7). See **17.78–17.91**.

258   HA 1996, s 193(3B). See **17.98–17.101**.

259   HA 1996, s 195(4B). See **17.126–17.128**.

260   For a 'private accommodation offer' (HA 1996, s 193(7AA)–(7AD)), see **17.104–17.108**.

261   See **17.49–17.50**, **17.78–17.91** and **17.98–17.108**.

it.[262] Given the serious consequences which may follow if an offer is refused but is later upheld as 'suitable', accepting the offer must usually be the advisable course of action.

18.170 Even if the applicant has not requested a review of a decision that accommodation offered in one of these two ways is suitable, he or she is still entitled to a review of any later decision (if one is made) that the duty on the local housing authority has ended by reason of the refusal of that accommodation.[263] If the applicant's reasons for refusing the offer are that the accommodation is not suitable, the local housing authority must consider his or her representations to that effect on review.

18.171 It should be noted that the general rules governing what facts, law and other circumstances the reviewing officer should consider are modified in relation to reviews of decisions to end duty as a result of the applicant having refused an offer of accommodation that the local housing authority has considered to be suitable for the applicant and his or her household. The reviewing officer is required to look at the facts that existed at the date of the applicant's refusal of the offer, albeit that some of those facts might only come to the local housing authority's attention after the refusal.[264]

Legal challenges

18.172 Where the local housing authority decides on review that the accommodation was suitable for the applicant, it has a duty to give reasons for that decision. Those reasons must be adequate and intelligible to the applicant.[265] If the review decision confirms that the accommodation offered was suitable, the applicant's remedy is to appeal to the county court on a point of law.[266]

18.173 An applicant can only seek to challenge a particular decision that the accommodation was suitable for his or her needs. The courts will not entertain a challenge to the local housing authority's policy on certain types of offers in abstract.[267]

18.174 If the local housing authority agrees that the accommodation is not suitable for the needs of the applicant and members of his or her household but does not secure any alternative accommodation, the applicant's remedy is to

---

[262] HA 1996, s 202(1A). See **19.27–19.35** and **19.39–19.47**.

[263] HA 1996, s 202(1)(b); and see *Warsame v Hounslow London Borough Council* (2000) 32 HLR 335, CA. See also **19.14–19.15**.

[264] *Oseilly v Westminster City Council* [2007] EWCA Civ 1108, [2008] HLR 18, CA; and *Omar v Westminster City Council* [2008] EWCA Civ 421, [2008] HLR 36, CA. See **17.47** and **19.102–19.109**.

[265] HA 1996, s 203(4). See **10.68–10.74** and **19.111**.

[266] HA 1996, s 204. See **19.141–19.210**.

[267] *R v Westminster City Council ex p Tansey* (1988) 21 HLR 57, CA.

bring a claim in judicial review for a mandatory order requiring the local housing authority to secure suitable accommodation.[268]

18.175 If the dispute between the applicant and the local housing authority as to the suitability of accommodation does not attract a right to request a review,[269] the applicant's remedy is to bring a claim by way of judicial review proceedings arguing that the local housing authority's decision is wrong in law, or to invoke the local housing authority's complaints procedure.[270]

Handling 'suitability' disputes

18.176 The general conduct of reviews, appeals and court challenges is dealt with in Chapter 19, but several specific points can be made about the conduct of cases which concern 'suitability' issues.

18.177 Where an applicant pursuing a review raises new information as part of his or her argument that the accommodation is unsuitable, the reviewing officer must take that information into account. If the fact that the information was not previously raised causes the reviewing officer to disbelieve the applicant, the reviewing officer must put its concerns to the applicant and give him or her an opportunity to deal with them.[271] If the reviewing officer is relying on inconsistencies in the applicant's account, those too should be put to the applicant for explanation.[272] If a reviewing officer, in the course of its deliberations into whether or not accommodation offered was suitable, obtains information from a third party causing it to believe that the accommodation was suitable, it should put that information to the applicant and give him or her a chance to comment.[273]

18.178 Where both medical and non-medical considerations are raised as reasons for the refusal of an offer, the local housing authority must take an overall or composite view of those reasons as affecting the suitability of the accommodation for the individual applicant.[274] If there is conflicting medical evidence or opinion, the local housing authority is under a duty to act fairly and not merely to rely on the view of its medical adviser without explaining why it had rejected the contrary views of other medical practitioners.[275] It should also put to the applicant for comment any adverse medical views on

---

[268] *R v Newham London Borough Council ex p Mashuda Begum* (1999) 32 HLR 808, QBD. See also **18.24** and **19.211–19.237**.
[269] See **18.18**.
[270] See **19.211–19.237** for judicial review, and **19.238–19.245** for complaints.
[271] *R v Hackney London Borough Council ex p Decordova* (1995) 27 HLR 108, QBD.
[272] *R v Camden London Borough Council ex p Mohammed* (1998) 30 HLR 315, QBD.
[273] *R v Southwark London Borough Council ex p Ryder* (1995) September *Legal Action*, p 15, CA (refusal of permission to appeal).
[274] *R v Lewisham London Borough Council ex p Dolan* (1993) 25 HLR 68, QBD.
[275] *R v Kensington and Chelsea Royal London Borough Council ex p Assister* (1996) September *Legal Action*, p 13, QBD.

which it is proposing to rely.[276] Where a consultant's report was rejected after referral to the local housing authority's medical adviser, the subsequent decision of the local housing authority was quashed because it had failed to give reasons for rejecting the report.[277] Where the local housing authority does not make its own investigations into the applicant's medical condition or obtain its own medical advice, it is bound by the medical evidence on suitability submitted by the applicant.[278]

18.179 Where an applicant has accepted the accommodation and simultaneously sought a review of the suitability, the reviewing officer should consider all the circumstances at the date of the review.[279] It follows that, if there have been any developments between the date of the request for a review and the reviewing officer's decision, and those developments might render the accommodation unsuitable, they should be considered.[280]

---

[276] *R v Newham London Borough Council ex p Lumley* (2001) 33 HLR 124, QBD; and *R (Amirun Begum) v Tower Hamlets London Borough Council* [2002] EWHC 633 (Admin), (2003) 33 HLR 8, Admin Ct.

[277] *R v Kensington and Chelsea Royal London Borough Council ex p Campbell* (1996) 28 HLR 160, QBD.

[278] *R v Haringey London Borough Council ex p Karaman* (1997) 29 HLR 366, QBD.

[279] *Mohamed v Hammersmith & Fulham London Borough Council* [2001] UKHL 57, [2002] 1 AC 547, HL. See *Omar v Westminster City Council* [2008] EWCA Civ 421, [2008] HLR 36, CA, and **17.47** and **19.102–19.109** for the relevant considerations when an applicant has refused an offer of accommodation.

[280] *Omar v Westminster City Council* [2008] EWCA Civ 421, [2008] HLR 36, CA, at [25], per Waller LJ.

Chapter 19

REVIEWING AND APPEALING HOMELESSNESS DECISIONS

INTRODUCTION

19.1   Inevitably, some applicants are disappointed with the decisions made by local housing authorities on their applications for assistance under the Housing Act 1996 (HA 1996) Part 7 ('Homelessness'). Others may be concerned at the way in which they have been treated by a local housing authority or the way in which it has performed its obligations.

19.2   Disputes about the content of decisions were not addressed at all in the earliest versions of the statutory homelessness provisions. From 1977 onwards, those who were disappointed sought recourse to the courts, initially by ordinary civil claims in the county courts and in the Chancery and Queen's Bench Divisions of the High Court. But from the early 1980s, challenges to decisions could only be made by bringing judicial review proceedings in the Crown Office List of the High Court. As a result, challenges were confined to claims alleging breach by the local housing authority of administrative law principles.

19.3   Only a modest number of judicial review applications were ever brought, but, partly at least to reduce the numbers of those challenges, later versions of the Codes of Guidance encouraged local housing authorities to establish and operate their own in-house mechanisms to review disputed decisions. Applicants who expressed concern about decisions on their applications could then request an extra-statutory, internal review of those decisions by the relevant local housing authority. The approach was widely adopted by local housing authorities, but in practice did little to diminish the numbers of judicial review applications to the courts.

19.4   The current regime in HA 1996, Part 7 has built on both approaches (in-house reviews and access to the courts to challenge the contents of unlawful decisions). First, HA 1996, Part 7 contains a statutory scheme for internal review by a local housing authority of some of its own decisions. Second, most legal challenges are diverted away from the High Court to the county court, where there is a limited right of appeal against those decisions capable of being subject to statutory review. Third, judicial review remains available for a residual category of HA 1996, Part 7 disputes, in particular those relating to non-reviewable decisions. Concerns that this three-pronged arrangement for challenging decisions might not comply with the 'fair hearing' requirements of the European Convention on Human Rights were quickly put to rest by the House of Lords.[1] More recently, in February 2010, the Supreme Court held that decision-making on an application for homelessness assistance did not involve a determination of the applicant's 'civil rights' and therefore that Art 6(1) of the European Convention on Human Rights did not apply.[2]

---

[1]   European Convention on Human Rights, Art 6; Human Rights Act 1998, Sch 1. *Runa Begum v Tower Hamlets London Borough Council* [2003] UKHL 5, [2003] 2 AC 430, HL.

[2]   *Tomlinson & others v Birmingham City Council* [2010] UKSC 8, SC.

19.5 Where the applicant's concern is over the way in which his or her application has been handled, or the way in which the duties owed have been performed, HA 1996, Part 7 provides no means of redress. For that, the applicant must look first to the local housing authority's own complaints procedure. That procedure is underscored by:

(1) a right of further complaint to the Local Commissioner for Administration;[3]

(2) the local housing authority's own monitoring officer, who deals with alleged maladministration or unlawful conduct;[4]

(3) an enhanced statutory power permitting local authorities to give compensation to complainants.[5]

19.6 Of course, in the process of delivering its HA 1996, Part 7 service, the local housing authority may also infringe the applicant's rights under the European Convention on Human Rights (giving rise to a possible claim under the Human Rights Act 1998) or be guilty of discrimination on grounds of race, sex or disability (giving rise to possible claims under the Race Relations Act 1976, Sex Discrimination Act 1975, or the Disability Discrimination Act 1995). A full consideration of such specialist claims is beyond the scope of this book. However, if the local housing authority is not performing its acknowledged duty under HA 1996, Part 7, or is failing to consider exercising an available power, the Administrative Court can grant a mandatory order in judicial review proceedings, requiring it to perform its statutory obligations. Examples of such cases are given in this book.

19.7 Any particular homelessness application may trigger more than one of the different possibilities for redress. This chapter considers each potential remedy in turn. The reader will need to consider the portfolio as a whole before deciding which remedy, or which selection of remedies, to pursue.

REVIEWS

Statutory reviews

An overview

19.8 Where an applicant is disappointed with a decision made by the local housing authority on his or her application for homelessness assistance, the statutory review process provided by HA 1996, Part 7 may give that applicant an opportunity to have all the relevant facts and the law reconsidered by the

---

3   Commonly called 'the Local Government Ombudsman' (LGO): www.lgo.org.uk in England; or in Wales, the Pubic Services Ombudsman for Wales, www.ombudsman-wales.org.uk.

4   Local Government and Housing Act 1989, s 5.

5   Local Government Act 2000, s 92.

local housing authority.[6] In most cases, the reviewing officer must look at all the circumstances afresh, and as they exist at the date of the review decision. The process is not confined to considering matters as they stood when the applicant first applied or as at the date of the initial decision.[7] The statutory review is, therefore, the opportunity for the applicant to have his or her case completely re-examined by the local housing authority itself.[8]

19.9   There is no free-standing right to a review of *every* adverse decision made by a local housing authority under HA 1996, Part 7. The statutory review scheme applies only to a specific band of decisions.[9] However, nothing in HA 1996, Part 7 prevents a local housing authority from adopting its own informal arrangements enabling it to look again at any other decisions about which applicants express concern. Such informal reviews are no part of the statutory scheme, but can nevertheless help to reduce the number of formal complaints or claims for judicial review. HA 1996, Part 7 only permits one statutory review of any particular decision. A review decision cannot itself be the subject of a statutory review.[10]

19.10   When the scheme of statutory reviews was introduced by HA 1996, Part 7, it was hoped that this new regime would be monitored so as to establish its success or failure. Regrettably, there has been very little feedback on whether or not the scheme of statutory reviews has been a success.

19.11   The first government-commissioned research targeted a geographic area in which there had been relatively little review activity.[11] The little empirical information that is available has come mainly through independent academic research.[12]

---

6   HA 1996, ss 202–203.
7   *Mohammed v Hammersmith and Fulham London Borough Council* [2001] UKHL 57, [2002] 1 AC 547, HL.
8   Case law has developed two exceptions to the general rule that a reviewing officer considers all the circumstances at the date of the review decision. The first exception is where the HA 1996, s 184 decision was unlawful, and had deprived the applicant of rights that he or she would have had if there had been a lawful decision, so the reviewing officer should restore those rights (*Robinson v Hammersmith & Fulham London Borough Council* [2006] EWCA Civ 1122, [2007] HLR 7, CA). See **13.115** and **19.108**. The second exception is where the review relates to a decision that the local housing authority's duty to the applicant has come to an end, because the applicant has refused an offer of suitable accommodation (HA 1996, s 193(5) and (7)). In those circumstances, the reviewing officer should consider the facts and circumstances at the date of the refusal (*Omar v Westminster City Council* [2008] EWCA Civ 421, [2008] HLR 36, CA). See **17.47–17.48**, **18.176–18.179** and **19.109**.
9   See **19.12–19.25**.
10   HA 1996, s 202(2). See also **19.128**.
11   Atkinson et al *A Regional Study of Local Authority and Court Processes in Homelessness Cases* (Faculty of Law, University of Leicester, Department of Constitutional Affairs 9/99, www.dca.gov.uk/research/1999/999esfr.htm).
12   D Cowan, S Halliday and C Hunter 'Homelessness reviews – findings published' (2002) July *Legal Action*, p 6; and 'Homeless applicants and internal reviews' (2003) March *Legal Action*, p 8.

Which decisions can be reviewed?

19.12 An applicant who is dissatisfied with a local housing authority's decision in his or her case can only request a review if the decision falls into one of seven specified categories.[13] Between them, these categories encompass many of the most important decisions that a local housing authority is likely to make on an application. We consider each of the seven categories in turn.

(1) Any decision as to the applicant's 'eligibility' for assistance[14]

19.13 'Eligibility' is primarily a matter of immigration status and is fully discussed in Chapter 12. The decision capable of statutory review is the decision of the local housing authority, not any decision of the immigration or benefits authorities on essentially the same subject matter.

(2) Any decision as to what duty (if any) is owed to the applicant[15]

19.14 The right to a review is only available in respect of decisions as to whether a duty is owed under HA 1996, Part 7, ss 190, 191, 192, 193, 195 and 196.[16] The list of sections included here is a little odd. The references to ss 191 and 196 are redundant, as they contain definitions,[17] not duties, and other sections of HA 1996, Part 7, which may also give rise to duties, are omitted. Several other sections carry separate rights to seek a review, but do not feature in this general right.[18] Moreover, the following sections all contain duties, yet are omitted from any right to request a review: ss 184,[19] 188,[20] 200,[21] 202,[22] 211[23] and 213A.[24]

19.15 This category is, however, broad enough to include a right to a review of any decision that a duty once owed (under one of the specified sections) is no longer owed.[25]

---

[13] HA 1996, s 202(1).
[14] HA 1996, s 202(1)(a).
[15] HA 1996, s 202(1)(b).
[16] HA 1996, s 190, duty to persons becoming homeless intentionally; HA 1996, s 192, duty to persons not in priority need who have not become homeless intentionally; HA 1996, s 193, duty to persons with priority need who have not become homeless intentionally; HA 1996, s 195, duties in cases of threatened homelessness.
[17] HA 1996, s 191 defines 'becoming homeless intentionally'; HA 1996, s 196 defines 'becoming threatened with homelessness intentionally'.
[18] For example, HA 1996, s 198, dealing with 'conditions for referral'.
[19] Duty to carry out inquiries and notify decisions. See Chapter 10.
[20] Duty to provide pre-decision accommodation. See **16.11–16.24**.
[21] Duty to accommodate in a referral situation. See **15.136–15.139** and **16.43–16.50**.
[22] Duty to carry out a review.
[23] Duty to protect possessions. See **17.163–17.184**.
[24] Duty to notify social services. See **17.155–17.162**.
[25] *Warsame v Hounslow London Borough Council* (2000) 32 HLR 335, CA. Note the special rules regarding the scope of the review where the decision is that an accommodation duty has come to an end as a result of the applicant having refused an offer of accommodation. See **17.47–17.48, 18.176–18.179** and **19.109**.

(3) Any decision to notify another local housing authority under HA 1996, s 198(1)[26]

19.16 Under HA 1996, s 198(1) ('conditions for referral'), a local housing authority can initiate the procedure for the referral of an application for homelessness assistance to another local housing authority.[27] The procedure starts when the local housing authority that has received the application notifies the other local housing authority that it believes the conditions for a referral are made out.

19.17 The applicant must be given a notice by the notifying local housing authority that such a notification to another local housing authority is going to be made or has been made. That notice must also inform him or her of the right to seek a review of the decision to notify.[28]

19.18 The sequence of events here is important. The applicant has the right to request a review once the notifying local housing authority has made two decisions on his or her application:

(1)   that it considers that the conditions for referral are met; and

(2)   that it is going to exercise its discretion to notify the other local housing authority on that basis.

19.19 The applicant's request for a review can cause both or either of those decisions to be reconsidered.

19.20 It follows that the review request can be made before the notification is actually sent from the first to the second local housing authority. In those circumstances, it may be sensible for the first local housing authority to conduct and determine the review before it notifies the second local housing authority, as, if the review is successful and the decision set aside, there may be no need to notify. This is particularly true if the applicant is challenging a decision as to which (of several) local housing authorities he or she should be referred.[29]

---

[26]   HA 1996, s 202(1)(c).

[27]   Outlined at **15.130–15.135**.

[28]   HA 1996, s 184(4) and (5).

[29]   In *Berhane v Lambeth London Borough Council* [2007] EWHC 2702 (QBD), (2008) March *Legal Action*, p 28, QBD, the High Court criticised a county court judge's decision to adjourn the applicant's appeal against a decision to notify another local housing authority until the two local housing authorities had resolved their dispute as to whether or not the conditions for referral were made out. Where there has been undue delay on the part of the notifying local housing authority, it was wrong, and deprived the applicant of effective access to the courts, to wait for the referee's decision. This decision emphasises that the applicant's right to challenge a decision to refer him or her to another local housing authority is entirely separate from the procedure used by two local housing authorities to resolve disputes between themselves. See **15.130–15.135**, **15.140–15.152** and **15.153–15.160**.

19.21 Where the second local housing authority is notified before a review is requested, or concluded, any response it makes does not affect the applicant's right to a review or the conclusions of that review.

19.22 There is no right available, either under this category or any other, to review a decision *not* to notify another local housing authority under the referral provisions.[30]

(4) Any decision under HA 1996, s 198(5) as to whether the conditions for referral are met[31]

19.23 The right to request a review of the decision set out in the preceding category enables an applicant to challenge the opinion of the notifying local housing authority that the conditions for referral under the local connection provisions are made out. This additional category confers a right to a review of the *final decision* as to whether the referral conditions are actually made out.

19.24 The final decision arises *after* the first local housing authority has notified the second local housing authority. They may either agree between them that the conditions are made out (or that they are not), or, if they cannot agree, they may invite a referee to decide the matter under the disputes procedure.

19.25 There are special modifications made to the ordinary review procedures where the request for a review is in respect of either a joint decision or a referee's decision.[32]

(5) Any decision under HA 1996, s 200(3) or (4)[33]

19.26 In the light of amendments made to HA 1996, s 200(3) and (4) by the Homelessness Act 2002, this category is redundant. The only decision to which these two subsections now refer is the final decision that the conditions for referral are or are not met. That decision is the subject matter of the review category just described.

(6) Any decision as to the suitability of accommodation[34]

19.27 This category concerns decisions as to the suitability of accommodation offered to the applicant in performance of duties owed under HA 1996, ss 190,

---

[30] *Sareen v Hackney London Borough Council* [2003] EWCA Civ 351, [2003] HLR 54, CA.
[31] HA 1996, s 202(1)(d).
[32] HA 1996, s 202(4); Allocation of Housing and Homelessness (Review Procedures) Regulations 1999, SI 1999/71, regs 6–9. *Homelessness Code of Guidance for local authorities* (Communities and Local Government, Department for Education and Skills, Department of Health, July 2006) (English Code), para 19.9. *Code of Guidance for local housing authorities on allocation of accommodation and homelessness for Wales* (National Assembly for Wales, April 2003) (Welsh Code), para 21.8; and see **15.162–15.166**.
[33] HA 1996, s 202(1)(e).
[34] HA 1996, s 202(1)(f).

191, 192, 193, 195, 196, 200(3) or (4), or as to the suitability of accommodation under HA 1996, Part 6 ('Allocation of Housing Accommodation') relied upon to release the local housing authority from the main housing duty under HA 1996, s 193(7).

19.28 The meaning of 'suitability' in respect of the accommodation offered under the statutory provisions referred to in this category is considered in Chapter 18.

19.29 The selection of sections listed in this category is, again, a little odd. The references to HA 1996, ss 191 and 196 are redundant.[35] The references to subsections 200(3) and (4) are superfluous as they merely trigger the HA 1996, s 193 duty under which the offer will be made.

19.30 Those provisions of HA 1996, Part 7 giving the local housing authority *powers* to provide accommodation, or obliging the local housing authority to provide some form of *interim* accommodation, are omitted from this category.

19.31 As a result, there is no right to review a decision as to the suitability of accommodation provided:

(1)   under the duty to provide pre-decision accommodation;[36]

(2)   under the duty to provide accommodation pending the outcome of a local connection referral;[37]

(3)   under the power to accommodate pending review;[38]

(4)   under the power to accommodate the non-priority homeless who have not become homeless intentionally;[39]

(5)   under the power to accommodate the non-priority homeless who have not become threatened with homelessness intentionally;[40]

(6)   under the power to accommodate pending a referral review;[41] or

(7)   under the power to accommodate pending appeal.[42]

---

[35]   They contain definitions and not duties. HA 1996, s 191 defines 'becoming homeless intentionally' and HA 1996, s 196 defines 'becoming threatened with homelessness intentionally'.
[36]   HA 1996, s 188(1).
[37]   HA 1996, s 200(1).
[38]   HA 1996, s 188(3).
[39]   HA 1996, s 192(3).
[40]   HA 1996, s 195(9).
[41]   HA 1996, s 200(5).
[42]   HA 1996, s 204(4).

19.32 Finally, this review category does not give everyone made an offer of accommodation under HA 1996, Part 6 a right to a review of its suitability. The only HA 1996, Part 6 offer addressed here is a final offer made to an applicant owed the main housing duty under Part 7, where the refusal of that offer may bring that duty to an end.[43] If other offers, not expressed as 'final offers' of Part 6 accommodation, and therefore not bringing the s 193(2) duty to an end, have been made, there is no right to request a review of the accommodation's suitability.

(7) For 'restricted cases' only, any decision as to the suitability of accommodation contained in a private accommodation offer[44]

19.33 This provision applies to applications to local housing authorities made on or after 2 March 2009. For 'restricted cases', see **12.30–12.39 and 17.98–17.99**. For 'private accommodation offer', see **17.104–17.108**. For 'suitability', see Chapter 18.

19.34 As with other disputes over the suitability of an offer of accommodation, the applicant has the right both to accept the offer and to request a review of its suitability. This must always be the safest course of action. Here, the applicant is being required to enter into a fixed-term assured shorthold tenancy. He or she will need a break clause to be contained in the tenancy, so as to permit the applicant to terminate the tenancy before the end of the fixed term upon notice to the landlord, if the outcome of the review (or any subsequent appeal) is a decision that the private accommodation offer was unsuitable.

19.35 If a local housing authority's decision does not fall into one of the seven specified categories, there is no right to request a statutory review, and any legal challenge to the decision itself can only be by way of judicial review.

Notifying review rights

19.36 It might be expected that, whenever a local housing authority takes *any* decision that carries a statutory right to a review, it should be required to notify the applicant not only of the decision, but also of the applicant's right to request a review and the time limit within which he or she should make the request.

19.37 However, that is only strictly true of decisions on an initial application for accommodation.[45] Even in those cases, there is no requirement that the applicant should also be informed of any advice or other help available to assist him or her in pursuing a review.

---

[43] HA 1996, s 193(7). For rights to accept the offer of Part 6 accommodation and simultaneously request a review, see **19.39–19.47**.

[44] HA 1996, s 202(1)(g), as inserted by Housing and Regeneration Act 2008, s 314 and Sch 15, in force 2 March 2009.

[45] HA 1996, s 184(5). See also **10.67**.

19.38 The Codes recommend that the local housing authority informs the applicant about the procedure involved in a review, if a request for review were to be made, but there is no statutory obligation to do so at this stage.[46] Nor is there any obligation to provide a pro-forma on which the applicant can request a review.[47]

Seeking a review and accepting accommodation

19.39 Where an applicant requests:[48]

- a review of the suitability of accommodation provided for him or her under the main housing duty;[49] or

- a review of the suitability of a final offer of accommodation offered under HA 1996, Part 6;[50] or

- a review of the suitability of accommodation offered under a 'private accommodation offer',[51]

he or she has the right both to accept the offer and to request the review.[52]

19.40 Although it is not a statutory requirement, the Codes advise that where an offer is being made in these specific circumstances, the offer should be accompanied both by an explanation that the applicant has a right to request a review of suitability and by an indication that the applicant can both accept the offer and request such a review.[53]

19.41 The way in which the applicant's options might be put in the notification has been neatly summarised as follows:

'[T]he choice which has to be presented to a person to whom an offer is made has to be in substance to this effect: you may accept or refuse a house. In either event you are entitled to seek a review of the decision to make this offer to you. If, though, you refuse to accept this accommodation you will not be able to retract

---

46   English Code, para 19.3; Welsh Code, para 21.2.

47   Only when a review has been requested is the local housing authority obliged to notify the applicant of the procedure: Allocation of Housing and Homelessness (Review Procedures) Regulations 1999, SI 1999/71, reg 6(3)(b).

48   HA 1996, s 202(1)(f).

49   HA 1996, s 193(2) and (5).

50   HA 1996, s 193(7).

51   HA 1996, s 193(7AC), as inserted by Housing and Regeneration Act 2008, s 314 and Sch 15, and in force for applications made on or after 2 March 2009.

52   HA 1996, s 202(1A), added by Homelessness Act 2002 and effective from 26 February 2002 (England and Wales) overturning *Alghile v City of Westminster* [2001] EWCA Civ 363, (2001) 33 HLR 627, CA.

53   English Code, para 19.3; Welsh Code, para 21.2. The guidance in the Codes refers to the first two types of circumstances. There is no guidance for restricted cases, since both Codes were published prior to the introduction of restricted cases by the Housing and Regeneration Act 2008 amendments to HA 1996, Part 7.

your refusal, so that if the review goes against you, we shall be discharged of any duty towards you. On the other hand, if the review goes in your favour, we shall, in the light of the review decision, have to make you a different offer or reconsider our position.'[54]

19.42 If the local housing authority fails to provide this information, it risks a subsequent complaint that the whole procedure has been unfair.[55]

19.43 Since the consequences of refusing an offer of suitable accommodation in any of these cases will be that the local housing authority's main housing duty to provide accommodation for the applicant will end, acceptance of the accommodation whilst simultaneously requesting a review of its suitability must always be the cautiously correct approach. For restricted cases, where the applicant is being required to enter into a fixed term assured shorthold tenancy, the terms of the tenancy should contain a break clause, so as to permit the applicant to terminate the tenancy before the end of the fixed term upon notice to the landlord, if the outcome of the review (or any subsequent appeal) is a decision that that the private accommodation offer was unsuitable.

19.44 However, it is only in the case of these three specific offers of accommodation[56] that the right to request a review whilst also accepting the offer is available.[57] In the case of offers made under the other provisions[58] there is no statutory right both to accept the accommodation and request a review. It may be that a local housing authority will permit applicants who are offered the other categories of accommodation the right both to accept and to request a review, but that would be entirely a matter for the local housing authority.[59]

19.45 Where an applicant has rejected accommodation offered under the main housing duty or as a final offer under HA 1996, Part 6, has requested a review of its suitability and then subsequently sought to accept the offer, the decision whether to re-offer the accommodation or not is one for the local housing authority. There is no requirement on the local housing authority to keep the accommodation available for the applicant during the review process.[60]

19.46 What happens if an applicant accepts accommodation offered under the main housing duty or as a final offer under HA 1996, Part 6 (or, in restricted cases, a private accommodation offer) without requesting any review, and then subsequently decides to request a review of its suitability? HA 1996,

---

[54] *R v Tower Hamlets London Borough Council ex p Mbidi* (2000) April *Legal Action*, p 32, QBD, per Jowitt J.

[55] See *Akhtar & Naseem v Manchester City Council* (2003) April *Legal Action*, p 28, Manchester County Court, but also *Ali-Ahmed v Islington London Borough Council* [2004] EWCA Civ 128, (2004) April *Legal Action*, p 35, CA, where the process was not unfair, although the offer letter did not contain this information.

[56] HA 1996, s 193(5), (7) and (7AA)–(7AD).

[57] HA 1996, s 202(1A).

[58] Referred to at **19.31**.

[59] English Code, para 17.45; Welsh Code, para 19.12.

[60] *Oseilly v Westminster City Council* [2007] EWCA Civ 1108, [2008] HLR 18, CA.

s 193(6)(c) provides that the main housing duty has ended as a result of the acceptance of the HA 1996, Part 6 offer, which implies that the right to request a review would also have ended.[61] However, the present tense used in s 202(1A)[62] suggests that the express statutory right to request a review, whilst also accepting the accommodation, remains open for the period of the statutory time limit in which to request a review.[63]

19.47   Where the applicant has accepted the offer of accommodation and also requested a review of its suitability, the reviewing officer should consider all the facts and circumstances as at the date of the review.[64]

Who may seek a review?

19.48   The statutory review rights are only available to 'an applicant'.[65] No member of the applicant's household has that statutory right. Nor can the review process be activated by others who may have an interest in challenging the local housing authority's decision, eg a different local housing authority, a registered social landlord (RSL), or another homeless person.

19.49   An applicant's request for review does not need to be made personally. It may be made by someone else as the applicant's formal or informal agent (by a solicitor or anyone else asked to act on the applicant's behalf).[66]

How to seek a review

19.50   The obligation on a local housing authority to carry out a review is triggered 'on a request being duly made to them'.[67]

19.51   Beyond those words HA 1996, Part 7 says nothing about the form or content of the request. In particular:

- the request need not be in writing;

- there is no prescribed form;

- the applicant need not use a form provided by the local housing authority (even if a form is available);

---

[61]   HA 1996, s 193(7AA)(a), dealing with private accommodation offers for restricted cases, makes the same provision.

[62]   HA 1996, s 202(1A): 'an applicant … may'.

[63]   21 days beginning with the date on which the applicant is notified of the local housing authority's decision: HA 1996, s 202(3); and see **19.56** and **19.62**.

[64]   *Omar v Westminster City Council* [2008] EWCA Civ 421, [2008] HLR 36, CA, at [25], per Waller LJ.

[65]   HA 1996, s 202(1).

[66]   As happened in *R (Sederati) v Enfield London Borough Council* [2002] EWHC 2423 (Admin), (2003) January *Legal Action*, p 23, Admin Ct, where the manager of the applicant's temporary accommodation made the request on his behalf.

[67]   HA 1996, s 202(4).

- no grounds or reasons for requesting the review need be given;[68] and

- no particular office or officer is the specified recipient of the request.

19.52 However, it must be tolerably clear that the applicant is asking for a review of the decision made and not, for example, requesting a disciplinary investigation into the conduct of the officer(s) who took the decision.[69]

19.53 There are a number of examples of written review requests available as precedents.[70]

19.54 The use of the words 'made to them' suggests that the request must not only have been made to, but also received by, the local housing authority.[71] Simply posting a letter containing a written request for a review will probably not suffice (although a local housing authority might agree to extend the time limit for requesting a review if it was satisfied that the request had been posted in good time but not subsequently received in time or at all).[72]

19.55 The local housing authority to which the request is to be made is normally the local housing authority that made the decision sought to be reviewed.[73] Where review is sought under the fourth category,[74] the request is to be made to the 'notifying local housing authority' which made the referral.[75]

Time in which to request a review

19.56 The applicant has 21 days, 'beginning with the day on which he [or she] is notified of the authority's decision', in which to make the request to the local housing authority for a review.[76] Because it is relatively short, the time limit needs careful consideration.

19.57 The time limit begins with the day on which the original decision is 'notified'.[77] So, for example, if the local housing authority's decision is received by the applicant on 2 April, the review request must be made to the local

---

68 English Code, para 19.10; Welsh Code, para 21.9.
69 For example, *R (Taylor) v Commissioner for Local Administration* [2003] EWCA Civ 1088, (2003) September *Legal Action*, p 28, CA.
70 For example, Holbrook and Luba 'Challenging homelessness decisions under the Housing Act 1996' (1997) January *Legal Action*, p 21 and in Astin *Housing Law, an adviser's handbook* (LAG, 2008).
71 See *R (Lester) v London Rent Assessment Committee* [2003] EWCA Civ 319, [2003] 33 HLR 53, [2003] 1 WLR 1449, CA – a rent is not 'referred' to the RAC until notice of referral is received by it.
72 HA 1996, s 202(3). See **19.59–19.62**.
73 Allocation of Housing and Homelessness (Review Procedures) Regulations 1999, SI 1999/71, reg 6(1)(a).
74 Of a decision made by a referee or by two local housing authorities jointly that the conditions for referral are met: HA 1996, s 202(1)(d); see **19.23–19.25**.
75 SI 1999/71, reg 6(1)(b).
76 HA 1996, s 202(3) and (4).
77 Which may be different from the day on which the decision was actually taken, and the day on

housing authority by midnight on 22 April.[78] Provided that it is physically delivered to the local housing authority's offices before midnight, it will be in time, even if 22 April is not a working day, or if the office has already closed.[79]

19.58   The local housing authority may take the view that a particular request for review was not made in time and that it therefore has no duty to conduct a review. If it will not agree to extend the time, the applicant can apply for judicial review of the refusal to carry out the review. The issue of whether a request was made and, if so, whether it was made in time, will have to be resolved by the High Court as a matter of fact.[80]

19.59   The local housing authority has a discretion to agree a longer period in which an applicant can request a review.[81] When a local housing authority receives a request to accept a review out of time, it should consider the explanation offered for the applicant's delay in making the request and the prospects of success on the review. The precise weight to be given to the balance between these two factors, and all other relevant considerations, is a matter for the local housing authority.[82] Nothing in HA 1996, Part 7, or in the regulations made under it, requires the decision on extending time to be taken by the person who would be conducting the review. As a matter of fairness and good practice, however, it probably should *not* be taken by the original decision-maker.[83]

19.60   Most (but not all) notifications of decisions carrying rights of review, will spell out the time limit.[84] A failure on the part of the local housing authority to comply with the obligation to notify (where it applies) would be a powerful factor in support of a request to extend time. On the other hand, if the time limit was notified and emphasised in the notification letter, any request to extend time will be more difficult to sustain.

---

which it was put in writing. See *Robinson v Hammersmith & Fulham London Borough Council* [2006] EWCA Civ 1122, [2007] HLR 7, CA, and **10.61–10.62**.

[78]   The phrase 'beginning with' includes the day of notification as the first day of the period: *Trow v Ind Coope (West Midlands) Ltd* [1967] 2 QB 899, CA.

[79]   *Van Aken v Camden London Borough Council* [2002] EWCA Civ 1724, (2003) 35 HLR 33, CA.

[80]   *R (Sederati) v Enfield London Borough Council* [2002] EWHC 2423 (Admin), (2003) January *Legal Action*, p 23, Admin Ct; and *R (Casey) v Restormel Borough Council* [2007] EWHC 2554 (Admin), (2008) January *Legal Action*, p 38, Admin Ct.

[81]   HA 1996, s 202(3).

[82]   *R (C) v Lewisham London Borough Council* [2003] EWCA Civ 927, [2004] HLR 4, CA; and *R (Slaiman) v Richmond upon Thames London Borough Council* [2006] EWHC 329 (Admin), [2006] HLR 20, Admin Ct.

[83]   It should be noted, however, that the Administrative Court, in *R (Abdi) v Lambeth London Borough Council* [2007] EWHC 1565 (Admin), [2008] HLR 5, Admin Ct, held that there was nothing in HA 1996, Part 7, the relevant regulations or the general law on issues of bias that prevented an original decision-maker from deciding a request for accommodation pending review.

[84]   HA 1996, s 184(5).

19.61 If the local housing authority accedes to the request to extend time, it must notify the applicant in writing accordingly.[85] This curious provision (not mirrored by any obligation to give written notice of a refusal to extend time) is presumably intended to avoid applicants suggesting that they were verbally given an indication that a late request would be allowed.

19.62 If the local housing authority refuses to extend the time limit for a review, where the request has been made late, the only challenge to that decision would be by way of judicial review.[86] A refusal to extend time is not itself a decision that can be subject to statutory review. If the decision to refuse to extend time was irrational, or for some other reason unlawful, it will be quashed and the local housing authority will be required to take the decision again on whether to extend time. In an exceptional case, the Administrative Court may even grant a mandatory order requiring the local housing authority to extend the time limit.[87]

Procedure on receipt of a request for review

Procedure locally

19.63 Only the barest outline of the procedure to be followed on review is set out in HA 1996, Part 7 itself.[88] Little more detail is given in the current version of the procedure regulations[89] which apply in both England and Wales. Accordingly, the day-to-day procedural operation of the review process is largely left to each local housing authority to determine with the benefit of the guidance given in HA 1996, Part 7, and the regulations and in the respective Codes.

19.64 The expectation is that each local housing authority will formulate and apply a written statement of its own procedure. Upon receipt of the review request the local housing authority must, if it has not earlier done so, notify the applicant of the 'procedure to be followed in connection with the review'.[90] Failure to comply with that obligation may undermine the fairness of the whole review process.

---

[85] HA 1996, s 202(3).
[86] As happened in *R (Casey) v Restormel Borough Council* [2007] EWHC 2554 (Admin), (2008) January *Legal Action*, p 38, Admin Ct.
[87] *R v Newham London Borough Council ex p P* (2001) January *Legal Action*, p 28, QBD, reported as *R (Patrick) v Newham London Borough Council* (2001) 4 CCLR 48, QBD.
[88] HA 1996, ss 202–203.
[89] Allocation of Housing and Homelessness (Review Procedures) Regulations 1999, SI 1999/71.
[90] Allocation of Housing and Homelessness (Review Procedures) Regulations 1999, SI 1999/71, reg 6(2)(b).

19.65 If the review is being sought of a referee's decision,[91] the person appointed to conduct the review must notify the applicant of the procedure that he or she is going to follow.[92]

Inviting written representations

19.66 As already noted,[93] there is no requirement that the applicant should set out any grounds or reasons in the request for review. Accordingly, not least so that any particular issues can be drawn out, the regulations require that once the request for a review has been received, the local housing authority which received it must notify the applicant that he or she, or a representative, may make written representations to the local housing authority in connection with the review.[94]

19.67 This invitation must be issued in every case. The local housing authority cannot assume that the applicant has made all the submissions he or she wants to make in the request for review, however comprehensive the request appears to be. Whether the request for a review has come directly from the applicant, or from someone acting on the applicant's behalf, the invitation to make written representations must be sent to the applicant personally.[95]

19.68 If the review is being sought of a referee's decision,[96] the person appointed to conduct the review will notify the applicant of the right to make written representations direct to him or her and not to the local housing authority.[97]

19.69 There is no obligation on the applicant to respond to the invitation to make written representations. The review will take place whether or not a response is received. Neither HA 1996, Part 7 nor the regulations provide any deadline for the receipt of written representations, and therefore they can be submitted at any stage before the decision on review is actually made.

19.70 Self-evidently, if the applicant has specific criticisms of the original decision, those criticisms should be set out in writing at the earliest possible stage so as to ensure that they are properly considered. The review process is

---

91   HA 1996, s 202(1)(d). See **15.146–15.152** and **19.23–19.25**.
92   Allocation of Housing and Homelessness (Review Procedures) Regulations 1999, SI 1999/71, reg 6(3)(b).
93   See **19.50–19.55**.
94   Allocation of Housing and Homelessness (Review Procedures) Regulations 1999, SI 1999/71, reg 6(2)(a). A notification which read 'you will be given an opportunity to make oral and/or written representations to the Panel' was described as wording which the local housing authority would be 'well advised' to reconsider, but was sufficient for the applicant to know that a review was under way and of his right to make representations (*Jama v Islington London Borough Council* [2006] EWCA Civ 45, (2006) June *Legal Action*, p 36, CA).
95   Allocation of Housing and Homelessness (Review Procedures) Regulations 1999, SI 1999/71, reg 6(2)(a).
96   HA 1996, s 202(1)(d). See **15.146–15.152** and **19.23–19.25**.
97   Allocation of Housing and Homelessness (Review Procedures) Regulations 1999, SI 1999/71, reg 6(3)(a).

the applicant's last opportunity to have the facts relevant to his or her application re-considered. The applicant, or his or her advisers, should therefore ensure that any fact that he or she believes might be relevant, and ought to be considered by the reviewing officer, is specifically brought to the reviewing officer's attention. It can often be helpful for the applicant, or his or her adviser, to ensure that the whole of the applicant's circumstances and representations are put together in one, full, letter, even if some or all of those representations have previously been put to the local housing authority in a more piecemeal fashion.

19.71 However, this does not mean that the reviewing officer is excused from considering points the applicant has not made. For example, even if the review request is primarily disputing whether an applicant did or did not personally do something that caused him or her to become homeless intentionally, and the reviewing officer is satisfied that the applicant did do the act in question, he or she must then go on, whether or not this point has been raised, to look at whether or not that act was 'deliberate'. That is true even if the applicant is professionally represented by experienced solicitors and has made detailed written representations which do not raise that point.[98]

19.72 A failure to inform the applicant of the right to make representations would make the review process unfair, particularly if the applicant would have responded with representations. The resultant review decision would be likely to be quashed on an appeal to the county court.

The identity of the reviewing officer

19.73 The review decision must be made by the local housing authority which made the original decision or, in the case of a review of a joint decision under the fourth category,[99] by the two or more local housing authorities which made that decision.[100]

19.74 Neither HA 1996, Part 7 nor the regulations prescribe that a particular officer or committee of the local housing authority (or authorities) should undertake the review. It is therefore for the local housing authority (or authorities) to decide whether:

---

[98] *O'Connor v Kensington and Chelsea Royal London Borough Council* [2004] EWCA Civ 394, [2004] HLR 37, CA. A later Court of Appeal decision held that it was only those issues that fell within 'the circumstances of obviousness' that should be considered by the reviewing officer if they had not been raised by the applicant or his or her representatives (*Aw-Aden v Birmingham City Council* [2005] EWCA Civ 1834, (2005) July *Legal Action*, p 29, CA, at [12b], per Kay LJ). For another example, see *Black v Wandsworth London Borough Council* (2008) February *Legal Action*, p 41, Lambeth County Court, where the reviewing officer was obliged to consider the questions of causation and intervening settled accommodation, even though the applicant had not raised the issues, because those issues arose from the established facts before the reviewing officer.

[99] HA 1996, s 202(1)(d); see **19.23–19.25**.

[100] HA 1996, s 202(4).

- to delegate the task to an officer; or

- to devolve it to a committee or subcommittee of the council;[101] or

- to contract the function out.[102]

19.75　If the original decision (subject of the request for a review) was made by an officer of the local housing authority, and the local housing authority has decided that the review will also be carried out by an officer, then the local housing authority is required to ensure that the person conducting the review was not involved in the original decision and is senior to the original decision-maker.[103]

19.76　The original decision-maker is not excluded from assisting the reviewing officer or reviewing committee by, for example, writing and receiving letters, making further inquiries, or even attending a further interview or review hearing, but the review decision must be made by the reviewing officer or committee.[104]

19.77　If the decision subject to review was made in the fourth category,[105] that decision will have been made either by agreement between two local housing authorities or by a referee.[106] If the decision was one made by agreement between two local housing authorities, then the review must be made by them jointly.[107] Presumably this will mean an arrangement for a joint committee or a joint panel of officers.

19.78　If a referee made the original decision,[108] then the reviewing officer should be a person jointly appointed by the local housing authorities within 5 working days from the day on which the review request was received by the notifying local housing authority.[109] This appointee could be anyone to whom both local housing authorities are prepared to entrust the review process.[110] If an appointment is not agreed within that time frame, the notifying local housing authority (which has received the review request) has a further 5 working days to ask the chair of the Local Government Association (LGA)

---

[101]　But not to an individual councillor.

[102]　*De-Winter Heald v Brent London Borough Council* [2009] EWCA Civ 930, (2009) October *Legal Action*, p 26, CA. See **21.20–21.23**.

[103]　HA 1996, s 203(2)(a); Allocation of Housing and Homelessness (Review Procedures) Regulations 1999, SI 1999/71, reg 2.

[104]　*Butler v Fareham Borough Council* (2001) May *Legal Action*, p 24, CA.

[105]　Where the decision is whether the conditions are met for the referral of an applicant to another local housing authority under the conditions for referral: HA 1996 s 202(1)(d); see **19.23–19.25**.

[106]　English Code, para 19.17; Welsh Code, para 21.7.

[107]　SI 1999/71, reg 1(2)(b)(i).

[108]　See also **15.146–15.152**.

[109]　SI 1999/71, reg 7(1) and (2).

[110]　English Code, para 18.34; Welsh Code, para 21.16.

to appoint another referee.[111] The chair must then appoint a referee within a further 7 (working or non-working) days[112] from among the membership of a panel appointed by the LGA.[113] That person then undertakes the review. Although this may appear to be a very tight time frame,[114] the membership of the panel comprises only a handful of referees, one of whom is already eliminated because he or she took the original decision.[115] Whether the reviewing officer is appointed by the local housing authorities or by the LGA chair, in this chapter we will refer to that person as the 'appointed' reviewing officer.[116]

19.79 In some local housing authorities, all reviews are conducted by a single senior officer. This can cause difficulties. For example, where an earlier review decision has been quashed on appeal, the same officer would be taking the new review decision. Likewise, the review might be a second one in the history of a single application where the first review decision was withdrawn. An applicant may be aggrieved if the reviewing officer on the second review is the same officer who considered his or her case at an earlier stage and reached an adverse decision on a different issue. The courts have considered how fairness might be achieved in such circumstances. In *Feld v Barnet London Borough Council*[117] and *Poor v Westminster City Council*[118] it was decided that neither the regulations nor the need to avoid bias required that any second review be conducted by a different reviewing officer. Applying the test of a 'fair-minded and intelligent observer', such an observer would conclude that reviewing officers were competent, conscientious, able to engage with issues on a reasonable and intelligent basis, and able to change their position on particular issues.[119]

Conduct of the review

The paper review

19.80 The reviewing officer's first task will be to gather together the relevant documents. These will consist of:

---

[111] SI 1999/71, reg 7(2) and (3).

[112] English Code, para 19.17; Welsh Code, para 21.16: both Codes say 5 'working days'. However, the current version of Local Authorities' Agreement (at English Code, Annex 18) refers to the 5-day period as 'working days' and to the 7-day period simply as 'seven days', which suggests that 7 non-working days is intended. See **15.163**.

[113] Allocation of Housing and Homelessness (Review Procedures) Regulations 1999, SI 1999/71, reg 7(2) and (3).

[114] The regulations even define 'working day': SI 1999/71, reg 7(7).

[115] SI 1999/71, reg 7(6).

[116] SI 1999/71, reg 7(4) refers to the reviewing officer appointed in these circumstances as 'the appointed person'.

[117] *Feld v Barnet London Borough Council* [2004] EWCA Civ 1307, [2005] HLR 9, CA.

[118] *Poor v Westminster City Council* [2004] EWCA 1307, [2005] HLR 9, CA.

[119] *Feld v Barnet London Borough Council, Poor v Westminster City Council* [2004] EWC Civ 1307, [2005] HLR 9, CA, at [44]–[46], per Ward LJ. The test of a 'fair-minded and intelligent observer' is derived from *Porter v Magill* [2001] UKHL 67, [2002] 2 AC 257, [2002] HLR 16, HL.

(1)   the original decision;

(2)   the request for review (if in writing);

(3)   the local housing authority's file relating to the application;

(4)   any written representations the applicant or his or her representative has
       made;

(5)   the Code of Guidance; and

(6)   the local homelessness strategy.

19.81   An 'appointed' reviewing officer[120] will, within 5 working days of his or
her appointment, receive files from each of the local housing authorities
involved containing the original decision and the 'information and evidence on
which that decision was based'.[121] Presumably, if the 'appointed' reviewing
officer is reviewing a referee's decision, she or he will ask for the documents that
the referee had.

19.82   The reviewing officer is required by HA 1996, Part 7 and regulations to
consider in every case:

(a)   any representations made;[122] and

(b)   the Code of Guidance;[123] and

(c)   the local homelessness strategy.[124]

19.83   Additionally, an 'appointed' reviewing officer must distribute any
representations received from the applicant to the two or more local housing
authorities involved,[125] and must then consider any representations they
make.[126]

*The initial opinion and special procedure where there might be a deficiency
or irregularity*

19.84   A reviewing officer must consider, on review of this material, whether
there was a deficiency or irregularity in the original decision or in the manner

---

120   See **19.73–19.79**.
121   Allocation of Housing and Homelessness (Review Procedures) Regulations 1999, SI 1999/71,
        reg 7(4).
122   SI 1999/71, reg 8(1).
123   HA 1996, s 182.
124   Homelessness Act 2002, s 1(5).
125   Allocation of Housing and Homelessness (Review Procedures) Regulations 1999, SI 1999/71,
        reg 7(5).
126   SI 1999/71, reg 8(1)(a).

in which it was made.[127] If the reviewing officer decides that there was a deficiency or irregularity, special provisions apply.

19.85 If the reviewing officer is satisfied that there was a deficiency or irregularity in the original decision, but is minded to make a decision in favour of the applicant, the reviewing officer may immediately proceed to make that review decision.

19.86 If, however, the reviewing officer is satisfied that there was a deficiency or irregularity in the original decision or in the manner in which it was made, but is still minded to make a decision that is against the interests of the applicant, the reviewing officer must notify the applicant:

(1)   of his or her intention; and

(2)   the reasons why he or she is so minded; and

(3)   give the applicant an opportunity to make representations, either orally or in writing, or both.[128]

19.87 This preliminary notification ('minded-to') letter gives the applicant a final opportunity to persuade the reviewing officer away from an expressed intention to reach a substituted, but nevertheless unfavourable, decision.[129] When the applicant receives this notification, he or she could respond by requesting an oral hearing, or could choose simply to make further representations in writing.

19.88 This is a mandatory obligation on the reviewing officer. There is no room for the reviewing officer to decide, if these two circumstances apply, not to send a 'minded-to' letter because there is no apparent benefit to the applicant. The wording of the Regulations makes it clear that the duty must be complied with.[130] One Court of Appeal judge has said:

> 'The minded-to notice gives an opportunity to the applicant to try to persuade the review officer that his reasoning for his provisional conclusion is mistaken and is,

---

[127]   *Lambeth London Borough Council v Johnston* [2008] EWCA Civ 690, [2009] HLR 10, CA.

[128]   HA 1996, s 203(2)(b); Allocation of Housing and Homelessness (Review Procedures) Regulations 1999, SI 1999/71, reg 8(2).

[129]   In one case, the reviewing officer had given the applicant a deadline for the submission of written representations of a week from the date of the letter inviting representations. That was held to be 'unreanobly short' a period by the judge, particularly since the letter took 5 days to arrive, so the 2 days' actual notice was 'manifestly too short': *Harman v Greenwich London Borough Council* (2010) January *Legal Action*, p 36, Lambeth County Court.

[130]   *Lambeth London Borough Council v Johnston* [2008] EWCA Civ 690, [2009] HLR 10, CA, at [51], per Rimer LJ.

at the very least, potentially of great benefit to an applicant, and to be deprived of that right is or may be seriously prejudicial.'[131]

19.89 The Codes provide some guidance as to the types of deficiencies or irregularities that a reviewing officer might consider render the original decision flawed. Examples given are:

(1) failure to take into account relevant considerations;

(2) taking into account irrelevant considerations;

(3) failure to base the decision on the facts;

(4) bad faith or dishonesty;

(5) a mistake of law;

(6) decisions that run contrary to the policy of HA 1996, Part 7;

(7) irrationality or unreasonableness; and

(8) procedural unfairness, eg where an applicant has not been given a chance to comment on relevant matters.[132]

19.90 In *Hall v Wandsworth London Borough Council*,[133] the Court of Appeal considered what was meant by 'deficiency'. It held that it meant 'something lacking' and was not limited to failings which would provide grounds for legal challenge, although it must be something sufficiently important to the fairness of the process to justify the operation of these special provisions and the 'minded-to' notification. In the two linked cases considered by the Court of Appeal, there was a deficiency in one (in that it was unclear whether the original decision-maker had applied the correct test for vulnerability). The reviewing officer should have understood that failing to be a 'deficiency' and should have applied the special provisions.

19.91 The English Code, accordingly, advises that the reviewing officer must consider whether there is 'something lacking' in the decision under review. It suggests that significant issues which were not addressed, or addressed inadequately, which could have to led to unfairness, constitute 'something lacking'.[134]

---

[131] *Banks v Royal Borough of Kingston-upon-Thames* [2008] EWCA Civ 1443, [2009] HLR 29, CA, per Lawrence Collins LJ at [67], following *Lambeth London Borough Council v Johnston* [2008] EWCA Civ 690, [2009] HLR 10, CA.

[132] English Code, para 19.13; Welsh Code, para 21.12.

[133] [2004] EWCA Civ 1740, [2005] HLR 23, CA.

[134] English Code, para 19.14.

19.92   Examples from case law as to when there may have been 'something lacking' include:

- where it is unclear, from the wording of the original decision, whether or not the decision-maker had applied the correct legal test;[135]

- where the original decision-maker had failed to make adequate inquiries of the applicant's medical advisers and had failed to give a reasoned explanation for preferring the in-house medical advice against that of the applicant's advisers;[136]

- where the original decision had not mentioned the medical evidence that had been submitted by the applicant;[137]

- where the original decision had been made 11 months after the applicant had been interviewed, and by a different officer from the one who had interviewed the applicant;[138]

- on a 'broad reading' of the Regulations, where the original decision had become 'deficient' simply because it did not deal with a matter raised by a changed factual situation since the original decision was made;[139] and

- where the original decision had simply set out the statutory elements necessary for the ending of the main housing duty under HA 1996, s 193(5), and had not given any reasons for the decision.[140]

19.93   The last point in the list above arose in *Banks v Kingston-upon-Thames Royal London Borough Council*.[141] In that case, the original decision had been that the applicant was not homeless. The applicant requested a review. Before the reviewing officer had completed the review, the applicant had been served with a notice to quit. The reviewing officer decided that the applicant was homeless but that he did not have a priority need. The Court of Appeal held that, once it was decided that the applicant was homeless, the original decision had become deficient because it had not addressed his priority need. As a result, where the reviewing officer is minded to decide the review against the interests of the applicant, reg 8(2) should operate so as to ensure that the applicant should be given the opportunity to make representations.

---

[135]   *Hall v Wandsworth London Borough Council* [2004] EWCA Civ 1740, [2005] HLR 23, CA.

[136]   *Benson v Lewisham London Borough Council* (2007) October *Legal Action*, p 26, Central London County Court.

[137]   *Al-Kabi v Southwark London Borough Council* (2008) March *Legal Action*, p 21, Lambeth County Court.

[138]   *Lambeth London Borough Council v Johnston* [2008] EWCA Civ 690, [2009] HLR 10, CA.

[139]   *Banks v Kingston upon Thames Royal London Borough Council* [2008] EWCA Civ 1443, [2009] HLR 29, CA.

[140]   *Makisi v Birmingham City Council* (2010) February *Legal Action*, p 33, Birmingham County Court.

[141]   [2008] EWCA Civ 1443, [2009] HLR 29, CA.

Oral hearing

19.94   The reviewing officer must obviously adopt and apply a fair procedure at the review stage. There is, however, no general right for the applicant to have an oral hearing, or even to have a meeting or interview with the reviewing officer. It will generally be for the reviewing officer to determine whether the facts or circumstances of the particular case warrant an oral hearing.

19.95   There is one circumstance in which 'an oral hearing'[142] must be convened. That occurs when:

(1)   the reviewing officer has issued a 'minded-to' letter;[143] and

(2)   the applicant responds indicating that she or he wishes to make representations orally (either personally or through a representative).[144]

19.96   Neither HA 1996, Part 7, nor the regulations specify how an oral hearing is to be conducted, if one takes place at all.[145] Indeed, 'hearing' may be an exaggerated description of what takes place, albeit that this is the term used in HA 1996, Part 7.[146] Even where the applicant has taken advantage of the right to make oral representations, the reviewing officer is only compelled to consider those representations. The applicant has no right to call or examine witnesses and there is no requirement that any other officers of the local housing authority (including the original decision-maker) should be present.

Fairness

19.97   The reviewing officer will consider not only the material originally before the decision-maker but also any further relevant material received. If a reviewing officer is minded to draw an adverse inference, or to call into question the applicant's credibility, or hold matters against the applicant, those should be put to the applicant for comment, especially if he or she has not already had an opportunity to comment prior to the original decision.[147]

19.98   Neither HA 1996, Part 7, nor the regulations specifically require or encourage the reviewing officer to make further inquiries at his or her own initiative. The reviewing officer should, however, be prepared to make further inquiries, if necessary, and to consider asking the applicant to agree to extend

---

[142]   HA 1996, s 203(2)(b)
[143]   See **19.84–19.93**.
[144]   Allocation of Housing and Homelessness (Review Procedures) Regulations 1999, SI 1999/71, reg 8(2)(b). See *Harman v Greenwich London Borough Council* (2010) January *Legal Action*, p 36, Lambeth County Court.
[145]   In *Makisi v Birmingham City Council* (2010) February *Legal Action*, p 33, Birmingham County Court, a judge decided that a telephone conversation was sufficient for the requirements of an oral hearing at reg 8(2) to be satisfied.
[146]   HA 1996, s 203(2)(b).
[147]   For general principles of fairness, see *Doody v Secretary of State for the Home Department* [1994] 1 AC 531, HL.

the time for a review to be completed if further inquiries need to be made, or an oral hearing needs to be arranged.[148] It is a decision for the reviewing officer as to what inquiries, if any, are necessary before the reviewing officer can complete and notify the review.[149]

Independence in the conduct of the review

19.99 Review decisions are ultimately made by the very local housing authorities which made the original decisions and are usually made by staff or councillors of the local housing authorities concerned. Only where the review is conducted by an 'appointed' reviewing officer[150] will there be anything resembling independence in the review process.[151]

19.100 The review procedure itself is therefore not compliant with the requirements of Art 6 of the European Convention on Human Rights, which provides that:

> '... everyone is entitled to a fair and public hearing within a reasonable time by an independent and impartial tribunal established by law.'

19.101 However, the opportunity of an appeal to the county court on a point of law against the eventual review decision (and the judicial control exercisable within the appeal) safeguards the fairness of the proceedings and renders the process compliant with Art 6(1) of the Convention.[152] Indeed, the Supreme Court held in February 2010 that decision-making on an application for homelessness assistance did not involve a determination of an applicant's 'civil rights' and so the procedure at Art 6(1) did not apply.[153]

Scope of review

19.102 It is not possible for an applicant to restrict the scope of the review only to a specific part of the decision she or he has asked to be reviewed. This

---

148 English Code, para 19.16; Welsh Code, para 21.15.
149 *Cramp v Hastings Borough Council, Phillips v Camden London Borough Council* [2005] EWCA Civ 1005, [2005] HLR 48, CA. See Chapter 10 on inquiries.
150 See **19.77–19.78**.
151 In *Runa Begum v Tower Hamlets London Borough Council* [2003] UKHL 5, [2003] 2 AC 430, HL, the House of Lords held that reviewing officers employed by local housing authorities were not independent of the local housing authority. In *De-Winter Heald v Brent London Borough Council* [2009] EWCA Civ 930, (2009) October *Legal Action*, p 26, CA, the Court of Appeal held that a reviewing officer contracted by the local housing authority to carry out the review (instead of being employed by the local housing authority) was not necessarily any more or less independent of the local housing authority than its employees were (per Stanley Burnton LJ at [52]–[54]).
152 *Runa Begum v Tower Hamlets London Borough Council* [2003] UKHL 5, [2003] 2 AC 430, HL. Subsequent to the House of Lords decision in *Begum*, the European Court of Human Rights held that local housing authorities' housing benefit review panels (as constituted to July 2001) were not independent or impartial and, despite the availability of judicial review, were therefore not compliant with Art 6(1) of the Convention: *Tsfayo v UK* [2007] HLR 19, ECHR.
153 *Tomlinson v Birmingham City Council* [2010] UKSC 8, SC.

is particularly important where the original decision falls under the second category of reviewable decisions, ie a decision as to 'what duty, if any' is owed to the applicant.[154] The general rule is that the reviewing officer is charged with the task of considering the whole matter (of whether any duty is owed) afresh on the latest material available. There are two senses in which this can create difficulties for applicants.

19.103   First, an applicant owed the benefit of a duty as a result of the original decision may find that the reviewing officer concludes (on consideration of the same material) that he or she is owed not a higher but a lesser duty. For example, the original decision may have been that the applicant was eligible, homeless, and in priority need, but had become homeless intentionally. The reviewing officer on reconsideration may conclude that the applicant did not become homeless intentionally but has never had a priority need, and that therefore there is no accommodation duty at all. The 'minded-to' procedure ought to ensure that the applicant is not taken by surprise by such a decision.[155]

19.104   Second, the applicant may find that new information, or a change of circumstances between the original decision and the conclusion of the review, undermines the benefits of the original decision. For example, the original decision may have been that the applicant was eligible, homeless, and had a priority need but had become homeless intentionally. The reviewing officer may be satisfied (by either new information or a change of circumstances) that the applicant is not eligible or no longer has a priority need. Even if the original decision was correct on the facts available at the time, the new information or change of circumstances renders the original decision subject to a 'deficiency'. The reviewing officer should send a 'minded-to' letter inviting the applicant to make representations if the reviewing officer is minded to decide the review against the interests of the applicant.[156]

19.105   The most difficult situation occurs where the applicant is not provided with accommodation pending review[157] and therefore has obtained his or her own accommodation before the conclusion of the review. If the applicant has managed to obtain something better than emergency accommodation, the reviewing officer will be entitled – indeed required – to conclude that the applicant is not homeless as at the date of the review.[158]

19.106   Obviously, any new information or change of circumstances could equally well work in an applicant's favour. Between the request for, and conclusion of, the review, he or she may have acquired priority need status, established a new local connection or had any other change of circumstance

---

[154]   HA 1999, s 202(1)(b); see **19.14–19.15**.
[155]   See **19.84–19.93**.
[156]   SI 1999/71, reg 8(2). *Banks v Kingston-upon-Thames Royal London Borough Council* [2008] EWCA Civ 1443, [2009] HLR 29, CA. See **19.84–19.93**.
[157]   See **16.26–16.36**.
[158]   See Chapter 11.

which could produce a more favourable review decision.[159] Provided that this material comes to the attention of the reviewing officer, it must be taken into account.

19.107 There are two exceptions to the general rule that the reviewing officer must consider the whole matter on the latest material available.

19.108 First, the Court of Appeal has held that, where the original decision was unlawful and had deprived the applicant of a benefit to which he or she would have been entitled had the original decision been lawfully taken, the reviewing officer should take a different approach from the normal course of considering all the facts and law at the date of the review decision. In those circumstances, the reviewing officer should restore to the applicant the rights he or she would have had if the decision had been lawful, even if the applicant's circumstances have changed such that he or she would normally not be entitled to that benefit.[160] The obvious example, and that considered by the Court of Appeal, is where a 17-year-old is notified that he or she does not have a priority need, requests a review and the review is decided after his or her eighteenth birthday.[161] These unusual circumstances apply where the original decision was unlawful, in this case because the 17-year-old could not have been anything other than in priority need at the date of the decision. The position if, for example, the original decision had been that the 17-year-old had a priority need but had become homeless intentionally, and a reviewing officer is considering the position after the applicant's eighteenth birthday, is much more difficult. The original decision was not unlawful, certainly as far as the priority need part of the decision is concerned. Should the reviewing officer confine him- or herself to considering the part of the decision that did not relate to priority need? The Court of Appeal's approach in *Crawley Borough Council v B*[162] suggests not and that all of the circumstances that go towards a decision as to what duty, if any, is owed to the applicant should be considered by the reviewing officer as at the date of the review. In those circumstances, reg 8(2)[163] requires the reviewing officer to send the applicant a 'minded-to' letter if he or she is minded to decide the review against the interests of the applicant.[164]

19.109 Second, where the reviewing officer is considering the applicant's reasons for refusing an offer of accommodation, the reviewing officer should consider the facts and circumstances that existed at the date of the refusal, not at the date of the review. Some of those facts may only come to the attention of

---

[159] *Mohammed v Hammersmith and Fulham London Borough Council* [2001] UKHL 57, [2002] 1 AC 547, HL.

[160] *Robinson v Hammersmith & Fulham London Borough Council* [2006] EWCA Civ 1122, [2007] HLR 7, CA, at [32], per Waller LJ, drawing on dicta in *Crawley Borough Council v B* [2000] 32 HLR 636, CA, at 651, per Chadwick LJ.

[161] See **13.115**.

[162] (2000) 32 HLR 636, CA.

[163] SI 1999/71

[164] *Banks v Kingston-upon-Thames Royal London Borough Council* [2008] EWCA Civ 1443, [2009] HLR 29, CA. See **19.89–19.93**.

the local housing authority after the date of the refusal, but the correct question for the reviewing officer is what facts existed at the date of the refusal.[165]

Notification of the review decision

19.110 Every review decision must be notified to the applicant by the local housing authority or authorities concerned, even if the review has been conducted by an 'appointed' reviewing officer.[166] That notice must be given in writing.[167] If the local housing authority is for some reason unable to give the applicant the written notice, it may make the review decision available for collection at its office for a reasonable period, and that can constitute notification.[168]

19.111 If the review decision is:

- to confirm the original decision against the interests of the applicant on any issue; or

- to confirm the original decision to give a notice of referral under the conditions for referral;[169] or

- to confirm the original decision that the conditions are met for referral of the applicant's case,[170]

the local housing authority must notify the applicant of the reasons for the review decision.[171] In any other case, where applicants would be expected to be pleased with the review decision, reasons are unnecessary and would be superfluous. It might, however, be expected that an 'appointed' reviewing officer[172] would have given written reasons to the local housing authorities involved and that they would be passed on to the applicant.

19.112 If reasons are to be given, the same notice of the review decision must also inform the applicant of the right to appeal to the county court on a point of law and of the 21-day period in which the appeal must be made.[173]

---

[165] *Oseilly v Westminster City Council* [2007] EWCA Civ 1108, [2008] HLR 18, CA; *Omar v Westminster City Council* [2008] EWCA Civ 421, [2008] HLR 36, CA. See **17.47–17.48** and **18.176–18.179**.
[166] HA 1996, s 203(3).
[167] HA 1996, s 203(8).
[168] HA 1996, s 203(8).
[169] See **19.16–19.22**.
[170] See **19.23–19.25**.
[171] HA 1996, s 203(4).
[172] See **19.77–19.78**.
[173] HA 1996, s 203(5).

19.113 A review decision notification that fails to provide either the reasons for the decision or the information about rights to appeal (where those are required) will not be effective as a review decision.[174] This will mean that the review has not been concluded.

19.114 The applicant's remedy in that case might be to appeal on a point of law against the original decision (because there is no review decision).[175] However, the better course might be to invite the reviewing officer to conclude the review properly by giving the required notice whilst seizing the opportunity to put forward any additional material before that notice is given.[176]

Time scale for completion of review

19.115 There is no time scale for the completion of the review in HA 1996, Part 7 itself, but there is a provision allowing for regulations to be made to govern both the period for completion of the review and, separately, the period for notification of the decision on review.[177]

19.116 The regulations set a composite time limit, referring only to the overall period ending with the giving of the written notice of the review decision, rather than dividing the period up.[178] The importance of this approach is that it emphasises not only that the review must be concluded and the review decision notified within the prescribed time limit, but also that the review process is not completed until the review decision is actually given in writing.

19.117 As indicated, any representations made, new material received or changes of circumstance occurring before notification is given should be taken into account by the reviewing officer.

19.118 In most cases, the time limit is that the review must be completed within 8 weeks from the receipt of the request for a review.[179]

19.119 Different time limits apply if the review has been sought under the fourth review category.[180] If the review is of a decision made by the two local housing authorities involved, the review period is 10 weeks.[181] If the review is of a decision made by a referee, the period is 12 weeks.[182] In the latter case, in order to give the local housing authorities concerned time to notify a review

---

174 HA 1996, s 203(6).
175 HA 1996, s 204(1)(b). See **19.148**.
176 See **19.122–19.125**.
177 HA 1996, s 203(7).
178 Allocation of Housing and Homelessness (Review Procedures) Regulations 1999, SI 1999/71, reg 9(1).
179 SI 1999/71, reg 9(1)(a).
180 A review of a decision that the conditions for a referral to another local housing authority are met. See HA 1996, s 202(1)(d) and see **19.23–19.25**.
181 Allocation of Housing and Homelessness (Review Procedures) Regulations 1999, SI 1999/71, reg 9(1)(b).
182 SI 1999/71, reg 9(1)(c).

decision within the 12-week period, the 'appointed' reviewing officer must notify them of his or her decision within 11 weeks.[183]

19.120 The period for completion of a review can be longer than these prescribed periods if both the applicant and local housing authority agree in writing that the period should be extended.[184] This important provision allows flexibility. It also eliminates the possibility of the local housing authority unilaterally extending time, and ensures a written record of the agreement to extend time and of the period of that extension.

19.121 The time limit of 21 days for bringing an appeal to the county court against a review decision[185] runs from the date of written notification of the review decision to the applicant.[186] That must mean the date on which the review decision is received if it is sent by post, and not the date of posting or the date on the letter itself.[187]

Remedies if the local housing authority fails to complete the review in time

19.122 If no review decision is notified at the end of the prescribed (or any agreed extended) period, the applicant has 21 days from the end of that period in which to bring an appeal against the original decision on a point of law.[188]

19.123 It may be, however, that pursuing an appeal on a point of law against the original decision is not the most appropriate option available to the applicant. The original decision may have been one that the local housing authority was lawfully entitled to take. But the applicant may disagree with the factual conclusions or may have submitted new information within the course of the review process which might alter the local housing authority's approach. In these cases, what the applicant requires is a reconsideration of the facts relevant to his or her application, not an appeal on a point of law. The local housing authority's failure to complete the review will have prevented the applicant from having his or her case reconsidered on its facts.

---

[183] SI 1999/71, reg 9(3).

[184] SI 1999/71, reg 9(2).

[185] See **19.174–19.178**.

[186] HA 1996, s 204(2).

[187] *Demetri v Westminster City Council* (1999) 32 HLR 470, CA, at 471, in which the review decision was posted on 7 December but not received until 17 December. See *Lambeth London Borough Council v Namegembe* [2006] EWHC 3608 (Ch), (2007) February *Legal Action*, p 31, ChD, for an example of a judge having to determine a conflict of fact between the parties as to when the review decision had been received by the applicant.

[188] HA 1996, s 204(1)(b) and (2).

19.124 The appropriate procedure in these circumstances would be for the applicant to apply by way of judicial review proceedings for a mandatory order requiring the local housing authority to complete the review and to notify the applicant of its decision on review.[189]

19.125 It may be sensible for the applicant to lodge an appellant's notice against the original decision in any event,[190] and then request that the HA 1996, s 204 appeal is adjourned until the judicial review application (seeking a review decision) has been determined.[191] If the applicant does not succeed in obtaining a review decision through the judicial review process, his or her appeal against the original decision will still have been issued at the court within the time limit.

Extra-statutory reviews

Preliminary reviews

19.126 As already noted,[192] prior to the introduction of HA 1996, Part 7, many local housing authorities had adopted informal local review procedures where decisions were disputed.

19.127 Since 1997, as the statutory review process has become more familiar, the operation of these informal preliminary reviews and of multi-layered reviewing has declined and, to the best of the authors' knowledge, no local housing authority in England or Wales operates a multi-staged scheme. Of course, local housing authorities may still offer informal extra-statutory reviews of those decisions which carry no right to a statutory review.[193]

Second reviews

19.128 There is no statutory provision for any further review of a review decision to be undertaken, and there is no right to request a statutory review of a review decision.[194]

19.129 Although the concept of a 're-review' is deployed in the case law, and is familiar to practitioners in the field, it has no statutory grounding. It is merely a convenient shorthand which refers to the exercise of the discretion enjoyed by any public authority to look again at a decision it has made.

19.130 A local housing authority is not precluded from reconsidering its decision on review, just as it is not precluded from reconsidering any other

---

[189] *R (Aguiar) v Newham London Borough Council* [2002] EWHC 1325 (Admin), (2002) September *Legal Action*, p 31, Admin Ct.

[190] HA 1996, s 204(1)(b).

[191] See **19.229–19.231**.

[192] See **19.3**.

[193] See **19.128–19.136**.

[194] HA 1996, s 202(2).

decision.[195] But if the review is reconsidered, the exercise is simply an extra-statutory reconsideration. It is not a review, and is not, and cannot be, a second statutory review.

19.131 The local housing authority may be prepared voluntarily to carry out an additional, extra-statutory reconsideration if, for example:

(1) new relevant information has come to light since the review decision; or

(2) an appeal against the review decision is likely to be mounted so that an early reconsideration would be a sensible opportunity to ensure the review decision is likely to survive judicial scrutiny; or

(3) there is some other good reason to justify looking at the matter again.

19.132 If the applicant is requesting that the local housing authority look again at the review decision, he or she should seek to dissuade the local housing authority from conducting only an informal or extra-statutory reconsideration. Instead, the applicant should ask the local housing authority to agree to treat the first review decision as withdrawn and the statutory review process as re-opened. The applicant should ask that the local housing authority confirms in writing that it is proceeding on this basis. That confirmation should also contain written agreement to any necessary extension of the time limit for completion of that review (if the original time limit has expired or is about to expire).

19.133 The applicant will need to take this course because only a true review decision, and not an extra-statutory reconsideration, can be subject to an appeal to the county court.[196]

19.134 If the local housing authority only agrees to an informal reconsideration, the applicant who wishes to preserve his or her position should bring an appeal against the statutory review decision. That appeal must be lodged within the normal 21-day period, even if the local housing authority has agreed to carry out an informal reconsideration of the review decision.

19.135 Theoretically, the decisions not to withdraw a review decision and/or not to undertake an extra-statutory reconsideration are amenable to judicial review. However, save in the most exceptional case, any such challenge is highly unlikely to be successful.[197] The better course would be to bring an appeal against the review decision or, if necessary, apply for an extension of time within which to bring that appeal.[198]

---

[195] *R v Westminster City Council ex p Ellioua* (1998) 31 HLR 440, CA.

[196] *Demetri v Westminster City Council* (2000) 32 HLR 470, CA.

[197] Exceptionally, a claim for judicial review succeeded in quashing the local housing authority's informal reconsideration in *R (Van Der Stolk) v Camden London Borough Council* [2002] EWHC 1261 (Admin), (2002) July *Legal Action*, p 26, Admin Ct. In *R v Westminster City Council ex p Ellioua* (1999) 31 HLR 440, CA, the applicant's claim for judicial review of a

19.136 Of course, a review decision only affects the position between the applicant and the particular reviewing local housing authority. An applicant unable or unwilling to challenge an adverse review decision of a local housing authority in the county court is always free to apply to a different local housing authority.

Accommodation pending determination of the review

19.137 The local housing authority has a discretion, but not a duty, to provide accommodation for the applicant and the members of his or her household during the review process.[199] The discretion is available whether or not the applicant has been accommodated prior to the original decision.[200]

19.138 The local housing authority is under no obligation to consider, in every case, whether it should exercise the power. An applicant who wants accommodation pending the review should ask for it.[201]

19.139 If the local housing authority declines to exercise this power, a court will only intervene if the local housing authority has made an error of law in considering the exercise of its discretion (or has failed to consider the request for accommodation at all). Any challenge to the local housing authority's exercise or non-exercise of discretion can only be made by way of judicial review proceedings.[202]

19.140 A full description of the power to accommodate pending review, its various features and the scope for challenges to decisions is given in Chapter 16.[203]

---

refusal to reconsider did not succeed; the county court was the correct forum for an appeal against the statutory review decision. In *R (C) v Lewisham London Borough Council* [2003] EWCA Civ 927, (2004) 36 HLR 4, CA, the Court of Appeal held that the local housing authority's exercise of its extra-statutory discretion in considering an extension of time in which to request a review, a further reconsideration of a review decision or a further extension of time is close to being an absolute discretion and unlikely to be amenable to challenge by judicial review; and see *R (Slaiman) v Richmond upon Thames London Borough Council* [2006] EWHC 329 (Admin), [2006] HLR 20, Admin Ct, where a similar challenge failed.

[198] See **19.141–19.142** and **19.179–19.182**.

[199] HA 1996, ss 188(3) and 200(5). See also English Code, paras 15.12–15.20; Welsh Code, 21.20–21.24. See **16.24–16.36** and **16.49**.

[200] This important extension of the power was made by HA 1996, ss 188(3) and 200(5), amended by Homelessness Act 2002, Sch 1, para 8.

[201] *R (Ahmed) v Waltham Forest London Borough Council* [2001] EWHC 540 (Admin), (2001) October *Legal Action*, p 17, Admin Ct.

[202] See **19.211–19.236**.

[203] See **16.24–16.36**.

APPEALS
Right to appeal

19.141 As already noted,[204] prior to HA 1996, Part 7 all legal challenges to local housing authority decisions made under the statutory homelessness provisions were brought by way of judicial review. Since 20 January 1997, challenges to most decisions are pursued instead by way of an appeal on a point of law to the county court.[205]

19.142 However, there is no free-standing or general right of appeal to the county court against every decision made under HA 1996, Part 7. The prerequisites (examined in more detail below) for a county court appeal against a substantive Part 7 decision are that:

(1)   the initial decision must have been a reviewable decision;[206] and

(2)   the applicant must have made a request for a review;[207] and

(3)   the review decision must have been properly notified;[208] or

(4)   the time limit for proper notification of a review decision must have expired;[209] and

(5)   the appeal must be on a point of law;[210] and

(6)   the appeal must be brought within the prescribed time limit (or such extension of it as the court may allow).[211]

But there is no need for the applicant to first obtain permission to appeal from the court (or from anyone else).[212]

Was the initial decision a reviewable decision?

19.143 An appeal can only be brought against one of the decisions set out in the seven categories of decision conferring the right to request a review which are listed at HA 1996, s 202(1).[213]

---

204   See **19.2–19.3**.
205   HA 1996, s 204(1). See also English Code, paras 19.21–19.24; Welsh Code, paras 21.25–21.32.
206   See **19.12–19.35** and **19.143–19.144**.
207   See **19.50–19.55** and **19.145–19.146**.
208   See **19.110–19.114**.
209   See **19.115–19.125** and **19.147–19.150**.
210   See **19.151–19.159**.
211   See **19.174–19.182**.
212   See *Buxton v Charnwood District Council* [2004] EWCA Civ 612, (2004) July *Legal Action*, p 19, CA, where the Court of Appeal made clear its disapproval of a local county court's practice of holding a preliminary consideration of the merits of HA 1996, s 204 appeals.
213   *Hackney London Borough Council v Sareen* [2003] EWCA Civ 351, (2003) 35 HLR 54, CA. See also **19.12–19.35**.

19.144 If the decision does not fall into one of the categories specified, the applicant had no right to request a statutory review and has no right to bring a county court appeal. The appropriate challenge to any such decision is made by a claim for judicial review.[214]

Who can appeal?

19.145 The statutory appeal rights are only available to 'an applicant'.[215] No member of the applicant's household, however closely related, has that statutory right. In the case of *Lewis v Brent London Borough Council*,[216] one of two joint applicants appealed to the county court, relying on the strength of the other joint applicant's case (her husband). The appeal was dismissed and the Court of Appeal refused permission to appeal, holding that the husband was not a party to the proceedings and the wife could not pray in aid, in her own case, any error in the decision relating to her husband. Nor can the appeal process be activated by others who may have an interest in challenging the local housing authority's original or review decision, eg a different local housing authority, Registered Social Landlord ('RSL'), or another homeless person.

19.146 In addition, the applicant must actually have requested a statutory review in order to be able to bring an appeal.[217] If the applicant did not request a review of a reviewable decision, no appeal is available. The applicant in that situation could only reinstate his or her appeal rights by first asking the local housing authority to review its original decision. If the time limit for making a review request has expired, the local housing authority will also have to agree to extend the time limit for the making of the review request.[218]

Which decision to appeal?

19.147 Because the right of appeal is only available to an applicant who has sought a review, the appeal will normally be brought against the review decision.[219]

19.148 However, if the local housing authority has failed to notify the applicant of its review decision within the prescribed time limit (or any agreed extension of that time limit), the applicant can bring an appeal against the original decision, which was the subject of the request for the review.[220] This important provision prevents the applicant from being denied access to the courts by the local housing authority unduly prolonging the review procedure.

---

214 See **19.229–19.231**.
215 HA 1996, s 204(1).
216 [2005] EWCA Civ 605, (2005) July *Legal Action*, p 29, CA.
217 HA 1996, s 204(1).
218 See **19.56–19.62**.
219 HA 1996, s 204(1)(a).
220 HA 1996, s 204(1)(b).

19.149   Even if the local housing authority has attempted to notify a review decision in time, a negative review decision is of no effect unless it has been communicated by written notice:

- containing reasons for the review decision; and

- informing the applicant of the right to appeal; and

- setting out the time limit for an appeal.[221]

19.150   Faced with a review decision which is invalid by reason of non-compliance with one or more of these provisions, the applicant can appeal against the original decision (although adding an appeal against the defective review decision in the alternative in the Appellant's Notice might be a sensible precaution).[222]

What is a point of law?

19.151   Appeals can only be brought on a point of law 'arising from the decision' appealed against.[223]

19.152   Points of law include any of the grounds of challenge that would normally be available in judicial review proceedings. Traditionally those grounds for judicial review have been classified as 'illegality', 'irrationality' and 'procedural impropriety'.[224]

19.153   A point of law can be properly said to arise from any decision that:

- is based on a misconstruction of HA 1996, Part 7 or the regulations;

- is ultra vires the local housing authority's powers (ie beyond or in excess of its powers);

- is irrational;

- is taken in breach of natural justice;

---

[221]   See **19.110–19.114**.

[222]   In *Bellamy v Hounslow London Borough Council* (reported under the name of *William v Wandsworth London Borough Council, Bellamy v Hounslow London Borough Council* [2006] EWCA Civ 535, [2006] HLR 42, CA), no review decision had been notified within the statutory time limits and the applicant appealed against the original HA 1996, s 184 decision. Before the appeal was heard in the county court, the local housing authority notified the applicant of its review decision. The appeal was then made against both the original and the review decision. The Court of Appeal, considering an appeal against the decision of the county court judge, doubted whether HA 1996, s 204 conferred a right of appeal against the original decision once the review decision had been notified (albeit late), and approved the first-instance judge's decision to treat the appeal as being against the review decision.

[223]   HA 1996, s 204(1).

[224]   *Council of Civil Service Unions v Minister for the Civil Service* [1985] AC 374, HL.

- is the result of bias or bad faith;

- is reached without all necessary inquiries having been undertaken;

- is reached where there is no evidence to support factual findings made;

- is reached without regard to relevant factors;

- has failed to have regard to relevant factors; or

- gives inadequate reasons.[225]

19.154 Questions of fact, as distinct from questions of law, are for the local housing authority to decide,[226] unless the local housing authority's decision cannot be supported (in which case it will have made an error of law). Lord Millett in *Runa Begum v Tower Hamlets London Borough Council*[227] summarised the distinction between disputes of law and disputes of fact:

> 'A decision may be quashed if it is based on a finding of fact or inference from the facts which is perverse or irrational; or there was no evidence to support it; or it was made by reference to irrelevant factors or without regard to relevant factors. It is not necessary to identify a specific error of law; if the decision cannot be supported the court will infer that the decision-making authority misunderstood or overlooked relevant evidence or misdirected itself in law. The court cannot substitute its own findings of fact for those of the decision-making authority if there was evidence to support them; and the questions as to the weight to be given to a particular piece of evidence and the credibility of witnesses are for the decision-making authority and not the court.'

19.155 Chadwick LJ put it succinctly in *Williams v Wandsworth London Borough Council*:[228]

> 'where what is alleged is a misconstruction of ascertained facts, "obvious perversity" is required before the court can properly interfere with the authority's findings of fact.'

19.156 What happens when the appellant is arguing that the review decision was based on a mistake of fact? In administrative law, there are two competing lines of authority. One argues that the issue of a mistaken fact should be absorbed into a traditional error of law approach, in that the decision-maker must have taken account of an irrelevant consideration, or failed to provide adequate or intelligible reasons, or failed to base the decision upon any

---

[225] *Nipa Begum v Tower Hamlets London Borough Council,* (2000) 32 HLR 445, CA; see also *Runa Begum v Tower Hamlets* [2003] UKHL 5, [2006] AC 430, HL, at 439, per Lord Bingham, and at 426, per Lord Millett.

[226] *Puhlhofer v Hillingdon London Borough Council* [1986] AC 484, HL.

[227] [2003] UKHL 5, [2006] 2 AC 430, HL, at 462, per Lord Millett. See also Wall LJ in *Wandsworth London Borough Council v Allison* [2008] EWCA Civ 354, (2008) June *Legal Action*, p 33, CA, at [65].

[228] [2006] EWCA Civ 535, [2006] HLR 42, CA, at [20], per Chadwick LJ.

evidence.[229] The other, more modern, approach holds that a mistake of fact giving rise to unfairness to the applicant can be a separate head of challenge in an appeal on a point of law. This latter view has recently prevailed in the context of asylum appeals.[230] Where there has been a mistake as to an existing 'established' fact,[231] that had not been brought about by the fault of the applicant or his or her advisers, and had played a material part in the decision-maker's decision, the decision-maker may have made an error of law.

19.157   Procedural errors in the making of inquiries, or in the making of the decision or review decision, are errors of law and can render the relevant decision unlawful. However, procedural unfairness in the appeal process, such as a failure to provide a copy of the applicant's housing file until 6 days before the county court hearing, does not render the decision under appeal wrong in law.[232]

Fresh evidence

19.158   A local housing authority will not generally be said to have made an error of law if it failed to take into account information that was not put before it during its decision-making process, but is subsequently put, as new information, to the county court. Indeed, the starting-point is that a county court will not generally admit fresh evidence on an appeal at all. However, if an applicant is seeking to argue that the local housing authority made a mistake of fact or that it failed to carry out all necessary inquiries, he or she may have to present new information to the court in order to show that one of the local housing authority's factual conclusions was based on a mistake of fact, or a failure to carry out necessary inquiries.[233] The authorities on the presentation of new information have been described as 'unusually fact-sensitive' rather than laying down general propositions of law.[234] The traditional test for the submission of new information on an appeal is found in *Ladd v Marshall*,[235] which provides that the court will only permit new evidence to be produced at appeal if:

(1)   it is evidence that could not have been obtained without reasonable diligence for use at trial (or, in a homelessness context, at the review or decision stage); and

---

[229]   *Wandsworth London Borough Council v A* [2000] 1 WLR 1246, CA, at1255, per Buxton LJ, and *R v London Residuary Body ex p Inner London Education Authority* (1987) The Times, July 24, CA, per Watkins LJ.

[230]   *E v Home Office* [2004] EWCA Civ 49, [2004] QB 1044, CA.

[231]   'Established' meaning 'uncontentious and objectively verifiable': *E v Home Office* [2004] EWCA Civ 49, [2004] QB 1044, CA, at [66], per Carnwath LJ.

[232]   *Goodger v Ealing London Borough Council* [2002] EWCA Civ 751, (2003) 35 HLR 6, CA.

[233]   In *Cramp v Hastings Borough Council* [2005] EWCA Civ 1005, [2005] HLR 48, CA, the Court of Appeal overturned first-instance decisions that inadequate inquiries had been made, and noted that the inquiries said by the appellants' solicitors to be necessary in the grounds of appeal had not been suggested by those same solicitors during the review process.

[234]   *E v Home Office* [2004] EWCA Civ 49, [2004] QB 1044, CA, at [88], per Carnwath LJ.

[235]   [1954] 1 WLR 1489, CA.

(2)   the evidence would probably have an important (although it need not be decisive) influence on the outcome; and

(3)   the evidence is such as is presumably to be believed.

19.159   In *Cramp v Hastings Borough Council*,[236] the Court of Appeal warned that:

> 'judges in the county court need to be astute to ensure that evidential material over and above the contents of the housing file and the reviewing officer's decision is limited to that which is necessary to illuminate the points of law that are to be relied on in the appeal, or the issue of what, if any, relief ought to be granted. An undisciplined approach to the admission of new evidence may lead to the danger that the reviewing officer is found guilty of an error of law for not taking into account evidence that was never before her, notwithstanding the applicant's opportunity to make representations about the original decision.'[237]

Paying for an appeal

19.160   Taking cases to court is not cheap, and an appeal in the county court is no exception. The court fee alone is £120,[238] and the normal rule is that the unsuccessful party will pay the other party's legal costs, so there is a considerable financial risk.

19.161   Because appeals can only be pursued on a point of law, it is very unusual for an appeal to be brought by an individual acting in person. The services of solicitors and/or counsel will usually be required. Usually, appeals take a day, or half a day, of court time and require considerable preparation.

19.162   Most applicants will qualify for free preliminary advice from a lawyer or legal adviser under the Legal Help scheme. If an appeal is thought to have merit, application can be made for full public funding (Certificate for Legal Representation) to fund the appeal. Specialist housing solicitors and agencies with Legal Services Commission (LSC) contracts will be able to grant emergency public funding so that work on an appeal can start quickly. The criteria under which the LSC will grant public funding for homelessness appeals is set out in the Funding Code (Section 7, 'Judicial Review') and in the Funding Code Guidance (Section 16, 'Judicial Review').[239]

---

[236]   [2005] EWCA Civ 1005, [2005] HLR 48, CA.

[237]   At [71], per Brooke LJ.

[238]   At the time of writing, although it may increase. This can be waived where a litigant in person is in receipt of qualifying benefits: Civil Proceedings Fees Order 2008, SI 2008/1053, reg 5 and Sch 2. The up-to-date figures are at www.hmcourts-service.gov.uk/publications/guidance/fees/index.htm.

[239]   Further information for lawyers and advisers on funding homelessness appeals is given in the Legal Services Commission Manual, available at the Legal Services Commission website http://www.legalservices.gov.uk/civil/guidance/lsc_manual.asp.

19.163 As already noted, the normal rule is that the unsuccessful party will pay the other party's legal costs. This rule was applied in *Waltham Forest London Borough Council v Maloba.*[240]

Powers of the county court on an appeal

19.164 If the court concludes that there has been an error of law, it may confirm, quash or vary the decision which is the subject of the appeal;[241] if there is no error of law, it will dismiss the appeal.

Confirming the decision

19.165 The court is only entitled to confirm a decision that contains an error of law in one of two circumstances:

(1) if it is satisfied that a properly directed local housing authority, which did not make the same error of law, would inevitably have reached the same decision;[242] or

(2) if it is satisfied that the bringing of the appeal was an abuse of process in the sense that bringing the appeal was for practical purposes 'pointless', even though there was some irregularity in the decision appealed against.[243]

Quashing the decision

19.166 Normally, where there is an error of law, the court will simply quash the decision that has been the subject of the appeal.

19.167 If a review decision is quashed on appeal, then the review process will not have been concluded because no legally correct review decision has been reached. The reviewing officer will need to re-open the review and the applicant and the local housing authority will need to agree in writing a new deadline for

---

[240] [2007] EWCA Civ 1281, [2008] HLR 26, CA, where the local housing authority argued unsuccessfully that there should be a general practice on HA 1996, s 204 appeals that any order for costs made against a local housing authority should be subject to a stay until after the re-determination of the decision under appeal and any subsequent appeal from that re-determination.

[241] HA 1996, s 204(3).

[242] The test is one of inevitability: if there is any real possibility of a different conclusion being reached, it is wrong for the court to confirm the decision: *Ali and Nessa v Newham London Borough Council* [2001] EWCA Civ 73, [2002] HLR 20, CA.

[243] *O'Connor v Kensington and Chelsea Royal London Borough Council* [2004] EWCA Civ 394 [2004] HLR 37, CA, at [42]–[43], per Waller LJ and Carnwath LJ, giving majority judgments on this point (Sedley LJ dissenting). In *Ugiagbe v Southwark London Borough Council* [2009] EWCA Civ 31, [2009] HLR 35, CA, by the time the appeal reached the Court of Appeal the applicant had found herself accommodation. The Court of Appeal rejected the local housing authority's submission that the appeal was academic, and because there was a risk that the applicant might again become homeless, it quashed the review decision; see Lloyd LJ at [30]–[32].

the completion of the review (as the original prescribed time limit will inevitably have expired by this stage).[244]

19.168 If the decision quashed on appeal is the original decision, then the local housing authority will have to take a fresh decision, having carried out such further inquiries as it considers necessary.

19.169 It is by no means inevitable that, following a successful appeal, the new decision reached will be different in effect from the one quashed. In either case the reviewing officer or the local housing authority must make the fresh decision on the basis of the facts and information as they stand at the date of that new decision, which may be very different from how they stood at the date of the quashed decision or even at the date of the quashing.

Varying the decision

19.170 It is unusual for the court to exercise its power to *vary* the decision appealed against. It may do so where it is satisfied on the evidence that there was only one lawful conclusion for the local housing authority to have reached, or, as Sedley LJ has put it: 'where the decision was erroneous in law and only a contrary decision was lawfully possible'.[245] In *Bond v Leicester City Council*,[246] the Court of Appeal held that, had the local housing authority asked itself the right question, it was 'more likely than not' that it would have found that the applicant was homeless and the court varied the decision accordingly. In *Ekwuru v Westminster City Council*,[247] the Court of Appeal held that, where the local housing authority had conceded that three successive statutory review decisions had been wrong in law, and there was no material which would entitle it to reach a conclusion other than that the applicant had not become homeless intentionally, it would exceptionally vary the latest decision rather than quash it.[248] It may also be appropriate to use this power where the behaviour of the

---

[244] See **19.115–19.121**. If, however, the local housing authority has applied for permission to bring a second appeal, the Court of Appeal has suggested that both parties should agree that the new review decision should not be notified until the appeal process has been concluded: *William v Wandsworth London Borough Council* [2006] EWCA Civ 535, [2006] HLR 42, CA, at [42], per Chadwick LJ.

[245] *Ozbek v Ipswich Borough Council* [2006] EWCA Civ 534, [2006] HLR 41 CA, at [63], per Sedley LJ. See, as one example, *Mohammed v Waltham Forest London Borough Council* (2002) October *Legal Action*, p 30, Bow County Court.

[246] [2001] EWCA Civ 1544, [2002] HLR 6, CA.

[247] *Ekwuru v Westminster City Council* [2003] EWCA Civ 1293 [2004] HLR 13, CA.

[248] See also the following cases in which the power to vary was used: *Woodrow v Lewisham London Borough Council* (2000) November *Legal Action*, p 23, Woolwich County Court, where the local housing authority conceded that it had applied the wrong test of vulnerability where HHJ Welchman varied the decision to that of the applicant being in priority need, holding that the evidence was 'particularly powerful and uncontroversial'; *Yousif v Newham London Borough Council* (2002) December *Legal Action*, p 22, Bow County Court; *Bond v Leicester City Council* [2001] EWCA Civ 1544, [2002] HLR 6, CA; *Lane and Ginda v Islington London Borough Council* (2001) April *Legal Action*, p 21, Clerkenwell County Court; *Houghton v Sheffield City Council* [2006] EWCA Civ 1799, (2007) March *Legal Action*, p 18, CA; *Benson v Lewisham London Borough Council* (2007) October *Legal Action*, p 26, Central London

local housing authority has been open to criticism, e g where it has repeatedly made and then withdrawn defective decisions.[249]

19.171　More recently, the Court of Appeal has upheld two first-instance decisions where the judge had varied the review decision. In *Tower Hamlets London Borough Council v Deugi*,[250] the local housing authority had conceded that its decision that the applicant was not eligible was wrong, and the Court of Appeal held that varying the decision would provide some enduring benefit to the applicant, and so the first-instance judge was correct to vary it. In *Slater v Lewisham London Borough Council*,[251] the Court of Appeal agreed with the first-instance judge that there was no real prospect that the local housing authority, acting rationally and with the benefit of any further inquiries it might make, could conclude that it was reasonable for an offer of accommodation to be accepted, and it upheld the first-instance judge's decision to vary a review decision to a finding that the duty to provide accommodation had not been discharged.

19.172　The House of Lords varied a review decision in *Moran v Manchester City Council*,[252] having found that the applicant could not have become homeless intentionally from a women's refuge, because the refuge in that case had not been reasonable for the applicant to continue to occupy.[253]

19.173　The county court does not have any power to make a mandatory order to require that certain steps are taken or procedures are followed: in contrast to the power available to the Administrative Court on judicial review. So that where a county court judge had allowed an appeal and ordered that a further review be conducted by a different reviewing officer, he had exceeded his powers.[254] In any event, there should be no need for any additional order or direction. The statutory scheme makes it tolerably clear what should occur after a decision is confirmed, varied or quashed.

County Court; *Bolah v Croydon London Borough Council* (2008) February *Legal Action*, p 40, Central London County Court; *Quaid v Westminster City Council* (2008) February *Legal Action*, p 41, Central London County Court; *Adekunle v Islington London Borough Council* (2009) November *Legal Action*, p 25, Mayor's and City of London County Court; and *Villiers v Lewisham London Borough Council* (2009) November *Legal Action*, p 26, Central London County Court.

[249]　*Mohamud v Lambeth London Borough Council* (2002) May *Legal Action*, p 30, Wandsworth County Court. In *Wandsworth London Borough Council v Brown* [2005] EWCA Civ 907, (2005) *Legal Action*, p 16, CA, the first-instance judge varied a decision that the appellant was not 'vulnerable', which he held to be perverse, to a decision that he was 'vulnerable'. The local housing authority was refused permission to bring a second appeal, as no important point of principle was raised; see **19.201–19.207**.

[250]　[2006] EWCA Civ 159, [2006] HLR 28, CA.

[251]　[2006] EWCA Civ 394, [2006] HLR 37, CA.

[252]　*Ali & others v Birmingham City Council, Moran v Manchester City Council* [2009] UKHL 36, [2009] 1 WLR 1506, HL, at [65]–[66], per Baroness Hale.

[253]　See **11.109–11.110**.

[254]　*Adan v Newham London Borough Council* [2001] EWCA Civ 1916, (2002) 34 HLR 28, CA.

Time limits

19.174 If the appeal is being made against a decision reached on review, the appeal must be brought within 21 days of the appellant being notified of the review decision.[255] The time limit therefore begins to run on the date that the notice of review decision is actually received rather than the date on the review decision letter or the date it is sent.[256] The last day of the 21-day period is the twenty-first day from the date of receipt, so that if a review decision is received on 4 July, the last day for bringing the appeal is 25 July.

19.175 If the appeal is being made in respect of an original decision, the appeal must be brought within 21 days of the date on which the review of that decision should have been notified. This time limit will therefore be calculated from the last day of the time limit for the conclusion of the review.[257] As already noted,[258] that will usually be a date 8 weeks after the date on which the request for a review was made, meaning that an appeal against an original decision should be brought within 21 days after the end of the 8-week period

19.176 An appeal is brought when an Appellant's Notice (court form N161) is filed at the county court.[259] 'Filing' means 'delivering it, by post or otherwise, to the court office'.[260] The form can be sent by fax or, in certain specified courts, by email or online form.[261] Although criticised by the Court of Appeal, Practice Directions 5 and 5B specify that, where a fax or email is received after 4pm on a working day, the document sent should not be recorded as 'filed' until the next working day. However, documents physically posted through a court's letterbox after close of business on a working day, but before midnight, are 'filed' on that day, and not on the following working day.[262] Where the final day falls on a non-working day, the period in which the form must be filed ends on the next day on which the court office is open.[263]

19.177 If there is any dispute over the date on which the appellant was notified of the review decision (or as to the date on which the time limit for review expired), the court itself will have to decide the question of the correct date, and go on to decide whether or not the appeal was filed within the 21-day time limit.[264]

---

[255] HA 1996, s 204(2).

[256] *Aadan v Brent London Borough Council* (1999) 32 HLR 848, CA, at 851, per Chadwick LJ. See also *Barrett v Southwark London Borough Council* [2008] EWCA Civ 1568 (Comm), (2008) September *Legal Action*, p 26, QBD, where the 21 days began to run, not from the date of the review decision or the date when it was received by the applicant's advisers, but from the date when the applicant herself received it.

[257] HA 1996, s 204(2).

[258] See **19.115–19.121**.

[259] CPR, r 52.4(2) and PD 52, para 5.1.

[260] CPR, r 2.3(1).

[261] CPR, PD 5, para 5.3 and 5B. The facility to file electronically is not available where a fee is payable.

[262] *Van Aken v Camden London Borough Council* [2002] EWCA Civ 1724, (2003) 35 HLR 33, CA.

[263] CPR, r 2.8(5); *Aadan v Brent London Borough Council* (2000) 32 HLR 848, CA.

[264] See *Bakare v Waltham Forest London Borough Council* (1998) December *Legal Action*, p 27,

19.178 As already noted,[265] notification is treated as having occurred if the decision has been made available at the local housing authority's office for a reasonable period for collection.[266] However, this deeming provision only applies where the review decision has *not* been sent to the appellant.

Extending the time limit[267]

19.179 The county court may give permission for an appeal to be brought after the end of the 21-day period if it is satisfied that there was a good reason for the failure to bring the appeal in time and for any delay in applying for permission to extend time.[268] Permission may be applied for either during the 21-day period, or after it has ended.[269]

19.180 The court may give permission to extend time before the expiry of the 21-day period. This provision might be thought helpful where it is appreciated that the time limit is about to expire but an Appellant's Notice cannot be prepared in time. But if the applicant can manage to lodge an application to extend the time limit, it is a little difficult to envisage a case in which the applicant (or his or her advisers) could not have filed even a very basic Appellant's Notice. Indeed, a professional adviser may be in difficulties if no such Appellant's Notice is filed in time, because it is always possible that a time extension, for which an application is made instead, will be refused.

19.181 If the concern is that it is getting late on a working day, and that day is the last day of the 21-day time limit, some comfort can be taken from the Court of Appeal's decision in *Van Aken v Camden London Borough Council*.[270] The appellant's advisers, confronted with the imminent expiry of the 21-day period, should aim to file the notice of appeal by posting it through the letterbox of the court (if one exists) at any time until midnight of that twenty-first day, rather than apply for permission to extend time.

19.182 In *Short v Birmingham City Council*,[271] the High Court upheld the first-instance judge's approach to whether or not to grant permission to appeal out of time. The court should first consider the reasons for delay and only consider the merits of the appeal, and the hardship to the applicant, if there

---

Bow County Court, where the local housing authority put in evidence as to the method and likely date of delivery and the appellant had no contrary evidence, the court held that he had been notified more than 21 days before the appeal had been filed; and *Lambeth London Borough Council v Namegembe* [2006] EWHC 3608 (Ch), (2007) February *Legal Action*, p 31, ChD.

265 See **19.110–19.114**.
266 HA 1996, s 203(8).
267 See Holbrook 'Appeals under the Homelessness Act 2002 – Part 2' (2002) December *Legal Action*, p 31.
268 HA 1996, s 204(2A).
269 HA 1996, s 204(2A).
270 *Van Aken v Camden London Borough Council* [2002] EWCA Civ 1724, [2003] 35 HLR 33, CA. See also **19.176**.
271 [2004] EWHC 2112 (QB), [2005] HLR 6, QBD.

were good reasons for that delay. In *Barrett v Southwark London Borough Council*,[272] the judge said 'good reason is a phrase in common parlance, which ... does not need elaboration'[273] and that all the circumstances were relevant.[274] Once it had been decided that there was 'good reason', permission should be given, unless the appeal is 'hopeless'.[275]

Procedure

19.183 The Civil Procedure Rules (CPR) and Practice Directions (PD) (particularly CPR 52 and PD 52) govern the procedure for the county court appeal. The appellant should file and serve with his or her Appellant's Notice a copy of the decision being appealed and a skeleton argument.[276] If the appellant is seeking permission to extend time, the application should be made in the appellant's notice and should be supported by a witness statement explaining the good reason for the failure to bring the appeal in time and for any delay since the time limit expired.[277] The appellant should also file a bundle of documents, which would normally include the relevant local housing authority's file on the application for homelessness assistance and any other correspondence.[278]

19.184 If the appellant has not received the whole of the homelessness file from the local housing authority, then an application should be made in the Appellant's Notice for a direction requiring the local housing authority (which in the appeal will be described as 'the respondent') to disclose it.

19.185 The respondent should serve and file its skeleton argument, and any witness statement which it has been directed to serve, within 14 days of service

---

272 [2008] EWHC 1568 (Comm), QBD.
273 *Barrett v Southwark London Borough Council* [2008] EWHC 1568 (Comm), (2008) September *Legal Action*, p 26, QBD, at [24], per Sir Thomas Morrison.
274 In *Barrett v Southwark London Borough Council* [2008] EWHC 1568 (Comm), (2008) September *Legal Action*, p 26, QBD, permission was given to bring an appeal 4 weeks late, where a profoundly deaf applicant had made diligent and wide attempts to obtain legal advice and had continued to try to find legal representation, even though she had received unfavourable advice.
275 *Barrett v Southwark London Borough Council* [2008] EWHC 1568 (Comm), (2008) September *Legal Action*, p 26, QBD, at [28], per Sir Thomas Morrison.
276 CPR 52 and PD 52, paras 5.6(2) and 5.6A. If it is impracticable for the skeleton argument to accompany the Appellant's Notice, it must be lodged and served within 14 days of filing: CPR, PD 52, para 5.9(2).
277 CPR 52 and PD 52 para 5.2.
278 CPR 52 and PD 52, para 5.6A. In *Cramp v Hastings Borough Council* [2005] EWCA Civ 1005, [2005] HLR 48, CA, the Court of Appeal stated that it was 'thoroughly bad practice to state the barest possible grounds in the original notice of appeal ... and then to delay formulating and serving very substantial amended grounds of appeal for five months so that they surfaced for the first time less than a week before the appeal hearing' (Brooke LJ at [72]). They also said that the appeal bundle should be limited to the grounds of appeal, the decision being appealed and only those documents which the appellant reasonably considers necessary to enable the appeal court to reach its decision on the hearing. Documents extraneous to the issues to be considered on appeal must be excluded, and it was quite wrong to photocopy the entire contents of a bulky housing file regardless of whether it was necessary to do so.

of the appellant's skeleton argument, or any such longer time as the court may direct.[279] Although the rules enable a local housing authority to file and serve a Respondent's Notice,[280] this is usually unnecessary, because the respondent will be trying to uphold the appealed decision on the basis of the reasoning which it contains (rather than on some different basis).

19.186   It is common practice for local housing authorities to put in witness statements, usually by the decision-maker, to explain or elucidate the reasons contained in the written decision. The purpose and admissibility of those witness statements (formerly affidavits) was considered in detail by the Court of Appeal in *R v Westminster City Council ex p Ermakov*.[281] Where the contents of the witness statement serve to elucidate the reasons contained in the decision letter, they will be admissible. Examples of circumstances in which evidence might elucidate, rather than alter, the original decision were said to include where: 'an error has been made in transcription or expression, or a word or words inadvertently omitted, or where the language used may be in some way lacking in clarity.'[282] Where, however, the contents fundamentally alter the reasons in the decision letter, they should not be admitted.

19.187   In *Bellamy v Hounslow London Borough Council*,[283] the Court of Appeal made some cautionary remarks about the use of witness statements in second appeals,[284] which also hold true for first-instance appeals to the county court:

> 'Witness statements are a proper vehicle for relevant and admissible evidence going to the issue before the court, and for nothing else. Argument is for advocates. Innuendo has no place at all.'[285]

19.188   There should usually be no need for witness statements to be filed by either party. If the points of law raised can be determined solely on contents of the review letter and the relevant parts of the homelessness file, there will be no need for any witness statement by the applicant. If, on the other hand, one of

---

[279]   CPR 52.5(4) and PD 52, paras 7.11–7.13.

[280]   CPR, r 52.5.

[281]   *R v Westminster City Council ex p Ermakov* [1996] 2 All ER 302, CA.

[282]   *R v Westminster City Council ex p Ermakov* [1996] 2 All ER 302, CA, at 315H, per Hutchison LJ; and see also *R v Westminster City Council ex p Khanam* (unreported) 9 May 1997, QBD, and *Hijazi v Kensington and Chelsea Royal London Borough Council* [2003] EWCA Civ 692, [2003] HLR 72, CA. In *Swords v Secretary of State for Communities and Local Government* [2007] EWCA Civ 795, [2008] HLR 17, CA, the Court of Appeal approved five reasons for admitting a witness statement into evidence, including '[i] it must, as a matter of common sense, be easier for a decision-maker to secure permission to make a belated assertion that she took into account a factor to which she had not previously referred but gave it no weight than that she gave weight to a factor to which she had not previously referred; for in the former case the lack of previous reference would be inherently less significant' (Wilson LJ at [47]).

[283]   Reported under the name of *William v Wandsworth London Borough Council, Bellamy v Hounslow London Borough Council* [2006] EWCA Civ 535, [2006] HLR 42, CA.

[284]   See **19.201–19.210**.

[285]   *Bellamy v Hounslow London Borough Council* [2006] EWCA Civ 535, [2006] HLR 42, CA, at [80], per Sedley LJ.

the points of law is that the local housing authority has failed to make all necessary inquiries, it can be helpful for the applicant to make a witness statement in which he or she sets out what inquiries should have been made and, if possible, what the results of those inquiries would have been. If the local housing authority is satisfied that its review decision is correct, there will normally be no need for a witness statement from the reviewing officer or any other officer.

19.189 Once the homelessness file has been disclosed, any witness statements and skeleton arguments have been filed, and a bundle of documents has been prepared,[286] the appeal will generally be ready for hearing. The hearing itself will consist of oral argument, based on the skeleton arguments. Since the appeal is on a point of law, there is not generally any need for live evidence to be given.

19.190 Homelessness appeals may only be heard by a circuit judge, not a district judge.[287]

Accommodation pending appeal

19.191 The local housing authority has a power, but not a duty, to provide accommodation pending the making or determination of the county court appeal. The scope and exercise of the power is detailed in Chapter 16,[288] but a brief outline is given here for ease of reference.

19.192 The power is triggered as soon as the period for an appeal starts to run, so the applicant need not actually have lodged an appeal before inviting the local housing authority to provide accommodation (or to continue accommodation). The local housing authority can only exercise its discretion to provide accommodation,[289] if it previously owed the appellant a duty to provide accommodation under HA 1996, ss 188,[290] 190,[291] or 200,[292] or had the power to provide accommodation under HA 1996, s 195(8).[293] When considering whether or not to exercise its discretion to provide accommodation pending an appeal, the local housing authority should take into account the

---

[286] See **19.183**.

[287] CPR 2 and PD 2B, para 9.

[288] See **16.37–16.42**.

[289] HA 1996, s 204(4).

[290] Interim accommodation duty pending decision or power to accommodate pending review. See **16.11–16.36**.

[291] Accommodation for those who have a priority need and have become homeless intentionally. See **17.111–17.118**.

[292] Duty to accommodate applicant pending referral. See **15.136–15.139**.

[293] Accommodation for those threatened with homelessness, pending review.

factors set out in *R v Camden London Borough Council ex p Mohammed*,[294] ie the prospects of success on appeal,[295] the appellant's personal circumstances, and any new information.[296]

19.193 If the local housing authority refuses to provide accommodation pending the determination of the appeal, or decides to provide accommodation only for a limited period, the appellant may appeal to the county court against that decision on a point of law.[297] This is a separate appeal from the main homelessness appeal and, for ease of reference, is referred to by the section number which contains the right to appeal: 'section 204A'. The principles to be applied in a HA 1996, s 204A appeal are the same as those applied in s 204 appeals and in judicial review.

19.194 Prior to 30 September 2002, any challenges to a refusal to provide accommodation pending appeal could only be brought by judicial review and the case law from that period is still instructive.[298] The Court of Appeal in *R v Brighton & Hove Council ex p Nacion*[299] held that where the local housing authority had followed the guidance in *Mohammed*,[300] any challenges arguing that the refusal to provide accommodation was wrong in law were likely to be futile, and applications should be strongly discouraged. The appropriate remedy for an appellant would normally be to apply to expedite the county court homelessness appeal, rather than bring judicial review proceedings.

19.195 After the HA 1996, s 204A appeal procedure was introduced,[301] the Court of Appeal considered the scope of those appeals in *Francis v Kensington and Chelsea Royal London Borough Council*.[302] In that case, the Court of Appeal applied its previous decision in *Nacion*[303] to appeals against the refusal of accommodation pending a homelessness appeal. It held that, unless the court considers that the local housing authority has failed to direct itself in accordance with *Mohammed*,[304] it should not intervene. Where the local housing authority has not properly directed itself, the decision should be quashed and the court should consider whether to exercise its power to order

---

294   *R v Camden London Borough Council ex p Mohammed* (1998) 30 HLR 315, QBD.
295   *R v Newham London Borough Council ex p Lumley* (2001) 33 HLR 124, QBD.
296   This power to provide accommodation pending appeal to the county court is not available to certain applicants from other EEA states, failed asylum-seekers, or people unlawfully present in the UK, unless the local housing authority considers it necessary in order to prevent a breach of rights under the European Convention on Human Rights or European Community law: Nationality Immigration and Asylum Act 2002, s 54 and Sch 3, para 1, in force from 8 January 2003. See **16.35, 16.41, 20.46–20.48** and **20.65–20.72**.
297   HA 1996, s 204A.
298   *Ali v Westminster City Council* (1999) 31 HLR 349, CA.
299   (1999) 31 HLR 1095, CA.
300   *R v Camden London Borough Council ex p Mohammed* (1998) 30 HLR 315, QBD. See **16.31–16.34**.
301   By Homelessness Act 2002, s 11, with effect from 30 September 2002.
302   [2003] EWCA Civ 443, (2003) 35 HLR 50, CA.
303   *R v Brighton & Hove Council ex p Nacion* (1999) 31 HLR 1095, CA.
304   *R v Camden London Borough Council ex p Mohammed* (1998) 30 HLR 315, QBD. See **16.31–16.34**.

the local housing authority to provide accommodation pending the determination of the appeal.³⁰⁵ The court should not embark on a review of the merits of the main appeal. The local housing authority is required to consider the applicant's grounds of appeal, as part of its consideration of the merits of the case, but would not normally be expected to refer to any of the grounds of appeal in its decision letter unless there is some important and striking ground which requires specific comment.³⁰⁶

19.196 In the light of the pronouncements made in these judicial review and Court of Appeal cases, if the local housing authority has considered the *Mohammed*³⁰⁷ factors and applied them to the appellant's circumstances, an appeal against the refusal to accommodate pending appeal is unlikely to be successful. That is not to suggest that on an HA 1996, s 204A appeal in an appropriate case a court would not quash a decision to refuse to accommodate.³⁰⁸ There must be proper consideration of the *Mohammed*³⁰⁹ factors. Simply referring to them was described in one case as paying only 'lip-service', and a refusal to accommodate pending review was quashed.³¹⁰ The HA 1996, s 204A appeal is only available in respect of a 'decision' not to accommodate pending an appeal. Where a local housing authority has failed altogether to make a decision on a request for accommodation pending appeal, the appropriate procedure is to seek a judicial review of the failure to make a decision. This has been described as a 'serious weakness' in the drafting of the section.³¹¹

*Procedure for an HA 1996, s 204A appeal*³¹²

19.197 There is no statutory time limit for the filing of an Appellant's Notice in an HA 1996, s 204A appeal against a refusal to accommodate pending appeal. The limit is therefore the 21-day period generally applied by the procedure rules to statutory appeals.³¹³ If possible, the appellant should file one Appellant's Notice (form N161) containing both the main homelessness appeal and the s 204A appeal. Otherwise, the s 204A appeal can be brought on a separate form N161.³¹⁴ The appellant should comply with CPR 52 and PD 52

---

³⁰⁵ Confirmed again by the Court of Appeal in *Brookes v Croydon London Borough Council* [2004] EWCA Civ 439, (2004) June *Legal Action*, p 31, CA.

³⁰⁶ *Lewis v Havering London Borough Council* [2006] EWCA Civ 1793, [2007] HLR 20, CA.

³⁰⁷ *R v Camden London Borough Council ex p Mohammed* (1998) 30 HLR 315, QBD. See **16.31–16.34**.

³⁰⁸ See *Onyaebor v Newham London Borough Council* (2004) May *Legal Action*, p 27, Bow County Court, for an example of a successful s 204A appeal.

³⁰⁹ *R v Camden London Borough Council ex p Mohammed* (1998) 30 HLR 315, QBD.

³¹⁰ *R (Paul-Coker) v Lewisham London Borough Council* [2006] EWHC 497 (Admin), [2006[HLR 32.

³¹¹ Robert Duddridge 'House of Bricks or House of Sticks: Some thoughts on the new s 204A of the Housing Act 1996' [2003] JHL 11.

³¹² See Jon Holbrook 'Appeals under the Homelessness Act 2002 – Part 1' (2002) November *Legal Action*, p 26.

³¹³ CPR 52 and PD 52, para 17.3.

³¹⁴ CPR 52 and PD 52, para 24.2.

and file and serve a copy of the decision under appeal, any witness statement and a skeleton argument with the Appellant's Notice.

19.198 If an HA 1996, s 204A appeal is brought, the need for a speedy decision is obvious. The whole point is to provide accommodation urgently. An application can therefore be made for an interim injunction requiring that the local housing authority provide accommodation until the s 204A appeal is determined. The matters to be considered on the application for an interim injunction would include:

(1)   the merits of the HA 1996, s 204A appeal itself and whether the applicant has a strong prima facie case;[315]

(2)   whether or not the appellant's ability to pursue the main homelessness appeal would be substantially prejudiced if no interim order was made; and

(3)   the balance of convenience as between the appellant and the local housing authority as at the date of the hearing of the application for an interim injunction.[316]

19.199 Appeals under HA 1996, s 204A can only be heard by a circuit judge.[317] The appeal may not be brought after the determination of the main homelessness appeal.[318]

19.200 At the final hearing of the HA 1996, s 204A appeal, the court may either confirm or quash the decision made by the local housing authority (refusing accommodation pending the main appeal). Variation is not a possibility. If the court quashes the decision, it may order that the local housing authority provides that accommodation is available for the appellant until the main appeal has been determined, or any earlier specified time. It can only order the local housing authority to provide accommodation if it is satisfied that the appellant's ability to pursue the main appeal would otherwise be substantially prejudiced.[319]

---

[315]   *Putans v Tower Hamlets London Borough Council* [2006] EWHC 1634 (Ch), [2007] HLR 10, ChD at [52], per Michael Briggs QC.

[316]   Applying *American Cyanamid Co v Ethicon Ltd* [1975] AC 396, HL, principles to HA 1996, s 204A. See also *R v Kensington & Chelsea Royal London Borough Council ex p Hammell* [1989] 1 QB 518, CA.

[317]   CPR 2 and PD 2B, para 9.

[318]   HA 1996, s 204A(3).

[319]   HA 1996, s 204A(5) and (6).

Appeal to the Court of Appeal

19.201 Any appeals against orders of the county court determining a main homelessness appeal or an HA 1996, s 204A appeal are *second* appeals and can only be made to the Court of Appeal.[320]

19.202 Such appeals require permission to appeal. Permission can be given only by the Court of Appeal itself and will only be given if the appeal raises 'an important point of principle or practice', or there is 'some other compelling reason' for the Court of Appeal to hear it.[321]

19.203 In *Uphill v BRB (Residuary) Ltd*,[322] the Court of Appeal considered the general principles to be applied when deciding whether to give permission to bring a second appeal.

19.204 It held that permission should only be granted in exceptional cases. When permission was sought under the first limb ('an important point of principle or practice'), it could be granted where such an important point had not yet been determined by a higher court, but would not be granted where the contention was merely that an established point of principle or practice had not been correctly applied. As far as the second limb was concerned ('some other compelling reason'), the starting point was that the prospects of success had to be very high. Even if they were very high, the decision against which the appellant sought permission to appeal had to be inconsistent with the authority of a higher court or tainted with some procedural irregularity leading to unfairness before permission would be given.

19.205 The Court of Appeal considered the second limb of the test ('some other compelling reason') in *Cramp v Hastings Borough Council*.[323] It held that there was a good prospect of success on a second appeal because the first-instance judge had appeared to substitute his own view for that of the local housing authority. There was evidence before the Court of Appeal that the extent of inquiries needed to be undertaken by the local housing authority was a matter of great concern to it and had implications for its resources. Those two points together were 'compelling reasons' sufficient to justify a second appeal.[324]

19.206 In *Camden London Borough Council v Phillips*,[325] the Court of Appeal granted the local housing authority permission to appeal (having heard the full appeal in *Cramp v Hastings Borough Council*, which had been listed for hearing

---

[320] *Azimi v Newham London Borough Council* (2001) 33 HLR 51, CA.

[321] CPR, r 52.13.

[322] [2005] EWCA Civ 60, [2005] I WLR 2070, CA.

[323] The permission hearing is at [2005] EWCA Civ 439, CA.

[324] Carnwath LJ quoted by Brooke LJ in the full appeal: *Cramp v Hastings Borough Council* [2005] EWCA Civ 1005, [2005] HLR 48, CA, at [34].

[325] Heard with the full appeal of *Cramp v Hastings Borough Council* [2005] EWCA Civ 1005, [2005] HLR 48, CA.

on the same day). It noted that the guidance in *Uphill v BRB Residuary Board Ltd*[326] was not exhaustive and should not require the Court of Appeal to feel that there is a:

> 'fetter on its power to put things right if it has occasion to believe that things are going wrong in an important way in the practical operation of the statutory scheme in Part 7 of the 1996 Act.'

19.207 *Camden London Borough Council v Phillips* raised an important point of practice in that both it and *Cramp v Hastings Borough Council* evidenced:

> 'a worrying tendency in judges at that level to overlook the fact that it will never be easy for a judge to say that an experienced senior housing officer on a homelessness review, who has considered all the reports readily available, and all the representations made by the applicant's solicitors, has made an error of law when she considered that it was unnecessary to put in train further detailed inquiries, not suggested by the applicant's solicitors, before she could properly make a decision on the review. The need to correct that tendency raises an important point of practice.'[327]

19.208 In *William v Wandsworth London Borough Council*,[328] the Court of Appeal was concerned with a second appeal which had been brought by the local housing authority. Noting that the local housing authority had made a new review decision between the date of the county court appeal and the date on which permission to bring a second appeal was given, the Court of Appeal criticised the local housing authority's failure to inform the court that it had carried out a further review as 'verging on abuse' and doubted that permission would have been given, had the Court of Appeal been informed that a new review decision had been made. The new review decision had been made because both the applicant's lawyers and the local housing authority's lawyers believed that HA 1996, s 202(4) and the regulations required it to be made, once the previous review decision had been quashed by the county court judge. Chadwick LJ described this as an unsatisfactory position and said that:

> 'the parties should ... take the sensible and obvious course of agreeing that performance of the duty imposed on the authority by section 202(4) of the Act should await the outcome of the application [for permission], or the appeal (as the case may be).'[329]

19.209 An application for permission to bring a second appeal should be made within the Appellant's Notice, and must be filed at the Court of Appeal within 21 days of the judgment or order appealed from.[330] The county court does not have the power to grant or refuse permission to appeal, but does have

---

[326] [2005] EWCA Civ 60, [2005] 1 WLR 2070, CA.
[327] Brooke LJ at [68].
[328] [2006] EWCA Civ 535, [2006] HLR 42, CA.
[329] *William v Wandsworth London Borough Council* [2006] EWCA Civ 535, [2006] HLR 42, CA, at [42]–[43], per Chadwick LJ.
[330] CPR, r 52.4.

the power to order that the time within which an Appellant's Notice is to be filed is extended.[331] Applications for permission do not need to be supported by witness statements, but if a witness statement is filed in support of the application for permission, or any other application, 'fairness requires it to be sent to the intended respondent' and, if it is the local housing authority which is seeking permission to appeal, it should bear in mind that the other party is likely to be without legal representation at the time and so those preparing a witness statement have a particular responsibility 'to ensure that it is relevant to the specific question whether permission to appeal should be granted, and that it is not argumentative and so far as practicable not contentious'.[332]

19.210 The local housing authority's power to provide accommodation for the appellant continues until any second appeal is finally determined, and so it may agree to provide accommodation until the determination of an appeal to the Court of Appeal.[333] If the local housing authority refuses to provide accommodation pending an appeal to the Court of Appeal, there is no power under HA 1996, s 204A for the county court to entertain an appeal against that refusal. Nor is there any other obvious power available to the county court or the Court of Appeal which would enable it to order the local housing authority to accommodate pending the Court of Appeal hearing. In the absence of such a power, the more straightforward course is for the applicant to challenge by way of judicial review the decision not to provide accommodation pending the second appeal to the Court of Appeal.

JUDICIAL REVIEW

Introduction

19.211 Local housing authority decisions made under HA 1996, Part 7 that do not carry with them a right to request a review can only be challenged (in the courts) in judicial review proceedings.

19.212 Complaints that the applicant has been treated unsatisfactorily, but where no error of law in the actual decision reached is alleged, should be raised within the local housing authority's internal complaints procedure.[334] If the treatment amounts to maladministration, the Local Government Ombudsman can investigate, once the internal complaints procedure has been exhausted.[335]

---

[331] CPR, r 52.4(2)(a).
[332] *William v Wandsworth London Borough Council* [2006] EWCA Civ 535, [2006] HLR 42, CA, at [80]–[81], per Sedley LJ; see **19.186–19.188** on contents of witness statements in general.
[333] HA 1996, s 204(4)(b).
[334] See **19.238–19.240**.
[335] See **19.241–19.245**.

Procedure

19.213 The procedure for judicial review is set out in the Civil Procedure Rules at CPR 54 and PD 54. Only a short summary of that procedure can be given here. Before the procedure is adopted, it will be expected that any applicant has complied with the Pre-Action Protocol for Judicial Review.[336]

19.214 In order to bring a claim by way of judicial review, the applicant must obtain permission from the Administrative Court.[337] The application for permission[338] is first considered on the papers. The local housing authority has an opportunity to put its brief case to the judge on paper in an Acknowledgment of Service.[339] If permission is refused on the papers, the applicant has the right to renew his or her application for permission at an oral hearing.[340]

19.215 Claims should be brought promptly, and in any event within 3 months of the decision being challenged (although the court does have the discretion to extend time where there is a good reason for the delay).[341] Delay can be a reason in itself for refusing permission. Judicial review is not available, and permission will be refused, if there is an alternative avenue for redress available to the applicant.

19.216 If permission is granted, the local housing authority has the opportunity to put in its own evidence and submissions, and a full hearing will take place.

19.217 If the court finds that the decision was made in breach of the usual administrative law principles, it can:

(1) quash the decision and remit the matter back to the local housing authority for reconsideration; or

(2) make a mandatory order requiring the local housing authority to act in a certain way; or

(3) make a prohibitory order setting out how the local housing authority may not act; or

(4) make an injunction.[342]

---

[336] Available at http://www.justice.gov.uk/civil/procrules_fin/contents/protocols/prot_jrv.htm.
[337] CPR 54.4
[338] Made on claim form N461.
[339] Form N462.
[340] CPR 54.12(3)
[341] CPR, r 54.5 and CPR, r 3.1(2)(a)
[342] CPR, r 54.2.

19.218 Judicial review is a discretionary remedy and, even if the court finds that an error of law was made, it may still decide in all the circumstances not to make any order.

19.219 Since 2 October 2000, when the Human Rights Act 1998 came into force, it has also been possible to claim damages for breach of human rights within judicial review proceedings.[343] Judicial review proceedings cannot, however, be brought solely to claim damages.[344]

Obtaining interim relief

19.220 In many judicial review claims relating to a local housing authority's decisions under HA 1996, Part 7, the applicant will have an immediate need for accommodation. The judicial review claim is likely to wait months before a full hearing. Even the application for permission to bring the claim may not be considered for several weeks.

19.221 At all times during the progress of the judicial review claim, the Administrative Court has a discretion to grant an interim injunction requiring the local housing authority whose decision is under challenge to accommodate the applicant, and his or her household, until the judicial review claim has been heard or determined.[345] Indeed, in cases of extreme urgency, it is possible to obtain an interim injunction out-of-hours from the duty judge, upon the applicant and his or her legal advisers undertaking to issue the judicial review claim within a specified period (usually less than 24 hours).

19.222 The principles on which an Administrative Court judge will decide whether or not to make an interim injunction would include:

(1) the merits of the judicial review claim itself and whether the claimant has made out a strong prima facie case;[346] and

(2) the balance of convenience.[347]

19.223 Where the application for an interim injunction is made in an emergency, and without notice to the local housing authority, the following principles should be borne in mind:

---

[343] See **19.233–19.237**.
[344] CPR, r 54.3(2).
[345] The power to make an injunction is at CPR 54.2. The Administrative Court's interim powers are at CPR 25.1(1) and include the power to make an interim injunction (CPR 25.1(1)(a)).
[346] *R v Kensington & Chelsea Royal London Borough Council ex p Hammell* [1989] QB 518.
[347] *American Cyanamid Co v Ethicon Ltd* [1975] AC 396, HL.

(1)   that the granting of an injunction without notice is 'an exceptional remedy',[348] and normally appropriate only if the case is genuinely one of emergency or other great urgency;

(2)   even then it should normally be possible to give some informal notice to the other party;

(3)   the claimant applying for an injunction, and his or her legal representatives, are under a heavy duty to make full and frank disclosure of all matters relevant to the claim, whether matters of fact or of law;

(4)   the duty to make full and frank disclosure includes a duty to make proper inquiries before making the application, so that the claimant, or his or her legal representatives, discloses all the material facts; and

(5)   proper disclosure means identifying all relevant documents for the judge, taking the judge to the particular passages in those documents, and taking appropriate steps to ensure that the judge appreciates the significance of what he or she is being asked to read, or is being told.[349]

19.224 Legal representatives are also reminded of the importance of complying with the Pre-Action Protocol for Judicial Review,[350] which requires that the claimant's representatives give notice of the intention to bring judicial review proceedings to the local housing authority's legal department. Even if the matter is too urgent to comply with the time limits required in the protocol, some warning to the legal department should be given.[351]

19.225 An interim injunction obtained without notice to the local housing authority will usually contain a provision permitting the local housing authority to apply to vary or discharge the injunction upon a short period of notice to the claimant or his or her legal representatives. Such applications should be considered relatively urgently by the Administrative Court.[352]

Judicial review as a substitute for county court appeal

19.226 Where an appeal to the county court is available, it is only in really exceptional circumstances that the Administrative Court will give permission for a judicial review claim to be brought.[353] Missing the 21-day deadline for the

---

[348] *R (Lawer) v Restormel Borough Council* [2007] EWHC 2299 (Admin), [2008] HLR 20, Admin Ct, at [62], per Munby J, quoting *Moat Housing Group South Ltd v Harris* [2005] EWCA Civ 287, [2006] QB 606, CA.

[349] *R (Lawer) v Restormel Borough Council* [2007] EWHC 2299 (Admin), [2008] HLR 20, Admin Ct, at [62]–[69], per Munby J.

[350] Available at http://www.justice.gov.uk/civil/procrules_fin/contents/protocols/prot_jrv.htm.

[351] *R (Lawer) v Restormel Borough Council* [2007] EWHC 2299 (Admin), [2008] HLR 20, Admin Ct, at [81]–[82], per Munby J.

[352] *R (Casey) v Restormel Borough Council* [2007] EWHC 2554 (Admin), (2008) January *Legal Action*, p 38, Admin Ct.

[353] *R v Brent London Borough Council ex p O'Connor* (1998) 31 HLR 923, QBD.

county court appeal[354] is not generally an exceptional circumstance,[355] and particularly so now that the county court has power to extend that deadline.

19.227 In one case, permission to bring a claim in judicial review was given where there was an arguable error of law and the applicant had unsuccessfully tried to issue a notice of appeal in the county court (but had wrongly made an application within possession proceedings instead).[356] In another case, permission was given, and the judicial review claim succeeded, where the local housing authority had refused to consider fresh information, produced after the review decision, concerning the applicant's mental health, which was relevant to the decision that he had become homeless intentionally.[357]

19.228 However, permission was refused to an applicant who had been found to have become homeless intentionally, had then withdrawn his request for a review, made a fresh application and then claimed that the local housing authority had failed to provide him with interim accommodation in accordance with the interim pre-decision duty.[358] Likewise, permission will be refused in cases where the applicant seeks to dispute the suitability of accommodation and where a right to a review of suitability is available under the sixth review category at HA 1996, s 202(1)(f).[359] An applicant also failed in judicial review where she sought to challenge an original decision which contained inadequate reasons. The Administrative Court held that the proper route to challenge such deficiencies was by requesting a review and subsequently appealing to the county court.[360]

Judicial review where there can be no county court appeal

19.229 There may be several reasons why a county court appeal is not available and the applicant may need to bring a claim for judicial review. They include:

(1) where he or she wishes to challenge a decision which does not carry the right to request a statutory review; or

---

[354] See **19.174–19.182**.

[355] *R v Brent London Borough Council ex p O'Connor* (1999) 31 HLR 923, QBD; *R v Waltham Forest London Borough Council ex p Abdullahi* (1999) May *Legal Action*, p 29, QBD; and *R v Hillingdon London Borough Council ex p Rahim* (2000), (2000) May *Legal Action*, p 30, QBD.

[356] *R v Lambeth London Borough Council ex p Alleyne* (1999), (1999) June *Legal Action*, p 24, CA.

[357] *R (Van der Stolk) v Camden London Borough Council* [2002] EWHC 1261 (Admin), (2002) July *Legal Action*, p 26, Admin Ct.

[358] *R (Campbell) v Enfield London Borough Council* [2001] EWHC 357 (Admin), Admin Ct.

[359] *R (Cano) v Kensington and Chelsea Royal London Borough Council* [2002] EWHC 1922 (Admin), (2002) December *Legal Action*, p 22, Admin Ct. See also **19.27–19.32**.

[360] *R (Lynch) v Lambeth London Borough Council* [2006] EWHC 2737 (Admin), [2007] HLR 15, Admin Ct. Unusually, the claimant had also issued an HA 1996, s 204 appeal to the county court, which was transferred to the High Court and heard with the judicial review claim.

(2)   if the local housing authority fails to comply with its acknowledged statutory duty, a judicial review claim can be brought for a mandatory order requiring the local housing authority to comply; or

(3)   if the local housing authority simply fails to take a decision on a request or application made to it, a judicial review claim can be brought for a mandatory order requiring the local housing authority to make the decision.

19.230   Subjects for judicial review can therefore include:

(1)   a local housing authority refusing to accept an application under HA 1996, Part 7;[361]

(2)   a local housing authority's failure to make the necessary inquiries or to notify the applicant of the decision on those inquiries;[362]

(3)   a local housing authority's refusal to provide interim accommodation pending an initial decision;[363]

(4)   a local housing authority's decision not to provide accommodation pending a decision on review;[364]

(5)   any dispute as to whether or not accommodation provided under an interim duty is suitable;[365]

(6)   any failure to provide suitable accommodation in discharge of any of its statutory duties (where the local housing authority either fails to provide accommodation at all or provides accommodation that it is agreed is unsuitable for the needs of the applicant and his or her household);[366]

(7)   any dispute as to the length of the period that would provide an applicant who has a priority need and who had become homeless intentionally with 'a reasonable opportunity of securing accommodation';[367]

---

[361]   HA 1996, s 183(1). For a recent example of a successful challenge to such a decision, see *R (G) v Haringey London Borough Council* [2009] EWHC 2699 (Admin), (2009) December *Legal Action*, p 17, Admin Ct.

[362]   HA 1996, s 184.

[363]   HA 1996, s 188(1).

[364]   HA 1996, s 188(3). *R v Camden London Borough Council ex p Mohammed* (1998) 30 HLR 315, QBD.

[365]   *R (Sacupima) v Newham London Borough Council* (2001) 33 HLR 2, CA.

[366]   *R v Newham London Borough Council ex p Begum (Mashuda)* (2000) 32 HLR 808, QBD. See also *R (Dumbaya) v Lewisham London Borough Council* [2008] EWHC 1852 (Admin), (2008) September *Legal Action*, p 25, Admin Ct, where the local housing authority had failed to provide short-term accommodation under HA 1996, s 190(2)(a) to the claimant, whom it had found to have a priority need and to have become homeless intentionally. The local housing authority was ordered to pay the claimant's costs of bringing the judicial review.

[367]   HA 1996, s 190(2)(a). *R (Conville) v Richmond upon Thames London Borough Council* [2006] EWCA Civ 718, [2006] HLR 45, CA, a decision of the Court of Appeal, contains, in the

(8) any failure to assess the applicant's housing needs before providing advice and assistance in discharge of the statutory duty;[368]

(9) any challenge to the assessment of the applicant's housing needs;

(10) any decision not to provide accommodation for those homeless who are not in priority need and did not become homeless intentionally;[369]

(11) any refusal to consider whether or not the conditions are met for the referral of the applicant's case to another local housing authority;[370]

(12) any decision not to allow the applicant to request a review outside the 21-day period;[371] and

(13) any failure to complete a statutory review or to notify the applicant of the decision on review.[372]

19.231 The last of these provides a good example of the usefulness of judicial review in the operation of HA 1996, Part 7. Where an applicant has requested a review, but the local housing authority has failed to complete the review or to notify him or her of the review decision, the applicant can appeal to the county court if there was an error of law in the original decision.[373] However, if there is no error of law in the original decision, but the applicant wants his or her case reconsidered, or has provided new information, then an appeal to the county court will not be the appropriate course. The applicant's remedy in those circumstances is to apply for a mandatory order in judicial review proceedings requiring the local housing authority to complete the review and notify him or her of the review decision.

19.232 Judicial review may also be available where the applicant is challenging the local housing authority's policy on some aspect of HA 1996, Part 7.[374] Although the court retains a discretion to consider disputes on policy matters

---

authors' opinion, the correct approach on forum; and *R (Nipyo) v Croydon London Borough Council* [2008] EWHC 847, [2008] HLR 37, Admin Ct. See **17.111–17.118**.

[368] HA 1996, ss 190(4), 192(4) and 195(6).

[369] HA 1996, s 192(3).

[370] *Hackney London Borough Council v Sareen* [2003] EWCA Civ 351, [2003] HLR 54, CA.

[371] *R (C) v Lewisham London Borough Council* [2003] EWCA Civ 927, [2004] HLR 4, CA; *R (Slaiman) v Richmond upon Thames London Borough Council* [2006] EWHC 329 (Admin), [2006] HLR 20, Admin Ct; and *R (Casey) v Restormel Borough Council* [2007] EWHC 2554 (Admin), (2008) January *Legal Action*, p 38, Admin Ct.

[372] HA 1996, s 203.

[373] HA 1996, s 204(1)(b).

[374] For example, *R (Khatun) v Newham London Borough Council* [2004] EWCA Civ 55, [2004] HLR 29, CA, where the applicants challenged the local housing authority's policy that offers of accommodation made under HA 1996, s 193 had to be accepted or rejected before they were viewed; *R (Calgin) v Enfield London Borough Council* [2005] EWHC 1716 (Admin), [2006] HLR 4, Admin Ct, where the challenge was to the local housing authority's policy of securing accommodation outside its district; and *Ali & others v Birmingham City Council* [2009] UKHL 36, [2009] 1 WLR 1506, HL, where the challenge was to the local housing authority's policy.

that have become academic for the individual applicant (because matters have moved on, or the local housing authority has conceded the applicant's claim), it should only do so if that would be in the public interest and the appropriate procedural steps have been taken.[375]

Claim for damages

19.233 If an applicant for accommodation under HA 1996, Part 7 is not dealt with properly by a local housing authority, he or she may suffer considerable personal loss and hardship. Ordinarily, the law would provide a right to recompense through an award of financial compensation or damages at the suit of the individual who had suffered loss. That is *not* the case for applicants seeking assistance under HA 1996, Part 7.

19.234 The House of Lords decision in *O'Rourke v Camden London Borough Council*[376] established that damages were not available at common law for a local housing authority's breach of its statutory duty owed to a homeless person. The local housing authority, when dealing with an application for homelessness assistance, is implementing a scheme of social welfare that is intended to confer benefits at public expense on the grounds of public policy. To implement the scheme involves the local housing authority making discretionary decisions as to how to provide accommodation and the type of accommodation to be provided. The House of Lords decided that it was unlikely that Parliament had intended that any errors of judgment made by the local housing authority in those circumstances would give rise to an obligation to make financial reparation.

19.235 Since 2 October 2000, it has been possible for damages to be claimed for breach of an applicant's human rights where the court is satisfied that the award is necessary to afford 'just satisfaction' to the applicant.[377] This has been used to explore possible compensation claims in recent years. A failure to provide suitable accommodation does not breach the applicant's right to respect for his or her home.[378] It can, however, breach the applicant's right to respect for his or her family or private life under Art 8 of the European Convention on Human Rights.[379] Damages should be assessed on the basis that they should not be a lesser amount than damages that would be awarded for a

---

[375] *R (Tshikangu) v Newham London Borough Council* (2001) The Times, April 27, QBD. See *R (Morris) v Westminster City Council* [2004] EWHC 1199 (Admin) for an example of permission to continue a claim for judicial review which had become academic. The substantive point was subsequently decided by the Court of Appeal in *R (Morris) v Westminster City Council* [2005] EWCA Civ 1184, [2006] HLR 8, CA.

[376] *O'Rourke v Camden London Borough Council* [1998] AC 188, HL.

[377] Human Rights Act 1998, s 8(1) and (2). See J Compton 'Claiming Damages: a public law perspective' (2006) March *Legal Action*, p 23.

[378] *R (Morris) v Newham London Borough Council* [2002] EWHC 1262 (Admin); and *Chapman v UK* (2001) 33 EHRR 18, ECHR.

[379] Human Rights Act 1998, Sch 1, art 8. See *R (Bernard) v Enfield London Borough Council* [2002] EWHC 2282 (Admin), (2003) 35 HLR 2, Admin Ct.

claim in tort, and using the amount of compensation awarded by the Local Government Ombudsmen as a reference point.

19.236 The Court of Appeal in *Anufrijeva v Southwark London Borough Council*[380] considered the circumstances in which damages should be awarded for breach of an applicant's rights under Art 8. In considering the extent to which Art 8(1) imposed a positive obligation on states to provide public assistance, it concluded that generally a failure to provide welfare support was unlikely to infringe a single applicant's rights under Art 8 if it did not also infringe his or her rights under Art 3 not to be subjected to inhuman or degrading treatment. However, where families were involved, the applicant's right to respect for his or her family life might be more easily infringed. Before a local housing authority could be held to have failed to respect an applicant's private or family life, there had to be an element of culpability, involving at the very least knowledge by the local housing authority that the applicant's private or family life was at risk. For maladministration to infringe an applicant's Art 8 rights, the consequences (that the maladministration would lead to lack of respect for the applicant's private or family life) must be serious and foreseeable. Damages would be awarded, taking into account Judicial Studies Board Guidelines, Criminal Injuries Compensation awards, and awards by the Parliamentary and Local Government Ombudsmen for maladministration.

19.237 In a case relating to prisoners' rights, the House of Lords considered generally the principles under which damages for breach of Convention rights should be awarded. They held that in many cases, the finding that there had been a violation should be 'just satisfaction' for the applicant. Where the finding in itself was not sufficient for there to be 'just satisfaction', damages should be assessed in accordance with the amounts awarded by the European Court of Human Rights.[381]

COMPLAINTS

Local complaints procedures

19.238 Every local housing authority will have a procedure for entertaining complaints made by those using its services, including the homeless. A procedure leaflet and complaint form should be readily available on request. This process will enable the HA 1996, Part 7 applicant to log concerns which do not attack the merits of local housing authority decisions, but rather raise matters such as staff (mis)conduct, unfair treatment, delay, incompetence and the like.

---

[380] *Anufrijeva v Southwark London Borough Council* [2003] EWCA Civ 1406, [2004] HLR 22, CA.

[381] *R (Greenfield) v Secretary of State for the Home Department* [2005] UKHL 14, [2005] 1 WLR 673, HL; and *Van Colle v Chief Constable of Hertfordshire Police* [2007] EWCA Civ 325, [2007] 1 WLR 1821, CA.

19.239 Every local housing authority will have designated one of its most senior officials as the statutory monitoring officer.[382] That person is responsible for ensuring that the local housing authority's services are administered lawfully and without maladministration. Advisers assisting those who have been poorly dealt with under HA 1996, Part 7 should direct their complaints to the monitoring officer. For example, in one case a local housing authority reached an incorrect decision and resisted an appeal which had overwhelming merit. On receipt of a complaint from the trial judge, the local monitoring officer engaged an independent firm of solicitors to scrutinise what had gone wrong. As a result of their report, procedures were changed and the complainant received compensation.[383]

19.240 Since July 2001, every local housing authority has had a specific power to pay compensation, or provide some other suitable remedy, to any complainant who has been adversely affected by council action or inaction which may amount to maladministration.[384] In order to assist local housing authorities in determining how much to award, the Local Government Ombudsmen have published guidance.[385] This deals with both monetary and other redress.[386]

Complaints to the Ombudsmen

19.241 Complaints can be made to the Local Government Ombudsman (or Public Services Ombudsman for Wales) where it is alleged that the applicant has been subject to maladministration.[387] The complaint can be made informally, but the Local Government Ombudsman publishes a useful information booklet which contains a pro-forma complaint.[388]

19.242 A complaint to the Local Government Ombudsman must be made within 12 months of the maladministration complained of, and the applicant should first complain through the local housing authority's internal complaints procedure.[389] If the applicant has not made an internal complaint before complaining to the Local Government Ombudsman, the Ombudsman will refer the complaint to the local housing authority's internal complaints procedure before investigating it.

19.243 The Local Government Ombudsman has the power to make recommendations, if he or she concludes that maladministration has occurred, and can recommend that the local housing authority compensate the applicant.

---

[382] Local Government and Housing Act 1989, s 5.

[383] *Mohamud v Lambeth London Borough Council* (2003) March *Legal Action*, p 31.

[384] Local Government Act 2000, s 92.

[385] *Guidance on Good Practice*, Vol 6: Remedies, January 2006.

[386] *Guidance on Good Practice*, Vol 6, pp 19–21 for the guidance applicable to homelessness complaints.

[387] See English Code, paras 19.26–19.28; Welsh Code, paras 5.24–5.26 and 21.38.

[388] Available from www.lgo.org.uk. The Public Services Ombudsman for Wales is at www.ombudsman-wales.org.uk.

[389] See **19.238–19.240**.

The level of compensation is usually modest, but the current rate for the 'distress' element alone in homelessness cases is in the general range of £500–£2000.[390]

19.244 Reports of individual investigations by the Local Government Ombudsman can be found at the Local Government Ombudsman's website and many are noted in Recent Developments in Housing Law in *Legal Action*. Each year the Local Government Ombudsmen gather a selection of homelessness cases in an Annual Digest. The housing chapters of the digests for the last 7 years are on the Local Government Ombudsman website.

19.245 For complaints involving Welsh local housing authorities, applicants should, having exhausted the local housing authority's internal complaints procedure, seek an investigation by the Public Services Ombudsman for Wales.[391] In 2006, the Public Services Ombudsman for Wales produced a comprehensive report on the practices of Welsh local housing authorities relating to homelessness[392] and the Ombudsman has since published many investigative report on homelessness complaints.

---

[390] £750 in 2001 for 300 days in bed and breakfast accommodation (99/C/4261 2001 Annual Report); £1,500 for 7 months spent in temporary accommodation (99/B/3040); £2,000 for 15 months when no accommodation was provided and the applicant and her family were frequently moving around friends and relatives (99/B/752); £2,700 for 3 years in bed and breakfast accommodation (00/A/5127); £3,000 for the distress of an eviction and nearly 18 months of homelessness caused by the local housing authority's housing benefit maladministration (03/B/13808); £1,000 for the distress of a failure to provide interim accommodation for 6 weeks (04/C/373); £7,200 in 2005 for an applicant who had to sleep rough and suffered considerable hardship (03/A/15819); and £3,000 in 2007 to a family denied interim accommodation for 7 weeks (06/B/07896, (2007) November *Legal Action*, p 38).See more generally the LGO *Guidance on Good Practice*, Vol 6: Remedies (http://www.lgo.org.uk/guidance.htm).

[391] See www.ombudsman-wales.org.uk.

[392] *Housing Allocations and Homelessness, a special report by the Local Government Ombudsman for Wales*, Public Services Ombudsman for Wales, 2006 at http://www.ombudsman-wales.org.uk/en/publications/?pID=76. See **7.23–7.24**.

Chapter 20

OTHER HELP WITH ACCOMMODATION FROM LOCAL AUTHORITIES

INTRODUCTION

20.1	The *homelessness* provisions in Housing Act 1996 ('HA 1996'), Part 7 are intended to ensure that local housing authorities provide short-term accommodation for those in the most urgent housing need. The *allocation* provisions in HA 1996, Part 6 are intended to facilitate the sensible distribution of longer-term homes in social housing by local housing authorities.

20.2	Taken together, the objective of these two Parts is to ensure that local housing authorities can help most people in housing need by providing them with temporary accommodation and/or by helping them find alternative homes.

20.3	Although these two Parts of HA 1996 are the primary statutory means by which local authorities meet housing need, they are not the only statutory provisions that allow local authorities to help with accommodation.

20.4	This chapter focuses on help that local authorities (both local housing authorities and other authorities) can, and in some cases must, give to those needing accommodation, either by the local authorities providing accommodation themselves, or by helping applicants to find it. Initially, the chapter outlines the general power to help (available in almost all cases) before turning separately to consider the special powers and duties that apply, in turn, to adults, young people and children. The chapter concludes with a brief review of the duties to accommodate those displaced from their homes in emergencies, in other circumstances of involuntary displacement, and under the Human Rights Act 1998.

20.5	This chapter cannot, however, cover all the help available to meet housing need. Apart from the powers and duties reviewed here, both central and local government departments have developed other arrangements to assist people in housing need.[1] For example, they have promoted schemes of self-build and for low cost home-purchase. Central government has also improved help available to 'key workers' to enable them to buy low cost homes, to help them with rents, or a combination of the two.[2] Those in need of accommodation can also apply directly to other social sector providers such as registered social landlords (RSLs), charitable trusts and co-operatives, and to private landlords.[3] For those on low incomes wishing to become tenants, housing benefit is available to help with the cost of renting. On a more limited basis, the cost of mortgage interest can be claimed through the income support scheme, so that the poorest owner-occupiers can remain in their homes, and

---

[1]	See *Homelessness Code of Guidance For Local Authorities* (Communities and Local Government, Department for Education and Skills, Department of Health, July 2006) (the English Code), chapter 3.

[2]	See www.communities.gov.uk.

[3]	See English Code, Annex 5, on the duties on RSLs to co-operate with local housing authorities and Chapter 6 of this book.

there are several schemes to assist those on low incomes with house purchase.[4] There is also a wholly separate statutory scheme that provides accommodation for individuals seeking asylum in the UK.[5] It is not possible to set out here the details of all these different arrangements. Rather this chapter concentrates on the powers and duties of local authorities to provide directly, or secure the provision of, accommodation.

GENERAL POWER TO HELP WITH ACCOMMODATION

20.6 Because they are statutory bodies, local authorities can only undertake functions conferred on them by legislation. The legislative provision concerned with accommodation has developed incrementally for over a century. This produced a veritable hotchpotch of powers and duties enabling local authorities to give help with housing and other social needs, including the provisions of what are now HA 1996, Parts 6 and 7. However, for cases falling outside the major provisions of those Parts, a local authority would have to scrabble about to identify some other discrete source of statutory power before it could know whether, when and how it could help to provide accommodation.[6]

20.7 Parliament adopted a wholly new approach when it enacted the Local Government Act 2000 ('LGA 2000'). This gives local authorities wide-ranging statutory powers to meet local social needs, expressed as a power to promote economic, social and environmental 'well-being'.[7] The government guidance suggests that this general power in LGA 2000, s 2 should be seen as a 'power of first resort' which could be 'wide ranging' and would lead to the abandonment of the 'traditionally cautious approach'.[8] The power is intended to 'broaden the scope for local authority action'.[9] Research on different local authorities' use of the LGA 2000, s 2 power has been published by Communities and Local Government.[10]

---

4   See 'Affordable Homes' in *Adviser*, Issue 114, March and April 2006, p 7. See also http://www.communities.gov.uk/housing/buyingselling/ownershipschemes/ for a summary of government policy promoting home ownership.

5   Immigration and Asylum Act 1999, Part 6, which set up the scheme formerly known as the National Asylum Support Service (NASS) and was operated by the UK Borders Agency on behalf of the Home Office. The extent of that scheme is outside the scope of this book, except in so far as there is an interplay with statutory powers and duties exercised by local housing authorities. A detailed guide can be found at Willman & Knafler *Support for Asylum Seekers and other Migrants, a guide to legal and welfare rights* (LAG, 3rd edn, 2009).

6   There is now a useful summary of some (not all) of the statutory powers in chapter 5 of the English Code.

7   Local Government Act 2000, s 2.

8   *Power to promote or improve economic, social or environmental well-being* (ODPM Guidance, 2000), chapter 1, paras 6–7 and 10.

9   LGA 2000, Explanatory notes, para 15, available at www.opsi.gov.uk/acts/en2000/2000en22. htm.

10   *Practical use of the well-being power* (CLG, November 2008) at http://www.communities.gov. uk/publications/localgovernment/practicalwellbeingpower, and Formative *Evaluation of the*

20.8 So an individual who needs accommodation (or aid with obtaining accommodation), and is unable or unwilling to obtain help through HA 1996, Parts 6 or 7, can ask any local authority (including a local housing authority) to provide assistance under the general power in LGA 2000, s 2. There is no prescribed application process governing the request for help (no statutory form and not even a requirement that an application be made in writing). However, it makes good sense for any request for help to include a reference to it.

20.9 Under LGA 2000, s 2, all local authorities have the power to do 'anything' that they consider is likely to achieve the improvement or promotion of the 'social well-being' of their area.[11] That includes 'anything' for the benefit of, or in relation to, any person resident in, or simply present in, the local authority's area.[12]

20.10 To put the scope for assistance with housing beyond doubt, the LGA 2000 specifically provides that the power includes a power to give 'financial assistance to any person'[13] (so as to enable that person to find his or her own accommodation) and a power to provide 'accommodation to any person'.[14]

20.11 Local authorities can therefore be asked to exercise this power in order to provide accommodation either directly or indirectly, or to assist with financial help in obtaining accommodation, e g with the costs of rental deposits or rent-in-advance, etc. In *R (J) v Enfield London Borough Council*,[15] the court found that the power under LGA 2000, s 2 permitted the local authority to help with payments so that a family could obtain accommodation. The power has also been used to offer financial assistance for travel arrangements to an applicant who could not afford to fund those travel arrangements.[16] The power

---

Take-Up and Implementation of the Well Being Power: Annual Report 2006 (CLG, July 2006), at www.communities.gov.uk/publications/localgovernment/formativeevaluation.

[11] LGA 2000, s 2(1)(b).

[12] LGA 2000, s 2(2)(b).

[13] LGA 2000, s 2(4)(b).

[14] LGA 2000, s 2(4)(f).

[15] *R (J) v Enfield London Borough Council* [2002] EWHC 432 (Admin), (2002) 34 HLR 38, Admin Ct.

[16] *R (Grant) v Lambeth LBC* [2004] EWCA Civ 1171, [2005] HLR 27, CA. Providing financial assistance with travel costs usually arises in circumstances where the provisions of Nationality, Immigration and Asylum Act 2002, s 54 and Sch 3 exclude certain assistance to be given to people who fall within one of five classes of persons from abroad and who have approached a local authority asking for assistance under certain statutory powers and duties. For the restrictions on providing support to people who have asked for assistance under National Assistance Act 1948, s 21, see **20.46–20.48**. For the restriction on providing support to people who have asked for assistance meeting the needs of their children under Children Act 1989, s 17, see **20.65–20.72**. For restrictions on providing accommodation to an applicant for homelessness assistance pending review or pending appeal, under HA 1996, ss 188(3) and 204(4), see **16.35** and **16.41**.

is by no means restricted to local housing authorities – others (eg county councils and local councils) have equal access to the power.[17]

20.12   It must be emphasised that LGA 2000, s 2 contains only a power and not a duty. A local authority cannot be compelled to provide help under this section. The LGA 2000 contains no mechanism for statutory review or appeal against decisions about whether to exercise the power or how to exercise it. Nor does it provide any quality criteria, such as a requirement that any accommodation provided must be reasonable or suitable.

20.13   Anyone disappointed by the refusal to exercise the power, or a decision to exercise it in a particular way, can invoke the local authority's own complaints procedure and, if still dissatisfied, complain to the Local Government Ombudsmen. Alternatively, if the local authority is behaving irrationally, or in some other way unlawfully, a challenge could be brought in judicial review proceedings.[18]

20.14   However, there is an important qualification. Local authorities cannot use LGA 2000, s 2 to do anything that they are prevented from doing by a prohibition, restriction or limitation contained in some other enactment.[19] So, for example, a local housing authority cannot use the power to allocate an individual a secure tenancy if such an allocation would be outside the terms of the local housing authority's own allocation scheme, because to do so would breach a statutory prohibition.[20] Likewise, the power cannot be used by a social services authority to assist with housing (or with the costs of housing) for an adult who is barred from help with accommodation under the National Assistance Act 1948.[21] Nor is it available to a social services authority to assist with accommodating a child or young person where the Children Act 1989 prohibits such assistance.[22]

POWERS AND DUTIES UNDER THE NATIONAL ASSISTANCE ACT 1948

The primary power/duty

20.15   Part 3 of the National Assistance Act 1948 ('NAA 1948') originally gave a power to social services authorities to make arrangements for providing residential accommodation for those who, 'by reason of':

---

[17]   LGA 2000, s 1, as amended by Local Government and Public Involvement in Health Act 2002, s 77, defines 'local authority'.

[18]   See *R (Theophilus) v Lewisham London Borough Council* [2002] EWHC 1371, [2002] 3 All ER 851, QBD as an example of a successful challenge to the refusal of an application for LGA 2000, s 2 assistance.

[19]   LGA 2000, s 3(1).

[20]   The prohibition in HA 1996, s 167(8).

[21]   *R (Khan) v Oxfordshire County Council* [2004] EWCA 309, [2004] HLR 41, CA. See also **20.43–20.45**.

[22]   See **20.65–20.72**.

- age;

- illness;

- disability; or

- any other circumstances,

were 'in need of care and attention which is not otherwise available to them'.[23]

20.16 NAA 1948 also contains a power to make arrangements for providing residential accommodation to pregnant women and breast-feeding mothers[24] who 'are in need of care and attention which is not otherwise available to them'.[25]

20.17 For historic reasons, and given the use of the terms 'age', 'illness' and 'disability', this power had been traditionally used to make places available in residential care homes and similar residential facilities (becoming colloquially known as 'Part 3 accommodation').

20.18 But the term 'residential accommodation', used in NAA 1948, Part 3, is also apt to describe a perfectly ordinary house, flat or any other form of housing provision. This is, therefore, a long-standing statutory power under which social services authorities can meet ordinary housing needs for those who have unmet needs for care and attention.[26]

20.19 By direction of the Secretary of State, the power at NAA 1948, s 21(1)(a) and (aa) has been converted into a duty.[27] So, provided that an individual is 'in need of care and attention which is not otherwise available' to him or her, by reason of one of the four matters prescribed,[28] residential accommodation must be provided by the social services authority *either* if the applicant is ordinarily resident in its area *or* if he or she is in 'urgent need'.

---

[23] National Assistance Act 1948, s 21(1)(a).
[24] Described in NAA 1948, s 21(1)(b) as 'expectant and nursing mothers'.
[25] NAA 1948, s 21(1)(aa). For an example of the use of this power, see *R (AG) v Leeds City Council* [2007] EWHC 3275, (2008) March *Legal Action*, p 22, Admin Ct.
[26] *R (Wahid) v Tower Hamlets London Borough Council* [2002] EWCA Civ 287, [2003] HLR 2, CA.
[27] Local Authority Circular 93/10, para 2(1), at http://www.dh.gov.uk/en/ Publicationsandstatistics/Lettersandcirculars/LocalAuthorityCirculars/AllLocalAuthority/ DH_4004121. It should be noted that the power to provide residential accommodation to expectant and nursing mothers who are in need of care and attention which is not otherwise available to them (NAA 1948, s 21(1)(aa)) remains a power and not a duty.
[28] See **20.15**.

20.20 Guidance on the exercise of the power/duty is provided by the Secretary of State in *The Policy Guidance, Fair Access to Care Services.*[29] Local social services authorities are required to take account of the guidance when making decisions under NAA 1948, Part 3.[30]

Restrictions on the power/duty

20.21 Prior to 6 December 1999, the duty to arrange accommodation under NAA 1948, s 21(1)(a) was owed to anyone who had the requisite 'need for care and attention'. Even people unlawfully in the UK could benefit from the duty if otherwise they risked serious injury to health.[31]

20.22 Since 6 December 1999, people subject to immigration control whose need for care and attention has arisen solely because of destitution or because of the physical effects or of the anticipated physical effects of destitution cannot be provided with residential accommodation under NAA 1948, Part 3.[32] Accommodation for those who are seeking asylum has become the responsibility of the Home Office. There is a further prohibition on providing residential accommodation to persons who fall within one of five specified classes of persons from abroad.[33]

20.23 Also the duty is now owed to adults only. The responsibility for arranging accommodation for children no longer falls under NAA 1948, Part 3, but is dealt with by the Children Act 1989.[34]

20.24 The duty does not extend to a requirement that a local authority should meet the needs of the applicant's family.[35] Family members should instead consider what other statutory provisions are available for their assistance.[36]

The duty to assess

20.25 Presented with an application for residential accommodation, the local social service authority's first task is to carry out an assessment of the applicant's needs.[37] The threshold triggering the obligation to assess is a very low one. The social services authority is under a mandatory duty to assess the

---

[29] Department of Health, 2002, www.dh.gov.uk/assetRoot/04/01/27/16/04012716.pdf.

[30] *R v Islington London Borough Council ex p Rixon* (1998) 1 CCLR 119, QBD.

[31] *R v Brent London Borough Council ex p D* (1998) 1 CCLR 234, QBD ; and *R v Lambeth London Borough Council ex p Sarhangi* (1999) 2 CCLR 145, QBD.

[32] National Assistance Act 1948, s 21(1A), inserted by Immigration and Asylum Act 1999, s 116. See **20.44–20.45** for the legal test as to whether or not a 'need for care and assistance' is said to have arisen solely as a result of being destitute or of the anticipated physical effects of being destitute.

[33] Nationality, Immigration and Asylum Act 2002, s 54 and Sch 3. See **20.46–20.48** and **20.65–20.72**.

[34] See **20.55–20.82**.

[35] *R (O) v Haringey London Borough Council* [2004] EWCA Civ 535, [2004] HLR 44, CA.

[36] Such as Housing Act 1996; Children Act 1989; Immigration and Asylum Act 1999.

[37] National Health Service and Community Care Act 1990, s 47.

needs of anyone who 'may be in need' of any community care services (including the provision of accommodation).[38] The local social services authority has a discretionary power to provide services while the assessment is being carried out.[39]

20.26   A failure to carry out an assessment, if the threshold is made out, is a breach of the social services authority's statutory duty. It can be enforced by bringing a claim by way of judicial review seeking a mandatory order requiring the social services authority to carry out an assessment.[40]

Which local authority?

20.27   The duty to assess is owed by the local authority in whose area the applicant is ordinarily resident.[41] Any dispute as to which local authority owes the duty to assess should be decided by the Secretary of State for Health.[42] If there is an urgent need for accommodation pending the resolution of the dispute as to which local authority is responsible, the local authority within whose area the applicant is physically present should provide the accommodation.[43] The same test of physical presence applies if the applicant has no settled residence.[44]

Assessing needs

20.28   Whether an applicant is 'in need of care and attention' by reason of one of the four statutory matters at NA 1948, s 21(1)(a)[45] is a factual decision for the social services authority to take. Social services authorities should ensure that the circumstances of each individual applicant are separately considered, and not apply blanket policies. The House of Lords has held that a 'need for care and attention' occurs where a person needs 'looking after', or, in other words:

> 'doing something for the person being cared for which he cannot or should not be expected to do for himself: it might be household tasks which an old person can no longer perform or can only perform with great difficulty; it might be protection

---

38   *R v Bristol City Council ex p Penfold* (1998) 1 CCLR 315, QBD; *R (Patrick) v Newham London Borough Council* (2001) 4 CCLR 48, QBD; and *R (Bempoa) v Southwark London Borough Council* [2002] EWHC 153 (Admin).

39   National Health Service and Community Care Act 1990, s 47(5); *R (AA) v Lambeth London Borough Council* [2001] EWHC 471 (Admin), (2002) 5 CCLR 36, QBD.

40   See **19.211–19.237** on practice and procedure for judicial review claims.

41   NAA 1948, s 24(1)

42   NAA 1948, s 32(3).

43   *R (Kromah) v Southwark London Borough Council* CO/2032/2008 permission application (2008) August *Legal Action*, p 44, Admin Ct.

44   NAA 1948, s 24(3); *R (S) v Lewisham London Borough Council* [2008] EWHC 1290 (Admin), (2008) July *Legal Action*, p 23, Admin Ct.

45   See **20.15**.

from risks which a mentally disabled person cannot perceive; it might be personal care, such as feeding, washing or toileting.'[46]

20.29 NAA 1948, Part 3 does not establish a scheme for the accommodation of everyone who is short of housing or resources.[47] Many of the cases considering the application of this test related to destitute asylum-seekers who, prior to 6 December 1999, could be provided with residential accommodation if they fell within the condition at NAA 1948, s 21(1)(a). They were also decided before the House of Lords' decision in *R (M) v Slough Borough Council*[48] defining the test for 'in need of care and attention'.

20.30 An able-bodied man, who was not entitled to welfare benefits but could work and was entitled to work, would not be likely to be considered to be 'in need of care and attention' even if he spoke no English and had nowhere to live.[49] However, in the case of an asylum-seeker who had lost her employment,[50] the social services authority could not dismiss her application without considering whether there was any realistic possibility of her finding work.[51] Where a person needs medical care, but not other services, he or she will not be a person 'in need of care and attention' for the purposes of NAA 1948, s 21(1).[52]

20.31 Since the House of Lords' decision in *R (M) v Slough Borough Council*,[53] the High Court has held that a blind man, who received help with shopping, laundry, cooking and getting around, was 'in need of care and attention'.[54] Other applicants, one of whom required a 'low-level care package'[55] and one who had medical needs,[56] have been held not to fall within the definition of having a 'need for care and attention'.

20.32 A person may have the requisite degree of 'need' for care and attention, even if he or she already has some accommodation.[57] Again, the question for the social services authority is simply one as to whether the applicant has the

---

[46] *R (M) v Slough Borough Council* [2008] UKHL 52, [2008] 1 WLR 1808, HL, at [33], per Baroness Hale. This is not an exhaustive list of 'looking after' functions.

[47] *R v Hammersmith and Fulham London Borough Council ex p M* (1998) 30 HLR 10, CA, at 20–21.

[48] [2008] UKHL 52, [2008] 1 WLR 1808, HL.

[49] *R v Newham London Borough Council ex p Plastin* (1997) 30 HLR 261, QBD.

[50] Prior to the implementation of Immigration and Asylum Act 1999, Part VI.

[51] *R v Southwark London Borough Council ex p Hong Cui* (1999) 31 HLR 639, QBD.

[52] *R (M) v Slough London Borough Council* [2008] UKHL 52, [2008] 1 WLR 1808, HL.

[53] [2008] UKHL 52, [2008] 1 WLR 1808, HL.

[54] *R (Zarzour) v Hillingdon London Borough Council* [2009] EWHC 1398 (Admin), (2009) August *Legal Action*, p 37, Admin Ct.

[55] *R (Walcott) v Lambeth London Borough Council* [2008] EWHC 2745 (Admin), (2009) March *Legal Action*, p 26, Admin Ct.

[56] *R (N) v Coventry City Council* [2008] EWHC 2786 (Admin), (2009) March *Legal Action,* p 26, Admin Ct. In *R (S) v Coventry City Council* [2009] EWHC 2191 (Admin), there was no error of law in the local authority's decision not to re-assess the needs of a person who was diagnosed with cancer, but was in remission and had no present need for services.

[57] *R v Newham London Borough Council ex p Gorenkin* (1998) 30 HLR 278, QBD.

requisite need. In one case, a secure tenant suffering from schizophrenia who occupied overcrowded accommodation was assessed not to be in need of care and attention, as support was available to address his mental health needs and the risk of the overcrowding causing a breakdown was relatively small.[58]

20.33   The duty to make arrangements for accommodation is only triggered if the applicant is in need of care and attention and the means of satisfying those needs are 'not otherwise available' to him or her.[59] The provisions of NAA 1948, Part 3 are not therefore available to an applicant who simply chooses not to take up provision available and accessible from another source.

Services provided to meet the needs

20.34   If the applicant is assessed to be 'in need of care and attention' for one of the prescribed reasons, and no means of satisfying those needs is otherwise available, residential accommodation and any necessary ancillary services must be provided. The accommodation must be suitable so as to meet the applicant's needs.

20.35   The type of accommodation to be provided is not confined to institutions such as care homes. It can include bed and breakfast emergency type accommodation[60] or 'ordinary accommodation', if that is appropriate to meet the applicant's needs.[61] The restriction imposed by HA 1996, Part 7 on the use of bed and breakfast accommodation[62] does not apply here.

20.36   Many of the court decisions as to the extent of services to be provided under NAA 1948, Part 3 concern destitute asylum-seekers (who were eligible for NAA 1948, Part 3 services prior to 6 December 1999), but the principles they establish apply to anyone meeting the statutory criteria.[63]

20.37   If the conclusion on assessment is that the applicant is 'in need of care and attention' in that he or she needs accommodation but no other services, then accommodation alone can be provided.[64] Likewise, the social services authority can give the applicant financial assistance to meet the costs of his or

---

[58]   *R (Wahid) v Tower Hamlets London Borough Council* [2002] EWCA Civ 287, (2003) 35 HLR 2, CA; See *R (Mooney) v Southwark London Borough Council* [2006] EWHC 1912 (Admin), (2006) September *Legal Action*, p 14, Admin Ct; and *Lambeth London Borough Council v Ireneschild* [2007] EWCA Civ 234, [2007] HLR 34, CA, for other cases involving secure tenants said to be in need of care and attention.

[59]   NAA 1948, s 21(1)(a) and (aa).

[60]   *R v Newham London Borough Council ex p C* (1999) 31 HLR 567, QBD; and *R v Richmond London Borough Council ex p T* (2001) January *Legal Action*, p 28, QBD.

[61]   *R (Wahid) v Tower Hamlets London Borough Council* [2002] EWCA Civ 287, (2003) 35 HLR 2, CA.

[62]   See **18.93–18.113**.

[63]   *R v Westminster City Council ex p M, P, A and X* (1997) 1 CCLR 85, CA.

[64]   *R v Newham London Borough Council ex p Medical Foundation for the Care of Victims of Torture* (1998) 30 HLR 955, QBD.

her own accommodation.[65] However, services cannot be provided without accommodation. If the applicant is in need of food vouchers or other services, he or she must also be provided with accommodation in order to get that additional assistance under NAA 1948, Part 3.[66]

20.38 The duty to provide accommodation and related services to those who meet the statutory criteria is an absolute and mandatory one. Social services authorities may not rely on lack of funds to excuse them from fulfilling their duty and providing the relevant services to meet the applicant's needs.[67] Nor can they argue that they only have certain ways of providing accommodation, for example by only offering accommodation in residential care homes.

20.39 Once an applicant's needs have been assessed, social services authorities should consider how best to meet those needs. This will involve reviewing options such as:

(1)   supported or sheltered housing;

(2)   helping the applicant to rent accommodation in the private sector;

(3)   paying an applicant's rent in his or her private or public sector accommodation so as to prevent his or her eviction; or

(4)   moving the applicant from accommodation that does not meet his or her needs to accommodation that does.

20.40 The duty is a duty to meet the applicant's *needs*. It does not oblige the social services authority to meet the applicant's preferences as to type or location of accommodation. Although the social services authority is entitled to take the applicant's views as to his or her needs into account, its only duty is to provide those services that it has concluded meet the applicant's needs.[68] It is for the social services authority to assess the extent of the applicant's needs and the services that will be provided to meet those needs.

20.41 As long as the need for care and attention remains, the social services authority has a continuing obligation to provide accommodation to meet that need. A social services authority is entitled to treat its duty as ended, and to decline to provide further accommodation, where the applicant refuses the accommodation offered, or has manifested by his or her conduct a persistent and unequivocal refusal to observe the reasonable requirements of the accommodation. However, even in those latter circumstances, there should be a

---

65   Health and Social Care Act 2001, s 57.

66   *R v Newham London Borough Council ex p Gorenkin* (1998) 30 HLR 278, QBD.

67   *R v Sefton Metropolitan Borough Council ex p Help the Aged* (1997) 1 CCLR 57, CA; and *R v Islington London Borough Council ex p Batantu* (2001) 4 CCLR 445, QBD.

68   *R (Khana and Karim) v Southwark London Borough Council* [2001] EWCA Civ 999, (2002) 34 HLR 31, CA.

reassessment of the applicant's needs and a careful consideration of the nature of his or her conduct before the social services authority could decide that its duty had been discharged.[69]

Disputes

20.42 Any applicant disappointed by a social services authority's response to his or her application can invoke the local authority's complaints procedure. But any legal challenge to the local social service authority's conclusions on the assessment, or as to the services provided, can only be brought in proceedings for judicial review. Damages are not available for breach of statutory duty, but where the social services authority's unlawful conduct has resulted in an infringement of an applicant's rights under the European Convention on Human Rights, Art 8(1), damages for breach of those Convention rights may be claimed within judicial review proceedings.[70]

Persons from abroad

Adults subject to immigration control

20.43 From 6 December 1999, people subject to immigration control who are excluded from benefits[71] cannot fall within the scope of NAA 1948, Part 3 if their need for care and attention arises solely from their being destitute, or from the physical effects or anticipated physical effects of being destitute.[72]

20.44 If such a person has a need for care and attention that has not arisen solely from being destitute, or the physical effects of being destitute, he or she remains entitled to a service under NAA 1948, Part 3. People in this position are colloquially referred to as experiencing 'destitution plus'. In *R (Westminster City Council) v National Asylum Support Service*,[73] an asylum-seeker suffering from cancer was not excluded from NAA 1948, Part 3 entitlement as her need for care and attention did not arise solely as a result of her being destitute. In *R v Wandsworth London Borough Council ex p O*[74] and in *R (Mani) v Lambeth London Borough Council*,[75] the Court of Appeal held that the exclusion did not apply where the applicant's need for care and attention had been rendered more acute by circumstances other than his or her destitution. Destitution can therefore contribute to the applicant having a need for care and attention, but if it is the sole cause, then a person subject to

---

69   *R v Kensington and Chelsea Royal London Borough Council ex p Kujtim* [1999] 4 All ER 161, CA; and *R (Patrick) v Newham London Borough Council* (2000) 4 CCLR 48, QBD.

70   *R (Bernard) v Enfield London Borough Council* [2002] EWHC 2882 (Admin), (2003) 35 HLR 27, Admin Ct; and *Anufrijeva v Southwark London Borough Council* [2003] EWCA Civ 1406, [2004] 2 WLR 603, CA. See also discussion at **19.233–19.237**.

71   Under Immigration and Asylum Act 1999, s 115.

72   NAA 1948, s 21(1A) added by Immigration and Asylum Act 1999, s 116.

73   *R (Westminster City Council) v National Asylum Support Service* [2001] EWCA Civ 512, [2002] UKHL 38, [2002] 1 WLR 2956, HL.

74   *R v Wandsworth London Borough Council ex p O* [2000] 1 WLR 2539, CA.

75   *R (Mani) v Lambeth London Borough Council* [2003] EWCA Civ 836, [2004] HLR 5, CA.

immigration control will be excluded from assistance under NAA 1948, Part 3 and reliant on support, if available, from the Home Office. Baroness Hale, giving the lead judgment in the House of Lords in *R (M) v Slough Borough Council*[76] said that she still considered it likely that O was in need of care and attention.[77]

20.45 In *R (Khan) v Oxfordshire County Council*,[78] the social services authority was held not to have misdirected itself in law when it took the view that a woman who was subject to immigration control, destitute and also fleeing domestic violence fell within the exclusion. The domestic violence could be a circumstance making her need for care and attention more acute, but the social services authority had considered that and decided that it had not had that effect on her.

Certain classes of persons from abroad

20.46 From 8 January 2003, five additional classes of people have been excluded from accommodation provision under NAA 1948, Part 3:

- refugees granted refugee status by another state of the European Economic Area (EEA);[79]

- nationals of another state of the EEA;

- asylum-seekers whose claims for asylum have failed and who have failed to co-operate with removal directions;

- persons who are not asylum-seekers and are unlawfully present in the UK; and

- failed asylum-seekers with dependent children, where those families have been certified by the Secretary of State as not having taken reasonable steps to leave the UK.[80]

20.47 There is a general prohibition on providing support to *adults without dependent children* who fall into one of those classes. There are two exceptions to that general prohibition:

---

[76] [2008] UKHL 52, [2008] 1 WLR 1808, HL.

[77] *R (M) v Slough Borough Council* [2008] UKHL 52, [2008] 1 WLR 1808, HL, at [32]–[33] per Baroness Hale.

[78] *R (Khan) v Oxfordshire County Council* [2004] EWCA Civ 309, [2004] HLR 41, CA.

[79] For a list of EEA states, see **12.56**, Box 2.

[80] Nationality, Immigration and Asylum Act 2002, s 54 and Sch 3; Withholding and Withdrawal of Support (Travel Assistance and Temporary Accommodation) Regulations 2002, SI 2002/3078. The same exclusion applies to the discretionary powers to secure accommodation pending review or appeal. See **16.35** and **16.41**.

(1)   where the support is necessary to prevent an interference with a person's human rights under the European Convention;[81] or

(2)   for the first two classes of people, provision of support can be made only in the form of assistance with travel arrangements to their home countries.[82]

20.48 *Adults with dependent children* may receive limited temporary accommodation while they await implementation of the travel arrangements.[83] If a request is made for support by anyone falling within one of the third, fourth or fifth classes, the local authority is obliged to inform the Home Office.[84]

POWERS AND DUTIES UNDER THE MENTAL HEALTH ACT 1983

20.49 Special statutory provision is made to meet the accommodation needs of adults who are, or who have recently been, mentally ill. The Mental Health Act 1983, s 117 ('MHA 1983') imposes a duty on social services authorities to provide after-care services for any person who has left hospital, having been detained, or who has been subject to certain hospital orders made in criminal proceedings.[85] This duty rests jointly on the relevant primary care trust or local health board and on the local social services authority, and they are expected to co-operate in ensuring that services are provided.

20.50 Guidance on this duty is provided in *After-Care Under the Mental Health Act 1983: section 117 after-care services*.[86]

---

[81]   Nationality, Immigration and Asylum Act 2002, Sch 3, para 3. See *R (Limbuela) v Secretary of State for the Home Department* [2005] UKHL 66, [2006] 1 AC 396, HL, as to the operation of this threshold. For cases raising issues as to breach of human rights (which generally involve adults with dependent children), see **20.70–20.72**. Where there is an outstanding claim for leave to remain in the UK, not yet determined by the Home Office or the courts, the local authority should not determine the merits of the claim for leave, unless it takes the view that the claim is 'manifestly unfounded': *R (Binomugisha) v Southwark London Borough Council* [2006] EWHC 2254 (Admin), (2006) November *Legal Action*, p 33, Admin Ct.

[82]   SI 2002/3078, reg 3; there is no obligation to provide assistance with travel arrangements to the third and fourth classes, who are expected to comply with removal directions.

[83]   See **20.65–20.67**. Financial assistance with travel costs may also be provided under Local Government Act 2000, s 2; see *R (Grant) v Lambeth LBC* [2004] EWCA Civ 1171, [2005] HLR 27, CA, and **20.7–20.14**.

[84]   Nationality, Immigration and Asylum Act 2002, Sch 3, para 14.

[85]   A description of the much broader provision in the Mental Health Act 1983, as amended by the Mental Capacity Act 2005 and Mental Health Act 2007, consolidating the health services to which mentally ill patients are entitled, is beyond the scope of this book.

[86]   LAC (2000) 3, Department of Health, at www.dh.gov.uk/PublicationsAndStatistics/ LettersAndCirculars/LocalAuthorityCirculars/AllLocalAuthorityCirculars/ AllLocalAuthority/DH_4003625; Health Service Circular (1999) 223; Local Authority Circular (1999) 34; and chapter 27 of the Department of Health *Code of Practice: Mental*

20.51 It is unlawful for a primary care trust, health authority or social services authority to fail to take steps to prepare a package of after-care services so as to enable discharge to take place from residential accommodation provided under the MHA 1983.[87] However, the duty at MHA 1983, s 117 is not absolute; all that social services authorities are required to do is to use their best endeavours to provide after-care services. In those circumstances, if no package is set up despite the social services authority using its best endeavours, and the consequence is that the patient remains detained rather than being released into the community, there is no illegality or breach of the patient's human rights.[88] Similarly, where there is a genuine inability to provide accommodation, because of the particular needs of the applicant and the absence of suitable accommodation, no unlawfulness or illegal detention will arise.[89]

20.52 The after-care services can include the provision of ordinary accommodation.[90] Importantly, social services authorities are not permitted to charge for after-care services provided under MHA 1983, s 117 and are not permitted to refuse to provide accommodation on the grounds of lack of resources.[91]

20.53 If the person has left hospital subject to supervised community treatment, the duty continues for the whole of the supervision period.[92] If he or she is not subject to supervision, the duty continues until the social services authority is satisfied that he or she is no longer in need of MHA 1983, s 117 services.

20.54 Voluntary patients and those patients detained for assessment under MHA 1983, s 2 are not entitled to the benefit of the MHA 1983, s 117 duty. If, on leaving hospital, they are in need of community care services and accommodation, they can require that the social services authority assesses their needs under s 47 of the National Health Service and Community Care Act 1990 and that the social services authority then provides community care services to meet those needs, which may include assistance with finding accommodation.[93]

Health Act 1983, 7 May 2008, in force November 2008, available at http://www.dh.gov.uk/en/Healthcare/NationalServiceFrameworks/Mentalhealth/DH_4132161.

[87] *R v Ealing London Borough Council ex p Fox* [1993] 3 All ER 170, QBD.

[88] *R (K) v Camden and Islington Health Authority* [2001] EWCA Civ 240, (2001) 4 CCLR 170, CA.

[89] *R (W) v Doncaster Metropolitan Borough Council* [2004] EWCA Civ 378, CA.

[90] *Clunis v Camden and Islington Health Authority* [1998] QB 978, (1998) 1 CCLR 215, CA.

[91] *R v Richmond London Borough Council ex p Watson, R v Manchester City Council ex p Stennett* [2002] UKHL 34, [2002] 2 AC 1127, HL.

[92] See Mental Health Act 1983, ss 17A–17G for provision about supervised community treatment.

[93] *R (B) v Camden London Borough Council and Camden & Islington Mental Health and Social Care Trust* [2005] EWHC 1366 (Admin), [2005] MHLR 258, Admin Ct. See **20.25–20.26**.

ACCOMMODATION FOR CHILDREN AND YOUNG PEOPLE – POWERS AND DUTIES IN THE CHILDREN ACT 1989

20.55 Local social services authorities have a duty, under s 17(1) of the Children Act 1989 ('CA 1989'), to safeguard and promote the welfare of children[94] within their area who are in need. So far as is consistent with that duty, they must promote the upbringing of such children by their families by providing a range and level of services appropriate to those children's needs. This duty is a target duty, meaning that it is owed generally to children within the social services authority's area. The social services authority has a substantial discretion as to how it performs that duty.

Assessment

20.56 Social services authorities must first assess whether or not a child is 'in need'. The social services authority is under a duty to take reasonable steps to assess the needs of any child within its area who appears to be in need. If it fails to do so, a mandatory order can be sought in judicial review compelling it to do so.[95]

20.57 The concept of being 'in need' is defined at CA 1989, s 17(10). A child is in need if he or she is disabled or if, without the provision of local authority services, the child is unlikely to achieve or maintain a reasonable standard of health or development, or his or her health or development is likely to be significantly impaired. Guidance is provided in the *Framework for assessment of children in need and their families*.[96] It is well established that a child without accommodation can be a 'child in need' and that the provision of accommodation can be a service to meet that need.[97]

20.58 The duty imposed on a social services authority by CA 1989, s 17(1) is to provide services appropriate to the needs of children within its area. 'Within their area' means that the child must be actually physically present. So the duty will be owed by the social services authority for the area where the child lives or where he or she attends school.

---

[94]   Children Act 1989, s 105 defines a child as 'a person under the age of 18'.

[95]   *R (AB and SB) v Nottinghamshire County Council* (2001) 4 CCLR 295, QBD.

[96]   *Framework for assessment of children in need and their families* (Department of Health, 2000), at   www.dh.gov.uk/PublicationsAndStatistics/Publications/PublicationsPolicyAndGuidance/ DH_4008144, to be read along with the *Common Assessment Framework* (Department for Children, Schools and Families, 2009) at http://www.dcsf.gov.uk/everychildmatters/strategy/ deliveringservices1/caf/cafframework/.

[97]   CA 1989, s 17(6) and (10). See also *R v Northavon District Council ex p Smith* [1994] 2 AC 402, HL; and *R (G) v Barnet London Borough Council, R (W) v Lambeth London Borough Council, R (A) v Lambeth London Borough Council* [2003] UKHL 57, [2004] 2 AC 208, [2003] 3 WLR 1194, HL.

20.59 Where a homeless family with children is found not to be eligible for assistance under HA 1996, Part 7, or the adults are found to have become intentionally homeless intentionally or to have become threatened with homelessness intentionally so that there is no main housing duty on the local housing authority to provide accommodation, the local housing authority must ask the applicant to consent to the family being referred to the local social services authority or department.[98] Even if the applicant refuses, the local housing authority must still make the referral if it considers that the child is, or may be, at risk of significant harm.[99] When a referral is received, the social services authority is entitled to request advice and assistance from the local housing authority.[100] It follows, therefore, that a local housing authority that has placed a homeless family outside its own district[101] should refer the family (if it is found to be ineligible or the adult members are found to have become homeless intentionally) to its own social services department or authority. It may, of course, also seek the assistance of the social services authority for the district in which the family has been placed, under the general provisions for co-operation in HA 1996, s 213.

20.60 Once the social services department is aware that the child may be in need, the child's needs *must* be assessed. If the child appears to be 'in need', there is a mandatory duty to assess, which should not be deferred.[102]

20.61 If a homeless applicant with dependent children has been found not to be 'eligible' for assistance under HA 1996, Part 7,[103] or there is no priority need because the dependent child or children are not 'eligible',[104] the local authority could consider using its powers under CA 1989, s 17 to provide accommodation.[105]

Services

20.62 After the assessment has been carried out, services to meet the child's identified needs must be provided. Services for the child's family or any member of his or her family may also be provided, with a view to safeguarding or promoting the child's welfare.[106] Those services can include drawing up and

---

[98] HA 1996, s 213A. See **17.155–17.162**.

[99] HA 1996, s 213A(4). See also English Code, chapter 13. *Code of Guidance for local housing authorities on allocation of accommodation and homelessness for Wales* (National Assembly for Wales, April 2003) (the Welsh Code), chapter 17.

[100] HA 1996, s 213A(5).

[101] See **15.205–15.211**.

[102] *R (J) v Newham London Borough Council* [2001] EWHC 992 (Admin), (2002) 5 CCLR 303.

[103] See Chapter 12.

[104] See **12.24–12.29**.

[105] For examples of applicants who were found not to be eligible, see *R (Rekiouak) v Southwark LBC CO/4836/2005*, (2005) December *Legal Action*, p 22, Admin Ct; *R (Badu) v Lambeth London Borough Council* [2005] EWCA Civ 1184, [2006] HLR 8, CA. See also *R (Bangura) v Southwark London Borough Council* [2007] EWHC 1681 (Admin), (2007) September *Legal Action*, p 18.

[106] CA 1989, s 17(3).

implementing plans to remedy inadequate accommodation,[107] or the provision of a roof over the child's head if he or she is facing literal homelessness. Cash can, in exceptional circumstances, be provided.[108] Therefore, in practice, a child's need for accommodation with his or her family could result in the social services authority assisting the family financially with a deposit or rent guarantee so that they can find accommodation in the private sector.[109] Other forms of assistance could include moving a child and his or her family from inadequate to adequate accommodation.[110] However, it is now common practice for social services' authorities to offer accommodation to the child, or children, alone under CA 1989, s 20[111] rather than offer assistance to the whole of the family. This practice was first considered by the House of Lords in *R (A) v Lambeth London Borough Council, R (W) v Lambeth London Borough Council and R (G) v Barnet London Borough Council*[112] and found, in principle, to be lawful.

20.63　The three cases considered by the House of Lords in *R (A) v Lambeth London Borough Council, R (W) v Lambeth London Borough Council and R (G) v Barnet London Borough Council*[113] illustrate the types of assistance with housing need that can be sought under CA 1989, s 17. In *A*, two severely disabled children, whose mother was a secure tenant, needed to move to larger and safer accommodation. In *W*, the child's mother had been found to have become homeless intentionally. She argued that her child was in need of emergency accommodation (and that it was in the child's best interests for the two of them to be accommodated together). In *G*, the child's mother was homeless and not eligible for homelessness assistance, as she was not habitually resident in the UK. The assessment of the child's needs had resulted in the social services authority offering to pay for travel to the family's home country, which the mother had refused. The children in *W* and *G*, therefore, both had immediate needs for accommodation with (it was argued) their parents, and the children in *A* had a need for suitable long-term accommodation. In both *W* and *G*, the social services authorities were offering accommodation to the children alone, without their mothers, pursuant to their duty under CA 1989, s 20.

20.64　The House of Lords confirmed that accommodation could be provided under CA 1989, s 17 powers, a position also legislated for by Parliament, which

---

[107]　*R v Ealing London Borough Council ex p C (A Minor)* (2000) 3 CCLR 132, CA.

[108]　CA 1989, s 17(6).

[109]　*R v Barking and Dagenham London Borough Council ex p Ebuki* (2001) March *Legal Action*, p 30, Admin Ct.

[110]　*R v Tower Hamlets London Borough Council ex p Bradford* (1997) 1 CCLR 294, CA. See also *R (Mooney) v Southwark London Borough Council* [2006] EWHC 1912 (Admin), (2006) September *Legal Action*, p 14, Admin Ct.

[111]　See **20.73–20.79**.

[112]　*R (G) v Barnet London Borough Council, R (W) v Lambeth London Borough Council, R (A) v Lambeth London Borough Council* [2003] UKHL 57, [2004] 2 AC 208, HL.

[113]　*R (G) v Barnet London Borough Council, R (W) v Lambeth London Borough Council, R (A) v Lambeth London Borough Council* [2003] UKHL 57, [2004] 2 AC 208, HL.

had amended s 17(6) to include specific reference to 'accommodation'.[114] It held, however, that the duty under CA 1989, s 17 was a 'target duty' and therefore there was no means by which an individual child could require that the social services authority provide him or her with particular services under that section. In *A*'s case, there was no power for the court to order that the social services authority obtain suitable accommodation for the children. The House of Lords also emphasised that the decisions, as to whether a child was in need and what services should be provided to meet those needs, were decisions for the social services authority. In particular, social services authorities are entitled to operate certain policies such as (in the case of *G*) offering to return the family to their home country and providing accommodation only for the child if the offer is refused. In *W*, the social services authority had not been acting unreasonably when it decided that the child was not in need of accommodation (as her mother had relatives with whom they could stay) and that, if the mother failed to make her own arrangements for accommodation, it would provide accommodation for the child but not the family. Social services authorities remain under an obligation to consider the individual circumstances of each applicant, but to operate a general policy normally providing accommodation for the children alone is not, in itself, unlawful.

Children of persons from abroad

20.65 There used to be no general prohibition on providing services under CA 1989, s 17 to children who were persons from abroad, or whose parents were persons from abroad. Prior to 6 December 1999, asylum-seekers whose families included dependent children were provided with accommodation and services by social services authorities under CA 1989, s 17. As from 6 December 1999, the statutory basis for providing accommodation and services fell under the Asylum Support (Interim Provisions) Regulations 1999[115] and, from 3 April 2000, social services authorities have been prevented from providing CA 1989, s 17 assistance to the children of asylum-seekers.[116] Even if the children have needs that would normally bring them within the scope of CA 1989, s 17(1) (eg disability), the provision of adequate accommodation and support for the family remains the responsibility of the Home Office.[117]

20.66 On 8 January 2003, s 54 and Sch 3 of the Nationality, Immigration and Asylum Act 2002 came into force, along with the Withholding and Withdrawal of Support (Travel Assistance and Temporary Accommodation) Regulations 2002.[118] These provisions apply to five classes of people:

---

[114] Adoption and Children Act 2002, s 116(1), in force from 7 November 2002 and enacted after the Court of Appeal decision in *R (A) v Lambeth London Borough Council* [2002] EWCA Civ 540, (2002) 34 HLR 13, CA, which had held that there was no such power and was subsequently overturned by the House of Lords.

[115] Asylum Support (Interim Provisions) Regulations 1999, SI 1999/3056.

[116] Immigration and Asylum Act 1999, s 122(5), to be substituted by s 122(3), but not yet in force (Nationality, Immigration and Asylum Act 2002, s 47).

[117] *R (A) v NASS and Waltham Forest London Borough Council* [2003] EWCA Civ 1473, [2004] HLR 24, CA.

[118] SI 2002/3078.

(1)   refugees given refugee status by another state of the EEA;

(2)   nationals of another state of the EEA;

(3)   asylum-seekers whose claims for asylum have failed and who have failed to co-operate with removal directions;

(4)   persons who are not asylum-seekers and are unlawfully present in the UK; and

(5)   failed asylum-seekers with dependent children where those families have been certified by the Secretary of State as not having taken reasonable steps to leave the UK.[119]

20.67   People in the first, second and fourth categories who have dependent children are entitled to limited support under CA 1989, s 17.[120] Social services authorities can provide assistance with travel arrangements for families in the first two categories to return to their home countries and can provide support and accommodation until they travel.[121] They may also provide support and accommodation for families in the fourth category until those people make their own arrangements to travel.[122] If the families do not leave the UK, accommodation and support will cease. The children will be entitled to accommodation and support under CA 1989, s 20, but their parents will not be entitled to any services. If a request is made for support by anyone falling within one of the third, fourth or fifth classes, the local authority is obliged to inform the Home Office.[123]

20.68   In all of those three categories of people for whom limited accommodation provision may be made, guidance issued by the Secretary of State (to which social services authorities must have regard)[124] states that it is preferable that accommodation is only provided for a limited period, with maximum periods suggested of 5 days for families falling within the first two categories and 10 days for families falling into the fourth category from the date when they first presented to the local authority for support.[125]

---

119   Nationality Immigration and Asylum Act 2002, s 54 and Sch 3; and SI 2002/3078. See also **20.46–20.48**. For a list of EEA states, see **12.56**, Box 2. The fifth category was added by s 9(1) of the Asylum and Immigration (Treatment of Claimants etc) Act 2004 and came into force on 1 December 2004.

120   SI 2002/3078, reg 3(2) and (3).

121   SI 2002/3078, reg 3(1).

122   Or travel assistance is provided by the local authority under some other statutory power such as Local Government Act 2000, s 2; see *R (Grant) v Lambeth London Borough Council* [2004] EWCA 1711, [2005] HLR 27, CA; and see **20.9–20.14**.

123   Nationality Immigration and Asylum Act 2002, Sch 3, para 14.

124   SI 2002/3078, reg 4(4).

125   See also *Guidance to Local Authorities and Housing Authorities on Nationality Immigration and Asylum Act 2002, s 54 and Sch 3 and the Withholding and Withdrawal of Support (Travel Assistance and Temporary Accommodation) Regulations 2002, SI 2002/3078* at www. asylumsupport.info/withholdingand withdrawing.htm.

20.69 Failed asylum-seeker families with dependent children (the fifth category) are the responsibility of the Home Office and remain eligible for support and accommodation from the Home Office until they are deported.[126]

20.70 Social services authorities are not prevented from providing accommodation and support to anyone falling within one of these five categories if it is necessary to do so in order to prevent a breach of that individual's European Convention rights or European Union Treaty rights.[127] They should also take into account Home Office policy where the claimant might potentially be entitled to remain in the UK.[128] They should not, however, be seeking to decide the merits of the claimant's immigration claim unless such a claim is 'manifestly unfounded.'[129]

20.71 In *R (M) v Islington London Borough Council*,[130] the social services authority's decision to provide support by returning the mother and child to the mother's home country of Guyana was held to be wrong in law because the social services authority had failed to consider the child's right to respect for her family life, in that she might lose contact with her father, who was to remain in the UK and thus it might be necessary to provide support in order to prevent a breach of the child's European Convention rights.[131] Furthermore, the Court of Appeal considered that it was not open to social services authorities to exercise the power in a way that encourages a family's expulsion before the immigration authorities have determined the family's status. The majority of the Court of Appeal held that the periods of 5 and 10 days suggested in the Secretary of State's guidance did not preclude a social services authority from providing accommodation for a longer period.[132]

20.72 In *R (Conde) v Lambeth London Borough Council*,[133] the court considered the position of an EEA national who was seeking work, and held

---

[126] Immigration and Asylum Act 1999, s 94(5), to be repealed by the Nationality, Immigration and Asylum Act 2002, s 44(1) and (5).

[127] Nationality, Immigration and Asylum Act 2002, Sch 3, para 3.

[128] *R (Clue) v Birmingham City Council* [2008] EWHC 3036 (Admin), (2009) January *Legal Action*, p 28, Admin Ct.

[129] *R (Binomugisha v Southwark London Borough Council* [2006] EWHC 2254 (Admin), (2006) November *Legal Action*, p 33, Admin Ct.

[130] *R (M) v Islington London Borough Council* [2004] EWCA Civ 235, [2004] 4 All ER 709, CA.

[131] In *R (K) v Lambeth London Borough Council* [2003] EWCA Civ 1150, [2004] HLR 15, CA, the Court of Appeal held that neither Art 3 nor Art 8 of the European Convention on Human Rights imposed a duty on the UK to provide support to foreign nationals who are permitted to enter the country but are in a position freely to return home. See also *R (Blackburn-Smith) v Lambeth London Borough Council* [2007] EWHC 767 (Admin), (2007) October *Legal Action*, p 27, Admin Ct.

[132] See also *R (McDonagh) v Hounslow London Borough Council* [2004] EWHC 511 (Admin), (2004) April *Legal Action*, p 35, Admin Ct, where the court declined to interfere with a decision to assist a family by financing the return to the Republic of Ireland; and *R (Grant) v Lambeth London Borough Council* [2004] EWCA 1711, [2005] HLR 27, CA, where the Court of Appeal held that the local authority's offer to provide temporary accommodation and financial assistance under LGA 2000, s 2 for travel for someone who was unlawfully present in the UK was not a breach of her, or her children's Convention rights.

[133] [2005] EWHC 62 (Admin), [2005] HLR 29, Admin Ct. See also **12.181**.

that social services authorities considering applications from EEA nationals should always ensure that those applicants are not exercising any rights under European Union Treaties, although it was unlikely that work-seekers applying for housing or Children Act accommodation would be exercising European Union Treaty rights.

Individual children

20.73 By CA 1989, s 20, social services authorities are required to provide accommodation for any children in need within their area who appear to them to require accommodation as a result of:

(1)   there being no one who has parental responsibility for them; or

(2)   their having been lost or abandoned; or

(3)   the person who had been caring for them being prevented from providing suitable accommodation or care.

20.74 In *R (M) v Gateshead Metropolitan Borough Council*,[134] Dyson LJ described the duty as:

> 'an absolute duty to provide accommodation for any child in need where one of the specified circumstances exists. It is a precise and specific duty. There is no scope of discretion as to whether or not to provide accommodation at all. Thus where it appears to the local authority that there is a child in need, for example, as a result of there being no person who has parental responsibility, the local authority has an absolute obligation to provide some accommodation for that child. Section 20 says nothing about the type of accommodation that must be provided: that is left to the discretion of the local authority.'[135]

20.75 CA 1989, s 20 poses a series of questions for the local authority to ask and answer:

(1)   Is the applicant a child?

(2)   If so, is the applicant a child in need, which might mean that he or she lacks accommodation?

(3)   If so, is the child within the local authority's area?[136]

---

[134] [2006] EWCA Civ 221, [2006] QB 650, CA.

[135] *R (M) v Gateshead Metropolitan Borough Council* [2006] EWCA Civ 221, [2006] 1 QB 650, CA, at [33], per Dyson LJ.

[136] See *R (Liverpool City Council) v Hillingdon London Borough Council and AK* [2008] EWCA Civ 43, [2009] LGR 289, CA, and *R (A) v Leicester City Council and Hillingdon London Borough Council* [2009] EWHC 2351 (Admin), (2009) November *Legal Action*, p 26, Admin Ct, for examples of disputes between local authorities.

(4) If so, does he or she appear to the local authority to require accommodation?

(5) If so, is that because of one of the three statutory reasons, which can include the circumstance where a child is excluded from the parental home by his or her parent?

(6) If so, what are the child's wishes and feelings regarding the provision of accommodation for him or her?

(7) What consideration should be given to the child's wishes and feelings?[137]

If the answers to those questions indicate that the child falls within the statutory criteria at CA 1989, s 20(1), accommodation must be provided by the local authority. The local authority should not be 'side-stepping' its responsibilities, for example by simply advising a child to make a homelessness application.[138]

20.76 The duty is owed to the individual child, and for these purposes a child is defined as a person who is not yet 18 years old.[139] The social services authority will initially assess whether or not a person claiming to be a child without parental support is in fact aged less than 18. Useful guidance on the assessment of the child's age is provided by *R (B) v Merton London Borough Council*.[140] However, if the child disagrees with the social services authority's assessment of his or her age, he or she can bring judicial review proceedings

---

[137] *R (G) v Southwark London Borough Council* [2009] UKHL 26, [2009] 1 WLR 2399, HL, at [28], per Baroness Hale.

[138] *R (G) v Southwark London Borough Council* [2009] UKHL 26, [2009] 1 WLR 2399, HL; *R (MM) v Lewisham London Borough Council* [2009] EWHC 416 (Admin), (2009) April *Legal Action*, p 23, Admin Ct. Similarly, a homeless child who has a priority need may also be a 'child in need' for the purposes of CA 1989 and local housing authorities should refer children who approach them for assistance with homelessness to social services as well as complying with their duties under HA 1996, Part 7 (*R (M) v Hammersmith & Fulham London Borough Council* [2008] UKHL 14, 1 WLR 535, HL). See *R (J) v Caerphilly County Borough Council* [2005] EWHC 586 (Admin), [2005] 2 FCR 153, Admin Ct for guidance on dealing with unco-operative children. See *R (L) v Nottinghamshire County Council* [2007] EWHC 2364 (Admin), and *R (S) v Sutton London Borough Council* [2007] EWHC 1196 (Admin), [2007] Fam Law 699, Admin Ct for guidance on determining whether the child appears to require accommodation. See *R (Liverpool City Council) v Hillingdon London Borough Council and AK* [2008] EWCA Civ 43, [2009] LGR 289, CA, on the extent to which the child's wishes and feelings should be taken into account. For one example where the local authority was guilty of maladministration, see *LGO Complaint against Waltham Forest London Borough Council* 08 016 986, 21 October 2009, at (2010) February *Legal Acgtion*, p 34, where £7,000 compensation was recommended by the LGO in respect of the local authority's failure to assess her and to provide her with services under CA 1989, s 20 and then under the leaving-care provisions. See also **13.124–13.130**.

[139] CA 1989, s 105.

[140] *R (B) v Merton London Borough Council* [2003] EWHC 1689 (Admin), [2003] 4 All ER 280, Admin Ct.

and, unlike most claims in judicial review, ask the court to review the evidence available and make its own decision as to what age he or she is.[141]

20.77 There are no restrictions on the grounds of immigration status to providing CA 1989, s 20 accommodation to children. Asylum-seeking children who are unaccompanied are entitled to the same care and after-care duties as any other children.[142]

20.78 Children who are provided with accommodation under CA 1989, s 20 are entitled to certain assistance beyond their eighteenth birthday.[143] This is not the case for children provided with help with accommodation under CA 1989, s 17. In *R (H) v Wandsworth London Borough Council*,[144] the court held that where a local authority actually provided accommodation to a child whom it had identified as a 'child in need', that accommodation was provided under CA 1989, s 20 and it was not for the local authority, or even the child, to characterise that accommodation as provided under CA 1989, s 17.[145]

Young people

20.79 Children falling within the duties at CA 1989, s 20 are entitled to accommodation until the age of 18 and thereafter (subject to certain conditions) to the benefits of the amendments to CA 1989 made by the Children (Leaving Care) Act 2000 and the regulations and guidance made under CA 1989. As the child approaches 18, the social services authority must prepare a pathway plan assessing the child's need for advice, assistance and support both before and after the authority ceases to look after the child.[146] The social services authority must also provide a personal adviser and pay for certain education-related expenses.[147] The social services authority continues to be under this obligation until the child reaches 21. Precisely because these young people, who have been in the care of the social services, are owed continuing duties as care-leavers they are not entitled to priority need under the provisions of HA 1996, Part 7 simply by virtue of their age.[148]

---

[141] *R (A) v Croydon London Borough Council, R (M) v Lambeth London Borough Council* [2009] UKSC 8, [2009] 1 WLR 2557, SC.

[142] *R (Berhe) v Hillingdon London Borough Council* [2003] EWHC 2075 (Admin), [2004] 1 FLR 439, Admin Ct; and *R (W) v Essex County Council* [2003] EWHC 3175 (Admin), [2003] All ER (D) 402 (Dec).

[143] See **13.125** and **20.79**.

[144] [2007] EWHC 1082 (Admin), [2007] 2 FCR 378, Admin Ct. See also *R (S) v Sutton London Borough Council* [2007] EWCA Civ 790, (2007) September *Legal Action*, p 19, CA.

[145] See also *R (LW) v North Lincolnshire Council* [2008] EWHC 2299 (Admin), [2008] 2 FLR 2150, Admin Ct.

[146] CA 1989, s 23E.

[147] CA 1989, ss 23C–23D.

[148] See **13.107–13.143** for English Priority Need Order; and see **13.175–13.184** for Welsh Priority Need Order.

20.80 There are no restrictions on the grounds of immigration status to these services provided to young people.[149]

Performing obligations under the Children Act 1989

20.81 Once a social services authority has identified a child's need for accommodation and has either acknowledged a duty to provide it (under CA 1989, s 20) or decided to exercise a power to provide it (under CA 1989, s 17) the crucial next step is to find that accommodation. The social services authority is most unlikely to have units of residential accommodation simply standing ready to meet demand.

20.82 Where what is needed is ordinary housing provision, the social services authority (or department) needs to be able to call upon others. Co-operation can be expected from the local housing authority (or department) as a result of the statutory requirement upon local housing authorities to assist, on request.[150] Similar expectations as to co-operation are imposed on local registered social landlords (RSLs), not least by the requirements of their regulatory body (formerly the Housing Corporation).[151] Beyond assistance from local housing authorities and RSLs, a social services authority will either need to pay for housing itself (by purchase or renting from the private sector) or help to finance the acquisition by the child, or his or her family, of suitable accommodation, usually by assisting with a deposit and rent guarantee.

DISPLACED OCCUPIERS

20.83 Quite apart from the requirements of HA 1996, Parts 6 and 7, local housing authorities can be required, in certain circumstances, to provide accommodation to existing tenants, or owner-occupiers who are faced with loss of their homes.

20.84 If the local housing authority is the landlord of a secure tenant, and is bringing possession proceedings against that tenant under statutory grounds 9–16 inclusive,[152] it must make suitable alternative accommodation available for the tenant and his or her family in order to obtain an order for possession from the court. The accommodation need not be provided by that, or any, local housing authority landlord; it may be provided by an RSL or even by a private landlord on an assured tenancy. What is 'suitable' accommodation for these purposes is determined by Sch 2, Part 4 of the Housing Act 1985. If no suitable accommodation is available from another provider, the local housing authority itself will have to provide the accommodation if it wishes to obtain possession.

---

[149] *R (Binomughisa) v Southwark London Borough Council* [2006] EWHC 2254 (Admin), [2007] 1 FLR 916.
[150] CA 1989, s 27.
[151] See English Code, Annex 5.
[152] Housing Act 1985, Sch 2.

20.85 More generally, where any person is 'displaced from residential accommodation' as a result of a local housing authority compulsorily purchasing land, making a housing order or making improvements to or redeveloping land, the local housing authority will be under a duty to provide suitable alternative residential accommodation on reasonable terms, if no such accommodation is otherwise available to the person displaced.[153] That duty does not require the local housing authority to put the displaced person to the top of its allocation scheme, thereby achieving priority over those who may have been waiting some considerable time. The provision of temporary accommodation until more permanent housing becomes available is sufficient to comply with the duty.[154] In order to give local housing authorities maximum flexibility, suitable alternative accommodation provided under this duty does not constitute an 'allocation', and the local housing authority does not have to comply with the requirements of HA 1996, Part 6 or its own allocation scheme.[155]

DEFECTIVE DWELLING-HOUSES

20.86 Special statutory provision is made for the re-housing of those who currently occupy, but need to leave, defective homes which were purchased from local housing authorities under right-to-buy arrangements. Local housing authorities have to take responsibility for those defective dwelling-houses in their areas,[156] including the re-purchase of a defective dwelling-house where an individual is entitled to that assistance.[157] Where such a property is occupied, the local housing authority will then become subject to housing obligations towards that occupier. If the property is occupied by its owner or by a statutory Rent Act 1977 tenant, the local housing authority is required to grant the occupier a secure tenancy of that property or, if the dwelling-house is not safe for occupation or the local housing authority intends to demolish or reconstruct it within a reasonable time, a different property.[158] If the property is occupied by a contractual tenant, who is either protected under the Rent Act 1977 or an assured tenant protected by the Housing Act 1988, the local housing authority acquires the landlord's interest under the tenancy and the status of the tenancy changes to that of a secure tenancy.[159] Again, if there is to be reconstruction or the house is unsafe, the tenant must be re-housed.

---

[153] Land Compensation Act 1973, s 39(1).

[154] *R v Bristol Corporation ex p Hendy* [1974] 1 All ER 1047, CA; *R v East Hertfordshire District Council ex p Smith* (1990) 23 HLR 26, CA.

[155] Allocation of Housing (England) Regulations 2002, SI 2002/3264, reg 3(2); and Allocation of Housing (Wales) Regulations 2003, SI 2003/239 (W 36), reg 3(a), both made under HA 1996, s 160(4). See also **1.26**.

[156] Housing Act 1985, Part XVI, 'Assistance for Owners of Defective Housing'.

[157] Housing Act 1985, ss 547–553 and Sch 20.

[158] These provisions only apply if the occupier makes a written request for the grant of a tenancy: Housing Act 1985, ss 554–557.

[159] Housing Act 1985, s 553.

20.87 The grant of a secure tenancy to a former owner-occupier or statutory tenant in these circumstances does not constitute an 'allocation' for the purposes of HA 1996, Part 6, and so the local housing authority is not obliged to offer the accommodation to those applicants entitled to reasonable preference under the statute or its allocation scheme.[160]

HELP WITH HOUSING UNDER THE HUMAN RIGHTS ACT 1998

20.88 Since 2 October 2000, all local housing authorities, along with all other public authorities, have had to refrain from acting in a way which is incompatible with the main provisions of the European Convention on Human Rights. RSLs may constitute public authorities for the purposes of allocating and terminating tenancies of social housing.[161]

20.89 Two Articles of the European Convention are particularly relevant to the subject of this book: an individual's absolute right not to be subjected to inhuman or degrading treatment (Art 3) and the qualified right to respect for his or her home, family life, private life and correspondence (Art 8).[162]

20.90 Each of these Articles may give an individual the right to insist on a local authority or other public authority providing adequate accommodation where he or she has none.

Article 3

20.91 For a breach of Art 3 of the European Convention to be made out, there must be either:

'... ill-treatment that attains a minimum level of severity and involves actual bodily injury or intense physical or mental suffering',

or treatment that:

'... humiliates or debases an individual showing lack of respect for, or diminishing, his or her human dignity or arouses feelings of fear, anguish or inferiority capable of breaking an individual's moral and physical resistance.'[163]

20.92 If the failure to provide accommodation would reduce an individual to this condition, then public authorities may have to take measures to avoid that situation arising.[164]

---

[160] SI 2003/3264, reg 3(3); SI 2003/239, reg 3(b), both made under HA 1996, s 160(4).
[161] *R (Weaver) v London & Quadrant Housing Trust* [2009] EWCA Civ 587, [2009] HOR 40, CA.
[162] Human Rights Act 1998, s 6 and Sch 1.
[163] *Pretty v UK* (2002) 35 EHRR 1, ECHR.
[164] But see **20.96**.

20.93 Prior to the implementation of the Human Rights Act 1998, the European Court of Human Rights considered the application of Art 3 in the case of a homeless person who was entitled to work and to claim benefits. He had been evicted from a night shelter due to his behaviour and had thereafter spent 14 months on the streets (essentially by his own choice). It was held that he had not demonstrated a minimum level of suffering sufficient to breach Art 3.[165]

20.94 An attempt, in *R (Bernard) v Enfield London Borough Council*,[166] to establish that the provision of grossly unsuitable temporary accommodation which failed to meet the assessed needs of a disabled woman was in breach of Art 3 was not successful.

20.95 More recently, the courts have considered the extent to which the failure of public authorities to provide shelter and subsistence can infringe Art 3 (in the context of destitute asylum-seekers).[167] It is not enough for there to be a risk, or even a real risk, of Art 3 suffering occurring; it must actually be occurring or be about to occur.[168] Physical ill health or psychological disturbance arising from a lack of a roof over the individual's head can constitute a condition that amounts to inhuman or degrading treatment.[169] Public authorities have to ask whether the entire package of deprivation is so severe that it can properly be described as inhuman or degrading treatment. The threshold of severity would, in the ordinary way, be crossed where a person deprived of subsistence and restricted from work is obliged to sleep in the street, or is seriously hungry, or is unable to sustain the most basic level of hygiene.[170]

20.96 Since local authorities, as public authorities, are subject to the obligation not to submit an individual to inhuman or degrading treatment, arguably they have a responsibility to provide accommodation to anyone in their area whose suffering is verging on being inhuman or degrading treatment.[171] It is important to note, however, that the threshold is a strict one. A person must have no access to any form of support (including welfare

---

[165] *O'Rourke v UK (Application No 39022/97)* (2001), ECHR.

[166] *R (Bernard) v Enfield London Borough Council* [2002] EWHC 2282 (Admin), (2003) 35 HLR 27, Admin Ct.

[167] *R (Limbuela) v Secretary of State for the Home Department* [2005] UKHL 66, [2006] 1 AC 396, HL.

[168] *R (Q) v Secretary of State for the Home Department* [2003] EWCA Civ 364, [2004] QB 36, CA.

[169] *R (T) v Secretary of State for the Home Department* [2003] EWCA Civ 1285, (2003) 7 CCLR 53, CA, at [17], per Kennedy LJ, referring to the condition of S, an applicant in the first instance decision.

[170] *R (Limbuela) v Secretary of State for the Home Department* [2005] UKHL 66, [2006] 1 AC 396, HL.

[171] However, in *R (Limbuela) v Secretary of State for the Home Department* [2005] UKHL 66, [2006] 1 AC 396, HL, the Secretary of State was under a statutory duty to provide support to an asylum-seeker in order to avoid a breach of his or her European Convention rights. The issue was therefore whether destitution constituted a breach of Art 3 and the House of Lords held that it did so. In *R (EW) v Secretary of State for the Home Department* [2009] EWHC 2957, (2010) January *Legal Action*, p 35, Admin Ct, at [90] Hickinbottom J said (relying on

benefits) and not be able to work, whether through physical or legal incapacity. The human rights obligation to support destitute asylum-seekers is undertaken by the Secretary of State; a local authority's obligation, therefore, would only extend to a destitute person in its area who was not entitled to asylum support or any other statutory scheme providing support, was prohibited from claiming welfare benefits, who had no access to employment, and was without any form of shelter or private means of subsistence.

Article 8

20.97   Claims centering on a public authority's obligation not to interfere with an individual's right to respect for his or her home, family, private life and correspondence under Art 8 of the European Convention have had rather more success since the introduction of the Human Rights Act 1998. Art 8:

'... concerns rights of central importance to the individual's identity, self-determination, physical and moral integrity, maintenance of relationships with others and a settled and secure place in the community.'[172]

20.98   It is well established in European human rights law that Art 8 does not contain a positive general obligation on central or local government to provide every individual with a home.[173] But where accommodation is provided by public authorities it must not be of such standard or condition as to amount to a lack of respect within Art 8. Nor must it be allowed to fall to such a standard once occupied.[174] Furthermore, if an individual is left without any accommodation, with the result that his or her family is fractured or private life is adversely affected, Art 8 may be engaged. This possibility has already been explored by the European Court of Human Rights in relation to a severely disabled individual.[175]

20.99   The conditions of the accommodation provided by the local authority in *R (Bernard) v Enfield London Borough Council*[176] were sufficiently demeaning to breach the applicant's right to respect for her private and family life under Art 8. However, in *R (Anufrijeva) v Southwark London Borough Council*,[177] a social services authority was found not to have interfered with an elderly woman's right to respect for her home, or for her family and private life, by virtue of the nature of temporary accommodation it had provided. The

---

R (Limbuela)) that Art 3 does 'not require a member state to provide accommodation for all within its jurisdiction, nor provide a minimum standard of living ... and it required more than a state's passivity for breach'.

172   *Connors v UK* [2004] HLR 52, ECHR, at 82.
173   See, amongst others, *Marzari v Italy* [1999] 28 EHRR CD 175, ECHR; *O'Rourke v UK* (*Application No 00039022/97*), ECHR.
174   *Lee v Leeds City Council* [2002] 1 WLR 1488, [2002] HLR 17, CA.
175   *Marzari v Italy* [1999] 28 EHRR CD 175, ECHR.
176   *R (Bernard) v Enfield London Borough Council* [2002] EWHC Admin 2282, (2003) 35 HLR 27, Admin Ct.
177   *R (Anufrijeva) v Southwark London Borough Council* [2003] EWCA Civ 1406, [2004] 2 WLR 603, CA.

court held that before a public authority could be held to have failed to respect an applicant's private or family life, there had to be an element of culpability, involving (at the very least) knowledge by the public authority that the applicant's private or family life was at risk.

Chapter 21

CONTRACTING OUT OF HOMELESSNESS AND ALLOCATION FUNCTIONS

INTRODUCTION

21.1 The major duties and powers discussed in this book are those which are the responsibility of local housing authorities under the provisions of the Housing Act 1996 (HA 1996), Parts 6 ('Allocation of Housing Accommodation') and 7 ('Homelessness'). Those local housing authorities must ensure that:

(1) they comply with the law;

(2) they perform those duties required by HA 1996; and

(3) they lawfully exercise the powers given to them by HA 1996.

21.2 If a local housing authority refuses to carry out its duties or to exercise its powers, or if there is a dispute as to the lawfulness of how it has carried out a duty or exercised a power, it will be the local housing authority itself that is answerable to the courts or the Local Government Ombudsmen (LGO).[1] The local housing authority cannot escape that responsibility by reference to, or reliance upon, some other body.

THE MOVE TOWARDS CONTRACTING OUT

21.3 A local housing authority is free to decide for itself how it wishes to organise the performance of its duties and the exercise of its powers. Traditionally, staff directly employed by the local housing authority would carry out those functions on behalf of the local housing authority.

21.4 In recent years, however, more and more local housing authorities have chosen to employ private contractors, frequently local registered social landlords (RSLs), to carry out those functions for them. Even when they engage contractors, local housing authorities remain responsible for those contractors' actions and also remain responsible to applicants for homelessness assistance, and to applicants for social housing, for any lapses made either by their own staff or by the contractors' staff. Therefore, in order to protect their position, local housing authorities are sensibly advised to build into the contracts between themselves and the private contractors robust penalty and escape clauses, in case of poor performance by the contractors.[2] So assured, more and more local housing authorities have been contracting out their homelessness and allocation functions.

---

[1]   In Wales to the Public Services Ombudsman for Wales (www.ombudsman-wales.org.uk).

[2]   *Homelessness Code of Guidance for Local Authorities* (Communities and Local Government, Department of Education and Skills, Department of Health, July 2006) (English Homelessness Code), para 21.10; *Code of Guidance for Local Housing Authorities on Allocation of Accommodation and Homelessness for Wales* (National Assembly for Wales, April 2003) (Welsh Code), Annex 21.

THE RELEVANCE OF STOCK TRANSFER

21.5 Over 150 local housing authorities have also chosen (with the consent of their tenants and the approval of the Secretary of State) to transfer all of their own housing stock to RSLs.[3] The law and guidance governing stock transfer itself is complex and outside the scope of this book. However, three particular points arise concerning homelessness and allocation of social housing following such a stock transfer.

21.6 *First*, even though a local housing authority no longer has any housing stock, and therefore cannot grant secure or introductory tenancies, it is still responsible for receiving and determining applications for homelessness assistance and for deciding (in response to an application for an allocation) who is to be nominated to RSLs for the granting of any assured tenancies (including nominations to any landlords who have acquired the local housing authority's own stock). It must, therefore, still have an allocation scheme and make those nominations in accordance with that scheme.

21.7 *Second,* some local housing authorities, having transferred the whole of their housing stock, have also contracted out their homelessness and/or allocation functions, usually to the transferee RSL. Applicants may find that, for all intents and purposes, they appear to be dealing exclusively with staff working for an RSL, from the moment that they apply (for homelessness assistance or under the local housing authority's allocation scheme), up to receiving an offer of accommodation from that same RSL. Despite that appearance, decisions that are made under one of the local housing authority's statutory functions remain the responsibility of the local housing authority.

21.8 *Third*, the statutory duties on an RSL to co-operate with a local housing authority from which it has acquired housing stock[4] do not mean that the purchasing RSL is itself obliged to operate an allocation scheme in the same terms as that which would have been operated by the local housing authority. An RSL will normally be required by the terms of the stock transfer contract to ensure that a certain proportion of its housing stock is available for the local housing authority to nominate applicants to. However, the RSL may also operate its own policies governing which applicants it will accept in relation to the rest of its stock.[5]

---

[3]   H Pawson et al *The impacts of housing stock transfers in urban Britain* (Joseph Rowntree Press, 2009); as at July 2008 there had been over 270 housing stock transfers (www.communities.gov. uk).

[4]   For example, Housing Act 1996, s 213.

[5]   English Homelessness Code, Annex 5. Paragraph 9 of Annex 5 refers to RSLs being required to offer at least 50% of vacancies in their stock to local housing authority nominations. This is out of date. The guidance in the current Regulatory Code refers to making 'a proportion of their stock' available, to such extent as is reasonable in the circumstances (para 3.6c of the *Housing Corporation Regulatory Code and Guidance 2005*, at www.housingcorp.gov.uk/server/ show/nav.493). Of course, many local housing authorities will make provision for a certain proportion, often 50%, of RSL stock to be made available to them in their contractual arrangements. See **6.31–6.34**.

THE DIFFERENT LEGAL STRUCTURES GOVERNING CONTRACTING OUT

21.9 When local housing authorities deliver their own homelessness and allocation services, they do so under HA 1996, Parts 6 and 7 and the Codes of Guidance issued by the Secretary of State and the Welsh Assembly Government pursuant to those statutory provisions. Guidance on contracting out (and stock transfer) is also available to local housing authorities from the Department of Communities and Local Government[6] and the Audit Commission.[7] The legal basis for contracting out to any contractor is explained below under sub-headings that deal separately with allocation and homelessness functions. In practice, most of the contractors engaged by local housing authorities (for either or both of the functions) are RSLs.

21.10 RSLs do not have the same statutory powers and duties as local housing authorities. They are simply required by HA 1996 to 'co-operate' in the delivery of the local housing authority's homelessness and allocation functions 'to such extent as is reasonable in the circumstances', if requested to do so by the local housing authority.[8] That requirement is amplified by the Housing Corporation's Regulatory Code, which emphasises that RSLs should be working with local housing authorities to enable the local housing authorities' statutory duties to be fulfilled. In particular, the guidance provides that RSLs should make a proportion of their vacancies available for nomination by their local housing authorities.[9] We refer in this chapter to statutory guidance issued by the Housing Corporation, albeit that that organisation closed down on 1 November 2008. This is because until April 2010 that guidance remains applicable (statutory responsible for it having passed, in England, to the Tenant Services Authority).[10] Likewise, for RSLs operating in Wales, the statuory guidance contained in the Welsh Assembly Government's *Regulatory Code for Housing Associations Registered in Wales*[11] will remain applicable until new regulatory arrangements are established later in 2010.[12]

21.11 Whether or not the local housing authority has disposed of its stock, if it has contracted out the HA 1996, Part 6 and/or HA 1996, Part 7 functions, the instrument regulating each RSL's (or other contractor's) relationship with the local housing authority is the contract by which the RSL or other contractor agrees to deliver the local housing authority's homelessness or allocation service (or both) at a price. Again, guidance is provided by government and the Housing Corporation on the contents of that contract,

---

6   http://www.communities.gov.uk.
7   http://www.audit-commission.gov.uk/.
8   HA 1996, ss 170 and 213(1).
9   Paragraph 3.6c of the *Housing Corporation Regulatory Code and Guidance 2005*, at www.housingcorp.gov.uk/server/show/nav.493. See **6.31–6.34**.
10   http://www.tenantservicesauthority.org/.
11   Published by the Welsh Assembly Government in March 2006, at http://wales.gov.uk/topics/housingandcommunity/housing/publications/regulatorycodehas?lang=en.
12   See **6.2–6.3** and **6.83–6.90**.

particularly where it forms part of an overall arrangement for stock transfer.[13] Clearly, the terms of the contract will govern the standard of the service to be provided and, in cases of stock transfer, the extent to which the RSL must make its vacancies available for nomination by the local housing authority.

21.12   Where, exceptionally, the local housing authority contracts out its HA 1996, Part 6 or Part 7 functions to another local authority, the legal basis for that process is given by the Local Government Act 1972, s 101 and the exact scope of the functions contracted out will be shown in the contract itself.

21.13   Any complaints by members of the public about the services provided by contractors acting on behalf of local housing authorities are made against the local housing authorities themselves, not the contractors. Accordingly, any member of the public wishing to complain should use first the local housing authority's complaints procedure[14] and then complain to the Local Government Ombudsmen.[15]

HOMELESSNESS (HOUSING ACT 1996, PART 7)

The statutory basis governing contracting out of homelessness functions

Background to the present arrangements

21.14   As a matter of strict law, a local housing authority consists only of its elected councillors. In practice, no local housing authority, whatever its size, expects the majority of its functions (except general policy-making) to be carried out by its elected councillors. The Local Government Act 1972 permits the elected councillors to delegate the performance of the local housing authority's duties to its own officers (staff employed directly by the local housing authority) and to other local authorities.[16]

21.15   In the homelessness context, by 1985 the statutory regime recognised a form of quasi-delegation.[17] The legislation provided that where a local housing authority requested a registered housing association to assist it with the

---

13   See *Housing Allocation, Homelessness and Stock Transfer: A guide to key issues* (ODPM, 2004), at www.communities.gov.uk/publications/housing/housingallocationhomelessness; *Housing Transfer Manual* (ODPM, 2005), at www.communities.gov.uk/publications/housing/housingtransfermanual; *Housing after Transfer: the Local Authority Role*, (Audit Commission, 2002), at www.audit-commission.gov.uk/reports/NATIONAL-REPORT.asp?CategoryID=&ProdID=2E04A056-F229-409F-BC87-9C27283356B0.

14   See **19.238–19.240**.

15   See **19.241–19.245**. Note that a local housing authority was found guilty of serious maladministration by a Local Government Ombudsman when a housing association to whom it had contracted out some of its homelessness responsibilities advised an applicant that complaints should be made to the Independent Housing Ombudsman and not to the Local Government Ombudsman (Local Government Ombudsman 05/B/08409).

16   Local Government Act 1972, s 101.

17   Housing Act 1985, s 72, repealed by HA 1996, s 227, Sch 19 (with effect from 20 January 1997).

discharge of its homelessness functions, the association should co-operate in rendering such assistance as was reasonable in the circumstances.

21.16 However, in recent years, many local housing authorities have actually employed either RSLs or other private contractors to assist with the performance of their duties (and some have gone so far as to transfer the whole or part of their housing stock to the same or different contractors).[18]

21.17 In 1994 and 1995, the High Court considered the extent to which a local housing authority could contract out its homelessness functions. In *R v West Dorset District Council and West Dorset Housing Association ex p Gerrard*,[19] the local housing authority had transferred all its stock to the housing association with which it also contracted for the provision of a homelessness advice and investigation service. On receipt of a summary report from the association, a local housing authority officer decided that the applicant in that case was not homeless. A deputy High Court judge held that the local housing authority remained responsible for taking 'an active and dominant part in the investigative process' even after contracting out. Since the local housing authority had not itself carried out any part of the inquiries into the applicant's application for homelessness assistance (and, in addition, relevant representations made by the applicant's solicitor had not been brought to the officer's attention), the decision was quashed. Indeed, the whole administration of the local housing authority's homelessness duties was held to be unlawful. A subsequent appeal against that judgment was dismissed by consent in the Court of Appeal.

21.18 Some 10 months later, another deputy High Court judge considered the same issue in *R v Hertsmere Borough Council ex p Woolgar*.[20] That local housing authority had transferred its stock to two housing associations. A different decision (the suitability of accommodation offered) was under scrutiny, but the judge held that the same statutory framework applied. He went on to consider Housing Act 1985, s 72,[21] the guidance offered in the Code,[22] and government guidelines on transfer of housing stock,[23] all of which clearly envisaged that:

- both the homelessness functions and a local housing authority's housing stock could be transferred;

- that the local housing authority should retain responsibility for decisions made under its homelessness duties; and

---

18 Governed by separate statutory powers: see **21.36–21.39**.
19 (1995) 27 HLR 150, QBD.
20 (1995) 27 HLR 703, QBD.
21 See **21.15**.
22 At that time Department of Environment's *Code of Guidance*, para 11.7.
23 *Large Scale Voluntary Transfers Guidelines* (Department of the Environment, December 1993).

• that the local housing authority should retain at least some nomination rights to its former housing.

21.19 Having considered those materials, he held that the decision in *Gerrard* had been made without any scrutiny of the government's guidelines and was therefore made *per incuriam*.[24] As a result, Hertsmere Borough Council's scheme for delivering its homelessness duties, which amounted to its homelessness functions being carried out by an RSL and the accommodation offered being provided by that same landlord, was held to be lawful.

The modern framework

21.20 The judicial uncertainty created by these two conflicting decisions was soon resolved by Parliament. The modern legislative framework permitting a local housing authority to contract out its homelessness functions is found in the Deregulation and Contracting Out Act 1994, s 70. Under that Act, the Secretary of State has made the Local Authorities (Contracting Out of Allocation of Housing and Homelessness Functions) Order 1996.[25] Local housing authorities are now permitted to contract out the bulk of their homelessness functions.[26]

21.21 Particular conditions related to the carrying out of those functions can be (and should be) included in the contract itself, so that standards of performance are prescribed. The Deregulation and Contracting Out Act 1994 provides that the contract cannot be for a period of more than 10 years, and may be for any shorter period.[27] The contract must also provide that it can be revoked at any time by the Minister or by the local housing authority.[28] The local housing authority remains responsible for any acts or omissions made by the contractor in the performance of the local housing authority's homelessness functions, unless the contractor is in breach of the conditions specified in the contract or the contractor has committed a criminal offence.

21.22 In *Runa Begum v Tower Hamlets London Borough Council*,[29] the House of Lords considered whether such a contractor could be considered 'independent' of the local housing authority for the purposes of the European Convention on Human Rights, Art 6(1).[30] If contractors were held to be 'independent' for those purposes, review decisions that were being taken by

---

[24] Without awareness of authority that might have made a difference to the court's decision.

[25] SI 1996/3205. See also English Homelessness Code, chapter 21; Welsh Code, Annex 21 for guidance.

[26] Except those listed at **21.23**.

[27] Deregulation and Contracting Out Act 1994, s 69(5)(a).

[28] Deregulation and Contracting Out Act 1994, s 69(5)(b).

[29] *Runa Begum v Tower Hamlets London Borough Council* [2003] UKHL 5, [2003] 2 AC 430, HL.

[30] Which provides that civil rights are to be determined by a body independent of the parties. Recently, in February 2010, the Supreme Court decided that decision-making on applications for homelessness assistance does not involve a determination of an applicant's 'civil rights' and so Art 6(1) does not apply (*Tomlinson & others v Birmingham City Council* [2010] UKSC 8, SC).

officers employed by the local housing authority (who were obviously not independent) could, instead, be taken by contracted individuals or organisations in order to obtain the necessary measure of independence. The Lords held that a contractor, whose services could be dispensed with, was probably no more independent than an officer employed directly by the local housing authority. However, Lord Bingham, in an obiter paragraph, added that he had very considerable doubt whether the resolution of applications for review fell within a local housing authority's relevant functions and therefore could be contracted out at all.[31] Since then, the Court of Appeal has held that the making of review decisions is a function that can be contracted by a local housing authority in *De-Winter Heald v Brent London Borough Council*.[32]

21.23 The local housing authority may *not* contract out four specified functions:

(1)   its power to provide finance to a person or organisation so that housing advice and information is provided on the local housing authority's behalf;[33]

(2)   its power to assist such a person or organisation by providing premises, furniture, or its own housing staff;[34]

(3)   its power to finance, or provide premises, furniture or the services of its staff, to a voluntary organisation concerned with homelessness or matters relating to homelessness;[35]

(4)   its obligation to render such assistance as is reasonable if asked by another local housing authority to assist it in the discharge of that local housing authority's HA 1996, Part 7 functions.[36]

Contracting to use a contractor's accommodation for the homeless

21.24 Different statutory provisions govern a local housing authority's ability to use accommodation from other sectors in order to perform its HA 1996, Part 7 duties to applicants for homelessness assistance. As an alternative to providing the applicant with its own accommodation, the HA 1996, Part 7[37] permits a local housing authority to perform its duty to provide accommodation for an applicant and members of his or her household, by securing that the applicant obtains suitable accommodation 'from some other person' or, even, merely by 'giving him such advice and assistance as will secure

---

[31]   [2003] UKHL 5, [2003] 2 AC 430, HL, at [10], per Lord Bingham.
[32]   [2009] EWCA Civ 930, (2009) October *Legal Action*, p 26, CA.
[33]   HA 1996, s 179(2); Local Authorities (Contracting Out of Allocation of Housing and Homelessness Functions) Order 1996, SI 1996/3205, art 3 and Sch 2.
[34]   HA 1996, s 179(3); SI 1996/3205, art 3 and Sch 2.
[35]   HA 1996, s 180; SI 1996/3205, art 3 and Sch 2.
[36]   HA 1996, s 213; SI 1996/3205, art 3 and Sch 2.
[37]   HA 1996, s 206.

that suitable accommodation is available from some other person'.[38] If the latter course is taken, then the local housing authority must ensure that the advice and assistance does actually secure that suitable accommodation is obtained. If not, the local housing authority's duty to secure accommodation from its own stock or from some other person remains.[39] These provisions have given local housing authorities considerable flexibility to arrange for accommodation for the homeless to be supplied, under contract, by RSLs and other private contractors.

21.25 The ability to secure accommodation 'from some other person' allows a local housing authority to arrange for a private landlord or RSL to grant a tenancy directly to an applicant.[40] The English Homelessness Code recommends that accommodation obtained from a private landlord or RSL for the provision of 'temporary' accommodation (usually the main housing duty at HA 1996, s 193(2)) should, if possible, be turned into 'settled' accommodation by negotiating with the landlord to offer the applicant an assured shorthold tenancy of the accommodation as a 'qualifying offer'.[41]

Ensuring that the private contractor maintains the appropriate level of service

21.26 Given that the local housing authority remains responsible for the calibre and correctness of its homelessness decisions, even when the inquiries and recommendations leading to those decisions have been made by a private contractor, it is vital for a local housing authority to be able to rely upon the quality of the service provided by the contractor. That safeguard should be contained in the contract between the local housing authority and the contractor. The Audit Commission notes (in the context of stock transfer):

> '... few [authorities] have experience of contracting out these services, and there is rarely time during the hectic [stock] transfer process to review them, decide their best location and draw up a good contract. As a result, some contracts are poorly written or difficult to monitor. Attention can focus on "maintaining" minimum service rather than improvement.'[42]

21.27 The Audit Commission recommends that, before a decision to contract out the service is made, the local housing authority should:

(1)   undertake a scrutiny report or best value review;

(2)   consult users;

---

[38]   HA 1996, s 206(1)(b) and (c).
[39]   See **18.7**.
[40]   HA 1996, s 206(1)(b) and see *R (on the application of Khatun) v Newham London Borough Council* [2004] EWCA Civ 55, [2004] HLR 29, CA, at [91], per Laws LJ.
[41]   English Homelessness Code, paras 16.39–16.43. See **17.92–17.97**.
[42]   *Housing after Transfer, the Local Authority Role* (The Audit Commission, 2002), at www.audit-commission.gov.uk, chapter 3, para 64.

(3)   consider more than one provider; and

(4)   take into account the impact that contracting out the service will have on retained housing services.

21.28 The contract should include targets for improvements in the service, quality control and workable monitoring arrangements.[43]

21.29 The Office of the Deputy Prime Minister (ODPM)[44] provided non-statutory guidance in *Housing Allocation, Homelessness and Stock Transfer: A guide to key issues*.[45] Particular guidance is provided on drafting the contract. Detailed service standards, monitoring of those standards, performance indicators and targets need to be specified, along with a procedure for reviewing and altering the contract. Power should be reserved for the local housing authority to terminate the contract for poor performance.

ALLOCATION OF ACCOMMODATION (HOUSING ACT 1996, PART 6)

21.30 The same statutory framework applies to the contracting out of the functions of the allocation of social housing. The Local Authorities (Contracting Out of Allocation of Housing and Homelessness Functions) Order 1996, made by the Secretary of State under Deregulation and Contracting Out Act 1994, s 70, permits local housing authorities to contract out the bulk of their functions involved in the allocation of social housing under HA 1996, Part 6. Many local housing authorities have disposed of the whole of their housing stock to local RSLs, so that the local housing authority's allocations are made by nomination to RSLs for assured tenancies.

21.31 The overall policy of the allocation scheme is for the local housing authority to decide, subject to complying with HA 1996, Part 6, the regulations and the Code. The House of Lords has noted that '[h]ousing allocation policy is a difficult exercise which requires not only social and political sensitivity and judgment, but also local expertise and knowledge'.[46] The overall policy decisions are political decisions.

21.32 It follows that the local housing authority is responsible for general policy decisions on:

---

[43]   *Housing after Transfer, the Local Authority Role* (The Audit Commission, 2002), at www.audit-commission.gov.uk, chapter 3.

[44]   At that time the government department responsible for housing and homelessness.

[45]   *Housing Allocation, Homelessness and Stock Transfer: A guide to key issues* (ODPM, January 2004), at www.communities.gov.uk/publications/housing/housingallocationhomelessness.

[46]   *Ahmad v Newham London Borough Council* [2009] UKHL 14, (2009) April *Legal Action*, p 21, HL, at [47], per Lord Neuberger.

(1)   whether or not it will offer 'choice' in its allocation scheme, or provide applicants with the opportunity to express preferences;[47]

(2)   whether it will frame the scheme so as to give additional preferences within the reasonable preference categories and, if so, on what criteria;[48]

(3)   on what principles it will prioritise different applicants within the reasonable preference categories;[49] and

(4)   whether it will provide for the allocation of accommodation to persons of a particular description and, if so, what accommodation, and to whom.[50]

Functions

21.33   Having drawn up its allocation scheme, the local housing authority may contract out nearly all of its *functions* under HA 1996, Part 6 to a contractor. The contractor's staff, therefore, could receive an application, ensure that the applicant is given the information to which he or she is entitled, provide advice and assistance with the making of an application, process the application, make any decisions required to be made in respect of the application and, in accordance with the policy, arrange for the grant of a secure or introductory tenancy, or nominate the applicant to an RSL for an assured tenancy. At each stage the contractor will be taking the practical steps, but the local housing authority remains liable for the decisions.

21.34   The local housing authority cannot contract out the duties:

(1)   to determine the terms of its allocation scheme;

(2)   to allocate in accordance with that scheme; and

(3)   to make the scheme available for inspection.[51]

21.35   If the contractor's staff fail to treat an applicant in accordance with the local housing authority's scheme, it is the local housing authority that will be answerable for that failure.

Stock transfers and nominations to RSLs[52]

21.36   Where a local housing authority is proposing a large scale voluntary transfer of its own stock, so that there will no longer be any council-owned

---

47   HA 1996, s 167(2E).
48   HA 1996, s 167(2).
49   HA 1996, s 167(2).
50   HA 1996, s 167(2E).
51   HA 1996, s 167 (in so far as it relates to adopting or altering an allocation scheme and to consulting RSLs), and s 168(2); SI 1996/3205, art 2 and Sch 1.
52   See Chapter 6 of this book.

accommodation in its district, any future allocation made under its allocation scheme will be by way of a nomination to an RSL for an assured tenancy. In order to ensure that it can continue to comply with its statutory duty to maintain an allocation scheme, and to allocate accommodation, the local housing authority must ensure that the purchasing RSL(s) will accept its nominations.

21.37 There are statutory duties, contractual obligations and Housing Corporation and government guidance requiring that RSLs co-operate with local housing authorities to ensure that a certain amount of their available accommodation is provided to people nominated by local housing authorities. If a local housing authority requests that an RSL co-operates with it by offering accommodation to people on the local housing authority's allocation scheme, the RSL is under a statutory duty to co-operate 'to such extent as is reasonable in the circumstances'.[53] In addition, when the local housing authority has transferred its own stock to the RSL, after the process of government approval, consultation and balloting, it will have done so in a contract. The local housing authority should ensure that the terms of the contract provide that the RSL will make a certain proportion of its empty properties available for people nominated by the local housing authority under its allocation scheme.[54] Any proposed transfer that does not include a contractual obligation on the RSL to make a specified proportion of empty accommodation available for allocation is unlikely to receive government approval. In addition, the Housing Corporation expected RSLs to make a reasonable proportion of their stock available for local housing authority nominations and for temporary accommodation for homelessness applicants.[55]

21.38 RSLs, including stock transfer associations, can therefore operate quotas under which a proportion (which can be up to 100%) of their vacancies will be allocated on the basis of the local housing authority's nominations. The remaining part of their vacancies will be allocated by the RSL itself, either to its own tenants seeking transfers or to people who have applied directly to the RSL for accommodation.

21.39 Generally, if an RSL gives over a proportion of its empty stock to local housing authority nominations, it should not impose its own conditions on the type of applicant nominated, and should be contractually obliged to accept whoever the authority nominates. However, when it comes to the remainder of the vacancies, RSLs will make their own decisions as to who is to be offered each vacancy. Each RSL, therefore, must have its own policy governing transfer applications (from its own tenants) and any applications made to it directly rather than through the local housing authority. The Housing Corporation's Regulatory Code requires RSLs to use their housing stock only for social

---

[53]   HA 1996, s 170.

[54]   *Housing Allocation, Homelessness and Stock Transfer: A guide to key issues* (ODPM, January 2004), at www.communities.gov.uk/publications/housing/housingallocationhomelessness.

[55]   Housing Corporation *The Regulatory Code and Guidance* (August 2005), at www.housingcorp. gov.uk/server/show/nav.493.

housing purposes, to seek to offer a choice of home whilst giving reasonable preference to those with a priority housing need and to use lettings policies that are fair and reflect the diversity of their tenants and applicants.[56] They are also required to work with local housing authorities to enable them to fulfil their statutory duty to applicants for homelessness assistance, to people with priority housing need and to the vulnerable. When it comes to their own lettings policies, the Housing Corporation Regulatory Code requires RSLs to exclude only those applicants whose 'unacceptable behaviour is serious enough to make them unsuitable to be a tenant and only in circumstances that are not unlawfully discriminating', effectively applying the same test as local housing authorities must apply.[57]

---

[56]   See *Tenancy Management: Eligibility and Evictions* (Housing Corporation Regulatory Circular 2/07, April 2007) for further guidance, at www.housingcorp.gov.uk/server/show/nav.539.

[57]   Housing Corporation *The Regulatory Code and Guidance* (August 2005), at www.housingcorp. gov.uk/server/show/nav.493.

Appendix 1

ENGLAND: ALLOCATION

Housing Act 1996

1996 c 52

CONTENTS

PART 6
ALLOCATION OF HOUSING ACCOMMODATION

Introductory

Eligibility for allocation of housing accommodation

Applications for housing accommodation

The allocation scheme

Supplementary

PART 8
MISCELLANEOUS AND GENERAL PROVISIONS

General

PART 6
ALLOCATION OF HOUSING ACCOMMODATION
Introductory
159 Allocation of housing accommodation

(1) A local housing authority shall comply with the provisions of this Part in allocating housing accommodation.

(2) For the purposes of this Part a local housing authority allocate housing accommodation when they –

  (a) select a person to be a secure or introductory tenant of housing accommodation held by them,
  (b) nominate a person to be a secure or introductory tenant of housing accommodation held by another person, or
  (c) nominate a person to be an assured tenant of housing accommodation held by a registered social landlord.

(3) The reference in subsection (2)(a) to selecting a person to be a secure tenant includes deciding to exercise any power to notify an existing tenant or licensee that his tenancy or licence is to be a secure tenancy.

(4) The references in subsection (2)(b) and (c) to nominating a person include nominating a person in pursuance of any arrangements (whether legally enforceable or not) to require that housing accommodation, or a specified amount of housing accommodation, is made available to a person or one of a number of persons nominated by the authority.

[(5) The provisions of this Part do not apply to an allocation of housing accommodation to a person who is already a secure or introductory tenant unless the allocation involves a transfer of housing accommodation for that person and is made on his application.

(6) ...]¹

(7) Subject to the provisions of this Part, a local housing authority may allocate housing accommodation in such manner as they consider appropriate.

AMENDMENT

¹ Sub-sections substituted: Homelessness Act 2002, s 13.

160 Cases where provisions about allocation do not apply

(1) The provisions of this Part about the allocation of housing accommodation do not apply in the following cases.

(2) They do not apply where a secure tenancy –

  (a) vests under section 89 of the Housing Act 1985 (succession to periodic secure tenancy on death of tenant),
  (b) remains a secure tenancy by virtue of section 90 of that Act (devolution of term certain of secure tenancy on death of tenant),

    (c)   is assigned under section 92 of that Act (assignment of secure tenancy by way of exchange),

    (d)   is assigned to a person who would be qualified to succeed the secure tenant if the secure tenant died immediately before the assignment, or

    (e)   vests or is otherwise disposed of in pursuance of an order made under –

        (i)   section 24 of the Matrimonial Causes Act 1973 (property adjustment orders in connection with matrimonial proceedings),

        (ii)   section 17(1) of the Matrimonial and Family Proceedings Act 1984 (property adjustment orders after overseas divorce, &c), ...[1]

        (iii)   paragraph 1 of Schedule 1 to the Children Act 1989 (orders for financial relief against parents)[, or

        (iv)   Part 2 of Schedule 5, or paragraph 9(2) or (3) of Schedule 7, to the Civil Partnership Act 2004 (property adjustment orders in connection with civil partnership proceedings or after overseas dissolution of civil partnership, etc)][2].

(3) They do not apply where an introductory tenancy –

    (a)   becomes a secure tenancy on ceasing to be an introductory tenancy,

    (b)   vests under section 133(2) (succession to introductory tenancy on death of tenant),

    (c)   is assigned to a person who would be qualified to succeed the introductory tenant if the introductory tenant died immediately before the assignment, or

    (d)   vests or is otherwise disposed of in pursuance of an order made under –

        (i)   section 24 of the Matrimonial Causes Act 1973 (property adjustment orders in connection with matrimonial proceedings),

        (ii)   section 17(1) of the Matrimonial and Family Proceedings Act 1984 (property adjustment orders after overseas divorce, &c), ...[3]

        (iii)   paragraph 1 of Schedule 1 to the Children Act 1989 (orders for financial relief against parents)[, or

        (iv)   Part 2 of Schedule 5, or paragraph 9(2) or (3) of Schedule 7, to the Civil Partnership Act 2004 (property adjustment orders in connection with civil partnership proceedings or after overseas dissolution of civil partnership, etc)][4].

(4) They do not apply in such other cases as the Secretary of State may prescribe by regulations.

(5) The regulations may be framed so as to make the exclusion of the provisions of this Part about the allocation of housing accommodation subject to such restrictions or conditions as may be specified.

In particular, those provisions may be excluded –

    (a)   in relation to specified descriptions of persons, or

(b)   in relation to housing accommodation of a specified description or a specified proportion of housing accommodation of any specified description.

AMENDMENT

[1] Word repealed: Civil Partnership Act 2004, s 261(4), Sch 30.

[2] Paragraph inserted: Civil Partnership Act 2004, s 81, Sch 8, para 60.

[3] Word repealed: Civil Partnership Act 2004, s 261(4), Sch 30.

[4] Paragraph inserted: Civil Partnership Act 2004, s 81, Sch 8, para 60.

[Eligibility for allocation of housing accommodation

160A Allocation only to eligible persons

[(1) A local housing authority shall not allocate housing accommodation –

(a)   to a person from abroad who is ineligible for an allocation of housing accommodation by virtue of subsection (3) or (5);

(b)   to a person who the authority have decided is to be treated as ineligible for such an allocation by virtue of subsection (7); or

(c)   to two or more persons jointly if any of them is a person mentioned in paragraph (a) or (b).

(2) Except as provided by subsection (1), any person may be allocated housing accommodation by a local housing authority (whether on his application or otherwise).

(3) A person subject to immigration control within the meaning of the Asylum and Immigration Act 1996 (c 49) is (subject to subsection (6)) ineligible for an allocation of housing accommodation by a local housing authority unless he is of a class prescribed by regulations made by the Secretary of State.

(4) No person who is excluded from entitlement to housing benefit by section 115 of the Immigration and Asylum Act 1999 (c 33) (exclusion from benefits) shall be included in any class prescribed under subsection (3).

(5) The Secretary of State may by regulations prescribe other classes of persons from abroad who are (subject to subsection (6)) ineligible for an allocation of housing accommodation, either in relation to local housing authorities generally or any particular local housing authority.

(6) Nothing in subsection (3) or (5) affects the eligibility of a person who is already –

(a)   a secure or introductory tenant;

(b)   an assured tenant of housing accommodation allocated to him by a local housing authority.

(7) A local housing authority may decide that an applicant is to be treated as ineligible for an allocation of housing accommodation by them if they are satisfied that –

(a) he, or a member of his household, has been guilty of unacceptable behaviour serious enough to make him unsuitable to be a tenant of the authority; and

(b) in the circumstances at the time his application is considered, he is unsuitable to be a tenant of the authority by reason of that behaviour.

(8) The only behaviour which may be regarded by the authority as unacceptable for the purposes of subsection (7)(a) is –

(a) behaviour of the person concerned which would (if he were a secure tenant of the authority) entitle the authority to a possession order under section 84 of the Housing Act 1985 (c 68) on any ground mentioned in Part 1 of Schedule 2 to that Act (other than ground 8); or

(b) behaviour of a member of his household which would (if he were a person residing with a secure tenant of the authority) entitle the authority to such a possession order.

(9) If a local housing authority decide that an applicant for housing accommodation –

(a) is ineligible for an allocation by them by virtue of subsection (3) or (5); or

(b) is to be treated as ineligible for such an allocation by virtue of subsection (7),

they shall notify the applicant of their decision and the grounds for it.

(10) That notice shall be given in writing and, if not received by the applicant, shall be treated as having been given if it is made available at the authority's office for a reasonable period for collection by him or on his behalf.

(11) A person who is being treated by a local housing authority as ineligible by virtue of subsection (7) may (if he considers that he should no longer be treated as ineligible by the authority) make a fresh application to the authority for an allocation of housing accommodation by them.][1]

AMENDMENT

[1] Heading and section inserted: Homelessness Act 2002, s 14(2); for transitional provisions see s 14(3), (4) thereof.

161–165...[1]

AMENDMENT

[1] Sections repealed: Homelessness Act 2002, ss 14(1), 18(2), Sch 2; for transitional provisions see s 14(3), (4) thereof.

[Applications for housing accommodation

166 Applications for housing accommodation

[(1) A local housing authority shall secure that –

(a) advice and information is available free of charge to persons in their district about the right to make an application for an allocation of housing accommodation; and

(b) any necessary assistance in making such an application is available free of charge to persons in their district who are likely to have difficulty in doing so without assistance.

(2) A local housing authority shall secure that an applicant for an allocation of housing accommodation is informed that he has the rights mentioned in section 167(4A).

(3) Every application made to a local housing authority for an allocation of housing accommodation shall (if made in accordance with the procedural requirements of the authority's allocation scheme) be considered by the authority.

(4) The fact that a person is an applicant for an allocation of housing accommodation shall not be divulged (without his consent) to any other member of the public.

(5) In this Part 'district' in relation to a local housing authority has the same meaning as in the Housing Act 1985 (c 68).]¹

AMENDMENT

¹ Heading and section substituted: Homelessness Act 2002, s 15.

The allocation scheme

167 Allocation in accordance with allocation scheme

(1) Every local housing authority shall have a scheme (their 'allocation scheme') for determining priorities, and as to the procedure to be followed, in allocating housing accommodation.

For this purpose 'procedure' includes all aspects of the allocation process, including the persons or descriptions of persons by whom decisions are to be taken.

[(1A) The scheme shall include a statement of the authority's policy on offering people who are to be allocated housing accommodation –

(a) a choice of housing accommodation; or

(b) the opportunity to express preferences about the housing accommodation to be allocated to them.]¹

[(2) As regards priorities, the scheme shall[, subject to subsection (2ZA),]² be framed so as to secure that reasonable preference is given to –

(a) people who are homeless (within the meaning of Part 7);

(b) people who are owed a duty by any local housing authority under section 190(2), 193(2) or 195(2) (or under section 65(2) or 68(2) of the Housing Act 1985) or who are occupying accommodation secured by any such authority under section 192(3);

(c)　people occupying insanitary or overcrowded housing or otherwise living in unsatisfactory housing conditions;

(d)　people who need to move on medical or welfare grounds [(including grounds relating to a disability)][3]; and

(e)　people who need to move to a particular locality in the district of the authority, where failure to meet that need would cause hardship (to themselves or to others).

The scheme may also be framed so as to give additional preference to particular descriptions of people within this subsection (being descriptions of people with urgent housing needs).

[(2ZA) People are to be disregarded for the purposes of subsection (2) if they would not have fallen within paragraph (a) or (b) of that subsection without the local housing authority having had regard to a restricted person (within the meaning of Part 7).][4]

(2A) The scheme may contain provision for determining priorities in allocating housing accommodation to people within subsection (2); and the factors which the scheme may allow to be taken into account include –

(a)　the financial resources available to a person to meet his housing costs;

(b)　any behaviour of a person (or of a member of his household) which affects his suitability to be a tenant;

(c)　any local connection (within the meaning of section 199) which exists between a person and the authority's district.

(2B) Nothing in subsection (2) requires the scheme to provide for any preference to be given to people the authority have decided are people to whom subsection (2C) applies.

(2C) This subsection applies to a person if the authority are satisfied that –

(a)　he, or a member of his household, has been guilty of unacceptable behaviour serious enough to make him unsuitable to be a tenant of the authority; and

(b)　in the circumstances at the time his case is considered, he deserves by reason of that behaviour not to be treated as a member of a group of people who are to be given preference by virtue of subsection (2).

(2D) Subsection (8) of section 160A applies for the purposes of subsection (2C)(a) above as it applies for the purposes of subsection (7)(a) of that section.

(2E) Subject to subsection (2), the scheme may contain provision about the allocation of particular housing accommodation –

(a)　to a person who makes a specific application for that accommodation;

(b)　to persons of a particular description (whether or not they are within subsection (2)).][5]

(3) The Secretary of State may by regulations –

(a)　specify further descriptions of people to whom preference is to be given as mentioned in subsection (2), or

(b) amend or repeal any part of subsection (2).

(4) The Secretary of State may by regulations specify factors which a local housing authority shall not take into account in allocating housing accommodation.

[(4A) The scheme shall be framed so as to secure that an applicant for an allocation of housing accommodation –

(a) has the right to request such general information as will enable him to assess –

(i)   how his application is likely to be treated under the scheme (including in particular whether he is likely to be regarded as a member of a group of people who are to be given preference by virtue of subsection (2)); and

(ii) whether housing accommodation appropriate to his needs is likely to be made available to him and, if so, how long it is likely to be before such accommodation becomes available for allocation to him;

(b) is notified in writing of any decision that he is a person to whom subsection (2C) applies and the grounds for it;

(c) has the right to request the authority to inform him of any decision about the facts of his case which is likely to be, or has been, taken into account in considering whether to allocate housing accommodation to him; and

(d) has the right to request a review of a decision mentioned in paragraph (b) or (c), or in section 160A(9), and to be informed of the decision on the review and the grounds for it.][6]

(5) As regards the procedure to be followed, the scheme shall be framed in accordance with such principles as the Secretary of State may prescribe by regulations.

(6) Subject to the above provisions, and to any regulations made under them, the authority may decide on what principles the scheme is to be framed.

(7) Before adopting an allocation scheme, or making an alteration to their scheme reflecting a major change of policy, a local housing authority shall –

(a) send a copy of the draft scheme, or proposed alteration, to every registered social landlord with which they have nomination arrangements (see section 159(4)), and

(b) afford those persons a reasonable opportunity to comment on the proposals.

(8) A local housing authority shall not allocate housing accommodation except in accordance with their allocation scheme.

AMENDMENT

[1] Sub-section inserted: Homelessness Act 2002, s 16(1), (2).

² Words inserted: Housing and Regeneration Act 2008, s 314, Sch 15, Pt 1, paras 1, 2(1), (2), with effect from 2 March 2009 (except in relation to applications for an allocation of social housing or housing assistance (homelessness) or for accommodation made before that date) (SI 2009/415, art 2).

³ Words inserted: Housing Act 2004, s 223, with effect from 27 April 2005 in England (SI 2005/1120), and as from a date to be appointed in Wales.

⁴ Sub-section inserted: Housing and Regeneration Act 2008, s 314, Sch 15, Pt 1, paras 1, 2(1), (3), with effect from 2 March 2009 (except in relation to applications for an allocation of social housing or housing assistance (homelessness) or for accommodation made before that date) (SI 2009/415, art 2).

⁵ Sub-sections substituted: Homelessness Act 2002, s 16(1), (3).

⁶ Sub-section inserted: Homelessness Act 2002, s 16(1), (4).

168 Information about allocation scheme

(1) A local housing authority shall publish a summary of their allocation scheme and provide a copy of the summary free of charge to any member of the public who asks for one.

(2) The authority shall make the scheme available for inspection at their principal office and shall provide a copy of the scheme, on payment of a reasonable fee, to any member of the public who asks for one.

(3) When the authority make an alteration to their scheme reflecting a major change of policy, they shall within a reasonable period of time [take such steps as they consider reasonable to bring the effect of the alteration to the attention of those likely to be affected by it]¹.

AMENDMENT

¹ Words substituted: Homelessness Act 2002, s 18(1), Sch 1, paras 2, 4.

Supplementary

169 Guidance to authorities by the Secretary of State

(1) In the exercise of their functions under this Part, local housing authorities shall have regard to such guidance as may from time to time be given by the Secretary of State.

(2) The Secretary of State may give guidance generally or to specified descriptions of authorities.

170 Co-operation between registered social landlords and local housing authorities

Where a local housing authority so request, a registered social landlord shall co-operate to such extent as is reasonable in the circumstances in offering accommodation to [people with priority under the authority's allocation scheme]¹.

AMENDMENT

¹ Words substituted: Homelessness Act 2002, s 18(1), Sch 1, paras 2, 5.

171 False statements and withholding information

(1) A person commits an offence if, in connection with the exercise by a local housing authority of their functions under this Part –

(a) he knowingly or recklessly makes a statement which is false in a material particular, or

(b) he knowingly withholds information which the authority have reasonably required him to give in connection with the exercise of those functions.

(2) A person guilty of an offence under this section is liable on summary conviction to a fine not exceeding level 5 on the standard scale.

172 Regulations

(1) Regulations under this Part shall be made by statutory instrument.

(2) No regulations shall be made under section 167(3) (regulations amending provisions about priorities in allocating housing accommodation) unless a draft of the regulations has been laid before and approved by a resolution of each House of Parliament.

(3) Any other regulations under this Part shall be subject to annulment in pursuance of a resolution of either House of Parliament.

(4) Regulations under this Part may contain such incidental, supplementary and transitional provisions as appear to the Secretary of State appropriate, and may make different provision for different cases including different provision for different areas.

173 Consequential amendments: Part 6

The enactments mentioned in Schedule 16 have effect with the amendments specified there which are consequential on the provisions of this Part.

174 Index of defined expressions: Part 6

The following Table shows provisions defining or otherwise explaining expressions used in this Part (other than provisions defining or explaining an expression used in the same section) –

allocation (of housing)	section 159(2)
allocation scheme	section 167
assured tenancy	section 230
[district (of local housing authority)	section 166(5)][1]
...	...[2]
introductory tenancy and introductory tenant	section 230 and 124
local housing authority	section 230

...   ...[3]

registered social landlord   section 230 and 2

secure tenancy and secure tenant   section 230

AMENDMENT

[1] Entry inserted: Homelessness Act 2002, s 18(1), Sch 1, paras 2, 6.

[2] Entry repealed: Homelessness Act 2002, s 18(2), Sch 2.

[3] Entry repealed: Homelessness Act 2002, s 18(2), Sch 2.

PART 8
MISCELLANEOUS AND GENERAL PROVISIONS

General

****

230 Minor definitions: general

In this Act –

'assured tenancy', 'assured shorthold tenancy' and 'assured agricultural
occupancy' have the same meaning as in Part I of the Housing Act 1988;

'enactment' includes an enactment comprised in subordinate legislation
(within the meaning of the Interpretation Act 1978);

'housing action trust' has the same meaning as in the Housing Act 1988;

'housing association' has the same meaning as in the Housing Associations
Act 1985;

'introductory tenancy' and 'introductory tenant' have the same meaning as
in Chapter I of Part V of this Act;

'local housing authority' has the same meaning as in the Housing Act 1985;

'registered social landlord' has the same meaning as in Part I of this Act;

'secure tenancy' and 'secure tenant' have the same meaning as in Part IV of
the Housing Act 1985.

Allocation of Accommodation: Code of Guidance for Local Housing Authorities, November 2002

CONTENTS

Appendix 1
England: Allocation

CHAPTER 1: INTRODUCTION

AMENDMENT

This Chapter was replaced by the Guidance contained in *Fair and flexible: statutory guidance on social housing allocations for local authorities in England* with effect from 4 December 2009: see paragraph 3 of the 2009 Guidance.

CHAPTER 2: OVERVIEW OF THE AMENDMENTS TO PART 6 OF THE 1996 ACT MADE BY THE HOMELESSNESS ACT 2002

AMENDMENT

This Chapter was replaced by the Guidance contained in *Fair and flexible: statutory guidance on social housing allocations for local authorities in England* with effect from 4 December 2009: see paragraph 3 of the 2009 Guidance.

CHAPTER 3: ALLOCATIONS: GENERAL

Partnership working

3.1.   Most social housing is provided by housing authorities using their own stock and by RSLs. Even where a housing authority has transferred its stock to an RSL, it retains responsibility for its statutory housing duties. A housing authority has a strategic responsibility for meeting its districts housing needs and the Secretary of State regards it as essential that housing authorities work closely with RSLs, other housing providers and voluntary agencies to meet those needs.

3.2.   Housing authorities will need to develop working relationships with other organisations at a strategic and operational level to ensure that the housing, care and support needs of vulnerable people are appropriately met. These organisations will include Supporting People teams, Connexions partnerships, housing related support providers, health authorities, social services authorities, the police and probation service.

3.3.   There need to be effective mechanisms in place for developing an interface with other services and providers. The Supporting People process provides a useful model (see www.spkweb.org.uk). Housing authorities will also wish to take advantage of the partnership working arrangements which they develop in drawing up their homelessness strategies.

Definition of allocation

3.4.   For the purposes of Part 6 the allocation of housing accommodation by housing authorities is defined in s 159 as:

(a)   selecting a person to be a secure or introductory tenant of housing accommodation held by a housing authority;

(b)   nominating a person to be a secure or introductory tenant of housing accommodation held by another person (ie one of the authorities or bodies fulfilling the landlord condition mentioned in the Housing Act 1985, s 80); or

(c)   nominating a person to be an assured tenant of housing accommodation held by an RSL.

Transfers

3.5.   Provisions in relation to transfers are now contained in s 159(5). As a result, Part 6 now applies to most allocations to existing tenants of housing authorities and RSLs seeking to move to other social housing. This entitles existing social housing tenants to apply to transfer to other social housing stock, which may be in the same district or in another housing authority's district. However, s 167(2A) of the 1996 Act means that housing authorities may take into account any local connection which exists between the applicant and the housing authority's district in determining priorities in relation to applicants who fall within the reasonable and additional preference categories (see Chapter 5, para 5.23).

3.6.   Those applying for a transfer must be treated on the same basis as other applicants in accordance with the provisions set out in the housing authority's allocation scheme, which should reflect a sensible balance between meeting the housing needs of existing tenants and new applicants, whilst ensuring the efficient use of stock. Transfers that the housing authority initiates for management purposes do not fall within Part 6. These would include a temporary decant to allow repairs to a property to be carried out. Mutual exchanges between existing tenants also do not fall within Part 6 (see annex 1 for a full list of exemptions).

Joint tenants

3.7.   The Secretary of State considers joint tenancies can play an important role in the effective use and equitable allocation of housing. Where household members have long term commitments to the home, for example, when adults share accommodation as partners (including same sex partners), friends or unpaid live-in carers, housing authorities should normally grant a joint tenancy. In this way the ability of other adult household members to remain in the accommodation on the death of the tenant would not be prejudiced. Housing authorities should ensure that there are no adverse implications from the joint tenancy for the good use of their housing stock and for their ability to continue to provide for housing need.

3.8.   Housing authorities should ensure that applicants, including where they are existing tenants, are made aware of the option of joint tenancies. When doing so, the legal and financial implications and obligations of joint tenancies must be made clear, including the implications for succession rights of partners and children. Where housing authorities refuse an application for a joint tenancy, clear, written reasons for the refusal should be given.

3.9.   Where a joint tenant serves notice to quit, housing authorities have a discretion to grant a sole tenancy to the remaining tenant. In exercising this discretion, they should ensure that there are no adverse implications for the good use of their housing stock and their ability to continue to provide for housing need. Where housing authorities decide that they may wish to exercise their discretion in this respect, they must reflect this in their allocation scheme.

3.10.   Where a tenant dies and another household member (who does not have succession rights to the tenancy) has:

(a)   been living with the tenant for the year prior to the tenants death; or
(b)   been providing care for the tenant; or
(c)   accepted responsibility for the tenants dependants and needs to live with them in order to do so;

housing authorities should consider granting a tenancy to the remaining person or persons, either in the same home or in suitable alternative accommodation, provided the allocation has no adverse implications for the good use of the housing stock and has sufficient priority under the allocation scheme. In the case of (a) and (b), the accommodation in question must be the principal or only residence of the survivor at the time the tenant dies.

Period for considering an offer of accommodation

3.11.   Applicants must be allowed a reasonable period to make a decision about accommodation offered to them under Part 6. There is no statutory time limit but it is important that applicants are given sufficient time for careful consideration. Applicants who have had the opportunity to make an informed, positive decision to accept an offer are more likely to be committed to making a success of the tenancy.

3.12.   Some applicants may require longer than others depending on their circumstances: they may wish to take advice in making their decision particularly in the case of vulnerable applicants; or they may be unfamiliar with the property. Longer periods may be required, for example, where the applicant is currently in hospital, on in some form of temporary accommodation, such as a hostel or refuge.

CHAPTER 4: ELIGIBILITY FOR AN ALLOCATION OF ACCOMMODATION

General overview

4.1.   Section 166(3) places an obligation on housing authorities to consider all applications for social housing that are made in accordance with the procedural requirements of the housing authority's allocation scheme. In considering applications, however, housing authorities must ascertain if an applicant is eligible for accommodation or whether he is excluded from allocation under s 160A (1)(a), (3) or (5). Housing authorities may decide to treat the applicant as ineligible for an allocation under s 160A(7) (unacceptable behaviour). Otherwise, housing authorities must treat all applicants as eligible.

Nationality and immigration status/persons from abroad

4.2.   Under s 160A (3) persons from abroad who are subject to immigration control within the meaning of the Asylum and Immigration Act 1996 are ineligible for allocations, but the Secretary of State has prescribed classes of persons who are subject to immigration control but are nonetheless to be eligible for an allocation. Under s 160A (5) the Secretary of State has also prescribed that certain persons from abroad, who are not subject to immigration control, have to be habitually resident in the Common Travel Area (CTA) (ie the UK, the Channel Islands, the Isle of Man and the Republic of Ireland) in order to be eligible (see annex 6).

4.3.   The following are the main categories of applicants to whom a housing authority may allocate accommodation taking account of nationality and immigration status (see also annex 4):

a)   **Existing tenants:** all existing secure and introductory tenants of a housing authority and assured tenants of accommodation allocated by a housing authority;

b)   **British Nationals:** British Nationals, who are habitually resident in the CTA;

c)   **EEA Nationals:** any person, who is a national of any of the countries in the European Economic Area (EEA), and is habitually resident in the CTA; or is a worker, or has a right to reside in the UK;

d)   **Persons subject to immigration control** who have been granted:

i)   **Refugee status;**

ii)   **Exceptional leave to remain** provided that there is no condition that they shall not be a charge on public funds; or

iii)   **Indefinite leave to remain** provided that they are habitually resident in the CTA and their leave to remain was not granted in the previous 5 years on the basis of a sponsorship given in relation to maintenance and accommodation (or, if so, that their sponsor has (or in the case of more than one sponsor, all of them have) died);

e)   **Persons subject to immigration control who are nationals of a country that has ratified the European Convention on Social and Medical Assistance (ECSMA) or the European Social Charter (ESC)** provided that they are habitually resident in the CTA and are lawfully present in the UK (see also annex 6).

The habitual residence test

4.4.   While the majority of the categories eligible for housing require the applicant to be habitually resident in the CTA, most applicants for social housing will not be persons from abroad and there will be no reason to apply the test. It is also likely that persons who have been resident in the CTA continuously during the 2 years prior to their housing application will be habitually resident in the CTA. In such cases, therefore, housing authorities may consider it unnecessary to make further enquiries to establish habitual residence, unless there are other circumstances that need to be taken into account. A period of continuous residence in the CTA might include visits abroad e.g. for holidays or to visit relatives. Where 2 years continuous residency in the UK is not established, housing authorities may need to conduct further enquiries to determine whether the applicant is habitually resident in the CTA.

4.5.   The term habitual residence is intended to convey a degree of permanence in the persons residence in the CTA; it implies an association between the individual and the country and relies substantially on fact. When deciding whether an applicant is habitually resident, housing authorities should take account of the applicants period of residence and its continuity, his employment prospects, his reason for coming to the UK, his future intentions and his centre of interest.

4.6.   A person cannot claim to be habitually resident in any country unless he has taken up residence and lived there for a period. There will be cases where the person concerned is not coming to the UK for the first time, but is resuming a habitual residence previously had. Annex 11 provides detailed guidance on the factors which a housing authority should consider in determining whether an applicant is habitually resident in these circumstances. However, the fact that a person has ceased to be habitually resident in another country does not imply habitual residence in the country to which he has travelled.

4.7.   A person who is in stable employment is more likely to be able to establish habitual residence than someone whose employment is, for whatever reason, transitory (ie an au pair or someone who is on a fixed short-term contract). Equally, a person, one of whose apparent aims in coming to the UK is to claim benefits, is less likely to be able to establish habitual residence.

4.8.   A person who intends to take up permanent work is more likely to be able to establish habitual residence, as is a person who can show that he has immediate family or other ties in the UK.

4.9.   The habitual residence test does not apply to:

    a)   a worker for the purposes of EC law (see Council Regulation (EEC) No 1612/68 or (EEC) No 1251/70);

    b)   a person with a right to reside in the United Kingdom under treaty rights (see Council Directive No 68/360/EEC or No 73/148/EEC); or

    c)   a person who left the territory of Montserrat after 1 November 1995 because of the effect of the volcanic activity there.

4.10.   On 21 May 2002 most British Overseas Territories Citizens, including all citizens of Montserrat, became British Citizens. Since their new EU-style passport will not identify that they are from Montserrat, it has been recommended that they should also retain their old British Overseas Territories Citizen passport, to help them demonstrate eligibility for social security benefits and social housing in the UK.

Eligible categories

4.11. Existing tenants – Section 160A(6) provides that none of the provisions relating to the eligibility of tenants with respect to their immigration status is to affect the eligibility of an applicant who is already a secure or introductory tenant or an assured tenant of housing accommodation allocated to him by a housing authority. It is therefore the case that where such a tenant applies for an allocation the housing authority does not need to question eligibility and an allocation can be made regardless of immigration status or habitual residence.

4.12. British Nationals – Where a British National arrives from abroad, as with all nationals of an EEA country, he must establish habitual residence in order to be eligible for an allocation, even in cases where he was born in the CTA.

4.13. EEA Nationals – These are the Nationals of the EU countries plus Iceland, Norway and Liechtenstein. They are not subject to immigration control, but are not eligible for accommodation unless they can establish habitual residence.

4.14. Persons subject to immigration controls prescribed as eligible – Generally, persons subject to immigration control are not eligible for housing accommodation. However, under s 160A (3) the Secretary of State has prescribed classes of person who are to be eligible and they are:

i) Persons granted refugee status A person is granted refugee status when his request for asylum is accepted.

ii) Persons granted exceptional leave to enter or remain (ELR) This will be either someone who has failed in his request for asylum, but nonetheless been given leave to remain, or someone who has been granted leave to remain where there are compelling, compassionate circumstances. However, it may be the case that when ELR was granted it was on condition that the applicant should not be a charge on public funds. If that is the case, the applicant is not eligible for an allocation.

iii) Persons granted indefinite leave to enter or remain (ILR) This will be someone who has permission to remain in the UK for an indefinite period and is regarded as having settled status. In order to be eligible, however, the applicant will still have to be able to establish habitual residence. It is also the case that if ILR status was obtained as a result of sponsorship five years must have elapsed since the persons arrival in the UK or the date of the sponsorship undertaking, whichever is later. However, where a sponsor dies (or where there is more than one sponsor, where all of them die) within the first five years, the applicant will be eligible provided he can establish habitual residence.

iv) Persons subject to immigration control who are nationals of a country that has ratified ECSMA or ESC Such persons have to be lawfully present in the UK as well as habitually resident. This means that the applicant must have leave to enter or remain in the UK.

4.15. Annex 8 provides guidance on identifying persons subject to immigration control who are eligible for an allocation. Annex 7 lists classes of persons subject to immigration control who are not eligible for an allocation. Annex 9 identifies the countries which have ratified ECSMA and ESC, and lists other European groupings.

4.16. The provisions on eligibility are complex and housing authorities will need to ensure that they have procedures in place to carry out appropriate checks on housing applicants.

4.17. If there is any uncertainty about an applicants immigration status, housing authorities are recommended to contact the Home Office Immigration and Nationality Directorate, using the procedures set out in annex 10. Before doing so, the applicant should be advised that an inquiry will be made; if at this stage the applicant prefers to withdraw his or her application, no further action will be required. Where there is reason to believe that the applicant may be an asylum seeker, they should be referred to the National Asylum Support Service (see annex 10).

4.18. Housing authorities should ensure that staff who are required to screen housing applicants about eligibility for an allocation are given training in the complexities of the housing provisions, the housing authority's duties and responsibilities under the race relations legislation and how to deal with applicants in a sensitive manner. Housing authorities may wish to refer to annex 5, which provides model questions that can provide a pathway to determining eligibility. Annex 12 provides a pathway for determining eligibility in the form of a flow chart.

Unacceptable behaviour

4.19. Most applicants for social housing will not be persons from abroad, and will have been resident in the UK (or elsewhere in the CTA) for 2 years prior to their application. Such applicants, together with those eligible applicants from abroad may nonetheless be treated as ineligible by the housing authority on the basis of unacceptable behaviour.

4.20. Where a housing authority is satisfied that an applicant (or a member of the applicants household) is guilty of unacceptable behaviour serious enough to make him unsuitable to be a tenant, section 160A(7) permits the authority to decide to treat the applicant as ineligible for an allocation.

4.21. Section 160A(8) provides that the only behaviour which can be regarded as unacceptable for these purposes is behaviour by the applicant or by a member of his household that would if the applicant had been a secure tenant of the housing authority at the time have entitled the housing authority to a possession order under s 84 of the Housing Act 1985 in relation to any of the grounds in Part I of Schedule 2, other than Ground 8. These are fault grounds and include behaviour such as conduct likely to cause nuisance or annoyance, and use of the property for immoral or illegal purposes. Housing authorities should note that it is not necessary for the applicant to have actually been a tenant of the housing authority when the unacceptable behaviour occurred.

The test is whether the behaviour would have entitled the housing authority to a possession order if, whether actually or notionally, the applicant had been a secure tenant.

4.22.   Where a housing authority has reason to believe that s 160A(7) may apply; there are a number of steps that will need to be followed.

i)   They will need to satisfy themselves that there has been unacceptable behaviour which falls within the definition in s 160A(8). In considering whether a possession order would be granted in the circumstances of a particular case, the housing authority would have to consider whether, having established the grounds, the court would decide that it was reasonable to grant a possession order. It has been established in case law that, when the court is deliberating, reasonable means having regard to the interests of the parties and also having regard to the interests of the public. So, in deciding whether it would be entitled to an order the housing authority would need to consider these interests, and this will include all the circumstances of the applicant and his or her household. In practice, courts are unlikely to grant possession orders in cases which have not been properly considered and are not supported by thorough and convincing evidence. It is acknowledged that in cases involving noise problems, domestic violence, racial harassment, intimidation and drug dealing, courts are likely to grant a possession order. Rent arrears would probably lead to a possession order, although in many cases it will be suspended giving the tenant the opportunity to pay the arrears. In taking a view on whether it would be entitled to a possession order, the housing authority will need to consider fully all the factors that a court would take into account in determining whether it was reasonable for an order to be granted. In the Secretary of States view, a decision reached on the basis of established case law would be reasonable.

ii) Having concluded that there would be entitlement to an order, the housing authority will need to satisfy itself that the behaviour is serious enough to make the person unsuitable to be a tenant of the housing authority. For example, the housing authority would need to be satisfied that, if a possession order were granted, it would not be suspended by the court. Behaviour such as the accrual of rent arrears which have resulted from factors outside the applicants control for example, delays in housing benefit payments; or liability for a partners debts, where the applicant was not in control of the households finances or was unaware that arrears were accruing should not be considered serious enough to make the person unsuitable to be a tenant.

iii) The housing authority will need to satisfy itself that the applicant is unsuitable to be a tenant by reason of the behaviour in question in the circumstances at the time the application is considered. Previous unacceptable behaviour may not justify a decision to consider the applicant as unsuitable to be a tenant where that behaviour can be shown to have improved.

4.23. The housing authority must be satisfied on all three aspects set out in para 4.22. Only then can the housing authority consider exercising its discretion to decide that the applicant is to be treated as ineligible for an allocation. In reaching a decision on whether or not to treat an applicant as ineligible, the housing authority will have to act reasonably, and will need to consider all the relevant matters before it. This will include all the circumstances relevant to the particular applicant, whether health, dependants or other factors. In practice, the matters before the housing authority will normally mean the information provided with the application.

4.24. If an applicant, who has, in the past, been deemed by the housing authority to be ineligible, considers his unacceptable behaviour should no longer be held against him as a result of changed circumstances, he can make a fresh application. Unless there has been a considerable lapse of time it will be for the applicant to show that his circumstances or behaviour have changed.

4.25. Where a housing authority has reason to believe that an applicants unacceptable behaviour is due to a physical, mental or learning disability, they must not treat that person as ineligible for an allocation without first considering whether he would be able to maintain a tenancy with appropriate care and support. In considering the applicants case, the housing authority will need to consult with relevant agencies, including social services, health professionals, and providers of suitable housing, care and housing related support services.

4.26. Housing authorities should note, however, that they are not required to treat an applicant as ineligible where they are satisfied that he is guilty of unacceptable behaviour serious enough to make him unsuitable to be a tenant; instead they may decide to proceed with the allocation but give the applicant no preference for an allocation. This option is considered further at Chapter 5, paras 5.19 to 5.22.

4.27. A housing authority may also take into account the behaviour of an applicant (or a member of his household) which affects his suitability to be a tenant when determining priorities in relation to applicants who fall within the reasonable preference categories. This option is considered further at Chapter 5, para 5.23(b).

Joint tenancies

4.28. Under s 160A(1)(c), a housing authority shall not grant a joint tenancy to two or more people if any one of them is a person from abroad who is ineligible or is a person who is being treated as ineligible because of unacceptable behaviour.

Reviews of decisions on eligibility

4.29. Under s 160A(9) and (10), and s 167(4A) housing authorities, who decide that applicants are ineligible by virtue of s 160A(3) or (5) or are to be treated as ineligible because of unacceptable behaviour, must give them written notification of the decision. The notification must give clear grounds for the decision which must be based firmly on the relevant facts of the case.

4.30. Under s 167(4A)(d) applicants have the right to request a review under the allocation scheme of any decision as to eligibility and a right to be informed of the decision on review and the grounds for that decision.

CHAPTER 5: ALLOCATION SCHEME

5.1–5.12 ...

AMENDMENT

These paragraphs were replaced by the Guidance contained in *Fair and flexible: statutory guidance on social housing allocations for local authorities in England* with effect from 4 December 2009: see paragraph 3 of the 2009 Guidance.

Medical and welfare grounds

5.13. Where it is necessary to take account of medical advice, housing authorities should contact the most appropriate health or social care professional who has direct knowledge of the applicants condition, as well as the impact his condition has on his housing needs.

5.14. Welfare grounds is intended to encompass not only care or support needs, but also other social needs which do not require ongoing care and support, such as the need to provide a secure base from which a care leaver or other vulnerable person can build a stable life. It would include vulnerable people (with or without care and support needs) who could not be expected to find their own accommodation.

5.15. Where accommodation is allocated to a person who needs to move on medical or welfare grounds, it is essential to assess any support and care needs, and housing authorities will need to liaise with social services, the Supporting People team and other relevant agencies, as necessary, to ensure the allocation of appropriate accommodation. Housing authorities should also consider, together with the applicant, whether his needs would be better served by staying put in his current accommodation if appropriate aids and adaptations were put in place.

Hardship grounds

5.16. This would include, for example, a person who needs to move to a different locality in order to give or receive care, to access specialised medical treatment or to take up a particular employment, education or training opportunity.

5.17. Possible indicators of the criteria which apply to categories (c) and (d) are given in annex 3.

5.18. ...

AMENDMENT

This paragraph was replaced by the Guidance contained in *Fair and flexible: statutory guidance on social housing allocations for local authorities in England* with effect from 4 December 2009: see paragraph 3 of the 2009 Guidance.

Unacceptable behaviour

5.19.   By virtue of s 167(2B) and (2C) an allocation scheme may provide that no preference is given to an applicant where the housing authority is satisfied that he, or a member of his household, has been guilty of unacceptable behaviour serious enough to make him unsuitable to be a tenant of the housing authority; and the housing authority is satisfied that, in the circumstances at the time the case is considered, he deserves not to be treated as a person who should be given reasonable preference.

5.20.   By virtue of s 167(2D), the same provisions apply for determining what is unacceptable behaviour for the purposes of deciding whether to give preference to an applicant, as apply to a decision on eligibility, that is to say s 160A(8).

5.21.   Section 160A(8) provides that the only behaviour which can be regarded as unacceptable for these purposes is behaviour by the applicant or by a member of his household that would if the applicant had been a secure tenant of the housing authority at the time have entitled the housing authority to a possession order under s 84 of the Housing Act 1985 in relation to any of the grounds in Part I of Schedule 2, other than Ground 8.

5.22.   Chapter 4, paras 4.21 and 4.22 provide guidance, for the purposes of determining eligibility under s 160A(7), on what constitutes unacceptable behaviour serious enough to make an applicant unsuitable to be a tenant, and sets out the steps which housing authorities should take to satisfy themselves in this regard. This guidance applies equally to decisions under s 167(2B) and (2C).

5.23–5.32   ...

AMENDMENT

These paragraphs were replaced by the Guidance contained in *Fair and flexible: statutory guidance on social housing allocations for local authorities in England* with effect from 4 December 2009: see paragraph 3 of the 2009 Guidance.

Children in need

5.33.   Households may include a child with a need for settled accommodation on medical or welfare grounds.

5.34.   Under s 27 of the Children Act 1989, housing authorities are required to respond to social services authorities, who have duties towards children under that Act (see s 18). Section 17 of that Act imposes a general duty on social services authorities to safeguard and promote the welfare of children within their area who are in need. Consistent with that duty, they must promote the upbringing of such children by their families, by providing a range and level of services appropriate to those children's needs. Subject to an amendment in the Adoption and Children Bill, families in this context are to include adoptive families, and prospective adoptive families.

5.35.   A child in need is defined in the Children Act 1989 as someone who is unlikely to achieve or maintain, or to have the opportunity of achieving or maintaining, a reasonable standard of health or development without the provision of certain services by a local authority; or someone whose health or development is likely to be significantly impaired, or further impaired, without the provision of such services; or someone who is disabled. A child in need may require settled accommodation on medical or welfare grounds.

5.36.   Housing authorities will need to consult with social services about the appropriate level of priority for an allocation in such cases, and how any support needs will be met.

Carers

5.37.   In making accommodation offers to applicants who receive support from carers who do not reside with them, housing authorities should, wherever possible, take account of the applicants need for a spare bedroom.

Lone teenage parents under 18

5.38.   The provision of suitable accommodation with support for lone parents under 18 is a key part of the Governments Teenage Pregnancy Strategy. While lone teenage parents will normally be young women which is why this guidance uses the terms she and her in this section housing authorities need to recognise that there may be some occasions when the applicant is a young man.

5.39.   The Governments objective is that all 16 and 17 year-old lone parents who cannot live with their parents or partner and who require social housing should be offered semi-independent accommodation with support. Housing authorities should work with social services, Supporting People teams, RSLs and relevant voluntary organisations in their district to ensure that the Governments objective is met.

5.40.   The allocation of appropriate housing and support should be based on consideration of the young persons housing and support needs, her individual circumstances and her views and preferences. Housing authorities must ensure that the accommodation is suitable for babies and young children. Wherever possible, housing authorities should take account of the education and employment needs and opportunities of the applicant when identifying suitable accommodation.

5.41.   Where an application for housing is received from a lone parent aged 16 or 17, the Secretary of State recommends that housing authorities have arrangements in place to ensure that they can undertake a joint assessment of the applicants housing, care and support needs with social services. Housing authorities should obtain the consent of the young parent before involving social services, unless child protection concerns are present and to seek such consent might endanger the welfare of the child of the young parent.

5.42.   Where RSLs in the district have vacancies in a suitable supported housing scheme, housing authorities should use their nomination rights to secure accommodation for young parents in such accommodation. Support may be provided on site or on a floating basis.

5.43.   Where there is no suitable RSL accommodation available, housing authorities should consider allocating the young parent a place in other similar accommodation where appropriate support is available.

5.44.   The Secretary of State believes that the young person should not normally be allocated an independent tenancy without floating support. In exceptional cases, however, it may be decided that supported housing would not be appropriate. Such a decision should only be made after careful consideration of the housing and support needs of that individual and her views and preferences. In such circumstances, housing authorities should ensure that the young person is aware of relevant sources of support and advice and how to access them. This might include social services, health visitors, the Connexions service, and relevant voluntary agencies and local providers.

5.45.   Housing authorities should also, in consultation with the relevant RSLs in their district, make provision for appropriate move-on accommodation for young parents who have been assessed as ready to leave supported accommodation and live independently. In some cases, where the young parent has made good progress, it may be appropriate for her to live independently before she reaches the age of 18. When allocating move-on accommodation to a young parent, the housing authority should consider whether the parent or child have any continuing support needs, in consultation with the young person, social services and relevant providers.

5.46.   If, with the young persons consent, a joint assessment is carried out with social services of the housing, care and support needs of a lone parent aged 16 or 17, it may be considered more appropriate for her to be accommodated by social services, for example, in foster care.

5.47.   Young parents under the age of 16 must always be referred to social services so that their social care needs may be assessed.

5.48.   Further guidance is set out in *Guidelines for Good Practice in Supported Accommodation for Young Parents* published jointly by DTLR and the Teenage Pregnancy Unit in September 2001 (available from www.teenagepregancyunit. gov.uk or www.housingcorp.gov.uk).

Tenancies for minors

5.49.   In some circumstances, social services authorities may consider it appropriate to underwrite a tenancy agreement for an applicant who is under 18. There are legal complications associated with the grant of a tenancy to a minor because a minor cannot hold a legal estate in land. However, if a tenancy is granted, it probably takes effect as a contract for a lease and would be fully enforceable as a contract for necessaries (ie the basic necessities of life) under common law. Any guarantee given in those circumstances would remain valid in respect of any liability incurred by the minor notwithstanding that he or she may repudiate the agreement on or shortly after reaching 18.

Rough sleeping

5.50.   Housing authority's homelessness strategies have a key role to play in preventing homelessness and rough sleeping. Access to good quality, affordable housing will be vital for rough sleepers and people at risk of sleeping rough.

5.51.   Housing authorities should ensure that allocation schemes make provision to enable access to housing authority and RSL accommodation for this client group. Where appropriate, schemes should also ensure that vulnerable people have access to the assistance they need to apply for housing. Often, people at risk of homelessness will require support, for example to address mental health, alcohol or drug problems, or simply to cope with bill paying and basic life skills. Allocation schemes should be developed with strong links to such support services provided under local homelessness strategies and Supporting People.

Sex offenders

5.52.   Where sex offenders are allocated accommodation, this should be in the light of considered decisions about managing any risks associated with their release from prison into the community, involving multi-agency arrangements with the police, probation services, social services, health professionals and other relevant bodies. Housing authorities should have regard to DETR guidance issued to Chief Housing Officers in November 1999 about the management of risk in such cases.

Rent (Agriculture) Act 1976

5.53.   The Rent (Agriculture) Act 1976 (referred to as the 1976 Act) requires housing authorities to use their best endeavours to provide accommodation for displaced agricultural workers. Section 27 of the 1976 Act requires the housing authority to be satisfied that:

  (a)   the dwelling-house from which the worker is displaced is needed to accommodate another agricultural worker;
  (b)   the farmer cannot provide suitable alternative accommodation for the displaced worker; and
  (c)   the displaced worker needs to be re-housed in the interests of efficient agriculture.

5.54.   In reaching a decision, the housing authority must have regard to advice of an Agricultural Dwelling-House Advisory Committee (ADHAC). The ADHAC's role is to provide advice on whether the interests of efficient agriculture are served by re-housing the worker, and on the applications urgency. If the housing authority is satisfied that the applicants case is substantiated, it is its duty under s 28 of the 1976 Act to use its best endeavours to provide suitable alternative accommodation for the displaced worker. In assessing the applications priority the housing authority is required to consider (a) the cases urgency; (b) the competing claims on the accommodation; and (c) its resources.

5.55.   A housing authority would not be properly discharging its duty under s 28 of the 1976 Act if it refused, on the grounds of the displaced worker having insufficient priority under the allocation scheme, to offer that person suitable alternative accommodation. There must be proper consideration of all relevant s 28 factors in the light of the ADHAC's advice. It is important, where relevant, for housing authorities to include in their allocation scheme a policy statement in respect of cases arising under the 1976 Act.

General information about particular applications

5.56.   Under s 167(4A)(a), allocation schemes must be framed so as to give applicants the right to request from housing authorities general information that will enable them to assess:

(a)   how their application is likely to be treated under the scheme and, in particular, whether they are likely to fall within the reasonable preference categories;

(b)   whether accommodation appropriate to their needs is likely to be made available and, if so, how long it is likely to be before such accommodation becomes available.

5.57.   Housing authorities which operate an open advertising scheme, whereby applicants can apply for particular properties, would usually be expected to provide information about the properties which have been let; for example, what level of priority the successful applicants had, or the date on which they had applied to go on the housing authority's waiting list. Such feedback is crucial as it enables applicants to assess their chances of success in subsequent applications. It can also assist applicants in refining their preferences, and all housing authorities are therefore recommended to consider the extent to which they are able to provide information about properties which have been let. However, s 166(4) prohibits housing authorities from divulging to other members of the public that a particular individual is an applicant for social housing, unless they have the applicants consent, and therefore personal information about applicants should always be kept confidential.

Notification about decisions and the right to a review of a decision

5.58.   Under s 167(4A), allocation schemes must also be framed so as to give applicants the following rights about decisions which are taken in respect of their application:

(a)   the right to be notified in writing of any decision not to give an applicant any preference under the scheme because of unacceptable behaviour serious enough to make him unsuitable to be a tenant of the housing authority;

(b)   the right, on request, to be informed of any decision about the facts of the applicants case which has been, or is likely to be, taken into account in considering whether to make an allocation to him; and

(c)   the right, on request, to review a decision mentioned in (a) or (b) above, or a decision to treat the applicant as ineligible because of unacceptable behaviour serious enough to make him unsuitable to be a tenant of the housing authority. The applicant also has the right to be informed of the decision on the review and the grounds for it.

CHAPTER 6: ALLOCATION SCHEME MANAGEMENT

AMENDMENT

This Chapter was replaced by the Guidance contained in *Fair and flexible: statutory guidance on social housing allocations for local authorities in England* with effect from 4 December 2009: see paragraph 3 of the 2009 Guidance.

CHAPTER 7: CONTRACTING OUT AND STOCK TRANSFER

Contracting out

7.1.   The Local Authorities (Contracting Out of Allocation of Housing and Homelessness Functions) Order 1996 (SI 1996 No 3205) enables housing authorities to contract out certain functions under Part 6 of the 1996 Act. The Order is made under s 70 of the Deregulation and Contracting Out Act 1994 (the 1994 Act). In essence, the Order allows the contracting out of executive functions, while leaving the responsibility for making strategic decisions with the housing authority.

7.2.   Schedule 1 to the Order lists the allocation functions which may not be contracted out:

i)   adopting or altering the allocation scheme, including the principles on which the scheme is framed, and consulting RSLs; and

ii)   making the allocation scheme available at the authority's principal office.

7.3.   The Order therefore provides that the majority of functions under Part 6 may be contracted out. These include:

i)   making enquiries about and deciding a persons eligibility for an allocation;

ii)   carrying out reviews of decisions;

    iii)   making arrangements to secure that advice and information is available free of charge to persons within the housing authority's district on how to apply for housing;

    iv)   making arrangements to secure that any necessary assistance is made available free of charge to anyone who is likely to have difficulty in making a housing application without such assistance; and

    v)   making individual allocations in accordance with the allocation scheme.

7.4.   The 1994 Act provides that a contract made:

    i)   may authorise a contractor to carry out only part of the function concerned;

    ii)   may specify that the contractor is authorised to carry out functions only in certain cases or areas specified in the contract;

    iii)   may include conditions relating to the carrying out of the functions, e g prescribing standards of performance;

    iv)   shall be for a period not exceeding 10 years and may be revoked at any time by the Minister or the housing authority. Any subsisting contract is to be treated as having been repudiated in these circumstances;

    v)   shall not prevent the authority from itself exercising the functions to which the contract relates.

7.5.   The 1994 Act also provides that the authority is responsible for any act or omission of the contractor in exercising functions under the contract, except:

    i)   where the contractor fails to fulfil conditions specified in the contract relating to the exercise of the function; or

    ii)   where criminal proceedings are brought in respect of the contractors act or omission.

7.6.   Where there is an arrangement in force under s 101 of the Local Government Act 1972 by virtue of which one authority exercises the functions of another, the 1994 Act provides that the authority exercising the function is not allowed to contract it out without the principal authoritys consent.

Stock transfer

7.7.   Housing authorities that have transferred all or part of their housing stock, or are in the process of transferring their stock, are still required under Part 6 to have an allocation scheme where they continue to allocate housing within the meaning of s 159 of the 1996 Act. The requirement in s 167(7) of the 1996 Act to consult RSLs before adopting or altering their allocation scheme will be particularly important in the case of a transferring housing authority. Whilst transfer RSLs must operate as independent bodies, housing authorities seeking to transfer may wish to consider including in the contract an obligation on the transfer RSL to consult the housing authority if the RSL wishes to amend its allocation policy.

7.8.   Nomination arrangements between the transferring housing authority and the transfer RSL must reflect the requirement that nominations of assured tenancies must be to eligible persons in accordance with the housing authoritys allocation scheme. It is important to remember that the housing authority may have nomination arrangements with other RSLs in the district, and these should be included in any agreement to contract out the allocation function.

7.9. The transfer agreement will need to include monitoring arrangements. Monitoring arrangements will be important, to ensure that housing authorities can demonstrate that they are meeting their statutory obligations under Part 6, and in particular the requirement to give reasonable preference to persons in the categories set out in s 167(2). The monitoring arrangements will also need to cover nominations to all RSL stock.

7.10. Where a housing authority has delegated or contracted out the operation of its allocation functions to an external contractor, the contractor must be made aware of the provisions of Part 6 and advised how the legislation and this guidance may apply to them.

7.11. Good practice guidance on arrangements for contracting out homelessness and allocation functions will be published in Autumn 2003.

ANNEX 1: SCOPE OF PART 6 EXEMPTIONS

1. Part 6 of the 1996 Act (as amended) does not apply to mutual exchanges within a RSLs stock or between housing authorities and RSLs.

Primary Legislation Exemptions

2. The 1996 Act (as amended), s 159(5) states that Part 6 provisions do not apply to a person who is already a secure or introductory tenant unless the allocation involves a transfer of housing accommodation for that person and is made on his application.

3. Similarly, s 160 (as amended) exempts from Part 6 provisions cases:

   a) where a secure tenant dies, the tenancy is a periodic one, and there is a person qualified to succeed the tenant under the Housing Act 1985, s 89;

   b) where a secure tenant with a fixed term tenancy dies and the tenancy remains secure by virtue the Housing Act 1985, s 90;

   c) where a secure tenancy is assigned by way of exchange under the Housing Act 1985, s 92;

   d) where a secure tenancy is assigned to someone who would be qualified to succeed to the tenancy if the secure tenant died immediately before the assignment; or

   e) where a secure tenancy vests or is otherwise disposed of in pursuance of an order made under:
      - the Matrimonial Causes Act 1973, s 24 (property adjustment orders in connection with matrimonial proceedings);
      - the Matrimonial and Family Proceedings Act 1984, s 17(1) (property adjustment orders after overseas divorce); or

- the Children Act 1989, Schedule 1, paragraph 1 (orders for financial relief against parents), or
(f) where an introductory tenancy:
    i) becomes a secure tenancy on ceasing to be an introductory tenancy;
    ii) vests under the 1996 Act, s 133(2) (succession to an introductory tenancy on death of tenant); or
    iii) is assigned to someone who would be qualified to succeed the introductory tenancy if the introductory tenant died immediately before the assignment; or
    iv) meets the criteria in paragraph 3(e) above.

Secondary Legislation Exemptions

4. The Allocation of Housing Regulations 1996 SI 1996 No 2753, Regulation 3 exempts the following allocations from Part 6 provisions:

a) cross-border transfers of secure or assured tenants belonging to the Northern Ireland Housing Executive; Scottish local authorities; housing associations registered with Scottish Homes; or housing companies who acquired the said accommodation from a Scottish local authority, or from Scottish Homes;

b) where a housing authority secure the provision of suitable alternative accommodation under the Land Compensation Act 1973, s 39 (duty to re-house residential occupiers); and

c) the grant of a secure tenancy under the Housing Act 1985, s 554 or s 555 (grant of a tenancy to a former owner-occupier or statutory tenant of defective dwelling-house).

ANNEX 2: AMENDING AND SECONDARY LEGISLATION

AMENDMENT

This Annex was replaced by the Guidance contained in *Fair and flexible: statutory guidance on social housing allocations for local authorities in England* with effect from 4 December 2009: see paragraph 3 of the 2009 Guidance.

ANNEX 3: INDICATORS OF THE CRITERIA IN THE REASONABLE PREFERENCE CATEGORIES (SECTION 167(2)(C) AND (D))

Local housing authorities may devise their own indicators of the criteria in the reasonable preference categories in the 1996 Act (as amended), s 167(2). The following list is included for illustrative purposes and to assist housing authorities in this task: it is by no means comprehensive or exhaustive, and local housing authorities may have other, local factors to consider and include as indicators of the categories.

Unsanitary, overcrowded and unsatisfactory housing conditions

Lacking bathroom or kitchen

Lacking inside WC

Lacking cold or hot water supplies, electricity, gas, or adequate heating

Lack of access to a garden for children

Overcrowding

Sharing living room, kitchen, bathroom/WC

Property in disrepair

Property unfit

Poor internal or external arrangements

Under-occupation

Children in flats or maisonettes above ground floor.

People who need to move on medical or welfare grounds (criteria may apply to any member of the household)

A mental illness or disorder

A physical or learning disability

Chronic or progressive medical conditions (e g MS, HIV/AIDS)

Infirmity due to old age

The need to give or receive care

The need to recover from the effects of violence (including racial attacks) or threats of violence, or physical, emotional or sexual abuse

Ability to fend for self restricted for other reasons

Young people at risk

People with behavioural difficulties

Need for adapted housing and/or extra facilities, bedroom or bathroom

Need improved heating (on medical grounds)

Need sheltered housing (on medical grounds)

Need ground floor accommodation (on medical grounds)

Need to be near friends/relatives or medical facility on medical grounds.

ANNEX 4: CLASSES OF APPLICANTS WHO ARE ELIGIBLE FOR AN ALLOCATION OF HOUSING

AMENDMENT

This Annex was replaced by the Guidance contained in *Fair and flexible: statutory guidance on social housing allocations for local authorities in England* with effect from 4 December 2009: see paragraph 3 of the 2009 Guidance.

ANNEX 5: ELIGIBILITY PATHWAY: MODEL QUESTIONS AND PROCEDURES

AMENDMENT

This Annex was replaced by the Guidance contained in *Fair and flexible: statutory guidance on social housing allocations for local authorities in England* with effect from 4 December 2009: see paragraph 3 of the 2009 Guidance.

ANNEX 6: ALLOCATION OF HOUSING (ENGLAND) REGULATIONS 2002

AMENDMENT

This Annex was replaced by the Guidance contained in *Fair and flexible: statutory guidance on social housing allocations for local authorities in England* with effect from 4 December 2009: see paragraph 3 of the 2009 Guidance.

ANNEX 7: PERSONS SUBJECT TO IMMIGRATION CONTROL WHO ARE NOT ELIGIBLE FOR AN ALLOCATION OF HOUSING

AMENDMENT

This Annex was replaced by the Guidance contained in *Fair and flexible: statutory guidance on social housing allocations for local authorities in England* with effect from 4 December 2009: see paragraph 3 of the 2009 Guidance.

ANNEX 8: HOW TO IDENTIFY THE MAIN CLASSES OF PERSONS SUBJECT TO IMMIGRATION CONTROL WHO WILL BE ELIGIBLE FOR AN ALLOCATION

AMENDMENT

This Annex was replaced by the Guidance contained in *Fair and flexible: statutory guidance on social housing allocations for local authorities in England* with effect from 4 December 2009: see paragraph 3 of the 2009 Guidance.

ANNEX 9: EUROPEAN GROUPINGS (EU, EEA, ECSMA, ESC)

AMENDMENT

This Annex was replaced by the Guidance contained in *Fair and flexible: statutory guidance on social housing allocations for local authorities in England* with effect from 4 December 2009: see paragraph 3 of the 2009 Guidance.

ANNEX 10: HOW TO CONTACT THE HOME OFFICE'S IMMIGRATION AND NATIONALITY DIRECTORATE

1. The Home Office's Immigration and Nationality Directorate (IND) will exchange information with housing authorities subject to relevant data protection and disclosure policy requirements being met and properly managed, provided that the information is required to assist with the carrying out of statutory functions or prevention and detection of fraud.

2. The Evidence and Enquiries Unit (EEU) will provide a service to housing authorities to confirm the immigration status of an applicant from abroad (Non Asylum Seekers). In order to take advantage of the service, housing authorities first need to register with the Evidence and Enquiries Unit, Immigration and Nationality Directorate, C Block 3rd Floor, Whitgift Centre, Wellesley Road, Croydon, CR9 2AT either by letter or Fax: 020 8604 5783.

3. Registration details required by the EEUs Local Authorities Team are:

   (a) Name of enquiring housing authority on headed paper,
   (b) Job title/status of officer registering on behalf of the housing authority,
   (c) Names of housing authority staff and their respective job titles/status who will be making enquiries on behalf of the housing authority.

4. Once the housing authority is registered with the EEU, then the authorised personnel can make individual enquiries by letter or fax, but replies will be returned by post.

5. In cases where the EEU indicate that the applicant may be an asylum seeker, enquiries of their status can be made to the National Asylum Support Service (NASS) by **Fax: 020 8633 0014**. Copies of the EEUs correspondence must accompany the request.

ANNEX 11: HABITUAL RESIDENCE TEST

Allocation of Housing (England) Regulations 2002 provide that some classes of applicant will be eligible for an allocation subject to their being habitually resident in the Common Travel Area (CTA). However, in practice, when considering applications from these classes of applicant it is only necessary to investigate habitual residence if the applicant has entered the UK in the last two years.

Appendix 1
England: Allocation

A person can satisfy the Habitual Residence Test (HRT) if they are habitually resident in the CTA. The CTA includes:

- the UK
- Channel Islands
- Isle of Man
- Republic of Ireland

Action on receipt of an application

Applicant came to live in the UK in the last two years

If it appears that the applicant came to live in the UK in the last two years, make further enquiries to decide if the applicant is habitually resident, or can be treated as such.

If it appears that the applicant came to live in the UK in the last two years, make further enquiries to decide if the applicant is habitually resident, or can be treated as such.

Factors to consider

It is important to consider the applicants stated reasons and intentions for coming to the UK.

If the applicants stated intention is to live in the UK, and not return to the country from which they came, that intention must be consistent with their actions. To decide whether an applicant is habitually resident in the UK, consider the following factors.

Why has the applicant come to the UK?

A. If the applicant is returning to the UK after a period spent abroad, where it can be established that the applicant was previously habitually resident in the UK and is returning to resume his former period of habitual residence, he is immediately habitually resident. In determining whether an applicant is returning to resume a former period of habitual residence consider:

- When did the applicant leave the UK?
- How long did the applicant live in the UK before leaving?
- Why did the applicant leave the UK?
- How long did the applicant intend to remain abroad?
- Why did the applicant return?
- Did the applicant's partner and children, if any, also leave the UK?
- Did the applicant keep accommodation in the UK?
- If the applicant owned property, was it let, and was the lease timed to coincide with the applicants return to the UK?
- What links did the applicant keep with the UK?
- Have there been other brief absences? If yes, obtain details.
- Why has the applicant come to the UK?

B.   If the applicant has arrived in the UK within the previous two years and is not resuming a period of habitual residence, consideration should be given to his reasons for coming to the UK, and in particular to the factors set out below.

Work arrangements

If the applicant states that they have a job, consider:

- Is the work full time or part time?
- How many hours do/will they work?
- Is the work short-term employment, e g au pair, seasonal work?
- Is the applicant on a short-term contract with a current employer?

The applicant's employment record and in particular the nature of any previous occupation and plans for the future are relevant. A person with the offer of genuine and effective work in the UK, whether full time or part time, is likely to be habitually resident here.

Pattern of work

Consider the pattern of work, ie:

- Has the applicant had a succession of casual or short term jobs either in the UK or the previous country? Be aware that a history of working in short term jobs does not always mean an applicant is not habitually resident.
- What is the name and address of the employer are they well known for employing casual labour?
- Was the applicant worked in the UK previously? If so:
  - How long ago?
  - For what period, either casual or short term?
- Has the applicant work prospects? If the applicant has come to the UK to seek work:
  - Has a job been arranged?
  - Who has the job been arranged with?
  - If a job has not been secured, have enquiries been made about a job?
  - Who were the enquiries made with?
  - Does the applicant have qualifications to match their job requirements?
  - Does the applicant, in your opinion, have realistic prospects of finding work?
  - Are prospects of finding work in the UK any better than in the country they have left?

Joining family or friends

If the applicant has come to the UK to join or rejoin family or friends, consider:

- Has the applicant sold or given up any property abroad?
- Has the applicant bought or rented accommodation or are they staying with friends?
- Is their move to the UK permanent?

Applicant's plans

Consider the applicant's plans, ie:

- If the applicant plans to remain in the UK, is their stated plan consistent with their actions?
- Were any arrangements made for employment and accommodation before the applicant arrived in the UK?
- Did they buy a one-way ticket?
- Did they bring all their belongings with them?
- Is there any evidence of links with the UK, e.g. membership of clubs?

The fact that a person may intend to live in the UK for the foreseeable future does not, of itself, mean that habitual residence has been established. However, the applicant's intentions along with other factors, for example the purchase of a home in the UK and the disposal of property abroad may indicate that the applicant is habitually resident in the UK.

An applicant who intends to reside in the UK for only a short period, for example on holiday, to visit friends or for medical treatment, is unlikely to be habitually resident in the UK.

Length of residence in another country

Consider the length and continuity of an applicant's residence in another country:

- How long did the applicant live in the previous country?
- Have they lived in the UK before, if so for how long?
- Are there any remaining ties with their former country of residence?
- Has the applicant stayed in different countries outside the UK?

It is possible that a person may own a property abroad but still be habitually resident in the UK. A person who has a home or close family in another country would normally retain habitual residence in that country. A person who has previously lived in several different countries but has now moved permanently to the UK may be habitually resident here.

Centre of interest

An applicant is likely to be habitually resident in the CTA, despite spending time abroad, if their centre of interest is located in the CTA.

People who maintain their centre of interest in the UK, for example a home, a job, friends, membership of clubs, are likely to be habitually resident in the UK.

People who have retained their centre of interest in another country and have no particular ties here are unlikely to be habitually resident in the UK.

Take the following into account when deciding the centre of interest:

- Home
- Family ties
- Club memberships
- Finance accounts

If the centre of interest appears to be in the CTA but the applicant has a home abroad, consider the applicant's intentions regarding that property.

In certain cultures, e g the Asian culture, it is quite common for a person to have property abroad which they do not intend to sell, even if they have lived in the CTA for many years and do not intend to leave. This does not mean that an applicants centre of interest is anywhere but in the CTA.

Definition of habitually resident

The term habitually resident is not defined in legislation. Always consider the overall circumstances of a case to determine whether someone is habitually resident in the CTA.

The above is not an exhaustive check list of questions or factors which will need to be considered. Further enquiries may be needed. The circumstances of each case will dictate what information is needed, and it is vital all relevant factors are taken into account.

General principles

When deciding whether a person is habitually resident in a place consideration must be given to all the facts of each case in a common sense way. It should be remembered that:

- the test focuses on the fact and nature of residence and not the legal right of abode;
- a person who is not resident in this country at all cannot be habitually resident. Residence is a more settled state than mere physical presence in a country. To be resident a person must be seen to be making a home. It need not be the only home or a permanent home but it must be a genuine home for the time being. For example a short stay visitor or a person receiving short term medical treatment is not resident;
- it is a question of fact whether a person who has established residence in a country has also become habitually resident; this must be decided by reference to all the circumstances of the particular case;
- the most important factors for habitual residence are the length, continuity and general nature of actual residence;
- the practicality of a persons arrangements for residence is a necessary part of determining whether it can be described as settled and habitual; AND

- established habitual residents of this country who have periods of temporary or occasional absence of long or short duration may still be habitually resident during such absences.

ANNEX 12: ELIGIBILITY PATHWAY FLOW CHART

AMENDMENT

This Annex was replaced by the Guidance contained in *Fair and flexible: statutory guidance on social housing allocations for local authorities in England* with effect from 4 December 2009: see paragraph 3 of the 2009 Guidance.

ANNEX 13: INFORMATION ABOUT DECISIONS AND THE RIGHT TO A REVIEW OF A DECISION

Information about decisions

1. Under s 160(A)(9) and s 167(4A)(b), a housing authority must notify an applicant in writing of any decision

 (i) to treat him as ineligible by virtue of s 160A(3) or (5) (ie persons from abroad);

 (ii) to treat him as ineligible because of unacceptable behaviour serious enough to make him unsuitable to be a tenant of the housing authority;

 (iii) not to give an applicant any preference under the scheme because of unacceptable behaviour serious enough to make him unsuitable to be a tenant of the housing authority.

2. The notification must give clear grounds for the decision, which must be based firmly on the relevant facts of the case.

3. An applicant also has the right, on request, to be informed of any decision about the facts of the applicants case which has been, or is likely to be, taken into account in considering whether to make an allocation to him.

The right to a review of a decision

4. Under s 167(4A)(d) an applicant has the right to request a review of a decision:

 (i) to treat him as ineligible because of unacceptable behaviour serious enough to make him unsuitable to be a tenant of the housing authority;

 (ii) not to give him any preference under the scheme because of unacceptable behaviour serious enough to make him unsuitable to be a tenant of the housing authority;

 (iii) about the facts of his case which has been, or is likely to be taken into account in considering whether to make an allocation to him.

and to be informed of the decision on the review and the grounds for it.

5.   By virtue of s 166(2), a housing authority must inform an applicant that he has the rights set out in s 1674A, that is to say the right to a review of a decision, and the right to be informed of any decision about the facts of his case.

Allocation of Accommodation: Choice Based Lettings
Code of Guidance for Local Housing Authorities, August 2008

CONTENTS

CHAPTER 1

Purpose of the code

1.1 The Secretary of State is issuing this guidance to local housing authorities in England (referred to in this guidance as 'housing authorities') under s 169 of the Housing Act 1996 (the 1996 Act). Housing authorities must have regard to this guidance for the purposes of exercising their functions under sections 167(1A) and 167(2E) of the 1996 Act. This guidance is also relevant to the duties in sections 193(3A) and 195(3A) of the 1996 Act.

1.2 This code of guidance ('the Code')provides information about those factors which housing authorities should take into account in framing their allocation scheme to offer a choice of accommodation to applicants, and factors which they may wish to consider. Accordingly the guidance is primarily for those authorities which have in place or propose to have in place a policy of offering choice to applicants. It is not a substitute for legislation and in so far as it comments on the law can only reflect the Department's understanding at the time of issue. Housing authorities will still need to keep up to date with any developments in the law in this area.

1.3 Housing authorities which offer a choice of accommodation to applicants continue to allocate accommodation within the meaning of Part 6 of the 1996 Act and must comply with the provisions of Part 6. This guidance is therefore supplementary to the Allocation of Accommodation Code of Guidance for Local Housing Authorities[1] issued in November 2002 (referred to in this guidance as the 'Allocations Code').

Who the guidance is for

1.4 This guidance is specifically for housing authority members and staff. It is also of direct relevance to registered social landlords (referred to as RSLs). Where a housing authority requests it, RSLs have a duty under section 170 of the 1996 Act to co-operate to such extent as is reasonable in the circumstances in offering accommodation to people with priority under the authority's allocation scheme. Other private landlords may also work in partnership with housing authorities to enable applicants to be offered a choice of accommodation and this guidance may be of interest to these landlords.

1.5 Many of the activities covered by this guidance require joint planning and operational co-operation between housing authorities and other bodies. These are likely to include social services departments, health authorities, other referral agencies and voluntary sector organisations, and RSL 'HomeBuy Agents',[2] although this list is not exhaustive. This guidance will be relevant to these organisations as well.

---

[1]   Allocation of Accommodation Code of Guidance for Local Housing Authorities, ODPM 2002.

[2]   HomeBuy Agents are appointed RSLs which provide a point of contact for affordable housing options in a given area in England and handle the application process for the Open Market and New Build Homebuy products.

Legislation in context

1.6   In framing their allocation scheme to offer a choice of accommodation to applicants, housing authorities should ensure that their policies and procedures are compatible with obligations imposed on them by other existing legislation, in addition to Part 6 of the 1996 Act, including but not limited to:

- The Race Relations Act 1976 (in particular s 71)
- The Disability Discrimination Act 1995 (in particular s 49A)
- The Sex Discrimination Act 1975 (in particular s 76A)
- The Equality Act (Sexual Orientation) Regulations 2007 (in particular regulations 5 and 8)
- The Human Rights Act 1998
- The Freedom of Information Act 2000 (in particular s 19)
- The Data Protection Act 1998 (see paragraph 5.36 below)

1.7   Section 71 of the Race Relations Act 1976 (as amended by the Race Relations (Amendment) Act 2000) requires specified bodies, including local authorities, to have due regard to the need to eliminate unlawful racial discrimination and to promote equality of opportunity and good relations between people of different racial groups. The aim of this provision is to make the promotion of racial equality central to the way relevant services are designed and delivered. Local authorities are also required to publish a race equality scheme which must be reviewed every three years. Policies and procedures on offering choice to housing applicants should have regard both to wider duties imposed on public bodies in terms of race relations, and to the local authority's own race equality scheme.

1.8   Section 49A of the Disability Discrimination Act 1995 (inserted by the Disability Discrimination Act 2005) introduces a new duty to promote disability equality which is applicable to all public bodies, including housing authorities. This duty came into force in December 2006. It includes, amongst other things, the requirement to have due regard to:

- the need to promote equality of opportunity between disabled persons and other persons
- the need to eliminate unlawful discrimination and
- the need to take steps to take account of disabled persons disabilities, even where that involves treating disabled persons more favourably than other persons

1.9   The Equality Act (Sexual Orientation) Regulations 2007 (which are made under section 81 of the Equality Act 2006) make it unlawful to discriminate on the grounds of sexual orientation in the provision of goods, facilities and services, the disposal and management of premises and the exercise of public functions (amongst other things). Sexual orientation is defined in section 35 of the Equality Act 2006 as meaning an individual's sexual orientation towards persons of the same sex as him or her, persons of the opposite sex, or both. Lesbian, gay and bisexual applicants may often be reluctant to access services, including social housing, for fear of discrimination and/or fear of a lack of awareness or sensitivity to their issues among housing and support providers.

Housing authorities should be aware of this when framing their allocation policies and when considering the support and assistance available to applicants (see further Chapter 5).

1.10   Section 19 of the Freedom of Information Act 2000 requires public authorities to adopt and maintain a scheme which relates to the publication of information by the authority, and to publish information in accordance with that scheme. The publication scheme must specify the classes of information which the authority publishes or intends to publish; the manner in which information of each class is, or is intended to be, published; and whether the material is, or is intended to be, available to the public free of charge or on payment. The type of information covered by a publication scheme would include the authority's allocation scheme. This is in addition to the duties under section 168 of the Housing Act 1996 to make information available about the authority's allocation scheme.

1.11   The following guidance on the equalities duties is available on the Equality and Human Rights Commission website at www.equalityhuman rights.com:

- The Duty to Promote Equality: Statutory Code of Practice
- Housing and the Disability Equality Duty: A guide to the Disability Equality Duty and Disability Discrimination Act 2005 for the social housing sector
- Gender Equality Duty: Code of Practice for England and Wales
- The gender equality duty and local government: Guidance for public authorities in England
- The Statutory Code of Practice on Racial Equality in Housing (England).

1.12   The policies and procedures on offering a choice of accommodation should be seen in the context of the authority's other housing functions. They should be compatible with the local authority's housing strategy and the relevant regional (and sub-regional) housing strategy. Since the allocation of accommodation under Part 6 is one of the ways in which the main homelessness duty can be discharged, the policies and procedures on choice should also be considered as part of the housing authority's homelessness strategy.

1.13   For a wide range of vulnerable people, housing, care and support are inextricably linked, and housing authorities will want to consider how their policies on offering choice to applicants interacts with other programmes of care and support.

CHAPTER 2

Overview of the legislative provisions in Part 6 of the 1996 Act relating to offering choice to applicants and the Government's 'choice based lettings' policy

Introduction

2.1   This chapter provides an overview of the Government's policy on offering social housing tenants a choice of accommodation and sets out the obligations imposed on, and powers granted to, housing authorities under Part 6 of the 1996 Act which are particularly relevant to offering choice.

Housing authority's obligations under s 167(1A) of the 1996 Act and powers under section 167(2E)

2.2   Sections 167(1A) and 167(2E) of the 1996 Act were inserted by section 16 of the Homelessness Act 2002 ('the 2002 Act').

2.3   Section 167(1A) provides that an allocation scheme must include a statement as to the housing authority's policy on offering people who are to be allocated housing accommodation a choice of accommodation, or the opportunity to express preferences about the accommodation to be allocated to them. This means that the housing authority must take a policy decision on this issue and address it within their allocation scheme.

2.4   A policy of allowing applicants an opportunity to express their preferences on areas or types of property is not the same as offering applicants a choice of accommodation. In the Secretary of State's view all housing authorities should adopt an allocation scheme which offers a choice of accommodation and she has set a target for all housing authorities to have done so by 2010. In the meantime, however, housing authorities which do not offer a choice of accommodation should consider giving the applicant an opportunity to express preferences in relation to accommodation. This means allowing the applicant to express a preference about, for example, the location and type of accommodation to be allocated. Wherever possible, such preferences should be taken into account in allocating accommodation to that person.

2.5   Section 167(2E) provides that an allocation scheme may contain provision about the allocation of particular accommodation to a person who makes a specific application for that accommodation. This is intended to facilitate choice by providing for the adoption of 'advertising schemes' whereby applicants can apply for particular properties which have been advertised as vacant by the housing authority.

2.6   Section 167(2E) does not specify how authorities should offer a choice of accommodation. However, in the Secretary of State's view the most effective way of doing so is by adopting an advertising scheme and accordingly she expects that all housing authorities will adopt allocation policies and procedures which incorporate an advertising scheme.

Definition of 'choice based lettings scheme'

2.7   The term 'choice based lettings scheme' will be used in this guidance to mean that an authority has adopted allocation policies and procedures which incorporate an advertising scheme.

The Government's policy on offering a choice of accommodation to applicants

2.8   The Secretary of State believes that allocation policies for social housing should provide for applicants to be given more of a say and a greater choice over the accommodation which they are allocated, while continuing to ensure that the primary purpose of social housing is to meet housing need. This is the best way to ensure sustainable tenancies and to build settled, viable and inclusive communities. Research carried out for Communities and Local Government[3] into the longer impact of choice based lettings found that tenants who were offered a choice of accommodation were more likely to be satisfied with their home and remain in that home for a longer period. Satisfied tenants, it is suggested, are more likely to meet their tenancy obligations and maintain the property in good condition.

2.9   In January 2005, ODPM published *Sustainable Communities: Homes for All*.[4] Paragraphs 5.18 to 5.21 of that document set out the Government's choice based lettings policy objectives. These objectives are:

- to make it as easy as possible for applicants and tenants to move between local authority, housing association and privately owned accommodation by encouraging the extension of choice based lettings to cover low cost home ownership options and properties for rent from private landlords, as well as social housing
- to develop choice based lettings schemes on a regional and/or sub-regional basis, recognising that housing markets do not follow local authority boundaries
- to support prospective applicants to choose the housing option which is best for them, including: promoting a wide range of options within the district (including low cost home ownership, mutual exchange, the private sector); providing information about 'staying put' options such as aids and adaptations; mobility schemes, including moves from high to low demand areas; property shops and housing advice centres

---

[3]   *Monitoring the Longer Term Impact of Choice Based Lettings*, Heriot-Watt University and BMRB, October 2006

[4]   *Sustainable Communities: Homes for All*, Office of the Deputy Prime Minister, January 2005.

CHAPTER 3

Choice based lettings: general

The extent of a policy to offer choice to applicants

3.1　Where housing authorities adopt a policy of offering a choice of accommodation, the policy should, as far as possible, extend to all applicants and to all available accommodation. Policies which restrict choice to certain categories of applicant or certain types of dwelling are likely to be more difficult for applicants to understand, and may be regarded as less open and transparent. Local authorities should ensure that any policy of restricting choice does not have a discriminatory impact on a particular group or community.

3.2　The fact that certain applicants – for example, people with physical or mental impairments – may have difficulty in making an application for accommodation without assistance, should not preclude them from being offered a choice of accommodation. Instead applicants should have access to any necessary assistance to enable them to make an application (see paragraphs 5.22 to 5.28). Likewise, the fact that certain applicants may have difficulty in living independently in the community without care and/or support should not preclude them from being offered a choice of accommodation. Rather housing authorities should work together with other relevant agencies and providers to ensure that people can apply for appropriate accommodation and receive the support and care necessary to allow them to live as independently as possible. To this end, wherever practicable, specialist and supported accommodation should be advertised to extend choice to as many people as possible. However, where specialist or supported accommodation is advertised alongside other accommodation, it is important to make clear that only those applicants with relevant housing and/or support needs may apply for it. This may be done, for example, by making clear in the details of the advert that only certain categories of applicants will be considered for the accommodation (see paragraphs 4.62, 4.72 and 4.73).

3.3　There may be occasions, however, when it is not advisable or practicable to offer a choice of accommodation to a particular applicant or category of applicants. This category could include sexual or violent offenders where the need to manage the risk which they pose to other individuals or the community in general could limit the amount of choice they can reasonably be allowed. Applicants who pose a risk should not necessarily be precluded from taking part in a choice based lettings scheme but it may be necessary to restrict the properties they can apply for or reserve the right to reject their bid[5] in certain circumstances. Housing authorities must ensure that they have given due consideration to any application made in accordance with the procedural requirements of their allocation scheme (see s 166(3) of the 1996 Act). It therefore follows that, where an authority decides to reject a bid on risk

---

[5]　For a definition of 'bid' see paragraph 3.7 below.

grounds which would otherwise have been successful, the applicant should be informed of the reasons for the decision and preferably informed of the properties they can bid for.

3.4   Local authorities may wish to reserve the right to make direct lets to manage the risk posed by some applicants or for other management reasons.[6] Examples might include: people whose property has been compulsorily purchased (where the local authority is required to offer a specific property to meet the legal requirements) or reluctant decants (ie people who have been required to leave their original property to facilitate an area regeneration scheme, for example, and who are reluctant to participate in the bidding process to move out of temporary into permanent accommodation); people seeking a move under a witness mobility scheme; and MAPPA[7] clients who pose a very serious risk to the community.

3.5   Housing authorities should try to keep to a minimum the circumstances in which choice may have to be restricted and should ensure that these are clearly set out in the published allocation scheme.

Applications for housing accommodation

3.6   Section 166(3) of the 1996 Act requires a housing authority to consider every application for an allocation of accommodation, provided it is made in accordance with the procedural requirements of the allocation scheme.

3.7   Applying for an allocation of accommodation where an authority operates a choice based lettings scheme will normally involve applicants in a two-stage process: in the first instance they will be required to apply to join the scheme; and in the second stage they will be required to express an interest in particular accommodation (a process which may be referred to as 'bidding') if they wish to be considered for an allocation of that accommodation. It is important that the procedural requirements of the allocation scheme cover both parts of this process and distinguish clearly between them.

Open v closed advertising

3.8   Housing authorities are encouraged to adopt an 'open advertising' approach whereby all applicants and interested members of the wider local population can find out about vacancies which are advertised (eg in a local newspaper or on a public website). Open advertising is more likely to engender trust and confidence in the choice based lettings scheme. It also helps ensure that applicants, and those who may be considering applying for social housing,

---

6   For the purposes of this guidance, the term 'direct let' refers to accommodation which is not let through the authority's choice based lettings scheme, that is to say where the applicant is not offered a choice of accommodation. Where a letting does not constitute an allocation under Part 6 of the 1996 Act (eg, where an existing tenant is moved for management reasons, rather than at his/her own request, or where the letting is excluded from Part 6 by virtue of regulations made under s 160(4) of the 1996 Act) it will be referred to as a 'management let'.

7   Multi Agency Public Protection arrangements for assessing and managing the risks posed by sexual and violent offenders.

are aware of what accommodation is, or is likely to become, available, thus making it easier for authorities to manage expectations.

Eligibility

3.9　　Housing authorities must ascertain if an applicant is eligible for an allocation of accommodation, or whether he or she is excluded from an allocation under s 160(A)(1), (3) or (5) of the 1996 Act. Housing authorities may also decide to treat an applicant as ineligible for an allocation because of serious unacceptable behaviour under s 160A(7) of the 1996 Act.

3.10　　Section 160A of the 1996 Act prevents an authority from allocating housing to a person who is not eligible. In the Secretary of State's view, an authority should consider an applicant's eligibility, both:

    a.　　at the time he or she applies to join the choice based lettings scheme; and

    b.　　at the point at which he or she is considered for an allocation of particular accommodation.

It is important to consider whether an applicant is eligible at registration because an applicant who is accepted onto a choice based lettings scheme has a reasonable expectation that he or she will be eligible to be allocated accommodation under that scheme. However, it is also important to check again on the applicant's eligibility when considering making an allocation to him or her, particularly where a substantial amount of time has elapsed since the applicant registered with the scheme.

3.11　　Where a housing authority concludes, at the time that the applicant joins the scheme, that he or she is a person from abroad but is nonetheless eligible for housing, it is recommended that the authority inform the applicant that changes to his or her immigration status or the statutory eligibility criteria prior to an allocation could affect his or her eligibility.

Offers of accommodation and refusals

3.12　　As a general rule, accommodation which has been advertised should be offered to the bidder who:

- has the highest priority under the allocation scheme, and
- matches the lettings criteria for that property

So, for example, a couple without children will not usually be permitted to bid successfully for property which has more than one bedroom. In some circumstances, it may be appropriate to attach more restrictive lettings criteria to individual properties, for example, where a s 106 agreement is in place, or where the property belongs to an RSL which operates different and more restrictive eligibility criteria. Where this is the case, the advert should, wherever possible, set out clearly the particular criteria which apply to that property (see paragraph 4.71). However, there may be other reasons why it would be necessary or advisable to reject a bid which would otherwise have been successful: where, for example, the property would not be suitable for that particular applicant (see paragraphs 3.3 and 4.77 about applicants who pose a risk to others and themselves). However, an authority should not reject such a bid, unless there are sound reasons for doing so, in accordance with the allocation scheme. Where an authority does pass over a bid which would otherwise have been successful, they should provide the applicant with the reasons for this decision.

3.13   Housing authorities should not, as a matter of course, impose penalties on applicants who refuse an offer of accommodation which they have applied for under a choice based lettings scheme.[8] This is particularly the case where applicants are expected to apply for properties before they have had a chance to view them. Rather, authorities should ensure that applicants receive sufficient information about the property which is advertised to enable them to make an informed decision as to whether or not to bid for it. This is the best way to ensure that applicants do not bid for properties which do not meet their needs or aspirations.

3.14   The Secretary of State is aware that some authorities restrict the number of bids which applicants can make at any particular time. There may be sound reasons for doing this: for example, to limit the number of refusals; and to minimise the administrative burden, and/or potential for delay, associated with managing a large number of bids. However, authorities are reminded that such an approach may restrict the amount of choice available to applicants, and may distort the feedback on properties which have been let. Authorities should also bear in mind that some applicants will be better equipped than others to use their limited bids to the best effect. Where authorities decide to restrict the number of bids which applicants can make, they should ensure that applicants who might be disadvantaged by such an approach have access to the appropriate advice and assistance to enable them to participate effectively.

3.15   As stated at paragraph 3.11 of the Allocations Code, applicants must be allowed a reasonable period to make a decision about accommodation offered to them under Part 6 of the 1996 Act. This applies equally to accommodation offered under a choice based lettings scheme. The Secretary of State considers that the fact that an applicant has expressed an interest in particular accommodation by bidding for it should not be treated as meaning that he or she has made a final decision to accept it. This is particularly the case where applicants have not had the opportunity to view the property before submitting an application.

3.16   Some applicants may require a longer period than others. For example, applicants requiring additional assistance and/or support may wish to take advice in making their decision. Housing authorities should allow sufficient time for such applicants to arrange for an adviser or advocate (who may be a friend or family member) to accompany them when viewing accommodation. This would be in line with a housing authority's duty to make reasonable

Appendix 1
England: Allocation

---

8   For further advice on offers of accommodation to applicants owed the main homelessness duty, see paragraphs 4.50 to 4.59.

adjustments for disabled people, including changes to their practices policies and procedures. Applicants may also need more time to view properties, where they need to travel long distances to do so (see further at paragraph 7.17).

CHAPTER 4

Choice based lettings: policy content and scheme design

4.1–4.49 ...

AMENDMENT

These paragraphs were replaced by the Guidance contained in *Fair and flexible: statutory guidance on social housing allocations for local authorities in England* with effect from 4 December 2009: see paragraph 4 of the 2009 Guidance.

Choice for applicants owed the main homelessness duty

4.50 By virtue of sections 193(3A) and 195(3A) of the 1996 Act, housing authorities are required to give people, to whom they owe a homelessness duty under sections 193 or 195, a copy of the statement included in their allocation scheme under s 167(1A) about their policy on offering choice or the opportunity to express preferences about Part 6 housing accommodation. Housing authorities must therefore ensure that their allocation scheme addresses the extent to which they are able to offer choice (or the ability to express preferences) to people to whom they owe one of these homelessness duties (see paragraph 5.7 of the Allocations Code of Guidance).

4.51 The Secretary of State considers that people owed the main homelessness duty (under s 193(2)) should, wherever possible, be offered a choice of Part 6 accommodation where they are awaiting an allocation that will bring the homelessness duty to an end.

4.52 Authorities are reminded that the main homelessness duty may also be brought to an end where the applicant accepts a 'qualifying offer' of an assured shorthold tenancy made by a private landlord (in accordance with section 193(7B)–(7F)).

4.53 Some people owed the main homelessness duty may need advice and assistance in order to participate actively in a choice based lettings scheme. Authorities are, therefore, advised to pay particular attention to the guidance in paragraphs 5.22 to 5.28 to ensure that people owed the main homelessness duty are not disadvantaged under a choice based lettings system.

4.54 The Secretary of State recognises that in certain circumstances (for example, where there is a shortage of social housing and/or where applicants owed the main homelessness duty do not have high priority under an authority's allocation scheme) providing choice for applicants owed the main homelessness duty for an unrestricted period could mean that such applicants wait an unreasonably long time before they are offered suitable Part 6 accommodation. This is unlikely to be in the best interests of applicants or authorities, particularly where it leads to extended periods in temporary accommodation. Accordingly, authorities will need to consider whether, in these circumstances, it would be appropriate to limit the period during which applicants can exercise choice and refuse offers without bringing the homelessness duty to an end.

4.55 Applicants should not be put under pressure so that they feel constrained to bid for accommodation that may not be suitable for them and their household. This would be unacceptable for the applicant and would not discharge the homelessness duty (which requires that the authority is satisfied that the accommodation offered is suitable). Accordingly, the period during which they are allowed to take part in the choice based lettings scheme (referred to hereafter as 'the bidding period') should be realistic. In determining how long the bidding period should be, authorities should take into account the pressure on social housing in the district and the time it would normally take before an opportunity to bid on a suitable property became available for someone with similar priority under the scheme. Larger households and those with special needs which are difficult to meet (eg those who need accessible accommodation) may need a longer time to bid for properties since the availability of suitable vacancies is likely to be limited.

4.56 It is important that there is a process for examining why an applicant has failed to be successful in being offered a suitable CBL property during the bidding period. Where it becomes clear that nothing suitable has been advertised during the bidding period; that the applicant has not fully understood what he or she was expected to do under the scheme; or that the applicant was incapable of accessing the scheme without advice and assistance, the authority should consider extending the period. The authority should also address any need for further advice and assistance to enable the applicant to participate effectively in the choice based lettings scheme.

4.57 Where the authority does not extend the bidding period, they should ensure that the applicant is aware that the period has ended and that he or she will no longer be able to bid for properties. The authority should also ensure that the applicant is aware of what is to happen next. Since the authority is still under a duty to secure that accommodation is available for occupation by the applicant, the options available to the authority are to offer the applicant:

- an allocation of suitable accommodation under Part 6 in accordance with the applicant's priority under the allocation scheme or
- a 'qualifying offer' of an assured shorthold tenancy in the private rented sector

The tenant should be made aware that the offer of Part 6 accommodation is a 'final' offer which will bring the authority's duty to an end (see following paragraph). In respect of a qualifying offer the duty only ends where the tenant accepts the offer.

4.58 Where the authority makes a 'final' offer of accommodation under Part 6, the main homelessness duty will come to an end if:

- the applicant accepts the offer, or

- having been informed of the possible consequences of refusal and of the right to request a review of the suitability of the accommodation, the applicant refuses the offer

Under section 193(7A), an offer of accommodation is a 'final' offer of accommodation only if it is in writing and states that it is a 'final' offer for the purposes of section 193(7). However, by section 193(7F) of the 1996 Act, an authority cannot make a 'final' offer unless they are satisfied that the accommodation is suitable for the applicant and that it is reasonable for the applicant to accept the offer.

4.59   Where the homelessness duty has come to an end following refusal of a final offer, applicants should not be precluded from participating in the choice based lettings scheme – although it should be made clear to them that they will no longer have the reasonable preference which had been accorded to them as a person who was owed the main homelessness duty.

Providing choice for disabled people with access needs

4.60   Section 167(2)(d) of the 1996 Act provides that people who need to move on 'medical and welfare' grounds must be given reasonable preference for an allocation. Section 167(2) has been revised (by section 223 of the Housing Act 2004) to make clear that 'medical and welfare grounds' include grounds relating to a disability. The amendment, which came into effect on 27 April 2005, is intended to ensure that disabled people with access needs are given appropriate priority for social housing.

4.61   The Secretary of State encourages housing authorities to include accessible properties (ie housing which has been designed or adapted to meet the needs of disabled people) within their choice based lettings scheme. She believes that this is the best way to ensure that disabled people have the widest possible choice of accommodation.

4.62   The Secretary of State believes that accessible housing should be allocated to people with relevant access needs. Accordingly, the Secretary of State encourages housing authorities to design their choice based lettings scheme in such a way that priority for accessible accommodation is given to people who have access needs. This is consistent with the duty to promote disability equality. One way to do this would be by means of the advertising criteria.

4.63   While it would be lawful to provide that only disabled people can apply for accessible vacancies, it would not be lawful to provide that disabled people can only apply for accessible property. However, where a disabled applicant applies for accommodation which does not meet his or her access needs, the housing authority will need to take into account whether it is reasonable and practicable to adapt that property when assessing his or her bid (and must do so in accordance with their duties under the Disability Discrimination Act 1995 and the Housing Grants, Construction and Regeneration Act 1996). If it is reasonable and practicable for the property to be adapted, the disabled applicant should be considered for the vacancy on the same basis as other applicants who have submitted a bid. Where there is a shortage of accessible property, and failure to adapt a property would lead to unreasonable delays in housing for a disabled person then the local authority should take steps to identify properties which are suitable to be adapted, and consider giving priority to disabled persons who bid for such properties.

4.64   Where an accessible property is advertised, it is important that the property is identified as such in the advertisement and that the advertisement gives sufficient information about the level of adaptations and/or accessibility features in the accommodation for disabled applicants to make an informed decision on whether or not to apply for the particular property. In the Secretary of State's view, this is the best way to ensure that:

- the most effective and efficient use is made of accessible housing stock; and
- disabled people are allocated accommodation which meets their needs, while giving them the widest possible choice and a greater say over where they live

4.65   In the case of accessible accommodation, it is also particularly important to include information about external access to the property (eg whether there is a ramp up to the property and whether there is accessible parking nearby) and relevant information about the surrounding area (eg are local shops and public transport easily accessible).

4.66   Housing authorities are also encouraged to maintain lists or databases of accessible housing within their district. This is likely to be of assistance to disabled applicants even where property is allocated under a choice based lettings scheme. Disabled applicants should be able to see the full range of accessible properties (the number and type of properties; accessibility features and level of adaptations of each property; and location) and be informed about the time they are likely to wait for any type of property to become available. Such information can assist people in determining whether to apply for a particular vacancy which is advertised.

4.67   Disabled people may need additional assistance and support to participate in a choice based lettings scheme on an equal footing with other applicants. The nature and degree of assistance they require will depend on the nature and degree of their disability. The following is a non-exhaustive list of the type of assistance and support which housing authorities should consider making available, some of which they will, in any case, be required to do under disability equality legislation:

- advising individual disabled applicants when suitable accessible property is about to or has been advertised
- making arrangements to enable applicants with disabilities to visit properties
- ensuring that websites are accessible for people who have visual impairments or learning disabilities
- using symbols rather than words in adverts
- providing large print maps on websites

- enabling text messaging for people who have hearing impairments
- providing documents in large or clear print, Moon or Braille
- making information available on computer disk or audiotape
- training appropriate staff in the use of British Sign Language and/or Makaton
- ensuring that advice and information is available over the telephone – for those who cannot use a website or cannot get to a property or advice shop easily
- mailing out literature to the housebound and physically disabled
- ensuring that people with learning disabilities who do not have support from any other source (eg friend, relative or social worker) are assigned a suitably trained member of staff to support them.

Local lettings policies and advertising criteria, labelling

4.68–4.71 ...

AMENDMENT

These paragraphs were replaced by the Guidance contained in *Fair and flexible: statutory guidance on social housing allocations for local authorities in England* with effect from 4 December 2009: see paragraph 4 of the 2009 Guidance.

Advertising criteria – 'restrictive labelling'

4.72 Where accommodation is allocated by means of a choice based lettings scheme, housing authorities may wish to attach criteria (known as 'advertising criteria' or 'restrictive labelling') to particular accommodation which is advertised specifying, for example, that:

- only people of a particular description may apply for that particular accommodation or
- people of a particular description will be given preference for that particular accommodation

4.73 Restrictive labelling may be used, for example, to give effect to a local lettings policy (see paragraphs 4.67 to 4.71) or to a target-based system (see paragraph 4.38 to 4.43), or to match people with access needs to accessible accommodation. It is important that the practical application of such labelling should be operated in accordance with criteria or policies which are set out clearly in the authority's allocation scheme, and that the effect should not be directly or indirectly discriminatory. Where an authority uses restrictive labelling, it should monitor the impact to ensure that it continues to comply with its duty to give reasonable preference to applicants in the reasonable preference categories.

Restricting choice

4.74 The fact that a housing authority adopts a policy of offering choice does not mean that applicants should be able to express an interest in and be considered for any and every available vacancy.

4.75 In framing and operating a policy of choice, a housing authority should be mindful of the need to ensure that there are no adverse implications for the good use of their stock and that it does not conflict with their ability to continue to provide for housing need.

4.76 So, for example, applicants should not be permitted to apply for vacancies which would result in statutory overcrowding. Conversely authorities will normally wish to ensure that applicants are not permitted to apply for vacancies which would result in under-occupation, although there may be occasions where this makes good housing management sense (eg in the case of hard-to-let properties or where the authority wishes to bring down the child density ratio on an estate). The information which is provided when a property is advertised ('the advertising criteria') should assist applicants in establishing whether or not they are entitled to express an interest in a particular vacancy.

4.77 The duty to confer reasonable preference on certain categories of people means that an authority should ensure that they are allocated accommodation which meets their identified needs. It is for the authority to make a final judgment on whether it is appropriate to allocate particular accommodation to a particular individual even under a choice based lettings scheme. So, for example, an authority may decide that it is inappropriate to house a drug user on an estate which is known to have a large proportion of other users or where there is a known drug dealer. However, it is important that an authority does not second-guess an individual's needs and should normally take into account his or her views before making a final decision. The authority may find that the drug user's main source of support lives on that estate as well.

4.78 There may be policy justification for designing a choice based lettings scheme to ensure that not all the popular properties go to those in greater housing need (eg by providing that priority cards will cease to have effect where more than a specified number of bids are received for an advertised vacancy). However, such an approach may limit the scope for those who must be given reasonable preference for an allocation to access housing which meets their needs, and may, for example, inadvertently lead to concentrations of homeless applicants in unpopular areas or in areas where there is already a high concentration of deprivation. Where authorities do adopt such an approach, it should be monitored carefully to ensure, for example, that it does not produce outcomes which are discriminatory on racial or other grounds, or conflict with the authority's ability to continue to provide for housing need. Such an approach is not recommended in areas where there is high demand for social housing or where a large proportion of housing applicants are in housing need.

Choice and mobility

4.79–4.80 ...

AMENDMENT

These paragraphs were replaced by the Guidance contained in *Fair and flexible: statutory guidance on social housing allocations for local authorities in England* with effect from 4 December 2009: see paragraph 4 of the 2009 Guidance.

CHAPTER 5

Managing a Choice Based Lettings scheme

Consultation

5.1 Paragraphs 6.4–6.6 of the Allocations Code provide guidance on considerations which authorities should take into account when consulting on changes to their allocation scheme, or before they adopt a new scheme, and this will include the adoption of a policy of offering choice to applicants.

5.2 Authorities are required to consult RSLs with which they have nomination arrangements. When considering whether to adopt a policy of offering choice to applicants, authorities are urged to go further than the statutory requirement to consult and explore the possibility of entering into partnership with all or most of the RSLs in their district so as to offer all those who are seeking social housing the widest possible choice of accommodation. It is important to do this at an early stage, so that RSLs are given the opportunity to contribute to the design of the choice based lettings scheme.

5.3 Organisations and individuals who provide advice and support to applicants will be crucial to the success of a choice based lettings scheme. In addition to their relevant statutory partners (such as social services, prisons, probation and primary care trusts) and voluntary bodies which provide care and support, authorities should consider whether there are other organisations which represent the interests of existing or potential applicants who may be socially excluded or disadvantaged by a choice based lettings system. Examples may include groups which represent ethnic minority communities, the gypsy and traveller community, veterans, ex-offenders, and drug or alcohol misusers. Bodies which represent the views of older people and people with physical and learning disabilities and mental health problems, and their carers, should also be included. Involving these groups will help authorities meet their race equality, disability and gender equality duties.

5.4 Authorities are also urged to consult existing tenants, applicants and residents. It may also be helpful to involve users in designing and testing various aspects of the scheme, in particular any supporting technology (eg a website). It will be particularly helpful to involve users who may have particular communication requirements, for example, people with visual impairments, those with learning disabilities, or those who cannot understand or speak English well, as well as people with poor literacy and computer skills.

Information, advice and assistance/support

5.5 Section 166(1) of the 1996 Act provides that housing authorities must ensure that advice and information about the right to apply for accommodation is available free of charge to everyone in their district.

5.6 Housing authorities should also ensure that sufficient information is available to all applicants to enable them to apply for accommodation. This includes general information about the procedures for applying to go on the scheme and for applying for advertised vacancies; information about how applicants are prioritised under the scheme and how successful applicants are selected; and the rationale for advertising criteria, for example that priority for bungalows is given to older people or those with disabilities (see paragraphs 4.72 to 4.73 above). Information about review procedures should also be included. If RSL vacancies are included in the scheme, it will be helpful for applicants to know whether each RSL operates specific exclusion policies and, if so, what these are. Information should be easy to understand and should be available in translation where relevant and in alternative formats (Braille; large print, and audiotapes etc).

5.7   It is also important that information can be accessed by all applicants. Choice based lettings schemes which rely entirely, or to a large extent, on web-based information, for example, may restrict participation by applicants who have difficulty accessing or operating a computer. Likewise, authorities which rely on local papers or freesheets to advertise accommodation should ensure that they are widely available at locations across the district, or directly mailed to applicants who would otherwise have difficulty accessing them (eg the housebound). Prisoners are a particular group who are likely to have difficulty accessing information. This is because many prisoners cannot obtain newspapers or access the internet, neither can they contact the choice based lettings scheme directly. One way around this might be to arrange for housing advice surgeries in prison. Such outreach work might also be appropriate in the case of other applicants who are traditionally considered to be hard to reach, such as the gypsy and traveller community.

5.8   Ideally information should be available using a variety of media, including printed hard copy form, on a website or via the telephone. While authorities should provide user-friendly information about their choice based lettings scheme, this is in addition to, rather than an alternative to, the duties in sections 167 and 168 to have and publish an allocation scheme. However, in the spirit of openness and to ensure that applicants have access to as much information as possible, authorities are also encouraged to publish their allocation scheme on their website as well as in hard copy form.

5.9   Applicants also need information about particular vacancies which are advertised in order to determine:

- whether they are entitled to bid for the property
- whether the property meets their needs and any other requirements and
- what their likelihood of success would be if they expressed an interest for the property

information in the advert will be important and should include basic details about the property such as:

- location
- type (flat, bungalow etc)
- size (eg number of bedrooms)
- floor, and whether or not it has a lift

- type of heating
- whether it has a garden
- the amount of rent payable

The information required will depend on the nature of the applicant. So, for example, disabled applicants will need to know about the type and level of adaptations. The more information provided (eg about the condition of the property or about access to services) the easier it is for applicants to make an informed decision. Information about local services and opportunities, such as transport, education and employment, may be provided through signposting to other websites, for example. Advertising criteria could be used to indicate what type of applicant is entitled or excluded from bidding for a property, or who will be given preference for a property. Authorities must be careful to ensure that advertising criteria are not unlawfully discriminatory. Adverts should be unambiguous and easy to understand. Authorities should consider how to address the needs of applicants, for example, who are deaf, who are blind or partially sighted, who have learning disabilities, or who cannot read English. Symbols rather than words, the use of Braille and translations may all assist; or information on available vacancies could be provided to applicants by telephone.

Information and advice about stock availability and other housing options

5.10 Many housing authorities have found that the introduction of choice based lettings has led to an immediate and significant increase in the number of applications for social housing. In some areas, this has included a marked rise in the numbers of applications from people who are traditionally under-represented in social housing, such as people in employment, indicating that choice based lettings schemes can have a positive impact on the way social housing is viewed. However, it is also clear that housing authorities which introduce choice based lettings schemes need to put in place strategies to manage expectations, recognising that those who bid unsuccessfully over a long period of time may become frustrated or disillusioned.

5.11 An applicant has the right to information to help him or her assess whether accommodation appropriate to his or her needs is likely to be made available and, if so, how long this is likely to take. 'Feedback' about advertised properties which have been let (see paragraphs 5.14 to 5.18 below) may assist applicants to assess how long they are likely to have to wait for a particular type of property or property in a particular location. Authorities should also consider making available general information about the profile of their stock. This might include the type, size and location of the stock, whether it is accessible or could be adapted, whether there is access to a shared or private garden, and how old it is. In the case of stock which is in short supply, an indication of how frequently it is likely to become available would also be helpful.

5.12   Some applicants may have to wait a considerable time before appropriate accommodation is made available to them, particularly in areas of high demand for social housing and/or where the applicant has low priority. In some cases, applicants may have little prospect of ever being allocated accommodation. It could assist such applicants to know about other appropriate housing options which might be available to them. This might include:

- private rented accommodation
- low cost home ownership options
- mobility schemes which enable applicants to move out of the district
- home improvement schemes or aids and adaptations services which enable applicants to remain in their existing accommodation for longer

Authorities are encouraged to make general information about housing options available to all applicants, for example, when they apply to join a choice based lettings scheme, or more generally via the website or weekly freesheets. Authorities are also encouraged to offer more specialised housing options advice to individual applicants whenever this may be appropriate (for example, in the case of applicants who bid frequently but without success).

Advice

5.13   A choice based lettings approach requires applicants to be more proactive than a traditional allocations approach in which allocation decisions are made by housing officers on the basis of need. For this reason all applicants may need advice as well as information to assist them to participate successfully. This is likely to be particularly important for applicants when they first join a choice based lettings scheme. Advice could be provided by staff of the authority or another partner landlord, or by the voluntary sector. It is likely to be most effective if the person providing the advice has appropriate housing related experience and is properly trained to sensitively meet the needs of a diverse client group.

Information about accommodation which has been allocated under a choice based lettings scheme – 'Feedback' information

5.14   It is recommended that housing authorities publish information about accommodation which has been allocated through a choice based lettings scheme (more commonly known as 'feedback'). This might specify the number of applications/bids received for the property and give an indication of the reason why the property was allocated to the successful applicant which will normally relate to their level of priority under the scheme. An example might be the band and waiting time of the applicant, or their points level. This information can be extremely useful both to those applicants who have expressed an interest in the vacancy, because it notifies them that the particular vacancy has been let, and to applicants generally, because it assists them to make judgments about what sort of property to bid for in future. Since this information is likely to be of interest to most if not all applicants, it should be easily accessible and authorities may want to consider using a variety of media, such as the local newspaper and website.

5.15   However, housing authorities need to bear in mind that section 166(4) prohibits them from divulging to other members of the public that a person is an applicant for social housing, unless they have the applicant's consent. Furthermore, authorities should process any personal data which they hold about applicants consistently with the Data Protection Act 1998. This means that, where housing authorities publish information about particular accommodation which has been allocated under a choice based lettings scheme, they must be careful not to provide information which would enable a member of the public to ascertain the identity of the individual applicant who has been allocated the accommodation. In particular, housing authorities should guard against providing information which might put the successful applicant at risk of violence or intimidation by other individuals or members of the public. In extreme cases, it may be advisable not to publish the fact that a property has been let. However, authorities should avoid doing this unnecessarily as it is likely to detract from the transparency of the scheme.

5.16   Where direct lettings are made for whatever reason, information about these lettings should normally be published alongside information about lettings made through the choice based lettings scheme. If providing information about individual lettings could lead to intimidation or harassment, or otherwise put vulnerable tenants at risk, then it might be preferable to generalise the feedback information, for example by publishing the number of direct lets made in any period.

5.17   Individual applicants who have expressed an interest in a particular vacancy but are unsuccessful may want more personalised feedback, for example, about their relative position on the shortlist, or on why they were unsuccessful. It would be helpful if authorities were able to provide this wherever possible. Authorities should also consider providing more detailed feedback to all unsuccessful bidders at regular intervals – perhaps after they have submitted a certain number of unsuccessful bids. This might involve advising applicants about the need to change their bidding strategy, or providing them with advice about alternative housing options available to them, eg low cost home ownership options or the private rented sector (see paragraph 5.12 above).

5.18   Authorities may wish to go further and extract generalised information from feedback data to help inform applicants' bidding strategies generally. For example, authorities could produce and publish tables giving estimated waiting times by estate or parish and/or property type.

Application form

5.19   While application forms should not be so complex/complicated that applicants have difficulty in completing them, it is important that they are drafted to obtain sufficient information from applicants to enable authorities to identify those applicants who are likely to have:

- priority under the authority's scheme and/or
- difficulty in making an application or choosing their accommodation without additional assistance

and to assess an applicant's access or support needs, or at least to alert authorities to the need to make further inquiries.

5.20 Application forms should also obtain sufficient information to enable authorities to determine applicants' eligibility and to monitor the fairness of allocations and compliance with equal opportunities requirements. So, for example, information about ethnicity, disability and gender should be collected through the application form. Best practice might also encourage the collection of data by age, religion and sexual orientation.

5.21 Where application forms obtain sufficiently detailed information, they can be a useful tool in assessing the housing needs of the district.

Support and assistance

5.22 Section 166(1)(b) of the 1996 Act requires a housing authority to secure that any necessary assistance is made available free of charge to persons in its district who are likely to have difficulty in making an application without assistance. Paragraph 6.9 of the Allocations Code provides that, where authorities adopt an allocation policy which requires the active participation of housing applicants in choosing their accommodation, the level of assistance needed by those who are likely to have difficulty in making an application will normally be greater, and housing authorities will need to provide for this. In providing for this, authorities are advised to consider:

- which individuals or group of applicants are likely to have difficulty in making an application without assistance
- how to identify individuals who need assistance
- what type and level of assistance are they likely to require and
- whether that assistance is currently available and from what organisation

5.23 Some people in the reasonable preference categories may need a high level of additional assistance. In such cases failure to provide such assistance could result in an individual failing to participate in the choice based letting scheme. Authorities must ensure that applicants are given the assistance they need to make certain they receive the reasonable preference to which they are entitled.

5.24 However, housing authorities are advised not to equate those who may have difficulty in participating in a choice based lettings scheme with those who are in the reasonable preference categories. It is not necessarily the case that only those in the reasonable preference categories will have difficulty participating in a choice based lettings scheme; neither is it necessarily the case that everyone in the reasonable preference categories will need assistance to participate. The following is a list of people who may have difficulty in making an application without assistance of some sort – the list is illustrative and not exhaustive:

- those for whom English is not their first language (eg refugees)
- people who have literacy problems
- people with learning disabilities
- people who lead chaotic lifestyles, such as those who misuse drugs or alcohol
- people with mental health problems
- those who are currently undergoing a crisis in their lives and for whom their housing situation may be only one of many problems, such as victims of domestic violence
- those who are socially excluded such as rough sleepers
- the gypsy and traveller community
- older people and those suffering from a long-term disability
- vulnerable young people

5.25   The appropriate type and level of assistance will depend on the type of difficulty the applicant is likely to experience. In some cases it may simply be a matter of ensuring that information and advice is available in translation or that people are given information about translation services; or that any relevant written material is delivered to those who are housebound. However, someone with a severe learning disability or acute mental health problem is likely to require intensive support throughout the process.

5.26   It is important that housing authorities work together with social services, prisons, probation and relevant health bodies and professionals, other housing providers, the community and voluntary sector, and carers and users groups to:

- identify which applicants are likely to need assistance in order to choose accommodation that is appropriate to their needs and
- ensure that suitable assistance is available

5.27   An authority may provide assistance itself. This could include a range of activities, from training applicants on use of the website, for example, to operating housing advice surgeries in prisons, making home visits to those with chaotic lifestyles, or making bids on applicants' behalf (with their agreement). However, while, under s 166(1)(a), an authority must secure that assistance is available, there is no requirement for the authority to provide that assistance itself. Where an authority relies on other organisations and individuals to provide such assistance, the authority will need to be very careful to ensure that the support needs of all applicants can be addressed. Authorities should consider and provide for the training needs of organisations and individuals (eg social services, prisons, probation, mental health teams, voluntary agencies, advocates and carers) about how the choice based lettings scheme operates in order to help them advise and assist their clients, friends and family.

5.28   Authorities should consider maintaining a list of applicants who require assistance and support. In many cases it may be relatively simple to identify those individuals who need assistance at the initial application stage. However, this may not always be the case. Similar considerations are likely to apply as those set out in paragraph 4.6 about assessing need. Otherwise, an applicant's behaviour may give an indication that they have a need for assistance which is not being met. So, for example, the fact that an applicant in priority housing need has failed to bid at all or bids for inappropriate accommodation is a good indication that the person may be experiencing difficulties.

Undue influence

5.29   Housing authorities should ensure that, when providing information, advice and assistance, they do not seek to unduly influence an applicant's choice of accommodation. So, for example, authorities which act as 'proxy bidders' on behalf of vulnerable applicants, will need to safeguard against bidding for properties which do not meet the applicants' needs and aspirations.

Monitoring

5.30   Authorities are encouraged to monitor their choice based lettings schemes. Monitoring will assist authorities in assessing:

- whether the scheme is meeting its aims and objectives and working well or
- whether changes need to be made

Data collected may help to inform the authority's homelessness strategy as well as its wider housing strategy. In particular, data on which types of properties are hard to let or in short supply, and which areas are unpopular, will feed decisions on new stock, redevelopment and redesignation, or demolition. Data – appropriately generalised – could also form part of customer feedback at regular intervals.

5.31   Monitoring is crucial to ensure that authorities comply with:

- the duty to give reasonable preference to certain applicants
- the various equality duties

5.32   The following is a range of matters which authorities could usefully include in their monitoring arrangements – it is illustrative and not exhaustive:

- **Housing management performance** – relet times, refusals
- **Support mechanisms** – are the mechanisms which are put in place to support applicants to participate in choice based lettings effective?
- **Nomination arrangements** – the number of successful nominations, proportion going to people in the reasonable preference categories, number of failed nominations and reasons for the failure
- **Lettings outcomes, policies and quotas** – the proportion of lettings (and separately, direct lettings outside CBL)[9] overall going to, for example: homeless applicants and other applicants in the reasonable preference

---

9   See footnote 6 for the meaning of 'direct let'.

categories; applicants on the "assisted list"; transferring tenants and new applicants; and the size and quality of properties going to each group. More specifically the proportion of disabled applicants let accessible properties, and conversely the proportion of accessible properties let to disabled applicants

- **Comparative data** about applicants on the waiting list should also be collected. Taken together the waiting list and lettings data may be used to determine whether existing lettings policies and quotas are effective or whether they need to be revised. For example, are existing policies having a disproportionate impact on certain groups or communities, are disabled people having to wait disproportionately long for suitable property, is the authority still able to give effect to its duty to give reasonable preference?
- **Ethnicity data** – particularly numbers on the waiting list, lettings outcomes, and bidding behaviour. The website of the Equalities and Human Rights Commission provides good practice on monitoring ethnicity and the categories to use
- **New communities** – authorities should identify the existence of any new communities within the district and monitor their involvement in choice based lettings. Authorities which use the census categories to define ethnicity may need to reconsider their ethnicity categories as the census categories do not capture this level of detail
- **Community cohesion issues** – whether ethnic minority applicants are moving into predominantly white areas and vice versa
- **Other equality and diversity data** – in particular disability, age and gender. Again this should include numbers on the waiting list, lettings outcomes, and bidding behaviour
- **Potentially disadvantaged/assisted list applicants** – given the pro-active nature of CBL, it is particularly important to monitor the activity levels (ie bidding) and lettings outcomes for potentially disadvantaged groups. Authorities may be able to use demographic and socio-economic data on new applicants to assist in identifying potentially disadvantaged applicants
- **Tenancy sustainment** – are tenancies lasting longer or are there more applications to transfer
- **Bidding behaviour** – ie the number or proportion of households which are actively bidding in any given period. This can be compared to the numbers on the housing waiting list; and can also be used to look at patterns of bidding over time. Also the proportion of applicants in various categories (eg homeless households, other reasonable preference categories, on the 'assisted list', and minority ethnic applicants) who are not bidding or bidding infrequently and what reasons they are giving for not bidding
- **Inter-authority, or inter-regional mobility** – ie numbers/proportions of out-of-borough applicants on the waiting list, making bids, and achieving lettings

- **Customer satisfaction** – do applicants find the system easy to understand and to use, are ethnic minority applicants and/or disabled applicants as satisfied with the system and/or outcomes as other groups

5.33 Authorities which are introducing a choice based lettings scheme are strongly encouraged to establish a baseline to monitor from; and to retain historical data from the period before the choice based lettings scheme is introduced for comparative purposes.

5.34 Rigorous management of the waiting list is important to ensure that the usefulness of waiting list numbers, as a measure of local housing need and/or an indicator of demand, is not compromised. Authorities are also reminded that data protection legislation (see following paragraphs) requires that personal information is kept up-to-date and is not held for longer than necessary. It is, therefore, strongly recommended that authorities review their waiting list on an annual basis.

Information sharing and data protection

5.35 Housing authorities may need to share information about applicants with other agencies and organisations, for example, to ensure that applicants are properly assisted to participate in a choice based lettings scheme and that they are housed appropriately. Such organisations could include social services, other statutory agencies, and voluntary agencies. Information sharing between housing authorities and partner RSLs will be particularly important and failure to get this right could undermine the success of a choice based lettings scheme. Adopting effective information sharing protocols can help ensure that housing authorities and other agencies are clear about the type of information which can be shared with whom and for what purposes.

5.36 In devising information sharing protocols, and when passing on information about individual applicants, housing authorities will need to be mindful of their responsibilities under the Data Protection Act 1998. However, this should not be seen as a complete barrier to sharing any information. If landlords are unclear about their obligations and responsibilities under the Act they should contact the Information Commissioner. Advice on data sharing can also be found on the website for the Department for Constitutional Affairs: www.dca.gov.uk/foi/sharing/toolkit/infosharing.htm

CHAPTER 6

Delivering choice in partnership with Registered Social Landlords (RSLs) and Private Sector Landlords

Joint/partnership CBL schemes with RSLs

6.1 The Secretary of State recommends that housing authorities work together with RSLs in their district to provide joint choice based lettings schemes which extend to all or the majority of the social housing vacancies to ensure that:

- best use is made of the available social housing in the district and
- applicants are offered the widest choice of accommodation and, as far as possible, a single point of access to that accommodation

6.2 However, where RSLs are involved in choice based lettings schemes with one or more housing authorities, the housing authorities will need to ensure that this does not affect their ability to meet their statutory obligations under Part 6 of the 1996 Act.

Statutory framework for co-operation

6.3 Section 170 of the 1996 Act provides that where a housing authority so request, an RSL must co-operate to such extent as is reasonable in the circumstances in offering accommodation to people with priority under the authority's allocation scheme. Similarly, s 213 of the 1996 Act provides that where an RSL has been requested by a housing authority to assist them in the discharge of their homelessness functions under Part 7, it must also co-operate to the same extent.

6.4 The Housing Corporation has issued regulatory guidance which sets out the requirements on RSLs in respect of local authority nominations (Housing Corporation Regulatory Circular 02/03, February 2003). This provides that in areas where evidence of local housing need is reflected in local planning criteria for affordable housing provision, nomination agreements should provide for 50 per cent or more of true voids for nominations. The circular recognises that agreed percentages may be considerably higher in areas of housing stress.

6.5 Housing authorities which have, or plan to adopt, a choice based lettings scheme will want to ensure that RSLs agree that those vacancies to which the authority has nomination rights are made available through the scheme. The Secretary of State would also encourage housing authorities to negotiate with RSLs to make their other vacancies available through a joint choice based lettings scheme as well. However, it is important that where RSLs let all or the majority of their stock through a joint choice based lettings scheme, there is a means for distinguishing those RSL vacancies to which the authority has nomination rights. It is in the interest of housing authorities, RSLs, applicants and tenants to be clear about the basis on which a tenancy is being allocated, not least in those instances where an applicant may seek to challenge the basis on which a property has been let. One way of distinguishing between the different types of letting would be to have one section of the newsletter or website for local authority lettings which would include 'nomination' lettings, and a separate section for other RSL lettings. In the local authority section, the relevant RSL landlord would be identified in the advertisement for each individual 'nomination' letting.

Applicant prioritisation and eligibility criteria

6.6   Housing authorities must comply with the requirements of Part 6 of the 1996 Act when they nominate an applicant to be the tenant of an RSL. This means that when advertising vacancies through a choice based lettings scheme to which the authority has nomination rights, it is important that applicants for those vacancies are prioritised in accordance with s 167 of the 1996 Act.

6.7   Under s 160A(7) of the 1996 Act, housing authorities are entitled to treat applicants as ineligible (ie to exclude them from an allocation) where they have been guilty of serious unacceptable behaviour. RSLs may operate exclusion policies which are wider than the provisions in s 160A(7). Where this is the case, the exclusion policy of each participating RSL should be clearly set out in the published CBL scheme details. In addition, where this is feasible, the exclusion criteria applied by an RSL should be stated in the advertisement of any relevant vacancy, so that applicants are clear about the basis on which the property is offered.

Nomination agreements

6.8   A local authority nominates a person to RSL accommodation when it does so 'in pursuance of any arrangements (whether legally enforceable or not) to require that housing accommodation, or a specified amount of housing accommodation, is made available to a person or one of a number of persons nominated by the authority', (s 159(4)).

6.9   It is important that nomination agreements are in place between the housing authority and all RSLs participating in a joint choice based lettings scheme. This is the case even where RSL partners have agreed to put all or the majority of their stock through the choice based lettings scheme.

6.10   Such agreements should set out the proportion of lettings that will be made available; any criteria which the RSLs have adopted, following consultation with the housing authority, for accepting or rejecting nominees; and how any disputes about suitability and eligibility will be resolved.

6.11   When negotiating nominations agreements, housing authorities should try to ensure that criteria for rejecting nominees are kept to a minimum. This will be particularly important where the housing authority have transferred their housing stock.

6.12   Housing authorities should ensure that the details of nominated households given to RSLs are accurate, comprehensive and up-to-date, and in particular provide information about any vulnerability, support needs and arrangements for support, where this information is available. To prevent new tenancies from failing and to minimise the likelihood of the RSL rejecting a nomination, housing authorities should ensure, wherever possible, that adequate support packages are in place for applicants who need them before a nominee is expected to take up their tenancy.

6.13   Housing authorities should ensure that robust monitoring arrangements are in place to monitor effective delivery of the terms of the nomination agreement or protocol. This will be crucial, to ensure that housing authorities can demonstrate that they are meeting their statutory obligations under Part 6, and in particular the requirement to give reasonable preference to persons in the categories set out in s 167(2). Monitoring arrangements should cover successful and 'failed' nominations.

6.14   A 'failed' nomination occurs when an RSL applies its own criteria to reject an applicant who has applied for particular accommodation and who would otherwise be allocated that accommodation, because he or she has appropriate priority under the choice based lettings scheme and is eligible for an allocation under Part 6. It is particularly important to monitor failed nominations to identify whether any particular applicants in the reasonable preference categories are being consistently denied access to accommodation for which they should be given priority.

6.15   The monitoring arrangements will also need to cover nominations to any RSL stock which is not included in the joint choice based lettings scheme.

Common housing registers

6.16   Where housing authorities and RSLs pool together their available accommodation in a single choice based lettings scheme, they are advised to consider developing a single list or database of all applicants who have applied and been accepted onto the joint choice based lettings scheme (referred to here as 'a common housing register').

6.17   A common housing register is a useful administrative tool which facilitates the operation of a joint choice based lettings scheme and improves co-ordination between participating landlords. For applicants, a common housing register, together with a single application form, provides a single point of access to all participating landlords and obviates the need to register separately with each of them. For housing authorities, a common housing register provides a more reliable assessment of housing need in their district, providing important information for the development of their housing strategy, and enabling the best use to be made of existing stock. However, it is important to remember that applicants on the common housing register who wish to bid for local authority allocations (including RSL vacancies to which the local authority has nomination rights) will need to meet the section 160A eligibility criteria.

Stock transfer, contracting out

6.18   Choice based lettings schemes which involve a housing authority and partner RSLs may operate in different contexts, including where the housing authority has contracted out some of its allocation functions and/or where the housing authority has transferred part or all of its stock.

6.19   Housing authorities which have transferred all or part of their stock, as well as those which have contracted out allocation functions, retain their statutory obligations regarding the allocation of accommodation, homelessness and the provision of housing advice. They also retain the responsibility for broader strategic duties such as the duty to undertake a periodic review of housing conditions and to consider aggregate housing needs.

6.20   All housing authorities are required to have an allocation scheme regardless of whether or not they retain ownership of the housing stock and whether or not they contract out the delivery of any of their allocation functions. Authorities are prohibited from contracting out certain allocation functions, including adopting and altering the allocation scheme, which includes the principles on which the scheme is framed.

6.21   In so far as a joint choice based lettings scheme applies to accommodation which is allocated within the meaning of s 159, housing authorities must ensure that:

- the principles of the choice based lettings scheme, and in particular the principles for determining priorities between applicants, comply with the requirements of Part 6 of the 1996 Act
- the principles of the choice based lettings scheme are set out in the authority's allocation scheme and
- accommodation which is allocated within the meaning of s 159 under a choice based lettings scheme is allocated in accordance with the authority's allocation scheme and in accordance with the requirements of Part 6

6.22   In circumstances where a stock transfer landlord – or an RSL to which a housing authority has contracted out some of its allocation functions – has, or proposes to, set up or participate in a choice based lettings scheme, housing authorities are strongly advised to actively participate in the scheme as well. This is the best way to ensure that they can properly carry out their statutory allocation and homelessness functions and duties as well as their strategic housing responsibilities.

Private sector landlords

6.23   Private rented sector housing already performs an important role in providing accommodation for those in housing need. In particular, the private rented sector can provide types and sizes of dwellings which may not be readily available within the social rented sector. For those who have lower priority under an authority's allocation scheme, and who may have to wait a considerable time before they are allocated a social tenancy, a vacancy in the private rented sector may offer a quicker and equally suitable housing solution. The private rented sector can also provide a way into independent living for vulnerable households, particularly where it is coupled with appropriate housing related support. Accordingly, the Secretary of State is of the view that it is appropriate and beneficial for vacancies in the private rented sector to be advertised through an authority's choice based lettings scheme, wherever possible, in order to ensure that all applicants have the widest possible range of housing options.

6.24 Where private rented sector vacancies are advertised in a choice based lettings scheme, authorities should consider putting in place appropriate safeguards to ensure that the housing on offer meets satisfactory standards of condition and management. Where authorities make extensive use of the private rented sector in their housing options approach, appropriate safeguards are likely to be in place already. In these circumstances, the Secretary of State believes private rented vacancies should be included, wherever possible, within the choice based lettings scheme.

6.25 Otherwise, housing authorities should consider putting in place such safeguards with a view to incorporating private rented vacancies within their choice based lettings scheme as soon as this is appropriate.

6.26 A nomination to a private sector landlord is outside the scope of Part 6 of the 1996 Act, and the letting is likely to take the form of an assured shorthold tenancy. Accordingly, where vacancies in the private rented sector are advertised as part of a choice based lettings scheme, the differences between the types of tenure should be made clear to applicants. In particular, authorities should ensure that applicants are aware of:

- the fact that the tenant will acquire more limited tenancy rights than in respect of local authority or RSL accommodation and
- the basis on which the landlord will select the successful bid, if this differs from the basis on which successful bids for social housing vacancies are selected

6.27 When advertising private sector vacancies, authorities will want to ensure that the advertisement includes broadly the same information about the particular vacancy – in terms of the size and nature of the property and level of rent – as for social rented vacancies (see paragraph 5.9). Additional information which it would be helpful to provide in the advertisement include:

- the name of the landlord or letting agent responsible for managing the property
- the form of the tenancy
- any restrictions on who may apply for the property, in particular whether applicants in receipt of Local Housing Allowance will be considered

6.28 In order to minimise confusion for applicants, authorities should consider creating within their advertising a separate and distinct section for private rented vacancies, rather than advertising them together with social rented vacancies. This might include general information about matters which would be of interest to applicants, such as:

Appendix 1
England: Allocation

- the particular features of assured shorthold tenancies
- a summary of the accreditation scheme, or other standards or safeguards in place
- the availability of rent deposits/bonds and guarantees
- information about tenancy deposit protection
- any housing related support available for private tenants
- any dispute resolution/mediation service (between landlord and tenant)
- an explanation of Local Housing Allowance and current rates

CHAPTER 7

Regional and sub-regional choice based lettings schemes

Policy objective

7.1   The Government's policy objective is for choice based lettings schemes to develop on a sub-regional and/or regional basis. The Secretary of State believes that such schemes, involving a partnership of housing authorities and registered social landlords – and working together with private landlords wherever possible – are the best way to achieve the greatest choice and flexibility in meeting tenants' housing needs.

7.2   There are likely to be a number of benefits from larger, sub-regional or regional schemes which span housing authorities' boundaries:

- they bring together a larger pool of available housing, giving tenants more choice and helping to ease localised problems of high demand
- they break down artificial boundaries and recognise existing housing and labour markets
- they enable greater mobility
- for RSLs, they reduce the costs and complexities associated with being involved in several different schemes and
- they enable partners to share the costs associated with developing and implementing choice based lettings schemes

Different models of sub-regional and regional CBL

7.3   The Secretary of State recognises that housing authorities which plan to set up a sub-regional or regional choice based lettings scheme should have the flexibility to determine how far they wish to coordinate their allocation functions with partner authorities, in line with local policy objectives. In some instances, authorities may decide to retain their own individual allocation schemes. In other circumstances, authorities may decide to adopt a single regional or sub-regional allocation scheme.

Delegating functions to a central body

7.4 A common feature of most sub-regional or regional choice based lettings schemes is likely to be the designation of a single body or organisation to carry out some of the administrative tasks in relation to the scheme. There are two principal options available to housing authorities seeking to delegate their allocation functions to a central body. The constitution of the central body will depend to a large extent on who the partners to the scheme are and which functions the partners choose to delegate to the body.

7.5 Firstly, housing authorities have powers to delegate some of their allocations functions to another body under the Local Authorities (Contracting Out of Allocation of Housing and Homelessness Functions) Order 1996 ('the Contracting Out Order'). Schedule 1 of the Order lists the allocation functions which cannot be contracted out, namely: adopting or altering an allocation scheme; consulting with relevant RSLs before adopting or altering an allocation scheme; and making the allocation scheme available at the authority's principal office, or providing a copy of the scheme on request.

7.6 Housing authorities may wish to use the powers under the Contracting Out Order to delegate allocation functions to an RSL or to a special purpose vehicle set up specifically for this purpose. The functions which could be delegated would include, for example, the central advertising of available properties on behalf of all partners, processing of applications and the compiling of a shortlist of bids for each advertised vacancy. Alternatively, housing authorities have the power to delegate to another housing authority under s 101 of the Local Government Act 1972.

7.7 Secondly, local authorities have general powers to work together in the discharge of their functions.[10] Subject to the constitutional arrangements of the authorities concerned, an authority may be able to arrange for the discharge of its functions by another authority, or two or more authorities may be able to arrange for the joint discharge of their functions by a joint committee. These powers could be used to establish a regional or sub-regional choice based lettings scheme involving two or more housing authorities which could be operated either by a lead authority discharging the functions of the other authorities, or by a joint committee set up by all the partner authorities. If the authorities wished to do so, they could delegate all of their Part 6 functions to this type of central CBL body.

7.8 Housing authorities may not use these general powers to operate a regional or sub-regional choice based lettings scheme together with RSLs or private sector landlords as partners to the scheme. However, it would be

---

[10] In most cases, the relevant statutory powers will be sections 19 and 20 of the Local Government Act 2000. These sections apply to local authorities which have adopted new constitutions which provide for 'executive arrangements'. Local authorities which have not adopted executive arrangements have similar powers under s 101 of the Local Government Act 1972. In practice, most local authorities in England do now have executive arrangements in place.

possible to include within such a scheme RSL vacancies to which a local authority had nomination rights (see paragraphs 6.8 to 6.15).

Regional and sub-regional allocation schemes

7.9   Where two or more housing authorities operate a choice based lettings scheme on a regional or sub-regional basis, they are encouraged to consider the benefits of adopting a single, common allocation scheme across all the participating authorities. Such an approach should have a number of advantages for local authorities and RSL partners, and for applicants. For instance, it is likely to:

- be more efficient and cost-effective for landlords
- be more transparent and simpler to understand for applicants, particularly those seeking to move between local authority districts
- promote greater mobility and thus provide greater choice for applicants

7.10   In the Secretary of State's view, the requirements:

- in section 167(1) for every local housing authority to have an allocation scheme, and
- in section 167(8) to allocate in accordance with that scheme

can be effectively discharged by two or more local authorities acting jointly to produce a common allocation scheme. Where a joint regional or sub-regional allocation scheme is adopted by partner authorities, it is important that this is clearly stated on the face of the document. The allocation scheme should explain, for example, that it is a joint scheme for the region or sub-region made up of the named authorities. The role of any central body allocating on behalf of the partner authorities should also be outlined in the joint allocation scheme.

7.11   When framing a joint allocation scheme, housing authorities must ensure that reasonable preference is secured for all applicants to the partner authorities who are entitled to it under section 167 of the 1996 Act. In particular, the joint allocation scheme will still need to meet the requirement for reasonable preference to be secured for 'people who need to move to a particular locality in the district of the housing authority, where failure to meet that need would cause hardship (to themselves or to others)' (section 167(2)(e)). One way this could be achieved in the context of a sub-regional or regional allocation scheme would be to give reasonable preference to an applicant who needs to live in a specific area within the region or sub-region when the applicant bids for a property advertised in that area.

7.12   Where authorities enter into a joint scheme, the same allocations criteria will apply to all allocations in the region, since authorities can only allocate in accordance with their scheme (s 167(8)). The only exception to this will be where the common allocations scheme itself makes provision for local differences under s 167(2E) (ie where the scheme provides for local lettings policies). This would allow authorities to continue to give priority to people with a local connection when allocating accommodation in certain rural parishes, for example.

7.13   Where authorities have adopted a joint allocation scheme, a person who applies for housing under the scheme should be treated as applying to all of the partner housing authorities. This would argue strongly for the partner authorities adopting a common housing register and a single application form. Once the application was accepted, the applicant would then be entitled to bid for vacancies advertised by all of the partner authorities, including partner authorities with which the applicant had no previous connection.

7.14   Another option would be for partner authorities to maintain separate allocation schemes but for each authority to adopt the same banding scheme or points system, preferably together with a common housing register, across the partner authorities. This would have a number of benefits, particularly where partner authorities also delegate their allocation functions to a central body. For partner authorities and the central body, it would be more cost-effective and easier to administer. For applicants, it would be easier to understand and to operate, particularly for those seeking to move across local authority boundaries. It could also be the first step towards a common allocation policy across the region or sub-region.

Cross-boundary mobility

7.15   Housing authorities which are partners in a regional or sub-regional scheme may wish to maintain separate allocation schemes but provide for cross-boundary mobility, that is to say they may wish to make it easier for applicants living within one partner authority's district to apply for and be allocated accommodation in the district of another partner authority. Authorities who have chosen not to adopt a joint allocation scheme are strongly urged to consider the advantages to applicants of facilitating mobility in this way.

7.16   The arrangements for cross-boundary mobility must be capable of being operated in line with the statutory requirements of Part 6. Authorities should note the following points in particular:

- if allocations under a particular allocation scheme are usually subject to a local connection rule, the scheme should make specific provision for dealing with cross-boundary moves
- an authority cannot rely on its partner authority's assessment of the applicant's priority, since it can only allocate in accordance with its own scheme. In practice, both authorities may have delegated some of their allocation functions to a central body (see paragraphs 7.4 to 7.8 above). Where this is the case, since the central body only has the powers which are delegated to it, it will still have to consider each application in accordance with the allocation scheme of the allocating authority

- any provision for cross-boundary moves must not affect the authority's ability to ensure reasonable preference for the classes of person specified in s 167(2). This is unlikely to be a problem if the cross-boundary applicants are all persons who are entitled to reasonable preference
- the basis for determining priority between cross-boundary applicants should be set out in the allocation scheme

7.17   Applicants who are looking to make longer distance moves may need information and support to help them do so. This may simply mean access to information about the new area which they are less likely to be familiar with. This might include information on schools, health facilities, transport, training and employment. Applicants may also need more time to view properties, where they need to travel long distances; and authorities should consider whether there is other support which it would be appropriate to offer. Partner authorities should build these factors into the sub-regional or regional choice based lettings scheme. Partner authorities should ensure that there is close co-operation between the choice based lettings scheme and other statutory and voluntary agencies, to ensure that applicants with care and support needs can be enabled to move across local authority boundaries. Housing authorities should also consider developing links with the providers of other services operating in partner authority areas. Examples might be training and education providers, as well as employers.

RSL involvement in regional CBL schemes

7.18   Where RSL property is advertised through a joint choice based lettings scheme by housing authorities which each have their own allocation scheme, the partners in the scheme should be clear as to which housing authority is the nominating authority. There should be clear information available for applicants as to which authority's allocation scheme applies to that property (and therefore how priority will be determined).

7.19   Housing authorities are encouraged to work with their local HomeBuy Agents on sub-regional or regional choice based lettings schemes. HomeBuy Agents are appointed RSLs funded by the Housing Corporation (in future the Homes and Community Agency) who provide a 'one stop shop' and point of contact in a given area in England for all applicants for the Government funded HomeBuy programme.

Housing Allocations – Members of the Armed Forces

Communities & Local Government Circular 04/2009　　　　　*9 April 2009*

INTRODUCTION

1.   This circular is guidance by the Secretary of State for Communities and Local Government under section 169 of the Housing Act 1996 (the 1996 Act). Local housing authorities are required to have regard to it in exercising their functions under Part 6 of the 1996 Act.

2.   In addition to the Code of Guidance for Local Authorities on the Allocation of Accommodation (the Code of Guidance) issued in November 2002, this circular provides updated guidance to housing authorities to which they should have regard when considering applications for an allocation of accommodation made by members of Her Majesty's Armed Forces or by persons who were formerly serving in the Armed Forces. The purpose of this circular is twofold:

(a)   to give effect to a commitment in: 'The Nation's Commitment: Cross-Government Support to our Armed Forces, their Families and Veterans' (the Command Paper) issued by the Ministry of Defence in July 2008; and

(b)   to take account of amendments to section 199 of the 1996 Act made by section 315 of the Housing and Regeneration Act 2008 (the 2008 Act) which change the application of the local connection test in respect of members of the armed forces.

BACKGROUND

3.   The Command Paper sets out a framework for action across Government Departments to:

a)   remove any disadvantage that Service personnel, their families, and veterans may suffer as a result of service in the Armed Forces, and particularly as a consequence of being required to move around the country and the world; and

b)   support those existing and former members of the Armed Forces who have been injured in the service of their country.

4.   The Command Paper contains a number of housing related commitments. Paragraph 2.15 sets out the Government's view that seriously injured personnel should be given high priority for social housing and contains a commitment to issue statutory guidance to reinforce this message. Paragraph 2.19 refers to the amendment to the local connection provision in s 199 of the 1996 Act in relation to members of the Armed Forces (as amended by section 315 of the 2008 Act).

Seriously injured and disabled servicemen

5. The Secretary of State believes that it is important that Service personnel who have been seriously injured or disabled in action and who have an urgent need for social housing should be given high priority within local authorities' allocation schemes in recognition of their service.

6. Section 167(2) of the 1996 Act provides that, in framing their allocation scheme so as to determine priorities in the allocation of accommodation, housing authorities must ensure that reasonable preference is given to specified categories of applicants, including people who need to move on medical or welfare grounds, including grounds relating to a disability. Section 167(2) further provides that housing authorities may frame their allocation scheme so as to give additional preference to people who fall within the reasonable preference categories and who have urgent housing needs.

7. Paragraph 5.18 of the Code of Guidance provides advice on the additional preference provision in s 167(2). It states that housing authorities must consider, in the light of local circumstances, the need to give effect to this provision. It also provides examples of people with urgent housing needs to whom housing authorities should consider giving additional preference within their allocation scheme including those who need to move because of urgent medical reasons.

8. The Secretary of State is of the view that, where an allocation scheme is framed to provide for additional preference to be given to applicants in urgent housing need, housing authorities should ensure that the categories of applicants to be given additional preference include the following:

– any applicant who needs to move to suitable adapted accommodation because of a serious injury, medical condition or disability which he or she, or a member of their household, has sustained as a result of service in the Armed Forces.

Section 315 of the Housing Act 2008 – local connection

9. Section 167(2A) of the 1996 Act allows allocation schemes to make provision for determining priorities in relation to applicants who fall within the reasonable preference and additional preference categories. It gives examples of factors which may be taken into account in determining priorities, including any local connection between the applicant and the authority's district. For these purposes, local connection is defined by reference to s 199 of the 1996 Act.

10. Paragraph 5.23 of the Code of Guidance provides advice on implementing s 167(2A) and sub-paragraph (c) sets out a brief summary of the local connection provisions in s 199. It states that, broadly speaking, a person has a local connection with the district of a housing authority if he has a connection because of normal residence there (either current or previous) of his own choice, employment there, family connections or special circumstances.

It goes on to state that residence in an area is not of a person's own choice if it is the consequence of serving in the Armed Forces. This exemption no longer applies.

11. Section 315 of the 2008 Act amends s 199 of the 1996 Act so that a person serving in the Armed Forces can establish a local connection with a district through residence or employment there, in the same way as a civilian person. The amendments apply in respect of all applications for housing under Part 6 made on or after 1 December 2008.

12. Where housing authorities frame their allocation scheme to give greater priority to applicants with a local connection, the effect of the amendments to section 199 of the 1996 Act will be:

(a) applicants who are serving in the Armed Forces and who are either employed or resident in the district will be able to establish a local connection with the district

(b) when considering applications from serving or former members of the Armed Forces, who are not currently employed or resident in the district, the local housing authority will need to consider whether they have a local connection through previous residence in the district as a result of a former posting in the area while serving in the Armed Forces.

13. Such authorities should also consider whether there is a need to revise their allocation scheme in light of the amendments to s 199.

OTHER INFORMATION

14. This Circular can be purchased from The Stationery Office (telephone 0870 600 5533) or viewed on the housing pages of the CLG website at www.communities.gov.uk

15. Telephone number for enquiries about the circular is: 020 7944 3666

Fair and Flexible: Statutory Guidance on Social Housing Allocations for Local Authorities in England, December 2009

CONTENTS

Appendix 1
England: Allocation

Foreword

Building more homes that people can afford to rent or buy is one of the highest priorities for the Government. We are investing to build the 12,000 new affordable homes over two years that we set out in the Government's plan, Building Britain's Future, in June.

As well as building more homes, we must enable local areas to respond to housing pressures in different ways. I want local councils to be more able to reflect the needs, demands and aspirations of their area in the way that they allocate housing. And I want the management of council waiting lists in every area to be better understood and seen ss fairer.

By issuing his new guidance, the Government sets out more clearly the freedoms and flexibilities that local authorities should use when developing allocations policies in their area.

I am reaffirming the Government's commitment to giving priority to those in the greatest housing need, through the reasonable preference categories.

Nevertheless, this guidance concerns greater scope for councils to meet local needs and priorities through their allocation policies. It strengthens councils' freedom to give greater weighting to specific local needs alongside those households who have 'reasonable preference'. In some areas this will mean giving more priority to people who have been on waiting lists for a long time or more priority for people with strong local or family connections. Elsewhere, there may be a greater need to support people in low paid work. Councils should work closely with the housing associations in their area to meet local priorities.

The system for allocating housing is complex and poorly understood. The demands and pressures on housing in an area are rarely well explained to local people. This helps give rise to the perception that the system is inflexible and unfair and the mistaken view that such public housing goes to those who have no legitimate right to it.

I want to see such myths and misunderstandings challenged. It is part of a council's responsibility to do so. Greater understanding will only come if councils do more to inform their communities about who is getting housing and do more to consult tenants and residents on their policies. This new guidance makes clear the responsibilities councils have to do exactly this when deciding how they allocate their housing.

This guidance is an important part of the Government's commitment to meet housing need across the country and we recognise that need is different in different places.

The Rt Hon John Healey MP
Minister for Housing and Planning

Summary

1.   This statutory guidance covers a number of issues:

(i)   It sets out the Government's strategic view of the objectives and outcomes which local authorities must and those they should seek to achieve in their allocation policies. These are:

- providing support for those in greatest housing need, including people who have experienced homelessness
- ensuring allocation policies comply with equality legislation
- promoting greater choice for prospective and existing tenants
- creating more mixed and sustainable communities
- promoting greater mobility for existing tenants
- making better use of the housing stock
- supporting people in work or seeking work
- delivering policies which are fair and considered to be fair

(ii)   It sets out the importance of local authorities' responsibilities under the Local Government Act 1999 (as amended by the Local Government and Public Involvement in Health Act 2007) to involve, inform and consult with local people; and it draws attention to the main legislative provisions governing the allocation of social housing, including the requirement to provide for 'reasonable preference'.

(iii) It emphasises the importance of communicating facts about allocations (including regular updates on how properties have been allocated), to tackle false perceptions which may arise about the way social housing is allocated.

(iv)   It highlights the implications of the House of Lords judgment in the case of *R (on application of Ahmad) v Newham LBC*,[11] which, among other things, removes the requirement to provide for cumulative preference to be taken into account in prioritising applicants.

(v)   It reinforces the flexibilities local authorities have within the allocation legislation to meet local pressures by:

- adopting local priorities alongside the statutory reasonable preference categories
- taking into account other factors in prioritising applicants, including waiting time and local connection
- operating local lettings policies

(vi)   It emphasises the importance of close working between authorities and registered social landlords.

Scope of the guidance

2.   This is statutory guidance provided under s 169 of the Housing Act 1996 (the 1996 Act). It applies to local authorities in England. Local authorities are required to have regard to this guidance in exercising their functions under Part 6 of the 1996 Act. In so far as this guidance comments on the law it can

---

[11]   [2009] UKHL 14.

Appendix 1
England: Allocation

only reflect the Department's understanding of the law at the time of issue. Local authorities will still need to keep up to date on any developments in the law in these areas.

3. This guidance replaces the following parts of the *Code of Guidance on the Allocation of Accommodation* which was issued in November 2002[12] (the 2002 code):

- chapters 1, 2 and 6
- paragraphs 5.1 to 5.12 , paragraph 5.18 and paragraphs 5.23 to 5.32 of chapter 5
- annexes 2, 4, 5, 6, 7, 8, 9 and 12

4. This guidance also replaces the following paragraphs of the *Code of Guidance on Choice Based Lettings* which was issued in August 2008[13] (the 2008 code):

- 4.1 to 4.49
- 4.68 to 4.71
- 4.79 and 4.80

5. *Circular 04/2009: Housing Allocations – Members of the Armed Forces* remains in effect.

6. This guidance is specifically for local authority Members and staff. It is also of direct relevance to registered social landlords[14] (referred to as RSLs). On a local authority's request, RSLs have a duty under s.170 of the 1996 Act to co-operate with local authorities to such extent as is reasonable in the circumstances in offering accommodation to people with priority under the authority's allocation scheme.

7. For local authorities, developing their allocation scheme and carrying out their allocation functions often requires joint planning and operational co-operation between local authorities and other bodies. These are likely to include social services departments, health authorities, the probation service, children's services, other referral agencies and voluntary sector organisations, although this list is not exhaustive. This guidance will be of interest to these organisations as well.

8. We believe that local authorities will welcome the additional flexibilities which this guidance promotes and would encourage them to review their existing policies as soon as possible and to revise them, where appropriate, in the light of this guidance.

---

[12] *Allocation of Accommodation: Code of Guidance for Local Housing Authorities*, ODPM, November 2002.

[13] *Allocation of Accommodation: Choice Based Lettings: Code of Guidance for Local Housing Authorities*, CLG, August 2008.

[14] Subject to Parliamentary approval, from April 2010 RSLs will cease to exist in England. Any references to RSLs will after that date be understood as references to private registered providers.

9. The Audit Commission will consider, through its agreed programmes of monitoring and inspection, which will be reflected in comprehensive area assessments, how well local authorities allocate social housing and therefore their response to this guidance.

Introduction

10. Social rented housing is an asset of great significance to the country, to local communities, to families and to individual people. It provides an essential part of the welfare safety net that supports many of the most vulnerable in our society. It provides a firm foundation, with the security and stability that can help people to overcome disadvantage and to build successful lives for themselves and their families. And it can help to create prosperous, healthy local communities, as part of a balanced housing market.

11. In any circumstances, the way that social housing is allocated would be a matter of real importance. That importance is greatly increased by the pressure of demand that we currently face in all parts of England. Almost every local authority has experienced significant growth in applications for social housing over the past five or six years. In *Building Britain's Future*, we set out ambitious plans to invest a further £1.5bn in building thousands of new affordable homes over this year and the next. In total we are committing more than £7.5bn over these years (2009/2011) to deliver 112,000 affordable homes, including 63,000 homes for social rent to be delivered by the Homes and Communities Agency (HCA) over the next two years. However, despite this ambitious programme of affordable housing delivery we can expect continued excess of demand over supply to continue for the medium term.

12. High levels of demand, often from families with pressing needs, mean decisions on the allocation of social housing need to be taken carefully. Because of the impact such decisions may have, people care deeply about how they are made. Whilst many local authorities are responding positively to this increased demand, we must ensure not only that decisions taken achieve the best overall outcomes for our communities: but also that they are made fairly, and in ways that can be explained and justified to all concerned.

13. The Government takes the view that decisions on the allocation of social housing – having, as they do, profound impacts at national and at local level – should rightly be taken in a framework which balances national and local interests.

14. It is important that local authorities continue to play a strong role in housing. They are best placed to assess housing need across the district, in light of demographic and economic change. Councils now have access to specific grant funding to build new council homes. We have also proposed a devolved system of accountability and funding for the existing stock. This would give more power to councils to plan long term, manage their assets and meet the housing needs of local people. They should also be working with partners to address such needs, including ensuring that the best use is made of existing housing stock. Local authorities also have responsibility for framing local

allocation policies within the context set by legislation and taking into account the reality of their local circumstances. It is only at local level that many of the key decisions can be taken, and balances can be struck between competing priorities. Many people find allocation policies complex and confusing. While the Government has a role to play in dispelling the myths which can arise around the allocation of social housing, the task of explaining local allocation policies to local people ultimately depends on effective communication and engagement by local authorities with their communities.

15.   In recent years, many local authorities have felt constrained in their decisions on allocations and the way in which their allocation scheme is devised because of the way in which the legislation has been interpreted by the courts. A recent judgment by the House of Lords (see paragraph 58), which we strongly welcome, provides clarity on the allocation legislation and the extent of local authorities' discretion under the legislation. The Government's view is that this is an opportune time, as well as an important one, for local authorities to re-examine their allocation policies and to make changes which take full advantage of the scope for local decision-making.

Objectives and outcomes which allocation policies must achieve

16.   There are a number of objectives and outcomes which local authorities must achieve when framing their allocation schemes.

Support for those in greatest housing need

17.   We believe it is right that social housing – which brings with it the dual benefits of security of tenure and sub-market rents – should continue to provide a stable base for those who are likely to have more difficulty fending for themselves in the private market. For this reason, we remain of the view that, overall, priority for social housing should go to those in greatest housing need. The current statutory reasonable preference categories are set out in s 167(2) of the 1996 Act. These were rationalised in the Homelessness Act 2002 (and further refined by the Housing Act 2004) to ensure that they are squarely based on housing need. The reasonable preference categories are:

(a)   people who are homeless (within the meaning of Part 7 of the 1996 Act); this includes people who are intentionally homeless, and those who do not have a priority need for accommodation

(b)   people who are owed a duty by any local authority under section 190(2), 193(2) or 195(2) of the 1996 Act (or under section 65(2) or 68(2) of the Housing Act 1985) or who are occupying accommodation secured by any local authority under section 192(3)

(c)   people occupying insanitary or overcrowded housing or otherwise living in unsatisfactory housing conditions

(d)   people who need to move on medical or welfare grounds, including grounds relating to a disability

(e)   people who need to move to a particular locality in the district of the local authority, where failure to meet that need would cause hardship (to themselves or to others)

18.   This means that a scheme must be framed to give reasonable preference to applicants who fall within the categories set out in s 167(2), over those who do not. While local authorities must demonstrate that, overall, reasonable preference is given to applicants in all the reasonable preference categories, this does not mean that they must give equal weight to each of the reasonable preference categories. Local authorities may wish to take into account local pressures. So, for example, where overcrowding is a particularly serious problem, they may wish to give more priority to overcrowded households in their allocation scheme. Authorities might give effect to this policy objective, for example, by assigning overcrowded households to a higher band, or by including a specific target in respect of overcrowded households in their annual lettings plan.

19.   In addition, s 167(2) gives local authorities the power to frame their allocation scheme so as to give additional preference to particular descriptions of people who fall within the reasonable preference categories and who have urgent housing needs. While there is no requirement for an allocation scheme to be framed to provide for additional preference, all local authorities should consider, in the light of local circumstances, whether there is a need to give effect to this provision.

Providing settled homes for people who have experienced homelessness

20.   The Government places great emphasis on the prevention of homelessness and local authorities are generally responding very positively to this agenda. Through their housing options services, local authorities are increasingly helping people at risk of homelessness by intervening earlier to resolve their difficulties before they reach crisis point. This is reflected by the significant reduction in the number of households accepted as owed the main duty to secure accommodation under the homelessness legislation since acceptances peaked in 2003–04. Local authorities are increasingly harnessing the private rented sector to help meet housing needs and we are looking at how this work could be extended and made more effective. Nevertheless, there are people at risk of homelessness or living in temporary accommodation for whom an allocation of social housing continues to be the most appropriate option to meet their need for a settled home. It is right, therefore, that people who are homeless or placed in temporary accommodation under the homelessness legislation should continue to be entitled to reasonable preference for social housing.

Promoting greater equality and clearly meeting equalities duties

21.   In framing their allocation scheme, local authorities need to ensure that it is compatible with the requirements in the equality legislation. In particular, as

well as the other duties to eliminate unlawful discrimination, local authorities are reminded that they are subject to a duty to promote equality of opportunity and good relations between people of different racial groups, as well as a duty to promote equality of opportunity between disabled persons and other persons, and between men and women. Local authorities are strongly recommended to carry out an equality impact assessment of any change to their allocation policies to ensure compliance with the local authority's legal equality duties; and to monitor lettings outcomes under the allocation scheme and ensure that this information is made regularly and publicly available.

22.　Local authorities should bear in mind that, subject to Parliamentary approval, the general public sector equality duty in the Equality Bill will mean that they will need, when carrying out their allocation function and reviewing and revising their allocation policies, to consider the impact of their decisions on people with the protected characteristics of age, race, disability, sex, pregnancy and maternity, sexual orientation, religion or belief or gender reassignment. Local authorities should also be aware of the provision in the Equality Bill which will require all local authorities to give due regard to the desirability of tackling socio-economic inequalities, when making strategic decisions about how to exercise their functions. The Government believes that the way in which local authorities frame their allocation scheme will be significant in ensuring they discharge this duty.

Objectives and outcomes which the Government believes allocation policies should achieve

23.　There are also a number of objectives and outcomes which local authorities should seek to achieve when framing their allocation schemes.

Greater choice and wider options for prospective and existing tenants

24.　The Government believes that allocation policies for social housing should provide for applicants to be given more of a say and a greater choice over the accommodation which they are allocated. This is the best way to ensure sustainable tenancies and to build settled, viable and inclusive communities. Research carried out for Communities and Local Government into the longer term impact of choice based lettings[15] found that tenants who were offered a choice of accommodation were more likely to be satisfied with their home and remain in that home for a longer period. Satisfied tenants are more likely to meet their tenancy obligations and maintain the property in good condition.

---

[15]　*Monitoring the Longer Term Impact of Choice Based Lettings*, Heriot-Watt University and BMRB, October 2006.

25.   It is also important that the allocation of social housing is set within a wider enhanced housing options approach, so that people receive joined-up advice and information about all the options open to them across sectors, including:

- renting in the private sector
- low cost home ownership options
- mobility schemes which enable applicants to move out of the district
- mutual exchange options for existing social tenants
- home improvement schemes or adaptations services which enable applicants to remain in their existing accommodation and
- supported/sheltered housing for older and disabled people

Creating more mixed and sustainable communities

26.   The way in which social housing is allocated can be instrumental in helping to create safe, prosperous and cohesive communities in which people want to live and work, now and in the future. The research into the longer term impacts of CBL suggests that the policy is encouraging applicants to think more flexibly about their housing options. It found that, where applicants have the opportunity to see details about all available vacancies, they will consider moving to areas beyond their immediate locality and beyond areas which, under a traditional allocations system, they would have specified as their 'preferred area'.

27.   Alongside CBL, making greater use of the existing flexibilities within the allocation legislation can help to tackle concentrations of deprivation, creating more mixed and sustainable communities. This might include:

- setting local priorities alongside the reasonable preference categories, such as promoting job-related moves
- setting aside a small proportion of lettings to enable existing tenants to move even where they do not have reasonable preference
- using local lettings policies to achieve a wide variety of policy objectives, including dealing with concentrations of deprivation or creating mixed communities by setting aside a proportion of vacancies for applicants who are in employment, or to enable existing tenants to take up an offer of employment.

Greater mobility

28.   Providing social housing tenants with greater opportunities to move within the social sector can help to promote social and economic mobility, as well as meeting individual tenants' specific needs and aspirations. It can also help make the best use of social housing stock.

29.   One way of increasing the opportunities for mobility between local authority areas is to develop choice based lettings schemes on a regional or sub-regional basis and our aim is to expand choice based lettings so that people can move nationwide. However, even where local authorities do not participate

in regional or sub-regional choice based lettings schemes, there are ways in which they can frame their allocation scheme to increase the opportunities for mobility across local authority boundaries. So, for example, authorities could use local lettings policies to allow for a small proportion of properties to be prioritised for essential workers (or people with skills in short supply) to attract them into the district; or they could develop arrangements with other authorities or RSLs to make a proportion of their lettings available for cross-boundary nominations.

Making better use of the housing stock

30.   Making better use of the social housing stock could mean giving existing tenants who are under-occupying social housing appropriate priority to secure a transfer within an authority's allocation scheme and ensuring that scarce accessible and adapted accommodation is prioritised for people with access needs. This might be coupled with personal support, incentives and financial payments to encourage people who under-occupy family-sized homes to downsize or vacate adapted homes they no longer need. Authorities may want to consider other approaches such as 'chain lets' – an approach under which a large property released by an under-occupying household can be reserved for existing overcrowded social rented tenants, where the resulting vacancy is then used to house another household with priority under the allocation scheme. For overcrowded households waiting for an allocation of larger accommodation, authorities can assist in mitigating the impacts through a range of measures. Improvements can be made to existing properties in order to improve liveability: additional toilets or wash basins, partitions or space saving furniture can all contribute to alleviating the pressures of overcrowding.

Policies which are fair and considered to be fair

31.   There are widespread perceptions that the current allocation system is unfair and favours certain groups (such as the unemployed or migrants). An Ipsos MORI survey carried out for Communities and Local Government in 2008 showed that less than a quarter (23%) of the public agreed that the way social housing is allocated is fair. One in three (32%) did not agree that it is fair. Just under a half (45%) said they did not know if it is fair or were unwilling to give an opinion and opted for 'neither agree nor disagree'.[16] While these perceptions may not always be founded on fact, we recognise that they are strongly felt.

32.   It is important that local authorities engage fully with their local community in developing their allocation priorities and drawing up their allocation scheme; and in providing regular, accurate, and generalised information on how housing is being allocated, working actively to dispel any myths and misperceptions which may arise. Policies which are easily

---

[16]   Communities and Local Government (2009) *Attitudes to housing: Findings from Ipsos MORI Public Affairs Monitor Omnibus Survey (England).*

understood and sensitive to local needs and local priorities are more likely to achieve acceptance across the wider community and to be, not just fair, but seen to be fair.[17]

Support for people in work or seeking work

33. Local authorities should consider how they can use their allocation policies to support those who are in work or who are seeking work. This could involve using local lettings policies to ensure that particular properties are allocated to essential workers or to those who have skills which are in short supply, regardless of whether they are currently resident in the authority's district. Alternatively, authorities may choose to give some preference within their scheme to existing tenants who are willing to move to take up employment or training opportunities – where, for example, the authority has identified a need to address skills shortages and worklessness, perhaps as part of their skills strategy.

Involving, consulting and raising awareness with local communities

34. For many people, the frustration engendered by long waiting times for social housing, the complexity and lack of transparency of many allocation policies, and poorly trained or supported front line housing officers, can contribute to false perceptions of unfairness or generate myths about 'queue jumping' by other groups. These myths and false perceptions need to be countered through effective, transparent communication.

35. Local authorities need to do more to help people locally understand how social housing is allocated.[18] The public are more likely to accept that allocation policies are fair if they have a clear understanding of what those policies are and what the justification for those policies is. Clarity about why social housing is prioritised for certain groups is key. To give a specific example, if an authority provided information about the amount of housing they have which is, not only accessible, but capable of being made accessible, and explained why priority for this accommodation is given to those with access needs, it is likely that people would view it as a fair and sensible use of that stock.

36. That is why it is important to engage fully with the whole community in developing allocation policies. It is also why it is important to provide feedback on properties let through choice based lettings,[19] and wider statistics about who

---

[17] An Ipsos MORI survey for Inside Housing shows that people consider the most important factors for prioritising social housing (where demand is greater than supply) as: how long someone has been on the waiting list (23%); whether they are currently living in inadequate accommodation (22%); how long someone has lived in the local area (15%); and being a key worker (e g nurse or teacher) (14%). Inside Housing, 6 June 2008, pp 22–25.

[18] The Ipsos Mori survey reports that 8% of the general public said they know a lot about the way social housing is allocated, 48% know a little and 41% said they know nothing, with 3% giving a 'don't know' response.

[19] Further guidance on feedback in the context of choice based lettings is provided at paragraphs 5.14–5.18 of the 2008 code.

is actually accessing social housing. Simple banding schemes play a role here too, since they can be more easily explained to applicants. Front line staff need to be properly trained and supported so that they provide accurate and consistent messages about how social housing is allocated, and elected members need to take a leading role in explaining to local people how social housing is being allocated and managed in their district – and what their local authority is doing to help increase availability of social housing.

The requirement to have an allocation scheme

37.   Local authorities must have an allocation scheme for determining priorities and the procedures to be followed in allocating housing accommodation; and they must allocate in accordance with that scheme (s 167 of the 1996 Act).

38.   The requirement to have an allocation scheme applies to all local authorities, regardless of whether or not they retain ownership of the housing stock and whether or not they contract out the delivery of any of their allocation functions. Authorities are prohibited from contracting out certain allocation functions, including adopting and altering the allocation scheme, which includes the principles on which the scheme is framed. 'Procedure' includes all aspects of the allocation process, including the people, or descriptions of people, by whom decisions are taken. It is essential that the scheme reflects all the local authority's policies and procedures, including information on whether the decisions are taken by elected members or officers acting under delegated powers.

Involving and consulting about the allocation scheme

39.   Part 6 of the 1996 Act imposes certain requirements on local authorities when consulting on changes to their allocation scheme, or before they adopt a new scheme. Authorities are required to consult with RSLs with which they have nomination arrangements (s 167(7)); while anyone likely to be affected by an alteration to the allocation scheme which reflects a major change of policy must be notified of it (s 168(3)).

40.   Under section 3 of the Local Government Act 1999 (as amended by the Local Government and Public Involvement in Health Act 2007) an authority is under a general duty to make arrangements to secure continuous improvement in the way in which its functions are exercised, having regard to a combination of economy, efficiency and effectiveness. Under s 3A of the Local Government Act 1999, where an authority considers it appropriate for representatives of local persons to be involved in the exercise of any of its functions by being provided with information, consulted or involved in another way, it must take such steps as it considers appropriate to secure that such representatives are involved in the exercise of the function in that way. Statutory guidance

published by the Government in July 2008[20] sets out the issues which local authorities should consider under the 'duty to involve'.

41. Engaging with and involving local communities in the development of allocation policies will contribute to:

- better awareness among local people of the facts around social housing, including a clearer understanding of the amount of housing available
- reduced opportunities for the circulation of misunderstandings and myths about the ways in which social housing is allocated
- local allocation policies which better reflect local pressures and priorities
- a greater sense among local people that housing is allocated fairly
- stronger community cohesion

42. Some local authorities currently make significant efforts to engage with local communities in the development of allocation policies, using techniques such as questionnaires and surveys aimed at residents or those on the waiting list, citizens' panels and focus groups. There is scope for all authorities to develop their approaches further, drawing on good practice from within the housing sector and more broadly.[21]

43. Anyone who is affected by or interested in the way social housing is allocated should be included when consulting on changes to an authority's allocation scheme. It will be important to engage with a wide range of stakeholders in the statutory and voluntary and community sector, as well as applicants and the general public. Consultation gives people the opportunity to have their views heard but it also gives local authorities the opportunity to engage the community, to raise awareness about the pressures on social housing, and to ensure that people have a better understanding of why certain groups are prioritised for social housing.

44. However, authorities should also engage with and involve the wider community before they produce their allocation scheme so that people are given the opportunity to contribute to the development of the allocation priorities. Only in this way can authorities ensure that the allocation scheme properly reflects local priorities and issues. An important aspect of engagement will be managing expectations. Providing clear information about allocations, including which households must be given priority under the allocation legislation and what social housing is available in the district, may be helpful here; as also ensuring that any consultation on allocation priorities is set firmly within the context of the local authority's overarching strategic priorities.

45. It will be important to take action to ensure that all groups within the area are engaged. Voluntary and community organisations can be useful here as they often have strong links with their particular communities or client groups. Authorities will need to give particular thought to how to engage those who

Appendix 1
England: Allocation

---

[20] *Creating Strong and Prosperous Communities*, July 2008.

[21] *The Duty to Involve: Making it Work* published by the Community Development Foundation (2009) provides advice and examples of effective engagement.

can often be marginalised but for whom social housing may be particularly relevant (such as substance misusers, gypsies and travellers and ex-offenders). Again, the voluntary and community sector may be in touch with hard to reach groups and can help ensure that they are involved in the consultation process. For this reason, it is particularly important that third sector organisations are involved at an early stage in the consultation process.

46.   Where local authorities involve individuals or groups in developing their allocation priorities or consult them on their allocation scheme, they should consider how they can feed back the outcomes of such involvement or consultation. In doing so they should make clear how the input to consultation and involvement has contributed to the published allocation scheme.

Information about allocations

47.   It is important that applicants and the wider community understand what social housing is available in their district, how social housing is allocated, and who is getting that social housing. Accordingly local authorities are encouraged to make appropriate information about allocations widely available in a way which is easy to access and to understand.[22] This is in addition to the duty in s 168 to make the full allocation scheme available for inspection and a summary of the scheme available free of charge. However, to ensure that local people have access to as much information as possible, authorities should publish their full allocation scheme on their website as well as in hard copy.

48.   Local authorities must ensure that advice and information is available free of charge to everyone in their district about the right to apply for an allocation of accommodation (s 166(1)). This includes general information about the procedures for making an application; as well as information about how applicants are prioritised under the allocation scheme.

49.   If applicants are to view the system as fair, they need to know how their application will be treated under the allocation scheme, what their rights and expectations are under the scheme, and they need reassurance that the scheme is being complied with and applied consistently across all applicants. So, for example, applicants have the right to be informed of certain decisions in relation to their application[23] and the right to a review of such decisions (s 167(4A)(d)). It is important that applicants have clear information about these rights as well as the procedure upon review. Applicants should also be provided with information about any other relevant complaints procedures which are available to them.

---

[22]   Chapter 5 of the 2008 code provides detailed guidance on how to ensure that information is provided in a way which is accessible and that advice, assistance and support are available to those who need them in order to apply for social housing.

[23]   Applicants have the right to be informed of any decision and the grounds for it, relating to their eligibility (s 160A(9)) and to be informed of a decision not to give them preference on grounds of unacceptable behaviour (s 167(4A(b))). Applicants also have the right on request to be informed of any decision about the facts of their case which are likely to be, or have been, taken into account in considering whether to allocate accommodation to them (s 167(4A)(c)).

50.   However, information about allocations should go beyond publication of the allocation scheme itself or information about how to apply for an allocation. Most applicants will want to know how long they are likely to have to wait to be allocated accommodation which meets their needs and aspirations (this is in line with their rights under s 167(4A)). Authorities can help applicants assess whether particular accommodation is likely to be available and how long they are likely to wait for it, by making available general information about the profile of their stock (amount, type, size, location and accessibility); together with information about how often property of that type/size/location becomes available and estimated waiting times. Information should be kept up-to-date and published on a regular basis. It should be widely available as it may be of interest to people who may be considering applying for social housing as well as those who are already on the waiting list.

51.   It is important that local authorities go wider than simply informing applicants, and consider how they can share information about allocation policies and outcomes with the wider community. Where tensions are associated with housing allocations, communication may need to be part of a wider community cohesion strategy.

52.   Key individuals and organisations need information and training to ensure that they understand how the allocation system works and that they provide consistent messages both to applicants and to the wider public. Training needs to be ongoing, recognising that allocation policies change over time and that council staff and other personnel move on. When communicating messages about why certain groups have access to social housing, it is important to work together with the statutory bodies or community organisations which support those groups and individuals. So, for example, local authorities should work together with local drug action teams and crime and disorder reduction partnerships to explain why providing a stable base for substance misusers or ex-offenders can reduce crime and anti-social behaviour.

Monitoring and evaluation

53.   Monitoring and evaluation systems should be put in place and lettings outcomes published so that people can see that the allocation scheme is being complied with and is fair, and that the authority is meeting its duties under the equality legislation (see paragraph 21). Local authorities should give people the opportunity to feedback comments about how the allocation scheme is working. This might include periodically carrying out surveys of people on the waiting list to find out about their experience over time, or people who have bid for social housing through a choice based lettings scheme (both successfully and unsuccessfully).

Framing an allocation scheme

54.   An authority's allocation priorities should be developed in the context of the authority's other housing functions. Consideration should be given to the wider objectives of meeting the district's housing needs, as set out in the

strategic housing market assessment. The allocation scheme should also be compatible with the local authority's housing strategy and the relevant regional housing strategy. Furthermore, since the allocation of accommodation under Part 6 of the 1996 Act is one of the ways in which the main homelessness duty can be discharged, allocation policies and procedures should also be consistent with the local authority's homelessness strategy.

55. It is also important that the allocation scheme is compatible with and flows from the authority's sustainable community strategy[24] which sets the overall strategic direction and long-term vision for the economic, social and environmental well-being of the local area.

56. It is strongly recommended that local authorities put in place allocation schemes which, not only meet the requirements in the legislation to ensure that reasonable preference for an allocation goes to those in the reasonable preference categories, but also:

- reflect the Government's objectives, and
- take into account the particular needs and priorities of the local area

57. We recognise that getting the balance right will be challenging, particularly given the constraints within which local authorities operate in terms of the supply of and demand for social housing. Nevertheless, we believe that there is considerable flexibility within the existing statutory framework, particularly following the recent decision in *Ahmad*.

R (on application of Ahmad) v London Borough of Newham

58. In March 2009 the House of Lords gave judgment in the case of *R (on application of Ahmad) v Newham LBC*[25] (*'Ahmad'*). The case has significant implications for the way local authorities frame their allocation scheme. In particular the House of Lords found:

- there is no requirement for local authorities to frame their allocation scheme to provide for cumulative preference, ie affording greater priority to applicants who fall into more than one reasonable preference category.
- an allocation scheme which allows for priority to be determined between applicants in the reasonable preference categories on the basis of waiting time (alone) is not unlawful or irrational
- an allocation scheme is not unlawful if it allows for a small percentage of lets to be allocated to existing social housing tenants who wish to transfer and who do not fall within any of the reasonable preference categories
- where a local authority's allocation scheme complies with the requirements of section 167 and any other statutory requirements, the courts should be very slow to interfere on the ground that it is irrational

---

[24] Section 4 of the Local Government Act 2000.
[25] [2009] UKHL 14.

59. Through their judgment in the *Ahmad* case, the House of Lords have recognised the complexity of allocation policy and the need for local decision-making.

60. The following paragraphs consider the factors which local authorities should consider in developing their allocation priorities and the different tools and mechanisms available to them to allow for greater flexibility within their allocation scheme and to adapt their scheme to respond to local needs.

Removal of the requirement to provide for 'cumulative preference'

61. The House of Lords decision in *Ahmad* reverses a line of Court of Appeal authority that has held that allocation schemes were required to provide for cumulative preference. This means that it is no longer necessary to distinguish between degrees of housing need, or to provide that those applicants who fall within more than one reasonable preference category are given greater priority for an allocation than those who have reasonable preference on a single, non-urgent basis (indeed there is no requirement for any system of determining priority between those in the reasonable preference groups). In the light of the decision in *Ahmad*, what is important is that an allocation scheme makes an appropriate distinction between those applicants in the reasonable preference categories and those who are not. It is no longer necessary to make a detailed prioritisation of applicants within the reasonable preference categories (instead it is open to local authorities to determine between applicants in the reasonable preference categories by waiting time alone (see paragraph 65).

62. Removing the requirement to provide for cumulative preference gives scope for local authorities to develop simpler, more transparent, systems of applicant prioritisation which are easier for applicants to understand and for housing staff to operate.

Determining priorities between households with a similar level of need

63. For practical purposes, allocation schemes will need to have some mechanism for determining priorities between applicants with a similar level of need, for example between applicants who are in the same band.

64. Section 167(2A) provides that authorities may frame their allocation scheme to take into account certain factors for the purposes of determining relative priorities between applicants in the reasonable (or additional) preference categories. Examples of factors which may be taken into account are given in the legislation: local connection,[26] financial resources and behaviour. However, these examples are not exclusive and authorities may take into account other factors instead or as well as these.

___
[26] For these purposes, local connection is defined in accordance with s 199 of the 1996 Act.

Waiting time

65.   The simplest way of determining priorities between those with a similar level of need would be to take into account the length of time which applicants have been waiting for an allocation (in the case of new applicants this will normally be the date of their original application or date into band, and in the case of transferring tenants, the date they applied to transfer).

66.   Waiting time has the benefits of being simple, transparent, and easy to understand. It also accords with the view held by some sections of the public about how social housing should be prioritised. Of course, we recognise that waiting time will already play a role in most allocation schemes. However, authorities may wish to consider the scope for giving more weight to it in the light of *Ahmad*, where this is seen locally as the fairest means of distinguishing between otherwise similar applicants.

Behaviour

67.   This would allow local authorities to take account of good as well as bad behaviour. So, for example, authorities could provide for greater priority to be given to applicants who can demonstrate that they have been model tenants or whose actions have directly benefited other residents on their estate or the community more generally. Bad behaviour would include unacceptable behaviour which was not serious enough to justify a decision to treat the applicant as ineligible, or to give him no preference for an allocation, but which could be taken into account in assessing the level of priority which was deserved relative to other applicants. An example could be minor rent arrears or low level anti-social behaviour.

Local connection

68.   Some local authorities may wish to give more priority to 'local connection', ensuring that, wherever possible, social housing goes to those people who live or work in the district, or to those who have close family associations with it or have other special circumstances. While local authorities cannot exclude people who do not have a local connection from applying for social housing, there is nothing to prevent them from framing their allocation scheme to include local connection as a policy priority, provided that overall the scheme continues to meet the reasonable preference requirements in s 167.

69.   An allocation scheme which attaches particular weight to local connection could disadvantage individual applicants. One example might be someone who has been placed out of the district they would normally live in for a period of time, while being looked after by children's services – although each case would need to be considered on its merits (care leavers might be able to establish a local connection through family association or special circumstances). Local authorities may wish to provide for circumstances such as these by setting aside a proportion of lettings (eg by including a specific

target in their lettings plan, or by means of an appropriate local lettings policy) to help meet the housing needs of such applicants where they meet the reasonable preference criteria.

Banding schemes

70.   An appropriate method of applicant prioritisation could be a system that groups applicants into a number of 'bands' that reflect different levels of housing need or relative priorities within a housing authority's allocation scheme. Such systems are commonly referred to as 'banding schemes'.

71.   The House of Lords in *Ahmad* recognised that simple banding schemes could have a number of advantages over more nuanced systems. They are clear, relatively simple to administer and highly transparent. Whereas banding schemes, which involve a large number of bands based on degrees of housing need, are likely to be more expensive and time consuming to operate, more based on value judgment, more open to argument, and more opaque. The House of Lords also considered that more complex banding systems may need to be monitored more closely to take account of the fact that applicants' circumstances are liable to change over time.

72.   In addition to the benefits identified in *Ahmad*, simpler banding schemes may also make it easier for authorities to work together to put in place sub-regional and regional choice based lettings schemes.

73.   Authorities should bear in mind that a banding scheme must be consistent with and give effect to the principles in the authority's allocation scheme for determining priorities for an allocation. The greater the number and complexity of these principles, the more complex the banding scheme will normally need to be.

Points based approaches

74.   Many local authorities have adopted a points-based approach to the prioritisation of applicants. Points-based systems can be complex and consequently lacking in transparency and difficult for applicants to understand. Local authorities that wish to continue with a points-based system should consider whether there is any scope to simplify it.

Including local priorities alongside the statutory reasonable preference categories

75.   Section 167(6) of the Housing Act 1996 makes it clear that, subject to the reasonable preference requirements, it is for local authorities to decide on what principles their allocation scheme is to be framed.

76.   An allocation scheme may provide for other factors than those set out in s 167(2) to be taken into account in determining which applicants are to be given preference under a scheme, provided they do not dominate the scheme and that overall the scheme operates to give reasonable preference to people in

the reasonable preference categories. This means that an allocation scheme may include other policy priorities, such as promoting job-related mobility, prioritising under-occupiers, or providing move-on accommodation for people leaving supported housing, provided that:

- they do not dominate the scheme and
- overall, the scheme operates to give reasonable preference to those in the statutory reasonable preference categories over those who are not

77.   The House of Lords in *Ahmad* accepted that local authorities are entitled to allocate to people who do not fall within the reasonable preference groups. For example, Newham's very favourable treatment of under-occupiers was not unlawful, notwithstanding the fact that they were unlikely to fall within any of the reasonable preference groups. It was accepted that account could be taken of wider housing management considerations (as well as the needs of those in the reasonable preference categories), and the judgment made the point that encouraging people in larger homes to transfer to smaller ones could be to the advantage of those in housing need because it produces an overall increase in the accommodation available.

78.   Lettings outcomes should be evaluated over time to ensure that the authority is able to meet the priorities and principles set out in its allocation scheme and the reasonable preference requirements in s 167(2). Robust monitoring systems are essential here.

Existing tenants seeking a move

79.   Part 6 of the 1996 Act extends to existing tenants of local authorities and RSLs who apply to transfer within the social rented sector. This means existing tenants applying for a transfer must be treated on the same basis as other applicants in accordance with the reasonable preference requirements in s 167. However, the House of Lords in *Ahmad* recognised that there could be good housing management reasons for enabling existing tenants to move, even where they do not have reasonable preference – provided that overall those in the reasonable preference categories continued to receive some preference. This is because such moves are broadly stock neutral (every transfer creates another void which can be used to meet housing needs). The House of Lords also recognised that people who are allowed to move to properties or locations which they prefer are likely to be happier and, as a result, better tenants.

80.   In the light of *Ahmad* we consider that authorities have the scope to provide within their allocation scheme for existing tenants to transfer to similar sized accommodation where they can demonstrate good reason for seeking a move, for example, where they want to move to take up an offer of employment. The extent to which there is scope to allow existing tenants to move within the stock will depend on the particular circumstances in the district, taking into account the demand from other applicants in greater housing need and the effect which this could have on lost revenue from increased void periods. In *Ahmad*, the court considered that setting aside a small proportion of lettings for transferring tenants was not unreasonable.

Quotas, targets and lettings plans

81.   An authority may want to set targets for the proportion of properties which it expects to allocate to the various groups within the allocation scheme as part of an annual lettings plan. So, for example, this might set a target for the proportion of large family-sized accommodation to be allocated to overcrowded households, or for the proportion of lettings to be given to transferring tenants.

82.   Authorities should avoid setting rigid quotas which cannot be amended in the light of changing circumstances. However, they may wish to set broad targets which should be published alongside the authority's allocation scheme. Targets should be published as part of an annual lettings plan and monitored, and lettings outcomes against the targets should be published. Published targets, together with information about lettings outcomes, help make the allocation process more transparent.

83.   In setting targets, authorities should take into account:

- the size and composition of the waiting list
- the profile of their stock and the vacancies which are likely to become available.

Local lettings policies

84.   Section 167(2E) of the 1996 Act enables local authorities to allocate particular accommodation to people of a particular description, whether or not they fall within the reasonable preference categories, provided that overall the authority is able to demonstrate compliance with the requirements of s 167. This is the statutory basis for so-called 'local lettings policies'. This could mean setting aside houses on a particular estate, or certain types of property across the stock, for applicants who meet specified criteria.

85.   A study carried out by Heriot Watt University[27] for Communities and Local Government in 2008, based in two regions, found that about half of responding authorities (23 out of 52) operated local lettings policies. This would suggest that local authorities may not be making as much use as they could of the flexibilities which the allocation legislation allows them.

86.   Local lettings policies may be used to achieve a wide variety of policy objectives. So for example, they may be used to:

- deal with concentrations of deprivation or create more mixed communities by setting aside a proportion of vacancies for applicants who are in employment or to enable existing tenants to take up an offer of employment
- attract essential workers into the district by giving them priority for a small number of properties even though they may not fall within any of the reasonable preference categories

---

[27]   *Exploring local authority policy and practice on allocations* (Hal Pawson and Anwen Jones) (CLG 2009).

Appendix 1
England: Allocation

- deal sensitively with lettings in rural villages and on s 106 exception sites by giving priority to those with a local connection to the parish
- ensure that properties which are particularly suited to being made accessible (e g ground floor flats) are prioritised for those with access needs
- set aside a proportion of properties to help meet the housing needs of people whose employment requires them to be mobile, such as members of the Armed Forces[28]

88.   Where a number of local authorities have agreed a common allocation policy or common prioritisation criteria, as part of a sub-regional CBL scheme, local lettings policies can be useful as a means of incorporating local priorities.

89.   Before adopting a local lettings policy, authorities should consult with those who are likely to be affected by it. So for example, where a local lettings policy is to apply to a particular estate, they should consult with tenants and residents on that estate. RSLs should also be consulted in relation to and, where appropriate (e g where stock they own is included in a relevant estate) involved in developing local lettings policies.

90.   The proportion of stock or lettings which may be made available through a local lettings policy to people who are not in the reasonable preference categories will depend on the particular circumstances and factors at play in the district. Authorities will need to take into account factors such as: the size and composition of the waiting list (ie the proportion of applicants in the reasonable preference categories); the stock profile; and the number and type/size of vacancies which are available overall.

91.   In the interests of transparency, local lettings policies should be published. Since they will often be time limited, it may not be practicable for the detailed policies to be included in the allocation scheme. One way to get around this would be for the allocation scheme to include a general statement about the intention to implement local lettings policies and to set out the detail in a separate published document or documents which could be revoked or revised as appropriate. Authorities should include an explanation of the local lettings policy which should be evidence-based wherever possible. Where it is intended that the policy is time limited, it should include an appropriate exit strategy.

92.   Local lettings policies should also be monitored as to their effectiveness and reviewed regularly so that they can be revised or revoked where they are no longer appropriate or necessary.

---

[28]   For further information on the Government's commitment to ensure that Service personnel are not disadvantaged when accessing public services, authorities are referred to *The Nation's Commitment to the Armed Forces Community: Consistent and Enduring Support*, Cm7674, published 16 July 2009.

Partnership working with RSLs

93.   It is important that local authorities take a strong strategic approach to meeting housing needs in their district. To do this, they will need to develop close working partnerships – both at the strategic and operational level – with RSLs, given their key role in the supply and management of social housing, to ensure that:

- best use is made of the available social housing in the district and
- applicants are offered the widest choice of accommodation

94.   This will be important for all local authorities but for those who have transferred their stock it will be crucial.

95.   RSLs should be involved at an early stage in developing allocation priorities and must be consulted on the allocation scheme. RSLs which manage a large number of properties in the district are likely to be well informed about the general housing needs of the area; while specialist RSLs may have significant knowledge of the needs of minority or marginalised groups. Allocation policies which are framed to take account of local needs and priorities are more likely to gain the support of RSLs.

96.   RSLs have a duty under s 170 of the 1996 Act to co-operate with local authorities – where the authority requests it – to such extent as is reasonable in the circumstances – in offering accommodation to people with priority under the authority's allocation scheme. This is reflected in the Tenant Services Authority's (TSA) draft allocation standard (issued for consultation on 12 November) which requires 'registered providers' to co-operate with local authorities' strategic function and their duties to meet identified housing needs, including meeting obligations in nomination agreements.

97.   Local authorities should ensure that they have nomination agreements in place with RSLs in their district and these should be updated regularly to ensure that they reflect changing housing markets.[29] Nomination agreements should set out the proportion of lettings that will be made available which should reflect the existing housing market circumstances; any criteria which the RSLs have adopted, following consultation with the housing authority, for accepting or rejecting nominees; and how any disputes about suitability and eligibility will be resolved. The TSA's draft allocation standard requires registered providers to clearly set out, and give reasons for, the criteria they use for excluding actual and potential tenants from consideration for allocations, mobility or mutual exchange schemes. When negotiating nominations agreements, local authorities should try to ensure that the criteria for rejecting nominees are kept to a minimum. This will be particularly important where the housing authority has transferred its housing stock. Robust monitoring arrangements should be put in place to measure the effectiveness of the nomination agreement.

---

[29]   *Effective Co-operation in Tackling Homelessness: Nomination Agreements and Exclusions*, published by CLG in November 2004 and available on the CLG website, identifies good practice in co-operation between housing authorities and RSLs in relation to nomination agreements and exclusions.

98.   Authorities should also agree information sharing protocols with RSLs in their district, covering issues such as rent arrears, anti-social behaviour and support needs. Information sharing between local authorities and RSLs is particularly important and failure to get this right could undermine the nomination process or the success of a joint choice based lettings scheme; while effective information sharing should help ensure that tenancies have the best chance of being sustained. The former Housing Corporation issued a national standard protocol for sharing information about applicants which authorities may wish to follow.[30] Amongst other things, it provides helpful advice on data protection issues.

99.   Local authorities are strongly encouraged to consider – together with RSLs in their district – the scope for developing common approaches to the allocation of social housing. This could include the adoption of a common housing register and a common allocation policy, and local lettings policies which cover RSLs as well as local authority stock. Providing a single point of access to social housing and one set of rules, should help make the process of applying for social housing simpler and more transparent for applicants, and can reduce wasteful duplication of effort by social landlords and applicants. This may help remove some of the confusion and frustration which applicants currently experience. The TSA made clear in *Building a new regulatory framework – a discussion paper* (June 2009), that it views agreement locally between social landlords and local authorities on how accommodation should be allocated as desirable and important for fairness and transparency within local areas.

100.   Common housing registers and common allocation policies are particularly relevant in the context of choice based lettings. Developing common approaches requires trust between the partners which can be built by partnerships agreeing clear accountable governance structures and cost sharing arrangements and by delivering a high quality service which is viewed by applicants and by all partner landlords as an improvement on those delivered by local authorities and RSLs on their own.[31]

---

[30]   *Access to Housing: Information Sharing Protocol*, Campbell Tickell for the Housing Corporation, November 2007.

[31]   Further guidance on partnership working with both RSLs and private landlords is provided in chapter 6 of the 2008 code.

Appendix 1
England: Allocation

SI 1996 No 3205

Local Authorities (Contracting Out of Allocation of Housing and Homelessness Functions) Order 1996

Made	*20th December 1996*
Coming into force	
Articles 1 and 3	*20th January 1997*
Article 2	*1st April 1997*

The Secretary of State for the Environment, as respects England, and the Secretary of State for Wales, as respects Wales, in exercise of the powers conferred on them by sections 70(2) and (4) and 77(1) of the Deregulation and Contracting Out Act 1994 and of all other powers enabling them in that behalf, after consultation with such representatives of local government as they consider appropriate, hereby make the following Order, a draft of which has been laid before and approved by resolution of each House of Parliament:

1 Citation, commencement and interpretation

(1) This Order may be cited as the Local Authorities (Contracting Out of Allocation of Housing and Homelessness Functions) Order 1996.

(2) This article and article 3 of this Order shall come into force on 20th January 1997 and article 2 of this Order shall come into force on 1st April 1997.

(3) In this Order –

'the Act' means the Housing Act 1996;
'an authority' means a local housing authority as defined in the Housing Act 1985.

(4) Any expressions used in this Order which are also used in the Act have the same meaning as they have in the Act.

2 Contracting out of allocation of housing functions

Any function of an authority which is conferred by or under Part 6 of the Act (allocation of housing accommodation), except one which is listed in Schedule 1 to this Order, may be exercised by, or by employees of, such person (if any) as may be authorised in that behalf by the authority whose function it is.

3 Contracting out of homelessness functions

Any function of an authority which is conferred by or under Part 7 of the Act (homelessness), except one which is listed in Schedule 2 to this Order, may be exercised by, or by employees of, such person (if any) as may be authorised in that behalf by the authority whose function it is.

Schedule 1
Allocation of Housing Functions of a Local Housing Authority Excluded from Contracting Out

Article 2

Functions conferred by or under any of the following provisions of the Act:

(a)   section 161(4) (classes of persons qualifying for allocations);

(b)   section 162 (the housing register) so far as they relate to any decision about the form of the register;

(c)   section 167 (allocation in accordance with allocation scheme) so far as they relate to adopting or altering an allocation scheme (including decisions on what principles the scheme is to be framed) and to the functions in subsection (7) of that section;

(d)   section 168(2) (information about allocation scheme) so far as they relate to making the allocation scheme available for inspection at the authority's principal office.

Schedule 2
Homelessness Functions of a Local Housing Authority Excluded from Contracting Out

Article 3

Functions conferred by or under any of the following provisions of the Act:

(a)   section 179(2) and (3) (duty of local housing authority to provide advisory services);

(b)   section 180 (assistance for voluntary organisations);

(c)   section 213 (co-operation between relevant housing authorities and bodies).

SI 1997 No 483

Allocation of Housing (Procedure) Regulations 1997

Made	*26th February 1997*
Laid before Parliament	*27th February 1997*
Coming into force	*1st April 1997*

The Secretary of State, in exercise of the powers conferred on him by sections 167(5) and 172(4) of the Housing Act 1996 and of all other powers enabling him in that behalf, hereby makes the following Regulations:

1 Citation and commencement

These Regulations may be cited as the Allocation of Housing (Procedure) Regulations 1997 and shall come into force on 1st April 1997.

2 Interpretation

In these Regulations –

'allocation decision' means a decision to allocate housing accommodation;
'authority' means a local housing authority in England;
'decision-making body' means an authority or a committee or sub-committee of an authority.

3 Allocation scheme procedure

(1) As regards the procedure to be followed, an authority's allocation scheme shall be framed in accordance with the principle prescribed in this regulation.

(2) A member of an authority who has been elected for the electoral division or ward in which –

(a) the housing accommodation in relation to which an allocation decision falls to be made is situated, or

(b) the person in relation to whom that decision falls to be made has his sole or main residence,

shall not, at the time the allocation decision is made, be included in the persons constituting the decision-making body.

SI 2002 No 3264

Allocation of Housing (England) Regulations 2002

Made	*18th December 2002*
Laid before Parliament	*10th January 2003*
Coming into force	*31st January 2003*

The Secretary of State, in exercise of the powers conferred upon him by sections 160(4), 160A(3) and (5) and 172(4) of the Housing Act 1996 hereby makes the following Regulations:

1 Citation, commencement and application

(1) These Regulations may be cited as the Allocation of Housing (England) Regulations 2002 and shall come into force on 31st January 2003.

(2) These Regulations apply in England only.

2 Interpretation

In these Regulations—

'the Act' means the Housing Act 1996;
'the Common Travel Area' means the United Kingdom, the Channel Islands, the Isle of Man and the Republic of Ireland collectively; and
'the immigration rules' means the rules laid down as mentioned in section 3(2) of the Immigration Act 1971 (general provisions for regulation and control).

3 Cases where the provisions of Part 6 of the Act do not apply

(1) The provisions of Part 6 of the Act about the allocation of housing accommodation do not apply in the following cases.

(2) They do not apply where a local housing authority secures the provision of suitable alternative accommodation under section 39 of the Land Compensation Act 1973 (duty to rehouse residential occupiers).

(3) They do not apply in relation to the grant of a secure tenancy under sections 554 and 555 of the Housing Act 1985 (grant of tenancy to former owner-occupier or statutory tenant of defective dwelling-house).

4 Classes prescribed under section 160A(3) who are eligible persons

AMENDMENT

Regulation revoked: SI 2006/1294, reg 7, Sch, with effect from 1 June 2006, subject to transitional provisions see SI 2006/1294, reg 8 (see Appendix 2).

5 Classes prescribed under section 160A(5) who are ineligible persons

AMENDMENT

Regulation revoked: SI 2006/1294, reg 7, Sch, with effect from 1 June 2006, subject to transitional provisions see SI 2006/1294, reg 8 (see Appendix 2).

6 Revocation

The Allocation of Housing (England) Regulations 2000 are revoked.

Revision of the Code of Guidance on the allocation of accommodation: Letter to Directors of all local authorities in England

OFFICE OF THE DEPUTY PRIME MINISTER

Frances Walker
Housing Policy Advisor
HHM
Eland House
Bressenden Place
London
SW1E 5DU

To Directors of Housing of all local authorities in England & other interested bodies (see Annex [not reproduced])

Direct line: 3666
Fax: 3489
GTN: 3533

Web site: www.odpm.gov.uk

11 November 2002

Code of Guidance on the Allocation of Accommodation

The attached Code of Guidance relates to the allocation of accommodation; and is issued to housing authorities under s 169 of the Housing Act 1996 (the 1996 Act) by the First Secretary of State. All housing authorities are required to have regard to the guidance when exercising their functions under Part 6 of the 1996 Act.

The guidance reflects changes to Part 6 of the 1996 Act contained in the Homelessness Act 2002 (the 2002 Act). The Government intends to bring the allocation provisions of the 2002 Act into force on 31 January 2003. This Code of Guidance will have statutory force on the same date, and will supersede all guidance previously issued under s 169 of the 1996 Act.

A consultative draft of this guidance was issued in May 2002; and the final version has been revised to take account of responses to the consultation wherever possible. The guidance also reflects, at paragraph 5.9, the key points arising from the recent Court of Appeal judgment in the conjoined cases of *R (on the application of A) v Lambeth London Borough Council and R (on the application of Lindsay) v Lambeth London Borough Council* on 23 July 2002.

The guidance addresses the issue of how to offer applicants a choice of accommodation while continuing to give reasonable preference to those with the most urgent housing need, at paragraphs 5.10 to 5.12. We will be providing more detailed guidance on this issue towards the end of next year, once the ODPM choice based lettings pilot scheme has been properly evaluated.

The Code does not contain detailed guidance on the procedures which housing authorities should adopt when carrying out reviews of decisions under Part 6 of the 1996 Act. The issue of local authorities' review procedures under Parts 5 and 7 of the 1996 Act has been considered on more than one occasion recently by the Court of Appeal. We understand that one of those cases may be the subject of an appeal to the House of Lords. We will consider whether it would be appropriate to bring out further guidance to cover review procedures under Part 6 of the 1996 Act as the law continues to develop. In the meantime, housing authorities should ensure that the procedure for any review carried out at the request of an applicant as mentioned in paragraphs 4.30, 5.58 and 6.13 of, and annex 13 to, this guidance is fair and compatible with the Convention for the Protection of Human Rights and Fundamental Freedoms (commonly known as the European Convention on Human Rights) (see sections 1 and 6(1) of, and Schedule 1 to, the Human Rights Act 1998). In doing so, they will wish to have regard to relevant judgments of the domestic courts and the European Court on Human Rights.

New regulations on the eligibility for an allocation of accommodation under s 160A(3) and (5) of the 1996 Act will come into force on 31 January 2003, and will replace the current regulations in SI 2000/702. A copy of the new regulations, and the commencement order, will be sent to housing authorities well in advance of the commencement date.

A copy of the Code of Guidance has been placed on the ODPM web-site.

Yours faithfully,

Frances Walker
Housing Management Division
Tel: 020 7944 3666
Fax: 020 7944 3489
E-mail: frances.walker@odpm.gsi.gov.uk

Appendix 1
England: Allocation

Appendix 2

ENGLAND: HOMELESSNESS

Housing Act 1996

1996 c 52

CONTENTS

PART 7
HOMELESSNESS

Homelessness and threatened homelessness

General functions in relation to homelessness or threatened homelessness

Application for assistance in case of homelessness or threatened homelessness

Eligibility for assistance

Interim duty to accommodate

Duties to persons found to be homeless or threatened with homelessness

Referral to another local housing authority

PART 8

MISCELLANEOUS AND GENERAL PROVISIONS

General

PART 7
HOMELESSNESS

Homelessness and threatened homelessness

175 Homelessness and threatened homelessness

(1)   A person is homeless if he has no accommodation available for his occupation, in the United Kingdom or elsewhere, which he –

(a)   is entitled to occupy by virtue of an interest in it or by virtue of an order of a court,

(b)   has an express or implied licence to occupy, or

(c)   occupies as a residence by virtue of any enactment or rule of law giving him the right to remain in occupation or restricting the right of another person to recover possession.

(2)   A person is also homeless if he has accommodation but –

(a)   he cannot secure entry to it, or

(b)   it consists of a moveable structure, vehicle or vessel designed or adapted for human habitation and there is no place where he is entitled or permitted both to place it and to reside in it.

(3)   A person shall not be treated as having accommodation unless it is accommodation which it would be reasonable for him to continue to occupy.

(4)   A person is threatened with homelessness if it is likely that he will become homeless within 28 days.

176 Meaning of accommodation available for occupation

Accommodation shall be regarded as available for a person's occupation only if it is available for occupation by him together with –

(a)   any other person who normally resides with him as a member of his family, or

(b)   any other person who might reasonably be expected to reside with him.

References in this Part to securing that accommodation is available for a person's occupation shall be construed accordingly.

177 Whether it is reasonable to continue to occupy accommodation

(1)   It is not reasonable for a person to continue to occupy accommodation if it is probable that this will lead to domestic violence [or other violence]¹ against him, or against –

(a)   a person who normally resides with him as a member of his family, or

(b)   any other person who might reasonably be expected to reside with him.

[(1A)   For this purpose 'violence' means –

(a)   violence from another person; or

(b)   threats of violence from another person which are likely to be carried out;

and violence is 'domestic violence' if it is from a person who is associated with the victim.]²

(2)   In determining whether it would be, or would have been, reasonable for a person to continue to occupy accommodation, regard may be had to the general circumstances prevailing in relation to housing in the district of the local housing authority to whom he has applied for accommodation or for assistance in obtaining accommodation.

(3)   The Secretary of State may by order specify –

   (a)   other circumstances in which it is to be regarded as reasonable or not reasonable for a person to continue to occupy accommodation, and
   (b)   other matters to be taken into account or disregarded in determining whether it would be, or would have been, reasonable for a person to continue to occupy accommodation.

AMENDMENT

¹ Words inserted: Homelessness Act 2002, s 10(1)(a).

² Sub-section substituted: Homelessness Act 2002, s 10(1)(b).

178 Meaning of associated person

(1)   For the purposes of this Part, a person is associated with another person if –

   (a)   they are or have been married to each other;
   [(aa) they are or have been civil partners of each other;]¹
   (b)   they are cohabitants or former cohabitants;
   (c)   they live or have lived in the same household;
   (d)   they are relatives;
   (e)   they have agreed to marry one another (whether or not that agreement has been terminated);
   [(ea) they have entered into a civil partnership agreement between them (whether or not that agreement has been terminated);]²
   (f)   in relation to a child, each of them is a parent of the child or has, or has had, parental responsibility for the child.

(2)   If a child has been adopted or [falls within subsection (2A)]³, two persons are also associated with each other for the purposes of this Part if –

   (a)   one is a natural parent of the child or a parent of such a natural parent, and
   (b)   the other is the child or a person –
      (i)   who has become a parent of the child by virtue of an adoption order or who has applied for an adoption order, or
      (ii) with whom the child has at any time been placed for adoption.

[(2A)   A child falls within this subsection if –

   (a)   an adoption agency, within the meaning of section 2 of the Adoption and Children Act 2002, is authorised to place him for adoption under section 19 of that Act (placing children with parental consent) or he has become the subject of an order under section 21 of that Act (placement orders), or

(b) he is freed for adoption by virtue of an order made –
    (i)   in England and Wales, under section 18 of the Adoption Act 1976,
    (ii) in Scotland, under section 18 of the Adoption (Scotland) Act 1978, or
    (iii) in Northern Ireland, under Article 17(1) or 18(1) of the Adoption (Northern Ireland) Order 1987.][4]

(3) In this section –

'adoption order' has the meaning given by section 72(1) of the Adoption Act 1976;

['adoption order' means an adoption order within the meaning of section 72(1) of the Adoption Act 1976 or section 46(1) of the Adoption and Children Act 2002;][5]

'child' means a person under the age of 18 years;

['civil partnership agreement' has the meaning given by section 73 of the Civil Partnership Act 2004;][6]

'cohabitants' means a man and a woman who, although not married to each other, are living together as husband and wife, and 'former cohabitants' shall be construed accordingly;

['cohabitants' means –
    (a)   a man and a woman who, although not married to each other, are living together as husband and wife, or
    (b)   two people of the same sex who, although not civil partners of each other, are living together as if they were civil partners;

and 'former cohabitants' shall be construed accordingly;][7]

'parental responsibility' has the same meaning as in the Children Act 1989; and

'relative', in relation to a person, means –
    (a)   the father, mother, stepfather, stepmother, son, daughter, stepson, stepdaughter, grandmother, grandfather, grandson or grand-daughter of that person or of that person's [spouse, civil partner, former spouse or former civil partner][8], or
    (b)   the brother, sister, uncle, aunt, niece or nephew (whether of the full blood or of the half blood or by [marriage or civil partnership])[9] of that person or of that person's [spouse, civil partner, former spouse or former civil partner][10],

and includes, in relation to a person who is living or has lived with another person as husband and wife, a person who would fall within paragraph (a) or (b) if the parties were married to each other.

AMENDMENT

[1] Sub-section inserted: Civil Partnership Act 2004, s 81, Sch 8, para 61(1), (2).

[2] Sub-section inserted: Civil Partnership Act 2004, s 81, Sch 8, para 61(1), (3).

[3] Words substituted: Adoption and Children Act 2002, s 139(1), Sch 3, paras 89, 90.

[4] Sub-section inserted: Adoption and Children Act 2002, s 139(1), Sch 3, paras 89, 91.

[5] Definition substituted: Adoption and Children Act 2002, s 139(1), Sch 3, paras 89, 92.

[6] Definition inserted: Civil Partnership Act 2004, s 81, Sch 8, para 61(1), (4).

[7] Definition substituted: Civil Partnership Act 2004, s 81, Sch 8, para 61(1), (5).

[8] Words substituted: Civil Partnership Act 2004, s 81, Sch 8, para 61(1), (6).

[9] Words substituted: Civil Partnership Act 2004, s 81, Sch 8, para 61(1), (7).

[10] Words substituted: Civil Partnership Act 2004, s 81, Sch 8, para 61(1), (6).

General functions in relation to homelessness or threatened homelessness

179 Duty of local housing authority to provide advisory services

(1)   Every local housing authority shall secure that advice and information about homelessness, and the prevention of homelessness, is available free of charge to any person in their district.

(2)   The authority may give to any person by whom such advice and information is provided on behalf of the authority assistance by way of grant or loan.

(3)   A local housing authority may also assist any such person –

    (a)   by permitting him to use premises belonging to the authority,
    (b)   by making available furniture or other goods, whether by way of gift, loan or otherwise, and
    (c)   by making available the services of staff employed by the authority.

180 Assistance for voluntary organisations

(1)   The Secretary of State or a local housing authority may give assistance by way of grant or loan to voluntary organisations concerned with homelessness or matters relating to homelessness.

(2)   A local housing authority may also assist any such organisation –

    (a)   by permitting them to use premises belonging to the authority,
    (b)   by making available furniture or other goods, whether by way of gift, loan or otherwise, and
    (c)   by making available the services of staff employed by the authority.

(3)   A 'voluntary organisation' means a body (other than a public or local authority) whose activities are not carried on for profit.

181 Terms and conditions of assistance

(1)   This section has effect as to the terms and conditions on which assistance is given under section 179 or 180.

(2) Assistance shall be on such terms, and subject to such conditions, as the person giving the assistance may determine.

(3) No assistance shall be given unless the person to whom it is given undertakes –

(a) to use the money, furniture or other goods or premises for a specified purpose, and

(b) to provide such information as may reasonably be required as to the manner in which the assistance is being used.

The person giving the assistance may require such information by notice in writing, which shall be complied with within 21 days beginning with the date on which the notice is served.

(4) The conditions subject to which assistance is given shall in all cases include conditions requiring the person to whom the assistance is given –

(a) to keep proper books of account and have them audited in such manner as may be specified,

(b) to keep records indicating how he has used the money, furniture or other goods or premises, and

(c) to submit the books of account and records for inspection by the person giving the assistance.

(5) If it appears to the person giving the assistance that the person to whom it was given has failed to carry out his undertaking as to the purpose for which the assistance was to be used, he shall take all reasonable steps to recover from that person an amount equal to the amount of the assistance.

(6) He must first serve on the person to whom the assistance was given a notice specifying the amount which in his opinion is recoverable and the basis on which that amount has been calculated.

182 Guidance by the Secretary of State

(1) In the exercise of their functions relating to homelessness and the prevention of homelessness, a local housing authority or social services authority shall have regard to such guidance as may from time to time be given by the Secretary of State.

(2) The Secretary of State may give guidance either generally or to specified descriptions of authorities.

Application for assistance in case of homelessness or threatened homelessness

183 Application for assistance

(1) The following provisions of this Part apply where a person applies to a local housing authority for accommodation, or for assistance in obtaining accommodation, and the authority have reason to believe that he is or may be homeless or threatened with homelessness.

(2) In this Part –

Appendix 2
England: Homelessness

'applicant' means a person making such an application,

'assistance under this Part' means the benefit of any function under the following provisions of this Part relating to accommodation or assistance in obtaining accommodation, and

'eligible for assistance' means not excluded from such assistance by section 185 (persons from abroad not eligible for housing assistance) [or section 186 (asylum seekers and their dependants)][1].

(3)   Nothing in this section or the following provisions of this Part affects a person's entitlement to advice and information under section 179 (duty to provide advisory services).

AMENDMENT

[1] Words repealed: Immigration and Asylum Act 1999, s 169(1), (3), Sch 14, para 116, Sch 16, as from a date to be appointed.

184 Inquiry into cases of homelessness or threatened homelessness

(1)   If the local housing authority have reason to believe that an applicant may be homeless or threatened with homelessness, they shall make such inquiries as are necessary to satisfy themselves –

(a)   whether he is eligible for assistance, and

(b)   if so, whether any duty, and if so what duty, is owed to him under the following provisions of this Part.

(2)   They may also make inquiries whether he has a local connection with the district of another local housing authority in England, Wales or Scotland.

(3)   On completing their inquiries the authority shall notify the applicant of their decision and, so far as any issue is decided against his interests, inform him of the reasons for their decision.

[(3A)   If the authority decide that a duty is owed to the applicant under section 193(2) or 195(2) but would not have done so without having had regard to a restricted person, the notice under subsection (3) must also –

(a)   inform the applicant that their decision was reached on that basis,

(b)   include the name of the restricted person,

(c)   explain why the person is a restricted person, and

(d)   explain the effect of section 193(7AD) or (as the case may be) section 195(4A).][1]

(4)   If the authority have notified or intend to notify another local housing authority under section 198 (referral of cases), they shall at the same time notify the applicant of that decision and inform him of the reasons for it.

(5)   A notice under subsection (3) or (4) shall also inform the applicant of his right to request a review of the decision and of the time within which such a request must be made (see section 202).

(6)   Notice required to be given to a person under this section shall be given in writing and, if not received by him, shall be treated as having been given to him if it is made available at the authority's office for a reasonable period for collection by him or on his behalf.

[(7)   In this Part 'a restricted person' means a person –

(a)   who is not eligible for assistance under this Part,

(b)   who is subject to immigration control within the meaning of the Asylum and Immigration Act 1996, and

(c)   either –

  (i)   who does not have leave to enter or remain in the United Kingdom, or

  (ii)   whose leave to enter or remain in the United Kingdom is subject to a condition to maintain and accommodate himself, and any dependants, without recourse to public funds.]²

AMENDMENT

¹ Paragraph inserted: Housing and Regeneration Act 2008, s 314, Sch 15, Pt 1, paras 1, 3(1), (2), with effect from 2 March 2009 (except in relation to applications for an allocation of social housing or housing assistance (homelessness) or for accommodation made before that date) (SI 2009/415, art 2).

² Paragraph inserted: Housing and Regeneration Act 2008, s 314, Sch 15, Pt 1, paras 1, 3(1), (3), with effect from 2 March 2009 (except in relation to applications for an allocation of social housing or housing assistance (homelessness) or for accommodation made before that date) (SI 2009/415, art 2).

Eligibility for assistance

185 Persons from abroad not eligible for housing assistance

(1)   A person is not eligible for assistance under this Part if he is a person from abroad who is ineligible for housing assistance.

(2)   A person who is subject to immigration control within the meaning of the Asylum and Immigration Act 1996 is not eligible for housing assistance unless he is of a class prescribed by regulations made by the Secretary of State.

[(2A)   No person who is excluded from entitlement to housing benefit by section 115 of the Immigration and Asylum Act 1999 (exclusion from benefits) shall be included in any class prescribed under subsection (2).]¹

(3)   The Secretary of State may make provision by regulations as to other descriptions of persons who are to be treated for the purposes of this Part as persons from abroad who are ineligible for housing assistance.

(4)   A person from abroad who is not eligible for housing assistance shall be disregarded in determining for the purposes of this Part whether [a person falling within subsection (5)]² –

(a)   is homeless or threatened with homelessness, or

(b)   has a priority need for accommodation.

[(5)   A person falls within this subsection if the person –

Appendix 2
England: Homelessness

   (a)   falls within a class prescribed by regulations made under subsection (2); but

   (b)   is not a national of an EEA State or Switzerland.][3]

AMENDMENT

[1] Sub-section: substituted by the Homelessness Act 2002, s 18(1), Sch 1, paras 2, 7(1).

[2] Words substituted: Housing and Regeneration Act 2008, s 314, Sch 15, Pt 1, paras 1, 4(1), (2), with effect from 2 March 2009 (except in relation to applications for an allocation of social housing or housing assistance (homelessness) or for accommodation made before that date) (SI 2009/415, art 2).

[3] Sub-section inserted: Housing and Regeneration Act 2008, s 314, Sch 15, Pt 1, paras 1, 4(1), (3), with effect from 2 March 2009 (except in relation to applications for an allocation of social housing or housing assistance (homelessness) or for accommodation made before that date) (SI 2009/415, art 2).

[186 Asylum-seekers and their dependants

(1)　An asylum-seeker, or a dependant of an asylum-seeker who is not by virtue of section 185 a person from abroad who is ineligible for housing assistance, is not eligible for assistance under this Part if he has any accommodation in the United Kingdom, however temporary, available for his occupation.

(2)　For the purposes of this section a person who makes a claim for asylum –

   (a)   becomes an asylum-seeker at the time when his claim is recorded by the Secretary of State as having been made, and

   (b)   ceases to be an asylum-seeker at the time when his claim is recorded by the Secretary of State as having been finally determined or abandoned.

(3)　For the purposes of this section a person –

   (a)   becomes a dependant of an asylum-seeker at the time when he is recorded by the Secretary of State as being a dependant of the asylum-seeker, and

   (b)   ceases to be a dependant of an asylum-seeker at the time when the person whose dependant he is ceases to be an asylum-seeker or, if it is earlier, at the time when he is recorded by the Secretary of State as ceasing to be a dependant of the asylum-seeker.

(4)　In relation to an asylum-seeker, 'dependant' means a person –

   (a)   who is his spouse or a child of his under the age of eighteen, and

   (b)   who has neither a right of abode in the United Kingdom nor indefinite leave under the Immigration Act 1971 to enter or remain in the United Kingdom.

(5)　In this section a 'claim for asylum' means a claim made by a person that it would be contrary to the United Kingdom's obligations under the Convention relating to the Status of Refugees done at Geneva on 28th July 1951 and the Protocol to that Convention for him to be removed from, or required to leave, the United Kingdom.][1]

Appendix 2
England: Homelessness

AMENDMENT

[1] Section repealed: Immigration and Asylum Act 1999, ss 117(5), 169(3), Sch 16, as from a date to be appointed.

187 Provision of information by Secretary of State

(1)   The Secretary of State shall, at the request of a local housing authority, provide the authority with such information as they may require –

   (a)   as to whether a person is [a person to whom section 115 of the Immigration and Asylum Act 1999 (exclusion from benefits) applies][1], and

   (b)   to enable them to determine whether such a person is eligible for assistance under this Part under section 185 (persons from abroad not eligible for housing assistance).

(2)   Where that information is given otherwise than in writing, the Secretary of State shall confirm it in writing if a written request is made to him by the authority.

(3)   If it appears to the Secretary of State that any application, decision or other change of circumstances has affected the status of a person about whom information was previously provided by him to a local housing authority under this section, he shall inform the authority in writing of that fact, the reason for it and the date on which the previous information became inaccurate.

AMENDMENT

[1] Words substituted: Immigration and Asylum Act 1999, s 117(6).

Interim duty to accommodate

188 Interim duty to accommodate in case of apparent priority need

(1)   If the local housing authority have reason to believe that an applicant may be homeless, eligible for assistance and have a priority need, they shall secure that accommodation is available for his occupation pending a decision as to the duty (if any) owed to him under the following provisions of this Part.

(2)   The duty under this section arises irrespective of any possibility of the referral of the applicant's case to another local housing authority (see sections 198 to 200).

(3)   The duty ceases when the authority's decision is notified to the applicant, even if the applicant requests a review of the decision (see section 202).

The authority may [secure][1] that accommodation is available for the applicant's occupation pending a decision on a review.

AMENDMENT

[1] Word substituted: Homelessness Act 2002, s 18(1), Sch 1, paras 2, 8.

189 Priority need for accommodation

(1)   The following have a priority need for accommodation –

(a)   a pregnant woman or a person with whom she resides or might reasonably be expected to reside;

(b)   a person with whom dependent children reside or might reasonably be expected to reside;

(c)   a person who is vulnerable as a result of old age, mental illness or handicap or physical disability or other special reason, or with whom such a person resides or might reasonably be expected to reside;

(d)   a person who is homeless or threatened with homelessness as a result of an emergency such as flood, fire or other disaster.

(2)   The Secretary of State may by order –

(a)   specify further descriptions of persons as having a priority need for accommodation, and

(b)   amend or repeal any part of subsection (1).

(3)   Before making such an order the Secretary of State shall consult such associations representing relevant authorities, and such other persons, as he considers appropriate.

(4)   No such order shall be made unless a draft of it has been approved by resolution of each House of Parliament.

Duties to persons found to be homeless or threatened with homelessness

190 Duties to persons becoming homeless intentionally

(1)   This section applies where the local housing authority are satisfied that an applicant is homeless and is eligible for assistance but are also satisfied that he became homeless intentionally.

(2)   If the authority are satisfied that the applicant has a priority need, they shall –

(a)   secure that accommodation is available for his occupation for such period as they consider will give him a reasonable opportunity of securing accommodation for his occupation, and

(b)   provide him with [(or secure that he is provided with) advice and assistance][1] in any attempts he may make to secure that accommodation becomes available for his occupation.

(3)   If they are not satisfied that he has a priority need, they shall provide him with [(or secure that he is provided with) advice and assistance][2] in any attempts he may make to secure that accommodation becomes available for his occupation.

[(4)   The applicant's housing needs shall be assessed before advice and assistance is provided under subsection (2)(b) or (3).

(5)   The advice and assistance provided under subsection (2)(b) or (3) must include information about the likely availability in the authority's district of types of accommodation appropriate to the applicant's housing needs (including, in particular, the location and sources of such types of accommodation).][3]

AMENDMENT

[1] Words substituted: Homelessness Act 2002, s 18(1), Sch 1, paras 2, 9.

[2] Words substituted: Homelessness Act 2002, s 18(1), Sch 1, paras 2, 9.

[3] Sub-sections inserted: Homelessness Act 2002, s 18(1), Sch 1, paras 2, 10.

191 Becoming homeless intentionally

(1) A person becomes homeless intentionally if he deliberately does or fails to do anything in consequence of which he ceases to occupy accommodation which is available for his occupation and which it would have been reasonable for him to continue to occupy.

(2) For the purposes of subsection (1) an act or omission in good faith on the part of a person who was unaware of any relevant fact shall not be treated as deliberate.

(3) A person shall be treated as becoming homeless intentionally if –

(a) he enters into an arrangement under which he is required to cease to occupy accommodation which it would have been reasonable for him to continue to occupy, and

(b) the purpose of the arrangement is to enable him to become entitled to assistance under this Part,

and there is no other good reason why he is homeless.

(4) ...[1]

AMENDMENT

[1] Sub-section repealed: Homelessness Act 2002, s 18(2), Sch 2.

192 Duty to persons not in priority need who are not homeless intentionally

(1) This section applies where the local housing authority –

(a) are satisfied that an applicant is homeless and eligible for assistance, and

(b) are not satisfied that he became homeless intentionally,

but are not satisfied that he has a priority need.

(2) The authority shall provide the applicant with [(or secure that he is provided with) advice and assistance][1] in any attempts he may make to secure that accommodation becomes available for his occupation.

[(3) The authority may secure that accommodation is available for occupation by the applicant.][2]

[(4) The applicant's housing needs shall be assessed before advice and assistance is provided under subsection (2).

(5) The advice and assistance provided under subsection (2) must include information about the likely availability in the authority's district of types of

accommodation appropriate to the applicant's housing needs (including, in particular, the location and sources of such types of accommodation).][3]

AMENDMENT

[1] Words substituted by the Homelessness Act 2002, s 18(1), Sch 1, paras 2, 11.

[2] Sub-section inserted: Homelessness Act 2002, s 5(1).

[3] Sub-sections inserted: Homelessness Act 2002, s 18(1), Sch 1, paras 2, 12.

193 Duty to persons with priority need who are not homeless intentionally

(1)   This section applies where the local housing authority are satisfied that an applicant is homeless, eligible for assistance and has a priority need, and are not satisfied that he became homeless intentionally.

…[1]

(2)   Unless the authority refer the application to another local housing authority (see section 198), they shall secure that accommodation is available for occupation by the applicant.

[(3)   The authority are subject to the duty under this section [in a case which is not a restricted case][2] until it ceases by virtue of any of the following provisions of this section.][3]

[(3A)   The authority shall, on becoming subject to the duty under this section, give the applicant a copy of the statement included in their allocation scheme by virtue of section 167(1A) (policy on offering choice to people allocated housing accommodation under Part 6).][4]

[(3B)   In this section 'a restricted case' means a case where the local housing authority would not be satisfied as mentioned in subsection (1) without having had regard to a restricted person.][5]

(4)   …[6]

(5)   The local housing authority shall cease to be subject to the duty under this section if the applicant, having been informed by the authority of the possible consequence of refusal [and of his right to request a review of the suitability of the accommodation][7], refuses an offer of accommodation which the authority are satisfied is suitable for him and the authority notify him that they regard themselves as having discharged their duty under this section.

(6)   The local housing authority shall cease to be subject to the duty under this section if the applicant –

(a)   ceases to be eligible for assistance,
(b)   becomes homeless intentionally from the accommodation made available for his occupation,
(c)   accepts an offer of accommodation under Part 6 (allocation of housing), or
[(cc)   accepts an offer of an assured tenancy (other than an assured shorthold tenancy) from a private landlord,][8]

(d)   otherwise voluntarily ceases to occupy as his only or principal home the accommodation made available for his occupation.

[(7)   The local housing authority shall also cease to be subject to the duty under this section if the applicant, having been informed of the possible consequence of refusal and of his right to request a review of the suitability of the accommodation, refuses a final offer of accommodation under Part 6.

(7A)   An offer of accommodation under Part 6 is a final offer for the purposes of subsection (7) if it is made in writing and states that it is a final offer for the purposes of subsection (7).][9]

[(7AA)   In a restricted case the authority shall also cease to be subject to the duty under this section if the applicant, having been informed of the matters mentioned in subsection (7AB) –

(a)   accepts a private accommodation offer, or
(b)   refuses such an offer.

(7AB)   The matters are—

(a)   the possible consequence of refusal of the offer, and
(b)   that the applicant has the right to request a review of the suitability of the accommodation.

(7AC)   For the purposes of this section an offer is a private accommodation offer if –

(a)   it is an offer of an assured shorthold tenancy made by a private landlord to the applicant in relation to any accommodation which is, or may become, available for the applicant's occupation,
(b)   it is made, with the approval of the authority, in pursuance of arrangements made by the authority with the landlord with a view to bringing the authority's duty under this section to an end, and
(c)   the tenancy being offered is a fixed term tenancy (within the meaning of Part 1 of the Housing Act 1988) for a period of at least 12 months.

(7AD)   In a restricted case the authority shall, so far as reasonably practicable, bring their duty under this section to an end as mentioned in subsection (7AA).][10]

[(7B)   The authority shall also cease to be subject to the duty under this section if the applicant accepts a qualifying offer of an assured shorthold tenancy which is made by a private landlord in relation to any accommodation which is, or may become, available for the applicant's occupation.

(7C)   The applicant is free to reject a qualifying offer without affecting the duty owed to him under this section by the authority.

(7D)   For the purposes of subsection (7B) an offer of an assured shorthold tenancy is a qualifying offer if –

(a)   it is made, with the approval of the authority, in pursuance of arrangements made by the authority with the landlord with a view to bringing the authority's duty under this section to an end;

  (b)   the tenancy being offered is a fixed term tenancy (within the meaning of Part 1 of the Housing Act 1988 (c 50)); and

  (c)   it is accompanied by a statement in writing which states the term of the tenancy being offered and explains in ordinary language that –

      (i)   there is no obligation to accept the offer, but

      (ii)   if the offer is accepted the local housing authority will cease to be subject to the duty under this section in relation to the applicant.

(7E)   An acceptance of a qualifying offer is only effective for the purposes of subsection (7B) if the applicant signs a statement acknowledging that he has understood the statement mentioned in subsection (7D).

(7F)   The local housing authority shall not –

  (a)   make a final offer of accommodation under Part 6 for the purposes of subsection (7); or

  [(ab) approve a private accommodation offer;][11]

  (b)   approve an offer of an assured shorthold tenancy for the purposes of subsection (7B),

unless they are satisfied that the accommodation is suitable for the applicant and that it is reasonable for him to accept the offer.][12]

(8)   For the purposes of [subsection (7F)][13] an applicant may reasonably be expected to accept an offer ...[14] even though he is under contractual or other obligations in respect of his existing accommodation, provided he is able to bring those obligations to an end before he is required to take up the offer.

(9)   A person who ceases to be owed the duty under this section may make a fresh application to the authority for accommodation or assistance in obtaining accommodation.

AMENDMENT

[1] Words repealed: Homelessness Act 2002, s 18(2), Sch 2.

[2] Words inserted: Housing and Regeneration Act 2008, s 314, Sch 15, Pt 1, paras 1, 5(1), (2), with effect from 2 March 2009 (except in relation to applications for an allocation of social housing or housing assistance (homelessness) or for accommodation made before that date) (SI 2009/415, art 2).

[3] Sub-section substituted: Homelessness Act 2002, s 6(1); for transitional provision see s 6(2) thereof.

[4] Sub-section inserted: Homelessness Act 2002, s 18(1), Sch 1, paras 2, 13.

[5] Sub-section inserted: Housing and Regeneration Act 2008, s 314, Sch 15, Pt 1, paras 1, 5(1), (3), with effect from 2 March 2009 (except in relation to applications for an allocation of social housing or housing assistance (homelessness) or for accommodation made before that date) (SI 2009/415, art 2).

[6] Sub-section substituted (by sub-section (3)): Homelessness Act 2002, s 6(1); for transitional provision see s 6(2) thereof.

[7] Words inserted: Homelessness Act 2002, s 8(1).

[8] Sub-section inserted: Homelessness Act 2002, s 7(1), (2); for transitional provision see s 7(6) thereof.

[9] Sub-sections substituted: Homelessness Act 2002, s 7(1), (3); for transitional provision see s 7(6) thereof.

[10] Sub-sections inserted: Housing and Regeneration Act 2008, s 314, Sch 15, Pt 1, paras 1, 5(1), (4), with effect from 2 March 2009 (except in relation to applications for an allocation of social housing or housing assistance (homelessness) or for accommodation made before that date) (SI 2009/415, art 2).

[11] Words inserted: by the Housing and Regeneration Act 2008, s 314, Sch 15, Pt 1, paras 1, 5(1), (6). Date in force: 2 March 2009 (except in relation to applications for an allocation of social housing or housing assistance (homelessness) or for accommodation made before that date): see SI 2009/415, art 2

[12] Sub-sections inserted: Homelessness Act 2002, s 7(1), (4); for transitional provision see s 7(6) thereof.

[13] Words substituted: Homelessness Act 2002, s 7(1), (5); for transitional provision see s 7(6) thereof.

[14] Words repealed: Homelessness Act 2002, ss 7(1), (5), 18(2), Sch 2; for transitional provision see s 7(6) thereof.

194 ...[1]

AMENDMENT

[1] Section repealed: Homelessness Act 2002, ss 6(3), 18(2), Sch 2; for transitional provision see s 6(4) thereof.

195 Duties in case of threatened homelessness

(1)   This section applies where the local housing authority are satisfied that an applicant is threatened with homelessness and is eligible for assistance.

(2)   If the authority –

  (a)   are satisfied that he has a priority need, and
  (b)   are not satisfied that he became threatened with homelessness intentionally,

they shall take reasonable steps to secure that accommodation does not cease to be available for his occupation.

...[1]

(3)   Subsection (2) does not affect any right of the authority, whether by virtue of a contract, enactment or rule of law, to secure vacant possession of any accommodation.

[(3A)   The authority shall, on becoming subject to the duty under this section [in a case which is not a restricted threatened homelessness case][2], give the applicant a copy of the statement included in their allocation scheme by virtue of section 167(1A) (policy on offering choice to people allocated housing accommodation under Part 6).][3]

(4)   Where[, in a case which is not a restricted threatened homelessness case,][4] in pursuance of the duty under subsection (2) the authority secure that accommodation other than that occupied by the applicant when he made his application is available for occupation by him, the provisions of section 193(3) to (9) (period for which duty owed) ...[5] apply, with any necessary modifications, in relation to the duty under this section as they apply in relation to the duty under section 193 [in a case which is not a restricted case (within the meaning of that section)][6].

[(4A)   Where, in a restricted threatened homelessness case, in pursuance of the duty under subsection (2) the authority secure that accommodation other than that occupied by the applicant when he made his application is available for occupation by him, the provisions of section 193(3) to (9) (period for which duty owed) apply, with any necessary modifications, in relation to the duty under this section as they apply in relation to the duty under section 193 in a restricted case (within the meaning of that section).

(4B)   In subsections (3A) to (4A) 'a restricted threatened homelessness case' means a case where the local housing authority would not be satisfied as mentioned in subsection (1) without having had regard to a restricted person.][7]

(5)   If the authority –

   (a)   are not satisfied that the applicant has a priority need, or
   (b)   are satisfied that he has a priority need but are also satisfied that he became threatened with homelessness intentionally,

they shall [provide him with (or secure that he is provided with) advice and assistance][8] in any attempts he may make to secure that accommodation does not cease to be available for his occupation.

[(6)   The applicant's housing needs shall be assessed before advice and assistance is provided under subsection (5).

(7)   The advice and assistance provided under subsection (5) must include information about the likely availability in the authority's district of types of accommodation appropriate to the applicant's housing needs (including, in particular, the location and sources of such types of accommodation).][9]

[(8)   If the authority decide that they owe the applicant the duty under subsection (5) by virtue of paragraph (b) of that subsection, they may, pending a decision on a review of that decision –

   (a)   secure that accommodation does not cease to be available for his occupation; and
   (b)   if he becomes homeless, secure that accommodation is so available.][10]

[(9)   If the authority –

   (a)   are not satisfied that the applicant has a priority need; and
   (b)   are not satisfied that he became threatened with homelessness intentionally,

the authority may take reasonable steps to secure that accommodation does not cease to be available for the applicant's occupation.]¹¹

AMENDMENT

¹ Words repealed: Homelessness Act 2002, s 18(2), Sch 2.

² Words inserted: Housing and Regeneration Act 2008, s 314, Sch 15, Pt 1, paras 1, 6(1), (2), with effect from 2 March 2009 (except in relation to applications for an allocation of social housing or housing assistance (homelessness) or for accommodation made before that date) (SI 2009/415, art 2).

³ Sub-section inserted: Homelessness Act 2002, s 18(1), Sch 1, paras 2, 14(a).

⁴ Words inserted: Housing and Regeneration Act 2008, s 314, Sch 15, Pt 1, paras 1, 6(1), (3)(a), with effect from 2 March 2009 (except in relation to applications for an allocation of social housing or housing assistance (homelessness) or for accommodation made before that date) (SI 2009/415, art 2).

⁵ Words repealed: Homelessness Act 2002, s 18(2), Sch 2.

⁶ Words inserted: Housing and Regeneration Act 2008, s 314, Sch 15, Pt 1, paras 1, 6(1), (3)(b), with effect from 2 March 2009 (except in relation to applications for an allocation of social housing or housing assistance (homelessness) or for accommodation made before that date) (SI 2009/415, art 2).

⁷ Words inserted: Housing and Regeneration Act 2008, s 314, Sch 15, Pt 1, paras 1, 6(1), (4), with effect from 2 March 2009 (except in relation to applications for an allocation of social housing or housing assistance (homelessness) or for accommodation made before that date) (SI 2009/415, art 2).

⁸ Words substituted: Homelessness Act 2002, s 18(1), Sch 1, paras 2, 14(b).

⁹ Sub-sections inserted: Homelessness Act 2002, s 18(1), Sch 1, paras 2, 14(c).

¹⁰ Sub-section inserted: Homelessness Act 2002, s 18(1), Sch 1, paras 2, 14(d).

¹¹ Sub-section inserted: Homelessness Act 2002, s 5(2).

196 Becoming threatened with homelessness intentionally

(1)   A person becomes threatened with homelessness intentionally if he deliberately does or fails to do anything the likely result of which is that he will be forced to leave accommodation which is available for his occupation and which it would have been reasonable for him to continue to occupy.

(2)   For the purposes of subsection (1) an act or omission in good faith on the part of a person who was unaware of any relevant fact shall not be treated as deliberate.

(3)   A person shall be treated as becoming threatened with homelessness intentionally if –

    (a)   he enters into an arrangement under which he is required to cease to occupy accommodation which it would have been reasonable for him to continue to occupy, and

    (b)   the purpose of the arrangement is to enable him to become entitled to assistance under this Part,

Appendix 2
England: Homelessness

and there is no other good reason why he is threatened with homelessness.

(4)   ...[1]

AMENDMENT

[1] Sub-section repealed: Homelessness Act 2002, s 18(2), Sch 2.

197 ...[1]

AMENDMENT

[1] Section repealed: Homelessness Act 2002, ss 9(1), 18(2), Sch 2; for transitional provision see s 9(2), (3) thereof.

Referral to another local housing authority

198 Referral of case to another local housing authority

(1)   If the local housing authority would be subject to the duty under section 193 (accommodation for those with priority need who are not homeless intentionally) but consider that the conditions are met for referral of the case to another local housing authority, they may notify that other authority of their opinion.

...[1]

(2)   The conditions for referral of the case to another authority are met if –

- (a)   neither the applicant nor any person who might reasonably be expected to reside with him has a local connection with the district of the authority to whom his application was made,
- (b)   the applicant or a person who might reasonably be expected to reside with him has a local connection with the district of that other authority, and
- (c)   neither the applicant nor any person who might reasonably be expected to reside with him will run the risk of domestic violence in that other district.

[(2A)   But the conditions for referral mentioned in subsection (2) are not met if –

- (a)   the applicant or any person who might reasonably be expected to reside with him has suffered violence (other than domestic violence) in the district of the other authority; and
- (b)   it is probable that the return to that district of the victim will lead to further violence of a similar kind against him.

(3)   For the purposes of subsections (2) and (2A)[, *and for the purpose of subsection (4A)(c)]*[3] 'violence' means –

- (a)   violence from another person; or
- (b)   threats of violence from another person which are likely to be carried out;

and violence is 'domestic violence' if it is from a person who is associated with the victim.]²

(4) The conditions for referral of the case to another authority are also met if –

(a) the applicant was on a previous application made to that other authority placed (in pursuance of their functions under this Part) in accommodation in the district of the authority to whom his application is now made, and

(b) the previous application was within such period as may be prescribed of the present application.

[*(4A) The conditions for referral of the case to another authority are also met if –*

(a) the local housing authority to whom the application has been made and another housing authority have agreed that the case should be referred to that other authority;

(b) that other authority has provided written confirmation of the agreement to the local housing authority; and

(c) neither the applicant nor any person who might reasonably be expected to reside with him will run the risk of domestic violence in the district of that other authority.

(4B) When reaching the agreement referred to in subsection (4A)(a), the local housing authority to whom the application was made and the other authority need not have regard to –

(a) any preference that the applicant, or any person who might reasonably be expected to reside with him, may have as to the locality in which the accommodation is to be secured; or

(b) whether the applicant, or any person who might reasonably be expected to reside with him, has a local connection with the district of any local housing authority.]⁴

(5) The question whether the conditions for referral of a case are satisfied shall be decided by agreement between the notifying authority and the notified authority or, in default of agreement, in accordance with such arrangements as the Secretary of State may direct by order.

(6) An order may direct that the arrangements shall be –

(a) those agreed by any relevant authorities or associations of relevant authorities, or

(b) in default of such agreement, such arrangements as appear to the Secretary of State to be suitable, after consultation with such associations representing relevant authorities, and such other persons, as he thinks appropriate.

(7) No such order shall be made unless a draft of the order has been approved by a resolution of each House of Parliament.

AMENDMENT

¹ Words repealed: Homelessness Act 2002, s 18(2), Sch 2.

² Sub-sections substituted: Homelessness Act 2002, s 10(2).

MODIFICATION

³ Original sub-section (3) as modified: SI 1999/3126, art 1(2), 2, 3(a).

⁴ Modifying sub-sections 4A and 4B: SI 1999/3126, art 1(2), 2, 3(b).

For England only, this section is modified in relation to asylum-seekers who are eligible for housing assistance as a result of regulations made under s 185(2) of the Housing Act 1996, and who are not made ineligible by s 186 (or any other provision) of that Act: Homelessness (Asylum-Seekers) (Interim Period) (England) Order 1999, SI 1999/3126, arts 1(2), 2, 3. That Order shall cease to have effect on the date on which s 186 of the Housing Act 1996 is repealed by the Immigration and Asylum Act 1999, s 117(5).

199 Local connection

(1) A person has a local connection with the district of a local housing authority if he has a connection with it –

- (a) because he is, or in the past was, normally resident there, and that residence is or was of his own choice,
- (b) because he is employed there,
- (c) because of family associations, or
- (d) because of special circumstances.

(2) ...¹

(3) Residence in a district is not of a person's own choice if –

- (a) ...²
- (b) he, or a person who might reasonably be expected to reside with him, becomes resident there because he is detained under the authority of an Act of Parliament.

(4) ...³

(5) The Secretary of State may by order specify *other*⁴ circumstances in which –

- (a) a person is not to be treated as employed in a district, or
- (b) residence in a district is not to be treated as of a person's own choice.

[(6) A person has a local connection with the district of a local housing authority if he was (at any time) provided with accommodation in that district under section 95 of the Immigration and Asylum Act 1999 (support for asylum-seekers).

(7) But subsection (6) does not apply –

- (a) to the provision of accommodation for a person in a district of a local housing authority if he was subsequently provided with accommodation in the district of another local housing authority under section 95 of that Act, or

(b) to the provision of accommodation in an accommodation centre by virtue of section 22 of the Nationality, Immigration and Asylum Act 2002 (c 41) (use of accommodation centres for section 95 support).][5]

AMENDMENT

[1] Sub-sections repealed: Housing and Regeneration Act 2008, s 315(a), 321(1), Sch 16. Date in force (in relation to England): 1 December 2008; SI 2008/3068, arts 1(2), 4(2), (10), 5, Schedule; for transitional provisions and savings see arts 6, 9, 10 thereof. Date in force (in relation to Wales): 30 March 2009: see SI 2009/773, art 2.

[2] Paragraph repealed by Housing and Regeneration Act 2008, s 315(b), 321(1), Sch 16. Date in force (in relation to England): 1 December 2008; SI 2008/3068, arts 1(2), 4(2), (10), 5, Schedule; for transitional provisions and savings see arts 6, 9, 10 thereof. Date in force (in relation to Wales): see SI 2009/773, art 2.

[3] Words substituted: Armed Forces Act 2001, s 34, Sch 6, Pt 5, para 30; sub-section repealed by Housing and Regeneration Act 2008, s 315(b), 321(1), Sch 16. Date in force (in relation to England for certain purposes): 1 December 2008; SI 2008/3068, arts 1(2), 4(2), (10), 5, Schedule; for transitional provisions and savings see arts 6, 9, 10 thereof. Date in force (in relation to Wales for certain purposes): 30 March 2009: see SI 2009/773, art 2. Date in force (for remaining purposes): to be appointed: see the Housing and Regeneration Act 2008, s 325(3)(b), (4), s 315(b), 321(1), Sch 16.

[4] Word repealed by Housing and Regeneration Act 2008, s 315(b), 321(1), Sch 16. Date in force (in relation to England): 1 December 2008; SI 2008/3068, arts 1(2), 4(2), (10), 5, Schedule; for transitional provisions and savings see arts 6, 9, 10 thereof. Date in force (in relation to Wales): 30 March 2009: see SI 2009/773, art 2.

[5] Sub-sections inserted: Asylum and Immigration (Treatment of Claimants, etc) Act 2004, s 11(1).

200 Duties to the applicant whose case is considered for referral or referred

(1) Where a local housing authority notify an applicant that they intend to notify or have notified another local housing authority of their opinion that the conditions are met for the referral of his case to that other authority –

(a) they cease to be subject to any duty under section 188 (interim duty to accommodate in case of apparent priority need), and

(b) they are not subject to any duty under section 193 (the main housing duty),

but they shall secure that accommodation is available for occupation by the applicant until he is notified of the decision whether the conditions for referral of his case are met.

(2) When it has been decided whether the conditions for referral are met, the notifying authority shall notify the applicant of the decision and inform him of the reasons for it.

The notice shall also inform the applicant of his right to request a review of the decision and of the time within which such a request must be made.

[(3) If it is decided that the conditions for referral are not met, the notifying authority are subject to the duty under section 193 (the main housing duty).

Appendix 2
England: Homelessness

(4)   If it is decided that those conditions are met, the notified authority are subject to the duty under section 193 (the main housing duty).][1]

(5)   The duty under subsection (1), ...[2] ceases as provided in that subsection even if the applicant requests a review of the authority's decision (see section 202).

The authority may [secure][3] that accommodation is available for the applicant's occupation pending the decision on a review.

(6)   Notice required to be given to an applicant under this section shall be given in writing and, if not received by him, shall be treated as having been given to him if it is made available at the authority's office for a reasonable period for collection by him or on his behalf.

AMENDMENT

[1] Sub-sections substituted: Homelessness Act 2002, s 18(1), Sch 1, paras 2, 15(a).

[2] Words repealed: Homelessness Act 2002, s 18(2), Sch 2.

[3] Word substituted: Homelessness Act 2002, s 18(1), Sch 1, paras 2, 15(b).

201 Application of referral provisions to cases arising in Scotland

Sections 198 and 200 (referral of application to another local housing authority and duties to applicant whose case is considered for referral or referred) apply –

(a)   to applications referred by a local authority in Scotland in pursuance of sections 33 and 34 of the Housing (Scotland) Act 1987, and

(b)   to persons whose applications are so transferred,

as they apply to cases arising under this Part (the reference in section 198 to this Part being construed as a reference to Part II of that Act).

Right to request review of decision

202 Right to request review of decision

(1)   An applicant has the right to request a review of –

(a)   any decision of a local housing authority as to his eligibility for assistance,

(b)   any decision of a local housing authority as to what duty (if any) is owed to him under sections 190 to 193 and 195 [and 196][1] (duties to persons found to be homeless or threatened with homelessness),

(c)   any decision of a local housing authority to notify another authority under section 198(1) (referral of cases),

(d)   any decision under section 198(5) whether the conditions are met for the referral of his case,

(e)   any decision under section 200(3) or (4) (decision as to duty owed to applicant whose case is considered for referral or referred), or

(f)   any decision of a local housing authority as to the suitability of accommodation offered to him in discharge of their duty under any of the provisions mentioned in paragraph (b) or (e) [or as to the suitability of accommodation offered to him as mentioned in section 193(7)]²[, or

(g) any decision of a local housing authority as to the suitability of accommodation offered to him by way of a private accommodation offer (within the meaning of section 193)]³.

[(1A) An applicant who is offered accommodation as mentioned in section 193(5)[, (7) or (7AA)]⁴ may under subsection (1)(f) [or (as the case may be) (g)]⁵ request a review of the suitability of the accommodation offered to him whether or not he has accepted the offer.]⁶

(2) There is no right to request a review of the decision reached on an earlier review.

(3) A request for review must be made before the end of the period of 21 days beginning with the day on which he is notified of the authority's decision or such longer period as the authority may in writing allow.

(4) On a request being duly made to them, the authority or authorities concerned shall review their decision.

AMENDMENT

¹ Words substituted: Homelessness Act 2002, s 18(1), Sch 1, paras 2, 16.

² Words inserted: Homelessness Act 2002, s 8(2)(a).

³ Sub-section inserted: Housing and Regeneration Act 2008, s 314, Sch 15, Pt 1, paras 1, 7(1), (2). Date in force: 2 March 2009 (except in relation to applications for an allocation of social housing or housing assistance (homelessness) or for accommodation made before that date): see SI 2009/415, art 2.

⁴ Words substituted: Housing and Regeneration Act 2008, s 314, Sch 15, Pt 1, paras 1, 7(1). Date in force: 2 March 2009 (except in relation to applications for an allocation of social housing or housing assistance (homelessness) or for accommodation made before that date): see SI 2009/415, art 2.

⁵ Words inserted: Housing and Regeneration Act 2008, Sch 15, Pt 1, paras 1, 7(1). Date in force: 2 March 2009 (except in relation to applications for an allocation of social housing or housing assistance (homelessness) or for accommodation made before that date): see SI 2009/415, art 2.

⁶ Sub-section inserted: Homelessness Act 2002, s 8(2)(b).

203 Procedure on a review

(1) The Secretary of State may make provision by regulations as to the procedure to be followed in connection with a review under section 202.

Nothing in the following provisions affects the generality of this power.

(2) Provision may be made by regulations –

(a) requiring the decision on review to be made by a person of appropriate seniority who was not involved in the original decision, and

(b)   as to the circumstances in which the applicant is entitled to an oral hearing, and whether and by whom he may be represented at such a hearing.

(3)   The authority, or as the case may be either of the authorities, concerned shall notify the applicant of the decision on the review.

(4)   If the decision is –

(a)   to confirm the original decision on any issue against the interests of the applicant, or

(b)   to confirm a previous decision –

(i)   to notify another authority under section 198 (referral of cases), or

(ii)   that the conditions are met for the referral of his case,

they shall also notify him of the reasons for the decision.

(5)   In any case they shall inform the applicant of his right to appeal to a county court on a point of law, and of the period within which such an appeal must be made (see section 204).

(6)   Notice of the decision shall not be treated as given unless and until subsection (5), and where applicable subsection (4), is complied with.

(7)   Provision may be made by regulations as to the period within which the review must be carried out and notice given of the decision.

(8)   Notice required to be given to a person under this section shall be given in writing and, if not received by him, shall be treated as having been given if it is made available at the authority's office for a reasonable period for collection by him or on his behalf.

204 Right of appeal to county court on point of law

(1)   If an applicant who has requested a review under section 202 –

(a)   is dissatisfied with the decision on the review, or

(b)   is not notified of the decision on the review within the time prescribed under section 203,

he may appeal to the county court on any point of law arising from the decision or, as the case may be, the original decision.

(2)   An appeal must be brought within 21 days of his being notified of the decision or, as the case may be, of the date on which he should have been notified of a decision on review.

[(2A)   The court may give permission for an appeal to be brought after the end of the period allowed by subsection (2), but only if it is satisfied –

(a)   where permission is sought before the end of that period, that there is a good reason for the applicant to be unable to bring the appeal in time; or

(b) where permission is sought after that time, that there was a good reason for the applicant's failure to bring the appeal in time and for any delay in applying for permission.]¹

(3) On appeal the court may make such order confirming, quashing or varying the decision as it thinks fit.

(4) Where the authority were under a duty under section 188, 190 or 200 to secure that accommodation is available for the applicant's occupation[, or had the power under section 195(8) to do so, they may]² secure that accommodation is so available –

(a) during the period for appealing under this section against the authority's decision, and
(b) if an appeal is brought, until the appeal (and any further appeal) is finally determined.

AMENDMENT

¹ Sub-section inserted: Homelessness Act 2002, s 18(1), Sch 1, paras 2, 17(a).

² Words substituted: Homelessness Act 2002, s 18(1), Sch 1, paras 2, 17(b).

[204A Section 204(4): appeals

(1) This section applies where an applicant has the right to appeal to the county court against a local housing authority's decision on a review.

(2) If the applicant is dissatisfied with a decision by the authority –

(a) not to exercise their power under section 204(4) ('the section 204(4) power') in his case;
(b) to exercise that power for a limited period ending before the final determination by the county court of his appeal under section 204(1) ('the main appeal'); or
(c) to cease exercising that power before that time,

he may appeal to the county court against the decision.

(3) An appeal under this section may not be brought after the final determination by the county court of the main appeal.

(4) On an appeal under this section the court –

(a) may order the authority to secure that accommodation is available for the applicant's occupation until the determination of the appeal (or such earlier time as the court may specify); and
(b) shall confirm or quash the decision appealed against,

and in considering whether to confirm or quash the decision the court shall apply the principles applied by the High Court on an application for judicial review.

(5) If the court quashes the decision it may order the authority to exercise the section 204(4) power in the applicant's case for such period as may be specified in the order.

(6)   An order under subsection (5) –

    (a)   may only be made if the court is satisfied that failure to exercise the section 204(4) power in accordance with the order would substantially prejudice the applicant's ability to pursue the main appeal;

    (b)   may not specify any period ending after the final determination by the county court of the main appeal.]¹

AMENDMENT

¹ Section inserted: Homelessness Act 2002, s 11.

Supplementary provisions

205 Discharge of functions: introductory

(1)   The following sections have effect in relation to the discharge by a local housing authority of their functions under this Part to secure that accommodation is available for the occupation of a person –

    section 206 (general provisions),
    …¹
    section 208 (out-of-area placements),
    section 209 (arrangements with private landlord).

(2)   In [sections 206 and 208]² those functions are referred to as the authority's 'housing functions under this Part'.

AMENDMENT

¹ Words repealed: Homelessness Act 2002, s 18(2), Sch 2.

² Words substituted: Homelessness Act 2002, s 18(1), Sch 1, paras 2, 18.

206 Discharge of functions by local housing authorities

(1)   A local housing authority may discharge their housing functions under this Part only in the following ways –

    (a)   by securing that suitable accommodation provided by them is available,

    (b)   by securing that he obtains suitable accommodation from some other person, or

    (c)   by giving him such advice and assistance as will secure that suitable accommodation is available from some other person.

[*(1A   In discharging their housing functions under this Part, a local housing authority shall have regard to the desirability, in general, of securing accommodation in areas in which there is a ready supply of accommodation.*]¹

(2)   A local housing authority may require a person in relation to whom they are discharging such functions –

    (a)   to pay such reasonable charges as they may determine in respect of accommodation which they secure for his occupation (either by making it available themselves or otherwise), or

(b) to pay such reasonable amount as they may determine in respect of sums payable by them for accommodation made available by another person.

MODIFICATION

[1] For England only, this section is modified in relation to asylum-seekers who are eligible for housing assistance as a result of regulations made under s 185(2) of the Housing Act 1996, and who are not made ineligible by s 186 (or any other provision) of that Act: Homelessness (Asylum-Seekers) (Interim Period) (England) Order 1999, SI 1999/3126, arts 1(2), 2, 4. That Order shall cease to have effect on the date on which s 186 of the Housing Act 1996 is repealed by the Immigration and Asylum Act 1999, s 117(5).

207 ...[1]

AMENDMENT

[1] Section repealed: Homelessness Act 2002, s 18(2), Sch 2.

208 Discharge of functions: out-of-area placements

(1) So far as reasonably practicable a local housing authority shall in discharging their housing functions under this Part secure that accommodation is available for the occupation of the applicant in their district.

(1A) Subsection (1) shall not apply where –

(a) the local housing authority and another housing authority have agreed that the local housing authority may secure that accommodation is available for the occupation of all or an agreed number of asylum-seekers who are section 185(2) persons in that other authority's district; and

(b) that other authority has provided written confirmation of the agreement to the local housing authority.][1]

(2) If they secure that accommodation is available for the occupation of the applicant outside their district, they shall give notice to the local housing authority in whose district the accommodation is situated.

(3) The notice shall state –

(a) the name of the applicant,
(b) the number and description of other persons who normally reside with him as a member of his family or might reasonably be expected to reside with him,
(c) the address of the accommodation,
(d) the date on which the accommodation was made available to him, and
(e) which function under this Part the authority was discharging in securing that the accommodation is available for his occupation.

(4) The notice must be in writing, and must be given before the end of the period of 14 days beginning with the day on which the accommodation was made available to the applicant.

MODIFICATION

¹ For England only, this section is modified in relation to asylum-seekers who are eligible for housing assistance as a result of regulations made under s 185(2) of the Housing Act 1996, and who are not made ineligible by s 186 (or any other provision) of that Act: Homelessness (Asylum-Seekers) (Interim Period) (England) Order 1999, SI 1999/3126, arts 1(2), 2, 5. That Order shall cease to have effect on the date on which s 186 of the Housing Act 1996 is repealed by the Immigration and Asylum Act 1999, s 117(5).

[209 Discharge of interim duties: arrangements with private landlord]

[(1)   This section applies where in pursuance of any of their housing functions under section 188, 190, 200 or 204(4) (interim duties) a local housing authority make arrangements with a private landlord to provide accommodation.

(2)   A tenancy granted to the applicant in pursuance of the arrangements cannot be an assured tenancy before the end of the period of twelve months beginning with –

   (a)   the date on which the applicant was notified of the authority's decision under section 184(3) or 198(5); or

   (b)   if there is a review of that decision under section 202 or an appeal to the court under section 204, the date on which he is notified of the decision on review or the appeal is finally determined,

unless, before or during that period, the tenant is notified by the landlord (or in the case of joint landlords, at least one of them) that the tenancy is to be regarded as an assured shorthold tenancy or an assured tenancy other than an assured shorthold tenancy.]¹

AMENDMENT

¹ Section substituted: Homelessness Act 2002, s 18(1), Sch 1, paras 2, 19.

210 Suitability of accommodation

(1)   In determining for the purposes of this Part whether accommodation is suitable for a person, the local housing authority shall have regard to *Parts IX, X and XI* [Parts 9 and 10]¹ of the Housing Act 1985 (slum clearance; overcrowding; houses in multiple occupation [and overcrowding) and Parts 1 to 4 of the Housing Act 2004]².

[*(1A)   In determining for the purposes of this Part whether accommodation is suitable for an applicant, or any person who might reasonably be expected to reside with him, the local housing authority –*

   (a)   shall also have regard to the fact that the accommodation is to be temporary pending the determination of the applicant's claim for asylum; and

   (b)   shall not have regard to any preference that the applicant, or any person who might reasonably be expected to reside with him, may have as to the locality in which the accommodation is to be secured.]³

(2)   The Secretary of State may by order specify –

(a) circumstances in which accommodation is or is not to be regarded as suitable for a person, and

(b) matters to be taken into account or disregarded in determining whether accommodation is suitable for a person.

AMENDMENT

[1] Words in italics repealed and words in square brackets substituted: Housing Act 2004, s 265(1), Sch 15, paras 40, 43(a).

[2] Words in italics repealed and words in square brackets substituted: Housing Act 2004, s 265(1), Sch 15, paras 40, 43(b).

MODIFICATION

[3] For England only, this section is modified in relation to asylum-seekers who are eligible for housing assistance as a result of regulations made under s 185(2) of the Housing Act 1996, and who are not made ineligible by s 186 (or any other provision) of that Act: Homelessness (Asylum-Seekers) (Interim Period) (England) Order 1999, SI 1999/3126, arts 1(2), 2, 6. That Order shall cease to have effect on the date on which s 186 of the Housing Act 1996 is repealed by the Immigration and Asylum Act 1999, s 117(5).

211 Protection of property of homeless persons and persons threatened with homelessness

(1) This section applies where a local housing authority have reason to believe that –

(a) there is danger of loss of, or damage to, any personal property of an applicant by reason of his inability to protect it or deal with it, and

(b) no other suitable arrangements have been or are being made.

(2) If the authority have become subject to a duty towards the applicant under –

section 188 (interim duty to accommodate),

section 190, 193 or 195 (duties to persons found to be homeless or threatened with homelessness), or

section 200 (duties to applicant whose case is considered for referral or referred),

then, whether or not they are still subject to such a duty, they shall take reasonable steps to prevent the loss of the property or prevent or mitigate damage to it.

(3) If they have not become subject to such a duty, they may take any steps they consider reasonable for that purpose.

(4) The authority may decline to take action under this section except upon such conditions as they consider appropriate in the particular case, which may include conditions as to –

(a) the making and recovery by the authority of reasonable charges for the action taken, or

(b) the disposal by the authority, in such circumstances as may be specified, of property in relation to which they have taken action.

Appendix 2
England: Homelessness

(5) References in this section to personal property of the applicant include personal property of any person who might reasonably be expected to reside with him.

(6) Section 212 contains provisions supplementing this section.

212 Protection of property: supplementary provisions

(1) The authority may for the purposes of section 211 (protection of property of homeless persons or persons threatened with homelessness) –

(a) enter, at all reasonable times, any premises which are the usual place of residence of the applicant or which were his last usual place of residence, and

(b) deal with any personal property of his in any way which is reasonably necessary, in particular by storing it or arranging for its storage.

(2) Where the applicant asks the authority to move his property to a particular location nominated by him, the authority –

(a) may, if it appears to them that his request is reasonable, discharge their responsibilities under section 211 by doing as he asks, and

(b) having done so, have no further duty or power to take action under that section in relation to that property.

If such a request is made, the authority shall before complying with it inform the applicant of the consequence of their doing so.

(3) If no such request is made (or, if made, is not acted upon) the authority cease to have any duty or power to take action under section 211 when, in their opinion, there is no longer any reason to believe that there is a danger of loss of or damage to a person's personal property by reason of his inability to protect it or deal with it.

But property stored by virtue of their having taken such action may be kept in store and any conditions upon which it was taken into store continue to have effect, with any necessary modifications.

(4) Where the authority –

(a) cease to be subject to a duty to take action under section 211 in respect of an applicant's property, or

(b) cease to have power to take such action, having previously taken such action,

they shall notify the applicant of that fact and of the reason for it.

(5) The notification shall be given to the applicant –

(a) by delivering it to him, or

(b) by leaving it, or sending it to him, at his last known address.

(6) References in this section to personal property of the applicant include personal property of any person who might reasonably be expected to reside with him.

213 Co-operation between relevant housing authorities and bodies

(1) Where a local housing authority –

(a) request another relevant housing authority or body, in England, Wales or Scotland, to assist them in the discharge of their functions under this Part, or

(b) request a social services authority, in England, Wales or Scotland, to exercise any of their functions in relation to a case which the local housing authority are dealing with under this Part,

the authority or body to whom the request is made shall co-operate in rendering such assistance in the discharge of the functions to which the request relates as is reasonable in the circumstances.

(2) In subsection (1)(a) 'relevant housing authority or body' means –

(a) in relation to England and Wales, a local housing authority, a new town corporation, a registered social landlord or a housing action trust;

(b) in relation to Scotland, a local authority, a development corporation, a registered housing association or Scottish Homes.

Expressions used in paragraph (a) have the same meaning as in the Housing Act 1985; and expressions used in paragraph (b) have the same meaning as in the Housing (Scotland) Act 1987.

(3) Subsection (1) above applies to a request by a local authority in Scotland under section 38 of the Housing (Scotland) Act 1987 as it applies to a request by a local housing authority in England and Wales (the references to this Part being construed, in relation to such a request, as references to Part II of that Act).

[213A Co-operation in certain cases involving children

(1) This section applies where a local housing authority have reason to believe that an applicant with whom a person under the age of 18 normally resides, or might reasonably be expected to reside –

(a) may be ineligible for assistance;

(b) may be homeless and may have become so intentionally; or

(c) may be threatened with homelessness intentionally.

(2) A local housing authority shall make arrangements for ensuring that, where this section applies –

(a) the applicant is invited to consent to the referral of the essential facts of his case to the social services authority for the district of the housing authority (where that is a different authority); and

(b) if the applicant has given that consent, the social services authority are made aware of those facts and of the subsequent decision of the housing authority in respect of his case.

(3)   Where the local housing authority and the social services authority for a district are the same authority (a 'unitary authority'), that authority shall make arrangements for ensuring that, where this section applies –

   (a)   the applicant is invited to consent to the referral to the social services department of the essential facts of his case; and
   (b)   if the applicant has given that consent, the social services department is made aware of those facts and of the subsequent decision of the authority in respect of his case.

(4)   Nothing in subsection (2) or (3) affects any power apart from this section to disclose information relating to the applicant's case to the social services authority or to the social services department (as the case may be) without the consent of the applicant.

(5)   Where a social services authority –

   (a)   are aware of a decision of a local housing authority that the applicant is ineligible for assistance, became homeless intentionally or became threatened with homelessness intentionally, and
   (b)   request the local housing authority to provide them with advice and assistance in the exercise of their social services functions under Part 3 of the Children Act 1989,

the local housing authority shall provide them with such advice and assistance as is reasonable in the circumstances.

(6)   A unitary authority shall make arrangements for ensuring that, where they make a decision of a kind mentioned in subsection (5)(a), the housing department provide the social services department with such advice and assistance as the social services department may reasonably request.

(7)   In this section, in relation to a unitary authority –

   'the housing department' means those persons responsible for the exercise of their housing functions; and
   'the social services department' means those persons responsible for the exercise of their social services functions under Part 3 of the Children Act 1989.][1]

AMENDMENT

[1] Section inserted: Homelessness Act 2002, s 12.

General provisions

214 False statements, withholding information and failure to disclose change of circumstances

(1)   It is an offence for a person, with intent to induce a local housing authority to believe in connection with the exercise of their functions under this Part that he or another person is entitled to accommodation or assistance in accordance with the provisions of this Part, or is entitled to accommodation or assistance of a particular description –

(a) knowingly or recklessly to make a statement which is false in a material particular, or

(b) knowingly to withhold information which the authority have reasonably required him to give in connection with the exercise of those functions.

(2) If before an applicant receives notification of the local housing authority's decision on his application there is any change of facts material to his case, he shall notify the authority as soon as possible.

The authority shall explain to every applicant, in ordinary language, the duty imposed on him by this subsection and the effect of subsection (3).

(3) A person who fails to comply with subsection (2) commits an offence unless he shows that he was not given the explanation required by that subsection or that he had some other reasonable excuse for non-compliance.

(4) A person guilty of an offence under this section is liable on summary conviction to a fine not exceeding level 5 on the standard scale.

215 Regulations and orders

(1) In this Part 'prescribed' means prescribed by regulations of the Secretary of State.

(2) Regulations or an order under this Part may make different provision for different purposes, including different provision for different areas.

(3) Regulations or an order under this Part shall be made by statutory instrument.

(4) Unless required to be approved in draft, regulations or an order under this Part shall be subject to annulment in pursuance of a resolution of either House of Parliament.

216 Transitional and consequential matters

(1) The provisions of this Part have effect in place of the provisions of Part III of the Housing Act 1985 (housing the homeless) and shall be construed as one with that Act.

(2) Subject to any transitional provision contained in an order under section 232(4) (power to include transitional provision in commencement order), the provisions of this Part do not apply in relation to an applicant whose application for accommodation or assistance in obtaining accommodation was made before the commencement of this Part.

(3) The enactments mentioned in Schedule 17 have effect with the amendments specified there which are consequential on the provisions of this Part.

217 Minor definitions: Part 7

(1) In this Part, subject to subsection (2) –

Appendix 2
England: Homelessness

['private landlord' means a landlord who is not within section 80(1) of the Housing Act 1985 (c 68) (the landlord condition for secure tenancies);][1]

'relevant authority' means a local housing authority or a social services authority; and

'social services authority' means a local authority for the purposes of the Local Authority Social Services Act 1970, as defined in section 1 of that Act.

(2) In this Part, in relation to Scotland –

   (a) 'local housing authority' means a local authority within the meaning of the Housing (Scotland) Act 1988, and

   (b) 'social services authority' means a local authority for the purposes of the Social Work (Scotland) Act 1968.

(3) References in this Part to the district of a local housing authority –

   (a) have the same meaning in relation to an authority in England or Wales as in the Housing Act 1985, and

   (b) in relation to an authority in Scotland, mean the area of the local authority concerned.

AMENDMENT

[1] Definition: inserted: Homelessness Act 2002, s 18(1), Sch 1, paras 2, 20.

218 Index of defined expressions: Part 7

The following Table shows provisions defining or otherwise explaining expressions used in this Part (other than provisions defining or explaining an expression used in the same section) –

accommodation available for occupation	section 176
applicant	section 183(2)
assistance under this Part	section 183(2)
associated (in relation to a person)	section 178
assured tenancy and assured shorthold tenancy	section 230
district (of local housing authority)	section 217(3)
eligible for assistance	section 183(2)
homeless	section 175(1)
housing functions under this Part (in sections [206 and 208][1])	section 205(2)
intentionally homeless	section 191
intentionally threatened with homelessness	section 196
local connection	section 199
local housing authority–	
– in England and Wales	section 230

– in Scotland	section 217(2)(a)
...	...²
Prescribed	section 215(1)
priority need	section 189
[private landlord	section 217(1)]³
Reasonable to continue to occupy accommodation	section 177
registered social landlord	section 230
relevant authority	section 217(1)
[restricted person	section 184 (7)]⁴
social services authority	section 217(1) and (2)(b)
threatened with homelessness	section 175(4)

AMENDMENT

¹ Words substituted: Homelessness Act 2002, s 18(1), Sch 1, paras 2, 21(a).

² Entry repealed: Homelessness Act 2002, s 18(2), Sch 2.

³ Entry inserted: Homelessness Act 2002, s 18(1), Sch 1, paras 2, 21(b).

⁴ Entry inserted: Housing and Regeneration Act 2008, s 314, Sch 15, Pt 1, paras 1, 8. Date in force: 2 March 2009 (except in relation to applications for an allocation of social housing or housing assistance (homelessness) or for accommodation made before that date): see SI 2009/415, art 2.

PART 8
MISCELLANEOUS AND GENERAL PROVISIONS

General

****

230 Minor definitions: general

In this Act –

'assured tenancy', 'assured shorthold tenancy' and 'assured agricultural occupancy' have the same meaning as in Part I of the Housing Act 1988;

'enactment' includes an enactment comprised in subordinate legislation (within the meaning of the Interpretation Act 1978);

'housing action trust' has the same meaning as in the Housing Act 1988;

'housing association' has the same meaning as in the Housing Associations Act 1985;

'introductory tenancy' and 'introductory tenant' have the same meaning as in Chapter I of Part V of this Act;

'local housing authority' has the same meaning as in the Housing Act 1985;

'registered social landlord' has the same meaning as in Part I of this Act;

'secure tenancy' and 'secure tenant' have the same meaning as in Part IV of the Housing Act 1985.

Homelessness Act 2002

2002 c 7

CONTENTS

Homelessness reviews and strategies

Supplementary

Homelessness reviews and strategies

1 Duty of local housing authority to formulate a homelessness strategy

(1)   A local housing authority ('the authority') may from time to time –

  (a)   carry out a homelessness review for their district; and
  (b)   formulate and publish a homelessness strategy based on the results of that review.

(2)   The social services authority for the district of the authority (where that is a different local authority) shall give such assistance in connection with the exercise of the power under subsection (1) as the authority may reasonably require.

(3)   The authority shall exercise that power so as to ensure that the first homelessness strategy for their district is published within the period of twelve months beginning with the day on which this section comes into force.

(4)   The authority shall exercise that power so as to ensure that a new homelessness strategy for their district is published within the period of five years beginning with the day on which their last homelessness strategy was published.

(5)   A local housing authority shall take their homelessness strategy into account in the exercise of their functions.

(6)   A social services authority shall take the homelessness strategy for the district of a local housing authority into account in the exercise of their functions in relation to that district.

(7)   Nothing in subsection (5) or (6) affects any duty or requirement arising apart from this section.

MODIFICATION

Article 3 of the Local Authorities' Plans and Strategies (Disapplication) (England) Order 2005, SI 2005/157, as amended by the Local Authorities' Plans and Strategies (Disapplication) (England) (Amendment) Order 2009, SI 2009/714, arts 2 and 4, disapplies the requirement to publish homelessness strategies under s 1(4) above for those local housing authorities in England which are categorised as excellent, 4 stars or 3 stars authorities.

2 Homelessness reviews

(1)   For the purposes of this Act 'homelessness review' means a review by a local housing authority of –

  (a)   the levels, and likely future levels, of homelessness in their district;
  (b)   the activities which are carried out for any purpose mentioned in subsection (2) (or which contribute to their achievement); and
  (c)   the resources available to the authority, the social services authority for their district, other public authorities, voluntary organisations and other persons for such activities.

(2)   Those purposes are –

  (a)   preventing homelessness in the district of the authority;

   (b)   securing that accommodation is or will be available for people in the district who are or may become homeless;

   (c)   providing support for people in the district –
      (i)   who are or may become homeless; or
      (ii) who have been homeless and need support to prevent them becoming homeless again.

(3)   A local housing authority shall, after completing a homelessness review –

   (a)   arrange for the results of the review to be available at its principal office for inspection at all reasonable hours, without charge, by members of the public; and

   (b)   provide (on payment if required by the authority of a reasonable charge) a copy of those results to any member of the public who asks for one.

3 Homelessness strategies

(1)   For the purposes of this Act 'homelessness strategy' means a strategy formulated by a local housing authority for –

   (a)   preventing homelessness in their district;

   (b)   securing that sufficient accommodation is and will be available for people in their district who are or may become homeless;

   (c)   securing the satisfactory provision of support for people in their district –
      (i)   who are or may become homeless; or
      (ii) who have been homeless and need support to prevent them becoming homeless again.

(2)   A homelessness strategy may include specific objectives to be pursued, and specific action planned to be taken, in the course of the exercise of –

   (a)   the functions of the authority as a local housing authority; or

   (b)   the functions of the social services authority for the district.

(3)   A homelessness strategy may also include provision relating to specific action which the authority expects to be taken –

   (a)   by any public authority with functions (not being functions mentioned in subsection (2)) which are capable of contributing to the achievement of any of the objectives mentioned in subsection (1); or

   (b)   by any voluntary organisation or other person whose activities are capable of contributing to the achievement of any of those objectives.

(4)   The inclusion in a homelessness strategy of any provision relating to action mentioned in subsection (3) requires the approval of the body or person concerned.

(5)   In formulating a homelessness strategy the authority shall consider (among other things) the extent to which any of the objectives mentioned in subsection (1) can be achieved through action involving two or more of the bodies or other persons mentioned in subsections (2) and (3).

(6) The authority shall keep their homelessness strategy under review and may modify it from time to time.

(7) If the authority modify their homelessness strategy, they shall publish the modifications or the strategy as modified (as they consider most appropriate).

(8) Before adopting or modifying a homelessness strategy the authority shall consult such public or local authorities, voluntary organisations or other persons as they consider appropriate.

(9) The authority shall –

(a) make a copy of [everything published under section 1 or]¹ this section available at its principal office for inspection at all reasonable hours, without charge, by members of the public; and

(b) provide (on payment if required by the authority of a reasonable charge) a copy of [anything]² so published to any member of the public who asks for one.

AMENDMENT

¹ Words substituted: Local Government Act 2003, s 127(1), Sch 7, para 81(a).

² Word substituted: Local Government Act 2003, s 127(1), Sch 7, para 81(b).

4 Sections 1 to 3: interpretation

In sections 1 to 3 –

'homeless' and 'homelessness' have the same meaning as in Part 7 of the Housing Act 1996 (c 52) (in this Act referred to as 'the 1996 Act');
'local housing authority' and 'district' have the same meaning as in the Housing Act 1985 (c 68);
'social services authority' means a local authority for the purposes of the Local Authority Social Services Act 1970 (c 42);
'support' means advice, information or assistance; and
'voluntary organisation' has the same meaning as in section 180(3) of the 1996 Act.

****

Supplementary

17 Wales

(1) The reference to the 1996 Act in Schedule 1 to the National Assembly for Wales (Transfer of Functions) Order 1999 (SI 1999/672) is to be treated as referring to that Act as amended by this Act.

(2) Subsection (1) does not affect the power to make further Orders varying or omitting that reference.

18 Minor and consequential amendments and repeals

(1)   Schedule 1 (which contains minor and consequential amendments) has effect.

(2)   Schedule 2 (which contains repeals) has effect.

19 Financial provision

There shall be paid out of money provided by Parliament any increase attributable to this Act in the sums payable out of money so provided under any other Act.

20 Commencement, transitional provision and general saving

(1)   The preceding provisions of this Act (and the Schedules), other than section 8 and paragraphs 3 and 7 of Schedule 1, come into force on such day as the Secretary of State may by order made by statutory instrument appoint; and different days may be appointed for different purposes.

(2)   The Secretary of State may by order made by statutory instrument make such transitional provisions and savings as he considers appropriate in connection with the coming into force of any provision of this Act.

(3)   The powers conferred by subsection (1) and (2) are exercisable as respects Wales by the National Assembly for Wales (and not the Secretary of State).

(4)   Nothing in this Act affects the operation of section 216(2) of the 1996 Act in relation to persons who applied for accommodation or assistance in obtaining accommodation before the commencement of Part 7 of that Act.

21 Short title, extent and application to Isles of Scilly

(1)   This Act may be cited as the Homelessness Act 2002.

(2)   This Act extends to England and Wales only.

(3)   This Act applies to the Isles of Scilly subject to such exceptions, adaptations and modifications as the Secretary of State may by order direct.

(4)   The power to make such an order is exercisable by statutory instrument subject to annulment in pursuance of a resolution of either House of Parliament.

****

Homelessness Code of Guidance for Local Authorities (July 2006)

CONTENTS

Appendix 2
England: Homelessness

OVERVIEW OF THE HOMELESSNESS LEGISLATION

This overview provides a summary of the homelessness legislation and the duties, powers and obligations on housing authorities and others towards people who are homeless or at risk of homelessness. This overview does not form part of the statutory code of guidance and is not a legal commentary.

Introduction

1. The homelessness legislation – that is, Part 7 of the Housing Act 1996 – provides the statutory under-pinning for action to tackle homelessness.

2. The Government's strategy for tackling homelessness is outlined in *Sustainable Communities: Homes for All* and *Sustainable Communities: settled homes; changing lives*, published in 2005. The strategy aims to expand housing opportunities, including for those who need additional support, and for disadvantaged sections of society by offering a wider range of preventative measures and increasing access to settled homes.

The homelessness legislation

3. The homelessness legislation places a general duty on housing authorities to ensure that advice and information about homelessness, and preventing homelessness, is available to everyone in their district free of charge. The legislation also requires authorities to assist individuals and families who are homeless or threatened with homelessness and apply for help.

4. In 2002, the Government amended the homelessness legislation through the *Homelessness Act 2002* and the *Homelessness (Priority Need for Accommodation) (England) Order 2002* to:

- ensure a more strategic approach to tackling and preventing homelessness, in particular by requiring a homelessness strategy for every housing authority district, and
- strengthen the assistance available to people who are homeless or threatened with homelessness by extending the priority need categories to homeless 16 and 17 year olds; care leavers aged 18, 19 and 20; people who are vulnerable as a result of time spent in care, the armed forces, prison or custody, and people who are vulnerable because they have fled their home because of violence.

5. The legislation places duties on housing authorities, and gives them powers, to meet these aims. But it also emphasises the need for joint working between housing authorities, social services and other statutory, voluntary and private sector partners in tackling homelessness more effectively.

6. The Government continues to supplement housing authorities' resources with specific programmes to help them deliver effective homelessness strategies and services, prevent homelessness, reduce use of temporary accommodation and end the worst manifestations of homelessness such as people sleeping rough and families with children living in bed and breakfast hotels.

Appendix 2
England: Homelessness

The homelessness review and strategy

7. Under the *Homelessness Act 2002* all housing authorities must have in place a homelessness strategy based on a review of all forms of homelessness in their district. The first strategy was required by July 2003 and it must be renewed at least every 5 years (unless this duty has been disapplied by the *Local Authorities Plans and Strategies (Disapplication) (England) Order 2005*). The social services authority must provide all reasonable assistance.

8. The strategy must set out the local authority's plans for the prevention of homelessness and for securing that sufficient accommodation and support are or will be available for people who become homeless or who are at risk of becoming so. Housing authorities will therefore need to ensure that all organisations, within all sectors, whose work can help to prevent homelessness and/or meet the needs of homeless people in their district are involved in the strategy. This will need to include not just housing providers (such as housing associations and private landlords) but also other statutory bodies such as social services, the probation service, the health service and the wide range of organisations in the private and voluntary sectors whose work helps prevent homelessness or meet the needs of people who have experienced homelessness.

9. Housing authorities will also need to give careful consideration to the scope for joint working between social services and the many other key players in the district who are working to meet the needs of people who are homeless or have experienced homelessness.

General duty to provide advice on homelessness

10. The housing authority can provide advice and information about homelessness – and the prevention of homelessness – themselves or arrange for another agency to do it on their behalf. Either way, the advice and assistance provided will need to be up to date and robust if it is to be effective and help achieve the housing authority's strategic aim of preventing homelessness. The service will need to be wide-ranging so that it offers advice and information about not only housing options but also the broad range of factors that can contribute to homelessness. This might include, for example, advice on social security benefits, household budgeting, tenancy support services and family mediation services. The advice provided should also act as a signpost to other, more specialist advice such as debt management, health care and coping with drug and alcohol misuse, where this is needed.

The main homelessness duty

11. Under the legislation, certain categories of household, such as families with children and households that include someone who is vulnerable, for example because of pregnancy, old age, or physical or mental disability, have a priority need for accommodation. Housing authorities must ensure that suitable accommodation is available for people who have priority need, if they are eligible for assistance and unintentionally homeless (certain categories of persons from abroad are ineligible.) This is known as the main homelessness duty. The housing authority can provide accommodation in their own stock or arrange for it to be provided by another landlord, for example, a housing association or a landlord in the private rented sector.

12. If settled accommodation is not immediately available, accommodation must be made available in the short term until the applicant can find a settled home, or until some other circumstance brings the duty to an end, for example, where the household voluntarily leaves the temporary accommodation provided by the housing authority. A settled home to bring the homelessness duty to an end could include the offer of a suitable secure or introductory tenancy in a local authority's housing stock (or nomination for a housing association assured tenancy) allocated under Part 6 of the 1996 Act or the offer of a suitable tenancy from a private landlord made by arrangement with the local authority.

13. Under the *Homelessness (Suitability of Accommodation) (England) Order 2003*, housing authorities can no longer discharge a homelessness duty to secure suitable accommodation by placing families with children, and households that include a pregnant woman, in Bed & Breakfast accommodation for longer than six weeks – and then only if more suitable accommodation is not available.

Applications and inquiries

14. Housing authorities must give proper consideration to all applications for housing assistance, and if they have reason to believe that an applicant may be homeless or threatened with homelessness, they must make inquiries to see whether they owe them any duty under Part 7 of the 1996 Act. This assessment process is important in enabling housing authorities to identify the assistance which an applicant may need either to prevent them from becoming homeless or to help them to find another home. In each case, the authority will need to decide whether the applicant is eligible for assistance, actually homeless, has a priority need, and whether the homelessness was intentional (see below). If they wish, housing authorities can also consider whether applicants have a local connection with the local district, or with another district. Certain applicants who are persons from abroad are not eligible for any assistance under Part 7 except free advice and information about homelessness and the prevention of homelessness.

Interim duty to accommodate

15. If an authority have reason to believe that an applicant may be homeless or threatened with homelessness, they must also decide if they also have reason to believe that the applicant may be eligible for assistance and have a priority need for accommodation. They must do this even before they have completed their inquiries. If there is reason to believe the applicant meets these criteria, the housing authority have an immediate duty to ensure that suitable accommodation is available until they complete their inquiries and decide whether a substantive duty is owed under Part 7. This is an important part of the safety net for people who have a priority need for accommodation and are unintentionally homeless.

When is someone homeless?

16. Broadly speaking, somebody is statutorily homeless if they do not have accommodation that they have a legal right to occupy, which is accessible and physically available to them (and their household) and which it would be reasonable for them to continue to live in. It would not be reasonable for someone to continue to live in their home, for example, if that was likely to lead to violence against them (or a member of their family).

Intentional homelessness

17. A person would be homeless intentionally where homelessness was the consequence of a deliberate action or omission by that person (unless this was made in good faith in ignorance of a relevant fact). A deliberate act might be a decision to leave the previous accommodation even though it would have been reasonable for the person (and everyone in the person's household) to continue to live there. A deliberate omission might be non-payment of rent that led to rent arrears and eviction.

Local connection and referrals to another authority

18. Broadly speaking, for the purpose of the homelessness legislation, people may have a local connection with a district because of residence, employment or family associations in the district, or because of special circumstances. (There are exceptions, for example residence in a district while serving a prison sentence there does not establish a local connection.) Where applicants are found to be eligible for assistance, unintentionally homeless and in priority need (ie they meet the criteria for the main homelessness duty) and the authority consider the applicant does not have a local connection with the district but does have one somewhere else, the housing authority dealing with the application can ask the housing authority in that other district to take responsibility for the case. However, applicants cannot be referred to another housing authority if they, or any member of their household, would be at risk of violence in the district of the other authority.

Other homelessness duties

19. If applicants are homeless but do not have a priority need, or if they have brought homelessness on themselves, the housing authority must ensure that they are provided with advice and assistance to help them find accommodation for themselves – but the authority does not have to ensure that accommodation becomes available for them. The housing authority can provide advice and assistance itself or arrange for another agency to do this. The housing authority must ensure that this includes a proper assessment of their housing needs and information about where they are likely to find suitable accommodation. Again, it will be crucial that the advice and assistance is effective and up to date if the housing authority's strategic aim of preventing homelessness is to be achieved.

20. Where people have a priority need but have brought homelessness on themselves, the housing authority must also ensure they have suitable accommodation available for a period that will give them a reasonable chance of finding accommodation for themselves. Sometimes, this may be for only a few weeks.

Intentionally homeless families with children

21. So, families with children who have been found intentionally homeless will not be owed a main homelessness duty; they will be entitled to advice and assistance and temporary accommodation for a short period only. If homelessness persists, any children in the family could be in need and the family could seek assistance from the social services authority under the Children Act 1989. It is therefore important that social services are made aware of such cases as soon as possible. Consequently, where a housing authority are dealing with a family that includes a child under 18 and they consider the family may be found intentionally homeless, they must make social services aware of the case. Where the family are found to be intentionally homeless by the housing authority, and social services decide the child's needs would best be met by helping the family to obtain accommodation, social services can ask the housing authority for reasonable assistance and the housing authority must respond.

Notifications/reviews of decisions/appeals to county court

22. Where authorities have reason to believe an applicant may be homeless or threatened with homelessness and make inquiries into the case, they must give the applicant written notification of their decision on the case, and the reasons for it insofar as it goes against the applicant's interests. Applicants can ask the housing authority to review most aspects of their decisions, and, if still dissatisfied, can appeal to the county court on a point of law. The county court can confirm or quash a housing authority's decision.

Power to accommodate pending a review or appeal

23. Housing authorities have the power to accommodate applicants pending a review or appeal to the county court, and they must consider whether to exercise this power in all cases. If the housing authority decide not to exercise this power pending a review, and the applicant wishes to appeal to the courts, he or she would need to seek permission to ask the High Court to judicially review the decision. If the housing authority decide not to exercise this power pending an appeal to the county court, the applicant can appeal to the county court to review the decision not to accommodate, and the court can require the housing authority to accommodate the applicant, pending the appeal on the substantive homelessness decision if the court considers this is necessary.

INTRODUCTION

Purpose of the code

1. The Secretary of State for Communities and Local Government is issuing this Code of Guidance to local housing authorities (referred to as housing authorities) in England under s 182 of the *Housing Act 1996* ('the 1996 Act'). Under s 182(1) of the 1996 Act, housing authorities are required to have regard to this guidance in exercising their functions under Part 7 of the 1996 Act and under the *Homelessness Act 2002* ('the 2002 Act'). This Code of Guidance replaces the previous version published in 2002.

2. Under s 182(1), social services authorities in England are also required to have regard to the guidance when exercising their functions relating to homelessness and the prevention of homelessness. The guidance applicable to social services authorities is issued jointly with the Secretary of State for Health and the Secretary of State for Education and Skills.

3. The Code gives guidance on how local authorities should exercise their homelessness functions and apply the various statutory criteria in practice. It is not a substitute for legislation and in so far as it comments on the law can only reflect the Department's understanding at the time of issue. Local authorities will still need to keep up to date on any developments in the law in these areas.

4. In addition to this Code, there is issued a range of good practice publications to assist local authorities in exercising their functions relating to homelessness and the prevention of homelessness (see Annex 1).

Who is the code for?

5. The Code is issued specifically for local authority members and staff. It is also of direct relevance to registered social landlords (RSLs). RSLs have a duty under the 1996 Act to co-operate with housing authorities in exercising their homelessness functions. RSLs are subject to the Housing Corporation's Regulatory Code and guidance and they need to take this into account when assisting housing authorities. Many of the activities discussed in the Code require joint planning and operational co-operation between housing authorities and social services authorities, health authorities, other referral agencies, voluntary sector organisations and the diverse range of bodies working in the rented sectors – so the Code is also relevant to these agencies.

The homelessness legislation

6. Part 7 of the 1996 Act sets out the powers and duties of housing authorities where people apply to them for accommodation or assistance in obtaining accommodation. The 2002 Act places a requirement on housing authorities to formulate and publish a homelessness strategy based on a review of homelessness in their district. The 2002 Act also amends a number of provisions in Part 7 of the 1996 Act to strengthen the safety net for vulnerable people.

Equality and diversity

7. When exercising their functions relating to homelessness and the prevention of homelessness, local authorities are under a statutory duty to ensure that their polices and procedures do not discriminate, directly or indirectly, on grounds of race, sex or gender, or disability. Authorities should also ensure that their policies and procedures do not discriminate on the basis of any other ground which is not material to a person's housing application, including grounds of sexual orientation or religion or belief. Authorities should observe relevant codes of practice and adopt a formal equality and diversity policy relating to all aspects of their homelessness service, to ensure equality of access and treatment for all applicants. Appropriate provision will need to be made to ensure accessibility for people with particular needs, including those with mobility difficulties, sight or hearing loss and learning difficulties, as well as those for whom English is not their first language.

8. The Race Relations Act 1976 now places a general duty on local authorities to promote race equality. This means that they must have due regard to the need to:

- eliminate unlawful racial discrimination; and
- promote equality of opportunity and good relations between people of difference racial groups.

In practice, this means building racial equality considerations into the day-to-day work of policy-making, service delivery, employment practice and other functions. The duty is a positive rather than a reactive one.

9. There are also specific duties relating to policy and service delivery. One of these concerns publishing a Race Equality Scheme every three years. Authorities' Race Equality Schemes should include their arrangements for:

- assessing and consulting on the likely impact of homelessness strategies on the promotion of race equality;
- monitoring homelessness policies for any adverse impact on the promotion of race equality;
- publishing the results of assessments, consultations and monitoring;
- ensuring access to homelessness information, advice and services.

The Commission for Racial Equality will publish a statutory Code of Practice on Racial Equality in Housing later this year (see Annex 1).

10. People from ethnic minority groups are around three times more likely than other households to be accepted as unintentionally homeless and in priority need.[1] Housing authorities need to ensure that their homelessness

Appendix 2
England: Homelessness

---

[1]   Source: ODPM data based on the P1E statistical returns completed by local authorities.

strategies and homelessness services pay particular attention to the needs of the ethnic minority communities they serve, for example, by ensuring that advice and information about homelessness and the prevention of homelessness is available in a range of ethnic languages appropriate to the district. ODPM published a Development Guide for local authorities on *Tackling Homelessness Amongst Ethnic Minority Households* (see Annex 1).

11. Section 49A of the *Disability Discrimination Act 1995* (added by the *Disability Discrimination Act 2005*) introduces a new duty to promote equality for disabled people. It requires public authorities to exercise their functions with due regard to the need to:

- eliminate unlawful discrimination against disabled people;
- eliminate harassment of disabled people that is related to their disabilities;
- promote equality of opportunity between disabled people and other persons;
- take steps to take account of disabled people's disabilities (even where that involves treating disabled people more favourably than other persons);
- promote positive attitudes towards disabled people; and
- encourage participation by disabled people in public life.

Authorities will be required to publish a Disability Equality Scheme every three years setting out how they will implement the duty to promote equality in their own context.

As with the duty to promote race equality, this is a positive duty rather than a reactive one and authorities will need to consider the implications for the delivery of their homelessness services.

The Disability Rights Commission has published a statutory Code of Practice on the Duty to Promote Disability Equality which will come into force in December 2006 (see Annex 1).

12. Authorities should also inform themselves of the provisions of Council Directives 2000/43/EC (the Race Directive) and 2000 78/EC (the Equality Directive). Under the *Equalities Act 2006* the Commission for Equality and Human Rights (CEHR) will bring together the Disability Rights Commission and the Equal Opportunities Commission from October 2007. The Act imposes a positive duty on public authorities to promote equality of opportunity and the elimination of discrimination on grounds of age; colour; race, nationality or ethnic origins; disability; family status; gender reassignment; marital status; pregnancy; religion or belief; sex; and sexual orientation. Discrimination on any such grounds in the carrying out by a public authority of its functions would be made unlawful. The *Gender Recognition Act 2004*, the *Employment Equality (Sexual Orientation) (Amendment) Regulations 2003* and the *Employment Equality (Religion or Belief) Regulations 2003* outlaw discrimination on the grounds of gender reassignment, sexual orientation or religion in the fields of employment and vocational training. In addition, the *Employment*

Equality (Age) Regulations, which are due to come into force in October 2006, will outlaw discrimination on the grounds of age in the fields of employment and vocational training.

13. Housing authorities should ensure that their homelessness strategies and homelessness services comply with existing equality and diversity legislation and new legislation as it comes into force.

Definitions

Throughout the Code,

'the 1996 Act' means the Housing Act 1996;

'the 2002 Act' means the Homelessness Act 2002;

'the housing authority' means the local housing authority.

CHAPTER 1: HOMELESSNESS REVIEWS & STRATEGIES

This chapter provides guidance on housing authorities' duties to carry out a homelessness review and to formulate and publish a strategy based on the results of that review.

Duty to formulate a homelessness strategy

1.1. Section 1(1) of the *Homelessness Act 2002* ('the 2002 Act') gives housing authorities the power to carry out a homelessness review for their district and formulate and publish a homelessness strategy based on the results of the review. This power can be exercised from time to time, however s 1(3) required housing authorities to publish their first homelessness strategy by 31 July 2003. Section 1(4) requires housing authorities to publish a new homelessness strategy, based on the results of a further homelessness review, within the period of five years beginning with the day on which their last homelessness strategy was published (there is an exemption from this requirement for local authorities categorised as an 'excellent authority', see paragraph 1.42). However, it is open to a housing authority to conduct homelessness reviews and strategies more frequently, if they wish.

1.2. For a homelessness strategy to be effective housing authorities need to ensure that it is consistent with other local plans and strategies and takes into account any wider relevant sub-regional or regional plans and strategies. There will be a lot of common ground between an authority's housing strategy (whether its own or a sub-regional one produced with neighbouring authorities) and its homelessness strategy. It is open to authorities to produce either separate housing and homelessness strategies or combine these in a single document where it is consistent to do so. It is also open to authorities, again where it would be consistent to do so, to consider producing a wider composite plan that includes not only the housing and homelessness strategies but also their Housing Revenue Account Business Plans and Home Energy

Appendix 2
England: Homelessness

Conservation Act report. The homelessness strategy should also link with other strategies and programmes that address the wide range of problems that can cause homelessness (see indicative list at Annex 2). It will be important to consider how these strategies and programmes can help achieve the objectives of the homelessness strategy and vice-versa.

1.3. Housing authorities are encouraged to take a broad view and consider the benefits of cross-boundary, sub-regional and regional co-operation. A county-wide approach will be particularly important in non-unitary authorities, where housing and homelessness services are provided by the district authority whilst other key services, such as social services and Supporting People, are delivered at the county level. Housing authorities should ensure that the homelessness strategy for their district forms part of a coherent approach to tackling homelessness with neighbouring authorities. Authorities may wish to collaborate with neighbouring housing authorities to produce a joint homelessness strategy covering a sub-regional area. London boroughs are encouraged to work closely with the Greater London Authority when formulating their homelessness strategies.

1.4. When carrying out a review and formulating a strategy, housing authorities are encouraged to refer to *Homelessness Strategies: A good practice handbook, Local Authorities' Homelessness Strategies: Evaluation and Good Practice* and other relevant good practice documents published by the Office of the Deputy Prime Minister (see list of publications at Annex 1).

1.5. Housing authorities are reminded that when drawing up their strategies for preventing and tackling homelessness, they must consider the needs of all groups of people in their district who are homeless or likely to become homeless, including Gypsies and Travellers. Under s 225 of the *Housing Act 2004*, which supplements s 8 of the *Housing Act 1985*, when undertaking a review of housing needs in their district, local authorities are required to carry out an assessment of the accommodation needs of Gypsies and Travellers residing in or resorting to their district. Draft guidance on accommodation needs assessment for Gypsies and Travellers is available on the DCLG website, and will be finalised after further consultation in 2006.

Assistance from social services

1.6. In non-unitary districts, where the social services authority and the housing authority are different authorities, section 1(2) of the 2002 Act requires the social services authority to give the housing authority such assistance as may be reasonably required in carrying out a homelessness review and formulating and publishing a homelessness strategy. **Since a number of people who are homeless or at risk of homelessness will require social services support, it is unlikely that it would be possible for a housing authority to formulate an effective homelessness strategy without assistance from the social services authority. It will be necessary therefore in all cases for housing authorities to seek assistance from the social services authority.** In unitary authorities the authority will need to ensure that the social services department assists the housing department in carrying out a homelessness review and formulating and publishing a homelessness strategy.

1.7. The social services authority must comply with all requests for assistance from housing authorities within their district which are reasonable. Examples of the type of assistance that a housing authority may reasonably require from the social services authority when carrying out a review and formulating a strategy may include:

- information about current and likely future numbers of social services client groups who are likely to be homeless or at risk of homelessness e g young people in need, care leavers and those with community care needs;
- details of social services' current programme of activity, and the resources available to them, for meeting the accommodation needs of these groups;
- details of social services' current programme of activity, and the resources available to them, for providing support for vulnerable people who are homeless or likely to become homeless (and who may not currently be social services clients).

1.8. Effective co-operation will benefit both housing and social services authorities. See Chapter 5 for guidance on joint working with other agencies and Chapter 13 for guidance on co-operation in cases involving children.

Taking the strategy into account

1.9. Sections 1(5) and (6) of the 2002 Act require housing and social services authorities to take the homelessness strategy into account when exercising their functions.

1.10. For a homelessness strategy to be effective it will need to be based on realistic assumptions about how it will be delivered in practice. Whilst this will apply in respect of all the agencies and organisations involved, the key players will be the housing authority and the social services authority. Both authorities will therefore need to ensure that, on the one hand, the assumptions in the strategy about their future activities are realistic and, on the other, that in practice these activities are actually delivered through the operation of their statutory functions. When the strategy is formulated, the social services authority (or social services department within a unitary authority) will need to work closely with the housing authority (or department) to ensure that this can be achieved. All contributors will need to take ownership of the strategy if it is to be effective. Again, because of its crucial role in delivering the strategy, this will be particularly important in the case of the social services authority (or department).

Homelessness reviews

1.11. Under section 2(1) of the 2002 Act a homelessness review means a review by a housing authority of:

  a)　the levels, and likely future levels, of homelessness in their district;
  b)　the activities which are carried out for any the following purposes (or which contribute to achieving any of them):
    i)　preventing homelessness in the housing authority's district;
    ii)　securing that accommodation is or will be available for people in the district who are or may become homeless; and
    iii)　providing support for people in the district:
      −　who are or may become homeless; or
      −　who have been homeless and need support to prevent them becoming homeless again;
  c)　the resources available to the housing authority, the social services authority for the district, other public authorities, voluntary organisations and other persons for the activities outlined in (b) above.

1.12. The purpose of the review is to establish the extent of homelessness in the district, assess its likely extent in the future, and identify what is currently being done, and by whom, and what level of resources are available, to prevent and tackle homelessness.

a)　current levels, and likely future levels, of homelessness

1.13. Homelessness is defined by sections 175 to 178 of the 1996 Act (see Chapter 8 for guidance). The review must take account of **all** forms of homelessness within the meaning of the 1996 Act, not just people who are unintentionally homeless and have a priority need for accommodation under Part 7. The review should therefore consider a wide population of households who are homeless or at risk of homelessness, including those who might be more difficult to identify, including people sleeping rough, or those whose accommodation circumstances make them more likely than others to become homeless or to resort to sleeping rough.

1.14. The housing authority's own records of its activity under the homelessness legislation (Part 7 of the 1996 Act) will provide a baseline for assessing the number of people who are likely to become homeless and seek help directly from the housing authority. These records should give some indication as to why those accepted as statutorily homeless became homeless. Other useful sources of data on potential homelessness in the district may include:

  •　records on rough sleeping;
  •　estimates of people staying with friends/family on an insecure basis;
  •　court records on possession orders;
  •　records of evictions by the local authority and registered social landlords (RSLs);
  •　local advice service records on homelessness cases;

- hospital records of people homeless on discharge;
- armed forces records of those homeless on discharge;
- prison/probation service records of ex-prisoners homeless on discharge;
- social services records of homeless families with children;
- social services records of young people leaving care and children in need requiring accommodation;
- records of Supporting People clients;
- records available from hostels and refuges;
- voluntary sector records, eg day centres, advice services;
- records of asylum seekers being accommodated in the district by the National Asylum Support Service;
- data from the national population census and housing authorities' own household surveys.

1.15. Some groups of people are likely to be more at risk of homelessness than others. These may include:

- young people who have become estranged from their family; have been in care; have a history of abuse, running away or school exclusions; or whose parents have had mental health, alcohol or drug problems; (see Chapter 12)
- people from ethnic minority groups;
- people with an institutionalised background, for example where they have spent time in prison or the armed forces;
- former asylum seekers who have been given permission to stay in the UK and are no longer being accommodated by the National Asylum Support Service;
- people who have experienced other problems that may increase the risk of homelessness including family/relationship breakdowns; domestic, racial or other violence; poor mental or physical health; drug and alcohol abuse; age-related problems and debt.

1.16. As part of the process of mapping and understanding the extent of current homelessness in the district, housing authorities may wish to develop a profile of those who have experienced homelessness. Elements within a profile may include:

- location of homelessness;
- reason(s) for homelessness;
- housing history including previous tenures and length of homelessness;
- ethnic background;
- other background (eg care provided by the local authority or other institution);
- age;
- gender and sexuality;
- disabilities;
- levels and types of debts;
- employment/benefits history;

Appendix 2
England: Homelessness

- composition of household;
- vulnerability of applicant (or household members);
- support needs (housing-related or other);
- health/drug problems;
- immigration status;
- trends in any of these elements.

1.17. Housing authorities will also need to consider the range of factors which could affect future levels of homelessness in their district. Many of these will be similar to factors taken into account for the purpose of assessing housing needs in the district (eg as part of a broader housing strategy). Relevant factors in the district may include:

- the availability of affordable accommodation including housing provided by the housing authority and by RSLs;
- housing market analyses, including property prices and rent levels;
- the supply of accommodation in the private rented sector;
- the provision and effectiveness of housing advice;
- local voluntary and community sector services;
- the allocation policy of the housing authority;
- the lettings policies of RSLs;
- the effectiveness of nomination agreements between the housing authority and RSLs;
- the policy of the housing authority and RSLs on management of tenants' rent arrears and on seeking repossession;
- the efficiency of the housing authority's administration of housing benefit;
- the provision and effectiveness of housing-related support services;
- redevelopment and regeneration activity;
- unemployment;
- strength of the local economy;
- the local population (and demographic trends);
- the level of overcrowding;
- the rate of new household formation in the district;
- the level of inward migration (both national and international);
- the flow of itinerant population (ie Gypsies and Travellers) and availability of authorised sites;
- the number of people likely to be in housing need on leaving:
  - the armed forces,
  - residential care,
  - local authority care,
  - prison,
  - hospital or
  - accommodation provided by the National Asylum Support Service.

1.18. Individual cases of homelessness are often the result of a complex matrix of problems that may develop over time. In many cases homelessness may be triggered by individual circumstances (for example, relationship breakdown or unemployment) but it can also be the result of a failure in the housing market (for example, high rents in the private sector and a shortage of accommodation in the social sector) or a failure of the administrative system (for example, delays in the payment of housing benefit). In districts where the housing market and administrative systems are functioning well, the levels of homelessness are likely to be lower. All these factors will need to be taken into account when assessing the likely future levels of homelessness in the district.

b) activities which are carried out

1.19. The public, private and voluntary sectors can all contribute, directly or indirectly, to the prevention of homelessness, the provision of accommodation and the provision of support for homeless people. When reviewing the activities which are being carried out for these purposes, the housing authority should consider the activities of all the various agencies and organisations, across all sectors, which are providing, or contributing to the provision of accommodation, support or relevant services in the district (Annex 3 provides an indicative list).

1.20. Having mapped all the current activities, the housing authority should consider whether these are appropriate and adequate to meet the aims of the strategy, and whether any changes or additional provision are needed.

Preventing homelessness

1.21. Gaining a good understanding of the causes of homelessness during the homelessness review process will help to inform the range of preventative measures that need to be put in place. Many statutory and non-statutory services can contribute to preventing homelessness. Housing authorities should adopt an open approach and recognise that there will be a broad range of organisations operating in fields other than housing, including, for example, health, education and employment, whose activities may help to prevent homelessness. Activities that contribute to preventing homelessness may include:

- advice services;
- mediation and reconciliation services;
- tenancy support schemes;
- proactive liaison with private sector landlords;
- rent deposit/guarantee schemes;
- management of social housing by the housing authority and by RSLs;
- debt counselling;
- Supporting People programme;
- social services support for vulnerable people;
- housing benefit administration;
- benefit liaison to young people delivered through Connexions;
- 'Sanctuary Schemes' to enable victims of domestic violence to stay in their homes;
- planning for the housing needs of people leaving institutions – e g local authority care, prison and the armed services.

Further guidance on preventing homelessness is provided in Chapter 2.

Securing accommodation

1.22.   Housing authorities need to consider that a range of accommodation is likely to be required for people who are, or may become, homeless. Landlords, accommodation providers and housing developers across all sectors can contribute to the provision of accommodation in the district. Activities that contribute to securing that accommodation will be available for people who are homeless, or at risk of becoming homeless, may include:

- initiatives to increase the supply of new affordable accommodation in the district (eg: affordable housing secured through the planning system);
- provision of new housing for owner occupation;
- initiatives to increase the supply of specialist and/or supported accommodation;
- provision of accommodation from the housing authority's own stock;
- the proportion of lettings RSLs make available to the housing authority and to homeless people generally;
- programmes for the provision of hostel, foyer and refuge spaces;
- initiatives for maximising use of the private rented sector (eg rent deposit guarantee schemes and landlord/tenant mediation services);
- schemes for maximising access to affordable accommodation (eg rent guarantee schemes);
- local, regional and national mobility schemes (eg to assist tenants or homeless households to move to other areas, incentives to reduce under-occupation, and assistance to move into home ownership).

Further guidance on ensuring a sufficient supply of accommodation is provided in Chapter 3.

Providing support

1.23.   As part of the review housing authorities should consider all the current activities which contribute to the provision of support for people in the district who are, or may become, homeless and people in the district who have been homeless and need support to prevent them becoming homeless again. The range of providers whose activities will be making a contribution to this area are likely to embrace the public, private and voluntary sectors.

1.24.   As a starting point, the housing authority may wish to consider the level of services being provided under the Supporting People programme. Other activities which may be relevant are:

- social services support under the community care programme;
- social services support for children in need who require accommodation;
- social services support for young people at risk;
- housing advice services;
- tenancy support services;

- schemes which offer practical support for formerly homeless people (eg furniture schemes);
- day centres for homeless people;
- supported hostel provision;
- women's refuges;
- support for people to access health care services (eg registration with a GP practice);
- support for people with problems of alcohol or substance abuse;
- support for people with mental health problems;
- support for people with learning disabilities;
- support for people seeking employment, eg personal adviser through Connexions, Jobcentre Plus, voluntary sector organisations dealing with homelessness and worklessness;
- advocacy support.

Further guidance on securing support services is provided in Chapter 4.

c) resources available for activities

1.25. As part of the homelessness review, the housing authority should consider the resources available for the activities set out in paragraph 1.11. The housing authority should consider not only its own resources (ie housing funding whether provided by central government or from authorities' own sources) but also those available for these purposes to the social services authority for their district, other public authorities, voluntary organisations and other persons. Annex 3 provides an indicative list of other authorities, organisations and persons whose activities may contribute to preventing and tackling homelessness.

Preventing homelessness

1.26. Housing authorities should invest their own resources in prevention services and measures since these are likely to produce direct net savings for the authority, for example through reduced processing of repeat homelessness applications, lower use of temporary accommodation and fewer social services interventions. Resources allocated to preventing homelessness will also help to reduce pressures on wider services, such as housing, health and employment, in the longer-term.

1.27. Resources available for the prevention of homelessness may include:

- staff or administrative budgets and resources available to the housing authority (eg related to the homeless persons unit, the housing advice service, the Supporting People programme, tenancy support etc);
- the resources allocated within the housing authority for rent guarantee schemes and other preventative measures;
- the availability and quality of housing and homelessness advice in the district (eg number and location of advice centres);

- staff or administrative budgets and resources within other public bodies (eg social services authority, Primary Care Trust, local education authority) dedicated to activities that help prevent/tackle homelessness; and
- staff or administrative budgets and resources available to other agencies working to prevent homelessness in the district (eg housing advice services in the voluntary sector and agencies working with young people).

Securing accommodation

1.28. Resources available for securing that accommodation is, or will be, available may include:

- initiatives to increase the supply of new affordable accommodation in the district (eg bids for resources through the Regional Housing Strategy and Housing Corporation Approved Development Programme, cash incentive schemes, affordable housing secured through the planning system, other RSL developments, Private Finance Initiative or regeneration developments, self-funded developments, self build schemes, shared ownership schemes, Homebuy);
- initiatives to increase the supply of specialist and/or supported accommodation;
- staff or administrative budgets and resources to make better use of the existing social housing stock (eg working with RSLs, managing own housing stock, mobility schemes);
- staff or administrative budgets and resources for maximising use of the private rented sector (eg landlord fora and accreditation schemes, rent deposit/guarantee schemes);
- initiatives to enable people to remain in their homes (eg through housing renewal assistance and disabled facilities grants).

Providing support

1.29. Resources available for providing support may include:

- staff or administrative budgets and resources available through the Supporting People programme;
- other staff or administrative budgets and resources available to the housing authority, for example through general fund expenditure or the Housing Revenue Account;
- staff or administrative budgets and resources available to the social services authority (eg personnel working to meet the support needs of homeless people);
- staff or administrative budgets and resources available to other public authorities and voluntary and community sector agencies (eg Primary Care Trusts, Drug Action Teams, Sure Start, Connexions and others listed at Annex 3); and
- availability of supported accommodation units and floating support for homeless people.

Results of the review

1.30. Having completed a homelessness review, housing authorities must arrange for a copy of the results of the review to be made available at their principal office; these must be available to the public for inspection at all reasonable hours without charge. A copy of the results must also be made available to any member of the public, on request (for which a reasonable charge can be made).

Homelessness strategies

1.31. Having carried out a homelessness review the housing authority will be in a position to formulate its homelessness strategy based on the results of that review as required by s 1(1)(b) of the 2002 Act. In formulating its strategy a housing authority will need to consider the necessary levels of activity required to achieve the aims set out in the paragraph below and the sufficiency of the resources available to them as revealed by the review.

1.32. Under s 3(1) of the 2002 Act a homelessness strategy means a strategy for:

  i) preventing homelessness in the district (see Chapter 2 for further guidance);

  ii) securing that sufficient accommodation is and will be available for people in the district who are or may become homeless (see Chapter 3 for further guidance);

  iii) securing the satisfactory provision of support for people in the district who are or may become homeless or who have been homeless and need support to prevent them becoming homeless again (see Chapter 4 for further guidance).

Specific objectives and actions for housing and social services authorities

1.33. A homelessness strategy may include specific objectives to be achieved and actions planned to be taken in the course of the exercise of the functions of the housing authority and the social services authority. This will apply equally in areas where the social services authority is not also the housing authority (for example, in district councils in county areas). Examples of specific objectives and actions for housing and social services authorities that might be included in a strategy are set out in Annex 4.

Specific action by others

1.34. A homelessness strategy can also include specific action which the housing authority expects to be taken by:

  i) other public authorities;

  ii) voluntary organisations; and

Appendix 2
England: Homelessness

iii)   other persons whose activities could contribute to achieving the strategy's objectives.

1.35. In all housing authority districts there will be a significant number of agencies whose activities address the wide range of needs and problems that can be linked to homelessness. These will be found across all sectors: public, private and voluntary. Housing authorities will need to seek the participation of all relevant agencies in the district in order to assist them in formulating and delivering an effective homelessness strategy that includes specific action that the housing authority expects to be taken by others.

1.36. In particular, housing authorities should enter into constructive partnerships with RSLs operating in their district. See Annex 5 for guidance on co-operation between housing authorities and RSLs.

1.37. An indicative list of the other public authorities, voluntary organisations and persons whose activities could contribute to achieving the strategy's objectives is at Annex 3. However, s 3(4) provides that a housing authority cannot include in a homelessness strategy any specific action expected to be taken by another body or organisation without their approval.

1.38. Examples of specific action that the housing authority might expect to be taken by others are provided at Annex 6.

Joint action

1.39. Section 3(5) of the 2002 Act requires housing authorities, when formulating a homelessness strategy, to consider (among other things) the extent to which any of the strategy's objectives could be achieved through joint action involving two or more of the persons or other bodies tackling homelessness in the district. This could include the housing authority, the social services authority, neighbouring housing authorities and any other public bodies working to alleviate homelessness within the district, for example, the National Offender Management Service. It might also include any other organisation or person whose activities could contribute to achieving the objectives of the homelessness strategy, for example, voluntary sector organisations working with homeless people, registered social landlords, and private landlords. The most effective strategies will be those which harness the potential of all the organisations and persons working to prevent and alleviate homelessness in the district, and which ensure that all the activities concerned are consistent and complementary. It will be important for all such organisations to take ownership of the strategy if they strive to help meet its objectives. See Chapter 5 for guidance on joint working with other agencies.

Action plans

1.40. As part of the homelessness strategy housing authorities should develop effective action plans, to help ensure that the objectives set out in the homelessness strategy are achieved. Action plans could include, for example, targets, milestones and arrangements for monitoring and evaluation. Good practice guidance on developing action plans is provided in the ODPM publication *'Local Authorities' Homelessness Strategies: Evaluation and Good Practice (2004)'*.

Need to consult on a strategy

1.41. Housing authorities must consult such public or local authorities, voluntary organisations or other persons as they consider appropriate before adopting or modifying a homelessness strategy. For a strategy to be effective it will need to involve every organisation and partnership whose activities contribute, or could contribute, in some way to achieving its objectives. As a minimum, therefore, it will be appropriate for all such organisations to be consulted on the strategy before it is adopted. It will be important to consult service users and homeless people themselves, or organisations representing their interests. Consultation with ethnic minority and faith-based groups will also be important in addressing the disproportionate representation of people from ethnic minority communities amongst homeless households. Annex 3 provides an indicative list of the types of authorities, organisations and people that the housing authority may wish to consult about a strategy.

Publishing a strategy

1.42. Under s 1(3) of the 2002 Act, housing authorities were required to publish their first homelessness strategy by 31 July 2003. Section 1(4) requires housing authorities to publish a new homelessness strategy, based on the results of a further homelessness review, within the period of five years beginning with the day on which their last homelessness strategy was published. However, those authorities which are categorised as an 'excellent authority' by the Secretary of State by virtue of the *Local Authorities' Plans and Strategies (Disapplication) (England) Order 2005* are exempt from this requirement. Housing authorities must make a copy of the strategy available to the public at their principal office, and this is to be available for inspection at all reasonable hours without charge. A copy must also be made available to any member of the public, on request (for which a reasonable charge can be made).

Keeping a strategy under review and modifying it

1.43. Housing authorities must keep their homelessness strategy under review and may modify it from time to time. Before modifying the strategy, they must consult on the same basis as required before adopting a strategy (see paragraph 1.41). If a strategy is modified, the housing authority must publish the modifications or the modified strategy and make copies available to the public on the same basis as required when adopting a strategy (see paragraph 1.42).

1.44. Circumstances that might prompt modification of a homelessness strategy include: transfer of the housing authority's housing stock to an RSL; the setting up of an Arms Length Management Organisation; a review of other, relevant local plans or strategies; new data sources on homelessness

Appendix 2
England: Homelessness

becoming available; a significant change in the levels or causes of homelessness; changes in either housing/homelessness/social security policy or legislation, or new factors that could contribute to a change in the levels or nature of homelessness in the district such as significant changes to the local economy (eg housing markets or levels of employment).

CHAPTER 2: PREVENTING HOMELESSNESS

2.1. This chapter provides guidance on housing authorities' duties to have a strategy to prevent homelessness in their district and to ensure that advice and information about homelessness, and the prevention of homelessness, are available free of charge to anyone in their district. The chapter also provides some examples of the action housing authorities and their partners can take to tackle the more common causes of homelessness and to prevent homelessness recurring.

2.2. Preventing homelessness means providing people with the ways and means to meet their housing, and any housing-related support, needs in order to avoid experiencing homelessness. Effective prevention will enable a person to remain in their current home, where appropriate, to delay a need to move out of current accommodation so that a move into alternative accommodation can be planned in a timely way; to find alternative accommodation, or to sustain independent living.

2.3. The prevention of homelessness should be a key strategic aim which housing authorities and other partners pursue through the homelessness strategy. It is vital that individuals are encouraged to seek assistance at the earliest possible time when experiencing difficulties which may lead to homelessness. In many cases early, effective intervention can prevent homelessness occurring. Housing authorities are reminded that they must not avoid their obligations under Part 7 of the 1996 Act (including the duty to make inquiries under s 184, if they have reason to believe that an applicant may be homeless or threatened with homelessness), but it is open to them to suggest alternative solutions in cases of potential homelessness where these would be appropriate and acceptable to the applicant.

2.4. The Secretary of State considers that housing authorities should take steps to prevent homelessness wherever possible, offering a broad range of advice and assistance for those in housing need. It is also important that, where homelessness does occur and is being tackled, consideration is given to the factors which may cause repeat homelessness and action taken to prevent homelessness recurring.

2.5. Homelessness can have significant negative consequences for the people who experience it. At a personal level, homelessness can have a profound impact on health, education and employment prospects. At a social level, homelessness can impact on social cohesion and economic participation. Early intervention to prevent homelessness can therefore bring benefits for those concerned, including being engaged with essential services and increasing the likelihood that children will live in a more secure environment. Investment in prevention services can also produce direct cost savings for local authorities, for example through lower use of temporary accommodation and fewer social services interventions. Furthermore, measures to prevent homelessness will also help to reduce longer-term pressures on wider services, such as health and employment.

2.6.   There are three stages where intervention can prevent homelessness:

early identification – by identifying categories of people who are at risk of homelessness and ensuring that accommodation and any necessary support are available to them in time to prevent homelessness. Early identification can target people who fall within known indicator groups (eg those leaving local authority care, prison, secure accommodation or the armed forces, or people at known or observed risk due to mental or physical health problems) even though they may not currently have a need for housing but for whom timely intervention can avoid homelessness when they leave their institutional environment and before they reach a crisis point;

pre-crisis intervention – this can take the form of: advice services and proactive intervention such as negotiation with landlords to enable people to retain their current tenancies. Such intervention is important even if it only delays the date when a person has to leave their home, as this may allow time to plan and manage a move to alternative accommodation;

preventing recurring homelessness – ensuring tenancy sustainment can be central to preventing repeat homelessness where there is an underlying need for support and the provision of accommodation by itself is insufficient to prevent homelessness.

Strategy to prevent homelessness

2.7.   Under s 1 of the 2002 Act, local housing authorities must formulate and publish a homelessness strategy based on a review of homelessness for their district, and they must take the strategy into account when exercising their functions. (See Chapter 1 for guidance.) Under section 3(1)(a) of the 2002 Act a homelessness strategy must include, among other things, a strategy for preventing homelessness in the district. Gaining a thorough understanding of the causes of homelessness in a local area through the review process will help to inform the range of measures required to prevent homelessness. As part of the review, housing authorities must consider all the current activities in their area that contribute to the prevention of homelessness. They must also consider the resources available. Both activities and resources are likely to involve a wide range of providers working in the public, private and voluntary sectors.

2.8.   In developing their homelessness strategies, housing authorities should consider the range of measures that need to be put in place to prevent homelessness. These will depend on local circumstances. Housing authorities are advised to adopt an open approach and recognise that there will be a broad range of organisations operating in fields other than housing, for example, in education, health and employment, whose activities may help to prevent

Appendix 2
England: Homelessness

homelessness. (See Chapter 1 for further guidance on carrying out a homelessness review and formulating a homelessness strategy).

Advice and information about homelessness and the prevention of homelessness

2.9. Under s 179(1) of the 1996 Act, housing authorities have a duty to secure that advice and information about homelessness, and the prevention of homelessness, are available free of charge to any person in their district. The provision of comprehensive advice will play an important part in delivering the housing authority's strategy for preventing homelessness in their district.

2.10. There is an enormous variety of reasons why people become homeless or find themselves threatened with homelessness. And, in many cases, there can be multiple reasons, and a complex chain of circumstances, that lead to homelessness. Some of these may relate to the housing market, for example, high rents and a shortage of affordable accommodation in the area, or to administrative systems, for example delays in the payment of benefits. Others may relate to personal circumstances, for example, relationship breakdown, a bereavement, long-term or acute ill health or loss of employment. The provision of advice and information to those at risk of homelessness will need to reflect this. It will need to be wide-ranging and comprehensive in its coverage and may require a full multi-disciplinary assessment.

2.11. Many people who face the potential loss of their current home will be seeking practical advice and assistance to help them remain in their accommodation or secure alternative accommodation. Some may be seeking to apply for assistance under the homelessness legislation without being aware of other options that could help them to secure accommodation. Advice services should provide information on the range of housing options that are available in the district. This might include options to enable people to stay in their existing accommodation, delay homelessness for long enough to allow a planned move, or access alternative accommodation in the private or social sectors. This 'housing options' approach is central to addressing housing need as a means of preventing homelessness.

2.12. Advice on the following issues may help to prevent homelessness:

- tenants' rights and rights of occupation;
- leaseholders' rights and service charges;
- what to do about harassment and illegal eviction;
- how to deal with possession proceedings;
- rights to benefits (eg housing benefit) including assistance with making claims as required;
- current rent levels;
- how to retrieve rent deposits;
- rent and mortgage arrears;
- how to manage debt;
- grants available for housing repair and/or adaptation;

- how to obtain accommodation in the private rented sector – e g details of landlords and letting agents within the district, including any accreditation schemes, and information on rent guarantee and deposit schemes;
- how to apply for an allocation of accommodation through the social housing waiting list or choice-based lettings scheme;
- how to apply to other social landlords for accommodation.

The advisory service might also include an advocacy service, which may include providing legal representation for people facing the loss of their home.

2.13. Housing authorities will need to ensure that the implications and likely outcomes of the available housing options are made clear to all applicants, including the distinction between having priority need for accommodation under Part 7 and having priority for an allocation of social housing under Part 6.

2.14. Advice services will need to be effectively linked to other relevant statutory and non-statutory service providers. As noted in paragraph 2.10 above, it is often a combination of factors that lead to homelessness, and housing authorities are advised to ensure that people who require advice of a wider or more specialist nature, for example, to address family and relationship breakdown, mental or physical health problems, drug and alcohol abuse, or worklessness are directed to other agencies who can provide the service they need. In situations where there is a history of child abuse or where there are child protection concerns, homelessness and housing organisations will need to work closely with the Local Safeguarding Children Board (LSCB).

2.15. The effectiveness of authorities' housing advice in preventing homelessness or the threat of homelessness is measured by Best Value Performance Indicator BVPI 213. Guidance on BVPI 213 is available at www.communities.gov.uk.

Accessibility

2.16. It is recommended that advisory services are well publicised and accessible to everyone in the district. Appropriate provision will need to be made to ensure accessibility for people with particular needs, including those with mobility difficulties, sight or hearing loss and learning difficulties, as well as those for whom English is not their first language.

Who provides the advice and information?

2.17. The legislation does not specify how housing authorities should ensure that advice and information on homelessness and the prevention of homelessness are made available. They could do this in a number of ways, for example:

i) provide the service themselves;
ii) ensure that it is provided by another organisation; or
iii) ensure that it is provided in partnership with another organisation.

Appendix 2
England: Homelessness

2.18. The housing authority must ensure that the service is free of charge and available and accessible to everyone in their district. Securing the provision of an independent advisory service may help to avoid conflicts of interest. Private sector tenants may not naturally look to the housing authority for advice. Some young people may be reluctant to approach a statutory authority for advice, but they may feel more at ease in dealing with a more informal advisory service provided by the voluntary sector. People from different ethnic minority groups might also find advice more accessible if it is delivered through community or faith organisations. (See Chapter 21 for guidance on contracting out homelessness functions).

2.19. Under s 179(2), housing authorities may give grants or loans to other persons who are providing advice and information about homelessness and the prevention of homelessness on behalf of the housing authority. Under s 179(3), housing authorities may also assist such persons (eg voluntary organisations) by:

 i) allowing them to use premises belonging to the housing authority,
 ii) making available furniture or other goods, by way of gift, loan or some other arrangement, and
 iii) making available the services of staff employed by the housing authority.

Standards of advice

2.20. Housing authorities should ensure that information provided is current, accurate and appropriate to the individual's circumstances. To ensure they are providing an effective service to a high standard, housing authorities may wish to refer to the quality assurance systems applied by the National Association of Citizens Advice Bureaux, the Shelter network of housing advice centres, the National Disabled Housing Services Ltd (HoDis) accreditation scheme and the Community Legal Service Quality Mark. Housing authorities are also advised to monitor the provision of advisory services to ensure they continue to meet the needs of all sections of the community and help deliver the aims of their homelessness strategy.

Preventing homelessness in specific circumstances

2.21. Some groups of people are likely to be more at risk of homelessness than others. These may include:

 • young people who have become estranged from their family; have been in care and/or secure accommodation; have a history of abuse, running away or school exclusions; or whose parents have had mental health, alcohol or drug problems (see Chapter 12 for further guidance on 16 and 17 year olds);
 • people from ethnic minority groups;
 • people with an institutionalised background, for example where they have spent time in care, in prison or in the armed forces;

- former asylum seekers who have been given permission to stay in the UK and are no longer being accommodated by the National Asylum Support Service;
- people who have experienced other problems that may increase the risk of homelessness including family/relationship breakdowns; domestic, racial or other violence; poor mental or physical health; drug and alcohol misuse; age-related problems and debt.

2.22. In many cases homelessness can be prevented by identifying people who are in circumstances which put them at risk of homelessness, and by providing services which can enable them to remain in their current home. Homelessness can also be prevented by ensuring assistance is available at known risk points such as discharge from prison or hospital. Table 2.1 below gives examples of some of the measures that may help tackle some of the more common causes of homelessness. More detailed guidance is provided in Annex 7.

2.23. Housing authorities should also work with housing providers to encourage them to seek to maintain and sustain tenancies by employing effective strategies for the prevention and management of rent arrears. Landlords should be encouraged to make early and personal contact with tenants in arrears and to assess whether there are any additional support needs and, where relevant, to establish that all benefits to which tenants are entitled are being claimed. Landlords should offer assistance and advice on welfare benefits and in making a claim, debt counselling and money advice either in-house or through a referral to an external agency and implement ways for recovering the money such as debt management plans or attachment to benefits or earnings orders. Possession action should only be taken as a last resort. See Annex 1 for ODPM guidance on *Improving the Effectiveness of Rent Arrears Management*.

Table 2.1: Tackling common causes of homelessness

Cause	Action
Parents, relatives or friends not being able or willing to provide accommodation	Mediation services, usually contracted out by local authority to, for example, Relate, Youth Crime prevention and parenting programmes.
Relationship breakdown, including domestic violence	'Sanctuary' schemes, which allow domestic violence victims to remain in their homes where they choose to do so once security measures are in place.

Cause	Action
Discharge from an institutional situation eg hospital, custody, residential treatment/care	Early planning for discharge between institutional staff and local housing providers, including assessing support needs. Proactive provision of advice by local housing authority on housing options (prior to discharge).
End of assured shorthold tenancy	Housing advice. Rent deposit or bond schemes to encourage landlords to let to potentially homeless people. Landlord-tenant mediation services, to resolve disputes about behaviour or repairs.
Mortgage and rent arrears	Debt counselling. Advocacy services in county court. Fast tracking housing benefit claims.
Person ill-equipped to sustain a tenancy	Advice and support under the Supporting People programme for vulnerable people at risk of homelessness, for example improving budgeting and 'life' skills.
Lack of information	Early and proactive intervention from local authority homelessness services to discuss options and offer assistance and advice.

Preventing homelessness recurring

2.24. The underlying problems which led to homelessness in the first place have to be addressed in order to provide long-term solutions. Failure to address these root causes can lead to repeated episodes of homelessness. Recurring homelessness may be indicative of problems that are not being resolved by the provision of accommodation alone.

2.25. An effective approach to tackling recurring homelessness is likely to be based on:

- effective monitoring that identifies housing applicants who are homeless or threatened with homelessness and who have previously been secured accommodation under the homelessness legislation (either by the same authority or another authority in a different area);
- an analysis of the main causes of homelessness among housing applicants who have experienced homelessness more than once; and

- the existence of support services (and, in particular, strong links with the local Supporting People strategy and services) for housing applicants who have experienced homelessness more than once, which tackle these causes and help the applicants to sustain tenancies or other forms of settled accommodation in the longer term.

2.26. Tenancy sustainment is central to preventing repeat homelessness and can include a range of interventions. It is closely linked with good housing management and the Supporting People programme. See Chapter 4 for further guidance on securing support services and the housing-related support services that can be funded through Supporting People.

2.27. Whilst tenancy sustainment is the eventual objective, there are some individuals who may not be able to sustain accommodation due to personal circumstances, for example mental health or substance misuse difficulties. Support will need to be provided to progress towards the time when they are able to maintain accommodation.

CHAPTER 3: ENSURING A SUFFICIENT SUPPLY OF ACCOMMODATION

3.1. **This chapter provides guidance on options available to housing authorities to help increase the supply of new housing and maximise the use of the housing stock in their district.**

3.2. Section 3(1)(b) of the *Homelessness Act 2002* provides that a homelessness strategy is a strategy for, amongst other things, securing that sufficient accommodation is and will be available for people who are or may become homeless. Chapter 16 provides guidance on the different ways in which housing authorities can ensure that suitable accommodation is available for applicants, for example by providing the accommodation themselves or by securing it from a private landlord or a registered social landlord.

3.3. Homelessness is significantly influenced by the availability of housing, and in particular affordable housing. A shortage of affordable housing can lead to increasing numbers of people being accommodated in temporary accommodation whilst waiting for settled housing to bring the main homelessness duty to an end. 'Settled housing' in this context will primarily be social housing and good quality private sector accommodation (see Chapter 14 for further guidance on bringing the main homelessness (s 193(2)) duty to an end.)

3.4. Although, in 2005, over 80% of people living in temporary accommodation were in self-contained homes they often lack certainty over how long they will live there. This can cause disruption to their lives, make it hard for them to put roots down in the community or to access important services. For example, they may face real difficulties in gaining access to a local GP or in enrolling their children in a local school. Many may already have faced disruption and become disconnected or moved away from existing services and support networks as a result of homelessness.

3.5. The Government's current target is to halve the number of households living in temporary accommodation by 2010. Increasing the supply of new affordable housing and making better use of existing social and private rented stock to provide settled homes will be critical for achieving this target, as will measures to prevent homelessness.

Increase supply of new housing

3.6. The *Sustainable Communities Plan* and *Sustainable Communities: Homes for All* set out how the Government is creating new communities and expanding existing communities in four areas in the wider South East. Taken together, these areas are expected to deliver an extra 200,000 homes above current planning totals.

3.7. At a regional level, local authorities have a key role to play to identify the priorities for housing in their region, to ensure these are reflected in regional housing strategies and to secure funding for their plans. Housing authorities will also need to ensure that housing strategies are aligned with regional economic and planning strategies.

3.8. There are a number of ways housing authorities can increase the supply of new housing. The main source of funding for the provision of affordable housing is the Housing Corporation's national Affordable Housing Programme (AHP), known formerly as the Approved Development Programme (ADP). From the 2006–2008 biannual bidding round, the AHP is open to both registered social landlords and non-registered bodies (eg developers). Bids continue to be assessed against a range of criteria including housing quality and value for money, and against regional and local priorities. Housing authorities will need to work closely with RSLs and others to make best use of this funding.

3.9. Another important means of providing affordable housing is through planning obligations, which are usually negotiated in the context of granting planning permission for new housing development. Planning obligations are generally secured by agreements made between a local authority and a developer under s 106 of the *Town and Country Planning Act 1990* and they are commonly referred to as 's 106 agreements'. Obligations may be appropriate where, for example, a planning objection to a proposed development cannot be overcome by the imposition of a condition. More detailed guidance on the use of s 106 agreements is contained in ODPM Circular 05/2005: Planning Obligations.

3.10. National guidance on planning and affordable housing is currently contained in Planning Policy Guidance Note 3 (PPG3): Housing, as supplemented by Circular 06/98. These documents provide advice to planning authorities about securing the provision of affordable housing either in kind or by financial contribution. They also remind local authorities when formulating local policy or determining planning applications to take account of the need to cater for a range of housing needs and to encourage the development of mixed and balanced communities in order to avoid areas of social exclusion.

3.11. PPG3 and Circular 06/98 are presently under review and a draft Planning Policy Statement 3 (PPS3): Housing was issued for consultation in December 2005. Following the publication of final PPS3, local planning authorities will be expected to ensure that policies in their Local Development Frameworks take into account the updated national planning policy framework for delivering the Government's housing objectives.

3.12. Planning authorities will need to ensure that their affordable housing policies are evidence-based, kept up to date over time, and applied consistently across developments to ensure that affordable housing is effectively and fairly delivered through this route.

Maximising the use of existing housing stock

3.13. A number of options are discussed below for how housing authorities might maximise the use of current housing stock.

The private rented sector

3.14. Some people living in the private rented sector can experience homelessness, but this sector can also provide solutions to homelessness. Homelessness statistics routinely show that the end of an assured shorthold tenancy (AST) is one of the top three reasons for loss of a settled home. Authorities are encouraged to work with landlords in their area to see how this can be addressed, for example, by offering mediation between landlord and tenant where relations have broken down, and negotiating to extend or renew ASTs where appropriate.

3.15. For many, renting in the private sector may offer a practical solution to their housing need (for example, it may offer more choice over location and type of property). Authorities are therefore encouraged to consider providing rent deposits, guarantees or rent in advance, to help households access this sector. They may also consider establishing Accreditation Schemes, whereby landlords voluntarily agree to a set of standards relating to the management or physical condition of privately rented accommodation to help increase the supply of private rented accommodation.

3.16. Many local authorities have used the private rented sector as a source of good quality, self-contained temporary accommodation. However, the private rented sector can also provide a source of settled accommodation, where qualifying offers of ASTs are accepted by households who are owed the main homelessness duty.

3.17. There is scope to make greater use of the private rented sector, either to help households avoid homelessness or to provide more settled homes for people living in temporary accommodation. Authorities are recommended to establish and maintain good relations with private sector landlords, for example through landlord fora. This can be effective in securing an improved supply of properties in the private rented sector for homeless, or potentially homeless, households.

Appendix 2
England: Homelessness

3.18. It is also recommended that authorities review the extent to which qualifying offers of ASTs are being made to households in temporary accommodation in their area; whether there are any barriers to such offers being made or accepted and, if so, what additional steps would need to be taken to address those barriers.

Social housing

3.19. The Secretary of State considers that, generally, it is inappropriate for general needs social housing to be used as temporary accommodation for long periods, especially where such properties are able to be let as settled homes.

3.20. It is important that housing authorities work effectively with RSLs to help them prevent and tackle homelessness in the district. RSLs have a key role to play in sustaining tenancies, reducing evictions and abandonment, and preventing homelessness through their housing management functions. To ensure effective collaboration between themselves and partner RSLs operating in their district housing authorities are advised to consider establishing a nominations agreement. This would include the proportion of lettings that will be made available, any conditions that will apply, and how any disputes about suitability or eligibility will be resolved. Housing authorities are also advised to aim for any exclusion criteria (that may be applied to nominees by the RSL) to be kept to a minimum. Further guidance on co-operation between RSLs and housing authorities is at Annex 5.

3.21. There are a number of schemes and policies that social housing providers can implement to facilitate the effective management and use of the existing housing stock and to keep voids and re-let times to a minimum.

- **Mobility**: 'moveUK' (formerly Housing Employment and Mobility Services) has been developed to offer social housing tenants and jobseekers more choice about where they live and work around the UK. Its services will open up new opportunities for people who wish to move. 'moveUK' will have three main service components:
  - (i) facilitated mobility services to social landlords and their tenants and applicants to help tenants and applicants to find new homes. This will continue and enhance the provision of the grant funded mobility previously provided by Housing Mobility and Exchange Services (HOMES) and LAWN (the Association of London Government scheme that helps tenants who want to, move out of London to areas of low demand);
  - (ii) 'one stop shop' web-based information about available housing, neighbourhoods and job vacancies;
  - (iii) web access to information on vacancies in social housing.
- **Cash Incentive Scheme** (CIS): although there is no obligation for a housing authority to provide a scheme, the main objectives of the Cash Incentive Scheme (CIS) are to release local authority accommodation required for letting to those in housing need, and to encourage

sustainable home ownership. This is achieved by the payment of a grant to a local authority tenant to assist them in buying a property in the private sector.

- **The new HomeBuy scheme**: this scheme, which commenced on 1st April 2006, provides people with the opportunity to own a home based on equity sharing, whilst protecting the supply of social housing. Existing social tenants are one of the priority groups helped under the scheme, and any rented housing association/local authority home vacated by them will then be made available to others in priority housing need. The Social HomeBuy option, which allows housing association and local authority tenants to purchase a share in their rented home, will be voluntary. Landlords will be able to reinvest the proceeds in replacement social homes.

3.22. The Secretary of State also considers that where local authority or RSL stock is provided as temporary accommodation to discharge a main homelessness duty (owed under section 193(2)) the housing authority should give very careful consideration to the scope for allocating the accommodation as a secure or assured tenancy, as appropriate, especially where a household has been living in a particular property for anything other than a short-term emergency stay.

Choice-based Lettings schemes

3.23. The expansion of choice-based lettings policy aims to achieve nationwide coverage by 2010. Local authorities are encouraged to work together, and with RSL partners, to develop sub-regional and regional choice-based lettings schemes which provide maximum choice and flexibility. Local authorities are encouraged to offer choice to homeless households, while ensuring that their schemes are designed so as not to provide a perverse incentive to applicants to make a homelessness application in order to increase their priority for housing. Housing authorities should also consider involving the private rented sector in their choice-based lettings schemes in order to maximise the housing options available.

Empty homes

3.24. Housing authorities are encouraged to adopt positive strategies for minimising empty homes, and other buildings that could provide residential accommodation, across all housing sectors and tenures within their district. A strategy for minimising empty homes might include schemes for tackling low demand social housing, bringing empty private sector properties back into use and bringing flats over shops into residential use.

3.25. Under the *Housing Act 2004* new provisions on Empty Dwelling Management Orders (EDMOs) are expected to be brought into force. EDMOs are a discretionary power for local authorities to use as part of their empty homes strategy. The new powers will allow local authorities to apply to a residential property tribunal for approval to make an interim EDMO lasting for up to 12 months. During this interim period, the authority may only place tenants in the house with the consent of the owner.

3.26.　Local authorities also have the discretion to set the council tax discount on long term empty properties at any point between 50% and 0%, as well as at any point between 50% and 10% on second homes, taking into account local conditions.

Housing renewal

3.27.　Housing renewal assistance can also assist in meeting the aims of the homelessness strategy. Under the *Regulatory Reform (Housing Assistance) (England and Wales) Order 2002*, local authorities have power to promote housing renewal assistance to landlords, private homeowners and others to increase the supply of a particular type of accommodation through converting under-utilised accommodation to meet identified housing need within the district. Empty homes, vacant accommodation above shops or commercial buildings can be targeted for assistance. Housing renewal assistance can also enable private homeowners to carry out essential repairs or improvements, and remain in their home.

Disabled facilities grant

3.28.　Uptake of the Disabled Facilities Grant – a mandatory entitlement administered by housing authorities for eligible disabled people in all housing tenures – can enable homeowners to remain living an independent life at home, and should be considered as part of an effective homelessness strategy. Authorities are required to give a decision within six months of receiving an application. The grant is subject to a maximum limit and is means tested to ensure that funding goes to those most in need.

CHAPTER 4: SECURING SUPPORT SERVICES

4.1.　**This chapter provides guidance on the importance of support services in preventing and tackling homelessness and outlines the types of housing-related and other support services that might be required.**

4.2.　A homelessness strategy is defined in section 3(1)(c) of the 2002 Act as (among other things) a strategy for securing the satisfactory provision of support for people in their district:

i)　　who are or may become homeless; or
ii)　　who have been homeless and need support to prevent them from becoming homeless again.

4.3.　In formulating their homelessness strategies, housing authorities need to recognise that for some households, homelessness cannot be tackled, or prevented, solely through the provision of accommodation. Some households will require a range of support services, which may include housing-related support to help them sustain their accommodation, as well as personal support relating to factors such as relationship breakdown, domestic violence, mental health problems, drug and alcohol addiction, poverty, debt and unemployment.

4.4. Support can help to prevent people who are at risk of homelessness from becoming homeless at all. In other cases, where people have experienced homelessness and been placed in temporary accommodation, the provision of support may be essential to ensure that they are able to continue to enjoy a reasonable quality of life and access the range of services they need to rebuild their lives. The provision of support can also be important in helping formerly homeless households to sustain settled housing and prevent homelessness from recurring.

4.5. Solutions to homelessness should be based on a thorough assessment of the household's needs, including support needs. Housing authorities will need to establish effective links with the Supporting People team, the social services authority and other agencies (for example, Primary Care Trusts, the Criminal Justice Service, and voluntary and community organisations) to ensure that a joint assessment of an applicant's housing and support needs can be made where necessary. Such assessments should inform decisions on intervention to enable a household to remain in their home, placements in temporary accommodation and options for the provision of more settled accommodation that will bring the main homelessness duty to an end.

4.6. Where children and young people are involved, it is important that any solutions to homelessness address the issues they are facing and do not undermine any support they may already be receiving. In particular, housing authorities will need to establish effective links with children's services authorities[2] and establish whether a Common Assessment Framework has been undertaken, and, if so, which agency will have relevant information about the child's or young person's needs.

Strategy to secure provision of support services

4.7. Section 1 of the 2002 Act requires housing authorities to carry out a homelessness review for their district. Gaining a thorough understanding of the causes of homelessness through the review process will help to inform the range of support provision required. As part of the review, housing authorities must consider all the current activities in their area which contribute to the provision of support for households who are, or may become, homeless, as well as people in the district who have been homeless and need support to prevent them becoming homeless again. They must also consider the resources available. Both activities and resources are likely to involve a range of providers working in the public, private and voluntary sectors. (See Chapter 1 for further guidance on carrying out a homelessness review and formulating a homelessness strategy).

---

[2] All authorities should have a children's services authority, delivering through a children's trust, by April 2008. All Directors of Children's Services will be in post by 2008.

4.8. In formulating their homelessness strategies housing authorities will need to consider the different types and level of support that households may require. Households who have experienced homelessness or who are at risk of homelessness may have diverse needs. Some households may only need information and advice in order to avoid experiencing homelessness, or becoming homeless again. Others, however, will need greater assistance including housing-related support and in some cases may require intensive support from a range of services.

Individuals at risk of homelessness

4.9. Housing authorities should be aware that some individuals may be at particular risk of homelessness, for example young people leaving care, ex-offenders, former members of the armed forces, refugees, people with mental health problems or individuals leaving hospital, and may require a broader package of resettlement support. When developing their homelessness strategies, housing authorities should consider carefully how to work effectively to prevent homelessness amongst these groups and ensure that appropriate support is available. Early identification of people at risk will be crucial to preventing homelessness. Housing authorities should consider agreeing protocols for joint action with local agencies in order to assist with early identification and prevention measures.

4.10. Individuals at risk of homelessness may also include those who have never experienced homelessness in the past and for whom, with the appropriate support, homelessness can be avoided. These individuals may be at risk of homelessness due to specific problems such as managing debt or accessing benefits and require specialist advice which may be delivered through partner agencies such as Citizens Advice Bureaux or Jobcentre Plus. See Chapter 2 for guidance on preventing homelessness.

Young people

4.11. Many young people who have experienced homelessness may lack skills in managing their affairs and require help with managing a tenancy and operating a household budget. Those estranged from their family, particularly care leavers, may lack the advice and support normally available to young people from family, friends and other mentors. 16 and 17 year olds who are homeless and estranged from their family will be particularly vulnerable and in need of support. See Chapter 12 for further guidance on 16 and 17 year olds.

Housing-related support services

4.12. Housing-related support services have a key role in preventing homelessness occurring or recurring. The types of housing-related support that households who have experienced homelessness may need include:

- **support in establishing a suitable home** – help, advice and support in finding and maintaining suitable accommodation for independent living in the community;
- **support with daily living skills** – help, advice and training in the day-to-day skills needed for living independently, such as budgeting and cooking;
- **support in accessing benefits, health and community care services** – information, advice and help in claiming benefits or accessing community care or health services;
- **help in establishing and maintaining social support** – help in rebuilding or establishing social networks that can help counter isolation and help support independent living.

4.13. Services might be delivered through:

- **floating support services** – using support workers who travel to clients' accommodation in order to provide support. These services can operate across all tenures and generally provide time-limited and low intensity support;
- **short and medium stay housing with support** – including direct access schemes, night shelters, hostels, transitional housing and supported lodgings. Some of these services may specialise in supporting particular groups of individuals at risk of homelessness, such as vulnerable young people;
- **long-stay supported housing services** – to provide ongoing support to those who are unable to live independently in the community.

4.14. Housing-related support can be funded through the Supporting People programme, and close co-operation between housing authorities and the Supporting People team will be essential for ensuring effective support for households who have experienced homelessness, particularly through the local Commissioning Body and Core Strategy Group. Further information on housing-related support services is provided in separate guidance, *Supporting People – Guide to Accommodation and Support Options for Homeless Households* (ODPM, 2003).

Other support services

4.15. Households who have experienced homelessness may need additional support services which are not directly housing-related and fall outside the scope of the Supporting People programme funding. Housing authorities will need to co-operate and work collaboratively with other departments within the authority and a wide range of statutory, voluntary and private sector agencies in order to ensure that the support which is required is provided. Joint working with commissioners/planners and providers of the following services will be particularly important:

- health services;
- drug/alcohol services including Drug Action Teams;
- social services;

Appendix 2
England: Homelessness

- children's and young persons' services (eg Connexions, Sure Start children's centres, child care services);
- voluntary and community sector service providers;
- National Offender Management Service (incorporating the Prison Service and the Probation Service);
- Youth Offending Teams;
- Crime and Disorder Reduction Partnerships;
- the Police;
- education and training services;
- the Employment Service (Jobcentre Plus);
- grant making charities and trusts;
- local strategic partnerships.

Support for households in temporary accommodation

4.16. The provision of support to households placed in temporary accommodation is essential to ensure that they are able to continue to enjoy a reasonable quality of life and access the range of services they need. In formulating their homelessness strategies, housing authorities should consider what arrangements need to be in place to ensure that households placed in temporary accommodation, within their district or outside, are able to access relevant support services. In particular households will need to be able to access:

- primary care services such as health visitors and GPs;
- appropriate education services;
- relevant social services; and
- employment and training services.

4.17. Housing authorities will need to liaise and work collaboratively with the relevant service providers to ensure that appropriate arrangements are put in place and monitored. When households are placed in temporary accommodation, it is recommended that housing authorities offer to liaise with the relevant health, education and social services departments in the area in which the households are temporarily housed. Liaison will be particularly important in cases where households have to be accommodated in the district of another housing authority.

4.18. The Secretary of State recommends that housing authorities offer to liaise with the appropriate Primary Care Trust of all families with babies or young children who are placed in temporary accommodation, to ensure that they have the opportunity to receive health and developmental checks from health visitors and/or other primary health care professionals and can participate in vaccination programmes. It would be insufficient for an authority simply to provide such a family with details of health centres and GP practices in the area.

Notify

4.19. Authorities are encouraged to participate in any regional or sub-regional arrangements which facilitate the notification of other authorities and agencies about the location and support needs of households in temporary accommodation. When considering procedures for notifying the relevant agencies of placements in temporary accommodation, housing authorities may wish to have regard to NOTIFY – a web-based notification and information system administered by the Greater London Authority (GLA).

4.20. NOTIFY is designed to improve access to services for households placed in temporary accommodation. Its primary role is to notify relevant services of the placement or movement of households placed in temporary accommodation by London boroughs under the homelessness legislation. The system uses information provided by London borough housing departments to notify housing, education, social services and Primary Care Trusts about households placed in, moving between or leaving temporary accommodation. Information is contained in a database and updated weekly. Authorised users of the NOTIFY notifications website can view information held on NOTIFY at any time, by accessing that website. Relevant services receive a weekly email alert from NOTIFY, informing them of any unviewed notifications and reminding them to access the website. NOTIFY will also shortly provide access for each borough to its own operational management data. The system also has the capacity to analyse aggregated data both at borough and London level. For further information on NOTIFY see notifylondon.gov.uk or contact notify@london.gov.uk.

CHAPTER 5: WORKING WITH OTHERS

5.1. This chapter provides guidance to housing authorities on working in partnership with other agencies to deliver co-ordinated and effective services to tackle homelessness. It considers the range of organisations and people that contribute to preventing and tackling homelessness and provides examples of types of joint working. It also sets out the statutory provisions that require co-operation between various authorities.

5.2. Under s 3(5) of the 2002 Act, when formulating a homelessness strategy the housing authority must consider, among other things, the extent to which any of the strategy's objectives could be achieved through joint action involving two or more of the organisations tackling homelessness in the district. Whilst housing authorities are best placed to take the strategic lead in tackling homelessness, it is vital that as part of their homelessness strategies effective partnerships are developed with other organisations to deliver co-ordinated and more effective approaches to tackling homelessness locally that address not only housing need but all aspects of social need.

Why joint working?

5.3. At its best, joint working can result in higher quality and more efficient and cost-effective services. Joint working can:

- expand the knowledge and expertise of partner agencies;
- help to provide higher quality integrated services to clients with multiple needs;
- help to ensure people who are homeless or at risk of homelessness do not fall through the net because no one agency can meet all their needs;
- reduce wasteful referrals and duplicated work between agencies. For example, common procedures for assessing clients and exchanging information mean homeless people do not have to be repeatedly assessed by different agencies.

Organisations/people working to prevent and tackle homelessness

5.4. The most effective homelessness strategies will be those which harness the potential of all the organisations and persons working to prevent and tackle homelessness in the district, and which ensure that all the activities concerned are consistent and complementary. Joint working could involve the social services authority, the Primary Care Trust, other public bodies such as the National Offender Management Service, voluntary and community sector organisations, registered social landlords, private landlords, and any other relevant organisations. Housing authorities should also consider joint working with other agencies, for example, the Police and voluntary and community sector organisations, to tackle issues related to homelessness such as street drinking, begging, drug misuse and anti-social behaviour. Such collaborative working can help reduce the numbers of people sleeping rough and provide effective services targeted at those who are homeless or at risk of becoming homeless. Annex 3 provides an indicative list of other authorities, organisations and persons whose activities may contribute to preventing and tackling homelessness. Chapter 2 provides guidance on the range of activities that housing authorities might undertake in conjunction with other bodies in order to prevent homelessness.

5.5. Housing authorities should also consider developing cross-boundary partnerships to help tackle homelessness, for example with neighbouring local authorities and local strategic partnerships. Initiatives at regional, cross-regional and sub-regional level that address issues which cut across administrative boundaries may also be relevant – for example regional strategies for refugee integration or reducing re-offending.

Types of joint working

5.6. Joint working can take many forms. Examples of types of collaborative working that could help to achieve the objectives of a homelessness strategy might include:

- establishment of a multi-agency forum for key practitioners and providers to share knowledge, information, ideas and complementary practices;
- clear links between the homelessness strategy and other key strategies such as Supporting People, and the NHS Local Delivery Plan;
- protocols for the referral of clients between services and sharing information between services – for example a joint protocol between hospital-based social workers and housing officers to address the housing needs of patients to be discharged from hospital;
- joint consideration of the needs of homeless people by housing and social services authorities under Part 7, the *Children Act 1989* and community care legislation;
- establishment of formal links with other services – for example with those provided by voluntary and community sector organisations;
- joint planning and commissioning of services;
- joint training;
- funding of joint posts, for example with the social services authority;
- senior housing representation on key corporate groups such as the Local Strategic Partnership (LSP) and the Crime and Disorder Reduction Partnership (CDRP);
- senior commitment from all stakeholders to joined-up working to ensure the homelessness strategy action plan is carried out;
- appropriate user involvement and consultation.

5.7. When offering housing advice and assistance, housing authorities should consider devising screening procedures that identify at an early stage those cases where there is a need for case-specific joint working. Authorities may also wish to encourage their partner agencies to develop similar procedures. Where there is a need for such an approach, authorities are encouraged to adopt agreed protocols to ensure that appropriate action can be quickly initiated. Early appraisal of all clients who may require multiple assessments, by whichever authority is first approached, with agreed triggers and procedures for further action, may help to prevent duplication of enquiries.

5.8. *Homelessness Strategies – A good practice handbook* (DTLR, March 2002) provides advice on successful joint working and the establishment of good links between different agencies and programmes that can prevent and alleviate homelessness. The handbook also signposts to other sources of guidance, for example, on joint protocols, joint commissioning and joint assessments.

The statutory framework

5.9. The need for co-operation between statutory authorities is recognised in legislation:

- s 213, s 213A and s 170 of the *Housing Act 1996*;
- s 1 of the *Homelessness Act 2002*;
- s 2 of the *Local Government Act 2000*;
- s 27 of the *Children Act 1989*;

- s 10, s 11 and s 13 of the *Children Act 2004*;
- s 47 of the *National Health Service and Community Care Act 1990*;
- s 27 and s 31 of the *Health Act 1999*.

These provisions are outlined in more detail below. However, the absence of a formal legal duty should not act as a barrier to joint working. Rather this should be predicated on meeting local needs and effectively implementing the homelessness strategy.

Housing Act 1996

Section 213

5.10. Where housing or inquiry duties arise under the 1996 Act a housing authority may seek co-operation from another relevant housing authority or body or a social services authority in England, Scotland or Wales. The authority or body to whom the request is made must co-operate to the extent that is reasonable in the circumstances. For this purpose, 'relevant housing authority or body' will include:

in England and Wales:

– another housing authority,

– a registered social landlord,

– a housing action trust, and

in Scotland:

– a local authority,

– a registered social landlord, and

– Scottish Homes.

5.11. The duty on the housing authority, body or social services authority receiving such a request to co-operate will depend on their other commitments and responsibilities. However, they cannot adopt a general policy of refusing such requests, and each case will need to be considered in the circumstances at the time.

5.12. Section 170 of the 1996 Act also provides that where a registered social landlord (RSL) has been requested by a housing authority to offer accommodation to people with priority under its allocation scheme, the RSL must co-operate to such extent as is reasonable in the circumstances. RSLs have a key role to play in preventing and tackling homelessness. See Annex 5 for guidance on co-operation between RSLs and housing authorities.

Section 213A

5.13. Section 213A applies where the housing authority has reason to believe than an applicant with whom a person under the age of 18 resides, or might normally be expected to reside, may be ineligible for assistance, or homeless, or threatened with homelessness, intentionally. Housing authorities are required to have arrangements in place to ensure that all such applicants are invited to agree to the housing authority notifying the social services authority of the essential facts of their case. This will give social services the opportunity to consider the circumstances of the child(ren) and family and plan any response that may be deemed by them to be appropriate. See Chapter 13 for further guidance on s 213A.

Local Government Acts

5.14. The promotion of well-being power contained in s 2 of the *Local Government Act 2000* gives local authorities substantial capacity for cross-boundary partnership working with other authorities and partners, such as the health and social services sectors. In particular, the power provides local authorities with increased scope to improve the social, economic and environmental well-being of their communities. Section 2(5) of the *Local Government Act 2000* makes it clear that local authorities may act in relation to and for the benefit of any person or area outside their own area if they consider that to do so is likely to promote or improve the social, economic or environmental well-being of their own area. This, therefore, provides scope for:

- co-operation between neighbouring local authorities and local strategic partnerships; and
- initiatives at regional, cross-regional and sub-regional level that address issues which cut across administrative boundaries.

It should be noted, however, that the s 2 power cannot be used by authorities to delegate, or contract out their functions. In order to do this, authorities will need to make use of specific powers such as those in s 101 of the *Local Government Act 1972* which provides for the joint exercise of functions between local authorities.

Children Act 1989

5.15. Under s 27 of the Children Act 1989 ('the 1989 Act'), a local authority can ask a range of other statutory authorities, including a housing authority, to help them in delivering services for children and families, under their functions in Part 3 of the 1989 Act. Authorities must comply with such a request to the extent that it is compatible with their own statutory duties and other obligations, and does not unduly prejudice the discharge of any of their own functions. They cannot adopt a general policy of refusing such requests, and each case will need to be considered according to the circumstances at the time.

5.16. Children and young people should not be sent to and fro between different authorities (or between different departments within authorities). To provide an effective safety net for vulnerable young people who are homeless or at risk of homelessness, housing and social services will need to work together. Effective collaborative working will require clear corporate policies and departmental procedures agreed between the relevant departments. These should make provision for speedy resolution of any dispute as to which department should take responsibility for a particular case. Joint agreements

Appendix 2
England: Homelessness

should cover not only the assessment of clients, but should also reflect the strategic planning and delivery of provision to be set out in the local Children and Young People's Plan. Local Safeguarding Children Boards, which will co-ordinate and ensure the effectiveness of local work to safeguard and promote the welfare of children, may also be involved in drawing up policies and procedures to ensure effective inter-agency co-operation (see also paragraphs 5.17–5.20 below) and Chapter 13.

5.17. Under the 1989 Act, young people leaving care and 16/17 year old children assessed as in need are owed duties which may extend to the provision of accommodation. Where social services approach a housing authority for assistance in housing a young person, the housing authority must co-operate subject to the conditions referred to above in para 5.16. Whether a young person is accommodated under the auspices of the social services authority or the housing authority is a matter for individual authorities to determine in each case. Ideally the relationship of the two authorities should be symbiotic, with jointly agreed protocols in place in respect of the assessment of needs. In many cases the social services authority will have a continuing responsibility for the welfare of vulnerable young people and for assisting them in the transition to adulthood and independent living. Under the 1989 Act, these responsibilities can extend until the young person is aged 18 and in the case of care leavers until the age of 21 (or beyond that age if they are in an agreed programme of education and training). Thus, social services authorities can request assistance from housing authorities in meeting their obligations to provide accommodation for a young person and housing authorities can look to social services authorities to provide the support that young homeless applicants may require. In some cases, housing and social services authorities will both have responsibilities towards young people and will need to work together in order to ensure that an appropriate combination of housing and support is arranged to help the young person to live independently successfully.

Children Act 2004

5.18. The *Children Act 2004* ('the 2004 Act') provides the legislative support for the *Every Child Matters: Change for Children* programme which sets out a national framework for local change programmes to build services around the needs of children and young people. Improved outcomes for children will be driven by an analysis of local priorities and secured through more integrated front-line delivery such as multi-agency working, integrated processes such as the Common Assessment Framework, integrated strategy with joint planning and commissioning, and governance arrangements such as the creation of a Director of Children's Services and lead member for children's services.

5.19. To support the integration of systems to improve outcomes for children and young people by the creation of children's trusts, s 10 of the 2004 Act establishes a duty on county level and unitary authorities[3] to make

---

3   Section 65 of the Children Act 2004 uses the term 'children's services authority' to define these authorities as: a county council in England; a metropolitan district council; a

arrangements to promote co-operation between the authority, relevant partners (including district councils) and other persons or bodies engaged in activities in relation to children, to improve the well-being of children and young people in the authority's area. Relevant partners are required to co-operate with the authority. Section 11 of the 2004 Act requires a range of agencies – including county level and unitary authorities and district authorities where there are two tiers of local government – to make arrangements for ensuring that their functions are discharged having regard to the need to safeguard and promote the welfare of children. Section 13 of the 2004 Act requires county level and unitary authorities to set up a Local Safeguarding Children Board (LSCB) incorporating key organisations including district councils where relevant. As set out in s 14, the objective of the LSCB is to co-ordinate and ensure the effectiveness of what is done by each person or body represented on the board to safeguard and promote the welfare of children in that area.

5.20. The 2004 Act also makes provision for indexes containing basic information about children and young people to enable better sharing of information. In addition, each local authority is required to draw up a Children and Young People's Plan (CYPP) by April 2006. The CYPP will be a single, strategic, over-arching plan for all services affecting children and young people. The CYPP and the process of joint planning should support local authorities and their partners as they work together. An integrated inspection framework is also being created with Joint Area Reviews assessing local areas' progress in improving outcomes.

The Department for Education and Skills has produced statutory guidance on the *Children Act 2004* which is available from **www.everychildmatters.gov.uk**.

National Health Service and Community Care Act 1990

5.21. Under the National Health Service (NHS) and Community Care Act 1990 ('the 1990 Act'), social services authorities are required to carry out an assessment of any person who may have a need for community care services. The purpose of the legislation is to ensure that the planning and assessment processes identify a person's full range of needs, including housing needs. Section 47 of the 1990 Act requires social service authorities to notify the housing authority if there appears to be a housing need when the assessment is carried out. The 'housing need', for example, may be for renovation or adaptation of the person's current accommodation or for alternative accommodation.

5.22. An assessment of vulnerability under the homelessness legislation will not necessarily mean that a client is eligible for social care services. Policy guidance on fair access to care services (FACS) was published on 2 June 2002 under guidance of local authority circular (LAC) (2002) 13. The guidance

Appendix 2
England: Homelessness

---

non-metropolitan district council for an area where there is no county council; a London borough council; the Common Council of the City of London and the Council of the Isles of Scilly.

provides authorities with an eligibility framework for adult social care for them to use when setting and applying their eligibility criteria.

Health Act 1999

5.23. Section 27 of the Health Act 1999 ('the 1999 Act') requires NHS bodies and local authorities to co-operate with one another in exercising their respective functions in order to secure and advance the health and welfare of the people of England and Wales.

5.24. Under s 31 of the 1999 Act, partnership arrangements can be designed to help break down the barriers between NHS and local authority services by removing existing constraints in the system and increasing flexibility in the provision and commissioning of services. The legislation introduces three flexibilities: pooled budgets, lead commissioning and integrated provision. Any health-related local authority function can be included in these partnerships, for example, housing, social services, education and leisure services.

National Standards, Local Action: Health and Social Care Standards and Planning Framework 2005/06–2007/08

5.25. This document sets out the framework for all NHS organisations and social services authorities to use in planning over the financial years 2005/06–2007/08. It looks to Primary Care Trusts (PCTs) and local authorities to lead community partnership by even closer joint working to take forward the NHS Improvement Plan. Building on joint work on Local Strategic Partnerships (LSPs), they will need to work in partnership with other NHS organisations in preparing Local Delivery Plans (LDPs) for the period 2005/06 to 2007/08.

Mental health

5.26. The Mental Health National Service Framework (NSF 30/09/1999) addresses the mental health needs of working age adults up to 65. It sets out national standards; national service models; local action and national underpinning programmes for implementation; and a series of national milestones to assure progress, with performance indicators to support effective performance management. An organisational framework for providing integrated services and for commissioning services across the spectrum is also included.

5.27. The Government wants to ensure that people suffering from mental illness receive appropriate care and assistance, particularly those whose illness is severe and enduring. Research has shown that provision of suitable, settled housing is essential to the well-being of this vulnerable group. A key element in the spectrum of care and support is the development of a care plan under the Care Programme Approach (CPA). The initial assessment and ongoing reviews under the CPA must include an assessment of an individual's housing needs. It is essential that housing authorities liaise closely with social services authorities so that any provision of housing is appropriate to the needs of the individual, and meshes with the social and health care support that may be an essential part of the person's care programme.

5.28. This is equally important for young people up to the age of 18. Chapter 9 of the National Service Framework for Children, Young People and Maternity Services published in 2004 makes clear that use of the CPA is also a key marker of good practice for child and adolescent mental health services working with young people with high levels of mental health need.

CHAPTER 6: APPLICATIONS, INQUIRIES, DECISIONS AND NOTIFICATIONS

6.1. **This chapter provides guidance on dealing with applications for accommodation or assistance in obtaining accommodation; a housing authority's duty to carry out inquiries (where it has reason to believe an applicant may be homeless or threatened with homelessness); and, following inquiries, an authority's duty to notify an applicant of its decision.**

Applications for assistance

6.2. Under s 184 of the 1996 Act, if a housing authority has reason to believe that a person applying to the authority for accommodation or assistance in obtaining accommodation may be homeless or threatened with homelessness, the authority must make such inquiries as are necessary to satisfy itself whether the applicant is eligible for assistance and if so, whether any duty, and if so what duty, is owed to that person under Part 7 of the 1996 Act. The definitions of 'homeless' and 'threatened with homelessness' are discussed in Chapter 8.

Preventing homelessness

6.3. Under s 179, housing authorities have a duty to ensure that advice and information about homelessness and the prevention of homelessness are available free of charge to anyone in their district (see Chapter 2 for further guidance on providing advice and information to prevent homelessness). In many cases early, effective intervention can prevent homelessness occurring. Many people who face the potential loss of their current home will be seeking practical advice and assistance to help them remain in their accommodation or secure alternative accommodation. Some may be seeking to apply for assistance under the homelessness legislation without being aware of other options that could help them to secure accommodation. Authorities should explain the various housing options that are available. These might include:

- advice and assistance (eg legal advice or mediation with a landlord) to enable them to remain in their current home;
- assistance (eg rent deposit or guarantee) to obtain accommodation in the private rented sector;

- an application for an allocation of long term social housing accommodation through a social housing waiting list or choice-based lettings scheme; or
- advice on how to apply to another social landlord for accommodation.

6.4. Housing authorities should ensure that the implications and likely outcomes of the available housing options are made clear to all applicants, including the distinction between having a priority need for accommodation under Part 7 and being in a 'reasonable preference' category for an allocation of housing under Part 6. Authorities must not avoid their obligations under Part 7 (especially the duty to make inquiries under s 184), but it is open to them to suggest alternative solutions in cases of potential homelessness where these would be appropriate and acceptable to the applicant.

Interim duty to accommodate

6.5. If a housing authority has reason to believe that an applicant may be eligible for assistance, homeless and have a priority need, the authority will have **an immediate duty under s 188 to ensure that suitable accommodation is available for the applicant** (and his or her household) pending the completion of the authority's inquiries and its decision as to what duty, if any, is owed to the applicant under Part 7 of the Act. Chapter 7 provides guidance on the interim duty to accommodate. Authorities are reminded that 'having reason to believe' is a lower test than 'being satisfied'.

Form of the application

6.6. Applications can be made by any adult to any department of the local authority and expressed in any particular form; they need not be expressed as explicitly seeking assistance under Part 7. Applications may also be made by a person acting on behalf of the applicant, for example, by a social worker or solicitor acting in a professional capacity, or by a relative or friend in circumstances where the applicant is unable to make an application themselves.

Applications to more than one housing authority

6.7. In some cases applicants may apply to more than one housing authority simultaneously and housing authorities will need to be alert to cases where an applicant is doing this. In such cases, where a housing authority has reason to believe that the applicant may be homeless or threatened with homelessness, it may wish to contact the other housing authorities involved, to agree which housing authority will take responsibility for conducting inquiries. Where another housing authority has previously made decisions about an applicant's circumstances, a housing authority considering a fresh application may wish to have regard to those decisions. However, housing authorities should not rely solely on decisions made by another housing authority and will need to make their own inquiries in order to reach an independent decision on whether any duty, and if so which duty, is owed under Part 7. Any arrangements for the discharge of any of their functions by another housing authority must comply with s 101 of the *Local Government Act 1972*.

Service provision

6.8. A need for accommodation or assistance in obtaining accommodation can arise at any time. Housing authorities will therefore need to provide access to advice and assistance at all times during normal office hours, and have arrangements in place for 24-hour emergency cover, eg by enabling telephone access to an appropriate duty officer. The police and other relevant services should be provided with details of how to access the service outside normal office hours.

6.9. In the interests of good administration, it is recommended that housing authorities should give proper consideration to the location of, and accessibility to, advice and information about homelessness and the prevention of homelessness, including the need to ensure privacy during interviews. Details of the service including the opening hours, address, telephone numbers and the 24-hour emergency contact should be well publicised within the housing authority's district.

6.10. Housing authorities should provide applicants with a clear and simple explanation of their procedures for handling applications and making decisions. It is recommended that this is provided in written form, for example as a leaflet, as well as orally. In order to ensure advice and assistance are accessible to everyone in the district, it is recommended that information is made available in the main languages spoken in the area, and that for languages less frequently spoken there is access to interpreters. Applicants should be kept informed of the progress of their application and the timescales involved for making a decision on their case. They should also be given a realistic expectation of the assistance to which they may be entitled.

6.11. Under s 214, it is an offence for a person, knowingly or recklessly to make a false statement, or knowingly to withhold information, with intent to induce the authority to believe that he or she, or another person, is entitled to accommodation under Part 7. If, before the applicant receives notification of a decision, there is any change of facts material to his or her case, he or she must inform the housing authority of this as soon as possible. Housing authorities must ensure that all applicants are made aware of these obligations and that they are explained in ordinary language. Housing authorities are advised to ensure that the obligations are conveyed sensitively to avoid intimidating applicants.

Inquiries

6.12. Under s 184, where a housing authority has reason to believe that an applicant may be homeless or threatened with homelessness, it must make inquiries to satisfy itself whether the applicant is eligible for assistance (see Chapter 9) and, if so, whether any duty and if so what duty is owed to him or her under Part 7. In order to determine this, the authority will need to establish whether the applicant is homeless or threatened with homelessness (see Chapter 8), whether he or she became homeless, or threatened with homelessness, intentionally (see Chapter 11) and whether he or she has a priority need for accommodation (see Chapter 10).

6.13. In addition to determining whether an applicant is owed any duty under Part 7, housing authorities are reminded that they have a **power** to provide further assistance to applicants who are eligible for assistance, homeless (or threatened with homelessness) unintentionally and do not have a priority need. Under s 192(3), housing authorities may secure that accommodation is available for applicants who are eligible, unintentionally homeless and do not have a priority need (see Chapter 15 for further guidance). Under s 195(9), housing authorities may take reasonable steps to secure that accommodation does not cease to be available for applicants who are eligible for assistance, unintentionally threatened with homelessness and do not have a priority need for accommodation (see paragraph 14.7 for guidance on steps to secure that accommodation does not cease to be available).

6.14. Under s 184(2), housing authorities may also make inquiries to decide whether the applicant has a local connection with another housing authority district in England, Wales or Scotland, but they are not required to do so. The possibility of a referral of an applicant to another housing authority can only arise where the applicant has been accepted as eligible for assistance, unintentionally homeless and having a priority need for accommodation (see Chapter 18 for guidance on local connection and referrals).

6.15. The obligation to make inquiries, and satisfy itself whether a duty is owed, rests with the housing authority and it is not for applicants to 'prove their case'. Applicants should always be given the opportunity to explain their circumstances fully, particularly on matters that could lead to a decision against their interests, for example, a decision that an applicant is intentionally homeless.

6.16. Housing authorities should deal with inquiries as quickly as possible, whilst ensuring that they are thorough and, in any particular case, sufficient to enable the housing authority to satisfy itself what duty, if any, is owed or what other assistance can be offered. Housing authorities are obliged to begin inquiries as soon as they have reason to believe that an applicant may be homeless or threatened with homelessness and should aim to carry out an initial interview and preliminary assessment on the day an application is received. An early assessment will be vital to determine whether the housing authority has an immediate duty to secure accommodation under s 188 (see Chapter 7 for guidance on the interim duty to accommodate). Wherever possible, it is recommended that housing authorities aim to complete their inquiries and notify the applicant of their decision within 33 working days of accepting a duty to make inquiries under s 184. In many cases it should be possible for authorities to complete the inquiries significantly earlier.

Violence

6.17. Under s 177, it is not reasonable for a person to continue to occupy accommodation if it is probable that this will lead to domestic or other violence against him or her, or against a person who normally resides with him or her as a member of his or her family, or any other person who might reasonably be expected to reside with him or her. Violence includes threats of violence from another person which are likely to be carried out. Inquiries into cases where violence is alleged will need careful handling. It is essential that inquiries do not provoke further violence. It is not advisable for the housing authority to approach the alleged perpetrator, since this could generate further violence, and may delay the assessment. Housing authorities may, however, wish to seek information from friends and relatives of the applicant, social services and the police, as appropriate. In some cases, corroborative evidence of actual or threatened violence may not be available, for example, because there were no adult witnesses and/or the applicant was too frightened or ashamed to report incidents to family, friends or the police. In many cases involving violence, the applicant may be in considerable distress and an officer trained in dealing with the particular circumstances should conduct the interview. Applicants should be given the option of being interviewed by an officer of the same sex if they so wish.

6.18. In cases where violence is a feature and the applicant may have a local connection elsewhere, the housing authority, in considering whether to notify another housing authority about a possible referral of the case, must be aware that s 198 provides that an applicant cannot be referred to another housing authority if he or she, or any person who might reasonably be expected to reside with him or her, would be at risk of violence in the district of the other housing authority (see Chapter 18 for guidance on referrals to another housing authority).

Support needs

6.19. 16 and 17 year olds (including lone parents) who apply for housing assistance may also have care and support needs that need to be assessed. The Secretary of State recommends that housing authorities and social services authorities (and the relevant departments within unitary authorities) have arrangements in place for joint consideration of such young people's needs, whether the application is made initially to the housing department or social services department. See Chapter 12 for further guidance on 16 and 17 year olds.

Assistance from another authority or body

6.20. Under s 213, a housing authority may request another relevant housing authority or body to assist them in the discharge of their functions under Part 7. In such cases the authority or body must co-operate in rendering such assistance in the discharge of the functions to which the request relates as is reasonable in the circumstances. For example, a housing authority may request another housing authority to co-operate in providing information about a previous application. See paragraph 5.10 for further guidance on s 213.

Decisions/notifications

6.21. When a housing authority has completed its inquiries under s 184 it must notify the applicant in writing of its decision on the case. Where the decision is against the applicant's interests, eg a decision that he or she is ineligible for assistance, not homeless, not in priority need or homeless intentionally, the notification must explain clearly and fully the reasons for the decision. If the housing authority has decided that the conditions for referring the applicant's homelessness case to another housing authority have been met, they must notify the applicant of this and give their reasons for doing so.

6.22. All notifications must inform applicants of their right to request a review of the housing authority's decision and the time within which such a request must be made. At this stage, it is also recommended that housing authorities explain the review procedures. (See Chapter 19 for guidance on reviews of decisions and appeals to the county court).

6.23. It will be important to ensure that the applicant fully understands the decision and the nature of any housing duty that is owed. In cases where the applicant may have difficulty understanding the implications of the decision, it is recommended that housing authorities consider arranging for a member of staff to provide and explain the notification in person.

6.24. Under s 193(3A), where the housing authority accepts a duty to secure accommodation for an applicant under s 193(2), they must give the applicant a copy of the statement included in their allocation scheme of the housing authority's policy on offering people a choice of housing or the opportunity to express their preferences about the accommodation to be allocated to them. This statement is required to be included in the allocation scheme under s 167(1A).

6.25. Section 184(6) provides that where a notification is not received by an applicant, it can be treated as having been given to him or her, if it is made available at the housing authority's office for a reasonable period that would allow it to be collected by the applicant or by someone acting on his or her behalf.

Withdrawn applications

6.26. It is recommended that housing authorities have procedures in place for dealing with applications that are withdrawn or where someone fails to maintain contact with the housing authority after making an application. The Secretary of State considers that it would be reasonable to consider an application closed where there has been no contact with the applicant for three months or longer. Any further approach from the applicant after this time may need to be considered as a fresh application. Where an applicant renews contact within three months the housing authority will need to consider any change of circumstances that may affect the application.

Further applications

6.27. There is no period of disqualification if someone wants to make a fresh application. Where a person whose application has been previously considered and determined under Part 7 makes a fresh application, the authority will need to decide whether there are any new facts in the fresh application which render it different from the earlier application. If no new facts are revealed, or any new facts are of a trivial nature, the authority would not be required to consider the new application. However, where the fresh application does reveal substantive new facts, the authority must treat the fresh application in the same way as it would any other application for accommodation or assistance in obtaining accommodation. Therefore, if the authority has reason to believe that the person is homeless, or threatened with homelessness, the authority should make inquiries under s 184 and decide whether any duty is owed under s 188(1).

CHAPTER 7: INTERIM DUTY TO ACCOMMODATE

7.1. **This chapter provides guidance on housing authorities' interim duty to secure that accommodation is available for an applicant if they have reason to believe that the applicant may be homeless, eligible for assistance and has a priority need.**

7.2. Section 188(1) imposes an interim duty on housing authorities to secure that accommodation is available for an applicant (and his or her household) pending their decision as to what duty, if any, is owed to the applicant under Part 7 of the Act if they have reason to believe that the applicant may:

a)   be homeless,
b)   be eligible for assistance, and
c)   have a priority need.

7.3. The threshold for the duty is low as the local authority only has to have a reason to believe that the applicant **may** be homeless, eligible for assistance and have a priority need. (See paragraph 6.5 for guidance on the 'reason to believe' test.)

7.4. The s 188(1) duty applies even where the authority considers the applicant may not have a local connection with their district and may have one with the district of another housing authority (s 188(2)). Applicants cannot be referred to another housing authority unless the housing authority dealing with the application is satisfied that s 193 applies (ie the applicant is eligible for assistance, unintentionally homeless and has a priority need). (See Chapter 18 for guidance on referrals to other housing authorities.)

Suitability of accommodation

7.5. The accommodation provided under s 188(1) must be suitable for the applicant and his or her household and the suitability requirements under s 206(1) and s 210(1) apply (see Chapter 17 for guidance on the suitability of accommodation). The applicant does not have the right to ask for a review of the housing authority's decision as to the suitability of accommodation secured under the interim duty, but housing authorities are reminded that such decisions could be subject to judicial review.

7.6. Housing authorities should avoid using Bed &Breakfast (B&B) accommodation wherever possible. Where B&B accommodation has been used in an emergency situation, applicants should be moved to more suitable accommodation as soon as possible. The *Homelessness (Suitability of Accommodation) (England) Order 2003* provides that B&B accommodation is not suitable accommodation for families with children and households that include a pregnant woman unless there is no alternative accommodation available and then only for a maximum of six weeks.

Discharging the interim duty

7.7. Where the s 188(1) interim duty is being discharged, inquiries should be completed as quickly as possible to minimise uncertainty for the applicant and the period for which accommodation needs to be secured by the housing authority. (See Chapter 6 for guidance on inquiries).

7.8. Housing authorities can discharge their interim duty to secure accommodation by providing their own accommodation or by arranging that it is provided by some other person, or by providing advice and assistance so that it will be provided by some other person. (See Chapter 16 for more information on discharging the duty to secure accommodation).

Ending the interim duty

7.9. The s 188(1) interim duty ends once the housing authority has notified the applicant of its decision as to what duty, if any, is owed to him or her under Part 7, even if the applicant requests a review of the decision.

7.10. Where, having completed their inquiries, the housing authority is satisfied that they are under no further duty to secure accommodation, they should give the applicant a reasonable period of notice to vacate the accommodation to enable him or her to make alternative accommodation arrangements for him/herself. The time allowed should be reasonable when judged against the circumstances of the applicant. Housing authorities should give the applicant time to consider whether to request a review of their decision and, if a review is requested, will need to consider whether to exercise their discretionary power under s 188(3) to secure that accommodation is available (see paragraph 7.13 below).

7.11. It has been established that, as a general rule, accommodation provided pending inquiries under s 184 does not create a tenancy or a licence under the *Protection from Eviction Act 1977*. The courts have applied this principle in cases where the accommodation provided was B&B accommodation in a hotel and where it was a self-contained flat. Consequently, where this general rule applies, housing authorities are required only to provide an applicant with reasonable notice to vacate accommodation provided under the interim duty, and do not need to apply for a possession order from the court. Authorities should note, however, that this general rule may be displaced by an agreement between the housing authority and the applicant, or if the occupation of the accommodation is allowed to continue on more than a transient basis.

7.12. In cases involving applicants who have children under 18 where the housing authority are satisfied that the applicant is ineligible for assistance, the housing authority must alert the social services authority, or social services department, as appropriate, to the case (see Chapter 13 for further guidance on co-operation with social services). Applicants should be invited to consent to social services being notified of the case, but in certain circumstances, for example where the housing authority are concerned about the welfare of the child, they should disclose information about the case even where consent has not been given.

Accommodation pending a review

7.13. Where a review of a decision of a housing authority is requested under s 202, although there is no duty under s 188(1), under s 188(3) the housing authority has a discretionary power to provide accommodation pending the outcome of the review. Failure to consider exercising this discretionary power could be the subject of challenge by judicial review proceedings. Housing authorities are reminded that applicants have 21 days in which to request a review of a decision. (See Chapter 19 for guidance on review of decisions and Chapter 15 for guidance on powers to accommodate pending a review).

CHAPTER 8: HOMELESS OR THREATENED WITH HOMELESSNESS

8.1. This chapter provides guidance on how to determine whether a person is 'homeless' or 'threatened with homelessness' for the purposes of Part 7.

8.2. Under s 184 of the 1996 Act, if a housing authority has reason to believe that a person applying to the housing authority for accommodation, or assistance in obtaining accommodation, may be homeless or threatened with homelessness, the housing authority must make inquiries to satisfy itself whether the applicant is eligible for assistance and if so, whether a duty is owed to that person under Part 7 of the 1996 Act (see Chapter 6 for guidance on applications for assistance).

Threatened with homelessness

8.3. Under s 175(4), a person is 'threatened with homelessness' if he or she is likely to become homeless within 28 days. In many cases, effective intervention can enable homelessness to be prevented or the loss of the current home to be delayed sufficiently to allow for a planned move. The Secretary of State considers that housing authorities should take steps to prevent homelessness wherever possible, offering a broad range of advice and assistance for those in housing need. Authorities should not wait until homelessness is a likelihood or is imminent before providing advice and assistance. (See Chapter 2 for guidance on preventing homelessness).

Homeless

8.4. There are a number of different factors that determine whether a person is homeless. Under s 175, a person is homeless if he or she has no accommodation in the UK or elsewhere which is available for his or her occupation and which that person has a legal right to occupy. A person is also homeless if he or she has accommodation but cannot secure entry to it, or the accommodation is a moveable structure, vehicle or vessel designed or adapted for human habitation (such as a caravan or house boat) and there is no place where it can be placed in order to provide accommodation. A person who has accommodation is to be treated as homeless where it would not be reasonable for him or her to continue to occupy that accommodation.

Available for occupation

8.5. Section 176 provides that accommodation shall be treated as available for a person's occupation only if it is available for occupation by him or her together with:

i)   any other person who normally resides with him or her as a member of the family, or

ii) any other person who might reasonably be expected to reside with him or her.

The first group covers those members of the family who normally reside with the applicant. The phrase 'as a member of the family' although not defined, will include those with close blood or marital relationships and cohabiting partners (including same sex partners), and, where such a person is an established member of the household, the accommodation must provide for him or her as well. The second group relates to any other person, and includes those who may not have been living as part of the household at the time of the application, but whom it would be reasonable to expect to live with the applicant as part of his or her household. Persons in the second group might include a companion for an elderly or disabled person, or children who are being fostered by the applicant or a member of his or her family. The second group will also include those members of the family who were not living as part of the household at the time of the application but who nonetheless might reasonably be expected to form part of it.

8.6. It is for the housing authority to assess whether any other person might reasonably be expected to live with the applicant and there will be a range of situations that the authority will need to consider. Persons who would normally live with the applicant but who are unable to do so because there is no accommodation in which they can all live together should be included in the assessment. When dealing with a family which has split up, housing authorities will need to take a decision as to which members of the family normally reside, or might be expected to reside, with the applicant. A court may have made a residence order indicating with whom the children are to live, but in many cases it will be a matter of agreement between the parents and a court will not have been involved.

Legal right to occupy accommodation

8.7. Under s 175(1), a person is homeless if he or she has no accommodation which he or she can legally occupy by virtue of:

i)   an interest in it (eg as an owner, lessee or tenant) or by virtue of a court order;

ii)   an express or implied licence to occupy it (eg as a lodger, as an employee with a service occupancy, or when living with a relative); or

iii) any enactment or rule of law giving him or her the right to remain in occupation or restricting the right of another person to recover possession (eg a person retaining possession as a statutory tenant under the Rent Acts where that person's contractual rights to occupy have expired or been terminated).

8.8. A person who has been occupying accommodation as a licensee whose licence has been terminated (and who does not have any other accommodation available for his or her occupation) is homeless because he or she no longer has a legal right to continue to occupy, despite the fact that that person may continue to occupy but as a trespasser. This may include, for example:

i)   those required to leave hostels or hospitals; or

ii)   former employees occupying premises under a service occupancy which is dependent upon contracts of employment which have ended.

People asked to leave accommodation by family or friends

8.9. Some applicants may have been asked to leave their current accommodation by family or friends with whom they have been living. In such cases, the housing authority will need to consider carefully whether the applicant's licence to occupy the accommodation has in fact been revoked. Housing authorities may need to interview the parents or friends to establish whether they are genuinely revoking the licence to occupy and rendering the applicants homeless. Authorities are encouraged to be sensitive to situations where parents or carers may have been providing a home for a family member with support needs (for example a person with learning difficulties) for a number of years and who are genuinely finding it difficult to continue with that arrangement, but are reluctant to revoke their licence to occupy formally until alternative accommodation can be secured.

8.10. In some cases the applicant may be unable to stay in his or her accommodation and in others there may be scope for preventing or postponing homelessness, and providing the applicant with an opportunity to plan their future accommodation and pursue various housing options with assistance from the housing authority. However, housing authorities will need to be sensitive to the possibility that for some applicants it may not be safe for them to remain in, or return to, their home because of a risk of violence or abuse.

8.11. In areas of high demand for affordable housing, people living with family and friends may have genuine difficulties in finding alternative accommodation that can lead to friction and disputes within their current home, culminating in a threat of homelessness. In some cases external support, or the promise of assistance with alternative housing, may help to reduce tension and prevent homelessness. The use of family mediation services may assist here.

8.12. Housing authorities will also need to be alert to the possibility of collusion where family or friends agree to revoke a licence to occupy accommodation as part of an arrangement whose purpose is to enable the applicant to be entitled to assistance under Part 7. Some parents and children, for example, may seek to take advantage of the fact that 16 and 17 year old applicants have a priority need for accommodation (see also Chapter 11 on intentional homelessness).

16 and 17 year olds

8.13. The Secretary of State considers that, generally, it will be in the best interests of 16 and 17 year olds to live in the family home, unless it would be unsafe or unsuitable for them to do so because they would be at risk of violence or abuse. See Chapter 12 for further guidance on 16 and 17 year olds.

Tenant given notice

8.14. With certain exceptions, a person who has been occupying accommodation as a tenant and who has received a valid notice to quit, or notice that the landlord requires possession of the accommodation, would have the right to remain in occupation until a warrant for possession was executed (following the granting of an order for possession by the court). The exceptions are tenants with resident landlords and certain other tenants who do not benefit from the *Protection from Eviction Act 1977*. **However, authorities should note that the fact that a tenant has a right to remain in occupation does not necessarily mean that he or she is not homeless.** In assessing whether an applicant is homeless in cases where he or she is a tenant who has a right to remain in occupation pending execution of a warrant for possession, the housing authority will also need to consider whether it would be reasonable for him or her to continue to occupy the accommodation in the circumstances (see paragraphs 8.30–8.32 below).

8.15. Some tenants may face having to leave their accommodation because their landlord has defaulted on the mortgage of the property they rent. Where a mortgage lender starts possession proceedings, the lender is obliged to give written notice of the proceedings to the occupiers of the property before an order for possession is granted. The notice must be given after issue of the possession summons and at least 14 days before the court hearing. As for tenants given notice that the landlord requires possession of the accommodation (see paragraph 8.14 above), authorities will need to consider whether it would be reasonable for a tenant to continue to occupy the accommodation after receiving notice of possession proceedings from the lender.

Inability to secure entry to accommodation

8.16. Under s 175(2), a person is homeless if he or she has a legal entitlement to accommodation, but is unable to secure entry to it, for example:

- those who have been evicted illegally, or
- those whose accommodation is being occupied illegally by squatters.

Although legal remedies may be available to the applicant to regain possession of the accommodation, housing authorities cannot refuse to assist while he or she is actually homeless.

Accommodation consisting of a moveable structure

8.17. Section 175(2)(b) provides that a person is homeless if he or she has accommodation available for his or her occupation which is a moveable structure, vehicle or vessel designed or adapted for human habitation (eg a caravan or houseboat), and there is nowhere that he or she is entitled or permitted to place it and reside in it. The site or mooring for the moveable structure need not be permanent in order to avoid homelessness. In many cases the nature of the structure may reflect the itinerant lifestyle of the applicant, who may not be looking for a permanent site but somewhere to park or moor on a temporary basis.

Reasonable to continue to occupy

8.18. Section 175(3) provides that a person shall not be treated as having accommodation unless it is accommodation which it would be reasonable for him or her to continue to occupy. There are a number of provisions relating to whether or not it is reasonable for someone to continue to occupy accommodation and these are discussed below. There is no simple test of reasonableness. It is for the housing authority to make a judgment on the facts of each case, taking into account the circumstances of the applicant.

Domestic violence or other violence

8.19.   Section 177(1) provides that it is not reasonable for a person to continue to occupy accommodation if it is probable that this will lead to domestic violence or other violence against:

   i)   the applicant;
   ii)   a person who normally resides as a member of the applicant's family; or
   iii)   any other person who might reasonably be expected to reside with the applicant.

Section 177(1A) provides that violence means violence from another person or threats of violence from another person which are likely to be carried out. Domestic violence is violence from a person who is associated with the victim and also includes threats of violence which are likely to be carried out. Domestic violence is not confined to instances within the home but extends to violence outside the home.

8.20.   Section 178 provides that, for the purposes of defining domestic violence, a person is associated with another if:

   (a)   they are, or have been, married to each other;
   (b)   they are or have been civil partners of each other;
   (c)   they are, or have been, cohabitants (including same sex partners);
   (d)   they live, or have lived, in the same household;
   (e)   they are relatives, ie father, mother, stepfather, stepmother, son, daughter, stepson, stepdaughter, grandmother, grandfather, grandson, granddaughter, brother, sister, uncle, aunt, niece or nephew (whether of full blood, half blood or by affinity) of that person or of that person's spouse or former spouse. A person is also included if he or she would fall into any of these categories in relation to cohabitees or former cohabitees if they were married to each other;
   (f)   they have agreed to marry each other whether or not that agreement has been terminated;
   (g)   they have entered into a civil partnership agreement between them whether or not that agreement has been terminated;
   (h)   in relation to a child, each of them is a parent of the child or has, or has had, parental responsibility for the child (within the meaning of the *Children Act 1989*). A child is a person under 18 years of age;
   (i)   if a child has been adopted or freed for adoption (s 16(1) *Adoption Act 1976*), two persons are also associated if one is the natural parent or grandparent of the child and the other is the child of a person who has become the parent by virtue of an adoption order (s 72(1) *Adoption Act 1976*) or has applied for an adoption order or someone with whom the child has been placed for adoption.

8.21.   The Secretary of State considers that the term 'violence' should not be given a restrictive meaning, and that 'domestic violence' should be understood to include threatening behaviour, violence or abuse (psychological, physical, sexual, financial or emotional) between persons who are, or have been, intimate partners, family members or members of the same household, regardless of gender or sexuality.

8.22. An assessment of the likelihood of a threat of violence being carried out should not be based on whether there has been actual violence in the past. An assessment must be based on the facts of the case and devoid of any value judgments about what an applicant should or should not do, or should or should not have done, to mitigate the risk of any violence (eg seek police help or apply for an injunction against the perpetrator). Inquiries into cases where violence is alleged will need careful handling. See Chapter 6 for further guidance.

8.23. In cases involving violence, housing authorities may wish to inform applicants of the option of seeking an injunction, but should make clear that there is no obligation on the applicant to do so. Where applicants wish to pursue this option, it is advisable that they obtain independent advice as an injunction may be ill-advised in some circumstances. Housing authorities should recognise that injunctions ordering a person not to molest, or enter the home of, an applicant may not be effective in deterring perpetrators from carrying out further violence or incursions, and applicants may not have confidence in their effectiveness. Consequently, applicants should not be expected to return home on the strength of an injunction. To ensure applicants who have experienced actual or threatened violence get the support they need, authorities should inform them of appropriate organisations in the area such as agencies offering counselling and support as well as specialist advice.

8.24. When dealing with cases involving violence, or threat of violence, from outside the home, housing authorities should consider the option of improving the security of the applicant's home to enable him or her to continue to live there safely, where that is an option that the applicant wishes to pursue. In some cases, immediate action to improve security within the victim's home may prevent homelessness. A fast response combined with support from the housing authority, police and the voluntary sector may provide a victim with the confidence to remain in their home. When dealing with domestic violence within the home, where the authority is the landlord, housing authorities should consider the scope for evicting the perpetrator and allowing the victim to remain in their home. **However, where there would be a probability of violence if the applicant continued to occupy his or her present accommodation, the housing authority must treat the applicant as homeless and should not expect him or her to remain in, or return to, the accommodation. In all cases involving violence the safety of the applicant and his or her household should be the primary consideration at all stages of decision making as to whether or not the applicant remains in their own home.**

8.25. The effectiveness of housing authorities' services to assist victims of domestic violence and prevent further domestic violence is measured by Best Value Performance Indicator BVPI 225. Guidance on BVPI 225 is available at www.communities.gov.uk.

Appendix 2
England: Homelessness

General housing circumstances in the district

8.26. Section 177(2) provides that, in determining whether it is reasonable for a person to continue to occupy accommodation, housing authorities may have regard to the general housing circumstances prevailing in the housing authority's district.

8.27. This would apply, for example, where it was suggested that an applicant was homeless because of poor physical conditions in his or her current home. In such cases it would be open to the authority to consider whether the condition of the property was so bad in comparison with other accommodation in the district that it would not be reasonable to expect someone to continue to live there.

8.28. Circumstances where an applicant may be homeless as a result of his or her accommodation being overcrowded should also be considered in relation to the general housing circumstances in the district. Statutory overcrowding, within the meaning of Part 10 of the *Housing Act 1985*, may not by itself be sufficient to determine reasonableness, but it can be a contributory factor if there are other factors which suggest unreasonableness.

Affordability

8.29. One factor that **must** be considered in all cases is affordability. The *Homelessness (Suitability of Accommodation) Order 1996* (SI 1996 No 3204) requires the housing authority to consider the affordability of the accommodation for the applicant. The Order specifies, among other things, that in determining whether it would be (or would have been) reasonable for a person to continue to occupy accommodation, a housing authority must take into account whether the accommodation is affordable for him or her and must, in particular, take account of:

  (a)   the financial resources available to him or her;
  (b)   the costs in respect of the accommodation;
  (c)   maintenance payments (to a spouse, former spouse or in respect of a child); and
  (d)   his or her reasonable living expenses.

Tenant given notice of intention to recover possession

8.30. In cases where the applicant has been occupying accommodation as a tenant and has received a valid notice to quit, or a notice that the landlord intends to recover possession, housing authorities should consider the scope for preventing homelessness through consulting the landlord at an early stage to explore the possibility of the tenancy being allowed to continue or the tenant being allowed to remain for a reasonable period to provide an opportunity for alternative accommodation to be found. If the landlord is not persuaded to agree, the authority will need to consider whether it would be reasonable for the applicant to continue to occupy the accommodation once the valid notice has expired.

8.31. In determining whether it would be reasonable for an applicant to continue to occupy accommodation, the housing authority will need to consider all the factors relevant to the case and decide the weight that individual factors should attract. As well as the factors set out elsewhere in this chapter, other factors which may be relevant include the general cost to the housing authority, the position of the tenant, the position of the landlord, the likelihood that the landlord will actually proceed with possession proceedings, and the burden on the courts of unnecessary proceedings where there is no defence to a possession claim (see paragraphs 8.14 and 8.15 above for guidance on the right to occupy where notice of possession proceedings has been given).

8.32. Each case must be decided on its facts, so **housing authorities should not adopt a general policy of accepting – or refusing to accept – applicants as homeless or threatened with homelessness when they are threatened with eviction but a court has not yet made an order for possession or issued a warrant of execution**. In any case where a housing authority decides that it would be reasonable for an applicant to continue to occupy their accommodation after a valid notice has expired – and therefore decides that he or she is not yet homeless or threatened with homelessness – that decision will need to be based on sound reasons which should be made clear to the applicant in writing (see Chapter 6 for guidance on housing authorities' duties to inform applicants of their decisions). **The Secretary of State considers that where a person applies for accommodation or assistance in obtaining accommodation, and:**

    (a)   the person is an assured shorthold tenant who has received proper notice in accordance with s 21 of the *Housing Act 1988*;

    (b)   the housing authority is satisfied that the landlord intends to seek possession; and

    (c)   there would be no defence to an application for a possession order;

then it is unlikely to be reasonable for the applicant to continue to occupy the accommodation beyond the date given in the s 21 notice, unless the housing authority is taking steps to persuade the landlord to withdraw the notice or allow the tenant to continue to occupy the accommodation for a reasonable period to provide an opportunity for alternative accommodation to be found.

8.32a. Authorities are reminded that an applicant cannot be treated as intentionally homeless unless it would have been reasonable for him or her to have continued to occupy the accommodation. Guidance on 'intentional homelessness' is provided in Chapter 11.

Former armed forces personnel required to leave service accommodation

8.33. The Ministry of Defence recognises that housing authorities will need to be satisfied that entitlement to occupy service accommodation will end on a certain date, in order to determine whether applicants who are service personnel and who are approaching their date of discharge may be homeless or threatened with homelessness. For this purpose, the MOD issues a *Certificate of Cessation of Entitlement to Occupy Service Living Accommodation* six months before discharge (see examples at Annexes 14 and 15). These certificates indicate the date on which entitlement to occupy service accommodation ends, and the Secretary of State considers that housing authorities should not insist upon a court order for possession to establish that entitlement to occupy has ended. Authorities should take advantage of the six-month period of notice of discharge to ensure that service personnel receive timely and comprehensive advice on the housing options available to them when they leave the armed forces.

Other relevant factors

8.34. Other factors which may be relevant in determining whether it would be reasonable for an applicant to continue to occupy accommodation include:

physical characteristics: it would not be reasonable for an applicant to continue to occupy accommodation if the physical characteristics of the accommodation were unsuitable for the applicant because, for example, he or she was a wheelchair user and access was limited.

type of accommodation: some types of accommodation, for example women's refuges, direct access hostels, and night shelters are intended to provide very short-term, temporary accommodation in a crisis and it should not be regarded as reasonable to continue to occupy such accommodation in the medium and longer-term.

people fleeing harassment: in some cases severe harassment may fall short of actual violence or threats of violence likely to be carried out. Housing authorities should consider carefully whether it would be, or would have been, reasonable for an applicant to continue to occupy accommodation in circumstances where they have fled, or are seeking to leave, their home because of non-violent forms of harassment, for example verbal abuse or damage to property. Careful consideration should be given to applicants who may be at risk of witness intimidation. In some criminal cases the police may provide alternative accommodation for witnesses, but usually this will apply for the duration of the trial only. Witnesses may have had to give up their home or may feel unable to return to it when the trial has finished.

This is not an exhaustive list and authorities will need to take account of all relevant factors when considering whether it is reasonable for an applicant to continue to occupy accommodation.

CHAPTER 9: ELIGIBILITY FOR ASSISTANCE

General

9.1. Part 7 of the 1996 Act includes provisions that make certain persons from abroad ineligible for housing assistance. Housing authorities will therefore need to satisfy themselves that applicants are eligible before providing housing assistance. The provisions on eligibility are complex and housing authorities will need to ensure that they have procedures in place to carry out appropriate checks on housing applicants.

9.2. Housing authorities should ensure that staff who are required to screen housing applicants about eligibility for assistance are given training in the complexities of the housing provisions, the housing authority's duties and responsibilities under the race relations legislation and how to deal with applicants in a sensitive manner.

9.3. Local authorities are reminded that Schedule 3 to the *Nationality, Immigration and Asylum Act 2002* provides that certain persons shall not be eligible for support or assistance provided through the exercise of local housing authorities' powers to secure accommodation pending a review (s 188(3)) or pending an appeal to the county court (s 204(4)). See paragraph 9.22 below.

Persons from abroad

9.4. A person will not be eligible for assistance under Part 7 if he or she is a person from abroad who is ineligible for housing assistance under s 185 of the 1996 Act. There are two categories of 'person from abroad' for the purposes s 185:

(i) *a person subject to immigration control* – such a person is not eligible for housing assistance unless he or she comes within a class prescribed in regulations made by the Secretary of State, and

(ii) *a person from abroad other than a person subject to immigration control* – the Secretary of State can make regulations to provide for other descriptions of person from abroad who, although they are not subject to immigration control, are to be treated as ineligible for housing assistance.

9.5. The regulations that set out which classes of persons from abroad are eligible or ineligible for housing assistance are the *Allocation of Housing and Homelessness (Eligibility) (England) Regulations 2006* (SI 2006 No 1294) ('the Eligibility Regulations'). Persons subject to immigration control are not eligible for housing assistance unless they fall within a class of persons prescribed in **regulation 5** of the Eligibility Regulations. Persons who are not subject to immigration control will be eligible for housing assistance unless they fall within a description of persons who are to be treated as persons from abroad who are ineligible for assistance by virtue of **regulation 6** of the Eligibility Regulations.

Persons subject to immigration control

9.6. The term 'person subject to immigration control' is defined in s 13(2) of the *Asylum and Immigration Act 1996* as a person who requires leave to enter or remain in the United Kingdom (whether or not such leave has been given).

9.7. Only the following categories of person do **not** require leave to enter or remain in the UK:

(i) British citizens;

(ii) certain Commonwealth citizens with a right of abode in the UK;

   (iii)   citizens of an EEA country, ('EEA nationals') and their family members, who have a right to reside in the UK that derives from EC law. The question of whether an EEA national (or family member) has a particular right to reside in the UK (or in another Member State eg the Republic of Ireland) will depend on the circumstances, particularly the economic status of the EEA national (eg whether he or she is a worker, self-employed, a student, or economically inactive etc). See Annex 12 for further guidance on rights to reside;

   (iv)   persons who are exempt from immigration control under the Immigration Acts, including diplomats and their family members based in the United Kingdom, and some military personnel.

For the purposes of this guidance, 'EEA nationals' means nationals of any of the EU member states (excluding the UK), and nationals of Iceland, Norway, Liechtenstein and Switzerland.

9.8. Any person who **does not** fall within one of the 4 categories in paragraph 9.7 above will be a person subject to immigration control and will be ineligible for housing assistance unless they fall within a class of persons prescribed by regulation 5 of the Eligibility Regulations (see paragraph 9.10 below).

9.9. If there is any uncertainty about an applicant's immigration status, it is recommended that authorities contact the Home Office Immigration and Nationality Directorate, using the procedures set out in Annex 8. In some circumstances, local authorities may be under a duty to contact the Immigration and Nationality Directorate (see paragraph 9.24).

Persons subject to immigration control who are eligible for housing assistance

9.10. Generally, persons subject to immigration control are not eligible for housing assistance. However, by virtue of regulation 5 of the Eligibility Regulations, the following classes of person subject to immigration control are eligible for housing assistance:

   (i)   *a person granted refugee status*: a person is granted refugee status when his or her request for asylum is accepted. Persons granted refugee status are granted 5 years' limited leave to remain in the UK. (Prior to 30 August 2005, it was the policy to provide immediate settlement (indefinite leave to remain) for persons granted refugee status.)

   (ii)   *a person granted exceptional leave to enter or remain in the UK without condition that they and any dependants should make no recourse to public funds*: this status is granted to persons, including some persons whose claim for asylum has been refused, for a limited period where there are compelling humanitarian and/or compassionate circumstances for allowing them to stay. However, if leave was granted on condition that the applicant and any dependants should not be a charge on public funds, the applicant will not be eligible for homelessness assistance. Since April 2003, exceptional leave to remain (which is granted at the Secretary of State's discretion outside the Immigration Rules) has taken the form of either humanitarian protection or discretionary leave.

(iii) *a person with current leave to enter or remain in the UK with no condition or limitation, and who is habitually resident in the UK, the Channel Islands, the Isle of Man or the Republic of Ireland*: such a person will have indefinite leave to enter (ILE) or remain (ILR) and will be regarded as having settled status. However, where ILE or ILR status was granted as a result of an undertaking that a sponsor would be responsible for the applicant's maintenance and accommodation, the person must have been resident in the UK, the Channel Islands, the Isle of Man or the Republic of Ireland for five years since the date of entry – or the date of the sponsorship undertaking, whichever is later – for the applicant to be eligible. Where a sponsor has (or, if there was more than one sponsor, all of the sponsors have) died within the first five years, the applicant will be eligible for housing assistance;

(iv) *a person who left the territory of Montserrat after 1 November 1995 because of the effect on that territory of a volcanic eruption.* (See paragraph 9.19 below.)

Asylum seekers

9.11. Asylum seekers will almost always be persons subject to immigration control.

Asylum seekers who are persons subject to immigration control and whose claim for asylum was made after 2 April 2000 are not eligible for assistance under Part 7 of the 1996 Act. Some asylum seekers whose claim for asylum was made before 3 April 2000 would be eligible for assistance under Part 7 in certain limited circumstances, but the number of persons who fall in these classes is likely to be very small (if any). Annex 9 provides guidance on the limited categories of asylum seekers eligible for assistance under Part 7 of the 1996 Act.

9.12. Under s 186 of the 1996 Act, an asylum seeker who would otherwise be eligible for assistance under the Eligibility Regulations, will be ineligible, if he or she has any accommodation available in the UK for his or her occupation, however temporary.

Other persons from abroad who may be ineligible for assistance

9.13. By virtue of regulation 6 of the Eligibility Regulations, a person who is not subject to immigration control and who falls within one of the following descriptions of persons is to be treated as a person from abroad who is ineligible for housing assistance:

(i) a person who is not habitually resident in the UK, the Channel Islands, the Isle of Man or the Republic of Ireland (subject to certain exceptions – see paragraph 9.14 below);

(ii) a person whose only right to reside in the UK is derived from his status as a jobseeker (or his status as the family member of a jobseeker). For this purpose, 'jobseeker' has the same meaning as for the purpose of regulation 6(1)(a) of the *Immigration (European Economic Area) Regulations 2006* (SI 2006 No 1003) ('the EEA Regulations');

(iii) a person whose only right to reside in the UK is an initial right to reside for a period not exceeding three months under regulation 13 of the EEA Regulations;

(iv) a person whose only right to reside in the Channel Islands, the Isle of Man or the Republic of Ireland is a right equivalent to one of the rights mentioned in (ii) or (iii) above and which is derived from the Treaty establishing the European Community ('the EC Treaty').

See Annex 12 for guidance on rights to reside in the UK derived from EC law.

Persons exempted from the requirement to be habitually resident

9.14. Certain persons from abroad (not being persons subject to immigration control) will be eligible for housing assistance even though they are not habitually resident in the UK, the Channel Islands, the Isle of Man or the Republic of Ireland. Such a person will be eligible for assistance even if not habitually resident, if he or she is:

(a) an EEA national who is in the UK as a worker (which has the same meaning as it does for the purposes of regulation 6(1) of the EEA Regulations);

(b) an EEA national who is in the UK as a self-employed person (which has the same meaning as it does for the purposes of regulation 6(1) of the EEA Regulations);

(c) a person who is an accession state worker requiring registration who is treated as a worker for the purposes of regulation 6(1) of the EEA Regulations, pursuant to the *Accession (Immigration and Worker Registration) Regulations 2004*, as amended;

(d) a person who is a family member of a person referred to in (a) to (c) above;

(e) a person with a right to reside permanently in the UK by virtue of regulation 15(c), (d) or (e) of the EEA Regulations (see Annex 12);

(f) a person who left Montserrat after 1 November 1995 because of the effect of volcanic activity there (see paragraph 9.19 below);

(g) a person who is in the UK as a result of his or her deportation, expulsion or other removal by compulsion of law from another country to the UK (see paragraph 9.21 below).

On (a) and (b), authorities should note that a person who is no longer working or no longer in self-employment will retain his or her status as a worker or self-employed person in certain circumstances. (See Annex 12 for further guidance.) On (c), authorities should note that accession state workers requiring registration will generally only be treated as a worker when they are actually working and will not retain 'worker' status in the circumstances referred to above. (See annexes 12 and 13 for further guidance.) On (d), authorities should note that 'family member' does not include a person who is an extended family member who is treated as a family member by virtue of regulation 7(3) of the EEA Regulations (see Annex 12 for further guidance).

The habitual residence test

9.15. The term 'habitual residence' is intended to convey a degree of permanence in the person's residence in the UK, the Channel Islands, the Isle of Man or the Republic of Ireland; it implies an association between the individual and the place of residence and relies substantially on fact.

9.16. The Secretary of State considers that it is likely that applicants who have been resident in the UK, Channel Islands, the Isle of Man or the Republic of Ireland continuously during the 2-year period prior to their housing application will be habitually resident. In such cases, therefore, housing authorities may consider it unnecessary to make further enquiries to determine whether the person is habitually resident, unless there are other circumstances that need to be taken into account. A period of continuous residence in the UK, Channel Islands, the Isle of Man or the Republic of Ireland might include periods of temporary absence, eg visits abroad for holidays or to visit relatives. Where two years' continuous residency has not been established, housing authorities will need to conduct further enquiries to determine whether the applicant is habitually resident.

9.17. A person will not generally be habitually resident anywhere unless he or she has taken up residence and lived there for a period. There will be cases where the person concerned is not coming to the UK for the first time, and is resuming a previous period of habitual residence.

9.18. Annex 10 provides guidance on the factors that a housing authority should consider in determining whether an applicant is habitually resident.

Persons from Montserrat

9.19. The classes of persons (not being persons subject to immigration control) who are not required to be habitually resident in order to be eligible for assistance under Part 7 include a person who left Montserrat after 1 November 1995 because of the effect of volcanic activity there.

9.20. On 21 May 2002 most British overseas territories citizens, including those from Montserrat, became British Citizens. Since their new EU-style passport will not identify that they are from Montserrat, it has been recommended that they should also retain their old British Overseas Citizen passport, to help them demonstrate eligibility for, among other things, housing assistance in the UK.

Appendix 2
England: Homelessness

Persons deported, expelled or removed to the UK from another country

9.21. Persons who are in the UK as a result of their deportation, expulsion or other removal by compulsion of law from another country to the UK will generally be UK nationals. (However, such persons could include EEA nationals, where the UK immigration authorities were satisfied that the person was settled in the UK and exercising EC Treaty rights prior to deportation from the third country.) Where deportation occurs, most countries will signal this in the person's passport and provide them with reasons for their removal. This should enable such persons to identify their circumstances when making an application for housing assistance.

Persons ineligible under certain provisions by virtue of Schedule 3 to the Nationality, Immigration and Asylum Act 2002

9.22. Section 54 of, and Schedule 3 to, the *Nationality, Immigration and Asylum Act 2002* have the effect of making certain applicants for housing assistance ineligible for accommodation under s 188(3) (*power to accommodate pending a review*) or s 204(4) (*power to accommodate pending an appeal to the county court*) of the 1996 Act. The following classes of person will be ineligible for assistance under those powers:

(i) *a person who has refugee status abroad*, ie a person:
   – who does not have the nationality of an EEA State, and
   – who the government of an EEA State other than the UK has determined is entitled to protection as a refugee under the Refugee Convention;

(ii) *a person who has the nationality of an EEA State other than the UK* (but see paragraph 9.23 below);

(iii) *a person who was (but is no longer) an asylum seeker and who fails to cooperate with removal directions* issued in respect of him or her;

(iv) *a person who is in the UK in breach of the immigration laws* (within the meaning of s 11 of the *Nationality, Immigration and Asylum Act 2002*) *and is not an asylum seeker*;

(v) *certain persons who are failed asylum seekers with dependent children*, where the Secretary of State has certified that, in his opinion, such a person has failed without reasonable excuse to take reasonable steps to leave the UK voluntarily or place himself or herself in a position where he or she is able to leave the UK voluntarily, and that person has received the Secretary of State's certificate more than 14 days previously;

(vi) *a person who is the dependant of a person who falls within class (i), (ii), (iii) or (v) above.*

9.23. However, s 54 and Schedule 3 do not prevent the exercise of an authority's powers under s 188(3) and s 204(4) of the 1996 Act to the extent that such exercise is necessary for the purpose of avoiding a breach of a person's rights under the European Convention of Human Rights or rights under the EC

Treaties. Among other things, this means that a local authority can exercise these powers to accommodate an EEA national who has a right to reside in the UK under EC law (see Annex 12).

9.24. Paragraph 14 of Schedule 3 provides, among other things, that authorities must inform the Secretary of State where the powers under s 188(3) or s 204(4) apply, or may apply, to a person who is, or may come, within classes (iii), (iv) or (v) in paragraph 9.22 (by contacting the Home Office Immigration and Nationality Directorate).

9.25. For further guidance, local authorities should refer to Guidance to Local Authorities and Housing Authorities about the *Nationality, Immigration and Asylum Act*, Section 54 and Schedule 3, and the *Withholding and Withdrawal of Support (Travel Assistance and Temporary Accommodation) Regulations 2002*, issued by the Home Office.

Eligibility – List of related Annexes:

Annex 8   How to contact the Home Office Immigration and
            Nationality Directorate

Annex 9   Asylum seekers

Annex 10   The habitual residence test

Annex 11   European groupings (EU, A8, EEA, Switzerland)

Annex 12   Rights to reside in the UK derived from EC law

Annex 13   Worker registration scheme

CHAPTER 10: PRIORITY NEED

This chapter provides guidance on the categories of applicant who have a priority need for accommodation under the homelessness legislation.

10.1. Under the homelessness legislation, housing authorities must have a strategy for preventing homelessness and ensuring that accommodation and support are available to anyone in their district who is homeless or at risk of homelessness. They must also provide advice and assistance on housing and homelessness prevention to anyone in their district, free of charge. Stronger duties to secure accommodation exist for households who have a priority need for accommodation. Since 2002, the priority need categories have embraced a wider range of people whose age or background puts them at greater risk when homeless, including more single people.

10.2. The main homelessness duties in s 193(2) and s 195(2) of the 1996 Act (to secure accommodation or take reasonable steps to prevent the loss of accommodation) apply only to applicants who have a priority need for accommodation. Section 189(1) and the *Homelessness (Priority Need for Accommodation) (England) Order 2002* provide that the following categories of applicant have a priority need for accommodation:

Appendix 2
England: Homelessness

i)   a pregnant woman or a person with whom she resides or might reasonably be expected to reside (see paragraph 10.5);

ii)   a person with whom dependent children reside or might reasonably be expected to reside (see paragraphs 10.6–10.11);

iii)   a person who is vulnerable as a result of old age, mental illness or handicap or physical disability or other special reason, or with whom such a person resides or might reasonably be expected to reside (see paragraphs 10.12–10.18);

iv)   a person aged 16 or 17 who is not a 'relevant child' or a child in need to whom a local authority owes a duty under section 20 of the *Children Act 1989* (see paragraphs 10.36–10.39);

v)   a person under 21 who was (but is no longer) looked after, accommodated or fostered between the ages of 16 and 18 (except a person who is a 'relevant student') (see paragraphs 10.40–10.41);

vi)   a person aged 21 or more who is vulnerable as a result of having been looked after, accommodated or fostered (except a person who is a 'relevant student') (see paragraphs 10.19–10.20);

vii)   a person who is vulnerable as a result of having been a member of Her Majesty's regular naval, military or air forces (see paragraphs 10.21–10.23);

viii)   a person who is vulnerable as a result of:
(a)   having served a custodial sentence,
(b)   having been committed for contempt of court or any other kindred offence, or
(c)   having been remanded in custody;
(see paragraphs 10.24–10.27)

ix)   a person who is vulnerable as a result of ceasing to occupy accommodation because of violence from another person or threats of violence from another person which are likely to be carried out (see paragraphs 10.28–10.29);

x)   a person who is vulnerable for any other special reason, or with whom such a person resides or might reasonably be expected to reside (see paragraphs 10.30–10.35);

xi)   a person who is homeless, or threatened with homelessness, as a result of an emergency such as flood, fire or other disaster (see paragraph 10.42).

10.3. Inquiries as to whether an applicant has a priority need must be carried out in all cases where the housing authority has reason to believe that an applicant may be homeless or threatened with homelessness, and is eligible for assistance (s 184). Moreover, where the housing authority has reason to believe that the applicant is homeless, eligible for assistance and in priority need, they will have an immediate duty to secure interim accommodation, pending a decision on the case (see Chapter 7).

10.4. Once a housing authority has notified an applicant that he or she has a priority need and has been accepted as owed the main homelessness duty (s 193(2)) it cannot – unless the decision is subject to a request for a review – change the decision if the applicant subsequently ceases to have a priority need (eg because a dependent child leaves home). Any change of circumstance prior to the decision on the homelessness application should be taken into account. However, once all the relevant inquiries are completed, the housing authority should not defer making a decision on the case in anticipation of a possible change of circumstance. (See Chapter 19 for guidance on reviews.)

Pregnant women

10.5. A pregnant woman, and anyone with whom she lives or might reasonably be expected to live, has a priority need for accommodation. This is regardless of the length of time that the woman has been pregnant. Housing authorities should seek normal confirmation of pregnancy, eg a letter from a medical professional, such as a midwife, should be adequate evidence of pregnancy. If a pregnant woman suffers a miscarriage or terminates her pregnancy during the assessment process the housing authority should consider whether she continues to have a priority need as a result of some other factor (eg she may be vulnerable as a result of an other special reason – see paragraph 10.30).

Dependent children

10.6. Applicants have a priority need if they have one or more dependent children who normally live with them or who might reasonably be expected to live with them. There must be actual dependence on the applicant, although the child need not be wholly and exclusively dependent on him or her. There must also be actual residence (or a reasonable expectation of residence) with some degree of permanence or regularity, rather than a temporary arrangement whereby the children are merely staying with the applicant for a limited period (see paragraphs 10.9 and 10.10). Similarly, the child need not be wholly and exclusively resident (or expected to reside wholly and exclusively) with the applicant.

10.7. The 1996 Act does not define dependent children, but housing authorities may wish to treat as dependent all children under 16, and all children aged 16–18 who are in, or are about to begin, full-time education or training or who for other reasons are unable to support themselves and who live at home. The meaning of dependency is not, however, limited to financial dependency. Thus, while children aged 16 and over who are in full-time employment and are financially independent of their parents would not normally be considered to be dependants, housing authorities should remember that such children may not be sufficiently mature to live independently of their parents, and there may be sound reasons for considering them to be dependent. Each case will need to be carefully considered according to the circumstances.

10.8. Dependent children need not necessarily be the applicant's own children but could, for example, be related to the applicant or his or her partner or be adopted or fostered by the applicant. There must, however, be some form of parent/child relationship.

10.9. Housing authorities may receive applications from a parent who is separated from his or her former spouse or partner. In some cases where parents separate, the court may make a residence order indicating with which parent the child normally resides. In such cases, the child may be considered to reside with the parent named in the order, and would not normally be expected to reside with the other parent. However, in many cases the parents come to an agreement themselves as to how the child is to be cared for, and a court order will not be made or required.

10.10. Residence does not have to be full-time and a child can be considered to reside with either parent even where he or she divides his or her time between both parents. However, as mentioned above, there must be some regularity to the arrangement. If the child is not currently residing with the applicant, the housing authority will need to decide whether, in the circumstances, it would be reasonable for the child to do so. An agreement between a child's parents, or a joint residence order by a court, may not automatically lead to a conclusion that it would be reasonable for the child to reside with the parent making the application, and housing authorities will need to consider each case individually. However, housing authorities should remember that where parents separate, it will often be in the best interests of the child to maintain a relationship with both parents.

10.11. Where the applicant's children are being looked after by a social services authority – for example, they are subject to a care order or are being accommodated under a voluntary agreement – and they are not currently living with the applicant, liaison with the social services authority will be essential. Joint consideration with social services will ensure that the best interests of the applicant and the children are served. This may, for example, enable a family to be reunited subject to suitable accommodation being available.

Vulnerability

10.12. A person has a priority need for accommodation if he or she is vulnerable as a result of:

   i)   old age;
   ii)   mental illness or learning disability (mental handicap) or physical disability;
   iii)   having been looked after, accommodated or fostered and is aged 21 or more;
   iv)   having been a member of Her Majesty's regular naval, military or air forces;
   v)   having been in custody or detention;
   vi)   ceasing to occupy accommodation because of violence from another person or threats of violence from another person which are likely to be carried out; or
   vii)   any other special reason.

In the case of i), ii) and vii) only, a person with whom a vulnerable person lives or might reasonably be expected to live also has a priority need for accommodation and can therefore make an application on behalf of themselves and that vulnerable person.

10.13. It is a matter of judgment whether the applicant's circumstances make him or her vulnerable. When determining whether an applicant in any of the categories set out in paragraph 10.12 is vulnerable, the local authority should consider whether, when homeless, the applicant would be less able to fend for him/herself than an ordinary homeless person so that he or she would suffer injury or detriment, in circumstances where a less vulnerable person would be able to cope without harmful effects.

10.14. Some of the factors which may be relevant to determining whether a particular category of applicant is vulnerable are set out below. The assessment of an applicant's ability to cope is a composite one taking into account all of the circumstances. The applicant's vulnerability must be assessed on the basis that he or she is or will become homeless, and not on his or her ability to fend for him or herself while still housed.

Old age

10.15. Old age alone is not sufficient for the applicant to be deemed vulnerable. However, it may be that as a result of old age the applicant would be less able to fend for him or herself as provided in paragraph 10.13 above. All applications from people aged over 60 need to be considered carefully, particularly where the applicant is leaving tied accommodation. However, housing authorities should not use 60 (or any other age) as a fixed age beyond which vulnerability occurs automatically (or below which it can be ruled out); each case will need to be considered in the light of the individual circumstances.

Mental illness or learning disability or physical disability

10.16. Housing authorities should have regard to any advice from medical professionals, social services or current providers of care and support. In cases where there is doubt as to the extent of any vulnerability authorities may also consider seeking a clinical opinion. However, the final decision on the question of vulnerability will rest with the housing authority. In considering whether such applicants are vulnerable, authorities will need to take account of all relevant factors including:

i)   the nature and extent of the illness and/or disability which may render the applicant vulnerable;

ii)   the relationship between the illness and/or disability and the individual's housing difficulties; and

iii)   the relationship between the illness and/or disability and other factors such as drug/alcohol misuse, offending behaviour, challenging behaviours, age and personality disorder.

10.17. Assessment of vulnerability due to mental health will require close co-operation between housing authorities, social services authorities and mental health agencies. Housing authorities should consider carrying out joint assessments or using a trained mental health practitioner as part of an assessment team. Mental Health NHS Trusts and local authorities have an express duty to implement a specifically tailored care programme (the Care Programme Approach – CPA) for all patients considered for discharge from psychiatric hospitals and all new patients accepted by the specialist psychiatric services (see *Effective care co-ordination in mental health services: modernising the care programme approach*, DH, 1999). **People discharged from psychiatric hospitals and local authority hostels for people with mental health problems are likely to be vulnerable.** Effective, timely, liaison between housing, social services and NHS Trusts will be essential in such cases but authorities will also need to be sensitive to direct approaches from former patients who have been discharged and may be homeless.

10.18. Learning or physical disabilities or long-term acute illnesses, such as those defined by the *Disability Discrimination Act 1995*, which impinge on the applicant's housing situation and give rise to vulnerability may be readily discernible, but advice from health or social services staff should be sought, wherever necessary.

Having been looked after, accommodated or fostered and aged 21 or over

10.19. A person aged 21 or over who is vulnerable as a result of having been looked after, accommodated or fostered has a priority need (other than a person who is a 'relevant student'). The terms 'looked after, accommodated or fostered' are set out in the *Children Act 1989* (s 24) and include any person who has been:

i)   looked after by a local authority (ie has been subject to a care order or accommodated under a voluntary agreement);

ii)   accommodated by or on behalf of a voluntary organisation;

iii)   accommodated in a private children's home;

iv)   accommodated for a consecutive period of at least three months:
   –   by a health authority, special health authority, primary care trust or local education authority, or
   –   in any care home or independent hospital or in any accommodation provided by a National Health Service trust; or

v)   privately fostered.

A 'relevant student' means a care leaver under 24 to whom section 24B(3) of the *Children Act 1989* applies, and who is in full-time further or higher education and whose term-time accommodation is not available during a vacation. Under s 24B(5), where a social services authority is satisfied that a person is someone to whom section 24B(3) applies and needs accommodation during a vacation they must provide accommodation or the means to enable it to be secured.

10.20. Housing authorities will need to make enquiries into an applicant's childhood history to establish whether he or she has been looked after, accommodated or fostered in any of these ways. If so, they will need to consider whether he or she is vulnerable as a result. In determining whether there is vulnerability (as set out in paragraph 10.13 above), factors that a housing authority may wish to consider are:

i) the length of time that the applicant was looked after, accommodated or fostered;

ii) the reasons why the applicant was looked after, accommodated or fostered;

iii) the length of time since the applicant was looked after, accommodated or fostered, and whether the applicant had been able to obtain and/or maintain accommodation during any of that period;

iv) whether the applicant has any existing support networks, particularly including family, friends or mentor.

Having been a member of the armed forces

10.21. A person who is vulnerable as a result of having been a member of Her Majesty's regular armed forces has a priority need for accommodation. Former members of the armed forces will include a person who was previously a member of the regular naval, military or air forces, including a person who has been released following detention in a military corrective training centre.

10.22. The principal responsibility for providing housing information and advice to Service personnel lies with the armed forces up to the point of discharge and these services are delivered through the Joint Service Housing Advice Office (telephone: 01722 436575). Some people, who have served in the armed forces for a long period, and those who are medically discharged, may be offered assistance with resettlement by Ministry of Defence (MOD) resettlement staff. The MOD issues a *Certificate of Cessation of Entitlement to Occupy Service Living Accommodation* (see examples at Annexes 14 and 15) six months before discharge. Applications from former members of the armed forces will need to be considered carefully to assess whether the applicant is vulnerable as a result of having served in the armed forces.

10.23. In considering whether former members of the armed forces are vulnerable (as set out in paragraph 10.13 above) as a result of their time spent in the forces, a housing authority may wish to take into account the following factors:

i) the length of time the applicant spent in the armed forces (although authorities should not assume that vulnerability could not occur as a result of a short period of service);

ii) the type of service the applicant was engaged in (those on active service may find it more difficult to cope with civilian life);

iii) whether the applicant spent any time in a military hospital (this could be an indicator of a serious health problem or of post-traumatic stress);

Appendix 2
England: Homelessness

iv)   whether HM Forces' medical and welfare advisers have judged an individual to be particularly vulnerable in their view and have issued a Medical History Release Form (F Med 133) giving a summary of the circumstances causing that vulnerability;

v)   the length of time since the applicant left the armed forces, and whether he or she had been able to obtain and/or maintain accommodation during that time;

vi)   whether the applicant has any existing support networks, particularly by way of family or friends.

Having been in custody or detention

10.24.   A person who is vulnerable as a result of having served a custodial sentence, been committed for contempt of court or remanded in custody has a priority need for accommodation. This category applies to applicants who are vulnerable as a result of having:

i)   served a custodial sentence within the meaning of the *Powers of Criminal Courts (Sentences) Act 2000*, s 76. (This includes sentences of imprisonment for those aged 21 or over and detention for those aged under 21, including children.);

ii)   been committed for contempt of court or any other kindred offence (kindred offence refers to statutory provisions for contempt as opposed to the inherent jurisdiction of the court, eg under the *Contempt of Court Act 1981*, s 12 (magistrates' court) and *County Court Act 1984*, s 118 (county court)). (Committal may arise, eg where an applicant has breached a civil injunction.);

iii)   been remanded in custody within the meaning of the *Powers of Criminal Courts (Sentencing) Act 2000*, s 88(1)(b), (c) or (d), ie remanded in or committed to custody by an order of a court; remanded or committed to housing authority accommodation under the *Children and Young Persons Act 1969* and placed and kept in secure accommodation; or, remanded, admitted or removed to hospital under the *Mental Health Act 1983*, ss 35, 36, 38 or 48.

10.25.   Applicants have a priority need for accommodation only if they are vulnerable (see paragraph 10.13 above) as a result of having been in custody or detention. In determining whether applicants who fall within one of the descriptions in paragraph 10.24 are vulnerable as a result of their period in custody or detention, a housing authority may wish to take into account the following factors:

i)   the length of time the applicant served in custody or detention (although authorities should not assume that vulnerability could not occur as a result of a short period in custody or detention);

ii)   whether the applicant is receiving supervision from a criminal justice agency eg the Probation Service, Youth Offending Team or Drug Intervention Programme. Housing authorities should have regard to any advice from criminal justice agency staff regarding their view of the applicant's general vulnerability, but the final decision on the question of vulnerability for the purposes of the homelessness legislation will rest with the housing authority;

iii) the length of time since the applicant was released from custody or detention, and the extent to which the applicant had been able to obtain and/or maintain accommodation during that time;

iv) whether the applicant has any existing support networks, for example family or friends, and how much of a positive influence these networks are likely to be in the applicant's life.

10.26. In many cases a housing needs assessment may have been completed in respect of offenders by the Probation Service, Prison Services, Youth Offending Team, Criminal Justice Intervention Team or a voluntary organisation acting on behalf of one of these agencies. Where such an assessment identifies an individual as needing help in finding accommodation and judges the individual to be particularly vulnerable and the applicant makes an application for housing assistance, this information will be made available to the relevant housing authority.

10.27. In addition to the question of priority need, when assessing applicants in this client group difficult issues may arise as to whether the applicant has become homeless intentionally. Housing authorities must consider each case in the light of all the facts and circumstances. **Housing authorities are reminded that they cannot adopt a blanket policy of assuming that homelessness will be intentional or unintentional in any given circumstances** (see Chapter 11 for guidance on intentional homelessness).

Having left accommodation because of violence

10.28. A person has a priority need if he or she is vulnerable (as set out in paragraph 10.13 above) as a result of having to leave accommodation because of violence from another person, or threats of violence from another person that are likely to be carried out. It will usually be apparent from the assessment of the reason for homelessness whether the applicant has had to leave accommodation because of violence or threats of violence (see Chapter 8 for further guidance on whether it is reasonable to continue to occupy accommodation). **In cases involving violence, the safety of the applicant and ensuring confidentiality must be of paramount concern.** It is not only domestic violence that is relevant, but all forms of violence, including racially motivated violence or threats of violence likely to be carried out. Inquiries of the perpetrators of violence should not be made. In assessing whether it is likely that threats of violence are likely to be carried out, a housing authority should only take into account the probability of violence, and not actions which the applicant could take (such as injunctions against the perpetrators). See Chapter 6 for further guidance on dealing with cases involving violence.

10.29. In considering whether applicants are vulnerable as a result of leaving accommodation because of violence or threats of violence likely to be carried out, a housing authority may wish to take into account the following factors:

i)   the nature of the violence or threats of violence (there may have been a single but significant incident or a number of incidents over an extended period of time which have had a cumulative effect);

ii)   the impact and likely effects of the violence or threats of violence on the applicant's current and future well being;

iii)   whether the applicant has any existing support networks, particularly by way of family or friends.

Other special reason

10.30. Section 189(1)(c) provides that a person has a priority need for accommodation if he or she is vulnerable for any 'other special reason'. A person with whom such a vulnerable person normally lives or might reasonably be expected to live also has a priority need. The legislation envisages that vulnerability can arise because of factors that are not expressly provided for in statute. Each application must be considered in the light of the facts and circumstances of the case. Moreover, other special reasons giving rise to vulnerability are not restricted to the physical or mental characteristics of a person. Where applicants have a need for support but have no family or friends on whom they can depend they may be vulnerable as a result of another special reason.

10.31. Housing authorities must keep an open mind and should avoid blanket policies that assume that particular groups of applicants will, or will not, be vulnerable for any 'other special reason'. Where a housing authority considers that an applicant may be vulnerable, it will be important to make an in-depth assessment of the circumstances of the case. Guidance on certain categories of applicants who may be vulnerable as a result of any 'other special reason' is given below. The list below is not exhaustive and housing authorities must ensure that they give proper consideration to every application on the basis of the individual circumstances. In addition, housing authorities will need to be aware that an applicant may be considered vulnerable for any 'other special reason' because of a combination of factors which taken alone may not necessarily lead to a decision that they are vulnerable (eg drug and alcohol problems, common mental health problems, a history of sleeping rough, no previous experience of managing a tenancy).

10.32. *Chronically sick people, including people with AIDS and HIV-related illnesses.* People in this group may be vulnerable not only because their illness has progressed to the point of physical or mental disability (when they are likely to fall within one of the specified categories of priority need) but also because the manifestations or effects of their illness, or common attitudes to it, make it very difficult for them to find and maintain stable or suitable accommodation. Whilst this may be particularly true of people with AIDS, it could also apply in the case of people infected with HIV (who may not have any overt signs or symptoms) if the nature of their infection is known.

10.33. *Young people.* The 2002 Order makes specific provision for certain categories of young homeless people (see paragraph 10.2). However, there are many other young people who fall outside these categories but who could become homeless and be vulnerable in certain circumstances. When assessing applications from young people under 25 who do not fall within any of the specific categories of priority need, housing authorities should give careful consideration to the possibility of vulnerability. Most young people can expect a degree of support from families, friends or an institution (eg a college or university) with the practicalities and costs of finding, establishing, and managing a home for the first time. But some young people, particularly those who are forced to leave the parental home or who cannot remain there because they are being subjected to violence or sexual abuse, may lack this back-up network and be less able than others to establish and maintain a home for themselves. Moreover, a young person on the streets without adequate financial resources to live independently may be at risk of abuse or prostitution. See Chapter 12 for further guidance on 16 and 17 year olds.

10.34. *People fleeing harassment.* Authorities should consider whether harassment falls under the general definition of domestic violence (see definition in Chapter 8 and paragraphs 10.28–10.29 above which give guidance on vulnerability as a result of violence). In some cases, however, severe harassment may fall short of actual violence or threats of violence likely to be carried out. Housing authorities should consider carefully whether applicants who have fled their home because of non-violent forms of harassment, for example verbal abuse or damage to property, are vulnerable as a result. Careful consideration should be given to applicants who may be at risk of witness intimidation. In some criminal cases the police may provide alternative accommodation for witnesses, but usually this will apply for the duration of the trial only. Witnesses may have had to give up their home or may feel unable to return to it when the trial has finished.

10.35. *Former asylum seekers.* Former asylum seekers who have been granted refugee status or exceptional leave to remain, humanitarian protection, or discretionary leave will be eligible for homelessness assistance and may be at risk of homelessness as a result of having to leave accommodation that had been provided for them (eg by the National Asylum Support Service) in the period before a decision was reached on their asylum claim. They may well have experienced persecution or trauma in their country of origin or severe hardship in their efforts to reach the UK and may be vulnerable as a result. In assessing applications from this client group, housing authorities should give careful consideration to the possibility that they may be vulnerable as a result of another special reason. Authorities should be sensitive to the fact that former asylum seekers may be reluctant to discuss, or have difficulty discussing, their potential vulnerability, if, for example, they have experienced humiliating, painful or traumatic circumstances such as torture, rape or the killing of a family member.

16 and 17 year olds

10.36. All 16 and 17 year old homeless applicants have a priority need for accommodation except those who are:

i)   a relevant child, or

Appendix 2
England: Homelessness

    ii)   a child in need who is owed a duty under s 20 of the *Children Act 1989*.

Relevant child or child in need owed a duty under s 20 of the 1989 Act

10.37.   A relevant child is a child aged 16 or 17 who has been looked after by a local authority for at least 13 weeks since the age of 14 and has been looked after at some time while 16 or 17 and who is not currently being looked after (ie an 'eligible child' for the purposes of paragraph 19B of Schedule 2 to the *Children Act 1989*). In addition, a child is also a relevant child if he or she would have been looked after by the local authority as an eligible child but for the fact that on his or her 16th birthday he or she was detained through the criminal justice system, or in hospital, or if he or she has returned home on family placement and that has broken down (see the *Children Act 1989*, s 23A and the *Children (Leaving Care) Regulations 2001* regulation 4).

10.38.   The *Children Act 1989* (s 20(3)) places a duty on children's services authorities to provide accommodation for a child in need aged 16 or over whose welfare is otherwise likely to be seriously prejudiced if they do not provide accommodation; and s 20(1) places a duty on children's services authorities to provide accommodation for children in need in certain other circumstances.

10.39.   Responsibility for providing suitable accommodation for a relevant child or a child in need to whom a local authority owes a duty under s 20 of the *Children Act 1989* rests with the children's services authority. In cases where a housing authority considers that a section 20 duty is owed, they should verify this with the relevant children's services authority. In all cases of uncertainty as to whether a 16 or 17 year old applicant may be a relevant child or a child in need, the housing authority should contact the relevant children's services authority and, where necessary, should provide interim accommodation under s 188, pending clarification. A framework for joint assessment of 16 and 17 year olds will need to be established by housing and children's services authorities (and housing and children's services departments within unitary authorities) to facilitate the seamless discharge of duties and appropriate services to this client group.

See Chapter 12 for more detailed guidance on 16 and 17 year olds.

Having been looked after, accommodated or fostered and aged under 21

10.40.   A person under 21 who was (but is no longer) looked after, accommodated or fostered between the ages of 16 and 18 has a priority need for accommodation (other than a person who is a 'relevant student'). The terms 'looked after', 'accommodated' or 'fostered' are set out in the *Children Act 1989* (s 24) and include any person who has been:

    i)   looked after by a local authority (ie has been subject to a care order or accommodated under a voluntary agreement);

ii) accommodated by or on behalf of a voluntary organisation;
iii) accommodated in a private children's home;
iv) accommodated for a consecutive period of at least three months:
- by a health authority, special health authority, primary care trust or local education authority, or
- in any care home or independent hospital or in any accommodation provided by a National Health Service trust; or
v) privately fostered.

A 'relevant student' means a care leaver under 24 to whom section 24B(3) of the *Children Act 1989* applies, and who is in full-time further or higher education and whose term-time accommodation is not available during a vacation. Under s 24B(5), where a social services authority is satisfied that a person is someone to whom s 24B(3) applies and needs accommodation during a vacation they must provide accommodation or the means to enable it to be secured.

10.41. Housing authorities will need to liaise with the social services authority when dealing with homeless applicants who may fall within this category of priority need.

Homeless as a result of an emergency

10.42. Applicants have a priority need for accommodation if they are homeless or threatened with homelessness as a result of an emergency such as fire, flood or other disaster. To qualify as an 'other disaster' the disaster must be in the nature of a flood or fire, and involve some form of physical damage or threat of damage. Applicants have a priority need by reason of such an emergency whether or not they have dependent children or are vulnerable for any reason.

CHAPTER 11: INTENTIONAL HOMELESSNESS

11.1. This chapter provides guidance on determining whether an applicant became homeless, or threatened with homelessness, *intentionally* or *unintentionally*.

11.2. The duty owed towards those who are homeless, or threatened with homelessness, and who have a priority need for accommodation will depend upon whether they became homeless, or threatened with homelessness, intentionally or unintentionally. Section 191 defines the circumstances in which an applicant is to be regarded as having become homeless intentionally. Section 196 frames the same definitions in regard to someone who is threatened with homelessness.

11.3. The duty owed to applicants who have a priority need for accommodation but have become homeless, or threatened with homelessness, intentionally is less than the duty owed to those who have a priority need for accommodation and have become homeless, or threatened with homelessness, unintentionally. This recognises the general expectation that, wherever possible, people should take responsibility for their own accommodation needs and ensure that they do not behave in a way which might lead to the loss of their accommodation.

11.4. Where a housing authority finds an applicant to be homeless, or threatened with homelessness, intentionally they have a duty to provide the applicant (or secure that the applicant is provided) with advice and assistance in any attempts he or she may make to secure that accommodation becomes available (or does not cease to be available) for his or her occupation. Before this advice and assistance is given, the authority must assess the applicant's housing needs. The advice and assistance must include information about the likely availability in the authority's district of types of accommodation appropriate to the applicant's housing needs (including, in particular, the location and sources of such types of accommodation). Authorities should consider what best advice and assistance the authoritiy could provide, for example, providing information about applying for social housing, local lettings in the private rented sector, rent deposit schemes or housing benefit eligibility – to help the applicant avoid homelessness or secure accommodation (see Chapter 2 for further guidance on preventing homelessness). Where such an applicant also has a priority need for accommodation the authority will also have a duty to secure accommodation for such period as will give the applicant a reasonable opportunity of securing accommodation for his or her occupation. See Chapter 14 for guidance on the main duties owed to applicants on completion of inquiries.

11.5. It is for housing authorities to satisfy themselves in each individual case whether an applicant is homeless or threatened with homelessness intentionally. Generally, it is not for applicants to 'prove their case'. The exception is where an applicant seeks to establish that, as a member of a household previously found to be homeless intentionally, he or she did not acquiesce in the behaviour that led to homelessness. In such cases, the applicant will need to demonstrate that he or she was not involved in the acts or omissions that led to homelessness, and did not have control over them.

11.6. Housing authorities must not adopt general policies which seek to pre-define circumstances that do or do not amount to intentional homelessness or threatened homelessness (for example, intentional homelessness should not be assumed in cases where an application is made following a period in custody – see paragraph 11.14). In each case, housing authorities must form a view in the light of all their inquiries about that particular case. Where the original incident of homelessness occurred some years earlier and the facts are unclear, it may not be possible for the housing authority to satisfy themselves that the applicant became homeless intentionally. In such cases, the applicant should be considered to be unintentionally homeless.

Definitions of intentional homelessness

11.7. Sections 191(1) and 196(1) provide that a person becomes homeless, or threatened with homelessness, intentionally if:

i)   he or she deliberately does or fails to do anything in consequence of which he or she ceases to occupy accommodation (or the likely result of which is that he or she will be forced to leave accommodation),

ii)   the accommodation is available for his or her occupation, and

iii)   it would have been reasonable for him or her to continue to occupy the accommodation.

However, for this purpose, an act or omission made in good faith by someone who was unaware of any relevant fact must not be treated as deliberate (see paragraph 11.20).

11.8.   Sections 191(3) and 196(3) provide that a person must be treated as homeless, or threatened with homelessness, intentionally if:

i)   the person enters into an arrangement under which he or she is required to cease to occupy accommodation which it would have been reasonable for the person to continue to occupy,

ii)   the purpose of the arrangement is to enable the person to become entitled to assistance under Part 7, and

iii)   there is no other good reason why the person is homeless or threatened with homelessness.

Whose conduct results in intentional homelessness?

11.9.   Every applicant is entitled to individual consideration of his or her application. This includes applicants where another member of their family or household has made, or is making, a separate application. It is the **applicant** who must deliberately have done or failed to do something which resulted in homelessness or threatened homelessness. Where a housing authority has found an applicant to be homeless intentionally, nothing in the 1996 Act prevents another member of his or her household from making a separate application. Situations may arise where one or more members of a household found to be intentionally homeless were not responsible for the actions or omissions that led to the homelessness. For example, a person may have deliberately failed to pay the rent or defaulted on the mortgage payments, which resulted in homelessness or threatened homelessness, against the wishes or without the knowledge of his or her partner. However, where applicants were not directly responsible for the act or omission which led to their family or household becoming homeless, but they acquiesced in that behaviour, then they may be treated as having become homeless intentionally themselves. In considering whether an applicant has acquiesced in certain behaviour, the Secretary of State recommends that the housing authority take into account whether the applicant could reasonably be expected to have taken that position through a fear of actual or probable violence.

Cessation of occupation

11.10.   For intentional homelessness to be established there must have been actual occupation of accommodation which has ceased. However, occupation need not necessarily involve continuous occupation at all times, provided the accommodation was at the disposal of the applicant and available for his or her occupation. The accommodation which has been lost can be outside the UK.

Consequence of a deliberate act or omission

11.11. For homelessness, or threatened homelessness, to be intentional it must be a consequence of a deliberate act or omission. Having established that there was a deliberate act or omission, the housing authority will need to decide whether the loss of the applicant's home, or the likelihood of its loss, is the reasonable result of that act or omission. This is a matter of cause and effect. An example would be where a person voluntarily gave up settled accommodation that it would have been reasonable for them to continue to occupy, moved into alternative accommodation of a temporary or unsettled nature and subsequently became homeless when required to leave the alternative accommodation. Housing authorities will, therefore, need to look back to the last period of settled accommodation and the reasons why the applicant left that accommodation, to determine whether the current incidence of homelessness is the result of a deliberate act or omission.

11.12. Where a person becomes homeless intentionally, that condition may persist until the link between the causal act or omission and the intentional homelessness has been broken. It could be broken, for example, by a period in settled accommodation which follows the intentional homelessness. Whether accommodation is settled will depend on the circumstances of the particular case. Factors such as security of tenure and length of residence will be relevant. It has been established that a period in settled accommodation after an incidence of intentional homelessness would make the deliberate act or omission which led to that homelessness irrelevant in the event of a subsequent application for housing assistance. Conversely, occupation of accommodation that was merely temporary rather than settled, for example, staying with friends on an insecure basis, may not be sufficient to break the link with the earlier intentional homelessness. However, a period in settled accommodation is not necessarily the only way in which a link with the earlier intentional homelessness may be broken: some other event, such as the break-up of a marriage, may be sufficient.

Probability of violence

11.13. In cases where there is a probability of violence against an applicant if they continue, or had continued, to occupy their accommodation, and the applicant was aware of measures that could have been taken to prevent or mitigate the risk of violence but decided not to take them, their decision cannot be taken as having caused the probability of violence, and thus, indirectly, having caused the homelessness. Authorities must not assume that measures which could have been taken to prevent actual or threatened violence would necessarily have been effective.

Ex-offenders

11.14. Some ex-offenders may apply for accommodation or assistance in obtaining accommodation following a period in custody or detention because they have been unable to retain their previous accommodation, due to that period in custody or detention. In considering whether such an applicant is homeless intentionally, the housing authority will have to decide whether, taking into account all the circumstances, there was a likelihood that ceasing to occupy the accommodation could reasonably have been regarded at the time as a likely consequence of committing the offence.

Former members of the armed forces

11.15. Where service personnel are required to vacate service quarters as a result of taking up an option to give notice to leave the service, and in so doing are acting in compliance with their contractural engagement, the Secretary of State considers that they should not be considered to have become homeless intentionally.

Deliberate act or omission

11.16. For homelessness to be intentional, the act or omission that led to homelessness must have been deliberate, and applicants must always be given the opportunity to explain such behaviour. An act or omission should not generally be treated as deliberate, even where deliberately carried out, if it is forced upon the applicant through no fault of their own. Moreover, an act or omission made in good faith where someone is genuinely ignorant of a relevant fact must not be treated as deliberate (see paragraph 11.24).

11.17. Generally, an act or omission should not be considered deliberate where:

i)   the act or omission was non-payment of rent which was the result of housing benefit delays, or financial difficulties which were beyond the applicant's control;

ii)   the housing authority has reason to believe the applicant is incapable of managing his or her affairs, for example, by reason of age, mental illness or disability;

iii) the act or omission was the result of limited mental capacity; or a temporary aberration or aberrations caused by mental illness, frailty, or an assessed substance abuse problem;

iv)   the act or omission was made when the applicant was under duress;

v)   imprudence or lack of foresight on the part of an applicant led to homelessness but the act or omission was in good faith.

11.18. An applicant's actions would not amount to intentional homelessness where he or she has lost his or her home, or was obliged to sell it, because of rent or mortgage arrears resulting from significant financial difficulties, and the applicant was genuinely unable to keep up the rent or mortgage payments even after claiming benefits, and no further financial help was available.

11.19.   Where an applicant has lost a former home due to rent arrears, the reasons why the arrears accrued should be fully explored. Similarly, in cases which involve mortgagors, housing authorities will need to look at the reasons for mortgage arrears together with the applicant's ability to pay the mortgage commitment when it was taken on, given the applicant's financial circumstances at the time.

11.20.   Examples of acts or omissions which may be regarded as deliberate (unless any of the circumstances set out in paragraph 11.17 apply) include the following, where someone:

   i)   chooses to sell his or her home in circumstances where he or she is under no risk of losing it;

   ii)   has lost his or her home because of wilful and persistent refusal to pay rent or mortgage payments;

   iii)   could be said to have significantly neglected his or her affairs having disregarded sound advice from qualified persons;

   iv)   voluntarily surrenders adequate accommodation in this country or abroad which it would have been reasonable for the applicant to continue to occupy;

   v)   is evicted because of his or her anti-social behaviour, for example by nuisance to neighbours, harassment etc;

   vi)   is evicted because of violence or threats of violence by them towards another person;

   vii) leaves a job with tied accommodation and the circumstances indicate that it would have been reasonable for him or her to continue in the employment and reasonable to continue to occupy the accommodation (but note paragraph 11.15).

Available for occupation

11.21.   For homelessness to be intentional the accommodation must have been available for the applicant and anyone reasonably expected to live with him or her. Further guidance on 'availability for occupation' is provided in Chapter 8.

Reasonable to continue to occupy the accommodation

11.22.   An applicant cannot be treated as intentionally homeless unless it would have been reasonable for him or her to have continued to occupy the accommodation. Guidance on 'reasonable to continue to occupy' is provided in Chapter 8. It will be necessary for the housing authority to give careful consideration to the circumstances of the applicant and the household, in each case, and with particular care in cases where violence has been alleged.

11.23.   Authorities are reminded that, where the applicant has fled his or her home because of violence or threats of violence likely to be carried out, and has failed to pursue legal remedies against the perpetrator(s) which might have prevented the violence or threat of violence, although these decisions (to leave the home and not pursue legal remedies) may be deliberate, the homelessness would not be intentional if it would not have been reasonable for the applicant to continue to occupy the home.

Acts or omissions in good faith

11.24. Acts or omissions made in good faith where someone was genuinely unaware of a relevant fact must not be regarded as deliberate. Provided that the applicant has acted in good faith, there is no requirement that ignorance of the relevant fact be reasonable.

11.25. A general example of an act made in good faith would be a situation where someone gave up possession of accommodation in the belief that they had no legal right to continue to occupy the accommodation and, therefore, it would not be reasonable for them to continue to occupy it. This could apply where someone leaves rented accommodation in the private sector having received a valid notice to quit or notice that the assured shorthold tenancy has come to an end and the landlord requires possession of the property, and the former tenant was genuinely unaware that he or she had a right to remain until the court granted an order and warrant for possession.

11.26. Where there was dishonesty there could be no question of an act or omission having been made in good faith.

11.27. Other examples of acts or omissions that could be made in good faith might include situations where:

i) a person gets into rent arrears, being unaware that he or she may be entitled to housing benefit or other social security benefits;

ii) an owner-occupier faced with foreclosure or possession proceedings to which there is no defence, sells before the mortgagee recovers possession through the courts or surrenders the property to the lender; or

iii) a tenant, faced with possession proceedings to which there would be no defence, and where the granting of a possession order would be mandatory, surrenders the property to the landlord.

In (iii) although the housing authority may consider that it would have been reasonable for the tenant to continue to occupy the accommodation, the act should not be regarded as deliberate if the tenant made the decision to leave the accommodation in ignorance of material facts, eg the general pressure on the authority for housing assistance.

Applicant enters into an arrangement

11.28. Housing authorities will need to be alert to the possibility of collusion by which a person may claim that he or she is obliged to leave accommodation in order to take advantage of the homelessness legislation. Some parents and children, for example, may seek to take advantage of the fact that 16 and 17 year old applicants have a priority need for accommodation. Collusion is not confined to those staying with friends or relatives but can also occur between landlords and tenants. Housing authorities, while relying on experience, nonetheless need to be satisfied that collusion exists, and must not rely on hearsay or unfounded suspicions. For collusion to amount to intentional homelessness, s 191(3) specifies that there should be no other good reason for the applicant's homelessness. Examples of other good reasons include overcrowding or an obvious breakdown in relations between the applicant and his or her host or landlord. In some cases involving collusion the applicant may not actually be homeless, if there is no genuine need for the applicant to leave the accommodation. See paragraphs 8.9–8.12 for further guidance on applicants asked to leave by family or friends.

Families with children under 18

11.29. It is important that social services are alerted as quickly as possible to cases where the applicant has children under 18 and the housing authority considers the applicant may be homeless, or threatened with homelessness, intentionally. Section 213A(2) therefore requires housing authorities to have arrangements in place to ensure that all such applicants are invited to agree to the housing authority notifying the social services authority of the essential facts of their case. The arrangements must also provide that, where consent is given, the social services authority are made aware of the essential facts and, in due course, of the subsequent decision on the homelessness case. See Chapter 13 for further guidance on section 213A.

Further applications for assistance

11.30. There is no period of disqualification if someone wants to make a fresh application after being found intentionally homeless. Where a person whose application has just been decided makes a fresh application, the authority will need to decide whether there are any new facts in the fresh application which render it different from the earlier application. If no new facts are revealed, or any new facts are of a trivial nature, the authority would not be required to consider the new application. However, where the fresh application does reveal substantive new facts, the authority must treat the fresh application in the same way as it would any other application for accommodation or assistance in obtaining accommodation. Therefore, if the authority have reason to believe that the person is homeless or threatened with homelessness, the authority must make inquiries under s 184 and decide whether any interim duty is owed under s 188(1). See Chapter 6 for guidance on inquiries and Chapter 7 for guidance on the interim duty.

CHAPTER 12: 16 & 17 YEAR OLDS

12.1. **This chapter provides guidance on specific duties towards 16 and 17 year old applicants.**

Priority need

12.2. All 16 and 17 year old homeless applicants have a priority need for accommodation except those who are:

i)   a relevant child, or

ii)   a child in need who is owed a duty under s 20 of the *Children Act 1989*.

See Chapter 10 for more detailed guidance on priority need.

Relevant child or child in need owed a duty under s 20 of the 1989 Act

12.3. A relevant child is a child aged 16 or 17 who has been looked after by a local authority for at least 13 weeks since the age of 14 and has been looked after at some time while 16 or 17 and who is not currently being looked after (ie an 'eligible child' for the purposes of paragraph 19B of Schedule 2 to the *Children Act 1989*). In addition, a child is also a relevant child if he or she would have been looked after by the local authority as an eligible child but for the fact that on his or her 16th birthday he or she was detained through the criminal justice system, or in hospital, or if he or she has returned home on family placement and that has broken down (see the *Children Act 1989*, s 23A and the *Children (Leaving Care) Regulations 2001*, Regulation 4).

12.4. The *Children Act 1989* (s 20(3)) places a duty on children's services authorities to provide accommodation for a child in need aged 16 or over whose welfare is otherwise likely to be seriously prejudiced if they do not provide accommodation; and s 20(1) places a duty on children's services authorities to provide accommodation for children in need in certain other circumstances.

12.5. Responsibility for providing suitable accommodation for a relevant child or a child in need to whom a local authority owes a duty under s 20 of the *Children Act 1989* rests with the children's services authority. In cases where a housing authority considers that a s 20 duty is owed, they should verify this with the relevant children's services authority.

12.6. In all cases of uncertainty as to whether a 16 or 17 year old applicant may be a relevant child or a child in need, the housing authority should contact the relevant children's services authority and, where necessary, should provide interim accommodation under s 188, pending clarification. A framework for joint assessment of 16 and 17 year olds will need to be established by housing and children's services authorities (and housing and children's services departments within unitary authorities) to facilitate the seamless discharge of duties and appropriate services to this client group.

Family relationships

12.7. The Secretary of State considers that, generally, it will be in the best interests of 16 and 17 year olds to live in the family home, unless it would be unsafe or unsuitable for them to do so because they would be at risk of violence or abuse. It is not unusual for 16 and 17 year olds to have a turbulent relationship with their family and this can lead to temporary disagreements and even temporary estrangement. Where such disagreements look likely to lead to actual or threatened homelessness the housing authority should consider the possibility of reconciliation with the applicant's immediate family, where appropriate, or the possibility of him or her residing with another member of the wider family.

Reconciliation

12.8. In all cases involving applicants who are 16 or 17 years of age a careful assessment of the young person's circumstances and any risk to them of remaining at home should be made at the first response. Some 16 and 17 year olds may be at risk of leaving home because of a temporary breakdown in their relationship with their family. In such cases, the housing authority may be able to effect a reconciliation with the family. In some cases, however, relationships may have broken down irretrievably, and in others it may not be safe or desirable for the applicant to remain in the family home, for example, in cases involving violence or abuse.

12.9. Therefore, any mediation or reconciliation will need careful brokering and housing authorities may wish to seek the assistance of social services in all such cases.

Collusion

12.10. Where homelessness can not be avoided, local authorities should work with 16 and 17 year olds, and their families where appropriate, to explore alternative housing options. Where the main homelessness duty is owed young people need to be given the chance to consider a range of housing options including but not limited to any accommodation to be offered under s 193. Clear and accurate information is essential to allow young people to identify the right housing solution for them.

12.11. Some parents and children may seek to take advantage of the fact that 16 and 17 year old applicants have a priority need for accommodation. Housing authorities will therefore need to be alive to the possibility of collusion when assessing applications from this client group. Section 191(3) (intentional homelessness) will apply in cases where there is no genuine basis for homelessness and parents have colluded with a child and fabricated an arrangement under which the child has been asked to leave the family home (see Chapter 11 for guidance on intentional homelessness).

Care and support needs

12.12. Where young people actually become homeless and are provided with accommodation, local authorities should consider whether they have any care or support needs. Many young people who have experienced homelessness may lack skills in managing their affairs and require help with managing a tenancy and operating a household budget. Those estranged from their family, particularly care leavers, may lack the advice and support normally available to young people from family, friends and other mentors. 16 and 17 year olds who are homeless and estranged from their family will be particularly vulnerable and in need of support.

12.13. Housing authorities will need to recognise that accommodation solutions for this client group are likely to be unsuccessful if the necessary support is not provided. Close liaison with social services, the Supporting People team and agencies working with young people will be essential. Most 16 and 17 year old applicants are likely to benefit from a period in supported accommodation before moving on to a tenancy of their own, but housing authorities should consider the circumstances of each case.

12.14. Housing authorities are reminded that Bed and Breakfast (B&B) accommodation is unlikely to be suitable for 16 and 17 year olds who are in need of support. Where B&B accommodation is used for this group it ought to be as a last resort for the shortest time possible and housing authorities will need to ensure that appropriate support is provided where necessary. See Chapter 17 on the suitability of accommodation for further guidance on the use of B&B accommodation.

12.15. 16 and 17 year olds (including lone parents) who apply for housing assistance may also have care and support needs that need to be assessed. **The Secretary of State recommends that housing authorities and social services authorities (and the relevant departments within unitary authorities) have arrangements in place for joint assessments of such young people's needs, whether the application is made initially to the housing department or social services department.** In all cases where an applicant may have care, health or other support needs, it is recommended that the housing authority liaise with the social services authority, the Supporting People team and other agencies (for example, the Primary Care Trust, Criminal Justice Services, and voluntary and community organisations), as appropriate, as part of their inquiries. A joint consideration of an applicant's housing and support needs may be crucial to assist the authority in establishing whether the applicant has a priority need for accommodation and any non-housing support needs (see Chapter 4 for guidance on securing support services and Chapter 5 for guidance on joint working).

Lone teenage parents under 18

12.16. The provision of suitable accommodation with support for lone parents under 18 is a key part of the Government's Teenage Pregnancy Strategy. Providing accommodation with support for 16 and 17 year old lone parents is important for a very vulnerable group at risk of social isolation. It increases the likelihood of them making a successful transition to an independent tenancy and reduces the risk of subsequent homelessness.

12.17. The Government's objective is that all 16 and 17 year old lone parents who cannot live with their parents or partner should be offered accommodation with support. Housing authorities should work with social services, RSLs, the local teenage pregnancy co-ordinator and relevant voluntary organisations in their district to ensure that the Government's objective is met. The allocation of appropriate housing and support should be based on consideration of the young person's housing and support needs, their individual circumstances and their views and preferences. Young parents under the age of 16 must always be referred to social services so that their social care needs may be assessed. Housing authorities may find it helpful to refer to *Guidelines for Good Practice in Supported Accommodation for Young Parents*, separate guidance published jointly by DTLR and the Teenage Pregnancy Unit in September 2001 (available from **www.teenagepregnancyunit.gov.uk**).

CHAPTER 13: CO-OPERATION IN CERTAIN CASES INVOLVING CHILDREN

13.1.   This chapter provides guidance on the duty housing authorities and social services authorities have to co-operate in certain cases involving children.

13.2.   Section 10 of the *Children Act 2004* establishes a duty on county level and unitary authorities[4] to make arrangements to promote co-operation between the authority, relevant partners (including district authorities) and other persons or bodies engaged in activities in relation to children, to improve the well-being of children and young people in the authority's area. Relevant partners are required to co-operate with the authority. Section 11 of the 2004 Act requires a range of agencies – including county level and unitary authorities and district authorities where there are two tiers of local government – to make arrangements for ensuring that their functions are discharged having regard to the need to safeguard and promote the welfare of children. See Chapter 5 for guidance on joint working.

13.3.   Where an applicant is eligible for assistance and unintentionally homeless, and has a priority need because there is one or more dependent child in his or her household, the housing authority will owe a main homelessness duty to secure that accommodation is available to them. However, not all applicants with dependent children will be owed a main homelessness duty. Applicants who are found to be ineligible for assistance are not entitled to homelessness assistance under Part 7 of the 1996 Act. Where an applicant with a priority need is found to be eligible but homeless intentionally, s 190(2) requires the housing authority to secure accommodation for such period as will give the applicant a reasonable opportunity to secure accommodation for him/herself and to ensure that the applicant is provided with advice and assistance in any attempts he or she may make to secure accommodation for his or her occupation. Where an applicant with a priority need is found to be

---

4   Section 65 of the *Children Act 2004* uses the term 'children's services authority' to define these authorities as: a county council in England; a metropolitan district council; a non-metropolitan district council for an area where there is no county council; a London borough council; the Common Council of the City of London and the Council of the Isles of Scilly.

eligible but threatened with homelessness intentionally, s 195(5) requires the housing authority to ensure that the applicant is provided with advice and assistance in any attempts he or she may make to secure that accommodation does not cease to be available for his or her occupation. See Chapter 14 for guidance on the main duties owed to applicants on completion of inquiries, including the duty to provide advice and assistance.

13.4. In each of the above cases, there is a possibility that situations could arise where families may find themselves without accommodation and any prospect of further assistance from the housing authority. This could give rise to a situation in which the children of such families might become children in need, within the meaning of the term as set out in s 17 of the *Children Act 1989*.

13.5. In such cases, it is important that local authority children's services are alerted as quickly as possible because the family may wish to seek assistance under Part 3 of the *Children Act 1989*, in circumstances in which they are owed no, or only limited, assistance under the homelessness legislation. This will give local authority children's services the opportunity to consider the circumstances of the child(ren) and family, and plan any response that may be deemed by them to be appropriate.

13.6. Section 213A of the 1996 Act applies where a housing authority has reason to believe that an applicant for assistance under Part 7 with whom a person under the age of 18 normally resides, or might reasonably be expected to reside:

a) may be ineligible for assistance;
b) may be homeless and may have become so intentionally; or
c) may be threatened with homelessness intentionally.

In these circumstances, a housing authority is required to have arrangements in place to ensure that the applicant is invited to consent to the referral of the essential facts of his or her case to the social services authority[5] for the district (or, in the case of a unitary authority, the social services department of the authority). The arrangements must also provide that, where consent is given, the social services authority or department is made aware of the essential facts and, in due course, of the subsequent decision in relation to the homelessness case.

13.7. The requirement to obtain the applicant's consent to the referral of the essential facts of his or her case under section 213A(2) or (3) does not affect any other power for the housing authority to disclose information about a homelessness case to the social services authority or department. For example, even where consent is withheld, the housing authority should disclose information about a homelessness case to the social services authority, if they have reason to believe that a child is, or may be, at risk of significant harm, as laid out in Chapter 5 of *Working Together to Safeguard Children: A guide to*

---

[5] 'Social services authority' is the term used in s 213A of the *Housing Act 1996*, and defined in s 217 of the *Housing Act 1996*. Such authorities are often now referred to as 'children's services authorities'. See footnote [4].

inter-agency working to safeguard and promote the welfare of children (2006). *Working Together* was recently revised to reflect developments in legislation, policy and practice. It was published in April 2006 and can be found on the *Every Child Matters* website at http://www.everychildmatters.gov.uk/socialcare/ safeguarding/workingtogether/

13.8. Where a family with one or more children has been found ineligible for assistance under Part 7 or homeless, or threatened with homelessness, intentionally and approaches the social services authority, that authority will need to decide whether the child is a 'child in need' under the terms of the *Children Act 1989*, by carrying out an assessment of their needs in accordance with the *Framework for the Assessment of Children in Need and their Families* (2000), Department of Health. The findings of the assessment should provide the basis for the decision as to whether the child is a 'child in need' and what, if any, services should be offered to the child in order to safeguard and promote his/her welfare. Section 17 of the *Children Act 1989* requires a local authority to promote the upbringing of children within their family, in so far as this is consistent with their general duty to safeguard and promote their welfare. The social services authority might wish to consider, for example, whether the best way of meeting the child's needs would be by assisting the family to obtain accommodation, for example by providing temporary accommodation or a rent deposit, as part of the exercise of its duty set out in s 17 of the *Children Act 1989. Local Authority Circular 2003(13): Guidance on accommodating children in need and their families* provides further guidance to social services authorities on the effect of s 17.

13.9. Where a social services authority has been made aware of a family found to be ineligible for assistance or homeless, or threatened with homelessness, intentionally by the housing authority, and they consider the needs of a child or children could best be met by helping the family to obtain accommodation, they can request the housing authority to provide them with such advice and assistance as is reasonable in the circumstances. Under s 213A(5), the housing authority must comply with such a request. Advice and assistance as is reasonable in the circumstances might include, for example, help with locating suitable accommodation and making an inspection of the property to ensure that it meets adequate standards of fitness and safety. However, the housing authority is not under a duty to provide accommodation for the family in these circumstances.

13.10. Section 213A(6) requires unitary authorities to have similar arrangements in place so that the housing department provide the social services department with such advice and assistance as they may reasonably request.

13.11. Housing authorities may also wish to consider alerting social services authorities to cases where an applicant whose household includes a child has refused an offer of accommodation which the authority is satisfied is suitable, and the authority has made a decision that it has discharged its homelessness duty under Part 7. In such cases the household could find itself without accommodation and any prospect of further assistance from the housing authority. The applicant would, however, need to consent to the housing authority notifying the social services authority of the essential facts of his or her case (unless the housing authority has any other powers to disclose the information without consent).

CHAPTER 14: MAIN DUTIES OWED TO APPLICANTS ON COMPLETION OF INQUIRIES

14.1. **This chapter provides guidance on the main duties owed to applicants where the housing authority has completed its inquiries and is satisfied that an applicant is eligible for assistance and homeless or threatened with homelessness. The chapter also provides guidance on the circumstances that will bring the s 193(2) duty ('the main homelessness duty') to an end.**

14.2. In many cases early, effective intervention can prevent homelessness occurring. The Secretary of State considers that housing authorities should take steps to prevent homelessness wherever possible, and offer a broad range of advice and assistance to those who face the prospect of losing their current home. However, where a housing authority has completed inquiries made under s 184 (see Chapter 6 for guidance on applications) and is satisfied that an applicant is eligible for assistance and homeless or threatened with homelessness, then one or more of the duties outlined in this chapter will apply under Part 7.

14.3. No duty is owed under Part 7 to applicants who are ineligible for assistance or not homeless or threatened with homelessness. However, homelessness strategies should aim to prevent homelessness amongst all households in the district and under s 179 advice and information about homelessness and the prevention of homelessness must be available free of charge to any person in the district, including these applicants. Housing authorities may also choose to offer other assistance to help them obtain accommodation, such as a rent deposit.

Duties to provide advice and assistance

14.4. Housing authorities have a duty to ensure that the applicant is provided with advice and assistance in a number of different circumstances, and these are dealt with below. These duties require an assessment to be made of the housing needs of the applicant before advice and assistance is provided. This assessment may need to range wider than the housing authority's inquiries into the applicant's homelessness carried out for the purpose of s 184, and should inform the provision of appropriate advice and assistance for that particular applicant. Among other things, the Secretary of State considers the assessment should identify any factors that may make it difficult for the applicant to secure accommodation for him or herself, for example, poverty, outstanding debt, health problems, disabilities and whether English is not a first language. In particular, housing authorities are advised to take account of the circumstances that led to the applicant's homelessness, or threatened homelessness, since these may impact on his or her ability to secure and maintain accommodation and may indicate what types of accommodation would be appropriate.

Duties owed to applicants who are threatened with homelessness

14.5. Under s 175(4), a person is 'threatened with homelessness' if he or she is likely to become homeless within 28 days. However, the Secretary of State considers that housing authorities should not wait until homelessness is a likelihood or is imminent before providing advice and assistance. Early intervention may enable homelessness to be prevented, or delayed sufficiently to allow for a planned move to be arranged. However, where a housing authority has completed its inquiries under s 184 and is satisfied that an applicant is eligible for assistance and threatened with homelessness, then the specific duties outlined in paragraphs 14.6–14.9 below will apply.

Unintentionally threatened with homelessness and has priority need (s 195(2))

14.6. Where the authority are satisfied that an applicant is threatened with homelessness unintentionally, eligible for assistance and has a priority need for accommodation, it has a **duty** under s 195(2) *to take reasonable steps to secure that accommodation does not cease to be available for the applicant's occupation.*

14.7. Such reasonable steps may include for example, negotiation with the applicant's landlord or, in cases where the applicant has been asked to leave by family and friends, by exploring the scope for mediation and the provision of support to the household in order to ease any pressures that may have led to the applicant being asked to leave. Where a housing authority is able to identify the precise reasons why the applicant is being required to leave his or her current accommodation – for example, by interviewing the applicant and visiting his or her landlord or family or friends (as appropriate) – there may be specific actions that the housing authority or other organisations can take, for example, addressing rent arrears due to delays in housing benefit payments or providing mediation services through the voluntary sector, that can prevent the threat of homelessness being realised. See Chapter 2 for further guidance on preventing homelessness.

14.8. Under s 195(3A), as soon as an authority has become subject to a duty under s 195(2), the authority must give the applicant a copy of the statement included in their allocation scheme about their policy on offering choice to people allocated housing accommodation under Part 6. Authorities are required to include such a statement in their allocation scheme by virtue of s 167(1A) of the 1996 Act.

14.9. Where the housing authority is under a duty under s 195(2) and they are unable to prevent the applicant losing his or her current accommodation, the authority will need to secure alternative suitable accommodation for the applicant. Authorities should not delay; arrangements to secure alternative accommodation should begin as soon as it becomes clear that it will not be possible to prevent the applicant from losing their current home. Section 195(4) provides that, where alternative suitable accommodation is secured, the provisions of s 193(3) to (9) will apply in relation to the duty under s 195(2) as they apply in relation to the duty under s 193(2) (see paragraphs 14.17 to 14.24 below).

Unintentionally threatened with homelessness, no priority need (s 195(5) and s 195(9))

14.10. Where the housing authority are satisfied that an applicant is threatened with homelessness, eligible for assistance and does not have a priority need for accommodation, it has a **duty** under s 195(5) *to ensure that the applicant is provided with advice and assistance in any attempts he or she may make to secure that accommodation does not cease to be available for his or her occupation.*

14.11. In addition, where the housing authority are satisfied that an applicant is threatened with homelessness unintentionally, it has a **power** under s 195(9) *to take reasonable steps to secure that accommodation does not cease to be available for the applicant's occupation.* See Chapter 2 for guidance on preventing homelessness and paragraph 14.7 above.

Intentionally threatened with homelessness and has priority need (s 195(5))

14.12. Where the authority are satisfied that an applicant is threatened with homelessness intentionally, eligible for assistance and has a priority need for accommodation, the housing authority has a **duty** under s 195(5) *to ensure that the applicant is provided with advice and assistance in any attempts he or she may make to secure that accommodation does not cease to be available for his or her occupation.* See Chapter 2 for guidance on preventing homelessness.

Duties owed to applicants who are homeless

14.13. Under s 175 a person is 'homeless' if he or she has no accommodation in the UK or elsewhere which is available for his or her occupation and which that person has a legal right to occupy. Where a housing authority has completed its inquiries under s 184 and is satisfied that an applicant is eligible for assistance and homeless then the specific duties outlined below will apply.

Unintentionally homeless and has priority need (s 193(2))

14.14. Where an applicant is unintentionally homeless, eligible for assistance and has a priority need for accommodation, the housing authority has a **duty** under s 193(2) *to secure that accommodation is available for occupation by the applicant* (unless it refers the application to another housing authority under s 198). This is commonly known as 'the main homelessness duty'. In all cases, the accommodation secured must be available for occupation by the applicant together with any other person who normally resides with him or her as a member of his or her family, or any other person who might reasonably be expected to reside, with him or her, and must be suitable for their occupation. See Chapter 16 for guidance on discharging the duty to secure accommodation and Chapter 17 for guidance on suitability of accommodation.

14.15. Acceptance of a duty under s 193(2) does not prevent an immediate allocation of accommodation under Part 6 of the 1996 Act if the applicant has the necessary priority under the housing authority's allocation scheme. Under s 193(3A), as soon as an authority has become subject to a duty under s 193(2), the authority must give the applicant a copy of the statement included in their allocation scheme about their policy on offering choice to people allocated housing accommodation under Part 6. Authorities are required to include such a statement in their allocation scheme by virtue of s 167(1A) of the 1996 Act.

14.16. If the housing authority has notified the applicant that it proposes to refer the case to another housing authority, the authority has a duty under s 200(1) to secure that accommodation is available for the applicant until he or she is notified of the decision whether the conditions for referral of his case are met. The duty under s 200(1) is therefore an interim duty only. Once it has been established whether or not the conditions for referral are met, a duty under s 193(2) will be owed by either the notified housing authority or the notifying housing authority. See Chapter 18 for guidance on referrals to another housing authority.

How the s 193(2) duty ends (this also applies where alternative accommodation has been secured under s 195(2))

14.17. The housing authority will cease to be subject to the duty under s 193(2) (the main homelessness duty) in the following circumstances:

i)   *the applicant accepts an offer of accommodation under Part 6 (an allocation of long term social housing)* (s 193(6)(c)): this would include an offer of an assured tenancy of a registered social landlord property via the housing authority's allocation scheme (see current guidance on the allocation of accommodation issued under s 169 of the 1996 Act);

ii)   *the applicant accepts an offer of an assured tenancy (other than an assured shorthold tenancy) from a private landlord* (s 193(6)(cc)): this could include an offer of an assured tenancy made by a registered social landlord;

iii) *the applicant accepts a qualifying offer of an assured shorthold tenancy from a private landlord* (s 193(7B)). The local authority must not approve an offer of an assured shorthold tenancy for the purposes of s 193(7B), unless they are satisfied that the accommodation is suitable and that it would be reasonable for the applicant to accept it (s 193(7F)) (see paragraph 14.25 below);

iv)   *the applicant refuses a final offer of accommodation under Part 6 (an allocation of long term social housing)*: the duty does not end unless the applicant is informed of the possible consequences of refusal and of his or her right to ask for a review of the suitability of the accommodation (s 193(7)), the offer is made in writing and states that it is a final offer (s 193(7A)), and the housing authority is satisfied that the accommodation is suitable and that it would be reasonable for the applicant to accept it (s 193(7F)) (see paragraph 14.25 below);

v) *the applicant refuses an offer of accommodation to discharge the duty which the housing authority is satisfied is suitable for the applicant* (s 193(5)): the duty does not end unless the applicant is informed of the possible consequences of refusal and of his or her right to ask for a review of the suitability of the accommodation. The housing authority must also notify the applicant that it regards itself as having discharged its duty, before it can end;

vi) *the applicant ceases to be eligible for assistance as defined in s 185 of the 1996 Act*;

vii) *the applicant becomes homeless intentionally from accommodation made available to him or her under s 193 or s 195*; see Chapter 11 for guidance on determining whether an applicant became homeless intentionally;

viii) *the applicant otherwise voluntarily ceases to occupy as his or her principal home accommodation made available under s 193 or s 195.*

14.18. The Secretary of State recommends that applicants are given the chance to view accommodation before being required to decide whether they accept or refuse an offer, and before being required to sign any written agreement relating to the accommodation (eg a tenancy agreement). Under s 202(1A), an applicant who is offered accommodation can request a review of its suitability whether or not he or she has accepted the offer. See Chapter 17 for guidance on suitability and Chapter 19 for guidance on reviews.

Qualifying offer of an assured shorthold tenancy

14.19. An offer of an assured shorthold tenancy is a qualifying offer if:

i) it is made, with the approval of the authority, in pursuance of arrangements made by the authority with the landlord with a view to bringing the authority's duty under s 193 to an end;

ii) it is for a fixed term within the meaning of Part 1 of the *Housing Act 1988* (ie not a periodic tenancy); and

iii) it is accompanied by a written statement that states the term of the tenancy being offered and explains in ordinary language that there is no obligation on the applicant to accept the offer, but if the offer is accepted the housing authority will cease to be subject to the s 193 duty.

14.20. The s 193 duty will not end with acceptance of an offer of a qualifying tenancy unless the applicant signs a statement acknowledging that he or she has understood the written statement accompanying the offer.

Reasonable to accept an offer

14.21. Housing authorities must not make a final offer under Part 6 or approve a qualifying offer of an assured shorthold tenancy unless they are satisfied that the accommodation is suitable for the applicant and that it is

Appendix 2
England: Homelessness

reasonable for him or her to accept the offer (s 193(7F)) (see Chapter 17 for guidance on suitability). Where an applicant has contractual or other obligations in respect of his or her existing accommodation (eg a tenancy agreement or lease), the housing authority can reasonably expect the offer to be taken up only if the applicant is able to bring those obligations to an end before he is required to take up the offer (s 193(8)).

14.22. Housing authorities must allow applicants a reasonable period for considering offers of accommodation made under Part 6 that will bring the homelessness duty to an end whether accepted or refused. There is no set reasonable period; some applicants may require longer than others depending on their circumstances, whether they wish to seek advice in making their decision and whether they are already familiar with the property in question. Longer periods may be required where the applicant is in hospital or temporarily absent from the district. In deciding what is a reasonable period, housing authorities must take into account the applicant's circumstances in each case.

Other circumstances that bring the s 193(2) duty to an end

14.23. Under s 193(6) the housing authority will also cease to be subject to the duty under s 193 in the following circumstances:

i) *the applicant ceases to be eligible for assistance as defined in s 185 of the 1996 Act*;

ii) *the applicant becomes homeless intentionally from accommodation made available to him or her under s 193 or s 195*: see Chapter 11 for guidance on determining whether an applicant became homeless intentionally;

iii) *the applicant otherwise voluntarily ceases to occupy as his or her only or principal home accommodation made available under s 193 or s 195*.

Further applications

14.24. Under s 193(9) a person who ceases to be owed a duty under s 193(2) can make a fresh application for accommodation or assistance in obtaining accommodation (see Chapter 6 for guidance on applications).

Unintentionally homeless and has no priority need (s 192(2) and s 192(3))

14.25. Where an applicant is unintentionally homeless, eligible for assistance and does not have a priority need for accommodation, the housing authority has a **duty** under s 192(2) *to ensure that the applicant is provided with advice and assistance in any attempts he or she may make to secure that accommodation becomes available for his or her occupation*. The housing authority might, for example, provide assistance with a rent deposit or guarantee to help the applicant to obtain accommodation in the private rented sector, or advice on applying for an allocation of accommodation through the social housing waiting list or through another social landlord (see Chapter 2 for guidance on advisory services).

14.26. In addition, housing authorities have a **power** under s 192(3) *to secure that accommodation is available for occupation by the applicant.* Authorities should consider whether to use this power in all relevant cases.

Intentionally homeless and has priority need (s 190(2))

14.27. Where an applicant is intentionally homeless, eligible for assistance and has a priority need for accommodation, the housing authority has a duty under s 190(2) to:

a) *secure that accommodation is available for the applicant's occupation for such period as it considers will give him or her a reasonable opportunity of securing accommodation for his or her occupation (s 190(2)(a)); and*

b) *provide the applicant, or secure that the applicant is provided with, advice and assistance in any attempts he or she may make to secure that accommodation becomes available for his or her occupation (s 190(2)(b)).*

14.28. The accommodation secured must be suitable. Housing authorities must consider each case on its merits when determining the period for which accommodation will be secured. A few weeks may provide the applicant with a reasonable opportunity to secure accommodation for him or herself. However, some applicants might require longer, and others, particularly where the housing authority provides pro-active and effective advice and assistance, might require less time. In particular, housing authorities will need to take account of the housing circumstances in the local area, including how readily other accommodation is available in the district, and have regard to the particular circumstances of the applicant, including the resources available to him or her to provide rent in advance or a rent deposit where this may be required by private landlords.

14.29. In addition to securing accommodation, the housing authority must ensure the applicant is provided with advice and assistance to help him or her secure accommodation for him/herself. This might include, for example, assistance with a rent deposit or guarantee to help the applicant to obtain accommodation in the private rented sector, or advice on applying for an allocation of long term social housing or accommodation through another social landlord. See Chapter 2 for guidance on advisory services.

Intentionally homeless and has no priority need (s 190(3))

14.30. Where an applicant is intentionally homeless, eligible for assistance and does not have a priority need for accommodation, the housing authority has a **duty** under s 190(3) *to ensure that the applicant is provided with advice and assistance in any attempts he or she may make to secure that accommodation becomes available for his or her occupation.* This might include, for example, assistance with a rent deposit or guarantee to help the applicant to obtain accommodation in the private rented sector, or advice on applying for an allocation of long term social housing accommodation or through another social landlord. See Chapter 2 for guidance on advisory services.

CHAPTER 15: DISCRETIONARY POWERS TO SECURE ACCOMMODATION

15.1. This chapter provides guidance on the discretionary *powers* housing authorities have to secure accommodation for a household where they do not have a *duty* to secure accommodation for that household (see Chapter 16 for guidance on discharge of duties to secure accommodation).

15.2. Housing authorities have powers to secure accommodation for:

i) applicants who are eligible for assistance, unintentionally homeless and do not have a priority need for accommodation;

ii) applicants who request a review of the housing authority's decision on their case and who satisfy the relevant conditions, pending a decision on the review; and

iii) applicants who appeal to the county court against the housing authority's decision and who satisfy the relevant conditions, pending the determination of the appeal.

15.3. The fact that a housing authority has decided that an applicant is ineligible for housing assistance under Part 7 does not preclude it from exercising its powers to secure accommodation pending a review or appeal. However, housing authorities should note that s 54 of, and Schedule 3 to, the *Nationality, Immigration and Asylum Act 2002* prevent them from exercising their powers to accommodate an applicant pending a review or appeal to the county court, where the applicant is a person who falls within one of a number of classes of person specified in Schedule 3. See paragraphs 9.20–9.23 in Chapter 9 on eligibility for assistance for further details.

Ways of securing accommodation

15.4. A housing authority may only discharge its housing functions under Part 7 in the following ways:

a) by securing that suitable accommodation provided by them is available for the applicant (s 206(1)(a));

b) by securing that the applicant obtains suitable accommodation from some other person (s 206(1)(b)); or

c) by giving the applicant such advice and assistance as will secure that suitable accommodation is available from some other person (s 206(1)(c)).

See Chapter 17 for guidance on the suitability of accommodation and Chapter 8 for guidance on when accommodation is available for occupation. In so far as is reasonably practicable, accommodation should be secured within the authority's own district (s 208(1)).

Power to secure accommodation for applicants who are unintentionally homeless and do not have priority need

15.5. Under s 192(3), housing authorities may secure that accommodation is made available for applicants who are eligible for assistance, unintentionally homeless and do not have a priority need for accommodation. Where a housing authority decides to exercise this power it will still have a duty under s 192(2) to provide advice and assistance to the applicant in any attempts that he or she may make to secure accommodation for him/herself. See Chapter 14 for guidance on this duty.

15.6. By virtue of paragraph 4 of Schedule 1 to the *Housing Act 1985*, a tenancy granted under the power in s 192(3) will not be a secure tenancy. Housing authorities are reminded that all secure and introductory tenancies must be allocated in accordance with their allocation scheme, as framed under Part 6.

15.7. Housing authorities should consider using this power in all relevant cases. Any exercise of, or decision not to exercise, a power may be open to challenge by way of judicial review. In considering the use of this power, housing authorities must have regard to the legitimate expectations of others in housing need who have applied for an allocation of housing under Part 6, and to any need for accommodation to meet their obligations under Part 7.

15.8. Housing authorities should, in particular, consider exercising the s 192(3) power in circumstances where to do so would enable compliance with the obligations imposed on them by virtue of s 6 of the *Human Rights Act 1998* and where not doing so would mean acting in a way that may be incompatible with the applicant's Convention rights. The same is true of the power in s 195(8) (see paragraph 15.17 below).

15.9. Housing authorities may also wish to consider exercising the s 192(3) power to provide accommodation for a limited period to applicants such as key workers who are unintentionally homeless but do not have priority need under Part 7, or priority for an allocation under Part 6. This would be particularly appropriate where it would be in the interests of the local community for such persons to be accommodated in the district.

15.10. Non-secure tenancies will generally be suitable for a limited period only. They should be provided as part of a managed programme of accommodation to give the applicant an opportunity to secure a more settled housing solution in due course. This should be explained to the applicant from the outset and the housing authority should assist him or her to secure alternative accommodation. Reasonable notice should be given of a decision to stop exercising the power.

15.11. Housing authorities should not provide accommodation under s 192(3) as an alternative to allocating accommodation under Part 6 and should not allow non-secure tenancies to continue over the long-term.

Powers to accommodate pending a review

15.12.   Under s 202, applicants have the right to ask for a review of a housing authority's decision on a number of issues relating to their case (see Chapter 19 for guidance on reviews). Housing authorities have three powers to accommodate applicants pending a decision on the review. The relevant powers are found in s 188(3), s 195(8)(b) and s 200(5).

15.13.   Under s 188(1), housing authorities must secure that accommodation is available for occupation by an applicant who they have reason to believe is:

(a)   homeless,
(b)   eligible for assistance, and
(c)   in priority need,

pending their decision as to what duty, if any, is owed to that applicant under Part 7. See Chapter 7 for further guidance on this interim duty. Under s 188(3), if the applicant requests a review of the housing authority's decision on the duty owed to them under Part 7, the authority has the power to secure that accommodation is available for the applicant's occupation pending a decision on the review.

15.14.   Section 188(3) includes a power to secure that accommodation is available where the applicant was found to be intentionally homeless and in priority need and:

(a)   a duty was owed under s 190(2)(a);
(b)   the s 190(2)(a) duty has been fully discharged; and
(c)   the applicant is awaiting a decision on a review.

15.15.   In considering whether to exercise their s 188(3) power, housing authorities will need to balance the objective of maintaining fairness between homeless persons in circumstances where they have decided that no duty is owed to them against proper consideration of the possibility that the applicant might be right. The Secretary of State is of the view that housing authorities should consider the following, although other factors may also be relevant:

(a)   the merits of the applicant's case that the original decision was flawed and the extent to which it can properly be said that the decision was one which was either contrary to the apparent merits or was one which involved a very fine balance of judgment;
(b)   whether any new material, information or argument has been put to them which could alter the original decision; and
(c)   the personal circumstances of the applicant and the consequences to him or her of a decision not to exercise the discretion to accommodate.

The Secretary of State considers that when determining the merits of the applicant's case that the original decision was flawed, housing authorities should take account of whether there may have been procedural irregularities in making the original decision which could have affected the decision taken.

15.16.   Housing authorities should give applicants reasonable notice to vacate accommodation provided under s 188(3) following an unsuccessful s 202 review. The Secretary of State considers that reasonableness should be judged against the particular applicant's circumstances. The applicant will require time to enable him or her to make alternative accommodation arrangements and housing authorities should take account of the fact that this may be easier for some applicants than others. Housing authorities may also require time to consider whether they should exercise their discretion under s 204(4) where the applicant appeals to the county court under s 204(1) (see paragraph 15.21).

15.17. Under s 195(5)(b), where a housing authority is satisfied that an applicant is:

(a)   threatened with homelessness,
(b)   eligible for assistance, and
(c)   has a priority need, but
(d)   became threatened with homelessness intentionally,

the authority is under a duty to provide the applicant (or secure that he or she is provided with) advice and assistance so that accommodation does not cease to be available for his or her occupation. Under s 195(8)(b), if the applicant requests a review of the housing authority's decision and, pending a decision on the review, becomes homeless, the housing authority may secure that accommodation is available for his or her occupation.

15.18. Under s 200(1), where a housing authority notifies another authority of its opinion that the conditions for the referral of an applicant's case to that authority are met, the authority has a duty to secure that accommodation is available for occupation by the applicant until a decision on the referral is reached. See Chapter 18 for guidance on local connection and referrals. If the applicant subsequently requests a review of the decision reached on the referral of his or her case, the notifying authority has the power under s 200(5) to secure that accommodation is available for the applicant's occupation pending the decision on that review.

15.19. Where, generally, only a small proportion of requests for a review are successful, it may be open to housing authorities to adopt a policy of deciding to exercise their powers to accommodate pending a review only in exceptional circumstances. However, such a policy would need to be applied flexibly and each case would need to be considered on its particular facts. In deciding whether there were exceptional circumstances, the housing authority would need to take account of all material considerations and disregard all those which were immaterial.

15.20. Where an applicant is refused accommodation pending a review, he or she may seek to challenge the decision by way of judicial review.

Power to accommodate pending an appeal to the county court

15.21. Applicants have the right to appeal to the county court on a point of law against a housing authority's decision on a review or, if they are not notified of the review decision, against the original homelessness decision (see

Chapter 19 for guidance on appeals). Under s 204(4), housing authorities have the power to accommodate certain applicants:

(a)   during the period for making an appeal against their decision, and

(b)   if an appeal is brought, until it and any subsequent appeals are finally determined.

This power may be exercised where the housing authority was previously under a duty to secure accommodation for the applicant's occupation under s 188 (interim duty pending initial inquiries), s 190 (duty owed to applicants intentionally homeless and in priority need), or s 200 (interim duty owed pending decision on a referral). The power may also be exercised in a case where the applicant was owed a duty under s 195(5)(b) (intentionally threatened with homelessness and in priority need), the applicant requested a review and subsequently become homeless, and, in consequence, the housing authority had a power under s 195(8)(b) to secure accommodation pending the decision on the review.

15.22.   The power under s 204(4) may be exercised whether or not the housing authority has exercised its powers to accommodate the applicant pending a review.

15.23.   In deciding whether to exercise this power, housing authorities will need to adopt the same approach, and consider the same factors, as for a decision whether to exercise their power to accommodate pending a review (see paragraph 15.12).

15.24.   Under s 204A, applicants have a right to appeal to the county court against a decision not to secure accommodation for them pending their main appeal. In deciding a s 204A appeal, the court must apply the principles that would be applied by the High Court on an application for judicial review. The county court cannot substitute its own decision as such. However, where the court quashes the decision of the housing authority, it may order the housing authority to accommodate the applicant, but only where it is satisfied that failure to do so would substantially prejudice the applicant's ability to pursue the main appeal on the homelessness decision.

CHAPTER 16: SECURING ACCOMMODATION

16.1.   This chapter provides guidance on the different ways in which housing authorities can ensure that suitable accommodation is available for applicants. In the case of the main homelessness duty the obligation to secure such accommodation will continue until such time as the duty ends in accordance with s 193.

Ways of securing accommodation

16.2.   Section 206(1) provides that a housing authority may only discharge its housing functions under Part 7 in the following ways:

(a)   by securing that suitable accommodation provided by them is available for the applicant (s 206(1)(a));

(b)   by securing that the applicant obtains suitable accommodation from some other person (s 206(1)(b)); or

(c)   by giving the applicant such advice and assistance as will secure that suitable accommodation is available from some other person (s 206(1)(c)).

16.3. Accommodation secured must be available for occupation by the applicant and any other person who normally resides with them as a member of their family, or might reasonably be expected to reside with them. The accommodation must also be suitable for their occupation. See Chapter 8 for guidance on when accommodation is available for occupation and Chapter 17 for guidance on the suitability of accommodation.

16.4. In deciding what accommodation needs to be secured housing authorities will need to consider whether the applicant has any support needs. Housing authorities will therefore need to make arrangements for effective links with the Supporting People team, the social services authority or other bodies (for example, Primary Care Trusts, Criminal Justice Services, RSLs and voluntary and community organisations) to ensure that a joint assessment of an applicant's housing and support needs can be made where necessary. See Chapter 4 for guidance on securing support services.

16.5. Where a housing authority has a duty under s 193(2) to secure accommodation for an applicant ('the main homelessness duty'), the Secretary of State recommends that the authority considers, where availability of suitable housing allows, securing settled (rather than temporary) accommodation that will bring the duty to an end in the immediate or short term. For example, an offer of accommodation under the housing authority's allocation scheme or a qualifying offer of an assured shorthold tenancy from a private landlord. See Chapter 14 for guidance on bringing the s 193(2) duty to an end.

16.6. The Secretary of State considers that, generally, it is inappropriate for social housing to be used as temporary accommodation for applicants other than for short periods (see paragraph 16.18 below). Except in limited circumstances where social housing is only going to be available for use for a short period, where an authority has placed a household in social housing as a temporary arrangement to fulfil a duty under s 193(2), the Secretary of State recommends that the authority considers offering the household a settled home under the terms of its allocation scheme as soon as possible.

Accommodation secured out of district

16.7. Section 208(1) requires housing authorities to secure accommodation within their district, in so far as is reasonably practicable. Housing authorities should, therefore, aim to secure accommodation within their own district wherever possible, except where there are clear benefits for the applicant of being accommodated outside of the district. This could occur, for example, where the applicant, and/or a member of his or her household, would be at risk of domestic or other violence in the district and need to be accommodated elsewhere to reduce the risk of further contact with the perpetrator(s) or where ex-offenders or drug/alcohol users would benefit from being accommodated outside the district to help break links with previous contacts which could exert a negative influence.

16.8. Where it is not reasonably practicable for the applicant to be placed in accommodation within the housing authority's district, and the housing authority places the applicant in accommodation elsewhere, s 208(2) requires the housing authority to notify the housing authority in whose district the accommodation is situated of the following:

i)   the name of the applicant;

ii)   the number and description of other persons who normally reside with the applicant as a member of his or her family or might reasonably be expected to do so;

iii) the address of the accommodation;

iv)   the date on which the accommodation was made available;

v)   which function the housing authority is discharging in securing the accommodation.

The notice must be given in writing within 14 days of the accommodation being made available to the applicant.

16.9. The Secretary of State considers that applicants whose household has a need for social services support or a need to maintain links with other essential services within the borough, for example specialist medical services or special schools, should be given priority for accommodation within the housing authority's own district. In particular, careful consideration should be given to applicants with a mental illness or learning disability who may have a particular need to remain in a specific area, for example to maintain links with health service professionals and/or a reliance on existing informal support networks and community links. Such applicants may be less able than others to adapt to any disruption caused by being placed in accommodation in another district.

Access to support services

16.10. The Secretary of State recommends that housing authorities consider what arrangements need to be in place to ensure that households placed in temporary accommodation, within their district or outside, are able to access relevant support services, including health, education and social services. The Secretary of State considers that all babies and young children placed in temporary accommodation, for example, should have the opportunity to receive health and developmental checks from health visitors and/or other primary health care professionals. See Chapter 4 for further guidance on securing support services.

Accommodation provided by the housing authority

16.11. Housing authorities may secure accommodation by providing suitable accommodation for the applicant themselves (s 206(1)(a)), in which case the housing authority will be the immediate landlord of the applicant, for example, where the housing authority place the applicant in:

i) a house or flat from its own stock (ie held under Part 2 of the *Housing Act 1985*);

ii) a hostel owned by the housing authority; or

iii) accommodation leased by the housing authority from another landlord (eg under a private sector leasing agreement) and sub-let to the applicant.

Housing authority's own stock

16.12. In considering whether to provide accommodation from their own stock, housing authorities will need to balance the requirements of applicants owed a duty under Part 7 against the need to provide accommodation for others who have priority for an allocation under Part 6 of the 1996 Act. **The Secretary of State considers that, generally, it is inappropriate for social housing to be used as temporary accommodation for applicants other than for short periods.**

16.13. Paragraph 4 of Schedule 1 to the *Housing Act 1985* provides that a tenancy granted by a housing authority in pursuance of any function under Part 7 is not a secure tenancy unless the housing authority notifies the tenant that it is such. Housing authorities are reminded that the allocation of secure and introductory tenancies must be made in accordance with their allocation scheme framed under the provisions of Part 6.

Housing authority hostels

16.14. Some housing authorities operate their own hostels and may wish to use these to accommodate certain applicants, particularly where they consider an applicant would benefit from a supported environment. See paragraphs 16.25 and 16.26 for further guidance on the use of hostel accommodation.

Accommodation leased from a private landlord

16.15. Accommodation leased from a private landlord can provide housing authorities with a source of good quality, self-contained accommodation which can be let to applicants. Where there is a need for temporary accommodation, housing authorities are encouraged to maximise their use of this type of leasing, in so far as they can secure cost-effective arrangements with landlords.

16.16. Under the prudential capital finance system (introduced by the *Local Government Act 2003* on 1 April 2004) local authorities are free to borrow without Government consent, provided that they can service the debts without

Appendix 2
England: Homelessness

extra Government support. The authority must determine how much it can afford to borrow. The new system ended the former financial disincentives to use leasing (and other forms of credit). Consequently, there is no longer any need for special concessions relating to leases of property owned by private landlords where that property is used to accommodate households owed a duty under Part 7. When entering into leases, as when borrowing, the capital finance rules simply require authorities to be satisfied that the associated liabilities are affordable.

Accommodation secured from another person

16.17.   Housing authorities may secure that the applicant obtains suitable accommodation from some other person (s 206(1)(b)). Housing authorities can make use of a wide range of accommodation, including housing in the private rented sector and accommodation held by RSLs. The following paragraphs outline a number of options for securing accommodation from another landlord, which are available to housing authorities.

Registered social landlords

16.18.   As the proportion of housing stock in the social sector held by RSLs increases, housing authorities should ensure that they maximise the opportunities for securing housing from RSLs. Under s 213 of the 1996 Act, where requested by a housing authority, an RSL must assist the housing authority in carrying out their duties under the homelessness legislation by co-operating with them as far as is reasonable in the circumstances. Housing Corporation regulatory guidance, issued with the consent of the Secretary of State under s 36 of the 1996 Act, requires RSLs, on request, to provide a proportion of their stock for nominations and as temporary accommodation for people owed a homelessness duty under Part 7 of the 1996 Act – to such extent as is reasonable in the circumstances. **The Secretary of State considers that, generally, it is inappropriate for social housing to be used as temporary accommodation other than for short periods** (see paragraph 16.6 above). Where a longer-term stay occurs or seems likely, the authority and RSL should consider offering an assured tenancy to bring the main homelessness duty to an end. See Annex 5 for further guidance on RSL co-operation with housing authorities.

16.19.   Housing authorities may wish to consider contracting with RSLs for assistance in discharging their housing functions under arrangements whereby the RSL lease and/or manage accommodation owned by private landlords, which can be let to households owed a homelessness duty and nominated by the housing authority. A general consent under s 25 of the *Local Government Act 1988* (*The General Consent under Section 25 of the Local Government Act 1988 for Financial Assistance to Registered Social Landlords or to Private Landlords to Relieve or Prevent Homelessness 2005*) allows housing authorities to provide RSLs with financial assistance in connection with such arrangements. Housing authorities must reserve the right to terminate such agreements, without penalty, after 3 years.

Private lettings

16.20. Housing authorities may seek the assistance of private sector landlords in providing suitable accommodation direct to applicants. A general consent under s 25 of the *Local Government Act 1988* (*The General Consent under Section 25 of the Local Government Act 1988 for Financial Assistance to Registered Social Landlords or to Private Landlords to Relieve or Prevent Homelessness 2005*) allows housing authorities to provide financial assistance to private landlords in order to secure accommodation for people who are homeless or at risk of homelessness. This could involve, for example, the authority paying the costs of leases; making small one-off grants ('finders' fees') to landlords to encourage them to let dwellings to households owed a homelessness duty; paying rent deposits or indemnities to ensure accommodation is secured for such households; and making one-off grant payments which would prevent an eviction. There is no limit set on the amount of financial assistance that can be provided, however authorities are obliged to act reasonably and in accordance with their fiduciary duty to local tax and rent payers. Housing authorities may also make Discretionary Housing Payments (DHP) to a private landlord to meet a shortfall between the rent and the amount of housing benefit payable to a person who is homeless or at risk of homelessness. DHPs are intended to provide extra financial assistance where there is a shortfall in a person's eligible rent and the housing authority consider that the claimant is in need of further financial assistance. They are governed by the *Discretionary Housing Payment (Grant) Order 2001*. Housing authorities should also consider working with private landlords to arrange qualifying offers of assured shorthold tenancies which would bring the main homelessness duty to an end if accepted by the applicant. See paragraph 14.19 for guidance on qualifying offers.

Tenancies granted by private landlords and registered social landlords to assist with interim duties

16.21. Section 209 governs security of tenure where a private landlord provides accommodation to assist a housing authority discharge an **interim** duty, for example, a duty under s 188(1), s 190(2), s 200(1) or 204(4). Any such accommodation is exempt from statutory security of tenure until 12 months from the date on which the applicant is notified of the authority's decision under s 184(3) or s 198(5) or from the date on which the applicant is notified of the decision of any review under s 202 or an appeal under s 204, unless the landlord notifies the applicant that the tenancy is an assured or assured shorthold tenancy.

16.22. Where a private landlord or RSL lets accommodation directly to an applicant to assist a housing authority discharge any other homelessness duty, the tenancy granted will be an assured shorthold tenancy unless the tenant is notified that it is to be regarded as an assured tenancy.

Other social landlords

16.23. Under s 213 other social landlords, ie new town corporations and housing action trusts, have a duty to co-operate, as far as is reasonable in the circumstances, with a housing authority in carrying out their housing functions under Part 7 of the 1996 Act, if asked to do so.

Lodgings

16.24. Lodgings provided by householders may be suitable for some young and/or vulnerable single applicants. Housing authorities may wish to establish a network of such landlords in their district, and to liaise with social services who may operate supported lodgings schemes for people with support needs.

Hostels

16.25. Some applicants may benefit from the supportive environment which managed hostels can provide. Hostels can offer short-term support to people who are experiencing a temporary crisis, and provide an opportunity for them to regain their equilibrium and subsequently move on to live independently. Where an applicant appears to need support, particularly on-going support, and there is no social worker or support worker familiar with their case, the housing authority should request a community care assessment by the social services authority. However, housing authorities should not assume that a hostel will automatically be the most appropriate form of accommodation for vulnerable people, particularly in relation to young people, people with mental health problems and those who have experienced violence and/or abuse. In addition, where hostel accommodation is used to accommodate vulnerable young people or families with children, the Secretary of State considers that it would be inappropriate to accommodate these groups alongside adults with chaotic behavioural problems.

16.26. Housing authorities will need to take into account that some hostels are designed to meet short-term needs only. In addition to the question of whether the hostel accommodation would be suitable for the applicant for other than a short period, housing authorities should have regard to the need to ensure that bed spaces continue to be available in hostels for others who need them.

Women's refuges

16.27. Housing authorities should develop close links with women's refuges within their district, and neighbouring districts, to ensure they have access to emergency accommodation for women applicants who are fleeing domestic or other violence or who are at risk of such violence. However, housing authorities should recognise that placing an applicant in a refuge will generally be a temporary expedient only, and a prolonged stay could block a bed space that was urgently needed by someone else at risk. Refuges should be used to provide accommodation for the minimum period necessary before alternative suitable accommodation is secured elsewhere. Housing authorities should not delay in securing alternative accommodation in the hope that the applicant might return to her partner.

Bed and breakfast accommodation

16.28. Bed and Breakfast (B&B) accommodation caters for very short-term stays only and generally will afford residents only limited privacy and may lack certain important amenities, such as cooking and laundry facilities. Consequently, where possible, housing authorities should avoid using B&B hotels to discharge a duty to secure accommodation for applicants, unless, in the very limited circumstances where it is likely to be the case, it is the most appropriate option for an applicant. The Secretary of State considers B&B hotels as particularly unsuitable for accommodating applicants with family commitments and applicants aged 16 or 17 years who need support. See paragraphs 17.23 et seq in Chapter 17 for guidance on suitability and Chapter 12 for more detailed guidance on 16 and 17 year olds.

Accommodation provided by other housing authorities

16.29. Other housing authorities experiencing less demand for housing may be able to assist a housing authority by providing temporary or settled accommodation for homeless applicants. This could be particularly appropriate in the case of applicants who would be at risk of violence or serious harassment in the district of the housing authority to whom they have applied for assistance. Other housing authorities may also be able to provide accommodation in cases where the applicant has special housing needs and the other housing authority has accommodation available which is appropriate to those needs. Under s 213(1), where one housing authority requests another to help them discharge a function under Part 7, the other housing authority must co-operate in providing such assistance as is reasonable in the circumstances. Housing authorities are encouraged to consider entering into reciprocal and co-operative arrangements under these provisions. See Chapter 5 for guidance on the statutory provisions on co-operation between authorities.

Mobile homes

16.30. Although mobile homes may sometimes provide emergency or short-term accommodation, eg to discharge an interim duty, housing authorities will need to be satisfied that the accommodation is suitable for the applicant and his or her household, paying particular regard to their needs, requirements and circumstances and the conditions and facilities on the site. Caravans designed primarily for short-term holiday use should not be regarded as suitable as temporary accommodation for applicants.

Appendix 2
England: Homelessness

Tenancies for minors

16.31. There are legal complications associated with the grant of a tenancy to a minor because a minor cannot hold a legal estate in land. However, if a tenancy is granted it is likely to be enforceable as a contract for necessaries (ie the basic necessities of life) under common law. In some circumstances, social services authorities may consider it appropriate to underwrite a tenancy agreement for a homeless applicant who is under 18.

Advice and assistance that will secure accommodation from another person

16.32. Housing authorities may secure accommodation by giving advice and assistance to an applicant that will secure that accommodation becomes available for him or her from another person (s 206(1)(c)). However, where an authority has a duty to secure accommodation, they will need to ensure that the advice and assistance provided results in suitable accommodation actually being secured. Merely assisting the applicant in any efforts that he or she might make to find accommodation would not be sufficient if suitable accommodation did not actually become available.

16.33. One example of securing accommodation in this way is where house purchase is a possibility for the applicant. Advice on all options for financing house purchase should be made available, especially those financial packages which may be suited to people on lower incomes.

16.34. One option to help people into home ownership is shared equity schemes (eg part buy/part rent or equity loans to assist with purchase). These schemes are mainly funded by the Housing Corporation and generally offered by RSLs. The Housing Corporation publishes booklets (available from their publication section) giving further details of the existing shared ownership and Homebuy schemes. A new HomeBuy scheme offering further opportunities for home ownership and building on the current schemes commenced on 1st April 2006.

16.35. In other cases, applicants may have identified suitable accommodation but need practical advice and assistance to enable them to secure it, for example the applicant may require help with understanding a tenancy agreement or financial assistance with paying a rent deposit.

16.36. Housing authorities should bear in mind that the advice and assistance must result in suitable accommodation being secured, and that applicants who wish to pursue this option may need alternative accommodation until this result is achieved.

Applicants who normally occupy moveable accommodation (eg caravans, houseboats)

16.37. Under s 175(2) applicants are homeless if the accommodation available for their occupation is a caravan, houseboat, or other movable structure and they do not have a place where they are entitled, or permitted, to put it and live in it. If a duty to secure accommodation arises in such cases, the housing authority is not required to make equivalent accommodation available (or provide a site or berth for the applicant's own accommodation). However, the authority must consider whether such options are reasonably available, particularly where this would provide the most suitable solution to the applicant's accommodation needs.

Gypsies and Travellers

16.38. The circumstances described in paragraph 16.37 will be particularly relevant in the case of Gypsies and Travellers. Where a duty to secure accommodation arises but an appropriate site is not immediately available, the housing authority may need to provide an alternative temporary solution until a suitable site, or some other suitable option, becomes available. Some Gypsies and Travellers may have a cultural aversion to the prospect of 'bricks and mortar' accommodation. In such cases, the authority should seek to provide an alternative solution. However, where the authority is satisfied that there is no prospect of a suitable site for the time being, there may be no alternative solution. Authorities must give consideration to the needs and lifestyle of applicants who are Gypsies and Travellers when considering their application and how best to discharge a duty to secure suitable accommodation, in line with their obligations to act consistently with the *Human Rights Act 1998*, and in particular the right to respect for private life, family and the home.

Temporary to settled accommodation

16.39. Housing authorities are encouraged to test new approaches that would enable temporary accommodation to become settled accommodation. This would reduce the uncertainty and lack of security that households in temporary accommodation can face, and provide them with a settled home more quickly. Such approaches could be developed with housing associations through a range of 'temporary to settled' housing initiatives.

16.40. Each year approximately a quarter to a third of all leases of private sector accommodation held by social landlords expire. This presents an opportunity for the leased accommodation to be converted from use as temporary accommodation to the provision of settled housing, through negotiation with the landlord and the tenant during the final months of the lease. Where the household would be content to remain in the accommodation when the lease ends if it could be provided on a more settled basis, and the landlord would be prepared to let directly to the household, the local authority may wish to arrange for the landlord to make a 'qualifying offer' of an assured shorthold tenancy, for the purposes of s 193(7B). See paragraph 14.19 for guidance on 'qualifying offer'.

16.41. Where scope for conversion of temporary accommodation to settled accommodation is explored, the interests of the household must take priority, and the household should not be pressured to accept offers of accommodation that would bring the homelessness duty to an end.

16.42. There may also be limited potential for converting temporary accommodation leased from the private sector to a qualifying offer of an assured shorthold tenancy at the beginning or mid-point of a lease. However, this would probably require the lease to include a break clause to facilitate early termination.

16.43. While the local authority holds the lease of accommodation owned by a private sector landlord, the accommodation would not be capable of being offered to a household as a qualifying offer of an assured shorthold tenancy under s 193(7B). However, where a registered social landlord held such a lease, the accommodation may be capable of being offered to a household as a qualifying offer of an assured shorthold tenancy under s 193(7B) during the period of the lease, if all the parties agreed and the qualifying offer met the terms of s 193(7D).

CHAPTER 17: SUITABILITY OF ACCOMMODATION

17.1. This chapter provides guidance on the factors to be taken into account when determining the suitability of temporary accommodation secured under the homelessness legislation. Key factors include: the needs, requirements and circumstances of each household; space and arrangement; health and safety considerations; affordability, and location. Annex 16 sets out the statutory definition of overcrowding and Annex 17 sets out the minimum recommended standards for Bed and Breakfast accommodation.

17.2. Section 206 provides that where a housing authority discharges its functions to secure that accommodation is available for an applicant the accommodation must be suitable. This applies in respect of all powers and duties to secure accommodation under Part 7, including interim duties such as those under s 188(1) and s 200(1). The accommodation must be suitable in relation to the applicant and to all members of his or her household who normally reside with him or her, or who might reasonably be expected to reside with him or her.

17.3. Suitability of accommodation is governed by s 210. Section 210(2) provides for the Secretary of State to specify by order the circumstances in which accommodation is or is not to be regarded as suitable for someone, and matters to be taken into account or disregarded in determining whether accommodation is suitable for someone.

17.4. Space and arrangement will be key factors in determining the suitability of accommodation. However, consideration of whether accommodation is suitable will require an assessment of all aspects of the accommodation in the light of the relevant needs, requirements and circumstances of the homeless person and his or her family. The location of the accommodation will always be a relevant factor (see paragraph 17.41).

17.5. Housing authorities will need to consider carefully the suitability of accommodation for applicants whose household has particular medical and/or physical needs. The Secretary of State recommends that physical access to and around the home, space, bathroom and kitchen facilities, access to a garden and modifications to assist sensory loss as well as mobility need are all taken into account. These factors will be especially relevant where a member of the household is disabled.

17.6. Account will need to be taken of any social considerations relating to the applicant and his or her household that might affect the suitability of accommodation. Any risk of violence or racial harassment in a particular locality must also be taken into account. Where domestic violence is involved and the applicant is not able to stay in the current home, housing authorities may need to consider the need for alternative accommodation whose location can be kept a secret and which has security measures and staffing to protect the occupants. For applicants who have suffered domestic violence who are accommodated temporarily in hostels or bed and breakfast accommodation, the accommodation may need to be gender-specific as well as have security measures.

17.7. Accommodation that is suitable for a short period, for example bed and breakfast or hostel accommodation used to discharge an interim duty pending inquiries under s 188, may not necessarily be suitable for a longer period, for example to discharge a duty under s 193(2).

17.8. As the duty to provide suitable accommodation is a continuing obligation, housing authorities must keep the issue of suitability of accommodation under review. If there is a change of circumstances of substance the authority is obliged to reconsider suitability in a specific case.

Standards of accommodation

17.9. Section 210(1) requires a housing authority to have regard to the following provisions when assessing the suitability of accommodation for an applicant:

- Parts 9 and 10 of the *Housing Act 1985* (the '1985 Act') (slum clearance and overcrowding), and
- Parts 1 to 4 of the *Housing Act 2004* (the '2004 Act') (housing conditions, licensing of houses in multiple occupation, selective licensing of other residential accommodation and additional control provisions in relation to residential accommodation.)

Fitness for habitation

17.10. Part 1 of the *Housing Act 2004* (the '2004 Act') contains provisions that replace the housing fitness regime in s 604 of the 1985 Act. From 6th April 2006, the fitness standard in the 1985 Act is replaced by a new evidence-based assessment of risks to health and safety in all residential premises (including HMOs), carried out using the Housing Health and Safety Rating System

(HHSRS). Part 9 of the 1985 Act is retained, with amendments, to deal with hazards for which demolition or area clearance is the most appropriate option.

Housing Health and Safety Rating System (HHSRS)

17.11. Action by local authorities is based on a three-stage consideration: (a) the hazard rating determined under HHSRS; (b) whether the authority has a duty or power to act, determined by the presence of a hazard above or below a threshold prescribed by Regulations (Category 1 and Category 2 hazards); and (c) the authority's judgment as to the most appropriate course of action to deal with the hazard.

17.12. The purpose of the HHSRS assessment is to generate objective information in order to determine and inform enforcement decisions. HHSRS allows for the assessment of twenty nine categories of housing hazard and provides a method for rating each hazard. It does *not* provide a single rating for the dwelling as a whole or, in the case of HMOs, for the building as a whole. A hazard rating is expressed through a numerical score which falls within a band, ranging from Band A to J. Scores in Bands A to C are Category 1 hazards. Scores in Bands D to J are Category 2 hazards. If a housing authority considers that a Category 1 hazard exists on any residential premises, they have a duty under the 2004 Act to take appropriate enforcement action in relation to the hazard. They also have a power to take particular kinds of enforcement action in cases where they consider that a Category 2 hazard exists.

17.13. The HHSRS assessment is based on the risk to the *potential occupant who is most vulnerable to that hazard*. For example, stairs constitute a greater risk to the elderly, so for assessing hazards relating to stairs they are considered the most vulnerable group. The very young as well as the elderly are susceptible to low temperatures. A dwelling that is safe for those most vulnerable to a hazard is safe for all.

17.14. Housing authorities should be familiar with the principles of the HHSRS and with the operational guidance issued under s 9 of the 2004 Act.

17.15. The Secretary of State recommends that when determining the suitability of accommodation secured under the homelessness legislation, local authorities should, as a minimum, ensure that all accommodation is free of Category 1 hazards. In the case of an out of district placement it is the responsibility of the placing authority to ensure that accommodation is free of Category 1 hazards.

Overcrowding

17.16. Part 10 of the 1985 Act is intended to tackle the problems of overcrowding in dwellings. Section 324 provides a definition of overcrowding which in turn relies on the room standard specified in s 325 and the space standard in s 326 (the standards are set out in Annex 17).

17.17. A room provided within an HMO may be defined as a 'dwelling' under Part 10 of the 1985 Act and the room and space standards will therefore apply.

Housing authorities should also note that 'crowding and space' is one of the hazards assessed by the HHSRS. Any breach of the room and space standards under Part 10 is likely to constitute a Category 1 hazard.

Houses in Multiple Occupation (HMOs)

17.18. Parts 2, 3 and 4 of the 2004 Act – which came into force on 6 April 2006 – contain provisions to replace Part 11 of the 1985 Act which relates to HMOs.

17.19. The 2004 Act introduces a new definition of an HMO. A property is an HMO if it satisfies the conditions set out in sections 254(2) to (4), has been declared an HMO under s 255 or is a converted block of flats to which s 257 applies.

17.20. Privately owned Bed and Breakfast or hostel accommodation that is used to accommodate a household pursuant to a homelessness function, and which is the household's main residence, will fall within this definition of an HMO. Buildings managed or owned by a public body (such as the police or the NHS), local housing authority, registered social landlord or buildings which are already regulated under other legislation (such as care homes or bail hostels) will be exempt from the HMO definition. Buildings which are occupied entirely by freeholders or long leaseholders, those occupied by only two people, or by a resident landlord with up to two tenants will also be exempt. Most student accommodation (housing students undertaking a course in higher or further education) will also be exempt if it is managed and controlled by the establishment in accordance with a code of management practice.

17.21. From 6 April 2006, local authorities have been required to undertake the mandatory licensing of all privately rented HMOs (except converted blocks of flats to which s 257 applies) of three or more storeys and occupied by five or more people who form two or more households. Local authorities will also have discretionary powers to introduce additional licensing schemes covering smaller HMOs. In order to be a licence holder, a landlord will have to be a 'fit and proper' person, as defined in s 89 of the Act and demonstrate that suitable management arrangements are in place in their properties.

17.22. In addition a local authority will have to be satisfied that the HMO is suitable for the number of occupants it is licensed for and meets statutory standards relating to shared amenities and facilities, e g that it has an adequate number, type and quality of shared bathrooms, toilets and cooking facilities. These standards are set out in Schedule 3 to the *Licensing and Management of Houses in Multiple Occupation and Other Houses (Miscellaneous Provisions) (England) Regulations 2006* (SI No 2006/373). These 'amenity standards' will run alongside the consideration of health and safety issues under HHSRS. The *Housing (Management of Houses in Multiple Occupation) Regulations 1990* are to be replaced by the *Management of Houses in Multiple Occupation (England) Regulations 2006* (SI 2006/372). Neither the amenity standards nor the new management regulations apply to HMOs that are converted blocks of flats to which s 257 applies. It is intended that separate regulations will be made by

July 6th to modify Part 2 of the 2004 Act (which deals with mandatory licensing) in so far as it relates to these types of HMO, and to extend, with modifications, the application of the new amenity standards and management regulations to these types of HMO. Until then they will continue to be subject to the registration schemes made under Part 11 of the 1985 Act. Transitional arrangements have been in place since April 2006 so that most HMOs that are registered in a 1985 scheme will automatically be licensed under the 2004 Act.

17.23. Local authorities also have discretion to extend licensing to privately rented properties in all, or part of, their area to address particular problems, such as low housing demand or significant incidence of anti-social behaviour. However, licensing in these selective circumstances is concerned only with property management and not the condition of the property.

Bed and breakfast accommodation

17.24. Bed and Breakfast (B&B) accommodation caters for very short-term stays only and generally will afford residents only limited privacy and may lack certain important amenities, such as cooking and laundry facilities. Consequently, where possible, housing authorities should avoid using B&B hotels to discharge a duty to secure accommodation for homeless applicants, unless, in the very limited circumstances where it is likely to be the case, it is the most appropriate option for the applicant.

17.25. Living in B&B accommodation can be particularly detrimental to the health and development of children. Under s 210(2), the Secretary of State has made the *Homelessness (Suitability of Accommodation) (England) Order 2003* (SI 2003 No 3326) ('the Order'). The Order specifies that when accommodation is made available for occupation under certain functions in Part 7, B&B accommodation is not to be regarded as suitable for applicants with family commitments.

17.26. Housing authorities should, therefore, use B&B hotels to discharge a duty to secure accommodation for applicants with family commitments only as a last resort. Applicants with family commitments means an applicant –

(a) who is pregnant;

(b) with whom a pregnant woman resides or might reasonably be expected to reside; or

(c) with whom dependent children reside or might reasonably be expected to reside.

17.27. For the purpose of the Order, B&B accommodation means accommodation (whether or not breakfast is included):

(a) which is not separate and self-contained premises; and

(b) in which any of the following amenities is shared by more than one household:

(i) a toilet;

(ii) personal washing facilities;

(iii) cooking facilities.

B&B accommodation does not include accommodation which is owned or managed by a local housing authority, a registered social landlord or a voluntary organisation as defined in section 180(3) of the *Housing Act 1996*.

17.28. B&B accommodation is not to be regarded as suitable for applicants with family commitments (except as specified in paragraph 17.29 below) for the purpose of discharging a duty under the following duties:

- section 188(1) (interim duty to accommodate in case of apparent priority need);
- section 190(2)(a) (duties to persons becoming homeless intentionally);
- section 193(2) (duty to persons with priority need who are not homeless intentionally);
- section 200(1) (duty to applicant whose case is considered for referral or referred); and
- section 195(2) (duties in cases of threatened homelessness) where the accommodation is other than that occupied by the applicant at the time of making his or her application.

17.29. The Order provides that if no alternative accommodation is available for the applicant the housing authority may accommodate the family in B&B for a period, or periods, not exceeding six weeks in result of a single homelessness application. **Where B&B accommodation is secured for an applicant with family commitments, the Secretary of State considers that the authority should notify the applicant of the effect of the Order, and, in particular, that the authority will be unable to continue to secure B&B accommodation for such applicants any longer than 6 weeks, after which they must secure alternative, suitable accommodation.**

17.30. When determining whether accommodation other than B&B accommodation is available for use, housing authorities will need to take into account, among other things, the cost to the authority of securing the accommodation, the affordability of the accommodation for the applicant and the location of the accommodation. An authority is under no obligation to include in its considerations accommodation which is to be allocated in accordance with its allocation scheme, published under s 167 of the 1996 Act.

17.31. If there is a significant change in an applicant's circumstances that would bring the applicant within the scope of the Order (eg a new pregnancy), the six week period should start from the date the authority was informed of the change of circumstances not the date the applicant was originally placed in B&B accommodation.

17.32. If the conditions for referring a case are met and another housing authority accepts responsibility for an applicant under s 200(4), any time spent in B&B accommodation before this acceptance should be disregarded in calculating the six week period.

17.33. B&B accommodation is also unlikely to be suitable for 16 and 17 year olds who are in need of support. Where B&B accommodation is used for this group it ought to be as a last resort for the shortest time possible and housing authorities will need to ensure that appropriate support is provided where necessary. See Chapter 12 for guidance on the use of B&B for 16 and 17 year olds.

17.34. The Secretary of State considers that the limited circumstances in which B&B hotels may provide suitable accommodation could include those where:

    (a)   emergency accommodation is required at very short notice (for example to discharge the interim duty to accommodate under s 188); or

    (b)   there is simply no better alternative accommodation available and the use of B&B accommodation is necessary as a last resort.

17.35. The Secretary of State considers that where housing authorities are unable to avoid using B&B hotels to accommodate applicants, they should ensure that such accommodation is of a good standard (see paragaphs 17.36–17.38 below) and is used for the shortest period possible. The Secretary of State considers that where a lengthy stay seems likely, the authority should consider other accommodation more appropriate to the applicant's needs.

Standards of B&B accommodation

17.36. Where housing authorities are unable to avoid using B&B hotels to accommodate applicants they should ensure that such accommodation is of a suitable standard. Where a B&B hotel is used to accommodate an applicant and is their main residence, it falls within the definition of an HMO. Paragraphs 17.18–17.23 above explain the legislation that applies to HMOs with regard to health and safety and overcrowding. Since April 2006, local authorities have a power under the 2004 Act to issue an HMO Declaration confirming HMO status where there is uncertainty about the status of a property.

17.37. The Government recognises that living conditions in HMOs should not only be healthy and safe but should also provide acceptable, decent standards for people who may be unrelated to each other and who are sharing basic facilities. As noted at paragraph 17.22 above, the Government has set out in regulation the minimum 'amenity standards' required for a property to be granted an HMO licence. These standards will only apply to 'high-risk' HMOs covered by mandatory licensing or those HMOs that will be subject to additional licensing, and will not apply to the majority of HMOs. However, housing authorities (or groups of authorities) can adopt their own local classification, amenity specification or minimum standards for B&B and other shared accommodation provided as temporary accommodation under Part 7. In London, for example, boroughs have, since 1988, had a code of practice on the use of B&B and other shared temporary accommodation used to accommodate households under Part 7. This establishes clear benchmarks for standards across the Capital. Under the code of practice, properties are graded from A to E, with the grading dependent upon a wide range of considerations and factors relating to the facilities and services provided by an establishment.

Placements are expected to be made only in those properties that meet the required standard. Setting the Standard (STS), a new automated system administered by the Greater London Authority (GLA), assists boroughs to comply with the code of practice. It collects and collates information from environmental health officers' annual inspections of properties and then makes this easily accessible to relevant borough officers across London. For further information on STS contact STS@london.gov.uk. The Secretary of State welcomes these arrangements and encourages other housing authorities to consider adopting similar systems to support the exchange of information and improve standards of temporary accommodation.

17.38. The Government considers that the size and occupancy levels of rooms, the provision and location of cooking, toilet and bathing facilities, and management standards are particularly important factors for determining whether B&B accommodation is suitable for accommodating households under Part 7. The Secretary of State therefore recommends that housing authorities have regard to the recommended minimum standards set out in Annex 17 when assessing whether B&B accommodation is suitable.

Affordability

17.39. Under s 210(2), the Secretary of State has made the *Homelessness (Suitability of Accommodation) Order 1996* (SI 1996 No 3204). The 1996 Order specifies that in determining whether it would be, or would have been, reasonable for a person to occupy accommodation that is considered suitable, a housing authority must take into account whether the accommodation is affordable by him or her, and in particular must take account of:

(a) the financial resources available to him or her *(ie all forms of income)*, including, but not limited to:

　　i)　salary, fees and other remuneration *(from such sources as investments, grants, pensions, tax credits etc)*;

　　ii)　social security benefits *(such as housing benefit, income support, income-based Jobseekers Allowances or Council Tax benefit etc)*;

　　iii)　payments due under a court order for the making of periodical payments to a spouse or a former spouse, or to, or for the benefit of, a child;

　　iv)　payments of child support maintenance due under the *Child Support Act 1991*;

　　v)　pensions;

　　vi)　contributions to the costs in respect of the accommodation which are or were made or which might reasonably be expected to be, or have been, made by other members of his or her household *(most members can be assumed to contribute, but the amount depends on various factors including their age and income. Other influencing factors can be drawn from the parallels of their entitlement to housing benefit and income support in relation to housing costs. Current rates should be available from housing authority benefit sections)*;

vii) financial assistance towards the costs in respect of the accommodation, including loans, provided by a local authority, voluntary organisation or other body;

viii) benefits derived from a policy of insurance *(such as cover against unemployment or sickness)*;

ix) savings and other capital sums *(which may be a source of income or might be available to meet accommodation expenses. However, it should be borne in mind that, again drawing from the parallel social securities assistance, capital savings below a threshold amount are disregarded for the purpose of assessing a claim)*;

(b) the costs in respect of the accommodation, including, but not limited to:

i) payments of, or by way of, rent *(including rent default/property damage deposits)*;

ii) payments in respect of a licence or permission to occupy the accommodation;

iii) mortgage costs *(including an assessment of entitlement to Income Support Mortgage Interest (ISMI))*;

iv) payments of, or by way of, service charges *(eg maintenance or other costs required as a condition of occupation of the accommodation)*;

v) mooring charges payable for a houseboat;

vi) where the accommodation is a caravan or a mobile home, payments in respect of the site on which it stands;

vii) the amount of council tax payable in respect of the accommodation;

viii) payments by way of deposit or security in respect of the accommodation;

ix) payments required by an accommodation agency;

(c) payments which that person is required to make under a court order for the making of periodical payments to a spouse or former spouse, or to, or for the benefit of, a child and payments of child support maintenance required to be made under the *Child Support Act 1991*; and

(d) his or her other reasonable living expenses.

17.40. In considering an applicant's residual income after meeting the costs of the accommodation, the Secretary of State recommends that housing authorities regard accommodation as not being affordable if the applicant would be left with a residual income which would be less than the level of income support or income-based jobseekers allowance that is applicable in respect of the applicant, or would be applicable if he or she was entitled to claim such benefit. This amount will vary from case to case, according to the circumstances and composition of the applicant's household. A current tariff of applicable amounts in respect of such benefits should be available within the authority's housing benefit section. Housing authorities will need to consider whether the applicant can afford the housing costs without being deprived of basic essentials such as food, clothing, heating, transport and other essentials. The Secretary of State recommends that housing authorities avoid placing applicants who are in low paid employment in accommodation where they would need to resort to claiming benefit to meet the costs of that accommodation, and to consider opportunities to secure accommodation at affordable rent levels where this is likely to reduce perceived or actual disincentives to work.

Location of accommodation

17.41. The location of the accommodation will be relevant to suitability and the suitability of the location for all the members of the household will have to be considered. Where, for example, applicants are in paid employment account will need to be taken of their need to reach their normal workplace from the accommodation secured. The Secretary of State recommends that local authorities take into account the need to minimise disruption to the education of young people, particularly at critical points in time such as close to taking GCSE examinations. Housing authorities should avoid placing applicants in isolated accommodation away from public transport, shops and other facilities, and, wherever possible, secure accommodation that is as close as possible to where they were previously living, so they can retain established links with schools, doctors, social workers and other key services and support essential to the well-being of the household.

Households with pets

17.42. Housing authorities will need to be sensitive to the importance of pets to some applicants, particularly elderly people and rough sleepers who may rely on pets for companionship. Although it will not always be possible to make provision for pets, the Secretary of State recommends that housing authorities give careful consideration to this aspect when making provision for applicants who wish to retain their pet.

Asylum seekers

17.43. Since April 2000 the National Asylum Support Service (NASS) has had responsibility for providing support, including accommodation, to asylum seekers who would otherwise be destitute, whilst their claims and appeals are being considered. Some local authorities may still be providing accommodation to asylum seekers who applied for asylum prior to April 2000 and whose cases have not yet been resolved. However, the number of these cases, if any, will be small and declining.

17.44. Section 210(1A) provides that, in considering whether accommodation is suitable for an applicant who is an asylum seeker, housing authorities:

(a) shall also have regard to the fact that the accommodation is to be temporary pending the determination of the applicant's claim for asylum; and

(b) shall not have regard to any preference that the applicant, or any person who might reasonably be expected to reside with him or her, may have as to the locality of the accommodation secured.

Right to request a review of suitability

17.45. Applicants may ask for a review on request of the housing authority's decision that the accommodation offered to them is suitable under s 202(1)(f), although this right does not apply in the case of accommodation secured under s 188, the interim duty to accommodate pending inquiries, or s 200(1), the interim duty pending the decision on a referral. Under s 202(1A) an applicant may request a review as to suitability regardless of whether or not he or she accepts the accommodation. This applies equally to offers of accommodation made under s 193(5) to discharge the s 193(2) duty and to offers of an allocation of accommodation made under s 193(7) that would bring the s 193(2) duty to an end. This means that the applicant is able to ask for a review of suitability without inadvertently bringing the housing duty to an end (see Chapter 19 for guidance on reviews). Housing authorities should note that although there is no right of review of a decision on the suitability of accommodation secured under s 188 or s 200(1), such decisions could nevertheless be subject to judicial review in the High Court.

CHAPTER 18: LOCAL CONNECTION AND REFERRALS TO ANOTHER HOUSING AUTHORITY

18.1. **This chapter provides guidance on the provisions relating to an applicant's 'local connection' with an area and explains the conditions and procedures for referring an applicant to another housing authority.**

18.2. Where a housing authority ('the notifying authority') decide that s 193 applies to an applicant (ie the applicant is eligible for assistance, unintentionally homeless and has a priority need) but it considers that the conditions for referral of the case to another housing authority are met, they may notify the other housing authority ('the notified authority') of their opinion.

18.3. Notwithstanding that the conditions for a referral are apparently met, it is the responsibility of the notifying authority to determine whether s 193 applies before making a reference. **Applicants can only be referred to another authority if the notifying authority is satisfied that the applicant is unintentionally homeless, eligible for assistance and has a priority need.** Applicants cannot be referred while they are owed only the interim duty under s 188, or any duty other than the s 193 duty (eg where they are threatened with homelessness or found to be homeless intentionally).

18.4. **Referrals are discretionary only: housing authorities are not required to refer applicants to other authorities. Nor are they, generally, required to make any inquiries as to whether an applicant has a local connection with an area.** However, by virtue of s 11 of the *Asylum and Immigration (Treatment of Claimants, etc)*

Act 2004, housing authorities will need to consider local connection in cases where the applicant is a former asylum seeker:

i) who was provided with accommodation in Scotland under s 95 of the *Immigration and Asylum Act 1999*, and

ii) whose accommodation was not provided in an accommodation centre by virtue of s 22 of the *Nationality, Immigration and Asylum Act 2002*.

In such cases, by virtue of s 11(2)(d) and (3) of the A*sylum and Immigration (Treatment of Claimants, etc) Act 2004*, local connection to a district in England, Wales or Scotland will be relevant to what duty is owed under s 193. (See paragraph 18.21 below.)

18.5. Housing authorities may have a policy about how they may exercise their discretion to refer a case. This must not, however, extend to deciding in advance that in all cases where there is a local connection to another district the case should be referred.

18.6. The Local Government Association (LGA) has issued guidelines for housing authorities about procedures for referring a case. These include guidance on issues such as local connection and invoking the disputes procedure when two housing authorities are unable to agree whether the conditions for referral are met. (A copy of the LGA guidelines is at Annex 18 for information).

Conditions for referral

18.7. Sections 198(2) and (2A) describe the conditions which must be satisfied before a referral may be made. A notifying authority may refer an applicant to whom s 193 applies to another housing authority if all of the following are met:

i) neither the applicant nor any person who might reasonably be expected to live with him or her has a local connection with its district; and

ii) at least one member of the applicant's household has a local connection with the district of the authority to be notified; and

iii) none of them will be at risk of domestic or non-domestic violence, or threat of domestic or non-domestic violence which is likely to be carried out, in the district of the authority to be notified.

Local connection

18.8. When a housing authority makes inquiries to determine whether an applicant is eligible for assistance and owed a duty under Part 7, it may also make inquiries under s 184(2) to decide whether the applicant has a local connection with the district of another housing authority in England, Wales or Scotland.

18.9. Section 199(1) provides that a person has a local connection with the district of a housing authority if he or she has a connection with it:

i) because he or she is, or was in the past, normally resident there, and that residence was of his or her own choice; or

ii) because he or she is employed there; or

iii) because of family associations there; or

iv) because of any special circumstances.

18.10. For the purposes of (i), above, residence in temporary accommodation provided by a housing authority under s 188 can constitute normal residence of choice and therefore contribute towards a local connection. With regard to (ii) the applicant should actually work in the district: it would not be sufficient that his or her employers' head office was located there. For the purposes of (iii), where the applicant raises family associations, the Secretary of State considers that this may extend beyond parents, adult children or siblings. They may include associations with other family members such as step-parents, grandparents, grandchildren, aunts or uncles provided there are sufficiently close links in the form of frequent contact, commitment or dependency. Family associations may also extend to unmarried couples, provided that the relationship is sufficiently enduring, and to same sex couples. With regard to (iv), special circumstances might include the need to be near special medical or support services which are available only in a particular district.

18.11. The grounds in s 199(1) should be applied in order to establish whether the applicant has the required local connection. However, the fact that an applicant may satisfy one of these grounds will not necessarily mean that he or she has been able to establish a local connection. For example, an applicant may be 'normally resident' in an area even though he or she does not intend to settle there permanently or indefinitely, and the local authority could therefore determine that he or she does not have a local connection. The overriding consideration should always be whether the applicant has a real local connection with an area – the specified grounds are subsidiary to that overriding consideration.

18.12. In assessing whether an applicant's household has a local connection with either its district or a district to which the case might be referred, a housing authority should also consider whether any person who might reasonably be expected to live with the applicant has such a connection.

18.13. A housing authority may not seek to transfer responsibility to another housing authority where the applicant has a local connection with their district but they consider there is a stronger local connection elsewhere. However, in such a case, it would be open to a housing authority to seek assistance from the other housing authority in securing accommodation, under s 213.

18.14. Where a person has a local connection with the districts of more than one other housing authority, the referring housing authority will wish to take account of the applicant's preference in deciding which housing authority to notify.

Ex-service personnel

18.15. Under s 199(2) and (3), serving members of the armed forces, and other persons who normally live with them as part of their household, do not establish a local connection with a district by virtue of serving, or having served, there while in the forces.

Ex-prisoners and detainees under the Mental Health Act 1983

18.16. Similarly, detention in prison (whether convicted or not) does not establish a local connection with the district the prison is in. However, any period of residence in accommodation prior to imprisonment may give rise to a local connection under s 199(1)(a). The same is true of those detained under the *Mental Health Act 1983*.

Former asylum seekers

18.17. Sections 199(6) and (7) were inserted by section 11 of the *Asylum and Immigration (Treatment of Claimants, etc) Act 2004*. Section 199(6) provides that a person has a local connection with the district of a housing authority if he or she was (at any time) provided with accommodation there under s 95 of the *Immigration and Asylum Act 1999* ('s 95 accommodation').

18.18. Under s 199(7), however, a person does not have a local connection by virtue of s 199(6):

(a)   if he or she has been subsequently provided with s 95 accommodation in a different area. Where a former asylum seeker has been provided with s 95 accommodation in more than one area, the local connection is with the area where such accommodation was last provided; or

(b)   if they have been provided with s 95 accommodation in an accommodation centre in the district by virtue of s 22 of the *Nationality, Immigration and Asylum Act 2002*.

18.19. A local connection with a district by virtue of s 199(6) does not override a local connection by virtue of s 199(1). Thus, a former asylum seeker who has a local connection with a district because he or she was provided with accommodation there under s 95 may also have a local connection elsewhere for some other reason, for example, because of employment or family associations.

Former asylum seekers provided with s 95 accommodation in Scotland

18.20. Under Scottish legislation, a person does not establish a local connection with a district in Scotland if he or she is resident there in s 95 accommodation. Consequently, if such a person made a homelessness application to a housing authority in England, and he or she did not have a local connection with the district of that authority, the fact that he or she had been provided with s 95 accommodation in Scotland would not establish conditions for referral to the relevant local authority in Scotland.

18.21.   Sections 11(2) and (3) of the *Asylum and Immigration (Treatment of Claimants, etc) Act 2004* provides that where a housing authority in England or Wales is satisfied that an applicant is eligible for assistance, unintentionally homeless and in priority need and:

i)   the applicant has been provided with s 95 accommodation in Scotland at any time;

ii)   the s 95 accommodation was not provided in an accommodation centre by virtue of s 22 of the *Nationality, Immigration and Asylum Act 2002*;

iii)   the applicant does not have a local connection anywhere in England and Wales (within the meaning of s 199 of the 1996 Act); and

iv)   the applicant does not have a local connection anywhere in Scotland (within the meaning of s 27 of the *Housing (Scotland) Act 1987*);

then the duty to the applicant under s 193 (the main homelessness duty) shall not apply. However, the authority:

(a)   may secure that accommodation is available for occupation by the applicant for a period giving him or her a reasonable opportunity of securing accommodation for his or her occupation; and

(b)   may provide the applicant (or secure that he or she is provided with) advice and assistance in any attempts he or she may make to secure accommodation for his or her occupation.

When dealing with an applicant in these circumstances, authorities will need to take into account the wishes of the applicant but should consider providing such advice and assistance as would enable the applicant to make an application for housing to the Scottish authority in the district where the s 95 accommodation was last provided, or to another Scottish authority of the applicant's choice. If such a person was unintentionally homeless and in priority need, it would be open to them to apply to any Scottish housing authority and a main homelessness duty would be owed to them.

No local connection anywhere

18.22.   If an applicant, or any person who might reasonably be expected to live with the applicant, has no local connection with any district in Great Britain, the duty to secure accommodation will rest with the housing authority that has received the application.

Risk of violence

18.23.   A housing authority cannot refer an applicant to another housing authority if that person or any person who might reasonably be expected to reside with him or her would be at risk of violence. The housing authority is under a positive duty to enquire whether the applicant would be at such a risk and, if he or she would, it should not be assumed that the applicant will take steps to deal with the threat.

18.24. Section 198(3) defines violence as violence from another person or threats of violence from another person which are likely to be carried out. This is the same definition as appears in s 177 in relation to whether it is reasonable to continue to occupy accommodation and the circumstances to be considered as to whether a person runs a risk of violence are the same.

18.25. Housing authorities should be alert to the deliberate distinction which is made in s 198(3) between actual violence and threatened violence. A high standard of proof of actual violence in the past should not be imposed. The threshold is that there must be:

(a)   no risk of domestic violence (actual or threatened) in the other district; and

(b)   no risk of non-domestic violence (actual or threatened) in the other district.

Nor should 'domestic violence' be interpreted restrictively (see definitions in the introduction to this Code).

Duties where case referred to another housing authority

18.26. If a housing authority decide to refer a case to another housing authority, they will need to notify the other housing authority that they believe the conditions for referral are met (s 198(1)). They must also notify the applicant that they have notified, or intend to notify, another housing authority that they consider that the conditions for referral are met (s 184(4)). At that point, the notifying authority would cease to be subject to the interim duty to accommodate under s 188(1) but will owe a duty under s 200(1) to secure that accommodation is available for the applicant until the question of whether the conditions for referral are met is decided.

18.27. Under s 200(4), if the referral is accepted by the notified authority they will be under a duty to secure accommodation for the applicant under s 193(2). Regardless of whether the notified authority had reached a different decision on a previous application, it is not open to it to re-assess the notifying authority's decision that the applicant is eligible, unintentionally homeless and in priority need. Nor may the notified authority rely on an offer of accommodation which was refused having been made in pursuance of a previous application to it.

18.28. Under s 200(3), if it is decided that the conditions for referral are not met, the notifying authority will be under a duty to secure accommodation for the applicant under s 193(2).

18.29. When the question of whether the conditions for referral to the notified authority are met has been decided, the notifying housing authority must notify the applicant of the decision and the reasons for it (s 200(2)). The notification must also advise the applicant of his or her right to request a review of the decision, and the timescale within which such a request must be made. The interim duty to accommodate under s 200(1) ends regardless of whether the applicant requests a review of the decision. However, where the applicant does request a review the notifying authority has a power under s 200(5) to secure that accommodation is available pending the review decision. (See Chapter 15 for guidance on powers to secure accommodation.)

18.30. Notifications to the applicant must be provided in writing and copies made available at the housing authority's office for collection by the applicant, or his or her representative, for a reasonable period.

Disputes

18.31. Applicants have the right to request a review of various decisions relating to local connection and referrals (see Chapter 19 for further guidance). There is not a right to request a review of a housing authority's decision not to refer a case, although a failure by a housing authority to consider whether it has the discretion to refer an applicant may be amenable to challenge by way of judicial review. The same is true of an unreasonable use of the discretion.

18.32. The question of whether the conditions for referral are met in a particular case should be decided by agreement between the housing authorities concerned. If they cannot agree, the decision should be made in accordance with such arrangements as may be directed by order of the Secretary of State (s 198(5)).

18.33. The *Homelessness (Decisions on Referrals) Order 1998* (SI 1998 No 1578) directs that the arrangements to be followed in such a dispute are the arrangements agreed between the local authority associations (ie the Local Government Association, the Convention of Scottish Local Authorities, the Welsh Local Government Association and the Association of London Government).

18.34. The arrangements are set out in the Schedule to the Order. Broadly speaking, they provide that in the event of two housing authorities being unable to agree whether the conditions for referral are met, they must agree on a person to be appointed to make the decision for them. If unable to agree on that, they should agree to request the LGA to appoint someone. In default of this, the notifying housing authority must make such a request of the LGA. In all cases the appointed person must be drawn from a panel established by the LGA for the purpose. The Local Government Association has issued guidelines for housing authorities on invoking the disputes procedure (a copy is at Annex 18 for information).

18.35. The arrangements set out in the Schedule to SI 1998 No 1578 apply where a housing authority in England, Wales or Scotland seek to refer a homelessness case to another housing authority in England or Wales, and they are unable to agree whether the conditions for referral are met. A similar Order, the *Homelessness (Decisions on Referrals) (Scotland) Order 1998*, SI 1998 No 1603 applies under the Scottish homelessness legislation. The arrangements in the latter apply in cases where a housing authority in England, Wales or

Scotland refer a homelessness case to a housing authority in Scotland, and they are unable to agree whether the conditions for referral are met.

18.36. Where an English or Welsh housing authority seek to refer a case to a Scottish housing authority, a request to the local authority association to appoint an arbitrator should be made to the Convention of Scottish Local Authorities.

18.37. A notified authority which wishes to refuse a referral because it disagrees on a finding as to the application of s 193 to the applicant must challenge the notifying authority's finding (for example as to intentionality) by way of judicial review.

CHAPTER 19: REVIEW OF DECISIONS AND APPEALS TO THE COUNTY COURT

19.1. This chapter provides guidance on the procedures to be followed when an applicant requests the housing authority to review their decision on the homelessness case.

Right to request a review

19.2. Applicants have the right to request the housing authority to review their decisions on homelessness cases in some circumstances. If the request is made in accordance with s 202 the housing authority must review the relevant decision.

19.3. When a housing authority have completed their inquiries into the applicant's homelessness case they must notify the applicant of:

(a) their decision and, if any decision is against the applicant's interest, the reasons for it;

(b) the applicant's right to request a review; and

(c) the time within which such a request must be made.

Housing authorities should also advise the applicant of his or her right to request a review of the suitability of any accommodation offered as a discharge of a homelessness duty, whether or not the offer is accepted. Authorities should also advise the applicant of the review procedures.

19.4. Under s 202 an applicant has the right to request a review of:

(a) any decision of a housing authority about his or her eligibility for assistance (ie whether he or she is considered to be a person from abroad who is ineligible for assistance under Part 7);

(b) any decision of a housing authority as to what duty (if any) is owed to him or her under s 190, s 191, s 192, s 193, s 195 and s 196 (duties owed to applicants who are homeless or threatened with homelessness);

(c) any decision of a housing authority to notify another housing authority under s 198(1) (ie a decision to refer the applicant to another housing authority because they appear to have a local connection with that housing authority's district and not with the district where they have made the application);

(d) any decision under s 198(5) whether the conditions are met for the referral of the applicant's case (including a decision taken by a person appointed under the *Homelessness (Decisions on Referrals) Order 1998* (SI 1998 No 1578));

(e) any decision under s 200(3) or (4) (ie a decision as to whether the notified housing authority or the notifying housing authority owe the duty to secure accommodation in a case considered for referral or referred);

(f) any decision of a housing authority as to the suitability of accommodation offered to the applicant under any of the provisions in (b) or (e) above or the suitability of accommodation offered under s 193(7) (allocation under Part 6). Under s 202(1A), applicants can request a review of the suitability of accommodation whether or not they have accepted the offer.

19.5. An applicant must request a review before the end of the period of 21 days beginning with the day on which he or she is notified of the housing authority's decision. The housing authority may specify, in writing, a longer period during which a review may be requested. Applicants do not have a right to request a review of a decision made on an earlier review.

19.6. In reviewing a decision, housing authorities will need to have regard to any information relevant to the period before the decision (even if only obtained afterwards) as well as any new relevant information obtained since the decision.

The review regulations

19.7. The *Allocation of Housing and Homelessness (Review Procedures) Regulations 1999* (SI 1999 No 71) set out the procedures to be followed by housing authorities in carrying out reviews under Part 7.

Who may carry out the review

19.8. A review may be carried out by the housing authority itself or by someone acting as an agent of the housing authority (see Chapter 21 on contracting out homelessness functions). Where the review is to be carried out by an officer of the housing authority, the officer must not have been involved in the original decision, and he or she must be senior to the officer (or officers) who took that decision. Seniority for these purposes means seniority in rank or grade within the housing authority's organisational structure. The seniority provision does not apply where a committee or sub-committee of elected members took the original decision.

19.9. Where the decision under review is a joint decision by the notifying housing authority and the notified housing authority as to whether the conditions of referral of the case are satisfied, s 202(4) requires that the review should be carried out jointly by the two housing authorities. Where the decision under review was taken by a person appointed pursuant to the arrangements set out in the Schedule to the *Homelessness (Decisions on Referrals) Order 1998* (SI 1998 No 1578), the review must be carried out by another person appointed under those arrangements (see paragraph 19.15).

Written representations

19.10. The applicant should be invited to make representations in writing in connection with his or her request for a review. The relevant provisions in Part 7 give a person an unfettered right to request a review of a decision, so he or she is not required to provide grounds for challenging the housing authority's decision. The purpose of the requirement is to invite the applicant to state his or her grounds for requesting a review (if he or she has not already done so) and to elicit any new information that the applicant may have in relation to his or her request for a review.

19.11. Regulation 6 requires the housing authority to notify the applicant that he or she, or someone acting on his or her behalf, may make written representations in connection with the request for a review. The notice should also advise the applicant of the procedure to be followed in connection with the review (if this information has not been provided earlier). Regulation 6 also provides that:

i)   where the original decision was made jointly by the notifying and notified housing authorities under s 198(5), the notification should be made by the notifying housing authority; and

ii)   where the original decision was made by a person appointed pursuant to the *Homelessness (Decisions on Referrals) Order 1998* (SI 1998 No 1578), the notification should be made by the person appointed to carry out the review.

Oral hearings

19.12. Regulation 8 provides that in cases where a review has been requested, if the housing authority, authorities or person carrying out the review consider that there is a deficiency or irregularity in the original decision, or in the manner in which it was made, but they are minded nonetheless to make a decision that is against the applicant's interests on one or more issues, they should notify the applicant:

(a)   that they are so minded and the reasons why; and,

(b)   that the applicant, or someone acting on his or her behalf, may, within a reasonable period, make oral representations, further written representations, or both oral and written representations.

19.13. Such deficiencies or irregularities would include:

i)   failure to take into account relevant considerations and to ignore irrelevant ones;

ii)   failure to base the decision on the facts;

iii) bad faith or dishonesty;
iv) mistake of law;
v) decisions that run contrary to the policy of the 1996 Act;
vi) irrationality or unreasonableness;
vii) procedural unfairness, e g where an applicant has not been given a chance to comment on matters relevant to a decision.

19.14. The reviewer must consider whether there is 'something lacking' in the decision, i e were any significant issues not addressed or addressed inadequately, which could have led to unfairness.

Period during which review must be completed

19.15. Regulation 9 provides that the period within which the applicant must be notified of the decision on review is:

i) eight weeks from the day of the request for a review, where the original decision was made by the housing authority;
ii) ten weeks, where the decision was made jointly by two housing authorities under s 198(5) (a decision whether the conditions for referral are met);
iii) twelve weeks, where the decision is taken by a person appointed pursuant to the *Schedule to the Homelessness (Decisions on Referrals) Order* (SI 1998 No 1578).

The regulations provide that in all of these cases it is open to the reviewer to seek the applicant's agreement to an extension of the prescribed period; any such agreement must be given in writing.

Late representations

19.16. The regulations require the reviewer(s) to consider any written representations received subject to compliance with the requirement to notify the applicant of the decision on review within the period of the review, i e the period prescribed in the regulations or any extended period agreed in writing by the applicant. It may in some circumstances be necessary to make further enquiries of the applicant about information he or she has provided. The reviewer(s) should be flexible about allowing such further exchanges, having regard to the time limits for reviews prescribed in the regulations. If this leads to significant delays, the applicant may be approached to agree an extension in the period for the review. Similarly, if an applicant has been invited to make oral representations and this requires additional time to arrange, the applicant should be asked to agree an appropriate extension.

Procedures for review of decisions made under the decisions on referrals order

19.17. Where the original decision under s 198(5) was made by a person appointed pursuant to the Schedule to the *Homelessness (Decisions on*

Referrals) Order 1998 (SI 1998 No 1578), regulation 7 provides that a review should be carried out by another person appointed by the notifying housing authority and the notified housing authority. This requirement applies even where the original decision was carried out by a person appointed from the panel by the chairman of the Local Government Association, or his or her nominee. If, however, the two housing authorities fail to appoint a person to carry out the review within five working days of the date of the request for a review, the notifying housing authority must request the chairman of the Local Government Association to appoint a person from the panel. The chairman, in turn, must within seven working days of that request appoint a person from the panel to undertake the review. The housing authorities are required to provide the reviewer with the reasons for the original decision, and the information on which that decision is based, within five working days of his or her appointment.

19.18. Any person thus appointed must comply with the procedures set out in regulations 6, 7, 8 and 9. Specifically, he or she must invite written representations from the applicant and send copies of these to the two housing authorities, inviting them to respond. The reviewer is also required to notify in writing the two housing authorities of his or her decision on review and the reasons for it at least a week before the end of the prescribed period of twelve weeks (or of any extended period agreed by the applicant). This allows the housing authorities adequate time to notify the applicant of the decision before expiry of the period.

Notification of decision on review

19.19. Section 203 requires a housing authority to notify the applicant in writing of their decision on the review. The authority must also notify the applicant of the reasons for their decision where it:

i) confirms the original decision on any issue against the interests of the applicant;

ii) confirms a previous decision to notify another housing authority under s 198; or,

iii) confirms a previous decision that the conditions for referral in s 198 are met in the applicant's case.

Where the review is carried out jointly by two housing authorities under s 198(5), or by a person appointed pursuant to the *Homelessness (Decisions on Referrals) Order 1998* (SI 1998 No 1578), the notification may be made by either of the two housing authorities concerned.

At this stage, the authority making the notification should advise the applicant of his or her right to appeal to the County Court against a review decision under s 204 and of the period in which to appeal.

Powers to accommodate pending a review

19.20. Sections 188(3) and 200(5) give housing authorities powers to secure accommodation for certain applicants pending the decision on a review. See Chapter 15 for guidance on powers to secure accommodation.

Appeals to the county court

19.21. Section 204 provides an applicant with the right of appeal on a point of law to the County Court if:

(a)   he or she is dissatisfied with the decision on a review; or

(b)   he or she is not notified of the decision on the review within the time prescribed in regulations made under s 203.

In the latter case, an applicant will be entitled to appeal against the original decision.

19.22. An appeal must be brought by an applicant within 21 days of:

(a)   the date on which he or she is notified of the decision on review; or

(b)   the date on which he or she should have been notified (ie the date marking the end of the period for the review prescribed in the regulations, or any extended period agreed in writing by the applicant).

19.23. The court may give permission for an appeal to be brought after 21 days, but only where it is satisfied that:

(a)   (where permission is sought within the 21-day period), there is good reason for the applicant to be unable to bring the appeal in time; or

(b)   (where permission is sought after the 21-day period has expired), there was a good reason for the applicant's failure to bring the appeal in time and for any delay in applying for permission.

19.24. On an appeal, the County Court is empowered to make an order confirming, quashing or varying the housing authority's decision as it thinks fit. It is important, therefore, that housing authorities have in place review procedures that are robust, fair, and transparent.

Power to accommodate pending an appeal to the county court

19.25. Section 204(4) gives housing authorities the power to accommodate certain applicants during the period for making an appeal, and pending the appeal and any subsequent appeal. Applicants have a right to appeal against a housing authority's decision not to secure accommodation for them pending an appeal to the County Court (s 204A). Applicants can also appeal against a housing authority's decision to secure accommodation for them for only a limited period which ends before final determination of the appeal. See Chapter 15 for guidance on powers to secure accommodation.

Local Government Ombudsman

19.26. Applicants may complain to a Local Government Ombudsman if they consider that they have been caused injustice as a result of maladministration by a housing authority. The Ombudsman may investigate the way a decision has been made, but may not question the merits of a decision properly reached. For example, maladministration would occur where a housing authority:

i)   took too long to do something;
ii)   did not follow their own rules or the law;
iii)   broke their promises;
iv)   treated the applicant unfairly;
v)   gave the applicant the wrong information.

19.27. There are some matters an Ombudsman cannot investigate. These include:

i)   matters the applicant knew about more than twelve months before he or she wrote to the Ombudsman or to a councillor, unless the Ombudsman considers it reasonable to investigate despite the delay;
ii)   matters about which the applicant has already taken court action against the housing authority, for example, an appeal to the County Court under s 204;
iii)   matters about which the applicant could go to court, unless the Ombudsman considers there are good reasons why the applicant could not reasonably be expected to do so.

19.28. Where there is a right of review the Ombudsman would expect an applicant to pursue the right before making a complaint. If there is any doubt about whether the Ombudsman can look into a complaint, the applicant should seek advice from the Ombudsman's office.

CHAPTER 20: PROTECTION OF PERSONAL PROPERTY

20.1.   This chapter provides guidance on the duty and powers housing authorities have to protect the personal property of an applicant.

20.2. Under s 211(1) and (2), where a housing authority has become subject to a duty to an applicant under specified provisions of Part 7 and it has reason to believe that:

i)   there is a danger of loss of, or damage to, the applicant's personal property because the applicant is unable to protect it or deal with it, and
ii)   no other suitable arrangements have been, or are being, made, then, whether or not the housing authority is still subject to such a duty, it must take reasonable steps to prevent the loss of, or to prevent or mitigate damage to, any personal property of the applicant.

20.3. The specified provisions are:

- s 188 (interim duty to accommodate);

- s 190, s 193 or s 195 (duties to persons found to be homeless or threatened with homelessness); or
- s 200 (duties to applicant whose case is considered for referral or referred).

20.4.   In all other circumstances, housing authorities have a power to take any steps they consider reasonable to protect in the same ways an applicant's personal property (s 211(3)).

20.5.   Section 212 makes provisions supplementing s 211. For the purposes of both s 211 and s 212, the personal property of an applicant includes the personal property of any person who might reasonably be expected to reside with him or her (s 211(5) and s 212(6)).

20.6.   A danger of loss or damage to personal property means that there is a likelihood of harm, not just that harm is a possibility. Applicants may be unable to protect their property if, for example, they are ill or are unable to afford to have it stored themselves.

20.7.   Under s 212(1), in order to protect an applicant's personal property, a housing authority can enter, at all reasonable times, the applicant's current or former home, and deal with the property in any way which seems reasonably necessary. In particular, it may store the property or arrange for it to be stored; this may be particularly appropriate where the applicant is accommodated by the housing authority in furnished accommodation for a period. In some cases, where the applicant's previous home is not to be occupied immediately, it may be possible for the property to remain there, if it can be adequately protected.

20.8.   Where a housing authority does take steps to protect personal property, whether by storing it or otherwise, it must take reasonable care of it and deliver it to the owner when reasonably requested to do so.

20.9.   The applicant can request the housing authority to move his or her property to a particular location. If the housing authority considers that the request is reasonable, they may discharge their responsibilities under s 211 by doing as the applicant asks. Where such a request is met, the housing authority will have no further duty or power to protect the applicant's property, and it must inform the applicant of this consequence before complying with the request (s 212(2)).

20.10.   Housing authorities may impose conditions on the assistance they provide where they consider these appropriate to the particular case. Conditions may include making a reasonable charge for storage of property and reserving the right to dispose of property in certain circumstances specified by the housing authority – eg if the applicant loses touch with them and cannot be traced after a certain period (s 211(4)).

20.11.   Where a request to move personal property to another location is either not made or not carried out, the duty or power to take any action under s 211 ends when the housing authority believes there is no longer any danger of loss or damage to the property because of the applicant's inability to deal with or protect it (s 212(3)). This may be the case, for example, where an applicant recovers from illness or finds accommodation where he or she is able to place his or her possessions, or becomes able to afford the storage costs him/herself. However, where the housing authority has discharged the duty under s 211 by placing property in storage, it has a discretionary power to continue to keep the property in storage. Where it does so, any conditions imposed by the housing authority continue to apply and may be modified as necessary.

20.12. Where the housing authority ceases to be under a duty, or ceases to have a power, to protect an applicant's personal property under s 211, it must notify the applicant of this and give the reasons for it. The notification must be delivered to the applicant or sent to his or her last known address (s 212(5)).

CHAPTER 21: CONTRACTING OUT HOMELESSNESS FUNCTIONS

21.1. This chapter provides guidance on contracting out homelessness functions and housing authorities' statutory obligations with regard to the discharge of those functions.

21.2. The *Local Authorities (Contracting Out of Allocation of Housing and Homelessness Functions) Order 1996* (SI 1996 No 3215) ('the Order') enables housing authorities to contract out certain functions under Parts 6 and 7 of the 1996 Act. The Order is made under s 70 of the *Deregulation and Contracting Out Act 1994* ('the 1994 Act'). In essence, the Order allows the contracting out of executive functions while leaving the responsibility for making strategic decisions with the housing authority.

21.3. The Order provides that the majority of functions under Part 7 can be contracted out. These include:

- making arrangements to secure that advice and information about homelessness, and the prevention of homelessness, is available free of charge within the housing authority's district;
- making inquiries about and deciding a person's eligibility for assistance;
- making inquiries about and deciding whether any duty, and, if so, what duty is owed to a person under Part 7;
- making referrals to another housing authority;
- carrying out reviews of decisions;
- securing accommodation to discharge homelessness duties.

21.4. Where decision-making in homelessness cases is contracted out, authorities may wish to consider retaining the review function under s 202 of the 1996 Act. This may provide an additional degree of independence between the initial decision and the decision on review.

21.5. The 1994 Act provides that a contract made:

i) may authorise a contractor to carry out only part of the function concerned;

ii) may specify that the contractor is authorised to carry out functions only in certain cases or areas specified in the contract;

iii) may include conditions relating to the carrying out of the functions, e g prescribing standards of performance;

iv) shall be for a period not exceeding 10 years and may be revoked at any time by the Minister or the housing authority. Any subsisting contract is to be treated as having been repudiated in these circumstances;

v) shall not prevent the housing authority from exercising themselves the functions to which the contract relates.

21.6. Schedule 2 to the Order lists the homelessness functions in Part 7 that may **not** be contracted out. These are:

- s 179(2) and (3): the provision of various forms of assistance to anyone providing advice and information about homelessness and the prevention of homelessness to people in the district, on behalf of the housing authority;
- s 180: the provision of assistance to voluntary organisations concerned with homelessness; and
- s 213: co-operation with relevant housing authorities and bodies by rendering assistance in the discharge of their homelessness functions.

21.7. Local authorities also **cannot** contract out their functions under the *Homelessness Act 2002* which relate to homelessness reviews and strategies. Chapter 1 provides guidance on homelessness reviews and strategies and outlines the main functions. These include:

- s 1(1): carry out a homelessness review for the district, and formulate and publish a homelessness strategy based on the results of that review;
- s 1(4): publish a new homelessness strategy within 5 years from the day on which their last homelessness strategy was published; and
- s 3(6): keep their homelessness strategy under review and modify it from time to time.

Reviews and the formulation of strategies can, however, be informed by research commissioned from external organisations.

21.8. The 1994 Act also provides that the housing authority is responsible for any act or omission of the contractor in exercising functions under the contract, except:

i) where the contractor fails to fulfil conditions specified in the contract relating to the exercise of the function; or,

ii) where criminal proceedings are brought in respect of the contractor's act or omission.

21.9. Where there is an arrangement in force under s 101 of the *Local Government Act 1972* by virtue of which one local authority exercises the functions of another, the 1994 Act provides that the authority exercising the function is not allowed to contract it out without the principal authority's consent.

21.10. Where a housing authority has contracted out the operation of any homelessness functions the authority remains statutorily responsible and accountable for the discharge of those functions. This is the case whether a housing authority contracts with a Large Scale Voluntary Transfer registered social landlord, an Arms Length Management Organisation or any other organisation. The authority will therefore need to ensure that the contract provides for delivery of the homelessness functions in accordance with both the statutory obligations and the authority's own policies on tackling and preventing homelessness. The performance of a housing authority's homelessness functions will continue to be part of its Comprehensive Performance Assessment and will need to be covered by Best Value reviews, whether or not it discharges the homelessness functions directly.

21.11. When contracting out homelessness functions, housing authorities will need to ensure that:

* proposed arrangements are consistent with their obligations under the 2002 Act to have a strategy for preventing homelessness and ensuring that accommodation and any necessary support will be available to everyone in their district who is homeless or at risk of homelessness;
* a high quality homelessness service will be provided, in particular the assessment of applicants and the provision of advice and assistance; and
* both short-term and settled accommodation services will be available for offer to all applicants owed the main homelessness duty.

21.12. Housing authorities should also ensure they have adequate contractual, monitoring and quality assurance mechanisms in place to ensure their statutory duties are being fully discharged.

21.13. In deciding whether to contract out homelessness functions, housing authorities are encouraged to undertake an options appraisal of each function to decide whether it would best be provided in-house or by another organisation. *Housing Allocation, Homelessness and Stock Transfer – A guide to key issues (ODPM 2004)* provides guidance on the key issues that housing authorities need to consider when deciding whether to retain or contract out the delivery of their homelessness functions.

ANNEX 1
GOOD PRACTICE/GUIDANCE PUBLICATIONS

Department for Communities and Local Government

Homelessness prevention: a guide to good practice (2006)

Office of the Deputy Prime Minister

Homelessness publications

www.communities.gov.uk/index.asp?id=1162505

Appendix 2
England: Homelessness

Sustainable Communities: settled homes, changing lives. A strategy for tackling homelessness (2005)

Tackling homelessness amongst ethnic minority households – a development guide (2005)

Resources for homeless ex-service personnel in London (2004)

Effective Co-operation in Tackling Homelessness: Nomination Agreements and Exclusions (2004)

Achieving Positive Shared Outcomes in Health and Homelessness (2004)

Local Authorities' Homelessness Strategies: Evaluation and Good Practice (2004)

Reducing B&B use and tackling homelessness – What's working: A Good Practice Handbook (2003)

Housing Associations and Homelessness Briefing (2003)

Achieving Positive Outcomes on Homelessness – A Homelessness Directorate Advice Note to Local Authorities (2003)

Addressing the health needs of rough sleepers (2002)

Care leaving strategies – a good practice handbook (2002)

Drugs services for homeless people – a good practice handbook (2002)

Homelessness Strategies: A Good Practice Handbook (2002)

More than a roof: a report into tackling homelessness (2002)

Helping rough sleepers off the streets: A report to the Homelessness Directorate – Randall, G and Brown, S (2002)

Preventing tomorrow's rough sleepers – Rough Sleepers Unit (2001)

Blocking the fast track from prison to rough sleeping – Rough Sleepers Unit (2000)

Homelessness and Housing Support Directorate Policy Briefings

Briefing 15: *Summary of Homelessness Good Practice Guidance* (June 2006)

Briefing 14: *Sustainable Communities: settled homes; changing lives – one year on* (March 2006)

Briefing 13: *Survey of English local authorities about homelessness* (December 2005)

Briefing 12: *Hostels Capital Improvement Programme (HCIP)* (September 2005)

Briefing 11: *Providing More Settled Homes* (June 2005)

Briefing 10: *Delivering on the Positive Outcomes* (December 2004)

Briefing 9: *Homelessness Strategies: Moving Forward* (November 2004)

Briefing 8: *Improving the Quality of Hostels and Other Forms of Temporary Accommodation* (June 2004)

Briefing 7: *Addressing the Health Needs of Homeless People Policy* (April 2004)

Briefing 6: *Repeat Homelessness Policy* (January 2004)

Briefing 5: *Improving Employment Options for Homeless People* (September 2003)

Briefing 4: *Prevention of Homelessness Policy* (June 2003)

Briefing 3: *Bed and Breakfast Policy* (March 2003)

Briefing 2: *Domestic Violence Policy* (December 2002)

Briefing 1: *Ethnicity and Homelessness Policy* (September 2002)

Supporting People publications

www.spkweb.org.uk

Supporting People: Guide to Accommodation and Support Options for People with Mental Health Problems (2005)

Guide to Housing and Housing Related Support Options for Offenders and People at Risk of Offending (2005)

Supporting People: Guide to Accommodation and Support Options for Homeless Households (2003)

Supporting People: The Support Needs of Homeless Households (2003)

Supporting People: Guide to Accommodation and Support Options for Households Experiencing Domestic Violence (2002)

Reflecting the Needs and Concerns of Black and Minority Ethnic Communities in Supporting People (2002)

Other ODPM publications

www.communities.gov.uk

Sustainable Communities: Homes for All. A Five Year Plan (2005)

Improving the Effectiveness of Rent Arrears Management (2005)

Housing Allocation, Homelessness and Stock Transfer – A guide to key issues (2004)

Guidance on Arms Length Management of Local Authority Housing (2004)

Allocation of Accommodation – Code of Guidance for local housing authorities (2002)

Appendix 2
England: Homelessness

Working together, Connexions and youth homelessness agencies, London, Department for Transport, Local Government and the Regions (DTLR) and Connexions (2001)

Other Government publications

Audit Commission

www.audit-commission.gov.uk

Homelessness: Responding to the New Agenda (2003)

ALMO Inspections. The Delivery of Excellent Housing Management Services (2003)

Housing Services After Stock Transfer (2002)

Department for Education and Skills

www.dfes.gov.uk

Safeguarding Children, The second joint Chief Inspectors' Report on arrangements to Safeguard Children, Commission for Social Care Inspection (2005)

Every Child Matters: Change for Children (2004)

Working with Voluntary and Community Organisations to Deliver Change for Children and Young People (2004)

Department of Health

www.dh.gov.uk/Home/fs/en

Our health, our care, our say: a new direction for community (2006)

Working together to safeguard children (2005)

Government response to Hidden Harm: the Report of an inquiry by the Advisory Council on the Misuse of Drugs (2005)

Making a Difference: Reducing Bureaucracy in Children, Young People and Family Services (2005)

Independence, well-being and choice: Our vision for the future of social care for adults in England (2005)

Commissioning a patient-led NHS (2005)

Health reform in England: update and next steps (2005)

National service framework for mental health: modern standards and service models (1999)

National service framework for children, young people and maternity services (2004)

From Vision to Reality: Transforming Outcomes for Children and Families (2004)

What to do if you're worried a child is being abused (2003)

Tackling Health Inequalities: a programme for action (2003)

Guidance on accommodating children in need and their families – Local Authority Circular 13 (2003)

Children Missing from Care and Home – a guide for good practice published in tandem with the Social Exclusion Unit's report *Young Runaways* (2002)

Getting it Right: good practice in leaving care resource pack (2000)

The framework for assessment of children in need and their families (2000)

Valuing People: A New Strategy for Learning Disability for the 21st Century (2000)

Working Together to Safeguard Children: a guide to interagency working to safeguard and promote the welfare of children (1999) Department of Health, Home Office and Department for Education and Employment

Home Office

www.homeoffice.gov.uk

Advice note on accommodation for vulnerable young people (2001)

Housing Corporation

www.housingcorp.gov.uk

Tenancy management: eligibility and evictions (2004)

Local Authority Nominations. Circular 02/03/Regulation (2003)

Non-Government publications

Centrepoint

www.centrepoint.org.uk

Joint protocols between housing and social services departments: a good practice guide for the assessment and assistance of homeless young people aged 16 and 17 years, Bellerby, N. London (2000)

Chartered Institute of Housing

www.cih.org

The Housing Manual (2005)

Housing and Support Services for asylum seekers and refugees: a good practice guide, John Perry (2005)

Strategic Approaches to Homelessness; Good Practice Briefing 24 (2002)

Commission for Racial Equality

www.cre.gov.uk

CRE Code of Practice on Racial Equality in Housing (2006)

Disability Rights Commission

www.drc-gb.org/

The Duty to Promote Disability Equality: Statutory Code of Practice (2005)

National Housing Federation

www.housing.org.uk

Level threshold: towards equality in housing for disabled people: good practice guide (2005)

Flexible allocation and local letting schemes (2000)

Homeless Link

www.homeless.org.uk

Hospital admission and discharge: Guidelines for writing a protocol for the hospital admission and discharge of people who are homeless (2006)

Shelter

http://england.shelter.org.uk/home/index.cfm

Sexual exclusion: issues and best practice in lesbian, gay and bisexual housing and homelessness (2005)

Youth housing: a good practice guide (2004)

Local authorities and registered social landlords – best practice on joint working (2002)

ANNEX 2
OTHER STRATEGIES AND PROGRAMMES THAT MAY ADDRESS HOMELESSNESS

- Local and Regional Housing Strategy
- Regional Homelessness Strategy
- Regional Economic Development Plan

- Local Strategic Partnership and Community Strategy
- Local Area Agreements
- Supporting People Strategy
- Children and Young People's Plan
- Sure Start
- Connexions
- Education and Employment programmes (eg The Princes Trust, New Deal, The Careers Service)
- Progress2work, for drug misusers, and where available, Progress2work-LinkUp for alcohol misusers, offenders and homeless people
- Local health schools programme
- Quality Protects
- NHS Local Delivery Plan
- Teenage Pregnancy Strategy
- Drug Action Team Plan
- Crime and Disorder Strategy
- Regional Reducing Reoffending Strategy
- Domestic Violence Strategy
- Anti-Social Behaviour Strategy
- Anti-Poverty Strategy
- Social Inclusion Strategy
- Valuing People Plan
- Town Centre Management Strategy
- Voluntary and community sector plans
- Gypsy and Traveller Accommodation Strategy (where required by s 225 *Housing Act 2004*)

ANNEX 3
OTHER AUTHORITES, ORGANISATIONS AND PERSONS WHOSE ACTIVITIES MAY CONTRIBUTE TO PREVENTING/TACKLING HOMELESSNESS

- Registered social landlords
- Private landlords
- Lettings agencies
- Self build groups
- Housing Co-operatives
- Housing Corporation
- Supported housing providers
- Home improvement agencies
- Primary Care Trusts, health centres and GP practices
- NHS Trusts – Acute and Mental Health
- Local mental health organisations (e.g. Mind)
- Local disability groups
- Care Services Improvement Partnership Regional Development Centres
- Learning Disability Partnership Boards

- Children's Trusts
- Youth Services and youth advice groups
- Education Welfare Services
- LEA Pupil Referral Units
- Schools
- Sure Start
- Connexions
- Youth Offending Team
- Police
- Crime and Disorder Reduction Partnerships
- Drug Action Teams
- National Offender Management Service (incorporating The Prison and Probation Services)
- Victim support groups
- Anti-Social Behaviour Team
- Street Wardens
- Jobcentre Plus
- Learning and Skills Councils
- Environmental Health Team
- Housing Management Team
- Housing Benefits Team
- Armed Forces resettlement services
- National Asylum Support Service
- Refugee Community Organisations
- Law Centres
- Advice/advocacy services (eg Citizens Advice Bureaux and Shelter)
- Local voluntary sector infrastructure bodies (eg CVS)
- Faith groups
- Women's groups
- Local domestic violence fora
- Ethnic minority groups
- Age groups (eg Age Concern, Help the Aged)
- Lesbian, gay and bisexual groups
- Emergency accommodation providers (such as the Salvation Army)
- Day centres for homeless people
- Refuges
- The Samaritans
- Mediation Services
- Local Strategic Partnerships
- Local businesses/Chambers of Commerce
- Regional Housing Board
- Regional planning bodies
- People living in insecure accommodation (and their representative bodies)
- Rough sleepers (and their representative bodies)
- Residents/tenants organisations
- Self help/user groups
- Services supporting sex workers

ANNEX 4

SPECIFIC OBJECTIVES AND ACTIONS FOR LOCAL AUTHORITIES THAT MIGHT BE INCLUDED IN A HOMELESSNESS STRATEGY

This Annex provides suggestions for objectives and actions that local authorities may wish to consider including in their homelessness strategies.

Housing authority

- **Facilitate the effective co-ordination of all service providers, across all sectors in the district, whose activities contribute to preventing homelessness and/or meeting the accommodation and support needs of people who are homeless or at risk of homelessness (objective).**
  - establish a homelessness forum to co-ordinate the activities of all the key players, across all sectors, who are contributing to meeting the aims of the homelessness strategy.
  - ensure the homelessness strategy is consistent with other relevant local plans and strategies and that all relevant stakeholders are aware of how they work together.
- **Ensure that people who are at risk of homelessness are aware of, and have access to, the services they may need to help them prevent homelessness (objective).**
  - provide comprehensive advice and information about homelessness and the prevention of homelessness, free to everyone in the district.
  - provide mediation and reconciliation services (eg to tackle neighbour disputes and family relationship breakdown).
  - implement an effective tenancy relations service (and good liaison with private landlords).
- **Ensure that the supply of accommodation, including affordable accommodation, in the district reflects estimated housing need (objective).**
  - in conjunction with RSLs operating in the district, maximise the number of social lettings available for people who have experienced homelessness or at risk of homelessness, consistent with the need to meet the reasonable aspirations of other groups in housing need.
  - ensure that provision of specialised and supported accommodation for people who have experienced homelessness or at risk of homelessness (eg refuges and wet hostels) reflects estimated need.
  - maximise the provision of affordable housing through planning requirements for new private developments.
- **Work with the social services authority to ensure that the needs of clients who have both housing and social services support needs are fully assessed and taken into account (objective).**

- develop a framework for effective joint working with the social services authority, including screening procedures to identify at an early stage where there is a need for case specific joint working.
- put in place arrangements for carrying out joint assessments of people with support needs who are homeless or have experienced homelessness.
- establish a protocol for the referral of clients and the sharing information between services.

Social services authority

- **Work with the housing authority to ensure that the needs of clients who have both housing and social services support needs are fully assessed and taken into account (objective).**
  - develop a framework for effective joint working with the housing authority, including screening procedures, to identify at an early stage where there is a need for case specific joint working.
  - put in place arrangements for carrying out joint assessments of people with support needs who are homeless or have experienced homelessness.
  - establish a protocol for the referral of clients and the sharing information between services.
- **Ensure that, subject to relevant eligibility criteria, vulnerable people who are homeless, or at risk of homelessness, receive the support they need to help them sustain a home and prevent homelessness recurring (objective).**
  - provide a reconciliation service for young people estranged from their families.
  - exercise powers under the *Children Act 1989* to make payments to assist young people who are homeless or at risk of homelessness to sustain/find accommodation.
  - operate a supported lodgings scheme for homeless 16 and 17 year olds who need a supportive environment.
  - provide assistance to enable families with children who have become homeless intentionally (or are ineligible for housing assistance) to secure accommodation for themselves (eg financial assistance with rent deposit/guarantees).

ANNEX 5
CO-OPERATION BETWEEN REGISTERED SOCIAL LANDLORDS AND HOUSING AUTHORITIES

Housing: the strategic context

1. Housing authorities have a statutory obligation to consider the housing needs of their district (s 8 Housing Act 1985). Under the *Homelessness Act 2002* ('the 2002 Act'), they also have a statutory duty to formulate a strategy for preventing homelessness and ensuring that accommodation and support are available for people who are homeless or at risk of homelessness in their district. A homelessness strategy may include actions which the authority expects to be taken by various other organisations, with their agreement.

2. Most social housing is provided by housing authorities and by Registered Social Landlords (RSLs). Virtually all provision of new social housing is delivered through RSLs and, under the transfer programme, ownership of a significant proportion of housing authority stock is being transferred from housing authorities to RSLs, subject to tenants' agreement. This means that, increasingly, RSLs will become the main providers of social housing. Consequently, it is essential that housing authorities work closely with RSLs, as well as all other housing providers, in order to meet the housing needs in their district and ensure that the aims and objectives of their homelessness strategy are achieved.

Statutory framework for co-operation

3. Section 170 of the *Housing Act 1996* ('the 1996 Act') provides that where an RSL has been requested by a housing authority to offer accommodation to people with priority under its allocation scheme, the RSL must co-operate to such extent as is reasonable in the circumstances. Similarly, s 213 provides that where an RSL has been requested by a housing authority to assist them in the discharge of their homelessness functions under Part 7, it must also co-operate to the same extent. Section 3 of the 2002 Act requires housing authorities to consult appropriate bodies and organisations before publishing a homelessness strategy, and this will inevitably need to include RSLs.

Housing corporation regulatory guidance

4. RSLs are regulated by the Housing Corporation which, under s 36 of the 1996 Act, and with the approval of the Secretary of State, has issued guidance to RSLs with respect to their management of housing accommodation. The Housing Corporation's Regulatory Code and guidance requires housing associations to work with local authorities to enable them to fulfil their statutory duties to, among others, homeless people and people who have priority for an allocation of housing. In particular, RSLs must ensure that:

- their lettings policies are flexible, non-discriminatory and responsive to demand while contributing to inclusivity and sustainable communities;
- they can demonstrate their co-operation with local authorities on homelessness reviews, homelessness strategies and the delivery of authorities' homelessness functions;
- when requested, and to such extent as is reasonable in the circumstances, they provide a proportion of their stock (at least 50% – see paragraph 9 below) to housing authority nominations and as temporary accommodation for people owed a homelessness duty;
- following consultation with local authorities, criteria are adopted for accepting or rejecting nominees and other applicants for housing;

- applicants are excluded from consideration for housing only if their unacceptable behaviour is serious enough to make them unsuitable to be a tenant; and
- their lettings policies are responsive to authorities' housing duties, take account of the need to give reasonable priority to transfer applicants, are responsive to national, regional and local mobility and exchange schemes, and are demonstrably fair and effectively controlled.

5. Therefore, the overriding requirement for RSLs in relation to homelessness is to demonstrate that they are co-operating with local authorities to enable them to fulfil their statutory duties.

Co-operation and partnerships

6. Housing authorities need to draw on these regulatory requirements to form constructive partnerships with RSLs. It is also recommended that authorities refer to the strategic document 'A Framework for Partnership' published jointly by the Local Government Association, the National Housing Federation and the Housing Corporation and available at www.lga.gov.uk/Documents/ Briefing/framework.pdf.

7. Where RSLs participate in choice-based lettings schemes, the Corporation will expect any protocols for joint working with housing authorities to make proper provision to meet the needs of vulnerable groups, and ensure that support is available to enable tenants and applicants to exercise choice. Housing authorities should involve RSLs in the implementation of choice-based lettings schemes at an early stage.

Nomination agreements

8. Whilst legislation provides the framework for co-operation between housing authorities and RSLs, nomination agreements set out the way in which this co-operation is given effect. It is crucial that a housing authority has a comprehensive nomination agreement with each of its partner RSLs to ensure that both sides know what is expected of them. The need for a robust nomination agreement applies in all circumstances, but will be particularly important where the housing authority has transferred ownership of its housing stock and is reliant on the transfer RSL (and any other partner RSLs) to provide housing for their applicants. ODPM guidance on *Housing Allocation, Homelessness and Stock Transfer – A Guide to Key Issues (2004)* sets out the policy and operational matters which the nomination agreement between the housing authority and their transfer RSL should cover.

9. RSLs are required to offer at least 50% of vacancies in their stock (net of internal transfers) to housing authority nominations, unless some lower figure is agreed between the two bodies.[6] In some circumstances, they may agree a substantially higher figure. However, housing authorities should bear in mind that RSLs are required to retain their independence. They must honour their

---

[6]   Housing Corporation Regulatory Circular, 02/03 Regulation, February 2003.

constitutional obligations under their diverse governing instruments, and will make the final decision on the allocation of their housing, within their regulatory framework.

10. Where requested by a housing authority, RSLs should consider the possible use of a proportion of their own stock to provide temporary accommodation for people owed a homelessness duty under Part 7 of the 1996 Act. This may be necessary in some areas, particularly those where demand for housing is very high and there is a significant number of homeless families with children who need to be placed in temporary accommodation. RSLs and housing authorities will have joint responsibility for determining the appropriate use of settled housing stock for temporary lettings, taking into account that such use will reduce the volume of RSL housing stock available for nominations into long-term tenancies. Housing authorities should ensure that their partnerships take maximum advantage of the flexibility that such arrangements can provide. The Secretary of State expects that, wherever possible, social housing should be allocated on a settled basis rather than used to provide temporary accommodation in the medium to long term. Where medium to long term accommodation is required, the authority and RSL should consider whether it is possible to offer a secure or an assured tenancy under the terms of the authority's allocations scheme.

11. Housing authorities should ensure that the details of nominated households given to RSLs are accurate and comprehensive. Details should include information about the applicant's priority status under the housing authority's policy, as well as indications of vulnerability, support needs and arrangements for support.

12. The Corporation expects that RSLs' approach to exclusions and evictions will generally reflect the principles to which housing authorities work. Housing Corporation Circular 07/04 *Tenancy management: eligibility and evictions* sets out the Corporation's expectations of RSLs when assessing the eligibility of applicants and when working to prevent or respond to breaches of tenancy.

Effective collaboration

13. It is important that housing authorities foster good partnership working with RSLs, to help them prevent and tackle homelessness in the district. The housing management and care and support approaches undertaken by RSLs are key to sustaining tenancies, reducing evictions and abandonment, and preventing homelessness. To ensure effective collaboration between themselves and partner RSLs operating in their district, housing authorities should consider the following:

nominations agreements: housing authorities should ensure that they have a formal nominations agreement with all partner RSLs and that there are robust arrangements in place to monitor effective delivery of the terms of the agreement. These should be clearly set out, and should include the proportion of lettings that will be made available, any conditions that will apply, and how any disputes about suitability or eligibility will be resolved. Housing authorities should negotiate for the maximum number of lettings that will be required to enable them to discharge their housing functions and which would be reasonable for the RSL to deliver.

exclusion criteria: when negotiating nominations agreements housing authorities should aim for any exclusion criteria (that may be applied to nominees by the RSL) to be kept to a minimum. To prevent new tenancies from failing and to minimise the likelihood of exclusion, housing authorities should also ensure that adequate support packages are in place for vulnerable applicants before a nominee is expected to take up their tenancy.

eviction policies: to help prevent homelessness, housing authorities should encourage RSLs to seek to minimise any need for eviction of their tenants by employing preventative strategies and taking early positive action where breaches of tenancy agreement have occurred. Associations should act to support and sustain, rather than terminate, a tenancy.

In cases involving anti-social behaviour eviction should, where possible, be used as a last resort, although in particularly serious cases or where perpetrators refuse to co-operate it may be necessary. A number of measures have been introduced which may be used to tackle anti-social behaviour without removing the perpetrator from their home and moving the problem to somewhere else. These include Acceptable Behaviour Contracts, Anti-Social Behaviour Orders, housing injunctions and demotion. Further information on the tools and powers available to tackle anti-social behaviour can be found on the TOGETHER website, a resource for practitioners working to tackle anti-social behaviour (www.together.gov.uk).

Similarly, in cases involving rent arrears eviction should, where possible, be used as a last resort. RSLs should employ strategies to maximise their income and to prevent and manage rent arrears. Where arrears have accrued they should seek early intervention through personal contact with the tenant(s) offering support and advice. They should offer practical ways for recovering the arrears through debt management plans, referrals to debt advice agencies and ensuring that tenants are claiming all the benefits to which they are entitled. ODPM published guidance for local authorities and RSLs on *Improving the Effectiveness of Rent Arrears Management* (June 2005).

Supporting People programme: housing authorities should ensure they work closely with RSLs in implementing the Supporting People programme to ensure that housing-related support can be delivered, where appropriate, for people who would be at risk of homelessness without such support.

mobility: housing authorities should work with RSLs in considering the scope for mobility – including moves to other areas, moves to other tenures, and joint action to reduce under-occupation and over-crowding – in meeting housing need and reducing homelessness. Larger RSLs, which operate in a number of different areas, may be uniquely placed to facilitate cross-boundary moves, including voluntary moves from high demand areas to areas of lower demand.

ODPM, in conjunction with the Housing Corporation, National Housing Federation and Local Government Association, published a good practice guide for local authorities and housing associations on *Effective Co-operation in Tackling Homelessness: Nomination Agreements and Exclusions (2004)*.

ANNEX 6
HOMELESSNESS STRATEGY: SPECIFIC ACTION THAT MIGHT BE EXPECTED TO BE TAKEN BY OTHERS

Public sector

Registered social landlords

- ensure allocation policies meet the needs of people accepted as homeless including specialist provision for vulnerable groups, eg drug misusers;
- ensure allocation policies are inclusive, defensible and do not operate 'blanket bans' for particular groups;
- ensure arrears policies take into account the aims of the homelessness strategy (and facilitate early access to money and housing advice).

Primary Care Trusts

- develop health services for homeless people, (eg Personal Medical Service pilots, walk-in centres, GP service that visits hostels and day centres);
- ensure access to primary health care for all homeless people including rough sleepers and those using emergency access accommodation;
- liaise with social services and special needs housing providers to ensure access to dependency and multiple needs services where needed;
- ensure that hospital discharge policies and protocols are developed and put in place for those leaving hospital who are in housing need;
- ensure access to mental health services, including counselling and therapy where needed.

Children's Trusts

- ensure children's services and housing strategies are integrated to achieve better outcomes for children.

Youth and Community Services

- develop peer support schemes;
- raise awareness of homelessness issues with young people at risk.

National Offender Management Service

- complete a basic housing needs assessment on entry to custody in all local establishments;

- share information with other agencies on risk of harm, potential homelessness and vulnerability;
- develop local protocols regarding dealing with potentially homeless offenders and information sharing;
- as part of the local Supporting People Commissioning bodies, provide specialist knowledge to help commission new services for vulnerable offender and victim groups.

Regional Offender Managers

- ensure regional strategic representation of the needs of offenders in custody and the community.

Community Safety Team/Anti-social Behaviour Team

- develop steps/interventions to reduce anti-social behaviour and therefore reduce the risk of evictions.

Youth Offending Team

- work with children and young people to prevent their offending, effectively integrate them and their families within the community and ultimately prevent evictions.

Drug Action Team

- consider the need to commission treatment for homeless people, or whether mainstream services can be extended to meet their needs;
- develop accommodation options for substance misusers including such provision as Rent Deposit Schemes;
- develop, in collaboration with Supporting People teams, specialist housing provision for substance misusers;
- ensure that the children of adults with substance misuse problems are taken into account when planning services.

Jobcentre Plus

- ensure that clients are helped to find and keep a job;
- ensure that clients claim and receive the benefits they are entitled to.

Connexions Service

- provide advice and information on housing and related benefits (or referral to other agencies where appropriate) to all 13 to 19 year olds who need it;
- ensure vulnerable young people have access to a personal adviser with the aim of preventing those young people becoming homeless.

National Asylum Support Service (NASS)

- ensure NASS accommodation providers notify local authorities of the planned withdrawal of NASS accommodation within two days of a positive asylum decision;
- encourage NASS accommodation providers to help prevent homelessness amongst new refugees (eg via tenancy conversion or delaying evictions);
- ensure that homelessness and housing pressures are taken into account by Regional Strategic Co-ordination Meetings when decisions are taken on future asylum seeker dispersal areas.

Voluntary sector

- Provision of a range of services including:
  - Rent in advance/deposit bond schemes;
  - Night stop schemes;
  - Supported lodgings schemes;
  - Homelessness awareness/preventative input to schools;
  - Advice services (housing/debt/benefits etc);
  - Counselling, mediation, reconciliation services;
  - Provision of floating support;
  - Lay advocacy services;
  - Dependency services;
  - Hospital discharge services;
  - Women's refuges;
  - Day Centres;
  - Outreach to those sleeping rough;
  - Provision of emergency accommodation (eg night shelters);
  - Hostels;
  - Foyers;
  - Resettlement services (including pre-tenancy, move-on accommodation and tenancy sustainment);
  - Mental health services;
  - Peer support, self-help and user groups;
  - Meaningful occupation/personal development work/job training/skills for employment/work placements;
  - Support for parents of young people at risk of homelessness;
  - Support for victims of crime.

Private sector

- provision of hostels;
- making lettings available to people who are homeless or at risk of homelessness (eg through landlord accreditation schemes);
- working with tenants to address rent arrears.

ANNEX 7
TACKLING COMMON CAUSES OF HOMELESSNESS

1. This annex provides guidance on how authorities might tackle some of the more common causes of homelessness at an early stage.

Parents, relatives or friends not being able to provide accommodation

2. Housing authorities are advised to consider a range of approaches aimed at avoiding the crisis of homelessness, resolving problems in the long-term or providing respite and time for a planned, and often more sustainable move. Home visits and mediation services can play an important role in delaying or preventing homelessness by helping people find solutions and resolve difficulties.

3. Family tensions can make living conditions intolerable for young people and their parents. Housing authorities are advised to work closely with children's trusts at strategic level to ensure that housing need and homelessness prevention are included in the strategic planning process through the Children and Young People's Plan. They are also advised to work closely with children's trusts at delivery level as part of local multi-agency teams that provide joined up services focusing on improving outcomes for children and young people. As part of this work, they may consider developing partnerships with key agencies in the voluntary sector who work with young people at risk of homelessness. Trained staff and peer mentors can often help young people in difficult relationships restore some links to their families or supporters, resolve family conflict or facilitate planned moves into alternative accommodation.

Relationship breakdown

4. Relationships may often be strained or break down due to periods of separation, eg long-term hospital or drug treatment or because of the behaviour of family members, eg offending or violence. Local authorities should develop systems for assessing appropriate forms of intervention and the assessment of risks to vulnerable family members to inform decisions about intervention, eg where domestic violence or child safety is involved.

5. Local authorities should consider the use of home visits, mediation and counselling services to help couples and families reconcile their differences or facilitate planned moves to alternative accommodation.

6. Housing authorities are advised to consider the provision of specialist advice targeted at young people at risk of homelessness. Local Connexions services, for example, can play a key role in reaching vulnerable young people; helping them access information and advice, providing one-to-one support or brokering appropriate specialist support from key services such as welfare, health, substance and/or alcohol misuse services, education and employment. Housing authorities might also consider working with local schools in order to provide young people with information about the implications of leaving home and the housing choices available to them.

Domestic violence

7. As well as being a direct and underlying cause of homelessness, it is becoming increasingly apparent that domestic violence is a major factor among people who experience 'repeat' homelessness. In many cases, the provision of advice and outreach services to support people who experience domestic violence before they reach crisis point, for example on ex-partner rent arrears, tenancy agreements and property rights, can help to prevent homelessness.

8. Housing authorities are encouraged to offer people who have experienced domestic violence a range of accommodation and support options. For some, escaping domestic violence will involve leaving their home, often as a last resort, and those who have experienced domestic violence may be placed in a refuge or another form of appropriate temporary accommodation where necessary. Many people who have experienced domestic violence would, however, prefer to remain in their own homes with their social and support networks around them. From 1 April 2005 local authorities have been strongly encouraged to develop, launch and promote a sanctuary type scheme in order to meet part of the revised domestic violence Best Value Performance Indicator 225. The scheme provides security measures to allow those experiencing domestic violence to remain in their own homes where they choose to do so, where safety can be assured and where the perpetrator no longer lives within the accommodation.

9. It is important that when developing policies, strategies and practice-based interventions, housing authorities work with all relevant bodies. For example, when considering the safety, security and confidentiality of people who have experienced domestic violence and their children, especially those children who may be vulnerable and/or at risk, housing authorities will need to work with Crime and Disorder Reduction Partnerships, the Local Domestic Violence Fora and with the Local Safeguarding Children Board. BVPI 225 encourages further work in this area.

End of an assured shorthold tenancy

10. The use of home visits, landlord-tenant mediation services and tenancy sustainment services may enable tenants who have been asked to leave their home to remain with their existing private landlords, through negotiation, mediation and the offer of practical solutions, such as clearing a debt, providing the tenant with advice on managing budgets or fast-tracking a Housing Benefit claim.

11. Housing authorities should also establish services to provide tenants in housing difficulties with advice and information about available housing options and, where necessary, assistance to help them access alternative accommodation. Advice might include, for example, advice about private landlords and letting agents, including any accreditation schemes, within the

Appendix 2
England: Homelessness

district; the availability of rent guarantee or rent deposit schemes; or how to apply for social housing through the local authority housing waiting list or from other social landlords).

Rent and mortgage arrears

12.   Early intervention by the housing authority could help prevent difficulties with rent or mortgage arrears from triggering a homelessness crisis for tenants or home owners.

Options might include:

- personal contact with tenants or homeowners to offer support and advice;
- mediation with private landlords;
- welfare benefits advice and assistance with making claims;
- debt counselling and money advice (either in-house or through referrals to specialist advice agencies);
- advice on practical ways of recovering rent arrears through debt management plans, attachment to earnings or benefits orders or by referrals to a debt advice agencies.

13.   Many approaches to the prevention and management of rent arrears among tenants can apply equally whether the landlord is a social sector or a private sector landlord. ODPM published guidance for local authorities and RSLs on *Improving the Effectiveness of Rent Arrears Management (June 2005)*.

14.   In some cases rent arrears may be the result of an underlying problem such as alcohol or drug misuse, death of a partner, relationship breakdown, change in employment status, or physical or mental health problems. In such cases the housing authority may wish to contact the appropriate health and social services departments and other relevant agencies for advice, assistance and specialist support. The Secretary of State considers that housing authorities should always consult the Children's Trust before considering the eviction of a family with children. Vital work helping vulnerable children can be affected if families with children are forced to move out of the local area. Effective, ongoing liaison arrangements and collaborative working will be important in such instances.

Housing Benefit administration

15.   Rent arrears can arise from delays in the calculation and payment of housing benefit. It is therefore in housing authorities' interests to develop prompt and efficient systems for the payment of benefit in order to avoid a risk of homelessness arising as a result of such delays. Where the administration of housing benefit and the provision of housing assistance are dealt with by different departments of the local authority, it will be necessary for the authority to ensure that effective liaison arrangements are in place. Efficient housing benefit payments systems can also help to increase the confidence of private sector landlords in letting accommodation to tenants who may rely on benefits to meet their rent costs.

Anti-Social Behaviour and Offending

16. Tenants may be at risk of becoming homeless as a result of their own or others' anti-social or offending behaviour. Housing authorities are urged to contact tenants in these circumstances at the earliest possible stage where they have received a complaint or where it has been brought to their attention that a tenant is causing a nuisance or annoyance. This will enable them to inform such tenants of the possible consequences of continuing with the reported behaviour and may prevent homelessness resulting in some instances. Authorities will need to be aware of the need for discretion about the source of any complaint, particularly where there is concern about threatening or aggressive behaviour.

17. In cases where a housing authority is satisfied that there is a substantive complaint of anti-social behaviour they will need to consider a range of options to address the problem with the tenant before embarking on action to terminate the tenancy. Housing authorities are advised, where possible, to use eviction as a last resort, although in particularly serious cases or where perpetrators refuse to co-operate it may be necessary.

18. Mediation services may help to resolve neighbour disputes which have led to complaints of anti-social behaviour. A number of measures have been introduced which may be used to tackle anti-social behaviour without removing the perpetrator from their home and simply moving the problem somewhere else. These include: Acceptable Behaviour Contracts, Anti-Social Behaviour Orders, housing injunctions and demotion. Further information can be found on the TOGETHER website, a resource for practitioners working to tackle anti-social behaviour (www.together.gov.uk).

19. Where local authority tenants are at risk of homelessness as a result of other tenants' anti-social behaviour, authorities should be aware of the powers they have to take action against the perpetrators and make urgent housing transfers to protect victims of violence or harassment, where requested.

20. Housing authorities will need to work closely with the National Offender Management Service (NOMS) and their partners in the voluntary and community sector to manage the housing arrangements of offenders in the community, and ensure they receive any support necessary to avoid a risk of homelessness. Where an authority may be considering the eviction of an offender, it will need to consult closely with NOMS to ensure this can be avoided wherever possible. This will also help reduce re-offending and promote community safety.

Leaving an institutional environment

21. People leaving an institutional environment can be particularly at risk of homelessness and may seek assistance from the housing authority to obtain

Appendix 2
England: Homelessness

accommodation when they move on. Authorities should have systems in place to ensure that they have advance notice of such people's needs for accommodation in such circumstances to allow them to take steps well in advance to ensure that arrangements are in place to enable a planned and timely move.

Young people leaving care

22. It is important that, wherever possible, the housing needs of care leavers are addressed before they leave care. All care leavers must have a pathway plan prepared by appropriate staff of the authority responsible for their care, setting out the support they will be provided with to enable them make a successful transition to a more independent lifestyle. Making arrangements for accommodation and ensuring that, where necessary, care leavers are provided with suitable housing support will be an essential aspect of the pathway plan. Where care leavers may require social housing, their housing and related support needs should be discussed with the appropriate agencies. Where necessary, arrangements will need to be made for joint assessment between social services and housing authorities, as part of a multi-agency assessment necessary to inform the pathway plan of individual young people.

23. Consideration of an individual care leaver's housing needs should take account of their need for support and reasonable access to places of education, employment, training and health care. As far as possible, pathway plans should include contingency plans in the event of any breakdown in the young person's accommodation arrangements. It is recommended that housing and social services authorities (and relevant departments within unitary authorities) develop joint protocols for meeting the needs of care leavers to ensure that each agency (or department) plays a full role in providing support to – and building trust with – this client group.

Custody or detention

24. Around a third of prisoners lose their housing on imprisonment, so it is important that prisoners receive effective advice and assistance about housing options, either prior to or when being remanded or sentenced to custody. Assessing an offender's housing needs at this point will help to identify those prisoners who may require assistance to bring to an end, sustain or transfer an existing tenancy, make a claim for Housing Benefit to meet rent costs while in prison, or to help a prisoner transfer or close down an existing tenancy appropriately. Local authorities are advised to assist the Prison Service in providing advice to prisoners and taking action to ensure they can sustain their accommodation while in custody.

25. It is recommended that housing advice be made available to offenders throughout the period of custody or detention to ensure that any housing needs are addressed. It is important that early planning takes place between prison staff and housing providers to identify housing options on release, to prevent homelessness and enable them to make a smooth transition from prison, or remand, to independent living.

26. All prisoners in local prisons and Category C prisons have access to housing advice. And, from April 2005 all local prisons have been required to carry out a housing needs assessment for every new prisoner, including those serving short sentences. Local authorities are advised to assist the Prison Service in delivering these services.

27. All Youth Offending Teams (YOTs) now have named accommodation officers. YOTs can offer both practical support to children, young people and their families and can increasingly play a key strategic role in ensuring that young offenders are effectively resettled through accessing mainstream provision and services.

28. Joint working between the National Offender Management Service/Youth Offending Teams and their local housing authorities is essential to help prevent homelessness amongst offenders, ex-offenders and others who have experience of the criminal justice system. Options might include:

- having a single contact point within the housing authority to provide housing advice and assistance for those who have experience of the criminal justice system;
- Probation staff offering information on securing or terminating tenancies prior to custody;
- running housing advice sessions in local prisons to further enable prisoners to access advice on housing options prior to their release;
- prisons granting prisoners Release On Temporary Licence to attend housing interviews with landlords;
- developing tenancy support services for those who have experienced the criminal justice system.

Armed forces

29. Members of Her Majesty's regular naval, military and air forces are generally provided with accommodation by the Ministry of Defence (MOD), but are required to leave this when they are discharged from the service. The principal responsibility for providing housing information and advice to Service personnel lies with the armed forces up to the point of discharge and these services are delivered through the Joint Service Housing Advice Office (telephone: 01722 436575). Some people, who have served in the armed forces for a long period, and those who are medically discharged, may be offered assistance with resettlement by Ministry of Defence (MOD) resettlement staff. The MOD issues a *Certificate of Cessation of Entitlement to Occupy Service Living Accommodation* (see examples at Annexes 14 and 15) six months before discharge.

30. Housing authorities that have a significant number of service personnel stationed in their area will need to work closely with relevant partners, such as the Joint Service Housing Advice Office and MOD's resettlement services, to ascertain likely levels of need for housing assistance amongst people leaving the forces and plan their services accordingly. In particular, housing authorities are advised to take advantage of the six-month period of notice of discharge to ensure that service personnel receive timely and comprehensive advice on the housing options available to them when they leave the armed forces. Authorities may also wish to consider creating links with the employment and business communities to assist people leaving the armed forces to find work or meaningful occupation, enabling them further to make a successful transition to independent living in the community.

31. The Veterans Agency should be the first point of contact for all former armed forces personnel who require information about housing issues. The agency provide a free help line (telephone: 0800 169 2277) which offers former armed forces personnel advice and signposting to ex-Service benevolent organisations who may be able to offer assistance with housing matters.

Hospital

32. Some people who are admitted to hospital – even for a short time – may be in housing need or at risk of homelessness. And some people who may not be in housing need when they are admitted may become at risk of losing their home during a protracted stay in hospital, for example, if they are unable to maintain their rent or mortgage payments. This can apply, in particular, to people admitted to hospital for mental health reasons and for whom family, tenancy or mortgage breakdown is an accompanying factor to the admission to hospital.

33. Housing authorities are advised to work closely with social services and NHS Trusts in order to establish good procedures for the discharge of patients, and to ensure that former patients are not homeless or at risk of homelessness on leaving hospital. This could involve agreeing joint protocols for hospital admissions and discharge of patients to ensure that the housing and support needs of inpatients are identified as early as possible after admission, and that arrangements are put in place to meet the needs of patients in good time prior to discharge. Measures might include, for example, setting up a multi-agency discharge team as part of the homelessness strategy action plan or funding a dedicated post to support patients who may be at risk of homelessness when discharged from hospital.

34. Further guidance is provided in Department of Health publications on *Achieving timely simple discharge from hospital: A toolkit for the multi-disciplinary team (2004)* and *Discharge from hospital: pathway, process and practice (2003)*.

Accommodation provided by National Asylum Support Service (NASS)

35. Asylum seekers who receive leave to remain in the UK must move on from their NASS accommodation within 28 days of the decision on their case.

Former asylum seekers will therefore have little time to find alternative accommodation and are unlikely to have had any experience of renting or buying accommodation in the UK, or experience of related matters such as claiming benefits or arranging essential services such as gas, water and electricity. These difficulties are likely to be compounded by the fact that many former asylum seekers may face cultural barriers such as language.

36. In order to prevent these factors leading to homelessness amongst former asylum seekers, housing authorities are advised to develop protocols with NASS accommodation providers, refugee support services and NASS regional managers to ensure that, where possible, a planned and timely move to alternative accommodation or the sustainment of existing accommodation can take place. Housing benefit, rent deposits, homeless prevention loans and discretionary housing benefit payments can all help to fund temporary extensions of the NASS notice period or longer-term tenancy conversion through the establishment of assured shorthold tenancies.

37. Former asylum seekers will need effective and timely advice on the range of housing options available. It is vital that housing authorities ensure that this advice and information can be readily translated into community languages and delivered in locations accessible to asylum seekers and refugees. Authorities are also advised to consider whether there may be a need for ongoing resettlement support in order to maximise the chances of tenancy sustainment. As standard, authorities are advised to ensure that new refugees are made fully aware of the steps that they need to take to maintain a UK tenancy.

38. Authorities may wish to refer to *Housing and Support Services for asylum seekers and refugees: a good practice guide (2005)* published by the Chartered Institute of Housing.

Ethnic minority populations

39. Statistics provided by local authorities show that people from ethnic minority backgrounds are around three times more likely to be accepted as owed a main homelessness duty than their White counterparts. This pattern is found across all regions in England and the reasons are varied and complex. It is therefore critical that housing authorities and their partner agencies develop comprehensive strategies to better prevent and respond to homelessness among people from ethnic minority communities.

40. ODPM published *Tackling homelessness amongst ethnic minority households – a development guide (2005)* to assist local authorities and their partner agencies in the development of inclusive, evidence-based and cost-effective homelessness services for their local ethnic minority populations.

Drug Users

41. Drug use can both precede and occur as a result of homelessness. Between half and three quarters of single homeless people have in the past been problematic drug misusers. Many have a wide range of support needs, which reinforce each other and heighten the risk of drug use and homelessness. For those who are engaging in drug treatment, or have stabilised their use, homelessness increases their chances of relapse and continued problematic drug use. Housing authorities are advised to work closely with Drug Action Teams (multi-agency partnerships who co-ordinate the drug strategy at the local level) to ensure that housing and homelessness strategies are aligned with DAT treatment plans and Supporting People strategies help address the needs of homeless drug users as a shared client group.

ANNEX 8
HOW TO CONTACT THE HOME OFFICE IMMIGRATION AND NATIONALITY DIRECTORATE

1. The Home Office's Immigration and Nationality Directorate (IND) will exchange information with housing authorities subject to relevant data protection and disclosure policy requirements being met and properly managed, provided that the information is required to assist with the carrying out of statutory functions or prevention and detection of fraud.

2. The Evidence and Enquiries Unit (EEU) will provide a service to housing authorities to confirm the immigration status of an applicant from abroad (Non-Asylum Seekers). In order to take advantage of the service, housing authorities first need to register with the Evidence and Enquiries Unit, Immigration and Nationality Directorate, 12th Floor Lunar House, Croydon, CR9 2BY either by letter or **Fax: 020 8196 3049**.

3. Registration details required by the EEU's Local Authorities' Team are:

(a) Name of enquiring housing authority on headed paper;

(b) Job title/status of officer registering on behalf of the local housing authority; and

(c) Names of housing authority staff and their respective job titles/status who will be making enquiries on behalf of the housing authority.

4. Once the housing authority is registered with the EEU, and this has been confirmed, then the authorised personnel can make individual enquiries by letter or fax, but replies will be returned by post.

5. The EEU will not usually indicate that someone is an asylum seeker unless the applicant has signed a disclaimer and it is attached to the enquiry or if the enquirer has specifically asked about asylum.

6. If a response indicates that the applicant has an outstanding asylum claim, or there are any queries regarding an ongoing asylum case, enquiries should be made to NASS LA Comms on 020 8760 4527. Local authorities will also need to be registered with this team before any information can be provided.

7. The Home Office (IND) can only advise whether an EEA/foreign national has a right of residence in the United Kingdom. IND does not decide whether an EEA/Foreign national qualifies for benefits or for local authority housing.

ANNEX 9
ASYLUM SEEKERS

Overview

1. Generally, asylum seekers can be expected to be *persons subject to immigration control* who have been given *temporary admission* but have not been granted leave to enter or remain in the UK.

2. Asylum seekers who are *persons subject to immigration control* and whose claim for asylum was made <u>after 2 April 2000</u> are not eligible for assistance under Part 7. However, some asylum seekers who are *persons subject to immigration control* and whose claim for asylum was made before 3 April 2000 may be eligible (see below).

3. Broadly speaking, an asylum seeker is a person claiming to have a well-founded fear of being persecuted for reasons of race, religion, nationality, membership of a particular social group, or political opinion, and who is unable or unwilling to avail him or her self of the protection of the authorities in his or her own country.

4. A person only becomes an asylum seeker when his or her claim for asylum has been recorded by the Home Secretary, and he or she remains an asylum seeker until such time as that application has been finally resolved (including the resolution of any appeal). The recording, consideration and resolution of such claims is a matter for the Home Office Immigration and Nationality Directorate (IND).

5. If there is any uncertainty about an applicant's immigration or asylum status, housing authorities should contact the Home Office Immigration and Nationality Directorate, using the procedures set out in Annex 8. Before doing so, the applicant should be advised that an inquiry will be made: if at this stage the applicant prefers to withdraw his or her application, no further action will be required.

Asylum seekers who are eligible for Part 7 assistance

6. The *Allocation of Housing and Homelessness (Eligibility) (England) Regulations 2006* (SI 2006 No 1294) ('the Eligibility Regulations') provide that asylum seekers who are *persons subject to immigration control* and who claimed asylum before 3 April 2000 are eligible for assistance under Part 7 in certain circumstances (set out below). However, by virtue of s 186(1), an asylum seeker is not eligible for Part 7 assistance if he or she has any accommodation in the UK – however temporary – available for his or her occupation. This would include a place in a hostel or bed and breakfast hotel.

7. Subject to s 186(1), such asylum seekers are eligible for assistance under Part 7, if they claimed asylum <u>before 3 April 2000</u>, and:

    i)   the claim for asylum was made at the port on initial arrival in the UK (but not on re-entry) from a country outside the United Kingdom, the Channel Islands, the Isle of Man or the Republic of Ireland; **or**

ii) the claim for asylum was made within 3 months of a declaration by the Secretary of State that he would not normally order the return of a person to the country of which he or she is a national because of a fundamental change of circumstances in that country, and the asylum seeker was present in Great Britain on the date the declaration was made; **or**

iii) the claim for asylum was made on or before 4 February 1996 and the applicant was entitled to housing benefit on 4 February 1996 under regulation 7A of the *Housing Benefit (General) Regulations 1987*.

8. Generally, a person ceases to be an asylum seeker for the purposes of the Eligibility Regulations when his claim for asylum is recorded by the Secretary of State as having been decided (other than on appeal) or abandoned. However, a person does not cease to be an asylum seeker in these circumstances for the purposes of paragraph 7(iii) if he continues to be eligible for housing benefit by virtue of:

– regulation 10(6) of the *Housing Benefit Regulations 2006* (SI 2006 No 213), or

– regulation 10(6) of the *Housing Benefit (persons who have attained the qualifying age for state pension credit) Regulations 2006* (SI 2006 No 214).

as amended by the *Housing Benefit and Council Tax Benefit (Consequential Provisions) Regulations 2006* (SI 2006 No 217).

Former asylum seekers

9. Where an asylum claim is successful – either initially or following an appeal – the claimant will normally be granted refugee status. If a claim is unsuccessful, leave to remain in the UK may still be granted, in accordance with published policies on Humanitarian Protection and Discretionary Leave. Former asylum seekers granted refugee status, or those granted Humanitarian Protection or Discretionary Leave which is not subject to a condition requiring him to maintain and accommodate himself without recourse to public funds will be eligible for homelessness assistance.

10. Prior to April 2003, Exceptional Leave to Remain was granted rather than Humanitarian Protection or Discretionary Leave. Those with Exceptional Leave to Remain which is not subject to a condition requiring him to maintain and accommodate himself without recourse to public funds will also be eligible for homelessness assistance.

Information

11. Under s 187 of the *Housing Act 1996*, the Home Office Immigration and Nationality Directorate (IND) will, on request, provide local housing authorities with the information necessary to determine whether a particular housing applicant is an asylum seeker, or a dependant of an asylum seeker, and whether he or she is eligible for assistance under Part 7. In cases where it is confirmed that a housing applicant is an asylum seeker, or the dependant of an asylum seeker, any subsequent change in circumstances which affect the applicant's housing status (eg a decision on the asylum claim) will be notified to the authority by the IND. The procedures for contacting the IND are set out in Annex 8.

ANNEX 10
THE HABITUAL RESIDENCE TEST

1. In practice, when considering housing applications from persons who are subject to the habitual residence test, it is only necessary to investigate habitual residence if the applicant has arrived or returned to live in the UK during the two year period prior to making the application.

Definition of habitually resident

2. The term 'habitually resident' is not defined in legislation. Local authorities should always consider the overall circumstances of a case to determine whether someone is habitually resident in the UK, the Channel Islands, the Isle of Man or the Republic of Ireland.

General principles

3. When deciding whether a person is habitually resident in a place, consideration must be given to all the facts of each case in a common sense way. It should be remembered that:

- the test focuses on the fact and nature of residence;
- a person who is not resident somewhere cannot be habitually resident there. Residence is a more settled state than mere physical presence in a country. To be resident a person must be seen to be making a home. It need not be the only home or a permanent home but it must be a genuine home for the time being. For example, a short stay visitor or a person receiving short term medical treatment is not resident;
- the most important factors for habitual residence are the length, continuity and general nature of actual residence rather than intention;
- the practicality of a person's arrangements for residence is a necessary part of determining whether it can be described as settled and habitual;
- established habitual residents who have periods of temporary or occasional absence of long or short duration may still be habitually resident during such absences.

Action on receipt of an application

Applicant came to live in the UK during the previous two years

4. If it appears that the applicant came to live in the UK during the previous two years, authorities should make further enquiries to decide if the applicant is habitually resident, or can be treated as such.

Factors to consider

5. The applicant's stated reasons and intentions for coming to the UK will be relevant to the question of whether he or she is habitually resident. If the applicant's stated intention is to live in the UK, and not return to the country from which they came, that intention must be consistent with their actions.

6. To decide whether an applicant is habitually resident in the UK, authorities should consider the factors set out below. However, these do not provide an exhaustive check list of the questions or factors that need to be considered. Further enquiries may be needed. The circumstances of each case will dictate what information is needed, and all relevant factors should be taken into account.

Why has the applicant come to the UK?

7. If the applicant is returning to the UK after a period spent abroad, and it can be established that the applicant was previously habitually resident in the UK and is returning to resume his or her former period of habitual residence, **he or she will be immediately habitually resident**.

8. In determining whether an applicant is returning to resume a former period of habitual residence authorities should consider:

- when did the applicant leave the UK?
- how long did the applicant live in the UK before leaving?
- why did the applicant leave the UK?
- how long did the applicant intend to remain abroad?
- why did the applicant return?
- did the applicant's partner and children, if any, also leave the UK?
- did the applicant keep accommodation in the UK?
- if the applicant owned property, was it let, and was the lease timed to coincide with the applicant's return to the UK?
- what links did the applicant keep with the UK?
- have there been other brief absences? If yes, obtain details.
- why has the applicant come to the UK?

9. If the applicant has arrived in the UK within the previous two years and is not resuming a period of habitual residence, consideration should be given to his or her reasons for coming to the UK, and in particular to the factors set out below.

Applicant is joining family or friends

10. If the applicant has come to the UK to join or rejoin family or friends, authorities should consider:

- has the applicant sold or given up any property abroad?
- has the applicant bought or rented accommodation or is he or she staying with friends?
- is the move to the UK intended to be permanent?

Applicant's plans

11. Authorities should consider the applicant's plans, eg:

- if the applicant plans to remain in the UK, is the applicant's stated plan consistent with his or her actions?
- were any arrangements made for employment and accommodation (even if unsuccessful) before the applicant arrived in the UK?
- did the applicant buy a one-way ticket?
- did the applicant bring all his or her belongings?
- is there any evidence of links with the UK, eg membership of clubs?

12. The fact that a person may intend to live in the UK for the foreseeable future does not, of itself, mean that habitual residence has been established. However, the applicant's intentions along with other factors, for example the disposal of property abroad, may indicate that the applicant is habitually resident in the UK.

13. An applicant who intends to reside in the UK for only a short period, for example for a holiday or to visit friends is unlikely to be habitually resident in the UK.

Length of residence in another country

14. Authorities should consider the length and continuity of an applicant's residence in another country:

- how long did the applicant live in the previous country?
- does the applicant have any remaining ties with his or her former country of residence?
- has the applicant stayed in different countries outside the UK?

15. It is possible that a person may own a property abroad but still be habitually resident in the UK. A person who has a home or close family in another country would normally retain habitual residence in that country. A person who has previously lived in several different countries but has now moved permanently to the UK may be habitually resident here.

Centre of interest

16. An applicant is likely to be habitually resident in the UK, the Channel Islands, the Isle of Man or the Republic of Ireland, despite spending time abroad, if his or her centre of interest is located in one of these places.

17. People who maintain their centre of interest in the UK, the Channel Islands, the Isle of Man or the Republic of Ireland, for example a home, a job, friends, membership of clubs, are likely to be habitually resident there. People who have retained their centre of interest in another country and have no particular ties with the UK, the Channel Islands, the Isle of Man or the Republic of Ireland, are unlikely to be habitually resident in the UK, the Channel Islands, the Isle of Man or the Republic of Ireland.

18. Authorities should take the following into account when deciding the centre of interest:

- home;
- family ties;
- club memberships;
- finance accounts.

19. If the centre of interest appears to be in the UK, the Channel Islands, the Isle of Man or the Republic of Ireland but the applicant has a home somewhere else, authorities should consider the applicant's intentions regarding the property.

20. In certain cultures, eg the Asian culture, it is quite common for a person to live in one country but have property abroad that they do not intend to sell. Where such a person has lived in the UK, the Channel Islands, the Isle of Man or the Republic of Ireland for many years, the fact that they have property elsewhere does not necessarily mean that they intend to leave, or that the applicant's centre of interest is elsewhere.

ANNEX 11
EUROPEAN GROUPINGS (EU, A8, EEA, SWITZERLAND)

The European Union (EU)

Austria, Belgium, Cyprus, the Czech Republic, Denmark, Estonia, Finland, France, Germany, Greece, Hungary, Ireland, Italy, Latvia, Lithuania, Luxembourg, Malta, the Netherlands, Poland, Portugal, Slovakia, Slovenia, Spain, Sweden, the United Kingdom and the A8 or Accession States.

The 'A8' or 'Accession States'

The 8 eastern European States that acceded to the EU in 2004 (and whose nationals may be subject to the UK Worker Registration Scheme for a transitional period): the Czech Republic, Estonia, Hungary, Latvia, Lithuania, Poland, Slovakia and Slovenia.

The European Economic Area (EEA)

All EU countries, plus: Iceland, Norway and Liechtenstein.

Switzerland

Note: Although not an EEA State, Switzerland should be treated as an EEA State for the purpose of this guidance. (See the *Immigration (European Economic Area) Regulations 2006* (SI 2006 No 1003), regulation 2(1).)

ANNEX 12
RIGHTS TO RESIDE IN THE UK DERIVED FROM EC LAW

1.   EEA nationals and their family members who have a right to reside in the UK that derives from EC law are not persons subject to immigration control. This means that they will be eligible for assistance under Part 7 of the *Housing Act 1996* ('housing assistance') unless they fall within one of the categories of persons to be treated as a person from abroad who is ineligible for assistance by virtue of regulation 6 of the *Allocation of Housing and Homelessness (Eligibility) (England) Regulations 2006* ('the Eligibility Regulations').

General

Nationals of EU countries

2.   Nationals of EU countries enjoy a number of different rights to reside in other Member States, including the UK. These rights derive from the EC Treaty, EC secondary legislation (in particular *Directive 2004/38/EC*), and the case law of the European Court of Justice.

3.   Whether an individual EU national has a right to reside in the UK will depend on his or her circumstances, particularly his or her economic status (e g whether employed, self-employed, seeking work, a student, or economically inactive etc).

The accession states

4.   A slightly different regime applies to EU nationals who are nationals of the accession states. For the purposes of this guidance, 'the accession states' are the 8 eastern European countries that acceded to the EU on 1 May 2004: Poland, Lithuania, Estonia, Latvia, Slovenia, Slovakia, Hungary and the Czech Republic.

The Immigration (European Economic Area) Regulations 2006

5.   The *Immigration (European Economic Area) Regulations 2006* ('the EEA Regulations') implement into UK domestic law EC legislation conferring rights of residence on EU nationals. Broadly, the EEA Regulations provide that EU

nationals have the right to reside in the UK without the requirement for leave to remain under the *Immigration Act 1971* for the first 3 months of their residence, and for longer, if they are a 'qualified person' or they have acquired a permanent right of residence.

Nationals of Iceland, Liechtenstein and Norway.

6. The EEA Regulations extend the same rights to reside in the UK to nationals of Iceland, Liechtenstein and Norway as those afforded to EU nationals (The EU countries plus Iceland, Liechtenstein and Norway together comprise the EEA.)

Nationals of Switzerland

7. The EEA Regulations also extend the same rights to reside in the UK to nationals of Switzerland.

8. For the purposes of this guidance, 'EEA nationals' means nationals of any of the EU member states (excluding the UK), and nationals of Iceland, Norway, Liechtenstein and Switzerland.

Initial 3 months of residence

9. Regulation 13 of the EEA Regulations provides that EEA nationals have the right to reside in the UK for a period of up to 3 months without any conditions or formalities other than holding a valid identity card or passport. Therefore, during their first 3 months of residence in the UK, EEA nationals will not be subject to immigration control (unless the right to reside is lost following a decision by an immigration officer in accordance with regulation 13(3) of the EEA Regulations).

10. However, regulations 6(1)(b)(i) and (c) of the Eligibility Regulations provide that a person who is not subject to immigration control is not eligible for housing assistance if:

(i)   his or her **only** right to reside in the UK is an initial right to reside for a period not exceeding 3 months under regulation 13 of the EEA Regulations, or

(ii)   his or her **only** right to reside in the Channel Islands, the Isle of Man or the Republic of Ireland is a right equivalent to the right mentioned in (i) above which is derived from the Treaty establishing the European Community.

On (ii), article 6 of *Directive 2004/38/EC* provides that EU citizens have the right of residence in the territory of another Member State (eg the Republic of Ireland) for a period of up to 3 months without any conditions or formalities other than holding a valid identity card or passport.

Rights of residence for 'qualified persons'

11. Regulation 14 of the EEA Regulations provides that 'qualified persons' have the right to reside in the UK so long as they remain a qualified person. Under regulation 6 of the EEA Regulations, 'qualified person' means:

a) a jobseeker,
b) a worker,
c) a self-employed person,
d) a self-sufficient person,
e) a student.

Jobseekers

12. For the purposes of regulation 6(1)(a) of the EEA Regulations, 'jobseeker' means a person who enters the UK in order to seek employment and can provide evidence that he or she is seeking employment and has a genuine chance of being employed.

13. Accession state nationals who need to register to work (see paragraph 20 below) do not have a right to reside in the UK as a jobseeker (see regulation 5(2) of the Accession Regulations, as amended). However, accession state nationals seeking work may have a right to reside by virtue of another status, eg as a self-sufficient person.

14. Although a person who is a jobseeker for the purposes of the definition of 'qualified person' in regulation 6(1)(a) of the EEA Regulations is not subject to immigration control, regulation 6 of the Eligibility Regulations provides that a person is not eligible for housing assistance if:

(i) his or her only right to reside in the UK is derived from his status as a jobseeker or the family member of a jobseeker, or
(ii) his or her only right to reside in the Channel Islands, the Isle of Man or the Republic of Ireland is a right equivalent to the right mentioned in (i) above which is derived from the Treaty establishing the European Community.

Workers

15. In order to be a worker for the purposes of the EEA Regulations, a person must be employed, that is, the person is obliged to provide services for another person in return for monetary reward and who is subject to the control of that other person as regards the way in which the work is to be done.

16. Activity as an employed person may include part-time work, seasonal work and cross-border work (ie where a worker is established in another Member State and travels to work in the UK). However, the case law provides that the employment must be effective and genuine economic activity, and not on such a small scale as to be regarded as purely marginal and ancillary.

17. Provided the employment is effective and genuine economic activity, the fact that a person's level of remuneration may be below the level of subsistence or below the national minimum wage, or the fact that a person may be receiving financial assistance from public benefits, would not exclude that person from being a 'worker'. Housing authorities should note that surprisingly small amounts of work can be regarded as effective and genuine economic activity.

18. Applicants in the labour market should be able to confirm that they are, or have been, working in the UK by providing, for example:

- payslips,
- a contract of employment, or
- a letter of employment.

Retention of worker status

19. A person who is no longer working does not cease to be treated as a 'worker' for the purpose of regulation 6(1)(b) of the EEA Regulations, if he or she:

- (a) is temporarily unable to work as the result of an illness or accident; or
- (b) is recorded as involuntarily unemployed after having being employed in the UK, provided that he or she has registered as a jobseeker with the relevant employment office, and:
    - (i) was employed for one year or more before becoming unemployed, or
    - (ii) has been unemployed for no more than 6 months, or
    - (iii) can provide evidence that he or she is seeking employment in the UK and has a genuine chance of being engaged; or
- (c) is involuntarily unemployed and has embarked on vocational training; or
- (d) has voluntarily ceased working and embarked on vocational training that is related to his or her previous employment.

Accession state workers requiring registration who are treated as workers

20. By virtue of the *Accession (Immigration and Worker Registration) Regulations 2004* (SI 2004/1219) ('the Accession Regulations'), accession state nationals (with certain exceptions) are required to register their employment in the UK until they have accrued a period of 12 months' continuous employment. The exceptions are set out in Annex 13.

21. An accession state national requiring registration is only treated as a worker if he or she is actually working and:

- (a) has registered his or her employment and is working in the UK for an authorised employer (see regulation 5(2) of the Accession Regulations, as amended), or
- (b) is not registered for employment, but has been working for an employer for less than one month (regulation 7(3) of the Accession Regulations), or

(c)   has applied to register under the Worker Registration Scheme and is working for the employer with whom he or she has applied to register (regulation 7(2)(b) of the Accession Regulations).

22.   To demonstrate eligibility for housing assistance, accession state workers requiring registration should be able to:

(a)   provide a valid worker registration card, and a valid worker registration certificate showing their current employer (see Annex 13 for specimens of these documents), or

(b)   (where the accession state worker has applied to register but not yet received the registration certificate) provide a copy of their application to register, or

(c)   show they have been working for their current employer for less than one month.

23.   Authorities may need to contact the employer named in the registration certificate, to confirm that the applicant continues to be employed.

24.   See Annex 13 for guidance on the Worker Registration Scheme.

25.   A person who is a 'worker' for the purposes of the definition of a qualified person in regulation 6(1) of the EEA Regulations is not subject to immigration control, and is eligible for housing assistance whether or not he or she is habitually resident in the UK, the Channel Islands, the Isle of Man or the Republic of Ireland.

Self-employed persons

26.   'Self-employed person' means a person who establishes himself in the UK in order to pursue activity as a self-employed person in accordance with Article 43 of the Treaty establishing the European Union.

27.   A self-employed person should be able to confirm that he or she is pursuing activity as a self-employed person by providing documents relating to their business such as:

a)   invoices,
b)   tax accounts, or
c)   utility bills.

28.   A person who is no longer in self-employment does not cease to be treated as a self-employed person for the purposes of regulation 6(1)(c) of the EEA regulations, if he or she is temporarily unable to pursue his or her activity as a self-employed person as the result of an illness or accident.

29.   Accession state nationals are not required to register in order to establish themselves in the UK as a self-employed person.

30.   A person who is a self-employed person for the purposes of the definition of a qualified person in regulation 6(1) of the EEA Regulations is not subject to immigration control, and is eligible for housing assistance whether or not he or she is habitually resident in the UK, the Channel Islands, the Isle of Man or the Republic of Ireland.

Self-sufficient persons

31.   Regulation 4(1)(c) of the EEA regulations defines 'self-sufficient person' as a person who has:

(i)   sufficient resources not to become a burden on the social assistance system of the UK during his or her period of residence, and

(ii)   comprehensive sickness insurance cover in the UK.

32.   By regulation 4(4) of the EEA Regulations, the resources of a person who is a self-sufficient person or a student (see below), and where applicable, any family members, are to be regarded as sufficient if they exceed the maximum level of resources which a UK national and his or her family members may possess if he or she is to become eligible for social assistance under the UK benefit system.

33.   Where an EEA national applies for housing assistance as a self-sufficient person and does not appear to meet the conditions of regulation 4(1)(c), the housing authority will need to consider whether he or she may have some other right to reside in the UK.

34.   Where the applicant does not meet the conditions of regulation 4(1)(c) but has previously done so during his or her residence in the UK, the case should be referred to the Home Office for clarification of their status.

35.   A person who is a self-sufficient person for the purposes of the definition of a qualified person in regulation 6(1) of the EEA Regulations is not subject to immigration control, but must be habitually resident in the UK, the Channel Islands, the Isle of Man or the Republic of Ireland to be eligible for housing assistance.

Students

36.   Regulation 4(1)(d) of the EEA regulations defines 'student' as a person who :

(a)   is enrolled at a private or public establishment included on the Department of Education and Skills' Register of Education and Training Providers, or is financed from public funds, for the principal purpose of following a course of study, including vocational training, and

(b)   has comprehensive sickness insurance cover in the UK, and

(c)   assures the Secretary of State, by means of a declaration or such equivalent means as the person may choose, that he or she (and if applicable his or her family members) has sufficient resources not to become a burden on the social assistance system of the UK during his or her period of residence.

37. A person who is a student for the purposes of the definition of a qualified person in regulation 6(1) of the EEA Regulations is not subject to immigration control. The eligibility of such a person for housing assistance should therefore be considered in accordance with regulation 6 of the Eligibility Regulations.

Permanent right of residence

38. Regulation 15 of the EEA Regulations provides that the following persons shall acquire the right to reside in the UK permanently:

(a) an EEA national who has resided in the UK in accordance with the EEA regulations for a continuous period of 5 years;

(b) a non-EEA national who is a family member of an EEA national and who has resided in the UK with the EEA national in accordance with the EEA regulations for a continuous period of 5 years;

(c) a worker or self-employed person who has ceased activity (see regulation 5 of the EEA Regulations for the definition of worker or self-employed person who has ceased activity);

(d) the family member of a worker or self-employed person who has ceased activity;

(e) a person who was the family member of a worker or self-employed person who has died, where the family member resided with the worker or self-employed person immediately before the death and the worker or self-employed person had resided continuously in the UK for at least 2 years before the death (or the death was the result of an accident at work or an occupational disease);

(f) a person who has resided in the UK in accordance with the EEA regulations for a continuous period of 5 years, and at the end of that period was a family member who has retained the right of residence (see regulation 10 of the EEA Regulations for the definition of a family member who has retained the right of residence).

Once acquired, the right of permanent residence can be lost through absence from the UK for a period exceeding two consecutive years.

39. A person with a right to reside permanently in the UK arising from (c), (d) or (e) above is eligible for housing assistance whether or not he or she is habitually resident in the UK, the Channel Islands, the Isle of Man or the Republic of Ireland. Persons with a permanent right to reside by virtue of (a), (b), or (f) must be habitually resident to be eligible.

Rights of residence for certain family members

The right to reside

40. Regulation 14 of the EEA Regulations provides that the following family members are entitled to reside in the UK:

(i) a family member of a qualified person residing in the UK;

(ii) a family member of an EEA national with a permanent right of residence under regulation 15; and

(iii) a family member who has retained the right of residence (see regulation 10 of the EEA Regulations for the definition).

41. A person who has a right to reside in the UK as the family member of an EEA national under the EEA Regulations will not be subject to immigration control. The eligibility of such a person for housing assistance should therefore be considered in accordance with regulation 6 of the Eligibility Regulations.

42. When considering the eligibility of a family member, local authorities should consider whether the person has acquired a right to reside in their own right, for example a permanent right to reside under regulation 15 of the EEA Regulations (see paragraph 38 above).

Who is a 'family member'?

43. Regulation 7 of the EEA regulations provides that the following persons are treated as the family members of another person (with certain exceptions for students – see below):

(a) the spouse of the person;

(b) the civil partner of the person (part of a registered partnership equivalent to marriage);

(c) a direct descendant of the person, or of the person's spouse or civil partner, who is under the age of 21;

(d) a direct descendant of the person, or of the person's spouse or civil partner, who is over 21 and dependent on the person, or the spouse or civil partner;

(e) an ascendant relative of the person, or of the person's spouse or civil partner, who is dependent on the person or the spouse or civil partner.

(f) a person who is an extended family member and is treated as a family member by virtue of regulation 7(3) of the EEA regulations (see below).

Family members of students

44. Regulation 7(2) of the EEA regulations provides that a person who falls within (c), (d) or (e) above shall not be treated as a family member of a student residing in the UK after the period of 3 months beginning on the date the student is admitted to the UK unless:

(i) in the case of paragraph 43 (c) and (d) above, the person is the dependent child of the student, or of the spouse or civil partner, or

(ii) the student is also a qualified person (for the purposes of regulation 6(1) of the EEA regulations) other than as a student.

Extended family members

45. Broadly, extended family members will be persons who :

(a)   do not fall within any of the categories (a) to (e) in paragraph 43 above, and

(b)   are either a relative of an EEA national (or of the EEA national's spouse or civil partner) or the partner of an EEA national, and

(c)   have been issued with an EEA family permit, a registration certificate or a residence card which is valid and has not been revoked.

Family members' eligibility for housing assistance

Relationship with other rights to reside

46.   This section concerns the eligibility of an applicant for housing assistance whose right to reside is derived from his or her status as the family member of an EEA national with a right to reside. In some cases, a family member will have acquired a right to reside in his or her own right. In particular, a person who arrived in the UK as the family member of an EEA national may have subsequently acquired a permanent right of residence under regulation 15 of the EEA Regulations, as outlined in paragraph 38(a)–(f) above. The eligibility for housing assistance of those with a permanent right of residence is discussed at paragraph 39.

Family members who must be habitually resident

47.   For family members with a right to reside under regulation 14 of the EEA Regulations, the following categories of persons must be habitually resident in the UK, the Channel Islands, the Isle of Man or the Republic of Ireland in order to be eligible for housing assistance:

a)   a person whose right to reside derives from their status as a family member of an EEA national who is a self-sufficient person for the purposes of regulation 6(1)(d) of the EEA regulations;

b)   a person whose right to reside derives from their status as a family member of an EEA national who is a student for the purposes of regulation 6(1)(e) of the EEA regulations;

c)   a person whose right to reside is dependent on their status as a family member of an EEA national with a permanent right to reside;

d)   a person whose right to reside is dependent on their status as a family member who has retained the right of residence.

Family members who are exempt from the habitual residence requirement

48.   A person with a right to reside under regulation 14 as a family member of an EEA national who is a worker or a self-employed person for the purposes of regulation 6(1) of the EEA regulations is exempted from the requirement to be habitually resident by regulation 6(2)(d) of the Eligibility Regulations. However, authorities should note that an extended family member (see above) is not counted as a family member for the purposes of regulation 6(2)(d) of the Eligibility Regulations (see regulation 2(3) of the Eligibility Regulations).

Family members of UK nationals exercising rights under the EC Treaty

49. There are some limited cases in which the non-EEA family member of a UK national may have a right to reside under EU law. Under regulation 9 of the EEA Regulations, the family member of a UK national should be treated as an EEA family member where the following conditions are met:

  (i)   the UK national is residing in an EEA State as a worker or self-employed person, or was so residing before returning to the UK; and

  (ii)   if the family member of the UK national is his spouse or civil partner, the parties are living together in the EEA State, or had entered into a marriage or civil partnership and were living together in that State before the UK national returned to the UK.

50. Where the family member of a UK national is to be treated as an EEA family member by virtue of regulation 9 of the EEA Regulations, that person is not subject to immigration control, and his or her eligibility for housing assistance should therefore be determined in accordance with regulation 6 of the Eligibility Regulations.

ANNEX 13
WORKER REGISTRATION SCHEME
Introduction

1. On 1 May 2004, 10 new countries acceded to the European Union: Cyprus, Malta, Poland, Lithuania, Estonia, Latvia, Slovenia, Slovakia, Hungary and the Czech Republic.

2. Nationals of all of these countries have the right to move freely among all member states. Nationals of 2 of the Accession countries – Malta and Cyprus – enjoyed full EU Treaty rights from 1 May 2004. These include the right to seek work and take up employment in another Member State.

3. However, under the EU Accession Treaties that apply to the other 8 Accession states ('the A8 Member States'), existing Member States can impose limitations on the rights of nationals of the A8 Member States to access their labour markets (and the associated rights of residence), for a transitional period. (The EU Accession Treaties do not allow existing Member States to restrict access to their labour markets by nationals of Malta or Cyprus.)

4. Under the *Accession (Immigration and Worker Registration) Regulations 2004* (SI 2004/1219) as amended ('the Accession Regulations'), nationals of the A8 Member States (with certain exceptions) are required to register with the Home Office if they work in the UK during the transitional period. While looking for work (or between jobs) their right to reside will be conditional on them being self-sufficient and not imposing an unreasonable burden on the UK social assistance system. These conditions cease to apply once they have worked in the UK continuously for 12 months.

The Accession (Immigration and Worker Registration) Regulations 2004

5. The *Accession (Immigration and Worker Registration) Regulations 2004* provide that, from 1 May 2004, nationals of the A8 Member States can take up employment in the UK provided they are authorised to work for their employer under the Worker Registration scheme.

6. The Accession Regulations also give workers from the A8 Member States the right to reside in the UK. Workers from the A8 Member States who are working lawfully have the same right to equal treatment as other EEA workers while they are working.

The Worker Registration scheme

7. The Worker Registration scheme applies only to nationals of: Poland, Lithuania, Estonia, Latvia, Slovenia, Slovakia, Hungary and the Czech Republic (the A8 Member States). It is a transitional scheme under which the UK Government allows nationals of the A8 Member States access to the UK labour market provided they comply with the registration scheme.

8. The derogation from EC law allowed by the Treaties of Accession does not apply to nationals of existing EEA states. Workers from those states, therefore, have an EC right to work and reside in the UK.

9. The Worker Registration scheme is a transitional measure. The *Accession (Immigration and Worker Registration) Regulations 2004* provide for the registration scheme to operate for up to five years from 1 May 2004 (ie until 30 April 2009). The Government reviewed the scheme within its first two years of operation and decided that the scheme will continue beyond 1 May 2006, and may continue throughout the second phase of the transitional arrangements. However, the need to retain the scheme during the whole of the second phase will be kept under review.

10. Nationals of A8 Member States who are self-employed are not required to register. (Under the Accession Treaties, there is no derogation from the right of EU citizens to establish themselves in another Member State (including the UK) as self-employed persons.) However, nationals of A8 Member States who are self-employed cannot take paid employment unless they register (unless they are exempt from registration, see below).

Registration under the scheme

11. Nationals of A8 Member States (except those who are exempt from the scheme, see below) must apply to register with the Home Office as soon as they start work in the UK, and within one month of taking up employment at the very latest. They will be issued with a **worker registration card** and a **worker registration certificate**, authorising them to work for the employer concerned.

12. If they change employers they will have to apply to for a new **registration certificate** authorising them to work for their new employer. They will then be provided with a new certificate for that employer. If they change employer or have a break in employment and resume working for the same employer, they must apply for a new registration certificate.

13. Workers from the A8 Member States have the same right to equal treatment as other EEA workers while they are working.

14. After 12 months' uninterrupted work in the UK, a worker from an A8 Member State will acquire full EU Treaty rights, and will be free from the requirement to register to work. At that stage, they will be able to apply to the Home Office for an EEA residence permit to confirm their right to equal treatment on the same basis as other EEA nationals.

15. The Worker Registration Team issues applicants with a secure **worker registration card** containing:

- Name;
- Date of Birth;
- Nationality;
- Date of issue;
- Unique identification number;
- A facial identifier (photograph);

and a **certificate** (on secure paper) which states:

- Worker's name;
- Worker's Date of Birth;
- Nationality;
- Worker's unique identification number;
- Name and address (head or main office) of employer;
- Job title;
- Start date;
- Date of issue.

16. The **registration card** is a secure document that provides applicants with a unique identification reference number. This is valid for as long as the applicant requires registration under the scheme.

17. The **registration certificate** is specific to a particular employer. The certificate expires as soon as the person stops working for that employer. If the person changes employers or has a break in employment and resumes working for the same employer, he or she must apply for a new registration certificate.

18. Specimen copies of the registration card and registration certificate are provided at the end of this annex.

12 months' uninterrupted work

19. A worker from an A8 Member State (who is subject to the registration scheme) must not be out of work more than a total of 30 days in a 12-month period, in order to establish '12 months' uninterrupted work'.

20. If a national of an A8 Member State has worked for a period of less than 12 months when the employment comes to an end, he or she will need to find another job within 30 days to be able to count the first period of work towards accruing a period of 12 months' uninterrupted employment.

21. If the worker's second (or subsequent) employment comes to an end before he or she has accrued a period of 12 months' uninterrupted employment, he or she must ensure that there has been no more than a total of 30 days between all of the periods of employment. If more than 30 days between periods of employment occur before a 12-month period of uninterrupted employment is established, a fresh period of 12 months' uninterrupted employment would need to commence from that point.

22. The Worker Registration scheme is based on continuity of employment – there is no restriction on the number of different jobs (or employers) that a worker can have during a 12-month period of continuous employment.

23. When an A8 Member State worker has worked for 12 months without interruption he or she can apply to the Home Office for an EEA residence permit. Evidence of 12 months' uninterrupted employment would include the worker registration card, registration certificates for each of the jobs they have undertaken, letters from employers and pay slips.

A8 nationals who must register

24. The Worker Registration Scheme applies to nationals of the following accession states: Poland; Lithuania; Estonia; Latvia; Slovenia; Slovakia; Hungary; and the Czech Republic.

25. Nationals of A8 Member States need to apply for a registration certificate under the Worker Registration Scheme, if they are a citizen of one of the countries listed above and they:

- start a new job on or after 1 May 2004;
- have been working in the UK before 1 May 2004 without authorisation or in breach of their immigration conditions;
- are working on a short-term or temporary basis; or
- are a student who is also working.

A8 nationals exempt from registration

26. The following are the categories of nationals of an A8 Member State who are not required to register under the Worker Registration Scheme:

- those working in a self-employed capacity;
- those who have been working with permission in the UK for 12 months or more without interruption;

Appendix 2
England: Homelessness

–   those who have been working with permission in the UK for their current employer since before 1 May 2004;

–   those who have leave to enter the UK under the *Immigration Act 1971* on 30 April 2004 and their leave was not subject to any condition restricting their employment; established in the UK;

–   those who are a citizen of the UK, another EEA state (other than an A8 state) or Switzerland;

–   those who are a family member (spouse, civil partner, or child under the age of 21 or dependant) of a Swiss or EEA national (other than an A8 national) who is working in the UK;

–   those who are a family member (spouse, civil partner or dependent child) of a Swiss or EEA national who is in the UK and is a student, self-employed, retired, or self-sufficient.

Home Office
BUILDING A SAFE, JUST
AND TOLERANT SOCIETY

[First Name] [Surname]
[House Number] [Street Name]
[Town]
[County]
[Post Code]

DATE OF ISSUE : [Issue Date]

REFERENCE No : [URN]

WORK CARD SERIAL No :

TELEPHONE : 0114 207 6022

Accession State Worker Registration Scheme

Thank you for your application to register on the Accession State Worker Registration scheme. I am pleased to inform you that we have approved your application and that you are now registered.

Your worker registration card is attached below. If you have any queries about this document, then please contact Work Permits (UK) on the telephone number above.

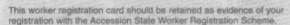

Accession State Worker Registration Scheme
Registration Card

SURNAME : [Surname]
FORENAME(S) : [First Name]
DATE OF BIRTH : [Date of Birth]
NATIONALITY : [Nationality]
REFERENCE No : [URN]
DATE OF ISSUE : [Issue Date]

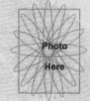

Photo
Here

This worker registration card should be retained as evidence of your registration with the Accession State Worker Registration Scheme.

PLEASE DO NOT LOSE - REPLACEMENTS MAY NOT BE ISSUED

WORK CARD SERIAL No

Appendix 2
England: Homelessness

Home Office
BUILDING A SAFE, JUST
AND TOLERANT SOCIETY

Managed Migration
Home Office
PO Box 3468
Sheffield S3 8WA

www.workingintheuk.gov.uk

[First Name] [Surname]
[House Number] [Street]
[Town]
[County]
[Post Code]

Date of Issue: [Issue Date]

ACCESSION STATE WORKER REGISTRATION SCHEME
REGISTRATION CERTIFICATE

Thank you for your application to register on the Accession State Worker Registration
Scheme. I am pleased to inform you that we have approved your application.

This is your worker registration certificate. It authorises you to work for the employer
specified in this certificate.

This certificate ceases to be valid if you are no longer working for the employer
specified in this certificate on the date on which it is issued.

This certificate expires on the date you cease working for the specified employer.

This certificate should be retained with your worker registration card.

Name	: [First Name] [Surname]
Date of Birth	: [Date of Birth]
Nationality	: [Nationality]
Unique Reference Number: [URN]	
Job start date	: [Date Started Employment]
Employer's Name	: [Employer Name]
Employer's Address	: [Unit Number] [Street Name] [Town] [County] [Post Code]

ANNEX 14
MOD CERTIFICATE: CERTIFICATE OF CESSATION OF ENTITLEMENT FOR SINGLE PERSONNEL TO OCCUPY SERVICE LIVING ACCOMMODATION

[crest]	**MINISTRY OF DEFENCE**	MOD Form 1166 *Introduced 5/97* *Revised 4/03*

CERTIFICATE OF CESSATION OF ENTITLEMENT FOR SINGLE PERSONNEL TO OCCUPY SERVICE LIVING ACCOMMODATION

I certify that (Name)

(Rank & Number)

Of (Unit)

Will cease to be entitled (Address)
to occupy Service Living
Accommodation

(Date)
From

By reason of

An application for housing was made to .... Housing

Authority/Housing Association on .... (copy of letter attached)

The person has the following special circumstances ....

....

Signed	UNIT STAMP
Name	
Position	
Date	

1. This certificate provides evidence of cessation of entitlement to occupy Service Living Accommodation.

2. The certificate should be completed by the unit admin authority and sent at the earliest possible date to the Housing Authority/Association to which application for accommodation has been made, preferably as soon as it is known that entitlement to occupy Service Living Accommodation will cease.

3. Copies of this form are published in the Homelessness Code of Guidance For Local Authorities issued by DCLG, and in guidance issued by the Welsh Assembly and Scottish Executive.

ANNEX 15
CERTIFICATE OF CESSATION OF ENTITLEMENT TO OCCUPY SERVICE FAMILIES ACCOMMODATION OR SUBSTITUTE SERVICE FAMILIES ACCOMMODATION (SFA/SSFA)

 MINISTRY OF DEFENCE | MOD Form *Introduced 4/03*

CERTIFICATE OF CESSATION OF ENTITLEMENT TO OCCUPY SERVICE FAMILIES ACCOMMODATION OR SUBSTITUTE SERVICE FAMILIES ACCOMMODATION(SFA/SSFA)

I certify that   (Name)

(Rank & Number) #

Of   (Unit) #
(# Omit if only family involved)

Will cease to be entitled (Address of SFA or
to occupy   SSFA)

From   (Date)
By reason of loss of entitlement to occupy Service Families Accommodation.

An application for housing was made to ....Housing Authority/
Housing Association on .... (copy of letter attached)

The following special circumstances apply ....
....

The household is as follows ....
....
....

	DHE STAMP
Signed	
Name	
Designation	
Date	

1. **This certificate provides evidence of cessation of entitlement to occupy Service Families Accommodation or Substitute Service Families Accommodation. Authorities should not insist on a Court Order for possession to establish a threat of homelessness.**

2. The certificate should be completed by the Licences Officer of the Defence Housing Executive and sent at the earliest possible date to the Housing Authority/Association to which application for accommodation has been made, preferably as soon as it is known that entitlement to occupy Service Families Accommodation will cease.

3. A period of at least six months notice should normally be allowed so that the appropriate arrangements can be made.

4. Copies of this form are published in the Homelessness Code of Guidance For Local Authorities issued by DCLG, and in guidance issued by the Welsh Assembly and Scottish Executive.

ANNEX 16
DEFINITION OF OVERCROWDING

Under s 324 of the *Housing Act 1985* a dwelling is overcrowded when the number of persons sleeping in the dwelling is such as to contravene –

(a)   the standard specified in s 325 (the room standard), or

(b)   the standard specified in s 326 (the space standard).

a)   The room standard

(1)   The room standard is contravened when the number of persons sleeping in a dwelling and the number of rooms available as sleeping accommodation is such that two persons of opposite sexes who are not living together as husband and wife must sleep in the same room.

(2)   For this purpose –

(a)   children under the age of ten shall be left out of account, and

(b)   a room is available as sleeping accommodation if it is of a type normally used in the locality either as a bedroom or as a living room.

b)   The space standard

(1)   The space standard is contravened when the number of persons sleeping in a dwelling is in excess of the permitted number, having regard to the number and floor area of the rooms of the dwelling available as sleeping accommodation.

(2)   For this purpose –

(a)   no account shall be taken of a child under the age of one and a child aged one or over but under ten shall be reckoned as one-half of a unit, and

(b)   a room is available as sleeping accommodation if it is of a type normally used in the locality either as a living room or as a bedroom.

(3)   The permitted number of persons in relation to a dwelling is whichever is the less of –

(a)   the number specified in Table I in relation to the number of rooms in the dwelling available as sleeping accommodation, and

(b)   the aggregate for all such rooms in the dwelling of the numbers specified in column 2 of Table II in relation to each room of the floor area specified in column 1.

No account shall be taken for the purposes of either Table of a room having a floor area of less than 50 square feet.

Appendix 2
England: Homelessness

Table I	
Number of rooms	*Number of persons*
1	2
2	3
3	5
4	7½
5 or more	2 for each room

Table II	
Floor area of room	*Number of persons*
110 sq ft or more	2
90 sq ft or more but less than 110 sq ft	1½
70 sq ft or more but less than 90 sq ft	1
50 sq ft or more but less than 70 sq ft	½

(4) The Secretary of State may by regulations prescribe the manner in which the floor area of a room is to be ascertained for the purposes of this section; and the regulations may provide for the exclusion from computation, or the bringing into computation at a reduced figure, of floor space in a part of the room which is of less than a specified height not exceeding eight feet.

(5) Regulations under subsection (4) shall be made by statutory instrument which shall be subject to annulment in pursuance of a resolution of either House of Parliament.

(6) A certificate of the local housing authority stating the number and floor areas of the rooms in dwelling, and that the floor areas have been ascertained in the prescribed manner, is prima facie evidence for the purposes of legal proceedings of the facts stated in it.

ANNEX 17
RECOMMENDED MINIMUM STANDARDS FOR BED AND BREAKFAST ACCOMMODATION

The Secretary of State recommends that housing authorities apply the standards set out below as minimum standards in deciding whether Bed and

Breakfast accommodation is suitable for an applicant for the purposes of Part 7 of the *Housing Act 1996* ('the homelessness leglislation') in the very limited circumstances where an authority may use such accommodation for this purpose.

Space Standards for Sleeping Accommodation

1.   *Room sizes where cooking facilities provided in a separate room/kitchen*

Floor Area of Room	*Maximum No of Persons*
Less than 70 sq ft (6.5 m²)	Nil persons
Not less than 70 sq ft (6.5 m²)	1 person
Not less than 110 sq ft (10.2 m²)	2 persons
Not less than 160 sq ft (14.9 m²)	3 persons
Not less than 210 sq ft (19.6 m²)	4 persons
Not less than 260 sq ft (24.2 m²)	5 persons

Room sizes where cooking facilities provided within the room

Floor Area of Room	*Maximum No of Persons*
Less than 110 sq ft (10.2 m²)	Nil persons
Not less than 110 sq ft (10.2 m²)	1 person
Not less than 150 sq ft (13.9 m²)	2 persons
Not less than 200 sq ft (18.6 m²)	3 persons
Not less than 250 sq ft (23.2 m²)	4 persons
Not less than 300 sq ft (27.9 m²)	5 persons

2.   In no case should a room be occupied by more than 5 persons. The standard is to be applied irrespective of the age of the occupants. The sharing of rooms in bed and breakfast accommodation is not desirable, but it is accepted that where accommodation is not self-contained families may find it preferable to share.

3.   No persons of the opposite sex who are aged 12 and over should have to share a room unless they are living together as partners and both are above the age of consent or are lawfully married.

4.   All rooms must have a minimum floor to ceiling height of at least 7 feet (2.14 metres) over not less than 75% of the room area. Any floor area where the ceiling height is less than 5 feet (1.53 metres) should be disregarded.

5.   Separate kitchens, bathrooms, toilets, shower rooms, communal rooms and en-suite rooms are deemed unsuitable for sleeping accommodation.

Installation for Heating

6. The premises should have adequate provision for heating. All habitable rooms and baths or shower rooms should be provided with a fixed space-heating appliance. The appliance must be capable of efficiently maintaining the room at a minimum temperature of 18°C when the outside temperature is –1°C. 'Fixed space heating appliance' means fixed gas appliance, fixed electrical appliance or an adequate system of central heating, operable at all times.

Facilities for the Storage, Preparation and Cooking of Food and Disposal of Waste Water

7. Wherever practicable, each household should have exclusive use of a full set of kitchen facilities including:

- cooking facilities – a gas or electric cooker with a four-burner hob, oven and grill. In single person lettings, a cooker with a minimum of two burners, oven and grill is permissible. Where the establishment caters for fewer than 6 persons, a small guest house for example, a microwave may be substituted for a gas or electric cooker for periods of stay not exceeding 6 weeks for any homeless household;
- sink and integral drainer – with a constant supply of hot and cold water and properly connected to the drainage system;
- storage cupboard, minimum capacity 0.4 m³ (400 litres/15 ft³). This provision is in addition to any base unit cupboards provided below the sink/drainer;
- refrigerator – minimum capacity 0.14 m³ (140 litres/5 ft³);
- electrical power sockets – minimum of two double 13 amp sockets situated at worktop height. These are in addition to electrical power sockets provided elsewhere in the letting;
- worktop – minimum surface area 1000 mm x 600 mm.

8. There may be circumstances where the housing authority is satisfied that the provision of kitchen facilities for exclusive use is not practicable or appropriate. These circumstances could, for example, include where a property is very small, no more than two or three letting rooms, or where the overall standard of the property is considered reasonable in all other respects and the costs of provision of exclusive use kitchens would be prohibitive or detrimentally affect the remaining amenity space. In circumstances such as these, the following standards for communal kitchens may be applied.

9. Kitchen facilities may be provided in the ratio of no less than one set for every 10 persons, irrespective of age. Such kitchen facilities should comprise a minimum of shared:

- gas or electric cooker with four burners, oven and grill. Where the establishment caters for fewer than 6 persons, a small guest house for example, a microwave may be substituted for a gas or electric cooker for periods of stay not exceeding 6 weeks for any homeless household;

- sink and integral drainer – with a constant supply of hot and cold water and properly connected to the drainage system;
- storage cupboard, minimum capacity 0.4 m^3 (400 litres/15 ft^3). This provision is in addition to any base unit cupboards provided below the sink/drainer;
- electrical power sockets – minimum of two double 13 amp sockets situated at worktop height. These are in addition to electrical power sockets provided elsewhere in the letting;
- worktop – minimum surface area 1000 mm x 600 mm;
- lockable storage cupboards, minimum capacity 0.14 m^3 (140 litres/5 ft^3) for each bedroom whose occupants use the kitchen. In calculating the required provision of storage cupboards, base unit cupboards below sinks/drainers should be discounted.

10. In addition, the following facilities should be provided within each bedroom, or within the total accommodation occupied exclusively by each household:

- worktop – minimum surface area 1000 mm x 600 mm;
- refrigerator – minimum capacity 0.14 m^3 (140 litres/5 ft^3);
- storage cupboard – minimum capacity 0.4 m^3 (400 litres/15 ft^3).

11. The kitchen used by management to provide breakfast may be included when calculating the one in ten ratio, unless it is not available, does not meet the conditions above or is deemed unsuitable for use by residents because:

- of the size of the kitchen and the equipment provided in it. In a commercial kitchen some equipment may be dangerous or unsatisfactory for use by residents; or
- the unsatisfactory location of the kitchen in relation to the accommodation it is supposed to serve.

12. In schemes providing a mix of kitchens for shared and exclusive use, one set of kitchen facilities should be provided for every 10 persons sharing. The number of persons who have kitchen facilities provided for their exclusive use should not be included in the calculations. Again, the kitchen used by management to provide breakfast may be included in the one in ten calculation subject to the above conditions.

13. Cooking facilities which are provided should be reasonably located in relation to the room(s) occupied by the person(s) for whom they are provided and in any event not more than one floor distant from these rooms. Please note the exception for smaller establishments described below.

14. In smaller establishments of not more than three storeys and not more than 30 bed spaces, communal cooking facilities may be provided in one area of the premises more than one floor distant from some bedrooms. In such cases, these kitchens must be provided in association with a suitable dining room or dining rooms of adequate size calculated on the basis of 1 m^2 per bed space. This should include one area of at least 15 m^2. Only effective usable space will be considered when calculating the areas for the purpose of this requirement. Dining room facilities should be provided with adequate seating provision.

Appendix 2
England: Homelessness

15. Kitchen facilities should be made available for use 24 hours per day, subject to any representation from the owner/manager, which must be agreed by the receiving and placing authorities.

Toilet and personal washing facilities

16. One internal water closet should be provided for every five persons irrespective of age. The water closet must be within a reasonable distance from its users and not more than one floor distant and, where practicable, a water closet should not be situated within a bathroom. At least 50% of the water closets that are required to be provided should be situated in separate accommodation. The number of persons occupying a bedroom where this facility is provided for their exclusive use should not be included in the calculations.

17. A suitable wash hand basin (minimum dimensions 500 mm x 400 mm) with constant hot and cold water supplies, should be provided in every bedroom, except where an en suite bathroom is available, when the wash hand basin may be provided in that bathroom.

18. Each separate water closet compartment and bathroom should be provided with a suitable wash hand basin (minimum dimensions 500 mm x 400 mm), together with constant supplies of hot and cold running water. A tiled splashback (minimum 300 mm high) is to be provided to each wash hand basin.

19. One bath (minimum dimensions 1700 mm x 700 mm) or one shower (minimum dimensions 800 mm x 800 mm) should be provided for every eight persons, irrespective of age. These facilities must be within a reasonable distance of each user and not more than one floor distant. The number of persons having the exclusive use of a bath or shower should not be included in the calculations.

20. Where the operator chooses to provide showers for the exclusive use of each separate household or the majority of households, a minimum provision of baths, rather than showers will always be required. In such circumstances a minimum of one communal bath should be provided for every 20 persons, irrespective of age, with a minimum of one bath per property. These facilities must be within a reasonable distance of each user and ideally no more than one floor distant.

Other facilities

21. In the case of families with young children, the facilities should include a safe play area(s) that is located away from sleeping accommodation and cooking areas.

Management Standards

22. In any B&B accommodation, suitability for the purposes of Part 7 will depend upon the management standards operated within an establishment as well as the adequate provision of basic amenities. The minimum management standards set out below should apply and it is the responsibility of the housing authority to monitor the management of the property.

- Operators are required to ensure the property complies with all relevant statutory and regulatory requirements especially in relation to fire, gas and electrical safety. The supply of gas or electricity to any resident should never be interfered with.
- A clear emergency evacuation plan should be in place setting out action upon hearing the fire alarm, escape routes and safe assembly points. The manager must ensure that each person newly arriving at the premises is told what to do in the event of a fire and about the fire precautions provided.
- Residents should have access to their rooms at all times except when rooms are being cleaned. Provision should be made to accommodate residents at these times.
- Refuse and litter should be cleared from the property and not allowed to accumulate in, or in the curtilage, of the property, except in adequately sized and suitable bulk refuse container(s).
- All communal areas (including, hallways, kitchens, bathrooms/showers, WCs, dining areas, lounges if provided) should be regularly cleaned.
- Appropriate officers of the authority in whose area the premises are situated should have access to inspect the premises as and when they consider necessary, to ensure that the requirements are being complied with. The manager should allow such inspections to take place, if necessary without notice.
- Officers of the health authority, local authority and authorised community workers for the area in which the premises are situated should have acess to visit the occupiers of the premises and interview them in private in the room(s) they occupy.
- A manager with adequate day to day responsibility to ensure the good management of the property should be contactable at all times. A notice giving the name, address and telephone number of the manager should be displayed in a readily visible position in the property.
- Procedures should be in place to deal with any complaints relating to harassment on racial, sexual or other discriminatory grounds by either residents or staff.
- There should be a clear complaints procedure for the resolution of disputes between residents and/or staff.
- There should be available within the premises a working telephone available for use by the occupiers and a notice should be displayed by the telephone with information on the address and telephone numbers of: the local Environmental Health Department, Fire Brigade, Gas Company, Electricity Company, Police Station and local doctors.

Appendix 2
England: Homelessness

ANNEX 18[7]
PROCEDURES FOR REFERRALS OF HOMELESS APPLICANTS ON THE GROUNDS OF LOCAL CONNECTION WITH ANOTHER LOCAL AUTHORITY

GUIDELINES FOR LOCAL AUTHORITIES AND REFEREES

Agreed by

ASSOCIATION OF LONDON GOVERNMENT (ALG)
CONVENTION OF SCOTTISH LOCAL AUTHORITIES (CoSLA)
LOCAL GOVERNMENT ASSOCIATION (LGA)
WELSH LOCAL GOVERNMENT ASSOCIATION (WLGA)
(*'the local authority associations'*)

Index

---

[7] This is not guidance issued by the Secretaries of State.

Standard notification form

Procedures for referrals of homeless applicants on the grounds of local connection with another local authority

Guidelines for local authorities on procedures for referral

Agreed by

> ASSOCIATION OF LONDON GOVERNMENT (ALG)
> CONVENTION OF SCOTTISH LOCAL AUTHORITIES (CoSLA)
> LOCAL GOVERNMENT ASSOCIATION (LGA)
> WELSH LOCAL GOVERNMENT ASSOCIATION (WLGA)
> (*'the local authority associations'*)

This procedure concerns the situation where, under Part 7 of the *Housing Act 1996*, a housing authority is satisfied that a housing applicant is eligible for assistance, homeless and has a priority need for accommodation, is not satisfied that the applicant is homeless intentionally and the authority consider that the conditions for referral of the case to another housing authority are met, and notifies the other housing authority of its opinion. Referrals are discretionary only. Housing authorities are not required to make inquiries as to whether an applicant has a local connection with another district, and where they decide to do so, there is no requirement to refer applicants to another authority, if the conditions for referral are met. Authorities may have a policy about how they may exercise their discretion. However, they cannot decide in advance that a referral will be made in all cases where an applicant who is eligible for assistance, unintentionally homeless and in priority need may have a local connection with another district.

1 Purpose of the guidelines

1.1 For English and Welsh authorities s 198 of the *Housing Act 1996* provides that:

> '(5) The question whether the conditions for referral of a case are satisfied shall be determined by agreement between the notifying authority and the notified authority or, in default of agreement, in accordance with such arrangements as the Secretary of State may direct by order.
>
> (6) An order may direct that the arrangements shall be:
>
> (a) those agreed by any relevant authorities or associations of relevant authorities, or
>
> (b) in default of such agreement, such arrangements as appear to the Secretary of State to be suitable, after consultation with such associations representing relevant authorities, and such other persons, as he thinks appropriate.'

1.2 Subsections 33(4) and (5) of the *Housing (Scotland) Act 1987* make the same provision for Scotland. However, s 8 of the *Homelessness (Scotland) Act 2003* gives Scottish ministers the power to suspend or vary the circumstances under which a homeless applicant may be referred by a Scottish local authority to another authority in Scotland. Please note any future orders made will need to be taken into account.

1.3 The ALG, CoSLA, LGA and the WLGA, the local authority associations in England, Scotland and Wales, have agreed guidelines for referrals which they recommend to local housing authorities. Section 198 *Housing Act 1996* and s 33 *Housing (Scotland) Act 1987* lay down the general procedures to be followed where it appears that s 192(2) (England and Wales) or s 31 (Scotland) applies to the applicant and the applicant does not have a local connection with the area of the authority receiving the housing application but does have one with another area in England, Scotland or Wales. There are, however, considerable areas of possible disagreement and dispute in determining whether the conditions of referral are met in any particular case. Although, in the last resort, disagreements can only be resolved by the courts, the associations are anxious to avoid, as far as possible, legal disputes between local authorities. The associations therefore issue these agreed guidelines on the procedures and criteria to be followed, and recommend them for general adoption by all their members. **These Guidelines are without prejudice to the duty of local authorities to treat each case on its merits and to take into account existing and future case law.** Furthermore, these Guidelines only apply to the issues of local connection and whether the conditions for referral are met for the purposes of Part 7 of the *Housing Act 1996* (England and Wales) and s 33 of the *Housing (Scotland) Act 1987*.

1.4 *In Re Betts (1983) the House of Lords considered the application of the referral arrangements agreed between the local authority associations. Their Lordships decided that a rigid application of the arrangements would constitute a fetter on an authority's discretion. The agreement could be taken into account, and applied as a guideline, provided its application to each case is given individual consideration.*

2 Definitions

2.1 All references in this agreement to an 'applicant' are to be taken as references to a housing applicant to whom s 193 of the *Housing Act 1996* (England and Wales) or s 28 *Housing (Scotland) Act 1987* or s 31 *Housing (Scotland) Act 1987* would apply but for the decision to refer the case to another authority. For the purposes of this agreement the 1996 Act and 1987 (Scotland) Act definitions apply.

2.2 The authority to whom the applicant applies for accommodation or assistance (for the purposes of s 183 *Housing Act 1996* or s 28 *Housing (Scotland) Act 1987*) and which decides to refer the case to another authority is the '*notifying authority*'.

2.3 Where the notifying authority consider that neither the applicant nor any person who might reasonably reside with the applicant, has a local connection with its district but does have one with another local authority district and notifies the other local authority of its opinion, the authority which they notify is known as the *'notified authority'*.

2.4 Section 199 *Housing Act 1996* and s 27 *Housing (Scotland) Act 1987* set out the circumstances when a person may have a 'local connection' with a district. These guidelines provide a framework within which the local connection referral procedures may be applied.

3 Criteria for notification

3.1 Before a local authority can consider referring an applicant to another local authority it must first be satisfied that the applicant is:

  (i)   eligible for assistance
  (ii) homeless, and
  (iii) in priority need,
  (iv) not homeless intentionally.

3.2 Before making a referral the notifying authority must be satisfied that the conditions of referral are met. Broadly, the conditions for referral will be met if:

  (a) neither the applicant nor any person who might reasonably be expected to reside with the applicant has a local connection with the district of the authority receiving the application,
  (b) either the applicant or any person who might reasonably be expected to reside with the applicant has a local connection with the district of another authority in England, Scotland or Wales,
  (c) neither the applicant nor any person who might reasonably be expected to reside with the applicant would run the risk of domestic violence/domestic abuse (Scotland) or face a probability of other violence in the district of the other authority (Refer to s 198 of the 1996 Act as amended by s 10 subsection (2&3) *Homelessness Act 2002* (England and Wales)). However, there are exceptions to these conditions, for example, where an applicant applies to an English or Welsh authority for assistance and has been provided with NASS support in Scotland.
  (d) **For Welsh authorities only**, the conditions for referral to another authority will also be met if the applicant was placed in accommodation in the district of the notifying authority by the other authority as a discharge of a duty to secure accommodation under Part 7 of the 1996 Act following an application to the other authority made within the last five years. (The period of 5 years is prescribed by the *Homelessness (Wales) Regulations 2000 SI 2000 No 1079*.)

3.3 3.2(a)(b) and (c) above apply to Scottish authorities. 3.2(d) above does not apply in Scotland.

Appendix 2
England: Homelessness

3.4 In deciding whether or not to make a referral authorities should also consider the court judgment in the case of *R v LB Newham ex parte LB Tower Hamlets* (1990). The notifying authority should have regard to any decisions made by the notified authority that may have a bearing on the case in question (e g a previous decision that the applicant was intentionally homeless) as well as any other material considerations, which should include the general housing circumstances prevailing in the district of the notifying authority and in the district of the notified authority. The notifying authority should also consider whether it is in the public interest to accept a duty to secure accommodation under s 193(2) (England and Wales).

3.5 Should a local authority wish to accept a duty to secure accommodation for an applicant who does not have a local connection with its district, nothing in this agreement shall prevent the authority from providing such assistance. The decision to make a referral is discretionary and could be challenged if the discretion was considered to have been exercised unreasonably.

3.6 Under s 202 of the 1996 Act, housing applicants in England and Wales have the right to request a review of certain decisions made by the local authority about their application, including a decision to notify another authority under s 198 and a decision that the conditions are met for referral of the case. The equivalent right to review in Scotland is set out in s 4 of the *Housing (Scotland) Act 2001*.

4 Local connection

4.1 The relevant date for deciding whether or not a local connection has been established is not the date when the application for housing assistance was made but the date of the decision or, if there is a review, the date of the review decision (cf House of Lords' judgment in *Mohamed v Hammersmith and Fulham London Borough Council 2001*). Moreover, if inquiries prior to a decision have been prolonged, the notifying authority should also consider whether there may have been any material change in circumstances that might affect the question of whether a local connection has been established. A local connection may be established where the following grounds apply, subject to the exceptions outlined in paragraph 4.2:

(i) the applicant or a person who might reasonably be expected to reside with the applicant is, or in the past was, normally resident in the district. It is suggested that a working definition of 'normal residence' should be residence for at least 6 months in the area during the previous 12 months, or for not less than 3 years during the previous 5 year period. The period taken into account should be up to the date of the authority's decision. This should include any periods living in temporary accommodation secured by the authority under s 188 (interim duty pending inquiries);

(ii) the applicant or a person who might reasonably be expected to reside with the applicant is at present employed in the district. The local authority should obtain confirmation from the employer that the person is in employment and that the employment is not of a casual nature;

(iii) the applicant or a person who might reasonably be expected to reside with the applicant has family associations in the district. Family associations normally arise where an applicant or a person who might reasonably be expected to reside with the applicant has parents, adult children or brothers or sisters who have been resident in the district for a period of at least 5 years at the date of the decision, and the applicant indicates a wish to be near them. Only in exceptional circumstances would the residence of relatives other than those listed above be taken to establish a local connection. The residence of dependent children in a different district from their parents would not be residence of their own choice and therefore would not establish a local connection with that district. However, a referral should not be made to another local authority on the grounds of a local connection because of family associations if the applicant objects to those grounds. **NB:** A Scottish authority, when considering the application of this clause, is advised to bear in mind the definition of 'family' in s 83 of the *Housing (Scotland) Act 1987* as amended;

(iv) there are special circumstances which the authority considers establish a local connection with the district. This may be particularly relevant where the applicant has been in prison or hospital and his or her circumstances do not conform to the criteria in (i)–(iii) above. Where, for example, an applicant seeks to return to a district where he or she was brought up or lived for a considerable length of time in the past, there may be grounds for considering that the applicant has a local connection with that district because of special circumstances. An authority must exercise its discretion when considering whether special circumstances apply.

4.2 A notifying authority should not refer an applicant to another authority on grounds of a local connection because of special circumstances without the prior consent of the notified authority. Alternatively, authorities may come to an informal arrangement in such cases on a reciprocal basis, subject to the agreement of the applicants.

4.3 There are certain circumstances where a local connection is not established because of residence or employment in a district. For these purposes:

(i) a person is not employed in a district if he or she is serving in the Regular Armed Forces of the Crown; and

(ii) residence in a district is not of a person's own choice if he or she (or anyone who might reasonably be expected to reside with them) becomes resident there because he or she is serving in the Regular Armed Forces of the Crown or is detained under the authority of any Act of Parliament (eg held in prison, or a secure hospital).

Appendix 2
England: Homelessness

4.4   For Welsh authorities only the conditions for referral to another authority are met if the applicant was placed in accommodation in the district of the notifying authority by the other authority as a discharge of a duty to secure accommodation under Part 7 of the 1996 Act following an application to the other authority made within the last five years. This is without prejudice to whether or not the applicant may have established a local connection with a particular district.

4.5   Former asylum seekers (England and Wales). Broadly, s 199(6) of the 1996 Act (inserted by s 11 of the *Asylum and Immigration (Treatment of Claimants, etc) Act 2004* ('the 2004 Act')) (England and Wales) provides that a person has a local connection with the district of a local housing authority if that person was provided with accommodation there under s 95 of the *Immigration and Asylum Act 1999* (NASS accommodation). Where a person has been provided with NASS accommodation in more than one area, the local connection is with the area where accommodation was last provided. A local connection with a district by virtue of s 199(6) does not override a local connection by virtue of s 199(1). So, a former asylum seeker who has a local connection with a district because he or she was provided with NASS accommodation there could also have a local connection elsewhere for some other reason, for example, because of employment or family associations.

4.6   Former asylum seekers (Scotland). Under s 27(2)(a)(iii) of the *Housing (Scotland) Act 2001*, as inserted by s 7 of the *Homelessness etc (Scotland) Act 2003*, residence in accommodation provided in pursuance of s 95 of the *Immigration and Asylum Act 1999* does not constitute a local connection as it is deemed to be residence which is not of the applicant's own choice. A local connection could be formed for other reasons, such as family association.

4.7   Former asylum seekers (cross-border arrangements). If a former asylum seeker who was provided with asylum support in England or Wales seeks homelessness assistance in Scotland the Scottish local authority could refer the application to another area where a local connection is established, if there was no local connection with the authority applied to. However under Scottish legislation, a local connection would not be formed by virtue of residence in accommodation provided in pursuance of s 95 of the *Immigration and Asylum Act 1999*.

4.8   This paragraph explains the position where a former asylum seeker who was provided with asylum support in Scotland seeks homelessness assistance in England or Wales. The provisions of s 11(2) and (3) of the 2004 Act provide that where a local housing authority in England or Wales are satisfied that an applicant is eligible for assistance, unintentionally homeless and in priority need, the s 193 duty to secure accommodation does not apply if the authority are satisfied that the applicant: has been provided with s 95 accommodation in Scotland at any time and does not have a local connection anywhere in England and Wales (within the meaning of s 199(1) of the 1996 Act) or anywhere in Scotland (within the meaning of s 27 of the *Housing (Scotland) Act 1987*). However, the authority may secure that accommodation is available for the applicant for a period giving him a reasonable opportunity of securing accommodation for himself, and provide the applicant (or secure that he is provided with) advice and assistance in any attempts he may make to secure accommodation for himself.

4.9 Subject to paragraphs 4.6 to 4.9 above (former asylum seekers), once the local authority is satisfied that the applicant is eligible, unintentionally homeless, falls within a priority need category, and does not have a local connection with the district , the authority may notify another authority under s 198 *Housing Act 1996* or s 33 *Housing (Scotland) Act 1987*, provided it is satisfied that all the conditions for referral set out in paragraph 3.3 above are met.

4.10 Once the local authority has established that the applicant is eligible, homeless, in a priority need category, not intentionally homeless and does not have any local connection in its own area it may notify another authority under s 198 *Housing Act 1996* or s 33 *Housing (Scotland) Act 1987*, provided it has satisfied itself that a local connection with the notified authority exists and that no member of the household would be at risk of domestic violence or threat of domestic violence in returning to that area. In determining whether or not there is such a risk authorities should have regard, where relevant, to the advice in the Homelessness Code of Guidance.

4.11 The notifying authority must consider that neither the applicant nor any person who might reasonably be expected to reside with the applicant has **any** local connection with its own district but **does** have a local connection with another local authority district in England, Scotland or Wales, in accordance with the criteria and exceptions listed above. The strength of local connection is irrelevant except where an applicant has no local connection with the notifying authority's district but has a local connection with more than one other local authority district. In such a scenario, the notifying authority must weigh up all the relevant factors in deciding to which authority it would be appropriate to refer the applicant.

4.12 Any relevant changes in an applicant's circumstances, eg obtaining employment, will need to be taken into account in determining whether the applicant has a local connection. Authorities should always consider whether special circumstances may apply.

5   *Procedures prior to making a referral*

5.1 If an authority considers that the conditions for referral s 198 *Housing Act 1996* or s 33 *Housing (Scotland) Act 1987* are likely to be met in a particular case it should make any necessary enquiries in the area/s where there may be a local connection. This should be undertaken as soon as possible. An authority that is considering making a referral must investigate all the circumstances of the case with the same thoroughness as if it were not considering a referral.

5.2 The notifying authority has a duty under s 200(1) (England and Wales) or s 34 *Housing (Scotland) Act 1987* to ensure that suitable accommodation is available for occupation by the applicant until the question of whether the conditions for referral are met have been decided.

5.3 Under section 184(4) *Housing Act 1996* or s 34 *Housing (Scotland) Act 1987*, if a housing authority notify, or intend to notify another authority that they consider that the conditions for referral of a case are met, the authority must notify the applicant of this decision, and the reasons for it, at the same time. For English and Welsh authorities, under s 184(5) of the 1996 Act, the notice must also inform the applicant of his right, under s 202, to request a review of the decision and that any request must be made within 21 days (or such longer period as the authority allows in writing). Regulations made under s 203 of the 1996 Act set out the procedure to be followed when making a review and the period within which a request for review must be carried out and the decision made. The *Allocation of Housing and Homelessness (Review Procedures) Regulations 1999 (SI 1999 No 71)* establishes for England and Wales the period within which the review must be carried out and the decision made. For England and Wales s 204 of the 1996 Act gives applicants the right to appeal to the county court on a point of law if dissatisfied with the decision on the review (or the initial decision, if a review decision is not made within the prescribed time limit).

5.4 Scottish local authorities have a duty to review homelessness decisions under s 35A of the *Housing (Scotland) Act 1987* as amended by s 4 of the *Housing (Scotland) Act 2001*. This process does not affect the rights of a homeless applicant to seek judicial review or to seek the redress of the Scottish Public Services Ombudsman.

5.5 Once the notifying authority is has decided that the applicant is eligible, unintentionally homeless, and in priority need, there is no provision for the notified authority to challenge the decision other than judicial review in the High Court. The local authority associations' disputes procedure should be used only where there is a disagreement over the question of whether the conditions for referral are met and not for resolving disagreement on any other matter.

6 *Making the notification*

6.1 All notifications and arrangements concerning an applicant should be made by telephone and then confirmed in writing. A specimen standard notification form is attached, which authorities are advised to use. If telephone contact cannot be made a fax or e-mail should be sent. Where the notified authority accepts the conditions for referral are met, it should not wait for the receipt of written confirmation of notification before making appropriate arrangements to secure accommodation for the applicant and his or her household.

6.2 Each authority should nominate an officer responsible for making decisions about applications notified by another authority. Appropriate arrangements should also be put in place to ensure cover during any absences of the designated officer.

6.3   The notified authority should normally accept the facts of the case relating to residence, employment, family associations etc, as stated by the notifying authority, unless they have clear evidence to the contrary. It is the notifying authority's duty to make inquiries into the circumstances of homelessness with the same degree of care and thoroughness before referring a case to another authority as it would for any other case.

6.4   Local authorities should try to avoid causing undue disruption to the applicant which could arise from the operation of the criteria and procedures set out above. For instance, where it is agreed that the conditions for referral are met two authorities involved could agree, subject to the applicants' consent, to enter into a reciprocal arrangement so as to avoid having to move a household which may already have made arrangements within the notifying authority's area for schooling, medical treatment etc. Such arrangements could involve provision via nominations to other social housing providers such as registered social landlords. Authorities are reminded that there is no requirement to refer applicants to another authority even where it is agreed that the conditions for referral are met.

6.5   Once written confirmation of notification has been received the notified authority should, within 10 days, reply to the notifying authority. If, despite reminders, there is an unreasonable delay by the notified authority in formally responding to the notification, the notifying authority may ask its local authority association to intercede on its behalf.

7   *Arrangements for securing accommodation*

7.1   As soon as the notifying authority has advised the applicant that it intends to notify, or has already notified, another authority that it considers that the conditions for referral are met, the notifying authority has a duty (under s 200 (1) of the 1996 Act) (England and Wales) and s 34 *Housing (Scotland) Act 1987* to secure accommodation until the applicant is informed of the decision whether the conditions for referral are met. During this period, the notifying authority also has a duty (under s 211) (England and Wales) and s 36 of the *Housing (Scotland) Act 1987* to take reasonable steps for the protection of property belonging to the applicant or anyone who might reasonably be expected to reside with the applicant.

7.2.1   When it has been decided whether the conditions for referral are met the notifying authority must inform the applicant of the decision and the reason for it (s 200(2), England and Wales or s 34 of the *Housing (Scotland) Act 1987*). The applicant must also be informed of his right to ask for a review of the decision and that any request must be made within 21 days or such longer period as the authority may allow in writing.

7.2.2   If it is decided that the conditions for referral are not met, under s 200(3) England and Wales or s 34(2) of the *Housing (Scotland) Act 1987* the notifying authority will be subject to the s 193 duty (England and Wales) or s 31 of the *Housing (Scotland) Act 1987* and must ensure that suitable accommodation is available for the applicant.

7.2.3 If it is decided that the conditions for referral are met, under s 200(4) or s 34(2) of the *Housing (Scotland) Act 1987*, the notified authority will be subject to the s 193 duty (England and Wales) s 31 of the *Housing (Scotland) Act 1987* and must ensure that suitable accommodation is available for the applicant.

7.3 The local authority associations recommend that once a notified authority has accepted that the conditions of referral are met it shall reimburse the notifying authority for any expenses which may reasonably have been incurred in providing temporary accommodation, including protection of property. If the notifying authority unduly delays advising an authority of its intention to refer an applicant then the notified authority shall only be responsible for expenses incurred after the receipt of notification. In normal circumstances a period of more than 30 working days, commencing from the date when the notifying authority had reason to believe that the applicant may be homeless or threatened with homelessness and commenced inquiries under s 184, (England & Wales), s 28 of the *Housing (Scotland) Act 1987*, should be considered as constituting undue delay.

8   *Right of review of referral decisions (England and Wales)*

8.1 Under s 202(1)(c) *Housing Act 1996*, applicants in England and Wales have the right to request a review of any decision by the authority to notify another authority of its opinion that the conditions for referral are met. And, under s 202(1)(d), applicants in England and Wales have the right to request a review of any decision whether the conditions for referral are met. In Scotland (under s 34(3A) and s 35A(2)(b) of the *Housing (Scotland) Act 1987*) as inserted by s 4 of the *Housing Scotland Act 2001* the applicant must be notified that they can request a review of any decision to refer their case to another authority, any determination reached following referral and the time within which this request should be made – the authority should also notify the applicant of advice and assistance available to him in connection with this review. In both cases the request for review will be made to the notifying authority.

9   *Statutory procedure on review*

9.1 **Review procedure for England** – The procedural requirements for a review are set out in the *Allocation of Housing and Homelessness (Review Procedures) Regulations 1999* (SI 1999 No 71).

9.2 The notifying authority shall notify the applicant:

(i)   that the applicant, or someone acting on the applicant's behalf, may make written representations,

(ii)   of the review procedures.

9.3 If the reviewer acting for the notifying authority considers that there is an irregularity in the original decision, or in the manner in which it was made, but is nevertheless minded to make a decision which is against the interests of the applicant, the reviewer shall notify the applicant:

(i) that the reviewer is so minded, and the reasons why,
(ii) that the applicant, or someone acting on the applicant's behalf, may make further written or oral representations.

9.4 In carrying out a review the reviewer shall:

(i)   consider any representations made by, or on behalf of, the applicant,
(ii) consider any further written or oral representations made by, or on behalf of, the applicant in response to a notification referred to in paragraph 9.2 (b) above,
(iii) make a decision on the basis of the facts known at the date of the review.

9.5 The applicant should be notified of the decision on a review within: eight weeks from the date on which a request for review was made under s 202(1)(c), ten weeks from the date on which a request for review was made under s 202(1)(d), or such longer period as the applicant may agree in writing.

9.6 Review procedure for Scotland – Procedures are set out in s 35A and s 35B of the *Housing (Scotland) Act 1987*. Good practice guidance on the procedures is set out in Chapter 11 of the Code of Guidance on Homelessness.

9.7 Review Procedure for Wales. The procedures are set out in *The Allocation of Housing and Homelessness (Review Procedures) Regulations 1999* (SI 1999 No 71).

9.8 Where the decision under review is a joint decision by the notifying housing authority and the notified housing authority s 202(4) requires that the review should be carried out jointly by the two housing authorities.

9.9 The notifying authority shall notify the applicant:

(i) that the applicant, or someone acting on the applicant's behalf, may make written representations,
(ii) of the review procedures.

9.10 If the reviewer acting for the notifying authority considers that there is an irregularity in the original decision, or in the manner in which it was made, but is nevertheless minded to make a decision which is against the interests of the applicant, the reviewer shall notify the applicant:

(i) that the reviewer is so minded, and the reasons why,
(ii) that the applicant, or someone acting on the applicant's behalf, may make further written and/or oral representations.

9.11 In carrying out a review the reviewer shall:

(i) consider any representations made by, or on behalf of, the applicant,
(ii) consider any further written or oral representations made by, or on behalf of, the applicant in response to a notification referred to in paragraph 9.9(ii) above,

(iii) make a decision on the basis of the facts known at the date of the review.

9.12 The applicant should be notified of the decision on a review within:

(i) eight weeks from the date on which a request for review, where the original decision was made by the housing authority,

(ii) ten weeks from the date on which a request for review was made where the decision was made jointly by two housing authorities,

(iii) twelve weeks, where the decision is taken by a person appointed pursuant to the Schedule to the *Homelessness (Decisions on Referrals) Order 1998* (SI 1998 No 1578).

In all these cases it is open to the reviewer to seek the applicant's agreement to an extension of the proscribed period; any such agreement must be given in writing.

10   *Disputes between authorities*

10.1 The *Homelessness (Decisions on Referrals) (Scotland) Order 1998* and the *Homelessness (Decisions on Referrals) Order 1998* (SI 1998 No 1578) (England and Wales) set out the arrangements for determining whether the conditions for referral are met, should the notifying and the notified authority fail to agree. These arrangements allow the question to be decided either by a person agreed between the two authorities concerned or, in default of such agreement, by a person appointed from a panel established by the LGA.

10.2 Where a notified authority considers the conditions for referral are not met it should write to the notifying authority giving its reasons in full, within 10 days. The letter should contain all the reasons for its opinion, to avoid delaying the appointment of a referee and to minimise any inconvenience for the applicant.

10.3 Where two authorities cannot reach agreement on whether the conditions for referral are met they must seek to agree on a referee who will make the decision. CoSLA and the LGA have jointly established an independent panel of referees for this purpose. A referee should be appointed within 21 days of the notified authority receiving the notification.

10.4 Authorities invoking the disputes procedure should, having first agreed on the proposed referee, establish that he or she is available and willing to accept the case. Each authority is then responsible for providing the referee with such information as he or she requires to reach a decision, making copies of the submission available to the applicant and ensuring prompt payment of fees and expenses. Sections 10–19 (Guidelines for Invoking the Disputes Procedure) set out in greater detail the requirements and timescale for the disputes procedure.

10.5 Authorities invoking the disputes procedure should be bound by the decision of the referee, including the apportionment of fees and expenses, subject to a further decision by a referee where the applicant asks for a review of the initial decision.

10.6 If the authorities are unable to agree on the choice of a referee, they must jointly request that CoSLA (for Scottish authorities) or the LGA (for English or Welsh authorities) appoint a referee on their behalf as outlined in paragraph 10.8 below.

10.7 If a referee has not been appointed within six weeks of the notified authority receiving the referral the notifying authority may request CoSLA or the LGA, as appropriate, to appoint a referee as outlined in paragraph 10.8 below.

10.8 Where two authorities fail to agree on the appointment of a referee CoSLA (if the dispute is between Scottish authorities) or the LGA (if the dispute is between English or Welsh authorities) may appoint a referee from the panel. Where the **notified** authority is Scottish then the local authority association responsible for appointing a referee will be CoSLA, even if the notifying authority is in England or Wales. The LGA will be the responsible association if the notified authority is English or Welsh.

10.9 The local authority associations should only be involved in the direct appointment of referees as a last resort. Under normal circumstances authorities should jointly agree the arrangements between themselves in accordance with the Guidelines for Invoking the Disputes Procedure.

Procedures for referrals of homeless applicants on the grounds of local connection with another local authority

Guidelines for invoking the disputes procedure

Agreed by

> ASSOCIATION OF LONDON GOVERNMENT (ALG)
> CONVENTION OF SCOTTISH LOCAL AUTHORITIES (CoSLA)
> LOCAL GOVERNMENT ASSOCIATION (LGA)
> WELSH LOCAL GOVERNMENT ASSOCIATION (WLGA)
> (*'the local authority associations'*)

11 Determining disputes

11.1 The local authority associations have been concerned to establish an inexpensive, simple, speedy, fair and consistent way of resolving disputes between authorities arising from the referral of homeless applicants under s 198 *Housing Act 1996* (England and Wales). In Scotland the provisions of s 33 *Housing (Scotland) Act 1987* apply.

11.2 For the purpose of this Disputes procedure, arbitrators are referred to as 'referees'. Referees will not normally be entitled to apply the criteria set out in

Appendix 2
England: Homelessness

this agreed procedure without the consent of the local authorities involved in the dispute. Where the issues in the case are evenly balanced, referees may have regard to the wishes of the applicant.

11.3 In determining disputes referees will need to have regard to:

a)   for English and Welsh authorities

- Part VII *Housing Act 1996*
- regulation 6 of the *Homelessness Regulations1996* (SI 1996 No 2754) for Wales
- the *Homelessness (Decisions on Referrals) Order 1998* (SI 1998 No 1578)
- the *Allocation of Housing and Homelessness (Review Procedures) Regulations 1999* (SI 1999 No 71)
- *Code of Guidance for Local Authorities on Allocation of Accommodation and Homelessness 2003 (Wales)* – currently under review
- *Homelessness Code of Guidance for Local Authorities 2006 (England)*

b)   for Scottish authorities

- *Housing (Scotland) Act 1987*
- the *Homelessness (Decisions on Referrals) (Scotland) Order 1998*
- the *Persons subject to Immigration Control (Housing Authority Accommodation and Homelessness) Order 2000* (SI 2000 706)
- *Homelessness etc (Scotland) Act 2003*
- *Code of Guidance on Homelessness: Guidance on legislation, policies and practices to prevent and resolve homelessness 2005 (Scotland)*

c)   for all authorities

- the *Procedures for s 198 (Local Connection) Homeless Referrals: Guidelines for Local Authorities and Referees* produced by the local authority associations
- *Asylum and Immigration (Treatment of Claimants, etc) Act 2004*

11.4 Where there is a cross border dispute between a Scottish authority and an English or Welsh authority then the legislation relevant to the location of the notified authority should be applied in determining whether the conditions for referral are met.

11.5 Scottish authorities need to be aware of any orders exercised by s 8 of the *Homelessness (Scotland) Act 2003* that may effect referrals between Scottish authorities in the future.

12   Arrangements for appointing referees

12.1 Referees will be approached by the authorities in dispute, both of which must agree that the referee should be invited to accept the appointment, to establish whether they are willing and able to act in a particular dispute. The referee should be appointed within 21 days of the notified authority receiving the referral. If the local authorities are unable to agree on the choice of referee they should contact CoSLA or the LGA, as appropriate, in accordance with section 10 of the Guidelines for Local Authorities on Procedures for Referral.

12.2 A referee will be given an initial indication of the reason for the dispute by the relevant authorities or the local authority association. The referee's jurisdiction is limited to the issue of whether the conditions for referral are met.

12.3 A referee must not have any personal interest in the outcome of the dispute and should not accept the appointment if he or she is, or was, employed by, or is a council tax payer in, one of the disputing local authorities, or if he or she has any connection with the applicant.

13   Procedures for determining the dispute

13.1 The general procedures to be followed by a referee in determining a dispute are outlined in the Schedule to the *Homelessness (Decisions on Referrals) Order 1998* (SI 1998 No 1578). (England and Wales) and SI 1998 No 1603 (Scotland). It is recommended that the following, more detailed, procedures are applied to *all* cases.

13.2 Following appointment, the referee shall invite the notifying and notified authorities to submit written representations within a period of *fourteen* working days, specifying the closing date, and requiring them to send copies of their submission to the applicant and to the other authority involved in the dispute. Authorities must have the opportunity to see each other's written statements, and should be allowed a further period of ten working days to comment thereon before the referee proceeds to determine the issue. The referee may also invite further written representations from the authorities, if considered necessary.

13.3 The homeless applicant to whom the dispute relates is not a direct party to the dispute but the referee may invite written or oral representations from the applicant, or any other person, which is proper and relevant to the issue. Where the referee invites representations from a person they may be made by another person acting on the person's behalf, whether or not the other person is legally qualified.

13.4 The disputing authorities should make copies of their submissions available to the applicant. The authorities should have the opportunity to comment on any information from the applicant (or any other source) upon which the referee intends to rely in reaching his/her decision.

13.5 Since the applicant's place of abode is in question, and temporary accommodation and property storage charges may be involved, it is important that a decision should be reached as quickly as possible – normally within *a month* of the receipt of the written representations and comments from the notifying and notified authority. This period will commence at the end of the process described in point 13.2. In the last resort, a referee may determine a dispute on the facts before him/her if one authority has, after reminders, failed to present its case without reasonable cause.

Appendix 2
England: Homelessness

14　Oral hearings

14.1　Where an oral hearing is necessary or more convenient (eg where the applicant is illiterate, English is not his/her first language or further information is necessary to resolve issues in dispute), it is suggested that the notifying authority should be invited to present its case first, followed by the notified authority and any other persons whom the referee wishes to hear. The applicant may be invited to provide information on relevant matters. The authorities should then be given a right to reply to earlier submissions.

14.2　The referee's determination must be in writing even when there is an oral hearing. The referee will have to arrange the venue for the hearing and it is suggested that the offices of the notifying authority would often be the most convenient location.

14.3　Where a person has made oral representations the referee may direct either or both authorities to pay reasonable travelling expenses. The notifying and notified authorities will pay their own costs.

15　Notification of determination

15.1　The written decision of the referee should set out:

  (a)　the issue(s) which he has been asked to determine
  (b)　the findings of fact which are relevant to the question(s) in issue
  (c)　the decision
  (d)　the reasons for the decision.

The referee's determination is binding upon the participating local authorities, subject to the applicant's right to ask for a review of the decision under s 202 of the 1996 Act (and possible right of appeal to the county court on a point of law under s 204). The statutory right to review does not apply to Scottish legislation.

16　Costs of determination

16.1　Referees will be expected to provide their own secretarial services and to obtain their own advice on points of law. The cost of so doing, however, will be costs of the determination and recoverable as such.

17　Circulation of determination

17.1　Referees should send copies of the determination to both disputing authorities and to the LGA. The LGA will circulate copies to other members of the Panel of Referees as an aid to settling future disputes and promoting consistency in decisions.

17.2　The notifying authority should inform the applicant of the outcome promptly.

18 Payment of fees and costs

18.1 The local authority associations recommend a flat rate fee of **£500** per determination (including determinations made on a review) which should be paid in full and as speedily as possible after the determination has been received. However, in exceptional cases where a dispute takes a disproportionate time to resolve, a referee may negotiate a higher fee. In addition, the referee may claim the actual cost of any travelling, secretarial or other incidental expenses which s/he has incurred, including any additional costs arising from the right of review or the right of appeal to a county court on a point of law.

18.2 The LGA will determine such additional fees as may be appropriate for any additional work which may subsequently arise should there be a further dispute or appeal after the initial determination has been made or should a referee be party to an appeal, under s 204 *Housing Act 1996*, to the county court on a point of law.

18.3 The referee's fees and expenses, and any third party costs, would normally be recovered from the unsuccessful party to the dispute, although a referee may choose to apportion expenses between the disputing authorities if he considers it warranted. Referees are advised, when issuing invoices to local authorities, to stipulate that payment be made within **28 days**.

19 Reopening a dispute

19.1 Once a determination on a dispute is made, a referee is not permitted to reopen the case, even though new facts may be presented to him or her, unless a fresh determination is required to rectify an error arising from a mistake or omission.

20 Right of review of referee's decision

20.1 Section 202(1)(d) *Housing Act 1996* gives an applicant the right to request a review of any decision made under these procedures. The right to review does not apply to Scottish legislation.

20.2 If an applicant asks for a review of a referee's decision the notifying and notified authority must, within five working days, appoint another referee ('the reviewer') from the panel. This applies even if the original referee was appointed by the LGA. The reviewer must be a different referee from the referee who made the initial decision. If the two authorities fail to appoint a reviewer within this period then the notifying authority must, within five working days, request the LGA to appoint a reviewer and the LGA must do so within seven days of the request.

20.3 The authorities are required to provide the reviewer with the reasons for the initial decision, and the information on which the decision is based, within five working days of his or her appointment. The two authorities should decide between them who will be responsible for notifying the applicant of the reviewer's decision, once received.

21 Statutory procedure on review

21.1 The procedural requirements for a review are set out in the *Allocation of Housing and Homelessness (Review Procedures) Regulations 1999* (SI 1999 No 71).

21.2 The reviewer is required to:

(i) notify the applicant that he or she, or someone acting on his or her behalf, may make written representations,

(ii) notify the applicant of the review procedures, and

(iii) send copies of the applicant's representations to the two authorities and invite them to respond.

21.3 If the reviewer considers that there is an irregularity in the original decision, or in the manner in which it was made, but is nevertheless minded to make a decision which is against the interests of the applicant, the reviewer shall notify the applicant:

(a) that the reviewer is so minded and the reasons why, and

(b) that the applicant, or someone acting on his behalf, may make further written or oral representations.

21.4 In carrying out a review, the reviewer is required to:

(i) consider any representations made by, or on behalf of, the applicant,

(ii) consider any responses to (i) above,

(iii) consider any further written or oral representations made by, or on behalf of, the applicant in response to a notification referred to in paragraph 21.3(b), and

(iv) make a decision on the basis of the facts known at the date of the review.

21.5 The applicant should be notified of the decision on a review within twelve weeks from the date on which the request for the review was made, or such longer period as the applicant may agree in writing. The two authorities should be advised in writing of the decision on the review, and the reasons for it, **at least a week before the end of the period** in order to allow them adequate time to notify the applicant. Copies of the decision should also be sent to the LGA.

Procedures for referrals of homeless applicants on the grounds of local connection with another local authority

Standard notification form

Agreed by

ASSOCIATION OF LONDON GOVERNMENT (ALG)
CONVENTION OF SCOTTISH LOCAL AUTHORITIES (CoSLA)
LOCAL GOVERNMENT ASSOCIATION (LGA)
WELSH LOCAL GOVERNMENT ASSOCIATION (WLGA)
(*'the local authority associations'*)

A   NOTIFYING AUTHORITY DETAILS

Contact Name _____

Authority _____

Telephone Number _____ Fax Number _____

E-mail _____

Address for Correspondence _____

_____

B   APPLICANT DETAILS

Name of Main Applicant _____ Date of Birth _____

Current Address _____

_____

_____

_____

_____

Appendix 2
England: Homelessness

C   FAMILY MEMBERS

Name   Relationship   Date of Birth

_____   _____   _____

_____   _____   _____

_____   _____   _____

_____   _____   _____

_____   _____   _____

_____   _____   _____

_____   _____   _____

_____   _____   _____

D   ADDRESSES IN LAST 5 YEARS (include dates and type of tenure)

_____

_____

_____

_____

_____

_____

_____

_____

_____

E   **PRESENT/PREVIOUS EMPLOYMENT DETAILS**

Employer _____ Tel No _____

Address _____

Contact Name _____ Job Title _____

Previous Employer _____

Date from _____ Date to _____

Address _____

F   **REASONS FOR HOMELESSNESS**

_____

_____

_____

_____

_____

H   **PRIORITY NEED CATEGORY**

_____

_____

I   **LOCAL CONNECTION DETAILS**

_____

_____

_____

_____

_____

_____

Appendix 2
England: Homelessness

J   WISHES OF THE APPLICANT(S) (in the context of the referral)

_____

_____

_____

_____

_____

_____

**K   THE NOTIFYING AUTHORITY CONSIDER THE CONDITIONS FOR
        REFERRAL ARE MET BECAUSE:**

_____

_____

_____

_____

_____

_____

L   ANY SUPPLEMENTARY INFORMATION
        (attach supporting documentation if relevant)

**I confirm that, in accordance with s.198 _Housing Act 1996_, this authority considers that
neither the applicant nor any person who might reasonably be expected to reside with
the applicant would run the risk of domestic violence or face a probability of other
violence in the district of your authority, if this referral is made.**

Signed _____ Date _____

Homelessness Code of Guidance for Local Authorities Supplementary Guidance on Intentional Homelessness

APPLICANTS WHO FACE HOMELESSNESS FOLLOWING DIFFICULTIES IN MEETING MORTGAGE COMMITMENTS

In response to the current economic climate, and the robust framework of financial support the Government has put in place to help homeowners in financial difficulty,[8] this note provides guidance on how local housing authorities should exercise their homelessness functions,and apply the various statutory criteria,when considering whether applicants who are homeless having lost their home because of difficulties in meeting mortgage commitments are intentionally or unintentionally homeless.

Introduction

1.   This guidance is issued by the Secretary of State under s 182 of the Housing Act 1996 ('the 1996 Act'). Under s 182(1) of the 1996 Act, housing authorities are required to have regard to this guidance in exercising their functions under Part 7 of the 1996 Act.

2.   This statutory guidance supplements Chapter 11 of the *Homelessness Code of Guidance for Local Authorities* issued in July 2006 ('the 2006 Code'), and should be read in conjunction with that chapter.

Homelessness following mortgage difficulties

3.   Homeowners may be at risk of homelessness if they experience difficulties in meeting their mortgage commitments, for example, because a member of the household loses their employment or suffers an income shock. Individual homeowners may respond in different ways when faced with such difficult circumstances.

4.   Some homeowners may voluntarily give up possession of the property (hand back the keys to the lender). Some homeowners may decide to sell the property. Others may seek help to remain in their home, including help under the Mortgage Rescue Scheme (MMRS) or Homeowner Mortgage Support (HHMS), but decide – if found eligible for the scheme – not to accept an offer because they consider that continuing with home ownership would be unsustainable or would entail unacceptable financial risk. Where homeowners who have experienced such circumstances become homeless or threatened with

---

8   The Mortgage Rescue Scheme and Homeowner Mortgage Support.

homelessness and apply to a local housing authority for assistance, the authority will need to give careful consideration to the substantive cause(s) of homelessness before coming to a decision on intentionality.

Definition of intentional homelessness

5. Authorities are reminded that by sections 191(1) and 196(1) of the 1996 Act, a person becomes homeless intentionally or threatened with homelessness intentionally, if:

i) the person deliberately does or fails to do anything in consequence of which the person ceases to occupy accommodation (or the likely result of which is that the person will be forced to leave accommodation);

ii) the accommodation is available for the person's occupation; and

iii) it would have been reasonable for the person to continue to occupy the accommodation.

However, an act or omission made in good faith by someone who was unaware of any relevant fact must not be treated as deliberate.

6. Authorities are also reminded that they must not adopt general policies that seek to pre-define circumstances that do or do not amount to intentional homelessness or threatened homelessness (see paragraph 11.55 of the *Homelessness Code of Guidance for Local Authorities*).

Principles established by case law

7. The broad thrust of section 191 is to ascribe intentional homelessness to a person who on the facts is responsible for his homelessness by virtue of his own act or omission. Whilst it is not part of the purpose of the legislation to require local authorities to house people whose homelessness is brought upon them by their own fault, equally, it is not part of the legislation that authorities should refuse to accommodate people whose homelessness has been brought upon them without fault on their part, for example, by an inability to make ends meet.

8. Nobody may be presumed to be intentionally homeless; the local housing authority must be satisfied of intentionality and must ask and answer the questions set out in the legislation. The decision maker in the local authority must look for the substantive cause of the homelessness and the effective cause will not always be the most immediate proximate cause.

9. Intentionality does not depend on whether applicants have behaved wisely or prudently or reasonably. Where an applicant's failure to seek help may have been foolish, imprudent or even unreasonable, this would not necessarily mean his or her conduct was not in good faith.

Some possible scenarios

10. As mentioned above, some former homeowners may seek housing assistance from a local housing authority having lost their home in one of the following circumstances:

i) having voluntarily surrendered the property (handed the keys back);
ii) having sold the property;
iii) where the property was repossessed after the applicant refused an offer under the MRS;
iv) where the property was repossessed after the applicant refused an offer of HMS;
v) where the property was repossessed and the applicant had not sought help.

There should be no general presumption that a homeowner will have brought homelessness on him or herself in any of the above scenarios. A person cannot be found to have become intentionally homeless from a property where he or she was already statutorily homeless: e g because it was not reasonable for him to continue to occupy the property (see paragraph 8.18 et seq of the *Homelessness Code of Guidance for Local Authorities*). Consequently, where someone was already homeless before surrendering or selling their home or refusing an offer under MRS or HMS, the 'acts' of surrender or sale, and the 'omission' of refusing an offer of MRS or HMS cannot be treated as the cause of homelessness.

11. In particular, authorities will need to satisfy themselves on two questions as applied at the point in time immediately before the applicant ceased to occupy accommodation (i e prior to the surrender, sale or refusal of help). First, was the applicant's home available as accommodation for the applicant, any other person who normally resides with him as a member of his family and any person who might reasonably be expected to reside with him? Second, did the applicant's home constitute accommodation that it would have been reasonable for him or her to continue to occupy? It would not have been reasonable for the applicant to continue to occupy his or her home, for example, if the home was not affordable, for example, because the applicant could not meet the cost of his or her mortgage commitments.

12. If the answer to either of the two questions above is in the negative, the applicant will have been homeless prior to the surrender or sale of the property or refusal of an offer of assistance under the MRS or HMS. In such a case, the authority may still consider whether the applicant's homelessness was intentional but will need to look at the substantive causes of that homelessness prior to surrender or sale of the property or refusal of an offer of assistance under the MRS or HMS.

SI 1996 No 3204

Homelessness (Suitability of Accommodation) Order 1996

Made	*19th December 1996*
Laid before Parliament	*23rd December 1996*
Coming into force	*20th January 1997*

The Secretary of State for the Environment, as respects England, and the Secretary of State for Wales, as respects Wales, in exercise of the powers conferred on them by sections 177(3)(b) and 210(2)(b) of the Housing Act 1996, and of all other powers enabling them in that behalf, hereby make the following Order:

1 Citation and commencement

This Order may be cited as the Homelessness (Suitability of Accommodation) Order 1996 and shall come into force on 20th January 1997.

2 Matters to be taken into account

In determining whether it would be, or would have been, reasonable for a person to continue to occupy accommodation and in determining whether accommodation is suitable for a person there shall be taken into account whether or not the accommodation is affordable for that person and, in particular, the following matters –

(a)　the financial resources available to that person, including, but not limited to, –

    (i)　salary, fees and other remuneration;

    (ii)　social security benefits;

    (iii)　payments due under a court order for the making of periodical payments to a spouse or a former spouse, or to, or for the benefit of, a child;

    (iv)　payments of child support maintenance due under the Child Support Act 1991;

    (v)　pensions;

    (vi)　contributions to the costs in respect of the accommodation which are or were made or which might reasonably be expected to be, or have been, made by other members of his household;

    (vii)　financial assistance towards the costs in respect of the accommodation, including loans, provided by a local authority, voluntary organisation or other body;

    (viii)　benefits derived from a policy of insurance;

    (ix)　savings and other capital sums;

(b)　the costs in respect of the accommodation, including, but not limited to, –

- (i)   payments of, or by way of, rent;
- (ii)   payments in respect of a licence or permission to occupy the accommodation;
- (iii) mortgage costs;
- (iv)   payments of, or by way of, service charges;
- (v)   mooring charges payable for a houseboat;
- (vi)   where the accommodation is a caravan or a mobile home, payments in respect of the site on which it stands;
- (vii) the amount of council tax payable in respect of the accommodation;
- (viii) payments by way of deposit or security in respect of the accommodation;
- (ix)   payments required by an accommodation agency;
- (c)   payments which that person is required to make under a court order for the making of periodical payments to a spouse or a former spouse, or to, or for the benefit of, a child and payments of child support maintenance required to be made under the Child Support Act 1991;
- (d)   that person's other reasonable living expenses.

[3 Circumstances in which accommodation is not to be regarded as suitable

For the purposes of section 197(1) of the Housing Act 1996 (duty where other suitable accommodation available), accommodation shall not be regarded as suitable unless the local housing authority are satisfied that it will be available for occupation by the applicant for at least two years beginning with the date on which he secures it.][1]

AMENDMENT

[1] Article inserted: SI 1997/1741, art 2.

LOCAL AUTHORITIES (CONTRACTING OUT OF ALLOCATION OF HOUSING AND HOMELESSNESS FUNCTIONS) ORDER 1996
SI 1996 NO 3205

See Appendix 1, p 955

Appendix 2
England: Homelessness

SI 1997 No 797

Homelessness (Isles of Scilly) Order 1997

Made	*12th March 1997*
Laid before Parliament	*13th March 1997*
Coming into force	*3rd April 1997*

The Secretary of State, in exercise of the powers conferred on him by section 225(1) of the Housing Act 1996, and of all other powers enabling him in that behalf, hereby makes the following Order:

1 Citation, commencement and interpretation

(1) This Order may be cited as the Homelessness (Isles of Scilly) Order 1997 and shall come into force on 3rd April 1997.

(2) In this Order –

'the Act' means the Housing Act 1996;
'the Council' means the Council of the Isles of Scilly.

2 Eligibility for assistance by the Council and local connection with the district of the Council

(1) Where –

   (a)   a person applies to the Council for assistance under Part 7 of the Act (homelessness); or

   (b)   a person applies to a local housing authority other than the Council for such assistance and, but for the provisions of paragraphs (2) and (3), the conditions specified in section 198(2) of the Act (referral of case to another authority) for referral of the case to the Council are satisfied,

sections 183 to 218 of the Act shall be subject to the following provisions of this article.

(2) A person is not eligible for assistance by the Council if he has not been resident in the district of the Council for a period of two years and six months during the period of three years immediately prior to his application.

(3) Where a person is not excluded from assistance by the Council by paragraph (2) –

   (a)   he has a local connection with the district of the Council; and

   (b)   section 199 of the Act (local connection) shall not apply for the purpose of determining whether he has a local connection with the district of the Council.

SI 1998 No 1578

Homelessness (Decisions on Referrals) Order 1998

Made	*25th June 1998*
Coming into force	*20th June 1998*

The Secretary of State for the Environment, Transport and the Regions, as respects England, and the Secretary of State for Wales, as respects Wales, in exercise of the powers conferred on them by section 198(5) and (6)(a) of the Housing Act 1996 and of all other powers enabling them in that behalf, hereby make the following Order, a draft of which has been laid before and approved by resolution of each House of Parliament:

1 Citation and commencement

This Order may be cited as the Homelessness (Decisions on Referrals) Order 1998 and shall come into force on the twenty-eighth day after the day on which it is approved by resolution of each House of Parliament.

2 Arrangements for deciding whether conditions for referral are satisfied

The arrangements set out in the Schedule to this Order are those agreed by the Local Government Association, the Welsh Local Government Association, the Association of London Government and the Convention of Scottish Local Authorities, and shall be the arrangements for the purposes of section 198(5) and (6)(a) of the Housing Act 1996.

3 Revocation of order

(1) Subject to paragraph (2), the Housing (Homeless Persons) (Appropriate Arrangements) Order 1978 ('the 1978 Order') is hereby revoked.

(2) The 1978 Order shall remain in force for any case where a notified authority has received a notification under section 67(1) of the Housing Act 1985 or section 198(1) of the Housing Act 1996 (referral to another local housing authority) prior to the date on which this Order comes into force.

Schedule

Article 2

The Arrangements

1 Appointment of person by agreement between notifying authority and notified authority

Where the question whether the conditions for referral of a case are satisfied has not been decided by agreement between the notifying authority and the notified authority, the question shall be decided by a person appointed by those authorities.

2 Appointment of person other than by agreement between notifying authority and notified authority

If within a period of 21 days commencing on the day on which the notified authority receives a notification under section 198(1) of the Housing Act 1996 a person has not been appointed in accordance with paragraph 1, the question shall be decided by a person –

    (a)   from the panel constituted in accordance with paragraph 3, and

    (b)   appointed in accordance with paragraph 4.

3

(1) Subject to sub-paragraph (2), the Local Government Association shall establish and maintain a panel of persons from which a person may be appointed to decide the question whether the conditions for referral of a case are satisfied.

(2) The Local Government Association shall consult such other associations of relevant authorities as they think appropriate before –

    (a)   establishing the panel,

    (b)   inviting a person to join the panel after it has been established, and

    (c)   removing a person from the panel.

4

(1) The notifying authority and the notified authority shall jointly request the Chairman of the Local Government Association or his nominee ('the proper officer') to appoint a person from the panel.

(2) If within a period of six weeks commencing on the day on which the notified authority receives a notification under section 198(1) of the Housing Act 1996 a person has not been appointed, the notifying authority shall request the proper officer to appoint a person from the panel.

5 Procedural requirements

(1) Subject to the following provisions of this paragraph, the procedure for deciding whether the conditions for referral of a case are satisfied shall be determined by the appointed person.

(2) The appointed person shall invite written representations from the notifying authority and the notified authority.

(3) The appointed person may also invite –

(a) further written representations from the notifying authority and the notified authority,

(b) written representations from any other person, and

(c) oral representations from any person.

(4) If the appointed person invites representations from any person, those representations may be made by a person acting on his behalf, whether or not legally qualified.

6 Notification of decision

The appointed person shall notify his decision, and his reasons for it, in writing to the notifying authority and the notified authority.

7 Costs

(1) The notifying authority and the notified authority shall pay their own costs incurred in connection with the arrangements set out in this Schedule.

(2) Where a person has made oral representations, the appointed person may give directions as to the payment by the notifying authority or the notified authority or both authorities of any travelling expenses reasonably incurred by that person.

8 Meaning of 'appointed person'

In this Schedule 'appointed person' means a person appointed in accordance with paragraph 1 or 4.

Appendix 2
England: Homelessness

SI 1999 No 71

Allocation of Housing and Homelessness (Review Procedures) Regulations 1999

Made	*14th January 1999*
Laid before Parliament	*21st January 1999*
Coming into force	*11th February 1999*

The Secretary of State for the Environment, Transport and the Regions, as respects England, and the Secretary of State for Wales, as respects Wales, in exercise of the powers conferred on them by sections 165(1), (2) and (5) and 203(1), (2) and (7) of the Housing Act 1996 and of all other powers enabling them in that behalf, hereby make the following Regulations:

PART I
GENERAL

1 Citation, commencement and interpretation

(1) These Regulations may be cited as the Allocation of Housing and Homelessness (Review Procedures) Regulations 1999 and shall come into force on 11th February 1999.

(2) In these Regulations –

'the authority' means the local housing authority which has made the decision whose review under section 164 or 202 has been requested;
'the Decisions on Referrals Order' means the Homelessness (Decisions on Referrals) Order 1998;
'the reviewer' means –
    (a)   where the original decision falls within section 202(1)(a), (b), (c), (e) or (f), the authority;
    (b)   where the original decision falls within section 202(1)(d) (a decision under section 198(5) whether the conditions are met for referral of a case) –
        (i)   the notifying authority and the notified authority, where the review is carried out by those authorities;
        (ii) the person appointed to carry out the review in accordance with regulation 7, where the case falls within that regulation.

(3) In these Regulations, references to sections are references to sections of the Housing Act 1996.

2 Who is to make the decision on the review

Where the decision of the authority on a review of an original decision made by an officer of the authority is also to be made by an officer, that officer shall be someone who was not involved in the original decision and who is senior to the officer who made the original decision.

PART II
THE HOUSING REGISTER

3 Notification of review procedure

Following a duly made request for a review under section 164, the authority shall –

(a) notify the person concerned that he, or someone acting on his behalf, may make representations in writing to the authority in connection with the review; and

(b) if they have not already done so, notify the person concerned of the procedure to be followed in connection with the review.

4 Procedure on a review

The authority shall, subject to compliance with the provisions of regulation 5, consider any representations made under regulation 3.

5 Notification of the decision on a review

The period within which the authority shall notify the person concerned of the decision on a review under section 164 is eight weeks from the day on which the request for a review is made to the authority or such longer period as the authority and the person concerned may agree in writing.

PART III
HOMELESSNESS

6 Request for a review and notification of review procedure

(1) A request for a review under section 202 shall be made –

(a) to the authority, where the original decision falls within section 202(1)(a), (b), (c), (e) or (f);

(b) to the notifying authority, where the original decision falls within section 202(1)(d) (a decision under section 198(5) whether the conditions are met for referral of a case).

(2) Except where a case falls within regulation 7, the authority to whom a request for a review under section 202 has been made shall –

(a) notify the applicant that he, or someone acting on his behalf, may make representations in writing to the authority in connection with the review; and

(b) if they have not already done so, notify the applicant of the procedure to be followed in connection with the review.

(3) Where a case falls within regulation 7, the person appointed in accordance with that regulation shall –

Appendix 2
England: Homelessness

(a) notify the applicant that he, or someone acting on his behalf, may make representations in writing to that person in connection with the review; and

(b) notify the applicant of the procedure to be followed in connection with the review.

7 Initial procedure where the original decision was made under the Decisions on Referrals Order

(1) Where the original decision under section 198(5) (whether the conditions are met for the referral of the case) was made under the Decisions on Referrals Order, a review of that decision shall, subject to paragraph (2), be carried out by a person appointed by the notifying authority and the notified authority.

(2) If a person is not appointed in accordance with paragraph (1) within five working days from the day on which the request for a review is made, the review shall be carried out by a person –

(a) from the panel constituted in accordance with paragraph 3 of the Schedule to the Decisions on Referrals Order ('the panel'), and

(b) appointed in accordance with paragraph (3) below.

(3) The notifying authority shall within five working days from the end of the period specified in paragraph (2) request the chairman of the Local Government Association or his nominee ('the proper officer') to appoint a person from the panel and the proper officer shall do so within seven days of the request.

(4) The notifying authority and the notified authority shall within five working days of the appointment of the person appointed ('the appointed person') provide him with the reasons for the original decision and the information and evidence on which that decision was based.

(5) The appointed person shall –

(a) send to the notifying authority and the notified authority any representations made under regulation 6; and

(b) invite those authorities to respond to those representations.

(6) The appointed person shall not be the same person as the person who made the original decision.

(7) For the purposes of this regulation a working day is a day other than Saturday, Sunday, Christmas Day, Good Friday or a bank holiday.

8 Procedure on a review

(1) The reviewer shall, subject to compliance with the provisions of regulation 9, consider –

(a) any representations made under regulation 6 and, in a case falling within regulation 7, any responses to them; and

(b) any representations made under paragraph (2) below.

(2) If the reviewer considers that there is a deficiency or irregularity in the original decision, or in the manner in which it was made, but is minded nonetheless to make a decision which is against the interests of the applicant on one or more issues, the reviewer shall notify the applicant –

(a)   that the reviewer is so minded and the reasons why; and

(b)   that the applicant, or someone acting on his behalf, may make representations to the reviewer orally or in writing or both orally and in writing.

9 Notification of the decision on a review

(1) The period within which notice of the decision on a review under section 202 shall be given under section 203(3) to the applicant shall be –

(a)   eight weeks from the day on which the request for the review is made, where the original decision falls within section 202(1)(a), (b), (c), (e) or (f);

(b)   ten weeks from the day on which the request for the review is made, where the original decision falls within section 202(1)(d) and the review is carried out by the notifying authority and the notified authority;

(c)   twelve weeks from the day on which the request for the review is made in a case falling within regulation 7.

(2) The period specified in paragraph (1) may be such longer period as the applicant and the reviewer may agree in writing.

(3) In a case falling within paragraph (1)(c), the appointed person shall notify his decision on the review, and his reasons for it, in writing to the notifying authority and the notified authority within a period of eleven weeks from the day on which the request for the review is made, or within a period commencing on that day which is one week shorter than that agreed in accordance with paragraph (2).

PART IV
REVOCATION

10 Revocation and transitional provisions

(1) Subject to paragraph (2), the following provisions are hereby revoked –

(a)   regulations 2 to 8 of the Allocation of Housing and Homelessness (Review Procedures and Amendment) Regulations 1996;

(b)   the definition of 'the Review Regulations' in regulation 1(3) of the Allocation of Housing and Homelessness (Amendment) Regulations 1997 and regulation 6 of those Regulations.

(2) The provisions revoked by paragraph (1) shall continue in force in any case where a request for a review under section 164 or 202 is made prior to the date these Regulations come into force.

SI 1999 No 3126

Homelessness (Asylum-Seekers) (Interim Period) (England) Order 1999

Made	*22nd November 1999*
Laid before Parliament	*22nd November 1999*
Coming into force	*6th December 1999*

The Secretary of State for the Environment, Transport and the Regions, in exercise of the powers conferred upon him by section 166(3) of, and paragraph 13 of Schedule 15 to, the Immigration and Asylum Act 1999, and of all other powers enabling him in that behalf, hereby makes the following Order:

1 Citation, commencement and extent

(1) This Order may be cited as the Homelessness (Asylum-Seekers) (Interim Period) (England) Order 1999 and shall come into force on 6th December 1999.

(2) This Order extends to England only.

AMENDMENT

This Order ceased to have effect by virtue of art 7 hereof.

2 Modification of Part 7 of the Housing Act 1996 for certain asylum-seekers

Part 7 of the Housing Act 1996 (homelessness) shall have effect in relation to asylum-seekers who are section 185(2) persons with the modifications specified in the following provisions of this Order.

AMENDMENT

This Order ceased to have effect by virtue of art 7 hereof.

3 Referrals to other local authorities

In section 198 (referral of case to another local housing authority) –

    (a)   in subsection (3), after 'this purpose', there shall be inserted ', and for the purpose of subsection (4A)(c),'; and

    (b)   after subsection (4), there shall be inserted –

    '(4A) The conditions for referral of the case to another authority are also met if –

        (a)   the local housing authority to whom the application has been made and another housing authority have agreed that the case should be referred to that other authority;

        (b)   that other authority has provided written confirmation of the agreement to the local housing authority; and

        (c)   neither the applicant nor any person who might reasonably be expected to reside with him will run the risk of domestic violence in the district of that other authority.

(4B) When reaching the agreement referred to in subsection (4A)(a), the local housing authority to whom the application was made and the other authority need not have regard to –

(a)   any preference that the applicant, or any person who might reasonably be expected to reside with him, may have as to the locality in which the accommodation is to be secured; or

(b)   whether the applicant, or any person who might reasonably be expected to reside with him, has a local connection with the district of any local housing authority.'.

AMENDMENT

This Order ceased to have effect by virtue of art 7 hereof.

4 Discharge of functions by local housing authorities

In section 206 (discharge of functions by local housing authorities), after subsection (1), there shall be inserted –

'(1A) In discharging their housing functions under this Part, a local housing authority shall have regard to the desirability, in general, of securing accommodation in areas in which there is a ready supply of accommodation.'.

AMENDMENT

This Order ceased to have effect by virtue of art 7 hereof.

5 Out-of-area placements

In section 208 (discharge of functions: out-of-area placements), after subsection (1), there shall be inserted –

(1A) Subsection (1) shall not apply where –

(a)   the local housing authority and another housing authority have agreed that the local housing authority may secure that accommodation is available for the occupation of all or an agreed number of asylum-seekers who are section 185(2) persons in that other authority's district; and

(b)   that other authority has provided written confirmation of the agreement to the local housing authority.'.

AMENDMENT

This Order ceased to have effect by virtue of art 7 hereof.

6 Suitability of accommodation

In section 210 (suitability of accommodation), after subsection (1), there shall be inserted –

'(1A) In determining for the purposes of this Part whether accommodation is suitable for an applicant, or any person who might reasonably be expected to reside with him, the local housing authority –

(a)   shall also have regard to the fact that the accommodation is to be temporary pending the determination of the applicant's claim for asylum; and

    (b)   shall not have regard to any preference that the applicant, or any person who might reasonably be expected to reside with him, may have as to the locality in which the accommodation is to be secured.'.

AMENDMENT

This Order ceased to have effect by virtue of art 7 hereof.

7 The interim period

This Order shall cease to have effect on the date on which section 186 of the Housing Act 1996 (asylum-seekers and their dependants) is repealed by the Immigration and Asylum Act 1999 (as to which see section 117(5) of that Act).

AMENDMENT

This Order ceased to have effect by virtue of art 7 hereof.

SI 2002 No 2051

Homelessness (Priority Need for Accommodation) (England) Order 2002

Made	*30th July 2002*
Coming into force	*31st July 2002*

The Secretary of State for Transport, Local Government and the Regions, in exercise of the powers conferred on him by section 189(2) of the Housing Act 1996, having consulted such associations representing relevant authorities, and such other persons as he considers appropriate, in accordance with section 189(3) of that Act, hereby makes the following Order –

1 Citation, commencement and interpretation

(1) This Order may be cited as the Homelessness (Priority Need for Accommodation) (England) Order 2002 and shall come into force on the day after the day on which it is made.

(2) This Order extends to England only.

(3) In this Order –

'looked after, accommodated or fostered' has the meaning given by section 24(2) of the Children Act 1989; and
'relevant student' means a person to whom section 24B(3) of that Act applies –
    (a)   who is in full-time further or higher education; and
    (b)   whose term-time accommodation is not available to him during a vacation.

2 Priority need for accommodation

The descriptions of person specified in the following articles have a priority need for accommodation for the purposes of Part 7 of the Housing Act 1996.

3 Children aged 16 or 17

(1) A person (other than a person to whom paragraph (2) below applies) aged sixteen or seventeen who is not a relevant child for the purposes of section 23A of the Children Act 1989.

(2) This paragraph applies to a person to whom a local authority owe a duty to provide accommodation under section 20 of that Act (provision of accommodation for children in need).

4 Young people under 21

(1) A person (other than a relevant student) who –

(a) is under twenty-one; and

(b) at any time after reaching the age of sixteen, but while still under eighteen, was, but is no longer, looked after, accommodated or fostered.

5 Vulnerability: institutional backgrounds

(1) A person (other than a relevant student) who has reached the age of twenty-one and who is vulnerable as a result of having been looked after, accommodated or fostered.

(2) A person who is vulnerable as a result of having been a member of Her Majesty's regular naval, military or air forces.

(3) A person who is vulnerable as a result of –

(a) having served a custodial sentence (within the meaning of section 76 of the Powers of Criminal Courts (Sentencing) Act 2000);

(b) having been committed for contempt of court or any other kindred offence;

(c) having been remanded in custody (within the meaning of paragraph (b), (c) or (d) of section 88(1) of that Act).

6 Vulnerability: fleeing violence or threats of violence

A person who is vulnerable as a result of ceasing to occupy accommodation by reason of violence from another person or threats of violence from another person which are likely to be carried out.

SI 2003 No 3326

Homelessness (Suitability of Accommodation) (England) Order 2003

Made	*19th December 2003*
Laid before Parliament	*23rd December 2003*
Coming into force	*1st April 2004*

The First Secretary of State, in exercise of the powers conferred upon him by sections 210(2)(a) and 215(2) of the Housing Act 1996 hereby makes the following Order:

1 Citation, commencement and application

(1) This Order may be cited as the Homelessness (Suitability of Accommodation) (England) Order 2003 and shall come into force on 1st April 2004.

(2) This Order applies in relation to the duties of local housing authorities in England to make accommodation available for occupation by applicants under Part 7 of the Housing Act 1996.

2 Interpretation

In this Order –

'applicant with family commitments' means an applicant –
- (a) who is pregnant;
- (b) with whom a pregnant woman resides or might reasonably be expected to reside; or
- (c) with whom dependent children reside or might reasonably be expected to reside;

'B&B accommodation' means accommodation (whether or not breakfast is included) –
- (a) which is not separate and self-contained premises; and
- (b) in which any one of the following amenities is shared by more than one household –
  - (i) a toilet;
  - (ii) personal washing facilities;
  - (iii) cooking facilities,

but does not include accommodation which is owned or managed by a local housing authority, a registered social landlord or a voluntary organisation as defined in section 180(3) of the Housing Act 1996; and any reference to a numbered section is a reference to a section of the Housing Act 1996.

3 Accommodation unsuitable where there is a family commitment

Subject to the exceptions contained in article 4, B&B accommodation is not to be regarded as suitable for an applicant with family commitments where accommodation is made available for occupation –

(a)   under section 188(1), 190(2), 193(2) or 200(1); or

(b)   under section 195(2), where the accommodation is other than that occupied by the applicant at the time of making his application.

4 Exceptions

(1) Article 3 does not apply –

(a)   where no accommodation other than B&B accommodation is available for occupation by an applicant with family commitments; and

(b)   the applicant occupies B&B accommodation for a period, or a total of periods, which does not exceed 6 weeks.

(2) In calculating the period, or total period, of an applicant's occupation of B&B accommodation for the purposes of paragraph (1)(b), there shall be disregarded –

(a)   any period before 1st April 2004; and

(b)   where a local housing authority is subject to the duty under section 193 by virtue of section 200(4), any period before that authority became subject to that duty.

SI 2006 No 1003

The Immigration (European Economic Area) Regulations 2006

Made	*30th March 2006*
Laid before Parliament	*4th April 2006*
Coming into force	*30th April 2006*

The Secretary of State, being a Minister designated for the purposes of section 2(2) of the European Communities Act 1972 in relation to measures relating to rights of entry into, and residence in, the United Kingdom, in exercise of the powers conferred upon him by that section, and of the powers conferred on him by section 109 of the Nationality, Immigration and Asylum Act 2002, makes the following Regulations:

PART 1
INTERPRETATION ETC

1 Citation and commencement

These Regulations may be cited as the Immigration (European Economic Area) Regulations 2006 and shall come into force on 30th April 2006.

2 General interpretation

(1) In these Regulations –

'the 1971 Act' means the Immigration Act 1971;
'the 1999 Act' means the Immigration and Asylum Act 1999;
'the 2002 Act' means the Nationality, Immigration and Asylum Act 2002;
'civil partner' does not include a party to a civil partnership of convenience;
'decision maker' means the Secretary of State, an immigration officer or an entry clearance officer (as the case may be);
['deportation order' means an order made pursuant to regulation 24(3);][1]
'document certifying permanent residence' means a document issued to an EEA national, in accordance with regulation 18, as proof of the holder's permanent right of residence under regulation 15 as at the date of issue;
'EEA decision' means a decision under these Regulations that concerns a person's –

(a)   entitlement to be admitted to the United Kingdom;
(b)   entitlement to be issued with or have renewed, or not to have revoked, a registration certificate, residence card, document certifying permanent residence or permanent residence card; or
(c)   removal from the United Kingdom;

Appendix 2
England: Homelessness

'EEA family permit' means a document issued to a person, in accordance with regulation 12, in connection with his admission to the United Kingdom;

'EEA national' means a national of an EEA State;

'EEA State' means –

(a)   a member State, other than the United Kingdom;

(b)   Norway, Iceland or Liechtenstein; or

(c)   Switzerland;

'entry clearance' has the meaning given in section 33(1) of the 1971 Act;

'entry clearance officer' means a person responsible for the grant or refusal of entry clearance;

['exclusion order' means an order made under regulation 19(1B);]²

'immigration rules' has the meaning given in section 33(1) of the 1971 Act;

'military service' means service in the armed forces of an EEA State;

'permanent residence card' means a card issued to a person who is not an EEA national, in accordance with regulation 18, as proof of the holder's permanent right of residence under regulation 15 as at the date of issue;

'registration certificate' means a certificate issued to an EEA national, in accordance with regulation 16, as proof of the holder's right of residence in the United Kingdom as at the date of issue;

'relevant EEA national' in relation to an extended family member has the meaning given in regulation 8(6);

'residence card' means a card issued to a person who is not an EEA national, in accordance with regulation 17, as proof of the holder's right of residence in the United Kingdom as at the date of issue;

'spouse' does not include a party to a marriage of convenience;

'United Kingdom national' means a person who falls to be treated as a national of the United Kingdom for the purposes of the Community Treaties.

(2) Paragraph (1) is subject to paragraph 1(a) of Schedule 4 (transitional provisions).

[(3) Section 11 of the 1971 Act (construction of references to entry) shall apply for the purpose of determining whether a person has entered the United Kingdom for the purpose of these Regulations as it applies for the purpose of determining whether a person has entered the United Kingdom for the purpose of that Act.]³

AMENDMENT

¹ Words inserted: SI 2009/1117, reg 2, Sch 1, para 1(a)(i).

² Words inserted: SI 2009/1117, reg 2, Sch 1, para 1(a)(ii).

³ Words inserted: SI 2009/1117, reg 2, Sch 1, para 1(b).

3 Continuity of residence

(1) This regulation applies for the purpose of calculating periods of continuous residence in the United Kingdom under regulation 5(1) and regulation 15.

(2) Continuity of residence is not affected by –

(a)   periods of absence from the United Kingdom which do not exceed six months in total in any year;

(b)   periods of absence from the United Kingdom on military service; or

(c)   any one absence from the United Kingdom not exceeding twelve months for an important reason such as pregnancy and childbirth, serious illness, study or vocational training or an overseas posting.

(3) But continuity of residence is broken if a person is removed from the United Kingdom under [these regulations].[1]

AMENDMENT

[1] Words substituted: SI 2009/1117, reg 2, Sch 1, para 2.

4 'Worker', 'self-employed person', 'self-sufficient person' and 'student'

(1) In these Regulations –

(a)'worker' means a worker within the meaning of Article 39 of the Treaty establishing the European Community;

(b)'self-employed person' means a person who establishes himself in order to pursue activity as a self-employed person in accordance with Article 43 of the Treaty establishing the European Community;

(c)'self-sufficient person' means a person who has –

(i)   sufficient resources not to become a burden on the social assistance system of the United Kingdom during his period of residence; and

(ii)   comprehensive sickness insurance cover in the United Kingdom;

(d)'student' means a person who –

(i)   is enrolled at a private or public establishment, included on the ...[1] Register of Education and Training Providers [maintained by the Department for Innovation, Universities and Skills][2] or financed from public funds, for the principal purpose of following a course of study, including vocational training;

(ii)   has comprehensive sickness insurance cover in the United Kingdom; and

(iii)   assures the Secretary of State, by means of a declaration, or by such equivalent means as the person may choose, that he has sufficient resources not to become a burden on the social assistance system of the United Kingdom during his period of residence.

(2) For the purposes of paragraph (1)(c), where family members of the person concerned reside in the United Kingdom and their right to reside is dependent upon their being family members of that person –

(a) the requirement for that person to have sufficient resources not to become a burden on the social assistance system of the United Kingdom during his period of residence shall only be satisfied if his resources and those of the family members are sufficient to avoid him and the family members becoming such a burden;

(b) the requirement for that person to have comprehensive sickness insurance cover in the United Kingdom shall only be satisfied if he and his family members have such cover.

(3) For the purposes of paragraph (1)(d), where family members of the person concerned reside in the United Kingdom and their right to reside is dependent upon their being family members of that person, the requirement for that person to assure the Secretary of State that he has sufficient resources not to become a burden on the social assistance system of the United Kingdom during his period of residence shall only be satisfied if he assures the Secretary of State that his resources and those of the family members are sufficient to avoid him and the family members becoming such a burden.

(4) For the purposes of paragraphs (1)(c) and (d) and paragraphs (2) and (3), the resources of the person concerned and, where applicable, any family members, are to be regarded as sufficient if they exceed the maximum level of resources which a United Kingdom national and his family members may possess if he is to become eligible for social assistance under the United Kingdom benefit system.

AMENDMENT

[1] Words revoked: SI 2007/3224, art 15, Schedule, Pt 2, para 60(a).

[2] Words inserted: SI 2007/3224, art 15, Schedule, Pt 2, para 60(b).

5 'Worker or self-employed person who has ceased activity'

(1) In these Regulations, 'worker or self-employed person who has ceased activity' means an EEA national who satisfies the conditions in paragraph (2), (3), (4) or (5).

(2) A person satisfies the conditions in this paragraph if he –

(a) terminates his activity as a worker or self-employed person and –
   (i) has reached the age at which he is entitled to a state pension on the date on which he terminates his activity; or
   (ii) in the case of a worker, ceases working to take early retirement;

(b) pursued his activity as a worker or self-employed person in the United Kingdom for at least twelve months prior to the termination; and

(c) resided in the United Kingdom continuously for more than three years prior to the termination.

(3) A person satisfies the conditions in this paragraph if –

    (a)   he terminates his activity in the United Kingdom as a worker or self-employed person as a result of a permanent incapacity to work; and

    (b)   either –

        (i)   he resided in the United Kingdom continuously for more than two years prior to the termination; or

        (ii)   the incapacity is the result of an accident at work or an occupational disease that entitles him to a pension payable in full or in part by an institution in the United Kingdom.

(4) A person satisfies the conditions in this paragraph if –

    (a)   he is active as a worker or self-employed person in an EEA State but retains his place of residence in the United Kingdom, to which he returns as a rule at least once a week; and

    (b)   prior to becoming so active in that EEA State, he had been continuously resident and continuously active as a worker or self-employed person in the United Kingdom for at least three years.

(5) A person who satisfies the condition in paragraph (4)(a) but not the condition in paragraph (4)(b) shall, for the purposes of paragraphs (2) and (3), be treated as being active and resident in the United Kingdom during any period in which he is working or self-employed in the EEA State.

(6) The conditions in paragraphs (2) and (3) as to length of residence and activity as a worker or self-employed person shall not apply in relation to a person whose spouse or civil partner is a United Kingdom national.

(7) For the purposes of this regulation –

    (a)   periods of inactivity for reasons not of the person's own making;

    (b)   periods of inactivity due to illness or accident; and

    (c)   in the case of a worker, periods of involuntary unemployment duly recorded by the relevant employment office,

shall be treated as periods of activity as a worker or self-employed person, as the case may be.

6 'Qualified person'

(1) In these Regulations, 'qualified person' means a person who is an EEA national and in the United Kingdom as –

    (a)   a jobseeker;

    (b)   a worker;

    (c)   a self-employed person;

    (d)   a self-sufficient person; or

    (e)   a student.

(2) A person who is no longer working shall not cease to be treated as a worker for the purpose of paragraph (1)(b) if –

    (a)   he is temporarily unable to work as the result of an illness or accident;

(b) he is in duly recorded involuntary unemployment after having been employed in the United Kingdom, provided that he has registered as a jobseeker with the relevant employment office and –

  (i) he was employed for one year or more before becoming unemployed;

  (ii) he has been unemployed for no more than six months; or

  (iii) he can provide evidence that he is seeking employment in the United Kingdom and has a genuine chance of being engaged;

(c) he is involuntarily unemployed and has embarked on vocational training; or

(d) he has voluntarily ceased working and embarked on vocational training that is related to his previous employment.

(3) A person who is no longer in self-employment shall not cease to be treated as a self-employed person for the purpose of paragraph (1)(c) if he is temporarily unable to pursue his activity as a self-employed person as the result of an illness or accident.

(4) For the purpose of paragraph (1)(a), 'jobseeker' means a person who enters the United Kingdom in order to seek employment and can provide evidence that he is seeking employment and has a genuine chance of being engaged.

7 Family member

(1) Subject to paragraph (2), for the purposes of these Regulations the following persons shall be treated as the family members of another person –

(a) his spouse or his civil partner;

(b) direct descendants of his, his spouse or his civil partner who are –

  (i) under 21; or

  (ii) dependants of his, his spouse or his civil partner;

(c) dependent direct relatives in his ascending line or that of his spouse or his civil partner;

(d) a person who is to be treated as the family member of that other person under paragraph (3).

(2) A person shall not be treated under paragraph (1)(b) or (c) as the family member of a student residing in the United Kingdom after the period of three months beginning on the date on which the student is admitted to the United Kingdom unless –

(a) in the case of paragraph (b), the person is the dependent child of the student or of his spouse or civil partner; or

(b) the student also falls within one of the other categories of qualified persons mentioned in regulation 6(1).

(3) Subject to paragraph (4), a person who is an extended family member and has been issued with an EEA family permit, a registration certificate or a residence card shall be treated as the family member of the relevant EEA national for as long as he continues to satisfy the conditions in regulation 8(2), (3), (4) or (5) in relation to that EEA national and the permit, certificate or card has not ceased to be valid or been revoked.

(4) Where the relevant EEA national is a student, the extended family member shall only be treated as the family member of that national under paragraph (3) if either the EEA family permit was issued under regulation 12(2), the registration certificate was issued under regulation 16(5) or the residence card was issued under regulation 17(4).

8 'Extended family member'

(1) In these Regulations 'extended family member' means a person who is not a family member of an EEA national under regulation 7(1)(a), (b) or (c) and who satisfies the conditions in paragraph (2), (3), (4) or (5).

(2) A person satisfies the condition in this paragraph if the person is a relative of an EEA national, his spouse or his civil partner and –

(a) the person is residing in an EEA State in which the EEA national also resides and is dependent upon the EEA national or is a member of his household;

(b) the person satisfied the condition in paragraph (a) and is accompanying the EEA national to the United Kingdom or wishes to join him there; or

(c) the person satisfied the condition in paragraph (a), has joined the EEA national in the United Kingdom and continues to be dependent upon him or to be a member of his household.

(3) A person satisfies the condition in this paragraph if the person is a relative of an EEA national or his spouse or his civil partner and, on serious health grounds, strictly requires the personal care of the EEA national, his spouse or his civil partner.

(4) A person satisfies the condition in this paragraph if the person is a relative of an EEA national and would meet the requirements in the immigration rules (other than those relating to entry clearance) for indefinite leave to enter or remain in the United Kingdom as a dependent relative of the EEA national were the EEA national a person present and settled in the United Kingdom.

(5) A person satisfies the condition in this paragraph if the person is the partner of an EEA national (other than a civil partner) and can prove to the decision maker that he is in a durable relationship with the EEA national.

(6) In these Regulations 'relevant EEA national' means, in relation to an extended family member, the EEA national who is or whose spouse or civil partner is the relative of the extended family member for the purpose of paragraph (2), (3) or (4) or the EEA national who is the partner of the extended family member for the purpose of paragraph (5).

9 Family members of United Kingdom nationals

(1) If the conditions in paragraph (2) are satisfied, these Regulations apply to a person who is the family member of a United Kingdom national as if the United Kingdom national were an EEA national.

(2) The conditions are that –

(a) the United Kingdom national is residing in an EEA State as a worker or self-employed person or was so residing before returning to the United Kingdom; and

(b) if the family member of the United Kingdom national is his spouse or civil partner, the parties are living together in the EEA State or had entered into the marriage or civil partnership and were living together in that State before the United Kingdom national returned to the United Kingdom.

(3) Where these Regulations apply to the family member of a United Kingdom national the United Kingdom national shall be treated as holding a valid passport issued by an EEA State for the purpose of the application of regulation 13 to that family member.

10 'Family member who has retained the right of residence'

(1) In these Regulations, 'family member who has retained the right of residence' means, subject to paragraph (8), a person who satisfies the conditions in paragraph (2), (3), (4) or (5).

(2) A person satisfies the conditions in this paragraph if –

(a) he was a family member of a qualified person when the qualified person died;

(b) he resided in the United Kingdom in accordance with these Regulations for at least the year immediately before the death of the qualified person; and

(c) he satisfies the condition in paragraph (6).

(3) A person satisfies the conditions in this paragraph if –

(a) he is the direct descendant of –
  (i) a qualified person who has died;
  (ii) a person who ceased to be a qualified person on ceasing to reside in the United Kingdom; or
  (iii) the person who was the spouse or civil partner of the qualified person mentioned in sub-paragraph (i) when he died or is the spouse or civil partner of the person mentioned in sub-paragraph (ii); and

(b) he was attending an educational course in the United Kingdom immediately before the qualified person died or ceased to be a qualified person and continues to attend such a course.

(4) A person satisfies the conditions in this paragraph if the person is the parent with actual custody of a child who satisfies the condition in paragraph (3).

(5) A person satisfies the conditions in this paragraph if –

(a) he ceased to be a family member of a qualified person on the termination of the marriage or civil partnership of the qualified person;

(b)   he was residing in the United Kingdom in accordance with these Regulations at the date of the termination;

(c)   he satisfies the condition in paragraph (6); and

(d)   either –

(i)   prior to the initiation of the proceedings for the termination of the marriage or the civil partnership the marriage or civil partnership had lasted for at least three years and the parties to the marriage or civil partnership had resided in the United Kingdom for at least one year during its duration;

(ii)   the former spouse or civil partner of the qualified person has custody of a child of the qualified person;

(iii) the former spouse or civil partner of the qualified person has the right of access to a child of the qualified person under the age of 18 and a court has ordered that such access must take place in the United Kingdom; or

(iv) the continued right of residence in the United Kingdom of the person is warranted by particularly difficult circumstances, such as he or another family member having been a victim of domestic violence while the marriage or civil partnership was subsisting.

(6) The condition in this paragraph is that the person –

(a)   is not an EEA national but would, if he were an EEA national, be a worker, a self-employed person or a self-sufficient person under regulation 6; or

(b)   is the family member of a person who falls within paragraph (a).

(7) In this regulation, 'educational course' means a course within the scope of Article 12 of Council Regulation (EEC) No 1612/68 on freedom of movement for workers.

(8) A person with a permanent right of residence under regulation 15 shall not become a family member who has retained the right of residence on the death or departure from the United Kingdom of the qualified person or the termination of the marriage or civil partnership, as the case may be, and a family member who has retained the right of residence shall cease to have that status on acquiring a permanent right of residence under regulation 15.

PART 2
EEA RIGHTS

11 Right of admission to the United Kingdom

(1) An EEA national must be admitted to the United Kingdom if he produces on arrival a valid national identity card or passport issued by an EEA State.

(2) A person who is not an EEA national must be admitted to the United Kingdom if he is a family member of an EEA national, a family member who has retained the right of residence or a person with a permanent right of residence under regulation 15 and produces on arrival –

    (a)   a valid passport; and

    (b)   an EEA family permit, a residence card or a permanent residence card.

(3) An immigration officer may not place a stamp in the passport of a person admitted to the United Kingdom under this regulation who is not an EEA national if the person produces a residence card or permanent residence card.

(4) Before an immigration officer refuses admission to the United Kingdom to a person under this regulation because the person does not produce on arrival a document mentioned in paragraph (1) or (2), the immigration officer must give the person every reasonable opportunity to obtain the document or have it brought to him within a reasonable period of time or to prove by other means that he is –

    (a)   an EEA national;

    (b)   a family member of an EEA national with a right to accompany that national or join him in the United Kingdom; or

    (c)   a family member who has retained the right of residence or a person with a permanent right of residence under regulation 15.

(5) But this regulation is subject to regulations 19(1) and (2).

12 Issue of EEA family permit

(1) An entry clearance officer must issue an EEA family permit to a person who applies for one if the person is a family member of an EEA national and –

    (a)   the EEA national –

        (i)   is residing in the UK in accordance with these Regulations; or

        (ii)   will be travelling to the United Kingdom within six months of the date of the application and will be an EEA national residing in the United Kingdom in accordance with these Regulations on arrival in the United Kingdom; and

    (b)   the family member will be accompanying the EEA national to the United Kingdom or joining him there and –

        (i)   is lawfully resident in an EEA State; or

        (ii)   would meet the requirements in the immigration rules (other than those relating to entry clearance) for leave to enter the United Kingdom as the family member of the EEA national or, in the case of direct descendants or dependent direct relatives in the ascending line of his spouse or his civil partner, as the family member of his spouse or his civil partner, were the EEA national or the spouse or civil partner a person present and settled in the United Kingdom.

(2) An entry clearance officer may issue an EEA family permit to an extended family member of an EEA national who applies for one if –

    (a)   the relevant EEA national satisfies the condition in paragraph (1)(a);

    (b)   the extended family member wishes to accompany the relevant EEA national to the United Kingdom or to join him there; and

(c)   in all the circumstances, it appears to the entry clearance officer appropriate to issue the EEA family permit.

(3) Where an entry clearance officer receives an application under paragraph (2) he shall undertake an extensive examination of the personal circumstances of the applicant and if he refuses the application shall give reasons justifying the refusal unless this is contrary to the interests of national security.

(4) An EEA family permit issued under this regulation shall be issued free of charge and as soon as possible.

(5) But an EEA family permit shall not be issued under this regulation if the applicant or the EEA national concerned [is subject to a deportation or exclusion order or]¹ falls to be excluded from the United Kingdom on grounds of public policy, public security or public health in accordance with regulation 21.

AMENDMENT

¹ Words inserted: SI 2009/1117, reg 2, Sch 1, para 3.

13 Initial right of residence

(1) An EEA national is entitled to reside in the United Kingdom for a period not exceeding three months beginning on the date on which he is admitted to the United Kingdom provided that he holds a valid national identity card or passport issued by an EEA State.

(2) A family member of an EEA national residing in the United Kingdom under paragraph (1) who is not himself an EEA national is entitled to reside in the United Kingdom provided that he holds a valid passport.

(3) But –

(a)   this regulation is subject to regulation 19(3)(b); and

(b)   an EEA national or his family member who becomes an unreasonable burden on the social assistance system of the United Kingdom shall cease to have the right to reside under this regulation.

14 Extended right of residence

(1) A qualified person is entitled to reside in the United Kingdom for so long as he remains a qualified person.

(2) A family member of a qualified person residing in the United Kingdom under paragraph (1) or of an EEA national with a permanent right of residence under regulation 15 is entitled to reside in the United Kingdom for so long as he remains the family member of the qualified person or EEA national.

(3) A family member who has retained the right of residence is entitled to reside in the United Kingdom for so long as he remains a family member who has retained the right of residence.

(4) A right to reside under this regulation is in addition to any right a person may have to reside in the United Kingdom under regulation 13 or 15.

Appendix 2
England: Homelessness

(5) But this regulation is subject to regulation 19(3)(b).

15 Permanent right of residence

(1) The following persons shall acquire the right to reside in the United Kingdom permanently –

- (a) an EEA national who has resided in the United Kingdom in accordance with these Regulations for a continuous period of five years;
- (b) a family member of an EEA national who is not himself an EEA national but who has resided in the United Kingdom with the EEA national in accordance with these Regulations for a continuous period of five years;
- (c) a worker or self-employed person who has ceased activity;
- (d) the family member of a worker or self-employed person who has ceased activity;
- (e) a person who was the family member of a worker or self-employed person where –
  - (i) the worker or self-employed person has died;
  - (ii) the family member resided with him immediately before his death; and
  - (iii) the worker or self-employed person had resided continuously in the United Kingdom for at least the two years immediately before his death or the death was the result of an accident at work or an occupational disease;
- (f) a person who –
  - (i) has resided in the United Kingdom in accordance with these Regulations for a continuous period of five years; and
  - (ii) was, at the end of that period, a family member who has retained the right of residence.

(2) Once acquired, the right of permanent residence under this regulation shall be lost only through absence from the United Kingdom for a period exceeding two consecutive years.

(3) But this regulation is subject to regulation 19(3)(b).

*****

SI 2006 No 1294

Allocation of Housing and Homelessness (Eligibility) (England) Regulations 2006

Made	*11th May 2006*
Laid before Parliament	*11th May 2006*
Coming into force	*1st June 2006*

The Secretary of State, in exercise of the powers conferred by sections 160A(3) and (5), 172(4), 185(2) and (3) and 215(2) of the Housing Act 1996 makes the following Regulations:

1 Citation, commencement and application

(1) These Regulations may be cited as the Allocation of Housing and Homelessness (Eligibility) (England) Regulations 2006 and shall come into force on 1st June 2006.

(2) These Regulations apply to England only.

2 Interpretation

(1) In these Regulations –

'the 1996 Act' means the Housing Act 1996;

['the Accession Regulations 2004' means the Accession (Immigration and Worker Registration) Regulations 2004;

'the Accession Regulations 2006' means the Accession (Immigration and Worker Registration) Regulations 2006;][1]

'the EEA Regulations' means the Immigration (European Economic Area) Regulations 2006;

'the Immigration Rules' means the rules laid down as mentioned in section 3(2) of the Immigration Act 1971 (general provisions for regulation and control);

'the Refugee Convention' means the Convention relating to the Status of Refugees done at Geneva on 28th July 1951, as extended by Article 1(2) of the Protocol relating to the Status of Refugees done at New York on 31st January 1967; and

'sponsor' means a person who has given an undertaking in writing for the purposes of the Immigration Rules to be responsible for the maintenance and accommodation of another person.

(2) For the purposes of these Regulations –

(a) 'jobseeker', 'self-employed person', and 'worker' have the same meaning as for the purposes of the definition of a 'qualified person' in regulation 6(1) of the EEA Regulations; and

(b)   subject to paragraph (3), references to the family member of a
       jobseeker, self-employed person or worker shall be construed in
       accordance with regulation 7 of those Regulations.

(3) For the purposes of regulations 4(2)(d) and 6(2)(d) 'family member' does
not include a person who is treated as a family member by virtue of
regulation 7(3) of the EEA Regulations.

[(4) For the purposes of regulations 4(2)(h) and 6(2)(h), 'the relevant period'
means the period beginning at 4 p.m. on 25th July 2006 and ending on 31st
January 2007.][2]

AMENDMENT

[1] Words substituted: SI 2006/3340, reg 2(1), (2).

[2] Paragraph inserted: The Allocation of Housing and Homelessness (Eligibility) (England)
(Amendment) Regulations 2006, SI 2006/2007, reg 2(2).

3 Persons subject to immigration control who are eligible for an allocation of housing accommodation

The following classes of persons subject to immigration control are persons
who are eligible for an allocation of housing accommodation under Part 6 of
the 1996 Act –

(a)   Class A –a person who is recorded by the Secretary of State as a
       refugee within the definition in Article 1 of the Refugee Convention
       and who has leave to enter or remain in the United Kingdom;
(b)   Class B –a person –
       (i)   who has exceptional leave to enter or remain in the United
              Kingdom granted outside the provisions of the Immigration
              Rules; and
       (ii)   who is not subject to a condition requiring him to maintain and
              accommodate himself, and any person who is dependent on him,
              without recourse to public funds;
(c)   Class C –a person who is habitually resident in the United Kingdom,
       the Channel Islands, the Isle of Man or the Republic of Ireland and
       whose leave to enter or remain in the United Kingdom is not subject to
       any limitation or condition, other than a person –
       (i)   who has been given leave to enter or remain in the United
              Kingdom upon an undertaking given by his sponsor;
       (ii)   who has been resident in the United Kingdom, the Channel
              Islands, the Isle of Man or the Republic of Ireland for less than
              five years beginning on the date of entry or the date on which his
              sponsor gave the undertaking in respect of him, whichever date is
              the later; and
       (iii) whose sponsor or, where there is more than one sponsor, at least
              one of whose sponsors, is still alive; and
[(d)   Class D –a person who has humanitarian protection granted under the
       Immigration Rules].[1]

AMENDMENT

¹ Paragraph substituted: SI 2006/2527, reg 2(1), (2).

4 Other persons from abroad who are ineligible for an allocation of housing accommodation

(1) A person who is not subject to immigration control is to be treated as a person from abroad who is ineligible for an allocation of housing accommodation under Part 6 of the 1996 Act if –

(a) subject to paragraph (2), he is not habitually resident in the United Kingdom, the Channel Islands, the Isle of Man, or the Republic of Ireland;

(b) his only right to reside in the United Kingdom –

    (i) is derived from his status as a jobseeker or the family member of a jobseeker; or

    (ii) is an initial right to reside for a period not exceeding three months under regulation 13 of the EEA Regulations; or

(c) his only right to reside in the Channel Islands, the Isle of Man or the Republic of Ireland is a right equivalent to one of those mentioned in sub-paragraph (b) which is derived from the Treaty establishing the European Community.

(2) The following are not to be treated as persons from abroad who are ineligible for an allocation of housing accommodation pursuant to paragraph (1)(a) –

(a) a worker;

(b) a self-employed person;

[(c) a person who is treated as a worker for the purpose of the definition of 'qualified person' in regulation 6(1) of the EEA Regulations pursuant to either –

    (i) regulation 5 of the Accession Regulations 2004 (application of the 2006 Regulations in relation to accession State worker requiring registration), or

    (ii) regulation 6 of the Accession Regulations 2006 (right of residence of an accession State national subject to worker authorisation);]¹

(d) a person who is the family member of a person specified in sub-paragraphs (a)–(c);

(e) a person with a right to reside permanently in the United Kingdom by virtue of regulation 15(c), (d) or (e) of the EEA Regulations;

(f) a person who left the territory of Montserrat after 1st November 1995 because of the effect on that territory of a volcanic eruption; …²

(g) a person who is in the United Kingdom as a result of his deportation, expulsion or other removal by compulsion of law from another country to the United Kingdom[; …]³

[(h) during the relevant period, a person who left Lebanon on or after 12th July 2006 because of the armed conflict there.]⁴; [and

(i) a person who –

(i)   arrived in Great Britain on or after 28th February 2009 but before 18th March 2011;

(ii)   immediately before arriving in Great Britain had been resident in Zimbabwe; and

(iii)   before leaving Zimbabwe, had accepted an offer, made by Her Majesty's Government, to assist that person to settle in the United Kingdom].[5]

AMENDMENTS

[1] Paragraph substituted: SI 2006/3340, reg 2(1), (3).

[2] Word omitted: The Allocation of Housing and Homelessness (Eligibility) (England) (Amendment) Regulations 2006, SI 2006/2007, reg 2(3).

[3] Word omitted: The Allocation of Housing and Homelessness (Eligibility) (England) (Amendment) Regulations 2006, SI 2006/2007, reg 2(4); word omitted revoked: SI 2009/358, reg 2(1), (2).

[4] Sub-paragraph inserted: The Allocation of Housing and Homelessness (Eligibility) (England) (Amendment) Regulations 2006, SI 2006/2007, reg 2(5).

[5] Paragraph inserted: SI 2009/358, reg 2(1), (3).

5 Persons subject to immigration control who are eligible for housing assistance

(1) The following classes of persons subject to immigration control are persons who are eligible for housing assistance under Part 7 of the 1996 Act –

(a)   Class A – a person who is recorded by the Secretary of State as a refugee within the definition in Article 1 of the Refugee Convention and who has leave to enter or remain in the United Kingdom;

(b)   Class B – a person –

(i)   who has exceptional leave to enter or remain in the United Kingdom granted outside the provisions of the Immigration Rules; and

(ii)   whose leave to enter or remain is not subject to a condition requiring him to maintain and accommodate himself, and any person who is dependent on him, without recourse to public funds;

(c)   Class C – a person who is habitually resident in the United Kingdom, the Channel Islands, the Isle of Man or the Republic of Ireland and whose leave to enter or remain in the United Kingdom is not subject to any limitation or condition, other than a person –

(i)   who has been given leave to enter or remain in the United Kingdom upon an undertaking given by his sponsor;

(ii)   who has been resident in the United Kingdom, the Channel Islands, the Isle of Man or the Republic of Ireland for less than five years beginning on the date of entry or the date on which his sponsor gave the undertaking in respect of him, whichever date is the later; and

(iii)   whose sponsor or, where there is more than one sponsor, at least one of whose sponsors, is still alive;

[(d) Class D – a person who has humanitarian protection granted under the Immigration Rules; and]¹

(e) Class E – a person who is an asylum-seeker whose claim for asylum is recorded by the Secretary of State as having been made before 3rd April 2000 and in the circumstances mentioned in one of the following paragraphs –

 (i) on arrival (other than on his re-entry) in the United Kingdom from a country outside the United Kingdom, the Channel Islands, the Isle of Man or the Republic of Ireland;

 (ii) within three months from the day on which the Secretary of State made a relevant declaration, and the applicant was in Great Britain on the day on which the declaration was made; or

 (iii) on or before 4th February 1996 by an applicant who was on 4th February 1996 entitled to benefit under regulation 7A of the Housing Benefit (General) Regulations 1987 (persons from abroad).

(2) For the purpose of paragraph (1)(e) –

(a) 'asylum-seeker' means a person who is at least 18 years old, who is in the United Kingdom, and who has made a claim for asylum;

(b) 'claim for asylum' means a claim that it would be contrary to the United Kingdom's obligations under the Refugee Convention for the claimant to be removed from, or required to leave, the United Kingdom;

(c) 'relevant declaration' means a declaration to the effect that the country of which the applicant is a national is subject to such a fundamental change of circumstances that the Secretary of State would not normally order the return of a person to that country; and

(d) subject to paragraph (3), a person ceases to be an asylum-seeker when his claim for asylum is recorded by the Secretary of State as having been decided (other than on appeal) or abandoned.

(3) For the purposes of paragraph (1)(e)(iii), a person does not cease to be an asylum-seeker as mentioned in paragraph (2)(d) while he is eligible for housing benefit by virtue of –

(a) regulation 10(6) of the Housing Benefit Regulations 2006; or

(b) regulation 10(6) of the Housing Benefit (Persons who have attained the qualifying age for state pension credit) Regulations 2006,

as modified in both cases by paragraph 6 of Schedule 3 to the Housing Benefit and Council Tax Benefit (Consequential Provisions) Regulations 2006.

AMENDMENT

¹ Sub-paragraph substituted: SI 2006/2527, reg 2(1), (3).

Appendix 2
England: Homelessness

6 Other persons from abroad who are ineligible for housing assistance

(1) A person who is not subject to immigration control is to be treated as a person from abroad who is ineligible for housing assistance under Part 7 of the 1996 Act if –

    (a)   subject to paragraph (2), he is not habitually resident in the United Kingdom, the Channel Islands, the Isle of Man, or the Republic of Ireland;

    (b)   his only right to reside in the United Kingdom –

        (i)   is derived from his status as a jobseeker or the family member of a jobseeker; or

        (ii)   is an initial right to reside for a period not exceeding three months under regulation 13 of the EEA Regulations; or

    (c)   his only right to reside in the Channel Islands, the Isle of Man or the Republic of Ireland is a right equivalent to one of those mentioned in sub-paragraph (b) which is derived from the Treaty establishing the European Community.

(2) The following are not to be treated as persons from abroad who are ineligible for housing assistance pursuant to paragraph (1)(a) –

    (a)   a worker;

    (b)   a self-employed person;

    [(c)   a person who is treated as a worker for the purpose of the definition of 'qualified person' in regulation 6(1) of the EEA Regulations pursuant to either –

        (i)   regulation 5 of the Accession Regulations 2004 (application of the 2006 Regulations in relation to accession State worker requiring registration), or

        (ii)   regulation 6 of the Accession Regulations 2006 (right of residence of an accession State national subject to worker authorisation);][1]

    (d)   a person who is the family member of a person specified in sub-paragraphs (a)–(c);

    (e)   a person with a right to reside permanently in the United Kingdom by virtue of regulation 15(c), (d) or (e) of the EEA Regulations;

    (f)   a person who left the territory of Montserrat after 1st November 1995 because of the effect on that territory of a volcanic eruption; ...[2]

    (g)   a person who is in the United Kingdom as a result of his deportation, expulsion or other removal by compulsion of law from another country to the United Kingdom[; ...][3]

    [(h)   during the relevant period, a person who left Lebanon on or after 12th July 2006 because of the armed conflict there.][4];[and

    (i)   a person who –

        (i)   arrived in Great Britain on or after 28th February 2009 but before 18th March 2011;

        (ii)   immediately before arriving in Great Britain had been resident in Zimbabwe; and

(iii)   before leaving Zimbabwe, had accepted an offer, made by Her Majesty's Government, to assist that person to settle in the United Kingdom].[5]

AMENDMENTS

[1] Paragraph substituted: SI 2006/3340, reg 2(1), (4).

[2] Word omitted: The Allocation of Housing and Homelessness (Eligibility) (England) (Amendment) Regulations 2006, SI 2006/2007, reg 2(6).

[3] Word omitted inserted: The Allocation of Housing and Homelessness (Eligibility) (England) (Amendment) Regulations 2006, SI 2006/2007, reg 2(7); word omitted revoked: SI 2009/358, reg 2(1), (4).

[4] Sub-paragraph inserted: The Allocation of Housing and Homelessness (Eligibility) (England) (Amendment) Regulations 2006, SI 2006/2007, reg 2(8).

[5] Sub-paragraph inserted: SI 2009/358, reg 2(1), (5).

7 Revocation

Subject to regulation 8, the Regulations specified in column (1) of the Schedule are revoked to the extent mentioned in column (3) of the Schedule.

8 Transitional provisions

The revocations made by these Regulations shall not have effect in relation to an applicant whose application for –

(a)   an allocation of housing accommodation under Part 6 of the 1996 Act; or

(b)   housing assistance under Part 7 of the 1996 Act,

was made before 1st June 2006.

Schedule

Regulation 7

Revocation schedule

(1)	(2)	(3)
Regulations Revoked	*References*	*Extent of revocation*
The Homelessness (England) Regulations 2000	SI 2000/701	The whole Regulations
The Allocation of Housing (England) Regulations 2002	SI 2002/3264	Regulations 4 and 5

Revocation schedule

(1) Regulations Revoked	(2) References	(3) Extent of revocation
The Allocation of Housing and Homelessness (Amendment) (England) Regulations 2004	SI 2004/1235	The whole Regulations
The Allocation of Housing and Homelessness (Amendment) (England) Regulations 2006	SI 2006/1093	The whole Regulations

SI 2006 No 2527

Allocation of Housing and Homelessness (Miscellaneous Provisions) (England) Regulations 2006

Made	*14th September 2006*
Laid before Parliament	*18th September 2006*
Coming into force	*9th October 2006*

The Secretary of State, in exercise of the powers conferred by sections 160A(3), 172(4), 185(2), 198(4) and 215(2) of the Housing Act 1996, makes the following Regulations:

1 Citation, commencement, interpretation and application

(1) These Regulations may be cited as the Allocation of Housing and Homelessness (Miscellaneous Provisions) (England) Regulations 2006 and shall come into force on 9th October 2006.

(2) In these Regulations, 'the 1996 Act' means the Housing Act 1996.

(3) These Regulations apply to England only.

2 Amendment of the classes of person from abroad who are eligible for an allocation of accommodation and for housing assistance

(1) The Allocation of Housing and Homelessness (Eligibility) (England) Regulations 2006 are amended as follows.

(2) For regulation 3(d), substitute –

'(d)   Class D –a person who has humanitarian protection granted under the Immigration Rules.'.

(3) For regulation 5(1)(d), substitute –

'(d)   Class D –a person who has humanitarian protection granted under the Immigration Rules; and'.

3 Prescribed period for referral of case to another local housing authority

For the purposes of section 198(4)(b) of the 1996 Act (referral of case to another local housing authority), the prescribed period is the aggregate of –

(a)   five years; and
(b)   the period beginning on the date of the previous application and ending on the date on which the applicant was first placed in pursuance of that application in accommodation in the district of the authority to whom the application is now made.

Appendix 2
England: Homelessness

4 Transitional provisions

The amendments made by these Regulations shall not have effect in relation to an applicant whose application for –

(a) an allocation of housing accommodation under Part 6 of the 1996 Act; or

(b) housing assistance under Part 7 of the 1996 Act,

was made before 9th October 2006.

Letter (Effective Homelessness Prevention) 12 April 2006

Chief Housing Officer

Yvette Cooper MP
Minister for Housing and Planning

Office of the Deputy Prime Minister
26 Whitehall
London SW1A 2WH

Tel: 020 7944 8931
FAX: 020 7944 8953
E-Mail:
yvette.cooper@odpm.gsi.gov.uk
www.odpm.gov.uk
12 April 2006

Dear colleague,

Effective Homelessness Prevention

In 2002 we published *More than a roof*, which set out a new approach to tackling homelessness, focussing on the personal problems that can cause homelessness as well as the bricks and mortar solutions.

Preventing homelessness more effectively remains at the heart of our work today and our strategy, *Sustainable Communities: settled homes; changing lives*, sets out the role prevention can play in meeting our aim to halve the number of households living in insecure temporary accommodation by 2010. We have set out plans to improve the supply of new private and social housing which will help greatly in this. But local authorities and their partners need to continue to provide an effective response to the social and personal causes of homelessness, to promote a wider range of housing options to meet people's housing needs, and to provide early and effective interventions that can stop a housing problem becoming a homelessness crisis.

Since local authorities first put in place homelessness strategies in 2003 the number of new cases of homelessness has been falling and 2005 saw the lowest number of annual acceptances since 1985. It seems clear that this reduction is the result of the positive work that local authorities and voluntary agencies are doing to help provide effective solutions to the housing needs of those who approach them for help. However, I have been concerned by some reports of bad practice in a handful of local authorities.

I want to take this opportunity to remind you of the importance and value of effective homelessness prevention schemes and to let you know that, to support your prevention work, we will shortly be publishing a revised *Homelessness Code of Guidance for Local Authorities*. This will provide clear statutory guidance on how local authorities should carry out their homelessness functions and will assist authorities in providing appropriate and effective

Appendix 2
England: Homelessness

responses to homelessness. The Code will be issued jointly by the Deputy Prime Minister and the Secretaries of State for Health and for Education and Skills.

We will also be publishing a good practice guide on homelessness prevention. This is based on an independent evaluation of a range of homelessness prevention activities which found that prevention has the potential to be highly cost-effective. The guide will offer good practice principles, as well as case study examples for you to consider when reviewing and updating your services and strategy for preventing homelessness. It will complement other guides and policy briefings already available, including the DVD produced by the seven Beacon councils, a copy of which you should already have received.

The statutory Code of Guidance and the good practice guide emphasise our message that homelessness prevention must focus on early intervention and on improving outcomes and options for those who seek help. I do want to see continued reductions in homelessness numbers, but that must be achieved through more effective help, not as a result of a 'gatekeeping' approach that discourages people from applying for housing assistance. It is critical that vulnerable households should not be denied the assistance they need.

In particular, I have been concerned by reports in some areas in relation to private sector tenancies, where households have reported being told to remain in properties when they have received a valid notice to quit or notice that a landlord intends to begin possession proceedings, on the basis that they cannot be helped until they are actually evicted. In these circumstances, authorities have to consider whether it would be reasonable for an applicant to remain in their accommodation, considering all the factors relevant to each individual case. But I would also like to see all authorities taking the approach of the best – acting immediately to explore all possible options for preventing homelessness, including negotiating with landlords to extend or renew tenancies, offering mediation services to resolve disputes over rent arrears or repairs, or providing households with help to find alternative housing before homelessness occurs. The statutory Code of Guidance and the good practice guide provide more detailed information on these approaches. ODPM will be keeping practice in this area under review to ensure that vulnerable households get proper support.

These different forms of advice, guidance and best practice have been produced to help you to strengthen the services your authority provides to help people avoid homelessness, wherever possible. My team of advisers and officials within the Homelessness and Housing Support Directorate are available to discuss your prevention work. Please get in touch with your regular contact there, or use the e-mail, tacklinghomelessness@odpm.gsi.gov.uk.

I look forward to hearing about your continuing success in tackling and preventing homelessness as we move towards achieving the target to halve the number of households in temporary accommodation by 2010.

YVETTE COOPER

Letter (Homelessness Legislation: Commencement of section 314 of, and Schedule 15 to, the Housing and Regeneration Act 2008) 16 February 2009

Alan Edwards

Department for Communities and
Local Government
Zone 1/B5
Eland House
Bressenden Place
London SW1E 5DU

Tel: 020 7944 3665
Email:
alan.edwards@communities.gsi.gov.uk
www.communities.gov.uk

16 February 2009

The chief housing officers of	Our Ref:
all local housing authorities in	Your Ref:
England	

Dear chief housing officer,

This letter informs local housing authorities in England that the Government intends to commence section 314 of, and Schedule 15 to, the Housing and Regeneration Act 2008 on 2 March 2009. This will remedy the incompatibility with the European Convention on Human Rights of section 185(4) of the Housing Act 1996 (a provision of the homelessness legislation).

I write further to my letter of 20 June 2008 (copy attached). Section 185(4) of the Housing Act 1996 currently requires local housing authorities in England (and Wales) to disregard household members (including dependent children) who are ineligible for housing assistance when considering whether an eligible housing applicant is homeless or has a priority need for accommodation.

The courts declared that section 185(4) is incompatible with Article 14 taken with Article 8 of the European Convention on Human Rights to the extent that it requires a dependent child or pregnant spouse of a British citizen, if both are habitually resident in the UK, to be disregarded when determining whether the British citizen has a priority need for accommodation, when the child or spouse is subject to immigration control. The Government has made provision to remedy the incompatibility, see section 314 of, and Schedule 15 to, the Housing and Regeneration Act 2008 (which amend Parts 6 and 7 of the Housing Act 1996). This letter is to inform local housing authorities that the Government intends to commence these provisions on 2 March 2009.

A guidance note about the new provisions is attached. Please arrange for any queries about this letter or the guidance to be directed to me.

Yours faithfully,

Alan Edwards

Annex
Part 1 of Schedule 15 to the Housing and Regeneration Act 2008:
Guidance for Local Housing Authorities in England

(*This guidance is not statutory guidance*)

INTRODUCTION

1.   The Government intends to commence section 314 of, and Schedule 15 to, the Housing and Regeneration Act 2008, on 2 March 2009. Part 1 of Schedule 15 to the Housing and Regeneration Act 2008 ('the 2008 Act') amends Parts 6 and 7 of the Housing Act 1996 ('the 1996 Act'). The amendments will apply to all applications for accommodation or assistance in obtaining accommodation, within the meaning of section 183 of the 1996 Act, made on or after 2 March 2009.

PRINCIPAL AMENDMENTS TO PART 7 OF THE 1996 ACT (HOMELESSNESS)

Section 185 (*persons from abroad not eligible for housing assistance*)

2.   Prior to Schedule 15 to the Housing and Regeneration Act 2008 ('the 2008 Act') coming into force, section 185(4) of the Housing Act 1996 ('the 1996 Act') required local housing authorities in England (and Wales) to disregard household members (including dependent children) who were ineligible for housing assistance when considering whether any eligible housing applicant was homeless or had a priority need for accommodation.

Eligible applicants who are a person subject to immigration control

3.   Schedule 15 to the 2008 Act amends section 185(4) so that it applies only to eligible applicants who are themselves a *person subject to immigration control*, for example, those granted refugee status, indefinite leave to remain, humanitarian protection or discretionary leave.

4.   Consequently, the changes introduced by Schedule 15 to the 2008 Act have no effect on the treatment of housing applicants who are eligible for assistance under Part 7 of the 1996 Act and are a *person subject to immigration control*.

5.   When considering an application from a *person subject to immigration control* who is eligible for assistance, local authorities should continue to disregard any dependants or other household members who are ineligible for assistance for any reason, when considering whether the applicant is homeless or has a priority need for accommodation.

All other eligible applicants (those who are not a person subject to immigration control)

6.　The effect of Schedule 15 to the 2008 Act is that section 185(4) no longer applies to eligible applicants who are not themselves a *person subject to immigration control* – that is, those who are a British citizen, a Commonwealth citizen with a right of abode in the UK, or an EEA national with a right to reside in the UK.

7.　This group of eligible applicants will therefore be able to rely on ineligible household members to convey homelessness or priority need, and thereby confer an entitlement to be secured suitable accommodation under section 193(2) of the 1996 Act. Typically, ineligible household members who could confer priority need in this way are likely to be dependent children and pregnant women who have immigration leave with a condition of 'no recourse to public funds'.

Section 193 (duty to persons with priority need who are not homeless intentionally)

A restricted case

8.　Section 193 is amended to make provision for a 'restricted case'. By section 193(3B), a 'restricted case' is a case where the local authority would not be satisfied that the applicant had a priority need for accommodation without having had regard to a 'restricted person'. A 'restricted person' (defined by section 184(7)) means a person who is not eligible for assistance under Part 7 of the 1996 Act and is subject to immigration control and either:

(i)　　does not have leave to enter or remain in the UK, or

(ii)　　does have leave but it is subject to a condition of no recourse to public funds.

9.　In a restricted case, by section 193(7AD) the local authority must, so far as reasonably practical, bring the section 193(2) duty to an end by arranging for an offer of an assured shorthold tenancy to be made to the applicant by a private landlord (a private accommodation offer).

Identifying restricted persons

10.　Where a local authority considers a household member of an applicant may be a restricted person who does not have leave to enter or remain in the UK, or if there is uncertainty about the immigration status of any household member, it is recommended that the authority contact the UK Border Agency at the Home Office, using the procedures set out in Annex 8 to the *Homelessness Code of Guidance for Local Authorities*, published by the Department for Communities and Local Government, July 2006.

A private accommodation offer

11.　Section 193 (7AC) defines a 'private accommodation offer' as an offer of an assured shorthold tenancy made by a private landlord to the applicant in relation to any accommodation which is, or may become, available for the applicant's occupation, and which:

Appendix 2
England: Homelessness

– is made with the approval of the authority, in pursuance of arrangements made by the authority with the landlord with a view to bringing the authority's duty under section 193(2) to an end, and

– the tenancy being offered is a fixed term tenancy (within the meaning of Part 1 of the Housing Act 1988) for a period of at least 12 months

Ending the section 193 duty in a restricted case

12.   In a restricted case, by section 193(7AA), the section 192(3) duty ends if the applicant, having been informed of certain matters specified in section 193(7AB), accepts or refuses a private accommodation offer. The matters in section 192(7AB) are:

(a)   the possible consequence of refusal of the offer, and

(b)   that the applicant has the right to request a review of the suitability of the accommodation.

13.   **Section 202**(1)(g) of the 1996 Act provides that applicants have a right to request a review of any decision of a local authority as to the suitability of accommodation offered to him by way of a private accommodation offer (within the meaning of section 193).

14.   In a restricted case, where it is not reasonably practical to bring the section 193(2) duty to an end with a private accommodation offer, the local authority may discharge the duty in accordance with the provisions of section 193 that are not specific to a restricted case. In practical terms this may require the provision of 'temporary accommodation', that is, accommodation which is not capable of bringing the section 193(2) duty to an end. In such a case, the effect of section 193(7AD) is that the authority should continue to try to bring the duty to an end with a private accommodation offer, so far as reasonably practicable.

AMENDMENTS TO PART 6 (ALLOCATION OF HOUSING ACCOMMODATION)

Section 167

15.   In a restricted case, where it has not been reasonably practical to bring the section 193(2) duty to an end with a private accommodation offer, it would be open to the local authority to bring the section 193(2) duty to an end with a final offer of accommodation under Part 6 of the 1996 Act, in accordance with section 193(7), (7F) and (8).

16.   However, authorities should note that, in a restricted case, an applicant owed the section 193(2) duty will not be entitled to reasonable preference for an allocation of housing under Part 6 by virtue of section 167(2)(a) or (b). Section 167(2ZA) provides that people are to be disregarded for the purposes of subsection (2) if they would not have fallen within paragraph (a) or (b) of that subsection without the local housing authority having had regard to a restricted person (within the meaning of Part 7).

17.   Consequently, if an authority is considering making an offer of Part 6 accommodation to an applicant in a restricted case, they will need to take

particular care to ensure that such an allocation would be in accordance with the priorities of their published allocation scheme.

OTHER AMENDMENTS TO PART 7 (HOMELESSNESS)

Section 195 (duties in the case of threatened homelessness)

18. Section 195(4B) provides that a 'restricted threatened homelessness case' means a case where the local housing authority would not be satisfied that the applicant had a priority need for accommodation without having had regard to a 'restricted person'.

19. Section 195(4A) provides that where, in a 'restricted threatened homelessness case', the authority secure that accommodation other than the accommodation occupied by the applicant when he made his application is available for occupation by the applicant, the provisions of section 193(3) to (9) apply, with any necessary modifications, to the duty under section 195 as they apply to the duty under section 193 in a restricted case.

Section 184 (*inquiry into cases of homelessness or threatened homelessness*)

20. Section 184(3A) provides that if the authority decide that a duty is owed to the applicant under section 193(2) or 195(2) but would not have done so without having had regard to a restricted person, the notice they are required to give the applicant under section 184(3) (on completing their inquires) must also:

(a) inform the applicant that their decision was reached on that basis,
(b) include the name of the restricted person,
(c) explain why the person is a restricted person, and
(d) explain the effect of section 193(7AD) or (as the case may be) section 195(4A) (requirement to being the duty to an end with a private accommodation offer, so far as reasonably practical).

21. As mentioned above, section 184(7) provides that a 'restricted person' means a person who is not eligible for assistance under Part 7 of the 1996 Act and is subject to immigration control and either:

(i) does not have leave to enter or remain in the UK, or
(ii) does have leave but it is subject to a condition of no recourse to public funds.

Appendix 2
England: Homelessness

Appendix 3

WALES: ALLOCATION AND HOMELESSNESS

HOUSING ACT 1996
1996 C 52

Part 6

Allocation of Housing Accommodation

See Appendix 1, p 852

HOUSING ACT 1996
1996 C 52

Part 7

Homelessness

See Appendix 2, p 965

HOMELESSNESS ACT 2002
2002 C 7

Sections 1–4 and 17–21

See Appendix 2, p 1002

CODE OF GUIDANCE FOR LOCAL AUTHORITIES ON ALLOCATION OF ACCOMMODATION AND HOMELESSNESS, APRIL 2003 (WALES)

See CD-ROM

HOMELESSNESS (SUITABILITY OF ACCOMMODATION) ORDER 1996
SI 1996/3204

See Appendix 2, p 1236

LOCAL AUTHORITIES (CONTRACTING OUT OF ALLOCATION OF HOUSING AND HOMELESSNESS FUNCTIONS) ORDER 1996
SI 1996/3205

See Appendix 1, p 955

SI 1997 No 45

Local Housing Authorities (Prescribed Principles for Allocation Schemes) (Wales) Regulations 1997

Made	*13th January 1997*
Laid before Parliament	*16th January 1997*
Coming into force	*7th February 1997*

The Secretary of State for Wales, in exercise of the powers conferred on him by sections 167(5) and 172(4) of the Housing Act 1996 and of all other powers enabling him in that behalf, hereby makes the following Regulations:

1 Citation, commencement and application

These Regulations may be cited as the Local Housing Authorities (Prescribed Principles for Allocation Schemes) (Wales) Regulations 1997 and shall come into force on 7th February 1997. They apply to Wales only.

2 Interpretation

In these Regulations –

'the Act' means the Housing Act 1996;
'allocation decision' means a decision to allocate housing accommodation;
'allocation scheme' means an allocation scheme within the meaning of section 167(1) of the Act;
'authority' means a Welsh local housing authority;
'delegation arrangements' means arrangements made under section 101(1) or (2) of the Local Government Act 1972 for the discharge of an authority's function of making allocation decisions;
'officer delegation arrangements' means delegation arrangements which arrange for the discharge (in whole or in part) of an authority's function of making allocation decisions, by an officer or a description of officers of the authority; and
'qualifying person', in relation to an authority, means a person who is qualified to be allocated housing accommodation by that authority.

3 Allocation scheme principles

As regards the procedure to be followed in allocating housing accommodation, the principles set out in the Schedule are prescribed as principles in accordance with which an authority's allocation scheme shall be framed.

Schedule
Allocation Scheme Principles

Regulation 3

(1) In relation to an allocation decision where either –

  (a)   the housing accommodation in question is situated in the electoral division for which a member is elected, or

  (b)   the qualifying person in question has his sole or main residence in the electoral division for which a member is elected,

that member shall not be included in the persons or descriptions of persons by whom the allocation decision is to be taken.

(2) An officer or a description of officers of the authority shall be included in the persons or descriptions of persons by whom allocation decisions, or descriptions of allocation decisions, may be taken, except where the authority or a committee or sub-committee of the authority, as the case may be, has determined that no officer delegation arrangements shall be made.

HOMELESSNESS (DECISIONS ON REFERRALS) ORDER 1998
SI 1998/1578

See Appendix 2, p 1239

ALLOCATION OF HOUSING AND HOMELESSNESS (REVIEW PROCEDURES) REGULATIONS 1999
SI 1999/71

See Appendix 2, p 1242

SI 2001 No 607

Homeless Persons (Priority Need) (Wales) Order 2001

Made	*27th February 2001*
Coming into force	*St David's Day 1st March 2001*

The National Assembly for Wales makes the following Order in exercise of the power conferred on the Secretary of State by section 189(2) of the Housing Act 1996 which is now exercisable by it in relation to Wales; after consultation with such associations representing relevant authorities and such other persons as it considers appropriate in accordance with section 189(3):

1 Name, commencement and application

(1) The name of this Order is the Homeless Persons (Priority Need) (Wales) Order 2001 and it shall come into force on St David's Day, March 1st 2001.

(2) This Order applies to Wales only.

2 Persons with priority need for accommodation

The descriptions of person specified in articles 3 to 7 have priority need for accommodation under section 189 of the Housing Act 1996.

3 A care leaver or person at particular risk of sexual or financial exploitation, 18 years or over but under the age of 21

(1) A person who

(a) is 18 years old or older but under the age of 21; and

(b) at any time while still a child was, but is no longer, looked after, accommodated or fostered; or

(c) is at particular risk of sexual or financial exploitation.

(2) In paragraph (1)(b) above 'looked after, accommodated or fostered' means:

(a) looked after by a local authority;

(b) accommodated by or on behalf of a voluntary organisation;

(c) accommodated in a private children's home;

(d) accommodated for a consecutive period of at least three months –

(i) by any health authority, special health authority or local education authority, or

(ii) in any residential care home, nursing home or mental nursing home or in any accommodation provided by a National Health Service Trust [or NHS foundation trust][1]; or

(e) privately fostered.

AMENDMENT

[1] Words inserted: SI 2004/696, art 3(2), Sch 2.

4 A 16 or 17 year old

A person who is 16 or 17 years old.

5 A person fleeing domestic violence or threatened domestic violence

A person without dependant children who has been subject to domestic violence or is at risk of such violence, or if he or she returns home is at risk of domestic violence.

6 A person homeless after leaving the armed forces

(1) A person formerly serving in the regular armed forces of the Crown who has been homeless since leaving those forces.

(2) In paragraph (1) above the expression 'regular armed forces of the Crown' has the meaning given to it in section 199(4) of the Housing Act 1996.

7 A former prisoner homeless after being released from custody

(1) A former prisoner who has been homeless since leaving custody and who has a local connection with the area of the local housing authority.

(2) A 'prisoner' means any person for the time being detained in lawful custody as the result of a requirement imposed by a court that he or she be detained.

SI 2003 No 239

Allocation of Housing (Wales) Regulations 2003

Made	*28th January 2003*
Coming into force	*29th January 2003*

The National Assembly for Wales makes the following Regulations in exercise of the powers given to the Secretary of State by sections 160(4), 160A(3) and (5) and 215(2) of the Housing Act 1996 which powers are now vested in the National Assembly for Wales so far as exercisable in relation to Wales:

1 Citation, commencement and application

(1) These Regulations may be cited as the Allocation of Housing (Wales) Regulations 2003 and shall come into force on 29 January 2003.

(2) These Regulations apply to Wales only.

2 Interpretation

In these Regulations –

'the Act' ('*y Ddeddf*') means the Housing Act 1996;

'the Common Travel Area' ('*Ardal Deithio Gyffredin*') means the United Kingdom, the Channel Islands, the Isle of Man and the Republic of Ireland collectively; and

'the immigration rules' ('*y rheolau mewnfudo*') mean the rules laid down as mentioned in section 3(2) of the Immigration Act 1971 (general provisions for regulation and control).

3 Cases where the provisions of Part 6 of the Act do not apply

The provisions of Part 6 of the Act about the allocation of housing accommodation do not apply in the following cases –

(a)   where a local housing authority secures the provision of suitable alternative accommodation under section 39 of the Land Compensation Act 1973 (duty to rehouse residential occupiers);

(b)   in relation to the grant of a secure tenancy under section 554 and 555 of the Housing Act 1985 (grant of tenancy to former owner-occupier or statutory tenant of defective dwelling-house).

4 Classes prescribed under section 160A(3) who are eligible persons

The following are classes of persons subject to immigration control prescribed for the purposes of section 160A(3) of the Act (persons prescribed as eligible for an allocation of housing accommodation by a local housing authority) –

(a)   Class A –a person recorded by the Secretary of State as a refugee within the definition in Article 1 of the Convention relating to the

Status of Refugees done at Geneva on 28th July 1951 as extended by Article 1(2) of the Protocol relating to the Status of Refugees done at New York on 31st January 1967;

(b)   Class B –a person –

     (i)   who has been granted by the Secretary of State exceptional leave to enter or remain in the United Kingdom outside the provisions of the immigration rules; and

     (ii)   whose leave is not subject to a condition requiring them to maintain and accommodate themselves, and any person who is dependent on them, without recourse to public funds;

(c)   Class C –a person who has current leave to enter or remain in the United Kingdom which is not subject to any limitation or condition and who is habitually resident in the Common Travel Area other than a person –

     (i)   who has been given leave to enter or remain in the United Kingdom upon an undertaking given by another person (that person's 'sponsor') in writing in pursuance of the immigration rules to be responsible for that person's maintenance and accommodation;

     (ii)   who has been resident in the United Kingdom for less than five years beginning on the date of entry or the date on which the above-mentioned undertaking was given in respect of that person, whichever date is the later; and

     (iii)   whose sponsor or, where there is more than one sponsor, at least one of whose sponsors, is still alive;

(d)   Class D –a person who is habitually resident in the Common Travel Area and who –

     (i)   is a national of a state which has ratified the European Convention on Social and Medical Assistance done at Paris on 11th December 1953 or a state which has ratified the European Social Charter done at Turin on 18th October 1961 and is lawfully present in the United Kingdom; or

     (ii)   before 3rd April 2000 was owed a duty by a housing authority under Part III of the Housing Act 1985 (housing the homeless) or Part 7 of the Act (homelessness) which is extant, and who is a national of a state which is a signatory to the European Convention on Social and Medical Assistance done at Paris on 11th December 1953 or a state which is a signatory to the European Social Charter done at Turin on 18th October 1961[;][1]

[(e)   Class D1 –a person who has humanitarian protection granted under the Immigration Rules.]

AMENDMENT

[1] Words inserted: SI 2006/2645, reg 2(1), 2(a).

[2] Words inserted: SI 2006/2645, reg 2(1), 2(b).

5 Classes prescribed under section 160A(5) who are not eligible persons

The following is a class of persons, not being persons subject to immigration control, prescribed for the purposes of section 160A(5) of the Act (persons prescribed as ineligible for an allocation of housing accommodation) –

Class E –a person who is not habitually resident in the Common Travel Area other than –

    (a)   a worker for the purposes of Council Regulation (EEC) No 1612/68 or (EEC) No 1251/70;

    (b)   a person with a right to reside in the United Kingdom pursuant to the Immigration (European Economic Area) Order 2000 and derived from Council Directive No 68/360/EEC or No 73/148/EEC;

    (c)   a person who left the territory of Montserrat after 1st November 1995 because of the effect on that territory of a volcanic eruption[;

    (d)   a person who –

        (i)   arrived in Great Britain on or after 28th February 2009 but before 18th March 2011;

        (ii)   immediately before arriving in Great Britain had been resident in Zimbabwe; and

        (iii)   before leaving Zimbabwe, had accepted an offer, made by Her Majesty's Government, to assist that person to settle in the United Kingdom].[1]

AMENDMENT

[1] Words inserted: SI 2009/393, reg 2.

6 Revocation

The Allocation of Housing (Wales) Regulations 2000 are revoked.

SI 2006 No 650

Homelessness (Suitability of Accommodation) (Wales) Order 2006

Made	*8 March 2006*
Coming into force	
Articles 1–3	*3 April 2006*
Articles 4–6	*2 April 2007*
Articles 7–10	*7 April 2008*

The National Assembly for Wales, in exercise of the powers conferred on the Secretary of State by sections 210(2) and 215(2) of the Housing Act 1996, and now vested in the National Assembly for Wales, hereby makes the following Order:

1 Title, commencement and application

(1) The title of this Order is the Homelessness (Suitability of Accommodation) (Wales) Order 2006.

(2) Save as provided in paragraphs (3) and (4) of this Article, this Order comes into force on 3 April 2006.

(3) Articles 4, 5 and 6 of, and the Schedule to this Order come into force on 2 April 2007.

(4) Articles 7, 8, 9 and 10 of this Order come into force on 7 April 2008.

(5) This Order applies in relation to the duties of local housing authorities in Wales under Part 7 of the Housing Act 1996 (homelessness).

2 Interpretation

In this Order –

'the 1996 Act' (*'Deddf 1996'*) means the Housing Act 1996; and any reference to a numbered section is a reference to a section of the Housing Act 1996;

'B&B accommodation' (*'llety Gwely a Brecwast'*) means commercially provided accommodation (whether or not breakfast is included) –

    (a) which is not separate and self-contained premises;

    (b) in which any of the following amenities is not available to the applicant or is shared by more than one household –

        (i) a toilet;

        (ii) personal washing facilities;

        (iii) cooking facilities;

(c)   which is not accommodation which is owned or managed by a local housing authority, a registered social landlord or a voluntary organisation as defined in section 180(3) of the Housing Act 1996; or

(d)   which is not an establishment registered under the provisions of the Care Standards Act 2000;

and 'B&B' (*'Gwely a Brecwast'*) is to be construed accordingly;

'basic standard accommodation' (*'llety o safon sylfaenol'*) means accommodation that –

(a)   complies with all statutory requirements (such as requirements relating to fire and gas safety, planning and licences for houses in multiple occupation, where applicable); and

(b)   has a manager deemed by the local housing authority to be a fit and proper person with the ability to manage B&B accommodation;

and 'basic standard' (*'safon sylfaenol'*) is to be construed accordingly;

'higher standard accommodation' (*'llety o safon uwch'*) means accommodation that meets –

(a)   the basic standard; and

(b)   the standards contained in the Schedule to this Order,

and 'higher standard' (*'safon uwch'*) is to be construed accordingly;

'shared accommodation' (*'llety a rennir'*) means accommodation –

(a)   which is not separate and self-contained premises; or

(b)   in which any of the following amenities is not available to the applicant or is shared by more than one household –

(i)   a toilet;

(ii)   personal washing facilities;

(iii)   cooking facilities; or

(c)   which is not an establishment registered under the provisions of the Care Standards Act 2000;

'small B&B' (*'llety Gwely a Brecwast bach'*) means –

B&B accommodation –

(i)   where the manager resides on the premises; and

(ii)   which has fewer than 7 bedrooms available for letting.

PART 1
ADDITIONAL MATTERS TO BE TAKEN INTO ACCOUNT IN DETERMINING SUITABILITY

3

In determining for the purposes of Part 7 of the 1996 Act whether accommodation is suitable for a person in priority need there must be taken into account the following matters –

(a)   the specific health needs of the person;

(b)   the proximity and accessibility of social services;

(c)　　the proximity and accessibility of the support of the family or other support services; or

(d)　　any disability of the person.

PART 2
CIRCUMSTANCES APPLYING FROM 2 APRIL 2007 IN WHICH ACCOMMODATION IS NOT TO BE REGARDED AS SUITABLE

4 B&B accommodation used for housing a homeless person to meet the basic standard

For the purposes of Part 7 of the 1996 Act, B&B accommodation is not to be regarded as suitable unless it meets at least the basic standard.

5 B&B accommodation not to be regarded as suitable for a minor or a pregnant woman

For the purposes of Part 7 of the 1996 Act and subject to the exceptions contained in article 6, B&B accommodation is not to be regarded as suitable for a person who is a minor or a pregnant woman.

6 Exceptions

(1) Article 5 does not apply where –

(a)　　the person occupies a basic standard B&B for a period, or a total of periods, which does not exceed 2 weeks;

(b)　　the person occupies a higher standard B&B for a period or a total of periods which does not exceed 6 weeks;

(c)　　the person occupies a basic standard small B&B for a period or a total of periods which does not exceed 6 weeks, and the local housing authority has, before the expiry of the two-week period referred to in sub-paragraph (a), offered suitable alternative accommodation, but the person has chosen to remain in the said B&B;

(d)　　the person occupies a basic standard small B&B after exercising the choice referred to in sub-paragraph (c) above, and the local housing authority has offered suitable alternative accommodation before the end of the six-week period referred to in sub-paragraph (c) above, but the person has chosen to remain in the said B&B; or

(e)　　the person occupies a higher standard small B&B, and the local housing authority has offered suitable alternative accommodation, before the expiry of the six-week period referred to in sub-paragraph (b) above, but the person has chosen to remain in the said B&B.

(2) If the suitable alternative accommodation offered for the purposes of paragraph (1) is shared, it must meet the higher standard.

(3) In the case of households with dependent children or a pregnant woman, the offer made under sub-paragraphs (d) or (e) must be of suitable self-contained accommodation. In the case of an applicant who is a minor, the offer must be of suitable accommodation with support.

(4) In calculating a period, or total period, of a person's occupation of B&B accommodation for the purposes of paragraph (1), there must be disregarded –

    (a)   any period before 2 April 2007; and

    (b)   where a local housing authority is subject to the duty under section 193 by virtue of section 200(4), any period before that authority became subject to that duty.

PART 3
EXTENSION FROM 7 APRIL 2008 TO ALL ACCOMMODATION PROVIDED IN DISCHARGE OF HOMELESSNESS FUNCTIONS

7 B&B accommodation not to be regarded as suitable for a homeless person in priority need

For the purposes of Part 7 of the 1996 Act and subject to the exceptions contained in article 9, B&B accommodation is not to be regarded as suitable for a person who is in priority need.

8 Shared accommodation to meet the higher standard

For the purposes of Part 7 of the 1996 Act and subject to the exceptions contained in articles 9 and 10, shared accommodation is not to be regarded as suitable for a person who is in priority need unless it meets the higher standard.

9 Exceptions

(1) Articles 7 and 8 do not apply where –

    (a)   the person occupies basic standard B&B for a period, or a total of periods, which does not exceed 2 weeks;

    (b)   the person occupies a higher standard B&B for a period or a total of periods which does not exceed 6 weeks;

    (c)   the person occupies a basic standard small B&B for a period or a total of periods which does not exceed 6 weeks, and the local housing authority has, before the expiry of the two-week period referred to in sub-paragraph (a), offered suitable alternative accommodation, but the person has chosen to remain in the said B&B;

    (d)   the person occupies a basic standard small B&B after exercising the choice referred to in sub-paragraph (c), and the local housing authority has offered suitable alternative accommodation before the end of the six-week period referred to in sub-paragraph (c) above, but the person has chosen to remain in the said B&B;

    (e)   the person occupies a higher standard small B&B, the local housing authority has offered suitable alternative accommodation, before the expiry of the six-week period referred to in sub-paragraph (b), but the person has chosen to remain in the said B&B; or

    (f)   the person occupies basic standard shared accommodation for a period, or a total of periods, which does not exceed 2 weeks;

    (g)   the person occupies, for a period or a total of periods which does not exceed 6 weeks, basic standard shared accommodation owned by a local housing authority or registered social landlord, and the local housing authority has offered suitable alternative accommodation before the expiry of the two-week period referred to in sub-paragraph (f), but the person has chosen to remain in the said accommodation.

(2) If the suitable alternative accommodation offered for the purposes of paragraph (1) is shared, it must meet the higher standard.

(3) In the case of households with dependent children or a pregnant woman, the offer made under sub-paragraphs (d) or (e) must be of suitable self-contained accommodation. In the case of an applicant who is a minor, the offer must be of suitable accommodation with support.

(4) In calculating a period, or total period, of a person's occupation of shared accommodation for the purposes of paragraph (1), there must be disregarded –

(a)   any period before 7 April 2008; and
(b)   where a local housing authority is subject to the duty under section 193 by virtue of section 200(4), any period before that authority became subject to that duty.

10 Delayed application to Social Housing

Article 7 is not to apply until 4 April 2011 to any property owned or managed by a local authority or registered social landlord and used for the purposes of Part 7 of the 1996 Act on 7 April 2008.

Schedule
Higher Standard

1 Minimum Space Standards

SPACE STANDARDS FOR SLEEPING ACCOMMODATION

Room sizes where cooking facilities provided in a separate room or kitchen

Floor Area of Room	Maximum No of Persons
Not less than 6.5 square metres	1 person
Not less than 10.2 square metres	2 persons
Not less than 14.9 square metres	3 persons
Not less than 19.6 square metres	4 persons

Room sizes where cooking facilities provided within the room

Floor Area of Room	Maximum No of Persons
Not less than 10.2 square metres	1 person
Not less than 13.9 square metres	2 persons

Floor Area of Room	Maximum No of Persons
Not less than 18.6 square metres	3 persons
Not less than 23.2 square metres	4 persons

For the purposes of the room size calculations above, a child less than 10 years old is treated as a half person.

(a) No room to be occupied by more than 4 persons, except where the occupants consent.

(b) No sharing of rooms for those of opposite genders, aged 10 or above unless they are living together as partners and both are over the age of consent, or where a parent or guardian elects to share with an older child.

(c) All rooms must have a floor to ceiling height of at least 2.1 metres over not less than 75% of the room area. Any part of the room where the ceiling height is less than 1.5 metres must be disregarded when calculating the floor area.

(d) Separate kitchens and bathrooms are unsuitable for sleeping accommodation.

2 Installation for heating

The premises must have adequate provision for heating. All habitable rooms and bath- or shower-rooms must have a heating system capable of maintaining the room at a minimum temperature of 18°C when the outside temperature is minus 1°C.

3 Facilities for the storage, preparation and cooking of food within the unit

(1) In a unit of accommodation accommodating more than one person, the food preparation area provided within the unit must include the following facilities:

(a) four burners or hobs, conventional oven and grill, or two burners or hobs and a microwave with a built in oven and grill,

(b) a sink and integral drainer, with a constant supply of hot water and cold drinking water,

(c) a storage cupboard of a minimum capacity 0.2 cubic metres excluding storage beneath the sink,

(d) a refrigerator,

(e) a minimum of four 13-amp sockets (single or double) situated over the worktop,

(f) a worktop for food preparation of minimum dimensions 1 metre x 0.6 metre, and

(g) a minimum of 1 metre circulation space from facilities to other furniture in the room.

(2) In a unit of accommodation accommodating one person, the food preparation area provided within the unit of accommodation must include the following facilities:

As (a)–(g) above but (a) to have a minimum of two burners or hobs.

4 Storage, preparation and cooking of food in a shared facility

(1) Where food preparation areas are shared between more than one household there must be one set of kitchen facilities for:

(a)   every 3 family households or fewer;

(b)   every 5 single-person households or fewer. (For between 6 and 9 single-person households an additional oven or microwave is required.)

(c)   every 10 persons or fewer where there is a mixture of family and single-person households within the same premises.

(2) Each set of shared facilities must provide the following facilities:

(a)   as for unit accommodating more than one person except that cooking facilities must consist of 4 burners or hobs, conventional oven, grill and microwave,

(b)   an electric kettle,

(c)   a toaster.

The food preparation area used by the management may be included when calculating the ratio, provided it meets the criteria for storage, preparation and cooking of food in a shared facility.

Where residents have no access to kitchen facilities and the proprietor provides at least a breakfast and evening-meal for residents, the requirements for shared kitchen facilities will be deemed to have been met.

Additional facilities to be provided in each bedroom or within the total accommodation occupied exclusively by each household must include:

(a)   a refrigerator; and

(b)   lockable storage.

Alternatively, these may be provided elsewhere within the building.

5 Toilet and washing facilities

(1) Facilities for the exclusive use of the occupant or household must include:

(a)   bath or shower,

(b)   a wash hand basin with a constant supply of hot and cold water, and

(c)   a water-closet either en-suite or in a separate room reserved for the exclusive use of individuals or households.

(2) Shared facilities must include:

(a)   One water closet and wash hand basin with a constant supply of hot and cold water within the building for every five households or fewer. This must be located not more than one floor away from the intended users. For the first five households the water closet and wash hand basin may be in the shower or bathroom. All additional water closets and wash hand basins for occupancies of six households or more must be in a separate compartment.

(b)   One bathroom or shower-room to be provided for every five persons. This must be located not more than one floor away from the intended users.

(c)   In premises accommodating children under the age of 10, at least half of the bathing facilities must contain baths suitable for children.

The number of persons occupying a unit of accommodation with a water closet facility provided for their exclusive use is not to be included in the calculation for shared water closets.

6 Security

The entrance door to each unit of accommodation must be lockable and be capable of being unlocked from inside without the use of a key.

7 Common Room(s)

Every premises must have a common room of at least 12 square metres unless all households have a living area separate from their sleeping area that is available for their exclusive use or the premises are for single person households only.

8 Management Standard

(a) Each household must be issued with written 'house rules' which include details as to how sanctions will be applied. This document is to be approved by the local authority placing homeless households in the premises.

(b) Each household must be issued with written information relating to the premises including how to operate all installations, for example heating and hot water appliances and fire fighting equipment.

(c) Written information must be made available to residents relating to the local area including the location or contact details of local facilities, laundrettes, doctors' surgeries and schools.

(d) Residents must have access to their rooms at all times except when rooms are being cleaned or otherwise maintained. Provision must be made to accommodate residents at these times.

(e) Access is allowed for the appropriate officers of the local housing authority in whose area the premises are situated, and officers of any authority placing homeless households in the premises, to inspect the premises as and when they consider necessary, to ensure that the requirements are being complied with; and that the manager will allow such inspections to take place, if necessary without notice.

(f) Access is allowed for the officers of the local authority and authorised health and community workers for the area in which the premises are situated, to visit the occupiers of the premises and interview them in private in the room(s) they occupy.

Appendix 3

Wales: Allocation and Homelessness

(g) A manager with adequate day to day responsibility to ensure the good management of the property can be contacted at all times and that a notice giving the name, address and telephone number of the manager must be displayed in a readily visible position in the property.

(h) A clear emergency evacuation plan is in place setting out action upon hearing the fire alarm, escape routes and safe assembly points. The managers must ensure that each person newly arriving at the premises is told what to do in the event of a fire and about fire precautions provided.

(i) Each household must be issued with a complaints procedure which specifies how a complaint can be made. This information must also include where the complainant can obtain further advice and assistance.

SI 2006 No 2646

Homelessness (Wales) Regulations 2006

Made	*3 October 2006*
Coming into force	*9 October 2006*

The National Assembly for Wales makes the following Regulations in exercise of the powers conferred upon the Secretary of State by sections 185(2) and (3) of the Housing Act 1996 which are now vested in the National Assembly so far as exercisable in Wales.

1 Title, commencement and application

(1) The title of these Regulations is the Homelessness (Wales) Regulations 2006 and they come into force on 9 October 2006.

(2) These Regulations apply to Wales

2 Interpretation

(1) In these Regulations

'the 1971 Act' (*'Deddf 1971'*) means the Immigration Act 1971;
'the 1995 Act' (*'Deddf 1995'*) means the Jobseekers Act 1995;
'the 1996 Act' (*'Deddf 1996'*) means the Housing Act 1996;
'asylum-seeker' (*'ceisydd lloches'*) means a person who is not under 18 and who made a claim for asylum which is recorded by the Secretary of State as having been made before 3 April 2000 but which has not been determined;
'claim for asylum' (*'hawliad lloches'*) means a claim that it would be contrary to the United Kingdom's obligations under the Refugee Convention for the claimant to be removed from, or required to leave, the United Kingdom;
'the Common Travel Area' (*'Ardal Deithio Gyffredin'*) means the United Kingdom, the Channel Islands, the Isle of Man and the Republic of Ireland collectively;
'the immigration rules' (*'y rheolau mewnfudo'*) means the rules laid down as mentioned in section 3(2) of the 1971 Act (general provisions for regulation and control);
'limited leave' (*'caniatâd cyfyngedig'*) means leave under the 1971 Act to enter or remain in the United Kingdom which is limited as to duration; and
'the Refugee Convention' (*'y Confensiwn ynglyn â Ffoaduriaid'*) means the Convention relating to the Status of Refugees done at Geneva on 28 July 1951, as extended by Article 1(2) of the Protocol relating to the Status of Refugees done at New York on 31 January 1967.

(2) For the purposes of the definition of 'asylum-seeker', a claim for asylum is determined at the end of such period beginning –

(a) on the day on which the Secretary of State notifies the claimant of the decision on the claim; or

(b) if the claimant has appealed against the Secretary of State's decision, on the day on which the appeal is disposed of,

as may be prescribed under section 94(3) of the Immigration and Asylum Act 1999.

(3) For the purposes of regulations 3(1)(i) (Class I) –

(a) 'an income-based jobseeker's allowance' ('*lwfans ceisio gwaith ar sail incwm*') means a jobseeker's allowance, payable under the 1995 Act, entitlement to which is based on the claimant satisfying conditions which include those set out in section 3 of the 1995 Act (the income-based conditions);

(b) 'income support' ('*cymhorthdal incwm*') has the same meaning as in section 124 of the Social Security Contributions and Benefits Act 1992 (income support); ...[1]

(c) a person is on an income-based jobseeker's allowance on any day in respect of which an income-based jobseeker's allowance is payable to that person and on any day –

  (i) in respect of which that person satisfies the conditions for entitlement to an income-based jobseeker's allowance but where the allowance is not paid in accordance with section 19 of the 1995 Act (circumstances in which jobseeker's allowance is not payable); or

  (ii) which is a waiting day for the purposes of paragraph 4 of Schedule 1 to the 1995 Act (waiting days) and which falls immediately before a day in respect of which an income-based jobseeker's allowance is payable to that person or would be payable to that person but for section 19 of the 1995 Act; [and

(d) 'an income-related employment and support allowance' means an employment and support allowance payable under Part 1 of the Welfare Reform Act 2007 entitlement to which is based on the claimant satisfying conditions which include those set out in Part 2 of Schedule 1 to that Act][2].

AMENDMENT

[1] Word revoked by SI 2008/1879, reg 31(1), (2)(a).

[2] Word inserted: para (3): SI 2008/1879, reg 31(1), (2)(b).

3 Classes of persons subject to immigration control who are eligible for housing assistance

(1) The following are classes of persons prescribed for the purposes of section 185(2) of the 1996 Act (persons subject to immigration control who are eligible for housing assistance) –

(a) Class A – a person recorded by the Secretary of State as a refugee within the definition in Article 1 of the Refugee Convention;

(b) Class B – a person –

    (i) who has been granted by the Secretary of State exceptional leave to enter or remain in the United Kingdom outside the provisions of the immigration rules; and

    (ii) whose leave is not subject to a condition requiring that person to maintain and accommodate themselves, and any person who is dependent on that person, without recourse to public funds;

(c) Class C – a person who has current leave to enter or remain in the United Kingdom which is not subject to any limitation or condition and who is habitually resident in the Common Travel Area other than a person –

    (i) who has been given leave to enter or remain in the United Kingdom upon an undertaking given by another person (that person's 'sponsor') in writing in pursuance of the immigration rules to be responsible for that person's maintenance and accommodation;

    (ii) who has been resident in the United Kingdom for less than five years beginning on the date of entry or the date on which the undertaking was given in respect of that person, whichever date is the later; and

    (iii) whose sponsor or, where there is more than one sponsor, at least one of whose sponsors, is still alive;

(d) Class D – a person who left the territory of Montserrat after 1 November 1995 because of the effect on that territory of a volcanic eruption;

(e) Class E – a person who is habitually resident in the Common Travel Area and who –

    (i) is a national of a state which has ratified the European Convention on Social and Medical Assistance done at Paris on 11 December 1953 or a state which has ratified the European Social Charter done at Turin on 18 October 1961 and is lawfully present in the United Kingdom; or

    (ii) before 3 April 2000 was owed a duty by a housing authority under Part III of the Housing Act 1985 (housing and homeless) or Part VII of the 1996 Act (homelessness) which is extant, and who is a national of a state which is a signatory to the European Convention on Social and Medical Assistance done at Paris on 11 December 1953 or a state which is a signatory to the European Social Charter done at Turin on 18 October 1961;

(f) Class F – a person who is an asylum-seeker and who made a claim for asylum –

    (i) which is recorded by the Secretary of State as having been made on his arrival (other than on his re-entry) in the United Kingdom from a country outside the Common Travel Area; and

    (ii) which has not been recorded by the Secretary of State as having been either decided (other than on appeal) or abandoned;

(g) Class G – a person who is an asylum-seeker and –

        (i)   who was in Great Britain when the Secretary of State made a
                declaration to the effect that the country of which that person is
                a national is subject to such a fundamental change in
                circumstances that the Secretary of State would not normally
                order the return of a person to that country;
        (ii)   who made a claim for asylum which is recorded by the Secretary
                of State as having been made within a period of three months
                from the day on which that declaration was made; and
        (iii)   whose claim for asylum has not been recorded by the Secretary
                of State as having been either decided (other than on appeal) or
                abandoned;
    (h) Class H – a person who is an asylum-seeker and –
        (i)   who made a relevant claim for asylum on or before 4 February
                1996; and
        (ii)   who was, on 4 February 1996, entitled to benefit under
                regulation 7A of the Housing Benefit (General) Regula-
                tions 1987 (persons from abroad);
        (i)   Class I – a person who is on an income-based jobseeker's
                allowance[, an income-related employment and support allow-
                ance][1] or in receipt of income support and is eligible for that
                benefit other than because –
        (i)   that person has limited leave to enter or remain in the United
                Kingdom which was given in accordance with the relevant
                immigration rules and that person is temporarily without funds
                because remittances to that person from abroad have been
                disrupted; or
        (ii)   that person has been deemed by regulation 3 of the Displaced
                Persons (Temporary Protection) Regulations 2005 to have been
                granted leave to enter or remain in the United Kingdom
                exceptionally for the purposes of the provision of means of
                subsistence; and
    (j) Class J – a person who has humanitarian protection granted under the
         Immigration Rules.

(2) In paragraph (1)(h)(i) (Class H), a relevant claim for asylum is a claim for
asylum which –

    (a) has not been recorded by the Secretary of State as having been either
         decided (other than on appeal) or abandoned; or
    (b) has been recorded as having been decided (other than on appeal) on or
         before 4 February 1996 and in respect of which an appeal is pending
         which –
        (i)   was pending on 5 February 1996; or
        (ii)   was made within the time limits specified in the rules of
                procedure made under section 22 of the 1971 Act (procedure).

(3) In paragraph (1)(i)(i) (Class I), 'relevant immigration rules' ('*rheolau
mewnfudo perthnasol*') means the immigration rules relating to –

    (a) there being or there needing to be no recourse

(b) there being no charge on public funds.

(4) In paragraph (1)(i) (Class I), 'means of subsistence' ('*moddion byw*') has the same meaning as in regulation 4 of the Displaced Persons (Temporary Protection) Regulations 2005.

AMENDMENT

¹ Words inserted: SI 2008/1879, reg 31 (1), (3).

4 Description of persons who are to be treated as persons from abroad ineligible for housing assistance

(1) The following are descriptions of persons, other than persons who are subject to immigration control, who are to be treated for the purposes of Part VII of the 1996 Act (homelessness) as persons from abroad who are ineligible for housing assistance –

(a) subject to paragraphs (2) and (3), a person who is not habitually resident in the United Kingdom, the Channel Islands, the Isle of Man or the Republic of Ireland;

(b) a person whose right to reside in the United Kingdom, the Channel Islands, the Isle of Man or the Republic of Ireland is derived solely from Council Directive No 90/364/EEC or Council Directive No 90/365/EEC.

(2) The following persons will not, however, be treated as persons from abroad who are ineligible pursuant to paragraph (1)(a) –

(a) a person who is a worker for the purposes of Council Regulation (EEC) No 1612/68 or (EEC) No 1251/70;

(b) a person who is an accession state worker requiring registration who is treated as a worker for the purpose of the definition of 'qualified person' in regulation 6 of the Immigration (European Economic Area) Regulations 2006 pursuant to regulation 5 of the Accession (Immigration and Worker Registration) Regulations 2004;

(c) a person with a right to reside pursuant to the Immigration (European Economic Area) Regulations 2006, which is derived from Council Directive No 68/360/EEC, No 73/148/EEC or No 75/34/EEC;

(d) a person who left the territory of Montserrat after 1 November 1995 because of the effect on that territory of a volcanic eruption[;

(e) a person who –
  (i) arrived in Great Britain on or after 28 February 2009 but before 18 March 2011;
  (ii) immediately before arriving in Great Britain had been resident in Zimbabwe; and
  (iii) before leaving Zimbabwe, had accepted an offer, made by Her Majesty's Government, to assist that person to settle in the United Kingdom].¹

(3) A person will not be treated as habitually resident in the United Kingdom, the Channel Islands, the Isle of Man or the Republic of Ireland for the

Appendix 3
Wales: Allocation and Homelessness

purposes of paragraph (1)(a) if he does not have a right to reside in the United Kingdom, the Channel Islands, the Isle of Man or the Republic of Ireland.

AMENDMENT

[1] Sub-paragraph inserted: SI 2009/393.

5 Transitional Provisions

The amendments made by these Regulations do not have effect in relation to an applicant whose application for housing assistance under Part VII of the 1996 Act was made before 9 October 2006.

6 Revocation

The Homelessness (Wales) Regulations 2000 are hereby revoked.

INDEX

References are to paragraph numbers.